PORTFOLIO

MUTUAL FUND INVESTOR'S GUIDE 2004

Kirk Kazanjian is a nationally recognized investment expert, mutual fund analyst, bestselling author, and lifelong entrepreneur. He spent several years as an award-winning television news anchor and business reporter before moving into various roles within the investment industry. Among other things, Kazanjian is the former Director of Research and Investment Strategy for two leading investment firms, where he performed investment manager research and due diligence, oversaw the creation of new investment programs, and developed strategies for managing more than $1.6 billion in client assets.

In addition to *Mutual Fund Investor's Guide 2004*, Kazanjian has written many other personal finance books, including *Wizards of Wall Street*, *Growing Rich with Growth Stocks*, and *Value Investing with the Masters*. He also coauthored *Making Dough: The 12 Secret Ingredients of Krispy Kreme's Sweet Success*.

Kazanjian regularly offers investment advice on CNBC, CNNfn, and Bloomberg, plus many other radio and television stations across the country. He has been featured in numerous publications, including *Barron's, Mutual Funds, Entrepreneur, The Christian Science Monitor*, and *USA Today*, and is a popular speaker and teacher on investment topics.

The author welcomes your comments and feedback. He can be reached through his Web site at www.kirkkazanjian.com.

MUTUAL FUND FUND INVESTOR'S GUIDE 2004

KIRK KAZANJIAN

Foreword by Reuben Gregg Brewer

PORTFOLIO
Published by the Penguin Group
Penguin Group (USA) Inc., 375 Hudson Street,
New York, New York 10014, U.S.A.
Penguin Books Ltd, 80 Strand,
London WC2R 0RL, England
Penguin Books Australia Ltd, 250 Camberwell Road, Camberwell,
Victoria 3124, Australia
Penguin Books Canada Ltd, 10 Alcorn Avenue,
Toronto, Ontario, Canada M4V 3B2
Penguin Books India (P) Ltd, 11 Community Centre, Panchsheel Park,
New Delhi - 110 017, India
Penguin Books (N.Z.) Ltd, Cnr Rosedale and Airborne Roads, Albany,
Auckland, New Zealand
Penguin Books (South Africa) (Pty) Ltd, 24 Sturdee Avenue,
Rosebank, Johannesburg 2196, South Africa

Penguin Books Ltd, Registered Offices:
80 Strand, London WC2R 0RL, England

This edition published by Portfolio, a member of Penguin Group (USA) Inc. 2004

10 9 8 7 6 5 4 3 2 1

Although the information in this book was obtained from sources believed to be reliable, neither the author, publisher, nor Value Line assumes responsibility for its accuracy. This publication is sold with the understanding that the publisher is not engaged in rendering financial, accounting, or other professional services. If you require financial advice or other expert assistance, you should seek the services of a competent professional. Under no circumstances does the information in this book represent a recommendation to buy or sell stocks or funds.

Charts and other materials used by permission of Value Line Publishing, Inc.; charts computer-generated by Fred Dahl, Inkwell Publishing.

ISBN 1-59184-031-7 / ISSN 1531-4545

Printed in the United States of America

To my Mom,
with love and admiration

CONTENTS

Chapter 7

The 25 Best Internet Sites for Mutual Fund Investors   262

Chapter 8

Value Line Performance Data for Thousands of Funds   271

FOREWORD

A valuable lesson. That's how I view both the erstwhile effervescent mega-bull market of the 1990s and the subsequent collapse into a prolonged bear market. I could look at my portfolio losses as both a painful rout of my wealth and the destruction of my aspirations for an early retirement, but that would be somewhat shortsighted.

Now, I don't mean to minimize anyone's financial pain. I certainly felt the sting of the market collapse along with just about everyone else. The point is if you burn your hand in an open fire, you deal with the wound and learn to be more careful with fire. If your portfolio gets hurt during a market collapse, you should accept the financial pain and learn to be more careful with your investment decisions.

That was, essentially, the crux of the problem. Many market participants in recent years had never been burned by a prolonged bear market and simply hadn't the chance to learn this valuable lesson. For this new group, the market only went up. That isn't how financial markets work. Indeed, it is an inescapable fact that a bear market follows every bull market.

It is also a fact that a bull market follows every bear market. And this is where you get to apply the lesson the market has taught you. I'd like to share some of my thoughts on how you can both protect yourself and profit in the coming years, no matter what happens with the market.

1. **Save, save, save.** During the bull market, many investors assumed that stock-market gains would make up for a low savings rate. This didn't happen and it never will. The one thing over which you have almost complete control is how much you save from your salary and other income. If you want to have more, save more. Age-old wisdom says you should save 10 percent of your salary, but I save much more than that and I believe you should, too. The key here is to live below your

means. It sounds corny, but it is the only way I know to truly build wealth.

2. **Have a financial roadmap.** If you wanted to get from New York (where I live) to California (where Kirk lives), you would probably get a map to find the best route. Far too often, investors go into the market without any goals or plans. The result is invariably a muddled portfolio that makes no logical sense (one full of Internet startups, for example). Know your goals, know your risk tolerance, and know your time horizon. Use these to build your financial plan.

3. **Diversify your portfolio.** At Value Line, we strongly believe in asset allocation. You needn't follow our model, but please don't bet on one horse. Spread your risk around, and when one basket of eggs falls, you'll still have others to fall back on.

4. **Knowledge is key.** You have taken the first step toward this end by purchasing this book. Now read the sage advice in *Mutual Fund Investor's Guide 2004* and apply it. Author Kirk Kazanjian's work expands on my points and will help you build a solid foundation for achieving your own goals.

If you can put these insights to work, I'm certain you will find that the market is less terrifying—even when those nasty bears are roaming around.

Reuben Gregg Brewer
Director of Mutual Fund Research
Value Line Publishing, Inc.

INTRODUCTION

Welcome to the *Mutual Fund Investor's Guide 2004*. This annually updated book contains everything you need for making smart decisions about investing in funds, whether you're a seasoned pro or just starting out. You'll find plenty of helpful advice for putting together a winning investment plan, including specific recommendations, model portfolios, and comprehensive performance data from the *Value Line Mutual Fund Survey*. (This information isn't found in any other book on the market today.) Plus, you'll discover 25 must-see Internet sites for fund investors loaded with information you can access absolutely free. It's like having the services of a trusted investment adviser at your fingertips all year long. You'll also find profiles of 100 Powerhouse Performers—funds for virtually every investment objective that appear to be especially well suited for the year ahead. Each fund is profiled in a research report that includes historical graphs and a multitude of performance data. When it comes to funds, there are plenty of dogs out there. Fortunately, the homework has already been done to help you uncover some real gems.

Without question, mutual funds are the investment of choice among today's smart consumers. In fact, figures from the Investment Company Institute, the fund industry trade association, show that one in three Americans now owns shares in at least one fund. Many books have been written on the subject of fund investing, but none contain the kind of specific and timely information found in this Guide. It will give you all the tools you need to build a comfortable financial future for yourself and your family. By the time you have finished reading this book, you will know:

- Precisely how mutual funds work
- What to look for when choosing them
- Which specific funds should do best in the year ahead

- How to construct your own personal portfolio plan
- Ways to make even more money using your computer

The book also contains exhaustive Value Line performance data for thousands of stock and bond funds, along with a glossary of commonly used investment terms that all fund investors should know. You'll want to refer to this valuable information again and again.

HOW TO USE THIS BOOK

If you're brand new to fund investing, you'll want to start with Chapter 1 and work your way through the book from the beginning. Along the way, you'll learn all about how funds work, determine whether you are better off in index or actively managed funds, discover the many ways to buy and sell funds, and get all of the tools you need to put together a winning investment plan. If, on the other hand, you are a more advanced fund investor, you might want to skip around a bit. Perhaps you can start off by reading the keys to finding great funds in Chapter 2. Then you can turn to Chapter 4, to learn about the only free lunch you'll find on Wall Street. (Hint: It's available only to fund investors.) After that, you can look through the "100 Powerhouse Performers" in Chapter 5, to uncover some new ideas for your portfolio in the year ahead, and be sure to check out the list of great Internet sites for fund investors in Chapter 7. Finally, everyone should spend some time going through the exhaustive list of Value Line data in Chapter 8. This wealth of information, found in no other book, will give you historical performance information on virtually every fund imaginable. That way you can compare what you own now with the many other choices available out there.

Don't forget, this book is updated each year, complete with new fund recommendations, model portfolios, Internet sites, fund manager interviews, performance data, and much more. Be on the lookout for *Mutual Fund Investor's Guide 2005* at a bookstore near you!

For now let's get started on the road to developing a mutual fund investment plan for the coming year that you can profit from for decades to come.

MUTUAL
FUND
INVESTOR'S
GUIDE 2004

1

MUTUAL FUNDS— TODAY'S INVESTMENT OF CHOICE

Access to the world's leading investment luminaries used to be reserved exclusively for the chosen few—those wealthy individuals with $1 million-plus portfolios. Even plain vanilla index funds were off limits to all but the largest institutions. Anyone else who wanted to participate in the fortunes of the stock market had to rely on tips from a commission-based broker, who was likely schooled in salesmanship, not investing. The only alternative was to put money in a bank, where it earned a comparatively inferior rate of interest.

How times have changed! Now, someone with just $1,000 to invest can tap into the same expertise that is available to a corporate CEO with a $20 million portfolio. This is made possible through arguably the greatest invention ever created for individual investors—mutual funds. Virtually every noted Wall Street money pro now either runs a fund of his or her own or is involved in the management of one. Therefore, it's possible for almost everyone to hire the leading brainpower in the business for a very small fee. In fact, owning funds is much cheaper and rewarding than buying individual stocks and bonds for most investors.

THE EXPLOSION OF MUTUAL FUNDS: A BRIEF HISTORY

For almost a decade now, investors around the world have been pouring money into funds at a record pace. But these investment vehicles have been around in one form or another much longer. The mutual fund industry

1

traces its roots back to 1868, when the Foreign and Colonial Government Trust ("the Trust") was formed in London. This British investment company, which issued a fixed number of shares, spread its portfolio across a number of different stocks. The Trust resembled today's closed-end funds: the daily price was determined by supply and demand, instead of by the actual underlying net asset value of the securities. (Closed-end funds trade on one of the stock exchanges and must be purchased and sold through a broker.)

The first open-end fund—the kind we will be focusing on in this book— was launched in 1924, when the Massachusetts Investors Trust opened for business. It began with a $50,000 portfolio containing 45 stocks. In an open-end fund, new shares are continuously offered to the public. Shares can be sold at any time, and their prices are based on the current net asset value of the portfolio's underlying holdings. It's pretty simple to calculate a fund's net asset value. Simply add up the value of every security in the portfolio, based on the closing market price, and divide that result by the number of outstanding shares. In other words, if you have a portfolio worth $100 and you own a total of 100 shares, the net asset value per share is $1.

TOUGH BEGINNINGS

The mutual fund industry got off to a rocky start in the United States. The 1929 stock market crash, and the resulting Great Depression, scared many investors away from equities in general. These events also caused Congress to enact a series of laws regulating the securities and financial markets, in an effort to protect investors. The Securities Act of 1933, for example, requires every fund sponsor to issue a prospectus describing how the portfolio would be invested. The most important law for fund investors is the Investment Company Act of 1940, which mandates that funds be priced based on the day's closing market value. It also prohibits transactions between a fund and its manager, sets up a statutory system of independent fund directors, requires funds to redeem shares upon demand, and sets out a series of rules that must be followed in the area of bookkeeping.

WHAT IS NET ASSET VALUE?

$$\text{Net Asset Value} = \frac{\text{Total Assets} - \text{Liabilities}}{\text{Number of Shares Outstanding}}$$

Mutual funds began to catch on with the American public during the 1940s and 1950s. In 1940, there were fewer than 80 funds, with total assets of around $500 million. Two decades later, there were 160 funds with collective assets of $17 billion. Almost all of these early funds had a front-end sales load and were peddled exclusively through stockbrokers. The "load" averaged around 8 percent and served as a commission taken right off the top to compensate the broker. Therefore, if you invested $100 in a fund with an 8 percent load, $8 immediately went into the broker's pocket, effectively putting only $92 to work. Even behemoth Fidelity Investments, which was formed in the 1930s, distributed its funds through brokers. That policy was changed after the brutal 1973–1974 bear market, which once again soured the public's appetite for mutual funds. In an effort to create new business, Ned Johnson, Fidelity's founder, came up with a unique idea. He introduced the first money market fund with a check-writing feature. These investments were touted as safe vehicles that offered investors easy access to their money. To keep the fund's yield as high as possible, Johnson decided to try selling it directly to the public by advertising a toll-free number in newspapers. The strategy was so successful, he soon converted many of his stock and bond funds to "no-loads" and began offering them through this channel as well.

There are now more than 12,000 mutual funds in the United States alone—including all share classes. That's more than the number of available individual stocks. The combined assets of these funds are more than $6.5 trillion. This amount is even more staggering when you realize that just one decade ago, total fund assets stood at a mere $1 trillion. Throughout the mid-1990s, money from individual investors flowed into funds at a feverish pace. While new contributions slowed in the face of the most recent bear market, the industry continues to grow. As of the latest statistics, 48 percent of total fund assets were in stocks, 18 percent were in bonds, and 34 percent were in money market funds. What's more, it's estimated that one in two Americans invests in mutual funds.

THE RIGHT IDEA FOR CHANGING TIMES

One reason funds have become so popular is that we are now being forced to invest. A generation ago, a recent graduate would go to work for a large company that promised to pay a sizable monthly pension after retirement. That pension, combined with a Social Security check, would surely pro-

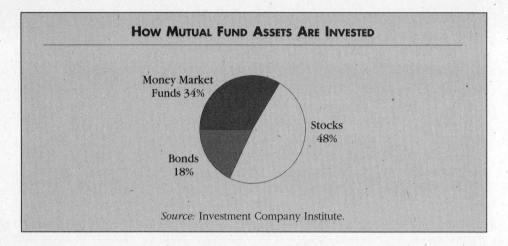

HOW MUTUAL FUND ASSETS ARE INVESTED

Money Market
Funds 34%

Stocks
48%

Bonds
18%

Source: Investment Company Institute.

vide enough income to live comfortably in one's sunset years, or so people thought.

For better or worse, things are much different now. Most companies, especially smaller ones, don't even have pensions. Instead, employees may be offered a chance to contribute to a retirement program such as a 401(k) or SEP-IRA, in which workers have a certain percentage of their income deducted and usually placed into a portfolio of funds. It's up to each employee to figure out how that money is invested, be it in stocks, bonds, or money market instruments. Therefore, millions of everyday folks have had to bone up on investing, since they are now required to make these integral decisions about how to save for their financial future. The other changing dynamic is that most younger Americans don't believe Social Security will be around when they need it, despite the federal government's assurances. Therefore, in addition to contributing to employer-sponsored retirement plans, wise individuals are setting up investment portfolios on their own, both regular and IRAs (individual retirement accounts), to make sure they are taken care of financially when they ultimately decide to leave the workforce. The really smart ones invest their money through carefully selected mutual funds.

WHY YOU SHOULD INVEST IN FUNDS

═══There are a number of reasons why funds make so much sense for most investors. We'll begin with a few of the obvious ones: diversification, low costs, professional management, ease of buying and selling, convenience, and a mix of asset classes.

DIVERSIFICATION

One of the first rules of investing is: Don't put all of your eggs in one basket. That's especially true with the stock market. In today's volatile trading environment, a small disappointment from even a blue-chip company can cause its stock to get hammered severely. What's more, a constant sector rotation is going on in the market. Financial stocks may do well this quarter, but technology companies may find favor with investors in the next quarter, followed by the pharmaceuticals, and so on. If you own a well-rounded list of stocks, you increase the odds that at least a portion of your portfolio will always be in the right place at the right time. Having a large list of holdings also reduces your "specific stock risk"—the danger that a company you own will see its share price get sliced as a result of some unforeseen bad news.

When you buy into a stock fund, you instantly tap into a portfolio that likely owns shares in dozens of different companies. Even the most concentrated funds usually contain at least 20 names. The same is true for bond and money market funds, which can spread their portfolios across a broad range of companies and maturities to smooth out volatility and increase overall returns. Unless you have at least a six-figure amount to invest, it would be cost-prohibitive to buy such a diversified basket of individual securities on your own. The commissions alone would kill you. When you invest in a fund, you instantly benefit from the economies of scale enjoyed by spreading these costs among a large base of shareholders. And even with a six-figure portfolio, most investors are still better off in funds. After all, when you go it alone, you're competing with the pros.

LOW COSTS

Every mutual fund, whether it has a sales load or not, comes with underlying management fees. These charges, expressed in the form of expense ratios, can be found near the front of every prospectus. The average expense ratio for actively managed stock funds is around 1.40 percent; for fixed-income portfolios, it is under 1 percent. If you have $1,000 in a stock fund with an expense ratio of 1.40 percent, you would pay the fund $14 a year for managing your money. The fund never sends you a bill for this charge. Instead, the fee is automatically deducted from the net asset value each day. Just think: for $14 a year (give or take a few bucks, depending on the particular fund you choose and the amount you invest), you can hire a highly educated investment expert, backed up by a team of equally smart research analysts, to make buy-and-sell decisions on your behalf.

Incidentally, do-it-yourself investors should stick with no-load funds, to save on unnecessary sales charges and expenses. In the pages that follow, you will be given an enormous amount of information you can use to put together a winning fund portfolio, including Chapter 5's list of 2004's "100 Powerhouse Performers." These funds were selected after doing an exhaustive amount of proprietary research. You'll notice that every one of these funds is offered on a no-load basis. You won't pay a penny to buy or sell them, so every cent of your investment dollar can work for you.

PROFESSIONAL MANAGEMENT

When you buy shares in a fund, you truly gain access to some of the sharpest minds on Wall Street. A few decades ago, this simply wasn't possible unless an investor placed a ton of money into an individually managed account. The expertise is similar, by the way, whether we're talking about actively managed funds (run by a human) or passive funds (index funds or similar offerings run solely by a computer). After all, it takes a high degree of intelligence to program a computer to properly replicate a given index in the first place. Over the past few years, it has been striking how many people became convinced they could do just as well, if not better, by choosing individual stocks on their own rather than using funds. This belief was exacerbated by the abnormally high returns offered by certain high-profile stocks in the late 1990s. If your attitude is "I can do a better job than these highly paid fund and well-connected fund managers," think about what you are really saying. You're contending that you have more brilliance and savvy than experts who spend 10 to 14 hours a day researching and watching the market. In an occasional streak of good luck, you might pick a stock that doubles or triples in a short period of time. But, as market veterans often warn, "Don't confuse brains with a bull market." We've seen that axiom at work during the recent bear market, as some previously high-flying stocks fell back down to earth. When you make individual stock selections on your own, you are competing against pros who have much more experience and clout than you do, and the results may prove to be disappointing.

MUTUAL FUND FEES AND EXPENSES

Two types of costs are involved in running a fund: (1) shareholder transaction expenses and (2) annual operating expenses.

1. **Shareholder transaction expenses** are fees charged directly to the investor for purchases, redemptions, or exchanges. For the most part, these expenses apply only to load funds. However, some no-load funds charge fees for early redemption, to discourage short-term trading. The following expenses can be expected:

   - *Front-end sales load.* This fee, charged at the time of purchase, compensates financial professionals for selling the fund to you. By law, this fee may not exceed 8.5 percent of the initial investment.
   - *Deferred sales charge.* Also called a "back-end load," this fee is charged at the time you sell shares in a fund. It is normally used as an alternative to a front-end load. In many funds, the deferred sales charge is reduced or eliminated over time.
   - *Redemption fee.* This is another type of back-end charge imposed for redeeming shares. It can be expressed as either a dollar amount or a percentage of the redemption price. It is occasionally imposed by no-load funds as a way of deterring short-term trading.
   - *Exchange fee.* This charge is imposed on shareholders when transferring money from one fund to another within the same family.

2. **Annual operating expenses** are the normal costs involved in operating a fund (i.e., for research, management, and equipment). Unlike transaction fees, these expenses are deducted directly from fund assets on a daily basis, instead of being billed to the investor. They are expressed as a percentage of the total net worth of the investment.

   - *Management fees.* This is what the fund's investment adviser charges for running the fund. Management fees are typically between 0.5 percent and 1 percent of assets, and ideally are reduced as the asset base increases.
   - *12b-1 fees.* This expense, named for the SEC rule that created it, is being charged by an increasing number of funds. It is used to pay for marketing, advertising, or sales costs. By law, 12b-1 fees cannot exceed 0.75 percent of net assets.
   - *Other expenses.* These include special charges for transfer agency and for accounting costs that are not included in any of the above expenses.

EASE OF BUYING AND SELLING

Mutual fund shares are highly liquid. With a single phone call, you can buy or sell as many shares as you want, and get a check for your proceeds in as little as one day (especially if you place your order through a discount broker). All shares are either purchased or redeemed at their net asset value at the close of business on the day the transaction takes place. It's true that most individual stocks and bonds are equally liquid, but you have to pay a commission when you convert these other instruments into cash. When you buy no-load funds, there is no fee on the way in or out.

CONVENIENCE

Mutual funds provide a clear element of convenience. Chances are you have a day job that doesn't involve selecting and monitoring investments. Maybe you're retired and spend your days improving your golf score or enjoying the great outdoors. In either case, you probably don't have a lot of time to research new investment ideas, follow the market, and continually analyze every one of your holdings. Investing truly is a full-time job, and an array of recordkeeping is involved when purchasing individual securities. When you buy a fund, the fund family or discount broker reduces your work to a minimum by doing most of this recordkeeping for you. Then, at tax-filing time, you only have to deal with a single 1099 form that gives you all the information you need to keep Uncle Sam satisfied. Most funds will gladly reinvest your dividends and capital gains distributions automatically, allowing you to profit from the magic of compounding. Often, you can get a money market fund from your discount broker or fund company as well with check-writing privileges and the ability to make exchanges from one fund to another.

MIX OF ASSET CLASSES

Finally, funds allow you to easily target specific asset classes, which is increasingly important in the current turbulent market environment. In a broad sense, you have various types of securities—stocks, bonds, and cash—available for investment. But there are subcategories within each of these classes. On the equity side, for example, you have small-caps, mid-caps, large-caps, and international securities. Informed investors have exposure to all of these areas in their portfolios. In fact, research has shown that having the right asset-class mix is even more important than security selection in determining long-term investment performance. It's virtually impossible to target specific

---

WHAT'S A MARKET CAP?

A stock's market capitalization is calculated by multiplying the number of outstanding shares by the price per share. For example, a stock trading for $1 with 10 million shares outstanding would have a market capitalization, or market cap, of $10 million. Stocks are categorized into four primary classes and have the following general guidelines:

1. **Micro-Cap.** Stocks with market capitalizations of $0 to $500 million.
2. **Small-Cap.** Stocks with market capitalizations of $500 million to $2 billion.
3. **Mid-Cap.** Stocks with market capitalizations of $2 billion to $5 billion.
4. **Large-Cap.** Stocks with market capitalizations of $5 billion or more.

---

asset classes like this through individual security selection. We'll delve deeper into the subject of asset allocation, and the categories that should be represented in your portfolio, in Chapter 6.

THE DRAWBACKS

Nothing in life is perfect, and that includes mutual funds. As wonderful as they are, funds do have a few shortfalls. For example, despite being closely regulated, funds still aren't held to high standards for disclosure. They don't have to tell you how much fund managers make, and only twice a year must they give you a list of the securities they own. Similarly, because you are hiring a manager to make all of your investment decisions, you have no say as to which stocks or bonds you own. (Some people hate letting go of that control.) Furthermore, although diversification is designed to give you smooth and respectable returns over the long haul, it prevents you from scoring any phenomenal home runs. If you own only one stock and it goes up 1,000 percent, you will become rich. But if you have a portfolio of 200 names and that same stock goes up 1,000 percent, it won't have much of an impact. Keep in mind that statistically stocks have the same chance of falling 100 percent as they do of rising 1,000 percent. This is why diversification makes so much sense. Even with modest returns of 8 to 10 percent a year, if you start early, save religiously, and use excellent funds, you will likely wind up with more money than you know what to do with.

The biggest disadvantage to owning funds rather than individual securities relates to taxes. By law, funds must pay out a majority of their built-in investment profits to shareholders at the end of each year. These profits are distributed in the form of dividends and capital gains. When you own individual securities, you don't have to pay taxes on any capital gains until you redeem your shares. With funds, you may incur a tax liability even if you hold on. This drawback has received a great deal of attention ever since Congress lowered the maximum rate for long-term gains. With funds, you don't always know in advance what percentage of your gains will be counted as long- or short-term, because some portfolio managers trade more frequently than others.

There are steps you can take to reduce your tax liability. One remedy is to buy tax-efficient funds. You can find out how tax-efficient a fund is by examining its past distribution record. Generally speaking, funds with low turnover rates are more tax-efficient than those which do a lot of trading. A fund's annual turnover rate can be found in the prospectus. Low-turnover funds generally hold on to their positions longer, allowing the gains to be carried on for years. Funds don't have to distribute gains to you until they have been realized, so low turnover usually, but not always, translates into greater tax efficiency. You can also buy index funds, which are inherently tax-efficient because they rarely do any trading among positions.

Remember, you will eventually have to pay taxes on your gains anyway. Holding on and building them up only delays the inevitable. You also get to add any fund distributions to the cost basis of your shares, which will reduce your capital gains liability when you finally sell out. So, although no one wants to share their profits with the IRS until they absolutely have to, the potential tax consequences shouldn't prevent investors from getting involved with funds. Taxes are a bigger issue in roaring bull markets, but, even then, they can be kept under control with proper planning and good fund selection.

SOME NOTES ON TAXES

Gains are typically paid out at the end of each calendar year, so you should avoid purchasing shares of a fund in December, until it has paid out its annual distribution. Otherwise, you will be taxed on the entire gain, even though you might have owned the fund for only a few weeks. Statistics show that 70 percent of all fund assets are in tax-deferred retirement accounts anyway. Therefore, in most cases, the one major argument against fund ownership doesn't even apply. That's because you don't have to worry about paying taxes until you make withdrawals from such accounts. For more information on the taxation of mutual funds, request Publications 550 (Investment Income and Expenses), 551 (Basis of Assets), and 564 (Mutual Fund Distributions) from the Internal Revenue Service. To get them, call (800) TAX-FORM, or visit www.irs.gov.

MAKING YOUR INITIAL INVESTMENT

══ In Chapter 2, you'll receive guidance on selecting individual funds. For now, let's assume you already have your list of fund choices from Chapter 5 and are ready to make an investment. Where do you go from here? Your first step is to order a prospectus, annual report, and application from the fund. Simply dial the toll-free number listed for the fund in Chapters 5 and 8, and ask for the information you need. Once you have the prospectus and report in hand, be sure to look them over, paying close attention to what really matters. For example, in the prospectus, you'll want to find out what the fund's expense ratio is. (See the box on page 7 for more on the various fees and expenses charged by funds.) You'll also want to learn about the manager's background, how long he or she has been at the fund, the types of investments he or she is allowed to buy, and the minimum amount required for initial and subsequent investments. Prospectuses are typically thick documents, full of incomprehensible legalese. Fortunately, the Securities and Exchange Commission (SEC) passed a "plain English" rule in 1998, requiring fund companies to use, whenever possible, common words, short sentences, and tables or bullet lists for complex material. They also must refrain from using highly technical legal jargon and multiple negatives.

Next, look through the annual report and read the list of specific securities in the portfolio. Examine whether the fund is properly diversified and whether it owns the kinds of investments you would expect it to. For example, if it's a small-cap fund and you find IBM among its list of holdings, you know something is wrong. By the same token, if it's supposed to be a large-cap, blue-chip fund, and you've never heard of any of the holdings, that should also trigger an alarm. This caution also applies if you are trying to determine how to invest your 401(k) money. You are normally given a list of at least a dozen funds to choose from. Demand a prospectus and report for

UNDERSTANDING THE EXPENSE RATIO

The following table is similar to an outline of a fund's various expenses, found in every fund prospectus:

Annual Portfolio Operating Expenses:

Management and Administrative Expenses	0.50%
Investment Advisory Expenses	0.25%
12b-1 Marketing Fees	0.25%
Other Expenses	None
Total Operating Expenses (Expense Ratio)	1.00%

The operating expenses for each fund will be different. In this example, the fund's total expense ratio is 1%, or $10 per $1,000 of assets.

each one, so you can make an informed decision about where to put your money.

After you have this information and can determine whether a particular fund is right for you (more help with this is on the way), you are then ready to make an investment. You can do it the traditional way: fill out the application that comes with your material, and mail a check directly to the fund. Or, you can purchase your shares through one of the major discount brokers, including Charles Schwab, Fidelity Investments, and TD Waterhouse. The latter method can work very well, especially if the funds you are considering are part of the broker's no-load, no-transaction-fee (NTF) programs. Chapter 4, which is devoted to these virtual fund supermarkets, will show you how to use them most effectively.

KEEPING TRACK OF YOUR HOLDINGS

After buying your funds, you'll want to keep track of how they perform on a regular basis, usually once a quarter. What you are looking for is how your funds compare to their peers. In other words, don't judge a bond fund next to the S&P 500. Do compare a small-cap fund to the Russell 2000 index, which is the benchmark for small-cap stocks. Find out whether your funds are keeping up with the averages. Ideally, your funds should be running

HOW TO READ THE NEWSPAPER FUND TABLES

② — Mutual Funds — ❸

Name	NAV	Net Chg	YTD % Ret
❶ WonderFund	7.24	−.03	+2.3
BestFund	10.04	+.13	+5.8
TechFund	8.54	−.01	+7.8
BondFund	3.32	+.22	+1.5

1. This is the name of the fund. In some papers, the listing begins with the name of the fund family in bold, with each individual fund printed below it.

2. This is the fund's net asset value (NAV).

3. This is the difference between the closing NAV price today versus yesterday.

4. This is the fund's year-to-date total return, expressed as a percentage.

ahead of them. If not, you must find out why. Is the manager just having a bad quarter? Is the fund overconcentrated in a lagging sector? Has the fund's manager changed? Have assets bloated the portfolio to the point where the fund is no longer nimble? Once you've answered these questions, you can determine whether to hang on or move on. It's normally not recommended that you sell a fund unless it has underperformed for at least 18 months. This particular timeline makes sense for two reasons: (1) you will be able to take advantage of the maximum 20 percent capital-gain rule when you sell, and (2) more important, all managers underperform at one point or another. Funds are designed to be a long-term investment. What's 18 months when your time horizon might be 20, 30, or even 40 years or more? Giving a good manager 18 months to get back into shape is often a wise investment decision.

2

FINDING THE FUND THAT'S RIGHT FOR YOU

Given that there are thousands of stock, bond, and money market funds currently available, finding the true gems in this enormous mix is a daunting task. After all, funds now outnumber stocks on all of the major exchanges combined. Not to worry. This chapter will give you some guidelines to help you narrow down the field of choices and make smart decisions about which funds are best for you.

This chapter offers several tips to keep in mind when you are scouring the field of contenders, broken down by the characteristics to look for in each asset class—namely, stocks, bonds, and money market funds. That's because traits you must find in stock funds don't necessarily apply for bond funds, and vice versa.

ALWAYS REMEMBER: GO NO-LOAD

The overriding rule you should adhere to, regardless of which type of fund you buy, is: Always stick with no-loads. There is no reason to pay a sales commission to purchase or sell a fund you have selected on your own. Nothing against the folks who peddle load funds. They're entitled to make a living. But that commission comes out of your pocket and goes into theirs. If you're making the selections on your own, there is no reason to pay them. When you buy a load fund, not only is some of your principal immediately wiped away, but you risk poor performance to boot. Without question, there are some fantastic load funds. Nevertheless, for every terrific load fund, you can almost always find an equally fine no-load alternative.

So, repeat this line: "I will never pay a load to buy or sell a fund that I have selected on my own." By following this rule, you can immediately cut in half the total number of funds you have to sift through when narrowing down your list of choices. This alone makes the job of analyzing funds much easier—and we haven't even delved into the good stuff yet!

STOCK FUND SELECTION

═══Let's begin with the process of finding equity funds. This is the asset class that requires the most analytical work on your part, because there are so many variables to consider. Remember, a mutual fund is nothing more than one large portfolio with the collective assets (stocks and other securities) of hundreds or even thousands of shareholders. You are paying for the manager's expertise in selecting the right investments for the portfolio. Therefore, the first thing to keep in mind when hunting for an actively managed stock fund is that *the manager is everything*.

PROVEN MANAGEMENT

You want a manager with a proven track record of beating his or her peers for a number of years—at least five and the longer the better. The manager doesn't necessarily have to be at a particular fund for five years. Some of the best investments available are new funds run by experienced managers who have a long history of outperformance. Tom Marsico is a good example. His Marsico Focus fund, one of the "100 Powerhouse Performers," began at the beginning of 1998. However, Marsico spent almost a decade running the Janus Twenty fund, where he racked up a tremendous record. So while it wasn't possible to go back five years to see how Marsico Focus performed when it first launched, you could evaluate manager Tom Marsico's record for a much longer period by studying the Janus fund. As it turned out, he has been able to continue his winning ways.

Some people fall into the trap of buying funds after reading an ad or article, without checking whether the manager who posted the touted numbers is still in place. Surprisingly, in many cases the manager has moved on. Make sure the manager of a fund you are considering has at least a five-year track record. If necessary, call and ask the fund. If you're told the manager has been at the fund for a shorter period of time, ask which fund he or she managed before that. If the answer is "only private accounts," demand to see the manager's performance record going back as far as possible. If you're told the manager just got out of school, move on to another selection.

A Record of Outperformance

A famous line appears in every fund advertisement and prospectus: "Past performance is no guarantee of future results." This is absolutely true. Just because a manager has been beating the market for the past five years doesn't mean he or she will continue to do so during the next five. But past perfor-

FUND MANAGERS: AN UP-CLOSE LOOK

What exactly happens to your hard-earned money after you send it to your favorite fund? To whom are you entrusting your financial future, and what do these folks do with your money? Beyond that, what does it take to become a fund manager? Brains, good looks, financial savvy, luck, good genes, an Ivy League education, or all of the above?

First, when most funds get your money, they place it with a custodian, like a bank, for safekeeping. Then the fund manager uses it to buy additional securities for the portfolio, based on the rules of the prospectus. (In other words, if it's a stock portfolio, the manager will buy stocks. If it's a fixed-income fund, bonds will most likely be added.)

The background of each fund manager is quite different. Some received degrees from prestigious universities, earned MBAs, and have a family pedigree of investment genius. Others are high school graduates who happened to be in the right place at the right time. No one trait tells you up front whether a fund manager is going to be a brilliant stock picker, but it is certainly encouraging to come across someone with good educational credentials and a pristine performance record to boot.

Also, the most successful managers remain true to their discipline. In other words, if they use value techniques, they never stray into growth stocks just because value happens to be temporarily out of favor. And, perhaps most importantly, great managers have a real passion for what they do.

mance is the only indicator of what the future might hold. It tells you what kind of ability a manager has. If the record shows his or her fund continually lags the market, there is no reason to believe that pattern will change anytime soon. On the other hand, if you find a manager who hits the lights out year after year, you know something is going right. Performance in sports is similar. If a certain player can be relied on for continually scoring, you expect that level of play during every game. Steady performance sets other standards as well. If you're a good driver with a track record of avoiding accidents, your insurance company will reduce the amount of your premium. If you're applying for a loan and have a clean credit report, you'll probably be approved. The lender will check your previous credit history to evaluate whether you're a good risk for the future. So, despite what the SEC-mandated warning tells us, a manager's past performance is our only indication of the future results we can expect. The returns from each fund vary, but we can determine that the manager has a demonstrated trend of outperformance.

In the earlier discussion about evaluating managers, we said to make sure they had a record of besting their *peers*, not the S&P 500 index, which is the benchmark most media sources and investment advisers refer to. The S&P 500 is a market-weighted index composed primarily of large-cap stocks. Broad market conditions affect all stocks (i.e., when one index goes up, the rest usually follow), but, during certain periods, small-caps and mid-caps can perform much differently than their large-cap brethren. Consider what happened with U.S. stocks in the late 1990s. Large-caps, as a group, far outshined small-caps. Therefore, if you compared a small-cap fund to the S&P 500 back then, you might have concluded that the manager fell asleep at the wheel. Instead, you must stack like against like. Large-cap funds should be evaluated next to the S&P 500, which is an appropriate benchmark. Small-cap funds, however, are better compared to the Russell 2000.

You also need to check how funds compare to their peers in the same category. Lipper Analytical maintains "category" indexes that are published regularly in the mutual fund section of *The Wall Street Journal*. For a quick feel for how a fund has stacked up against its peers, look at its overall Value Line rank, included as part of the performance data in Chapter 8. This number takes both performance and risk into consideration. On a scale of 1 through 5, all other things being equal, look for a fund ranked 1 or 2. A higher number may mean something is wrong. (The Value Line rank is based on performance over a five-year period, so make sure the manager who achieved it is still at the helm. If not, these performance statistics are essentially worthless as a predictor for how the fund might do in the future.)

REASONABLE EXPENSE RATIO

Up to this point, we have talked exclusively about evaluating actively managed funds. Let's review the parameters for selecting stock index funds. Because these investments are run by a computer, issues concerning management and performance are less important. After all, an index fund, by definition, can't beat its benchmark. Therefore, a key factor to look for in an index fund is its expense ratio. The lower, the better.

Now let's turn to actively managed funds. Low expense ratios are preferable here, too, though it's sometimes wise to pay a bit more for performance. In other words, if a manager consistently makes money and beats the competition, don't quibble too much over the expense ratio. Plenty of funds have low expense ratios and poor track records. On the other hand, there are funds with above-average costs that whip the socks off the competition. (Of course, there are plenty of high expense funds that are dogs, so do a careful analysis before investing.) Generally speaking, look for stock funds with expense ratios of less than 1.3 percent. For large-cap U.S. stocks, that number should be even lower. When the topic is international equity funds, the expense ratio often reaches toward 2 percent, because of the added cost of researching foreign securities. The lower, the better; but don't avoid a quality manager because of expenses alone.

LOW TURNOVER

Earlier, we discussed how low turnover often helps to reduce year-end capital gains distributions and keeps your tax liability down. But there's another reason to favor low-turnover funds. Each time a manager buys or sells a stock in the portfolio, a trading commission must be paid, and that fee is not reflected in the fund's expense ratio. Excessive trading can shave several percentage points off a fund's annual performance.

Low-turnover funds also tend to do better over time because buy-and-hold investors usually make more money in stocks than do frequent traders. If you don't believe that, just ask a guy named Warren Buffett. One of the most successful funds in history is the Sequoia Fund, which has a mere 4 percent annual turnover. Sequoia manager Bill Ruane adheres to Buffett's teachings in running the portfolio, and the fund's largest holding is Buffett's Berkshire Hathaway. Unfortunately, Sequoia has long been closed to new investors, which is why it's not one of the "100 Powerhouse Performers." Not all high-turnover funds are bad, but less frequent trading seems to be a huge advantage.

MANAGEABLE ASSET BASE

Is it possible for a mutual fund portfolio to grow too large? That's a debatable question that has yet to be decisively answered. There are plenty of tiny funds (in terms of asset size) that have been dismal performers for years. At the same time, a number of very large funds offer excellent returns. Still, at some point, size does seem to become an issue for funds, especially those investing in small-cap stocks. Several reasons can be offered. To begin with, the more money a fund attracts, the more stocks a manager normally has to buy. Each time another name is added, the performance punch provided by the biggest winners is diluted. As a portfolio grows in size, the research efforts get severely squeezed. It's hard for managers to do quality research on hundreds of different companies, while staying on top of every new development.

An even greater problem for small-cap funds is liquidity. Many companies in this universe have market capitalizations (market price multiplied by the number of shares outstanding) of less than $100 million. Diversified funds, by law, cannot have an ownership position of more than 5 percent in any one company, so a $1 billion small-cap fund will have to own a large number of names to meet this requirement. In addition, small-cap stocks tend to be less liquid than their larger counterparts. If a fund manager holds a significant position in any one company, it may be difficult for the fund to get out without severely lowering the share price—if buyers can even be found. Fidelity Investments, the fund giant, apparently concurs that, at some point, fund size is an issue. In 1997, the company closed its flagship Magellan Fund to new investors, after years of subpar performance. Then, in 1998, Fidelity shut the doors to its Contrafund and Low-Priced Stock funds, which also began to experience floundering returns after reaching assets of $30 billion and $10 billion, respectively. (Contrafund and Low-Priced Stock have since reopened.)

Large-cap funds often start to lose their ability to be effective after hitting around $10 billion in assets. However, for small-cap funds, that cutoff amount is much less. Most analysts grow uncomfortable when a small-cap fund gets larger than $500 million, put it on close watch after it hits the $1 billion mark, and almost always sell by the time it gets up to $2 billion. Many are convinced that small-cap funds with assets greater than $1 billion, and certainly above $2 billion, can provide shareholders with little more than average performance at best, because of the severe limitations placed on the manager. Almost every small-cap fund larger than $2 billion has been forced to change its focus from small-cap companies to either mid-cap or large-cap companies, which defeats the purpose of buying the fund in the first place.

Below small-caps is a category called micro-caps. In terms of market capitalization, these are the tiniest stocks available to investors. Some of these companies could have capitalizations as low as $10 million. It's advisable to avoid any micro-cap fund larger than $300 million in assets; the smaller, the better. As for mid-cap funds, the $2 billion mark is about the limit for maximum effectiveness because, again, there are liquidity issues.

TAX EFFICIENCY

We won't cover the whole issue of mutual funds and taxes again, other than to remind you that funds distribute taxable gains at the end of each year. You should favor funds that try to keep distributions to an absolute minimum when investing for a taxable account. In retirement plans, this isn't an issue because all distributions are tax-deferred anyway. Low-turnover funds generally have the highest tax efficiency.

AFFORDABLE INVESTMENT REQUIREMENT

When evaluating stock funds, the final item to check is the minimum investment amount needed to open an account. Although the average fund requires around $2,500, some let you in for as little as $100, and others make you pony up at least $1 million. You should also check the fund's minimum amount for additional contributions, especially if you want to set up a dollar-cost averaging program. Dollar-cost averaging calls for adding a set amount of money to your favorite funds on a regular basis, which enables you to take advantage of market fluctuations. We'll tell you more about this technique in Chapter 6, when we discuss how to structure your personal portfolio.

THE QUANTITATIVE VARIABLES

In addition to these more fundamental characteristics, you should also take a look at a slew of quantitative statistics for each fund. This analysis can be quite complex, and well beyond the means of most individual investors. The two numbers you should pay attention to are alpha and beta. To get these figures, you'll need to use one of the more advanced fund-screening tools on the market today, such as the *Value Line Mutual Fund Survey*. (Note that beta is provided for each of the "100 Powerhouse Performers" in this book.)

In essence, alpha tells you how much value the manager has added to performance, outside of just being in the market. In other words, when the overall market goes up, so do most stock funds. Alpha tells you how much of a fund's return was due to market forces versus stock picking brilliance on the part of the manager. The higher the alpha relative to the market, the better.

Beta gives you an idea of how volatile a fund is compared to the general market. For instance, the S&P 500 has a beta of 1. A fund with a beta below 1 is less volatile than the S&P, while a fund with a higher beta tends to be much riskier. Therefore, you should expect funds with high betas to go up more than the market in rising periods, and down more when stocks fall.

As an individual investor, beta will likely prove to be a much more useful number. If you want to temper the volatility of your portfolio, look for funds with a low beta. Similarly, if you're considering a fund with stellar returns but an extremely high beta, you should expect some wild and bumpy rides over time. In a perfect world, every fund you buy would have a rare combination of high performance with a low relative beta. And if the same funds had high alphas, too, you'd really be on to something!

BOND FUNDS

What should you look for when choosing a bond or fixed-income fund? Think of buying bonds as being the same as lending money to a company or a government. As a lender, you are paid a set interest rate, usually between 1 and 5 percent today, depending on the credit quality of the issuer. Short-term bonds are safer and fluctuate less, but they come with a lower yield. Long-term bonds pay more but are highly volatile, especially in times of rising interest rates. Bonds are most suitable for investors seeking to generate income in their portfolios. They can also serve as an added form of diversification, if you want to move away from stocks. When evaluating bond funds, look for low expense ratios, credit quality, and favorable maturities.

Low Expense Ratios

Choosing bonds for a portfolio doesn't take nearly as much analysis as is required for stocks. Therefore, you should expect to pay the manager of a bond fund less than a manager who picks stocks. As a result, all other things being equal, favor bond funds with the lowest expense ratios. Yields today are low to begin with, and high management fees can quickly eat up your overall returns. If you're investing in short-term Treasuries, for example, the portfolio might be expected to throw off little more than 3 percent a year in interest. If you're paying 1 percent of that for expenses, your return instantly drops to 2 percent or less. Look for bond funds with annual expenses below 0.5 percent and never pay higher than 1 percent of assets. Depending on your needs, you might also consider buying bonds directly from a discount broker, especially if you plan to hold on through maturity. In that way, you'll avoid paying management fees altogether. (The one exception, which we'll get to in a moment, is high-yield or "junk" bonds. Because these are so risky, you're often better off buying them through a fund.)

CREDIT QUALITY

It's pretty much a given that the higher the yield offered by a bond fund, the lower the credit quality of the securities in the portfolio. This stands to reason; high-risk companies are forced to pay a premium to borrow money. If you're determined to invest in high-yield bonds, the best way to do it is through a fund. Diversify widely in this area of the market, especially if it looks like the economy could be slowing down or even heading into a recession. Before getting in, understand that if you buy a portfolio of low credit quality, you can expect a heightened degree of volatility, similar to what you would get from a typical stock fund.

FAVORABLE MATURITIES

Bond funds have an inverse relationship to interest rates. As rates rise, bond prices fall. The opposite is also true. If this doesn't make sense at first glance, let's illustrate why this relationship exists: If you buy a bond today at par, or $1,000, offering a 4 percent yield, and tomorrow interest rates rise to 4.2 percent, no one will pay you $1,000 to buy that 4 percent bond. The value of the bond must fall, to compensate for the higher rate one can get on new issues. If a buyer gives you only $950 for that $1,000 bond, the 4 percent yield is suddenly worth more because you're still earning 4 percent annually on $1,000, which translates into an effective yield of 4.2 percent. The point here is: The longer the maturity on a bond or bond fund, the more interest rate risk you take. If you'll need your money in less than two years, by all means buy only short-term bond funds. In today's low-interest-rate environment, where the chances are that rates will go up before they go down much more, it makes sense to favor short-term and intermediate-term maturities, even if you have a long investment horizon. In addition to short-term bond and Treasury funds, you might also consider Ginnie Maes (GNMAs, or Government National Mortgage Association bonds), which are mortgage-backed securities with intermediate-term maturities.

MONEY MARKET FUNDS

═══With bank certificates of deposit and savings passbooks offering such paltry interest rates these days, you would be wise to consider putting your liquid cash into a carefully selected money market fund. Almost every major fund family, broker, and bank has at least one to choose from. You can select from regular taxable funds, U.S. government funds (which are often exempt from state taxes), and municipal funds (which may be exempt from both state and federal taxes). Money market portfolios are comprised primarily of short-term bonds and other cash-equivalent instruments, and are designed to offer higher returns while maintaining a steady per-share net asset value of $1. Unlike traditional bank accounts, these funds are not insured by the government, but they have historically been just as safe.

QUALITY COMPANIES

How do you choose a money market fund? For one thing, because money market deposits aren't insured, invest in funds sponsored by companies of integrity. You probably can't go wrong with any of the major brokers or recognized fund families. The reason that's important is this: Only twice in recent memory have credit defaults threatened to push a money market fund's net asset value below the magic $1 level. In both cases, the fund management company stepped in and made up the difference, preventing this from happening. Big firms know that letting their money market funds dip under $1 would do irreparable harm; clients would fear for the safety of the entire organization. Therefore, they simply won't let it happen.

HIGH YIELD

Do some research to find the fund with the highest yield. Because there isn't much wiggle room with the securities in a portfolio, funds with the lowest operating expenses almost always have the highest yields. Funds at the top of the yield list often waive some or all of their management fees to attract new assets. It's up to you to keep an eye on the date when those fees kick back in, so you can move to another fund if the yield becomes less competitive. You can find the highest yielding funds on a regular basis in publications like *The Wall Street Journal* or *Barron's*, and by visiting the iMoneyNet site at www.imoneynet.com (a profile of the IBC site is given in Chapter 7).

CONVENIENCE

Because money market funds are generally used as short-term parking places, you want those that give you easy access to your money. Most funds offer some kind of check-writing feature, but look at the rules for this very closely. A few funds cap the number of checks you can write each month; others impose a minimum amount ($500 or more) on each check. Some funds offer ATM card access to your account and other perks that make them more like regular bank checking accounts. You'll normally find that the more perks you are offered, the lower the yield. But that's not always the case, so be sure to shop around.

SELL STRATEGY

Up to this point, the sole focus of this chapter has been on what to look for when deciding to buy a fund. It's equally important to know when to sell. Here are several good reasons for getting rid of one fund and replacing it with another.

- **A new manager arrives**. If the manager of a fund you own moves on, you should, too, unless he or she is replaced by someone whose track record you admire just as much.

- **A better fund comes along**. If you stumble across a fund that's even more attractive than the one you currently own, it might make sense to switch, especially if the new fund is run by a seasoned manager.

- **You need the money**. This is a no-brainer reason. If you're saving money for a long-term goal such as retirement, you will have to sell your fund when your day of need ultimately arrives.

- **Expenses are too high**. Occasionally, funds will actually raise the expense ratio, usually for a nonsensical reason. If that happens with your fund, get out.

- **You spot underperformance**. Every manager goes through bad periods. It's reasonable to give managers 18 months to get their acts together. If they are still underperforming their peers and comparative benchmarks after that, they probably should get the boot.

- **Tax efficiency is missing.** If you're investing your money in a taxable account and the year-end distributions are unreasonably high, it might be wise to switch into a more tax-efficient fund.

- **Asset allocation is skewed.** We'll get into asset allocation in Chapter 6. Suffice it to say, if the particular fund you own no longer fits your desired asset mix, it's time to move on. (In other words, if you need to reduce your overall exposure to stocks, you may have to trade a stock fund for a bond fund to get things into balance.)

- **Style drifts occur.** If you bought a small-cap fund that has grown so large it now concentrates on mid-cap stocks, you may want to replace it with a true small-cap offering. Alternatively, if a manager who used to concentrate on value stocks suddenly turns into a growth investor, see the move as a red flag that something's wrong.

- **The fund has become too big.** As a general rule, funds with comparatively tiny asset bases have the potential to perform better than larger ones. This is especially true in the small-cap area. You should consider selling micro-cap funds if assets grow much past $500 million, small-caps after $1 billion, mid-caps after $2 billion, and most funds bigger than $10 billion. There are always exceptions to this rule, but these are good guidelines.

- **You own too many funds.** If you have a tendency to fall in love with funds, you might want to do some housecleaning. No matter how much money you have to invest, you probably don't need to own more than six to ten funds. If you're above that limit, consider cutting back.

THE SEVEN DEADLY SINS OF MUTUAL FUND INVESTING

1. BUYING LAST YEAR'S HOT PERFORMER

Many investors falsely believe that buying the fund that did best during the previous year is a smart move. They figure the manager will continue to post the same incredible numbers, and they don't want to miss the ride. The sad truth is: Time and time again, one year's winner turns into the next year's dog. Among the many reasons for this reversal: "star managers" tend to get inundated with new cash, which can disrupt the portfolio and hurt existing shareholders.

2. TIMING THE MARKET

This is clearly a loser's game. No one is able to consistently forecast the direction of the market. That's why it pays to stick with your strategy and stay fully invested at all times. In the 1980s, the annual return on stocks in the S&P 500 index was 17.6 percent. During that period, if you were in cash on the top ten trading days, your return dropped to 12.6 percent. Had you been on the sidelines for the 20 best days, you earned only 9.3 percent. And if you missed the 30 biggest advancing sessions, your return plummeted to 6.5 percent. Especially when it comes to stocks, not being fully invested is costly. It would be great to avoid major market declines and bear markets. Unfortunately, this cannot be done with any degree of accuracy.

3. BLINDLY FOLLOWING THE STARS

Based on all of the fund advertising that's out there today, you might think a fund with four or five stars from a rating service like Morningstar is a surefire winner. The truth is, even the president of Morningstar will tell you that the company's rating system is far from perfect, and that picking a fund solely because of the number of stars it has been given is a loser's game. The Morningstar system is based on risk-adjusted past performance, which has very little predictive value. The manager who earned the stars may no longer be there. Think in terms of buying managers, not funds, and never rely exclusively on a simplistic rating system for advice, especially without doing further research on your own. You might build a lousy portfolio by buying only five-star funds.

4. PURCHASING FUNDS, NOT MANAGERS

Looking at a fund's track record is not enough. Some of the best-performing funds are those that have been around for just a few years but are spearheaded by veteran managers who have outstanding long-term records. New funds run by seasoned talent can be some of the best. Good managers tend to get a lot of money sent their way, which can bloat their portfolios and hamper performance. When these luminaries launch a new fund, they're able to start with a clean slate. Take advantage of their talents while the fund is still small and nimble.

5. Falling for the Media's "Fund Darling of the Month"

Members of the media are extremely short-term oriented. The mainstream press usually won't feature a fund until it is poised to underperform. Here's why: They wait until a fund builds a hot short-term performance record, then they do a big write-up on it. Fresh money flows in, and the portfolio manager gets overwhelmed with new cash and underwhelmed with places to put it. As a result, performance usually plummets. It can take years for that situation to reverse itself.

6. Focusing on Quantity, Instead of Quality

It's a common belief that by simply owning eight or ten different funds, an investor is properly diversified. Unfortunately, that kind of portfolio may not be diversified at all. The reason: Funds with similar investment objectives often hold the same stocks. For example, suppose you own 10 different aggressive growth funds. Your diversification is very limited because you are exposed to only one area of the market. Without question, asset allocation decisions are a critical starting point for constructing a well-rounded investment plan.

7. Taking Your Eye Off the Ball

Investors often think they can buy a great fund and never look at it again. There are many flaws with that kind of logic. The fund industry is constantly changing, and you need to keep up with it. The manager running a fund when you bought it may move on and be replaced by a lesser practitioner. That's one of several good reasons to get out. Or, as we've already discussed, funds may grow too large for their own good. Some managers lose their focus or change their investment strategy, which often leads to abysmal results. You should always keep an eye on your fund and be ready to pull the trigger if necessary.

3

INDEX FUNDS—
BETTER THAN
ACTIVE MANAGEMENT?

Once considered inferior investments suitable only for those who didn't know any better, index funds are now among the darlings of the mutual fund industry. Index funds used to be publicly berated by mainstream money managers and stock brokerage houses alike. In fact, for almost two decades, the Vanguard Group was the only major fund company that even offered index funds to the public.

How things have changed! Index funds began to find big-time favor with both Main Street and Wall Street in the late 1990s. That's when investors started to realize what had been true all along: Index funds tend to outperform actively managed funds some 70 percent of the time. From 1996–1998, the percentage of outperformance, as measured by the Standard & Poor's 500 index, was closer to 90 percent.

Once this fact became evident, index funds really moved into the spotlight. They were soon touted on the covers of one personal finance magazine after another. Even mainstream magazines—such as *Time*, *Newsweek*, and *Esquire*—began to tell how wonderful index funds were. And, in a startling development, major actively managed fund sponsors—including Fidelity, T. Rowe Price, and Dean Witter—began to roll out and tout index fund offerings of their own. To show you how much favor index funds have found among investors, Vanguard's Index 500 Portfolio is now the second largest stock fund in the country.

WHAT ARE INDEX FUNDS ANYWAY?

≡≡≡Many people are talking about them, but most investors have no idea what index funds are, nor do they understand exactly how they work. They may know that their fund is tied to a benchmark like the Standard & Poor's 500 index (S&P 500, for short), but what does that mean?

First, it's important to realize that index funds are referred to in the industry as "passively managed" investments. In other words, they are based solely on computer models set up to replicate a given index. And there are plenty of indexes to choose from. On the stock side, some choices are: the S&P 500; Dow Jones Industrial Average; Russell 2000; Wilshire 4500; Wilshire 5000; Morgan Stanley International; and Europe, Australasia, and Far East (EAFE) index. The list goes on and on. (Incidentally, the vast majority of stock funds today are tied to the S&P 500.) Fixed-income investors also have several indexes to choose from, most notably the Lehman Brothers Aggregate Bond index.

An index fund is comprised of either a complete or a representative sample of the stocks or bonds found in the underlying index. For example, the ideal S&P 500 fund would hold proper weightings of each of the 500 funds found in the index.

A Look Inside the Indexes

As previously mentioned, there are many different market benchmarks out there. What follows are brief descriptions of several of the major indexes.

S&P 500

By far the most common index used in the fund industry, the S&P 500 holds a basket of 500 stocks. It is designed to mirror the large-capitalization sector of the U.S. equity market. The S&P 500 represents about 70 percent of the value of the entire market. But it's not necessarily composed of the 500 largest companies. Instead, an eight-member panel selected by Standard & Poor's is responsible for hand-picking which companies are listed in the index, and the list does change from time to time. The committee makes its selections based on market value, company financial conditions, and trading liquidity; it isn't looking for the next hot stock. The goal is to have the index properly represent the country's leading industries. At last check, the S&P

500 was comprised of about 380 industrial, 70 financial, 40 utility, and 10 transportation issues. The S&P 500 is a market-weighted index: the higher a company's market valuation, the more emphasis it is given in the index. Therefore, the stocks of the biggest companies are weighted more heavily and drive a large portion of the index's performance. Among the companies with the most substantial weightings in the S&P 500 are:

Microsoft	(3.3 percent)
General Electric	(3.2 percent)
ExxonMobil	(3.0 percent)
Wal-Mart Stores	(2.9 percent)
Pfizer	(2.4 percent)
Citigroup	(2.2 percent)
Johnson & Johnson	(2.2 percent)
IBM	(1.7 percent)
American Intl. Group	(1.6 percent)
Merck	(1.6 percent)

The largest 60 stocks make up about half of the value of the index. Therefore, if these 60 stocks were all down 20 percent for the year, and the remaining 440 were up 20 percent, the S&P 500 would merely break even.

DOW JONES INDUSTRIAL AVERAGE

The Dow Jones Industrial Average (DJIA, or "The Dow"), by contrast, is a price-weighted index. This means that the higher the share price of a stock in the index, the greater the influence it has. Accordingly, a big change in a single company can give a false reading for how the overall market is behaving. The Dow is the most often quoted index in the media today. It was born in 1884, when a journalist named Charles Dow compiled a list of 11 companies and tracked their performance. Two years later, he increased the number of stocks to 12 and began publishing their performance in the pages of a publication he called *The Wall Street Journal*. He wanted readers to get a better feel for what was going on in the stock market. Back then, most of the DJIA's representative companies were in the railroad industry. By 1916, the number of stocks in the DJIA had grown to 20, before leaping to 30 (the current number) in 1928. The 30 stocks listed have changed over the years, either to align with the economy or in response to acquisitions and other events that make previous choices all but irrelevant. As just one example, the DJIA now includes a number of technology companies, reflecting our evolution from a manufacturing-based to a technology-based economy.

RUSSELL 2000

This index is made up of the stocks of small, unseasoned U.S. companies. It is generally considered the best indicator of how the NASDAQ market, and small-cap stocks in general, are doing. NASDAQ stands for National Association of Securities Dealers Automated Quotation System. (You can see why they just call it NASDAQ.) This index is weighted by market value and represents domestic companies that are traded over-the-counter.

WILSHIRE 5000

Despite its name, the Wilshire 5000 tracks more than 6,000 publicly traded securities. It is therefore the most accurate measure of the health of the overall market, and the most diversified index available. Roughly 70 percent of the stocks in the Wilshire 5000 are large-caps; the remaining 30 percent are mid- and small-caps. This benchmark's cousin, the Wilshire 4500, tracks 4,500 stocks that are not part of the S&P 500.

A BRIEF HISTORY OF INDEX FUNDS

The formation of index funds can be traced back to July 1971, when Wells Fargo Bank launched a $6 million fund to manage the pension assets of luggage-maker Samsonite. This fund held an equal amount of every company listed on the New York Stock Exchange. Two years later, Wells Fargo began the first index fund tied to the S&P 500. Both funds were the creation of William Fouse, a jazz saxophonist-turned-banker from West Virginia. Fouse initially developed this electronically driven strategy for picking stocks while working at the Pittsburgh-based Mellon Bank in the late 1960s. But when he suggested that Mellon start a fund run entirely by computer, without analysis by a human manager, he was asked to leave. Ironically, Fouse later returned to Mellon, which now runs a number of index funds of its own under its Dreyfus Funds arm.

Retail investors were given their first chance to invest in index funds in

1976, when Vanguard launched the First Index Investment Trust, which was tied to the S&P 500. This fund was originally sold exclusively through brokers and carried a hefty 6 percent load. One year later, at the urging of Vanguard founder John Bogle, the fund became a no-load. Because of the Trust's limited assets in the beginning, the initial portfolio contained only 280 stocks—the 200 largest, plus 80 selected by various optimization models designed to roughly match the remaining companies in the index.

Bogle's timing couldn't have been worse. After outperforming nearly 70 percent of all equity funds from 1972 to 1976, index funds underperformed 75 percent of active managers from 1977 to 1979. "This sort of reversal in form, which seems to plague all new fund concepts, is hardly surprising," Bogle says in retrospect. By 1982, the Trust had $100 million in assets, but only because it merged with another fund. Fortunately for Vanguard, this was right at the start of a boom in the stock market that has continued to this day. Index funds soon bounced back to the top of the rankings. By 1990, there were 43 registered index funds, including two from Fidelity, which, before, touted nothing but the advantages of active management.

Still, index funds never quite caught on with the public until around 1995. By then, they had racked up a string of stellar returns. From 1994 to 1996, index funds tied to the S&P 500 outpaced 91 percent of all actively managed offerings. As usual, money followed performance. When this fact was noticed by the media, one story after another began proclaiming how index funds were the next best thing to nirvana. Suddenly, Vanguard's Bogle was a hero, even though he had been preaching the merits of indexing for several decades. And, as index funds rose in notoriety, so did the number of available funds. Today, there are dozens of index funds, tracking virtually every benchmark you can think of, including one just for socially-conscious investors.

Index fund investing is predicated on two beliefs: (1) the market is too efficient to beat, and (2) investors can do no better than the market because they are the market. This idea was further popularized in a 1973 book, *A Random Walk Down Wall Street*, by Princeton University Professor Burton S. Malkiel, who has long been a strong advocate of index funds.

WHY BUY INDEX FUNDS?

There are several reasons why you might want to include index funds in your portfolio. For one thing, most index funds operate at bare-bones expenses. Vanguard's Index 500 charges just .18 percent of assets. That's some

1 percent less than you would pay to own the average actively managed stock fund. The reason index funds are cheaper is simple—a computer runs the show. Fund companies don't have to pay computers the seven-figure salaries that good human managers pull down. As a result, index funds normally get a huge 1 percent head start right at the beginning.

Second, index funds are generally highly tax-efficient. As mentioned earlier, funds have to distribute all of their capital gains and dividends to shareholders at the end of each year. If your money is not in a tax-deferred account, this can add a significant bite to your tax bill. Index funds, on the other hand, rarely pay out any gains because their portfolio turnover is so low. (Managers of such funds sell a stock only when they must meet redemptions or make necessary adjustments to stay in line with the index.) Therefore, if you are looking to keep your year-end distributions to an absolute minimum, index funds make a lot of sense.

Third, fund managers change jobs with the speed of a Texas tornado these days. With an index fund, the manager is not as important because the fund is run entirely by a computer. Therefore, if you want to buy and hold and forget about your investments until you're ready to touch the money years down the line, index funds may be right for you.

Because you aren't paying for management expertise, a low expense ratio should be your number-one concern when selecting an index fund. All other things being equal, go with the fund that offers the lowest expenses for the benchmark you are trying to track. Index funds from the Vanguard Group are often very cost-efficient, although several other companies have been lowering their expenses to become more competitive. And *never* pay a sales load to buy an index fund.

THE DOWNSIDE OF INDEX FUNDS

The main argument against owning index funds is that, by definition, you will never be able to outperform the index you are tracking. By contrast, actively managed funds always have a shot at earning more. Granted, many actively managed funds underperform these passive indexes over time. However, a number of brilliant stock pickers have proven themselves capable of consistently managing to outperform the indexes. If you're willing to do the work to find them (this book will be an enormous help in that pursuit), over the long haul you will have the potential to outperform the indexes by a respectable margin. (Even a percentage or two, in the long term, can add significantly to your net worth.)

ENHANCED INDEX FUNDS

═══Some fund families have come up with a compromise between the active and passive approaches. They have introduced so-called "enhanced index" funds. In essence, such funds mirror most aspects of the index but try to do something different in an effort to produce market-beating returns. (Remember, true index funds can never outperform their benchmark.) The most common technique used by such funds is complicated and exotic: they buy futures contracts as a way of arbitraging the index. "An S&P 500 enhanced index fund might, for example, invest in the S&P 500 stocks and then switch the portfolio into S&P 500 futures contracts when those contracts are undervalued relative to the stocks," notes a study prepared by Ibbotson Associates, a fund consulting group in Chicago. The study is entitled "Are Enhanced Index Mutual Funds Worthy of Their Name?" Its conclusion? "No, most of them are not worthy." As the Ibbotson study also points out, an enhanced index fund is really actively managed. If you're not replicating the stated benchmark exactly, you're not really running an index fund. As for returns, Ibbotson found that a majority of the enhanced funds it examined underperformed their respective indexes—in some cases, by a considerable margin.

FINAL THOUGHTS ABOUT INDEXING

═══Is indexing right for you? That, of course, is a personal decision only you can make. By now, you should have a good feel for what indexing is, how it works, what kinds of stocks are in the various indexes, and the pros and cons of this approach. Before ending this chapter, here are some additional thoughts for you to consider.

For starters, index funds—particularly those tied to the U.S. market—will likely remain admirable performers in the future. This belief, in large part, is based on a conviction that the U.S. stock market will continue to rise over time, and those willing to take the risk of investing in equities will be richly rewarded. As a result, it makes perfect sense to hold an S&P 500 or Wilshire 5000 index fund as a core position in your portfolio. It's a fine substitute for almost any large-cap mutual fund you will come across. For small-cap and foreign investing, however, research shows you are generally better off with actively managed funds. Over the past 10 years, more than half of all diversified international stock funds have whipped the performance of the Morgan Stanley Capital International Europe, Australasia, Far East (EAFE) index. And U.S. small-caps are much less efficient than their large-cap brethren, making it possible for active managers to shoot the lights out with selected issues.

If you want a truly passive approach that will allow you to participate in the rise of the market without doing any research to uncover the most promising funds available, indexing may be right for you. Should you opt to go this route, here's a suggestion: If you're going to buy only one fund, consider one that tracks the Wilshire 5000, instead of the S&P 500. In that way, you'll get exposure to all areas of the market, not just large-cap stocks. The Wilshire 5000 is also much more diversified because the biggest companies are not weighted as heavily. The best funds in this category are Vanguard Total Stock Market and the Fidelity Spartan Total Market Index. Both are among the "100 Powerhouse Performers." As noted in the profile for these funds in Chapter 5, either could be the sole holding for the U.S. equity portion of your portfolio, especially if you have a relatively modest amount of money to invest.

With a little work on your part and with the help of this book, you can beat the indexes by investing in outstanding funds run by the best stock pickers in the business. A study compiled by a financial consulting firm, Evaluation Associates, affirms this. It found that the S&P 500, the index against which most funds are measured, beat less than half of all actively managed large-cap funds during rolling five-year periods from 1981 to 1996. So, while it makes good sense to consider putting a core position of your portfolio in an index fund, to ensure that you'll never significantly underperform the market, a more active approach to investing is not only more fun, but also offers the potential to produce greater results over time.

4

SHOPPING AT THE FUND SUPERMARKETS

We learn early that there's no such thing as a free lunch. But when it comes to buying mutual funds, America's leading discount brokers are trying to break this perennial rule.

You already know that one way to purchase shares in a fund is by calling the fund directly, ordering a prospectus and application, completing the necessary paperwork, and sending it all back to the fund with your initial investment to get the ball rolling. When you decide to redeem your shares, you once again have to phone the fund and then wait for your check to arrive. If you want to switch from one fund to another in a different family, you have to order the prospectus and application for the new fund, request a redemption from your old one, fill out a new set of paperwork, cash the check your old fund sends you, and write out a check for the new fund. This is not only a hassle, but valuable time is being consumed. Worse still, because transferring from one fund to another can take days or weeks, you risk missing out on gains in the market during the interim.

Now, however, this way of doing business with your favorite funds is a thing of the past. Top discount brokers, including Charles Schwab, Fidelity, and TD Waterhouse, have created virtual "no-load, no-transaction-fee supermarkets." These programs enable you to buy and sell hundreds of funds in a single account without paying a penny in commissions. The programs are convenient, cost-effective, and, arguably, the most important new development for fund investors in recent memory.

SHOPPING AT THE FUND SUPERMARKETS

THE START OF SOMETHING BIG

In 1984, San Diego (California) discount broker Jack White & Co. (now a part of TD Waterhouse) was the first to start selling no-load funds to clients. Rival Charles Schwab quickly did the same. Each offered about 150 funds that could be traded for a minimal transaction fee, similar to the commission charged on stocks.

Both brokers threw in a variety of services that were never before available to those dealing with no-loads—for example, statement consolidation and the ability to purchase shares without having to mail in an order form. However, initial public reaction to the concept, even with the small fee, was disappointing. Schwab soon realized that the transaction fee was a stumbling block, since people could still invest free by calling the funds directly. It was apparent that, for many clients, the convenience factor alone wasn't enough to overcome the $30 to $50 transaction fee they were being charged.

In 1990, Charles Schwab himself began working on a plan to get the fund companies to pay the transaction fee on behalf of his clients. He knew that he was on to something big, but he understood that investors wouldn't welcome the idea of buying funds through his brokerage until he completely got rid of the commission. What's now known as Schwab's OneSource program was born in 1992. Just as he had transformed the way people bought stocks 17 years earlier, Schwab dramatically changed the distribution channel for no-load funds with the birth of this program.

ONE-STOP SHOPPING

From the start, OneSource allowed clients to purchase and sell shares from a handful of large fund companies free of charge. How? By charging the participating fund companies anywhere from $.25 to $.35 for every $100 in assets that Schwab brought in. This was considered to be a marketing and distribution fee. Because the funds saved the cost of performing these functions on their own, Schwab argued that it was a good deal for them. Initially, the idea ran into resistance. Many fund families approached it with a "wait-and-see" attitude. They wanted to see how the competition reacted before taking the plunge themselves.

Jack White & Co. soon introduced a similar program, although founder and president Jack White had some doubts that it would ever take off. He knew many fund managers personally, and figured they would resist paying to be part of a program that made it so easy for investors to buy and sell their shares. Fund companies, as a rule, hate traders and market timers because frequent buying and selling disrupts the normal flow of funds. Just to meet redemptions, managers may have to sell positions they like, thus hurting other shareholders.

As it turned out, the concept caught on and spread like wildfire. One fund family after another started courting Schwab and Jack White to sign up. Before long, fund behemoth Fidelity Investments joined the party with a fund supermarket of its own and was closely followed by almost all of the other major discount brokers, including Muriel Siebert and TD Waterhouse.

WIDE AVAILABILITY

Today, no-load, no-transaction-fee (NTF) programs have amassed some $200 billion in assets. Almost all of the major no-load fund families participate, as do a number of smaller boutique funds that were formerly available only to high-net-worth institutional investors.

Noticeably absent from the current list of available offerings are funds from giants T. Rowe Price and Vanguard, which maintain that the cost of participation is simply too high. (Funds from these families can still be purchased from the brokers, although a small commission is charged for each transaction.) Even full-service brokers like Merrill Lynch and Smith Barney, once famous for bad-mouthing no-loads, are joining the NTF fund bandwagon to stem the flow of lost assets, as are some of the fund families themselves.

THE WAVE OF THE FUTURE

Some industry analysts predict that funds and brokers that refuse to join these programs will struggle to survive as NTF supermarkets become more popular. Many of the participating funds already get more than half of their assets from them. In fact, most start-up money managers are designing their new funds specifically around the supermarkets, to make sure they can get in right away.

THE ADVANTAGES

It seems inevitable that NTF supermarkets would gain such widespread acceptance. After all, with one phone call, clients can buy and sell hundreds of high-quality funds from dozens of different families, and all of their holdings are consolidated on one monthly statement. In addition, the brokers keep track of pertinent tax information, leaving clients to contend with only one 1099 form at the end of the year. Other advantages include fee-free IRAs and SEP retirement plans, which are perfect for small business owners; no-cost reinvestment of dividends and capital gains; around-the-clock account access by phone and computer; free check writing; and, in some cases, the ability to trade on margin.

The Drawbacks

There are a few drawbacks. When you buy shares through an NTF supermarket, the fund companies won't know you exist. Your investment gets lumped into one omnibus account registered in the name of your broker, so don't expect to get much promotional mail touting your fund companies' new products and services. Your annual reports and other information will likely arrive a few days later than normal, because everything must be sent through each discount broker's third-party mailing center.

In addition, most brokers have short-term trading rules, which require payment of a transaction fee if a fund position is sold before a given time period (usually, six months). The rules are designed to discourage frequent switching around. That's probably a good thing; such regular trading usually leads to lower returns anyway. But all in all, the downside is relatively minor.

GETTING STARTED

How can you take advantage of this first free lunch on Wall Street? Begin by opening an account with the broker of your choice. It usually takes at least $5,000 to get started, and the extra perks start to kick in at around the $10,000 level.

Which broker is best for you is a very personal decision. Your choice depends on your own needs and preferences. Let's say you want to do most of your trading online. Every broker offers a computerized trading program and/or Internet site, but Schwab and Fidelity currently have the most sophisticated products. If you desire personal face-to-face service, Schwab, Fidelity, TD Waterhouse, and Scottrade have branch offices located across the country. (Keep in mind that it's possible to conduct all of your business over the phone or by computer, so not having a branch office is no big deal.) Scottrade by far offers the most transaction-fee funds, but has the fewest perks.

You may also want to look at some of the smaller details. For example, Fidelity has the best-looking and most comprehensive monthly account statements. Meanwhile, some brokers charge for using the ATM debit card that comes with your money market account, while others don't.

YOUR ONE-STOP BANK, TOO

When you open a brokerage account, you can establish an entire cash management program that not only links all of your funds and other investments (including stocks and bonds), but also gives you easy access to an interest-bearing money market account. All of your available cash is automatically swept into this account at the end of each day. You can then write as many checks as your account balance allows, or use a debit card to get cash from automated teller machines (ATMs) around the world. For all intents and purposes, you could make this your primary checking account, and would be well advised to do so. You'll likely earn a much higher rate of interest than you'll get at your local bank, and this option makes it easy for you to invest in your favorite funds on a regular basis.

The beauty of these programs is that they cost you nothing, assuming you meet all of the minimum balance requirements, and the fact that you're getting a lot of free services should be an important consideration.

CHOOSING YOUR BROKER

Here's the best plan of action for deciding which broker is right for you: Call or visit each one and ask for more information and an application. (You'll find a list of names, toll-free numbers, and Internet addresses in the box on page 41.) Then, on paper, map out the products and services you are seeking. Next, determine which broker(s) offer most of the things on your list. Some of the more popular features include free IRAs and SEPs, large availability of NTF funds, strong computerized trading programs, and all-in-one asset management accounts. Also check out each broker's Internet site. If you plan to use your computer to keep track of your investments, see what each broker offers via online technology.

Regardless of which broker you ultimately choose, you're sure to find NTF supermarkets a convenient and less expensive way to buy no-load funds in the future. As for the free lunch, the fund families are picking up the tab, so eat and enjoy. Deals like this don't come along very often.

10 REASONS TO BUY YOUR MUTUAL FUNDS THROUGH THE NTF FUND SUPERMARKETS

1. Purchase hundreds of top-performing no-load funds from more than 90 different families without paying any commissions or transaction costs.

2. Have all of your investment holdings (stocks, bonds, cash, and funds) consolidated on one easy-to-read monthly statement.

3. Gain entry into exclusive funds once available only to high-net-worth institutional investors.

4. Get 24-hour-a-day access to your portfolio holdings and values by phone and computer, allowing you to keep constant tabs on your investments.

5. Buy into funds with minimum investment requirements of up to $1 million for as little as $1,000.

6. Receive a fee-free retirement account (IRA, SEP, Keogh, etc.) for yourself and your employees, while choosing from a plethora of no-load funds to build your wealth.

7. Enjoy same-day order execution of your fund transactions, and avoid having to rely on mail delivery and signature guarantees to redeem shares.

8. Let your discount broker keep track of all fund gains and losses, making tax time a breeze.

9. Get a free high-interest-bearing checking account linked directly to your investment portfolio.

10. Keep more money in your pocket by avoiding "loaded" funds, and benefit from the many services provided by America's top discount brokers.

NTF DISCOUNT BROKERS

Broker	Telephone	Internet Address
Ameritrade	(800) 454-9272	www.ameritrade.com
Charles Schwab & Co.	(800) 845-1714	www.schwab.com
E*Trade	(800) 387-2331	www.etrade.com
Fidelity Investments	(800) 343-3548	www.fidelity.com
Muriel Siebert & Co.	(800) 872-0711	www.msiebert.com
Scottrade	(800) 619-7283	www.scottrade.com
TD Waterhouse	(800) 934-4443	www.waterhouse.com

5

100 POWERHOUSE PERFORMERS FOR 2004

You've been given the tools you need to effectively select your own funds, but there are some 12,000 names to sift through and analyze, and the number keeps growing each day. Since you presumably bought this book to make your investment life easier, we've performed exhaustive research to uncover the 100 most attractive no-load stock and fixed-income funds for the year ahead. All have brilliant track records and are spearheaded by seasoned managers with a proven talent for picking winning investments. We call these funds the "100 Powerhouse Performers." Every Powerhouse Performer is profiled in a two-page report that starts with the fund's name, objective, and manager.

Within each group, the funds are arranged alphabetically by the first word of their name. Entries 1 through 91 represent the equity side; entries 92 through 100 represent the fixed-income side.

Each fund's investment style is described as precisely as possible, based on the manager's most recent portfolio composition. Style refers to the kinds of securities a fund holds. This information tells you whether a given fund will add an element of diversity to your portfolio. Having exposure to many different styles will help you to weather the market's constant fluctuations and sector rotations. You can find definitions for each of these investment styles in the Glossary in the back of the book.

Generally speaking, growth fund managers look for companies experiencing rapid earnings and/or sales growth. Shares in these companies frequently trade at a premium to the overall stock market. Value fund managers hunt for bargains, often buying slower growing or troubled businesses that are available at depressed prices.

Each Powerhouse Performer's report contains a brief overview of the fund, a description of how the manager invests the portfolio, and why the fund made the list. The accompanying tables show various returns and rankings. You'll find each fund's annualized return over the past one-, three-, and five-year periods (through May 31, 2003) where applicable. For updated performance numbers online, visit www.valueline.com.

Next come the fund's overall and risk rankings, according to Value Line. The overall ranking takes into account how a given fund has performed compared to its peers. Ranking is on a scale of 1 through 5, with 1 being best. The risk ranking gives you a feel for how volatile the portfolio is. On a scale of 1 through 5, 5 is the riskiest.

Also included are a handful of useful statistics, including the fund's annual turnover rate, expense ratio, 12b-1 fee, maximum sales load, and three-year beta coefficient. Beta is a measure of a fund's volatility in relation to its benchmark index (usually the S&P 500, for stocks). The S&P 500 has a beta of 1. Funds with a beta lower than 1 fluctuate less than the overall market; funds with a beta above 1 are more volatile. If you are conservative and seek to temper your market risk, you need to favor funds with low betas.

For each fund, we provide the minimum investment requirements for both regular and IRA accounts, the toll-free telephone number, and the fund's Internet address (where applicable). You can use this information to get a prospectus and/or more information, such as a listing of which discount brokers (if any) carry the fund through their NTF supermarket.

On the second page of every report are two graphs (courtesy of Value Line). The first graph shows the return on a $10,000 investment in the fund over a period of years compared to its benchmark index. The second graph is a measure of individual annual performance, illustrating, year by year, what kind of returns the fund has generated since its inception or since 1978, whichever is longer. (For some of the newer funds, this information is not available.) Finally, there is a box showing the fund's most recent top 10 portfolio holdings.

To keep this information updated on a monthly basis, consider subscribing to the *Value Line Mutual Fund Survey for Windows*. For a free trial of this product, be sure to check out the special offer exclusively for readers of *Mutual Fund Investor's Guide 2004* at the back of this book.

Coming up in Chapter 6, we'll help you put together a portfolio tailored to your individual needs, drawing from the lineup of Powerhouse Performers. For now, let's take a look at some of the most deserving candidates for your investment consideration in 2004.

100 POWERHOUSE PERFORMERS FOR 2004

ABN AMRO/MONTAG & CALDWELL GROWTH

OBJECTIVE:	*Large-Cap Growth*	*1*
MANAGER:	*Ronald E. Canakaris*	

FUND OVERVIEW:

ABN AMRO/Montag & Caldwell Growth manager Ronald Canakaris seeks to generate long-term capital appreciation by investing in a relatively concentrated portfolio of equities. He buys companies that he believes are undervalued based on both current earnings power and the ability to generate strong earnings growth over the next 12 to 18 months. Many of the names in the portfolio are established brands with long histories.

"We continue to be quite positive on the outlook for the shares of high-quality growth companies," Canakaris says. "Because we expect more moderate growth in the U.S. economy and corporate profits in the future, the superior and consistent earnings growth rates of these companies should become increasingly attractive." Many of his companies do business around the world, which Canakaris feels gives them a tremendous advantage. "With the U.S. economy already operating at a high level of activity, the multinational consumer, healthcare, and technology companies in the fund are particularly well positioned to benefit from the greater growth opportunities that exist in global markets," he adds.

ANNUALIZED RETURNS		PORTFOLIO STATISTICS	
1-Year	−10.20%	Beta	0.70
3-Year	−10.77%	Turnover	N/A
5-Year	−1.05%	12-Month Yield	0.00%
Overall Rank	3	12b-1 Fee	0.25%
Risk Rank	2	Expense Ratio	1.06%

MINIMUM INVESTMENT		CONTACT INFORMATION
Regular	$2,500	*ABN AMRO/Montag & Caldwell Growth Fund*
IRA	$500	*Telephone: (800) 992-8151*
		www.abnamro.com

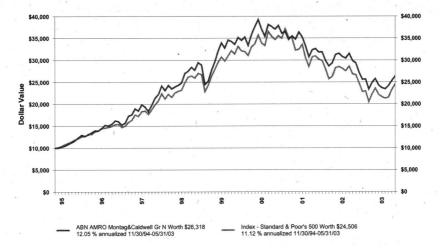

ABN AMRO Montag&Caldwell Gr N Worth $26,318
12.05 % annualized 11/30/94-05/31/03

Index - Standard & Poor's 500 Worth $24,506
11.12 % annualized 11/30/94-05/31/03

GROWTH OF $10,000

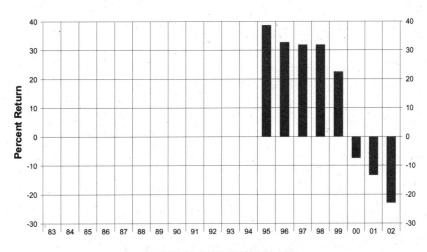

ANNUAL PERFORMANCE

TOP 10 HOLDINGS	
Johnson & Johnson	Amgen
Pfizer	Coca-Cola
Procter & Gamble	Schlumberger
Medtronic	3M
Colgate Palmolive	Gillette

ATLANTIC WHITEHALL GROWTH

OBJECTIVE: *Large-Cap Growth*
MANAGER: *Paul Blaustein*

2

FUND OVERVIEW:

You might call Atlantic Whitehall Growth manager Paul Blaustein a value-conscious growth investor. It's an approach known as GARP, or growth at a reasonable price. Blaustein is an infrequent trader who runs a fairly focused fund.

He keeps volatility down by limiting each stock position to around 3 percent of total assets. Still, although he holds between 30 and 40 names in the portfolio, he's not afraid to load up on stocks in a particular sector that happens to attract his fancy at any point in time.

Blaustein favors companies with products that stand out from the crowd, along with steady profit growth and consistent rates of return on invested capital. He also likes seasoned managers who are continually coming up with new, innovative product ideas that customers would have a hard time living without.

Blaustein tends to stay away from businesses lacking proprietary products, and avoids high-flying stocks in companies that have little or no profits to back them up.

ANNUALIZED RETURNS

1-Year	−9.20%
3-Year	−15.03%
5-Year	3.18%
Overall Rank	3
Risk Rank	4

MINIMUM INVESTMENT

Regular	$1,000
IRA	$250

PORTFOLIO STATISTICS

Beta	1.33
Turnover	32.00%
12-Month Yield	0.00%
12b-1 Fee	0.25%
Expense Ratio	1.38%

CONTACT INFORMATION

Atlantic Whitehall Growth Fund
Telephone: (800) 994-2533
www.thewhitehallfunds.com

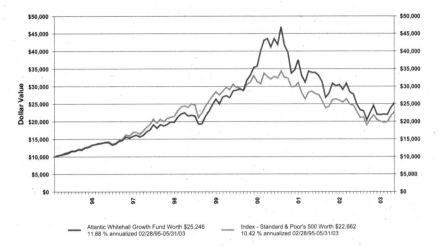

Atlantic Whitehall Growth Fund Worth $25,246
11.88 % annualized 02/28/95-05/31/03

Index - Standard & Poor's 500 Worth $22,662
10.42 % annualized 02/28/95-05/31/03

GROWTH OF $10,000

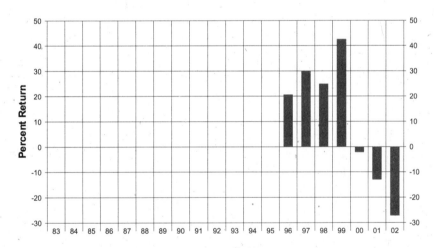

ANNUAL PERFORMANCE

TOP 10 HOLDINGS	
Comcast	Maxim Integrated
Fox Entertainment Group	Liberty Media
Amgen	Altera Corporation
Wells Fargo & Company	Cisco Systems
Pfizer	Cardinal Health

DREYFUS APPRECIATION

OBJECTIVE:	*Large-Cap Growth*	
MANAGER:	*Fayez Sarofim*	*3*

FUND OVERVIEW:

Since taking over management of Dreyfus Appreciation in 1990, manager Fayez Sarofim has turned this fund into a growth-oriented portfolio full of large-cap global names. Sarofim is no rookie to the investment scene. He founded his firm, Fayez Sarofim & Co., in 1958. The firm serves as subadviser to the fund and manages some $30 billion in assets. Sarofim and his comanager, Russell Hawkins, are convinced that overseas exposure by dominant blue-chip companies will give them an impressive earnings boost over the long run. That's why they are banking on such stocks. Because the top 20 names in the portfolio often account for 60 percent of assets, this can be a more volatile fund than others in the category.

Dreyfus Appreciation's emphasis is on U.S.-based companies that are easily recognized and get at least 35 to 40 percent of their income from international markets. Visibility of earnings is also important. Sarofim will occasionally buy American Depositary Receipts (ADRs) when he feels purchasing them is appropriate. The visibility of a company's future earnings growth is an important consideration, because Sarofim tends to stick with a buy-and-hold strategy.

ANNUALIZED RETURNS		PORTFOLIO STATISTICS	
1-Year	−9.60%	Beta	0.70
3-Year	−7.54%	Turnover	5%
5-Year	−0.05%	12-Month Yield	0.89%
Overall Rank	3	12b-1 Fee	0.00%
Risk Rank	2	Expense Ratio	0.91%
MINIMUM INVESTMENT		**CONTACT INFORMATION**	
Regular	$2,500	*Dreyfus Appreciation Fund*	
IRA	$750	*Telephone: (800) 782-6620*	
		www.dreyfus.com	

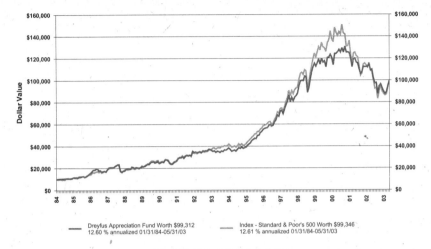

Dreyfus Appreciation Fund Worth $99,312
12.60 % annualized 01/31/84-05/31/03

Index - Standard & Poor's 500 Worth $99,346
12.61 % annualized 01/31/84-05/31/03

GROWTH OF $10,000

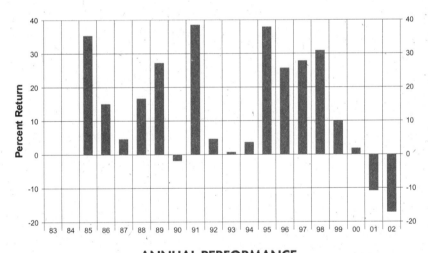

ANNUAL PERFORMANCE

TOP 10 HOLDINGS	
Pfizer	Altria Group
ExxonMobil	Procter & Gamble
Johnson & Johnson	Merck
Federal Natl. Mortgage	Wal-Mart Stores
General Electric	Coca-Cola

FIDELITY DIVIDEND GROWTH

OBJECTIVE:	*Large-Cap Growth*	4
MANAGER:	*Charles Mangum*	

FUND OVERVIEW:

Although it has the name "dividend" in its title, Fidelity Dividend Growth is actually most concerned with capital appreciation. Nevertheless, it pursues this goal by investing in companies with increasing dividend payout ratios, or those that manager Charles Mangum expects to start paying dividends in the near future. To Mangum, a stock's dividend yield is a measure of a company's soundness and prospects for future growth. Mangum also believes that dividend-paying companies can be safer investments, which helps to keep risk under control. But not every company has to pay a dividend to make it into the portfolio. Again, long-term growth is the main objective.

Mangum uses a bottom-up approach, focusing on firms with low price-earnings multiples and good business prospects. The fund's two goals are growth and safety. Even with his more cautious approach, Mangum has managed to significantly outperform his large-cap growth peers over time while paying a slim, yet consistent, dividend. Once more, if you're looking for dividend income alone, this fund probably isn't right for you. But if long-term growth is a bigger concern, this fund is a worthy candidate.

ANNUALIZED RETURNS

1-Year	−7.50%
3-Year	−3.62%
5-Year	3.45%
Overall Rank	2
Risk Rank	3

MINIMUM INVESTMENT

Regular	$2,500
IRA	$2,500

PORTFOLIO STATISTICS

Beta	0.97
Turnover	81.00%
12-Month Yield	0.90%
12b-1 Fee	0.00%
Expense Ratio	0.95%

CONTACT INFORMATION

Fidelity Dividend Growth Fund
Telephone: (800) 343-3548
www.fidelity.com

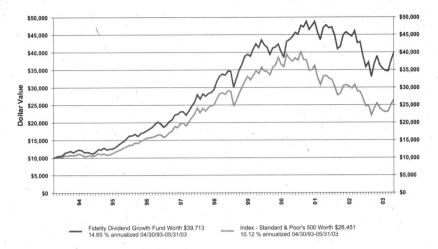

Fidelity Dividend Growth Fund Worth $39,713
14.65 % annualized 04/30/93-05/31/03

Index - Standard & Poor's 500 Worth $26,451
10.12 % annualized 04/30/93-05/31/03

GROWTH OF $10,000

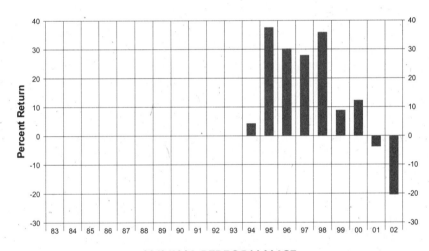

ANNUAL PERFORMANCE

TOP 10 HOLDINGS

Cardinal Health	Citigroup
Clear Channel Communications	Merck
General Electric	Pfizer
Federal Natl. Mortgage	Conoco Phillips
American International Group	Home Depot

GABELLI GROWTH

OBJECTIVE:	*Large-Cap Growth*
MANAGER:	*Howard Ward*

5

Fund Overview:

Gabelli Growth manager Howard Ward invests in a diversified portfolio of large, seasoned, well-managed companies that he believes have favorable earnings dynamics and price appreciation potential. His companies normally boast above-average or expanding market shares, high profit margins, and respectable returns on equity. Ward does a lot of hands-on research. He especially likes businesses with a demonstrated competitive advantage that benefit from one or more secular trends, such as the technology revolution, aging of the population, and globalization. He also focuses on valuation, hoping to buy these growers at attractive prices.

The fund's largest weightings are in the financial services, drug, technology, newspaper, and broadcasting sectors. "Virtually all of our companies occupy leading positions in their fields," Ward explains. "We should do well when large growth company stocks do well, and less well when they periodically stall." Ward is a strong advocate of diversification, but he doesn't believe in being spread out more than necessary. He expects to keep his portfolio at around 50 to 70 names, to prevent his best ideas from being unfairly diluted.

ANNUALIZED RETURNS

1-Year	−15.30%
3-Year	−21.82%
5-Year	−3.49%
Overall Rank	4
Risk Rank	4

MINIMUM INVESTMENT

Regular	$1,000
IRA	$250

PORTFOLIO STATISTICS

Beta	1.37
Turnover	29.00%
12-Month Yield	0.00%
12b-1 Fee	0.25%
Expense Ratio	1.39%

CONTACT INFORMATION

Gabelli Growth Fund
Telephone: (800) 422-3554
www.gabelli.com

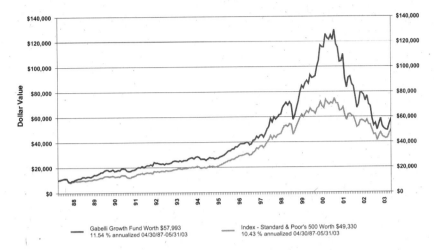

Gabelli Growth Fund Worth $57,993
11.54 % annualized 04/30/87-05/31/03

Index - Standard & Poor's 500 Worth $49,330
10.43 % annualized 04/30/87-05/31/03

GROWTH OF $10,000

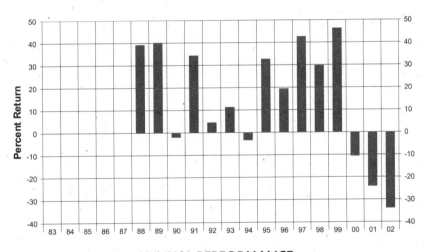

ANNUAL PERFORMANCE

TOP 10 HOLDINGS

Clear Channel Communications	Northern Trust
Viacom Class B	Microsoft
State Street Corporation	Pfizer
AOL Time Warner	Amgen
Home Depot	Walgreen

HARBOR CAPITAL APPRECIATION

OBJECTIVE:	Large-Cap Growth
MANAGER:	Spiros Segalas

6

FUND OVERVIEW:

Harbor Capital Appreciation is one of the more aggressive large-cap growth funds you will come across. Although Spiros Segalas fills his portfolio with blue-chip household names, he's not afraid to trade around his positions with frequency and will concentrate in specific sectors if he thinks that's the best course of action. Segalas is an admitted momentum player. If one of his companies fails to achieve or exceed his expected earnings target, he'll get rid of it, although he doesn't try to time the market itself.

Segalas's bottom-up management style seeks out growth at a reasonable price. He prefers companies with market capitalizations of at least $1 billion and with track records of superior sales growth, high returns on equity, and solid balance sheets. Earnings numbers are also critical, and he is constantly reevaluating his expectations.

Harbor Capital Appreciation has been a stellar long-term performer since Segalas took over in 1990. It has an extremely low expense ratio for a fund of this nature. Clearly, you can expect it to be volatile. But if you can stand these more frequent fluctuations, you will likely be rewarded.

ANNUALIZED RETURNS

1-Year	–12.40%
3-Year	–18.26%
5-Year	–1.71%
Overall Rank	3
Risk Rank	4

MINIMUM INVESTMENT

Regular	$2,000
IRA	$500

PORTFOLIO STATISTICS

Beta	1.20
Turnover	75.20%
12-Month Yield	0.16%
12b-1 Fee	0.00%
Expense Ratio	0.66%

CONTACT INFORMATION

Harbor Capital Appreciation
Telephone: (800) 422-1050
www.harborfund.com

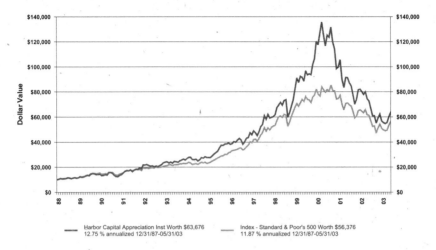

Harbor Capital Appreciation Inst Worth $63,676
12.75 % annualized 12/31/87-05/31/03

Index - Standard & Poor's 500 Worth $56,376
11.87 % annualized 12/31/87-05/31/03

GROWTH OF $10,000

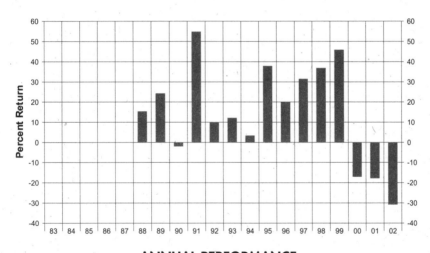

ANNUAL PERFORMANCE

TOP 10 HOLDINGS

Amgen	Kohls
Wal-Mart Stores	American International Group
Microsoft	3M
Cisco Systems	Intel
Viacom Class B	American Express

JENSEN PORTFOLIO

OBJECTIVE:	*Large-Cap Growth*	7
MANAGER:	*Team Managed*	

FUND OVERVIEW:

The Jensen Portfolio is on the lookout for a few good large-cap names. The management team, led by Val Jensen, keeps around 20 to 30 names in the portfolio, all of which are selected through a series of screens. As a first test, securities must have a return-on-equity of at least 15 percent annually for the prior 10 years. When you put the whole universe of stocks to that test, you come back with about 100 to 150 names. From there, managers look for those companies with excellent balance sheets, economies of scale in production, and those that have continually increased dividends to shareholders at a rate above inflation.

Stocks tend to stick around in the Jensen Portfolio for many years. The long-term-oriented management team will sell a position when it no longer meets their strict criteria or when they find a more attractive alternative. The fund's annual turnover rate is usually less than 25 percent, which should make the portfolio tax-efficient over time. Because of the management team's more conservative approach, this fund tends to do better than its peers in bear markets, while slightly underperforming more aggressive offerings in roaring bull cycles.

ANNUALIZED RETURNS

1-Year	−7.20%
3-Year	−0.94%
5-Year	7.45%
Overall Rank	2
Risk Rank	2

MINIMUM INVESTMENT

Regular	$1,000
IRA	$1,000

PORTFOLIO STATISTICS

Beta	0.64
Turnover	2.10%
12-Month Yield	0.43%
12b-1 Fee	0.10%
Expense Ratio	0.91%

CONTACT INFORMATION

Jensen Portfolio
Telephone: (800) 992-4144
www.jenseninvestment.com

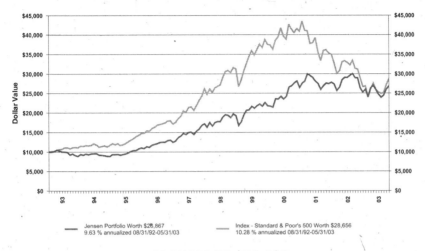

GROWTH OF $10,000

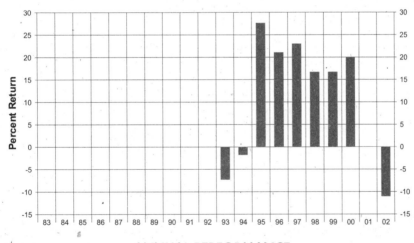

ANNUAL PERFORMANCE

TOP 10 HOLDINGS	
Stryker	Equifax
Pfizer	State Street Corporation
Johnson & Johnson	General Electric
3M	Procter & Gamble
Emerson Electric	Gannett

MARSICO FOCUS

OBJECTIVE:	*Large-Cap Growth*	*8*
MANAGER:	*Thomas Marsico*	

FUND OVERVIEW:

Tom Marsico built a stellar record at the Janus Twenty fund, steering it to a 22.38 percent annualized return from January 31, 1988 to August 7, 1997. (That compared favorably to an 18.20 percent return for the S&P 500.) He left Janus in late 1997 to start his own shop and launched Marsico Focus at the beginning of 1998. The portfolio looks almost identical to the old Janus Twenty, only better because he is working with a smaller asset base. Marsico Focus holds this proven manager's 20 to 30 favorite stocks. This added concentration increases both the fund's potential risks and rewards.

Marsico considers this to be a global portfolio, meaning he can invest in both U.S. and foreign securities. He prides himself in being an out-of-the-box thinker who looks for variables that aren't obvious from examining conventional financial analyses. He spends a lot of time talking with the management, suppliers, customers, competitors, and critics of the companies he owns. Among the characteristics he looks for in his high-growth, large-cap businesses are an element of change, a strong franchise, products with a global reach, and the potential to benefit from a positive emerging social or economic theme.

ANNUALIZED RETURNS		PORTFOLIO STATISTICS	
1-Year	−10.10%	Beta	0.86
3-Year	−10.27%	Turnover	117.00%
5-Year	2.14%	12-Month Yield	0.00%
Overall Rank	3	12b-1 Fee	0.25%
Risk Rank	3	Expense Ratio	1.35%

MINIMUM INVESTMENT		CONTACT INFORMATION
Regular	$2,500	*Marsico Focus Fund*
IRA	$1,000	*Telephone: (888) 860-8686*
		www.marsicofunds.com

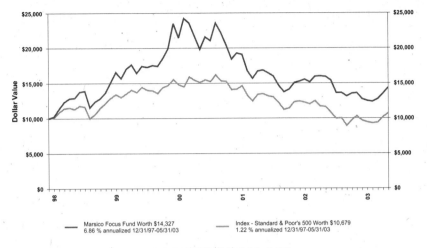

Marsico Focus Fund Worth $14,327
6.86 % annualized 12/31/97-05/31/03

Index - Standard & Poor's 500 Worth $10,679
1.22 % annualized 12/31/97-05/31/03

GROWTH OF $10,000

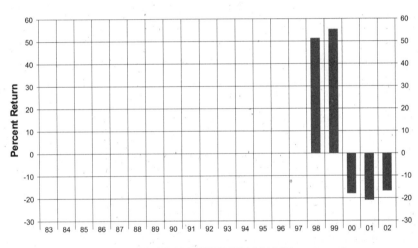

ANNUAL PERFORMANCE

TOP 10 HOLDINGS

United Health Group
SLM
Cisco Systems
Viacom Class B
Tiffany & Company

Quest Diagnostics
Citigroup
Amgen
Federal Natl. Mortgage
Microsoft

MOSAIC INVESTORS

OBJECTIVE:	*Large-Cap Growth*
MANAGER:	*Jay Sekelsky*

9

FUND OVERVIEW:

Mosaic Investors manager Jay Sekelsky invests primarily in companies with a stock market capitalization of $5 billion or more. He's a concentrated investor, typically keeping between 25 and 30 names in his portfolio. While primarily a growth manager, Sekelsky seeks stocks that, in his estimation, are undervalued. His strategy is known as GARP, or growth at a reasonable price. Among the characteristics he looks for when selecting stocks are a pattern of consistent, sustainable earnings; strong balance sheets; and solid cash flow.

When putting the overall portfolio together, Sekelsky does take sector and industry trends into consideration, though stocks are evaluated for their individual merits. He'll sell a position either when it reaches his valuation target, when the company's fundamentals deteriorate, or if he finds a better value elsewhere. Mosaic Investors has managed to outperform its peers under Sekelsky's management while keeping volatility relatively low. That makes the fund a good large-cap option for more risk-averse investors.

ANNUALIZED RETURNS		PORTFOLIO STATISTICS	
1-Year	−8.20%	Beta	0.80
3-Year	−0.30%	Turnover	88.00%
5-Year	3.08%	12-Month Yield	0.22%
Overall Rank	2	12b-1 Fee	0.00%
Risk Rank	2	Expense Ratio	1.00%
MINIMUM INVESTMENT		**CONTACT INFORMATION**	
Regular	$1,000	*Mosaic Investors Fund*	
IRA	$1,000	*Telephone: (800) 336-3063*	
		www.mosaicfunds.com	

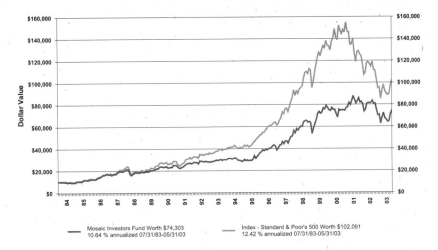

Mosaic Investors Fund Worth $74,303
10.64 % annualized 07/31/83-05/31/03

Index - Standard & Poor's 500 Worth $102,091
12.42 % annualized 07/31/83-05/31/03

GROWTH OF $10,000

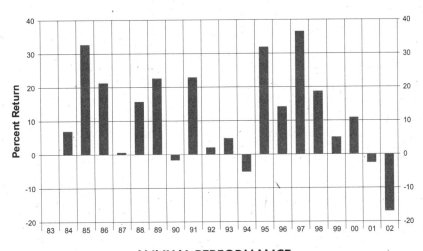

ANNUAL PERFORMANCE

TOP 10 HOLDINGS

Mohawk Industries	American International Group
Costco Wholesale	Pfizer
Freddie Mac	Merck
Liberty Media	Markel
MGIC Investment Corporation	Wells Fargo & Company

PAPP AMERICA ABROAD

OBJECTIVE:	*Large-Cap Growth*	*10*
MANAGER:	*L. Roy Papp and Rosellen Papp*	

FUND OVERVIEW:

Roy Papp knows there's a world of opportunity out there for investors. He's seen much of it with his own eyes, having traveled around the globe throughout his life. But he's too scared to trust any of his own money to one of the foreign stock exchanges. That's why he started a fund designed to profit from global growth through buying domestically domiciled companies. Papp America Abroad invests primarily in U.S. multinationals, most of which do more than half of their business overseas.

Among the many dangers of investing directly in foreign soil, Papp cites currency risk, varying accounting standards, higher transaction costs, political instability, and the loss of SEC protection. He also notes that U.S. companies tend to be more technologically advanced and competitive than their international counterparts, which means their profit potential is greater.

In addition to the international business component, Papp's ideal company is an industry leader—better yet, a monopoly. It is also growing at a rate of 20 to 25 percent a year, and trades at or near a market multiple at the time of initial purchase.

ANNUALIZED RETURNS		PORTFOLIO STATISTICS	
1-Year	−15.00%	Beta	1.11
3-Year	−17.03%	Turnover	4.00%
5-Year	−4.55%	12-Month Yield	0.00%
Overall Rank	4	12b-1 Fee	0.00%
Risk Rank	4	Expense Ratio	1.11%
MINIMUM INVESTMENT		**CONTACT INFORMATION**	
Regular	$5,000	*Papp America Abroad Fund*	
IRA	$1,000	*Telephone: (800) 421-4004*	
		www.roypapp.com	

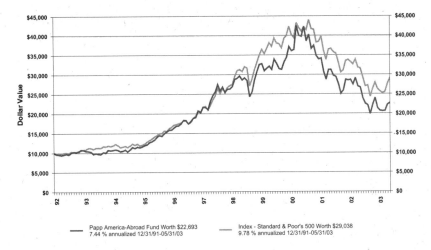

Papp America-Abroad Fund Worth $22,693
7.44 % annualized 12/31/91-05/31/03

Index - Standard & Poor's 500 Worth $29,038
9.78 % annualized 12/31/91-05/31/03

GROWTH OF $10,000

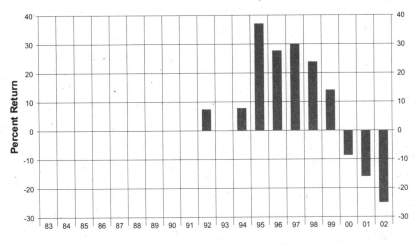

ANNUAL PERFORMANCE

TOP 10 HOLDINGS

Microsoft
State Street Corporation
Merck
Johnson & Johnson
Intel

Expeditors International
General Electric
American International Group
Omnicom Group
Eli Lilly

RAINIER CORE EQUITY

OBJECTIVE:	Large-Cap Growth	
MANAGER:	James R. Margard	*11*

FUND OVERVIEW:

Although the Rainier Core Equity portfolio is composed primarily of companies in the S&P 500 index, manager James Margard and his investment team can invest in stocks of all sizes. This highly diversified fund is spread across a broad range of industries. To reduce risk, Margard purposely makes sure not to overweight any single industry. He adheres to a "growth at a reasonable price" philosophy, believing it allows him to generate competitive returns in all market environments.

When evaluating individual securities, Margard emphasizes companies likely to experience superior earnings growth, relative to their peers. He also favors businesses with a competitive advantage operating in a favorable regulatory environment, and he wants them at the right price. Strong management, insider ownership, and financial integrity are other requirements. A stock is sold when it reaches a predetermined target price, or if Margard finds a more attractive idea and needs the money to purchase it.

Even though the minimum investment requirement is a steep $25,000, you can get in for much less through one of the NTF programs (see Chapter 4).

ANNUALIZED RETURNS

1-Year	−9.60%
3-Year	−10.01%
5-Year	−0.41%
Overall Rank	3
Risk Rank	3

MINIMUM INVESTMENT

Regular	$25,000
IRA	$25,000

PORTFOLIO STATISTICS

Beta	0.95
Turnover	79.92%
12-Month Yield	0.00%
12b-1 Fee	0.25%
Expense Ratio	1.12%

CONTACT INFORMATION

Rainier Core Equity Portfolio
Telephone: (800) 248-6314
www.rainierfunds.com

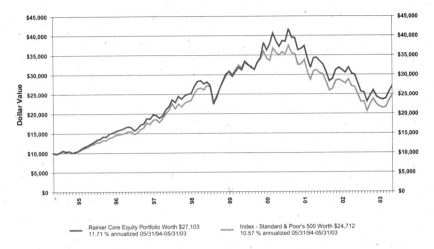

Rainier Core Equity Portfolio Worth $27,103
11.71 % annualized 05/31/94-05/31/03

Index - Standard & Poor's 500 Worth $24,712
10.57 % annualized 05/31/94-05/31/03

GROWTH OF $10,000

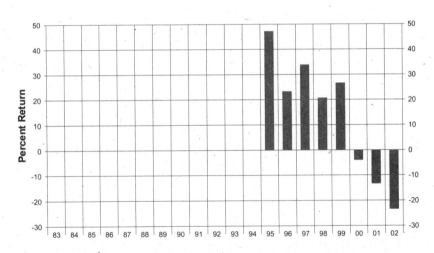

ANNUAL PERFORMANCE

TOP 10 HOLDINGS

Microsoft	American International Group
General Electric	Freddie Mac
Pfizer	Colgate Palmolive
Citigroup	Johnson & Johnson
Procter & Gamble	Cisco Systems

TCW GALILEO SELECT EQUITIES

OBJECTIVE:	Large-Cap Growth	*12*
MANAGER:	Glen Bickerstaff	

FUND OVERVIEW:

Glen Bickerstaff may be the biggest secret in the mutual fund industry. He has outperformed the S&P 500 in 13 of the 15 years he's been managing money, which is a terrific record. However, since he's only been running a publicly traded mutual fund for about the past eight years, he hasn't received the attention he deserves. After posting great results at the Transamerica Premier Equity Fund, Bickerstaff moved to Trust Company of the West in 1998 and now runs the TCW Galileo Select Equities Fund.

Bickerstaff uses a bottom-up approach and looks for high-quality companies with leadership positions in their respective industries. Among management, he seeks what he calls "patterns of perfection." He wants to make sure they have ownership positions in the companies along with specific plans to capitalize on positive fundamental changes. He also seeks businesses that use cash flow to generate the highest return for shareholders, and he doesn't want to pay too much for the future growth he expects. Bickerstaff keeps a somewhat concentrated portfolio of around 40 names. Because he doesn't do a lot of trading, the fund tends to be pretty tax-efficient.

ANNUALIZED RETURNS		PORTFOLIO STATISTICS	
1-Year	−0.60%	Beta	1.57
3-Year	−15.82%	Turnover	3.00%
5-Year	2.72%	12-Month Yield	0.00%
Overall Rank	3	12b-1 Fee	0.25%
Risk Rank	5	Expense Ratio	1.20%

MINIMUM INVESTMENT		CONTACT INFORMATION
Regular	$2,000	*TCW Galileo Select Equities Fund*
IRA	$500	*Telephone: (800) 386-3829*
		www.tcwgroup.com

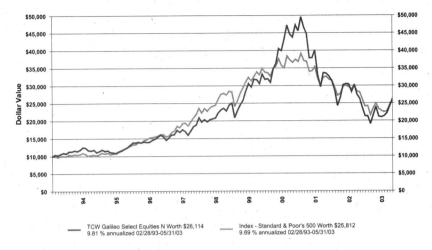

TCW Galileo Select Equities N Worth $26,114
9.81 % annualized 02/28/93-05/31/03

Index - Standard & Poor's 500 Worth $25,812
9.69 % annualized 02/28/93-05/31/03

GROWTH OF $10,000

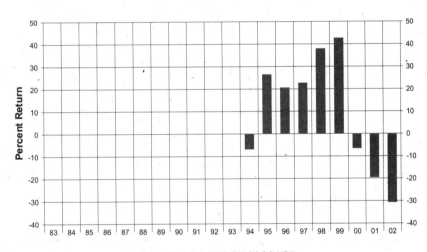

ANNUAL PERFORMANCE

TOP 10 HOLDINGS	
Progressive	Genentech
Amgen	Ebay
Maxim Integrated	Microsoft
Dell Computer	Amazon.com
Network Appliance	Eli Lilly

THOMPSON PLUMB GROWTH

OBJECTIVE: *Large-Cap Growth*
MANAGER: *John W. Thompson and John C. Thompson*

13

FUND OVERVIEW:

The father-and-son team of John W. Thompson and John C. Thompson runs a diversified portfolio of stocks designed to provide both growth and a degree of dividend income. To increase diversification, and therefore lower risk, the Thompson Plumb Growth fund invests in many types of stocks. While its primary focus is on larger companies, the Thompsons also buy smaller names.

Although they concentrate on growth stocks, they also are willing to buy value plays. They believe this more flexible approach will enable them to provide competitive returns under a variety of market environments.

The two attend a lot of research conferences and visit with company management to uncover promising investment ideas. They don't adhere to any specific sector allocations, although no industry represents more than 25 percent of net assets. Individual companies that make the cut generally have a leading market position, competitive advantages, and a low amount of debt.

ANNUALIZED RETURNS	
1-Year	−9.80%
3-Year	6.98%
5-Year	8.52%
Overall Rank	2
Risk Rank	4

MINIMUM INVESTMENT	
Regular	$2,500
IRA	$2,000

PORTFOLIO STATISTICS	
Beta	1.03
Turnover	63.00%
12-Month Yield	0.64%
12b-1 Fee	0.00%
Expense Ratio	1.19%

CONTACT INFORMATION

Thompson Plumb Growth Fund
Telephone: (800) 841-0199
www.thompsonplumb.com

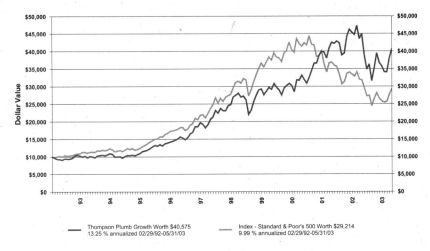

Thompson Plumb Growth Worth $40,575
13.25 % annualized 02/29/92-05/31/03

Index - Standard & Poor's 500 Worth $29,214
9.99 % annualized 02/29/92-05/31/03

GROWTH OF $10,000

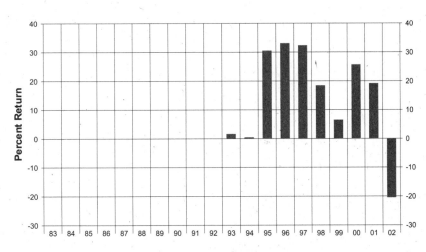

ANNUAL PERFORMANCE

TOP 10 HOLDINGS	
Pfizer	Bristol Myers Squibb
Microsoft	General Electric
Federal Natl. Mortgage	Coca-Cola
AOL Time Warner	Concord EFS
Cincinnati Financial	Tyco

VANGUARD HEALTH CARE

OBJECTIVE:	*Large-Cap Growth*	*14*
MANAGER:	*Edward P. Owens*	

FUND OVERVIEW:

While categorized as a large-cap growth fund, Vanguard Health Care is technically a sector fund. Although investing in sector funds isn't generally the best way to go, this fund has been a real standout and is worthy of consideration, at least for a small portion of your portfolio (maybe 5 percent or so). Having said that, one downside to this fund is its hefty minimum initial investment requirement of $25,000, meaning the stock portion of your portfolio should be at least $500,000 before giving this fund serious consideration.

Under the long-term management of Edward Owens, this has been one of the best-performing funds of any kind. The fund seeks capital appreciation through investing in healthcare companies. Owens uses a strict bottom-up investment approach that is often contrarian in nature. He looks for undervalued stocks that he believes have strong growth potential. The end result is a portfolio full of companies involved in various aspects of healthcare, from medical supply companies to biotechnology research firms, major and specialty pharmaceuticals, and hospitals.

ANNUALIZED RETURNS		PORTFOLIO STATISTICS	
1-Year	–3.60%	Beta	0.40
3-Year	6.08%	Turnover	25.00%
5-Year	13.09%	12-Month Yield	0.83%
Overall Rank	1	12b-1 Fee	0.00%
Risk Rank	2	Expense Ratio	0.28%

MINIMUM INVESTMENT		CONTACT INFORMATION	
Regular	$25,000	*Vanguard Health Care*	
IRA	$25,000	*Telephone: (800) 662-7447*	
		www.vanguard.com	

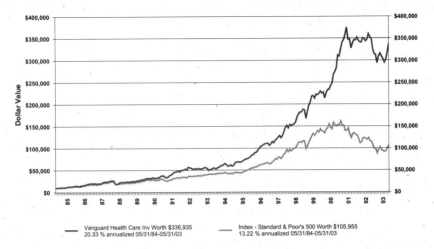

Vanguard Health Care Inv Worth $336,935
20.33 % annualized 05/31/84-05/31/03

Index - Standard & Poor's 500 Worth $105,955
13.22 % annualized 05/31/84-05/31/03

GROWTH OF $10,000

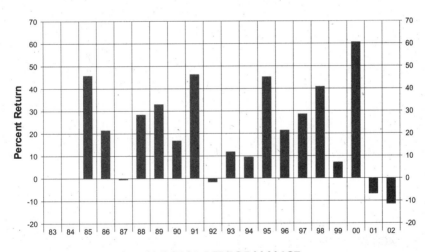

ANNUAL PERFORMANCE

TOP 10 HOLDINGS

Pharmacia	Astra Zeneca PLC
Shering Plough	Amgen
Genzyme	Wyeth
Pfizer	Abbott Laboratories
Eli Lilly	Merck

WHITE OAK GROWTH

| OBJECTIVE: | Large-Cap Growth | 15 |
| MANAGER: | James D. Oelschlager | |

FUND OVERVIEW:

This concentrated fund contains around 25 stocks focused in three primary market sectors: financials, technology, and drugs. Manager James Oelschlager has been investing in these areas for more than a decade, even before starting this fund. He believes in staying put and running with his winners, which makes the portfolio extremely tax-efficient. With such concentration comes volatility, however, and this fund can give investors a bumpy ride. It fared poorly during the recent bear market, though it has been a winner over time.

White Oak Growth owns established large-cap companies selling at attractive valuations based on expected future earnings. Stocks are monitored based on their five-year growth rates relative to their price-to-earnings multiple. Oelschlager doesn't try to time the market; he generally stays fully invested at all times. He continues to be excited about technology, his largest sector, believing that, going forward, it will be the strongest area for growth in the economy. Furthermore, he remains positive on the pipeline for new drugs and continuing consolidation in the financial services area.

ANNUALIZED RETURNS

1-Year	−8.40%
3-Year	−25.67%
5-Year	−3.79%
Overall Rank	4
Risk Rank	5

MINIMUM INVESTMENT

Regular	$2,000
IRA	$2,000

PORTFOLIO STATISTICS

Beta	1.87
Turnover	15.00%
12-Month Yield	0.00%
12b-1 Fee	0.00%
Expense Ratio	1.00%

CONTACT INFORMATION

White Oak Growth
Telephone: (888) 462-5386
www.oakassociates.com

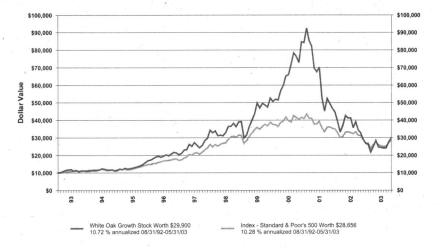

White Oak Growth Stock Worth $29,900
10.72 % annualized 08/31/92-05/31/03

Index - Standard & Poor's 500 Worth $28,656
10.28 % annualized 08/31/92-05/31/03

GROWTH OF $10,000

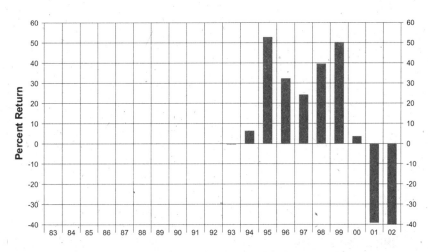

ANNUAL PERFORMANCE

TOP 10 HOLDINGS

MBNA	Cisco Systems
Pfizer	Medtronic
Microsoft	Eli Lilly
Morgan Stanley	Citigroup
Applied Materials	Linear Technology

WILSHIRE TARGET LARGE CO. GROWTH

| OBJECTIVE: | *Large-Cap Growth* | *16* |
| MANAGER: | *Thomas Stevens* | |

FUND OVERVIEW:

You might think of Wilshire Target Large Company Growth as a stylized index fund. The process of putting this portfolio together begins by culling through the 2,500 largest companies from the Wilshire 5000 index (a benchmark consisting of all publicly traded U.S. stocks). From here, manager Thomas Stevens picks 200 or so of the biggest names with above-average earnings or sales growth. Stevens further favors established companies with solid market recognition, as opposed to up-and-coming turnaround situations. He remains fully invested, opting to switch among holdings as economic conditions change, instead of raising cash.

Stevens reports that five-year earnings growth on the companies in his portfolio remains well above that of the S&P 500, demonstrating the high quality and record of success exemplified by his chosen companies. The fund's sector weighting makeup is also much different from the S&P 500, with almost half of the portfolio in technology and healthcare stocks. Its heavy exposure to these areas makes the portfolio more volatile than your average large-cap fund, but gives it the potential to outperform over time.

ANNUALIZED RETURNS		PORTFOLIO STATISTICS	
1-Year	−5.10%	Beta	1.10
3-Year	−13.44%	Turnover	47.00%
5-Year	0.17%	12-Month Yield	0.16%
Overall Rank	3	12b-1 Fee	0.25%
Risk Rank	3	Expense Ratio	0.82%

MINIMUM INVESTMENT		CONTACT INFORMATION
Regular	$2,500	*Wilshire Target Large Co. Growth*
IRA	$750	*Telephone: (888) 200-6796*
		www.wilfunds.com

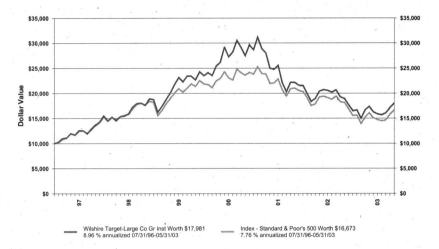

GROWTH OF $10,000

Wilshire Target-Large Co Gr Inst Worth $17,981
8.96 % annualized 07/31/96–05/31/03

Index - Standard & Poor's 500 Worth $16,673
7.76 % annualized 07/31/96–05/31/03

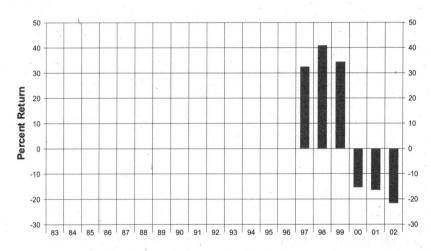

ANNUAL PERFORMANCE

TOP 10 HOLDINGS

Microsoft	International Business Machines
Wal-Mart Stores	Merck
Pfizer	Verizon Communications
Johnson & Johnson	Cablevision
Procter & Gamble	Intel

AMERICAN CENTURY EQUITY GROWTH

OBJECTIVE:	Large-Cap Value	
MANAGER:	William Martin and Jeff Tyler	*17*

FUND OVERVIEW:

American Century Equity Growth managers William Martin and Jeff Tyler use a quantitative approach to running their fund. They begin by combing through the 2,500 largest companies traded in the U.S., which means there are plenty of small caps represented as well. Using a portfolio optimization model, they make sure holdings in the fund match the risk characteristics of the S&P 500, while seeing to it that no more than 25 percent of all assets are invested in the same industry. "This gives the fund balance and stability, which are favorable characteristics during periods of increased market volatility," the managers note.

When it comes to picking individual stocks, the model takes many factors into consideration, including whether a company is underpriced based on earnings growth, business fundamentals, or intrinsic value. Martin and Tyler remain fully invested at all times and tend to focus on the largest names. However, they often include a number of small companies in an effort to enhance returns. They are also working to reduce turnover, which should make the portfolio more tax-efficient going forward.

ANNUALIZED RETURNS	
1-Year	–6.40%
3-Year	–10.39%
5-Year	–1.92%
Overall Rank	3
Risk Rank	3

MINIMUM INVESTMENT	
Regular	$2,500
IRA	$1,000

PORTFOLIO STATISTICS	
Beta	0.98
Turnover	100.00%
12-Month Yield	0.84%
12b-1 Fee	0.00%
Expense Ratio	0.68%

CONTACT INFORMATION
American Century Equity Growth Fund
Telephone: (800) 345-2021
www.americancentury.com

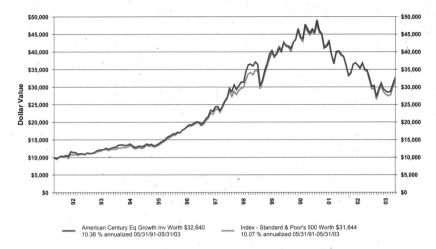

—— American Century Eq Growth Inv Worth $32,640
10.36 % annualized 05/31/91-05/31/03

—— Index - Standard & Poor's 500 Worth $31,644
10.07 % annualized 05/31/91-05/31/03

GROWTH OF $10,000

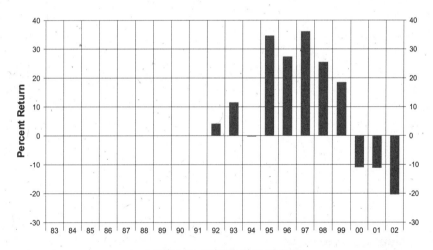

ANNUAL PERFORMANCE

TOP 10 HOLDINGS

Microsoft	ExxonMobil
Merck	Verizon Communications
Pfizer	General Electric
Bank of America	Intel
Johnson & Johnson	Citigroup

AMERISTOCK

OBJECTIVE:	Large-Cap Value	
MANAGER:	Nicholas D. Gerber	*18*

FUND OVERVIEW:

It's not surprising that Nicholas Gerber adheres to a strict combination of active and passive strategies when running his Ameristock mutual fund. After all, before going out on his own, Gerber managed a series of index funds for Bank of America. On the "active" side of the equation, he looks for stocks with low price-to-earnings ratios, high dividend yields, consistent sales growth, and impressive earnings track records. On the "passive" side, he adheres to a low turnover strategy, which keeps commissions and taxable gains down.

Gerber's universe is the largest and most successful companies, which he ranks according to value. He then buys those names that meet his "active" requirements. Gerber started Ameristock in 1995. Although he has recently brought on a few analysts to help him out, this fund remains a fairly small operation. In fact, if you call his firm for information, Gerber himself might answer the phone.

Nevertheless, Ameristock has everything you could want in a large-cap value fund: relatively low expenses, high tax efficiency, and excellent performance.

ANNUALIZED RETURNS		PORTFOLIO STATISTICS	
1-Year	−9.60%	Beta	0.73
3-Year	1.40%	Turnover	6.00%
5-Year	5.36%	12-Month Yield	1.15%
Overall Rank	2	12b-1 Fee	0.00%
Risk Rank	3	Expense Ratio	0.77%

MINIMUM INVESTMENT		CONTACT INFORMATION	
Regular	$1,000	*Ameristock Mutual Fund*	
IRA	$1,000	*Telephone: (800) 394-5064*	
		www.ameristock.com	

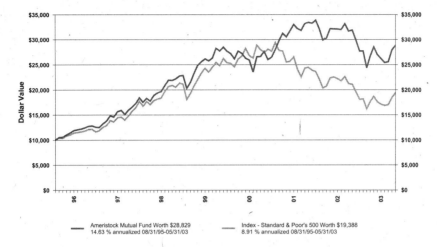

Ameristock Mutual Fund Worth $28,829
14.63 % annualized 08/31/95-05/31/03

Index - Standard & Poor's 500 Worth $19,388
8.91 % annualized 08/31/95-05/31/03

GROWTH OF $10,000

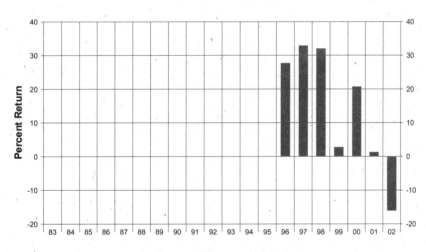

ANNUAL PERFORMANCE

TOP 10 HOLDINGS

Merck	Bristol Myers Squibb
Washington Mutual	Wyeth
Bank of America	Citigroup
General Electric	Sara Lee
Federal Natl. Mortgage	DuPont

CLIPPER FUND

OBJECTIVE:	*Large-Cap Value*	*19*
MANAGER:	*Team Managed*	

FUND OVERVIEW:

Clipper Fund lead skipper James Gipson runs a tight ship. He looks for a few select large-cap stocks that are priced right, and will hold hefty amounts of cash when he can't find any. His portfolio may contain as few as 10 to 15 names, especially when he's gloomy about the outlook for the overall market. A cautious approach? You bet. Yet Gipson has managed to beat the S&P 500 over time, a tough job for even the most aggressive fund.

Gipson is most concerned about preserving capital. He looks for industry leaders selling below intrinsic value. That number is determined either by using a dividend and cash flow discounting model, or by looking at price-to-earnings ratios and comparing the sales transactions of like businesses. Balance sheet strength and the ability to generate earnings are other key factors in the appraisal process. Gipson attempts to keep turnover down, to reduce taxes. But he won't hesitate to trim a holding when he feels the timing is right to do so. "Our first choice is to buy stock in a good company cheaply and then hold it forever," he says. "We will sell overvalued stocks, however, rather than expose [the] portfolio to potential loss."

ANNUALIZED RETURNS		PORTFOLIO STATISTICS	
1-Year	–6.90%	Beta	0.52
3-Year	13.15%	Turnover	48.10%
5-Year	10.66%	12-Month Yield	1.31%
Overall Rank	2	12b-1 Fee	0.00%
Risk Rank	2	Expense Ratio	1.07%
MINIMUM INVESTMENT		**CONTACT INFORMATION**	
Regular	$5,000	*Clipper Fund*	
IRA	$2,000	*Telephone: (800) 776-5033*	
		www.clipperfund.com	

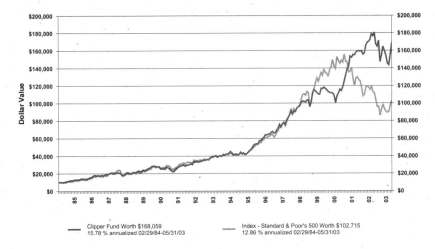

Clipper Fund Worth $168,059
15.78 % annualized 02/29/84-05/31/03

Index - Standard & Poor's 500 Worth $102,715
12.86 % annualized 02/29/84-05/31/03

GROWTH OF $10,000

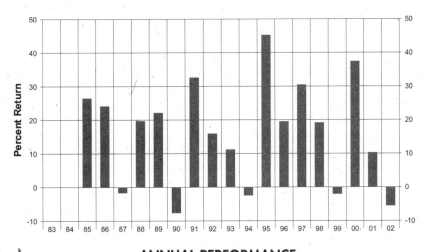

ANNUAL PERFORMANCE

TOP 10 HOLDINGS

Freddie Mac	Tenet Healthcare
Tyco	American Express
Electronic Data Systems	Equity Residential
Fannie Mae	El Paso Corporation
Altria Group	UST

DODGE & COX STOCK

| OBJECTIVE: | *Large-Cap Value* | *20* |
| MANAGER: | *Team Managed* | |

FUND OVERVIEW:

The Dodge & Cox Stock fund, founded in 1965, takes a price-disciplined approach to investing in large-cap companies. The management team won't buy or sell a stock unless it meets their projected price target. They use a bottom-up approach to company selection, emphasizing fundamental analysis. Still, several themes stand out. The fund has a high weighting in cyclically sensitive areas, such as chemicals, autos, paper/forest products, and transportation. It also maintains a lower exposure than the S&P 500 to the consumer products, healthcare, and telephone sectors, because valuations in these areas are too high, given the managers' assessment of future earnings potential. "We strive to invest in companies with strong business franchises, good prospects for improving profitability, and current valuations that we believe reflect relatively low investor expectations," notes fund president John A. Gunn.

Stocks in the portfolio generally have below-average price-to-earnings, price-to-book, and market cap-to-sales ratios. Because every investment is made with a three- to five-year time horizon, turnover is consistently low, which increases the overall tax efficiency of this time-tested performer.

ANNUALIZED RETURNS		PORTFOLIO STATISTICS	
1-Year	−4.90%	Beta	0.68
3-Year	5.87%	Turnover	13.33%
5-Year	7.79%	12-Month Yield	1.58%
Overall Rank	2	12b-1 Fee	0.00%
Risk Rank	2	Expense Ratio	0.54%

MINIMUM INVESTMENT		CONTACT INFORMATION	
Regular	$2,500	*Dodge & Cox Stock Fund*	
IRA	$1,000	*Telephone: (800) 621-3979*	
		www.dodgeandcox.com	

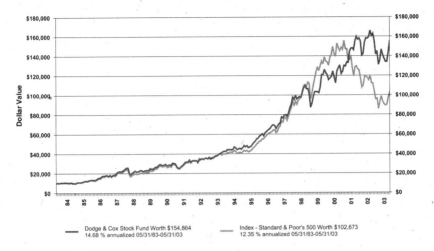

Dodge & Cox Stock Fund Worth $154,864
14.68 % annualized 05/31/83-05/31/03

Index - Standard & Poor's 500 Worth $102,673
12.35 % annualized 05/31/83-05/31/03

GROWTH OF $10,000

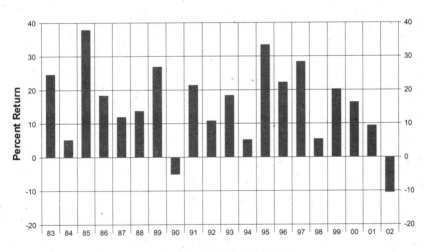

ANNUAL PERFORMANCE

TOP 10 HOLDINGS

Dow Chemical
Bank One
Comcast
News Corp
Schering Plough

Conoco Phillips
Hewlett Packard
Golden West Financial
FedEx
Xerox

EXCELSIOR VALUE AND RESTRUCTURING

OBJECTIVE: *Large-Cap Value*
MANAGER: *David Williams*

21

FUND OVERVIEW:

For years, David Williams's Excelsior Value and Restructuring Fund was one of the best kept secrets in the mutual funds world. Then word of his great performance started to trickle into the media. Even though the sudden exposure brought a huge inflow of new assets, Williams has been able to handle the fresh cash without a problem, doing well in both the growth and value markets.

This astute U.S. Trust manager looks for stocks that are predicted to benefit from either an expected restructuring or the redeployment of assets and operations. Such companies may include those involved in prospective mergers, consolidations, liquidations, spin-offs, or financial reorganizations. Because these stocks are troubled to begin with, Williams can usually pick them up on the cheap, often for less than 15 times earnings. But such a strategy is fraught with risk. After all, these businesses are often in bad shape to begin with. If the restructuring isn't successful, they might not survive. Williams increases his chances for success by first meeting with management. Then he makes sure the portfolio is diversified among close to 90 names. With that strategy, he surmises, there's a good chance something will always be working.

ANNUALIZED RETURNS	
1-Year	−7.80%
3-Year	−2.79%
5-Year	4.95%
Overall Rank	2
Risk Rank	3

MINIMUM INVESTMENT	
Regular	$500
IRA	$250

PORTFOLIO STATISTICS	
Beta	1.08
Turnover	8.00%
12-Month Yield	0.34%
12b-1 Fee	0.00%
Expense Ratio	0.98%

CONTACT INFORMATION

Excelsior Value and Restructuring Fund
Telephone: (800) 446-1012
www.excelsiorfunds.com

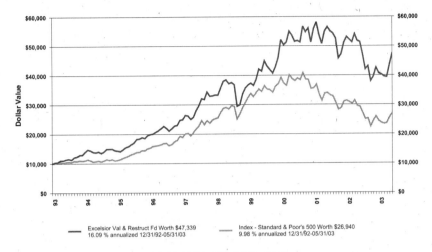

Excelsior Val & Restruct Fd Worth $47,339
16.09 % annualized 12/31/92-05/31/03

Index - Standard & Poor's 500 Worth $26,940
9.98 % annualized 12/31/92-05/31/03

GROWTH OF $10,000

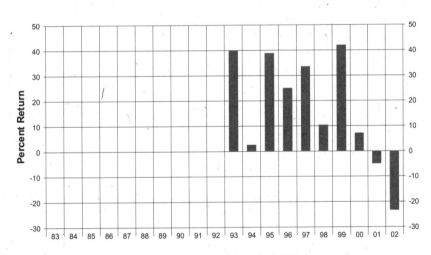

ANNUAL PERFORMANCE

TOP 10 HOLDINGS	
Centex	Harman International
Union Pacific	Avon Products
Black and Decker	Kraft Foods
Dean Foods	Harris Corporation
XM Satellite Radio	Citigroup

GABELLI WESTWOOD EQUITY

OBJECTIVE:	*Large-Cap Value*	*22*
MANAGER:	*Susan Byrne*	

FUND OVERVIEW:

Susan Byrne's number-one rule of investing is "Try not to ever lose money." It's a goal she doesn't always achieve, of course. But when she buys each stock for Gabelli Westwood Equity's portfolio, she first attempts to figure out how much it could go down. In her search for individual companies, Byrne employs a top-down approach, beginning with an analysis of overall economic trends to identify sectors or industries poised for growth. Once that work has been done, she starts looking for individual securities that are most likely to benefit.

Byrne's analysis includes searching for a catalyst that can drive a stock higher. When she finds one, she checks out what other analysts are saying about the company. She'll only buy if she feels her peers are underestimating the company's potential. Specifically, Byrne wants to invest in businesses that she is almost certain will come through with positive earnings surprises, surpassing all Wall Street estimates. She sets a target for every stock in the portfolio, and revises it up or down based on the actual reported numbers. This means that sometimes she gets out of high-fliers before they run out of steam. But she'd rather play it safe than risk being shocked by a disappointment.

ANNUALIZED RETURNS		PORTFOLIO STATISTICS	
1-Year	–11.80%	Beta	0.71
3-Year	–5.96%	Turnover	84.00%
5-Year	1.54%	12-Month Yield	1.06%
Overall Rank	3	12b-1 Fee	0.25%
Risk Rank	2	Expense Ratio	1.46%

MINIMUM INVESTMENT		CONTACT INFORMATION	
Regular	$1,000	*Gabelli Westwood Equity Fund*	
IRA	$250	*Telephone: (800) 422-3554*	
		www.gabelli.com	

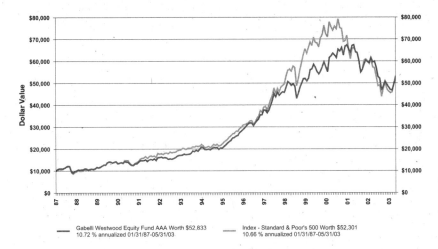

Gabelli Westwood Equity Fund AAA Worth $52,833
10.72 % annualized 01/31/87-05/31/03

Index - Standard & Poor's 500 Worth $52,301
10.66 % annualized 01/31/87-05/31/03

GROWTH OF $10,000

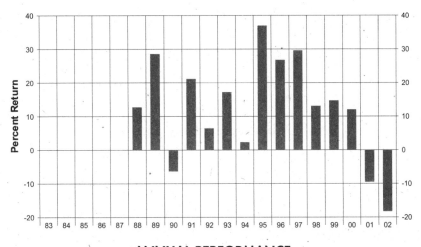

ANNUAL PERFORMANCE

TOP 10 HOLDINGS	
ExxonMobil	Washington Mutual
Bear Stearns	Federal Natl. Mortgage
Murphy Oil	Lockheed Martin
Procter & Gamble	M&T Bank
Pfizer	International Business Machines

LEGG MASON VALUE TRUST

OBJECTIVE:	*Large-Cap Value*	*23*
MANAGER:	*William Miller*	

FUND OVERVIEW:

Legg Mason Value Trust manager Bill Miller is a legend in the fund industry, with an unmatched record for consistently beating the S&P 500 (14 years and running so far). Miller has attracted both praise and criticism for the comparatively liberal way he defines "value." But you can't argue that he's led this fund to excellent returns thanks to shrewd stock picking and a low turnover style.

Miller is quick to point out that he is an investor, not a speculator. He doesn't try to guess the direction of the market or which industries are most likely to outperform. He builds his portfolio one name at a time. "We do intensive research on our holdings and try to buy companies whose prices represent large discounts to our assessment of the intrinsic value of the business," he says. "We use an economic value approach to our analytical process, which involves going well beyond simple accounting-based measures of value."

Miller runs a tightly focused portfolio of about 35 to 40 names, and will hold on to his biggest winners, even when they mature from being "value" stocks and become "growth" stocks.

ANNUALIZED RETURNS

1-Year	15.73%
3-Year	−5.42%
5-Year	5.98%
Overall Rank	2
Risk Rank	4

MINIMUM INVESTMENT

Regular	$1,000
IRA	$1,000

PORTFOLIO STATISTICS

Beta	1.19
Turnover	31.20%
12-Month Yield	0.00%
12b-1 Fee	1.00%
Expense Ratio	1.70%

CONTACT INFORMATION

Legg Mason Value Trust
Telephone: (800) 822-5544
www.leggmason.com

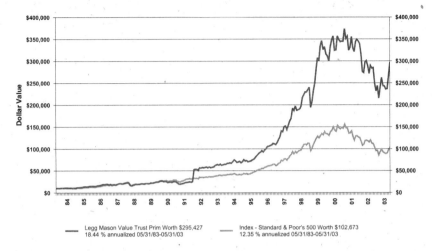

Legg Mason Value Trust Prim Worth $295,427
18.44 % annualized 05/31/83-05/31/03

Index - Standard & Poor's 500 Worth $102,673
12.35 % annualized 05/31/83-05/31/03

GROWTH OF $10,000

VALUE LINE ANNUAL PERFORMANCE CHART
NOT AVAILABLE FOR THIS FUND

ANNUAL PERFORMANCE

TOP 10 HOLDINGS

Nextel Communications
United Health Group
Amazon.com
Tyco
Washington Mutual

Eastman Kodak
Bank One
Waste Management
USA Interactive
MGIC Investment Corporation

LONGLEAF PARTNERS

OBJECTIVE:	*Large-Cap Value*	*24*
MANAGER:	*Team Managed*	

FUND OVERVIEW:

The Memphis-based team of managers at Longleaf Partners runs a non-diversified portfolio of between 20 and 30 companies that they view as being attractively priced. They look for these stocks using a rigid screening process. They first assess a company's net worth, by determining its level of free cash flow and analyzing its niche in the marketplace to make a prediction on future profitability. The decision to buy depends on whether the stock's current market price is at least 40 percent less than its net worth, or what Longleaf managers call "intrinsic value."

The Longleaf team, led by Mason Hawkins and Staley Cates, views equity investments as part ownership in business enterprises. They believe that buying stocks below intrinsic value will help to protect capital from significant loss, while allowing for substantial appreciation once the market ultimately recognizes this value. Longleaf's managers believe in concentrating assets in their best ideas and have been known to close funds when assets get to a level where future returns might be jeopardized.

ANNUALIZED RETURNS		PORTFOLIO STATISTICS	
1-Year	1.10%	Beta	0.64
3-Year	10.61%	Turnover	18.00%
5-Year	7.41%	12-Month Yield	0.33%
Overall Rank	1	12b-1 Fee	0.00%
Risk Rank	2	Expense Ratio	0.91%
MINIMUM INVESTMENT		**CONTACT INFORMATION**	
Regular	$10,000	*Longleaf Partners Fund*	
IRA	$10,000	*Telephone: (800) 445-9469*	
		www.longleafpartners.com	

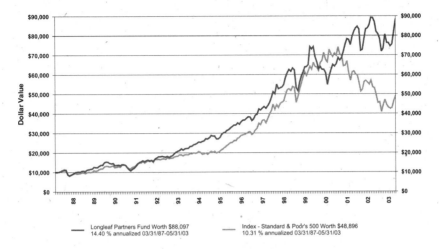

Longleaf Partners Fund Worth $88,097
14.40 % annualized 03/31/87-05/31/03

Index - Standard & Podr's 500 Worth $48,896
10.31 % annualized 03/31/87-05/31/03

GROWTH OF $10,000

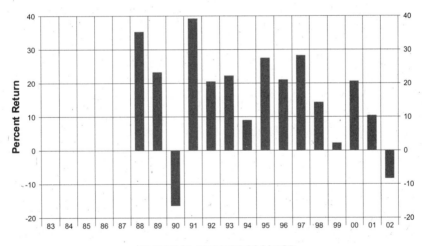

ANNUAL PERFORMANCE

TOP 10 HOLDINGS

Walt Disney	General Motors Class H
FedEx	Pioneer Natural Resource
Comcast	Yum! Brands
AON	Hilton Hotels
Marriott International	Vivendi Universal

NEUBERGER BERMAN FOCUS

OBJECTIVE:	*Large-Cap Value*	*25*
MANAGER:	*Kent Simons*	

FUND OVERVIEW:

Neuberger Berman Focus manager Kent Simons searches for companies with solid fundamentals that he considers to be undervalued by the market. He concentrates on industry leaders with above-average earnings growth and sound future prospects. Since he believes such companies come in all sizes, he doesn't limit his selections to any particular capitalization range, although his portfolio has historically owned mostly large blue-chip names.

Simons selects stocks from 13 different market sectors, but he generally narrows his list down to no more than six. That's because he's found that the conditions leading one stock to be undervalued often cause other companies in the same sector to be similarly cheap. As a result, the portfolio is generally concentrated in just a handful of industries, which can lead to added volatility.

Simons has been managing money for more than 40 years. He seeks companies that are industry leaders and temporarily undervalued, not those that are in the bargain bin because of poor management or limited growth prospects.

ANNUALIZED RETURNS		PORTFOLIO STATISTICS	
1-Year	–15.80%	Beta	1.87
3-Year	–7.84%	Turnover	38.00%
5-Year	1.32%	12-Month Yield	0.00%
Overall Rank	3	12b-1 Fee	0.10%
Risk Rank	5	Expense Ratio	1.09%

MINIMUM INVESTMENT		CONTACT INFORMATION
Regular	$1,000	*Neuberger Berman Focus*
IRA	$250	*Telephone: (800) 877-9700*
		www.nbfunds.com

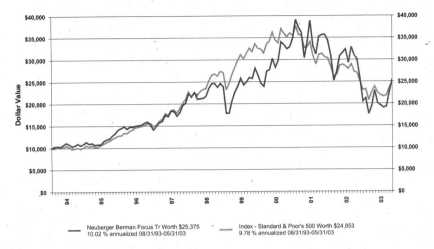

— Neuberger Berman Focus Tr Worth $25,375
10.02 % annualized 08/31/93-05/31/03

— Index - Standard & Poor's 500 Worth $24,853
9.78 % annualized 08/31/93-05/31/03

GROWTH OF $10,000

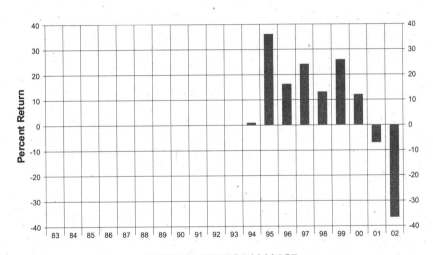

ANNUAL PERFORMANCE

TOP 10 HOLDINGS

Capital One
Citigroup
International Rectifier
Merrill Lynch
JP Morgan Chase

Lehman Brothers
Furniture Brands
TJX Companies
Morgan Stanley
Flextronics

OAK VALUE

OBJECTIVE:	Large-Cap Value	
MANAGER:	Team Managed	*26*

FUND OVERVIEW:

David Carr and his late business partner, George Brumley, didn't have a background in money management when they started their investment firm in 1986. What they did have was a keen interest in the teachings of Warren Buffett. They studied Buffett's Berkshire Hathaway annual reports and used them to help form the foundation of the investment discipline that Carr continues to follow today.

After Brumley's untimely death in 2003, Carr began running the fund with the help of two other managers. Like Buffett, they refer to their approach as looking for "good businesses with good management at attractive prices." Oak Value Fund seeks companies selling at a discount to intrinsic value. Carr and his team search for strong franchises and value stocks that can be had at a discount to the cash flow the business is expected to generate over the next several years. They personally visit dozens of companies each year, looking for new ideas. They strive to build a portfolio full of companies whose products or services they understand, and whose management they respect, just like Buffett. Not surprisingly, Buffett's Berkshire Hathaway is among the fund's top holdings.

ANNUALIZED RETURNS		PORTFOLIO STATISTICS	
1-Year	−10.50%	Beta	0.83
3-Year	1.29%	Turnover	63.00%
5-Year	0.53%	12-Month Yield	0.00%
Overall Rank	3	12b-1 Fee	0.00%
Risk Rank	3	Expense Ratio	1.36%
MINIMUM INVESTMENT		**CONTACT INFORMATION**	
Regular	$2,500	Oak Value Fund	
IRA	$1,000	Telephone: (800) 680-4199	
		www.oakvaluefund.com	

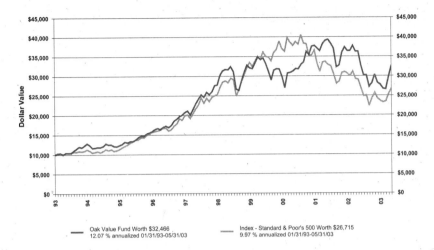

Oak Value Fund Worth $32,466
12.07 % annualized 01/31/93-05/31/03

Index - Standard & Poor's 500 Worth $26,715
9.97 % annualized 01/31/93-05/31/03

GROWTH OF $10,000

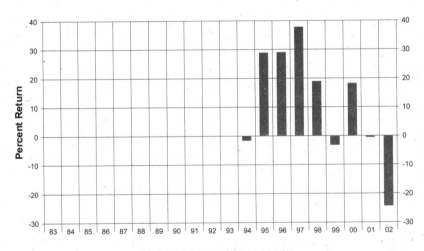

ANNUAL PERFORMANCE

TOP 10 HOLDINGS

Comcast	EW Scripps
Berkshire Hathaway	Constellation Brands
Cendant	AOL Time Warner
Ambac Financial	Merck
XL Capital	Dow Jones & Co.

OAKMARK

OBJECTIVE:	Large-Cap Value	27
MANAGER:	Bill Nygren and Kevin Grant	

FUND OVERVIEW:

Bill Nygren has built a terrific record picking value-oriented stocks for the concentrated Oakmark Select Fund. Unfortunately, that fund closed to new investors in mid-2001. Luckily you can still tap into his great investment skills through the flagship Oakmark Fund, which he took charge of in 2000.

Oakmark is a more diversified fund than Select, but Nygren applies his same value investment philosophy and process. This calls for buying companies trading at a significant discount to their true underlying business value.

The portfolio generally contains large, recognized companies with temporarily depressed share prices. In recent years, Nygren has even loaded up on technology companies and other previously high-flying growth names that were once far too pricey to meet his strict value discipline.

Nygren joined Harris Associates, the fund's adviser, in 1983. He was the firm's director of research for eight years before becoming its most prominent fund manager.

The fund usually holds around 50 stocks, which are purchased at what Nygren deems to be a 40 percent discount from their actual value.

ANNUALIZED RETURNS	
1-Year	−8.50%
3-Year	8.88%
5-Year	1.56%
Overall Rank	2
Risk Rank	2

MINIMUM INVESTMENT	
Regular	$1,000
IRA	$1,000

PORTFOLIO STATISTICS	
Beta	0.70
Turnover	21.00%
12-Month Yield	0.33%
12b-1 Fee	0.00%
Expense Ratio	1.14%

CONTACT INFORMATION

Oakmark Fund
Telephone: (800) 625-6275
www.oakmark.com

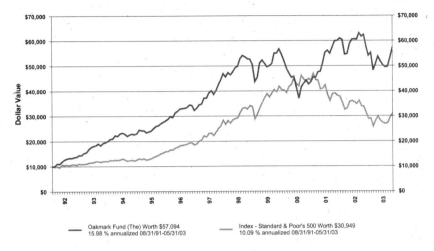

Oakmark Fund (The) Worth $57,094
15.98 % annualized 08/31/91-05/31/03

Index - Standard & Poor's 500 Worth $30,949
10.09 % annualized 08/31/91-05/31/03

GROWTH OF $10,000

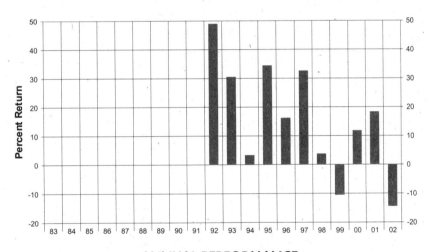

ANNUAL PERFORMANCE

TOP 10 HOLDINGS

Washington Mutual
H&R Block
Home Depot
Fannie Mae
AOL Time Warner

Bristol Myers Squibb
MGIC Investment Corporation
Yum! Brands
Liberty Media
First Data

SELECTED AMERICAN SHARES

OBJECTIVE:	*Large-Cap Value*	*28*
MANAGER:	*Christopher Davis and Kenneth Feinberg*	

FUND OVERVIEW:

If you had to make a short list of the best mutual fund managers of all time, there's no question that Shelby Davis would show up near the top. His New York Venture Fund has been an outstanding performer since its inception in 1969. Perhaps he inherited much of his investment skill from his late father, who was a Wall Street legend in his own right. Unfortunately, New York Venture is a load fund, meaning you pay a commission to get in. The good news is that Shelby took over management of Selected American Shares in 1993, which is a nearly identical fund that is available on a no-load basis. Shelby relinquished day-to-day portfolio management duties to his son, Chris, in 1997, although he remains the firm's chief investment officer. Shelby still spends his days providing guidance on investment themes, strategies, and individual stock selection, while Chris and comanager Kenneth Feinberg pull the trigger.

The Davis investment philosophy calls for finding overlooked, undervalued companies with promising long-term prospects and doing rigorous research, visiting with management, and actively managing risk. They also favor proven businesses with long histories of earnings growth.

ANNUALIZED RETURNS		PORTFOLIO STATISTICS	
1-Year	−6.40%	Beta	0.81
3-Year	−6.21%	Turnover	19.00%
5-Year	2.64%	12-Month Yield	0.71%
Overall Rank	2	12b-1 Fee	0.25%
Risk Rank	2	Expense Ratio	0.93%

MINIMUM INVESTMENT		CONTACT INFORMATION	
Regular	$1,000	*Selected American Shares*	
IRA	$250	*Telephone: (800) 243-1575*	
		www.selectedfunds.com	

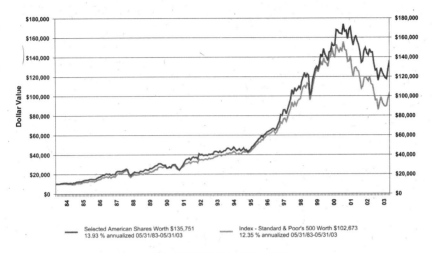

Selected American Shares Worth $135,751
13.93 % annualized 05/31/83-05/31/03

Index - Standard & Poor's 500 Worth $102,673
12.35 % annualized 05/31/83-05/31/03

GROWTH OF $10,000

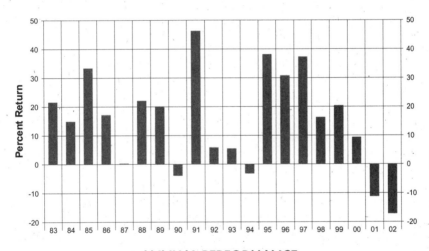

ANNUAL PERFORMANCE

TOP 10 HOLDINGS

American Express	Household International
Altria Group	Tyco
American International Group	Bank One
Wells Fargo & Company	Costco Wholesale
Citigroup	Golden West Financial

TORRAY FUND

| OBJECTIVE: | Large-Cap Value |
| MANAGER: | Robert E. Torray |

29

FUND OVERVIEW:

Robert Torray has long been well known in institutional money management circles. His retail fund has also earned increasing respect and notoriety in recent years. While clearly a value manager, Torray doesn't like labels, nor can he be easily pigeonholed into a clear-cut category.

Torray says his investment style is simple. He buys stocks in the best companies at a fair price and keeps them indefinitely. He'll consider small, medium, or large capitalization companies, although the latter have been getting most of his attention lately. His chosen companies have favorable economic characteristics, like rising sales and earnings, a strong competitive position, capable management, and a solid balance sheet. Torray runs a concentrated portfolio. More than half of all assets are placed in his top 20 holdings.

While his fund has received an ever-increasing inflow of new cash in recent years, Torray insists he's had no problem putting it to work. "So far, cash flow from shareholders has proven to be a tremendous advantage," he claims. "It has funded promising new investments and additions to existing holdings that otherwise could not have been made without selling stocks we prefer to maintain."

ANNUALIZED RETURNS		PORTFOLIO STATISTICS	
1-Year	−7.20%	Beta	0.91
3-Year	−2.12%	Turnover	27.30%
5-Year	2.22%	12-Month Yield	0.55%
Overall Rank	2	12b-1 Fee	0.00%
Risk Rank	3	Expense Ratio	1.36%
MINIMUM INVESTMENT		**CONTACT INFORMATION**	
Regular	$10,000	*Torray Fund*	
IRA	$10,000	*Telephone: (800) 443-3036*	
		www.torray.com	

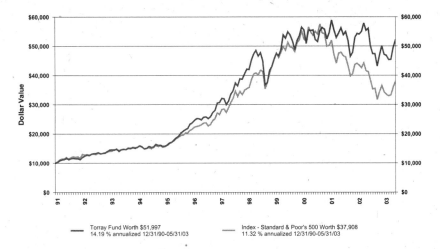

Torray Fund Worth $51,997
14.19 % annualized 12/31/90-05/31/03

Index - Standard & Poor's 500 Worth $37,908
11.32 % annualized 12/31/90-05/31/03

GROWTH OF $10,000

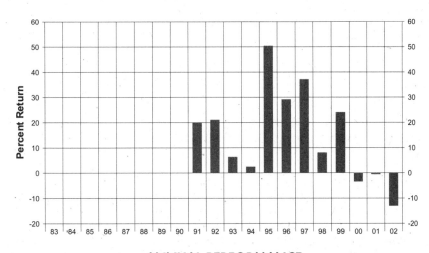

ANNUAL PERFORMANCE

TOP 10 HOLDINGS

Illinois Tool Works	Abbott Laboratories
United Technologies	Clear Channel Communications
General Motors Class H	Kimberly Clark
Tribune	Markel
Merck	Bank One

BONNEL GROWTH

		30
OBJECTIVE:	*Mid-Cap Growth*	
MANAGER:	*Art Bonnel*	

FUND OVERVIEW:

In Art Bonnel's mind, a company's financial numbers tell the whole story. That's why he places such an emphasis on locating companies with strong earnings and a solid balance sheet. Working out of his Reno, Nevada home, along with wife Wanda, Bonnel begins most mornings by going through all of the Wall Street earnings reports, in search of potential candidates for his portfolio. If the numbers look good, he'll dig deeper, making sure the company has a leading position in its market niche and a management team with a substantial ownership stake.

While Bonnel has the freedom to buy any stocks he wants, he usually focuses on companies with market capitalizations of under $5 billion. Bonnel has been managing money since 1970, and especially shines when investors are attracted to stocks with rising earnings momentum. He often loads up on specific sectors, which leads to frequent turbulence, and even moves completely into cash when he thinks the market outlook is unfavorable. But, over the long term, Bonnel has done a good job of staying ahead of the market. What's more, running this fund is the only thing Bonnel does, unlike many of his peers who are left juggling a couple of funds and a number of private accounts on the side.

ANNUALIZED RETURNS		PORTFOLIO STATISTICS	
1-Year	–21.00%	Beta	0.77
3-Year	–21.01%	Turnover	79.93%
5-Year	1.23%	12-Month Yield	0.00%
Overall Rank	4	12b-1 Fee	0.17%
Risk Rank	3	Expense Ratio	1.47%

MINIMUM INVESTMENT		CONTACT INFORMATION
Regular	$5,000	*Bonnel Growth Fund*
IRA	$0	*Telephone: (800) 873-8637*
		www.usfunds.com

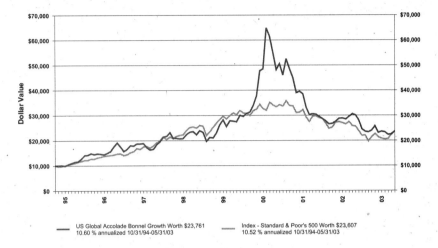

US Global Accolade Bonnel Growth Worth $23,761
10.60 % annualized 10/31/94-05/31/03

Index - Standard & Poor's 500 Worth $23,607
10.52 % annualized 10/31/94-05/31/03

GROWTH OF $10,000

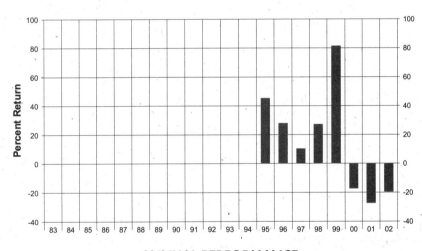

ANNUAL PERFORMANCE

TOP 10 HOLDINGS

Nvidia	Network Appliance
Intel	Cisco Systems
Nasdaq 100 Trust	Computer Associates
Fairchild Semiconductor	BEA Systems
Altera Corporation	Americredit

BRAMWELL GROWTH

| **OBJECTIVE:** | Mid-Cap Growth | *31* |
| **MANAGER:** | Elizabeth R. Bramwell | |

FUND OVERVIEW:

Elizabeth Bramwell uses a blended approach to find stocks for her Bramwell Growth Fund portfolio. She begins from a top-down perspective, looking at such macroeconomic variables as inflation and interest rates to help her determine which broad industries or themes are likely to benefit most from current conditions. From here, she does bottom-up analysis, focusing on company-specific variables like competitive industry dynamics, uniqueness of products and services, market leadership, and management expertise. On the financial side, Bramwell searches for stocks with high returns on sales and equity, favorable debt-to-equity ratios, and strong earnings and cash flow growth. She gets information from many sources, and she meets with management by attending the frequent analyst meetings held near her New York office.

Bramwell has been managing money for some three decades. Before launching her own fund in 1994, she built a great record at Gabelli Growth. Her present focus is on companies offering innovative new products and services that are beneficiaries of lower interest rates and effective users of technology. And while the fund is classified in the mid-cap growth category, lately Bramwell has been primarily favoring the stocks of larger companies.

ANNUALIZED RETURNS

1-Year	–13.40%
3-Year	–11.34%
5-Year	0.47%
Overall Rank	3
Risk Rank	2

MINIMUM INVESTMENT

Regular	$1,000
IRA	$500

PORTFOLIO STATISTICS

Beta	0.75
Turnover	66.00%
12-Month Yield	0.00%
12b-1 Fee	0.25%
Expense Ratio	1.67%

CONTACT INFORMATION

Bramwell Growth Fund
Telephone: (800) 272-6227
www.bramcap.com

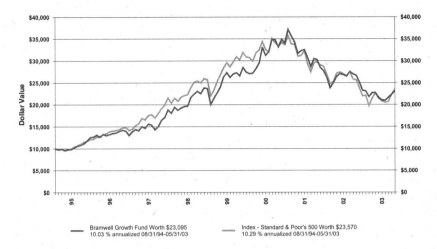

GROWTH OF $10,000

Bramwell Growth Fund Worth $23,095
10.03 % annualized 08/31/94-05/31/03

Index - Standard & Poor's 500 Worth $23,570
10.29 % annualized 08/31/94-05/31/03

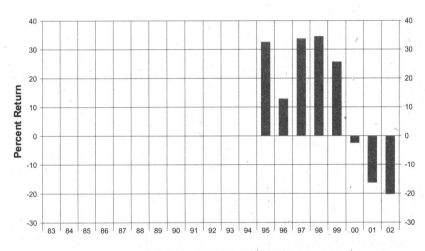

ANNUAL PERFORMANCE

TOP 10 HOLDINGS

Wal-Mart Stores	International Business Machines
Lowes Companies	Kohls
Dell Computer	Anthem
United Health Group	Microsoft
Affiliated Computer Services	Cardinal Health

MAIRS & POWER GROWTH

OBJECTIVE:	*Mid-Cap Growth*	*32*
MANAGER:	*George A. Mairs and William Frels*	

FUND OVERVIEW:

George Mairs likes to find investment ideas in his own backyard. That's why his Mairs & Power Growth fund has a large concentration of companies based in Minnesota. In fact, he and comanager William Frels focus their research efforts on finding good businesses in the upper Midwest. Their rationale is that this allows them to add value to the research process. After all, they understand these local firms better than Wall Street and can easily visit them in person. That doesn't mean they won't consider companies in other parts of the country. They will, but usually only when they can't find an equivalent idea in the same sector locally. This regional focus certainly hasn't hampered performance.

Mairs and Frels look for high-quality companies with predictable earnings, above-average return on equity, market dominance, and financial strength. They stay fully invested at all times and favor a buy-and-hold strategy. The managers will sell a holding once they believe it has become fully priced. They then use the proceeds either to establish a new position or add to an existing one. Although Mairs plans to retire next year, he will make himself available as a consultant to Frels, who shares an almost identical investment philosophy.

ANNUALIZED RETURNS		PORTFOLIO STATISTICS	
1-Year	−5.10%	Beta	0.53
3-Year	7.44%	Turnover	7.91%
5-Year	7.95%	12-Month Yield	0.83%
Overall Rank	1	12b-1 Fee	0.00%
Risk Rank	2	Expense Ratio	0.76%
MINIMUM INVESTMENT		**CONTACT INFORMATION**	
Regular	$2,500	*Mairs & Power Growth Fund*	
IRA	$1,000	*Telephone: (800) 304-7404*	
		www.mairsandpower.com	

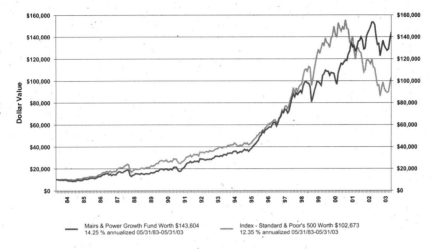

Mairs & Power Growth Fund Worth $143,604
14.25 % annualized 05/31/83-05/31/03

Index - Standard & Poor's 500 Worth $102,673
12.35 % annualized 05/31/83-05/31/03

GROWTH OF $10,000

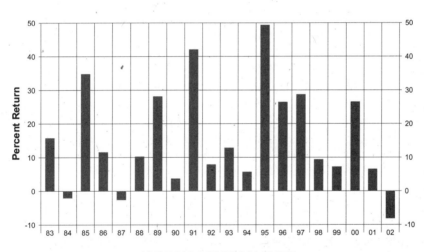

ANNUAL PERFORMANCE

TOP 10 HOLDINGS	
Medtronic	St. Jude Medical
Wells Fargo & Company	Pfizer
Target	Toro
TGF Financial	Graco
General Mills	Johnson & Johnson

MERIDIAN GROWTH

OBJECTIVE:	Mid-Cap Growth	*33*
MANAGER:	Richard Aster	

FUND OVERVIEW:

Meridian Growth manager Richard Aster looks for high-quality growth companies that he doesn't have to pay a lot of money for. Aster normally invests in companies with revenues between $100 million and $1.5 billion at the time of purchase that are growing by at least 15 percent annually. He prefers companies with significant market shares in growing industries, with high returns on equity and strong corporate management. He's always on the lookout for fundamentally sound and well-positioned companies that can be had at reasonable prices.

When such opportunities aren't immediately available, Aster is willing to sit on the sidelines in cash. He tries to limit the number of holdings in the portfolio to around 40. Although stocks are selected based on their own individual merits, he also considers the impact of macroeconomic factors on market performance when making investment decisions.

Aster started the Meridian Growth fund in 1984, following a career that included stops at both the U.S. Treasury and various investment banking firms.

ANNUALIZED RETURNS	
1-Year	−5.70%
3-Year	8.07%
5-Year	9.21%
Overall Rank	2
Risk Rank	3

MINIMUM INVESTMENT	
Regular	$1,000
IRA	$1,000

PORTFOLIO STATISTICS	
Beta	0.85
Turnover	26.00%
12-Month Yield	0.20%
12b-1 Fee	0.00%
Expense Ratio	0.94%

CONTACT INFORMATION

Meridian Growth Fund
Telephone: (800) 446-6662
www.meridianfund.com

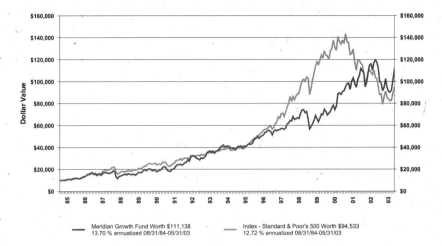

Meridian Growth Fund Worth $111,138
13.70 % annualized 08/31/84-05/31/03

Index - Standard & Poor's 500 Worth $94,533
12.72 % annualized 08/31/84-05/31/03

GROWTH OF $10,000

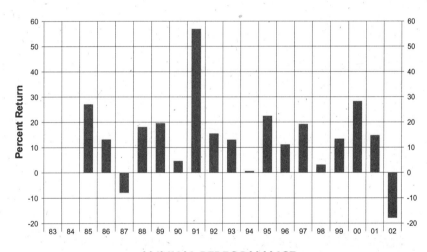

ANNUAL PERFORMANCE

TOP 10 HOLDINGS

Ruby Tuesday   Sonic Corporation
Republic Services   Mercury General
Davita   Applebee's International
Tektronix   Regis Corporation
Renal Care Group   Health Management Association

MOSAIC MID-CAP FUND

OBJECTIVE:	*Mid-Cap Growth*	*34*
MANAGER:	*Team Managed*	

FUND OVERVIEW:

Mosaic Mid-Cap's management team, led by Richard Eisinger and Jay Sekelsky, screens for both growth and value characteristics when searching for portfolio ideas. The fund typically holds 25 to 30 stocks, allowing the team to concentrate on its top ideas.

While growth is the fund's primary objective, each holding is also monitored for valuation. It's a discipline called growth-at-a-reasonable-price. The idea is that by avoiding the most expensive stocks and sectors, managers can temper volatility, especially in down markets.

Among the characteristics the Mosaic Mid-Cap team looks for is a pattern of consistent, sustainable earnings growth. Stock valuations are based on the projected growth rate of earnings and compared to the market in general and the company's historical patterns (they try to buy at the low end of historical valuations). The firm's fundamental screens normally lead to stocks in the financial, technology, healthcare, and consumer sectors. Generally no more than 25 percent of assets are placed into any one area of the market.

ANNUALIZED RETURNS		PORTFOLIO STATISTICS	
1-Year	−2.40%	Beta	0.69
3-Year	8.72%	Turnover	35.00%
5-Year	8.25%	12-Month Yield	0.77%
Overall Rank	1	12b-1 Fee	0.00%
Risk Rank	2	Expense Ratio	1.25%
MINIMUM INVESTMENT		**CONTACT INFORMATION**	
Regular	$1,000	*Mosaic Mid-Cap Fund*	
IRA	$500	*Telephone: (800) 336-3063*	
		www.mosaicfunds.com	

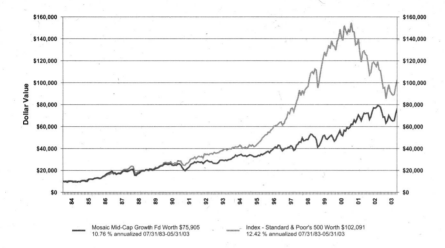

Mosaic Mid-Cap Growth Fd Worth $75,905
10.76 % annualized 07/31/83-05/31/03

Index - Standard & Poor's 500 Worth $102,091
12.42 % annualized 07/31/83-05/31/03

GROWTH OF $10,000

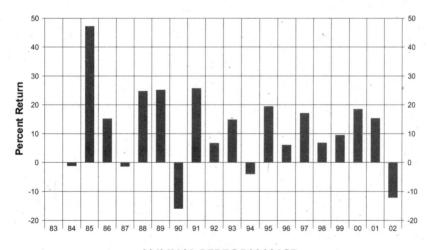

ANNUAL PERFORMANCE

TOP 10 HOLDINGS	
Markel	Liberty Media
White Mountains Insurance Group	Hasbro
Odyssey Reinsurance	Ethan Allen
Mohawk Industries	Dover Corporation
Costco Wholesale	Expeditors International

T. ROWE PRICE MID-CAP GROWTH

OBJECTIVE:	*Mid-Cap Growth*	*35*
MANAGER:	*Brian W. H. Berghuis*	

FUND OVERVIEW:

Brian Berghuis looks for stocks with market values in the $300 million to $4 billion range and with earnings that are growing at a faster-than-average rate. The manager of T. Rowe Price Mid-Cap Growth sticks mostly with domestic equities, although he'll occasionally buy foreign securities when compelling buying opportunities become available.

Berghuis invests based on the belief that good research—not opinions on the overall economic environment—is what leads to superior long-term results. "We devote our time to carefully researching and evaluating company fundamentals," he says. "While we typically examine a multitude of factors before we invest, and virtually never invest before a face-to-face meeting with a company's management, several of the criteria we focus on include the growth in the company's industry sector, the growth rate we foresee for the company over the next several years, the strength of a company's business model, management we respect, strong financial characteristics, and reasonable valuations."

Berghuis maintains a well-diversified portfolio and invests across multiple sectors to lower the fund's risk profile.

ANNUALIZED RETURNS		PORTFOLIO STATISTICS	
1-Year	−7.20%	Beta	1.13
3-Year	−2.00%	Turnover	36.00%
5-Year	5.54%	12-Month Yield	0.00%
Overall Rank	2	12b-1 Fee	0.00%
Risk Rank	4	Expense Ratio	0.91%

MINIMUM INVESTMENT		CONTACT INFORMATION
Regular	$2,500	*T. Rowe Price Mid-Cap Growth Fund*
IRA	$1,000	*Telephone: (800) 638-5660*
		www.troweprice.com

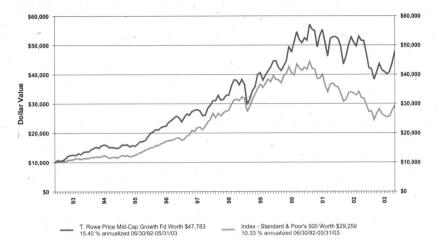

GROWTH OF $10,000

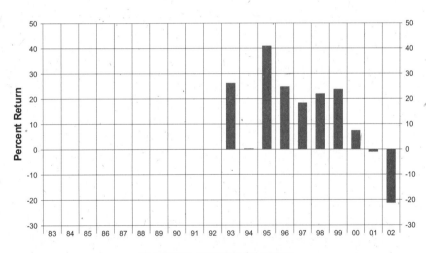

ANNUAL PERFORMANCE

TOP 10 HOLDINGS

Omnicare	Iron Mountain
Whole Foods Market	Choicepoint
BJ Services	Best Buy
Anthem	Waddell & Reed Financial
Gilead Sciences	Teva Pharmaceuticals

TCW GALILEO AGGRESSIVE GROWTH EQUITIES

OBJECTIVE:	Mid-Cap Growth	
MANAGER:	Christopher Ainley and Douglas Foreman	36

FUND OVERVIEW:

The TCW Galileo Aggressive Growth Equities Fund buys mid-sized companies that portfolio managers Christopher Ainley and Douglas Foreman believe are "reshaping the competitive landscape of the industries in which they compete." They believe investors are generally slow to recognize these trends, and feel if they can spot such companies early enough, they can profit handsomely once the rest of Wall Street catches on.

Ainley and Foreman narrow the mid-cap universe of more than 2,700 issues down to around 200 securities through a computerized screening process. They look for companies with earnings growth of at least 15 percent over the last three years and a similar return on equity. When all is said and done, they get a list of about 80 companies from which to choose.

This is among the most volatile funds in the mid-cap growth category, largely because the two managers often concentrate money in their favorite holdings. In fact, during the most recent period, almost half of the portfolio was invested in the fund's top 10 names. But the fund's long-term performance record has been admirable.

ANNUALIZED RETURNS		PORTFOLIO STATISTICS	
1-Year	5.00%	Beta	2.12
3-Year	−25.17%	Turnover	21.00%
5-Year	N/A	12-Month Yield	0.00%
Overall Rank	3	12b-1 Fee	0.25%
Risk Rank	5	Expense Ratio	1.62%

MINIMUM INVESTMENT		CONTACT INFORMATION	
Regular	$2,000	TCW Galileo Aggressive Growth Equities Fund	
IRA	$500	Telephone: (800) 386-3829	
		www.tcwgroup.com	

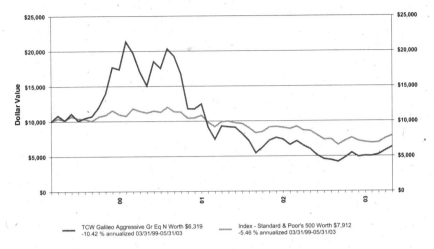

TCW Galileo Aggressive Gr Eq N Worth $6,319
-10.42 % annualized 03/31/99-05/31/03

Index - Standard & Poor's 500 Worth $7,912
-5.46 % annualized 03/31/99-05/31/03

GROWTH OF $10,000

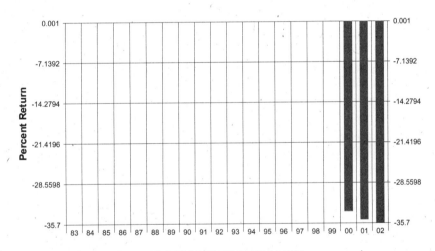

ANNUAL PERFORMANCE

TOP 10 HOLDINGS

Ebay
Maxim Integrated
Xilinx
Bed Bath & Beyond
Echostar Communications

Gilead Sciences
Westwood One
Univision
Expedia
Yahoo

TURNER MIDCAP GROWTH

OBJECTIVE:	*Mid-Cap Growth*
MANAGER:	*Christopher McHugh*

37

FUND OVERVIEW:

Chris McHugh selects stocks for the Turner Midcap portfolio based on the belief that earnings drive stock prices. His universe is equities with market capitalizations between $1 billion and $10 billion.

Unlike other funds in this category, McHugh attempts to keep his sector concentrations in line with the Russell Midcap Growth Index, which means you won't find him overweighted in any one area, including technology. In addition, by prospectus, the fund normally won't keep more than 2 percent of its assets in any one security. Such diversification is designed to lower risk, though this fund remains one of the category's most volatile offerings.

McHugh buys those stocks he believes will show impressive earnings and generally sells for one of two reasons: either the earnings don't pan out, or the stock grows outside of his capitalization range. As a result, there is a lot of trading going on in this portfolio, which can create some hefty year-end capital gains distributions. Therefore, this fund fits best into the tax-deferred portion of your investment portfolio.

ANNUALIZED RETURNS		PORTFOLIO STATISTICS	
1-Year	3.25%	Beta	1.66
3-Year	−19.68%	Turnover	260.00%
5-Year	7.17%	12-Month Yield	0.00%
Overall Risk	N/A	12b-1 Fee	0.00%
Risk Rate	N/A	Exchange Ratio	1.05%
MINIMUM INVESTMENT		**CONTACT INFORMATION**	
Regular	$2,500	*Turner Midcap Growth*	
IRA	$2,000	*Telephone: (800) 224-6312*	
		www.turner-invest.com	

VALUE LINE GROWTH OF $10,000 CHART
NOT AVAILABLE FOR THIS FUND

GROWTH OF $10,000

VALUE LINE ANNUAL PERFORMANCE CHART
NOT AVAILABLE FOR THIS FUND

ANNUAL PERFORMANCE

TOP 10 HOLDINGS

Gilead Sciences	Novellus Systems
MedImmune	St. Jude Medical
Aetna	Veritas Software
Yahoo	Legg Mason
VeriSign	KLA-Tencor

ARTISAN MID CAP VALUE

OBJECTIVE:	Mid-Cap Value	
MANAGER:	Scott Satterwhite and James Kieffer	*38*

FUND OVERVIEW:

Artisan Mid Cap Value managers Scott Satterwhite and James Kieffer troll around looking for undervalued companies with market capitalizations between $1.2 billion and $10 billion. Their value-oriented strategy general leads them to opportunities in one of the following: turnarounds (companies that appear capable of substantially improving earnings), undiscovered stocks (companies that aren't widely followed by Wall Street analysts), businesses with hidden assets (such as undervalued real estate or unrecognized product lines), and those in the process of major change (which may include new management, new product lines, or a cyclical uptrend in its industry).

From the list of potential candidates with the above characteristics, Satterwhite and Kieffer then concentrate on firms with low debt and positive cash flow, along with good returns on capital, to control risk. The fund generally holds 35 to 65 holdings and is broadly diversified across sectors and industries. Individual holdings typically don't exceed 5 percent of total assets.

Although this is a newer fund, Satterwhite has a solid track record managing similar portfolios using this winning approach.

ANNUALIZED RETURNS		PORTFOLIO STATISTICS	
1-Year	N/A	Beta	N/A
3-Year	N/A	Turnover	168.00%
5-Year	N/A	12-Month Yield	0.00%
Overall Rank	N/A	12b-1 Fee	0.25%
Risk Rank	N/A	Expense Ratio	1.95%

MINIMUM INVESTMENT		CONTACT INFORMATION	
Regular	$1,000	*Artisan Mid Cap Value Fund*	
IRA	$1,000	*Telephone: (800) 344-1770*	
		www.artisanfunds.com	

VALUE LINE GROWTH OF $10,000 CHART
NOT AVAILABLE FOR THIS FUND

GROWTH OF $10,000

VALUE LINE ANNUAL PERFORMANCE CHART
NOT AVAILABLE FOR THIS FUND

ANNUAL PERFORMANCE

TOP 10 HOLDINGS

Apache	Polo Ralph Lauren
Countrywide Financial	Republic Services A
Student Loan	XTO Energy
White Mountains Insurance Group	Nuveen Investment
Furniture Brands International	Zale

C&B MID CAP VALUE PORTFOLIO

OBJECTIVE:	Mid-Cap Value	**39**
MANAGER:	James Norris and Michael Meyer	

FUND OVERVIEW:

C&B Mid Cap Value, run by James Norris and Michael Meyer, invests primarily in the common stocks of companies with market capitalizations between $500 million and $5 billion. Stocks are selected based on analysis of a company's financial characteristics, the quality of management, and valuation. Norris and Meyer specifically look for companies with strong balance sheets, industry leading positions, an ability to generate excess cash flow that can be reinvested at attractive rates, and dividend and/or share repurchase policies that are beneficial to shareholders. They also seek stocks with a high return on equity and excellent fixed cost coverage ratios.

The evaluation process involves intensive research including interviews with a company's top executives and customers. Norris and Meyer determine a stock's value based on its future stream of anticipated cash flows. Stocks are sold when they are no longer attractively priced, the outlook for the company changes, or better alternatives are found. The portfolio generally contains 30 to 50 stocks, allowing for decent diversification, but with the potential to perform differently than the overall market.

ANNUALIZED RETURNS

1-Year	−0.12%
3-Year	15.57%
5-Year	13.03%
Overall Rank	N/A
Risk Rank	N/A

MINIMUM INVESTMENT

Regular	$2,500
IRA	$500

PORTFOLIO STATISTICS

Beta	0.69
Turnover	32.00%
12-Month Yield	0.11%
12b-1 Fee	0.00%
Expense Ratio	1.40%

CONTACT INFORMATION

C&B Mid Cap Value Portfolio
Telephone: (800) 336-7031
www.cooke-bieler.com

VALUE LINE GROWTH OF $10,000 CHART
NOT AVAILABLE FOR THIS FUND

GROWTH OF $10,000

VALUE LINE ANNUAL PERFORMANCE CHART
NOT AVAILABLE FOR THIS FUND

ANNUAL PERFORMANCE

TOP 10 HOLDINGS

Zale	Tommy Hilfiger
Big Lots	Hasbro
AON	Steelcase
Carlisle	CBRL Group
Pall	Snap-On

COHEN & STEERS REALTY

OBJECTIVE:	*Mid-Cap Value*	*40*
MANAGER:	*Martin Cohen and Robert Steers*	

FUND OVERVIEW:

Martin Cohen and Robert Steers started one of the first real estate funds in the 1980s. Like others in the category, Cohen & Steers Realty invests primarily in real estate investment trusts (REITs), which are publicly traded companies that own and operate real estate. Some specialize in commercial property; others, residential. In all cases, they pass through most of the rental income from properties to shareholders in the form of a dividend. Therefore, real estate funds like Cohen & Steers tend to have a high dividend yield, making them attractive to investors looking for regular investment income.

While its portfolio holdings generally fall into the mid-cap value category, Cohen & Steers Realty is technically a sector-specific fund. It's included in this book for two reasons: One, as previously stated, it may be of interest to those of you looking for regular dividend income. Second, real estate is an asset class of its own. Keeping 5 percent to 10 percent of your portfolio in a fund like this is an added form of diversification. Cohen & Steers Realty sticks mostly with blue-chip names and stays diversified across the various real estate industry sectors.

ANNUALIZED RETURNS		PORTFOLIO STATISTICS	
1-Year	3.50%	Beta	0.17
3-Year	13.17%	Turnover	37.30%
5-Year	6.62%	12-Month Yield	4.98%
Overall Rank	1	12b-1 Fee	0.00%
Risk Rank	2	Expense Ratio	1.08%

MINIMUM INVESTMENT		CONTACT INFORMATION	
Regular	$10,000	*Cohen & Steers Realty*	
IRA	$10,000	*Telephone: (800) 437-9912*	
		www.cohenandsteers.com	

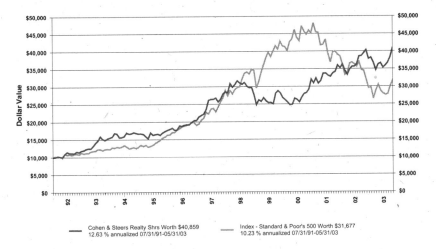

GROWTH OF $10,000

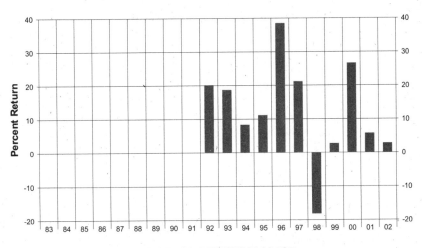

ANNUAL PERFORMANCE

TOP 10 HOLDINGS

Vornado Realty Trust
Boston Properties
Prologis
Simon Property Group
Rouse Company

Arden Realty
Brookfield Properties
Archstone Smith Trust
Equity Office Properties
Avalon Bay Communities

FIRST EAGLE FUND OF AMERICA

OBJECTIVE:	Mid-Cap Value	*41*
MANAGER:	Team Managed	

FUND OVERVIEW:

The focus of the First Eagle Fund of America is to find quality companies undergoing significant change. Lead portfolio manager Harold Levy contends that positive change can have a tremendous impact on a business, although the market is slow to realize that fact. This creates inefficiencies in the market, which he hopes to capitalize on. Among the changes Levy looks for: new management, acquisitions, share repurchases, divestitures, technological breakthroughs, or changes in strategy. Then, Levy figures out whether the stock is worth owning from a valuation perspective. "We look at a company as if we were buying the whole business, [which is] the way a rational businessman would price an acquisition," Levy says. He targets a return of 50 percent over a 12- to 18-month time frame for every idea under consideration. If he thinks a stock can achieve that ambitious goal, it will likely find its way into the portfolio.

You can never be certain that change will be good for a company. That's why Levy is constantly reevaluating his decisions. He hopes to limit his errors by doing extensive research and visiting his holdings on a regular basis to get a firsthand sense of how things are progressing.

ANNUALIZED RETURNS

1-Year	−3.10%
3-Year	4.99%
5-Year	4.96%
Overall Rank	2
Risk Rank	1

MINIMUM INVESTMENT

Regular	$2,500
IRA	$500

PORTFOLIO STATISTICS

Beta	0.52
Turnover	51.20%
12-Month Yield	0.00%
12b-1 Fee	0.25%
Expense Ratio	1.50%

CONTACT INFORMATION

First Eagle Fund of America
Telephone: (800) 451-3623
www.firsteaglefunds.com

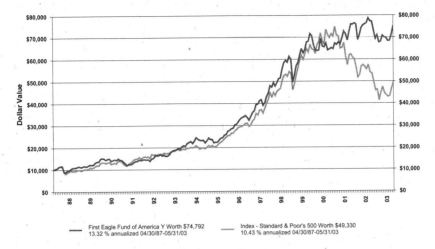

First Eagle Fund of America Y Worth $74,792
13.32 % annualized 04/30/87-05/31/03

Index - Standard & Poor's 500 Worth $49,330
10.43 % annualized 04/30/87-05/31/03

GROWTH OF $10,000

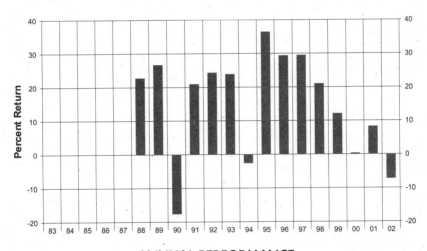

ANNUAL PERFORMANCE

TOP 10 HOLDINGS

General Dynamics
Packaging Corp. of America
Dean Foods
Storage Technology
Ball Corporation

Level-3 Communications
American Standard
Manor Care
Tyco
Laboratory Corp. America

GABELLI ASSET

| OBJECTIVE: | Mid-Cap Value | *42* |
| MANAGER: | Mario Gabelli | |

FUND OVERVIEW:

Mario Gabelli doesn't mind that some people view his investment style as being boring. He focuses on a company's free cash flow, defined as earnings before interest, taxes, depreciation, and amortization, less the capital expenditures needed to grow the business. "Rising free cash flow often foreshadows net earnings improvement," he says. "Unlike Wall Street's ubiquitous earnings momentum players, we do not try to forecast earnings with accounting precision and then trade stocks based on quarterly expectations and realities." Instead, he positions himself in front of long-term earnings uptrends.

Gabelli also closely analyzes assets and liabilities, paying attention to inventories, receivables, and potential legal issues. His goal is to come up with a private market value estimate of what a company is worth. He then wants to buy the company's stock for less than that number. Often, Gabelli finds a catalyst that leads him to believe earnings will rise, thus increasing the private market value. At other times, he's attracted by a management change or spin-off. Once he has put his money on the line, Gabelli tends to be patient, though vocal, in seeing that his companies perform up to expectations.

ANNUALIZED RETURNS

1-Year	−7.10%
3-Year	−1.54%
5-Year	4.24%
Overall Rank	1
Risk Rank	2

MINIMUM INVESTMENT

Regular	$1,000
IRA	$250

PORTFOLIO STATISTICS

Beta	0.83
Turnover	15.00%
12-Month Yield	0.03%
12b-1 Fee	0.25%
Expense Ratio	1.36%

CONTACT INFORMATION

Gabelli Asset Fund
Telephone: (800) 422-3554
www.gabelli.com

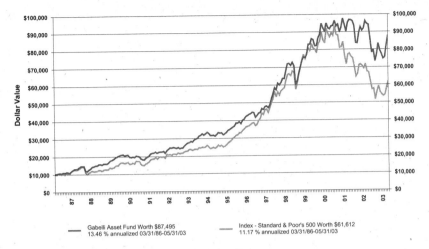

Gabelli Asset Fund Worth $87,495
13.46 % annualized 03/31/86-05/31/03

Index - Standard & Poor's 500 Worth $61,612
11.17 % annualized 03/31/86-05/31/03

GROWTH OF $10,000

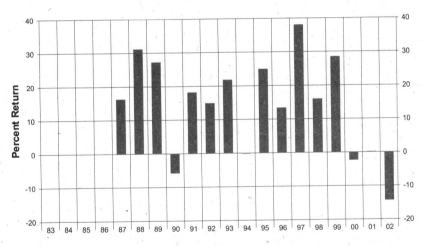

ANNUAL PERFORMANCE

TOP 10 HOLDINGS

News Corp.	USA Interactive
Liberty Media	Media General
Cablevision	Neiman Marcus
Viacom	Procter & Gamble
Telephone & Data Systems	Deere and Company

JANUS MID CAP VALUE

OBJECTIVE:	*Mid-Cap Value*	
MANAGER:	*Robert Perkins and Thomas Perkins*	*43*

FUND OVERVIEW:

Janus Mid Cap Value is run by brothers Robert and Tom Perkins out of their Chicago office. They start looking for stocks by poring over the new low lists in the paper. They want companies that have been beaten down by the market, but still offer strong upside potential. The Perkins brothers look for stocks with a low price relative to their assets, earnings, cash flow, or business franchise. They also seek businesses with products and services that give them a competitive advantage, along with quality balance sheets and strong management.

Both managers have been in the investment industry for a long time. Robert has 35 years of experience, while Tom has been in the industry for 30 years. The two also manage the Janus Small Cap Value Fund, which is closed to new investors. (Both funds were once part of the Berger funds family, but merged into the Janus fold in 2003.)

In addition to looking for promising companies, the managers keep an eye on risk. They will only buy a stock when they believe the appreciation potential is at least two times as great as the possible downside risk.

ANNUALIZED RETURNS

1-Year	−4.90%
3-Year	11.25%
5-Year	N/A
Overall Rank	1
Risk Rank	3

MINIMUM INVESTMENT

Regular	$2,000
IRA	$500

PORTFOLIO STATISTICS

Beta	0.84
Turnover	116.00%
12-Month Yield	0.18%
12b-1 Fee	0.25%
Expense Ratio	1.21%

CONTACT INFORMATION

Janus Mid Cap Value
Telephone: (800) 333-1001
www.janus.com

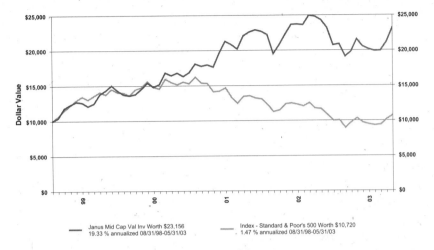

Janus Mid Cap Val Inv Worth $23,156
19.33 % annualized 08/31/98-05/31/03

Index - Standard & Poor's 500 Worth $10,720
1.47 % annualized 08/31/98-05/31/03

GROWTH OF $10,000

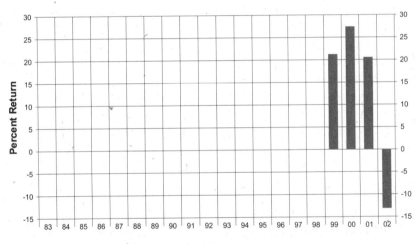

ANNUAL PERFORMANCE

TOP 10 HOLDINGS

Devon Energy	Genuine Participacoes
Furniture Brands	Republic Services
Southtrust	Mercantile Bankshares
Omnicare	Stone Energy
Cendant	Marathon Oil

LEGG MASON OPPORTUNITY TRUST

OBJECTIVE:	Mid-Cap Value
MANAGER:	William Miller

44

FUND OVERVIEW:

Among the list of Large-Cap Value "Powerhouse Performers," you may remember reading about the Legg Mason Value Trust run by Bill Miller. At the end of 1999, he was given a new fund to manage that gives him much more freedom to buy whatever stocks he wants, small or large. In fact, the fund's prospectus makes it clear that Miller's not limited by investment style, industry sector, location, size, or market capitalization.

As an added twist, he can also sell securities short, which is an aggressive maneuver. In essence, it's a bet that a stock's price is going to fall. Plus, since this fund is considerably smaller than Value Trust, Miller's able to be more flexible.

Miller looks for companies trading at a discount to their intrinsic value. Before buying a security, he and his team assess a potential holding's products, strategy, competitive positioning, and industry dynamics. A stock is sold for a variety of reasons, including when it no longer seems to offer long-term growth, when a more compelling investment opportunity comes around, to realize gains, or to limit losses.

ANNUALIZED RETURNS	
1-Year	14.20%
3-Year	2.85%
5-Year	N/A
Overall Rank	2
Risk Rank	5

MINIMUM INVESTMENT	
Regular	$1,000
IRA	$1,000

PORTFOLIO STATISTICS	
Beta	1.51
Turnover	44.00%
12-Month Yield	0.43%
12b-1 Fee	1.00%
Expense Ratio	1.90%

CONTACT INFORMATION

Legg Mason Opportunity Trust
Telephone: (800) 577-8589
www.leggmasonfunds.com

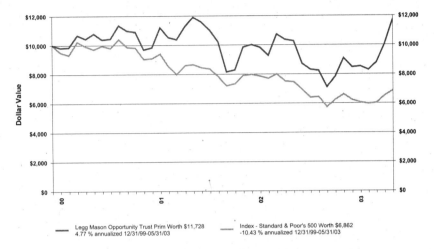

Legg Mason Opportunity Trust Prim Worth $11,728
4.77 % annualized 12/31/99–05/31/03

Index - Standard & Poor's 500 Worth $6,862
-10.43 % annualized 12/31/99–05/31/03

GROWTH OF $10,000

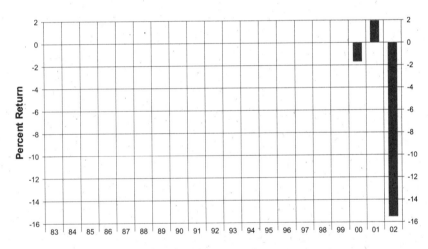

ANNUAL PERFORMANCE

TOP 10 HOLDINGS

Amazon.com	Abercrombie and Fitch
Tyco	Omnicare
Level-3 Communications	Acxiom
Providian Financial	Cott
Broadwing	VeriSign

MUHLENKAMP FUND

OBJECTIVE:	*Mid-Cap Value*	*45*
MANAGER:	*Ronald Muhlenkamp*	

FUND OVERVIEW:

Ron Muhlenkamp fills his portfolio with whatever he thinks will make the most money. That usually means a heavy weighting in stocks, although he'll emphasize bonds when interest rates exceed the return he expects to get from equities. Muhlenkamp doesn't believe in applying historical standards to today's market, because economic conditions are always changing. Instead, he constantly evaluates the current business cycle to see which industries appear to be most attractive.

Muhlenkamp is a value-oriented investor. He views a company's return on equity and price-to-book value ratio as important numbers for determining whether a stock is attractively priced. Instead of buying growth at a reasonable price, he wants profitability at a reasonable price.

Muhlenkamp strives to generate a maximum total return for shareholders consistent with taking a reasonable amount of risk. He will only invest in securities that he expects to outpace the rate of inflation by at least 5 to 6 percent for stocks, and at least 3 percent for bonds.

ANNUALIZED RETURNS		PORTFOLIO STATISTICS	
1-Year	−7.60%	Beta	1.28
3-Year	7.00%	Turnover	10.86%
5-Year	5.84%	12-Month Yield	0.00%
Overall Rank	2	12b-1 Fee	0.00%
Risk Rank	4	Expense Ratio	1.16%
MINIMUM INVESTMENT		**CONTACT INFORMATION**	
Regular	$1,500	*Muhlenkamp Fund*	
IRA	$1,500	*Telephone: (800) 860-3863*	
		www.muhlenkamp.com	

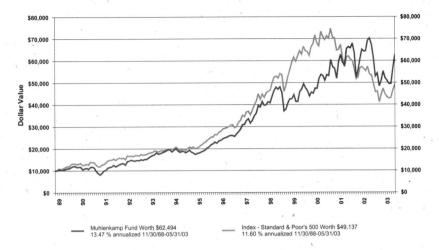

Muhlenkamp Fund Worth $62,494
13.47 % annualized 11/30/88-05/31/03

Index - Standard & Poor's 500 Worth $49,137
11.60 % annualized 11/30/88-05/31/03

GROWTH OF $10,000

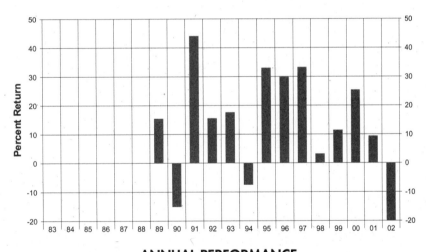

ANNUAL PERFORMANCE

TOP 10 HOLDINGS

NVR	Patterson UTI Energy
Centex	Arkansas Best
Fidelity National Financial	Meritage
Countrywide Credit	Tyco
Mohawk Industries	Citigroup

TCW GALILEO VALUE OPPORTUNITIES

OBJECTIVE:	*Mid-Cap Value*	*46*
MANAGER:	*Nicholas Galluccio and Susan Shottenfeld*	

FUND OVERVIEW:

TCW Galileo Value Opportunities managers Nicholas Galluccio and Susan Shottenfeld look for cheap mid-cap stocks that have the potential for big growth. They divide the fund's portfolio into three categories: undervalued growth plays, turnarounds, and asset values. In essence, they look for companies that are temporarily troubled and trading at bargain prices.

This fund is the offspring of a small-cap value trust portfolio Galluccio and Shottenfeld ran for some time at Trust Company of the West (TCW), a large institutional management company. They found that many of the stocks they liked most were graduating to mid-cap status, and started the TCW Galileo Value Opportunities Fund to give these stocks a home.

Galluccio and Shottenfeld have been managing money as a team for 19 years. They begin the process of finding stocks by using quantitative screens to look for companies trading at the low end of their historic price range or PE ratio. This is followed by in-depth fundamental analysis, including company visits and management interviews.

ANNUALIZED RETURNS		PORTFOLIO STATISTICS	
1-Year	–12.70%	Beta	N/A
3-Year	N/A	Turnover	N/A
5-Year	N/A	12-Month Yield	0.00%
Overall Rank	N/A	12b-1 Fee	0.25%
Risk Rank	N/A	Expense Ratio	1.29%

MINIMUM INVESTMENT		CONTACT INFORMATION
Regular	$2,000	*TCW Galileo Value Opportunities Fund*
IRA	$500	*Telephone: (800) 386-3829*
		www.tcwgroup.com

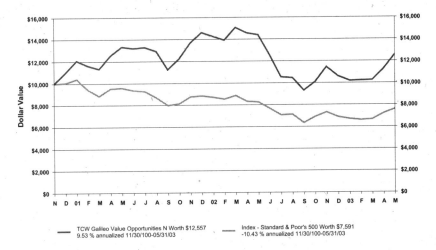

TCW Galileo Value Opportunities N Worth $12,557
9.53 % annualized 11/30/100-05/31/03

Index - Standard & Poor's 500 Worth $7,591
-10.43 % annualized 11/30/100-05/31/03

GROWTH OF $10,000

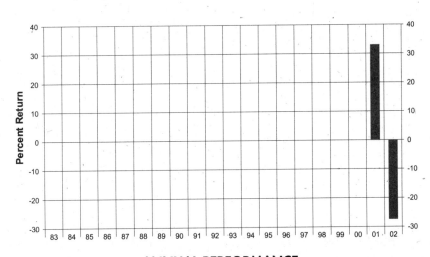

ANNUAL PERFORMANCE

TOP 10 HOLDINGS

National Semiconductor	Vishay Intertechnology
Hain Celestial Group	Silicon Valley Bancshares
Teradyne	Starwood Hotels & Resorts
Countrywide Credit	Pall
Mellon Financial	Emcor Group

TWEEDY, BROWNE AMERICAN VALUE

OBJECTIVE:	*Mid-Cap Value*	*47*
MANAGER:	*Team Managed*	

FUND OVERVIEW:

The managers of Tweedy, Browne American Value aren't shy about telling you they run their portfolio using the principles espoused in *Security Analysis*, the classic book written by the late Columbia University Business School Professor Benjamin Graham. Graham talked about evaluating companies based on their "intrinsic value," which is the amount a rational business-person would pay for the entire business. Graham claimed that investments made at a 40 to 50 percent discount to intrinsic value provided investors with a margin of safety. Graham recommended selling a stock once its market price reached intrinsic value and reinvesting the proceeds into other, more attractive ideas.

Therefore, Tweedy, Browne American Value holds stocks with one or more of the following characteristics: low stock price in relation to book value, low price-to-earnings ratio, low price-to-cash flow ratio, above-average dividend yield, and recent stock purchases by insiders. Managers Christopher Browne, John Spears, and William Browne own some 200 small, medium, and large stocks, including a few foreign companies. This conservative fund normally manages to at least keep up with the S&P 500 while incurring less risk.

ANNUALIZED RETURNS		PORTFOLIO STATISTICS	
1-Year	−11.50%	Beta	0.46
3-Year	1.73%	Turnover	6.00%
5-Year	1.16%	12-Month Yield	0.47%
Overall Rank	3	12b-1 Fee	0.00%
Risk Rank	2	Expense Ratio	1.36%
MINIMUM INVESTMENT		**CONTACT INFORMATION**	
Regular	$2,500	*Tweedy, Browne American Value Fund*	
IRA	$500	*Telephone: (800) 432-4789*	
		www.tweedy.com	

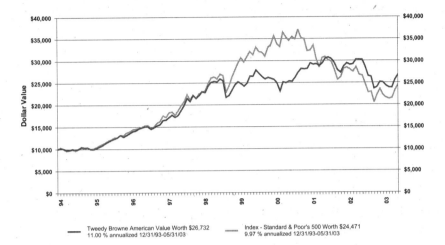

Tweedy Browne American Value Worth $26,732
11.00 % annualized 12/31/93-05/31/03

Index - Standard & Poor's 500 Worth $24,471
9.97 % annualized 12/31/93-05/31/03

GROWTH OF $10,000

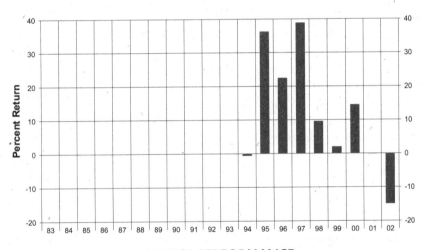

ANNUAL PERFORMANCE

TOP 10 HOLDINGS

Transatlantic Holdings	Torchmark
MBIA	Federated Investors
Pfizer	Freddie Mac
American Express	Rayonier
Panamerican Beverages	Proquest

WEITZ PARTNERS VALUE

OBJECTIVE:	*Mid-Cap Value*	*48*
MANAGER:	*Wallace Weitz*	

FUND OVERVIEW:

Weitz Partners Value is a non-diversified fund that seeks companies trading for half of their intrinsic value, or what they would be worth whole if bought out entirely by an interested suitor. This is the same philosophy espoused by both Warren Buffett and Benjamin Graham. Manager Wallace Weitz notes that he favors businesses he can understand, which keeps him from owning many technology companies. He also wants businesses with a niche or franchise that insulates them from competition. Next, a potential company must generate more cash flow than it needs to conduct operations.

To make the final cut, a business must have what Weitz calls "honest, intelligent management who treat shareholders as partners in the business, rather than necessary evils." Weitz is also quick to point out that he wants good companies, not just cheap stocks. Although he prefers to stay fully invested, he will hold cash reserves when he can't find enough promising ideas.

You'll notice this fund has a high minimum investment requirement of $25,000, even for IRAs. However, you can get in for much less by using a discount broker.

ANNUALIZED RETURNS

1-Year	−3.70%
3-Year	3.41%
5-Year	7.88%
Overall Rank	1
Risk Rank	2

MINIMUM INVESTMENT

Regular	$25,000
(less through some discount brokers)	
IRA	$25,000
(less through some discount brokers)	

PORTFOLIO STATISTICS

Beta	0.68
Turnover	16.00%
12-Month Yield	0.26%
12b-1 Fee	0.00%
Expense Ratio	1.09%

CONTACT INFORMATION

Weitz Partners Value Fund
Telephone: (800) 232-4161
www.weitzfunds.com

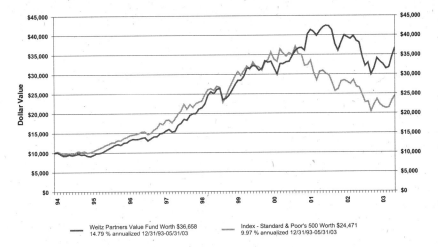

Weitz Partners Value Fund Worth $36,658
14.79 % annualized 12/31/93-05/31/03

Index - Standard & Poor's 500 Worth $24,471
9.97 % annualized 12/31/93-05/31/03

GROWTH OF $10,000

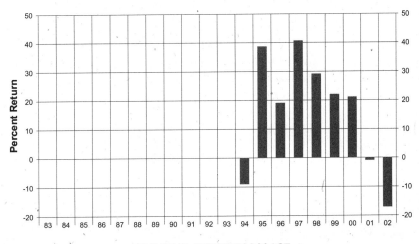

ANNUAL PERFORMANCE

TOP 10 HOLDINGS

Liberty Media	Host Marriott
Comcast	Hilton Hotels
Washington Mutual	Washington Post
Countrywide Credit	Berkshire Hathaway Class B
Park Place Entertainment	US Bancorp

YACKTMAN FUND

OBJECTIVE:	*Mid-Cap Value*	
MANAGER:	*Donald Yacktman*	*49*

FUND OVERVIEW:

Don Yacktman has never been shy about putting a lot of money in his favorite investments. While that's not a bad thing, understand that Yacktman tends to fall in love with companies that are out-of-favor by just about everyone else on Wall Street. He won't flinch at putting close to 10 percent of the portfolio in a single name. If he's right, shareholders of his fund are rewarded. But if he's wrong, which he has been in the past, shareholders definitely feel the pain. That's why this fund is only appropriate for those willing to stick with Yacktman for the long run.

Yacktman himself is a long-term investor who looks to buy traditional growth stocks after they have been whacked down in price. He wants businesses with high returns on tangible assets, shareholder-oriented management that spends cash wisely, and low valuations. Yacktman's goal is to provide the highest returns consistent with taking a minimal amount of risk. Remember, risk is a relative word with a concentrated portfolio like this. Don't expect the portfolio to move in line with the S&P 500. This fund is a big bet on a man who has proved to be a talented stock picker over time.

ANNUALIZED RETURNS

1-Year	14.30%
3-Year	23.05%
5-Year	6.05%
Overall Rank	1
Risk Rank	2

MINIMUM INVESTMENT

Regular	$2,500
IRA	$500

PORTFOLIO STATISTICS

Beta	0.69
Turnover	39.19%
12-Month Yield	0.74%
12b-1 Fee	0.00%
Expense Ratio	0.98%

CONTACT INFORMATION

Yacktman Fund
Telephone: (800) 525-8258
www.yacktman.com

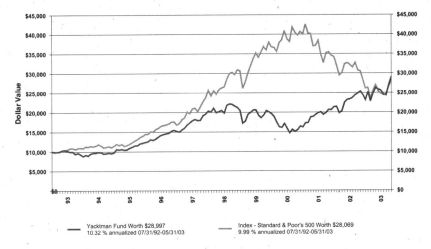

Yacktman Fund Worth $28,997
10.32 % annualized 07/31/92-05/31/03

Index - Standard & Poor's 500 Worth $28,069
9.99 % annualized 07/31/92-05/31/03

GROWTH OF $10,000

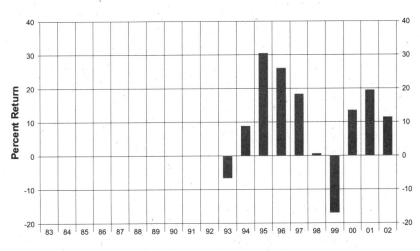

ANNUAL PERFORMANCE

TOP 10 HOLDINGS

Tyco	Bristol Myers Squibb
Liberty Media	Henkel KGAA
Kraft Foods	Electronic Data Systems
Lancaster Colony	Interpublic Group
Americredit	Trizec Properties

BARON SMALL CAP

OBJECTIVE: *Small-Cap Growth*
MANAGER: *Cliff Greenberg*

50

FUND OVERVIEW:

Even though Cliff Greenberg hasn't been managing a mutual fund for long, he has been making money in small-cap stocks for many years. Before joining Baron in 1997, Greenberg spent more than a decade running a prominent New York hedge fund. He tries to find companies with superior prospects that can be purchased at attractive prices. Greenberg won't buy a stock unless he thinks it can go up at least 50 percent over a two-year period, and he won't hesitate to overweight his favorite ideas in the portfolio.

Greenberg has an eclectic style. He says most of his investments fall into one of the following categories: growth stocks, fallen angels, or special situations. Growth companies either have new products or are involved in blossoming industries. They are also growing by at least 20 percent a year. Fallen angels are stocks that have tumbled dramatically in price. This often happens because Wall Street is concerned about current earnings prospects. Greenberg digs deeper to see whether the long-term fundamentals have materially changed. If not, he's interested. Finally, special situations encompass spin-offs, recapitalizations, equity stubs, and the like. One thing you won't find is many technology companies, since they rarely meet his price criteria.

ANNUALIZED RETURNS		PORTFOLIO STATISTICS	
1-Year	−8.00%	Beta	0.89
3-Year	0.71%	Turnover	55.07%
5-Year	6.69%	12-Month Yield	0.00
Overall Rank	2	12b-1 Fee	0.25%
Risk Rank	4	Expense Ratio	1.36%
MINIMUM INVESTMENT		**CONTACT INFORMATION**	
Regular	$2,000	*Baron Small Cap Fund*	
IRA	$2,000	*Telephone: (800) 992-2766*	
		www.baronfunds.com	

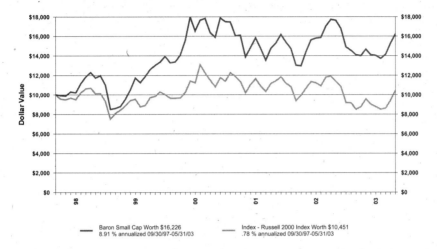

GROWTH OF $10,000

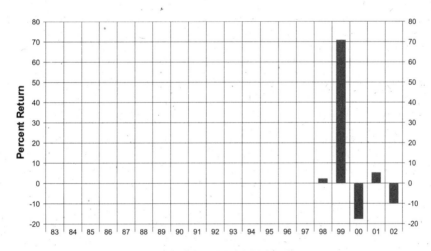

ANNUAL PERFORMANCE

TOP 10 HOLDINGS

Career Education	Radio One
Fair Isaac	Krispy Kreme Doughnuts
Choicepoint	Information Holdings
Iron Mountain	United Surgical Partners
Apollo Group	Interactive Data

BJURMAN, BARRY SMALL CAP GROWTH

OBJECTIVE:	*Small-Cap Growth*	*51*
MANAGER:	*Team Managed*	

FUND OVERVIEW:

The Bjurman Small Cap Growth Fund looks for high-growth companies with market capitalizations between $100 million and $1 billion at the time of initial investment. The management team, lead by O. Thomas Barry, seeks out undervalued stocks with superior earnings growth characteristics. They typically screen through a universe of 1,900 companies, using five different models. The models look at such attributes as earnings growth, earnings strength, and earnings revisions. They also take into account price-to-earnings, price-to-growth, and price-to-cash flow ratios. Then the managers perform a top-down analysis of the economy to identify the 10 to 15 most promising industries to be invested in over the next 12 to 18 months. With the two lists in hand, Barry and his associates select up to 200 of the most attractive companies and begin doing additional fundamental and technical research.

To make sure the portfolio is well diversified, no more than 5 percent of assets are placed in any one stock, nor more than 15 percent in a single industry. This fund is fairly new, although its adviser, Bjurman, Barry & Associates, has been managing money for more than 30 years. What's more, sister fund Bjurman, Barry Micro Cap, now closed to new investors, has been a category leader since its launch.

ANNUALIZED RETURNS		PORTFOLIO STATISTICS	
1-Year	N/A	Beta	N/A
3-Year	N/A	Turnover	N/A
5-Year	N/A	12-Month Yield	N/A
Overall Rank	N/A	12b-1 Fee	N/A
Risk Rank	N/A	Expense Ratio	N/A

MINIMUM INVESTMENT		CONTACT INFORMATION
Regular	$5,000	*Bjurman Small Cap Growth Fund*
IRA	$2,000	*Telephone: (800) 227-7264*
		www.bjurmanfunds.com

VALUE LINE GROWTH OF $10,000 CHART
NOT AVAILABLE FOR THIS FUND

GROWTH OF $10,000

VALUE LINE ANNUAL PERFORMANCE CHART
NOT AVAILABLE FOR THIS FUND

ANNUAL PERFORMANCE

TOP 10 HOLDINGS

Top 10 Holdings unavailable for this new fund.

FMI FOCUS FUND

| OBJECTIVE: | *Small-Cap Growth* | *52* |
| MANAGER: | *Richard Lane and Glenn Primack* | |

FUND OVERVIEW:

FMI Focus is one of the most concentrated small-cap funds you'll run across. Managers Richard Lane and Glenn Primack look for companies they consider to be undiscovered or undervalued by Wall Street. They follow a process designed to find good businesses at value prices. To uncover ideas, they go through computer databases, brokerage reports, newspapers, trade journals, and other outside sources. From here, they study each candidate's business model, determine whether a strong business franchise exists, and fill in the gaps by talking with management, competitors, customers, and industry experts.

Valuation is a critical factor in their process, although it's not a pure "value" fund. In fact, it falls into the small-cap growth category. Stocks are sold when they are considered to be overpriced, because of dramatic appreciation, or if the managers simply determine they were wrong about a story in the first place. Lane and Primack generally keep about 40 stocks in the portfolio, which is about half of what you'll find in most small-cap portfolios. But this concentration has provided category-beating returns over the long haul, even during periods when this style of investing has been out of favor.

ANNUALIZED RETURNS		PORTFOLIO STATISTICS	
1-Year	−8.40%	Beta	1.25
3-Year	−1.03%	Turnover	93.00%
5-Year	12.81%	12-Month Yield	0.00%
Overall Rank	2	12b-1 Fee	0.25%
Risk Rank	4	Expense Ratio	1.44%

MINIMUM INVESTMENTS		CONTACT INFORMATION	
Regular	$1,000	*FMI Focus Fund*	
IRA	$1,000	*Telephone: (800) 811-5311*	
		www.fiduciarymgt.com	

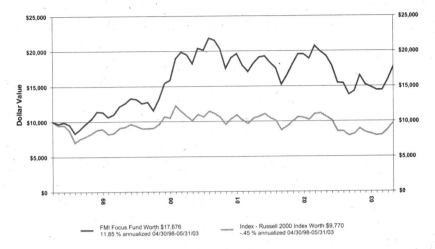

FMI Focus Fund Worth $17,676
11.85 % annualized 04/30/98-05/31/03

Index - Russell 2000 Index Worth $9,770
-.45 % annualized 04/30/98-05/31/03

GROWTH OF $10,000

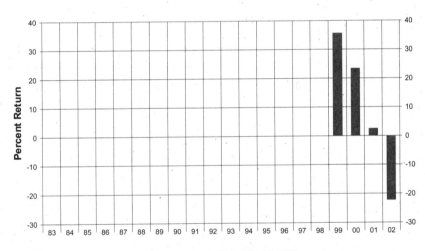

ANNUAL PERFORMANCE

TOP 10 HOLDINGS	
I Shares	Liberty Media
JD Edwards	Henry Schein
Young Broadcasting	Polo Ralph Lauren
Snap-On	Republic Services
Rockwell Automation	Kadant

HENLOPEN

OBJECTIVE:	*Small-Cap Growth*	*53*
MANAGER:	*Team Managed*	

FUND OVERVIEW:

Henlopen's managers look for dominant small companies with rapid earnings growth. Their eclectic investment philosophy calls for purchasing stocks with strong momentum that they believe can carry the share price significantly higher over a one- or two-year period. But this isn't a pure momentum play, since they will also buy cyclical and out-of-favor companies if the price is right. The fund's average holding in the portfolio reported annual gains over the past three years that were well ahead of companies in the S&P 500.

The fund's managers remain true to their convictions. They will overweight favorite names and quickly pull out of companies they no longer like. This "quick draw" approach means the fund is more volatile than many of its peers, but past performance has more than compensated for its inherently bumpy ride. Henlopen has landed among the top percentile of all small-cap funds since inception in 1992 and has easily surpassed its direct benchmark, the Russell 2000. Henlopen also has a small asset base, which gives it an extra advantage as it navigates through this risk-laden area of the market.

ANNUALIZED RETURNS	
1-Year	−4.70%
3-Year	−7.98%
5-Year	3.58%
Overall Rank	3
Risk Rank	5

MINIMUM INVESTMENT	
Regular	$2,000
IRA	$2,000

PORTFOLIO STATISTICS	
Beta	1.43
Turnover	132.00%
12-Month Yield	0.00%
12b-1 Fee	0.00%
Expense Ratio	1.60%

CONTACT INFORMATION

Henlopen Fund
Telephone: (800) 922-0224

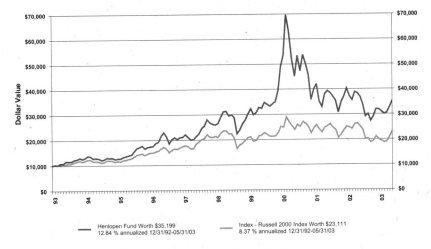

Henlopen Fund Worth $35,199
12.84 % annualized 12/31/92-05/31/03

Index - Russell 2000 Index Worth $23,111
8.37 % annualized 12/31/92-05/31/03

GROWTH OF $10,000

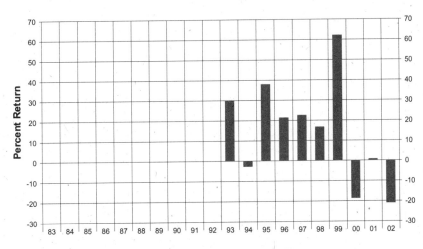

ANNUAL PERFORMANCE

TOP 10 HOLDINGS

Igen
Grey Wolf
Universal Compression
Acres Gaming
Patterson UTI Energy

Rite-Aid
Joseph A. Bank Clothiers
Penn-America
Doral Financial
WSFS Financial

MANAGERS SPECIAL EQUITY

OBJECTIVE:	Small-Cap Growth	
MANAGER:	Team Managed	54

FUND OVERVIEW:

Managers Special Equity gives you access to five leading small-cap stock pickers in one portfolio. It farms out 20 percent of the portfolio each to Bill Dutton of Skyline Asset Management, Andrew Knuth of Westport Asset Management, Gary Pilgrim of Pilgrim Baxter & Associates (who also runs the PBHG Growth Fund), Donald Smith of Donald Smith & Company, and Bob Kern of Kern Capital Management.

Each manager has a unique style and approach to small-cap investing. Dutton searches for companies with below-average valuations and strong growth prospects. Knuth will only buy stocks trading at or below the market's price-to-earnings multiple. Pilgrim focuses on companies with high earnings momentum. Smith buys out-of-favor small-cap stocks. And Kern, who also runs the closed Fremont U.S. Micro-Cap Fund, directs his efforts toward finding micro-cap stocks that are succeeding through new product innovation. Therefore, you get a blend of growth, earnings momentum, and value in one package.

Because of all the managers involved, Managers Special Equity's portfolio is quite diversified. This is a good fund for investors seeking to keep only one small-cap name in their portfolio.

ANNUALIZED RETURNS		PORTFOLIO STATISTICS	
1-Year	−11.40%	Beta	1.21
3-Year	−8.09%	Turnover	71.00%
5-Year	2.87%	12-Month Yield	0.00%
Overall Rank	3	12b-1 Fee	0.00%
Risk Rank	4	Expense Ratio	1.31%
MINIMUM INVESTMENT		**CONTACT INFORMATION**	
Regular	$2,000	Managers Special Equity Fund	
IRA	$500	Telephone: (800) 835-3879	
		www.managersfunds.com	

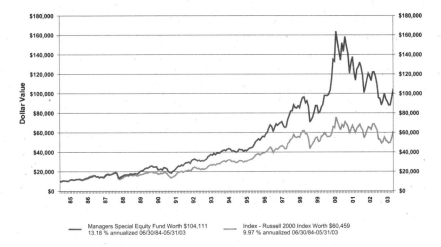

— Managers Special Equity Fund Worth $104,111
13.18 % annualized 06/30/84-05/31/03

Index - Russell 2000 Index Worth $60,459
9.97 % annualized 06/30/84-05/31/03

GROWTH OF $10,000

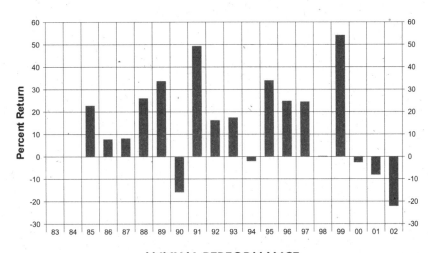

ANNUAL PERFORMANCE

TOP 10 HOLDINGS

ITT Educational Services	Pogo Producing
Airborne	Advanced Micro Devices
Emmis Communications	Getty Images
Massey Energy	Visteon
Ruby Tuesday	International Speedway

RESERVE SMALL-CAP GROWTH

OBJECTIVE:	Small-Cap Growth	
MANAGER:	Edwin Vroom and Adele Weisman	55

FUND OVERVIEW:

Edwin Vroom and Adele Weisman have been picking stocks together for more than 20 years. The two manage the little-known Reserve Small-Cap Growth Fund, which has an impressive track record. Vroom and Weisman tend to be aggressive and keep their portfolio heavily invested in technology companies, which has led to both volatility and outsized returns since the fund's inception in 1994. Even more impressive is that Reserve Small-Cap managed to stay ahead of the S&P 500 in the late 1990s, even though small company stocks in general were out of favor during that time.

On the quantitative side, Vroom and Weisman look for stocks with market caps below $2 billion that are poised to exceed Wall Street's earnings expectations. They also want companies capable of growing the bottom line by at least 25 percent a year. On the qualitative front, they try to understand where a company fits in to its own business environment. They also want to get a sense of what new products and services are in the pipeline that may add to the bottom line and help fuel future profitability.

ANNUALIZED RETURNS

1-Year	−14.20%
3-Year	−16.30%
5-Year	11.25%
Overall Rank	3
Risk Rank	5

MINIMUM INVESTMENT

Regular	$1,000
IRA	$250

PORTFOLIO STATISTICS

Beta	1.79
Turnover	15.00%
12-Month Yield	0.00%
12b-1 Fee	0.25%
Expense Ratio	1.56%

CONTACT INFORMATION

Reserve Small-Cap Growth
Telephone: (800) 637-1700
www.reservefunds.com

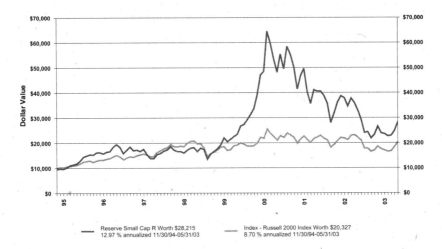

Reserve Small Cap R Worth $28,215
12.97 % annualized 11/30/94-05/31/03

Index - Russell 2000 Index Worth $20,327
8.70 % annualized 11/30/94-05/31/03

GROWTH OF $10,000

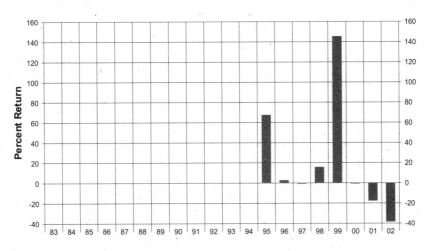

ANNUAL PERFORMANCE

TOP 10 HOLDINGS

XTO Energy	Chronimed
Caremark	Harman International
Accredo Health	Newfield Exploration
Fossil	Documentum
Fair Isaac	ATMI

RS DIVERSIFIED GROWTH

OBJECTIVE:	*Small-Cap Growth*	*56*
MANAGER:	*John Wallace and John Seabern*	

FUND OVERVIEW:

True to his flexible approach to stock picking, RS Diversified Growth manager John Wallace has the freedom to choose from the broad universe of small- and mid-cap stocks. But, more often than not, he latches on to the tinier names, which is why this fund is in the small-cap category.

Wallace and comanager John Seabern look for a catalyst in each company they buy that they believe will drive earnings and valuations higher over a one- to three-year time horizon. That catalyst could be new management, enhanced products, or expanding markets. The managers consider selling when a stock reaches their price objective, when it falls 15 percent from their purchase price, or when something negative happens with management, product definition, or the overall economic environment. They'll also unload one holding to replace it with another.

The overwhelming majority of the portfolio's assets are in technology-related companies, including the fast-growing biotech area. As a result, the fund has been known to give shareholders a rather volatile ride.

Before joining RS Investment Management, Wallace managed the Oppenheimer Main Street Income & Growth fund to great results.

ANNUALIZED RETURNS		PORTFOLIO STATISTICS	
1-Year	−14.90%	Beta	1.56
3-Year	−18.17%	Turnover	223.00%
5-Year	6.46%	12-Month Yield	0.00%
Overall Rank	3	12b-1 Fee	0.25%
Risk Rank	5	Expense Ratio	1.70%
MINIMUM INVESTMENT		**CONTACT INFORMATION**	
Regular	$5,000	*RS Diversified Growth*	
IRA	$1,000	*Telephone: (800) 766-3863*	
		www.rsfunds.com	

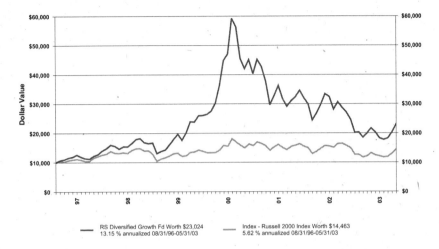

RS Diversified Growth Fd Worth $23,024
13.15 % annualized 08/31/96-05/31/03

Index - Russell 2000 Index Worth $14,463
5.62 % annualized 08/31/96-05/31/03

GROWTH OF $10,000

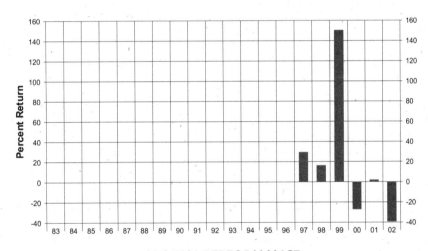

ANNUAL PERFORMANCE

TOP 10 HOLDINGS	
Regeneration Technology	SupportSoft
RMH Teleservices	Secure Computing
Imanage	Coinstar
Landstar	Quanex
NetFlix.com	Martek Biosciences

T. ROWE PRICE SMALL-CAP STOCK

OBJECTIVE:	*Small-Cap Growth*	*57*
MANAGER:	*Greg A. McCrickard*	

FUND OVERVIEW:

Although T. Rowe Price Small-Cap Stock is categorized as a growth fund, manager Greg McCrickard actually invests in both growth- and value-oriented securities. He says this flexible approach gives him access to more opportunities, and the value component helps to temper overall volatility. The fund is also highly diversified, with the average holding making up less than 1.5 percent of the portfolio. This is both good and bad. It reduces risk, but it can prevent the fund from reaping the full rewards of its biggest winners. McCrickard is prone to take his gains sooner than most (although he's not a frequent trader), and he generally avoids concentrating too heavily in any one sector or industry.

McCrickard uses a variety of fundamental checkpoints to evaluate potential holdings. Among other things, he wants companies with sound financial structures, good management, attractive niches, pricing flexibility, and strong insider ownership. Because of his value component, McCrickard keeps a close eye on how much he's willing to pay for a stock, checking to see whether price-to-cash flow and price-to-earnings ratios are attractive relative to estimated earnings growth.

ANNUALIZED RETURNS		PORTFOLIO STATISTICS	
1-Year	−7.90%	Beta	0.84
3-Year	4.20%	Turnover	11.20%
5-Year	4.19%	12-Month Yield	0.04%
Overall Rank	2	12b-1 Fee	0.00%
Risk Rank	3	Expense Ratio	0.97%

MINIMUM INVESTMENT		CONTACT INFORMATION	
Regular	$2,500	*T. Rowe Price Small-Cap Stock Fund*	
IRA	$1,000	*Telephone: (800) 638-5660*	
		www.troweprice.com	

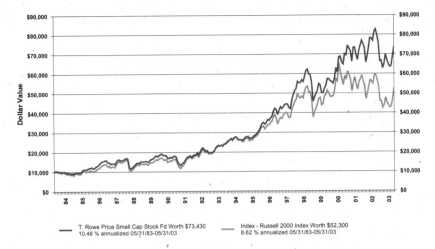

Dollar Value

—— T. Rowe Price Small Cap Stock Fd Worth $73,430
10.48 % annualized 05/31/83-05/31/03

Index - Russell 2000 Index Worth $52,300
8.62 % annualized 05/31/83-05/31/03

GROWTH OF $10,000

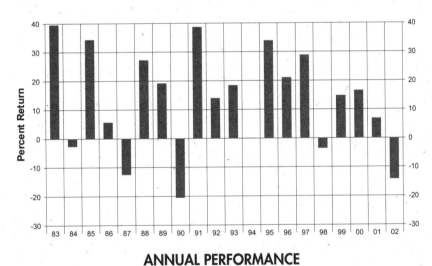

Percent Return

ANNUAL PERFORMANCE

TOP 10 HOLDINGS	
Harman International	AO Smith
Iron Mountain	Kronos
SCP Pool	Airgas
XTO Energy	WestAmerica Bancorporation
Chittenden	Minerals Technologies

AEGIS VALUE

OBJECTIVE:	*Small-Cap Value*	*58*
MANAGER:	*Team Managed*	

FUND OVERVIEW:

The managers of Aegis Value believe their success is due to following the timeless teachings of Benjamin Graham, Warren Buffett, and other value investing legends. They invest in small companies, with market capitalizations below $1 billion trading at prices below the fund management team's estimate of intrinsic value. Stocks are held until they achieve this estimate of value, as calculated by Aegis managers Bill Berno, Paul Gambal, and Scott Barbee. Purchases are limited to stocks with very low price-to-book or price-to-cash flow ratios. One reason for this price-conscious approach is that the management team strives to achieve long-term appreciation while minimizing losses.

Because of the fund's deep value strategy, it often takes positions in companies that are cheap because of an industry downturn, unfavorable news, poor economic conditions, an overall stock market decline, tax-loss selling, or anticipated negative developments. Given this reality, the managers invest based on the strength of company management, hidden assets, and likely catalysts that will turn the business around and make the stock price rise.

ANNUALIZED RETURNS

1-Year	5.50%
3-Year	20.14%
5-Year	14.75%
Overall Rank	1
Risk Rank	2

MINIMUM INVESTMENT

Regular	$10,000
IRA	$2,000

PORTFOLIO STATISTICS

Beta	0.50
Turnover	29.00%
12-Month Yield	0.13%
12b-1 Fee	0.00%
Expense Ratio	1.50%

CONTACT INFORMATION

Aegis Value Fund
Telephone: (800) 528-3780
www.aegisvaluefund.com

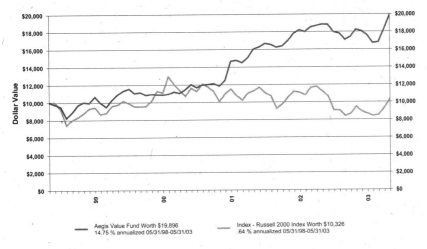

Aegis Value Fund Worth $19,896
14.75 % annualized 05/31/98-05/31/03

Index - Russell 2000 Index Worth $10,326
.64 % annualized 05/31/98-05/31/03

GROWTH OF $10,000

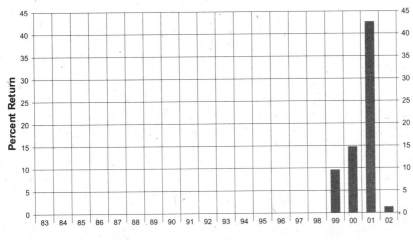

ANNUAL PERFORMANCE

TOP 10 HOLDINGS	
SCPIE Holdings	USEC
Audiovox	American Physicians Capital
OMI	Andersons
Aegis Realty	Allied Defense Group
American Pacific	PNM Resources

ARIEL FUND

OBJECTIVE:	*Small-Cap Value*	*59*
MANAGER:	*John Rogers*	

FUND OVERVIEW:

John Rogers runs a concentrated portfolio of undervalued, yet financially strong, small-cap companies. He specifically seeks names that are ignored by the rest of Wall Street. Still, they must be of high quality with distinct market niches. He further demands strong management teams and proven success records.

In addition, Rogers puts each stock through a series of social screens. For instance, he won't invest in companies involved in tobacco, weapons manufacturing, or the production of nuclear energy. He also wants to make sure each company in the portfolio does good things for the environment, although this isn't technically considered to be a socially conscious fund.

Rogers is more conservative than many of his peers in this category. He normally avoids technology companies and those in industries that are highly sensitive to business cycles or commodity prices. But conservatism aside, he believes in loading up on his best ideas. It's not unusual to find roughly half of the fund's assets in the top ten names.

ANNUALIZED RETURNS		PORTFOLIO STATISTICS	
1-Year	−8.40%	Beta	0.42
3-Year	13.21%	Turnover	6.00%
5-Year	7.84%	12-Month Yield	0.00%
Overall Rank	2	12b-1 Fee	0.25%
Risk Rank	2	Expense Ratio	1.18%

MINIMUM INVESTMENT		CONTACT INFORMATION	
Regular	$1,000	*Ariel Fund*	
IRA	$250	*Telephone: (800) 292-7435*	
		www.arielfunds.com	

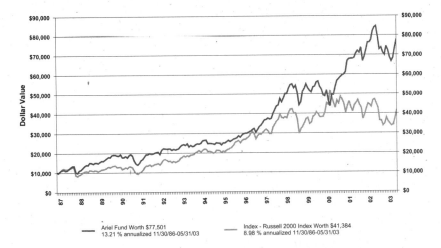

Ariel Fund Worth $77,501
13.21 % annualized 11/30/86-05/31/03

Index - Russell 2000 Index Worth $41,384
8.98 % annualized 11/30/86-05/31/03

GROWTH OF $10,000

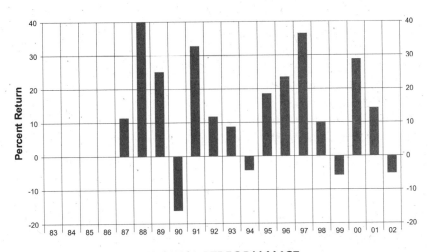

ANNUAL PERFORMANCE

TOP 10 HOLDINGS

Markel	Idex
Lee Enterprises	Rouse Company
Grey Global Group	Graco
American Greetings	HCC Insurance
Neiman Marcus	Hasbro

BRIDGEWAY ULTRA-SMALL COMPANY MARKET

OBJECTIVE:	*Small-Cap Value*	
MANAGER:	*John Montgomery*	*60*

FUND OVERVIEW:

This quantitatively driven, supercharged index fund seeks to approximate the return of the Cap-Based Portfolio 10 index published by the University of Chicago's Center for Research in Security Prices. This is an index of stocks in the smallest 10 percent of market capitalization. As a result, Bridgeway Ultra-Small Company Market manager John Montgomery normally keeps at least 80 percent of the portfolio in ultra-small company stocks, while matching the weighting, sector representation, and financial characteristics of the index.

Companies represented in the portfolio generally have 20 to 2,000 employees, produce revenues of $10 million to $500 million annually, and may be known for just one product or service. To keep the risk inherent in these companies down, Montgomery maintains a highly diversified portfolio. He uses a proprietary computer program to identify the most attractive stocks in the small-cap universe, and has the added goal of trading efficiently to avoid paying out a capital gain to shareholders. So far he's accomplished this goal, while keeping expenses low and posting some of the best returns in the small-cap value category.

ANNUALIZED RETURNS	
1-Year	16.10%
3-Year	19.33%
5-Year	12.52%
Overall Rank	1
Risk Rank	3

MINIMUM INVESTMENT	
Regular	$2,000
IRA	$2,000

PORTFOLIO STATISTICS	
Beta	0.84
Turnover	55.80%
12-Month Yield	0.00%
12b-1 Fee	0.00%
Expense Ratio	0.75%

CONTACT INFORMATION

Bridgeway Ultra-Small Company
Market Fund
Telephone: (800) 661-3550
www.bridgewayfunds.com

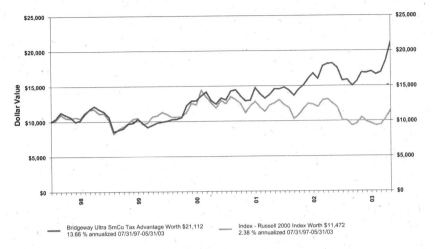

Bridgeway Ultra SmCo Tax Advantage Worth $21,112
13.66 % annualized 07/31/97-05/31/03

Index - Russell 2000 Index Worth $11,472
2.38 % annualized 07/31/97-05/31/03

GROWTH OF $10,000

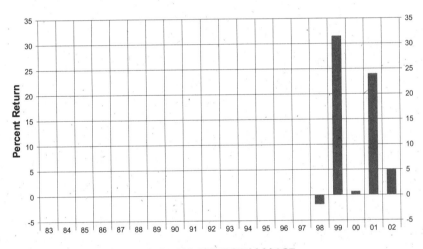

ANNUAL PERFORMANCE

TOP 10 HOLDINGS	
Ask Jeeves	Perry Ellis
Hi-Tech Pharmacal	Covest Bancshares
Anfi	Pervasive Software
Centro Euro Distribution	Quality Systems
First Niagara Financial	HTE

MERIDIAN VALUE

OBJECTIVE:	Small-Cap Value	*61*
MANAGER:	Richard Aster and Kevin O'Boyle	

FUND OVERVIEW:

When a growth stock messes up and gets sold off by the rest of Wall Street, it peaks the interest of Meridian Value managers Richard Aster and Kevin O'Boyle. O'Boyle discovered that once investors beat up a stock, it usually goes on to enjoy a period of positive results, especially during the subsequent two quarters. It's during this time that Aster and O'Boyle investigate to see whether the company's prospects have, in fact, improved. If so, they'll add the holding to their portfolio, hoping that what is now a value stock will become a growth stock once again. Given Wall Street's tendency to punish stocks that disappoint, the two never have a shortage of ideas to choose from.

Meridian Value's portfolio is concentrated in the handful of holdings these managers have the greatest conviction in. You might say that Aster and O'Boyle are often buying what the skippers of momentum-oriented small-cap funds are trying to sell. What's impressive is that they have been able to perform at the head of their asset class over the years, without loading up on any particular market sector. This is a good small-cap choice for more conservative investors.

ANNUALIZED RETURNS		PORTFOLIO STATISTICS	
1-Year	−3.70%	Beta	0.70
3-Year	8.66%	Turnover	54.00%
5-Year	15.16%	12-Month Yield	0.00%
Overall Risk	1	12b-1 Fee	0.00%
Risk Rank	2	Expense Ratio	1.12%

MINIMUM INVESTMENT		CONTACT INFORMATION	
Regular	$1,000	Meridian Value	
IRA	$1,000	Telephone: (800) 446-6662	
		www.meridianfund.com	

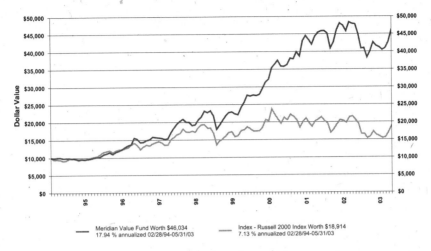

Meridian Value Fund Worth $46,034
17.94 % annualized 02/28/94-05/31/03

Index - Russell 2000 Index Worth $18,914
7.13 % annualized 02/28/94-05/31/03

GROWTH OF $10,000

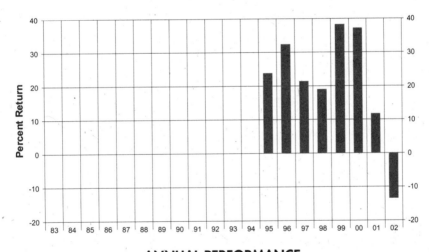

ANNUAL PERFORMANCE

TOP 10 HOLDINGS

Waste Management	Citizens Communications
Mylan Laboratories	Dial
Newmont Mining	Burlington Resources
Omnicare	Davita
Safeco	Becton Dickinson

ROYCE OPPORTUNITY

| **OBJECTIVE:** | *Small-Cap Value* | *62* |
| **MANAGER:** | *Boniface Zaino* | |

FUND OVERVIEW:

Royce Opportunity manager Boniface "Buzz" Zaino looks for companies with market capitalizations below $2 billion. Using a bottom-up approach, he focuses on those firms trading at a significant discount to their intrinsic value. He looks for "opportunistic situations" to buy distressed shares, such as turnarounds, firms with a temporary disruption in earnings, businesses with unrecognized asset values, and undervalued growth companies.

In order to remain diversified, Zaino holds many small positions (unlike his colleague Charlie Dreifus of fellow Powerhouse Performer Royce Special Equity), and each stock comprises no more than 1 percent of assets. Zaino will sell a stock if the fundamentals deteriorate, if a more compelling opportunity arises, or if the issue becomes overvalued.

In contrast to other small-cap value funds, Zaino does delve into technology on occasion. The fund has managed to post a gain in each full calendar year of its history, with the exception of 2002. It is slightly less volatile than others in the category, making it especially appealing to investors with a lower risk tolerance.

ANNUALIZED RETURNS	
1-Year	−9.80%
3-Year	6.95%
5-Year	11.66%
Overall Rank	2
Risk Rank	4

MINIMUM INVESTMENT	
Regular	$2,000
IRA	$500

PORTFOLIO STATISTICS	
Beta	1.11
Turnover	46.00%
12-Month Yield	0.00%
12b-1 Fee	0.00%
Expense Ratio	1.23%

CONTACT INFORMATION

Royce Opportunity Fund
Telephone: (800) 221-4268
www.roycefunds.com

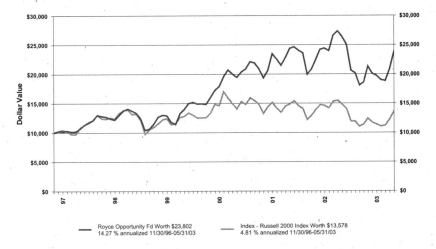

GROWTH OF $10,000

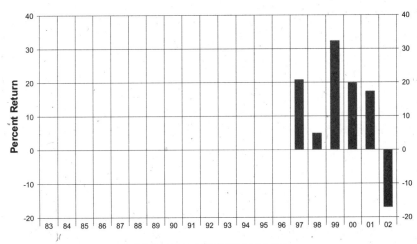

ANNUAL PERFORMANCE

TOP 10 HOLDINGS	
Memc Electronic Materials	Gundle/SLT Environmental
Comtech Telecom	Macdermid
Unova	Wild Oats Markets
Allen Telecom	Vishay Intertechnology
CTS	Circor International

ROYCE SPECIAL EQUITY

OBJECTIVE:	Small-Cap Value	
MANAGER:	Charles Dreifus	63

FUND OVERVIEW:

Royce Special Equity invests in small- and micro-cap companies with market capitalizations below $500 million. Manager Charlie Dreifus is a disciplined value investor who traces his roots to the teachings of Benjamin Graham. He attempts to find inexpensive stocks with high returns on assets and low leverage.

Specifically, Dreifus looks for companies with some or all of the following characteristics: unrecognized assets, the ability to operate effectively in adverse environments, recently changed management, substantial or growing cash flow, a large ownership stake by management, and conservative financial reporting policies.

Dreifus believes in concentration, even in this inherently volatile area of the market. This approach is much different from the one taken by his boss, Charles Royce, who has historically owned several hundred stocks in his portfolios. Royce Special Equity's largest industry sectors tend to be consumer and industrial products and services, while technology, financial services, and healthcare are nearly absent from the mix.

ANNUALIZED RETURNS		PORTFOLIO STATISTICS	
1-Year	0.80%	Beta	0.40
3-Year	20.25%	Turnover	41.00%
5-Year	9.66%	12-Month Yield	0.16%
Overall Rank	2	12b-1 Fee	0.00%
Risk Rank	2	Expense Ratio	2.12%
MINIMUM INVESTMENT		**CONTACT INFORMATION**	
Regular	$2,000	Royce Special Equity Fund	
IRA	$500	Telephone: (800) 221-4268	
		www.roycefunds.com	

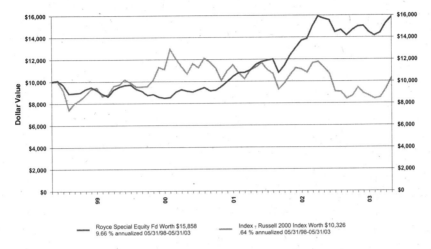

Royce Special Equity Fd Worth $15,858
9.66 % annualized 05/31/98-05/31/03

Index - Russell 2000 Index Worth $10,326
.64 % annualized 05/31/98-05/31/03

GROWTH OF $10,000

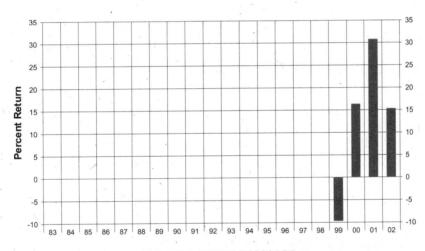

ANNUAL PERFORMANCE

TOP 10 HOLDINGS

Lancaster Colony
Lubrizol
Banta
Bob Evans Farms
Universal

Schweitzer Mauduit
Bandag
Russ Berrie
Farmer Brothers
CEC Entertainment

THIRD AVENUE VALUE

OBJECTIVE:	*Small-Cap Value*	
MANAGER:	*Martin J. Whitman*	*64*

FUND OVERVIEW:

Marty Whitman isn't offended when people refer to him as a vulture. After all, that's what he calls himself. Whitman is a dedicated value investor, but not in the traditional sense. He looks for special situations where he can get in cheap, often because investors worry about the businesses' ability to continue as going concerns. His ideal company has an exceptionally strong financial position, as measured by a lack of debt and the presence of high-quality assets.

To Whitman a perfect stock also has a "reasonable" management team, understandable business, and can be had for no more than 50 cents on the $1 for what it would be worth if taken over by another entity. "There are trade-offs involved in following our approach," Whitman admits. "In almost all cases, when we acquire a security, the near-term earnings outlook is terrible." But that, he believes, also reduces his downside; the stock is presumably trading at a low level because this bleak prognosis has already been factored in.

When Whitman can't find enough equities, he'll buy distressed bonds or even hold cash. He's even been known to close his funds to new investors when he can't find enough bargains.

ANNUALIZED RETURNS		PORTFOLIO STATISTICS	
1-Year	−11.20%	Beta	0.76
3-Year	0.65%	Turnover	19.00%
5-Year	5.20%	12-Month Yield	1.18%
Overall Rank	2	12b-1 Fee	0.00%
Risk Rank	2	Expense Ratio	1.07%

MINIMUM INVESTMENT		CONTACT INFORMATION	
Regular	$1,000	*Third Avenue Value Fund*	
IRA	$500	*Telephone: (800) 443-1021*	
		www.mjwhitman.com	

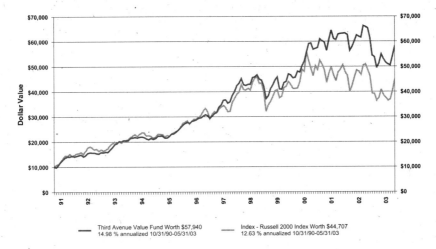

Third Avenue Value Fund Worth $57,940
14.98 % annualized 10/31/90-05/31/03

Index - Russell 2000 Index Worth $44,707
12.63 % annualized 10/31/90-05/31/03

GROWTH OF $10,000

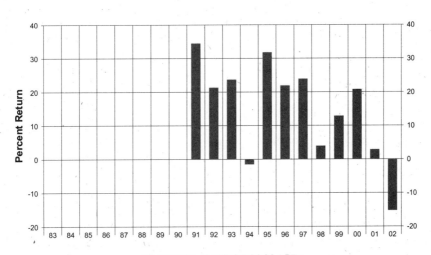

ANNUAL PERFORMANCE

TOP 10 HOLDINGS

Toyota	Forest City Enterprises
Tejon Ranch	St. Joe Company
MBIA	Radian Group
Millea Holdings	First American
AVX	Brascan

OAKMARK EQUITY & INCOME

OBJECTIVE:	*Equity Income*
MANAGER:	*Clyde McGregor and Edward Studzinski*

FUND OVERVIEW:

With a value-oriented portfolio of 60 percent equities and 40 percent fixed-income securities, Clyde McGregor and Edward Studzinski have steered the Oakmark Equity & Income fund to standout performance. On the equity side, the two look for stocks trading at a significant discount to what they call "intrinsic value," or what a rational buyer would pay for the entire company. They buy both common stocks and convertibles, focusing on businesses with free cash flows and a high level of ownership by management. There are no market capitalization restrictions and, despite its income orientation, not every stock the managers own pays a dividend. What's more, although they primarily buy domestic stocks, they can also purchase foreign securities.

On the bond side, McGregor and Studzinski generally buy U.S. Treasury or government agency securities. While the fund's dividend yield has typically been below the category average, risk-averse investors more interested in growth of capital than income would be well-served by this fund.

ANNUALIZED RETURNS		PORTFOLIO STATISTICS	
1-Year	2.10%	Beta	0.39
3-Year	12.69%	Turnover	60.00%
5-Year	11.06%	12-Month Yield	1.23%
Overall Rank	1	12b-1 Fee	0.00%
Risk Rank	1	Expense Ratio	0.93%

MINIMUM INVESTMENT		CONTACT INFORMATION	
Regular	$1,000	*Oakmark Equity & Income Fund*	
IRA	$1,000	*Telephone: (800) 625-6275*	
		www.oakmark.com	

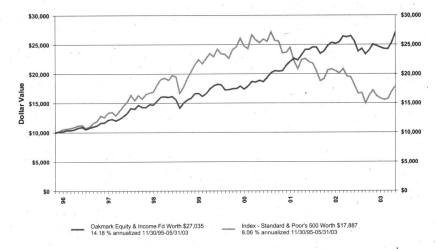

Oakmark Equity & Income Fd Worth $27,035
14.18 % annualized 11/30/95-05/31/03

Index - Standard & Poor's 500 Worth $17,887
8.06 % annualized 11/30/95-05/31/03

GROWTH OF $10,000

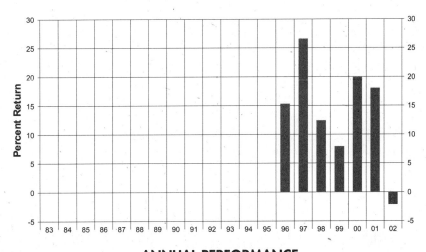

ANNUAL PERFORMANCE

TOP 10 HOLDINGS

Laboratory Corp. America
Burlington Resources
Synopsys
Guidant
Safeco

First Health Group
General Motors Class H
Watson Pharmaceuticals
Plum Creek Timber
Ceridian

T. ROWE PRICE EQUITY INCOME

OBJECTIVE:	*Equity Income*	
MANAGER:	*Brian Rogers*	*66*

FUND OVERVIEW:

T. Rowe Price Equity Income takes a conservative approach to generating both consistent income and long-term capital growth. It is managed by Brian Rogers, whose value-oriented strategy has made this fund a real standout. (You may be familiar with Rogers from his regular appearances as a rotating panelist on *Louis Rukeyser's Wall Street* on CNBC.) Rogers looks for dividend-paying stocks that appear to be temporarily undervalued for one reason or another. The yield component offers some downside protection against both overall market declines and potential future disappointments from these sometimes troubled companies.

Research is the cornerstone of Rogers's investment approach. He and his analysts screen through hundreds of stocks looking for promising candidates. They then do a bottom-up evaluation of each business to see whether the story really checks out. To make the cut, a company must have an established operating history, a high dividend, a low price-to-earnings ratio relative to the S&P, and a sound balance sheet. The portfolio contains mostly large blue-chip names and is extremely diversified, making it an attractive conservative equity investment.

ANNUALIZED RETURNS		PORTFOLIO STATISTICS	
1-Year	−8.10%	Beta	0.68
3-Year	1.98%	Turnover	7.80%
5-Year	2.97%	12-Month Yield	1.69%
Overall Rank	2	12b-1 Fee	0.00%
Risk Rank	2	Expense Ratio	0.81%

MINIMUM INVESTMENT		CONTACT INFORMATION	
Regular	$2,500	*T. Rowe Price Equity Income*	
IRA	$1,000	*Telephone: (800) 638-5660*	
		www.troweprice.com	

T. Rowe Price Equity Income Fd Worth $85,516
12.98 % annualized 10/31/85-05/31/03

Index - Standard & Poor's 500 Worth $78,830
12.46 % annualized 10/31/85-05/31/03

GROWTH OF $10,000

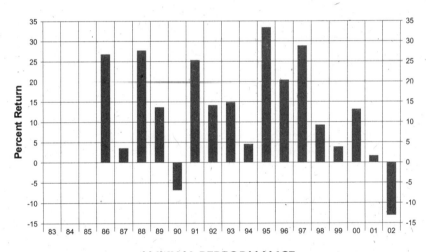

ANNUAL PERFORMANCE

TOP 10 HOLDINGS

Merck	Bristol Myers Squibb
ExxonMobil	Honeywell
Verizon Communications	Union Pacific
General Electric	Bank One
Chevron Texaco	Wyeth

AMERICAN CENTURY INCOME & GROWTH

| **OBJECTIVE:** | *Growth and Income* | *67* |
| **MANAGER:** | *Team Managed* | |

FUND OVERVIEW:

Armed with a computer database of 2,500 stocks, the managers of American Century Income & Growth search tirelessly for attractive ideas to put in their American Century Income & Growth portfolio. Every company is ranked according to earnings momentum and valuation characteristics, to make sure the fund pays a fair price for its holdings. The model also verifies that no more than 25 percent of the portfolio is put in any one industry. The overall goal of this quantitatively driven strategy is to beat the S&P 500 index while generating a yield that's at least 30 percent higher. This is a stiff challenge, but the fund has been able to meet it since inception.

Like most of the other funds in this category, this one doesn't have much of an income component. The portfolio does hold some high-yielding utility and energy stocks, but there are almost no bonds. In the past, the fund experienced a high degree of turnover stemming from strong new asset growth; fresh cash causes the model to reallocate holdings to keep everything in balance. However, the fund's managers have vowed to make an effort to reduce this frequent trading.

ANNUALIZED RETURNS		**PORTFOLIO STATISTICS**	
1-Year	−7.60%	Beta	0.95
3-Year	−8.65%	Turnover	67.00%
5-Year	−0.71%	12-Month Yield	1.44%
Overall Rank	3	12b-1 Fee	0.00%
Risk Rank	3	Expense Ratio	0.68%

MINIMUM INVESTMENT		**CONTACT INFORMATION**
Regular	$2,500	*American Century Income &*
IRA	$1,000	*Growth Fund*
		Telephone: (800) 345-2021
		www.americancentury.com

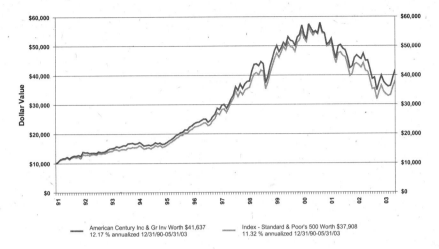

American Century Inc & Gr Inv Worth $41,637
12.17 % annualized 12/31/90-05/31/03

Index - Standard & Poor's 500 Worth $37,908
11.32 % annualized 12/31/90-05/31/03

GROWTH OF $10,000

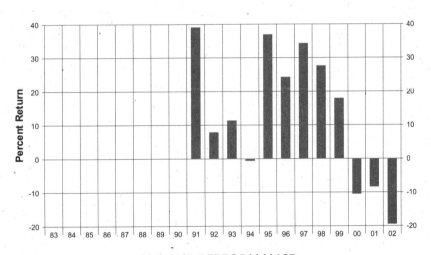

ANNUAL PERFORMANCE

TOP 10 HOLDINGS

Bank of America	Procter & Gamble
ExxonMobil	Verizon Communications
Citigroup	Merck
Microsoft	Pfizer
General Electric	Eastman Kodak

FIDELITY GROWTH & INCOME II

| OBJECTIVE: | Growth and Income | *68* |
| MANAGER: | Louis Salemy | |

Fund Overview:

The goal of Fidelity Growth & Income II is to provide both current income and capital appreciation by investing assets in dividend-paying common stocks. While the fund owns both growth and value stocks, manager Louis Salemy tends to be more cautious, which serves the fund well in tough markets. He's also allowed to invest in bonds, non-dividend paying stocks, and foreign companies, as he finds attractive opportunities.

Overall, Salemy favors companies with steady earnings and reasonable valuations, and relies on fundamental analysis when making investment decisions. As is the case with most funds in this category, Fidelity Growth & Income II really doesn't throw off that much "income," sporting a yield of under 1 percent. But it does offer investors a lower risk alternative to gaining stock exposure, along with the potential to enjoy a small but steady stream of regular dividend income.

Note that, like all Fidelity funds, Fidelity Growth & Income II must be purchased directly from Fidelity. That's because Fidelity does not currently make its funds available through the NTF programs of other discount brokers.

ANNUALIZED RETURNS		PORTFOLIO STATISTICS	
1-Year	−1.20%	Beta	0.77
3-Year	−5.33%	Turnover	52.00%
5-Year	N/A	12-Month Yield	0.83%
Overall Rank	2	12b-1 Fee	0.00%
Risk Rank	2	Expense Ratio	0.89%
MINIMUM INVESTMENT		**CONTACT INFORMATION**	
Regular	$2,500	*Fidelity Growth & Income II Portfolio*	
IRA	$2,500	*Telephone: (800) 343-3548*	
		www.fidelity.com	

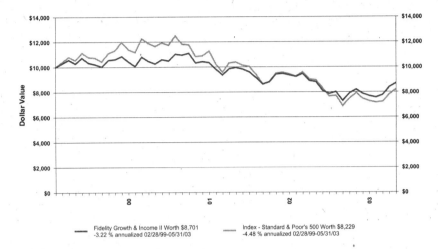

Fidelity Growth & Income II Worth $8,701
-3.22 % annualized 02/28/99-05/31/03

Index - Standard & Poor's 500 Worth $8,229
-4.48 % annualized 02/28/99-05/31/03

GROWTH OF $10,000

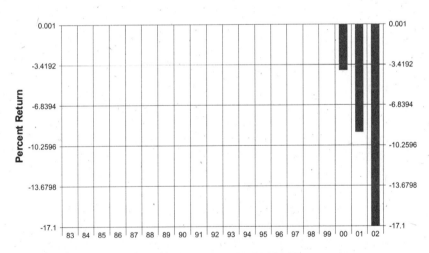

ANNUAL PERFORMANCE

TOP 10 HOLDINGS

Walgreen
Gillette
Omnicom Group
Morgan Stanley
Echostar Communications

Merrill Lynch
Wells Fargo & Company
Microsoft
Wal-Mart Stores
Freddie Mac

BRIDGEWAY BLUE CHIP 35 INDEX

OBJECTIVE:	*Index*
MANAGER:	*John Montgomery*

69

FUND OVERVIEW:

Bridgeway Blue Chip 35 Index calls itself a hybrid between the Dow and S&P 500. This unique offering, which has the lowest expense ratio of any fund in this book, consists of equal percentages of the 35 largest U.S. companies, excluding tobacco stocks and allowing for industry diversification. Holdings include Johnson & Johnson, Procter & Gamble, Fannie Mae, Coca-Cola, AT&T, Merck, Wal-Mart, Texas Instruments, AOL Time Warner, and General Electric. What's great about this fund, besides its bare-bones costs, is that manager John Montgomery runs it with an eye on keeping taxes to an absolute minimum. In fact, his goal is to never have a capital gains distribution. (The fund is fairly new, having been launched in July 1997, although so far Montgomery has achieved this objective.)

Bridgeway Blue Chip 35 Index has everything you could want in a fund: low expenses, tax efficiency, and quality management. By the way, you won't find the past performance of the index Montgomery follows anywhere. He made the index up, so the numbers aren't available through any other source. Nevertheless, this fund has done better than the S&P 500 since inception, an accomplishment few funds can boast about. (Note: This fund was formerly known as the Bridgeway Ultra-Large 35 Index fund.)

ANNUALIZED RETURNS		PORTFOLIO STATISTICS	
1-Year	−3.70%	Beta	0.96
3-Year	−10.16%	Turnover	40.80%
5-Year	1.63%	12-Month Yield	1.44%
Overall Rank	3	12b-1 Fee	0.00%
Risk Rank	3	Expense Ratio	0.14%

MINIMUM INVESTMENT		CONTACT INFORMATION
Regular	$2,000	*Bridgeway Blue Chip 35 Index*
IRA	$500	*Telephone: (800) 661-3550*
		www.bridgewayfunds.com

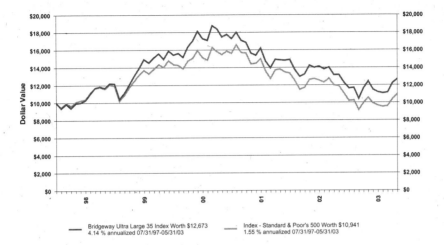

Bridgeway Ultra Large 35 Index Worth $12,673
4.14 % annualized 07/31/97-05/31/03

Index - Standard & Poor's 500 Worth $10,941
1.55 % annualized 07/31/97-05/31/03

GROWTH OF $10,000

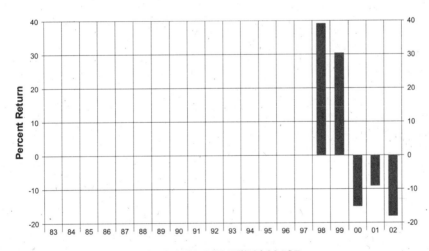

ANNUAL PERFORMANCE

TOP 10 HOLDINGS

Oracle	International Business Machines
Procter & Gamble	Cisco Systems
Johnson & Johnson	Verizon Communications
Wells Fargo & Company	Intel
Bank of America	Fannie Mae

CALIFORNIA INVESTMENT S&P 500 INDEX

OBJECTIVE:	*Index*
MANAGER:	*Roderick Baldwin*

70

FUND OVERVIEW:

California Investment S&P 500 Index may be the best index fund you've never heard of. This tiny fund has not only managed to track the S&P 500 with great precision, it slightly outperforms it during some periods, even after accounting for the portfolio's modest expense ratio. The fund is run by Rod Baldwin. Before taking the reins of the portfolio, Baldwin was vice president of index investing at Bank of America Capital Management.

This diverse portfolio contains stocks representing roughly 90 percent of the S&P 500 index. The index is made up of large companies, many of which are market leaders in their respective industries. Because these companies earn about 25 percent of total revenues from overseas operations, the fund also gives you impressive international exposure.

This fund has been around since 1992 and is clearly one of the best managed index funds in the industry. Still, few investors have heard of it, primarily because The California Funds don't have a large marketing budget. For those of you interested in an S&P 500 index fund, this one is definitely worth a look.

ANNUALIZED RETURNS		PORTFOLIO STATISTICS	
1-Year	−7.80%	Beta	0.98
3-Year	−10.59%	Turnover	9.00%
5-Year	−0.89%	12-Month Yield	1.46%
Overall Rank	3	12b-1 Fee	0.00%
Risk Rank	3	Expense Ratio	0.20%

MINIMUM INVESTMENT		CONTACT INFORMATION
Regular	$5,000	*California Investment S&P 500*
IRA	$0	*Index Fund*
		Telephone: (800) 225-8778
		www.caltrust.com

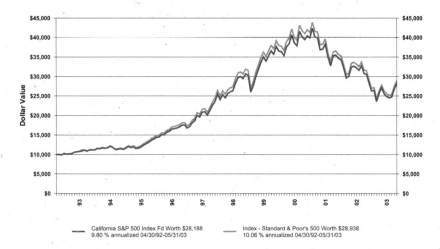

California S&P 500 Index Fd Worth $28,188
9.80 % annualized 04/30/92-05/31/03

Index - Standard & Poor's 500 Worth $28,938
10.06 % annualized 04/30/92-05/31/03

GROWTH OF $10,000

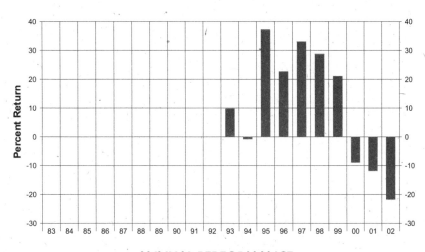

ANNUAL PERFORMANCE

TOP 10 HOLDINGS

General Electric	Citigroup
Microsoft	Johnson & Johnson
Wal-Mart Stores	American International Group
Pfizer	International Business Machines
ExxonMobil	Merck

DOMINI SOCIAL EQUITY

OBJECTIVE:	*Index*	
MANAGER:	*Team Managed*	*71*

FUND OVERVIEW:

Domini Social Equity is an index fund with a twist. It invests in a unique index made up of about 400 companies that pass multiple social screens. Specifically, to make it into the Domini Social Index, companies must have positive records for making safe and useful products, good employee relations, positive corporate citizenship, and good track records for protecting the environment. What's more, the index excludes companies deriving more than 2 percent of gross revenues from the sale of military weapons, and an included company must not have any revenue coming from tobacco products, alcoholic beverages, gambling operations, or nuclear power plants.

Clearly, if you are concerned about such social issues, this fund makes perfect sense. But investing with your conscience historically hasn't been very profitable, since most socially aware funds have lousy track records. Domini Social Equity is a rare exception. It has almost kept pace with the S&P 500 since inception. That's an amazing accomplishment for any fund, let alone one that requires its holdings to pass such rigorous and subjective requirements and has a higher expense ratio than most others in this category.

ANNUALIZED RETURNS

1-Year	−8.40%
3-Year	−11.75%
5-Year	−1.32%
Overall Rank	3
Risk Rank	3

MINIMUM INVESTMENT

Regular	$1,000
IRA	$250

PORTFOLIO STATISTICS

Beta	1.00
Turnover	9.00%
12-Month Yield	0.46%
12b-1 Fee	0.25%
Expense Ratio	0.92%

CONTACT INFORMATION

Domini Social Equity Fund
Telephone: (800) 582-6757
www.domini.com

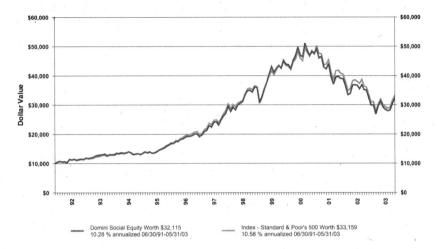

Domini Social Equity Worth $32,115
10.28 % annualized 06/30/91-05/31/03

Index - Standard & Poor's 500 Worth $33,159
10.58 % annualized 06/30/91-05/31/03

GROWTH OF $10,000

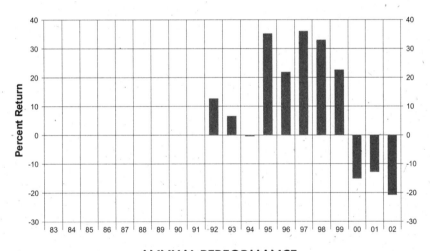

ANNUAL PERFORMANCE

TOP 10 HOLDINGS

Microsoft	Procter & Gamble
Johnson & Johnson	Bank of America
American International Group	Cisco Systems
Merck	Verizon Communications
Intel	Coca-Cola

RYDEX OTC

| **OBJECTIVE:** | *Index* | *72* |
| **MANAGER:** | *Michael Byrum* | |

FUND OVERVIEW:

Without question, the index everyone talked about in the late 1990s was the Nasdaq 100. After all, prior to its recent correction, it posted incredible returns, thanks to its large tech weighting. For many years, there weren't many ways to gain access to this index. But that has changed. There are now a number of no-load funds tracking the Nasdaq 100, plus the so-called "QQQ" Nasdaq tracking shares traded on the American Stock Exchange. The oldest fund following the Nasdaq 100 is Rydex OTC. It's also the largest.

The fund's manager, Mike Byrum, puts together a portfolio of stocks that he feels will adequately replicate the performance of the Nasdaq 100. While the fund's expense ratio is higher than most other index funds, investors aren't complaining because of the great performance.

Keep in mind that the Nasdaq 100 is basically an index of large technology stocks, such as Microsoft, Intel, Cisco Systems, Dell Computer, and Oracle. Although there are a few service companies and retailers thrown in—such as Starbucks, Costco, and Amazon.com—a bet on the Nasdaq 100 is a bet on technology stocks. Also note the fund's high minimum investment requirement of $25,000 for both individual accounts and IRAs (although you may be able to get in for less through some of the NTF programs).

ANNUALIZED RETURNS		PORTFOLIO STATISTICS	
1-Year	−2.20%	Beta	2.06
3-Year	−30.26%	Turnover	385.00%
5-Year	−1.28%	12-Month Yield	0.00%
Overall Rank	3	12b-1 Fee	0.00%
Risk Rank	5	Expense Ratio	1.08%
MINIMUM INVESTMENT		CONTACT INFORMATION	
Regular	$25,000	*Rydex OTC Fund*	
IRA	$25,000	*Telephone: (800) 820-0888*	
		www.rydexfunds.com	

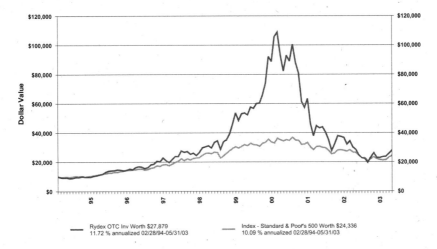

Rydex OTC Inv Worth $27,879
11.72 % annualized 02/28/94–05/31/03

Index - Standard & Poor's 500 Worth $24,336
10.09 % annualized 02/28/94–05/31/03

GROWTH OF $10,000

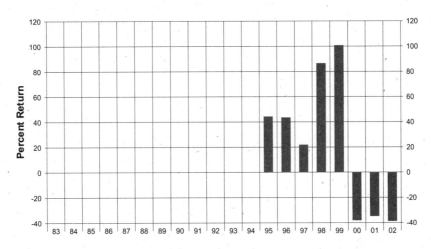

ANNUAL PERFORMANCE

TOP 10 HOLDINGS	
Microsoft	Comcast
Intel	Dell Computer
Cisco Systems	Oracle
Amgen	Ebay
Qualcomm	Maxim Integrated

SCHWAB 1000

OBJECTIVE:	*Index*	*73*
MANAGER:	*Geri Hom*	

FUND OVERVIEW:

Schwab 1000 is a proprietary index set up by discount broker Charles Schwab & Co. This fund is predictably designed to mimic that index. The index contains the 1,000 largest publicly traded companies in the U.S., in terms of market capitalization. Schwab calls it an index of both large- and mid-cap stocks. Interestingly enough, although there are more than 7,200 publicly traded American stocks, the companies in Schwab 1000 make up some 87 percent of the total value of all U.S. stocks.

Like most index funds, Schwab 1000 is very tax-efficient. In fact, the fund's goal is to never pay out a capital gains distribution, although it does distribute annual dividends that are taxed as ordinary income. To accomplish this goal, the fund may adjust its weightings of certain stocks and even continue to hold companies no longer included in the index to avoid having to realize gains.

Schwab offers this fund in two classes: investor shares and select shares. Select shares have a slightly lower expense ratio, but a much higher initial minimum investment requirement of $50,000.

ANNUALIZED RETURNS

1-Year	−7.90%
3-Year	−10.30%
5-Year	−0.81%
Overall Rank	3
Risk Rank	3

MINIMUM INVESTMENT

Regular	$1,000
IRA	$500

PORTFOLIO STATISTICS

Beta	1.00
Turnover	9.00%
12-Month Yield	1.17%
12b-1 Fee	0.00%
Expense Ratio	0.46%

CONTACT INFORMATION

Schwab 1000
Telephone: (800) 435-4000
www.schwab.com

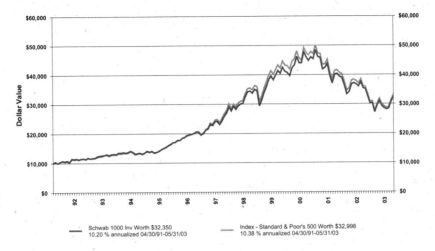

Schwab 1000 Inv Worth $32,350
10.20 % annualized 04/30/91-05/31/03

Index - Standard & Poor's 500 Worth $32,998
10.38 % annualized 04/30/91-05/31/03

GROWTH OF $10,000

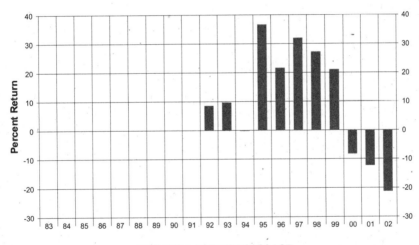

ANNUAL PERFORMANCE

TOP 10 HOLDINGS	
General Electric	Citigroup
Microsoft	Johnson & Johnson
Wal-Mart Stores	American International Group
Pfizer	International Business Machines
ExxonMobil	Merck

VANGUARD INDEX 500

OBJECTIVE: *Index*
MANAGER: *George Sauter*

74

FUND OVERVIEW:

Vanguard Index 500 is the granddaddy of all index funds. It is the largest and best performing of the portfolios that try to replicate the price and yield performance of the S&P 500. It does so by following a computer model that guides the fund to invest in all 500 stocks in the index in approximately the exact same proportions. (The S&P 500, as you probably know by now, is dominated by large blue-chip stocks and represents approximately 70 percent of the total capitalization of all U.S. equities.) By nature, the fund will be close to fully invested at all times, holding only a tiny level of cash to meet redemptions. The fund's returns since inception have been virtually identical to the S&P 500, less Vanguard's bare-bones expense ratio.

Assuming no mass redemption requests come in, this fund should be highly tax-efficient because turnover is low. It would make a nice large-cap core holding in almost any portfolio, although many analysts prefer the Vanguard Total Stock Market Portfolio (which we will discuss next) even more for those who want to own just one index fund. For more on the role indexing should play in your overall portfolio, you might want to reread Chapter 3.

ANNUALIZED RETURNS		PORTFOLIO STATISTICS	
1-Year	−8.10%	Beta	1.00
3-Year	−10.90%	Turnover	9.00%
5-Year	−1.09%	12-Month Yield	1.53%
Overall Rank	3	12b-1 Fee	0.00%
Risk Rank	3	Expense Ratio	0.17%

MINIMUM INVESTMENT		CONTACT INFORMATION
Regular	$3,000	*Vanguard Index 500 Portfolio*
IRA	$1,000	*Telephone: (800) 662-7447*
		www.vanguard.com

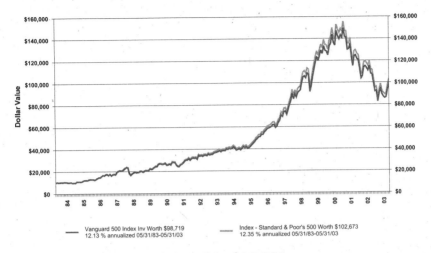

Vanguard 500 Index Inv Worth $98,719
12.13 % annualized 05/31/83-05/31/03

Index - Standard & Poor's 500 Worth $102,673
12.35 % annualized 05/31/83-05/31/03

GROWTH OF $10,000

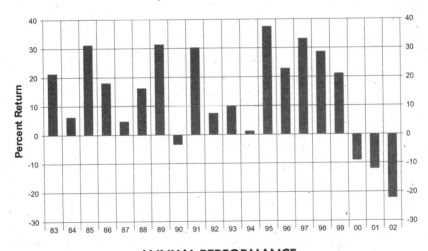

ANNUAL PERFORMANCE

TOP 10 HOLDINGS

Microsoft	Citigroup
General Electric	Johnson & Johnson
ExxonMobil	International Business Machines
Wal-Mart Stores	American International Group
Pfizer	Merck

VANGUARD TOTAL STOCK MARKET

| OBJECTIVE: | *Index* |
| MANAGER: | *George Sauter* |

75

FUND OVERVIEW:

Unlike the Vanguard Index 500 fund, which only gives you exposure to blue-chip America, Vanguard Total Stock Market allows you to invest in equities of all sizes—large and small. Although 70 percent of the portfolio looks just like the S&P 500, 20 percent is in mid-cap stocks and the remaining 10 percent is in small caps. This gives you access to the entire U.S. equity market. The fund is designed to parallel the performance of the Wilshire 5000 Index, which consists of all regularly traded U.S. stocks on the three major exchanges. However, it normally will hold only a representative sample of some 2,000 positions because the cost of owning all 5,000 would be quite high.

If you are looking for the simplest approach to gaining exposure to the entire stock market without having to do any work, this fund is a great choice. The actual manager isn't that important because this fund is run by a computer. As a result, this fund is the ultimate buy-and-hold investment. Plus, it is so diversified, it could technically be the only fund you own for your U.S. market exposure. (Similar funds are offered by such families as T. Rowe Price and Fidelity. If you already have an account with one of these firms, their total market stock index funds would make a fine substitute.)

ANNUALIZED RETURNS	
1-Year	−7.30%
3-Year	−9.71%
5-Year	−0.83%
Overall Rank	3
Risk Rank	3

MINIMUM INVESTMENT	
Regular	$3,000
IRA	$1,000

PORTFOLIO STATISTICS	
Beta	1.03
Turnover	4.00%
12-Month Yield	1.31%
12b-1 Fee	0.00%
Expense Ratio	0.20%

CONTACT INFORMATION

Vanguard Total Stock Market Portfolio
Telephone: (800) 662-7447
www.vanguard.com

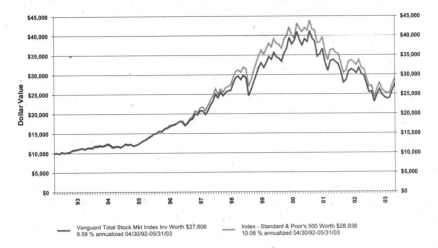

Vanguard Total Stock Mkt Index Inv Worth $27,606
9.59 % annualized 04/30/92-05/31/03

Index - Standard & Poor's 500 Worth $28,938
10.06 % annualized 04/30/92-05/31/03

GROWTH OF $10,000

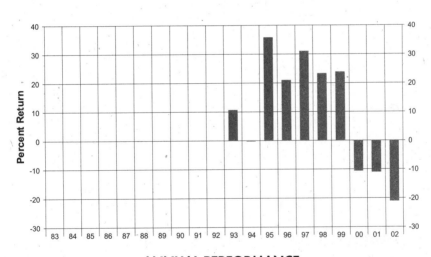

ANNUAL PERFORMANCE

TOP 10 HOLDINGS

Microsoft	Citigroup
General Electric	Johnson & Johnson
ExxonMobil	International Business Machines
Wal-Mart Stores	American International Group
Pfizer	Merck

ABN AMRO/MONTAG & CALDWELL BALANCED

| OBJECTIVE: | *Balanced* | *76* |
| MANAGER: | *Ronald E. Canakaris* | |

FUND OVERVIEW:

ABN AMRO/Montag & Caldwell Balanced takes a total return approach to investing by spreading the fund across blue-chip companies, corporate and U.S. government bonds, and a slight reserve of cash. Instead of worrying about which asset classes to put the money to work in, manager Ronald Canakaris focuses on finding the best investments for each area of the portfolio.

The fund's strategic target allocation calls for stocks to make up 50 to 70 percent of total assets, with the bulk of the rest in senior fixed-income securities. However, if Canakaris believes one asset class is exceedingly more attractive than another, he can navigate outside of these parameters.

Canakaris is positive on the outlook for stocks, assuming the economy and corporate profits continue to grow. On the bond side, he's keeping the duration of the portfolio shorter than normal, in anticipation of rising interest rates. On the equity side, he currently favors high-quality consumer staple and healthcare stocks, along with quality cyclical growth companies

ANNUALIZED RETURNS

1-Year	−2.50%
3-Year	−3.54%
5-Year	2.16%
Overall Rank	2
Risk Rank	1

MINIMUM INVESTMENT

Regular	$2,500
IRA	$500

PORTFOLIO STATISTICS

Beta	0.40
Turnover	38.86%
12-Month Yield	1.83%
12b-1 Fee	0.25%
Expense Ratio	1.12%

CONTACT INFORMATION

ABN AMRO/Montag &
Caldwell Balanced Fund
Telephone: (800) 992-8151
www.abnamro.com

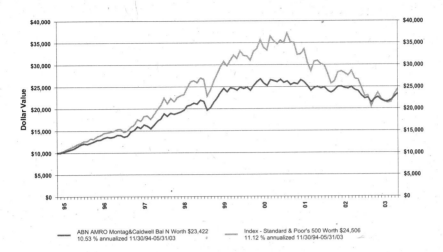

ABN AMRO Montag&Caldwell Bal N Worth $23,422
10.53 % annualized 11/30/94-05/31/03

Index - Standard & Poor's 500 Worth $24,506
11.12 % annualized 11/30/94-05/31/03

GROWTH OF $10,000

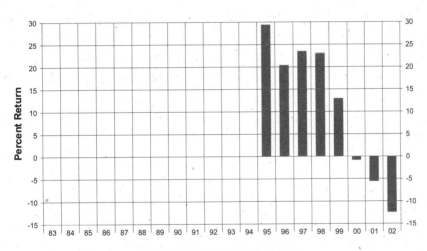

ANNUAL PERFORMANCE

TOP 10 HOLDINGS

Johnson & Johnson	3M
Pfizer	Amgen
Medtronic	Gillette
Colgate Palmolive	American International Group
Procter & Gamble	Coca-Cola

ATLANTIC WHITEHALL BALANCED

OBJECTIVE:	*Balanced*	77
MANAGER:	*Paul Blaustein and John Curry*	

FUND OVERVIEW:

Atlantic Whitehall Balanced fund managers Paul Blaustein and John Curry usually keep a ratio of 60 percent equities and 40 percent bonds in their portfolio. Blaustein is a bottom-up stock picker who oversees the equity portion of the portfolio. He also manages fellow large-cap growth Powerhouse Performer Atlantic Whitehall Growth. Blaustein places great emphasis on a company's business forecasts and competitive position, and seeks to buy stocks at reasonable valuations. Although Atlantic Whitehall Balanced has no market capitalization restrictions, holdings in the fund typically fall into the large-cap category because of Blaustein's preference for industry leaders with solid histories and earnings momentum.

On the fixed-income side, Curry strives to maintain an investment-grade rating for the bonds in the portfolio. As a result, he usually shuns high-yield bonds, and instead favors high-quality corporate, government, and agency issues. While the fund has outperformed its peers and delivers a competitive dividend yield, it is slightly more volatile than others in the balanced category.

ANNUALIZED RETURNS		PORTFOLIO STATISTICS	
1-Year	−3.40%	Beta	0.73
3-Year	−5.50%	Turnover	32.00%
5-Year	4.61%	12-Month Yield	1.22%
Overall Rank	2	12b-1 Fee	0.25%
Risk Rank	2	Expense Ratio	1.38%

MINIMUM INVESTMENT		CONTACT INFORMATION	
Regular	$1,000	*Atlantic Whitehall Balanced Fund*	
IRA	$250	*Telephone: (800) 994-2533*	
		www.thewhitehallfunds.com	

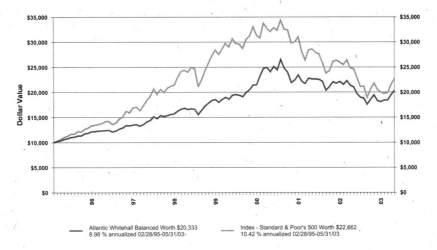

Atlantic Whitehall Balanced Worth $20,333
8.98 % annualized 02/28/95-05/31/03

Index - Standard & Poor's 500 Worth $22,662
10.42 % annualized 02/28/95-05/31/03

GROWTH OF $10,000

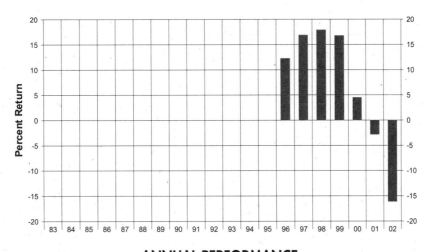

ANNUAL PERFORMANCE

TOP 10 HOLDINGS	
Maxim Integrated	Novellus Systems
ExxonMobil	Wells Fargo & Company
Amgen	Applied Materials
Altera Corporation	Comcast
Xilinx	Pfizer

GABELLI WESTWOOD BALANCED

OBJECTIVE:	*Balanced*	
MANAGER:	*Susan Byrne*	*78*

FUND OVERVIEW:

Gabelli Westwood Balanced manager Susan Byrne takes a top-down approach to investing. She begins by looking at the overall economic environment, paying special attention to inflation. If conditions seem right for equities, she'll place up to 70 percent of the portfolio in stocks, with the remainder in fixed-income instruments and cash. Byrne also buys preferreds, real estate investment trusts (REITs), and high-grade convertible securities.

Gabelli Westwood Balanced seeks to provide shareholders with both capital appreciation and current income. No less than 25 percent of the portfolio will be invested in bonds and other fixed-income instruments at all times. If Byrne believes the outlook for equities is bleak, she can temporarily put the entire portfolio in U.S. government securities, certificates of deposit, or other cash-equivalent investments to preserve capital.

A few years ago, Byrne entered into an agreement with prominent fund manager Mario Gabelli for the marketing of her Westwood family of funds. When you call for information, you'll be connected to Gabelli's office, even though Gabelli himself isn't involved with the fund's management.

ANNUALIZED RETURNS		PORTFOLIO STATISTICS	
1-Year	−2.30%	Beta	0.40
3-Year	0.28%	Turnover	78.00%
5-Year	3.89%	12-Month Yield	2.18%
Overall Rank	1	12b-1 Fee	0.25%
Risk Rank	1	Expense Ratio	1.16%

MINIMUM INVESTMENT		CONTACT INFORMATION	
Regular	$1,000	*Gabelli Westwood Balanced*	
IRA	$1,000	*Telephone: (800) 422-3554*	
		www.gabelli.com	

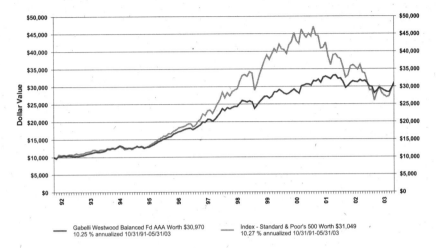

Gabelli Westwood Balanced Fd AAA Worth $30,970
10.25 % annualized 10/31/91-05/31/03

Index - Standard & Poor's 500 Worth $31,049
10.27 % annualized 10/31/91-05/31/03

GROWTH OF $10,000

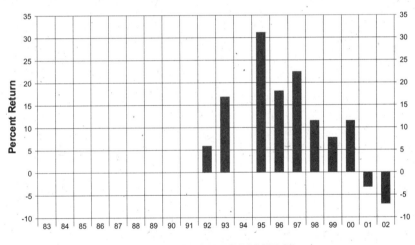

ANNUAL PERFORMANCE

TOP 10 HOLDINGS

Fannie Mae	Washington Mutual
ExxonMobil	Procter & Gamble
Bear Stearns	Merck
Pfizer	Lockheed Martin
Murphy Oil	Anadarko Petroleum

RAINIER BALANCED PORTFOLIO

OBJECTIVE:	*Balanced*	*79*
MANAGER:	*Team Managed*	

FUND OVERVIEW:

Rainier Balanced is designed to provide long-term capital appreciation and regular income, with less return and risk than the S&P 500. The portfolio is allocated among equities, fixed-income instruments, and short-term cash equivalents. Stocks will normally make up 35 to 65 percent of the portfolio, and bonds will constitute from 30 to 55 percent. The remainder will be in cash. The management team uses a strategic asset allocation approach, putting money where it is expected to do best, given short-term trends in the economy. Shifts from one asset to another are gradual, though, and aggressive market timing is avoided.

The equity portion of the portfolio is invested by Jim Margard, who also runs another Powerhouse Performer, Rainier Core Equity. This fund is appropriate for conservative investors who prefer to have their stock and bond exposure in one place. Note that the fund has a minimum initial investment requirement of $25,000, which is steep for most people. However, if you buy it through a no-load, no-transaction-fee program at one of the discount brokers, you can get in for as little as $2,500.

ANNUALIZED RETURNS		PORTFOLIO STATISTICS	
1-Year	−0.40%	Beta	0.55
3-Year	−2.60%	Turnover	71.26%
5-Year	2.60%	12-Month Yield	1.74%
Overall Rank	1	12b-1 Fee	0.25%
Risk Rank	1	Expense Ratio	1.18%

MINIMUM INVESTMENT		CONTACT INFORMATION	
Regular	$25,000	*Rainier Balanced Portfolio*	
IRA	$25,000	*Telephone: (800) 248-6314*	
		www.rainierfunds.com	

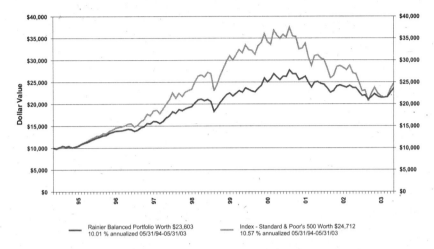

GROWTH OF $10,000

Rainier Balanced Portfolio Worth $23,603
10.01 % annualized 05/31/94-05/31/03

Index - Standard & Poor's 500 Worth $24,712
10.57 % annualized 05/31/94-05/31/03

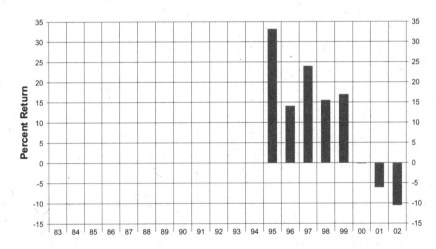

ANNUAL PERFORMANCE

TOP 10 HOLDINGS

Microsoft	Johnson & Johnson
General Electric	Freddie Mac
Pfizer	Colgate Palmolive
Citigroup	Procter & Gamble
American International Group	Cisco Systems

VALUE LINE ASSET ALLOCATION

OBJECTIVE:	*Balanced*	
MANAGER:	*Team Managed*	*80*

FUND OVERVIEW:

Unlike a traditional balanced fund, which maintains a pretty steady weighting of stocks, bonds, and cash, Value Line Asset Allocation's managers shift exposure to these asset classes, depending on what their computer model tells them. What's amazing is that even though the fund has averaged less than a 50 percent exposure to equities since inception, it has managed to outperform the S&P 500 all-stock index. And it has done so in spite of owning a highly diversified list of some 200 mostly small- and mid-cap companies across a wide variety of industries. "Our highly disciplined strategy is to invest exclusively in stocks with strong earnings and strong price momentum, quickly selling issues that fail to make the grade," fund chairperson Jean Bernhard Buttner notes.

Because Value Line's proprietary stock model is currently somewhat cautious, the fund's equity exposure is slightly below its neutral benchmark of 55 percent. Another 30 percent is in U.S. Treasuries, and the remainder is resting in cash. Value Line Asset Allocation is great for investors looking for both stock and bond diversification in one fund. But if you already have elements of both in your portfolio, this fund might be redundant.

ANNUALIZED RETURNS		PORTFOLIO STATISTICS	
1-Year	−7.20%	Beta	0.68
3-Year	−3.54%	Turnover	51.00%
5-Year	2.91%	12-Month Yield	0.06%
Overall Rank	2	12b-1 Fee	0.25%
Risk Rank	3	Expense Ratio	1.09%

MINIMUM INVESTMENT		CONTACT INFORMATION	
Regular	$1,000	*Value Line Asset Allocation Fund*	
IRA	$100	*Telephone: (800) 223-0818*	
		www.valueline.com	

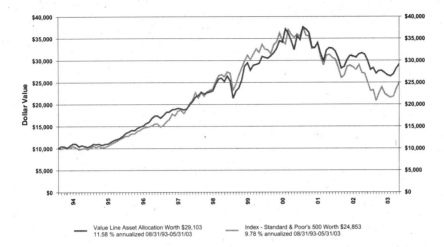

Value Line Asset Allocation Worth $29,103
11.58 % annualized 08/31/93-05/31/03

Index - Standard & Poor's 500 Worth $24,853
9.78 % annualized 08/31/93-05/31/03

GROWTH OF $10,000

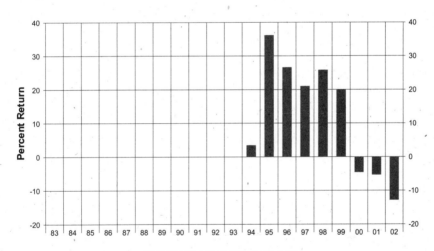

ANNUAL PERFORMANCE

TOP 10 HOLDINGS

Apollo Group	Brinker International
Career Education	Forest Laboratories
Chicos FAS	Progressive
Wal-Mart Stores	Harman International
UCBH Holdings	Varian Medical Systems

ARTISAN INTERNATIONAL

OBJECTIVE:	*International*	*81*
MANAGER:	*Mark Yockey*	

FUND OVERVIEW:

Mark Yockey begins the process of investing his Artisan International fund by looking around the world and figuring out where he would most like to put his money to work. He favors those countries with improving economic conditions, and avoids those that appear to be overvalued. He pays attention to such measures as gross domestic product growth, corporate profitability, current accounting and currency issues, and changes in interest rates. Having made those decisions, he looks for individual companies that are best positioned to profit from the current outlook. He concentrates on stocks with above-average financials and accelerating earnings per share. He also keeps an eye on price, avoiding businesses trading at unsustainable or unusually high valuations.

Yockey is presently most enthusiastic about Europe, where he has invested the biggest bulk of his assets. "To our mind, Europe offers the greatest investment potential in a generation," he insists. "The reasons include privatization, deregulation, increasing competition, merger activity, and a burgeoning commitment to enhancing shareholder value." Asia/Pacific and Latin America have relatively small weightings, as does Canada.

ANNUALIZED RETURNS

1-Year	−18.60%
3-Year	−14.33%
5-Year	3.24%
Overall Rank	4
Risk Rank	3

MINIMUM INVESTMENT

Regular	$1,000
IRA	$1,000

PORTFOLIO STATISTICS

Beta	0.84
Turnover	38.52%
12-Month Yield	0.85%
12b-1 Fee	0.00%
Expense Ratio	1.20%

CONTACT INFORMATION

Artisan International Fund
Telephone: (800) 344-1770
www.artisanfunds.com

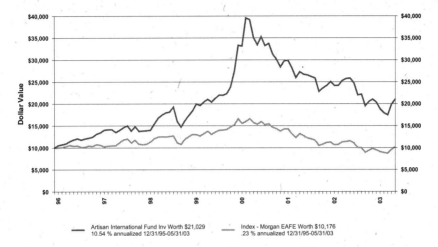

Artisan International Fund Inv Worth $21,029
10.54 % annualized 12/31/95-05/31/03

Index - Morgan EAFE Worth $10,176
.23 % annualized 12/31/95-05/31/03

GROWTH OF $10,000

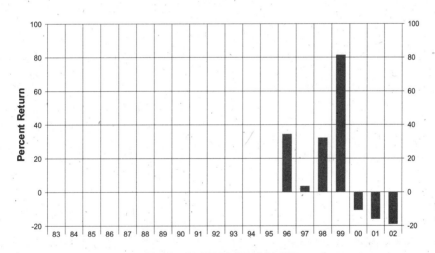

ANNUAL PERFORMANCE

TOP 10 HOLDINGS

Compass Group	Honda Motor
Nestle	Allianz
Diageo	Muenchener Rueckversicherungs
CIBA Speciality Chemicals	Lloyds TSP Group
Telefonos de Mexico	Fortis

JULIUS BAER INTERNATIONAL EQUITY

OBJECTIVE:	*International*	
MANAGER:	*Rudolph-Riad Younes and Richard C. Pell*	*82*

FUND OVERVIEW:

In selecting stocks for the Julius Baer International Equity fund, managers Rudolph-Riad Younes and Richard Pell generally focus on a minimum of five different countries. They normally keep at least 65 percent of the portfolio in no fewer than three different, non-U.S. countries, including the emerging markets. In fact, Younes and Pell invest more money in these smaller developing countries than any of the other broad-based international funds. They can also put up to 10 percent of the portfolio in high yielding debt securities.

Younes and Pell believe that well diversified international funds provide better risk-adjusted returns than overly concentrated portfolios. As a result, they typically own 150 to 200 stocks. While they are growth oriented, they buy stocks of all types and valuations, depending on where opportunities arise. Their research process is primarily based on a fundamental assessment of companies, sectors, and the macroeconomic influences on individual regions and countries. They can invest in companies of all sizes, though the portfolio emphasizes larger firms for the relative liquidity they provide.

ANNUALIZED RETURNS		PORTFOLIO STATISTICS	
1-Year	−4.70%	Beta	0.58
3-Year	−7.67%	Turnover	66.00%
5-Year	6.34%	12-Month Yield	1.49%
Overall Rank	2	12b-1 Fee	0.25%
Risk Rank	2	Expense Ratio	1.51%

MINIMUM INVESTMENT		CONTACT INFORMATION	
Regular	$2,500	*Julius Baer International Equity Fund*	
IRA	$100	*Telephone: (800) 435-4659*	
		us-funds.juliusbaer.com	

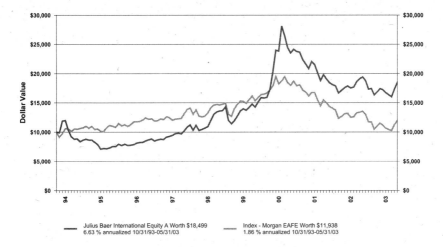

Julius Baer International Equity A Worth $18,499
6.63 % annualized 10/31/93-05/31/03

Index - Morgan EAFE Worth $11,938
1.86 % annualized 10/31/93-05/31/03

GROWTH OF $10,000

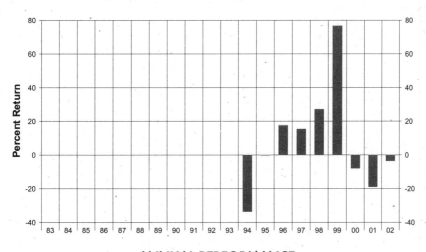

ANNUAL PERFORMANCE

TOP 10 HOLDINGS	
Komercni Banka	ENI
Bank Pekao	Encana
Vodafone	Nokia
Erste Bk Der Osterreichischen	Endesa SA
Total Fina	Unicredito Italiano

MANAGERS INTERNATIONAL EQUITY

| OBJECTIVE: | *International* | **83** |
| MANAGER: | *Team Managed* | |

FUND OVERVIEW:

Managers International Equity gives one third of the portfolio to each of three different managers: William Holzer of Deutsche Asset Management, Ted Tyson of Mastholm Asset Management, and Andrew Adelson of Bernstein Investment Research and Management. In essence, you get three approaches to selecting overseas investments in one fund.

Holzer is a top-down thematic investor who views the world as a single global economy. He first develops themes that target the fastest growing or most profitable segments. He then works with Scudder's analysts to identify companies that could benefit from the effects of these themes. Tyson and his team use a bottom-up growth style for investing in international equities of all sizes. They continually search for companies with growing earnings and visit with management teams around the world. Adelson describes Bernstein's investment approach as value-based and research driven. They look for companies with short-term problems that are available at bargain prices.

The end result is a broad portfolio of names from around the world. All three managers take a long-term view on investing, and are normally diversified across at least three countries.

ANNUALIZED RETURNS		PORTFOLIO STATISTICS	
1-Year	–15.70%	Beta	0.68
3-Year	–12.83%	Turnover	98.00%
5-Year	–5.65%	12-Month Yield	0.29%
Overall Rank	3	12b-1 Fee	0.00%
Risk Rank	2	Expense Ratio	1.54%

MINIMUM INVESTMENT		CONTACT INFORMATION
Regular	$2,000	*Managers International Equity*
IRA	$500	*Telephone: (800) 835-3879*
		www.managersfunds.com

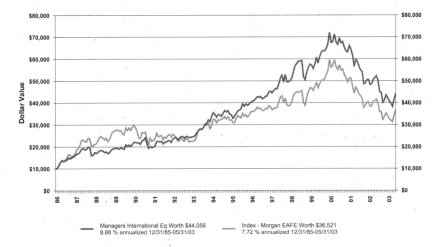

Managers International Eq Worth $44,056
8.88 % annualized 12/31/85-05/31/03

Index - Morgan EAFE Worth $36,521
7.72 % annualized 12/31/85-05/31/03

GROWTH OF $10,000

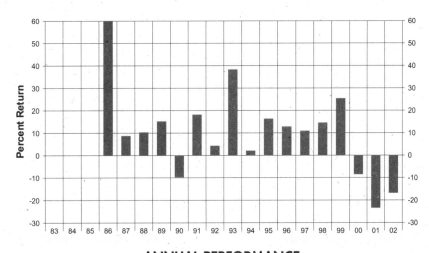

ANNUAL PERFORMANCE

TOP 10 HOLDINGS

Canon	Societe Generale
Vodafone	Grupo Dragados
Safeway	ENI
DSM	Bank Ireland
Banque Nationale de Paris	Six Continents

OAKMARK INTERNATIONAL

OBJECTIVE:	*International*	
MANAGER:	*David Herro and Michael Welsh*	*84*

FUND OVERVIEW:

Oakmark International's David Herro and Michael Welsh are very dedicated to their value-oriented investment style. They have strict guidelines for determining whether a stock is worth buying or selling. They choose companies from around the world that trade at a discount to current or potential free cash flow, with management they believe will use that money to enhance shareholder value. A stock must also sell at no less than a 15 percent discount from what Herro and Welsh consider to be its fair market value. Once a holding approaches fair value, they get rid of it. Herro and Welsh feel currency is a separate issue, and will only hedge when they think the portfolio will suffer if they don't.

When evaluating an individual business, Herro and Welsh consider the relative political and economic stability in the issuer's home country, the applicable accounting practices, and the company's ownership structure. The fund invests in mature markets (Japan, Canada, and the United Kingdom), as well as less developed areas (Mexico and Thailand), and select parts of the emerging markets. There are no limits on the fund's geographic distribution, though Herro and Walsh are normally spread over at least five countries outside the United States.

ANNUALIZED RETURNS		PORTFOLIO STATISTICS	
1-Year	–13.60%	Beta	0.92
3-Year	1.57%	Turnover	64.00%
5-Year	4.95%	12-Month Yield	0.88%
Overall Rank	3	12b-1 Fee	0.00%
Risk Rank	3	Expense Ratio	1.30%

MINIMUM INVESTMENT		CONTACT INFORMATION	
Regular	$1,000	*Oakmark International*	
IRA	$1,000	*Telephone: (800) 625-6275*	
		www.oakmark.com	

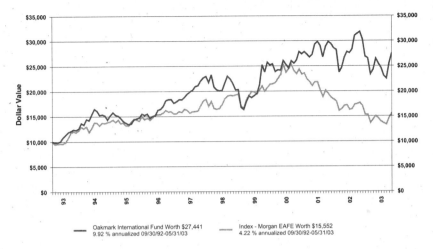

Oakmark International Fund Worth $27,441
9.92 % annualized 09/30/92-05/31/03

Index - Morgan EAFE Worth $15,552
4.22 % annualized 09/30/92-05/31/03

GROWTH OF $10,000

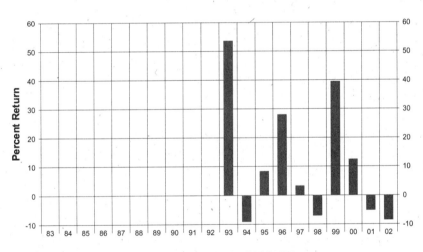

ANNUAL PERFORMANCE

TOP 10 HOLDINGS

Ericsson
Akzo Nobel
Vivendi Universal
Euronext NV Amsterdam
GlaxoSmithKline

Diageo
Aventis
Grupo Televisa
Banque Nationale
John Fairfax Holdings

ARTISAN INTERNATIONAL SMALL CAP

| OBJECTIVE: | *International Small-Cap* | *85* |
| MANAGER: | *Team Managed* | |

FUND OVERVIEW:

Artisan International Small Cap is the little sister to fellow Powerhouse Performer Artisan International. Managed by a team led by Mark Yockey, the fund buys the stocks of small and growing international companies. It concentrates on industries and themes that Yockey and his team believe present accelerating growth prospects and are well positioned to exploit this positive positioning in the future. They generally look for companies with market capitalizations of less than $3 billion and begin their search by first identifying global or regional industries and themes that may benefit from long-term positive catalysts.

In order to make it into the fund, a company must have sustainable growth potential, a reasonable valuation, effective management focused on shareholder value, and a dominant or increasing market share. The end result is a portfolio of names from developed and emerging economies. Smaller international stocks have performed far better than their larger brethren over time, although they come with much more volatility. To preserve the integrity of its small-cap focus, Artisan plans to close this fund once assets reach $500 million.

ANNUALIZED RETURNS		PORTFOLIO STATISTICS	
1-Year	12.69%	Beta	N/A
3-Year	N/A	Turnover	N/A
5-Year	N/A	12-Month Yield	0.00%
Overall Rank	N/A	12b-1 Fee	0.00%
Risk Rank	N/A	Expense Ratio	2.39%
MINIMUM INVESTMENT		**CONTACT INFORMATION**	
Regular	$1,000	*Artisan International Small Cap Fund*	
IRA	$1,000	*Telephone: (800) 344-1770*	
		www.artisanfunds.com	

VALUE LINE GROWTH OF $10,000 CHART
NOT AVAILABLE FOR THIS FUND

GROWTH OF $10,000

VALUE LINE ANNUAL PERFORMANCE CHART
NOT AVAILABLE FOR THIS FUND

ANNUAL PERFORMANCE

TOP 10 HOLDINGS

Telekom Austria	Vimpel-Communications
JD Wetherspoon	Sa Rodriguez Group
Precision Drilling	Stada Arzneimittel
Trinity Mirror	Fraser & Neave
Straumann Holdings	Scottish Media Group

DRIEHAUS INTERNATIONAL DISCOVERY

OBJECTIVE: *International Small-Cap*
MANAGER: *Emery Brewer and Eric Ritter*

86

FUND OVERVIEW:

The daring approach employed by Driehaus International Discovery managers Emery Brewer and Eric Ritter involves looking for small companies in international markets with rapidly accelerating sales and earnings growth. While there are no set restrictions on the size of companies they must buy, the two generally invest in stocks with market capitalizations of less than $1.5 billion. They normally keep the portfolio's assets in at least three different countries outside of the United States, and they can place a substantial portion in the more risky emerging markets when they feel the opportunity is right.

The style of investing practiced by Brewer and Ritter calls for looking for companies with dominant products or market niches, improving sales, demonstrated sales growth and earnings, a cost restructuring program that should further positively affect profitability, and new products or industry developments that will likely add to the bottom line. While this is the riskiest fund in the international small-cap category, Brewer and Ritter have done an excellent job of executing their momentum-driven strategy, and shareholders have been greatly rewarded.

ANNUALIZED RETURNS	
1-Year	3.20%
3-Year	−9.82%
5-Year	N/A
Overall Rank	N/A
Risk Rank	N/A

MINIMUM INVESTMENT	
Regular	$10,000
IRA	$2,000

PORTFOLIO STATISTICS	
Beta	N/A
Turnover	613.00%
12-Month Yield	0.00%
12b-1 Fee	0.00%
Expense Ratio	1.86%

CONTACT INFORMATION
Driehaus International Discovery Fund
Telephone: (800) 560-6111
www.driehaus.com

VALUE LINE GROWTH OF $10,000 CHART
NOT AVAILABLE FOR THIS FUND

GROWTH OF $10,000

VALUE LINE ANNUAL PERFORMANCE CHART
NOT AVAILABLE FOR THIS FUND

ANNUAL PERFORMANCE

TOP 10 HOLDINGS

Erste Bk Der Oester	Premier Oil
Merloni Elettrodomestic	Westjet Airlines
Komercni Banka	Taro Pharma Inds.
Stada Arzneimittel	Don Quijote
New Look Group	Recordati Ind. Chimica

VANGUARD INTERNATIONAL EXPLORER

OBJECTIVE:	*International Small-Cap*	*87*
MANAGER:	*Team Managed*	

FUND OVERVIEW:

Vanguard International Explorer invests in high-quality small companies headquartered outside of the U.S. with improving earnings and strong returns on equity. The management team utilizes fundamental research and a value-driven approach to build a diversified portfolio of between 150 and 170 stocks. They do keep regional weightings in mind, yet are willing to make sizable sector bets, based on where their research leads them.

When selecting stocks, the Vanguard International Explorer team considers whether a company is likely to have above-average earnings growth, whether it is attractively priced, and whether it has any competitive advantages. While companies in the fund are normally located in developing countries, the managers can also keep a limited amount of money in emerging markets securities.

This fund tends to be a bit tamer than other international small-cap funds, yet its performance has not been hurt by this lower volatility. Like most Vanguard funds, it also sports the lowest expense ratio in this category.

ANNUALIZED RETURNS		PORTFOLIO STATISTICS	
1-Year	−8.20%	Beta	0.83
3-Year	−10.28%	Turnover	40.00%
5-Year	6.28%	12-Month Yield	0.63%
Overall Rank	3	12b-1 Fee	0.00%
Risk Rank	3	Expense Ratio	0.75%

MINIMUM INVESTMENT		CONTACT INFORMATION	
Regular	$10,000	*Vanguard International Explorer Fund*	
IRA	$1,000	*Telephone: (800) 662-7447*	
		www.vanguard.com	

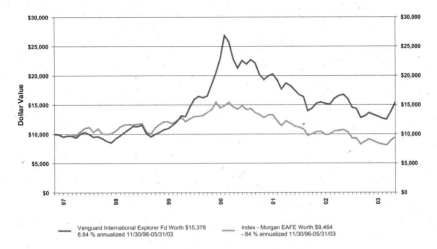

Vanguard International Explorer Fd Worth $15,378
6.84 % annualized 11/30/96-05/31/03

Index - Morgan EAFE Worth $9,464
-.84 % annualized 11/30/96-05/31/03

GROWTH OF $10,000

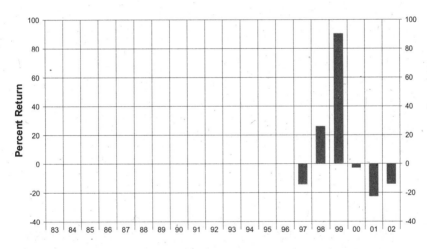

ANNUAL PERFORMANCE

TOP 10 HOLDINGS

Venture Mfg	Fountain Set Hldgs.
Paragon Grp UK	Enterprise Inns
Galen Holdings	Koram Bank
Lindt & Spruengli	BPP Holdings
Taylor Woodrow	Forth Ports

AMERICAN CENTURY GLOBAL GROWTH

OBJECTIVE: *Global*
MANAGER: *Team Managed*

88

FUND OVERVIEW:

The international investing team at American Century is talented, yet aggressive. This offering lets investors tap into their stock-picking powers both in the U.S. and abroad.

American Century Global Growth owns companies from around the world with accelerating earnings growth and strong revenue trends. Lead manager Henrik Strabo and his team also run American Century International Growth (a pure overseas fund) and American Century International Discovery Fund, which was closed to new investors in 2000.

Global Growth is newer, but it's off to a promising start. It has outperformed both the average international fund and the international fund benchmark, although it has underperformed the S&P 500. Because of this fund's strong diversification, it should be less risky than its two international siblings.

Why buy a global fund versus a pure international fund? It's really a matter of preference. For those looking to get some foreign exposure without taking undue risk, a global fund like this one is probably an excellent solution. But, as global funds go, this one will likely be more volatile than normal due to the managers' style of buying high-octane stocks.

ANNUALIZED RETURNS

1-Year	−13.90%
3-Year	−13.88%
5-Year	N/A
Overall Rank	4
Risk Rank	3

MINIMUM INVESTMENT

Regular	$2,500
IRA	$1,000

PORTFOLIO STATISTICS

Beta	0.81
Turnover	278.00%
12-Month Yield	0.00%
12b-1 Fee	0.00%
Expense Ratio	1.32%

CONTACT INFORMATION

American Century Global Growth
Telephone: (800) 345-3533
www.americancentury.com

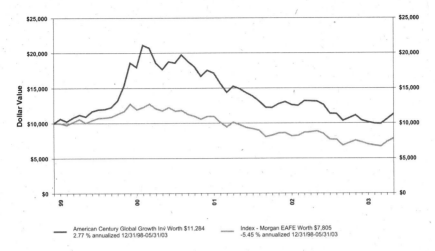

American Century Global Growth Inv Worth $11,284
2.77 % annualized 12/31/98-05/31/03

Index - Morgan EAFE Worth $7,805
-5.45 % annualized 12/31/98-05/31/03

GROWTH OF $10,000

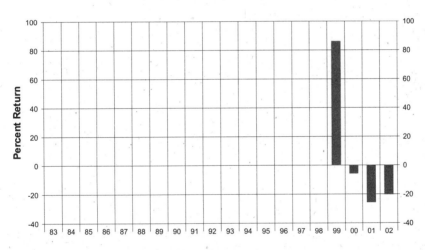

ANNUAL PERFORMANCE

TOP 10 HOLDINGS	
Pfizer	Affiliated Computer Services
Citigroup	American International Group
Microsoft	UBS AG
Merck	Nokia
Bank of America	Verizon Communications

CITIZENS GLOBAL EQUITY

OBJECTIVE:	*Global*	
MANAGER:	*Sevgi Ipek*	*89*

FUND OVERVIEW:

Sevgi Ipek proves that you don't have to sacrifice returns when investing with your heart. The Citizens Global Equity manager buys stocks in companies from around the world that pass a series of social screens. For instance, she avoids companies that pollute. She also makes sure that company management treats workers well, and that there is solid representation on the board by women. In addition, tobacco and arms manufacturers are automatically excluded. The result is a portfolio of widely varied companies with progressive management policies.

As it turns out, some of today's fastest growing companies often rate highest on Ipek's various social screens. These are also the companies that have been fueling the growth of the economy.

Citizens Global Equity is one of the only funds to apply this screening strategy to companies from around the world. Yet even with the strict criteria, the fund's performance has been excellent. For investors looking to add international exposure, without completely leaving the U.S., Citizens Global Equity is a fine, relatively conservative choice.

ANNUALIZED RETURNS		PORTFOLIO STATISTICS	
1-Year	−12.10%	Beta	1.03
3-Year	−20.50%	Turnover	30.00%
5-Year	−1.12%	12-Month Yield	0.00%
Overall Rank	4	12b-1 Fee	0.25%
Risk Rank	3	Expense Ratio	1.96%

MINIMUM INVESTMENT		CONTACT INFORMATION	
Regular	$2,500	*Citizens Global Equity*	
IRA	$1,000	*Telephone: (800) 223-7010*	
		www.citizensfunds.com	

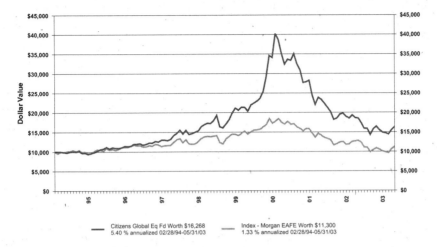

Citizens Global Eq Fd Worth $16,268
5.40 % annualized 02/28/94-05/31/03

Index - Morgan EAFE Worth $11,300
1.33 % annualized 02/28/94-05/31/03

GROWTH OF $10,000

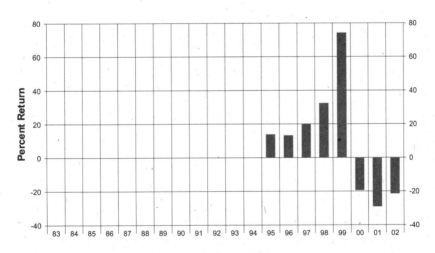

ANNUAL PERFORMANCE

TOP 10 HOLDINGS	
Vodafone	GlaxoSmithKline
Microsoft	Royal Bank of Scotland
Canon	HSBC Holdings
Citigroup	Marsh & McLennan
Encana	EOG Resources

OAKMARK GLOBAL

OBJECTIVE:	*Global*	
MANAGER:	*Greg Jackson and Michael Welsh*	*90*

FUND OVERVIEW:

Oakmark Global applies the winning value approach of the Oakmark family of funds to the entire world. Managers Greg Jackson and Michael Welsh hold a blend of domestic and international securities and seek to find bargains both in the U.S. and overseas. The fund's broad mandate allows them to invest in companies of all sizes and sectors. (Because Welsh also co-manages the Oakmark International Small Cap fund, a number of smaller foreign companies find their way into this portfolio.)

The Oakmark process involves searching for undervalued individual stocks, without regard to macroeconomic or market factors. They look for companies trading at a price below what they deem to be its intrinsic business value. Jackson and Welsh also seek companies with free cash flows and a high level of manager ownership.

This is a newer fund, but Oakmark has done a great job of managing both foreign and domestic portfolios in the past. The same research team involved in its other funds is a part of this portfolio, meaning it should contain their best ideas from around the globe.

ANNUALIZED RETURNS		PORTFOLIO STATISTICS	
1-Year	12.09%	Beta	N/A
3-Year	17.14%	Turnover	86.00%
5-Year	N/A	12-Month Yield	0.00%
Overall Rank	N/A	12b-1 Fee	0.00%
Risk Rank	N/A	Expense Ratio	1.86%

MINIMUM INVESTMENT		CONTACT INFORMATION	
Regular	$1,000	*Oakmark Global Fund*	
IRA	$1,000	*Telephone: (800) 625-6275*	
		www.oakmark.com	

VALUE LINE GROWTH OF $10,000 CHART
NOT AVAILABLE FOR THIS FUND

GROWTH OF $10,000

VALUE LINE ANNUAL PERFORMANCE CHART
NOT AVAILABLE FOR THIS FUND

ANNUAL PERFORMANCE

TOP 10 HOLDINGS

eFunds	Grupo Televisa ADR
Interpublic Group	Ceridian
Synopsys	Novell
Concord EFS	GlaxoSmithKline
Vivendi	First Health Group

TWEEDY, BROWNE GLOBAL VALUE

OBJECTIVE:	*Global*	
MANAGER:	*Team Managed*	*91*

FUND OVERVIEW:

Tweedy, Browne Global Value's three managers apply the time-tested value approach of the late Benjamin Graham to international investing. Graham, a former Columbia University Business School professor, wrote the 1934 classic *Security Analysis*. He suggested buying companies that could be had for a minimum 40 percent discount from their true intrinsic value. He also advised paying attention to price-to-earnings ratios, book value, and similar benchmarks. This is the same discipline these managers follow at their other Powerhouse Performer fund, Tweedy, Browne American Value. The difference is that this portfolio is made up mostly of foreign securities, although you will find a few U.S. companies inside as well.

You could argue that this is one of the less risky international offerings available, because all overseas investments are hedged back to the U.S. dollar. This eliminates currency risk, which can be either good or bad, depending on the direction of the dollar. When the dollar is declining, you're better off in an unhedged fund because the return from currency fluctuations alone will be impressive. Conservative investors wanting international exposure should feel very comfortable entrusting their money to Tweedy, Browne.

ANNUALIZED RETURNS		PORTFOLIO STATISTICS	
1-Year	−15.50%	Beta	0.52
3-Year	−2.47%	Turnover	7.00%
5-Year	2.68%	12-Month Yield	1.21%
Overall Rank	3	12b-1 Fee	0.00%
Risk Rank	2	Expense Ratio	1.37%

MINIMUM INVESTMENT		CONTACT INFORMATION	
Regular	$2,500	*Tweedy, Browne Global Value Fund*	
IRA	$500	*Telephone: (800) 432-4789*	
		www.tweedy.com	

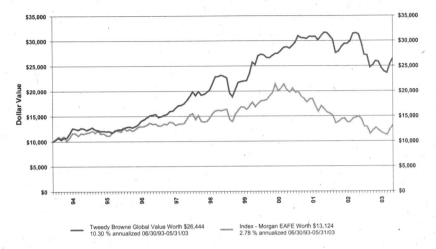

Tweedy Browne Global Value Worth $26,444
10.30 % annualized 06/30/93-05/31/03

Index - Morgan EAFE Worth $13,124
2.78 % annualized 06/30/93-05/31/03

GROWTH OF $10,000

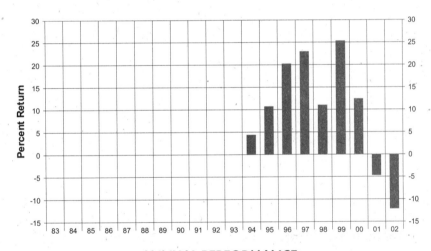

ANNUAL PERFORMANCE

TOP 10 HOLDINGS	
Nestle	Novartis AG
Merck KGAA	Trinity Mirror
Panamerican Beverages	ABM-AMRO
Kone	CNP Assurances
Pfizer	Diageo

VANGUARD SHORT-TERM CORPORATE

OBJECTIVE:	*Corporate Bond (Short-Term)*	
MANAGER:	*Ian MacKinnon and Robert Auwaerter*	*92*

FUND OVERVIEW:

Given that today's short-term bond rates are low to begin with, you want to invest your money in funds that are well managed and have ultra-low expense ratios. Vanguard Short-Term Corporate fits this bill. The fund invests in a variety of short-term bonds, including high-quality corporate and U.S. Treasury securities. Managers Ian MacKinnon and Robert Auwaerter currently maintain an average maturity of 1 to 3 years to reduce the risk of share-price fluctuations in response to changing interest rates. Nevertheless, they are able to adjust this duration based on their outlook for the direction of rates.

The managers further try to add value by focusing on market sectors and individual securities that represent good value, based on historical yield relationships. Of course, such shifts are made only after taking into consideration a bond's credit quality and average maturity. By prospectus, the fund can also invest up to 20 percent of its assets in futures contracts, and may buy repurchase agreements, foreign bonds, and a limited number of illiquid securities as well.

ANNUALIZED RETURNS		PORTFOLIO STATISTICS	
1-Year	6.30%	Beta	0.47
3-Year	7.78%	Turnover	69.00%
5-Year	6.30%	12-Month Yield	4.78%
Overall Rank	3	12b-1 Fee	0.00%
Risk Rank	1	Expense Ratio	0.23%

MINIMUM INVESTMENT		CONTACT INFORMATION	
Regular	$3,000	*Vanguard Short-Term Corporate Fund*	
IRA	$1,000	*Telephone: (800) 662-7447*	
		www.vanguard.com	

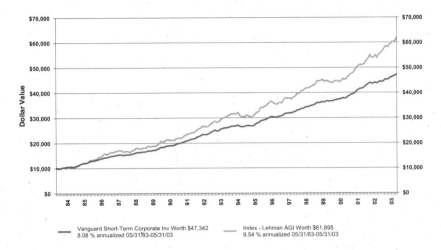

Vanguard Short-Term Corporate Inv Worth $47,342
8.08 % annualized 05/31/83-05/31/03

Index - Lehman AGI Worth $61,895
9.54 % annualized 05/31/83-05/31/03

GROWTH OF $10,000

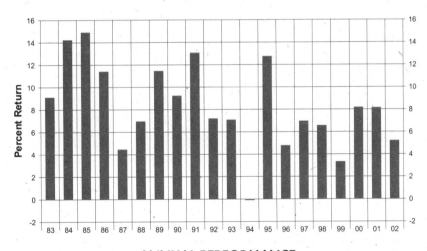

ANNUAL PERFORMANCE

TOP 10 HOLDINGS

US Treasury Note 12/04	Unilever 6.75% 11/01/03
Targeted Return Index 1/25/07	Fannie Mae 3.775% 8/01/32
US Treasury Note 8/15/07	Fannie Mae 3.678% 9/01/32
IBM 4.875% 10/01/06	Principal Life 6.25% 3/01/06
Mass Mutual Global 6/28/05	Spear Leeds & Kellogg 8.25% 8/15/05

FREMONT BOND

OBJECTIVE: *Corporate/Government Bond (Intermediate)*
MANAGER: *William Gross*

93

FUND OVERVIEW:

Bill Gross is widely considered to be one of the shrewdest bond managers in the business. He is most widely known for managing several PIMCO funds. Unfortunately, PIMCO funds carry a front-end sales charge, which is something you especially want to avoid when it comes to bond funds. Fortunately, we can tap into Gross's investment expertise through the back door, if you will, by buying the Fremont Bond fund. Fremont has hired Gross as a subadvisor to the fund. And he's continued his winning ways here.

Fremont Bond has held up well in a variety of markets, without taking much risk. Major shifts in Gross's portfolio strategy are driven by longer-term (three- to five-year) trends. He maintains consistency by avoiding extreme swings in portfolio maturity or duration. He also tends to own a combination of corporate, government, and mortgage-backed securities. "Successful bond investing is more than just clipping coupons," Gross says. "Active maturity/ duration management and sector and individual securities analysis add a considerable measure of value to the process."

ANNUALIZED RETURNS

1-Year	12.20%
3-Year	11.58%
5-Year	8.50%
Overall Rank	1
Risk Rank	3

MINIMUM INVESTMENT

Regular	$2,000
IRA	$1,000

PORTFOLIO STATISTICS

Beta	1.04
Turnover	176.00%
12-Month Yield	3.27%
12b-1 Fee	0.00%
Expense Ratio	0.58%

CONTACT INFORMATION

Fremont Bond Fund
Telephone: (800) 548-4539
www.fremontfunds.com

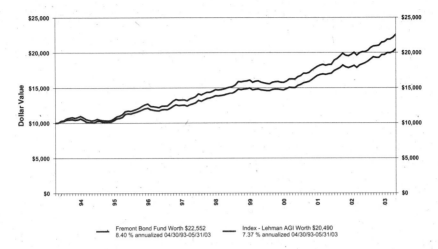

Fremont Bond Fund Worth $22,552
8.40 % annualized 04/30/93-05/31/03

Index - Lehman AGI Worth $20,490
7.37 % annualized 04/30/93-05/31/03

GROWTH OF $10,000

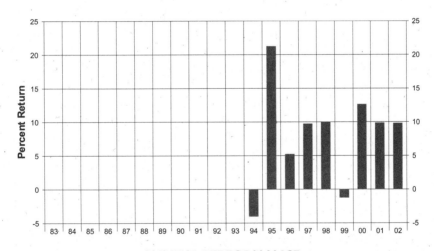

ANNUAL PERFORMANCE

TOP 10 HOLDINGS

Federal Home Loan Bks. 5/16/03
Federal Home Loan Mtg. 5/22/03
Federal Home Loan Mtg. 6/16/03
Federal Home Loan Mtg. 5/29/03
US Treasury Note 3.875% 1/15/09

US Treasury Bond 8.75% 5/15/17
Federal National Mtg. 5% 4/25/33
Ford Motor 2.53% 6/23/03
Federal Home Loan Mtg. 6.5% 8/15/31
Fannie Mae 5/14/03

LOOMIS SAYLES BOND

OBJECTIVE:	*Corporate/Government Bond (Intermediate)*	*94*
MANAGER:	*Daniel J. Fuss*	

FUND OVERVIEW:

Loomis Sayles Bond manager Daniel J. Fuss is one of the best fixed-income investors around. He strives to generate a high total return through a combination of current income and capital appreciation. He invests most of his fund's assets in bonds, although up to 20 percent of the portfolio can be placed in preferred stocks. The fixed-income side includes corporate and U.S. government obligations, plus commercial paper, zero coupon bonds, and mortgage-backed securities. In addition, the prospectus allows Fuss to invest up to 20 percent of the portfolio overseas and up to 35 percent in junk bonds. Fuss isn't shy about exploiting this flexibility when he thinks conditions warrant it. In 1998, for example, he was busy looking for battered bargains in Southeast Asia and Latin America.

Loomis Sayles Bond should be viewed as a long-term investment because the fund's issues tend to have extended maturities, and thus a heightened degree of volatility. You'll notice the fund's minimum investment is $25,000. However, that can be reduced to just $2,500 by going through one of the many no-load, no-transaction-fee programs offered by the nation's leading discount brokers.

ANNUALIZED RETURNS		PORTFOLIO STATISTICS	
1-Year	25.10%	Beta	0.84
3-Year	12.16%	Turnover	22.00%
5-Year	8.09%	12-Month Yield	6.07%
Overall Rank	3	12b-1 Fee	0.25%
Risk Rank	4	Expense Ratio	1.00%

MINIMUM INVESTMENT		CONTACT INFORMATION
Regular	$25,000	*Loomis Sayles Bond Fund*
IRA	$25,000	*Telephone: (800) 633-3330*
		www.loomissayles.com

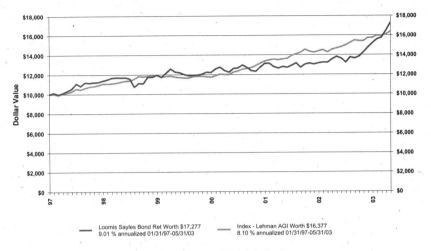

Loomis Sayles Bond Ret Worth $17,277
9.01 % annualized 01/31/97-05/31/03

Index - Lehman AGI Worth $16,377
8.10 % annualized 01/31/97-05/31/03

GROWTH OF $10,000

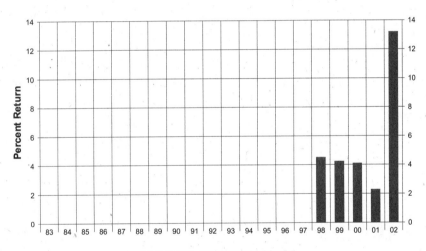

ANNUAL PERFORMANCE

TOP 10 HOLDINGS

Canada Govt. 6% 9/01/05	Time Warner 6.95% 1/15/28
Loews Corp. 3.125% 9/15/07	Manitoba Prov. Canada 7.75% 12/22/25
Analog Devices 4.75% 10/01/05	Canada Govt. 4.5% 9/01/07
Brazil Fed. 8% 4/15/14	Manitoba Prov. 6.5% 9/22/17
Intl. Bank for Recon. & Dev. 8/20/07	Fannie Mae 5.25% 6/15/06

VANGUARD TOTAL BOND MARKET INDEX

OBJECTIVE:	*Corporate/Government Bond (Intermediate)*
MANAGER:	*Ian MacKinnon and Kenneth Volpert*

FUND OVERVIEW:

Who says index funds are for stocks only? Vanguard, the king of index fund families, also offers an unmanaged bond fund that seeks to match the performance of the Lehman Brothers Aggregate Bond Index. This is a widely recognized measure representing an amalgamation of the entire taxable U.S. bond market. The Lehman index consists of more than 5,000 U.S. Treasury, federal agency, mortgage-backed, and high-quality corporate securities, valued at more than $4 trillion.

While the fund doesn't own every security in the index, it does invest in a large sample matching such key characteristics as market-sector weightings, coupon interest rates, credit quality, and maturity.

The fund further tries to boost returns by holding a higher percentage of high-quality, short-term corporate bonds and fewer short-term Treasury securities than are found in the index. It also uses futures contracts and options to keep cash on hand to meet shareholder redemptions, to make trading easier, and to reduce costs.

ANNUALIZED RETURNS	
1-Year	9.80%
3-Year	10.16%
5-Year	7.29%
Overall Rank	2
Risk Rank	2

MINIMUM INVESTMENT	
Regular	$3,000
IRA	$1,000

PORTFOLIO STATISTICS	
Beta	0.94
Turnover	67.00%
12-Month Yield	0.00%
12b-1 Fee	0.00%
Expense Ratio	0.22%

CONTACT INFORMATION

Vanguard Total Bond Market
Index Fund
Telephone: (800) 662-7447
www.vanguard.com

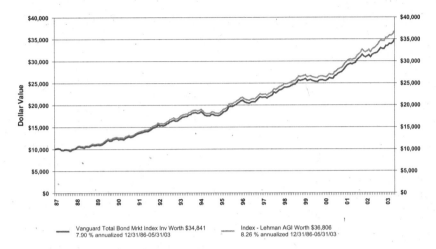

GROWTH OF $10,000

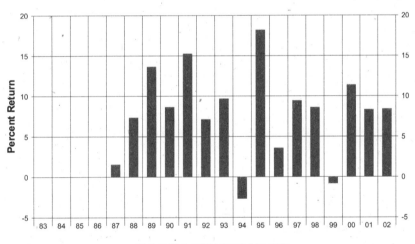

ANNUAL PERFORMANCE

TOP 10 HOLDINGS

Federal Home Loan Mtg. 7% 7/15/05	US Treasury Bond 8.125% 8/15/19
US Treasury Note 3.375% 4/30/04	Federal Home Loan Bks. 3.375% 6/15/04
US Treasury Note 5% 2/15/11	Fannie Mae 7.25% 5/15/30
US Treasury Bond 8.125% 8/15/21	Fannie Mae 7% 7/15/05
US Treasury Bond 11.875% 11/15/03	US Treasury Bond 10.375% 11/15/09

TCW GALILEO TOTAL RETURN BOND

OBJECTIVE: *Mortgage-Backed Securities (Intermediate)*
MANAGER: *Team Managed*

96

FUND OVERVIEW:

Trust Company of the West is one of the industry's most respected managers of mortgage-backed securities. This fund allows some of the firm's top talent in the sector—Jeffrey Gundalch, Philip Barach, and Frederick Horton—to put their skills to work. The TCW Total Return Bond fund seeks to maximize current income and achieve above-average performance by investing primarily in mortgage-backed securities of any maturity or type guaranteed by, or secured by collateral that is guaranteed by, the U.S. Government and its agencies. The fund also buys privately issued mortgage-backed securities rated Aa and higher by Moody's or AA and higher by S&P.

Except when maintaining a temporary defensive position, the fund will invest at least 80 percent of its assets in fixed-income securities with a weighted duration of no more than eight years. It has been a real standout in the category, and maintains a portfolio diversified primarily across adjustable rate mortgages, pass-throughs, agency collateralized mortgage obligations, and private collateralized mortgage obligations.

ANNUALIZED RETURNS		PORTFOLIO STATISTICS	
1-Year	8.90%	Beta	0.75
3-Year	11.50%	Turnover	26.00%
5-Year	7.04%	12-Month Yield	6.73%
Overall Rank	2	12b-1 Fee	0.25%
Risk Rank	2	Expense Ratio	0.93%

MINIMUM INVESTMENT		CONTACT INFORMATION	
Regular	$2,000	*TCW Galileo Total Return Bond Fund*	
IRA	$2,000	*Telephone: (800) 386-3829*	
		www.tcw.com	

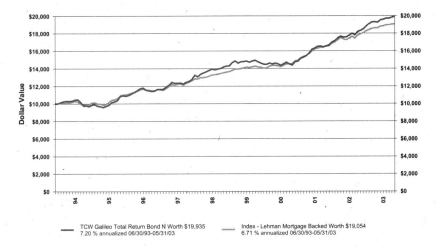

TCW Galileo Total Return Bond N Worth $19,935
7.20 % annualized 06/30/93-05/31/03

Index - Lehman Mortgage Backed Worth $19,054
6.71 % annualized 06/30/93-05/31/03

GROWTH OF $10,000

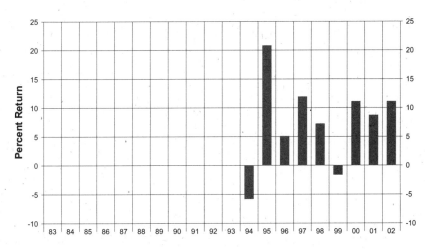

ANNUAL PERFORMANCE

TOP 10 HOLDINGS	
Fannie Mae 5.5% 2/02/23	Chase Mortgage 6.75% 10/25/31
Fannie Mae 4.74% 1/01/33	Fannie Mae 5.103% 2/01/33
Fannie Mae 5.183% 2/01/33	Federal Home Loan 4.888% 11/01/32
Fannie Mae 4.55% 2/01/33	Fannie Mae 4.952% 8/01/32
Federal Home Loan 7% 5/15/32	Federal Home Loan 7% 1/15/31

VANGUARD GNMA

OBJECTIVE:	*Mortgage-Backed Securities (Intermediate)*	*97*
MANAGER:	*Paul D. Kaplan*	

FUND OVERVIEW:

If you're looking for high current yield, credit safety, and liquidity, few investments compare to mortgage-backed Government National Mortgage Association (GNMA) certificates, or Ginnie Maes. The GNMA is a U.S. government agency that pools mortgages together and sells them in the form of certificates. Each certificate represents an undivided part-ownership in one of these pools. Every mortgage in the pool is guaranteed by a certain government agency, meaning they are very safe. In fact, Ginnie Maes and the other securities in the Vanguard GNMA portfolio are guaranteed by Uncle Sam as to the timely payment of principal and interest.

Still, the price and yield of shares in the fund fluctuate with interest rates. GNMAs are also subject to early prepayments from homeowners wishing to refinance their loans at lower rates. High prepayments will have a negative impact on the fund's relative performance. And because prepayments tend to get reinvested at lower yields, the dividend-per-share payouts will be reduced. You shouldn't expect to see much overall volatility in this fund, and you will enjoy a generous yield that currently comes in just below 5 percent.

ANNUALIZED RETURNS		PORTFOLIO STATISTICS	
1-Year	7.70%	Beta	0.66
3-Year	9.41%	Turnover	8.00%
5-Year	7.07%	12-Month Yield	5.18%
Overall Rank	2	12b-1 Fee	0.00%
Risk Rank	2	Expense Ratio	0.22%

MINIMUM INVESTMENT		CONTACT INFORMATION	
Regular	$3,000	*Vanguard GNMA Portfolio*	
IRA	$3,000	*Telephone: (800) 662-7447*	
		www.vanguard.com	

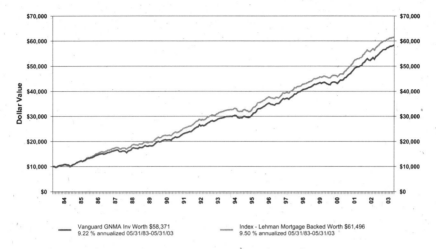

Vanguard GNMA Inv Worth $58,371
9.22 % annualized 05/31/83-05/31/03

Index - Lehman Mortgage Backed Worth $61,496
9.50 % annualized 05/31/83-05/31/03

GROWTH OF $10,000

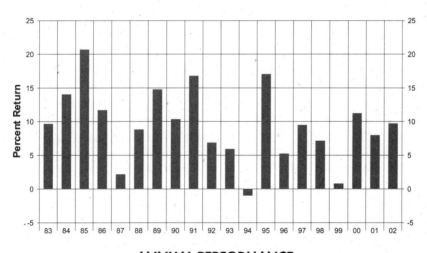

ANNUAL PERFORMANCE

TOP 10 HOLDINGS	
GNMA 5.5%	GNMA 5%
GNMA 5%	GNMA 5%
GNMA 6%	GNMA 5.5%
GNMA 5%	GNMA 6%
GNMA 5%	GNMA 6%

NORTHEAST INVESTORS TRUST

OBJECTIVE:	High-Yield Corporate	*98*
MANAGER:	Ernest Monrad and Bruce Monrad	

FUND OVERVIEW:

The father-and-son team of Ernest and Bruce Monrad tries to generate income for shareholders through investing in both corporate bonds and stocks. But, unlike other managers of funds of this nature, the Monrads also try to achieve as much capital appreciation as possible. The proportions of stocks and bonds vary based on market conditions. Since 1970, about 80 percent of all assets have been held in fixed-income securities, preferred stocks, and cash. Only a small portion has been put in common stocks, usually for liquidity purposes and to increase the potential for capital gains. The Monrads also avoid keeping more than 25 percent of the portfolio exposed to any one industry.

A combination of in-house and Wall Street research is used for selecting and evaluating securities for the fund. The Monrads place heavy emphasis on value. When they find an attractive bond, they'll also consider adding shares of the company's stock if the price is right. As an added booster, the Monrads can use leverage, borrowing up to 25 percent of the portfolio's net assets. This enhances the fund's buying power when they are bullish, and gives them adequate cash to meet redemptions without having to liquidate any holdings.

ANNUALIZED RETURNS		PORTFOLIO STATISTICS	
1-Year	−0.80%	Beta	−0.66
3-Year	1.61%	Turnover	18.00%
5-Year	−0.11%	12-Month Yield	7.92%
Overall Rank	4	12b-1 Fee	0.00%
Risk Rank	5	Expense Ratio	0.65%

MINIMUM INVESTMENT		CONTACT INFORMATION
Regular	$1,000	*Northeast Investors Trust*
IRA	$500	*Telephone: (800) 225-6704*
		www.northeastinvestors.com

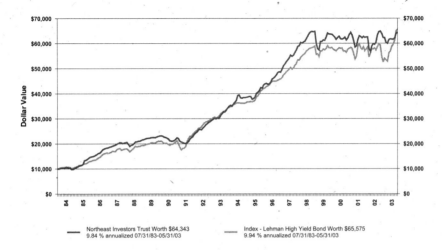

Northeast Investors Trust Worth $64,343
9.84 % annualized 07/31/83-05/31/03

Index - Lehman High Yield Bond Worth $65,575
9.94 % annualized 07/31/83-05/31/03

GROWTH OF $10,000

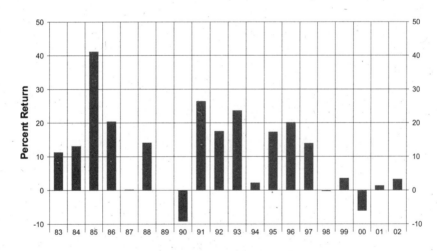

ANNUAL PERFORMANCE

TOP 10 HOLDINGS

US Treasury Bill 12/05/02	Boyd Gaming 9.5% 7/15/07
Trump Atlantic City 11.25% 5/01/06	Sterling Chemicals 12.375% 7/15/06
Southern CA Edison 8.95% 11/03/03	Universal Compression 9.875% 2/15/03
Venetian Casino 11% 6/15/10	Husky Oil 8/15/28
Advantica Restaurant 11.25% 1/15/08	Motors & Gears 10.75% 11/15/06

TCW GALILEO HIGH YIELD BOND

| OBJECTIVE: | High-Yield Corporate | *99* |
| MANAGER: | Melissa Weiler and James Hassett | |

FUND OVERVIEW:

While TCW Galileo High Yield Bond fund managers Melissa Weiler and James Hassett pursue above-average returns, they look for it at the lower-risk end of the junk-bond-grade investment spectrum. The fund keeps at least 80 percent of its assets in high-yielding, below-investment-grade bonds. But the managers look for securities issued by companies that appear to have improving business prospects. They also highly diversify the portfolio and conduct a careful analysis of each bond to determine the issuer's ability to make timely payments of principal and interest regardless of broad economic trends and corporate developments.

"While history suggests that there are brief periods where the highest risk segment of the market generates superior returns, over a full credit cycle, the high default rate and low level of recoveries associated with the lower-tier of the market ultimately produces inferior risk-adjusted returns," Weiler and Hassett say. In fact, the fund has been a standout performer in the category, even when compared to those funds that concentrate on the higher yielding segment of the market.

ANNUALIZED RETURNS		PORTFOLIO STATISTICS	
1-Year	6.50%	Beta	−0.14
3-Year	3.12%	Turnover	55.00%
5-Year	1.84%	12-Month Yield	8.59%
Overall Rank	5	12b-1 Fee	0.25%
Risk Rank	5	Expense Ratio	1.26%
MINIMUM INVESTMENT		CONTACT INFORMATION	
Regular	$2,000	TCW Galileo High Yield Bond Fund	
IRA	$2,000	Telephone: (800) 386-3829	
		www.tcw.com	

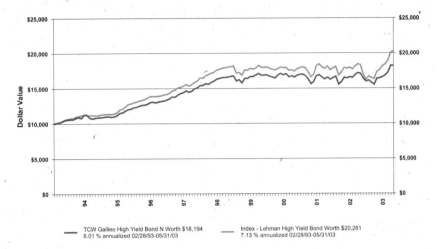

TCW Galileo High Yield Bond N Worth $18,194
6.01 % annualized 02/28/93-05/31/03

Index - Lehman High Yield Bond Worth $20,261
7.13 % annualized 02/28/93-05/31/03

GROWTH OF $10,000

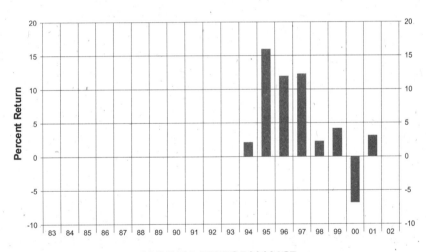

ANNUAL PERFORMANCE

TOP 10 HOLDINGS

DirectTV 8.375% 3/15/03
Nextel 9.375% 11/15/09
Allied Waste 10% 8/01/09
Sprint Capital 8.375% 3/15/12
Young Broadcasting 10% 3/01/11

Coastal Corp. 7.625% 9/01/08
Delhaize America 8.125% 4/15/11
Calpine 8.5% 2/15/11
CMS Energy 9.875% 10/15/07
Goldman Sachs 8.125% 5/15/11

FIDELITY NEW MARKETS INCOME

OBJECTIVE:	*International Bond*
MANAGER:	*John H. Carlson*

100

FUND OVERVIEW:

While it is often wise to invest your stock portfolio internationally, global diversification on the fixed-income side can also make sense. Fidelity New Markets Income seeks high current income and capital appreciation by investing most of its assets in bonds from foreign issuers, including many in the emerging markets. Manager John Carlson favors regions with the potential for growth and a relatively low per-capita gross national product. He also invests based on a country's monetary and fiscal policies, economic reform programs, local demographics, average level of education, infrastructure needs, savings rate, and outlook for the capital markets.

Fidelity New Markets generally buys lower-quality and longer-duration securities, and usually avoids currency hedging. Each security is analyzed based on current pricing, trading opportunities, and the issuer's credit, currency, and economic risks. Foreign bond investing clearly carries more risk, but it also has the potential for greater returns over time. This is definitely not a parking place for short-term money, but makes sense for a portion of the fixed-income side of your long-term portfolio.

ANNUALIZED RETURNS	
1-Year	26.00%
3-Year	17.39%
5-Year	11.83%
Overall Rank	1
Risk Rank	5

MINIMUM INVESTMENT	
Regular	$2,500
IRA	$2,500

PORTFOLIO STATISTICS	
Beta	−0.23
Turnover	219.00%
12-Month Yield	7.04%
12b-1 Fee	0.00%
Expense Ratio	1.00%

CONTACT INFORMATION

Fidelity New Markets Income Fund
Telephone: (800) 343-3548
www.fidelity.com

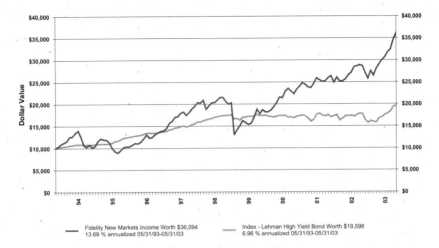

Fidelity New Markets Income Worth $36,094
13.69 % annualized 05/31/93-05/31/03

Index - Lehman High Yield Bond Worth $19,598
6.96 % annualized 05/31/93-05/31/03

GROWTH OF $10,000

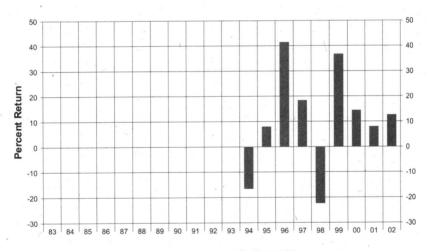

ANNUAL PERFORMANCE

TOP 10 HOLDINGS

Brazil 8% 4/15/04
Brazil 8.875% 4/15/24
Russian Federation 5% 3/31/30
Mexico-United Mexican States
   11.375% 9/15/16
Russia Govt. 11% 7/24/18

Colombia Rep. 10.5% 7/09/10
Petroleos Mexicanos 9.25% 3/30/18
Colombia Rep. 11.75% 2/25/20
Russian Federation 12.75% 6/24/28
Brazil 11% 8/17/40

6

PUTTING YOUR
PORTFOLIO TOGETHER

Now that you know what mutual funds are, how they work, what to look for when choosing them, and which ones appear to be most promising for the year ahead, it's time to put together your own personal investment plan. In a moment, you'll be given an asset allocation test, to help you determine which types of funds might be most appropriate for you, given your stage in life and your comfort level. Then you will find a number of sample portfolios (complete with sample percentage allocations to selected funds from the Powerhouse Performers list) that correspond to your score on the test.

WHAT IS ASSET ALLOCATION?

You may have heard the term "asset allocation" before. But what exactly does it mean? In a nutshell, asset allocation is the process of figuring out how much of your investment capital should be placed in each of the three main asset classes: stocks, bonds, and cash. (Other asset classes include real estate, precious metals, artwork, limited partnerships, commodities, options, futures, and various other possibilities.)

"Investment capital," for purposes of our continuing discussion in this chapter, includes only money you have set aside for the long term. It is an amount above and beyond the money you need to live on. It does not include a home that you own, cash in a savings account that you plan to spend soon (say, on a car or vacation), insurance policies, or any emergency funds you may have set aside to get you through rough financial periods. It does include your 401(k)s, 403(b)s, and IRAs, although you will probably have to assemble separate fund portfolios for these accounts, because most company retirement plans give you a select list to choose from. Nevertheless, the principles and allocation guidelines we are about to discuss apply to them as well.

RISK VERSUS REWARD

You've no doubt heard the cliché "No pain, no gain." It certainly applies to investing. Every investment comes with some degree of risk. With stocks, you risk that the overall market will fall or that your underlying companies will suffer financially—or even go out of business. The same is true for corporate bonds. Even bank savings accounts carry the risk that your financial institution will fail, and your balance may be above the amount covered by federal depository insurance. The only no-risk investments out there are Treasury bills, notes, and bonds, which will fluctuate in value as interest rates change (assuming you don't hold on through maturity).

The $150,000 Lunch?

You may have more money to invest than you think. Simply cutting back on some of life's indulgences can pump up your portfolio by almost $400,000 over time. Here are just a few examples:

Cut Back On	Savings per Month	Savings per Year	30-Year Growth
Eating lunch out	$ 65	$ 780	$148,702
Coffee	22	260	49,567
Impulse Purchases	43	520	99,135
Clothes	40	480	91,173
Total savings	$170	$2,040	$388,577

These hypothetical figures assume a 10 percent annual rate of return compounded at the same rate as contributions over a 30-year period in a tax-deferred account. All numbers are in today's dollars. The tabulation is for illustrative purposes only. Actual investment returns will vary.

As you might have guessed, the level of return you can expect to receive from an investment corresponds directly with the degree of risk you take. Small-company and foreign stocks, the most volatile of all, have historically showered investors with the highest returns. Equities in general have done much better than fixed-income investments. Corporate bonds pay higher rates than risk-free Treasuries. And insured bank savings accounts normally pay the least.

But there is another risk that most people don't think about: "opportunity risk." If you aren't willing to endure the volatility associated with stocks, at least for a portion of your portfolio, you risk suffering low returns that might not even keep up with the rate of inflation. Consider these statistics. Stocks have provided a rate of return far superior to that of any other asset class over time. For the past 10 years, the S&P 500 has returned an average of 9.8 percent annually, including reinvested dividends. That compares to 4.4 percent for money market funds and 7.4 percent for government bonds. The returns during the most recent 10-year bull market from 1989 to 2000 were even higher for stocks: 18.3 percent annually for the S&P, while money market funds provided a paltry 4.8 percent, and government bonds returned 7.9 percent. If this trend continues in the future, you will build more wealth from stocks than from any other asset class, while also accepting more risk.

It is generally assumed that the younger you are, the more you should have allocated to stocks. This makes sense for two reasons. First, equities generally don't provide much income, a disadvantage that becomes increasingly important in retirement. Second, stocks can be extremely volatile over the short term, so the longer your time horizon, the less you will be impacted by such fluctuations. Nevertheless, some astute elderly investors keep anywhere from 70 to 100 percent of their portfolios in equities at all

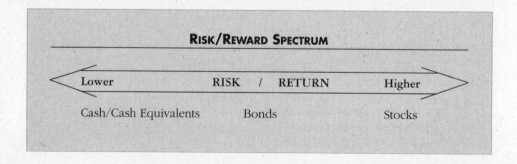

times, even as they near the age of eligibility to receive a televised happy birthday greeting from Willard Scott.

DOLLAR COST AVERAGING

Investors of all ages can profit from volatility by using a technique known as "dollar cost averaging." Simply put, this means investing a fixed amount in your favorite funds on a regular basis, regardless of what's going on with the market. In that way, you buy more shares when the market is down, and fewer shares when it is up. This is precisely what you do when you contribute to your 401(k), SEP-IRA, or 403(b) plan at work. Your company (or you, if you're self-employed) takes regular contributions out of your paycheck and sends them in to your selected funds each month or quarter. Dollar cost averaging doesn't necessarily increase your overall returns, especially during strong bull markets. But it certainly lessens your volatility, and it's often the only way people can afford to invest. (See below.)

DOLLAR COST AVERAGING AT WORK

Regular Investment	Per-Share Price	Shares Acquired
$ 200	$10	20
200	8	25
200	5	40
200	8	25
200	10	20
Total $1,000		130

Average Price Per Share=$7.69 ($1,000 / 130 shares)

By regularly investing the same dollar amount in your account, you take advantage of market fluctuations by buying more fund shares when prices are low, fewer as prices rise. This strategy, however, does not guarantee profit or protection against loss in declining markets. This is only a hypothetical illustration. It does not project the future performance of any particular investment.

By the way, don't think you can't get a monthly income check from your non-dividend-paying stock funds. You can. Simply sign up for what's called "systematic withdrawal." This program allows you to have a certain amount redeemed automatically from your funds each month. You might think of it as dollar cost averaging in reverse.

INVESTOR PROFILE

====Now back to that asset allocation test. Discount broker Charles Schwab & Co. created an investor profile quiz to help people determine which asset allocation plan is most appropriate for them. The quiz takes into consideration such things as age, personality, and tolerance for risk. In the end, you get an overall score, which can be matched up with the model portfolios that follow. (The portfolios are ours, not Schwab's.) Keep in mind that the test assumes we're talking about investment capital, or money being set aside for at least five years.

Take a few moments to circle the most appropriate answer for each question in the test. Better yet, make a copy of the test first, so that your spouse (or significant other) can take it, too.

Calculate your total and match it up with the appropriate model portfolio. Is this an accurate reflection of your actual investment risk tolerance? Read all five portfolio descriptions before you decide.

1. AGGRESSIVE ALL-STOCK PORTFOLIO: 86 TO 100 POINTS

====This portfolio is most appropriate for those under age 40, who have a 20- to 30-year time horizon before needing the money. It assumes you are looking for high growth and are willing to endure substantial year-to-year volatility in that pursuit. The suggested subasset class breakdown for this portfolio is as follows:

50% Large-Cap Funds
20% Mid-Cap Funds
20% Small-Cap Funds
10% International Funds

INVESTOR PROFILE TEST

Points

1. My current age is:
   a) under 31. 8
   b) 31 to 40. 6
   c) 41 to 50. 4
   d) 51 to 60. 2
   e) over 60. 0

2. Over the next few years, I expect my income to:
   a) decline. 0
   b) stay about the same. 1
   c) increase. 2
   d) fluctuate. 0

3. My investment experience is best described as follows:
   a) I've never invested in stocks, either directly or through stock
      mutual funds. 2
   b) I've invested a small amount of money in stocks or stock funds. 6
   c) I've occasionally invested a fair amount in stocks or stock funds. 10
   d) I've invested in commodities, options, international stocks, or
      limited partnerships. 14
   e) I have money in a company retirement plan (i.e., a 401(k) or
      SEP-IRA), but am not sure whether I'm invested in stock funds
      or other types of investments. 0

4. I plan to start withdrawing money from my investments in:
   a) less than 5 years. 0
   b) 5 to 10 years. 10
   c) 11 to 15 years. 20
   d) more than 15 years. 30

5. When I begin withdrawing the money I've accumulated, I plan to
   spend it in:
   a) less than a year. 0
   b) less than 5 years. 2
   c) less than 10 years. 8
   d) at least 10 years. 10

(Continued)

6. How might you respond to fluctuations in your investment?
   a) I'm very concerned any time my investments lose value and will
      sell quickly if they start to lose money. 0
   b) Day-to-day market moves make me uncomfortable. If an investment
      loses 5 percent or more over a full quarter, I am likely to sell it and
      look for a better alternative. 4
   c) I realize there are lots of random day-to-day movements in the
      market. I usually wait until I have watched the performance of an
      investment for at least a year before making changes. 10
   d) Even if poor market conditions result in losses of up to 20 percent
      in a given year, I try to follow a consistent, long-term investment
      plan. 14

7. Consider the range of high and low returns that might result from a
   $10,000 investment in four different areas over a 10-year period. Keep in
   mind that investments offering higher returns often involve greater risks.
   Which range of possible outcomes would be most acceptable to you?

   Value of $10,000 after 10 years:
   Investment A
   Best case $45,412
   Worst case   6,979 10
   Investment B
   Best case $82,425
   Worst case   4,186 15
   Investment C
   Best case $27,000
   Worst case   9,622 5
   Investment D
   Best case $12,689
   Worst case   10,118 2

8. When I buy car insurance, I:
   a) choose the lowest deductible amount to ensure maximum coverage
      even though my policy costs more. 0
   b) choose a moderate deductible level in order to reduce the premium. 2
   c) choose a high deductible in order to pay a low premium, even
      though many losses may not be covered. 5
   d) choose to carry no insurance. 7

   Your Total Points ....____

Now, take your total score and see which of the following portfolios it
matches up best with.

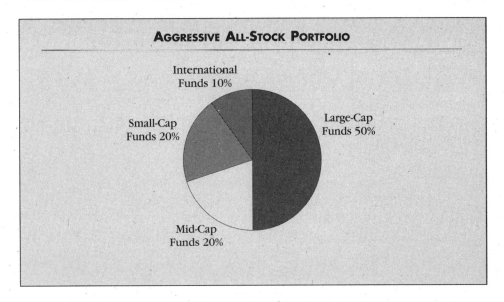

AGGRESSIVE ALL-STOCK PORTFOLIO

International Funds 10%

Small-Cap Funds 20%

Large-Cap Funds 50%

Mid-Cap Funds 20%

Sample Funds and Weightings:

TCW Galileo Select Equities (25%)

Excelsior Value & Restructuring (25%)

Meridian Growth (10%)

C&B Mid-Cap Value (10%)

Bjurman, Barry Small Cap Growth (10%)

Aegis Value (10%)

Julius Baer International (5%)

Artisan International Small Cap (5%)

2. MODERATE ALL-STOCK PORTFOLIO: 71 TO 85 POINTS

This portfolio is most appropriate for those ages 40 to 50 who have a 10- to 20-year time horizon, or for younger investors seeking a lower-risk approach to equity investing. It is fully invested, primarily in the stocks of more seasoned and value-oriented companies, yet it assumes you are willing to endure substantial year-to-year volatility in the pursuit of high growth. The suggested subasset class breakdown for this portfolio is as follows:

60% Large-Cap Funds
15% Mid-Cap Funds
15% Small-Cap Funds
10% International Funds

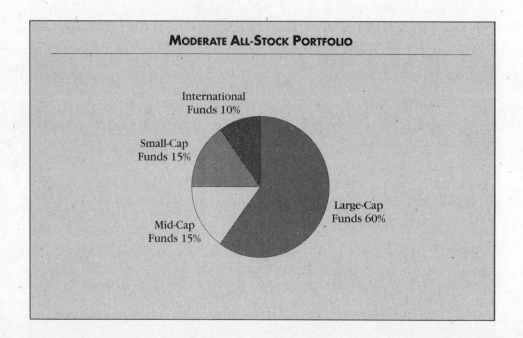

MODERATE ALL-STOCK PORTFOLIO

International Funds 10%

Small-Cap Funds 15%

Mid-Cap Funds 15%

Large-Cap Funds 60%

Sample Funds and Weightings:

Atlantic Whitehall Growth (30%)

Oakmark Fund (30%)

Artisan Mid-Cap Value (15%)

Bjurman, Barry Small Cap Growth (15%)

Julius Baer International (10%)

3. MODERATE STOCK AND BOND PORTFOLIO: 56 TO 70 POINTS

═══This portfolio is designed for those ages 50 to 70 who are looking to maintain a majority weighting in stocks, but with a solid fixed-income component to temper volatility. It assumes you are willing to enjoy slightly lower returns in exchange for less risk. The suggested subasset class fund breakdown for this portfolio is:

40% Large-Cap Funds

10% Mid-Cap Funds

10% International Funds

20% Corporate Bond Funds

20% Mortgage-Backed Securities Funds

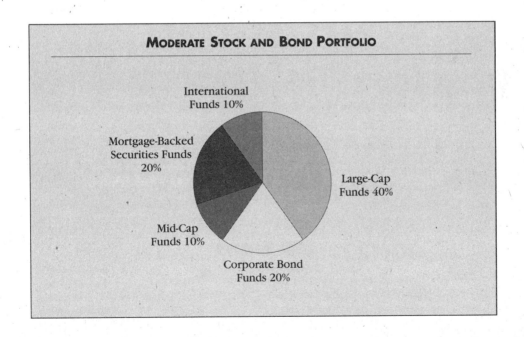

Sample Funds and Weightings:

Atlantic Whitehall Growth (20%)

Dodge & Cox Stock (20%)

Berger Mid-Cap Value (10%)

Julius Baer International (10%)

Fremont Bond (20%)

Vanguard GNMA (20%)

4. BALANCED STOCK AND BOND PORTFOLIO: 41 TO 55 POINTS

═══ This portfolio is most appropriate for those in retirement seeking a balanced portfolio with 50 percent stocks and 50 percent bonds. While it will provide a moderate degree of income, its primary goal is to grow capital without subjecting investors to a high degree of risk. The suggested subasset class breakdown for this portfolio is as follows:

35% Large-Cap Funds

10% Mid-Cap Funds

5% International Funds

20% Corporate Bond Funds

30% Mortgage-Backed Securities Funds

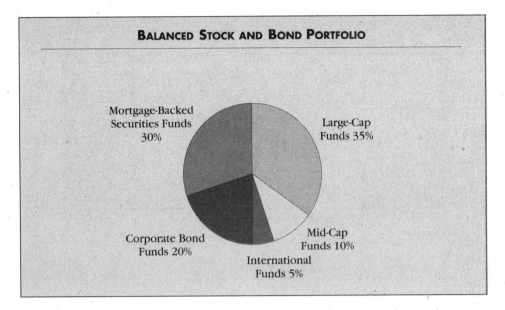

Sample Funds and Weightings:

Marsico Focus (17.5%)

Selected American Shares (17.5%)

C&B Mid-Cap Value (10%)

Julius Baer International (5%)

Fremont Bond (20%)

TCW Galileo Total Return Bond (30%)

5. CONSERVATIVE INCOME PRODUCER: 0 TO 40 POINTS

This portfolio maintains a small exposure to dividend-paying stocks for growth, but concentrates on bond investments to provide a steady stream of monthly income. It is most appropriate for people in retirement who are looking to live off their investments while enduring only a minimal amount of volatility. The suggested subasset class breakdown for this portfolio is:

30% Large-Cap Funds

30% Corporate Bond Funds

40% Mortgage-Backed Securities Funds

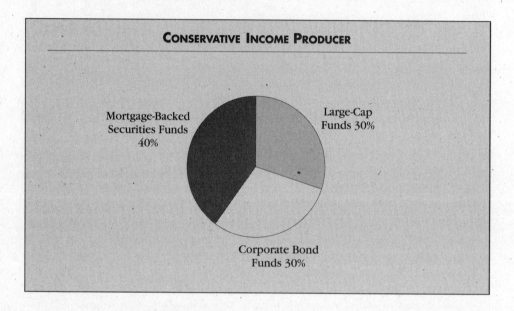

CONSERVATIVE INCOME PRODUCER

Mortgage-Backed Securities Funds 40%

Large-Cap Funds 30%

Corporate Bond Funds 30%

Sample Funds and Weightings:

Atlantic Whitehall Growth (15%)

Clipper Fund (15%)

Vanguard Total Bond Market Index (15%)

Fremont Bond (15%)

Vanguard GNMA (20%)

TCW Galileo Total Return Bond (20%)

HOW THE PORTFOLIOS WERE PUT TOGETHER

The funds in the five model portfolios are for illustration purposes only. Feel free to mix and match as necessary, based on your own research and preferences. Also keep in mind that you can substitute index funds in all of the above portfolios. Plus, if you're in a high tax bracket, you might consider replacing taxable bond funds with tax-free municipal funds instead. The key is to find an allocation you are comfortable with that you can stick to over the long haul.

Keep in mind that these portfolios, the recommended funds, and the entire "Powerhouse Performers" roster is updated in each annual edition of this book.

Most of the portfolios contain both "growth" and "value" funds. After all, growth and value aren't always in vogue at the same time. Therefore, part of your diversification plan should call for holding funds that adhere to both disciplines.

TIMING THE MARKET

After you have set your asset allocation plan, it makes sense to review it as you grow older and/or as your needs change. But once you have decided on the right program for you, stick with it and avoid trying to time the market. If you have made a decision to be 100 percent invested in a globally diversified equity portfolio, don't get creative by switching back and forth from stocks to bonds, based on whether you're bullish or bearish at the moment. The reason? While some are occasionally lucky, no one has proven that you can successfully time the market over the long haul.

The only thing we know for sure is that the market has an upward bias. It's impossible to know where it will be tomorrow, next week, or even next year, but odds are it will be higher 10 years from now than it is today. It would be great to be able to avoid every bear market. The problem is, those nasty bears creep up without warning. And study after study has shown that investors who simply stay put and ride out the inevitable market swings come out far ahead of traders who try to guess what will happen next by switching back and forth, which is an exercise in futility.

It's worth emphasizing that investment capital is money you are willing to put away for long periods of time. In this way, you can afford to ride out the sometimes grueling short-term volatility you will surely be forced to endure. One of the questions on the test you just took asked how you would feel if your $10,000 investment fell to a mere $4,186 over a 10-year period. If that kind of possibility scares you to death, lighten up on or entirely avoid stocks. But as the question also implies, that $10,000 could grow significantly. Again, the more risk you take, the greater your potential reward, but the more fluctuations you will be forced to endure.

IRA Facts

Every investor who qualifies should consider putting the maximum $2,000 a year into an IRA account. Even if you can't deduct the contribution, this money will compound tax-free until you withdraw it. Keep in mind that IRA stands for Individual *Retirement* Account, which means this money should not be touched until you need it in your golden years. If you try to tap into an IRA before you turn 59½, the government slaps you with a 10 percent penalty in addition to any income taxes due, unless you have a qualified reason.

There are now two types of IRAs: Traditional and Roth. What follows is a brief rundown of the benefits and requirements for both:

Eligibility

Traditional IRA: Individuals under age 70½ (and their spouses) who have earned income, regardless of the amount.

Roth IRA: Individuals of any age (and their spouses) with earned income and with adjusted gross income below $110,000 (for single filers) or $160,000 (for those filing a joint return).

Deductibility of Contribution

Traditional IRA: Contribution is fully deductible if the investor is not covered by an employer-sponsored retirement plan. If the investor is covered by an employer-sponsored retirement plan, a partial deduction may be permitted for those falling within these income guidelines: $30,000 to $40,000 for single filers; $50,000 to $60,000 for those filing jointly. Above these amounts, you can still contribute to a traditional IRA, but will not receive a tax deduction.

Roth IRA: No deduction permitted.

Annual Contribution Limits

Traditional IRA: Individuals (and their spouses) may contribute up to $3,000 per year (or 100 percent of compensation, whichever is less). If you're over 50, you can contribute up to $3,500 per year.

Roth IRA: Individuals (and their spouses) may contribute up to $3,000 (or 100 percent of compensation, whichever is less) with the following limits: The ability to contribute phases out at income levels between

$95,000 and $110,000 for individuals and between $150,000 and $160,000 for those filing joint returns. If you're over 50, the maximum contribution amount goes up to $3,500 per year.

Tax Treatment of Distributions

Traditional IRA: Total deductible contributions and interest taxed as ordinary income in the year of withdrawal. Nondeductible contributions are not taxed, although the interest earned from them is. Distributions made before age 59½ may be subject to a 10 percent penalty. Early penalty-free withdrawals can be made prior to age 59½ upon death, disability, the purchase of a first-time home (up to $10,000 lifetime maximum), to fund higher education expenses, to pay for medical expenses in excess of 7.5 percent of adjusted gross income, or for health insurance premiums if unemployed more than 12 weeks.

Roth IRA: Distributions made after age 59½ are tax-free if the Roth IRA has been held for more than five years. Distributions made before age 59½ may be subject to a 10 percent penalty. Early penalty-free withdrawals can be made prior to age 59½ upon death, disability, the purchase of a first home (up to $10,000 lifetime maximum), to fund higher education expenses, to pay for medical expenses in excess of 7.5 percent of adjusted gross income, or for health insurance premiums if unemployed more than 12 weeks. You can also withdraw your contributed principal from a Roth IRA without tax or penalty at any time.

Minimum Distribution Requirements

Traditional IRA: Distributions must start by age 70½.

Roth IRA: No requirements.

7

THE 25 BEST INTERNET SITES FOR MUTUAL FUND INVESTORS

If you have Internet access, you can now tap into more information about mutual funds than you ever dreamed possible by visiting the plethora of financial sites that pop up daily on the World Wide Web. These locations allow you to do research, download performance charts, track your portfolio online, and even chat in real time with other investors. The bad news is that most of these sites aren't worth your time. A majority of the so-called investment sites out there are mere advertisements for certain products or services. They contain little, if any, objective investment information. Others with more substance charge a subscription fee, which can get pretty steep.

This chapter reveals 25 of the best sites in cyberspace for mutual fund investors. The sites can be accessed absolutely free. A few have premium content you have to pay for, but you'll do fine just sticking with the stuff that's available at no cost.

A few caveats before you proceed: Anyone can set up and contribute to an Internet site, so always be suspicious of advice you receive online; much of it is self-serving. Occasionally, you'll find companies touting their own stock under the auspices of a seemingly legitimate financial column. Another thing: think twice before giving your e-mail address to anyone, unless you're open to being deluged with junk announcements. In some cases, you must reveal this information to gain access to a site. Otherwise, keep all personal data to yourself.

Finally, beyond what you can access through the Internet, a number of helpful computer software programs are available to help monitor and improve the results of your portfolio. Quicken and Microsoft Money, for example, will keep track of your cost basis for every fund. These programs are complete personal finance solutions, and they allow for such other features as check writing, budgeting, and financial planning. For fund analysis, you should consider the *Value Line Mutual Fund Survey for Windows*, which includes monthly CD-ROM updates on more than 12,000 funds along with on-line updates. The program has sophisticated sorting, screening, filtering, portfolio analysis, and graphics capabilities. A special free-trial offer to receive this service can be found at the back of this book.

Now that the formalities are out of the way, here (in no particular order) are our picks for the year's 25 best Web sites for mutual fund investors. Be sure to look for an updated list of new sites in each annual edition of this book.

1. **CBS MarketWatch**   www.marketwatch.com

   If you enjoy reading late-breaking business news and information, you'll love CBS MarketWatch. In addition to quotes and stock charting tools, the site has a dedicated mutual funds channel. This area contains insightful articles and fund manager interviews, plus profiles on new funds and fund industry commentary. There are also interesting perspectives on the industry by such columnists as Chuck Jaffe, Paul Merriman, and Paul Farrell. In addition, MarketWatch has some great fund monitoring and screening tools, plus links to various fund family sites. Best of all, everything is accessible at no charge.

2. **Morningstar.com**   www.morningstar.com

   Fund-rating service Morningstar has put together a rather impressive site full of fund manager interviews, financial news, chat rooms, market analysis, and snapshot fund profiles containing the company's trademark star ratings. For a fee, the site allows you to monitor your fund portfolio online, and an X-ray feature shows how broadly diversified your overall holdings are across various asset classes and investment styles. Of greatest value is the archive of reports and insightful articles on the personalities and trends within the fund industry.

3. **CNN/Money**   money.cnn.com

   While not strictly a site for fund investors, CNN/Money contains late-breaking financial information from CNN and such sister properties as Fortune.com and Business 2.0. In addition to the most recent market numbers, it contains the latest investment news and Web video segments containing interviews with CEOs and portfolio managers from CNN. The site also includes a "Money 101" section, where you can learn about such subjects as the basics of investing and buying a home.

4. **USA Today – Money**   www.usatoday.com/money

The money section of *USA Today* is always full of insightful articles. Now, you can access many of these stories online at no charge. Actually, the online version is much more up-to-date than the print edition of the newspapers and also offers free quotes and investment research. From this page, you can easily navigate through *USA Today*'s other sections as well, including general news and sports. Also helpful are the financial calculators, which enable you to work through various "what if" scenarios on everything from estimated living expenses 30 years in the future to the amount you must save to afford the home of your dreams.

5. **MutualFundsNet.com**   www.mutualfundsnet.com

Whether you're looking to find a mutual fund prospectus, or want to find a job in the fund industry, MutualFundsNet.com can link you to the exact right site for the information you need. This simple directory allows you to search for the Web site of almost every mutual fund family, with direct links to specific sections, such as career opportunities. A news section contains recent developments in the industry. While the site is of most interest to those actually in the fund industry, the information will also appeal to investors looking to research their favorite funds online.

6. **Investor Words**   www.investorwords.com

The glossary in the back of this book is pretty comprehensive, but it's nothing compared to what you'll find at the Investor Words site. Billed as "the biggest, best investing glossary on the Web," it contains definitions for some 4,000 investment-related words, from alpha to zero-coupon bond. Within most definitions, you will find links to other related words, to further your understanding of every concept. Given the financial industry's knack for throwing around confusing gobbledygook, this site is bound to be a frequent stop for every serious investor.

7. **Forbes.com**   www.forbes.com/funds

   This helpful site from *Forbes* magazine has everything from manager profiles to screening tools for fund investors. It also includes practical advice on building your portfolio, along with video feature stories and recent financial news. What's more, you can access information from *Forbes* magazine's annual mutual fund guide and search the archives for articles relating to the fund industry. This is definitely a site fund investors should check out, especially those who don't read the print edition of *Forbes* on a regular basis.

8. **Yahoo Finance**   www.finance.yahoo.com

   It's not that pretty to look at, but Yahoo Finance is a great source of comprehensive, up-to-the-minute investment information. On the stock side, it reports on the day's major corporate developments. It also has a page devoted exclusively to news relating to mutual funds, such as new fund launches, cash flow trends, and manager changes. Additionally, it includes links to fund-related stories by reporters from Reuters and Dow Jones. What's more, Yahoo Finance has a fund message board and can provide a quick printout of top performers across various time periods.

9. **MaxFunds.com**   www.maxfunds.com

   While some of this site's best information is now only available to paid subscribers, there is still plenty of free stuff here for your perusal. One stop should be MaxUniversity, home to courses on mutual fund investing. Among the contents: Everything you always wanted to know about mutual funds, but were afraid to ask; the lowdown on options and trading; and why investing in Beanie Babies is not really such a good idea. The site also contains links to articles on mutual fund investing from other publications written by MaxFunds founder, Jonas Ferris.

10. **TheStreet.com**   www.thestreet.com

    Once designed primarily for frequent traders, TheStreet.com now contains more articles of value to long-term investors. The site's mutual fund reporting has improved as well, including regular fund manager interviews, profiles, and recommendations. The site also includes a wealth of daily market analysis (including a separate subscription-based service called RealMoney), for those more interested in what's happening with the market on an hour-by-hour basis.

11. **MSN Money**   www.moneycentral.com

This site, run by Microsoft, no doubt can answer just about any money question you have. In addition to offering general financial news and quotes, by clicking on the investing section, and then going to "funds," you'll find information especially targeted to mutual fund investors. You can also screen for top-performing funds using data supplied by Morningstar. Also worth checking out: Jubak's Journal by financial writer Jim Jubak. Although he doesn't always write specifically about funds, his insights on the world of money are always enlightening and are proprietary to this site.

12. **ICI Mutual Fund Connection**   www.ici.org

Investment Company Institute is the trade association for the fund industry. Its Web site is packed with statistical fund information, along with the association's most recent press releases, speeches, and research reports. This site will give you a better understanding of the various issues affecting the fund industry. In addition, the "About Mutual Fund Shareholders" section contains some fascinating information on the demographic characteristics of the average fund investor.

13. **U.S. Securities and Exchange Commission**   www.sec.gov

By tapping in to the SEC Web site, you'll be able to access the huge database of legal documents that mutual funds are required to file with the government. You can pull down prospectuses and other detailed papers filed by every fund company. This is an effective and quick way to do research on funds you own or are considering. It can also lead you to brand-new funds that have registered with the SEC but are not yet available to the public. Incidentally, you can use this same database to search for 10-Ks, 10-Qs, and other material that must be filed with the SEC by public companies as well.

14. **Vanguard Online**   www.vanguard.com

Almost every major fund company now has its own Internet site, but this one from the Vanguard Group stands out. It is more than just a commercial message for the company's various funds. Instead, it contains a lot of educational material. Vanguard Online has an area called "The University," which features a series of ten courses answering such questions as "What is a mutual fund?" "How do you build a portfolio?" and "What are the best ways to rebalance your portfolio?" You'll also find helpful tools for retirement planning and a library of in-depth fund material.

15. **SmartMoney.com**   www.smartmoney.com

SmartMoney.com is the online site of *SmartMoney* magazine, which is one of the finest personal finance periodicals. The site includes daily market analysis, along with helpful feature articles and analytical tools. There is a special section devoted exclusively to mutual fund investing, along with tools for mapping various fund features, including asset style and comparative performance. You can also track the performance of your own portfolio at no extra charge.

16. **Mutual Fund Investor's Center**   www.mfea.com

This site, sponsored by the Mutual Fund Education Alliance, contains in-depth profiles of select fund managers, thoughts from leaders in the field, and a news center with recent developments in the industry. The education center teaches users about the basics of fund investing, goes over the various types of funds available, discusses the tax ramifications of fund ownership, and has a special feature on investing for women. Plus, the site's planning center lets you go through various scenarios to make informed decisions about everything from investing for college to retirement.

17. **Fund Alarm**   www.fundalarm.com

Almost every fund site gives you some kind of advice on buying funds. Fund Alarm is the only one specializing in telling you when to sell. It is updated at the beginning of each month and follows more than 1,900 funds. A fund is likely to earn a "three alarm" sell signal if it undergoes a bad change in management or its performance lags behind its benchmark over a consistent time period. Fund Alarm is run by Roy Weitz, an accountant by trade who is not even in the investment business. Still, his monthly commentary, in which he "tells it like it is" about the industry and its key players, is must reading, even if you don't always agree with him. Weitz has become the unofficial watchdog of the mutual fund industry and performs a valuable service.

18. **Bloomberg**   www.bloomberg.com

New York mayor Michael Bloomberg's investment information empire is into just about every medium imaginable now (radio, TV, print, computer terminals), so it's no surprise he has put up his own Internet address as well. The site is flush with news straight from the Bloomberg wires, including a section packed with mutual fund-related stories. If you're looking for the latest developments on fund companies and the industry in general, this is about the most comprehensive source around. The site also updates the equity indexes throughout the day and lets you tap into Bloomberg Radio and TV live.

19. **Fund $pot**   www.fundspot.com

Fund $pot is a site that connects you to other areas on the Internet that are of interest to fund investors. You'll find links to mutual fund news, portfolio manager interviews, and fund family Web sites. "Interactive Spot" takes you to worksheets and financial calculators useful for college, retirement, and general financial planning. If you feel like chatting about your newest fund discovery, the site can direct you to an investor forum where you can talk to your heart's content. To round things out, Fund $pot leads you to sites with portfolio tracking capabilities, research, and current quotes.

20. **Brill's Mutual Funds Interactive**   www.fundsinteractive.com

Mutual Funds Interactive is awash with useful information and articles written by its founder, Marla Brill, and a team of contributing fund experts. This isn't the best looking site around, but there are discussions here about everything from retirement planning to which Web sites users like the most. You'll also find the results of various fund-related surveys, manager profiles, and a news section with articles of interest to fund investors culled from numerous columnists and publications.

21. **WSJ.com Mutual Funds**   investing.wsj.com/mutualfunds

This section of The Wall Street Journal Online contains an online tutorial on choosing, sorting through, and screening mutual funds. You can also use this as a gateway for accessing content from the rest of *The Wall Street Journal* and sister publication *Barron's*. Although much of the remaining content is subscription-based, there is still a lot available here at no charge. It's probably not a site you'll want to visit every day (at least the mutual funds section), but at least one visit to the tutorial would be helpful in accelerating your learning curve into mutual funds and how they work.

22. **Kiplinger.com**   www.kiplinger.com/investing/funds

This online version of *Kiplinger's Personal Finance* contains a surprising amount of great articles and advice for fund investors. In addition to offering model portfolios and screening tools, regular users will learn about new funds, read interviews with leading fund managers, and discover important issues that all savvy investors should be aware of. In addition to recycling articles that previously appeared in the print edition of *Kiplinger's*, the site has a number of articles found exclusively online. It's by far one of the most regularly refreshed and content-intensive sites for mutual fund fans on the Web.

23. **iMoneyNet.com**   www.imoneynet.com

You'll notice that there are no money market funds among the list of "100 Powerhouse Performers." That's because money market yields change so often, it's hard to keep track of who is offering the best deals. One way to stay ahead of the curve is by visiting the iMoneyNet.com site. iMoneyNet is in the business of tracking money funds and yields. You can't access all of its services without paying a fee, but the freebies are all you need. A click of the mouse gives you a rundown of the highest yielding funds. Another section goes over the finer points of selecting and evaluating these cash-equivalent investments.

24. **IndexFunds.com**   www.indexfunds.com

If you opt to keep part of your portfolio in index funds, or just want to learn more about how these investments work, you'll find the content of IndexFunds.com to be of interest. The site, run by a diehard indexer, has articles on indexing and related pieces from various publications and books. It includes an area with information on each of the major global indexes (i.e., number of stocks included and market capitalizations), along with a listing of funds available to track these indexes. The site updates how well the various indexes have performed on a weekly basis, and contains articles about non-index funds as well.

25. **The Motley Fool** www.fool.com

Although Motley Fool founders Tom and David Gardner generally pan mutual funds (they prefer individual stocks), they have devoted a special section of their popular site to mutual fund investing. In fact, mutual funds have gained an increasing presence on the site in recent years. While by no means the best of the bunch, the Motley Fool does contain handy articles on how to select winning funds along with a glossary for fund investors. It also has a section on investing for retirement, which will no doubt be of interest to those of you getting ready to leave the workforce and wondering what to do with your 401(k)s, IRAs, and other pension programs.

8

VALUE LINE
PERFORMANCE DATA FOR
THOUSANDS OF FUNDS

What follows are comprehensive performance results and rankings for thousands of stock and bond mutual funds from the Value Line Mutual Fund Survey. This is the most exhaustive collection of fund data you will find in any book on the market today. The directory starts out with a listing of stock funds, and then gives a roster of bond offerings. The following information (where available) is provided for each entry:

Fund Name.   Funds are listed in alphabetical order, with stock funds up front, and bond funds in the back. Almost every fund you own or are considering can probably be found somewhere on these pages.

Objective.   This is a brief description of the fund's investment objective (i.e., growth, foreign, corporate bond, and so on).

Annualized Return for 1, 3, and 5 Years.   Here you will find every fund's average annual return over the past one-, three- and five-year periods, where applicable, as compiled by Value Line. (All performance data is as of May 31, 2003, unless otherwise noted.)

Overall Rank.   This number, compiled exclusively by Value Line, shows how a given fund stacks up next to its peers. Ratings are on a scale of 1 through 5. Funds with a 1 ranking have performed best, and those rated 5 have done the poorest.

271

Risk Rank.   Another proprietary Value Line statistic, the risk rank number tells you how much volatility a fund has subjected its investors to. It is also based on a scale of 1 through 5, with 1 being least risky, and 5 being riskiest.

Maximum Sales Load.   If a fund has a front-end sales load, it will be noted here. (Remember: If you're making fund selections on your own, you should favor no-load funds.) Also, many load funds have several share classes that come with back-ended redemption fees, instead of up-front sales commissions. In other words, you pay on the way "out" rather than on the way "in." Therefore, although some load funds in this directory may have several other share classes with "0" listed as the maximum sales load, be aware that you can almost always count on being hit with steep exit fees on these funds.

Expense Ratio.   Every fund has an expense ratio. This number represents the percentage that gets deducted from the fund's net asset value each year, to cover all charges related to managing your money.

Toll-Free (or Toll) Telephone.   This is the toll-free (or toll) telephone number you can call to request a prospectus and more information on the listed fund.

For up-to-date performance numbers on these funds, visit ValueLine.com. Also be sure to check out the special offer at the back of this book, which will give you a three-month subscription to the Value Line Mutual Fund Survey for Windows absolutely free.

Many thanks to the good folks at Value Line who helped to put this performance directory together. They, as always, truly did a first-rate job.

Stock Fund Name	Objective	Annualized Return for			Rank		Max Load	Expense Ratio	Toll-Free/(Toll) Telephone
		1 Year	3 Years	5 Years	Overall	Risk			

STOCK FUNDS

Stock Fund Name	Objective	1 Year	3 Years	5 Years	Overall	Risk	Max Load	Expense Ratio	Toll-Free/(Toll) Telephone
1838 International Equity Fund	Foreign	-13.2	-13.22	-4.95	4	2	0	1.1	877 367-1838
1st Source Monogram Dvrs Equity	Growth	-12.2	-14.18	-6.63	5	3	5	1.33	800 766-8938
1st Source Monogram Income Equity	Growth/Inc	-8.7	4.21	4.66	2	2	0	1.19	800 766-8938
1st Source Monogram Special Eq	Small Co	-10.2	4.46	7.94	3	4	5	1.29	800 766-8938
AAL Aggressive Growth A	Agg Growth	-11.3					5.5	2.21	800 553-6319
AAL Aggressive Growth B	Agg Growth	-12.4					0	3.33	800 553-6319
AAL Aggressive Growth I	Agg Growth	-9.9					0	1.15	800 553-6319
AAL Balanced A	Balanced	-1.5	-1.17	3.24	2	1	5.5	1.02	800 553-6319
AAL Balanced B	Balanced	-2.3	-2.04	2.29	2	1	0	1.92	800 553-6319
AAL Balanced I	Balanced	-1.2	-0.77	3.64	1	1	0	0.62	800 553-6319
AAL Capital Growth Fund A	Growth	-10.3	-9.75	0.4	3	2	5.5	0.95	800 553-6319
AAL Capital Growth Fund B	Growth	-11.3	-10.68	-0.64	3	2	0	1.97	800 553-6319
AAL Capital Growth Fund I	Growth	-9.8	-9.35	0.81	3	2	0	0.55	800 553-6319
AAL Equity Income A	Growth/Inc	-15.4	-6.94	-1.86	3	2	5.5	0.98	800 553-6319
AAL Equity Income B	Growth/Inc	-16.3	-7.88	-2.87	3	2	0	1.91	800 553-6319
AAL Equity Income I	Growth/Inc	-15	-6.51	-1.4	3	2	0	0.51	800 553-6319
AAL International A	Foreign	-17.9	-18.07	-6.99	4	3	5.5	1.56	800 553-6319
AAL International B	Foreign	-19.2	-19.1	-8.08	4	3	0	2.57	800 553-6319
AAL International I	Foreign	-17.2	-17.42	-6.32	5	3	0	0.78	800 553-6319
AAL Large Company Index I	Growth	-8.2	-11.14		3	3	0	0.49	800 553-6319
AAL Large Company Index II A	Growth	-8.3					5.5	0.54	800 553-6319
AAL Large Company Index II B	Growth	-9.3					0	0.68	800 553-6319
AAL Mid Cap Index I	Growth	-9.4	0.56		2	3	0	0.88	800 553-6319
AAL Mid Cap Index II A	Growth	-10.2					5.5	1.21	800 553-6319
AAL Mid Cap Index II B	Growth	-10.7					0	2.15	800 553-6319
AAL Mid Cap Stock A	Growth	-10	-4.2	1.6	3	3	5.5	1.23	800 553-6319
AAL Mid Cap Stock B	Growth	-11.1	-5.29	0.41	3	3	0	2.39	800 553-6319
AAL Mid Cap Stock I	Growth	-9.4	-3.68	2.16	2	3	0	0.7	800 553-6319
AAL Small Cap Index Fund II A	Small Co	-11.6					5.5	1.36	800 553-6319
AAL Small Cap Index Fund II B	Small Co	-12.4					0	2.07	800 553-6319
AAL Small Cap Stock A	Small Co	-12.5	0.77	3.64	3	4	5.5	1.37	800 553-6319
AAL Small Cap Stock B	Small Co	-13.3	-0.22	2.6	3	4	0	2.41	800 553-6319
AAL Small Cap Stock I	Small Co	-11.8	1.44	4.37	3	4	0	0.75	800 553-6319
AAL Small Cap Value A	Small Co	-10.3					5.5	1.66	800 553-6319
AAL Small Cap Value B	Small Co	-11					0	2.4	800 553-6319
AAL Small Cap Value I	Small Co	-9.4					0	1.63	800 553-6319
AAL Technology Stock A	Technology	-7.4					5.5	1.33	800 553-6319
AAL Technology Stock B	Technology	-8.2					0	1.75	800 553-6319
AAL Technology Stock I	Technology	-6.2					0	1.14	800 553-6319
ABN AMRO Balanced Fund N	Balanced	-2.7	-2.47	3.93	2	1	0	1.07	800 992-8151
ABN AMRO Equity Plus I	Growth	-7	-13.33	-1.2	3	3	0	0.49	800 992-8151
ABN AMRO Growth Fund C	Growth/Inc						0	1.93	800 992-8151
ABN AMRO Growth Fund N	Growth	-9.7	-9.15	2.2	3	3	0	1.11	800 992-8151
ABN AMRO Growth Fund R	Growth/Inc						0	1.38	800 992-8151
ABN AMRO Intl Equity N	Foreign	-17.6	-20.05	-7.44	4	3	0	1.41	800 992-8151
ABN AMRO Mid Cap Fund N	Growth	-1.7	6.95	8.09	2	4	0	1.3	800 992-8151
ABN AMRO Montag&Caldwell Bal I	Balanced	-2.3	-1.93		2	1	0		800 992-8151
ABN AMRO Montag&Caldwell Bal N	Balanced	-2.5	-3.54	2.16	2	1	0	1.13	800 992-8151
ABN AMRO Montag&Caldwell Gr I	Growth	-10	-10.53		3	2	0	0.78	800 992-8151
ABN AMRO Montag&Caldwell Gr N	Growth	-10.2	-10.77	-1.05	3	2	0	1.06	800 992-8151
ABN AMRO Montag&Caldwell Gr R	Growth						0	1.33	800 992-8151
ABN AMRO Real Estate N	Real Est	4.9	12.88	7.15	1	2	0	1.37	800 992-8151
ABN AMRO Select Small Cap N	Small Co	-10	2.54		3	3	0	1.03	800 992-8151
ABN AMRO TAMRO Lg Cap Val N	Growth	-5.2					0	1.2	800 992-8151
ABN AMRO TAMRO Small Cap N	Small Co	-6.3					0	1.3	800 992-8151

273

Stock Fund Name	Objective	Annualized Return for			Rank		Max Load	Expense Ratio	Toll-Free/(Toll) Telephone
		1 Year	3 Years	5 Years	Overall	Risk			
ABN AMRO Value N	Growth/Inc	-9.5	-6.54	-3.27	3	2	0	0.94	800 992-8151
ABN AMRO Veredus Agg Gr N	Agg Growth	-16	-11		3	4	0	1.4	800 992-8151
AFBA 5Star Balanced Fd	Balanced	-4.1	-0.2	1.41	1	2	0	1.06	800 243-9865
AFBA 5Star Large Cap I	Growth	-8.6	-8.46	-0.9	3	4	0	1.06	800 243-9865
AFBA 5Star USA Global Fd	Global	-13.6	-10.34	1.62	3	4	0	1.06	800 243-9865
AHA Balanced Portfolio	Balanced	-4.2	0.64	3.37	2	1	0	0.46	800 445-1341
AHA Diversified Equity	Growth	-9.7	-4.19	1.82	2	3	0	0.16	800 445-1341
AIC Acadian Emerging Mkts Inst	Foreign	-1.4	0.26	4.05	2	4	0	2.2	866 234-5426
AIC Chicago Asset Mgmt Val Contr I	Growth	-9.9	-5.5	-0.94	3	3	0		866 234-5426
AIC FMA Small Company Inst	Small Co	-12.5	5.74	2.29	3	3	0	0.86	866 234-5426
AIC ICM Small Company Inst	Small Co	-6	12.89	6.78	2	3	0	0.86	866 234-5426
AIC II Analytic Defensive Eq Instl	Growth/Inc	-2	-2.85	-3.45	2	1	0	0.98	800 374-2633
AIC Independence Small Cap Instl	Small Co	-15.9	3.66		3	4	0	1.48	866 450-3722
AIC McKee Intl Equity Portf Instl	Foreign	-14	-11.56	-2.1	4	3	0	1.02	866 234-5426
AIC Rice Hall James Micro Cap Inst	Small Co	-13.3	5.98	5.3	2	4	0	1.15	866 474-5669
AIC Rice Hall James Sm/Mid Cp Inst	Small Co	-15.2	0.05	3.74	3	4	0	1.21	866 474-5669
AIC Sirach Equity Inst	Growth	-12	-18.66	-7.29	5	3	0		866 234-5426
AIC Sirach Growth Inst	Growth	-10	-14.41	-3.39	4	3	0		866 234-5426
AIC Sirach Special Equity Inst	Small Co	-16.6	-16.73	0.17	5	4	0		866 234-5426
AIC Sirach Strategic Bal Inst	Balanced	-2.6	-5.04	0.93	2	1	0	1.08	866 234-5426
AIC TS&W Equity Portfolio Inst	Growth	-14.2	-6.17	-1.55	3	3	0		866 234-5426
AIC TS&W International Eq Inst	Foreign	-16.5	-16.3	-3.97	5	3	0	1.44	866 234-5426
AIM Aggressive Growth A	Agg Growth	-14.9	-16.51	-1.85	4	4	5.5	1.18	800 347-4246
AIM Aggressive Growth B	Agg Growth	-15.5	-17.14		4	4	0	1.93	800 347-4246
AIM Aggressive Growth C	Agg Growth	-15.5	-17.12		4	4	0	1.93	800 347-4246
AIM Asia Pacific Growth A	Pacific	-12.8	-11.4	2.2	3	3	5.5	2.37	800 347-4246
AIM Asia Pacific Growth B	Pacific	-13.2	-11.93	1.48	3	3	0	3.02	800 347-4246
AIM Asia Pacific Growth C	Pacific	-13.4	-12.01	1.41	3	3	0	3.02	800 347-4246
AIM Balanced Fund A	Balanced	-6	-7.95	-1.29	3	2	4.75	1.01	800 347-4246
AIM Balanced Fund B	Balanced	-6.7	-8.64	-2.06	3	2	0	1.76	800 347-4246
AIM Balanced Fund C	Balanced	-6.7	-8.63	-2.04	3	2	0	1.76	800 347-4246
AIM Basic Balanced A	Balanced	-3.8					4.75	1.47	800 347-4246
AIM Basic Balanced B	Balanced	-4.5					0	2.12	800 347-4246
AIM Basic Balanced C	Balanced	-4.5					0	2.12	800 347-4246
AIM Basic Value A	Growth	-13.5	-0.69	6.7	3	3	5.5	1.3	800 347-4246
AIM Basic Value B	Growth	-14	-1.35	6.01	3	3	0	1.95	800 347-4246
AIM Basic Value C	Growth	-14.1	-1.36		2	3	0	1.95	800 347-4246
AIM Blue Chip Fund A	Growth	-8.5	-16.85	-3.68	4	3	5.5	1.28	800 347-4246
AIM Blue Chip Fund B	Growth	-9.1	-17.41	-4.33	4	3	0	1.93	800 347-4246
AIM Blue Chip Fund C	Growth	-9.1	-17.39	-4.33	4	3	0	1.93	800 347-4246
AIM Capital Development A	Growth	-14.7	-6.03	1.52	3	3	5.5	1.34	800 347-4246
AIM Capital Development B	Growth	-15.2	-6.62	0.82	2	3	0	1.99	800 347-4246
AIM Capital Development C	Growth	-15.2	-6.62	0.81	3	3	0	1.99	800 347-4246
AIM Charter Fund A	Growth	-6.7	-14.51	-1.39	4	4	5.5	1.17	800 347-4246
AIM Charter Fund B	Growth	-7.4	-15.13	-2.12	3	4	0	1.87	800 347-4246
AIM Charter Fund C	Growth	-7.5	-15.14	-2.14	3	4	0	1.87	800 347-4246
AIM Constellation Fund A	Agg Growth	-10.1	-17.01	-2.16	4	4	5.5	1.14	800 347-4246
AIM Constellation Fund B	Agg Growth	-10.8	-17.6	-2.91	4	4	0	1.87	800 347-4246
AIM Constellation Fund C	Agg Growth	-10.7	-17.57	-2.91	4	4	0	1.87	800 347-4246
AIM Dent Demographic Trends A	Growth	-10.3	-22.37		4	5	5.5	1.66	800 347-4246
AIM Dent Demographic Trends B	Growth	-11	-22.89		4	5	0	2.31	800 347-4246
AIM Dent Demographic Trends C	Growth	-11	-22.89		4	5	0	2.31	800 347-4246
AIM Developing Markets A	Foreign	-10.4	-7.36	-5.33	3	4	4.75	1.76	800 347-4246
AIM Developing Markets B	Foreign	-10.9	-7.92	-5.91	3	4	0	2.35	800 347-4246
AIM Developing Markets C	Foreign	-10.9	-7.94		3	4	0	2.35	800 347-4246
AIM Diversified Dividend A	Growth/Inc	-7					5.5	1.72	800 347-4246
AIM Diversified Dividend B	Growth/Inc	-7.6					0	2.37	800 347-4246
AIM Diversified Dividend C	Growth/Inc	-7.7					0	2.37	800 347-4246

Stock Fund Name	Objective	Annualized Return for			Rank		Max Load	Expense Ratio	Toll-Free/(Toll) Telephone
		1 Year	3 Years	5 Years	Overall	Risk			
AIM Emerging Growth A	Agg Growth	-11.7	-14.74		3	5	5.5	1.83	800 347-4246
AIM Emerging Growth B	Agg Growth	-12.4	-15.26		4	5	0	2.48	800 347-4246
AIM Emerging Growth C	Agg Growth	-12.2	-15.26		4	5	0	2.48	800 347-4246
AIM European Growth A	European	-3.2	-10.35	4.01	3	3	5.5	1.84	800 347-4246
AIM European Growth B	European	-3.9	-10.94	3.29	3	3	0	2.49	800 347-4246
AIM European Growth C	European	-3.9	-10.96	3.29	3	3	0	2.49	800 347-4246
AIM European Small Company A	European	4.5					5.5	2.01	800 347-4246
AIM European Small Company B	European	3.8					0	2.66	800 347-4246
AIM European Small Company C	European	3.7					0	2.66	800 347-4246
AIM Global Aggr Growth Fund A	Global	-8.9	-17.1	-3.5	5	4	4.75	1.88	800 347-4246
AIM Global Aggr Growth Fund B	Global	-9.4	-17.53	-4.03	5	4	0	2.38	800 347-4246
AIM Global Aggr Growth Fund C	Global	-9.4	-17.53	-4.03	5	4	0	2.38	800 347-4246
AIM Global Energy A	Energy/Res	6.1	1.95	-1.89	2	4	4.75	2	800 347-4246
AIM Global Energy B	Energy/Res	5.5	1.42	-2.39	2	4	0	2.5	800 347-4246
AIM Global Energy C	Energy/Res	5.5	1.44		2	4	0	2.5	800 347-4246
AIM Global Financial Services A	Financial	-8.4	1.05	5.38	3	3	4.75	1.85	800 347-4246
AIM Global Financial Services B	Financial	-8.8	0.55	4.86	3	3	0	2.35	800 347-4246
AIM Global Financial Services C	Financial	-8.8	0.53		3	3	0	2.35	800 347-4246
AIM Global Growth Fund A	Global	-11.8	-19.23	-5.46	5	3	4.75	1.79	800 347-4246
AIM Global Growth Fund B	Global	-12.3	-19.64	-5.96	5	3	0	2.29	800 347-4246
AIM Global Growth Fund C	Global	-12.3	-19.64	-5.96	5	3	0	2.29	800 347-4246
AIM Global Health Care A	Health	-15.4	6.01	8.58	3	2	4.75	1.75	800 347-4246
AIM Global Health Care B	Health	-15.9	5.48	8.02	3	2	0	2.25	800 347-4246
AIM Global Health Care C	Health	-15.8	5.5		3	2	0	2.25	800 347-4246
AIM Global Science and Tech A	Technology	-12.3	-38.96	-16.94	4	5	4.75	2	800 347-4246
AIM Global Science and Tech B	Technology	-12.7	-39.24	-17.35	4	5	0	2.5	800 347-4246
AIM Global Science and Tech C	Technology	-12.7	-39.22		4	5	0	2.5	800 347-4246
AIM Global Trends A	Global	-3.2	-5.63	3.18	2	2	4.75	2	800 347-4246
AIM Global Trends B	Global	-3.7	-6.11	2.66	2	2	0	2.5	800 347-4246
AIM Global Trends C	Global	-3.8	-6.11	2.66	2	2	0	2.5	800 347-4246
AIM Global Utilities Fund A	Utilities	-12.1	-17.3	-3.91	3	3	5.5	1.13	800 347-4246
AIM Global Utilities Fund B	Utilities	-12.8	-17.94	-4.65	4	3	0	1.88	800 347-4246
AIM Global Utilities Fund C	Utilities	-12.7	-17.92	-4.65	4	3	0	1.88	800 347-4246
AIM Global Value A	Global	-1.5					5.5	2	800 347-4246
AIM Global Value B	Global	-2.2					0	2.65	800 347-4246
AIM Global Value C	Global	-2.1					0	2.65	800 347-4246
AIM International Core Eqty A	Foreign	-15.3	-9.25	-3.62	4	3	5.5	1.7	800 347-4246
AIM International Core Eqty B	Foreign	-15.9	-9.92	-4.33	4	3	0	2.35	800 347-4246
AIM International Core Eqty C	Foreign	-15.9	-9.93	-4.34	4	3	0	2.35	800 347-4246
AIM International Emerging Gr A	Foreign	3.5					5.5	2	800 347-4246
AIM International Emerging Gr B	Foreign	2.9					0	2.65	800 347-4246
AIM International Emerging Gr C	Foreign	2.8					0	2.65	800 347-4246
AIM International Growth A	Foreign	-12.3	-15.42	-5.08	5	3	5.5	1.57	800 347-4246
AIM International Growth B	Foreign	-12.9	-16.01	-5.78	5	3	0	2.27	800 347-4246
AIM International Growth C	Foreign	-13	-16.05	-5.79	5	3	0	2.27	800 347-4246
AIM Large Cap Basic Value A	Growth	-13	-1.11		3	3	5.5	1.38	800 347-4246
AIM Large Cap Basic Value B	Growth	-13.5					0	2.03	800 347-4246
AIM Large Cap Basic Value C	Growth	-13.4					0	2.03	800 347-4246
AIM Large Cap Growth A	Growth	-8	-20.21		4	4	5.5	1.57	800 347-4246
AIM Large Cap Growth B	Growth	-8.6	-20.69		4	4	0	2.22	800 347-4246
AIM Large Cap Growth C	Growth	-8.6	-20.71		4	4	0	2.22	800 347-4246
AIM Libra A	Growth						4.75	1.8	800 347-4246
AIM Libra B	Growth						0	2.45	800 347-4246
AIM Libra C	Growth						0	2.45	800 347-4246
AIM Mid Cap Basic Value A	Growth	-11.5					5.5	1.77	800 347-4246
AIM Mid Cap Basic Value B	Growth	-12.1					0	2.42	800 347-4246
AIM Mid Cap Basic Value C	Growth	-12.1					0	2.42	800 347-4246
AIM Mid Cap Core Equity A	Growth	-6.5	1.13	8.39	2	3	5.5	1.4	800 347-4246

275

Stock Fund Name	Objective	Annualized Return for			Rank		Max Load	Expense Ratio	Toll-Free/(Toll) Telephone
		1 Year	3 Years	5 Years	Overall	Risk			
AIM Mid Cap Core Equity B	Growth	-7.1	0.5	7.66	2	3	0	2.05	800 347-4246
AIM Mid Cap Core Equity C	Growth	-7.2	0.5		2	3	0	2.05	800 347-4246
AIM Mid Cap Growth A	Growth	-15.9	-18.94		4	4	5.5	1.67	800 347-4246
AIM Mid Cap Growth B	Growth	-16.5	-19.48		4	4	0	2.32	800 347-4246
AIM Mid Cap Growth C	Growth	-16.4	-19.46		4	4	0	2.32	800 347-4246
AIM New Technology A	Technology	-12.8					5.5	2	800 347-4246
AIM New Technology B	Technology	-13.3					0	2.65	800 347-4246
AIM New Technology C	Technology	-13.3					0	2.65	800 347-4246
AIM Opportunities I A	Small Co	-14.2	-7.19		3	4	5.5	1.14	800 347-4246
AIM Opportunities I B	Small Co	-14.9	-7.88		3	4	0	1.89	800 347-4246
AIM Opportunities I C	Small Co	-14.8	-7.88		3	4	0	1.89	800 347-4246
AIM Opportunities II A	Growth	-5.9	-11.98		3	3	5.5	1.25	800 347-4246
AIM Opportunities II B	Growth	-6.5	-12.61		3	3	0	2	800 347-4246
AIM Opportunities II C	Growth	-6.5	-12.61		3	3	0	2	800 347-4246
AIM Opportunities III A	Growth	-9.9	-12.56		3	3	5.5	2.13	800 347-4246
AIM Opportunities III B	Growth	-10.6	-13.18		4	3	0	2.88	800 347-4246
AIM Opportunities III C	Growth	-10.6	-13.18		4	3	0	2.88	800 347-4246
AIM Premier Equity A	Growth	-12.9	-16.57	-2.97	4	3	5.5	1.13	800 347-4246
AIM Premier Equity B	Growth	-13.5	-17.19	-3.72	4	3	0	1.88	800 347-4246
AIM Premier Equity C	Growth	-13.4	-17.17	-3.7	4	3	0	1.88	800 347-4246
AIM Premier Equity II A	Growth	-16.7					5.5	1.55	800 347-4246
AIM Premier Equity II B	Growth	-17.2					0	2.2	800 347-4246
AIM Premier Equity II C	Growth	-17.2					0	2.2	800 347-4246
AIM Real Estate A	Real Est	8.8	15.56	6.37	1	1	4.75	1.79	800 347-4246
AIM Real Estate B	Real Est	8	14.78	5.69	1	1	0	2.43	800 347-4246
AIM Real Estate C	Real Est	8	14.78	5.65	1	1	0	2.43	800 347-4246
AIM Select Equity Fund A	Growth	-17.5	-18.87	-1.64	5	4	5.5	1.25	800 347-4246
AIM Select Equity Fund B	Growth	-18.2	-19.5	-2.41	5	4	0	2	800 347-4246
AIM Select Equity Fund C	Growth	-18.2	-19.51	-2.43	5	4	0	2	800 347-4246
AIM Small Cap Equity A	Small Co	-14					5.5	1.39	800 347-4246
AIM Small Cap Equity B	Small Co	-14.5					0	2.04	800 347-4246
AIM Small Cap Equity C	Small Co	-14.5					0	2.04	800 347-4246
AIM Small Cap Growth A	Small Co	-10.7	-12.83	7.62	3	5	5.5	1.39	800 347-4246
AIM Small Cap Growth B	Small Co	-11.4	-13.47	6.83	3	5	0	2.04	800 347-4246
AIM Small Cap Growth C	Small Co	-11.4	-13.47		4	5	0	2.04	800 347-4246
AIM Summit Fund I	Growth	-13	-21.67	-4.15	5	4	8.5	0.8	800 347-4246
AIM Weingarten Fund A	Growth	-10.9	-25.64	-8.35	4	4	5.5	1.22	800 347-4246
AIM Weingarten Fund B	Growth	-11.5	-26.16	-9.02	4	4	0	1.92	800 347-4246
AIM Weingarten Fund C	Growth	-11.5	-26.14	-9.02	4	4	0	1.92	800 347-4246
API Trust Capital Income Fund	Income	-8.7	-10.09	-5.17	3	3	0	2.11	800 544-6060
API Trust Growth Fund	Global	-7.8	-14.31	-3.33	4	4	0	2.76	800 544-6060
API Trust-Multiple Index Trust	Global	-6.3	-13.47	-1.72	3	4	0	1.24	800 544-6060
API Yorktown Classic Value Trust	Growth	-9	-8.59	-2	3	5	0	2.48	800 544-6060
ARK Fds-Balanced Inst	Balanced	-2.4	-5.5	3.62	1	2	0	0.91	800 275-3863
ARK Fds-Balanced Retail A	Balanced	-2.6	-5.62	3.52	1	2	4.75	1.1	800 275-3863
ARK Fds-Balanced Retail B	Balanced	-3.3	-6.3	2.54	1	2	0	1.8	800 275-3863
ARK Fds-Blue Chip Equity Inst	Growth	-12.9	-15.43	-2.41	4	3	0	1.14	800 275-3863
ARK Fds-Blue Chip Equity Retail A	Growth	-13	-15.53	-2.54	4	3	4.75	1.06	800 275-3863
ARK Fds-Blue Chip Equity Retail B	Growth	-13.6	-16.17	-2.87	4	3	0	1.84	800 275-3863
ARK Fds-Capital Growth Inst	Growth	-7.2	-18.39	0.82	3	4	0	1	800 275-3863
ARK Fds-Capital Growth Retail A	Growth	-7.3	-18.5	0.69	3	4	4.75	1.19	800 275-3863
ARK Fds-Capital Growth Retail B	Growth	-7.9	-19.07	-0.34	3	4	0	1.89	800 275-3863
ARK Fds-Emerg Mkt Eqty Retail A	Foreign	-9.6	-12	-6.36	3	4	4.75	2.1	800 275-3863
ARK Fds-Equity Income Inst	Income	-13.2	-6.34	-1.32	3	2	0	1	800 275-3863
ARK Fds-Equity Income Retail A	Income	-13.5	-6.5	-1.47	3	2	4.75	1.18	800 275-3863
ARK Fds-Equity Index Inst	Growth	-8.4	-10.69	-0.9	3	3	0	0.25	800 275-3863
ARK Fds-Equity Index Retail A	Growth	-8.7	-10.93	-1.14	3	3	4.75	0.58	800 275-3863
ARK Fds-Intl Equity Inst	Foreign	-21.1	-18.03		4	3	0	2	800 275-3863

Stock Fund Name	Objective	Annualized Return for			Rank		Max Load	Expense Ratio	Toll-Free/(Toll) Telephone
		1 Year	3 Years	5 Years	Overall	Risk			
ARK Fds-Intl Equity Retail A	Foreign	-21.1	-18.12	-0.48	5	3	4.75	1.67	800 275-3863
ARK Fds-Mid-Cap Equity Inst	Growth	-7.6	-5.37	5.08	3	4	0	1.11	800 275-3863
ARK Fds-Mid-Cap Equity Retail A	Growth	-7.9	-5.53		3	4	4.75	1.29	800 275-3863
ARK Fds-Small-Cap Equity Inst	Small Co	-20.3	-9.35	13.99	3	4	0	1.17	800 275-3863
ARK Fds-Small-Cap Equity Retail A	Small Co	-20.5	-9.46	13.84	2	4	4.75	1.33	800 275-3863
ARK Fds-Value Equity Inst	Growth	-12.6	-9.75	-1.72	3	3	0	1.21	800 275-3863
ARK Fds-Value Equity Retail A	Growth	-12.8	-9.83	-1.84	3	3	4.75	1.38	800 275-3863
ARK Fds-Value Equity Retail B	Growth	-13.4	-10.51	-2.95	3	3	0	2.08	800 275-3863
ASAF ALGER All-Cap Growth A	Growth	-10.3					5.75	1.85	800 752-6342
ASAF ALGER All-Cap Growth B	Growth	-10.7					0	2.35	800 752-6342
ASAF ALGER All-Cap Growth C	Growth	-10.7					1	2.35	800 752-6342
ASAF ALGER All-Cap Growth X	Growth	-10.7					0	2.35	800 752-6342
ASAF All/Bern Growth + Value A	Growth	-8.5					5.75	1.85	800 752-6342
ASAF All/Bern Growth + Value B	Growth	-9.1					0	2.35	800 752-6342
ASAF All/Bern Growth + Value C	Growth	-9.1					1	2.35	800 752-6342
ASAF All/Bern Growth + Value X	Growth	-9					0	2.35	800 752-6342
ASAF Alliance Gr & Inc A	Growth/Inc	-7.4	-4.49	1.18	2	3	5.75	1.65	800 752-6342
ASAF Alliance Gr & Inc B	Growth/Inc	-8	-4.96	0.68	2	3	0	2.15	800 752-6342
ASAF Alliance Gr & Inc C	Growth/Inc	-7.9	-4.96	0.68	2	3	1	2.15	800 752-6342
ASAF Alliance Gr & Inc X	Growth/Inc	-7.9	-4.98	0.67	2	3	0	2.15	800 752-6342
ASAF Alliance Growth A	Growth	-10.6	-18.92	-3.25	4	4	5.75	1.8	800 752-6342
ASAF Alliance Growth B	Growth	-11	-19.3	-3.72	4	4	0	2.3	800 752-6342
ASAF Alliance Growth C	Growth	-11.1	-19.32	-3.77	4	4	1	2.3	800 752-6342
ASAF Alliance Growth X	Growth	-11	-19.3	-3.74	4	4	0	2.3	800 752-6342
ASAF American Century Intl Gr A	Foreign	-19.4	-20.07	-9.82	4	2	5.75	2.1	800 752-6342
ASAF American Century Intl Gr B	Foreign	-19.6	-20.46	-10.25	4	2	0	2.6	800 752-6342
ASAF American Century Intl Gr C	Foreign	-19.7	-20.46	-10.25	4	2	1	2.6	800 752-6342
ASAF American Century Intl Gr X	Foreign	-19.7	-20.46	-10.25	4	2	0	2.6	800 752-6342
ASAF American Century Strat Bal A	Balanced	-0.2	-3.08	2.41	2	1	5.75	1.65	800 752-6342
ASAF American Century Strat Bal B	Balanced	-0.7	-3.56	1.86	2	1	0	2.15	800 752-6342
ASAF American Century Strat Bal C	Balanced	-0.7	-3.56	1.86	2	1	1	2.15	800 752-6342
ASAF American Century Strat Bal X	Balanced	-0.8	-3.58	1.86	2	1	0	2.15	800 752-6342
ASAF DeAM International Equity A	Foreign	-14.1	-21.96	-6.54	5	3	5.75	2.2	800 752-6342
ASAF DeAM International Equity B	Foreign	-14.9	-22.44	-7.08	5	3	0	2.7	800 752-6342
ASAF DeAM International Equity C	Foreign	-14.9	-22.46	-7.13	5	3	1	2.7	800 752-6342
ASAF DeAM International Equity X	Foreign	-15	-22.44	-7.08	5	3	0	2.7	800 752-6342
ASAF DeAM Small Cap Growth A	Small Co	-8.4	-17.78		4	5	5.75	1.9	800 752-6342
ASAF DeAM Small Cap Growth B	Small Co	-8.7	-18.17		4	5	0	2.4	800 752-6342
ASAF DeAM Small Cap Growth C	Small Co	-8.9	-18.17		4	5	1	2.4	800 752-6342
ASAF DeAM Small Cap Growth X	Small Co	-8.7	-18.16		4	5	0	2.4	800 752-6342
ASAF Gabelli All-Cap Value A	Growth	-6.1					5.75	1.85	800 752-6342
ASAF Gabelli All-Cap Value B	Growth	-6.7					0	2.35	800 752-6342
ASAF Gabelli All-Cap Value C	Growth	-6.6					1	2.35	800 752-6342
ASAF Gabelli All-Cap Value X	Growth	-6.6					0	2.35	800 752-6342
ASAF Gabelli Small Cap Value A	Small Co	-4	7.74	2.79	1	3	5.75	1.9	800 752-6342
ASAF Gabelli Small Cap Value B	Small Co	-4.5	7.25	2.31	1	3	0	2.4	800 752-6342
ASAF Gabelli Small Cap Value C	Small Co	-4.5	7.19	2.27	1	3	1	2.4	800 752-6342
ASAF Gabelli Small Cap Value X	Small Co	-4.5	7.25	2.31	1	3	0	2.4	800 752-6342
ASAF Goldman Sachs Concen Gr A	Growth	-7.8	-24.08	-4.75	5	4	5.75	1.75	800 752-6342
ASAF Goldman Sachs Concen Gr B	Growth	-8.3	-24.46	-5.24	5	4	0	2.25	800 752-6342
ASAF Goldman Sachs Concen Gr C	Growth	-8.3	-24.5	-5.25	4	4	1	2.25	800 752-6342
ASAF Goldman Sachs Concen Gr X	Growth	-8.3	-24.46	-5.21	5	4	0	2.25	800 752-6342
ASAF Goldman Sachs Mid Cap Gr A	Growth	-8.1					5.75	1.9	800 752-6342
ASAF Goldman Sachs Mid Cap Gr B	Growth	-8.1					0	2.4	800 752-6342
ASAF Goldman Sachs Mid Cap Gr C	Growth	-8.4					1	2.4	800 752-6342
ASAF Goldman Sachs Mid Cap Gr X	Growth	-8.2					0	2.4	800 752-6342
ASAF INVESCO Capital Income A	Income	-8	-5.86	0.39	3	2	5.75	1.67	800 752-6342
ASAF INVESCO Capital Income B	Income	-8.3	-6.2	-0.16	3	2	0	2.17	800 752-6342

Stock Fund Name	Objective	Annualized Return for 1 Year	3 Years	5 Years	Rank Overall	Risk	Max Load	Expense Ratio	Toll-Free/(Toll) Telephone
ASAF INVESCO Capital Income C	Income	-8.4	-6.24	0.08	3	2	1	2.17	800 752-6342
ASAF INVESCO Capital Income X	Income	-8.4	-6.24	0.05	3	2	0	2.17	800 752-6342
ASAF INVESCO Health Science Fund A	Health	-6.5					5.75	1.9	800 752-6342
ASAF INVESCO Health Science Fund B	Health	-7					0	2.4	800 752-6342
ASAF INVESCO Health Science Fund C	Health	-7					1	2.4	800 752-6342
ASAF INVESCO Health Science Fund X	Health	-7					0	2.4	800 752-6342
ASAF INVESCO Technology A	Technology	-17.6					5.75	1.9	800 752-6342
ASAF INVESCO Technology B	Technology	-17.9					0	2.4	800 752-6342
ASAF INVESCO Technology C	Technology	-18.2					1	2.4	800 752-6342
ASAF INVESCO Technology X	Technology	-18.2					0	2.4	800 752-6342
ASAF MFS Growth with Income A	Growth/Inc	-9.9	-10.88		3	2	5.75	1.8	800 752-6342
ASAF MFS Growth with Income B	Growth/Inc	-10.3	-11.27		3	2	0	2.3	800 752-6342
ASAF MFS Growth with Income C	Growth/Inc	-10.4	-11.26		3	2	1	2.3	800 752-6342
ASAF MFS Growth with Income X	Growth/Inc	-10.4	-11.34		3	2	0	2.3	800 752-6342
ASAF Marsico Capital Growth A	Growth	-9.6	-10.28		3	3	5.75	1.8	800 752-6342
ASAF Marsico Capital Growth B	Growth	-10.1	-10.75		3	3	0	2.3	800 752-6342
ASAF Marsico Capital Growth C	Growth	-10.1	-10.76		3	3	1	2.3	800 752-6342
ASAF Marsico Capital Growth X	Growth	-10	-10.75		3	3	0	2.3	800 752-6342
ASAF Neuberger&Berman Mid Cap Gr A	Growth	-12.6	-18.16		4	5	5.75	1.85	800 752-6342
ASAF Neuberger&Berman Mid Cap Gr B	Growth	-13.1	-18.6		4	5	0	2.35	800 752-6342
ASAF Neuberger&Berman Mid Cap Gr C	Growth	-13.1	-18.6		4	5	1	2.35	800 752-6342
ASAF Neuberger&Berman Mid Cap Gr X	Growth	-13.1	-18.6		4	5	0	2.35	800 752-6342
ASAF Neuberger&Berman Mid Cp Val A	Growth	-6.1	4.57		2	2	5.75	1.85	800 752-6342
ASAF Neuberger&Berman Mid Cp Val B	Growth	-6.6	4.04		1	2	0	2.35	800 752-6342
ASAF Neuberger&Berman Mid Cp Val C	Growth	-6.6	4.04		2	2	1	2.35	800 752-6342
ASAF Neuberger&Berman Mid Cp Val X	Growth	-6.6	4.01		2	2	0	2.35	800 752-6342
ASAF PBHG Small Cap Growth A	Small Co	-14.4	-18.98	-1.54	4	5	5.75	1.8	800 752-6342
ASAF PBHG Small Cap Growth B	Small Co	-14.8	-19.37	-2.02	4	5	0	2.3	800 752-6342
ASAF PBHG Small Cap Growth C	Small Co	-14.8	-19.37	-2.02	4	5	1	2.3	800 752-6342
ASAF PBHG Small Cap Growth X	Small Co	-14.7	-19.37	-2	4	5	0	2.3	800 752-6342
ASAF ProFund Managed OTC A	Other	-4.7					5.75	1.75	800 752-6342
ASAF ProFund Managed OTC B	Other	-4.8					0	2.25	800 752-6342
ASAF ProFund Managed OTC C	Other	-5.2					1	2.25	800 752-6342
ASAF ProFund Managed OTC X	Other	-5.2					0	2.25	800 752-6342
ASAF Sanford Bernstein Core Val A	Growth	-6.1					5.75	1.7	800 752-6342
ASAF Sanford Bernstein Core Val B	Growth	-6.5					0	2.2	800 752-6342
ASAF Sanford Bernstein Core Val C	Growth	-6.6					1	2.2	800 752-6342
ASAF Sanford Bernstein Core Val X	Growth	-6.6					0	2.2	800 752-6342
ASAF Sanford Bernstein Mgd 500 A	Growth	-9.4	-9.52		3	2	5.75	1.5	800 752-6342
ASAF Sanford Bernstein Mgd 500 B	Growth	-9.9	-9.99		3	2	0	2	800 752-6342
ASAF Sanford Bernstein Mgd 500 C	Growth	-9.9	-9.99		3	2	1	2	800 752-6342
ASAF Sanford Bernstein Mgd 500 X	Growth	-9.9	-10.02		3	2	0	2	800 752-6342
ASAF Strong International Equity A	Foreign	-12.3	-18.01		5	3	5.75	2.1	800 752-6342
ASAF Strong International Equity B	Foreign	-12.6	-18.44		5	3	0	2.6	800 752-6342
ASAF Strong International Equity C	Foreign	-12.7	-18.5		5	3	1	2.6	800 752-6342
ASAF Strong International Equity X	Foreign	-12.6	-18.42		5	3	0	2.6	800 752-6342
ASAF T. Rowe Price Tax-Managed A	Growth	-6.6					5.75		800 752-6342
ASAF T. Rowe Price Tax-Managed B	Growth	-7.2					0		800 752-6342
ASAF T. Rowe Price Tax-Managed C	Growth	-7.1					1		800 752-6342
ASAF T. Rowe Price Tax-Managed X	Growth	-7.1					0		800 752-6342
ASAF William Blair Int Growth A	Foreign	-15.9	-21.8	-4.65	4	3	5.75	2.06	800 752-6342
ASAF William Blair Int Growth B	Foreign	-16.3	-22.21	-5.15	4	3	0	2.56	800 752-6342
ASAF William Blair Int Growth C	Foreign	-16.3	-22.19	-5.11	4	3	1	2.56	800 752-6342
ASAF William Blair Int Growth X	Foreign	-16.3	-22.19	-5.13	4	3	0	2.56	800 752-6342
AXA Premier Health Care A	Health	-4.7					5.5	2.11	866 231-8585
AXA Premier Health Care B	Health	-5					0	2.86	866 231-8585
AXA Premier Health Care C	Health	-5					0	2.86	866 231-8585
AXA Premier Health Care Z	Health	-4.7					0	1.86	866 231-8585

Stock Fund Name	Objective	Annualized Return for			Rank		Max Load	Expense Ratio	Toll-Free/(Toll) Telephone
		1 Year	3 Years	5 Years	Overall	Risk			
AXA Premier International Equity A	Global	-15.7					5.5	2.03	866 231-8585
AXA Premier International Equity B	Global	-15.7					0	2.78	866 231-8585
AXA Premier International Equity C	Global	-15.6					0	2.78	866 231-8585
AXA Premier International Equity Z	Global	-15.6					0	1.78	866 231-8585
AXA Premier Large Cap Core Equity A	Growth	-8.6					5.5	1.81	866 231-8585
AXA Premier Large Cap Core Equity B	Growth	-8.4					0	2.56	866 231-8585
AXA Premier Large Cap Core Equity C	Growth	-8.6					0	2.56	866 231-8585
AXA Premier Large Cap Core Equity Z	Growth	-8.5					0	1.56	866 231-8585
AXA Premier Large Cap Growth A	Growth	-7.6					5.5	1.81	866 231-8585
AXA Premier Large Cap Growth B	Growth	-7.7					0	2.56	866 231-8585
AXA Premier Large Cap Growth C	Growth	-7.7					0	2.56	866 231-8585
AXA Premier Large Cap Growth Z	Growth	-7.6					0	1.56	866 231-8585
AXA Premier Large Cap Value A	Growth/Inc	-11.4					5.5	1.81	866 231-8585
AXA Premier Large Cap Value B	Growth/Inc	-11.4					0	2.56	866 231-8585
AXA Premier Large Cap Value C	Growth/Inc	-11.4					0	2.56	866 231-8585
AXA Premier Large Cap Value Z	Growth/Inc	-11					0	1.56	866 231-8585
AXA Premier Sm/Mid Cap Growth A	Small Co	-16.2					5.5	2.01	866 231-8585
AXA Premier Sm/Mid Cap Growth B	Small Co	-16.8					0	2.76	866 231-8585
AXA Premier Sm/Mid Cap Growth C	Small Co	-17					0	2.76	866 231-8585
AXA Premier Sm/Mid Cap Growth Z	Small Co	-16					0	1.76	866 231-8585
AXA Premier Sm/Mid Cap Value A	Small Co	-13.9					5.5	2.01	866 231-8585
AXA Premier Sm/Mid Cap Value B	Small Co	-14					0	2.76	866 231-8585
AXA Premier Sm/Mid Cap Value C	Small Co	-14.1					0	2.76	866 231-8585
AXA Premier Sm/Mid Cap Value Z	Small Co	-13.9					0	1.76	866 231-8585
AXA Premier Technology A	Technology	-7.7					5.5	2.11	866 231-8585
AXA Premier Technology B	Technology	-8.2					0	2.86	866 231-8585
AXA Premier Technology C	Technology	-8.2					0	2.86	866 231-8585
AXA Premier Technology Z	Technology	-7.7					0	1.86	866 231-8585
AXA Rosenberg Intl Small Cap Inst	Foreign	4	-0.08	2.1	2	3	0.5	1.5	800 447-3332
AXA Rosenberg Intl Small Cap Inv	Foreign	3.8					0.5	1.78	800 447-3332
AXA Rosenberg US Lg/MidCap L/S Inst	Growth/Inc	-2.4	5.09		2	2	0	1.95	800 447-3332
AXA Rosenberg US Small Cap Adv	Small Co	-6.5	8.44	4.37	2	3	0	1.35	800 447-3332
AXA Rosenberg US Small Cap Instl	Small Co	-6.2	8.74	4.59	2	3	0	1.15	800 447-3332
AXA Rosenberg US Small Cap Inv	Small Co	-6.6	8.38	4.32	2	3	0.25	1.5	800 447-3332
AXA Rosenberg Value Lng/Shrt Inst	Growth	2.2	14.34	3.37	2	3	0	2.18	800 447-3332
AXA Rosenberg Value Lng/Shrt Inv	Growth	2	14.03	3.06	2	3	0	2.48	800 447-3332
AXP Blue Chip Advantage A	Growth	-9.5	-13.56	-3.56	4	3	5.75	0.99	800 328-8300
AXP Blue Chip Advantage B	Growth	-10.2					0	1.76	800 328-8300
AXP Discovery Fund Incorp. A	Small Co	-7.8	-10.81	-7.82	4	4	5.75	1.3	800 328-8300
AXP Discovery Fund Incorp. B	Small Co	-8.6	-11.55	-8.56	4	4	0	2.09	800 328-8300
AXP Diversified Equity Income A	Income	-10	-1.69	0.81	3	3	5.75	0.99	800 328-8300
AXP Diversified Equity Income B	Income	-10.9					0	1.76	800 328-8300
AXP Emerging Markets A	Foreign	-10.4					5.75	2.1	800 328-8300
AXP Emerging Markets B	Foreign	-11.1					0	2.88	800 328-8300
AXP Equity Select A	Growth	-7.7	-5.53	2.47	2	4	5.75	1.28	800 328-8300
AXP Equity Select B	Growth	-8.4	-6.25	1.71	3	4	0	2.03	800 328-8300
AXP Equity Value A	Growth/Inc	-14.1					5.75	0.93	800 328-8300
AXP Equity Value B	Growth/Inc	-14.7	-7.42	-3.2	3	3	0	1.71	800 328-8300
AXP European Equity A	European	-14.3					5.75	1.61	800 328-8300
AXP European Equity B	European	-15					0	2.39	800 328-8300
AXP Focused Growth A	Growth	-19					5.75	1.38	800 328-8300
AXP Focused Growth B	Growth	-19.7					0	2.14	800 328-8300
AXP Global Balanced A	Balanced	-0.2					5.75	1.46	800 328-8300
AXP Global Balanced B	Balanced	-0.9	-8.91	-2.47	3	1	0	2.22	800 328-8300
AXP Global Growth A	Global	-12.6	-18.35	-7.21	5	3	5.75	1.45	800 328-8300
AXP Global Growth B	Global	-13.3					0	2.23	800 328-8300
AXP Global Technology A	Technology	-0.7	-33.79	-4.07	3	5	5.75	2.13	800 328-8300
AXP Global Technology B	Technology	-0.8	-34.24	-4.74	3	5	0	2.94	800 328-8300

Stock Fund Name	Objective	Annualized Return for			Rank		Max Load	Expense Ratio	Toll-Free/(Toll) Telephone
		1 Year	3 Years	5 Years	Overall	Risk			
AXP Growth Dimensions A	Growth	-10.2					5.75	1.15	800 328-8300
AXP Growth Dimensions B	Growth	-10.4					0	1.92	800 328-8300
AXP Growth Fund A	Growth	-6.1	-22.3	-6.71	4	4	5.75	1.21	800 328-8300
AXP Growth Fund B	Growth	-6.8					0	1.99	800 328-8300
AXP International Fund A	Foreign	-18.3	-19.96	-9.64	4	3	5.75	1.61	800 328-8300
AXP International Fund B	Foreign	-19	-20.6	-10.33	4	3	0	2.4	800 328-8300
AXP Managed Allocation A	Flexible	-4.4	-4.75	-0.98	2	1	5.75	1.04	800 328-8300
AXP Managed Allocation B	Flexible	-5.2	-5.51	-1.76	2	1	0	1.81	800 328-8300
AXP Mutual A	Balanced	-3.1	-10	-4.62	3	2	5.75	0.95	800 328-8300
AXP Mutual B	Balanced	-3.8	-10.68	-5.37	3	2	0	1.73	800 328-8300
AXP New Dimensions Fund A	Growth	-7.7	-12.18	0.23	3	3	5.75	1.08	800 328-8300
AXP New Dimensions Fund B	Growth	-8.4	-12.85	-0.54	3	3	0	1.85	800 328-8300
AXP Partners Fundamental Value A	Growth	-6.7					5.75	1.34	800 328-8300
AXP Partners Fundamental Value B	Growth	-7.7					0	2.11	800 328-8300
AXP Partners Intl Aggressive Gr A	Other	-13.2					5.75	1.72	800 328-8300
AXP Partners Intl Aggressive Gr B	Other	-14					0	2.52	800 328-8300
AXP Partners Intl Aggressive Gr C	Other	-13.8					0	2.51	800 328-8300
AXP Partners Intl Select Value A	Other	-6.5					5.75	1.64	800 328-8300
AXP Partners Intl Select Value B	Other	-7.1					0	2.42	800 328-8300
AXP Partners Intl Select Value C	Other	-7.2					0	2.42	800 328-8300
AXP Partners Small Cap Growth A	Small Co	-16.8					5.75	1.55	800 328-8300
AXP Partners Small Cap Growth B	Small Co	-17.4					0	2.31	800 328-8300
AXP Partners Small Cap Value A	Growth	-11.9					5.75	1.6	800 328-8300
AXP Partners Small Cap Value B	Growth	-12.5					0	2.37	800 328-8300
AXP Partners Value A	Growth/Inc	-8.1					5.75	1.32	800 328-8300
AXP Partners Value B	Growth/Inc	-8.8					0	2.09	800 328-8300
AXP Precious Metals Fund A	Prec Metal	-14.3	22.51	6.23	2	5	5.75	1.59	800 328-8300
AXP Precious Metals Fund B	Prec Metal	-14.9	21.6	5.42	2	5	0	2.35	800 328-8300
AXP Progressive Fund A	Small Co	-6.9	-6.99	-4.95	3	4	5.75	1.17	800 328-8300
AXP Progressive Fund B	Small Co	-7.6	-7.66	-5.67	3	4	0	1.96	800 328-8300
AXP Research Opportunities Fund A	Growth	-10	-14.91	-3.97	5	3	5.75	1.27	800 328-8300
AXP Research Opportunities Fund B	Growth	-10.6	-15.5	-4.66	5	3	0	2.04	800 328-8300
AXP Small Cap Advantage A	Small Co	-7.2	-2.87		2	4	5.75	1.44	800 328-8300
AXP Small Cap Advantage B	Small Co	-7.8	-3.56		2	4	0	2.21	800 328-8300
AXP Small Company Index Fund A	Small Co	-11.5	2.5	2.24	3	3	5.75	0.98	800 328-8300
AXP Small Company Index Fund B	Small Co	-12.3	1.7	1.44	3	3	0	1.75	800 328-8300
AXP Stock Fund A	Growth/Inc	-9.6	-10.82	-2.64	4	2	5.75	0.93	800 328-8300
AXP Stock Fund B	Growth/Inc	-10.3	-11.51	-3.39	3	2	0	1.71	800 328-8300
AXP Strategy Aggressive A	Agg Growth	-11.8	-22.48	-9.33	4	5	5.75	1.31	800 328-8300
AXP Strategy Aggressive B	Agg Growth	-12.4	-23.07	-5.8	4	5	0	2.1	800 328-8300
AXP Utilities A	Utilities	-7.6	-8.27	-0.67	2	3	5.75	1.15	800 328-8300
AXP Utilities B	Utilities	-8.6	-9.01	-1.45	3	3	0	1.92	800 328-8300
Accessor Fd-Growth Portfolio Adv	Growth	-9.8	-17.32	-3.14	4	3	0	0.8	800 759-3504
Accessor Fd-Growth Portfolio Inv	Growth	-10	-17.69		4	3	0	1.25	800 759-3504
Accessor International Equity Adv	Foreign	-11.7	-15.75	-5.45	3	3	0	1.43	800 759-3504
Accessor International Equity Inv	Foreign	-11.9	-18.19		5	3	0	1.96	800 759-3504
Accessor Small to Mid Cap Adv	Growth	-6.1	-8.33	-2.14	3	4	0	1.13	800 759-3504
Accessor Small to Mid Cap Inv	Growth	-6.4	-10.61		3	4	0	1.52	800 759-3504
Accessor Value Adv	Growth/Inc	-7.7	-7.19	-3.16	3	3	0	0.87	800 759-3504
Activa Growth Fund	Growth	-12.2	-20.5		5	3	0	1.4	800 346-2670
Activa International Fund	Foreign	-14.8	-18.16		4	2	0	1.7	800 346-2670
Adv Inn Cir C & B Mid Cap Val Port	Growth	-7.2	14.5	11.21		2	0	1.4	866 450-3722
Adv Inn Cir CRA Realty Shares Inst	Real Est	4.1	13.77	6.62	1	2	0	1	866 450-3722
Adv Inn Cir Sterling Cap SmCap Val	Small Co	-9.8	7.34	3.58	2	3	0		866 450-3722
Adv Inn Cir-Sterling Cap Bal Fd	Balanced	-1.1	0.3	-0.23	2	1	0		866 450-3722
Advantus Cornerstone Fund A	Growth	-9.8	-5.24	-4.44	3	3	5.5	1.24	800 665-6005
Advantus Cornerstone Fund B	Growth	-10.6	-5.95	-5.16	3	3	0	1.99	800 665-6005
Advantus Cornerstone Fund C	Growth	-10.6	-5.94	-5.11	3	3	0	1.99	800 665-6005

Stock Fund Name	Objective	Annualized Return for			Rank		Max Load	Expense Ratio	Toll-Free/(Toll) Telephone
		1 Year	3 Years	5 Years	Overall	Risk			
Advantus Enterprise Fund A	Small Co	-8.7	-11.82	-3.95	3	5	5.5	1.46	800 665-6005
Advantus Enterprise Fund B	Small Co	-9.4	-12.53	-4.74	3	5	0	2.21	800 665-6005
Advantus Enterprise Fund C	Small Co	-9.4	-12.57	-4.75	3	5	0	2.21	800 665-6005
Advantus Horizon Fund A	Growth	-7.6	-20.55	-6.33	4	4	5.5	1.19	800 665-6005
Advantus Horizon Fund B	Growth	-8.3	-21.14	-7	4	4	0	1.94	800 665-6005
Advantus Horizon Fund C	Growth	-8.3	-21.16	-7.01	4	4	0	1.94	800 665-6005
Advantus Index 500 Fund A	Growth/Inc	-8.8	-11.53	-1.94	3	3	5.5	0.79	800 665-6005
Advantus Index 500 Fund B	Growth/Inc	-9.5	-12.26	-2.79	4	3	0	1.54	800 665-6005
Advantus Index 500 Fund C	Growth/Inc	-9.4	-12.25	-2.79	4	3	0	1.54	800 665-6005
Advantus International Balanced A	Foreign	3	0.23	1.58	2	2	5.5	1.62	800 665-6005
Advantus International Balanced B	Foreign	2.2	-0.52	0.81	2	2	0	2.42	800 665-6005
Advantus International Balanced C	Foreign	2.2	-0.55	0.78	2	2	0	2.42	800 665-6005
Advantus Real Estate Securities A	Real Est	6.8	15.02		1	2	5.5	1.52	800 665-6005
Advantus Spectrum Fund A	AssetAlloc	0.1	-8.5	-0.28	3	3	5.5	1.17	800 665-6005
Advantus Spectrum Fund B	AssetAlloc	-0.6	-9.18	-1.03	3	3	0	1.92	800 665-6005
Advantus Spectrum Fund C	AssetAlloc	-0.7	-9.21	0.11	3	3	0	1.92	800 665-6005
Advantus Venture Fund A	Small Co	-16.5	10.41	2.58	3	4	5.5	1.47	800 665-6005
Advantus Venture Fund B	Small Co	-17.1	9.5	1.72	3	4	0	2.22	800 665-6005
Advantus Venture Fund C	Small Co	-17.1	9.5	1.73	3	4	0	2.22	800 665-6005
Aegis Value Fund	Small Co	5.5	20.14	14.75	1	2	0	1.5	800 528-3780
Al Frank Fund (The)	Growth	-13.8	4.51	11.17	3	4	0	2.25	888 878-3944
Alger Balanced Port A	Balanced	-1.1	-5.08	5.42	1	1	5.25	1.28	800 992-3863
Alger Balanced Port B	Balanced	-1.8	-5.79	4.65	2	1	0	2.03	800 992-3863
Alger Balanced Port C	Balanced	-1.8	-5.79	4.65	2	1	1	2.03	800 992-3863
Alger Balanced Port Inst I	Balanced	-6.1					0		800 992-3863
Alger Balanced Port Inst R	Balanced						0		800 992-3863
Alger Capital Appr Port A	Growth	-11.3	-19.73	-0.56	4	4	5.25	1.53	800 992-3863
Alger Capital Appr Port B	Growth	-12.1	-20.28	-1.26	4	4	0	2.28	800 992-3863
Alger Capital Appr Port C	Growth	-12	-20.35	-1.31	4	4	1	2.28	800 992-3863
Alger Capital Appr Port Inst I	Agg Growth	-10.5	-18.51	4.9	3	4	0		800 992-3863
Alger Capital Appr Port Inst R	Growth						0	1.48	800 992-3863
Alger Health Sciences Port A	Health	8					5.25	2.15	800 992-3863
Alger Health Sciences Port B	Health	7.3					0	2.91	800 992-3863
Alger Health Sciences Port C	Health	7.3					1	2.9	800 992-3863
Alger LargeCap Growth Port A	Growth	-12.1	-16.25	-0.82	4	3	5.25	1.36	800 992-3863
Alger LargeCap Growth Port B	Growth	-12.8	-16.71	-1.44	4	3	0	2.11	800 992-3863
Alger LargeCap Growth Port C	Growth	-12.8	-16.92	-1.58	4	3	1	2.11	800 992-3863
Alger LargeCap Growth Port Inst I	Growth	-13.8	-16.55	0.01	4	4	0	1.09	800 992-3863
Alger LargeCap Growth Port Inst R	Growth						0	1.39	800 992-3863
Alger MidCap Growth Port A	Growth	-8.6	-8.6	6.24	3	4	5.25	1.41	800 992-3863
Alger MidCap Growth Port B	Growth	-9.3	-8.77	5.79	3	4	0	2.15	800 992-3863
Alger MidCap Growth Port C	Growth	-9.3	-9.32	5.41	3	4	1	2.16	800 992-3863
Alger MidCap Growth Port Inst I	Growth	-8.2	-6.66	9.9	3	4	0	1.12	800 992-3863
Alger MidCap Growth Port Inst R	Growth						0	1.42	800 992-3863
Alger SmallCap Port A	Small Co	-10.6	-24.26	-12.01	4	4	5.25	1.75	800 992-3863
Alger SmallCap Port B	Small Co	-11.2	-23.28	-11.56	4	4	0	2.49	800 992-3863
Alger SmallCap Port C	Small Co	-11.2	-24.92	-12.69	4	4	1	2.49	800 992-3863
Alger SmallCap Port Inst I	Small Co	-10.1	-19.32	-4.53	3	4	0	1.18	800 992-3362
Alger SmallCap Port Inst R	Small Co						0	1.5	800 992-3863
Alger SmallCap and MidCap Port A	Growth	-12.2					5.25	1.89	800 992-3863
Alger SmallCap and MidCap Port B	Growth	-12.8					0	2.64	800 992-3863
Alger SmallCap and MidCap Port C	Growth	-12.8					1	2.64	800 992-3863
Alger Social Resp Gr Port Inst I	Growth	-16.6					0		800 992-3863
Alger Social Resp Gr Port Inst R	Growth						0		800 992-3863
AllianceBernstein All-Asia Inv Adv	Pacific	-22.4	-26.07	-5.2	5	3	0	3.96	800 247-4154
AllianceBernstein All-Asia Invest A	Pacific	-22.4	-26.14	-5.45	5	3	4.25	4.26	800 247-4154
AllianceBernstein All-Asia Invest B	Pacific	-23.2	-26.71	-6.2	5	3	0	5.11	800 247-4154
AllianceBernstein All-Asia Invest C	Pacific	-22.8	-26.58	-6.12	5	3	0	5	800 247-4154

Stock Fund Name	Objective	Annualized Return for			Rank		Max Load	Expense Ratio	Toll-Free/(Toll) Telephone
		1 Year	3 Years	5 Years	Overall	Risk			
AllianceBernstein Bal Shrs Adv	Balanced	2	2.62	5.33	1	1	0	0.79	800 247-4154
AllianceBernstein Balanced Shares A	Balanced	1.7	2.35	5.05	1	1	4.25	1.07	800 247-4154
AllianceBernstein Balanced Shares B	Balanced	1	1.59	4.28	1	1	0	1.82	800 247-4154
AllianceBernstein Balanced Shares C	Balanced	1	1.59	4.29	1	1	0	1.81	800 247-4154
AllianceBernstein Consrv Inv A	Balanced	6.8	2.06	3.7	2	1	4.25	1.4	800 247-4154
AllianceBernstein Consrv Invest B	Balanced	6.1	1.35	2.97	2	1	0	2.1	800 247-4154
AllianceBernstein Consrv Invest C	Balanced	6.1	1.37	2.97	2	1	0	2.1	800 247-4154
AllianceBernstein Displd Value A	Growth	-6.3	2.18			4	4.25	1.59	800 247-4154
AllianceBernstein Displd Value B	Growth	-6.9	1.71			4	0	2.32	800 247-4154
AllianceBernstein Displd Value C	Growth	-6.9	1.75			4	0	2.3	800 247-4154
AllianceBernstein Emer Mkts Val	Foreign	2.7	-0.36		2	3	0	1.73	(212 756-4097)
AllianceBernstein Gbl Sm Cap A	Global	-17.4	-20.69	-8.24	5	4	4.25	3.26	800 247-4154
AllianceBernstein Gbl Sm Cap Adv	Global	-17.1	-20.5	-8.01	5	4	0	2.96	800 247-4154
AllianceBernstein Gbl Sm Cap B	Global	-18	-21.35	-8.98	5	4	0	4.09	800 247-4154
AllianceBernstein Gbl Sm Cap C	Global	-18	-21.32	-8.98	5	4	0	4.02	800 247-4154
AllianceBernstein Global Value A	Other	-7					4.25	1.76	800 247-4154
AllianceBernstein Global Value Adv	Other	-6.9					0	1.23	800 247-4154
AllianceBernstein Global Value B	Other	-7.1					0	2.45	800 247-4154
AllianceBernstein Global Value C	Other	-7					0	2.4	800 247-4154
AllianceBernstein Gr Invest Fd A	AssetAlloc	-3.3	-7.44	0.02	2	1	4.25	1.75	800 247-4154
AllianceBernstein Gr Invest Fd B	AssetAlloc	-4.1	-8.15	-0.71	3	1	0	2.49	800 247-4154
AllianceBernstein Gr Invest Fd C	AssetAlloc	-4	-8.11	-0.69	2	1	0	2.46	800 247-4154
AllianceBernstein Growth & Inc dv	Growth/Inc	-11	-5.01	2.49	2	3	0	0.86	800 247-4154
AllianceBernstein Growth & Income A	Growth/Inc	-11	-5.16	2.25	2	3	4.25	1.14	800 247-4154
AllianceBernstein Growth & Income B	Growth/Inc	-11.7	-5.94	1.42	3	3	0	1.88	800 247-4154
AllianceBernstein Growth & Income C	Growth/Inc	-11.9	-5.95	1.41	2	3	0	1.86	800 247-4154
AllianceBernstein Growth Fund A	Growth	-9.2	-19.71	-6.36	4	4	4.25	1.49	800 247-4154
AllianceBernstein Growth Fund Adv	Growth	-9	-19.48	-6.08	4	4	0	1.18	800 247-4154
AllianceBernstein Growth Fund B	Growth	-9.9	-20.3	-7.04	4	4	0	2.22	800 247-4154
AllianceBernstein Growth Fund C	Growth	-9.8	-20.28	-7.01	4	4	0	2.19	800 247-4154
AllianceBernstein Grtr China 97 A	Pacific	-9.9	-6.79	5.5	3	3	4.25	2.5	800 247-4154
AllianceBernstein Grtr China 97 Adv	Pacific	-9.5	-6.45	5.83	3	3	0	2.2	800 247-4154
AllianceBernstein Grtr China 97 B	Pacific	-10.5	-7.51	4.66	3	3	0	3.2	800 247-4154
AllianceBernstein Grtr China 97 C	Pacific	-10.5	-7.48	4.66	3	3	0	3.2	800 247-4154
AllianceBernstein Health Care A	Health	-3.8	-3.33		2	2	4.25	1.85	800 247-4154
AllianceBernstein Health Care B	Health	-4.4					0	2.6	800 247-4154
AllianceBernstein Health Care C	Health	-4.4	-4		2	2	0	2.57	800 247-4154
AllianceBernstein Intl Prem Gr A	Foreign	-15	-18.42	-6.44	4	3	4.25	2.47	800 247-4154
AllianceBernstein Intl Prem Gr Adv	Foreign	-14.5	-18.16	-6.15	4	3	0	2.18	800 247-4154
AllianceBernstein Intl Prem Gr B	Foreign	-15.5	-19.05	-7.12	5	3	0	3.2	800 247-4154
AllianceBernstein Intl Prem Gr C	Foreign	-15.4	-19	-7.08	5	3	0	3.2	800 247-4154
AllianceBernstein Intl Value A	Other	-5.3					4.25	1.2	800 247-4154
AllianceBernstein Intl Value Adv	Other	-5.2					0	0.9	800 247-4154
AllianceBernstein Intl Value B	Other	-5.6					0	1.9	800 247-4154
AllianceBernstein Intl Value C	Other	-5.6					0	1.9	800 247-4154
AllianceBernstein Mid-Cap Gr Adv	Growth	1.9	-11.83	-5.45	3	4	0	1.08	800 247-4154
AllianceBernstein Mid-Cap Growth A	Growth	1.9	-12.03	-5.66	3	4	4.25	1.34	800 247-4154
AllianceBernstein Mid-Cap Growth B	Growth	0.8	-12.78	-6.49	3	4	0	2.2	800 247-4154
AllianceBernstein Mid-Cap Growth C	Growth	1.1	-12.83	-6.58	3	4	0	2.16	800 247-4154
AllianceBernstein New Europe A	European	-12.9	-14.02	-6.37	5	4	4.25	2.47	800 247-4154
AllianceBernstein New Europe Adv	European	-12.7	-13.91	-6.17	5	4	0	2.16	800 247-4154
AllianceBernstein New Europe B	European	-13.7	-14.77	-7.12	4	4	0	3.27	800 247-4154
AllianceBernstein New Europe C	European	-13.7	-14.75	-7.11	4	4	0	3.19	800 247-4154
AllianceBernstein Prem Gr Adv	Growth	-13	-22.8	-6.24	5	4	0	1.45	800 247-4154
AllianceBernstein Prem Gr Instl A	Growth	-11.6	-21.42	-5.11	5	4	0	0.9	800 247-4154
AllianceBernstein Prem Gr Instl B	Growth	-12	-21.69	-5.42	5	4	0	1.2	800 247-4154
AllianceBernstein Premier Growth A	Growth	-13.2	-23.03	-6.54	5	4	4.25	1.73	800 247-4154
AllianceBernstein Premier Growth B	Growth	-13.9	-23.62	-7.2	5	4	0	2.47	800 247-4154

Stock Fund Name	Objective	Annualized Return for			Rank		Max Load	Expense Ratio	Toll-Free/(Toll) Telephone
		1 Year	3 Years	5 Years	Overall	Risk			
AllianceBernstein Premier Growth C	Growth	-13.9	-23.6	-7.2	5	4	0	2.45	800 247-4154
AllianceBernstein Quasar Fund A	Small Co	-13.4	-11.03	-9.32	4	5	4.25	1.92	800 247-4154
AllianceBernstein Quasar Fund Adv	Small Co	-13.2	-13.69	-10.85	4	5	0	1.6	800 247-4154
AllianceBernstein Quasar Fund B	Small Co	-14.2	-15.14	-12.11	5	5	0	2.72	800 247-4154
AllianceBernstein Quasar Fund C	Small Co	-14.2	-15.11	-12.1	5	5	0	2.71	800 247-4154
AllianceBernstein Quasar Instl A	Small Co	-11.5	-5.8	-4.82	3	5	0	1.2	800 247-4154
AllianceBernstein Quasar Instl B	Small Co	-12	-6.34	-5.24	3	5	0	1.5	800 247-4154
AllianceBernstein RE Inv Instl I	Real Est	3.9	11.68	4.45	2	1	0	1.19	800 247-4154
AllianceBernstein RE Inv Instl II	Real Est	3.5	11.34	4.13	2	1	0	1.49	800 247-4154
AllianceBernstein Real Est Iv A	Real Est	4.2	12.93	4.76	2	2	4.25	1.75	800 247-4154
AllianceBernstein Real Est Iv Adv	Real Est	4.4	13.27	5.05	1	2	0	1.51	800 247-4154
AllianceBernstein Real Est Iv B	Real Est	3.4	12.16	4.03	2	2	0	2.47	800 247-4154
AllianceBernstein Real Est Iv C	Real Est	3.5	12.17	4.05	2	2	0	2.46	800 247-4154
AllianceBernstein Sel Inv Prem A	Growth	-13.1	-20.55		5	4	4.25	1.86	800 247-4154
AllianceBernstein Sel Inv Prem B	Growth	-13.8	-21.12		5	4	0	2.57	800 247-4154
AllianceBernstein Sel Inv Prem C	Growth	-13.8	-21.12		5	4	0	2.59	800 247-4154
AllianceBernstein Sm Cap Value A	Small Co	-6.3					4.25	1.4	800 247-4154
AllianceBernstein Sm Cap Value Adv	Small Co	-6					0	1.1	800 247-4154
AllianceBernstein Sm Cap Value B	Small Co	-7					0	2.1	800 247-4154
AllianceBernstein Sm Cap Value C	Small Co	-7					0	2.1	800 247-4154
AllianceBernstein Tax-Mgd Intl Val	Foreign	-6.9	-3.79	-0.84	3	3	0	1.25	800 221-5672
AllianceBernstein Technology Adv	Technology	-17.2	-28.62	-2.35	4	5	0	1.49	800 247-4154
AllianceBernstein Technology Fund A	Technology	-17.4	-28.82	-2.64	4	5	4.25	1.85	800 247-4154
AllianceBernstein Technology Fund B	Technology	-18.1	-29.37	-5.51	4	5	0	2.58	800 247-4154
AllianceBernstein Technology Fund C	Technology	-18.1	-29.37	-3.37	4	5	0	2.55	800 247-4154
AllianceBernstein Utility Inc A	Utilities	-2.1	-7.19	2.45	2	2	4.25	1.5	800 247-4154
AllianceBernstein Utility Inc Adv	Utilities	-1.8	-6.92	2.75	2	2	0	1.2	800 247-4154
AllianceBernstein Utility Inc B	Utilities	-2.7	-7.84	1.73	3	2	0	2.2	800 247-4154
AllianceBernstein Utility Inc C	Utilities	-2.8	-7.83	1.72	3	2	0	2.2	800 247-4154
AllianceBernstein Value A	Income	-7					4.25	1.45	800 247-4154
AllianceBernstein Value Adv	Income	-6.7					0	1.23	800 247-4154
AllianceBernstein Value B	Income	-7.6					0	2.18	800 247-4154
AllianceBernstein Value C	Income	-7.6					0	2.16	800 247-4154
AllianceBernstein WW Priv A	Foreign	-4.4	-10.33	-1.79	3	3	4.25	2.27	800 247-4154
AllianceBernstein WW Priv Adv	Foreign	-4.2	-10.1	-1.53	3	3	0	1.97	800 247-4154
AllianceBernstein WorldWide Priv B	Foreign	-5.2	-11.02	-2.54	3	3	0	3.05	800 247-4154
AllianceBernstein WorldWide Priv C	Foreign	-5.2	-11	-2.54	3	3	0	3.04	800 247-4154
Alpha Analytics Value Fund	Growth	-6.6	1.03		2	3	0	1.3	877 257-4240
Alpha Select Target Select Equity	Growth	-17.6	-37.78	-9.8	4	5	0	1.21	800 224-6312
Alpine Intl Real Estate Y	Real Est	1.7	10.1	2.41	2	2	0	1.81	888 785-5578
Alpine Realty Inc & Growth Y	Real Est	10.7	17.82		1	1	0		888 785-5578
Alpine U.S. Real Estate Eq Y	Real Est	14.7	26.87	6.96	2	4	0	1	888 785-5578
AmSouth Aggressive Growth Port A	Agg Growth	-11.3	-7.57		3	3	5.5	0.79	800 451-8379
AmSouth Aggressive Growth Port B	Agg Growth	-11.9	-8.26		3	3	0	1.52	800 451-8379
AmSouth Aggressive Growth Port Tr	Agg Growth	-11.2	-7.51		3	3	0	0.72	800 451-8379
AmSouth Balanced A	Balanced	1	4.03	4	1	1	5.5	1.31	800 451-8379
AmSouth Balanced B	Balanced	0.2	3.24	3.22	1	1	0	2.06	800 451-8379
AmSouth Balanced Tr	Balanced	1.2	4.17	4.17	1	1	0	1.16	800 451-8379
AmSouth Cap Gr A	Growth	-10.2	-14.08	-1.17	3	3	5.5	1.3	800 451-8379
AmSouth Cap Gr B	Growth	-10.9	-14.68	-1.87	4	3	0	1.96	800 451-8379
AmSouth Cap Gr Tr	Growth	-10.2	-13.94	-3.2	3	3	0	1.11	800 451-8379
AmSouth Enhanced Market A	Growth	-9.7	-11.67		4	3	5.5	1.04	800 451-8379
AmSouth Enhanced Market B	Growth	-10.4	-12.33		4	3	0	1.8	800 451-8379
AmSouth Enhanced Market Tr	Growth	-9.6	-11.56		4	3	0	0.9	800 451-8379
AmSouth Gr & Inc Port A	Growth/Inc	-1	-0.7		1	1	5.5	0.63	800 451-8379
AmSouth Gr & Inc Port B	Growth/Inc	-1.8	-1.12		1	1	0	1.37	800 451-8379
AmSouth Gr & Inc Port Tr	Growth/Inc	-1.1	-0.32		1	1	0	0.57	800 451-8379
AmSouth Growth Port A	Growth	-4.7	-3.56		1	1	5.5	0.78	800 451-8379

Stock Fund Name	Objective	Annualized Return for			Rank		Max Load	Expense Ratio	Toll-Free/(Toll) Telephone
		1 Year	3 Years	5 Years	Overall	Risk			
AmSouth Growth Port B	Growth	-5.5	-4.29		1	1	0	1.53	800 451-8379
AmSouth Growth Port Tr	Growth	-4.7	-3.5		1	1	0	0.73	800 451-8379
AmSouth International Equity A	Foreign	-9.9	-11.81	-5.69	4	3	5.5	1.62	800 451-8379
AmSouth International Equity B	Foreign	-10.2	-12.32			3	0	2.38	800 451-8379
AmSouth International Equity Tr	Foreign	-9.4	-11.56	-5.54	4	3	0	1.47	800 451-8379
AmSouth Large Cap A	Growth	-8.8	-10.16	1.38	3	3	5.5	1.25	800 451-8379
AmSouth Large Cap B	Growth	-9.4	-10.83	-0.27	3	3	0	2	800 451-8379
AmSouth Large Cap Tr	Growth	-8.7	-10.02	1.47	3	3	0	1.1	800 451-8379
AmSouth Mid Cap A	Growth	-8.3	-13.86		5	4	5.5	1.57	800 451-8379
AmSouth Mid Cap B	Growth	-9	-14.6		5	4	0	2.32	800 451-8379
AmSouth Mid Cap Tr	Growth	-8.2	-13.83		4	4	0	1.42	800 451-8379
AmSouth Moder Gr & Inc Port A	Growth/Inc	0.6	1.71		1	1	5.5	0.77	800 451-8379
AmSouth Moder Gr & Inc Port B	Growth/Inc	-0.2	0.94		1	1	0	1.51	800 451-8379
AmSouth Moder Gr & Inc Port Tr	Growth/Inc	0.8	1.79		1	1	0	0.71	800 451-8379
AmSouth Select Equity Fund A	Growth	-1.8	8.27		2	2	5.5	1.71	800 451-8379
AmSouth Select Equity Fund B	Growth	-2.6	7.54		2	2	0	2.44	800 451-8379
AmSouth Select Equity Fund Tr	Growth	-1.7	8.46			2	0	1.56	800 451-8379
AmSouth Small Cap A	Small Co	-19.7	-14.97	-4.74	4	3	5.5	1.61	800 451-8379
AmSouth Small Cap B	Small Co	-20.3	-15.57		4	3	0	2.36	800 451-8379
AmSouth Small Cap Tr	Small Co	-19.6	-14.82	-4.54	4	3	0	1.46	800 451-8379
AmSouth Value Fd A	Growth	-19.5	-5.29	-1.65	3	3	5.5	1.34	800 451-8379
AmSouth Value Fd B	Growth	-20.1	-6.01	-2.41	3	3	0	2.09	800 451-8379
AmSouth Value Fd Tr	Growth	-19.4	-5.17	-1.48	3	3	0	1.19	800 451-8379
Amana Growth Fund	Growth	-9.7	-11.39		3	3	0	1.55	800 728-8762
Amana Mutual Fund-Income Fund	Income	-8.8	-5.79	-2.25	3	2	0	1.57	800 728-8762
American AAdvant Bal Inst	Balanced	-1.6	5.07	2.72	1	1	0	0.62	800 967-9009
American AAdvant Bal PlanAhead	Balanced	-1.5	4.98	2.54	1	1	0	0.84	800 967-9009
American AAdvant Intl Eq Inst	Foreign	-12.7	-6.7	-1.45	3	3	0	0.78	800 967-9009
American AAdvant Intl Eq PlanAhd	Foreign	-12.6	-6.83	-1.63	3	3	0	1.1	800 967-9009
American AAdvant Lg Cp Val Inst	Growth/Inc	-9	1.6	-0.3	3	3	0	0.64	800 967-9009
American AAdvant Lg Cp Val PlanAhd	Growth/Inc	-9.4	1.32	-0.59	3	3	0	0.89	800 967-9009
American AAdvant S&P 500 Inst	Growth	-8	-10.84	-1.12	3	3	0	0.15	800 967-9009
American AAdvant S&P 500 PlanAhd	Growth	-8.8	-11.49	-1.69	3	3	0	0.55	800 967-9009
American Century Balanced Adv	Balanced	0.7	-2.72	1.43	2	1	0	1.15	800 378-9878
American Century Balanced Inv	Balanced	1	-2.27	1.84	1	1	0	0.9	800 378-9878
American Century Emerging Mkts Inv	Foreign	-17	-13.92	-1.25	3	4	0	2.05	800 378-9878
American Century Eq Growth Adv	Growth	-6.6	-10.59	-2.14	3	3	0	0.61	800 378-9878
American Century Eq Growth Inst	Growth	-6.2	-10.19	-1.71	3	3	0	1.06	800 378-9878
American Century Eq Growth Inv	Growth	-6.4	-10.39	-1.92	3	3	0	0.69	800 378-9878
American Century Eq Income Adv	Income	0.8	10.66	7.79	1	1	0	1.25	800 378-9878
American Century Eq Income Inst	Income	1.2	11.39			1	0	0.8	800 378-9878
American Century Eq Income Inv	Income	1	11.11	8.17	1	1	0	1	800 378-9878
American Century Eq Index Inv	Income	-8.7	-11.25			3	0	0.49	800 378-9878
American Century Giftrust	Small Co	-16.3	-22.73	-5.82	5	5	0	1	800 378-9878
American Century Global Gold Adv	Prec Metal	-8.1	28.14	6.9	2	5	0	0.69	800 378-9878
American Century Global Gold Inv	Prec Metal	-7.9	28.76	7.33	2	5	0	0.94	800 378-9878
American Century Global Growth Inv	Global	-13.9	-13.88		4	3	0	1.32	800 378-9878
American Century Global Nat Res Fd	Energy/Res	-8.1	0.88	3.33	2	3	0	0.7	800 378-9878
American Century Growth Adv	Growth	-10.3	-17.71	-2.25	4	3	0	1.25	800 378-9878
American Century Growth Inst	Growth	-9.9	-17.26	-1.76	4	3	0	0.8	800 378-9878
American Century Growth Inv	Growth	-10.1	-17.48	-1.98	3	3	0	1	800 378-9878
American Century Heritage Adv	Growth	-14.2	-10.07	1.21	3	3	0	1.25	800 378-9878
American Century Heritage Inst	Growth	-13.9	-9.59	1.69	3	3	0	0.8	800 378-9878
American Century Heritage Inv	Growth	-14.1	-9.81	1.5	3	3	0	1	800 378-9878
American Century Inc & Gr Adv	Growth/Inc	-7.8	-8.96	-1.05	3	3	0	0.94	800 378-9878
American Century Inc & Gr Inst	Growth/Inc	-7.3	-8.52	-0.57	3	3	0	0.49	800 378-9878
American Century Inc & Gr Inv	Growth/Inc	-7.6	-8.65	-0.71	3	3	0	0.69	800 378-9878
American Century Intl Disc Adv	Foreign	-8.9	-15.9	-0.77	3	3	0	1.78	800 378-9878

284

Stock Fund Name	Objective	Annualized Return for 1 Year	3 Years	5 Years	Rank Overall	Risk	Max Load	Expense Ratio	Toll-Free/(Toll) Telephone
American Century Intl Disc Inst	Foreign	-8.5	-12.21	1.97	3	3	0	1.33	800 378-9878
American Century Intl Disc Inv	Foreign	-8.8	-12.38	1.8	3	3	0	1.53	800 378-9878
American Century Intl Gr A	Foreign						5.75	1.5	800 378-9878
American Century Intl Gr Adv	Foreign	-15.4	-17.3	-4.09	3	2	0	1.5	800 378-9878
American Century Intl Gr B	Foreign						0	2.25	800 378-9878
American Century Intl Gr C	Foreign						0	2.25	800 378-9878
American Century Intl Gr Inst	Foreign	-14.9	-16.91	-3.64	4	2	0	1.05	800 378-9878
American Century Intl Gr Inv	Foreign	-15.2	-17.12	-3.89	3	2	0	1.25	800 378-9878
American Century Life Sciences Adv	Other						0	1.75	800 378-9878
American Century Lrge Comp Val A	Growth						5.75		800 378-9878
American Century Lrge Comp Val Adv	Growth	-6.5					0	1.15	800 378-9878
American Century Lrge Comp Val B	Growth						0		800 378-9878
American Century Lrge Comp Val Inv	Growth	-6.3	3.56			2	0	0.9	800 378-9878
American Century New Opp Inv	Agg Growth	-17.6	-23.08	3.83	4	5	0	1.5	800 378-9878
American Century Real Estate Adv	Real Est	8					0	1.43	800 378-9878
American Century Real Estate Inst	Real Est	8.4	15.39	7.11	1	1	0	0.98	800 378-9878
American Century Real Estate Inv	Real Est	8.2	15.16	6.84	1	1	0	1.18	800 378-9878
American Century Select Adv	Growth	-8.6	-13.74	-1.59	3	2	0	1.25	800 378-9878
American Century Select Inst	Growth	-8.2	-13.3	-1.12	3	2	0	0.8	800 378-9878
American Century Select Inv	Growth	-8.4	-13.49	-1.34	3	2	0	1	800 378-9878
American Century Sm Cap Val Adv	Small Co	-8.4	18.89		2	3	0	1.5	800 378-9878
American Century Sm Cap Val Inv	Small Co	-8.2	18.19		2	3	0	1.25	800 378-9878
American Century Small Company Inv	Small Co	-2.6	5.98		2	3	0	0.88	800 378-9878
American Century Str Alloc:Agg Adv	AssetAlloc	-5.4	-6.04	2.33	2	2	0	1.45	800 378-9878
American Century Str Alloc:Agg Inv	AssetAlloc	-5.2	-5.79	2.6	1	2	0	1.2	800 378-9878
American Century Str Alloc:Con Adv	AssetAlloc	0.8	1.95	3.95	2	1	0	1.25	800 378-9878
American Century Str Alloc:Con Inv	AssetAlloc	1.2	2.25	4.24	2	1	0	1	800 378-9878
American Century Str Alloc:Mod Adv	AssetAlloc	-1.9	-2.31	3.12	2	1	0	1.35	800 378-9878
American Century Str Alloc:Mod Inv	AssetAlloc	-1.8	-1.9	3.45	2	1	0	1.1	800 378-9878
American Century Technology Adv	Technology	-10.5					0	1.75	800 378-9878
American Century Technology Fd	Technology	-10.6					0	1.5	800 378-9878
American Century Ultra Adv	Agg Growth	-10.7	-14.39	-1.14	4	3	0	1.24	800 378-9878
American Century Ultra Inst	Agg Growth	-10.2	-13.93	-0.72	3	3	0	0.79	800 378-9878
American Century Ultra Inv	Agg Growth	-10.4	-14.14	-0.93	4	3	0	0.99	800 378-9878
American Century Utilities Inv	Utilities	-5.7	-12.97	-2.29	3	2	0	0.69	800 378-9878
American Century VP Ultra I	Growth						0	0	800 378-9878
American Century VP Ultra Totl Inst	Agg Growth	-10.6					0		800 378-9878
American Century Value A	Growth/Inc						0		800 378-9878
American Century Value Adv	Growth/Inc	-5.1	7.84	4.04	2	2	0	1.25	800 378-9878
American Century Value B	Growth/Inc						0		800 378-9878
American Century Value C	Growth/Inc						0	2	800 378-9878
American Century Value Inst	Growth/Inc	-4.7	8.26	4.48	1	2	0	0.8	800 378-9878
American Century Value Inv	Growth/Inc	-5	8.15	4.33	1	2	0	1	800 378-9878
American Century Veedot Inv	Agg Growth	-8.9	-12.32			3	0	1.5	800 378-9878
American Century Vista Adv	Agg Growth	-8.4	-12.63	3.72	3	4	0	1.25	800 378-9878
American Century Vista Inst	Agg Growth	-8	-12.15	4.17	3	4	0	0.8	800 378-9878
American Century Vista Inv	Agg Growth	-8.2	-12.34	3.99	3	4	0	1.25	800 378-9878
American Funds AMCAP A	Growth	-2.9	-2.91	6.2	1	3	5.75	0.77	800 421-4120
American Funds AMCAP B	Growth	-3.7	-3.68		1	3	0	1.55	800 421-4120
American Funds AMCAP C	Growth	-3.7					0	1.59	800 421-4120
American Funds AMCAP F	Growth	-2.9	-3	6.12	1	3	0	0.82	800 421-4120
American Funds AMCAP R1	Growth	-3.7	-3.72	5.3		3	0	1.57	800 421-4120
American Funds AMCAP R2	Growth	-3.6	-3.68	5.36		3	0	1.52	800 421-4120
American Funds AMCAP R3	Growth	-3.2	-3.29	5.78		3	0	1.13	800 421-4120
American Funds AMCAP R4	Growth	-3	-2.99	6.12		3	0	0.8	800 421-4120
American Funds AMCAP R5	Growth						0	0.5	800 421-4120
American Funds Balanced A	Balanced	0	7.12	6.75	1	1	5.75	0.7	800 421-4120
American Funds Balanced B	Balanced	-0.7	6.33		1	1	0	1.46	800 421-4120

Stock Fund Name	Objective	Annualized Return for			Rank		Max Load	Expense Ratio	Toll-Free/(Toll) Telephone
		1 Year	3 Years	5 Years	Overall	Risk			
American Funds Balanced C	Balanced	-0.8					0	1.51	800 421-4120
American Funds Balanced F	Balanced	0	7.07	6.69	1	1	0	0.72	800 421-4120
American Funds Balanced R1	Balanced	-0.8	6.28	5.9		1	0	1.83	800 421-4120
American Funds Balanced R2	Balanced	-0.8	6.32	5.94		1	0	1.54	800 421-4120
American Funds Balanced R3	Balanced	-0.3	6.74	6.36		1	0	1.08	800 421-4120
American Funds Balanced R4	Balanced	0	7.08	6.7		1	0	0.75	800 421-4120
American Funds Balanced R5	Balanced						0	0.39	800 421-4120
American Funds Cap Inc Builder A	Income	0.1	7.98	5.4	1	1	5.75	0.67	800 421-4120
American Funds Cap Inc Builder B	Income	-0.7	6.79		1	1	0	1.44	800 421-4120
American Funds Cap Inc Builder C	Income	-0.8					0	1.52	800 421-4120
American Funds Cap Inc Builder F	Income	-0.1	7.82	5.28	1	1	0	0.79	800 421-4120
American Funds Cap Inc Builder R1	Income	-0.7	7.08	4.58		1	0	1.52	800 421-4120
American Funds Cap Inc Builder R2	Income	-0.7	7.12	4.62		1	0	1.47	800 421-4120
American Funds Cap Inc Builder R3	Income	-0.3	7.54	5.04		1	0	1.08	800 421-4120
American Funds Cap Inc Builder R4	Income	0.1	7.91	5.38		1	0	0.75	800 421-4120
American Funds Cap Inc Builder R5	Income	0.4	8.24	5.63		1	0	0.45	800 421-4120
American Funds Cap Wld Gr&Inc A	Global	-5.3	-1.1	5.03	1	2	5.75	0.82	800 421-4120
American Funds Cap Wld Gr&Inc B	Global	-6.1	-1.86		1	2	0	1.59	800 421-4120
American Funds Cap Wld Gr&Inc C	Global	-6.2					0	1.65	800 421-4120
American Funds Cap Wld Gr&Inc F	Global	-5.4	-1.19	4.94	1	2	0	0.91	800 421-4120
American Funds Cap Wld Gr&Inc R1	Global	-6.1	-1.93	4.12		2	0	1.64	800 421-4120
American Funds Cap Wld Gr&Inc R2	Global	-6.1	-1.88	4.19		2	0	1.59	800 421-4120
American Funds Cap Wld Gr&Inc R3	Global	-5.7	-1.51	4.58		2	0	1.2	800 421-4120
American Funds Cap Wld Gr&Inc R4	Global	-5.4	-1.14	4.95		2	0	0.87	800 421-4120
American Funds Cap Wld Gr&Inc R5	Global	-5.1	-0.86	5.25		2	0	0.56	800 421-4120
American Funds Endowments Gr & Inc	Growth/Inc	-3.5	4.57	5.28	1	2	0	0.66	800 421-4120
American Funds EuroPacific Gr A	Foreign	-11.6	-11.78	0.72	3	2	5.75	0.9	800 421-4120
American Funds EuroPacific Gr B	Foreign	-12.3	-12.47		3	2	0	1.68	800 421-4120
American Funds EuroPacific Gr C	Foreign	-12.3					0	1.74	800 421-4120
American Funds EuroPacific Gr F	Foreign	-11.6	-11.83	0.67	3	2	0	0.94	800 421-4120
American Funds EuroPacific Gr R1	Foreign	-12.2	-12.47	-0.07		2	0	1.7	800 421-4120
American Funds EuroPacific Gr R2	Foreign	-12.3	-12.47	-0.04		2	0	1.65	800 421-4120
American Funds EuroPacific Gr R3	Foreign	-12	-12.14	0.34		2	0	1.26	800 421-4120
American Funds EuroPacific Gr R4	Foreign	-12.1	-12	0.56		2	0	0.93	800 421-4120
American Funds EuroPacific Gr R5	Foreign						0	0.63	800 421-4120
American Funds Fundamental Inv A	Growth/Inc	-10.4	-7.01	2.04	3	3	5.75	0.67	800 421-4120
American Funds Fundamental Inv B	Growth/Inc	-11.1	-7.74		3	3	0	1.45	800 421-4120
American Funds Fundamental Inv C	Growth/Inc	-11.2					0	1.5	800 421-4120
American Funds Fundamental Inv F	Growth/Inc	-10.5	-7.07	2	3	3	0	0.72	800 421-4120
American Funds Fundamental Inv R1	Growth/Inc	-11.2	-7.79	1.21		3	0	1.5	800 421-4120
American Funds Fundamental Inv R2	Growth/Inc	-11.2	-7.75	1.26		3	0	1.46	800 421-4120
American Funds Fundamental Inv R3	Growth/Inc	-10.8	-7.38	1.65		3	0	1.08	800 421-4120
American Funds Fundamental Inv R4	Growth/Inc	-10.4	-7.05	2		3	0	0.73	800 421-4120
American Funds Fundamental Inv R5	Growth/Inc						0	0.41	800 421-4120
American Funds Gr Fnd of Amer A	Growth	-4.6	-8.77	7.83	2	3	5.75	0.75	800 421-4120
American Funds Gr Fnd of Amer B	Growth	-5.3	-9.48		3	3	0	1.52	800 421-4120
American Funds Gr Fnd of Amer C	Growth	-5.4					0	1.55	800 421-4120
American Funds Gr Fnd of Amer F	Growth	-4.6	-8.82	7.78	2	3	0	0.77	800 421-4120
American Funds Gr Fnd of Amer R1	Growth	-5.4	-9.51	6.95		3	0	1.52	800 421-4120
American Funds Gr Fnd of Amer R2	Growth	-5.4	-9.48	7		3	0	1.47	800 421-4120
American Funds Gr Fnd of Amer R3	Growth	-5	-9.14	7.42		3	0	1.08	800 421-4120
American Funds Gr Fnd of Amer R4	Growth	-4.6	-8.82	7.79		3	0	0.75	800 421-4120
American Funds Gr Fnd of Amer R5	Growth						0	0.45	800 421-4120
American Funds Inc Fnd of Amer A	Income	-0.1	6.17	4.51	1	1	5.75	0.61	800 421-4120
American Funds Inc Fnd of Amer B	Income	-0.9	5.36		1	1	0	1.37	800 421-4120
American Funds Inc Fnd of Amer C	Income	-0.9					0	1.48	800 421-4120
American Funds Inc Fnd of Amer F	Income	-0.1	6.08	4.44	1	1	0	0.73	800 421-4120
American Funds Inc Fnd of Amer R1	Income	-0.9	5.25	3.6		1	0	1.47	800 421-4120

286

Stock Fund Name	Objective	Annualized Return for 1 Year	3 Years	5 Years	Rank Overall	Risk	Max Load	Expense Ratio	Toll-Free/(Toll) Telephone
American Funds Inc Fnd of Amer R2	Income	-1.1	5.24	3.62		1	0	1.42	800 421-4120
American Funds Inc Fnd of Amer R3	Income	-0.5	5.7	4.05		1	0	1.03	800 421-4120
American Funds Inc Fnd of Amer R4	Income	-0.1	6.08	4.41		1	0	0.7	800 421-4120
American Funds Inc Fnd of Amer R5	Income						0	0.4	800 421-4120
American Funds Inv Co of Amer A	Growth/Inc	-7.3	-3.87	3.41	2	2	5.75	0.59	800 421-4120
American Funds Inv Co of Amer B	Growth/Inc	-8	-4.63		2	2	0	1.39	800 421-4120
American Funds Inv Co of Amer C	Growth/Inc	-8					0	1.45	800 421-4120
American Funds Inv Co of Amer F	Growth/Inc	-7.4	-3.97	3.31	2	2	0	0.7	800 421-4120
American Funds Inv Co of Amer R1	Growth/Inc	-8	-4.7	2.52		2	0	2.16	800 421-4120
American Funds Inv Co of Amer R2	Growth/Inc	-8	-4.65	2.56		2	0	1.56	800 421-4120
American Funds Inv Co of Amer R3	Growth/Inc	-7.7	-4.29	2.95		2	0	1.11	800 421-4120
American Funds Inv Co of Amer R4	Growth/Inc	-7.4	-3.97	3.29		2	0	0.72	800 421-4120
American Funds Inv Co of Amer R5	Growth/Inc	-7.1	-3.68	3.6		2	0	0.37	800 421-4120
American Funds Mutual Fund A	Growth/Inc	-6.6	2.81	3.31	2	2	5.75	0.6	800 421-4120
American Funds Mutual Fund B	Growth/Inc	-7.4	2.02		2	2	0	1.4	800 421-4120
American Funds Mutual Fund C	Growth/Inc	-7.5					0	1.48	800 421-4120
American Funds Mutual Fund F	Growth/Inc	-6.8	2.64	3.18	2	2	0	0.75	800 421-4120
American Funds Mutual Fund R1	Growth/Inc	-7.5	1.9	2.39		2	0	1.48	800 421-4120
American Funds Mutual Fund R2	Growth/Inc	-7.5	1.91	2.41		2	0	1.43	800 421-4120
American Funds Mutual Fund R3	Growth/Inc	-7.1	2.35	2.83		2	0	1.04	800 421-4120
American Funds Mutual Fund R4	Growth/Inc	-6.7	2.7	3.18		2	0	0.71	800 421-4120
American Funds Mutual Fund R5	Growth/Inc						0	0.41	800 421-4120
American Funds New Economy A	Growth	-8.1	-14.81	-0.44	3	4	5.75	0.89	800 421-4120
American Funds New Economy B	Growth	-8.8	-15.48		4	4	0	1.69	800 421-4120
American Funds New Economy C	Growth	-8.8					0	1.7	800 421-4120
American Funds New Economy F	Growth	-8.1	-14.86	-0.5	3	4	0	1	800 421-4120
American Funds New Economy R1	Growth	-8.7	-15.46	-1.21		4	0	1.64	800 421-4120
American Funds New Economy R2	Growth	-8.8	-15.43	-1.17		4	0	2	800 421-4120
American Funds New Economy R3	Growth	-8.4	-15.09	-0.79		4	0	1.2	800 421-4120
American Funds New Economy R4	Growth	-8.1	-14.81	-0.46		4	0	0.87	800 421-4120
American Funds New Economy R5	Growth						0	0.56	800 421-4120
American Funds New Perspective A	Global	-9.3	-8.83	3.54	3	3	5.75	0.82	800 421-4120
American Funds New Perspective B	Global	-10	-9.52		2	3	0	1.6	800 421-4120
American Funds New Perspective C	Global	-10					0	1.64	800 421-4120
American Funds New Perspective F	Global	-9.3	-8.89	3.47	3	3	0	0.88	800 421-4120
American Funds New Perspective R1	Global	-10.1	-9.61	2.64		3	0	1.63	800 421-4120
American Funds New Perspective R2	Global	-9.9	-9.52	2.72		3	0	1.58	800 421-4120
American Funds New Perspective R3	Global	-9.6	-9.18	3.12		3	0	1.19	800 421-4120
American Funds New Perspective R4	Global	-9.3	-8.9	3.47		3	0	0.86	800 421-4120
American Funds New Perspective R5	Global						0	0.56	800 421-4120
American Funds New World A	Global	-5.1					5.75	1.34	800 421-4120
American Funds New World B	Global	-5.8	-4.28		2	3	0	2.15	800 421-4120
American Funds New World C	Global	-5.8					0	2.14	800 421-4120
American Funds New World F	Global	-5.1	-3.64		2	3	0	1.38	800 421-4120
American Funds New World R1	Global	-5.8	-4.25			3	0	2.1	800 421-4120
American Funds New World R2	Global	-5.7	-4.2			3	0	2.05	800 421-4120
American Funds New World R3	Global	-5	-3.72			3	0	1.66	800 421-4120
American Funds New World R4	Global	-5.1	-3.54			3	0	1.33	800 421-4120
American Funds New World R5	Global						0	1.03	800 421-4120
American Funds SMALLCAP World A	Global	-10.9	-13.93	-1.57	4	4	5.75	1.17	800 421-4120
American Funds SMALLCAP World B	Global	-11.6	-14.61		5	4	0	1.95	800 421-4120
American Funds SMALLCAP World C	Global	-11.6					0	1.96	800 421-4120
American Funds SMALLCAP World F	Global	-10.9	-13.99	-1.62	4	4	0	1.2	800 421-4120
American Funds SMALLCAP World R1	Global	-11.6	-14.61	-2.35		4	0	1.91	800 421-4120
American Funds SMALLCAP World R2	Global	-11.5	-14.56	-2.29		4	0	1.86	800 421-4120
American Funds SMALLCAP World R3	Global	-11.2	-14.24	-1.92		4	0	1.47	800 421-4120
American Funds SMALLCAP World R4	Global	-10.9	-13.94	-1.6		4	0	1.14	800 421-4120
American Funds SMALLCAP World R5	Global						0	0.84	800 421-4120

Stock Fund Name	Objective	Annualized Return for			Rank		Max Load	Expense Ratio	Toll-Free/(Toll) Telephone
		1 Year	3 Years	5 Years	Overall	Risk			
American Funds Wash Mutual Inv A	Growth/Inc	-8.8	-0.19	2.12	3	2	5.75	0.65	800 421-4120
American Funds Wash Mutual Inv B	Growth/Inc	-9.6	-0.96		2	2	0	1.41	800 421-4120
American Funds Wash Mutual Inv C	Growth/Inc	-9.6					0	1.51	800 421-4120
American Funds Wash Mutual Inv F	Growth/Inc	-8.9	-0.28	2.04	3	2	0	0.78	800 421-4120
American Funds Wash Mutual Inv R1	Growth/Inc	-9.6	-1.03	1.28		2	0	1.49	800 421-4120
American Funds Wash Mutual Inv R2	Growth/Inc	-9.6	-1	1.32		2	0	1.44	800 421-4120
American Funds Wash Mutual Inv R3	Growth/Inc	-9.2	-0.57	1.71		2	0	1.05	800 421-4120
American Funds Wash Mutual Inv R4	Growth/Inc	-8.9	-0.26	2.06		2	0	0.72	800 421-4120
American Funds Wash Mutual Inv R5	Growth/Inc						0	0.42	800 421-4120
American Growth Fund A	Growth	-11.9	-28.17	-18.96	4	5	5.75	5.05	800 525-2406
American Growth Fund B	Growth	-12.8	-28.8	-19.62	4	5	0	5.81	800 525-2406
American Growth Fund C	Growth	-13.1	-28.87	-19.67	4	5	0	5.86	800 525-2406
American Growth Fund D	Growth	-11.7	-27.62	-18.48	4	5	5.75	4.86	800 525-2406
American Heritage Fund	Agg Growth	-45.4	-39.42	-42.2				12.6	800 828-5050
American Heritage Growth Fund	Growth	-12.5					0	14.7	800 828-5050
American Independence Stock Fd	Growth	-8.2	1.65	0.68	3	3	0	1.29	800 342-1223
American Performance Balanced	Balanced	-1.6	-2.64	1.62	2	1	5	0.7	800 762-7085
American Performance Equity Fund	Growth	-12.3	-11.58	-4.28	4	3	5	1.03	800 762-7085
American Performance Growth Equity	Growth	-9.4	-16.78		3	3	5	1.03	800 762-7085
American Trust Allegiance Fd	Growth	-10.7	-17.57	-0.65	3	4	0	1.45	800 385-7003
Amerindo Technology D	Technology	45.5	-30.64	2.77	3	5	0	2.25	888 832-4386
Ameristock Mutual Fund	Growth/Inc	-9.6	1.4	5.36	2	3	0	0.77	800 394-5064
Ameritor Investment	Agg Growth	-27.4					0	8.83	800 424-8570
Ameritor Security Trust	Agg Growth	-18.5					0	6.07	800 424-8570
Analysts Inv-Stock Fund	Growth	-6	-9.33	-1.44	3	3	0	2	(513 792-5402)
Apex Mid-Cap Growth Fund	Agg Growth	10	-29.37	-19.92	4	5	5.75		877 593-8637
Aquila Rocky Mountain Equity A	Growth	-6.3	-1.32	2.08	2	3	4.25	1.3	800 437-1020
Aquila Rocky Mountain Equity C	Growth	-6.9	-2.04	1.41	2	3	0	2.05	800 437-1020
Aquila Rocky Mountain Equity Y	Growth	-6	-1.07	2.33	2	3	0	1.05	800 437-1020
Aquinas Growth Fund	Growth	-13.2	-11.14	-0.57	2	3	0	1.5	800 423-6369
Aquinas Small-Cap Fund	Small Co	-17.1	-11.56	-5.45	4	3	0	1.95	800 423-6369
Aquinas Value Fund	Income	-13.4	-7.65	-4.8	3	2	0	1.49	800 423-6369
Ariel Appreciation Fund	Growth	-8.7	11.01	7.79	2	3	0	1.26	800 292-7435
Ariel Fund	Small Co	-8.4	13.21	7.84	2	2	0	1.19	800 292-7435
Ariston Convertible Secs	Converts	7	-17.1	1.27	3	5	0	2.25	888 387-2273
Armada Aggressive Allocation A	AssetAlloc	-8.7					4.75	1.37	800 622-3863
Armada Aggressive Allocation B	AssetAlloc	-9.3					0	1.98	800 622-3863
Armada Aggressive Allocation C	AssetAlloc	-9.3					0	1.98	800 622-3863
Armada Aggressive Allocation Inst	AssetAlloc	-8.6					0	1.12	800 622-3863
Armada Balanced Allocation A	Balanced	-4.8	-7.26			2	4.75	1.25	800 622-3863
Armada Balanced Allocation B	Balanced	-5.5	-7.79			1	0	1.96	800 622-3863
Armada Balanced Allocation C	Balanced	-5.5	-7.98			2	0	1.96	800 622-3863
Armada Balanced Allocation H	Balanced	-5.4					0	2.02	800 622-3863
Armada Balanced Allocation Inst	Balanced	-4.6	-3.85		2	1	0	1	800 622-3863
Armada Conservative Allocation A	AssetAlloc	0.9					4.75	1.27	800 622-3863
Armada Conservative Allocation B	AssetAlloc	0.3					0	1.88	800 622-3863
Armada Conservative Allocation C	AssetAlloc	0.3					0	1.88	800 622-3863
Armada Conservative Allocation Inst	AssetAlloc	1.2					0	1.02	800 622-3863
Armada Core Equity A	Growth	-11.2	-8.8	1.34	3	3	5.5	1.22	800 622-3863
Armada Core Equity B	Growth	-11.8					0	1.93	800 622-3863
Armada Core Equity C	Growth	-11.7	-9.4			3	0	1.93	800 622-3863
Armada Core Equity H	Growth	-11.8					0	1.94	800 622-3863
Armada Core Equity Inst	Growth	-10.9	-8.52	1.62	3	3	0	0.97	800 622-3863
Armada Equity Growth A	Growth	-12.3	-14.74	-2.58	4	3	5.5	1.17	800 622-3863
Armada Equity Growth B	Growth	-12.9					0	1.88	800 622-3863
Armada Equity Growth C	Growth	-12.9	-15.32			3	0	1.88	800 622-3863
Armada Equity Growth H	Growth	-12.9					0	1.88	800 622-3863
Armada Equity Growth Inst	Growth	-12	-14.5	-2.31	4	3	0	0.92	800 622-3863

Stock Fund Name	Objective	Annualized Return for			Rank		Max Load	Expense Ratio	Toll-Free/(Toll) Telephone
		1 Year	3 Years	5 Years	Overall	Risk			
Armada Equity Index A	Growth/Inc	-8.6	-11.31		3	3	3.75	0.58	800 622-3863
Armada Equity Index B	Growth/Inc	-9.4	-12.03		4	3	0	1.33	800 622-3863
Armada Equity Index C	Growth/Inc	-9.4	-12.02		4	3	0	1.33	800 622-3863
Armada Equity Index H	Growth/Inc	-9.4					0	1.27	800 622-3863
Armada Equity Index Inst	Growth/Inc	-8.5	-11.13		3	3	0	0.33	800 622-3863
Armada International Equity A	Foreign	-16.1	-16.6	-4.12	5	3	5.5	1.59	800 622-3863
Armada International Equity B	Foreign	-16.6	-18.96	-6.12		3	0	2.3	800 622-3863
Armada International Equity C	Foreign	-16.6	-18.96			3	0	2.3	800 622-3863
Armada International Equity H	Foreign	-16.6					0	2.14	800 622-3863
Armada International Equity Inst	Foreign	-15.9	-16.39	-3.91	5	3	0	1.34	800 622-3863
Armada Large Cap Ultra A	Growth/Inc	-13.2	-22.1	-5.87	5	4	4.5	1.25	800 622-3863
Armada Large Cap Ultra B	Growth/Inc	-13.8	-22.64	-6.54	5	4	0	1.96	800 622-3863
Armada Large Cap Ultra C	Growth/Inc	-13.8					0	1.96	800 622-3863
Armada Large Cap Ultra H	Growth/Inc	-13.8					0	1.88	800 622-3863
Armada Large Cap Ultra Inst	Growth/Inc	-13	-21.89	-5.59	4	4	0	1	800 622-3863
Armada Large Cap Value A	Growth/Inc	-9.8	-0.92	-0.3	3	2	5.5	1.17	800 622-3863
Armada Large Cap Value B	Growth/Inc	-10.4	-2.29	-1.67		2	0	1.88	800 622-3863
Armada Large Cap Value C	Growth/Inc	-10.4	-2.14			2	0	1.88	800 622-3863
Armada Large Cap Value H	Growth/Inc	-10.5					0	1.84	800 622-3863
Armada Large Cap Value Inst	Growth/Inc	-9.5	-0.64	-0.02	3	2	0	0.92	800 622-3863
Armada Midcap Growth A	Growth	-12.5	-18.94	-2.7	3	4	4.5	1.52	800 622-3863
Armada Midcap Growth B	Growth	-13	-19.53	-3.43	4	4	0	2.23	800 622-3863
Armada Midcap Growth C	Growth	-13.2					0	2.23	800 622-3863
Armada Midcap Growth H	Growth						0		800 622-3863
Armada Midcap Growth Inst	Growth	-12.2	-18.71	-2.47	3	4	0	1.27	800 622-3863
Armada Small Cap Growth A	Small Co	-16.3	-17.37	-6.29	4	4	5.5	1.49	800 622-3863
Armada Small Cap Growth B	Small Co	-17	-19.48	-8.17		4	0	2.2	800 622-3863
Armada Small Cap Growth C	Small Co	-16.9	-19.39			4	0	2.2	800 622-3863
Armada Small Cap Growth H	Small Co	-16.8					0	2.19	800 622-3863
Armada Small Cap Growth Inst	Small Co	-16.1	-17.17	-6.04	4	4	0	1.24	800 622-3863
Armada Small Cap Value A	Small Co	-9.9	11.97	8.58	2	3	5.5	1.41	800 622-3863
Armada Small Cap Value B	Small Co	-10.6	11.16	5.62		3	0	2.12	800 622-3863
Armada Small Cap Value C	Small Co	-10.5	11.16			3	0	2.12	800 622-3863
Armada Small Cap Value H	Small Co	-10.5					0	2.12	800 622-3863
Armada Small Cap Value Inst	Small Co	-9.7	12.24	8.96	2	3	0	1.16	800 622-3863
Armada Small/Midcap Value A	Small Co						5.5	1.49	800 622-3863
Armada Small/Midcap Value Inst	Small Co						0	1.24	800 622-3863
Armada Tax Managed Equity A	Growth	-14.2	-12.66	-0.66	4	2	5.5	1.18	800 622-3863
Armada Tax Managed Equity B	Growth	-14.8	-13.25	-1.36	4	2	0	1.89	800 622-3863
Armada Tax Managed Equity C	Growth	-14.7	-13.34		4	2	0	1.89	800 622-3863
Armada Tax Managed Equity H	Growth	-14.8					0	1.87	800 622-3863
Armada Tax Managed Equity Inst	Growth	-13.9	-12.42	-0.53	4	2	0	0.93	800 622-3863
Armstrong Associates	Growth	-4	-9.16	-0.14	3	2	0	1.3	(214 720-9101)
Artisan International Fund Inv	Foreign	-18.6	-14.33	3.24	4	3	0	1.21	800 344-1770
Artisan Mid Cap Fund	Growth	-9	-3.47	14.15	2	4	0	1.22	800 344-1770
Artisan Small Cap Fund	Small Co	-11	-2.02	-1.28	3	4	0	1.31	800 344-1770
Artisan Small Cap Value	Small Co	-2.3	12.69	7.57	1	2	0	1.2	800 344-1770
Atalanta Sosnoff Fund	Other	-3.7	-5.5		2	3	0	1.5	877 767-6633
Atlantic Whitehall Balanced	Balanced	-3.4	-5.5	4.16	2	2	0	1.39	800 994-2533
Atlantic Whitehall Growth Fund	Growth	-9.2	-15.03	3.18	3	4	0	1.33	800 994-2533
Atlas Balanced Fund A	Balanced	-5.5	-6.32	-5.58	3	2	3	1.22	800 933-2852
Atlas Global Growth Fund A	Global	-14.8	-9.5	3.87	3	3	0	1.55	800 933-2852
Atlas Growth & Income Fund A	Growth/Inc	-5.4	-9.49	1.68	3	3	0	1.09	800 933-2852
Atlas Strategic Growth Fund A	Growth	-12	-20.66	-6.66	4	4	3	1.26	800 933-2852
Austin Global Equity Fund	Global	-12.2	-16.37	-2.37	5	3	0	2.24	800 754-8759
Avatar Advantage Balanced Fund	Balanced	-2.4	-6.25	0.56	3	1	0	1.4	888 263-6452
Avatar Advantage Equity Alloc Fd	AssetAlloc	-10	-15.3	-4.21	3	2	0	1.46	888 263-6452
BB&K International Equity	Foreign	-8.6	-12.01	-4.79	4	2	0	1.34	800 882-8383

Stock Fund Name	Objective	Annualized Return for			Rank		Max Load	Expense Ratio	Toll-Free/(Toll) Telephone
		1 Year	3 Years	5 Years	Overall	Risk			
BB&T Balanced A	Balanced	-5.6	-3.66	-1.08	2	1	5.75	1.28	800 228-1872
BB&T Balanced B	Balanced	-6.3	-4.37	-1.83	2	1	0	2.04	800 228-1872
BB&T Balanced Tr	Balanced	-5.4	-3.41	-0.83	2	1	0	1.19	800 228-1872
BB&T Capital Manager Agg Gr A	Agg Growth	-11.3					5.75	0.9	800 228-1872
BB&T Capital Manager Agg Gr B	Agg Growth	-12.9					0	1.67	800 228-1872
BB&T Capital Manager Agg Gr C	Agg Growth	-12.8					0	1.94	800 228-1872
BB&T Capital Manager Conserv Gr A	Growth/Inc	-0.7	-1.18	1.76	2	1	5.75	1.21	800 228-1872
BB&T Capital Manager Conserv Gr B	Growth/Inc	-1.1	-1.44	1.44		1	0	1.53	800 228-1872
BB&T Capital Manager Conserv Gr C	Growth/Inc	-1.6	-1.43	1.53		1	0	1.52	800 228-1872
BB&T Capital Manager Conserv Gr Tr	Growth/Inc	-0.5	-0.54	2.27	2	1	0	0.71	800 228-1872
BB&T Capital Manager Growth A	Growth	-9.4	-8.61	-0.91		2	5.75	0.87	800 228-1872
BB&T Capital Manager Growth B	Growth	-10.2	-9.35	-2		2	0	1.62	800 228-1872
BB&T Capital Manager Growth C	Growth	-10.1	-9.23	-1.9		2	0	1.61	800 228-1872
BB&T Capital Manager Growth Tr	Growth	-9.2	-8.41	-1.28	3	2	0	0.66	800 228-1872
BB&T Capital Manager Mod Gr A	Growth/Inc	-5.6	-4.96	0.22		1	5.75	0.81	800 228-1872
BB&T Capital Manager Mod Gr B	Growth/Inc	-6.3	-5.7	-0.4		1	0	1.56	800 228-1872
BB&T Capital Manager Mod Gr C	Growth/Inc	-6.3	-5.79	-0.34		1	0	1.58	800 228-1872
BB&T Capital Manager Mod Gr Tr	Growth/Inc	-5.5	-4.75	0.39	2	1	0	0.71	800 228-1872
BB&T Equity Index A	Growth	-8.5					5.75	0.55	800 228-1872
BB&T Equity Index B	Growth	-9.2					0	1.3	800 228-1872
BB&T International Equity A	Foreign	-19.8	-16.32	-6.91	5	2	5.75	1.98	800 228-1872
BB&T International Equity B	Foreign	-20.2	-16.89	-7.54	4	2	0	2.48	800 228-1872
BB&T International Equity Tr	Foreign	-19.6	-16.1	-6.66	5	2	0	1.48	800 228-1872
BB&T Large Company Growth A	Growth	-9	-17.92	-3.12	4	3	5.75	1.28	800 228-1872
BB&T Large Company Growth B	Growth	-12.7	-18.64	-3.83	4	3	0	2.03	800 228-1872
BB&T Large Company Growth Tr	Growth	-8.7	-17.73	-2.81	4	3	0	1.19	800 228-1872
BB&T Large Company Value A	Growth/Inc	-13.1	-3.33	-0.81	3	2	5.75	1.23	800 228-1872
BB&T Large Company Value B	Growth/Inc	-13.7	-4.05	-1.59	3	2	0	1.98	800 228-1872
BB&T Large Company Value Tr	Growth/Inc	-12.9	-3.08	-0.57	3	2	0	1.94	800 228-1872
BB&T Mid Cap Growth A	Growth	-9.7	-8.97	8.52	3	4	5.75	1.17	800 228-1872
BB&T Mid Cap Growth B	Growth	-10.6	-17.55	-2.12	4	3	0	1.76	800 228-1872
BB&T Mid Cap Growth C	Growth	-10.4	-16.14	-1.37		3	0	1.81	800 228-1872
BB&T Mid Cap Growth Tr	Growth	-9.4	-15.28	-0.46		3	0	1.02	800 228-1872
BB&T Mid Cap Value A	Growth	-8.5	1.85	3.81		2	5.75	1.15	800 228-1872
BB&T Mid Cap Value B	Growth	-9.2	1.12	3.35		2	0	1.91	800 228-1872
BB&T Mid Cap Value C	Growth	-9.2	1.11	3.35		2	0	1.91	800 228-1872
BB&T Mid Cap Value Tr	Growth	-8.2	2.1	4.08		2	0	1.57	800 228-1872
BB&T Small Company Growth A	Small Co	-12.7	-23.73	-6.23	5	4	5.75	1.73	800 228-1872
BB&T Small Company Growth B	Small Co	-13.3	-24.3	-8.66	5	4	0	2.47	800 228-1872
BB&T Small Company Growth Tr	Small Co	-12.5	-23.55	-5.99	5	4	0	1.47	800 228-1872
BBH European Equity	European	-10.6	-13.58	-5.17	5	3	0	1.46	800 625-5759
BBH International Eq	Foreign	-14.4	-16.53	-4.59	5	2	0	1.24	800 625-5759
BBH Pacific Basin Eq	Pacific	-27	-24.62	-2.77	5	3	0	1.7	800 625-5759
BBH Tax Efficient Eq	Growth	-6.8	-14.44		4	3	0	1.2	800 625-5759
BNY Hamilton Equity Income Inst	Income	-8.7	-7.74	-0.66	3	2	0	0.89	800 426-9363
BNY Hamilton Equity Income Inv	Income	-8.9	-7.9	-0.84	3	2	0	1.15	800 426-9363
BNY Hamilton International Eq CRT	Other	-11.4	-15.82		5	2	0	1.22	800 426-9363
BNY Hamilton Intl Equity Inst	Foreign	-15.9	-17.73	-6.8	4	2	0	1.44	800 426-9363
BNY Hamilton Intl Equity Inv	Foreign	-16.1	-17.62	-6.83	4	3	0	1.69	800 426-9363
BNY Hamilton Large Cap Gr CRT	Growth	-7.5	-16.01		3	3	0	0.8	800 426-9363
BNY Hamilton Large Cap Gr Inst	Growth	-7.7	-15.84	-1.15	2	3	0	0.9	800 426-9363
BNY Hamilton Large Cap Gr Inv	Growth	-8	-16.05	-1.39	2	3	0	1.15	800 426-9363
BNY Hamilton Large Cap Value Inst	Growth	-3	-3.35		1	3	0	0.8	800 426-9363
BNY Hamilton Multi-Cap Equity Fd	Income	-10.6	-15.22	-1.4	3	4	0	1.3	(617 236-8900)
BNY Hamilton S&P 500 Index Inst	Growth	-8.4	-11.39		3	3	0	0.35	800 426-9363
BNY Hamilton Small Cap Gr CRT	Small Co	-11.4	-5.2		3	4	0	0.96	800 426-9363
BNY Hamilton Small Cap Gr Inst	Small Co	-10.3	-5.62	9.32	3	4	0	1.06	800 426-9363
BNY Hamilton Small Cap Gr Inv	Small Co	-10.3	-5.74	8.84	3	4	0	1.32	800 426-9363

Stock Fund Name	Objective	Annualized Return for			Rank		Max Load	Expense Ratio	Toll-Free/(Toll) Telephone
		1 Year	3 Years	5 Years	Overall	Risk			
Babson Enterprise Fund	Small Co	-6.4	14.92	4.75	1	3	0	1.08	866 409-2550
Babson Enterprise Fund II	Small Co	-12.3	5.16	2.25	3	3	0	1.3	866 409-2550
Babson Growth Fund	Growth	-12.9	-17.05	-5.08	4	4	0	0.85	866 409-2550
Babson Value Fund	Growth/Inc	-16.3	-0.26	-1.57	3	2	0	0.96	866 409-2550
Babson-Stewart Ivory International	Foreign	-18.6	-20.07	-8.75	4	3	0	1.65	866 409-2550
Banc Stock Group A	Financial	8.3					4	1.7	888 226-5595
Banknorth Large Cap Core	Growth	-8.3	-8	2.31	3	2	4	1.13	888 247-4505
Barclays Gbl Inv Asset All Fd	AssetAlloc	0.6	-3.87	2.43	2	2	0	0.75	888 204-3956
Barclays Gbl Inv LifePath 2010 Fd	AssetAlloc	-1.1	-0.72	2.87	2	1	0	0.89	888 204-3956
Barclays Gbl Inv LifePath 2020 Fd	AssetAlloc	-3.2	-4.66	1.15	2	1	0	0.89	888 204-3956
Barclays Gbl Inv LifePath 2030 Fd	AssetAlloc	-4.8	-7.12	0.11	2	2	0	0.89	888 204-3956
Barclays Gbl Inv LifePath 2040 Fd	AssetAlloc	-6.4	-10.01	-1.12	3	3	0	0.9	888 204-3956
Barclays Gbl Inv LifePath Inc Fd	AssetAlloc	2.5	3.35	4.26	2	1	0	0.95	888 204-3956
Barclays Gbl Inv S&P500 Stock Fd	Growth	-8.2	-11.03	-1.3	3	3	0	0.22	888 204-3956
Baron Asset Fund	Small Co	-15.5	-6.37	-1.93	3	4	0	1.38	800 992-2766
Baron Growth Fund	Growth	-7.7	5.45	8.3	2	3	0	1.36	800 992-2766
Baron Small Cap	Small Co	-8	0.71	6.69	2	4	0	1.37	800 992-2766
Baron iOpportunity Fund	Technology	15.2					0	1.5	800 992-2766
Barrett Growth Fund	Growth	-6.3	-15.75		3	3	0	1.25	(414 765-5519)
Bear Stearns Alpha Grth Ptfl A	Growth	-7.8	-0.92	6.48	3	2	5.5	0.56	800 766-4111
Bear Stearns Alpha Grth Ptfl B	Growth	-8	-1.32	5.95	3	2	0	0.56	800 766-4111
Bear Stearns Alpha Grth Ptfl C	Growth	-7.9	-1.3	5.98	3	2	0	0.56	800 766-4111
Bear Stearns Insiders Select A	Growth	-13	1.66	1.73	3	3	5.5	0.52	800 766-4111
Bear Stearns Insiders Select B	Growth	-13.4	1.14	0.16	3	3	0	0.52	800 766-4111
Bear Stearns Insiders Select C	Growth	-13.5	1.12	1.2	3	3	0	0.52	800 766-4111
Bear Stearns Insiders Select Y	Growth	-12.3	2.22	2.24	3	3	0	0.52	800 766-4111
Bear Stearns International Eq A	Foreign	-22.4	-21	-4.63	3	2	5.5	0.57	800 766-4111
Bear Stearns International Eq B	Foreign	-22.8	-21.39	-5.13	3	2	0	0.57	800 766-4111
Bear Stearns International Eq C	Foreign	-22.7	-21.37	-5.12	3	2	0	0.57	800 766-4111
Bear Stearns Intrinsic Value A	Growth	-10.1	3.08	2.37	2	3	5.5	0.43	800 766-4111
Bear Stearns Intrinsic Value B	Growth	-10.7					0	0.43	800 766-4111
Bear Stearns Intrinsic Value C	Growth	-10.6	2.56	1.86	2	3	0	0.43	800 766-4111
Bear Stearns Intrinsic Value Y	Growth	-9.2	3.75	3	2	3	0	0.43	800 766-4111
Bear Stearns S&P STARS A	Growth/Inc	-17.4	-18.6	-0.07	4	4	5.5	0.16	800 766-4111
Bear Stearns S&P STARS B	Growth/Inc	-17.8	-19	-0.56	4	4	0	0.16	800 766-4111
Bear Stearns S&P STARS C	Growth/Inc	-17.9	-19.01	-0.59	4	4	0	0.16	800 766-4111
Bear Stearns S&P STARS Opp Port A	Growth	-10.5					5.5	0.44	800 766-4111
Bear Stearns S&P STARS Opp Port B	Growth	-11.1					0	0.44	800 766-4111
Bear Stearns S&P STARS Opp Port C	Growth	-11					0	0.44	800 766-4111
Bear Stearns S&P STARS Y	Growth/Inc	-16.8	-18.16	0.46	4	4	0	1	800 766-4111
Bear Stearns Small Cap Value A	Small Co	-15.3	-3.75	-0.41	3	4	5.5	0.48	800 766-4111
Bear Stearns Small Cap Value B	Small Co	-15.9	-4.37	-0.54	3	4	0	0.48	800 766-4111
Bear Stearns Small Cap Value C	Small Co	-15.9	-4.33	-0.32	3	4	0	0.48	800 766-4111
Bear Stearns Small Cap Value Y	Small Co	-14.8	-3.27	0.05	3	4	0	0.48	800 766-4111
Berkshire Focus Fund	Growth	-21.6	-49.78	-10.38	4	5	0	1.97	877 526-0707
Berwyn Fund	Small Co	-7.5	15.26	0.27	2	3	0	1.33	800 992-6757
Berwyn Income Fund	Flexible	10.2	13.33	6.13	1	1	0	1.19	800 992-6757
Bishop Street Equity Inst	Growth	-7.6	-18.46	-5.58	4	3	0	1	800 262-9565
Bjurman Micro-Cap Growth Fund	Small Co	-3.8	12.35	20.89	2	4	0	1.8	800 227-7264
BlackRock Asia Pacific Equity A	Pacific	-21.7					5	1.92	800 441-7762
BlackRock Asia Pacific Equity B	Pacific	-22.6					0	2.65	800 441-7762
BlackRock Asia Pacific Equity C	Pacific	-22.5					0	2.67	800 441-7762
BlackRock Asia Pacific Equity Inst	Pacific	-21.4					0	1.45	800 441-7762
BlackRock Asia Pacific Equity Svc	Pacific	-21.4					0	1.75	800 441-7762
BlackRock Balanced Instl	Balanced	-0.9	-7.2	-0.9	2	1	0	0.92	800 441-7762
BlackRock Balanced Inv A	Balanced	-1.4	-7.65	-1.36	2	1	4.5	1.42	800 441-7762
BlackRock Balanced Inv B	Balanced	-2	-8.32	-2.1	2	1	0	2.16	800 441-7762
BlackRock Balanced Inv C	Balanced	-2.1	-8.41	-2.16	2	1	0	2.16	800 441-7762

Stock Fund Name	Objective	Annualized Return for			Rank		Max Load	Expense Ratio	Toll-Free/(Toll) Telephone
		1 Year	3 Years	5 Years	Overall	Risk			
BlackRock Balanced Svc	Balanced	-1.2	-7.49	-1.19	2	1	0	1.21	800 441-7762
BlackRock European Equity A	European	-19.6					5	1.92	800 441-7762
BlackRock European Equity B	European	-20.2					0	2.65	800 441-7762
BlackRock European Equity C	European	-20.2					0	2.67	800 441-7762
BlackRock European Equity Inst	European	-19.1					0	1.45	800 441-7762
BlackRock GNMA Portfolio Blrk	Other						0		800 441-7762
BlackRock Glb Science & Tech A	Technology	-7.6					5	1.67	800 441-7762
BlackRock Glb Science & Tech Instl	Technology	-7.3					0	1.2	800 441-7762
BlackRock Glb Science & Tech Svc	Technology	-7.7					0	1.5	800 441-7762
BlackRock Index Eq Inst	Growth/Inc	-8.2	-11.01	-1.27	3	3	0	0.18	800 441-7762
BlackRock Index Eq Inv A	Growth/Inc	-8.8	-11.55	-1.83	3	3	3	0.79	800 441-7762
BlackRock Index Eq Inv B	Growth/Inc	-9.4	-12.21	-2.56	4	3	0	1.53	800 441-7762
BlackRock Index Eq Inv C	Growth/Inc	-9.5	-12.22	-2.56	4	3	0	1.53	800 441-7762
BlackRock Index Eq Svc	Growth/Inc	-8.6	-11.4	-1.65	3	3	0	0.61	800 441-7762
BlackRock Intl Eq Inst	Foreign	-19	-20.76	-10.42	4	3	0	1.06	800 441-7762
BlackRock Intl Eq Inv A	Foreign	-19.3	-16.51	-7.76	5	2	5	1.55	800 441-7762
BlackRock Intl Eq Inv B	Foreign	-20	-21.87	-11.64	4	3	0	2.27	800 441-7762
BlackRock Intl Eq Inv C	Foreign	-19.4	-21.62	-11.46	4	3	0	2.31	800 441-7762
BlackRock Intl Eq Svc	Foreign	-19.2	-21.03	-10.73	4	3	0	1.36	800 441-7762
BlackRock Intl Opp Inv A	Foreign	-10.4	-8.08	11.08	3	2	5	1.8	800 441-7762
BlackRock Intl Opp Inv C	Foreign	-11	-8.77	8.26	3	2	4.5	2.55	800 441-7762
BlackRock Large Cap Gr Inst	Growth	-12.4	-27.05	-9.21	4	4	0	0.82	800 441-7762
BlackRock Large Cap Gr Inv B	Growth	-13.6	-27.96	-10.34	5	4	0	2.04	800 441-7762
BlackRock Large Cap Gr Svc	Growth	-12.8	-27.3	-9.55	5	4	0	1.12	800 441-7762
BlackRock Large Cap Val Inv A	Growth/Inc	-11.2	-6.13	-3.75	3	3	4.5	1.27	800 441-7762
BlackRock Large Cap Val Inv C	Growth/Inc	-11.8	-6.83	-4.49	3	3	0	2.01	800 441-7762
BlackRock Mid Cap Growth Eq A	Growth	-9.6	-21.03	4.44	3	4	4.5	1.62	800 441-7762
BlackRock Mid Cap Growth Eq C	Growth	-10.2	-21.53	3.7	3	4	0	2.37	800 441-7762
BlackRock Mid Cap Growth Eq Svc	Growth	-9.4	-20.89	4.63	3	4	0	1.45	800 441-7762
BlackRock Mid Cap Value Eq B	Growth/Inc	-15	-0.94	-2.27	3	2	0	2.37	800 441-7762
BlackRock Mid Cap Value Eq Inst	Growth/Inc	-13.9	0.28	-1.07	3	2	0	1.14	800 441-7762
BlackRock Select Eq Inst	Growth/Inc	-8.6	-16.62	-6.21	4	3	0	0.81	800 441-7762
BlackRock Select Eq Inv A	Growth/Inc	-9	-17.03	-6.66	3	3	4.5	1.29	800 441-7762
BlackRock Select Eq Inv B	Growth/Inc	-9.7	-17.64	-7.37	4	3	0	1.28	800 441-7762
BlackRock Select Eq Inv C	Growth/Inc	-9.7	-17.62	-7.37	4	3	0	2.03	800 441-7762
BlackRock Select Eq Svc	Growth/Inc	-8.9	-16.89	-6.51	4	3	0	1.11	800 441-7762
BlackRock Small Cap Gr Inst	Small Co	-3.8	-20.8	-2.72	3	4	0	0.85	800 441-7762
BlackRock Small Cap Gr Inv B	Small Co	-5	-21.73	-3.89	3	4	0	2.07	800 441-7762
BlackRock Small Cap Gr Svc	Small Co	-4.2	-21.01	-3.04	3	4	0	1.15	800 441-7762
BlackRock Small Cap Val Inv A	Small Co	-8.4	7.12	0.67	2	3	4.5	1.35	800 441-7762
BlackRock Small Cap Val Inv C	Small Co	-9	6.32	-0.08	2	3	0	2.1	800 441-7762
BlackRock U.S. Opportunities A	Small Co	-15.7	-17.73	16.64	4	5	5	1.92	800 441-7762
BlackRock U.S. Opportunities C	Small Co	-16.3	-18.32	15.78	4	5	0	2.67	800 441-7762
BlackRock U.S. Opportunities Svc	Small Co	-15.6	-17.57	16.82	4	5	0	1.75	800 441-7762
BlackRock-European Equity Svc	European	-19.4					0	1.75	800 441-7762
BlackRock-Intl Opp Inst	Foreign	-10	-7.65	7.57	3	2	0	1.33	800 441-7762
BlackRock-Intl Opp Inv B	Foreign	-11	-8.77	8.26	3	2	0	2.54	800 441-7762
BlackRock-Intl Opp Serv	Foreign	-10.2	-7.98	9.23	3	2	0	1.6	800 441-7762
BlackRock-Large Cap Gr Inv A	Growth	-12.8	-27.42	-9.65	5	4	4.5	1.29	800 441-7762
BlackRock-Large Cap Gr Inv C	Growth	-13.6	-28	-10.38	5	4	0	2.04	800 441-7762
BlackRock-Large Cap Val Inst	Growth/Inc	-10.8	-5.7	-3.33	3	3	0	0.79	800 441-7762
BlackRock-Large Cap Val Inv B	Growth/Inc	-11.9	-6.95	-4.54	3	3	0	2.01	800 441-7762
BlackRock-Large Cap Val Svc	Growth/Inc	-11.1	-6	-3.62	3	3	0	1.09	800 441-7762
BlackRock-Mid Cap Growth Eq B	Growth	-10.2	-21.6	3.68	3	4	0	2.37	800 441-7762
BlackRock-Mid Cap Growth Eq Inst	Growth	-9.1	-20.64	4.95	3	4	0	1.14	800 441-7762
BlackRock-Mid Cap Value Eq A	Growth/Inc	-14.3	-0.19	-1.54	3	2	4.5	1.62	800 441-7762
BlackRock-Mid Cap Value Eq C	Growth/Inc	-15	-0.94	-2.27	3	2	0	2.37	800 441-7762
BlackRock-Mid Cap Value Eq Svc	Growth/Inc	-14.2	-0.02	-1.38	3	2	0	1.45	800 441-7762

Stock Fund Name	Objective	Annualized Return for			Rank		Max Load	Expense Ratio	Toll-Free/(Toll) Telephone
		1 Year	3 Years	5 Years	Overall	Risk			
BlackRock-Small Cap Gr Inv A	Small Co	-4.3	-21.19	-3.2	3	4	4.5	1.33	800 441-7762
BlackRock-Small Cap Gr Inv C	Small Co	-5	-21.71	-3.89	3	4	0	2.07	800 441-7762
BlackRock-Small Cap Val Inst	Small Co	-8	7.63	1.12	2	3	0	0.88	800 441-7762
BlackRock-Small Cap Val Inv B	Small Co	-9	6.37	-0.08	2	3	0	2.1	800 441-7762
BlackRock-Small Cap Val Svc	Small Co	-8.2	7.32	0.83	2	3	0	1.18	800 441-7762
BlackRock-U.S Opportunities B	Small Co	-16.3	-18.32	15.81	4	5	0	2.67	800 441-7762
BlackRock-U.S Opportunities Inst	Small Co	-15.3	-17.32	17.19	4	5	0	1.45	800 441-7762
Boston Balanced Fund	Balanced	2	1.65	3	2	1	0	1	(617-726-7250)
Boston Ptrs Long/Short Equity Inst	Balanced	-7.1	16.3		2	2	0	2.5	888 261-4073
Boston Ptrs Long/Short Equity Inv	Balanced	-7.3	16.03		2	2	0	2.75	888 261-4073
Boston Ptrs Lrg Cap Value Inst	Growth/Inc	-10.8					0	1	888 261-4073
Boston Ptrs Lrg Cap Value Inv	Growth	-11.1					0	1.25	888 261-4073
Boston Ptrs Mid Cp Val Inst	Growth	-8					0	1	888 261-4073
Boston Ptrs Mid Cp Val Inv	Growth	-8.2					0	1.25	888 261-4073
Boston Ptrs Sm Cap Value II Inst	Small Co	-8.1	22.53		2	4	0	1.55	888 261-4073
Boston Ptrs Sm Cap Value II Inv	Small Co	-8.4					0	1.8	888 261-4073
Bramwell Growth Fund	Growth	-13.4	-11.34	0.47	3	2	0	1.68	800 272-6227
Brandes Instl Intl Equity Fund	Foreign	-16.2	-5.61	5.08	2	3	0	1.2	800 237-7119
Brandywine Advisors	Growth	-7.5					0	1.21	800 656-3017
Brandywine Blue Fund	Growth	-5.9	-9.34	3.06	2	2	0	1.13	800 656-3017
Brandywine Fund	Growth	-12.8	-11.52	2.64	3	2	0	1.1	800 656-3017
Brazos Micro Cap Portfolio B	Small Co	-20.1					0	2.55	800 426-9157
Brazos Micro Cap Portfolio II	Small Co	-20.1					0	2.55	800 426-9157
Brazos Micro Cap Portfolio N	Small Co	-19.5					5.75	1.9	800 426-9157
Brazos Micro Cap Portfolio Y	Small Co	-19.5	-2.31	6.83		4	0	1.6	800 426-9157
Brazos Mid Cap Portfolio N	Growth	-16.4	-5.78			3	5.75	1.47	800 426-9157
Brazos Mid Cap Portfolio Y	Growth	-15.9	-5.36			3	0	1.12	800 426-9157
Brazos Multi Cap Portfolio B	Growth	-23					0	2.2	800 426-9157
Brazos Multi Cap Portfolio II	Growth	-23					0	2.2	800 426-9157
Brazos Multi Cap Portfolio N	Growth	-22.6	-9.56			3	5.75	1.55	800 426-9157
Brazos Multi Cap Portfolio Y	Growth	-22.3	-9.21			3	5.75	1.2	800 426-9157
Brazos Real Estate Sec B	Real Est	4.5	12.4			2	0	2.3	800 426-9157
Brazos Real Estate Sec II	Real Est	4.6	12.38			1	0	2.3	800 426-9157
Brazos Real Estate Sec N	Real Est	5.2	13.16			2	5.75	1.65	800 426-9157
Brazos Real Estate Sec Y	Real Est	5.6	13.63	5.33	1	2	0	1.25	800 426-9157
Brazos Small Cap Portfolio B	Small Co	-16.5	-9.83			3	0	2.3	800 426-9157
Brazos Small Cap Portfolio II	Small Co	-16.5	-9.88			3	0	2.3	800 426-9157
Brazos Small Cap Portfolio N	Small Co	-16	-9.27			3	5.75	1.47	800 426-9157
Brazos Small Cap Portfolio Y	Small Co	-15.7	-8.81	0.28	3	3	0	1.12	800 426-9157
Bremer Growth Stock Fund	Growth	-10.2	-13.72	-1.86	4	3	0	0.93	800 595-5552
Bridges Investment Fund	Growth/Inc	-3	-12.32	-0.53	3	3	0	0.85	800 939-8401
Bridgeway Aggressive Investors 1	Agg Growth	-0.5	-2.47	18.85	3	4	0	1.81	800 661-3550
Bridgeway Micro-Cap Ltd	Small Co	-8.6	11.88		2	4	0	1.9	800 661-3550
Bridgeway Ultra Large 35 Index	Growth	-3.7	-10.16	1.63	3	3	0	0.15	800 661-3550
Bridgeway Ultra SmCo Tax Advantage	Small Co	16.1	19.32	12.52	1	3	0	0.75	800 661-3550
Bridgeway Ultra-Small Company	Small Co	15.7	24.96	15.82	1	3	0	1.26	800 661-3550
Brown Advisory Growth Equity Instl	Growth	-4.2	-12.33		3	4	0	1.6	800 540-6807
Brown Advisory International A	Other						0		800 540-6807
Brown Advisory International Instl	Other						0		800 540-6807
Brown Advisory Small-Cap Gr A	Small Co						0		800 540-6807
Brown Advisory Small-Cap Gr B	Small Co						0		800 540-6807
Brown Advisory Small-Cap Gr Instl	Small Co	-3.3	-15.57		3	5	0	1.64	800 540-6807
Brown Advisory Value Equity A	Other						0		800 540-6807
Brown Advisory Value Equity Instl	Other						0		800 540-6807
Brown Capital Mgmt Balanced	Flexible	-7	-8.14	-2.37	3	2	0	1.2	877 892-4226
Brown Capital Mgmt Equity	Growth	-12.7	-13.52	-4.94	5	3	0	1.2	877 892-4226
Brown Capital Mgmt Sm Co	Small Co	-14.5	-0.81	6.67	3	5	0	1.24	877 892-4226
Bruce Fund	Flexible	23	25.16	10.96	1	2	0	1.46	800 872-7823

Stock Fund Name	Objective	Annualized Return for			Rank		Max Load	Expense Ratio	Toll-Free/(Toll) Telephone
		1 Year	3 Years	5 Years	Overall	Risk			
Brundage Story & Rose Equity	Growth	-6.7	-7.09	1.58	2	2	0	1.15	800 543-8721
Buffalo Balanced Fund	Balanced	-3.5	-1.89	-1.14	2	3	0	1.08	800 492-8332
Buffalo Large Cap Fund	Growth	-7.4	-7.95	0.73	3	4	0	1.06	800 492-8332
Buffalo Small Cap Fund	Small Co	-14.4	9.17	15.4	2	4	0	1.01	800 492-8332
Buffalo USA Global Fund	Global	-11.5	-9.98	2.45	3	4	0	1.05	800 492-8332
Burnham Fund A	Growth/Inc	-11.6	-11	0.97	3	3	5	1.38	800 874-3863
Burnham Fund B	Growth/Inc	-13.3	-12.01	-0.02	3	3	0	2.1	800 874-3863
C & B Large Cap Value	Growth	-7.5	5.61	5.07	2	2	0	1.25	866 450-3722
C & B Tax Managed Value Portfolio	Growth	-3.2	3.81	5.41	1	2	0	1.25	866 450-3722
C/Fund	Growth/Inc	4.5	-3.29	-0.05	3	1	0		800 338-9477
CCMI Equity Fund	Income	-6.6					4.5	1.24	800 386-3111
CDC Nvest AEW Real Estate A	Real Est	4					5.75	1.5	800 225-5478
CDC Nvest AEW Real Estate B	Real Est	3.1					0	2.25	800 225-5478
CDC Nvest AEW Real Estate C	Real Est	3.2					1	2.25	800 225-5478
CDC Nvest AEW Real Estate Y	Real Est	4.2					0	1.25	800 225-5478
CDC Nvest Balanced A	Balanced	-3.8	-4.13	-4.54	2	1	5.75	1.65	800 225-5478
CDC Nvest Balanced B	Balanced	-4.5	-4.87	-5.28	2	1	0	2.4	800 225-5478
CDC Nvest Balanced C	Balanced	-4.6	-4.87	-5.28	2	1	1	2.4	800 225-5478
CDC Nvest Balanced Y	Balanced	-2.8	-3.37	-3.95	2	1	0	0.92	800 225-5478
CDC Nvest Capital Growth A	Growth	-12.5	-19.44	-5.84	5	4	5.75	1.71	800 225-5478
CDC Nvest Capital Growth B	Growth	-13.2	-20.03	-6.54	5	4	0	2.46	800 225-5478
CDC Nvest Capital Growth C	Growth	-13.2	-20.05	-6.58	5	4	1	2.46	800 225-5478
CDC Nvest Growth & Income A	Growth/Inc	-6.5	-8.94	-3.22	3	3	5.75	1.54	800 225-5478
CDC Nvest Growth & Income B	Growth/Inc	-7.2	-9.63	-3.93	3	3	0	2.29	800 225-5478
CDC Nvest Growth & Income C	Growth/Inc	-7.2	-9.61	-3.91	3	3	1	2.29	800 225-5478
CDC Nvest Growth & Income Y	Growth/Inc	-5.5	-8.25		3	3	0	0.94	800 225-5478
CDC Nvest Intl Equity A	Foreign	-14.7	-18.07	-3.89	5	3	5.75	2.32	800 225-5478
CDC Nvest Intl Equity B	Foreign	-15.5	-18.73	-4.66	5	3	0	3.07	800 225-5478
CDC Nvest Intl Equity C	Foreign	-15.5	-18.89	-4.75	5	3	1	3.07	800 225-5478
CDC Nvest Intl Equity Y	Foreign	-13.4	-17.25	-3.14	3	3	0	1.58	800 225-5478
CDC Nvest Large Cap Growth Fund A	Growth	-12.5	-20.16		4	4	5.75	1.37	800 225-5478
CDC Nvest Large Cap Growth Fund B	Growth	-13	-20.71		5	4	0	2.15	800 225-5478
CDC Nvest Large Cap Growth Fund C	Growth	-13	-20.71		5	4	1	2.12	800 225-5478
CDC Nvest Large Cap Growth Fund Y	Growth	-12.1	-19.89		5	4	0	1.12	800 225-5478
CDC Nvest Select A	Growth	-7.4					5.75	1.69	800 225-5478
CDC Nvest Select B	Growth	-8.1					0	2.44	800 225-5478
CDC Nvest Select C	Growth	-8					1	2.44	800 225-5478
CDC Nvest Star Advisers A	Growth	-10.3	-10.74	0.89	3	3	5.75	1.87	800 225-5478
CDC Nvest Star Advisers B	Growth	-11	-11.4	0.14	3	3	0	2.62	800 225-5478
CDC Nvest Star Advisers C	Growth	-11.1	-11.46	0.11	3	3	1	2.62	800 225-5478
CDC Nvest Star Advisers Y	Growth	-9.7	-10.21	1.35	3	3	0	1.27	800 225-5478
CDC Nvest Star Growth A	Growth	-12.4	-29.6	-7.7		4	5.75	1.5	800 225-5478
CDC Nvest Star Growth B	Growth	-13.1	-30.12			4	0	2.25	800 225-5478
CDC Nvest Star Growth C	Growth	-13.2	-30.14			4	1	2.25	800 225-5478
CDC Nvest Star Small Cap A	Small Co	-16	-15.33	-0.77	4	4	5.75	2.11	800 225-5478
CDC Nvest Star Small Cap B	Small Co	-16.7	-15.98	-1.52	3	4	0	2.86	800 225-5478
CDC Nvest Star Small Cap C	Small Co	-16.7	-15.96	-1.51	3	4	1	2.86	800 225-5478
CDC Nvest Star Value A	Growth/Inc	-8.7	-1.31	-2.89	3	3	5.75	1.63	800 225-5478
CDC Nvest Star Value B	Growth/Inc	-9.4	-2	-3.58	3	3	0	2.38	800 225-5478
CDC Nvest Star Value C	Growth/Inc	-9.2	-2.02	-3.62	3	3	1	2.38	800 225-5478
CDC Nvest Star Worldwide A	Global	-11.6	-6.95	-0.81	3	3	5.75	2.18	800 225-5478
CDC Nvest Star Worldwide B	Global	-12.2	-7.62	-1.55	3	3	0	2.93	800 225-5478
CDC Nvest Star Worldwide C	Global	-12.3	-7.65	-1.56	3	3	1	2.93	800 225-5478
CDC Nvest Targeted Equity A	Growth	-15.7	-10.63	-3.1	3	3	5.75	1.39	800 225-5478
CDC Nvest Targeted Equity B	Growth	-16.4	-11.28	-3.79	4	3	0	2.15	800 225-5478
CDC Nvest Targeted Equity C	Growth	-16.6	-11.33		4	3	1	2.15	800 225-5478
CDC Nvest Targeted Equity Y	Growth	-15	-10.08		3	3	0	0.84	800 225-5478
CG Cap Mkts Balanced	Balanced	-4.6	-3.66	-0.32	2	1	0	1	800 444-4273

Stock Fund Name	Objective	Annualized Return for			Rank		Max Load	Expense Ratio	Toll-Free/(Toll) Telephone
		1 Year	3 Years	5 Years	Overall	Risk			
CG Cap Mkts Emerging Mkts	Foreign	-9.9	-8.13	-2.87	3	4	0	2.04	800 444-4273
CG Cap Mkts Intl Equity Invts	Foreign	-13.8	-14.99	-4.12	5	3	0	1.23	800 444-4273
CG Cap Mkts Large Cap Growth	Growth	-5.3	-19.66	-4.29	3	4	0	0.94	800 444-4273
CG Cap Mkts Large Cap Val Eq	Growth/Inc	-9.9	-4.17	-1.05	3	3	0	0.96	800 444-4273
CG Cap Mkts Sm Cap Val Eqty	Small Co	-11.5	9.16	1.8	3	3	0	1.26	800 444-4273
CG Cap Mkts Small Cap Growth	Small Co	-10.1	-12.64	-2.85	4	5	0	1.39	800 444-4273
CGM Capital Development	Growth	-15.6	-11.83	-5.87	4	3	0	1.15	800 345-4048
CGM Focus Fund	Growth	-14.9	29.89	17.14	3	5	0	1.2	800 345-4048
CGM Mutual Fund	Balanced	-14.2	-6.84	-2.02	3	2	0	1.14	800 345-4048
CGM Realty Fund	Real Est	19.6	21.55	11.51	1	3	0	1.03	800 345-4048
CNI Charter Large Cap Growth Eq I	Growth	-6.8	-13.89		3	3	0	1.05	888 889-0799
CNI Charter Large Cap Value Eq I	Growth	-9.4	-5.83		3	3	0	1	888 889-0799
CNI Charter RCB Small Cap Value R	Small Co	-0.5	10.69		1	3	3.5	1.24	888 889-0799
CRM Small Cap Value Inv	Small Co	-14.5	11.48	3.54	3	3	0	1.29	800 276-2883
CSI Equity Fund	Global	-10.5	-8.47	2.91	2	2	5.75	1.45	800 527-9525
Calamos Convertible Fund A	Converts	0.8	3.5	8.34	1	1	4.75	1.2	800 823-7386
Calamos Convertible Fund B	Converts	0					0	1.95	800 823-7386
Calamos Convertible Fund C	Converts	0	2.95	7.79	1	1	0	1.95	800 823-7386
Calamos Convertible Fund I	Converts	1	3.68	8.69	1	1	0	0.97	800 823-7386
Calamos Global Growth & Income A	Converts	-0.7	-1.54	5.87	1	1	4.75	1.75	800 823-7386
Calamos Global Growth & Income B	Converts	-1.2					0	2.5	800 823-7386
Calamos Global Growth & Income C	Converts	-1.4	-1.81	5.5	1	1	0	2.5	800 823-7386
Calamos Global Growth & Income I	Converts	-0.1	-1.26	6.16		1	0	1.5	800 823-7386
Calamos Growth & Income A	Converts	4.6	4.91	13.03	1	2	4.75	1.28	800 823-7386
Calamos Growth & Income B	Converts	3.8					0	2.03	800 823-7386
Calamos Growth & Income C	Converts	3.8	4.66	12.66	1	2	0	2.03	800 823-7386
Calamos Growth & Income I	Converts	4.9	5.16	13.42		2	0	1.03	800 823-7386
Calamos Growth Fund A	Growth	-3.7	-2.39	18.28	1	4	4.75	1.4	800 823-7386
Calamos Growth Fund B	Growth	-4.5					0	2.15	800 823-7386
Calamos Growth Fund C	Growth	-4.4	-2.68	17.85	2	4	0	2.15	800 823-7386
Calamos Growth Fund I	Growth	-3.5	-1.44	19.17		4	0	1.23	800 823-7386
Calamos Market Neutral Fund A	Converts	8.8	8.02	9.52	1	1	4.75	1.53	800 823-7386
Calamos Market Neutral Fund B	Converts	8					0	2.28	800 823-7386
Calamos Market Neutral Fund C	Converts	8	8.18			1	0	2.27	800 823-7386
Calamos Market Neutral Fund I	Converts	9.1	8.76			1	0	1.04	800 823-7386
Calamos Mid Cap Value A	Growth	-8.9					0	1.75	800 823-7386
Calamos Mid Cap Value B	Growth	-9.5					0	2.5	800 823-7386
Calamos Mid Cap Value C	Growth	-9.6					0	2.5	800 823-7386
Caldwell & Orkin Mkt Opportunity	Flexible	1.9	3.2	6.13	1	1	0	1.29	800 237-7073
California Equity Income Fd	Income	-5.1					0	0.8	800 225-8778
California European Growth & Inc Fd	Foreign	-8.4	-13.33			3	0	0.95	800 225-8778
California S&P 500 Index Fd	Growth/Inc	-7.8	-10.59	-0.89	3	3	0	0.2	800 225-8778
California S&P MidCap Index Fd	Growth	-9.4	1.52	7.41	2	3	0	0.4	800 225-8778
California S&P SmallCap Index Fd	Small Co	-10.6					0	0.65	800 225-8778
Calvert Capital Accumulation A	Growth	-10.4					4.75	0.35	800 368-2745
Calvert Capital Accumulation B	Growth	-11.3	-10.64	-2.75		4	0	1	800 368-2745
Calvert Capital Accumulation C	Growth	-11.2					0	1	800 368-2745
Calvert Large Cap Growth A	Growth	-2.3					4.75	0.25	800 368-2745
Calvert Large Cap Growth B	Growth	-3.2					0	1	800 368-2745
Calvert Large Cap Growth C	Growth	-3.2					0	1	800 368-2745
Calvert Large Cap Growth I	Growth	-1.6	-14.28	2.08	3	3	0		800 368-2745
Calvert New Vision Small Cap A	Small Co	-20.4					4.75	0.25	800 368-2745
Calvert New Vision Small Cap B	Small Co	-21.2	-2.83	0.23		3	0	1	800 368-2745
Calvert New Vision Small Cap C	Small Co	-21.1					0	1	800 368-2745
Calvert Short Duration Income A	Income	10.6					2.75	1.66	800 368-2745
Calvert Social Inv Balanced A	Balanced	-1.5	-3.75	0.05	2	1	4.75	0.24	800 368-2745
Calvert Social Inv Balanced C	Balanced	-2.5	-7.33	-2.58	3	2	0	1	800 368-2745
Calvert Social Inv Equity A	Growth	-5.9	-1.41	5.66	1	3	4.75	1.24	800 368-2745

Stock Fund Name	Objective	Annualized Return for			Rank		Max Load	Expense Ratio	Toll-Free/(Toll) Telephone
		1 Year	3 Years	5 Years	Overall	Risk			
Calvert Social Inv Equity C	Growth	-6.7	-2.27	4.74	2	3	0	1	800 368-2745
Calvert Social Inv Equity I	Growth	-5.4	-1		1	3	0		800 368-2745
Calvert Social-Enhanced Eq A	Growth	-5.8	-8.17	0.46	3	3	4.75	0.25	800 368-2745
Calvert Social-Enhanced Eq B	Growth	-6.9	-8.98	-0.53	3	3	0		800 368-2745
Calvert Social-Enhanced Eq C	Growth	-6.8	-5.25		2	3	0	1	800 368-2745
Calvert Social-Index A	Other	-7.2					4.75	0.25	800 368-2745
Calvert Social-Index B	Other	-8.2					0	1	800 368-2745
Calvert Social-Index C	Other	-8.1					0	1	800 368-2745
Calvert Social-Index I	Other	-6.9					0		800 368-2745
Calvert World Values Intl Eqty A	Foreign	-10.6	-13.38	-5.79	4	3	4.75	2.02	800 368-2745
Calvert World Values Intl Eqty C	Foreign	-11.6	-14.31	-8.97	5	3	0	1	800 368-2745
Cambiar Opportunity Fund	Growth	-6.6	2.14		2	3	0	1.3	
Canandaigua Equity Fund	Growth	-10.1	-17.94	-2.95	4	4	0	1.35	888 693-9276
Capital Management Mid-Cap Inst	Growth	-14.4	-3.81	1.62	3	2	0	1.5	888 626-3863
Capital Management Mid-Cap Inv	Growth	-14.7	-4.42	1	3	3	3	2.25	888 626-3863
Capital Value Fund	AssetAlloc	-4.5	-10.49	0.22	3	2	3.5	2.48	800 773-3863
Capstone Growth Fund	Growth	-13.2	-12.91	-2.41	5	3	0	1.27	800 262-6631
Causeway International Value Instl	Foreign	-10.8					0		866 947-7000
Causeway International Value Inv	Foreign	-11					0		866 947-7000
Century Shares Trust	Financial	-6.5	6.54	2.33	2	2	0	1.18	800 321-1928
Century Small Cap Select Instl	Small Co	6.5	16.82			2	0	1.45	800 321-1928
Century Small Cap Select Inv	Small Co	5.8	17.57			2	0	1.8	800 321-1928
Chase Growth Fund	Growth	-9.2	-5.79	4.58	1	1	0	1.5	800 293-9104
Chesapeake Aggressive Growth Fund	Agg Growth	-10.6	-14.94	-4.87	4	5	3	1.56	800 430-3863
Chesapeake Core Growth Fund	Growth	-3.2	-8.52	6.91	2	4	0	1.16	800 430-3863
Chesapeake Growth Fund A	Growth	-15	-19.03	-3.66	4	5	3	1.78	800 430-3863
Chesapeake Growth Fund Instl	Growth	-14.1	-18.51	-3.14	4	5	0	1.18	800 430-3863
Chesapeake Growth Fund SuperInst	Growth	-14	-18.41	-3	4	5	0	1.03	800 430-3863
Citizens Balanced Fund	Balanced						0	1.3	800 223-7010
Citizens Core Growth Fd	Growth	-11.1	-17.71	-3.58	4	4	0	1.34	800 223-7010
Citizens Core Growth Inst	Growth	-10.5	-17.17	-2.91	4	4	0	0.68	800 223-7010
Citizens Emerg Gr Fd	Agg Growth	-16.5	-21.91	2.37	3	4	0	1.68	800 223-7010
Citizens Emerg Gr Inst	Agg Growth	-15.9	-21.96		5	4	0	1.2	800 223-7010
Citizens Global Eq Fd	Global	-12.1	-20.5	-1.12	4	3	0	1.82	800 223-7010
Citizens Global Eq Inst	Global	-11.6	-20.07		5	3	0	1.39	800 223-7010
Citizens International Growth	Other	-16.2					0	1.85	800 223-7010
Citizens Small Cap Core Growth Fd	Small Co	-11.2	-5.76		3	4	0	1.34	800 223-7010
Citizens Value Fund	Growth	-15.7	-8.83	0	3	4	0	1.95	800 410-3337
Clipper Fund	Growth	-6.9	13.15	10.66	2	2	0	1.07	800 432-2504
Cohen & Steers Equity Income A	Real Est	5	16.07	8.25	1	1	4.5	1.41	800 437-9912
Cohen & Steers Equity Income B	Real Est	4.3	15.14	7.58	1	1	0	2.04	800 437-9912
Cohen & Steers Equity Income C	Real Est	4.3	15.18	6.53	1	1	0	2.04	800 437-9912
Cohen & Steers Realty Shrs	Real Est	3.5	13.17	6.62	1	2	0	1.09	800 437-9912
Cohen & Steers Special Equity	Real Est	6.7	17.3	4.16	1	2	0	1.83	800 437-9912
Columbia Balanced A	Balanced						5.75	1.17	800 338-2550
Columbia Balanced B	Balanced						0	1.92	800 338-2550
Columbia Balanced D	Balanced						0	1.92	800 338-2550
Columbia Balanced Z	Balanced	-2.8	-5.08	1.79	2	1	0	0.69	800 338-2550
Columbia Common Stock A	Growth/Inc						5.75		800 338-2550
Columbia Common Stock B	Growth/Inc						0		800 338-2550
Columbia Common Stock D	Growth/Inc						0		800 338-2550
Columbia Common Stock Z	Growth/Inc	-11.1	-14.69	-1.57	4	3	0	0.83	800 338-2550
Columbia Growth A	Growth						5.75	1.12	800 338-2550
Columbia Growth B	Growth						0	1.85	800 338-2550
Columbia Growth D	Growth						0		800 338-2550
Columbia Growth G	Growth						0	1.8	800 338-2550
Columbia Growth Z	Growth	-13	-19.07	-4.79	4	4	0	0.75	800 338-2550
Columbia International Stock A	Foreign						5.5		800 338-2550

Stock Fund Name	Objective	Annualized Return for			Rank		Max Load	Expense Ratio	Toll-Free/(Toll) Telephone
		1 Year	3 Years	5 Years	Overall	Risk			
Columbia International Stock B	Foreign						0		800 338-2550
Columbia International Stock D	Foreign						0		800 338-2550
Columbia International Stock Z	Foreign	-13.2	-12.83	-2.41	4	2	0	1.55	800 338-2550
Columbia Real Estate Equity A	Real Est						5.75		800 338-2550
Columbia Real Estate Equity B	Real Est						0		800 338-2550
Columbia Real Estate Equity D	Real Est						0		800 338-2550
Columbia Real Estate Equity Z	Real Est	3.4	11.74	6.49	1	2	0	0.94	800 338-2550
Columbia Small Cap Z	Small Co	-5.7	-8.67	4.44	3	4	0	1.21	800 338-2550
Columbia Special A	Agg Growth						5.75	1.5	800 338-2550
Columbia Special B	Agg Growth						0	2.44	800 338-2550
Columbia Special D	Agg Growth						0	2.41	800 338-2550
Columbia Special G	Agg Growth						5.75	1.45	800 338-2550
Columbia Special T	Agg Growth						0	2.35	800 338-2550
Columbia Special Z	Growth	-9.5	-11.4	2.56	3	4	0	1.14	800 338-2550
Columbia Strategic Value A	Growth						5.5		800 338-2550
Columbia Strategic Value B	Growth						0		800 338-2550
Columbia Strategic Value D	Growth						0		800 338-2550
Columbia Strategic Value Z	Growth	-4.2					0	0.94	800 338-2550
Columbia Technology A	Technology						5.75		800 338-2550
Columbia Technology B	Technology						0		800 338-2550
Columbia Technology D	Technology						0		800 338-2550
Columbia Technology Z	Technology	-2.8					0	1.65	800 338-2550
Columbia Thermostat A	Other						5.75		800 338-2550
Columbia Thermostat B	Other						0		800 338-2550
Columbia Thermostat D	Other						1		800 338-2550
Columbia Thermostat Z	Other						0		800 338-2550
Commerce Asset Allocation Inst	AssetAlloc						0	0.35	800 995-6365
Commerce Asset Allocation Svc	AssetAlloc						0	0.6	800 995-6365
Commerce Growth Instl	Growth	-9.4	-15.61	-5.2	3	3	0	1.11	800 995-6365
Commerce Growth Svc	Growth	-9.7	-15.83	-9.98	4	3	3.5	1.36	800 995-6365
Commerce Intl Equity Instl	Foreign	-15.7	-15.86	-6	4	3	3.5	1.31	800 995-6365
Commerce Intl Equity Svc	Foreign	-15.9	-16.07	-6.25	4	3	3.5	1.72	800 995-6365
Commerce Mid Cap Growth Instl	Agg Growth	-10.8	-17.64	-5.46	4	4	0	1.14	800 995-6365
Commerce Mid Cap Growth Svc	Agg Growth	-11.1	-17.87	-9.35	4	4	3.5	1.39	800 995-6365
Commerce Value Fund Instl	Growth/Inc	-11.8	-3.29	-2.66	3	2	0	1.08	800 995-6365
Commerce Value Fund Svc	Growth/Inc	-12	-3.54	-2.91	3	2	3.5	1.33	800 995-6365
Commonwealth Australia/New Zealand	Foreign	19	15.74	8.85	1	3	0	5.7	800 262-6631
Commonwealth Japan Fund	Pacific	-16.6	-20.46	-5.83	4	2	0	5.5	888 345-1898
Concorde Value Fund	Growth	-11.8	-1.3	-0.02	3	2	0	1.5	800 294-1699
Conseco 20 Fund A	Growth	-9.4	-34.75	-11.61	3	5	5.75	1.69	800 825-1530
Conseco 20 Fund B	Growth	-10.1	-35.07	-12.03	3	5	0	2.19	800 825-1530
Conseco 20 Fund C	Growth	-10	-35.06	-12.01	3	5	0	2.19	800 825-1530
Conseco 20 Fund Y	Growth	-9.1	-34.42	-11.25	3	5	0	1.19	800 825-1530
Conseco Balanced Fund A	Balanced	-0.7	-2.29	5.11	1	2	5.75	1.5	800 825-1530
Conseco Balanced Fund B	Balanced	-1.2	-2.77	4.62	1	2	0	2	800 825-1530
Conseco Balanced Fund C	Balanced	-1.1	-2.74	4.67	1	2	0	2	800 825-1530
Conseco Balanced Fund Y	Balanced	-0.1	-1.79	5.62	1	2	0	1	800 825-1530
Conseco Convertible Sec A	Converts	12	-4.16		2	3	5.75	1.55	800 825-1530
Conseco Convertible Sec B	Converts	11.4	-4.63		2	3	0	2.05	800 825-1530
Conseco Convertible Sec C	Converts	11.4	-4.66		2	3	0	2.05	800 825-1530
Conseco Convertible Sec Y	Converts	12.5	-3.7		2	3	0	1.05	800 825-1530
Conseco Equity Fd A	Growth	-5.9	-4.37	8.4	2	4	5.75	1.5	800 825-1530
Conseco Equity Fd B	Growth	-6.4	-4.84	7.94	3	4	0	2	800 825-1530
Conseco Equity Fd C	Growth	-6.4	-4.8	8	2	4	0	2	800 825-1530
Conseco Equity Fd Y	Growth	-5.5	-3.89	8.91	2	4	0	1	800 825-1530
Conseco Fd Grp-Large Cap A	Growth	-9.8					5.75	1.5	800 825-1530
Conseco Fd Grp-Large Cap B	Growth	-10.5					0	2	800 825-1530
Conseco Fd Grp-Large Cap C	Growth	-10.4					0	2	800 825-1530

Stock Fund Name	Objective	Annualized Return for			Rank		Max Load	Expense Ratio	Toll-Free/(Toll) Telephone
		1 Year	3 Years	5 Years	Overall	Risk			
Conseco Fd Grp-Large Cap Y	Growth	-9.6					0	1	800 825-1530
Conseco Science & Tech A	Technology	-13.4					5.75	1.75	800 825-1530
Conseco Science & Tech B	Technology	-13.5					0	2.25	800 825-1530
Conseco Science & Tech C	Technology	-13.5					0	2.25	800 825-1530
Conseco Science & Tech Y	Technology	-12.8					0	1.25	800 825-1530
Copley Fund	Growth/Inc	-6.5	-0.11	1	2	2	0	0.97	(508 674-8459)
CornerCap Sm. Cap Value Fd	Growth	-14.2	10.91	2.43	3	3	0	1.49	888 813-8637
Country Growth Fund	Growth	-8	-6	3.06	2	2	0	1.27	800 245-2100
Country Trust Balanced Fund Y	Balanced	-1.8	-1.87	3.43	1	1	0	1.67	800 245-2100
Credit Suisse Capital Apprec A	Growth	-11.1					5.75	1.5	800 494-6847
Credit Suisse Capital Apprec Adv	Growth	-11.4	-18.96	-2.6	3	3	0	1.73	800 494-6847
Credit Suisse Capital Apprec B	Growth	-11.8					0	2.25	800 494-6847
Credit Suisse Capital Apprec C	Growth	-11.9					0	2.24	800 494-6847
Credit Suisse Capital Apprec Com	Growth	-11	-18.55	-2.08	3	3	0	1.24	800 494-6847
Credit Suisse Emerg Growth A	Small Co	-8.1					5.75	1.75	800 494-6847
Credit Suisse Emerg Growth Adv	Small Co	-8.2	-16.75	-5.51	3	4	0	2	800 494-6847
Credit Suisse Emerg Growth Com	Small Co	-7.7	-16.32	-5.05	3	4	0	1.5	800 494-6847
Credit Suisse Emerg Markets A	Foreign	-15					5.75	1.65	800 494-6847
Credit Suisse Emerg Markets Adv	Foreign	-14.8	-14.9	-5.57	4	4	0	1.95	800 494-6847
Credit Suisse Emerg Markets Com	Foreign	-14.4	-14.67	-4.83	3	4	0	1.71	800 494-6847
Credit Suisse Global Health Sci A	Health	-2.2					5.75	1.59	800 494-6847
Credit Suisse Global Health Sci Com	Health	-2.2	0.11	3.95	2	4	0	1.59	800 494-6847
Credit Suisse Global PostVen Cp A	Global	-19.4					5.75	1.65	800 494-6847
Credit Suisse Global PostVen Cp Adv	Global	-19.2	-23.82	1.61	5	4	0	1.9	800 494-6847
Credit Suisse Global PostVen Cp B	Global	-19.6					0	2.4	800 494-6847
Credit Suisse Global PostVen Cp C	Global	-19.6					0	2.4	800 494-6847
Credit Suisse Global PostVen Cp Com	Global	-18.9	-23.57	1.88	5	4	0	1.65	800 494-6847
Credit Suisse Global Tech A	Technology	-13.7					5.75	1.65	800 494-6847
Credit Suisse Global Tech Com	Technology	-13.6	-29.83	-0.83	4	5	0	1.65	800 494-6847
Credit Suisse Inst Cap Apprec	Growth	-10.8					0	0.75	800 494-6847
Credit Suisse Inst Internatl Inst	Foreign	-16.8	-19.39	-8.61	5	3	0	1.25	800 494-6847
Credit Suisse Inst Intl Focus Fd	Foreign	-15.3	-15.65	-5.29	5	3	0	0.95	800 494-6847
Credit Suisse Inst Small Cap Gr	Small Co	-10.8	-15.71	-2.58	3	5	0	0.99	800 494-6847
Credit Suisse Internatl Focus A	Foreign	-16.3					5.75	1.85	800 494-6847
Credit Suisse Internatl Focus Adv	Foreign	-16.7					0	2.1	800 494-6847
Credit Suisse Internatl Focus B	Foreign	-17.2					0	1.85	800 494-6847
Credit Suisse Internatl Focus C	Foreign	-17.2					0	2.6	800 494-6847
Credit Suisse Internatl Focus Com	Foreign	-16.2	-13.89	-2.49		3	0	1.6	800 494-6847
Credit Suisse Japan Growth A	Pacific	-31.9					5.75	1.75	800 494-6847
Credit Suisse Japan Growth Adv	Pacific	-32	-33.85	-11.13	4	5	0	2	800 494-6847
Credit Suisse Japan Growth Com	Pacific	-31.7	-33.46	-10.47	4	5	0	1.75	800 494-6847
Credit Suisse Large Cap Value A	Growth/Inc	-9.1	-3.12	2.08	2	2	5.75	1.03	800 494-6847
Credit Suisse Large Cap Value B	Growth/Inc	-9.5	-9.08	-2.04	3	2	0	1.78	800 494-6847
Credit Suisse Large Cap Value C	Growth/Inc	-9.8	-3.89			2	0	1.78	800 494-6847
Credit Suisse Large Cap Value Com	Growth/Inc	-9					0	1.03	800 494-6847
Credit Suisse Select Equity A	Growth	-13.4					5.75	1.19	800 494-6847
Credit Suisse Select Equity B	Growth	-14					0	1.94	800 494-6847
Credit Suisse Select Equity C	Growth	-14.2					0	1.94	800 494-6847
Credit Suisse Select Equity Com	Growth	-13.5	-12.98		3	3	0	1.19	800 494-6847
Credit Suisse Small Cap Gr A	Growth	-8.3					5.75	1.4	800 494-6847
Credit Suisse Small Cap Gr Com	Small Co	-8.3	-11.63	3.72	3	5	0	1.4	800 494-6847
Credit Suisse Small Cap Val A	Small Co	-9.8	9.46	4.99	2	2	5.75	1.32	800 494-6847
Credit Suisse Small Cap Val B	Small Co	-10.5	8.64	4.2	3	2	0	2.07	800 494-6847
Credit Suisse Small Cap Val C	Small Co	-10.6	8.65			2	0	2.07	800 494-6847
Credit Suisse Small Cap Val Com	Small Co	-9.9					0	1.32	800 494-6847
Credit Suisse Strategic Sm Cap A	Small Co						5.75	1.4	800 494-6847
Credit Suisse Strategic Sm Cap B	Small Co						0	2.15	800 494-6847
Credit Suisse Strategic Sm Cap C	Small Co						0	2.15	800 494-6847

Stock Fund Name	Objective	Annualized Return for			Rank		Max Load	Expense Ratio	Toll-Free/(Toll) Telephone
		1 Year	3 Years	5 Years	Overall	Risk			
Credit Suisse Strategic Value A	Growth/Inc	-12.1					5.75	1.63	800 494-6847
Credit Suisse Strategic Value Adv	Growth/Inc	-12.3	-3.29	-0.52	3	2	0	1.88	800 494-6847
Credit Suisse Strategic Value B	Growth/Inc	-12.8					0	2.4	800 494-6847
Credit Suisse Strategic Value C	Growth/Inc	-12.7					0	2.38	800 494-6847
Credit Suisse Strategic Value Com	Growth/Inc	-11.9	-2.02	0.44	3	2	0	1.38	800 494-6847
Credit Suisse Tax Efficient A	Growth	-10.8	-13.77	-1.21	4	3	5.75	1.35	800 494-6847
Credit Suisse Tax Efficient B	Growth	-11.6	-15.78	-3.29	4	3	0	2.1	800 494-6847
Credit Suisse Tr-Glb PstVent Cp	Growth	-18.3	-24.01	-6.99	4	4	0	1.4	800 494-6847
Credit Suisse Tr-Intl Focus	Foreign	-16.8	-17.57	-7.32	5	3	0	1.3	800 494-6847
Credit Suisse Tr-Large Cap Value	Growth/Inc	-14.6	-3.77	-0.98	3	2	0	1	800 494-6847
Credit Suisse Tr-Small Cap Growth	Small Co	-9.7	-15.56	-2.89	3	5	0	1.12	800 494-6847
Credit Suisse Tr-Small Cap Value	AssetAlloc	-8.7					0	0.98	800 494-6847
Croft-Leominster Value	Growth	-14.3	-4.04	-1.31	3	3	0	1.5	800 551-0990
Cutler Value Fund	Income	-13.2	-6.07	-0.71	3	3	0	1.25	888 288-5374
DEVCAP Shared Return Fund	Growth	-9.4	-11.93	-1.23	3	3	0	1.75	800 592-8890
DFA Continental Small Company	European	6.5	3.58	-0.14	2	3	0	0.79	800 342-6684
DFA Emerging Markets	Foreign	-0.3	-6.15	2.43	2	4	0	0.88	800 342-6684
DFA International High Book to Mkt	Foreign	-10.1	-3.25	-0.9	3	3	0	0.52	800 342-6684
DFA International Small Cap Value	Foreign	6.9	7.42	4.75	1	2	0	0.8	800 342-6684
DFA International Value I	Foreign	-10.1	-3.22	-0.91	3	3	0	0.53	800 342-6684
DFA Japanese Small Co	Pacific	-1.6	-4.11	1.14	3	4	0	0.73	800 342-6684
DFA Large Cap International	Foreign	-11.3	-12.35	-3.72	4	2	0	0.46	800 342-6684
DFA Large Cap Value I	Growth	-12	2.56	1.62	3	3	0	0.31	800 342-6684
DFA Pacific Rim Small Company	Pacific	4.9	7.2	9.75	1	3	0	0.76	800 342-6684
DFA Real Estate Securities Port	Real Est	5.4	14.96	7.79	1	1	0	0.42	800 342-6684
DFA Small Cap Value I	Small Co	-8.2	11.23	6	2	4	0	0.56	800 342-6684
DFA U.S Micro Cap Portfolio	Small Co	-4.8	7.24	6.12	2	4	0	0.55	800 342-6684
DFA U.S Small Cap Portfolio	Small Co	-6.6	3.74	3.93	2	4	0	0.41	800 342-6684
DFA US Large Company	Growth/Inc	-8.2	-10.99	-1.2	3	3	0	0.15	800 342-6684
DFA United Kingdom Small Co	European	-4.4	1.27	-0.65	3	3	0	0.72	800 342-6684
DLB Emerging Mkt Fd	Foreign	-2.4	0.45		1	3	0	1.75	888 722-2766
DLB Enhanced Index Core Equity	Income	-8.5					0	0.73	888 722-2766
DLB Enhanced Index Growth	Growth	-8.6					0	0.7	888 722-2766
DLB Enhanced Index Value	Growth	-7.6					0	0.7	888 722-2766
DLB International Fund	Foreign	-17.8					0	1	888 722-2766
DLB Small Capitalization Value	Small Co	-10					0	0.85	888 722-2766
DLB Value	Growth	-13.5					0	0.8	888 722-2766
Davis Convertible Securities A	Converts	5	-0.63	2.72	2	2	4.75	1.09	800 279-0279
Davis Convertible Securities B	Converts	4.8	-1.51	1.83	2	2	0	2.01	800 279-0279
Davis Convertible Securities C	Converts	4.8	-1.86	0.64	2	2	0	2.02	800 279-0279
Davis Convertible Securities Y	Converts	6.2	-0.05	3.25	1	2	0	0.88	800 279-0279
Davis Financial A	Financial	-9.1	-0.4	2.41	2	3	4.75	1.08	800 279-0279
Davis Financial B	Financial	-9.8	-1.25	1.55	2	3	0	1.9	800 279-0279
Davis Financial C	Financial	-9.8	-1.23	1.56	2	3	0	1.9	800 279-0279
Davis Financial Y	Financial	-8.9	-0.2	2.64	2	3	0	0.87	800 279-0279
Davis Growth Opportunity Y	Growth	-3.2	-8.91	-0.71	3	4	0	0.91	800 279-0279
Davis Intl Total Return A	Foreign	-17	-17.26	-11.22	4	3	4.75	1.47	800 279-0279
Davis Intl Total Return B	Foreign	-18.1	-18.23	-12.19	5	3	0	2.5	800 279-0279
Davis Intl Total Return C	Foreign	-18.1	-18.39	-12.17	5	3	0	2.5	800 279-0279
Davis Intl Total Return Y	Foreign	-17.6	-17.05		4	3	0	1.39	800 279-0279
Davis New York Venture Fund A	Growth	-6.6	-6.36	2.1	2	2	4.75	0.89	800 279-0279
Davis New York Venture Fund B	Growth	-7.3	-7.11	1.26	3	2	0	1.71	800 279-0279
Davis New York Venture Fund C	Growth	-7.3	-7.09	1.29	2	2	0	1.68	800 279-0279
Davis New York Venture Fund Y	Growth	-6.3	-6.05	2.41	2	2	0	0.62	800 279-0279
Davis Opportunity A	Growth	-3.6	-0.28	4.73	2	4	4.75	1.23	800 279-0279
Davis Opportunity B	Growth	-4.3	-1.12	3.91	2	4	0	2.06	800 279-0279
Davis Opportunity C	Growth	-4.3	-10.43	-2.14	3	4	0	2.08	800 279-0279
Davis Real Estate A	Real Est	9.2	13.84	5.29	1	1	4.75	1.19	800 279-0279

Stock Fund Name	Objective	Annualized Return for			Rank		Max Load	Expense Ratio	Toll-Free/(Toll) Telephone
		1 Year	3 Years	5 Years	Overall	Risk			
Davis Real Estate B	Real Est	8.2	14.26	5.16	1	1	0	1.99	800 279-0279
Davis Real Estate C	Real Est	8.2	13.09	4.53	1	1	0	1.97	800 279-0279
Davis Real Estate Y	Real Est	9.8	16.17	6.73	1	2	0	0.85	800 279-0279
Dean Balanced Fund A	Balanced	-6.8	-4.28	-4.16	2	3	5.25	1.85	888 899-8343
Dean Balanced Fund C	Balanced	-7.4	-6.04	-5.58	2	3	0	2.6	888 899-8343
Dean International Value A	Foreign	-13.5	-21.91	-7.12	4	4	5.25	2.1	888 899-8343
Dean International Value C	Foreign	-14.6	-22.14	-7.5	4	4	0	2.85	888 899-8343
Dean Large Cap Value A	Growth	-15.8	-6.59	-4.96	3	4	5.25	1.85	888 899-8343
Dean Large Cap Value C	Growth	-16.7	-7.29	-6.15	3	4	0		888 899-8343
Dean Small Cap Value A	Small Co	-13.8	10.16	-0.23	3	4	5.25	1.84	888 899-8343
Dean Small Cap Value C	Small Co	-13.7	9.88	-0.68	3	4	0	2.58	888 899-8343
Delafield Fund Inc	Small Co	-3.5	15.65	7.2	1	3	0	1.26	800 221-3079
Delaware American Services Fund A	Financial	3.2	15.61			3	5.75	1.45	800 523-1918
Delaware American Services Fund B	Financial	2.4					0	2.2	800 523-1918
Delaware American Services Fund C	Financial	2.4					0	2.2	800 523-1918
Delaware American Services Fund I	Financial	3.5	15.82			3	0	1.2	800 523-1918
Delaware Balanced A	Balanced	-4.5	-4.24	-3.6	2	2	5.75	1.37	800 523-1918
Delaware Balanced B	Balanced	-5.2	-4.96	-4.33	2	2	0	2.12	800 523-1918
Delaware Balanced C	Balanced	-5.2	-4.95	-4.33	2	2	0	2.12	800 523-1918
Delaware Balanced I	Balanced	-4.2	-4	-3.37	2	2	0	1.12	800 523-1918
Delaware Core Equity A	Growth	-9.6	-8.26	-3.43	3	2	5.75	1.54	800 523-1918
Delaware Core Equity B	Growth	-10.3	-8.96	-4.16	3	2	0	2.29	800 523-1918
Delaware Core Equity C	Growth	-10.3	-8.96	-4.16	3	2	0	2.29	800 523-1918
Delaware Core Equity I	Growth	-9.4	-8.05	-3.25	3	2	0	1.29	800 523-1918
Delaware Decatur Equity Income A	Income	-8.9	-1.12	-1.68	3	2	5.75	1.11	800 523-1918
Delaware Decatur Equity Income B	Income	-9.7	-1.87	-2.43	3	2	0	1.86	800 523-1918
Delaware Decatur Equity Income C	Income	-9.7	-1.88	-2.43	3	2	0	1.86	800 523-1918
Delaware Decatur Equity Income I	Income	-8.8	-0.9	-1.45	3	2	0	0.86	800 523-1918
Delaware Devon A	Growth	-8.3	-12.65	-8.18	4	3	5.75	1.5	800 523-1918
Delaware Devon B	Growth	-8.8	-13.25	-8.8	4	3	0	2.2	800 523-1918
Delaware Devon C	Growth	-8.9	-13.24	-8.8	4	3	0	2.2	800 523-1918
Delaware Devon I	Growth	-8	-12.38	-7.91	3	3	0	1.2	800 523-1918
Delaware Diversified Growth A	Growth	-9.3	-20.48	-8.32		4	5.75	0.95	800 523-1918
Delaware Diversified Growth B	Growth	-9.8					0	1.75	800 523-1918
Delaware Diversified Growth C	Growth	-9.6					0	1.75	800 523-1918
Delaware Diversified Growth I	Growth	-8.9	-20.39	-8.25		4	0	0.75	800 523-1918
Delaware Diversified Value A	Income	-9.5	-2.93			2	5.75	1	800 523-1918
Delaware Diversified Value B	Income	-10.7					0	1.75	800 523-1918
Delaware Diversified Value C	Income	-10.7					0	1.75	800 523-1918
Delaware Diversified Value I	Income	-9.4	-2.85			2	0	0.75	800 523-1918
Delaware Emerging Markets A	Foreign	-0.9	1.21	-0.85	2	3	5.75	1.5	800 523-1918
Delaware Emerging Markets B	Foreign	-1.6	0.46	-1.59	2	3	0	2.25	800 523-1918
Delaware Emerging Markets C	Foreign	-1.6	0.46	-1.61	2	3	0	2.25	800 523-1918
Delaware Emerging Markets I	Foreign	-0.6	1.43	-0.57	2	3	0	1.7	800 523-1918
Delaware Focus Growth A	Growth	-11	-12.13			4	5.75	0.75	800 523-1918
Delaware Focus Growth I	Growth	-11	-12.13			4	0	0.75	800 523-1918
Delaware Focus Value A	Other	-5.9	-7.05			3	5.75	1.2	800 523-1918
Delaware Focus Value I	Other	-5.9	-7.05			3	0	1.18	800 523-1918
Delaware Foundation Balancd Alloc A	Balanced	-0.1	-2	0.34	2	1	5.75	0.75	800 523-1918
Delaware Foundation Balancd Alloc B	Balanced	-0.8	-2.72	-0.39	2	1	0	1.55	800 523-1918
Delaware Foundation Balancd Alloc C	Balanced	-0.9	-2.72	-0.36	2	2	0	1.55	800 523-1918
Delaware Foundation Balancd Alloc I	Balanced	0.3	-1.72	0.57	2	1	0	0.55	800 523-1918
Delaware Foundation Growth Alloc A	Growth	-5.6	-6.98	-1.87	2	2	5.75	0.75	800 523-1918
Delaware Foundation Growth Alloc B	Growth	-6.3	-7.67	-2.6	3	2	0	1.55	800 523-1918
Delaware Foundation Growth Alloc C	Growth	-6.3	-7.7	-2.6	3	2	0	1.55	800 523-1918
Delaware Foundation Growth Alloc I	Growth	-5.3	-6.74	-1.37	2	2	0	0.55	800 523-1918
Delaware Foundation Income Alloc A	Income	2.9	0.97	1.39	1	1	5.75	0.75	800 523-1918
Delaware Foundation Income Alloc B	Income	2.1	0.2	0.68	1	1	0	1.55	800 523-1918

Stock Fund Name	Objective	Annualized Return for			Rank		Max Load	Expense Ratio	Toll-Free/(Toll) Telephone
		1 Year	3 Years	5 Years	Overall	Risk			
Delaware Foundation Income Alloc C	Income	2.1	0.16	0.6	1	1	0	1.55	800 523-1918
Delaware Foundation Income Alloc I	Income	3.2	1.22	1.66	1	1	0	0.55	800 523-1918
Delaware Growth & Income A	Growth/Inc	-10.6	-5.71	-4.24	3	3	5.75	1.4	800 523-1918
Delaware Growth & Income B	Growth/Inc	-11.3	-6.4	-4.91	3	3	0	2.1	800 523-1918
Delaware Growth & Income C	Growth/Inc	-11.2	-6.37	-4.9	3	3	0	2.1	800 523-1918
Delaware Growth & Income I	Growth/Inc	-10.4	-5.45	-3.95	3	3	0	1.1	800 523-1918
Delaware Growth Opportunities A	Growth	-6.9	-13	3.22	3	4	5.75	1.46	800 523-1918
Delaware Growth Opportunities B	Growth	-7.5	-13.59	2.5	3	4	0	2.46	800 523-1918
Delaware Growth Opportunities C	Growth	-7.6	-13.61	2.5	3	4	0	2.16	800 523-1918
Delaware Growth Opportunities I	Growth	-6.6	-12.75	3.54	3	4	0	1.16	800 523-1918
Delaware Health Care A	Health	7.7					5.75	0.75	800 523-1918
Delaware Health Care I	Health	7.7					0		800 523-1918
Delaware International Equity B	Foreign	-9.6	-3.95	-2.04	3	3	0	2.83	800 523-1918
Delaware International Equity C	Foreign	-9.7	-3.99	-2.04	3	3	0	2.83	800 523-1918
Delaware International Equity I	Foreign	-8.7	-3	-1	3	3	0	1.83	800 523-1918
Delaware Intl Small Cap Value A	Foreign	-8.7	0.69	0.9		2	5.75	1.5	800 523-1918
Delaware Intl Small Cap Value B	Foreign	-9.5					0	2.25	800 523-1918
Delaware Intl Small Cap Value C	Foreign	-9.3					0	2.25	800 523-1918
Delaware Intl Small Cap Value I	Foreign	-8.5	0.85	1		2	0	1.25	800 523-1918
Delaware Intl Value Equity A	Foreign	-9	-3.29	-1.28	3	3	5.75	2.13	800 523-1918
Delaware Pooled Tr-All Cap Gr Eq	Growth	-5.6	-17.1			5	0	1.64	800 523-1918
Delaware Pooled Tr-Emerging Mkts	Foreign	-0.1	2.89	0.36	2	3	0	2.55	800 523-1918
Delaware Pooled Tr-Glbl Equity	Global	-5.8	-2.79	-2.72	3	2	0	1.71	800 523-1918
Delaware Pooled Tr-Intl Equity	Foreign	-7.4	-1.13	1.37	3	2	0	0.75	800 523-1918
Delaware Pooled Tr-Intl Lrg Cap Eq	Foreign	-9.4	-3.95			3	0	1.71	800 523-1918
Delaware Pooled Tr-Intl Small Cap	Foreign	-7.9	1.73			2	0	2.2	800 523-1918
Delaware Pooled Tr-Labor Intl Eq	Foreign	-5.8	-0.28	0.98	3	2	0	1.71	800 523-1918
Delaware Pooled Tr-Lg Cap Val	Growth/Inc	-7.6					0	1.23	800 523-1918
Delaware Pooled Tr-Mid Cap Gr	Agg Growth	-6.4	-11.64	4.78	3	4	0	1.68	800 523-1918
Delaware Pooled Tr-REIT Port I	Real Est	2.1	14.02	7.87	2	1	0	1.1	800 523-1918
Delaware Pooled Tr-REIT Port II	Real Est	1.4	14.46	5.73	2	1	0	1.61	800 523-1918
Delaware Pooled Tr-Sm Cap Growth	Small Co	-3.8					0	1.64	800 523-1918
Delaware Pooled Tr-Sm Cap Val Eq	Small Co	-5	11.36		1	2	0	1.64	800 523-1918
Delaware REIT A	Real Est	1.8	13.75	8.02	2	1	5.75	1.38	800 523-1918
Delaware REIT B	Real Est	1.1	12.92	6.8	2	1	0	2.13	800 523-1918
Delaware REIT C	Real Est	1.1	12.92	6.8	2	1	0	2.13	800 523-1918
Delaware REIT I	Real Est	2.1					0	1.13	800 523-1918
Delaware S&P 500 Index Cons	Other	-8.5	-11.26		3	3	0	0.52	800 523-1918
Delaware S&P 500 Index I	Other	-8.5	-11.22		3	3	0	0.4	800 523-1918
Delaware Select Growth A	Agg Growth	-6.3	-18.26	0.83	3	5	5.75	1.5	800 523-1918
Delaware Select Growth B	Agg Growth	-7	-18.89	0.08	4	5	0	2.25	800 523-1918
Delaware Select Growth C	Agg Growth	-7	-18.89	0.1	4	5	0	2.25	800 523-1918
Delaware Select Growth I	Agg Growth	-6.1	-18.07	1.07	3	5	0	1.25	800 523-1918
Delaware Small Cap Value A	Small Co	-5.9	10.72	3.87	2	2	5.75	1.63	800 523-1918
Delaware Small Cap Value B	Small Co	-6.6	9.94	3.16	2	2	0	2.33	800 523-1918
Delaware Small Cap Value C	Small Co	-6.6	9.94	3.16	2	2	0	2.33	800 523-1918
Delaware Small Cap Value I	Small Co	-5.6	11.07	4.2	2	2	0	1.33	800 523-1918
Delaware Small-Cap Growth A	Small Co	5.4					5.75	1.6	800 523-1918
Delaware Small-Cap Growth B	Small Co	4.6					0	2.35	800 523-1918
Delaware Small-Cap Growth C	Small Co	4.6					0	2.35	800 523-1918
Delaware Small-Cap Growth I	Small Co	5.6					0	1.35	800 523-1918
Delaware Social Awareness A	Growth	-8.1	-10.83	-4.01	3	3	5.75	1.5	800 523-1918
Delaware Social Awareness B	Growth	-8.8	-11.5	-4.75	3	3	0	2.25	800 523-1918
Delaware Social Awareness C	Growth	-8.8	-11.48	-4.74	3	3	0	2.25	800 523-1918
Delaware Social Awareness I	Growth	-7.9	-10.61	-3.79	3	3	0	1.25	800 523-1918
Delaware Technology & Innovation A	Technology	-10.8	-43.57		4	5	5.75	1.45	800 523-1918
Delaware Technology & Innovation B	Technology	-11.6	-43.92		4	5	0	2.2	800 523-1918
Delaware Technology & Innovation C	Technology	-11.6	-43.92		4	5	0	2.2	800 523-1918

301

Stock Fund Name	Objective	Annualized Return for			Rank		Max Load	Expense Ratio	Toll-Free/(Toll) Telephone
		1 Year	3 Years	5 Years	Overall	Risk			
Delaware Technology & Innovation I	Technology	-10.1	-43.31		4	5	0	1.2	800 523-1918
Delaware Trend Fund A	Agg Growth	-5	-10.57	6.4	3	4	5.75	1.45	800 523-1918
Delaware Trend Fund B	Agg Growth	-5.7	-11.22	5.63	3	4	0	2.16	800 523-1918
Delaware Trend Fund C	Agg Growth	-5.7	-11.22	5.63	3	4	0	2.16	800 523-1918
Delaware Trend Fund I	Agg Growth	-4.8	-10.32	6.7	3	4	0	1.16	800 523-1918
Delaware US Growth A	Growth	-15.3	-17.26	-2.72	4	4	5.75	1.4	800 523-1918
Delaware US Growth B	Growth	-15.8	-17.82	-3.39	4	4	0	2.1	800 523-1918
Delaware US Growth C	Growth	-15.8	-17.82	-3.33	3	4	0	2.1	800 523-1918
Delaware US Growth I	Growth	-15	-17.01	-2.58	4	4	0	1.1	800 523-1918
Diversified Inst Aggress Equity	Agg Growth	-14.3	-22.62	-0.6		4	0	1.5	(914 697-8000)
Diversified Inst Balanced	Balanced	-0.8	-3.2	0.13		1	0	1.1	(914 697-8000)
Diversified Inst Equity Growth	Growth	-6.4	-15.89	-1.07		3	0	1.24	(914 697-8000)
Diversified Inst Growth & Income	Growth/Inc	-10.8	-16.94	-3.89		3	0	1.15	(914 697-8000)
Diversified Inst Interm Gov Bond	Other	7.3	7.86	6.16		1	0	0.99	(914 697-8000)
Diversified Inst Interm Horizon	AssetAlloc	-1.3					0	0.2	(914 697-8000)
Diversified Inst International Eq	Other	-14.5	-14.94	-2		3	0	1.4	(914 697-8000)
Diversified Inst Intrm-Long Hor SAF	AssetAlloc	-5.9					0	0.2	(914 697-8000)
Diversified Inst Long Horizon SAF	AssetAlloc	-11.3					0	0.2	(914 697-8000)
Diversified Inst Mid-Cap Growth	Growth	-7.9					0	1.35	(914 697-8000)
Diversified Inst Mid-Cap Value	Growth	-9.6					0	1.25	(914 697-8000)
Diversified Inst Short Horizon SAF	AssetAlloc	5.8					0	0.2	(914 697-8000)
Diversified Inst Shrt-Intrm Hor SAF	AssetAlloc	2.8					0	0.2	(914 697-8000)
Diversified Inst Special Equity	Other	-14.4	-7.16	-0.53		4	0	1.43	(914 697-8000)
Diversified Inst Stock Index	Other	-8.4	-11.11	-1.33		3	0	0.65	(914 697-8000)
Diversified Inst Value & Income	Income	-9.4	-0.4	1.62		2	0	1	(914 697-8000)
Diversified Inv Aggress Equity	Agg Growth	-14.4	-22.55	-0.63		4	0	1.5	(914 697-8000)
Diversified Inv Balanced	Balanced	-1.2	-3.52	-0.2		1	0	1.1	(914 697-8000)
Diversified Inv Equity Growth	Growth	-6.6	-16.19	-1.38		3	0	1.25	(914 697-8000)
Diversified Inv Growth & Income	Growth/Inc	-11.1	-17.05	-4.08		3	0	1.15	(914 697-8000)
Diversified Inv Interm Gov Bond	Other	7	3.77	2.02		1	0	0.99	(914 697-8000)
Diversified Inv Interm Horizon SAF	AssetAlloc	-1.2	-0.96	2.6		1	0	0.2	(914 697-8000)
Diversified Inv International Eq	Other	-14.7	-15.15	-2.25		3	0	1.4	(914 697-8000)
Diversified Inv Intrm-Long Horizon	AssetAlloc	-4.6	-4.57	1.35		2	0	0.2	(914 697-8000)
Diversified Inv Long Horizon SAF	AssetAlloc	-11.2	-9.74	-1.4		3	0	0.2	(914 697-8000)
Diversified Inv Mid-Cap Growth	Growth	-8.7					0	1.35	(914 697-8000)
Diversified Inv Mid-Cap Value	Growth	-10.1					0	1.25	(914 697-8000)
Diversified Inv Short Horizon SAF	AssetAlloc	5.6	6.28	4.76		1	0	0.2	(914 697-8000)
Diversified Inv Shrt-Intrm Horizon	AssetAlloc	3.1	2.45	3.6		1	0	0.2	(914 697-8000)
Diversified Inv Small Cap Value	Global						0	1.4	(914 697-8000)
Diversified Inv Special Equity	Other	-14.6	-7.45	-0.85		4	0	1.43	(914 697-8000)
Diversified Inv Stock Index	Other	-8.7	-11.47	-1.72		3	0	0.65	(914 697-8000)
Diversified Inv Value & Income	Income	-9.6	-0.66	1.37		2	0	1	(914 697-8000)
Dodge & Cox Balanced Fund	Balanced	2.2	8.66	8.41	1	1	0	0.53	800 621-3979
Dodge & Cox Stock Fund	Growth/Inc	-4.9	5.87	7.79	2	2	0	0.54	800 621-3979
Domini Institutional Social Eq	Other	-8.2	-11.31	-0.8	3	3	0	0.3	800 762-6814
Domini Social Equity	Growth	-8.4	-11.75	-1.32	3	3	0	0.92	800 762-6814
Dreyfus Appreciation Fund	Growth	-9.6	-7.54	-0.05	3	2	0	0.91	800 782-6620
Dreyfus Balanced Fund	Balanced	-4.8	-4.73	-0.07	2	2	0	1.01	800 782-6620
Dreyfus Basic S&P 500 Stock Idx	Growth/Inc	-8.3	-11.05	-1.3	3	3	0	0.2	800 782-6620
Dreyfus Disciplined Stock Fund	Growth/Inc	-10.7	-12.4	-2.93	4	3	0	1	800 782-6620
Dreyfus Emerging Leaders Fund	Small Co	-9.7	-4.51	4.29	2	4	0	1.34	800 782-6620
Dreyfus Founders Bal Fd F	Balanced	-5.4	-8.77	-5.57	3	2	0	1.23	800 645-6561
Dreyfus Founders Balanced Fund A	Balanced	-5.6	-9.39		3	2	5.75	2.33	800 645-6561
Dreyfus Founders Balanced Fund B	Balanced	-6.3	-9.93		3	2	0	2.9	800 645-6561
Dreyfus Founders Balanced Fund C	Balanced	-6.7	-10.27		3	2	0	4.6	800 645-6561
Dreyfus Founders Balanced Fund R	Balanced	-0.3	-9.52		3	3	0		800 645-6561
Dreyfus Founders Balanced Fund T	Balanced	-0.5	-8.8		3	3	4.5	1.29	800 645-6561
Dreyfus Founders Discovery Fund A	Small Co	-17.9	-18.03		5	5	5.75	1.21	800 645-6561

Stock Fund Name	Objective	Annualized Return for			Rank		Max Load	Expense Ratio	Toll-Free/(Toll) Telephone
		1 Year	3 Years	5 Years	Overall	Risk			
Dreyfus Founders Discovery Fund B	Small Co	-18.7	-18.73		5	5	0	2.1	800 645-6561
Dreyfus Founders Discovery Fund C	Small Co	-18.7	-18.73		5	5	0	2.1	800 645-6561
Dreyfus Founders Discovery Fund F	Small Co	-17.9	-18.05	2.97	4	5	0	1.25	800 645-6561
Dreyfus Founders Discovery Fund R	Small Co	-17.7	-17.82		5	5	0	0.98	800 645-6561
Dreyfus Founders Discovery Fund T	Small Co	-18.3	-18.46		5	5	4.5	2.22	800 645-6561
Dreyfus Founders Gr & Inc A	Growth/Inc	-9.8	-16.1		3	3	5.75	3.1	800 645-6561
Dreyfus Founders Gr & Inc B	Growth/Inc	-10.4	-16.23		4	3	0	2.45	800 645-6561
Dreyfus Founders Gr & Inc C	Growth/Inc	-10.5	-16.8		4	3	0	4.1	800 645-6561
Dreyfus Founders Gr & Inc F	Growth/Inc	-9.4	-15.36	-7.45	3	3	0	1.14	800 645-6561
Dreyfus Founders Gr & Inc R	Growth/Inc	-9.9	-15.76		3	3	0	4.49	800 645-6561
Dreyfus Founders Gr & Inc T	Growth/Inc	-10.2	-16.35		4	3	4.5	4.7	800 645-6561
Dreyfus Founders Growth Fund A	Growth	-10.7	-20.82		4	4	5.75	1.31	800 645-6561
Dreyfus Founders Growth Fund B	Growth	-11.5	-21.39		4	4	0	2.08	800 645-6561
Dreyfus Founders Growth Fund C	Growth	-11.5	-21.44		4	4	0	2.31	800 645-6561
Dreyfus Founders Growth Fund F	Growth	-10.6	-20.76	-7.51	3	4	0	1.31	800 645-6561
Dreyfus Founders Growth Fund R	Growth	-10.4	-20.67		4	4	0	1.86	800 645-6561
Dreyfus Founders Growth Fund T	Growth	-11.4	-21.55		4	4	4.5	3.64	800 645-6561
Dreyfus Founders Intl Equity A	Foreign	-19.8	-22.03		5	3	5.75	1.4	800 645-6561
Dreyfus Founders Intl Equity B	Foreign	-20.4	-22.62		5	3	0	2.15	800 645-6561
Dreyfus Founders Intl Equity C	Foreign	-20.4	-22.67		5	3	0	2.15	800 645-6561
Dreyfus Founders Intl Equity F	Foreign	-19.8	-22	-7.74	5	3	0	1.55	800 645-6561
Dreyfus Founders Intl Equity R	Foreign	-19.6	-21.85		5	3	0	1.15	800 645-6561
Dreyfus Founders Intl Equity T	Foreign	-20	-22.23		5	3	4.5	1.65	800 645-6561
Dreyfus Founders Mid-Cap Growth A	Agg Growth	-10.8	-18.07		5	4	5.75	3.26	800 645-6561
Dreyfus Founders Mid-Cap Growth B	Agg Growth	-11.8	-18.53		5	4	0	3.12	800 645-6561
Dreyfus Founders Mid-Cap Growth C	Agg Growth	-11.4	-18.82		5	4	0	4.06	800 645-6561
Dreyfus Founders Mid-Cap Growth F	Agg Growth	-10.6	-17.66	-7.8	4	4	0	1.39	800 645-6561
Dreyfus Founders Mid-Cap Growth R	Agg Growth	-10.4	-17.82		4	4	0	3.92	800 645-6561
Dreyfus Founders Mid-Cap Growth T	Agg Growth	-12.2	-18.96		5	4	4.5		800 782-6620
Dreyfus Founders Passport Fund A	Foreign	-8.9	-17.5		4	4	5.75	1.97	800 645-6561
Dreyfus Founders Passport Fund B	Foreign	-9.7	-18.19		5	4	0	3.07	800 645-6561
Dreyfus Founders Passport Fund C	Foreign	-9.6	-18.19		5	4	0	2.8	800 645-6561
Dreyfus Founders Passport Fund F	Foreign	-8.9	-17.51	-3.99	4	4	0	1.92	800 645-6561
Dreyfus Founders Passport Fund R	Foreign	-10.4	-18.46		5	4	0	4.31	800 645-6561
Dreyfus Founders Passport Fund T	Foreign	-9.6	-18.46		5	4	4.5	4.65	800 645-6561
Dreyfus Founders WW Growth F	Global	-14.1	-20	-8.47	5	3	0	1.61	800 645-6561
Dreyfus Founders Worldwide Grwth A	Global	-14.2	-20.25		5	3	5.75	2.47	800 645-6561
Dreyfus Founders Worldwide Grwth B	Global	-14.8	-20.71		5	3	0	2.8	800 645-6561
Dreyfus Founders Worldwide Grwth C	Global	-14.8	-21.21		5	3	0	4.5	800 645-6561
Dreyfus Founders Worldwide Grwth R	Global	-13.7	-19.69		5	3	0	1.25	800 645-6561
Dreyfus Founders Worldwide Grwth T	Global	-16.3	-21.57		5	3	4.5	4.62	800 645-6561
Dreyfus Fund	Growth/Inc	-10.5	-11.58	-3.06	4	3	0	0.73	800 782-6620
Dreyfus Growth & Income	Growth/Inc	-10.8	-9.67	-1.92	3	3	0	1.01	800 782-6620
Dreyfus Growth Opportunity	Growth	-8.6	-12.27	-3.74	4	3	0	1.05	800 782-6620
Dreyfus Intl Stock Index	Foreign	-14.1	-14.34	-5.26	4	3	0	0.6	800 782-6620
Dreyfus Inv Port-Emerging Leaders	Growth	-6.9	9.01		1	4	0	1.46	800 782-6620
Dreyfus Large Company Value	Growth	-10.4	-4.5	-0.85	3	2	0	1.25	800 782-6620
Dreyfus Lifetime Gr & Inc Inv	AssetAlloc	-2.5	-2.47	1.56	2	1	0	1.34	800 782-6620
Dreyfus Lifetime Gr & Inc Rest	AssetAlloc	-2.1					0	0.84	800 782-6620
Dreyfus Lifetime Growth Inv	AssetAlloc	-11.1					0	1.48	800 782-6620
Dreyfus Lifetime Growth Rest	AssetAlloc	-10.6					0	0.91	800 782-6620
Dreyfus Mid-Cap Value Plus	Global	-10.2					0	1.5	800 782-6620
Dreyfus MidCap Index Fund	Growth	-9.6	0.52	6.41	3	3	0	0.5	800 782-6620
Dreyfus Midcap Value	Growth	-7.8	1.47	6.2	2	5	0	1.2	800 782-6620
Dreyfus Premier Balanced Fd A	Balanced	-5.9	-7.08	-0.85	2	2	5.75	1.25	800 782-6620
Dreyfus Premier Balanced Fd B	Balanced	-6.6	-7.76	-1.58	2	2	0	2	800 782-6620
Dreyfus Premier Balanced Fd C	Balanced	-6.7	-7.76	-1.59	3	2	0	2	800 782-6620
Dreyfus Premier Balanced Fd R	Balanced	-5.7	-6.84	-0.59	2	2	0	1	800 782-6620

Stock Fund Name	Objective	Annualized Return for			Rank		Max Load	Expense Ratio	Toll-Free/(Toll) Telephone
		1 Year	3 Years	5 Years	Overall	Risk			
Dreyfus Premier Balanced Fd T	Balanced	-6.2					4.5	1.5	800 782-6620
Dreyfus Premier Core Equity A	Growth	-10.8					0	1.35	800 782-6620
Dreyfus Premier Core Equity B	Growth	-11.4					0	2.1	800 782-6620
Dreyfus Premier Core Equity C	Growth	-11.4					0	2.1	800 782-6620
Dreyfus Premier Core Equity R	Growth	-10.6					0	1.1	800 782-6620
Dreyfus Premier Core Equity T	Growth	-11.1					0	1.6	800 782-6620
Dreyfus Premier Core Value A	Growth	-13.4	-4.95	0.23	3	3	5.75	1.15	800 782-6620
Dreyfus Premier Core Value B	Growth	-14	-5.66	-0.53	3	3	0	1.9	800 782-6620
Dreyfus Premier Core Value C	Growth	-14	-5.66	-0.53	3	3	0	1.9	800 782-6620
Dreyfus Premier Core Value Inst	Growth	-13.3	-4.86	0.34	3	3	0	1.05	800 782-6620
Dreyfus Premier Core Value R	Growth	-13.2	-4.7	0.48	3	3	0	0.9	800 782-6620
Dreyfus Premier Core Value T	Growth	-13.6					4.5	1.4	800 782-6620
Dreyfus Premier Develop Markets A	Foreign	-6.2	-3.97	1.62	3	4	5.75	2.25	800 782-6620
Dreyfus Premier Develop Markets B	Foreign	-7	-4.75	0.76	3	4	0	3	800 782-6620
Dreyfus Premier Develop Markets C	Foreign	-6.9	-4.73	0.83	3	4	0	3	800 782-6620
Dreyfus Premier Develop Markets R	Foreign	-6	-3.93	3.16	3	4	0	2	800 782-6620
Dreyfus Premier Develop Markets T	Foreign	-6.3					4.5	2.25	800 782-6620
Dreyfus Premier Emerging Markets A	Foreign	-5.4	2.14	7.12	2	3	5.75	1.82	800 782-6620
Dreyfus Premier European Eq A	European	-12.1	-13.13		4	3	5.75	2.25	800 782-6620
Dreyfus Premier European Eq B	European	-12.8	-13.82		4	3	0	3	800 782-6620
Dreyfus Premier European Eq C	European	-12.6	-13.69		4	3	0	3	800 782-6620
Dreyfus Premier European Eq R	European	-11.9	-12.89		4	3	0	2	800 782-6620
Dreyfus Premier European Eq T	European	-9.2					4.5	2.5	800 782-6620
Dreyfus Premier Future Leaders A	Growth	-10.5					5.75	1.43	800 782-6620
Dreyfus Premier Future Leaders B	Growth	-11.2					0	2.19	800 782-6620
Dreyfus Premier Future Leaders C	Growth	-11.2					0	2.19	800 782-6620
Dreyfus Premier Future Leaders R	Growth	-10.2					0	1.1	800 782-6620
Dreyfus Premier Future Leaders T	Growth	-10.9					4.5	1.79	800 782-6620
Dreyfus Premier Greater China A	Pacific	-10.9	-6.82	8.86	3	3	5.75	2.25	800 782-6620
Dreyfus Premier Greater China B	Pacific	-11.5	-7.55	7.99	3	3	0	3	800 782-6620
Dreyfus Premier Greater China C	Pacific	-11.5	-7.54	8.01	3	3	0	3	800 782-6620
Dreyfus Premier Greater China R	Pacific	-10.5	-6.51	9.17	3	3	0	2	800 782-6620
Dreyfus Premier Greater China T	Pacific	-10.9					4.5	2.5	800 782-6620
Dreyfus Premier Growth & Inc A	Growth/Inc	-11.4	-10.27	-2.62	3	3	5.75	1.46	800 782-6620
Dreyfus Premier Growth & Inc B	Growth/Inc	-12.2	-10.98	-3.39	4	3	0	2.22	800 782-6620
Dreyfus Premier Growth & Inc C	Growth/Inc	-12.1	-10.93	-3.33	4	3	0	2.19	800 782-6620
Dreyfus Premier Growth & Inc R	Growth/Inc	-11.4	-10.24	-2.56	3	3	0	1.43	800 782-6620
Dreyfus Premier Growth & Inc T	Growth/Inc	-13					4.5	2.48	800 782-6620
Dreyfus Premier Health Care C	Health						0		800 782-6620
Dreyfus Premier Health Care Fd	Health	-0.1					0	1.65	800 782-6620
Dreyfus Premier Health Care R	Health						0		800 782-6620
Dreyfus Premier Health Care T	Health						4.5		800 782-6620
Dreyfus Premier High Income A	Income						0		800 782-6620
Dreyfus Premier High Income B	Income						0		800 782-6620
Dreyfus Premier High Income C	Income						0		800 782-6620
Dreyfus Premier High Income R	Income						0		800 782-6620
Dreyfus Premier Intl Equity A	Foreign						0		800 782-6620
Dreyfus Premier Intl Equity B	Foreign						0		800 782-6620
Dreyfus Premier Intl Equity C	Foreign						0		800 782-6620
Dreyfus Premier Intl Equity R	Foreign						0		800 782-6620
Dreyfus Premier Intl Equity T	Foreign						0		800 782-6620
Dreyfus Premier Intl Growth A	Foreign	-15.9	-21.71	-10.6	5	3	5.75	1.83	800 782-6620
Dreyfus Premier Intl Growth B	Foreign	-16.8	-22.44	-11.39	5	3	0	2.8	800 782-6620
Dreyfus Premier Intl Growth C	Foreign	-16.5	-22.39	-11.38	5	3	0	2.71	800 782-6620
Dreyfus Premier Intl Growth R	Foreign	-15.6	-21.37	-10.41	5	3	0	1.47	800 782-6620
Dreyfus Premier Intl Growth T	Foreign	-17					4.5	2.72	800 782-6620
Dreyfus Premier Intl Opp A	Foreign	-15.6	-6.78	-1.53	3	2	5.75	2	800 782-6620
Dreyfus Premier Intl Opp B	Foreign	-16.2	-7.51	-2.31	3	2	0	2.75	800 782-6620

Stock Fund Name	Objective	Annualized Return for			Rank		Max Load	Expense Ratio	Toll-Free/(Toll) Telephone
		1 Year	3 Years	5 Years	Overall	Risk			
Dreyfus Premier Intl Opp C	Foreign	-16.2	-7.5	-2.29	3	2	0	2.75	800 782-6620
Dreyfus Premier Intl Opp R	Foreign	-15.1	-6.45	-1.22	3	2	0	1.75	800 782-6620
Dreyfus Premier Intl Opp T	Foreign	-14.2					4.5	2.25	800 782-6620
Dreyfus Premier Intl Small Cap A	Foreign						0		800 782-6620
Dreyfus Premier Intl Small Cap B	Foreign						0		800 782-6620
Dreyfus Premier Intl Small Cap C	Foreign						0		800 782-6620
Dreyfus Premier Intl Small Cap R	Foreign						0		800 782-6620
Dreyfus Premier Intl Small Cap T	Foreign						0		800 782-6620
Dreyfus Premier Intl Value	Foreign	-15.2	-5.74	-1.25	3	3	0	1.39	800 782-6620
Dreyfus Premier Japan Fund A	Pacific	-23.2	-20.51		5	3	5.75	2.25	800 782-6620
Dreyfus Premier Japan Fund B	Pacific	-23.9	-21.16		5	3	0	3	800 782-6620
Dreyfus Premier Japan Fund C	Pacific	-23.8	-21.12		5	3	0	3	800 782-6620
Dreyfus Premier Japan Fund R	Pacific	-23	-20.3		5	3	0	2	800 782-6620
Dreyfus Premier Japan Fund T	Pacific	-23.6	-20.75		5	3	4.5	2.5	800 782-6620
Dreyfus Premier Large Co Stock A	Growth/Inc	-10.9	-12.58	-3.06	4	3	5.75	1.15	800 782-6620
Dreyfus Premier Large Co Stock B	Growth/Inc	-11.6	-13.25	-3.81	5	3	0	1.9	800 782-6620
Dreyfus Premier Large Co Stock C	Growth/Inc	-11.6	-13.24	-3.79	5	3	0	1.9	800 782-6620
Dreyfus Premier Large Co Stock R	Growth/Inc	-10.7	-12.39	-2.83	4	3	0	0.9	800 782-6620
Dreyfus Premier Large Co Stock T	Growth/Inc	-11.2					4.5	1.4	800 782-6620
Dreyfus Premier Micro-Cap Growth A	Growth	-3.2					5.75	2.8	800 782-6620
Dreyfus Premier Micro-Cap Growth B	Growth	-4					0	3.57	800 782-6620
Dreyfus Premier Micro-Cap Growth C	Growth	-3.9					0	3.56	800 782-6620
Dreyfus Premier Micro-Cap Growth T	Growth	-3.5					4.5	3.06	800 782-6620
Dreyfus Premier Midcap Stock A	Growth	-8.5	-1.45	2.27	2	3	5.75	1.35	800 782-6620
Dreyfus Premier Midcap Stock B	Growth	-9.2	-2.22	1.5	3	3	0	2.1	800 782-6620
Dreyfus Premier Midcap Stock C	Growth	-9.2	-2.2	1.51	3	3	0	2.1	800 782-6620
Dreyfus Premier Midcap Stock R	Growth	-8.3	-1.21	2.54	2	3	0	1.1	800 782-6620
Dreyfus Premier Midcap Stock T	Growth	-8.7					4.5	1.6	800 782-6620
Dreyfus Premier New Leaders A	Growth	-6	-2.64	3.29	2	3	5.75	1.16	800 782-6620
Dreyfus Premier New Leaders R	Growth						0	0.91	800 782-6620
Dreyfus Premier Nextech A	Growth	-15.6					5.75	1.61	800 782-6620
Dreyfus Premier Nextech B	Growth	-16.4					0	2.35	800 782-6620
Dreyfus Premier Nextech C	Growth	-16.4					0	2.36	800 782-6620
Dreyfus Premier Nextech T	Growth	-16					4.5	1.93	800 782-6620
Dreyfus Premier Select Growth A	Growth						0		800 782-6620
Dreyfus Premier Select Growth B	Growth						0		800 782-6620
Dreyfus Premier Select Growth C	Growth						0		800 782-6620
Dreyfus Premier Select Growth R	Growth						0		800 782-6620
Dreyfus Premier Select Growth T	Growth						0		800 782-6620
Dreyfus Premier Select Mid-Cap Gr A	Growth						0		800 782-6620
Dreyfus Premier Select Mid-Cap Gr B	Growth						0		800 782-6620
Dreyfus Premier Select Mid-Cap Gr C	Growth						0		800 782-6620
Dreyfus Premier Select Mid-Cap Gr T	Growth						0		800 782-6620
Dreyfus Premier Small Cap Eqty A	Small Co						0		800 782-6620
Dreyfus Premier Small Cap Eqty B	Small Co						0		800 782-6620
Dreyfus Premier Small Cap Eqty C	Small Co						0		800 782-6620
Dreyfus Premier Small Cap Eqty R	Small Co						0		800 782-6620
Dreyfus Premier Small Cap Eqty T	Small Co						0		800 782-6620
Dreyfus Premier Small Cap Val A	Small Co	-5.1	11.01	4.2	2	3	5.75	1.5	800 782-6620
Dreyfus Premier Small Cap Val B	Small Co	-5.8	10.22	3.45	2	3	0	2.25	800 782-6620
Dreyfus Premier Small Cap Val C	Small Co	-5.8	10.24	3.45	2	3	0	2.25	800 782-6620
Dreyfus Premier Small Cap Val R	Small Co	-4.8	11.33	4.37	1	3	0	1.25	800 782-6620
Dreyfus Premier Small Cap Val T	Small Co	-5.3					4.5	1.75	800 782-6620
Dreyfus Premier Strategic Value A	Agg Growth	-4.4	-1	2.74	2	4	5.75	1.48	800 782-6620
Dreyfus Premier Tax Mgd Grwth A	Growth	-10.2	-8.22	-0.56	3	2	5.75	1.35	800 782-6620
Dreyfus Premier Tax Mgd Grwth B	Growth	-10.9	-8.9	-1.32	3	2	0	2.1	800 782-6620
Dreyfus Premier Tax Mgd Grwth C	Growth	-10.9	-8.91	-1.32	3	2	0	2.1	800 782-6620
Dreyfus Premier Tax Mgd Grwth T	Growth	-10.4	-8.44	-0.82	3	2	4.5	1.6	800 782-6620

Stock Fund Name	Objective	Annualized Return for			Rank		Max Load	Expense Ratio	Toll-Free/(Toll) Telephone
		1 Year	3 Years	5 Years	Overall	Risk			
Dreyfus Premier Tech Growth A	Technology	-6	-28.6	7.32	3	5	5.75	1.28	800 782-6620
Dreyfus Premier Tech Growth B	Technology	-6.9	-29.23		4	5	0	2.43	800 782-6620
Dreyfus Premier Tech Growth C	Technology	-6.9	-29.19		4	5	0	2.38	800 782-6620
Dreyfus Premier Tech Growth R	Technology	-5.4	-28.28		4	5	0	1.15	800 782-6620
Dreyfus Premier Tech Growth T	Technology	-6.4	-28.94		4	5	4.5	1.99	800 782-6620
Dreyfus Premier Third Century A	Growth	-15					5.75	1.12	800 782-6620
Dreyfus Premier Third Century B	Growth	-15.6					0	1.93	800 782-6620
Dreyfus Premier Third Century C	Growth	-15.6					0	1.98	800 782-6620
Dreyfus Premier Third Century R	Growth	-14.5					0	0.81	800 782-6620
Dreyfus Premier Third Century T	Growth	-15.3					4.5	1.78	800 782-6620
Dreyfus Premier Third Century Z	Growth	-14.8	-18.85	-4.91	5	3	0	1.02	800 782-6620
Dreyfus Premier Value A	Growth	-10.1	-4.17	-0.7	3	2	5.75	1.28	800 782-6620
Dreyfus Premier Value B	Growth	-10.9	-4.96	-1.51	3	2	0	2.1	800 782-6620
Dreyfus Premier Value C	Growth	-10.9	-4.96	-1.56	3	2	0	2.11	800 782-6620
Dreyfus Premier Value R	Growth	-10.5	-4.54	-1.17	3	2	0	1.56	800 782-6620
Dreyfus Premier Value T	Growth	-11.4					4.5	2.38	800 782-6620
Dreyfus Premier Wrldwde Growth A	Global	-9.7	-10.49	-2.12	4	3	5.75	1.32	800 782-6620
Dreyfus Premier Wrldwde Growth B	Global	-10.4	-11.13	-2.83	4	3	0	2.03	800 782-6620
Dreyfus Premier Wrldwde Growth C	Global	-10.4	-11.09	-2.81	4	3	0	2.01	800 782-6620
Dreyfus Premier Wrldwde Growth R	Global	-9.5	-10.21	-1.83	4	3	0	0.93	800 782-6620
Dreyfus Premier Wrldwde Growth T	Global	-9.9					4.5	1.5	800 782-6620
Dreyfus S&P 500 Index Fund	Growth/Inc	-8.5	-11.3	-1.59	3	3	0	0.5	800 782-6620
Dreyfus Small Cap Stock Index Fd	Small Co	-11	3.08	2.87	3	3	0	0.5	800 782-6620
Dreyfus Small Company Value Fund	Small Co	-22.2	-1.57	1.19	3	5	0	1.2	800 782-6620
Dreyfus Stock Index Fund	Growth	-8.3	-11.55	-1.65	3	3	0	0.26	800 782-6620
Driehaus Emerging Markets Growth	Foreign	-3.1	-5.12	8.41	2	4	0	2.5	800 560-6111
Driehaus European Opportunity	European	11.2	-6.91		2	3	0	2.18	800 560-6111
Driehaus International Growth Fund	Foreign	-10	-22.51	-7.58	5	3	0	1.98	800 560-6111
Duncan-Hurst Agg Growth Fund I	Agg Growth	-13.3	-34.54		5	4	0	1.23	800 558-9105
Duncan-Hurst Internat'l Growth I	Foreign	-13.6	-22.85		5	3	0	1.48	800 558-9105
E*TRADE International Index Fund	Foreign	-13	-13.73		3	3	0	0.65	800 786-2575
E*TRADE Russell 2000 Index Fund	Small Co	-9					0	0.65	800 786-2575
E*TRADE S & P 500 Index Fund	Growth	-8.3	-11.28		3	3	0	0.4	800 786-2575
E*TRADE Technology Index Fund	Technology	-7.4	-30.3		4	5	0	0.85	800 786-2575
Eagle Growth Shares	Growth	-11.6	8.06	3.14	2	2	8.5	3.44	800 749-9933
Eaton Vance Asian Small Co A	Pacific	-6.9	-1.34		3	3	5.75	2.49	800 262-1122
Eaton Vance Asian Small Co B	Pacific	-7.4	-4		3	3	5.75	3	800 262-1122
Eaton Vance Balanced A	Balanced	-2	-1.27	-0.5	2	3	5.75	1.18	800 262-1122
Eaton Vance Balanced B	Balanced	-2.6	2	1.17	2	3	0	1.93	800 262-1122
Eaton Vance Emerging Mkts A	Foreign	-2.5	-0.98	2.97	2	3	5.75	2.95	800 262-1122
Eaton Vance Emerging Mkts B	Foreign	-3.1	-1.59	2.43	2	3	0	3.45	800 262-1122
Eaton Vance Greater China Gr A	Pacific	-13.4	-13.32	-1.14	3	3	5.75	2.37	800 262-1122
Eaton Vance Greater China Gr B	Pacific	-14	-14	-1.82	4	3	0	2.87	800 262-1122
Eaton Vance Greater China Gr C	Pacific	-14	-14.06	-1.87	4	3	0	2.87	800 262-1122
Eaton Vance Greater India A	Foreign	10.2	-11.91	-1.68	3	4	5.75	3.9	800 262-1122
Eaton Vance Greater India B	Foreign	9.7	-12.64	-2.37	3	4	0	4.4	800 262-1122
Eaton Vance Growth Fund A	Growth	-8.6	-8.25	-5.57	4	4	5.75	1.29	800 262-1122
Eaton Vance Growth Fund B	Growth	-9.4	-9.05	-6.34	4	4	0	2.04	800 262-1122
Eaton Vance Growth Fund C	Growth	-9.4	-9.02	-6.37	4	4	0	2.04	800 262-1122
Eaton Vance Info Age A	Technology	-12.5	-16.37	1.79	4	3	5.75	1.99	800 262-1122
Eaton Vance Info Age B	Technology	-13.2	-16.96	1.22	4	3	0	2.72	800 262-1122
Eaton Vance Info Age C	Technology	-13.2	-16.94	1.19	4	3	0	2.72	800 262-1122
Eaton Vance Info Age D	Technology	-13.2	-17.46	0.85	4	3	0	2.72	800 262-1122
Eaton Vance Large Cap Growth A	Growth	-11.6					5.75	1.4	800 262-1122
Eaton Vance Large Cap Value A	Growth/Inc	-9.9	0.34	3.2	3	2	5.75	1.13	800 262-1122
Eaton Vance Large Cap Value B	Growth/Inc	-10.6	0.78	3.14	3	2	0	1.88	800 262-1122
Eaton Vance Large Cap Value C	Growth/Inc	-10.6					0	1.88	800 262-1122
Eaton Vance Small Cap Growth A	Small Co	-11.9	-18.55	5.4	3	5	5.75	1.7	800 262-1122

306

Stock Fund Name	Objective	Annualized Return for			Rank		Max Load	Expense Ratio	Toll-Free/(Toll) Telephone
		1 Year	3 Years	5 Years	Overall	Risk			
Eaton Vance Small Cap Growth B	Small Co	-12.4					0	2.75	800 262-1122
Eaton Vance Small Cap Growth C	Small Co	-12.5					0	2.75	800 262-1122
Eaton Vance Small Cap Value A	Small Co	1					5.75	1.75	800 262-1122
Eaton Vance Special Equities A	Small Co	-11.4	-19.6	-4.49	4	5	5.75	1.29	800 262-1122
Eaton Vance Special Equities B	Small Co	-12.1	-20.32	-5.67	4	5	0	2.04	800 262-1122
Eaton Vance Special Equities C	Small Co	-12					0	2.04	800 262-1122
Eaton Vance Tax-Mgd Eqty A-Alloc A	AssetAlloc	-11.6					5.75	1.55	800 262-1122
Eaton Vance Tax-Mgd Eqty A-Alloc B	AssetAlloc	-12.1					0	2.3	800 262-1122
Eaton Vance Tax-Mgd Eqty A-Alloc C	AssetAlloc	-12.2					0	2.3	800 262-1122
Eaton Vance Tax-Mgd Growth 1.0	Growth/Inc	-10.2	-7.91	0.98	3	2	0	0.46	800 262-1122
Eaton Vance Tax-Mgd Growth 1.1 A	Growth	-10.5	-8	0.85	3	2	5.75	0.79	800 262-1122
Eaton Vance Tax-Mgd Growth 1.1 B	Growth	-11.1	-8.66	-0.16	3	2	0	1.54	800 262-1122
Eaton Vance Tax-Mgd Growth 1.1 C	Growth	-11.1	-8.69	0.05	3	2	0	1.54	800 262-1122
Eaton Vance Tax-Mgd Growth 1.1 I	Growth	-10.2	-7.62	1.06	2	2	0	0.54	800 262-1122
Eaton Vance Tax-Mgd Growth 1.2 A	Growth	-10.6	-8.23	0.7	3	2	5.75	1.03	800 262-1122
Eaton Vance Tax-Mgd Growth 1.2 B	Growth	-11.1	-8.96	-0.07	3	2	0	1.77	800 262-1122
Eaton Vance Tax-Mgd Growth 1.2 C	Growth	-11.2	-8.97	-0.13	3	2	0	1.77	800 262-1122
Eaton Vance Tax-Mgd Growth 1.2 D	Growth	-11.2	-8.96	-0.07	3	2	0	1.77	800 262-1122
Eaton Vance Tax-Mgd Growth 1.2 I	Growth	-10.4	-8.14	0.7	3	2	0	0.78	800 262-1122
Eaton Vance Tax-Mgd Intl Gr A	Foreign	-23.9	-25.44	-10.91	5	4	5.75	1.82	800 262-1122
Eaton Vance Tax-Mgd Intl Gr B	Foreign	-24.4	-25.98	-11.58	5	4	0	2.57	800 262-1122
Eaton Vance Tax-Mgd Intl Gr C	Foreign	-24.5	-25.98	-11.6	5	4	0	2.57	800 262-1122
Eaton Vance Tax-Mgd Intl Gr D	Foreign	-24.5	-25.26	-11.07	5	4	0	2.57	800 262-1122
Eaton Vance Tax-Mgd Mid-Cap Core A	Global	-8					5.75	1.65	800 262-1122
Eaton Vance Tax-Mgd Mid-Cap Core B	Global	-8.7					0	2.4	800 262-1122
Eaton Vance Tax-Mgd Mid-Cap Core C	Global	-8.6					0	2.3	800 262-1122
Eaton Vance Tax-Mgd MultiCap Opp A	Growth	-6.7					5.75	1.6	800 262-1122
Eaton Vance Tax-Mgd MultiCap Opp B	Growth	-7.4					0	2.35	800 262-1122
Eaton Vance Tax-Mgd MultiCap Opp C	Growth	-7.4					0	2.35	800 262-1122
Eaton Vance Tax-Mgd Sm Cp Gr 1.2 A	Growth	-12.8	-19.32	-4.21	4	5	5.75	1.24	800 262-1122
Eaton Vance Tax-Mgd Sm Cp Gr 1.2 B	Growth	-13.7	-19.92	-4.95	4	5	0	2.14	800 262-1122
Eaton Vance Tax-Mgd Sm Cp Gr 1.2 C	Growth	-13.7	-19.94	-5	4	5	0	2.14	800 262-1122
Eaton Vance Tax-Mgd SmCap Gr 1.1 A	Growth	-13	-19.19	-4.12	4	5	5.75	1.42	800 262-1122
Eaton Vance Tax-Mgd SmCap Gr 1.1 B	Growth	-13.7	-19.82	-4.88	5	5	0	1.99	800 262-1122
Eaton Vance Tax-Mgd SmCap Gr 1.1 C	Growth	-13.6	-19.82	-4.91	5	5	0	1.99	800 262-1122
Eaton Vance Tax-Mgd Small-Cap Val A	Global	-8.3					5.75	1.75	800 262-1122
Eaton Vance Tax-Mgd Small-Cap Val B	Global	-8.9					0	2.5	800 262-1122
Eaton Vance Tax-Mgd Small-Cap Val C	Global	-8.8					0	2.5	800 262-1122
Eaton Vance Tax-Mgd Value A	Growth	-10.2	1.45		2	2	5.75	1.26	800 262-1122
Eaton Vance Tax-Mgd Value B	Growth	-10.9	0.68		2	2	0	2.01	800 262-1122
Eaton Vance Tax-Mgd Value C	Growth	-10.9	0.67		2	2	0	2.01	800 262-1122
Eaton Vance Tax-Mgd Value D	Growth	-10.9	0.67		2	2	0	2.01	800 262-1122
Eaton Vance Utilities A	Utilities	0	-5.08	5.16	1	3	5.75	1.1	800 262-1122
Eaton Vance Utilities B	Utilities	-0.6	-5.78	4.41	2	3	0	1.85	800 262-1122
Eaton Vance Utilities C	Utilities	-0.8					0	1.85	800 262-1122
Eaton Vance WW Health Sciences A	Health	5.1	4.12	17.73	2	4	5.75	1.67	800 262-1122
Eaton Vance WW Health Sciences B	Health	4.2	3.33	16.87	2	4	0	2.42	800 262-1122
Eaton Vance WW Health Sciences C	Health	4.2	3.33	16.85	2	4	0	2.42	800 262-1122
Eaton Vance WW Health Sciences D	Health	4.1	3.33	16.85	2	4	0	2.42	800 262-1122
Eclipse Asset Manager Fund L	AssetAlloc						0	1.83	866 232-5477
Eclipse Asset Manager NL	AssetAlloc	-3.5	-3.66	2.02	2	1	0	0.83	866 232-5477
Eclipse Asset Manager Svc	AssetAlloc	-3.8					0	1.08	866 232-5477
Eclipse Balanced Fd	Balanced	2.1	9.25	4.69	1	1	0	0.94	866 232-5477
Eclipse Balanced L	Balanced						0	1.94	866 232-5477
Eclipse Balanced Serv	Balanced						0	1.19	866 232-5477
Eclipse Growth Equity Fd NL	Growth	-13.9	-18.3	-4.03	5	3	0	0.93	866 232-5477
Eclipse Growth Equity Fd Svc	Growth	-14.1					0	1.18	866 232-5477
Eclipse Indexed Equity Fund	Growth/Inc	-8.2	-10.91	-1.13	3	3	0	0.3	866 232-5477

| Stock Fund Name | Objective | Annualized Return for | | | Rank | | Max Load | Expense Ratio | Toll-Free/(Toll) Telephone |
		1 Year	3 Years	5 Years	Overall	Risk			
Eclipse Indexed Equity Fund Svc	Growth/Inc	-8.4					0	0.55	866 232-5477
Eclipse Int Broad Mkt Fd NL	Foreign	-14.9	-14.84	-5.66	5	2	0	0.94	866 232-5477
Eclipse Int Broad Mkt Fd Serv	Foreign	-14.5					0	1.19	866 232-5477
Eclipse Intl Equity Fd NL	Foreign	-1.9	-5.86	-0.41	3	2	0	1.03	866 232-5477
Eclipse Intl Equity Fd Svc	Foreign	-2.2	-6.04	-0.65	3	2	0	1.28	866 232-5477
Eclipse Mid Cap Core Fund	Growth	-7.2					0	1	866 232-5477
Eclipse Mid Cap Value Fd	Growth/Inc	-4.4	7.05	2	2	2	0	1.04	866 232-5477
Eclipse Mid Cap Value L	Growth						0	2.04	866 232-5477
Eclipse Mid Cap Value Serv	Growth						0	1.29	866 232-5477
Eclipse Small Cap Value Fd	Small Co	-4.4	7.24	1.88	2	2	0	1.19	866 232-5477
Eclipse Small Cap Value L	Small Co						0	2.19	866 232-5477
Eclipse Small Cap Value Serv	Small Co						0	1.44	866 232-5477
Eclipse Tax Managed Equity L	Income						0	1.95	866 232-5477
Eclipse Tax Managed Equity NL	Growth/Inc	-9.2					0	0.95	866 232-5477
Eclipse Ultra Short Duration Serv	Growth						0		866 232-5477
Eclipse Value Equity Fund	Growth/Inc	-15.1	-2.85	-2.56	3	3	0	0.94	866 232-5477
Eclipse Value Equity Fund Svc	Growth/Inc	-15.4					0	1.19	866 232-5477
Edgar Lomax Value Fund	Growth/Inc	-13.9	-1.59	-0.05	3	3	0		888 263-6443
Ehrenkrantz Growth Fund	Growth	7.6	-8.05	1.53	2	3	0		800 867-8600
Elfun Diversified Fund	Flexible	-0.1	-0.02	4.46	1	1	0	0.21	800 242-0134
Elfun International Fund	Foreign	-15.7	-13.74	-2.89	3	3	0	0.33	800 242-0134
Elfun Trusts	Growth	-7.2	-5.15	3.41	2	3	0	0.18	800 242-0134
Emerald Growth A	Small Co	-7.4	-6.7	2.12	3	4	4.75	1.7	800 232-0224
Emerald Select Banking & Finance A	Financial	11	22.75	9.89	1	1	4.75	1.96	800 232-0224
Emerald Select Technology C	Technology	-11.8	-33.64	-8.68	3	5	2.89	3	800 232-0224
Enterprise Capital Appreciation A	Growth	-9.8	-9.58	0.69	3	3	4.75	1.67	800 432-4320
Enterprise Capital Appreciation B	Growth	-10.3	-10.08	0.14	3	3	0	2.22	800 432-4320
Enterprise Capital Appreciation C	Growth	-10.3	-10.06	0.2	4	3	1	2.22	800 432-4320
Enterprise Capital Appreciation Y	Growth	-9.4					0	1.23	800 432-4320
Enterprise Equity Income A	Income	-11.9	-5.82	-1.96	3	2	4.75	1.5	800 432-4320
Enterprise Equity Income B	Income	-12.3	-6.29	-2.5	3	2	0	2.05	800 432-4320
Enterprise Equity Income C	Income	-12.3	-6.29	-2.7	3	2	1	2.05	800 432-4320
Enterprise Equity Income Y	Income	-11.5	-5.37	-1.52	3	2	0	1.05	800 432-4320
Enterprise Growth and Income A	Growth/Inc	-13.5	-12.56	-1.09	4	3	4.75	1.5	800 432-4320
Enterprise Growth and Income B	Growth/Inc	-14	-13.03	-1.61	4	3	0	2.05	800 432-4320
Enterprise Growth and Income C	Growth/Inc	-14	-13.02	-1.59	4	3	1	2.05	800 432-4320
Enterprise Growth and Income Y	Growth/Inc	-13.1					0	1.05	800 432-4320
Enterprise Multi-Cap Growth A	Agg Growth	-11.9	-19.48		5	4	4.75	1.85	800 432-4320
Enterprise Multi-Cap Growth B	Agg Growth	-12.4	-19.94		5	4	0	2.4	800 432-4320
Enterprise Multi-Cap Growth C	Agg Growth	-12.3	-19.94		5	4	1	2.4	800 432-4320
Enterprise Multi-Cap Growth Y	Agg Growth	-11.5	-19.14		5	4	0	1.4	800 432-4320
Enterprise Small Co Growth A	Small Co	-15.3	-5.9	1.57	3	4	4.75	1.65	800 432-4320
Enterprise Small Co Growth B	Small Co	-15.8	-6.38	0.93	3	4	0	2.2	800 432-4320
Enterprise Small Co Growth C	Small Co	-15.8	-6.37	1	3	4	1	2.2	800 432-4320
Enterprise Small Co Growth Y	Small Co	-14.9					0	1.2	800 432-4320
Enterprise Small Co Value A	Small Co	-4.9	3.39	4.17	1	3	4.75	1.64	800 432-4320
Enterprise Small Co Value B	Small Co	-5.4	2.83	3.6	1	3	0	2.19	800 432-4320
Enterprise Small Co Value C	Small Co	-5.4	2.79	3.68	1	3	1	2.19	800 432-4320
Enterprise Small Co Value Y	Small Co	-4.6					0	1.19	800 432-4320
Enterprise-Deep Value A	Growth	-11.3					4.75	1.5	800 432-4320
Enterprise-Deep Value B	Growth	-11.8					0	2.05	800 432-4320
Enterprise-Deep Value C	Growth	-11.8				1		2.05	800 432-4320
Enterprise-Deep Value Y	Growth	-10.9					0	1.05	800 432-4320
Enterprise-Equity Fund A	Growth	1.3	-14.73	-4.82	3	5	4.75	1.6	800 432-4320
Enterprise-Equity Fund B	Growth	0.6	-15.13	-5.15	3	5	0	2.15	800 432-4320
Enterprise-Equity Fund C	Growth	0.9	-15.09	-5.19	3	5	1	2.15	800 432-4320
Enterprise-Equity Fund Y	Growth	1.7					0	1.15	800 432-4320
Enterprise-Global Financial Serv A	Financial	-4.6	5.41		2	3	4.75	1.75	800 432-4320

Stock Fund Name	Objective	Annualized Return for			Rank		Max Load	Expense Ratio	Toll-Free/(Toll) Telephone
		1 Year	3 Years	5 Years	Overall	Risk			
Enterprise-Global Financial Serv B	Financial	-5.2	4.86		2	3	0	2.3	800 432-4320
Enterprise-Global Financial Serv C	Financial	-5.1	4.91		2	3	1	2.3	800 432-4320
Enterprise-Global Financial Serv Y	Financial	-4.2	5.87		2	3	0	1.3	800 432-4320
Enterprise-Global Socially Resp A	Global	-11.8					4.75	1.75	800 432-4320
Enterprise-Global Socially Resp B	Global	-12.2					0	2.3	800 432-4320
Enterprise-Global Socially Resp C	Global	-12.1					1	2.3	800 432-4320
Enterprise-Global Socially Resp Y	Global	-11.3					0	1.3	800 432-4320
Enterprise-Growth A	Growth	-10.6	-11.16	-1.45	3	2	4.75	1.58	800 432-4320
Enterprise-Growth B	Growth	-11.2	-11.66	-1.95	3	2	0	2.12	800 432-4320
Enterprise-Growth C	Growth	-11.2	-11.66	-1.97	3	2	1	2.13	800 432-4320
Enterprise-Growth Y	Growth	-10.3	-10.77	-0.9	3	2	0	1.13	800 432-4320
Enterprise-Internat'l Growth A	Foreign	-19.8	-18.1	-7.95	4	3	4.75	1.85	800 432-4320
Enterprise-Internat'l Growth B	Foreign	-20.4	-18.71	-8.58	4	3	5.75	2.4	800 432-4320
Enterprise-Internat'l Growth C	Foreign	-20.3	-18.71	-8.58	4	3	1	2.4	800 432-4320
Enterprise-Internat'l Growth Y	Foreign	-19.6					0	1.4	800 432-4320
Enterprise-Managed A	AssetAlloc	-9	-8.83	-5.04	3	2	4.75	1.45	800 432-4320
Enterprise-Managed B	AssetAlloc	-9.4	-9.31	-5.54	3	2	0	2	800 432-4320
Enterprise-Managed C	AssetAlloc	-9.5	-9.33	-5.69	3	2	1	2	800 432-4320
Enterprise-Managed Y	AssetAlloc	-8.3	-8.41	-5.7	3	2	0	1	800 432-4320
Enterprise-Mergers & Acquisition A	Growth	1					4.75	1.83	800 432-4320
Enterprise-Mergers & Acquisition B	Growth	0.4					0	2.38	800 432-4320
Enterprise-Mergers & Acquisition C	Growth	0.4					1	2.39	800 432-4320
Enterprise-Mergers & Acquisition Y	Growth	1.4					0	1.38	800 432-4320
Enterprise-Strategic Allocation A	AssetAlloc	-8.5					4.75	1.5	800 432-4320
Enterprise-Strategic Allocation B	AssetAlloc	-9					0	2.05	800 432-4320
Enterprise-Strategic Allocation C	AssetAlloc	-9					1	2.05	800 432-4320
Enterprise-Strategic Allocation Y	AssetAlloc	-8.1					0	1.05	800 432-4320
Enterprise-Technology Fund A	Technology	1	-32.03		4	5	4.75	1.9	800 432-4320
Enterprise-Technology Fund B	Technology	0.4	-32.39		4	5	0	2.45	800 432-4320
Enterprise-Technology Fund C	Technology	0.6	-32.35		4	5	1	2.45	800 432-4320
Enterprise-Technology Fund Y	Technology	1.5	-31.69		4	5	0	1.45	800 432-4320
EquiTrust Series Blue Chip Portf	Growth	-9.3	-10.25	-3.27	3	3	0	1.48	877 860-2904
EquiTrust Series Managed Portfolio	Flexible	0.1	8.51	1.69	1	1	0	1.92	877 860-2904
EquiTrust Series Value Growth Port	Growth/Inc	-4	4.53	-4.03	2	2	0	1.69	877 860-2904
Eureka Equity Fund A	Growth	-9.5	-11.99	-3.29		3	5	1.38	888 890-8121
Eureka Equity Fund B	Growth	-10	-12.53	-3.97		3	0	2.13	888 890-8121
Eureka Equity Fund Tr	Growth	-9	-11.69	-3	4	3	0	1.31	888 890-8121
Eureka Global Fund A	Balanced	-12.1	-9.16	-2.75		2	5	1.99	888 890-8121
Eureka Global Fund B	Balanced	-12.7	-9.63	-3.33		2	0	2.8	888 890-8121
Eureka Global Fund Tr	Balanced	-12	-8.94	-2.52	4	2	0	1.74	888 890-8121
Evergreen Aggressive Growth A	Agg Growth	-7.5	-16.48	1.71	3	4	5.75	1.5	800 343-2898
Evergreen Aggressive Growth B	Agg Growth	-8.2	-17.1	0.93	3	4	0	2.25	800 343-2898
Evergreen Aggressive Growth C	Agg Growth	-8.2	-17.07	0.91	3	4	1	2.25	800 343-2898
Evergreen Aggressive Growth I	Agg Growth	-7.2	-16.25	2.08	3	4	0	1.25	800 343-2898
Evergreen Asset Allocation A	AssetAlloc	1.7	6.67	5.911	5.75			1.16	800 343-2898
Evergreen Asset Allocation B	AssetAlloc	1.4	6.54	5.831	0			1.89	800 343-2898
Evergreen Asset Allocation C	AssetAlloc	1.5	6.58	5.861	1			1.9	800 343-2898
Evergreen Asset Allocation I	AssetAlloc	1.9	6.74	5.951	0			0.91	800 343-2898
Evergreen Balanced A	Balanced	-2.4	-3.77	1.09	2	1	5.75	0.98	800 343-2898
Evergreen Balanced B	Balanced	-3.1	-4.53	0.28	2	1	0	1.73	800 343-2898
Evergreen Balanced C	Balanced	-3.2	-4.53	0.3	2	1	1	1.73	800 343-2898
Evergreen Balanced I	Balanced	-2.2	-3.62	1.28	2	1	0	0.73	800 343-2898
Evergreen Blue Chip A	Growth	-11.5	-13.48	-2.83	4	2	5.75	1.52	800 343-2898
Evergreen Blue Chip B	Growth	-12.2	-14.13	-3.58	5	2	0	2.27	800 343-2898
Evergreen Blue Chip C	Growth	-12.1	-14.13	-3.58	5	2	1	2.27	800 343-2898
Evergreen Blue Chip I	Growth	-11.3	-13.25		4	2	0	1.27	800 343-2898
Evergreen Capital Growth A	Growth	-17.2	-8.42	-1.22	3	3	5.75	1.73	800 343-2898
Evergreen Capital Growth B	Growth	-17.8					0	2.48	800 343-2898

Stock Fund Name	Objective	Annualized Return for			Rank		Max Load	Expense Ratio	Toll-Free/(Toll) Telephone
		1 Year	3 Years	5 Years	Overall	Risk			
Evergreen Capital Growth C	Growth	-17.8	-9.1	-2.27	4	3	1	2.47	800 343-2898
Evergreen Capital Growth I	Growth	-16.9	-8.18	-0.4		3	0	1.49	800 343-2898
Evergreen Core Equity I	Growth	-13	-13.66	-5.29	5	3	0	0.76	800 343-2898
Evergreen Core Equity IS	Growth	-13.3	-13.89	-5.53	5	3	0	1.01	800 343-2898
Evergreen Emerging Growth A	Small Co	1.3	-11.83	-0.53	3	4	5.75	1.21	800 343-2898
Evergreen Emerging Growth B	Small Co	0.6	-12.44	-1.22	3	4	0	1.96	800 343-2898
Evergreen Emerging Growth C	Small Co	0.8	-12.48	-1.26	3	4	1	1.96	800 343-2898
Evergreen Emerging Growth I	Small Co	1.5	-11.61	-0.3	3	4	0	0.97	800 343-2898
Evergreen Emerging Markets Gr A	Foreign	-7.9	-6.01	-2.89	3	4	5.75	1.79	800 343-2898
Evergreen Emerging Markets Gr B	Foreign	-8.6	-6.69	-3.68	3	4	0	2.63	800 343-2898
Evergreen Emerging Markets Gr C	Foreign	-8.6	-6.67	-3.64	3	4	1	2.56	800 343-2898
Evergreen Emerging Markets Gr I	Foreign	-7.7	-5.73	-2.58	3	4	0	1.55	800 343-2898
Evergreen Equity Income A	Growth/Inc	-2	0.52	1.77	1	2	5.75	1.35	800 343-2898
Evergreen Equity Income B	Growth/Inc	-2.7	-0.25	0.98	1	2	0	2.1	800 343-2898
Evergreen Equity Income C	Growth/Inc	-2.8	-0.25	0.96	1	2	1	2.1	800 343-2898
Evergreen Equity Income I	Growth/Inc	-1.8	0.76	2	1	2	0	1.1	800 343-2898
Evergreen Equity Index Fund A	Growth	-8.7	-11.33	-1.64	3	3	5.75	0.57	800 343-2898
Evergreen Equity Index Fund B	Growth	-9.4	-11.97	-2.31	4	3	0	1.32	800 343-2898
Evergreen Equity Index Fund C	Growth	-9.4	-11.98	-2.2	4	3	1	1.32	800 343-2898
Evergreen Equity Index Fund I	Growth	-8.5	-11.09	-1.41	3	3	0	0.32	800 343-2898
Evergreen Equity Index Fund IS	Growth	-8.7	-11.32	-1.66	3	3	5.5	0.57	800 343-2898
Evergreen Foundation Fund A	Balanced	-1.6	-6.07	-0.73	2	1	5.75	1.41	800 343-2898
Evergreen Foundation Fund B	Balanced	-2.4	-6.78	-1.5	2	1	0	2.16	800 343-2898
Evergreen Foundation Fund C	Balanced	-2.4	-6.75	-1.5	2	1	1	2.16	800 343-2898
Evergreen Foundation Fund I	Balanced	-1.5	-5.83	-0.51	2	1	0	1.15	800 343-2898
Evergreen Fund A	Growth	-8.2	-14.46	-7.2	4	2	5.75	1.73	800 343-2898
Evergreen Fund B	Growth	-8.9	-15.09	-7.86	5	2	0	2.49	800 343-2898
Evergreen Fund C	Growth	-8.9	-15.09	-7.86	3	2	1	2.48	800 343-2898
Evergreen Fund I	Growth	-8	-14.24	-6.92	4	2	0	1.48	800 343-2898
Evergreen Global Leaders A	Global	-16.3	-11.84	-3.85	4	2	5.75	1.88	800 343-2898
Evergreen Global Leaders B	Global	-16.9	-12.5	-4.55	3	2	0	2.63	800 343-2898
Evergreen Global Leaders C	Global	-16.9	-12.5	-4.54	3	2	1	2.63	800 343-2898
Evergreen Global Leaders I	Global	-16	-11.61	-3.58	4	2	0	1.61	800 343-2898
Evergreen Global Opportunities A	Global	-8.2	-9.41	1.67	3	4	5.75	1.89	800 343-2898
Evergreen Global Opportunities B	Global	-8.9	-10.08	0.93	3	4	0	2.58	800 343-2898
Evergreen Global Opportunities C	Global	-8.9	-10.09	0.93	4	4	1	2.59	800 343-2898
Evergreen Global Opportunities I	Global	-8					0	1.59	800 343-2898
Evergreen Growth & Income Fund A	Growth/Inc	-8.4	-7.37	-4.08	4	3	5.75	1.63	800 343-2898
Evergreen Growth & Income Fund B	Growth/Inc	-9.1	-8.06	-4.79	4	3	0	2.38	800 343-2898
Evergreen Growth & Income Fund C	Growth/Inc	-9.1	-8.07	-4.79	4	3	1	2.38	800 343-2898
Evergreen Growth & Income Fund I	Growth/Inc	-8.2	-7.15	-3.81	3	3	0	1.38	800 343-2898
Evergreen Growth A	Small Co	-10.5	-6.51	0.51	3	4	5.75	1.38	800 343-2898
Evergreen Growth B	Small Co	-11.3					0	2.13	800 343-2898
Evergreen Growth C	Small Co	-11.2	-7.23	-0.23	3	4	1	2.13	800 343-2898
Evergreen Growth I	Small Co	-10.3	-6.29	0.75	3	4	0	1.14	800 343-2898
Evergreen Health Care Fund A	Health	9.1	11.13		1	4	5.75	2.03	800 343-2898
Evergreen Health Care Fund B	Health	8.2	10.31		1	4	0	2.78	800 343-2898
Evergreen Health Care Fund C	Health	8.2	10.28		1	4	1	2.78	800 343-2898
Evergreen Health Care Fund I	Health	9.3	11.4		1	4	0	1.8	800 343-2898
Evergreen International Growth A	Foreign	-14.8	-8.42	-3.31	3	2	5.75	1.12	800 343-2898
Evergreen International Growth B	Foreign	-15.3	-9.05	-3.97	3	2	0	1.87	800 343-2898
Evergreen International Growth C	Foreign	-15.3	-9.05	-3.97	3	2	1	1.87	800 343-2898
Evergreen International Growth I	Foreign	-14.4	-8.09	-3.06	3	2	0	0.88	800 343-2898
Evergreen Large Cap Value A	Growth	-10.6	0.75	1.86		2	5.75	0.78	800 343-2898
Evergreen Large Cap Value B	Growth	-10.9	0.67	1.81		2	0	2.15	800 343-2898
Evergreen Large Cap Value C	Growth	-10.9	0.64	1.8		2	1	2.14	800 343-2898
Evergreen Large Cap Value I	Growth	-10.6	0.76	1.87		2	0	1.21	800 343-2898
Evergreen Large Comp Growth A	Growth	-7.6	-17.21	-1.75	3	3	5.75	1.16	800 343-2898

Stock Fund Name	Objective	Annualized Return for			Rank		Max Load	Expense Ratio	Toll-Free/(Toll) Telephone
		1 Year	3 Years	5 Years	Overall	Risk			
Evergreen Large Comp Growth B	Growth	-8.4	-17.85	-2.5	3	3	0	1.91	800 343-2898
Evergreen Large Comp Growth C	Growth	-8.3	-17.82	-2.47	3	3	1	1.91	800 343-2898
Evergreen Large Comp Growth I	Growth	-7.4	-17	-1.7	4	3	0	0.91	800 343-2898
Evergreen Masters Fund A	Growth	-11.7	-14.19		4	4	5.75	2.15	800 343-2898
Evergreen Masters Fund B	Growth	-12.4	-14.88		5	4	0	2.9	800 343-2898
Evergreen Masters Fund C	Growth	-12.4	-14.86		5	4	1	2.89	800 343-2898
Evergreen Masters Fund I	Growth	-11.6	-14.01		4	4	0	1.9	800 343-2898
Evergreen Mid Cap Value A	Growth	-8.2	3.99	2.89		3	5.75	1.6	800 343-2898
Evergreen Mid Cap Value B	Growth	-8.2	3.99	2.89		3	0		800 343-2898
Evergreen Mid Cap Value C	Growth	-8.3	3.95	2.87		3	1		800 343-2898
Evergreen Mid Cap Value I	Growth	-8.2	3.99	2.89	3	3	0	1.3	800 343-2898
Evergreen Omega A	Agg Growth	-9.1	-17.39	0.65	3	3	5.75	1.65	800 343-2898
Evergreen Omega B	Agg Growth	-9.7	-18	-0.08	3	3	0	2.4	800 343-2898
Evergreen Omega C	Agg Growth	-9.7	-17.98	-0.08	3	3	1	2.4	800 343-2898
Evergreen Omega I	Agg Growth	-8.9	-17.17	0.93	3	3	0	1.4	800 343-2898
Evergreen Precious Metals A	Prec Metal	-3.8	31.23	10.77	2	5	5.75	1.61	800 343-2898
Evergreen Precious Metals B	Prec Metal	-4.5	30.26	9.96	2	5	0	2.35	800 343-2898
Evergreen Precious Metals C	Prec Metal	-4.4	30.21	9.93	2	5	1	2.33	800 343-2898
Evergreen Precious Metals I	Prec Metal	-3.5	31.57	10.69		5	0	1.34	800 343-2898
Evergreen Premier 20 A	Agg Growth	-13.7					5.75	1.91	800 343-2898
Evergreen Premier 20 B	Agg Growth	-14.5					0	2.66	800 343-2898
Evergreen Premier 20 C	Agg Growth	-14.3					1	2.65	800 343-2898
Evergreen Premier 20 I	Agg Growth	-13.3					0	1.7	800 343-2898
Evergreen Select Strategic Gr A	Growth	-7.9					5.75	1	800 343-2898
Evergreen Select Strategic Gr B	Growth	-8.6					0	1.76	800 343-2898
Evergreen Select Strategic Gr C	Growth	-8.6					1	1.76	800 343-2898
Evergreen Select Strategic Gr I	Growth	-7.7	-15.72	0.61	3	4	0	0.75	800 343-2898
Evergreen Select Strategic Gr IS	Growth	-7.9	-15.94	0.34	4	4	0	1	800 343-2898
Evergreen Small Cap Value Fd A	Small Co	-16.4	8.08	3.04	3	3	5.75	1.61	800 343-2898
Evergreen Small Cap Value Fd B	Small Co	-17	7.29	2.25	3	3	0	2.35	800 343-2898
Evergreen Small Cap Value Fd C	Small Co	-17	7.28	2.24	3	3	1	2.35	800 343-2898
Evergreen Small Cap Value Fd I	Small Co	-16.2	8.35	3.27	3	3	0	1.35	800 343-2898
Evergreen Small Cap Value Fd IS	Small Co	-16.4	8.1	3.14		3	0	1.6	800 343-2898
Evergreen Small Cap Value II B	Small Co	-9.5	10.4	6.13		2	0		800 343-2898
Evergreen Small Cap Value II C	Small Co	-9.5	10.4	6.13		2	1		800 343-2898
Evergreen Small Cap Value II I	Small Co	-9.4	10.41	6.15	2	2	0	1.4	800 343-2898
Evergreen Special Equity A	Growth	-9.5	-10.38		3	4	5.75	1.48	800 343-2898
Evergreen Special Equity B	Growth	-10.1	-11.02		3	4	0	2.22	800 343-2898
Evergreen Special Equity C	Growth	-10.1	-11.08		3	4	1	2.22	800 343-2898
Evergreen Special Equity I	Growth	-9.2	-10.17	4.03	3	4	0	1.22	800 343-2898
Evergreen Special Equity IS	Growth	-9.4	-10.36	3.77	3	4	5.5	1.46	800 343-2898
Evergreen Special Values A	Small Co	-7.6	10.38	5.91	2	2	5.75	1.2	800 343-2898
Evergreen Special Values B	Small Co	-8.4	9.52	5.29	2	2	0	1.95	800 343-2898
Evergreen Special Values C	Small Co	-8.3					1	1.96	800 343-2898
Evergreen Special Values I	Small Co	-7.4	10.64	6.16	2	2	0	0.95	800 343-2898
Evergreen Stock Selector A	Growth	-8.4	-10.81	-2.83	3	3	5.75	1.06	800 343-2898
Evergreen Stock Selector B	Growth	-9	-11.49	-3.58	3	3	0	1.81	800 343-2898
Evergreen Stock Selector C	Growth	-9.1	-11.5		3	3	1	1.81	800 343-2898
Evergreen Stock Selector I	Growth	-8.2	-10.61	-2.62	3	3	0	0.81	800 343-2898
Evergreen Stock Selector IS	Growth	-8.4	-10.82	-2.85		3	0	1.06	800 343-2898
Evergreen Strategic Value A	Growth	-6.7					5.75	1.07	800 343-2898
Evergreen Strategic Value B	Growth	-7					0	1.83	800 343-2898
Evergreen Strategic Value C	Growth	-7.1					1	1.83	800 343-2898
Evergreen Strategic Value I	Growth	-6.2	-3.47	-1.07	2	2	0	0.82	800 343-2898
Evergreen Strategic Value IS	Growth	-6.3	-3.7	-1.32	3	2	0	1.07	800 343-2898
Evergreen Tax Strat Foundation A	Balanced	1.1	-1.6	0.08	2	1	5.75	1.36	800 343-2898
Evergreen Tax Strat Foundation B	Balanced	0.3	-2.35	-0.68	2	1	0	2.11	800 343-2898
Evergreen Tax Strat Foundation C	Balanced	0.3	-2.33	-0.67	2	1	1	2.11	800 343-2898

Stock Fund Name	Objective	Annualized Return for			Rank		Max Load	Expense Ratio	Toll-Free/(Toll) Telephone
		1 Year	3 Years	5 Years	Overall	Risk			
Evergreen Tax Strat Foundation I	Balanced	1.3	-1.35	0.33	2	1	0	1.11	800 343-2898
Evergreen Technology Fund A	Technology	-12.2	-21.98		4	5	5.75	2.69	800 343-2898
Evergreen Technology Fund B	Technology	-12.8	-22.55		4	5	0	3.36	800 343-2898
Evergreen Technology Fund C	Technology	-12.8	-22.6		4	5	1	3.41	800 343-2898
Evergreen Technology Fund I	Technology	-11.9	-21.76			5	0	2.43	800 343-2898
Evergreen Utility and Telecom A	Utilities	-4.6	-14.77	-1.84	3	3	5.75	1.16	800 343-2898
Evergreen Utility and Telecom B	Utilities	-5.2	-15.4	-2.56	3	3	0	1.9	800 343-2898
Evergreen Utility and Telecom C	Utilities	-5.3	-15.41	-0.78	2	3	1	1.91	800 343-2898
Evergreen Utility and Telecom I	Utilities	-4.3	-14.52	0.59	3	3	0	0.91	800 343-2898
Excelsior Blended Equity Fd	Growth	-7.6	-12.74	-1.68	3	3	0	1.05	800 881-9358
Excelsior Energy & Nat Resrc Fd	Energy/Res	-7.5	-1.79	5.01	2	4	0	1.25	800 881-9358
Excelsior Institutional Equity	Growth	-4.8	-13.98	-2.37	3	3	0	0.68	800 881-9358
Excelsior Instl Intl Equity Inst I	Foreign	-17	-16.53	-4.98	5	3	0		800 881-9358
Excelsior International Fd	Foreign	-17	-19.44	-7.19	5	3	0	1.5	800 881-9358
Excelsior Large Cap Growth Fd	Growth	-15.3	-26.32	-5.66	5	4	0	1.05	800 881-9358
Excelsior Mid Cap Value Fd	Growth	-5.6	4.54	9.17	2	4	0	1.05	800 881-9358
Excelsior Optimum Growth Fd	Growth	-12.4	-24.37	-4.15	4	4	0	1.05	800 881-9358
Excelsior Pacific/Asia Fd	Pacific	-16	-13.44	2.24	4	3	0	1.5	800 881-9358
Excelsior Pan European Fd	European	-18.2	-18.98	-9.72	5	4	0	1.5	800 881-9358
Excelsior Real Estate Fd	Real Est	1	13.38	6.08	2	1	0	1.05	800 881-9358
Excelsior Small Cap Fd	Small Co	-13.7	-4.08	1.04	3	4	0	1.05	800 881-9358
Excelsior Val & Restruct Fd	Growth	-7.8	-2.79	4.95	2	3	0	0.99	800 881-9358
Exeter Blended Asset I	AssetAlloc	2.6	4.87	5.66	1	0		1.2	800 466-3863
Exeter Blended Asset II	AssetAlloc	1.6	3.91	5.65		2	0	1.19	800 466-3863
Exeter Defensive Series Fund	AssetAlloc	12	8.33	7.01	1	0		1	800 466-3863
Exeter Maximum Horizon Series A	AssetAlloc	-5.2	1.02	6.26		3	0	1.2	800 466-3863
Expedition Equity Fund A	Growth	-15.6	-15.18	-4.24	5	4	4	1.38	800 992-2085
Expedition Equity Fund B	Growth	-16.3	-15.85	-3.85	5	4	0	2.13	800 992-2085
Expedition Equity Fund Inst	Growth	-15.4	-15.01	-2.95	5	4	0	1.13	800 992-2085
FAM Equity-Income Fund	Income	-0.6	15.23	7.12	1	1	0	1.56	800 932-3271
FAM Value Fund	Growth	-4	12.41	5.66	1	2	0	1.21	800 932-3271
FBP Contrarian Balanced Fund	Balanced	-3.3	2.95	3.2	2	2	0	1	800 443-4249
FBP Contrarian Equity Fund	Growth	-10.5	-0.32	0.85	3	3	0	0.99	800 443-4249
FBR American Gas Index Fund	Utilities	-12.1	-2.22	2.6	3	3	0	0.85	888 888-0025
FBR Financial Services Fd	Financial	-6.4	11.67	3.35	2	2	0	1.95	888 888-0025
FBR Small Cap Financial Fd	Financial	12.1	30.87	11.13	1	1	0	1.52	888 888-0025
FBR Small Cap Value Fd	Small Co	23.8	14.06	11.19	1	3	0	1.93	888 888-0025
FMC Select Fd	Growth	-4.3	8.09	8.35	1	1	0	1.05	866 450-3722
FMI Common Stock Fund	Growth	-4.2	9	7.4	1	2	0	1.75	800 595-5519
FMI Focus Fund	Growth	-8.4	-1.03	12.81	2	4	0	1.45	800 595-5519
FMI Provident Trust Strategy Fd	Growth/Inc	-7	-14.03	-1.36	3	2	0	1.2	800 811-5311
FMI Sasco Contrarian Value Fund	Agg Growth	-15.1	9.26	3.95	3	3	0	1.3	800 811-5311
FMI Winslow Growth Fund	Growth	-8	-13.41	-2.99	3	4	0	1.3	800 811-5311
FMI Woodland Sm Cap Value Fund	Small Co	-19.1	6.75	0.27	3	3	0	1.3	800 811-5311
FPA Capital Fund	Small Co	-1.6	12.32	7.75	2	4	5.25	0.86	800 982-4372
FPA Crescent Fund	Financial	4.9	18.78	7.41	1	2	0		800 982-4372
FPA Paramount Fund	Small Co	-6.6	9.82	-5.23	3	3	5.25	0.29	800 982-4372
FPA Perennial Fund	Small Co	-5.1	8.18	9.89	2	3	5.25	0.9	800 982-4372
FTI European Smaller Companies	European	-16.7					0	1.19	888 343-8242
FTI Large Cap Growth and Income	Growth/Inc	-8.9	-9.91		3	3	0	1.03	888 343-8242
FTI Small Capitalization Equity	Small Co	-11.7	-12.56	0.26	4	4	0	1.3	888 343-8242
Fairport Growth & Income Fund	Growth/Inc	-14.4	-5.41	-6.05	3	2	0	1.5	800 332-6459
Fairport Growth Fund	Growth	-13.6					0	1.38	800 332-6459
Federated American Leaders A	Growth/Inc	-12.1	-4.92	-1.53	3	3	5.5	1.09	800 341-7400
Federated American Leaders B	Growth/Inc	-12.7	-5.63	-2.27	3	3	0	1.84	800 341-7400
Federated American Leaders C	Growth/Inc	-12.7	-5.63	-2.29	3	3	0	1.84	800 341-7400
Federated American Leaders F	Growth/Inc	-12.1	-4.92	-1.7	3	3	1	1.09	800 341-7400
Federated Capital Appreciation A	Growth/Inc	-10.8	-7.17	4.37	3	3	5.5	1.25	800 341-7400

Stock Fund Name	Objective	Annualized Return for			Rank		Max Load	Expense Ratio	Toll-Free/(Toll) Telephone
		1 Year	3 Years	5 Years	Overall	Risk			
Federated Capital Appreciation B	Growth/Inc	-11.5	-7.87	3.58	3	3	0	2	800 341-7400
Federated Capital Appreciation C	Growth/Inc	-11.5	-7.84	3.6	3	3	0	2	800 341-7400
Federated Capital Income Fund A	Utilities	-10.4	-13.33	-6.58	3	2	5.5	1.45	800 341-7400
Federated Capital Income Fund B	Utilities	-11.1	-14.01	-7.29	3	2	0	2.2	800 341-7400
Federated Capital Income Fund C	Utilities	-11.1	-13.99	-7.28	3	2	0	2.2	800 341-7400
Federated Capital Income Fund F	Utilities	-10.5	-13.36	-6.59	3	2	1	1.45	800 341-7400
Federated Comm Technology A	Technology	-10.2	-35.42		4	5	5.5	2	800 341-7400
Federated Comm Technology B	Technology	-11.1	-35.9		5	5	0	2.75	800 341-7400
Federated Comm Technology C	Technology	-10.9	-35.9		5	5	0	2.75	800 341-7400
Federated Equity Income A	Income	-7.8	-11.13	-2.62	3	3	5.5	1.18	800 341-7400
Federated Equity Income B	Income	-8.5	-11.78	-3.35	4	3	0	1.93	800 341-7400
Federated Equity Income C	Income	-8.4	-11.78	-3.33	4	3	0	1.93	800 341-7400
Federated Equity Income F	Income	-8	-11.32	-2.85	3	3	1	1.43	800 341-7400
Federated European Equity Fund A	European	-14.6	-16.53	-7.29	4	3	5.5	2.5	800 341-7400
Federated European Equity Fund B	European	-15.2	-17.14	-7.99	5	3	0	3.25	800 341-7400
Federated European Equity Fund C	European	-15.4	-17.12	-8	5	3	0	3.25	800 341-7400
Federated Global Equity A	Global	-17.6	-14.66		4	3	5.75	2.82	800 341-7400
Federated Global Equity B	Global	-18	-15.08		5	3	0	3.32	800 341-7400
Federated Global Equity C	Global	-18	-15.07		5	3	0	3.32	800 341-7400
Federated Global Financ Serv A	Financial	-8.3	4.25		2	3	5.5	2.55	800 341-7400
Federated Global Financ Serv B	Financial	-9	3.47		3	3	0	3.3	800 341-7400
Federated Global Financ Serv C	Financial	-9	3.45		3	3	0	3.3	800 341-7400
Federated Global Value Fund A	Utilities	-9.9	-13.58	-2.14	4	3	5.5	2.06	800 341-7400
Federated Global Value Fund B	Utilities	-10.6	-14.24	-2.87	4	3	0	2.81	800 341-7400
Federated Global Value Fund C	Utilities	-10.6	-14.24	-2.89	4	3	0	2.81	800 341-7400
Federated Growth Strategies A	Growth	-9	-15.32	-0.81	4	4	5.5	1.4	800 341-7400
Federated Growth Strategies B	Growth	-9.7	-15.97	-1.56	4	4	0	2.15	800 341-7400
Federated Growth Strategies C	Growth	-9.7	-15.97	-1.51	4	4	1	2.15	800 341-7400
Federated International Equity A	Foreign	-19.3	-21.26	-6.33	5	3	5.5	1.81	800 341-7400
Federated International Equity B	Foreign	-20	-21.85	-7.05	5	3	0	2.56	800 341-7400
Federated International Equity C	Foreign	-20	-21.85	-7.01	4	3	0	2.56	800 341-7400
Federated International Sm Co A	Foreign	-8.2	-18.21	-0.72	3	3	5.5	2.15	800 341-7400
Federated International Sm Co B	Foreign	-8.8	-18.78	-1.43	4	3	0	2.9	800 341-7400
Federated International Sm Co C	Foreign	-8.8	-18.8	-1.44	3	3	0	2.9	800 341-7400
Federated Internatl Cap Apprec A	Foreign	-14.6	-17.51	-5.67	5	3	5.5	2	800 341-7400
Federated Internatl Cap Apprec B	Foreign	-15.3	-18.17	-6.45	5	3	0	2.75	800 341-7400
Federated Internatl Cap Apprec C	Foreign	-15.3	-18.14	-6.44	5	3	1	2.75	800 341-7400
Federated Kaufmann A	Agg Growth	-6.1	2.52	5.91	2	3	5.5	1.95	800 341-7400
Federated Kaufmann B	Agg Growth	-6.6					0	2.5	800 341-7400
Federated Kaufmann C	Agg Growth	-6.6					0	2.5	800 341-7400
Federated Kaufmann K	Agg Growth	-6.1	2.52	5.91	2	3	0	1.95	800 341-7400
Federated Kaufmann Sm Cap A	Small Co						5.5		800 341-7400
Federated Kaufmann Sm Cap B	Small Co						0		800 341-7400
Federated Kaufmann Sm Cap C	Small Co						0		800 341-7400
Federated Large Cap Gr A	Growth	-15.6	-21.57		5	4	5.5	1.56	800 341-7400
Federated Large Cap Gr B	Growth	-16.2	-22.16		5	4	0	2.31	800 341-7400
Federated Large Cap Gr C	Growth	-16.2	-22.14		5	4	0	2.31	800 341-7400
Federated Managed Growth Port Inst	AssetAlloc	-5.7					0	1.46	800 341-7400
Federated Managed Growth Port Sel	AssetAlloc	-6.4					0	2.16	800 341-7400
Federated Market Opportunity A	Income	3.2					5.5	1.23	800 341-7400
Federated Market Opportunity B	Income	2.4					0	1.98	800 341-7400
Federated Market Opportunity C	Income	2.4					0	1.98	800 341-7400
Federated Max-Cap Index C	Growth/Inc	-9.4	-12.11	-2.49	4	3	0	1.34	800 341-7400
Federated Max-Cap Index Instl	Growth/Inc	-8.5	-11.24	-1.51	3	3	0	0.34	800 341-7400
Federated Max-Cap Index Instl-Svc	Growth/Inc	-8.7	-11.5	-1.81	3	3	0	0.64	800 341-7400
Federated Mid-Cap Index Fund	Growth	-9.7	0.34	6.25	3	3	0	0.49	800 341-7400
Federated Mini-Cap Index C	Small Co	-9.7	-3	-1.75	3	4	0	1.79	800 341-7400
Federated Mini-Cap Index Instl	Small Co	-8.9	-2.2	-0.92	3	4	0	0.91	800 341-7400

313

Stock Fund Name	Objective	Annualized Return for			Rank		Max Load	Expense Ratio	Toll-Free/(Toll) Telephone
		1 Year	3 Years	5 Years	Overall	Risk			
Federated Mngd Conserv Gr Instl	Balanced	4	0.63	2.47	1	1	0	1.22	800 341-7400
Federated Mngd Conserv Gr Sel	Balanced	3.3	-0.05	1.76	1	1	0	1.92	800 341-7400
Federated Mngd Moderate Gr Instl	AssetAlloc	0.2	-3.27	0.71	2	1	0	1.18	800 341-7400
Federated Mngd Moderate Gr Sel	AssetAlloc	-0.3	-3.89	0.04	2	1	0	1.88	800 341-7400
Federated Stock Trust	Growth/Inc	-11	-2.31	0.35	3	3	0	0.99	800 341-7400
Federated Stock and Bond Fund A	Balanced	-2	0.48	1.32	2	1	5.5	1.31	800 341-7400
Federated Stock and Bond Fund B	Balanced	-2.8	-0.27	0.56	2	1	0	2.06	800 341-7400
Federated Stock and Bond Fund C	Balanced	-2.7	-0.26	0.56	2	1	0	2.06	800 341-7400
Fidelity Adv Asset Allocation A	AssetAlloc	-3.5	-5.5		2	2	5.75	1.23	800 522-7297
Fidelity Adv Asset Allocation B	AssetAlloc	-4.3	-6.29		2	2	0	2.01	800 522-7297
Fidelity Adv Asset Allocation C	AssetAlloc	-4.2	-6.24		2	2	0	1.99	800 522-7297
Fidelity Adv Asset Allocation I	AssetAlloc	-3.3	-5.29		2	2	0	0.92	800 522-7297
Fidelity Adv Asset Allocation T	AssetAlloc	-3.9	-5.8		2	2	3.5	1.57	800 522-7297
Fidelity Adv Balanced Fund A	Balanced	3.5	-1.32	0.55	2	1	5.75	0.93	800 522-7297
Fidelity Adv Balanced Fund B	Balanced	2.6	-2.1	-0.26	2	1	0	1.74	800 522-7297
Fidelity Adv Balanced Fund C	Balanced	2.6	-2.1	-0.28	2	1	0	1.71	800 522-7297
Fidelity Adv Balanced Fund I	Balanced	3.7	-1.05	0.85	2	1	0	0.65	800 522-7297
Fidelity Adv Balanced Fund T	Balanced	3.2	-1.58	0.23	2	1	3.5	1.21	800 522-7297
Fidelity Adv Biotechnology A	Health	9.8					5.75	1.49	800 522-7297
Fidelity Adv Biotechnology B	Health	9.1					0	2.24	800 522-7297
Fidelity Adv Biotechnology C	Health	9.1					0	2.24	800 522-7297
Fidelity Adv Biotechnology I	Health	10					0	1.24	800 522-7297
Fidelity Adv Biotechnology T	Health	9.6					3.5	2.43	800 522-7297
Fidelity Adv Consumer Indust A	Growth	-11.5	-4.08	-0.11	3	2	5.75	1.49	800 522-7297
Fidelity Adv Consumer Indust B	Growth	-12.2	-4.01	-0.35	3	2	0	2.24	800 522-7297
Fidelity Adv Consumer Indust C	Growth	-12.2	-4.82	-0.88	3	2	0	2.24	800 522-7297
Fidelity Adv Consumer Indust I	Growth	-11.3	-3.79	0.2	3	2	0	1.24	800 522-7297
Fidelity Adv Consumer Indust T	Growth	-11.8	-3.52	0.16	3	2	3.5	2.01	800 522-7297
Fidelity Adv Cyclical Indust A	Growth	-11.7	0.4	0.86	3	3	5.75	1.5	800 522-7297
Fidelity Adv Cyclical Indust B	Growth	-12.3	-0.35	0.11	3	3	0	2.25	800 522-7297
Fidelity Adv Cyclical Indust C	Growth	-12.3	-0.34	0.11	3	3	0	2.25	800 522-7297
Fidelity Adv Cyclical Indust I	Growth	-11.4	0.68	1.14	3	3	0	1.25	800 522-7297
Fidelity Adv Cyclical Indust T	Growth	-12	0.14	0.64	3	3	3.5	2.26	800 522-7297
Fidelity Adv Developing Comm A	Technology	-3.3					5.75	1.46	800 522-7297
Fidelity Adv Developing Comm B	Technology	-3.9					0	2.21	800 522-7297
Fidelity Adv Developing Comm C	Technology	-3.9					0	2.21	800 522-7297
Fidelity Adv Developing Comm I	Technology	-3.1					0	1.2	800 522-7297
Fidelity Adv Developing Comm T	Technology	-3.5					3.5	1.7	800 522-7297
Fidelity Adv Diversified Intl A	Foreign	-6.1	-5.13		3	2	5.75	1.46	800 522-7297
Fidelity Adv Diversified Intl B	Foreign	-7	-5.98		2	2	0	2.3	800 522-7297
Fidelity Adv Diversified Intl C	Foreign	-6.9	-5.9		3	2	0	2.24	800 522-7297
Fidelity Adv Diversified Intl I	Foreign	-5.8	-4.82		2	2	0	1.12	800 522-7297
Fidelity Adv Diversified Intl T	Foreign	-6.5	-5.46			2	3.5	1.78	800 522-7297
Fidelity Adv Dividend Growth A	Growth	-7.9	-3.68		2	3	5.75	1.1	800 522-7297
Fidelity Adv Dividend Growth B	Growth	-8.5	-4.36		2	3	0	1.85	800 522-7297
Fidelity Adv Dividend Growth C	Growth	-8.5	-4.34		3	3	0	1.81	800 522-7297
Fidelity Adv Dividend Growth I	Growth	-7.6	-3.35		2	3	0	0.76	800 522-7297
Fidelity Adv Dividend Growth T	Growth	-8.1	-4.12		2	3	3.5	1.33	800 522-7297
Fidelity Adv Dynamic Cap App A	Growth	-3.6	-7.91		3	5	5.75	1.26	800 522-7297
Fidelity Adv Dynamic Cap App B	Growth	-4.2	-8.58		3	5	0	1.99	800 522-7297
Fidelity Adv Dynamic Cap App C	Growth	-4.2	-8.5		3	5	0	1.9	800 522-7297
Fidelity Adv Dynamic Cap App I	Growth	-3.1					0	0.89	800 522-7297
Fidelity Adv Dynamic Cap App T	Growth	-3.8	-8.11		3	5	5.75	1.58	800 522-7297
Fidelity Adv Electronics B	Technology	-25					0	2.23	800 522-7297
Fidelity Adv Electronics C	Technology	-24.9					0	2.23	800 522-7297
Fidelity Adv Electronics I	Technology	-24.2					0	1.23	800 522-7297
Fidelity Adv Emerging Asia A	Pacific	-18.5	-14.34		4	4	5.75	1.97	800 522-7297
Fidelity Adv Emerging Asia T	Pacific	-18.7	-14.59		3	4	3.5	2.22	800 522-7297

314

Stock Fund Name	Objective	Annualized Return for			Rank		Max Load	Expense Ratio	Toll-Free/(Toll) Telephone
		1 Year	3 Years	5 Years	Overall	Risk			
Fidelity Adv Equity Growth A	Growth	-12.1	-16.17	-0.69	4	4	5.75	1.09	800 522-7297
Fidelity Adv Equity Growth B	Growth	-12.8	-16.85	-1.46	4	4	0	1.87	800 522-7297
Fidelity Adv Equity Growth C	Growth	-12.8	-16.82	-1.44	4	4	0	1.81	800 522-7297
Fidelity Adv Equity Growth I	Growth	-11.8	-15.86	-0.34	4	4	0	0.72	800 522-7297
Fidelity Adv Equity Growth T	Growth	-12.3	-16.35	-0.9	4	4	3.5	1.26	800 522-7297
Fidelity Adv Equity Income A	Income	-9.8	0.08	1.25	3	2	5.75	0.95	800 522-7297
Fidelity Adv Equity Income B	Income	-10.5	-0.69	0.47	3	2	0	1.73	800 522-7297
Fidelity Adv Equity Income C	Income	-10.5	-4.28	-1.71	3	2	0	1.71	800 522-7297
Fidelity Adv Equity Income I	Income	-9.5	0.41	1.58	2	2	0	0.65	800 522-7297
Fidelity Adv Equity Income T	Income	-10	-0.13	1.04	3	2	3.5	1.19	800 522-7297
Fidelity Adv Equity Value A	Growth	-3.7					5.75	1.71	800 522-7297
Fidelity Adv Equity Value B	Growth	-4.4					0	2.47	800 522-7297
Fidelity Adv Equity Value C	Growth	-4.5					0	2.46	800 522-7297
Fidelity Adv Equity Value I	Growth	-3.4					0	1.46	800 522-7297
Fidelity Adv Equity Value T	Growth	-4					3.5	2.88	800 522-7297
Fidelity Adv Europe Cap App A	European	-13.4					5.75	1.95	800 522-7297
Fidelity Adv Europe Cap App B	European	-14.1					0	2.7	800 522-7297
Fidelity Adv Europe Cap App C	European	-14.2					0	2.7	800 522-7297
Fidelity Adv Europe Cap App I	European	-13.2	-8.5		3	3	0	1.69	800 522-7297
Fidelity Adv Europe Cap App T	European	-13.6					3.5	2.77	800 522-7297
Fidelity Adv Financial Serv A	Financial	-4.2	3.83	3.29	2	3	5.75	1.26	800 522-7297
Fidelity Adv Financial Serv B	Financial	-4.9	3.08	2.5	2	3	0	2	800 522-7297
Fidelity Adv Financial Serv C	Financial	-4.9	3.14	2.54	2	3	0	1.95	800 522-7297
Fidelity Adv Financial Serv I	Financial	-3.8	4.24	3.6	1	3	0	0.87	800 522-7297
Fidelity Adv Financial Serv T	Financial	-4.5	3.62	3.02	2	3	3.5	1.53	800 522-7297
Fidelity Adv Global Equity A	Global	-7.8	-9.02		3	2	5.75	1.96	800 522-7297
Fidelity Adv Global Equity B	Global	-8.5	-9.72		4	2	0	2.71	800 522-7297
Fidelity Adv Global Equity C	Global	-8.5	-9.71		4	2	0	2.71	800 522-7297
Fidelity Adv Global Equity I	Global	-7.4	-8.75		3	2	0	1.71	800 522-7297
Fidelity Adv Global Equity T	Global	-8.1	-9.27		3	3	3.5	2.92	800 522-7297
Fidelity Adv Gr Opportunities A	Growth	-6.2	-12.34	-6.37	3	3	5.75	0.75	800 522-7297
Fidelity Adv Gr Opportunities B	Growth	-6.9	-13.03	-7.09	3	3	0	1.54	800 522-7297
Fidelity Adv Gr Opportunities C	Growth	-6.9	-13.01	-7.08	3	3	0	1.5	800 522-7297
Fidelity Adv Gr Opportunities I	Growth	-5.8	-12	-6.04	3	3	0	0.37	800 522-7297
Fidelity Adv Gr Opportunities T	Growth	-6.3	-12.48	-6.53	3	3	3.5	0.9	800 522-7297
Fidelity Adv Growth & Income A	Growth/Inc	-3	-8.35	0.61	3	3	5.75	1	800 522-7297
Fidelity Adv Growth & Income B	Growth/Inc	-3.8	-9.05	-0.14	3	3	0	1.76	800 522-7297
Fidelity Adv Growth & Income C	Growth/Inc	-3.7	-9.01	-0.11	3	3	0	1.73	800 522-7297
Fidelity Adv Growth & Income I	Growth/Inc	-2.6	-8.02	0.94	3	3	0	0.67	800 522-7297
Fidelity Adv Growth & Income T	Growth/Inc	-3.2	-8.56	0.4	3	3	3.5	1.3	800 522-7297
Fidelity Adv Health Care A	Health	-3.7	-3.02	4.45	2	2	5.75	1.3	800 522-7297
Fidelity Adv Health Care B	Health	-4.4	-3.7	3.7	2	2	0	2.03	800 522-7297
Fidelity Adv Health Care C	Health	-4.3	-3.68	3.74	2	2	0	1.98	800 522-7297
Fidelity Adv Health Care I	Health	-3.3	-2.7	4.79	2	2	0	0.95	800 522-7297
Fidelity Adv Health Care T	Health	-4	-3.24	4.23	2	2	3.5	1.54	800 522-7297
Fidelity Adv Intl Cap Apprec A	Foreign	-11.4	-10.82	1.92	3	4	5.75	1.57	800 522-7297
Fidelity Adv Intl Cap Apprec B	Foreign	-12	-11.51	1.14	4	4	0	2.32	800 522-7297
Fidelity Adv Intl Cap Apprec I	Foreign	-11	-10.4	2.29	3	4	0	1.05	800 522-7297
Fidelity Adv Intl Cap Apprec T	Foreign	-11.6	-11	1.77	3	4	3.5	1.85	800 522-7297
Fidelity Adv Japan A	Pacific	-24.2	-22.14		5	3	5.75	1.84	800 522-7297
Fidelity Adv Japan B	Pacific	-24.8	-22.8		5	3	0		800 522-7297
Fidelity Adv Japan C	Pacific	-24.8	-22.75		5	3	0	2.55	800 522-7297
Fidelity Adv Japan I	Pacific	-24	-21.89		5	3	0	1.44	800 522-7297
Fidelity Adv Japan T	Pacific	-24.4	-22.44		5	3	3.5	2.21	800 522-7297
Fidelity Adv Large Cap Fund A	Growth	-11	-14.77	-1.78	5	3	5.75	1.2	800 522-7297
Fidelity Adv Large Cap Fund B	Growth	-11.7	-15.41	-2.49	5	3	0	1.94	800 522-7297
Fidelity Adv Large Cap Fund C	Growth	-11.7	-15.41	-2.56	5	3	0	1.91	800 522-7297
Fidelity Adv Large Cap Fund I	Growth	-10.7	-14.46	-1.41	4	3	0	0.82	800 522-7297

Stock Fund Name	Objective	Annualized Return for			Rank		Max Load	Expense Ratio	Toll-Free/(Toll) Telephone
		1 Year	3 Years	5 Years	Overall	Risk			
Fidelity Adv Large Cap Fund T	Growth	-11.2	-14.92	-1.93	5	3	3.5	1.42	800 522-7297
Fidelity Adv Leveraged Co Stk A	Growth	47.7					5.75	1.68	800 522-7297
Fidelity Adv Leveraged Co Stk B	Growth	47					0	2.43	800 522-7297
Fidelity Adv Leveraged Co Stk C	Growth	46.6					0	2.43	800 522-7297
Fidelity Adv Leveraged Co Stk I	Growth	48					0	1.43	800 522-7297
Fidelity Adv Leveraged Co Stk T	Growth	47.2					3.5	1.92	800 522-7297
Fidelity Adv Mid Cap Fund A	Growth	-5.6	-0.6	9.39	1	3	5.75	1.07	800 522-7297
Fidelity Adv Mid Cap Fund B	Growth	-6.2	-1.35	8.59	1	3	0	1.85	800 522-7297
Fidelity Adv Mid Cap Fund C	Growth	-6.2	-1.32	8.6	1	3	0	1.81	800 522-7297
Fidelity Adv Mid Cap Fund I	Growth	-5.2	-0.22	9.82	1	3	0	0.76	800 522-7297
Fidelity Adv Mid Cap Fund T	Growth	-5.8	-0.8	9.18	1	3	3.5	1.38	800 522-7297
Fidelity Adv Natural Resources A	Energy/Res	-7.8	-2.45	3.41	2	3	5.75	1.25	800 522-7297
Fidelity Adv Natural Resources B	Energy/Res	-8.4	-3.16	2.77	2	3	0	1.97	800 522-7297
Fidelity Adv Natural Resources C	Energy/Res	-8.4	-3.14	2.79	2	3	0	1.93	800 522-7297
Fidelity Adv Natural Resources I	Energy/Res	-7.4	-2.12	3.87	2	3	0	0.89	800 522-7297
Fidelity Adv Natural Resources T	Energy/Res	-7.9	-2.64	3.31	2	3	3.5	1.47	800 522-7297
Fidelity Adv Overseas Fund A	Foreign	-18.6	-15.52	-5.63	4	3	5.75	1.41	800 522-7297
Fidelity Adv Overseas Fund B	Foreign	-19.3	-16.23	-6.38	4	3	0	2.23	800 522-7297
Fidelity Adv Overseas Fund C	Foreign	-19.3	-19.16	-8.36	5	3	0	2.14	800 522-7297
Fidelity Adv Overseas Fund I	Foreign	-18.3	-15.21	-5.29	5	3	0	1.02	800 522-7297
Fidelity Adv Overseas Fund T	Foreign	-18.8	-15.68	-5.79	4	3	3.5	1.57	800 522-7297
Fidelity Adv Small Cap A	Growth	-7.8	-4.16		3	4	5.75	1.34	800 522-7297
Fidelity Adv Small Cap B	Growth	-8.5	-4.91		3	4	0		800 522-7297
Fidelity Adv Small Cap I	Growth	-7.3	-3.56		3	4	0	0.95	800 522-7297
Fidelity Adv Small Cap T	Growth	-8	-4.4		3	4	3.5	1.57	800 522-7297
Fidelity Adv Strategic Growth A	Growth	-23.6	-18.05	-4.53	4	3	5.75	1.26	800 522-7297
Fidelity Adv Strategic Growth B	Growth	-24.1	-18.71	-5.26	5	3	0	2.01	800 522-7297
Fidelity Adv Strategic Growth C	Growth	-24.2	-18.69	-5.26	5	3	0	2	800 522-7297
Fidelity Adv Strategic Growth I	Growth	-23.4	-17.89	-4.34	4	3	0	1	800 522-7297
Fidelity Adv Strategic Growth T	Growth	-23.8	-18.3	-4.79	3	3	3.5	2.21	800 522-7297
Fidelity Adv Tax Mgd Stock Fund A	Other	-11.4					0	1.69	800 522-7297
Fidelity Adv Tax Mgd Stock Fund B	Other	-12					0	2.44	800 522-7297
Fidelity Adv Tax Mgd Stock Fund C	Other	-12					0	2.45	800 522-7297
Fidelity Adv Tax Mgd Stock Fund I	Other	-11.2					0	1.43	800 522-7297
Fidelity Adv Tax Mgd Stock Fund T	Other	-11.6					0	1.94	800 522-7297
Fidelity Adv Technology A	Technology	-0.3	-26.1	0.11	3	5	5.75	1.46	800 522-7297
Fidelity Adv Technology B	Technology	-1	-26.67	-0.64	3	5	0	2.21	800 522-7297
Fidelity Adv Technology C	Technology	-1	-26.62	-0.59	3	5	0	2.17	800 522-7297
Fidelity Adv Technology I	Technology	0.3	-25.76	0.52	3	5	0	1.02	800 522-7297
Fidelity Adv Technology T	Technology	-0.6	-26.28	-0.11	3	5	3.5	1.71	800 522-7297
Fidelity Adv Telecom & Util Gr A	Utilities	-0.1	-18.53	-4.2	3	4	5.75	1.41	800 522-7297
Fidelity Adv Telecom & Util Gr B	Utilities	-0.6	-19.12	-4.87	3	4	0	2.17	800 522-7297
Fidelity Adv Telecom & Util Gr C	Utilities	-0.6	-19.07	-4.91	3	4	0	2.08	800 522-7297
Fidelity Adv Telecom & Util Gr I	Utilities	0.6	-18.14	-3.91	3	4	0	0.93	800 522-7297
Fidelity Adv Telecom & Util Gr T	Utilities	-0.3	-18.71	-4.4	3	4	3.5	1.7	800 522-7297
Fidelity Adv Value Strategies A	Growth	-7.5	4.45	5	3	4	5.75	1.16	800 522-7297
Fidelity Adv Value Strategies B	Growth	-8.3	3.62	4.2	3	4	0	1.92	800 522-7297
Fidelity Adv Value Strategies C	Growth	-8.3	3.68	4.25	3	4	0	1.86	800 522-7297
Fidelity Adv Value Strategies I	Growth	-7.2	4.83	5.41	3	4	0	0.58	800 522-7297
Fidelity Adv Value Strategies Init	Growth	-7.1					0	1.34	800 522-7297
Fidelity Adv Value Strategies T	Growth	-7.7	4.24	4.83	3	4	3.5	1.34	800 522-7297
Fidelity Aggressive Growth Fund	Agg Growth	-10.6	-33.35	-7.99	3	5	0	0.66	800 343-3548
Fidelity Aggressive Intl Fund	Foreign	-10.1	-10.19	-1.12	3	4	0	1.59	800 343-3548
Fidelity Asset Manager	AssetAlloc	1.6	-0.8	4.07	1	1	0	0.75	800 343-3548
Fidelity Asset Manager: Aggressive	Agg Growth	-15.6	-13.78		4	4	0	0.94	800 343-3548
Fidelity Asset Manager: Growth	AssetAlloc	-1.9	-4.45	0.95	2	2	0	0.83	800 343-3548
Fidelity Asset Manager: Income	Balanced	6.8	4.03	4.66	1	1	0	0.64	800 343-3548
Fidelity Balanced Fund	Balanced	1.8	3.1	5.69	1	1	0	0.68	800 343-3548

Stock Fund Name	Objective	Annualized Return for			Rank		Max Load	Expense Ratio	Toll-Free/(Toll) Telephone
		1 Year	3 Years	5 Years	Overall	Risk			
Fidelity Blue Chip Growth	Growth	-9.1	-14.16	-1.84	3	3	0	0.77	800 343-3548
Fidelity Canada Fund	Foreign	3	2.49	5.17	1	3	3	1.47	800 343-3548
Fidelity Capital Appreciation	Growth	-2.7	7.55	2.37	3	4	0	1.08	800 343-3548
Fidelity China Region Fund	Pacific	-12.8	-8.8	5.57	3	3	0	1.27	800 343-3548
Fidelity Congress Street	Growth	-7.1	-4.54	1.58	3	2	0	0.64	800 343-3548
Fidelity Contrafund	Growth	-6	-5.9	3.2	3	1	3	0.98	800 343-3548
Fidelity Contrafund II	Growth	-5.4	-8.36	4	2	3	3	1.11	800 343-3548
Fidelity Convertible Securities	Converts	2	1.7	9.08	1	3	0	0.84	800 343-3548
Fidelity Destiny I Class N	Growth	-10.8	-14.81		5	3	0	1.27	800 522-7297
Fidelity Destiny II Class N	Growth	-5.6	-9.22		3	3	0	1.44	800 522-7297
Fidelity Destiny Portf I Class O	Growth	-10.1	-14.08	-7.58	5	3	8.5	0.37	800 522-7297
Fidelity Destiny Portf II Class O	Growth	-4.7	-8.36	1.05	3	3	8.5	0.55	800 522-7297
Fidelity Disciplined Equity	Growth	-8.3	-9.9	-0.48	3	2	0	0.95	800 343-3548
Fidelity Diversified Intl Fund	Foreign	-6.5	-5.07	3.04	3	2	0	1.21	800 343-3548
Fidelity Dividend Growth Fund	Growth	-7.5	-3.62	3.45	2	3	0	0.98	800 343-3548
Fidelity Emerging Markets	Foreign	-10.5	-9.25	-2.7	3	4	3	1.44	800 343-3548
Fidelity Equity-Income Fund	Income	-9.9	-2.77	0.38	3	2	0	0.69	800 343-3548
Fidelity Equity-Income II Fund	Income	-3.2	-1.2	1.63	2	3	0	0.68	800 343-3548
Fidelity Europe	European	-11.2	-12.76	-5.48	5	4	0	1.25	800 343-3548
Fidelity Europe Cap Appreciation	European	-12.2	-7	-2.25	3	3	0	1.37	800 343-3548
Fidelity Exchange Fund	Growth	-7.2	-6.87	-1	3	2	0	0.62	800 343-3548
Fidelity Export & Multinational	Growth	-2.6	-2.52	8.5	1	3	0	0.89	800 343-3548
Fidelity Fifty Fund	Agg Growth	-2.8	-1.14	7.23	2	3	0	1.12	800 343-3548
Fidelity Focused Stock Fund	Growth	-26.6	-18.23	-4.58	5	3	0	1.34	800 343-3548
Fidelity Four In One Index Fund	Growth/Inc	-5	-7.37		2	2	0	0.32	800 522-7297
Fidelity Freedom 2000 Fund	AssetAlloc	3.3	2.14	5.37	1	1	0	0.68	800 544-8888
Fidelity Freedom 2010 Fund	AssetAlloc	1.9	-1.05	4.65	1	1	0	0.77	800 544-8888
Fidelity Freedom 2020 Fund	AssetAlloc	-2.2	-5.42	2.85	1	2	0	0.83	800 544-8888
Fidelity Freedom 2030 Fund	AssetAlloc	-4.8	-7.91	1.57	2	2	0	0.85	800 544-8888
Fidelity Freedom 2040 Fund	AssetAlloc	-6.6					0	0.88	800 544-8888
Fidelity Freedom Income Fund	Balanced	3.7	3.5	5.13	1	1	0	0.62	800 544-8888
Fidelity Fund	Growth/Inc	-8.4	-10.27	-0.72	3	3	0	0.59	800 343-3548
Fidelity Global Balanced Fund	Balanced	-3	-3.16	2.49	2	1	0	1.25	800 343-3548
Fidelity Growth & Income II	Growth/Inc	-1.2	-5.33		2	2	0	0.9	800 522-7297
Fidelity Growth & Income Portf	Growth/Inc	-8.2	-7.08	-0.2	2	2	0	0.69	800 343-3548
Fidelity Growth Company	Growth	-5.1	-17.44	3.12	3	4	0	1.06	800 343-3548
Fidelity Independence Fund	Growth	-12	-10.06	3.18	3	4	0	1.03	800 343-3548
Fidelity Intl Growth & Income	Foreign	-10.8	-9.06	0.25	3	3	0	1.14	800 343-3548
Fidelity Japan Fund	Pacific	-19.9	-22.39	1.25	3	3	0	1.61	800 343-3548
Fidelity Japan Smaller Companies	Pacific	-15.9	-16.98	11.25	4	4	0	1.26	800 343-3548
Fidelity Large Cap Stock Fund	Growth	-10.5	-14.61	-1.35	3	3	0	0.91	800 343-3548
Fidelity Latin American Fund	Foreign	-7.4	-5	-4.21	3	4	0	1.45	800 343-3548
Fidelity Leveraged Company Stock	Income	50.2					0	1.15	800 522-7297
Fidelity Low-Priced Stock	Small Co	-5.2	15.25	8.82	2	2	3	1.01	800 343-3548
Fidelity Magellan Fund	Growth	-8.9	-11.52	-0.34	3	3	3	0.89	800 343-3548
Fidelity Mid-Cap Stock Fund	Growth	-11.5	-5.13	6.74	2	4	0	0.94	800 343-3548
Fidelity New Millennium	Agg Growth	-5.4	-7.7	11.64	3	5	3	1.02	800 343-3548
Fidelity Nordic Fund	European	-10.4	-17.25	-1.22	3	4	3	1.32	800 343-3548
Fidelity OTC Portfolio	Agg Growth	-6.5	-19	0.42	3	5	0	1.09	800 343-3548
Fidelity Overseas Fund	Foreign	-17.9	-15.24	-5.2	5	3	0	1.26	800 343-3548
Fidelity Pacific Basin	Pacific	-17.4	-15.49	3.14	4	3	0	1.57	800 343-3548
Fidelity Puritan Fund	Balanced	-1.2	1.75	3.2	1	1	0	0.65	800 343-3548
Fidelity Real Estate Investment	Real Est	4.4	14.53	7.32	1	1	0	0.84	800 343-3548
Fidelity Select Air Transportation	Other	-21.5	-4.2	3.56	3	4	3	1.43	800 343-3548
Fidelity Select Automotive	Other	-14.5	5.07	-1.87	3	4	3	1.9	800 343-3548
Fidelity Select Biotechnology	Health	9.5	-10.9	10.39	3	5	3	1.11	800 343-3548
Fidelity Select Brokrg and Inv Mgt	Financial	-1.8	1.76	5.41	2	4	3	1.15	800 343-3548
Fidelity Select Bus Svcs & Outsrcng	Financial	-17.1	-1.51	5.83	3	4	3	1.34	800 343-3548

Stock Fund Name	Objective	Annualized Return for			Rank		Max Load	Expense Ratio	Toll-Free/(Toll) Telephone
		1 Year	3 Years	5 Years	Overall	Risk			
Fidelity Select Chemicals	Other	-8.3	5.48	1.29	2	3	3	1.34	800 343-3548
Fidelity Select Computers	Technology	-9	-28.83	1.93	3	5	3	1.19	800 343-3548
Fidelity Select Const & Housing	Other	-9.4	12.98	4.15	3	3	3	1.45	800 343-3548
Fidelity Select Consumer Inds	Other	-13.2	-4.01	-0.34	3	2	3	1.71	800 343-3548
Fidelity Select Cyclical Inds	Other	-12.7	-0.4	0.44	3	3	3	1.79	800 343-3548
Fidelity Select Defense & Aerospace	Technology	-16.9	3.02	3.64	3	2	3	1.23	800 343-3548
Fidelity Select Developing Commun	Technology	-3.7	-31.89	-0.11	3	5	3	1.31	800 343-3548
Fidelity Select Electronics	Technology	-24.3	-28.23	7.2	4	5	3	0.99	800 343-3548
Fidelity Select Energy Portfolio	Energy/Res	-6.7	-3.22	4.38	2	3	3	1.16	800 343-3548
Fidelity Select Energy Service	Energy/Res	-5.7	-2.5	3.12	2	5	3	1.13	800 343-3548
Fidelity Select Environmental	Other	-4	1.86	-7.54	2	3	3	2	800 343-3548
Fidelity Select Financial Services	Financial	-3.9	3.66	3.27	2	3	3	1.07	800 343-3548
Fidelity Select Food & Agriculture	Other	-15	5	1.2	2	2	3	1.24	800 343-3548
Fidelity Select Gold Portfolio	Prec Metal	-5.6	25.75	9.93	2	5	3	1.29	800 343-3548
Fidelity Select Health Care	Health	-3.6	-2.81	3.7	2	2	3	0.99	800 343-3548
Fidelity Select Home Finance	Financial	-3.9	17.46	2.47	2	3	3	1.15	800 343-3548
Fidelity Select Industrial Equip	Other	-18.1	-10.15	-2.75	4	4	3	1.46	800 343-3548
Fidelity Select Industrial Matls	Other	-12.4	7.36	0.35	2	3	3	1.57	800 343-3548
Fidelity Select Insurance	Financial	-2.2	11.61	9.02	2	3	3	1.2	800 343-3548
Fidelity Select Leisure	Other	-2.9	-5.95	2.87	3	4	3	1.12	800 343-3548
Fidelity Select Medcl Equip & Sys	Health	11	10.67	1	2	3		1.26	800 343-3548
Fidelity Select Medical Delivery	Health	-25.6	12.09	-2.7	3	3		1.22	800 343-3548
Fidelity Select Multimedia	Other	15.1	-4.12	6.25	3	4	3	1.13	800 343-3548
Fidelity Select Natural Gas	Energy/Res	1.5	-0.3	8.81	2	4	3	1.17	800 343-3548
Fidelity Select Natural Resources	Energy/Res	-8.2	-2.43	4.62	2	3	3	1.61	800 343-3548
Fidelity Select Paper&Forest Prods	Other	-18.4	3.06	2.27	3	4	3	1.82	800 343-3548
Fidelity Select Retailing	Other	-14.9	-5.66	-0.4	3	3	3	1.29	800 343-3548
Fidelity Select Software & Comp Svc	Technology	6.8	-10.52	9.51	3	5	3	1.09	800 343-3548
Fidelity Select Technology	Technology	0.8	-27.19	5.19	3	5	3	1.19	800 343-3548
Fidelity Select Telecommunications	Technology	9.6	-26.48	-7.48	3	5	3	1.29	800 343-3548
Fidelity Select Transportation	Other	-5.7	7.75	7.07	2	3	3	1.32	800 343-3548
Fidelity Select Utilities Growth	Utilities	-1	-18.16	-2.79	3	4	3	1.11	800 343-3548
Fidelity Select-Banking	Financial	-5.6	5.76	2.24	3	3	3	1.11	800 343-3548
Fidelity Small Cap Independence	Small Co	-16.6	-2	-1.04	3	3	0	1.06	800 343-3548
Fidelity Small Cap Stock Fund	Small Co	-11	1.51	6.73	2	3	0	1.12	800 343-3548
Fidelity Southeast Asia Fund	Pacific	-16.4	-10.6	5.86	4	4	3	1.51	800 343-3548
Fidelity Spartan 500 Idx Fund	Growth/Inc	-8.1	-10.93	-1.18	3	3	0	0.39	800 343-3548
Fidelity Spartan Extended Mkt Idx	Growth	-4.9	-6.87	-0.56	3	4	0	0.45	800 343-3548
Fidelity Spartan Intl Index	Foreign	-11.9	-13.4	-4.05	5	3	0	0.56	800 343-3548
Fidelity Spartan Total Mkt Index	Growth	-7.5	-9.77	-0.9	3	3	0	0.41	800 343-3548
Fidelity Spartan US Equity Index	Growth/Inc	-8.2	-10.96	-1.21	3	3	0	0.04	800 343-3548
Fidelity Stock Selector	Growth	-6	-10.64	-2.14	3	3	0	0.93	800 343-3548
Fidelity Structured Lg Cap Growth	Growth	-9.5					0	3.32	800 522-7297
Fidelity Structured Lg Cap Value	Other	-10.4					0	3.13	800 522-7297
Fidelity Structured Mid Cap Growth	Growth	-8.9					0	2.4	800 522-7297
Fidelity Structured Mid Cap Value	Growth	-9.3					0		800 522-7297
Fidelity Tax Managed Stock Fund	Growth	-10.8	-12.16		4	3	0	0.89	800 343-3548
Fidelity Trend Fund	Growth	-5.4	-9.77	-1.89	3	3	0	1.05	800 343-3548
Fidelity Utilities Fund	Utilities	0	-16.75	-3.74	3	3	0	0.94	800 343-3548
Fidelity Value Discovery Fund	Growth/Inc						0		800 522-7297
Fidelity Value Fund	Growth	-7	6.83	3.85	2	3	0	0.96	800 343-3548
Fidelity Worldwide Fund	Global	-10.3	-7.51	-1.95	3	3	0	1.17	800 343-3548
Fifth Third Balanced A	Balanced	-5.1	-6.91	1.05	2	2	5	1.31	800 282-5706
Fifth Third Balanced C	Balanced	-5.8	-7.63	0.4	3	2	0	2.04	800 282-5706
Fifth Third Balanced I	Balanced	-4.8	-6.66		2	2	0	1.04	800 282-5706
Fifth Third Discipl Large Cap Val A	Growth/Inc	-2.4	-2.16	-0.51	3	2	5	0.69	800 282-5706
Fifth Third Discipl Large Cap Val C	Growth/Inc	-3.2	-2.87	-1.12	3	2	0	2.11	800 282-5706
Fifth Third Discipl Large Cap Val I	Growth/Inc	-2.3	-1.93	-0.28	3	2	0	1.11	800 282-5706

Stock Fund Name	Objective	Annualized Return for			Rank		Max Load	Expense Ratio	Toll-Free/(Toll) Telephone
		1 Year	3 Years	5 Years	Overall	Risk			
Fifth Third Equity Index A	Growth	-8.5	-11.34	-1.62	3	3	5	0.66	800 282-5706
Fifth Third Equity Index Inst	Growth	-8.3	-11.11	-1.37	3	3	0	0.41	800 282-5706
Fifth Third Intl Equity A	Foreign	-12.8	-11.46	-6.25	4	2	5	1.63	800 282-5706
Fifth Third Intl Equity C	Foreign	-13.8	-12.3	-5.23	4	2	0	2.38	800 282-5706
Fifth Third Intl Equity Instl	Foreign	-12.8	-11.38		4	2	0	1.39	800 282-5706
Fifth Third Intl GDP A	Foreign	-12	-15.11	-5.84	4	3	5	1.3	800 282-5706
Fifth Third Intl GDP Instl	Foreign	-11.8	-14.84	-5.57	5	3	0	1.04	800 282-5706
Fifth Third Large Cap Core A	Growth/Inc	-11.3	-12.67	-2.93	4	3	5	1.18	800 282-5706
Fifth Third Large Cap Core Inst	Growth/Inc	-11	-12.44	-2.68	4	3	0	0.93	800 282-5706
Fifth Third Large Cap Opp A	Growth	-18.3	-21.62	-10.13	5	3	5	1.49	800 282-5706
Fifth Third Large Cap Opp C	Growth	-18.9					0	2.27	800 282-5706
Fifth Third Large Cap Opp I	Growth	-18.1	-21.42		5	3	0	1.27	800 282-5706
Fifth Third LifeModel Agg A	Agg Growth						5	0.75	800 282-5706
Fifth Third LifeModel Agg B	Agg Growth						0	1.5	800 282-5706
Fifth Third LifeModel Agg C	Agg Growth						0	1.5	800 282-5706
Fifth Third LifeModel Agg Inst	Agg Growth						0	0.5	800 282-5706
Fifth Third LifeModel Conserv A	AssetAlloc						5	0.75	800 282-5706
Fifth Third LifeModel Conserv B	AssetAlloc						0	1.5	800 282-5706
Fifth Third LifeModel Conserv C	AssetAlloc						0	1.5	800 282-5706
Fifth Third LifeModel Conserv Inst	AssetAlloc						0	0.5	800 282-5706
Fifth Third LifeModel Mod Agg A	Agg Growth						5	0.75	800 282-5706
Fifth Third LifeModel Mod Agg B	Agg Growth						0	1.5	800 282-5706
Fifth Third LifeModel Mod Agg C	Agg Growth						0	1.5	800 282-5706
Fifth Third LifeModel Mod Agg Inst	Agg Growth						0	0.5	800 282-5706
Fifth Third LifeModel Mod Cons A	AssetAlloc						5	0.75	800 282-5706
Fifth Third LifeModel Mod Cons B	AssetAlloc						0	1.5	800 282-5706
Fifth Third LifeModel Mod Cons C	AssetAlloc						0	1.5	800 282-5706
Fifth Third LifeModel Mod Cons Inst	AssetAlloc						0	0.5	800 282-5706
Fifth Third LifeModel Moderate A	Growth						5	0.75	800 282-5706
Fifth Third LifeModel Moderate B	Growth						0	1.5	800 282-5706
Fifth Third LifeModel Moderate C	Growth						0	1.5	800 282-5706
Fifth Third LifeModel Moderate Inst	Growth						0	0.5	800 282-5706
Fifth Third Micro Cap Value A	Agg Growth	11.2					5	1.62	800 282-5706
Fifth Third Micro Cap Value Inst	Agg Growth	11.5	18.44	14.1	1	4	0	1.37	800 282-5706
Fifth Third Mid Cap A	Growth/Inc	-11.8	-8.59	-1.26	3	4	5	1.33	800 282-5706
Fifth Third Mid Cap C	Growth/Inc	-12.5	-9.31	-1.9	3	4	0	2.05	800 282-5706
Fifth Third Mid Cap I	Growth/Inc	-11.6	-8.34		3	4	0	1.06	800 282-5706
Fifth Third Multi Cap Value A	Growth	-1.7					5	1.54	800 282-5706
Fifth Third Multi Cap Value Adv	Growth	-1.9	4.5	3.93	1	3	0	1.79	800 282-5706
Fifth Third Multi Cap Value Inst	Growth	-1.4	5	4.29		3	0	1.3	800 282-5706
Fifth Third Quality Growth A	Growth	-13.7	-15.64	-1.82	4	4	5	1.3	800 282-5706
Fifth Third Quality Growth C	Growth	-14.3	-16.23	-2.37	4	4	0	2.04	800 282-5706
Fifth Third Quality Growth I	Growth	-13.4	-15.41		4	4	0	1.04	800 282-5706
Fifth Third Small Cap Growth A	Small Co	-15.1	-6.51	-1.97	3	4	5	1.17	800 282-5706
Fifth Third Small Cap Growth Inst	Small Co	-14.9	-6.24	-1.71	3	4	0	0.92	800 282-5706
Fifth Third Strategic Income A	Flexible	10.5	12.39	7.4	1	1	0	1.84	800 282-5706
Fifth Third Strategic Income C	Flexible	9.9					0	2.39	800 282-5706
Fifth Third Strategic Income Inst	Flexible	11	12.92	7.74	1	1	0	1.26	800 282-5706
Fifth Third Technology A	Technology	8.8					5	1.77	800 282-5706
Fifth Third Technology C	Technology	8					0	2.49	800 282-5706
Fifth Third Technology Instl	Technology	9					0	1.52	800 282-5706
Fifth Third Worldwide Fund Adv	Growth/Inc	-13.4	-11.8	3.06	4	3	0	1.76	800 282-5706
Fifth Third Worldwide Fund C	Growth/Inc	-13.8					0	1.81	800 282-5706
Fifth Third Worldwide Fund Inst	Growth/Inc	-12.9	-11.49	5.37		3	0	1.13	800 282-5706
First American Balanced A	Balanced	-3	-3.77	0.73	2	2	5.5	1.05	800 677-3863
First American Balanced B	Balanced	-3.6	-5.65	-2.43	2	1	0	1.8	800 677-3863
First American Balanced C	Balanced	-3.8					1	1.8	800 677-3863
First American Balanced S	Balanced	-3					0	1.05	800 677-3863

Stock Fund Name	Objective	Annualized Return for			Rank		Max Load	Expense Ratio	Toll-Free/(Toll) Telephone
		1 Year	3 Years	5 Years	Overall	Risk			
First American Balanced Y	Balanced	-2.8	-4.82	-1.52	2	1	0	0.8	800 677-3863
First American Eqty Inc A	Income	-8.7	-1.76	0.98	2	2	5.5	1.15	800 677-3863
First American Eqty Inc B	Income	-9.5	-2.49	0.28	3	2	0	1.9	800 677-3863
First American Eqty Inc C	Income	-9.5	-2.5		3	2	1	1.9	800 677-3863
First American Eqty Inc S	Income	-8.8					0	1.15	800 677-3863
First American Eqty Inc Y	Income	-8.5	-1.5	1.28	2	2	0	0.9	800 677-3863
First American Eqty Indx A	Growth/Inc	-8.5	-11.25	-1.61	3	3	5.5	0.62	800 677-3863
First American Eqty Indx B	Growth/Inc	-9.1	-11.91	-2.35	3	3	0	1.37	800 677-3863
First American Eqty Indx C	Growth/Inc	-9.1	-11.94		4	3	1	1.37	800 677-3863
First American Eqty Indx S	Growth/Inc	-8.4					0	0.62	800 677-3863
First American Eqty Indx Y	Growth/Inc	-8.2	-11.06	-0.86	3	3	0	0.37	800 677-3863
First American International A	Foreign	-15.1	-17.78	-2.41	3	2	5.5	1.6	800 677-3863
First American International B	Foreign	-15.8	-18.37	-3.18	5	2	0	2.35	800 677-3863
First American International C	Foreign	-15.8					1	2.35	800 677-3863
First American International S	Foreign	-15.1	-16.3	-4.17	3	3	0	1.6	800 677-3863
First American International Y	Foreign	-14.9	-16.03	-3.85	3	3	0	1.35	800 677-3863
First American Lrg Cap Gr Opp A	Growth	-12.1	-15.27	-4.12	5	3	5.5	1.15	800 677-3863
First American Lrg Cap Gr Opp B	Growth	-12.8	-15.91		5	3	0	1.9	800 677-3863
First American Lrg Cap Gr Opp C	Growth	-12.8					1	1.9	800 677-3863
First American Lrg Cap Gr Opp S	Growth	-12.2					0	1.9	800 677-3863
First American Lrg Cap Gr Opp Y	Growth	-11.9	-15.07	-3.89	4	3	0	0.9	800 677-3863
First American Lrg Cap Select A	Growth						5.5	1.15	800 677-3863
First American Lrg Cap Select B	Growth						0	1.9	800 677-3863
First American Lrg Cap Select C	Growth						1	1.9	800 677-3863
First American Lrg Cap Select S	Growth						0	0.9	800 677-3863
First American Lrg Cap Select Y	Growth						0	0.9	800 677-3863
First American Lrg Cap Val A	Growth/Inc	-11.8	-8.3	-3.29	3	3	5.5	1.15	800 677-3863
First American Lrg Cap Val B	Growth/Inc	-12.5	-8.97	-4.01	4	3	0	1.9	800 677-3863
First American Lrg Cap Val C	Growth/Inc	-12.5	-8.98		3	3	1	1.9	800 677-3863
First American Lrg Cap Val S	Growth/Inc	-11.8					0	1.15	800 677-3863
First American Lrg Cap Val Y	Growth/Inc	-11.6	-8.06	0.11	3	3	0	0.9	800 677-3863
First American Mid Cap Gr Opp A	Growth	-8	0.22	2.52	1	3	5.5	1.2	800 677-3863
First American Mid Cap Gr Opp B	Growth	-8.6	-0.56	1	3	0		1.95	800 677-3863
First American Mid Cap Gr Opp C	Growth	-8.5				1		1.95	800 677-3863
First American Mid Cap Gr Opp S	Growth	-8					0	1.2	800 677-3863
First American Mid Cap Gr Opp Y	Growth	-7.7	0.46	2.77	1	3	0	0.95	800 677-3863
First American Mid Cap Index A	Growth	-9.8	-0.08		3	3	5.5	0.75	800 677-3863
First American Mid Cap Index B	Growth	-10.6	-0.8		3	3	0	1.5	800 677-3863
First American Mid Cap Index C	Growth	-10.6					1	1.5	800 677-3863
First American Mid Cap Index S	Growth	-9.9					0	0.75	800 677-3863
First American Mid Cap Index Y	Growth	-9.7	0.14		3	3	0	0.5	800 677-3863
First American Mid Cap Val A	Growth	-6.9	4.7	-2.12	2	2	5.5	1.2	800 677-3863
First American Mid Cap Val B	Growth	-7.5	3.97	-2.79	2	2	0	1.95	800 677-3863
First American Mid Cap Val C	Growth	-7.6	3.95		2	2	1	1.95	800 677-3863
First American Mid Cap Val S	Growth	-6.8					0	1.2	800 677-3863
First American Mid Cap Val Y	Growth	-6.6	4.92	2.54	2	2	0	0.95	800 677-3863
First American Real Est Secs A	Real Est	6.3	15.31	7.57	1	1	5.5	1.23	800 677-3863
First American Real Est Secs B	Real Est	5.6	14.92	7	1	1	0	1.98	800 677-3863
First American Real Est Secs C	Real Est	5.5	14.41	1		1	1	1.98	800 677-3863
First American Real Est Secs S	Real Est	6.2					0	1.23	800 677-3863
First American Real Est Secs Y	Real Est	6.6	16.14	8.13	1	1	0	0.98	800 677-3863
First American Short Tax Free A	Other						2.25	0.75	800 677-3863
First American Short Tax Free Y	Other						0	0.6	800 677-3863
First American Sm Cap Gr Opp A	Small Co	-7.4	-1.83	15.23	3	5	5.5	1.93	800 677-3863
First American Sm Cap Gr Opp B	Small Co	-8.2	-2.54		2	5	0	2.68	800 677-3863
First American Sm Cap Gr Opp C	Small Co	-8.1					1	2.68	800 677-3863
First American Sm Cap Gr Opp S	Small Co	-7.5					0	1.93	800 677-3863
First American Sm Cap Gr Opp Y	Small Co	-7.3	-1.6	15.53	3	5	0	1.68	800 677-3863

Stock Fund Name	Objective	Annualized Return for			Rank		Max Load	Expense Ratio	Toll-Free/(Toll) Telephone
		1 Year	3 Years	5 Years	Overall	Risk			
First American Sm Cap Index A	Small Co	-9.7	1.54		2	4	5.5	0.93	800 677-3863
First American Sm Cap Index B	Small Co	-10.2					0	1.68	800 677-3863
First American Sm Cap Index C	Small Co	-10.3					1	1.68	800 677-3863
First American Sm Cap Index S	Small Co	-9.8	1.45		2	4	0	0.93	800 677-3863
First American Sm Cap Index Y	Small Co	-9.4	1.79		2	4	5.5	0.68	800 677-3863
First American Sm Cap Select A	Small Co	-8.1	2.87	4.67	2	4	5.5	1.21	800 677-3863
First American Sm Cap Select B	Small Co	-8.8	2.12	3.97	2	4	0	1.96	800 677-3863
First American Sm Cap Select C	Small Co	-8.7					1	1.96	800 677-3863
First American Sm Cap Select S	Small Co	-8.1	2.97	4.75	2	4	0	1.21	800 677-3863
First American Sm Cap Select Y	Small Co	-7.8	3.16	5	2	4	4.5	0.96	800 677-3863
First American Sm Cap Val A	Small Co	-14.2	4.98	3.35	2	3	5.5	1.23	800 677-3863
First American Sm Cap Val B	Small Co	-14.9	4.12	0.91	2	3	0	1.98	800 677-3863
First American Sm Cap Val C	Small Co	-14.9	4.19		2	3	1	1.98	800 677-3863
First American Sm Cap Val S	Small Co	-14.2					0	1.23	800 677-3863
First American Sm Cap Val Y	Small Co	-14.1	5.23	1.97	2	3	0	0.98	800 677-3863
First American Strat-Agg Alloc A	Agg Growth	-9.1	-9.36	-1.72	3	2	5.5	0.4	800 677-3863
First American Strat-Agg Alloc B	Agg Growth	-9.9					0	1.15	800 677-3863
First American Strat-Agg Alloc C	Agg Growth	-9.9					1	1.15	800 677-3863
First American Strat-Agg Alloc S	Agg Growth	-9.2	-9.47	-1.8	3	2	0	0.4	800 677-3863
First American Strat-Agg Alloc Y	Agg Growth	-9					0	0.15	800 677-3863
First American Strat-Gr Alloc A	Growth/Inc	-5.6	-4.59	0.01	2	2	5.5	0.4	800 677-3863
First American Strat-Gr Alloc B	Growth/Inc	-6.4					0	1.15	800 677-3863
First American Strat-Gr Alloc C	Growth/Inc	-6.3					1	1.15	800 677-3863
First American Strat-Gr Alloc S	Growth/Inc	-5.8	-6.45	-0.55	2	2	0	0.4	800 677-3863
First American Strat-Gr Alloc Y	Growth/Inc	-5.4					0	0.15	800 677-3863
First American Strat-Gr&Inc Allc A	Growth	-2.5	-4.9	0.46	2	2	5.5	0.4	800 677-3863
First American Strat-Gr&Inc Allc B	Growth	-3.3					0	1.15	800 677-3863
First American Strat-Gr&Inc Allc C	Growth	-3.2					1	1.15	800 677-3863
First American Strat-Gr&Inc Allc S	Growth	-2.5	-3.37	0.79	2	1	0 /	0.4	800 677-3863
First American Strat-Gr&Inc Allc Y	Growth	-2.2					0	0.15	800 677-3863
First American Strat-Inc Alloc A	Flexible	3.9	4.75	3.83	1	1	5.5	0.4	800 677-3863
First American Strat-Inc Alloc B	Flexible	3.2					0	1.15	800 677-3863
First American Strat-Inc Alloc C	Flexible	3.2					1	1.15	800 677-3863
First American Strat-Inc Alloc S	Flexible	4	4.5	3.68	1	1	0	0.4	800 677-3863
First American Strat-Inc Alloc Y	Flexible	4.3					0	0.15	800 677-3863
First American Technology A	Technology	-11.5	-42.67	-9.98	4	5	5.5	1.23	800 677-3863
First American Technology B	Technology	-12.3	-43.14	-10.68	4	5	0	1.98	800 677-3863
First American Technology C	Technology	-12.2	-43.11		4	5	1	1.98	800 677-3863
First American Technology S	Technology	-12					0	1.23	800 677-3863
First American Technology Y	Technology	-11.2	-42.5	-9.72	4	5	0	0.98	800 677-3863
First Eagle Fund of America C	Growth	-3.8	4.17	4.17	1	1	0	2.26	800 334-2143
First Eagle Fund of America Y	Growth	-3.1	4.99	4.96	2	1	0	1.43	800 334-2143
First Eagle Global Fund A	Global	7.7	14.3	10.4	1	1	5	1.39	800 334-2143
First Eagle Global Fund C	Global	7					0	2.14	800 334-2143
First Eagle Global Fund I	Global	8	14.58		1	1	0	1.14	800 334-2143
First Eagle Gold Fund	Prec Metal	3.2	39.78	15.6	2	5	5	2.65	800 334-2143
First Eagle Overseas Fund A	Foreign	7.2	12.74	11.14	1	2	5	1.39	800 334-2143
First Eagle Overseas Fund C	Foreign	6.4					0	2.28	800 334-2143
First Eagle Overseas Fund I	Foreign	7.4	12.96		1	2	0	1.28	800 334-2143
First Eagle U.S. Value A	Small Co	-2.3					5	1.5	800 334-2143
First Eagle U.S. Value C	Small Co	-3.1					0	2.25	800 334-2143
First Eagle U.S. Value I	Small Co	-2.2					0	1.25	800 334-2143
First Fds-Cap Appreciation I	Growth	4.8	-4.16	0.05	2	4	0	1.27	800 442-1941
First Fds-Cap Appreciation II	Growth	4.6	-4.45	0.22	2	4	5.75	1.76	800 442-1941
First Fds-Cap Appreciation III	Growth	3.9	-5.25	-0.56	3	4	0	2.63	800 442-1941
First Fds-Growth & Income I	Growth/Inc	-5.5	-7.29	2.33	2	3	0	0.98	800 442-1941
First Fds-Growth & Income II	Growth/Inc	-5.7	-7.5	2.08	2	3	5.75	1.19	800 442-1941
First Fds-Growth & Income III	Growth/Inc	-6.4	-8.22	1.3	2	3	0	1.95	800 442-1941

321

Stock Fund Name	Objective	Annualized Return for			Rank		Max Load	Expense Ratio	Toll-Free/(Toll) Telephone
		1 Year	3 Years	5 Years	Overall	Risk			
First Focus Balanced Fund Instl	Balanced	2.6	4.26	0.8	1	1	0	1.32	800 662-4203
First Focus CO Tax Free Instl	AssetAlloc	10.7					0	0.9	800 662-4203
First Focus Core Equity Instl	Growth	-11	-1.4	-3.45	3	2	0	1.08	800 662-4203
First Focus Growth Opp Instl	Growth	-8	1.33	3.02		2	0	1.28	800 662-4203
First Focus Income Inst	AssetAlloc	10	9.8	6.01		1	0	0.86	800 662-4203
First Focus Small Company Instl	Small Co	-4.6	11.8	4.83	1	2	0	0.6	800 662-4203
First Inv All Cap Growth A	Agg Growth	-6.6					5.75	1.75	800 423-4026
First Inv All Cap Growth B	Agg Growth	-7.2					0	2.45	800 423-4026
First Inv Blue Chip A	Growth	-11.9	-14.99	-3.85	5	3	5.75	1.36	800 423-4026
First Inv Focused Equity A	Growth	-8.2	-13.08		3	3	5.75	1.75	800 423-4026
First Inv Global A	Global	-12.8	-13.31	-3.87	5	3	5.75	1.78	800 423-4026
First Inv Global B	Global	-13.3					0	1.48	800 423-4026
First Inv Growth & Income A	Growth/Inc	-10.3					5.75	1.36	800 423-4026
First Inv Mid-Cap Opp A	Growth	-12.2	-4.58	4.36	3	3	5.75	1.51	800 423-4026
First Inv Mid-Cap Opp B	Growth	-12.7	-6.96	2.5	3	4	0	2.21	800 423-4026
First Inv Special Situations A	Small Co	-15.7	-15.02	-5.37	5	4	5.75	1.54	800 423-4026
First Inv Special Situations B	Small Co	-16.2	-15.6	-6.04	5	5	0	2.24	800 423-4026
First Inv Total Return A	Balanced	-2.6	-5.62	1.18	2	1	5.75	1.37	800 423-4026
First Inv Utilities Income A	Utilities	-9.8	-13.48	-3.22	3	2	5.75	1.37	800 423-4026
Firsthand Global Technology	Technology	-12.6					0	1.94	888 884-2675
Firsthand-E-Commerce Fund (The)	Technology	-3.6	-39.68		4	5	0	1.95	888 884-2675
Firsthand-Technology Innovators	Technology	-7.2	-36.29	4.16	3	5	0	1.95	888 884-2675
Firsthand-Technology Leaders Fund	Technology	-8.6	-34.28	2.2	3	5	0	1.9	888 884-2675
Firsthand-Technology Value Fund	Technology	-13	-36.31	-0.73	3	5	0	1.84	888 884-2675
Flex-funds Highlands Growth Fd	Growth	-10.6	-12.65	-2.91	3	3	0	1.76	800 325-3539
Flex-funds Muirfield Fund	AssetAlloc	-6	-7.25	0.11	3	1	0	1.41	800 325-3539
Flex-funds Total Return Utilities	Utilities	-14.5	-10.18	-1.18	3	3	0	1.81	800 325-3539
Forester Discovery Fund	Other	1.4	2.75			1	0	1.79	800 388-0365
Forester Value Fund	Income	5.5	4.12			1	0	1.79	800 388-0365
Forum Equity Index Fund	Growth	-20.4	-15.13	-4	3	3	4	0.13	800 943-6786
Forward Hansberger Intl Grwth Fund	Foreign	-9.5	-11.34		4	3	0	1.68	800 999-6809
Forward Hoover Small Cap Equity	Small Co	-8.3	-0.25		2	4	0	1.65	800 999-6809
Forward Uniplan Real Estate Ret	Real Est	0.1	12.48		1	1	0	1.79	800 999-6809
Fountainhead Special Value Fund	Growth	-8.4	-14.22	0.33	3	4	0		800 298-1995
Franklin Aggressive Growth Fd A	Agg Growth	-13.6	-23.1		4	5	5.75	1.85	800 632-2350
Franklin Aggressive Growth Fd Adv	Agg Growth	-13.3	-22.87		3	5	0	1.5	800 632-2350
Franklin Aggressive Growth Fd B	Agg Growth	-14.1	-23.62		4	5	0	2.49	800 632-2350
Franklin Aggressive Growth Fd C	Agg Growth	-14.2	-23.62		4	5	1	2.49	800 632-2350
Franklin Aggressive Growth Fd R	Agg Growth	-13.8	-23.26		4	5	0	2	800 632-2350
Franklin Balance Sheet Investmt A	Small Co	-5.4	12.09	4.79	2	2	5.75	1	800 632-2350
Franklin Balance Sheet Investmt Adv	Small Co	-5.1	12.28	4.91	2	2	0	0.75	800 632-2350
Franklin Balance Sheet Investmt B	Small Co	-6.1					0	1.75	800 632-2350
Franklin Balance Sheet Investmt C	Small Co	-6.1					1	1.75	800 632-2350
Franklin Balance Sheet Investmt R	Small Co	-5.6	11.83	4.53	2	2	0	1.25	800 632-2350
Franklin Biotechnology Discovery A	Health	8	-9.39	10.86	3	5	5.75	1.5	800 632-2350
Franklin Blue Chip A	Growth	-8.7	-11.25	0.8	3	3	5.75	1.5	800 632-2350
Franklin Blue Chip B	Growth	-9.3	-11.83		3	3	0	2.14	800 632-2350
Franklin Blue Chip C	Growth	-9.3	-11.82		3	3	1	2.12	800 632-2350
Franklin Blue Chip R	Growth	-8.8	-11.36	0.64	3	3	0	1.65	800 632-2350
Franklin Capital Growth A	Growth/Inc	-7.9	-14.59	0.46	3	4	5.75	1.02	800 632-2350
Franklin Capital Growth Adv	Growth/Inc	-7.6	-14.38	0.69	3	4	0	0.77	800 632-2350
Franklin Capital Growth B	Growth/Inc	-8.6	-15.19		3	4	0	1.76	800 632-2350
Franklin Capital Growth C	Growth/Inc	-8.6	-15.26	-0.23	3	4	1	1.75	800 632-2350
Franklin Capital Growth R	Growth/Inc	-8.1	-14.81	0.2	3	4	0	1.27	800 632-2350
Franklin Convertible Securities A	Converts	0.4	1.57	5.09	1	3	5.75	1.02	800 632-2350
Franklin Convertible Securities C	Converts	-0.4	0.8	4.32	1	3	1	1.74	800 632-2350
Franklin DynaTech A	Technology	1.6	-10.99	2.91	3	3	5.75	1.04	800 632-2350
Franklin DynaTech B	Technology	0.8					0	1.79	800 632-2350

Stock Fund Name	Objective	Annualized Return for			Rank		Max Load	Expense Ratio	Toll-Free/(Toll) Telephone
		1 Year	3 Years	5 Years	Overall	Risk			
Franklin DynaTech C	Technology	0.8	-11.64	2.14	3	3	1	1.78	800 632-2350
Franklin Equity Inc A	Income	-12	0.54	1.41	3	2	5.75	1.03	800 632-2350
Franklin Equity Inc B	Income	-12.7	-0.2		3	2	0	1.78	800 632-2350
Franklin Equity Inc C	Income	-12.6	-0.2	0.67	3	2	1	1.76	800 632-2350
Franklin Equity Inc R	Income	-12.1	0.3	1.13		2	0	1.28	800 632-2350
Franklin Flex Cap Growth A	Growth	-8.5	-14.58	4.98	3	4	5.75	1.08	800 632-2350
Franklin Flex Cap Growth B	Growth	-9.2	-15.22		3	4	0	1.83	800 632-2350
Franklin Flex Cap Growth C	Growth	-9.2	-15.23	4.2	3	4	1	1.82	800 632-2350
Franklin Flex Cap Growth R	Growth	-8.6	-14.78	4.71	3	4	0	1.33	800 632-2350
Franklin Global Aggressive Gr A	Global	-16.2					5.75	1.75	800 632-2350
Franklin Global Aggressive Gr Adv	Global	-15.8					0	1.4	800 632-2350
Franklin Global Aggressive Gr B	Global	-16.5					0	2.24	800 632-2350
Franklin Global Aggressive Gr C	Global	-16.7					1	2.39	800 632-2350
Franklin Global Communications A	Technology	-5.7	-26.8	-11.31	3	4	5.75	1.45	800 632-2350
Franklin Global Communications B	Technology	-6.3	-27.32		4	4	0	2.2	800 632-2350
Franklin Global Communications C	Technology	-6.4	-27.32	-11.97	4	4	1	2.19	800 632-2350
Franklin Global Growth A	Global	-13.5					5.75	1.75	800 632-2350
Franklin Global Growth Adv	Global	-13.1					0	1.4	800 632-2350
Franklin Global Growth B	Global	-14					0	2.28	800 632-2350
Franklin Global Growth C	Global	-14					1	2.4	800 632-2350
Franklin Global Health Care A	Health	-12.7	-4.76	0.32	3	4	5.75	1.41	800 632-2350
Franklin Global Health Care B	Health	-13.4	-5.5		3	4	0	2.16	800 632-2350
Franklin Global Health Care C	Health	-13.4	-5.5	-0.41	3	4	1	2.15	800 632-2350
Franklin Gold & Prec Metals A	Prec Metal	-8.3	18.78	9.66	2	4	5.75	1.06	800 632-2350
Franklin Gold & Prec Metals Adv	Prec Metal	-8	19.07	10.06	2	4	0	0.82	800 632-2350
Franklin Gold & Prec Metals B	Prec Metal	-8.9	17.92		2	4	0	1.82	800 632-2350
Franklin Gold & Prec Metals C	Prec Metal	-8.8	17.96	8.74	2	4	1	1.76	800 632-2350
Franklin Growth A	Growth	-12.6	-9.56	-0.42	4	3	5.75	1	800 632-2350
Franklin Growth Adv	Growth	-12.4	-9.33	-0.17	4	3	0	0.75	800 632-2350
Franklin Growth B	Growth	-13.3	-10.23		4	3	0	1.75	800 632-2350
Franklin Growth C	Growth	-13.2	-10.23	-1.15	4	3	1	1.74	800 632-2350
Franklin Income A	Flexible	7.4	8.8	6.25	1	1	4.25	0.73	800 632-2350
Franklin Income Adv	Flexible	7.1	9	6.42	1	1	0	0.58	800 632-2350
Franklin Income B	Flexible	6.1	7.54		1	1	0	1.58	800 632-2350
Franklin Income C	Flexible	6.9	8.39	5.79	1	1	1	1.22	800 632-2350
Franklin Income R	Flexible	6.6	8.11	5.67	1	1	0	1.08	800 632-2350
Franklin Large Cap Value A	Growth/Inc	-8.5					5.75	1.46	800 632-2350
Franklin Large Cap Value B	Growth/Inc	-9					0	2.11	800 632-2350
Franklin Large Cap Value C	Growth/Inc	-9					1	2.08	800 632-2350
Franklin Large Cap Value R	Growth/Inc	-8.7					0	1.61	800 632-2350
Franklin MicroCap Value A	Small Co	-7.8	17.85	6.04	1	2	5.75	1.2	800 632-2350
Franklin Natural Resources A	Energy/Res	-9.2	-2.45	2.47	3	4	5.75	1.38	800 632-2350
Franklin Natural Resources Adv	Energy/Res	-8.8	-2.06	3.27	2	4	0	1.06	800 632-2350
Franklin Real Estate Sec A	Real Est	3	12.99	5.87	2	2	5.75	0.96	800 632-2350
Franklin Real Estate Sec Adv	Real Est	3.2	13.27	4.67	1	2	0	0.71	800 632-2350
Franklin Real Estate Sec B	Real Est	2.3	12.19		1	2	0	1.71	800 632-2350
Franklin Real Estate Sec C	Real Est	2.2	12.17	5.09	2	2	1	1.71	800 632-2350
Franklin Rising Dividends A	Growth/Inc	-5.1	10.71	4.94	2	2	5.75	1.4	800 632-2350
Franklin Rising Dividends B	Growth/Inc	-5.6	10.14		2	2	0	1.97	800 632-2350
Franklin Rising Dividends C	Growth/Inc	-5.6	10.08	4.34	2	2	1	1.89	800 632-2350
Franklin Rising Dividends R	Growth/Inc	-5.2	10.66	4.88	2	2	0	1.45	800 632-2350
Franklin Small Cap Growth II A	Agg Growth	-12.2	-5.61		3	5	5.75	1.29	800 632-2350
Franklin Small Cap Growth II Adv	Agg Growth	-11.9	-5.38		3	5	0	0.94	800 632-2350
Franklin Small Cap Growth II B	Agg Growth	-12.8	-6.19		3	5	0	1.94	800 632-2350
Franklin Small Cap Growth II C	Agg Growth	-12.8	-20.44		4	5	1	1.91	800 632-2350
Franklin Small Cap Growth II R	Agg Growth	-12.5	-5.04		3	5	0	1.44	800 632-2350
Franklin Small Cap Value A	Growth/Inc	-12.9	8.4	0.77	3	3	5.75	1.43	800 632-2350
Franklin Small Cap Value Adv	Growth/Inc	-12.6	8.76	1.12	3	3	0	1.08	800 632-2350

Stock Fund Name	Objective	Annualized Return for			Rank		Max Load	Expense Ratio	Toll-Free/(Toll) Telephone
		1 Year	3 Years	5 Years	Overall	Risk			
Franklin Small Cap Value B	Growth/Inc	-13.5	7.7		3	3	0	2.08	800 632-2350
Franklin Small Cap Value C	Growth/Inc	-13.5	7.67	0.11	3	3	1	2.05	800 632-2350
Franklin Small Cap Value R	Growth/Inc	-13.1	8.22	0.57		3	0	1.58	800 632-2350
Franklin Small-Mid Cap Growth A	Small Co	-9.4	-15.43	1.67	3	5	5.75	0.98	800 632-2350
Franklin Small-Mid Cap Growth Adv	Small Co	-9.1	-15.25	1.93	3	5	0	0.73	800 632-2350
Franklin Small-Mid Cap Growth B	Small Co						0	1.73	800 632-2350
Franklin Small-Mid Cap Growth C	Small Co	-10	-16.07	0.93	3	5	1	1.73	800 632-2350
Franklin Small-Mid Cap Growth R	Small Co	-9.6	-15.66	1.41	3	5	0	1.23	800 632-2350
Franklin Technology A	Technology	-12.7	-28.32		4	5	5.75	1.97	800 632-2350
Franklin Technology Adv	Technology	-12.3	-28.05		4	5	0	1.65	800 632-2350
Franklin Technology B	Technology	-13.1					0	2.64	800 632-2350
Franklin Technology C	Technology	-13.1					1	2.63	800 632-2350
Franklin Technology R	Technology	-12.5	-28.08		4	5	0	2.15	800 632-2350
Franklin Templeton Conserv Tgt A	Growth/Inc	0.9	1.75	4.44	1	1	5.75	0.89	800 632-2350
Franklin Templeton Conserv Tgt C	Growth/Inc	0.3	0.98	3.64	1	1	1	1.57	800 632-2350
Franklin Templeton Conserv Tgt R	Growth/Inc	0.7	1.5	4.16	1	1	0	1.14	800 632-2350
Franklin Templeton Growth Tgt A	Growth	-6.1	-7.3	0.94	2	3	5.75	0.9	800 632-2350
Franklin Templeton Growth Tgt C	Growth	-6.8	-8	0.2	2	3	1	1.62	800 632-2350
Franklin Templeton Growth Tgt R	Growth	-6.4	-7.55	0.67	2	3	0	1.15	800 632-2350
Franklin Templeton Moderate Tgt A	Growth	-1.1	-1.66	2.79	1	2	5.75	0.87	800 632-2350
Franklin Templeton Moderate Tgt C	Growth	-1.9	-2.39	2	1	2	1	1.56	800 632-2350
Franklin Templeton Moderate Tgt R	Growth	-1.4	-1.89	2.54	1	2	0	1.12	800 632-2350
Franklin U.S. Long-Short A	Growth	2.4	2.79		1	1	5.75	2.52	800 632-2350
Franklin Utilities A	Utilities	-1.7	5.91	3.62	2	3	4.25	0.83	800 632-2350
Franklin Utilities Adv	Utilities	-1.5	6.08	3.83	2	3	0	0.69	800 632-2350
Franklin Utilities B	Utilities	-2.2	5.33		1	3	0	1.34	800 632-2350
Franklin Utilities C	Utilities	-2.1	5.37	3.12	2	3	1	1.32	800 632-2350
Fremont Global Fund	Global	-1.8	-6.51	-0.05	2	2	0	0.94	800 548-4539
Fremont Instl U.S. Micro-Cap Fund	Small Co	-3	-7.79	15.23	3	5	0	1.29	800 548-4539
Fremont International Growth	Foreign	-16.3	-19.71	-5.92	5	3	0	1.5	800 548-4539
Fremont New Era Value Fund	Growth	-8.1					0	1.2	800 548-4539
Fremont Real Estate Sec Fund	Real Est	1.8	10.38	3.77	2	1	0	1.5	800 548-4539
Fremont Structured Core Fund	Growth	-12.7	-12.22	-3.83	4	3	0	1.01	800 548-4539
Fremont US Micro-Cap Fd	Small Co	-5	-8.77	11.32	3	5	0	1.57	800 548-4539
Froley Revy Convertible Sec A	Converts	2					4	1.5	800 441-6580
Frontier Fund-Equity	Small Co	-71.9	-56.2	-34.13	5	5	8	7.3	800 231-2901
GAM American Focus Fund A	Growth	-17	-8.81	-1.42	4	4	5	1.78	800 426-4685
GAM American Focus Fund B	Growth	-17.9	-9.67	-2.68	4	4	0	2.84	800 426-4685
GAM American Focus Fund C	Growth	-18	-9.83		4	4	0	3.11	800 426-4685
GAM Europe Fund A	European	-12.6	-11.69	-4.45	4	2	5	2.67	800 426-4685
GAM Europe Fund B	European	-13.8	-12.8	-5.61	4	2	0	3.73	800 426-4685
GAM Europe Fund C	European	-16	-14.08	-6.84	3	2	0	5.26	800 426-4685
GAM Gabelli Long/Short A	Other	-27.1					5	3.03	800 426-4685
GAM Gabelli Long/Short B	Other	-27.1					0	3.72	800 426-4685
GAM Gabelli Long/Short C	Other	-27.1					0	3.73	800 426-4685
GAM Global Fund A	Global	-12.4	-9.5	-8.46	4	2	5	3.18	800 426-4685
GAM Global Fund B	Global	-13.3	-10.28	-9.18	4	2	0	4.11	800 426-4685
GAM Global Fund C	Global	-13.6	-10.47	-9.33	4	2	0	4.44	800 426-4685
GAM Global Fund D	Global	-14	-10.47	-9.11	4	2	3.5	4.61	800 426-4685
GAM International Fund A	Foreign	-16.2	-13.18	-13.05	3	2	5	2.27	800 426-4685
GAM International Fund B	Foreign	-16.8	-13.81	-13.66	5	2	0	2.96	800 426-4685
GAM International Fund C	Foreign	-16.9	-13.83	-13.67	5	2	0	3.03	800 426-4685
GAM International Fund D	Foreign	-16.6	-13.43	-13.24	5	2	3.5	2.62	800 426-4685
GAM Japan Capital Fund A	Pacific	-27.9	-22.05	-5.74	4	3	5	4.27	800 426-4685
GAM Japan Capital Fund B	Pacific	-29.6	-23.25	-7.4	5	3	0	6.2	800 426-4685
GAM Japan Capital Fund C	Pacific	-31.2	-24.28	-8	5	3	0	7.96	800 426-4685
GAM Pacific Basin Fund A	Pacific	-21	-10.38	0.34	3	3	5	3.67	800 426-4685
GAM Pacific Basin Fund B	Pacific	-22.2	-11.52	-1.91	4	3	0	5.33	800 426-4685

Stock Fund Name	Objective	Annualized Return for			Rank		Max Load	Expense Ratio	Toll-Free/(Toll) Telephone
		1 Year	3 Years	5 Years	Overall	Risk			
GAM Pacific Basin Fund C	Pacific	-24.3	-13.26		4	3	0	7.61	800 426-4685
GAM Pacific Basin Fund D	Pacific	-22.7	-11.81	-1.1	4	3	3.5	5.75	800 426-4685
GAMNA Focus Fund A	Growth	-14.2					5.75	1.74	800 848-0920
GAMNA Focus Fund B	Growth	-14.2					0	1.77	800 848-0920
GAMNA Focus Fund C	Growth	-14.2					0	1.9	800 848-0920
GAMerica Capital A	Growth	0.4	-0.13	6.04	1	2	5	1.83	800 426-4685
GAMerica Capital B	Growth	-0.3	-0.83	5.2	1	2	0	2.56	800 426-4685
GAMerica Capital C	Growth	-0.3	-0.83	5.07	1	2	0	2.58	800 426-4685
GE Global Equity A	Global	-11.8	-13.16	-3.02	4	3	5.75	1.35	800 242-0134
GE Global Equity B	Global	-12.4	-13.78	-3.75	4	3	0	2.1	800 242-0134
GE Global Equity Y	Global	-11.5	-12.91	-2.77	4	3	0	1.1	800 242-0134
GE Institutional Intl Equity Inv	Foreign	-15.2	-14.06	-4.73	5	3	0	0.59	800 242-0134
GE Institutional S&P 500 Index Inv	Growth	-8.1	-11.05	-0.95	3	3	0	0.15	800 242-0134
GE Institutional Sm-Cap Val Eq Inv	Small Co	-13.4	5.21		3	2	0	0.7	800 242-0134
GE Institutional US Equity Inv	Growth	-9.3	-7.28	1.27	3	3	0	0.58	800 242-0134
GE Institutional Value Equity Inv	Growth/Inc	-8.7	-6.36	-3.08	2	2	0	0.42	800 242-0134
GE International Equity Fd A	Foreign	-21.6	-18.28	-8.33	4	3	5.75	1.35	800 242-0134
GE International Equity Fd B	Foreign	-22.2	-18.64	-8.84	4	3	0	2.1	800 242-0134
GE International Equity Fd Y	Foreign	-21.3	-18.05	-8.09	5	3	0	1.1	800 242-0134
GE Mid-Cap Growth A	Growth	-13	-7.15	-1.04	3	3	5.75	1.15	800 242-0134
GE Mid-Cap Growth B	Growth	-13.5	-7.79	-1.69	3	3	0	1.9	800 242-0134
GE Mid-Cap Growth Y	Growth	-12.9	-6.11	-0.22	3	3	0	0.9	800 242-0134
GE Premier Growth Equity A	Growth	-7.7	-8.59	4.41	3	3	5.75	1.03	800 242-0134
GE Premier Growth Equity B	Growth	-8.4	-9.27	3.64	3	3	0	1.78	800 242-0134
GE Premier Growth Equity Y	Growth	-7.5	-8.36	4.62	2	3	0	0.78	800 242-0134
GE S&S Program Mutual Fund	Growth/Inc	-8.2	-7.01	1.41	2	2	0	0.17	800 242-0134
GE Small Cap Value Equity B	Small Co	-14.7	3.75		3	2	0	1.9	800 242-0134
GE Strategic Investment Fd A	Flexible	-0.6	-0.7	3.81	1	1	5.75	0.88	800 242-0134
GE Strategic Investment Fd B	Flexible	-1.3	-1.43	3.04	2	1	0	1.63	800 242-0134
GE Strategic Investment Fd Y	Flexible	-0.3	-0.46	4.07	1	1	0	0.63	800 242-0134
GE US Equity Fund A	Growth	-9	-7.48	1	3	2	5.75	0.9	800 242-0134
GE US Equity Fund B	Growth	-9.7	-7.88	0.41	3	2	0	1.65	800 242-0134
GE US Equity Fund Y	Growth	-8.7	-7.21	1.27	3	2	0	0.65	800 242-0134
GE Value Equity Fund A	Growth/Inc	-9.3	-6.84	1.15	3	2	5.75	1.09	800 242-0134
GE Value Equity Fund B	Growth/Inc	-10.2	-7.45	0.53	3	2	0	1.84	800 242-0134
GE Value Equity Fund Y	Growth/Inc	-9.2	-8.42	0.28	3	2	0	0.84	800 242-0134
Gabelli ABC Fund	Small Co	1.3	4.46	6.69	1	1	0	1.46	800 422-3554
Gabelli Asset Fund	Growth	-7.1	-1.54	4.24	1	2	0	1.36	800 422-3554
Gabelli Blue Chip Value AAA	Growth	-5.1	-9.34		3	4	0	1.75	800 422-3554
Gabelli Comstck Partners Cap Val A	AssetAlloc	9.7	17.3	-0.44	2	4	4.5	1.75	800 422-3554
Gabelli Comstck Partners Cap Val B	AssetAlloc	8.8	16.28	-1.27	2	4	0	2.51	800 422-3554
Gabelli Comstck Partners Cap Val C	AssetAlloc	9.1	16.44	-1.12	2	4	0	2.5	800 422-3554
Gabelli Comstck Partners Cap Val R	AssetAlloc	9.6	17.37	-0.23	2	4	0	1.56	800 422-3554
Gabelli Equity Income	Income	-1.3	2.83	4.66	1	2	0	1.55	800 422-3554
Gabelli Global Convertible	Converts	-5.6	-12.85	-1.12	3	1	0	2.69	800 422-3554
Gabelli Global Growth Fund	Technology	-6.2	-21.37	1.03	3	4	0	1.75	800 422-3554
Gabelli Global Telecom	Technology	5	-18.37	0.82	3	4	0	1.5	800 422-3554
Gabelli Gold A	Prec Metal						0		800 422-3554
Gabelli Gold B	Prec Metal						0		800 422-3554
Gabelli Gold C	Prec Metal						0		800 422-3554
Gabelli Gold Fd	Prec Metal	-2.6	34.92	13.83	2	5	0	2.46	800 422-3554
Gabelli Growth Fund	Growth	-15.3	-21.82	-3.49	4	4	0	1.52	800 422-3554
Gabelli International Growth	Foreign	-13.3	-13.91	-3.25	4	2	0	2.41	800 422-3554
Gabelli Mathers Fund	Flexible	-4	-2.22	-0.71	2	1	0	1.35	800 422-3554
Gabelli Small Cap Growth	Small Co	-4.3	6.76	4.88	1	3	0	1.45	800 422-3554
Gabelli Value Fund	Agg Growth	-5.6	-1.38	5.62	2	3	5.5	1.4	800 422-3554
Gabelli Westwood Balanced Fd A	Balanced	-2.5	-0.08	3.54	2	1	4	1.42	800 937-8909
Gabelli Westwood Balanced Fd AAA	Balanced	-2.3	0.28	3.89	1	1	0	1.17	800 937-8909

Stock Fund Name	Objective	Annualized Return for			Rank		Max Load	Expense Ratio	Toll-Free/(Toll) Telephone
		1 Year	3 Years	5 Years	Overall	Risk			
Gabelli Westwood Equity Fund A	Growth/Inc	-12	-6.21	1.28	3	2	4	1.68	800 937-8909
Gabelli Westwood Equity Fund AAA	Growth/Inc	-11.8	-5.96	1.54	3	2	0	1.43	800 937-8909
Gabelli Westwood Mighty Mites AAA	Small Co	1.6	0.04	5.29	2	2	0	1.52	800 937-8909
Gabelli Westwood Realty AAA	Real Est	3.4	13.24	6.59	2	1	0	1.64	800 937-8909
Gabelli Westwood Sm Cap Equity Fd	Small Co	-19.9	-17.48	-3.95	5	4	0	1.59	800 937-8909
Gartmore Emerging Market A	Foreign	-7.9					5.75	2.75	800 848-0920
Gartmore Emerging Market B	Foreign	-8.6					0	3.5	800 848-0920
Gartmore Emerging Market Instl-Svc	Foreign	-7.6					0		800 848-0920
Gartmore Global Financial Svc A	Financial	-2.3					5.75	3	800 848-0920
Gartmore Global Financial Svc C	Financial	-3					0	3.75	800 848-0920
Gartmore Global Financial Svc Instl	Financial	-2					0	2.75	800 848-0920
Gartmore Global Health Science A	Global	2.6					5.75	1.55	800 848-0920
Gartmore Global Health Science B	Global	2					0	2.25	800 848-0920
Gartmore Global Health Science Inst	Global	2.9					0	1.3	800 848-0920
Gartmore Global Health Sciences C	Global						1	2.25	800 848-0920
Gartmore Global Tech & Com A	Technology	-6.5					5.75	1.68	800 848-0920
Gartmore Global Tech & Com B	Technology	-7.2					0	2.78	800 848-0920
Gartmore Global Tech & Com C	Global	-7.2					1	2.4	800 848-0920
Gartmore Global Tech & Com IS	Technology	-6.2					0	1.78	800 848-0920
Gartmore Global Utilities A	Utilities	-3.6					5.75	2.8	800 848-0920
Gartmore Global Utilities B	Utilities	-4.3					0	3.55	800 848-0920
Gartmore Global Utilities C	Utilities	-4.3					0	3.55	800 848-0920
Gartmore Growth Fund A	Growth	-11	-22.76	-12.85	5	4	5.75	1.13	800 848-0920
Gartmore Growth Fund B	Growth	-11.5	-23.94	-13.91	5	4	0	1.88	800 848-0920
Gartmore Growth Fund D	Growth	-10.7	-22.53	-12.63	5	4	4.5	0.96	800 848-0920
Gartmore Intl Growth A	Foreign	-15.8					5.75	1.83	800 848-0920
Gartmore Intl Growth B	Foreign	-16.3					0	4.32	800 848-0920
Gartmore Intl Growth Instl-Svc	Foreign	-15.5					0		800 848-0920
Gartmore Intl SmCap Gr A	Foreign	-18.9					5.75	1.8	800 848-0920
Gartmore Intl SmCap Gr B	Foreign	-19.5					0	4.32	800 848-0920
Gartmore Intl SmCap Gr Instl-Svc	Foreign	-18.6					0		800 848-0920
Gartmore Inv Dest Aggressive A	Global	-9.5	-8.91			3	5.75	0.48	800 848-0920
Gartmore Inv Dest Aggressive B	Global	-10.1	-9.51			3	0	1.23	800 848-0920
Gartmore Inv Dest Aggressive C	Global	-10.1					5.75	1.23	800 848-0920
Gartmore Inv Dest Aggressive Svc	Global	-9.6	-8.93			3	0	0.61	800 848-0920
Gartmore Inv Dest Conservative A	Global	3	3.16			1	5.75	0.52	800 848-0920
Gartmore Inv Dest Conservative B	Global	2.4	2.49			1	0	1.27	800 848-0920
Gartmore Inv Dest Conservative C	Global	2.4					5.75	1.27	800 848-0920
Gartmore Inv Dest Conservative Svc	Global	3	3.18			1	0	0.61	800 848-0920
Gartmore Inv Dest Mod Aggr A	Global	-6.6	-6.13			2	5.75	0.47	800 848-0920
Gartmore Inv Dest Mod Aggr B	Global	-7.3	-6.82			2	0	1.22	800 848-0920
Gartmore Inv Dest Mod Aggr C	Global	-7.2					5.75	1.22	800 848-0920
Gartmore Inv Dest Mod Aggr Svc	Global	-6.8	-6.13			2	0	0.61	800 848-0920
Gartmore Inv Dest Mod Conserv A	Global	0.4	0.44			1	5.75	0.49	800 848-0920
Gartmore Inv Dest Mod Conserv B	Global	-0.2	-0.16			1	0	1.24	800 848-0920
Gartmore Inv Dest Mod Conserv C	Global	-0.1					5.75	1.24	800 848-0920
Gartmore Inv Dest Mod Conserv Svc	Global	0.4	0.51			1	0	0.61	800 848-0920
Gartmore Inv Dest Moderate A	Global	-2.8	-2.93			1	5.75	0.47	800 848-0920
Gartmore Inv Dest Moderate B	Global	-3.5	-3.54			1	0	1.22	800 848-0920
Gartmore Inv Dest Moderate C	Global	-3.7					5.75	1.22	800 848-0920
Gartmore Inv Dest Moderate Svc	Global	-3	-2.89			1	0	0.61	800 848-0920
Gartmore Large Cap Value A	Growth	-8.8	-0.11		2	2	5.75	1.44	800 848-0920
Gartmore Large Cap Value B	Growth	-9.3	-0.81		3	2	0	2.04	800 848-0920
Gartmore Micro Cap Equity A	Income						5.75	1.85	800 848-0920
Gartmore Micro Cap Equity B	Income						0	2.55	800 848-0920
Gartmore Micro Cap Equity C	Income						1	2.55	800 848-0920
Gartmore Micro Cap Equity Instl	Income						0	1.55	800 848-0920
Gartmore Micro Cap Equity Instl Svc	Income						0	1.6	800 848-0920

Stock Fund Name	Objective	Annualized Return for			Rank		Max Load	Expense Ratio	Toll-Free/(Toll) Telephone
		1 Year	3 Years	5 Years	Overall	Risk			
Gartmore Millennium Growth A	Growth	-9.2	-20.19	-9.19	4	5	4.5	2.15	800 848-0920
Gartmore Millennium Growth B	Growth	-9.9	-21.28	-10.25	4	5	0	2.86	800 848-0920
Gartmore Millennium Growth D	Growth	-8.9	-19.87	-8.93	4	5	5.75	2.86	800 848-0920
Gartmore NW Leaders A	Global	-11.6					5.75	2.44	800 848-0920
Gartmore NW Leaders B	Global	-12.4					0	3.19	800 848-0920
Gartmore NW Leaders C	Global	-12.5					0	3.19	800 848-0920
Gartmore NW Leaders Instl-Svc	Global	-11.6					0	2.19	800 848-0920
Gartmore Nationwide A	Growth/Inc	-8.3	-8.91	-2.93	3	3	5.75	1.14	800 848-0920
Gartmore Nationwide B	Growth/Inc	-8.9	-9.66	-3.95	3	3	0	1.84	800 848-0920
Gartmore Nationwide C	Growth/Inc	-8.9					1	1.8	800 848-0920
Gartmore Nationwide D	Growth/Inc	-8.1	-8.72	-2.72	3	3	4.5	1.71	800 848-0920
Gartmore Nationwide Instl-Svc	Growth/Inc	-8					0	0.9	800 848-0920
Gartmore U.S. Gr Leaders A	Growth	7.6					5.75	1.56	800 848-0920
Gartmore U.S. Gr Leaders B	Growth	6.8					0	2.3	800 848-0920
Gartmore U.S. Gr Leaders Instl-Svc	Growth	7.9					0	1.32	800 848-0920
Gartmore Value Opp Fund A	Small Co	-9.2	3.2		1	3	5.75	1.43	800 848-0920
Gartmore Value Opp Fund B	Small Co	-9.9	2.62		2	3	0	2.18	800 848-0920
Gartmore Value Opp Fund IS	Small Co	-9.1	3.52		1	3	0	1.08	800 848-0920
Gartmore Worldwd Leaders A	Global	-16.3					5.75	2.44	800 848-0920
Gartmore Worldwd Leaders B	Global	-16.8					0	3.19	800 848-0920
Gartmore Worldwd Leaders Instl-Svc	Global	-15.9					0	1.42	800 848-0920
Gartmore Worldwide Leaders C	Foreign	-16.9					1	2.4	800 848-0920
Gateway Cincinnati Fund	Growth	-10.4	-1.59	-1.18	3	2	0	1.75	800 354-6339
Gateway Fund	Growth/Inc	2	-0.16	4.41	1	1	0	0.97	800 354-6339
General Securities Fund	Flexible	-12.3	-19.05	-5.08	4	4	0	1.49	800 577-9217
GenomicsFund,com	Health	10.4	-25.82		4	5	0	1.85	800 527-9525
George Putnam Fund of Boston A	Balanced	-2.3	2.27	2.16	1	1	5.75	0.92	800 354-2228
George Putnam Fund of Boston B	Balanced	-3.1	1.5	1.38	2	1	0	1.67	800 354-2228
George Putnam Fund of Boston C	Balanced	-3.1	1.48	1.37	2	1	0	1.67	800 354-2228
George Putnam Fund of Boston M	Balanced	-2.8	1.77	1.65	2	1	3.5	1.42	800 354-2228
Gintel Fund	Growth	-19.2	-15.41	-7.74	3	4	0	2.29	800 243-5808
Glenmede International Equity Fd	Foreign	-13.4	-7.17	-1.42	4	3	0	0.13	800 442-8299
Glenmede International I	Foreign	-14.3	-8.39	-2.74	4	3	0	0.11	800 442-8299
Glenmede Large Cap Value Fd	Growth	-8.9	-2.47	-0.8	3	2	0	0.21	800 442-8299
Glenmede Small Cap Equity I	Small Co	-5.8	4.29		2	3	0	0.7	800 442-8299
Glenmede Small Cap Value Adv	Small Co	-5.9	6.29	1.75	2	2	0	0.87	800 442-8299
Glenmede Strategic Equity	Growth/Inc	-9.8	-12.98	-2.91	3	2	0	0.12	800 442-8299
Globalt Growth Fund	Growth	-10.2					0	1.3	800 298-1995
Golden Oak Growth A	Agg Growth	-9.5	-20.71	-3.27	4	4	5.75	1.35	800 545-6331
Golden Oak Growth I	Agg Growth	-9.4	-20.53	-2.5	4	4	0	1.1	800 545-6331
Golden Oak International Equity A	Foreign	-16.1					5.75	1.75	800 545-6331
Golden Oak International Equity I	Foreign	-15.9					0	1.5	800 545-6331
Golden Oak Small Cap Value A	Small Co	-8.2	11.91			3	5.75	1.6	800 545-6331
Golden Oak Small Cap Value I	Small Co	-8	12.19			3	0	1.35	800 545-6331
Golden Oak Value A	Growth	-7.6	-5.66	-0.82	3	2	5.75	1.35	800 545-6331
Golden Oak Value I	Growth	-7.3	-5.44	-0.46	3	2	0	1.1	800 545-6331
Goldman Sachs Aggr Gr Strat A	Growth	-10.6	-9.91	-3.89	3	2	5.5	0.59	800 292-4726
Goldman Sachs Aggr Gr Strat B	Growth	-11.5	-10.64	-4.66	4	2	0	1.34	800 292-4726
Goldman Sachs Aggr Gr Strat C	Growth	-11.4	-10.61	-4.62	4	2	0	1.34	800 292-4726
Goldman Sachs Aggr Gr Strat Instl	Growth	-10.2					0	0.19	800 292-4726
Goldman Sachs Aggr Gr Strat Svc	Growth	-10.7					0	0.69	800 292-4726
Goldman Sachs Asia Growth A	Pacific	-20.6	-12.48	-0.81	3	3	5.5	2.05	800 292-4726
Goldman Sachs Asia Growth B	Pacific	-21.1	-12.91	-1.3	4	3	0	2.55	800 292-4726
Goldman Sachs Asia Growth C	Pacific	-21.2	-12.91	-1.36	4	3	0	2.55	800 292-4726
Goldman Sachs Asia Growth Inst	Pacific	-19.8					0	1.4	800 292-4726
Goldman Sachs Balanced A	Balanced	-0.3	-2.12	-1.97	2	1	5.5	1.36	800 292-4726
Goldman Sachs Balanced B	Balanced	-1	-2.85	-1.12	2	1	0	2.11	800 292-4726
Goldman Sachs Balanced C	Balanced	-1	-2.85	-1.1	2	1	0	2.11	800 292-4726

Stock Fund Name	Objective	Annualized Return for			Rank		Max Load	Expense Ratio	Toll-Free/(Toll) Telephone
		1 Year	3 Years	5 Years	Overall	Risk			
Goldman Sachs Balanced Inst	Balanced	0.1	-1.73	0.02	1	1	0	1.46	800 292-4726
Goldman Sachs Balanced Strat A	AssetAlloc	-1.8					4.5	0.59	800 292-4726
Goldman Sachs Balanced Strat B	AssetAlloc	-2.5					0	1.34	800 292-4726
Goldman Sachs Balanced Strat C	AssetAlloc	-2.4					0	1.34	800 292-4726
Goldman Sachs Balanced Strat Inst	AssetAlloc	-1.4					0	0.19	800 292-4726
Goldman Sachs Balanced Strat Svc	AssetAlloc	-1.9					0	0.69	800 292-4726
Goldman Sachs Balanced Svc	Balanced	-0.3	-2.2	-0.46	2	1	0	1.26	800 292-4726
Goldman Sachs CORE Intl Eq A	Foreign	-15.7	-12.72	-5.13	3	2	5.5	1.33	800 292-4726
Goldman Sachs CORE Intl Eq B	Foreign	-16.2	-13.14	-5.58	3	2	0	2.08	800 292-4726
Goldman Sachs CORE Intl Eq C	Foreign	-16.2	-13.15	-5.61	3	2	0	2.08	800 292-4726
Goldman Sachs CORE Intl Eq Inst	Foreign	-15.1	-12.1	-4.49	4	2	0	0.93	800 292-4726
Goldman Sachs CORE Intl Eq Svc	Foreign	-15.6	-12.57	-4.95	3	2	0	1.43	800 292-4726
Goldman Sachs CORE Lrg Cp Gr A	Growth	-8.8	-19.89	-5.33	4	4	5.5	1.24	800 292-4726
Goldman Sachs CORE Lrg Cp Gr B	Growth	-9.5	-20.48	-6.12	4	4	0	1.99	800 292-4726
Goldman Sachs CORE Lrg Cp Gr C	Growth	-9.4	-20.46	-6	4	4	0	1.99	800 292-4726
Goldman Sachs CORE Lrg Cp Gr Inst	Growth	-8.5	-19.55	-4.94	4	4	0	0.84	800 292-4726
Goldman Sachs CORE Lrg Cp Gr Svc	Growth	-8.9					0	1.34	800 292-4726
Goldman Sachs CORE Lrg Cp Val A	Growth/Inc	-10	-3.74		3	2	5.5	1.24	800 292-4726
Goldman Sachs CORE Lrg Cp Val B	Growth/Inc	-10.7	-4.26		3	2	0	1.99	800 292-4726
Goldman Sachs CORE Lrg Cp Val C	Growth/Inc	-10.8	-4.28		3	2	0	1.99	800 292-4726
Goldman Sachs CORE Lrg Cp Val Inst	Growth/Inc	-9.7	-3.37		3	2	0	0.84	800 292-4726
Goldman Sachs CORE Lrg Cp Val Svc	Growth/Inc	-10.1	-3.81		3	2	0	1.34	800 292-4726
Goldman Sachs CORE Sm Cap Eq A	Small Co	-8.4	1.75	0.63	3	3	5.5	1.24	800 292-4726
Goldman Sachs CORE Sm Cap Eq B	Small Co	-9	0.97	-0.11	3	4	0	1.99	800 292-4726
Goldman Sachs CORE Sm Cap Eq C	Small Co	-9.1	0.97	-0.11	3	3	0	1.99	800 292-4726
Goldman Sachs CORE Sm Cap Eq Inst	Small Co	-8	2.16	1.05	3	3	0	0.84	800 292-4726
Goldman Sachs CORE Sm Cap Eq Svc	Small Co	-8.4	1.68	0.55	3	3	0	1.34	800 292-4726
Goldman Sachs CORE Tax Mngd A	Growth	-10	-10.25		4	3	5.5	1.31	800 292-4726
Goldman Sachs CORE Tax Mngd B	Growth	-10.7	-10.94		3	3	0	2.06	800 292-4726
Goldman Sachs CORE Tax Mngd C	Growth	-10.7	-10.91		3	3	0	2.06	800 292-4726
Goldman Sachs CORE Tax Mngd Inst	Growth	-9.6	-9.86		3	3	0	0.91	800 292-4726
Goldman Sachs CORE Tax Mngd Svc	Growth	-10.1	-10.31		4	3	0	1.41	800 292-4726
Goldman Sachs CORE US Equity A	Growth/Inc	-9.2	-11.09	-2.1	3	3	5.5	1.24	800 292-4726
Goldman Sachs CORE US Equity B	Growth/Inc	-9.9	-11.75	-2.93	3	3	0	1.99	800 292-4726
Goldman Sachs CORE US Equity C	Growth/Inc	-9.8	-11.75	-2.93	3	3	0	1.99	800 292-4726
Goldman Sachs CORE US Equity Inst	Growth/Inc	-8.8					0	0.84	800 292-4726
Goldman Sachs CORE US Equity Svc	Growth/Inc	-9.3					0	1.34	800 292-4726
Goldman Sachs Capital Growth A	Growth	-9	-12.86	-1.04	3	3	5.5	1.46	800 292-4726
Goldman Sachs Capital Growth B	Growth	-9.6	-13.52	-1.78	3	3	0	2.21	800 292-4726
Goldman Sachs Capital Growth C	Growth	-9.6	-13.51	-1.76	3	3	0	2.21	800 292-4726
Goldman Sachs Capital Growth Inst	Growth	-8.6	-12.52	-0.65	3	3	0	1.06	800 292-4726
Goldman Sachs Capital Growth Svc	Growth	-9.1	-12.96	-1.26	3	3	0	1.56	800 292-4726
Goldman Sachs Emerg Mkts Eq A	Foreign	-11.8	-9.66	-2.93	3	4	5.5	1.8	800 292-4726
Goldman Sachs Emerg Mkts Eq B	Foreign	-12.2	-10.11	-3.39	3	4	0	2.3	800 292-4726
Goldman Sachs Emerg Mkts Eq C	Foreign	-12.3	-10.14	-3.37	3	4	0	2.3	800 292-4726
Goldman Sachs Emerg Mkts Eq Inst	Foreign	-11.3					0	1.15	800 292-4726
Goldman Sachs Emerg Mkts Eq Svc	Foreign	-11.6					0	1.65	800 292-4726
Goldman Sachs European Equity A	European	-8.8	-12.19		4	3	5.5	1.79	800 292-4726
Goldman Sachs European Equity B	European	-9.3	-12.71		3	3	0	2.29	800 292-4726
Goldman Sachs European Equity C	European	-9.3	-12.72		3	3	0	2.29	800 292-4726
Goldman Sachs European Equity Inst	European	-8.3					0	1.14	800 292-4726
Goldman Sachs European Equity Svc	European	-8.7					0	1.64	800 292-4726
Goldman Sachs Gr & Inc Strat A	Growth/Inc	-3.8	-3.72	-0.19	2	1	5.5	0.59	800 292-4726
Goldman Sachs Gr & Inc Strat B	Growth/Inc	-4.4	-4.41	-0.93	2	1	0	1.34	800 292-4726
Goldman Sachs Gr & Inc Strat C	Growth/Inc	-4.5	-4.44	-0.93	2	1	0	1.34	800 292-4726
Goldman Sachs Gr & Inc Strat Inst	Growth/Inc	-3.4					0	0.19	800 292-4726
Goldman Sachs Gr & Inc Strat Svc	Growth/Inc	-3.9					0	0.69	800 292-4726
Goldman Sachs Growth & Income A	Growth/Inc	-5.3	-6.67	-6.01	3	2	5.5	1.22	800 292-4726

328

Stock Fund Name	Objective	Annualized Return for			Rank		Max Load	Expense Ratio	Toll-Free/(Toll) Telephone
		1 Year	3 Years	5 Years	Overall	Risk			
Goldman Sachs Growth & Income B	Growth/Inc	-6.1	-7.38	-6.73	3	2	0	1.97	800 292-4726
Goldman Sachs Growth & Income C	Growth/Inc	-6.1	-7.37	-6.74	3	2	0	1.97	800 292-4726
Goldman Sachs Growth & Income Inst	Growth/Inc	-5					0	0.82	800 292-4726
Goldman Sachs Growth & Income Svc	Growth/Inc	-5.4					0	1.32	800 292-4726
Goldman Sachs Growth Opp A	Growth	-10.5	-1.08		2	4	5.5	1.46	800 292-4726
Goldman Sachs Growth Opp B	Growth	-11.2	-1.83		2	4	0	2.21	800 292-4726
Goldman Sachs Growth Opp C	Growth	-11.1	-1.8		2	4	0	2.21	800 292-4726
Goldman Sachs Growth Opp Inst	Growth	-10.1	-0.69		2	4	0	1.06	800 292-4726
Goldman Sachs Growth Opp Svc	Growth	-10.6	-1.19		2	4	0	1.56	800 292-4726
Goldman Sachs Growth Strategy A	Growth	-8.3	-7.63	-2.5	3	2	5.5	0.59	800 292-4726
Goldman Sachs Growth Strategy B	Growth	-8.9	-8.32	-3.24	3	2	0	1.34	800 292-4726
Goldman Sachs Growth Strategy C	Growth	-9	-8.32	-3.24	3	2	0	1.34	800 292-4726
Goldman Sachs Growth Strategy Inst	Growth	-7.8					0	0.19	800 292-4726
Goldman Sachs Growth Strategy Svc	Growth	-8.4					0	0.69	800 292-4726
Goldman Sachs Internet Tollkp A	Technology	-1.4	-28.94		4	5	5.5	1.5	800 292-4726
Goldman Sachs Internet Tollkp B	Technology	-2.1	-29.48		4	5	0	2.25	800 292-4726
Goldman Sachs Internet Tollkp C	Technology	-1.9	-29.48		4	5	0	2.25	800 292-4726
Goldman Sachs Internet Tollkp I	Technology	-0.8					0	1.1	800 292-4726
Goldman Sachs Internet Tollkp Svc	Technology	-1.4					0	1.6	800 292-4726
Goldman Sachs Intl Equity A	Foreign	-14.3	-15.92	-6.3	5	3	5.5	2.05	800 292-4726
Goldman Sachs Intl Equity B	Foreign	-14.7	-16.62	-6.96	5	3	0	2.55	800 292-4726
Goldman Sachs Intl Equity C	Foreign	-14.8	-16.32	-6.78	5	3	0	2.55	800 292-4726
Goldman Sachs Intl Equity Inst	Foreign	-13.8					0	1.4	800 292-4726
Goldman Sachs Intl Equity Svc	Foreign	-14.2	-15.78	-6.12	4	3	0	1.9	800 292-4726
Goldman Sachs Intl Gr Opp A	Foreign	-14.8	-16.46	-2.37	4	3	5.5	1.79	800 292-4726
Goldman Sachs Intl Gr Opp B	Foreign	-15.2	-16.89	-2.91	4	3	0	2.29	800 292-4726
Goldman Sachs Intl Gr Opp C	Foreign	-15.3	-16.89	-2.83	4	3	0	2.29	800 292-4726
Goldman Sachs Intl Gr Opp Inst	Foreign	-14.3					0	1.14	800 292-4726
Goldman Sachs Intl Gr Opp Serv	Foreign	-14.7					0	1.64	800 292-4726
Goldman Sachs Japanese Equity A	Pacific	-28.4	-24.67	-5.12	5	3	5.5	1.79	800 292-4726
Goldman Sachs Japanese Equity B	Pacific	-28.9	-25.1	-5.62	5	3	0	2.29	800 292-4726
Goldman Sachs Japanese Equity C	Pacific	-28.9	-25.07	-5.61	5	3	0	2.29	800 292-4726
Goldman Sachs Japanese Equity Inst	Pacific	-28.2					0	1.14	800 292-4726
Goldman Sachs Japanese Equity Svc	Pacific	-28.4					0	1.64	800 292-4726
Goldman Sachs Large Cap Value A	Growth/Inc	-6.1	-0.86		1	2	5.5	1.37	800 292-4726
Goldman Sachs Large Cap Value B	Growth/Inc	-6.8					0	2.12	800 292-4726
Goldman Sachs Large Cap Value C	Growth/Inc	-6.8					0	2.12	800 292-4726
Goldman Sachs Large Cap Value Inst	Growth/Inc	-5.7	-0.44		1	2	0	0.97	800 292-4726
Goldman Sachs Large Cap Value Svc	Growth/Inc	-6.2	-0.82		1	2	0	1.47	800 292-4726
Goldman Sachs Mid Cap Value A	Growth	-7.8	11.13	4.57	2	2	5.5	1.37	800 292-4726
Goldman Sachs Mid Cap Value B	Growth	-8.5	10.43	3.87	2	2	0	2.12	800 292-4726
Goldman Sachs Mid Cap Value C	Growth	-8.5	10.41	3.83	2	2	0	2.12	800 292-4726
Goldman Sachs Mid Cap Value Inst	Growth	-7.5					0	1.47	800 292-4726
Goldman Sachs Mid Cap Value Svc	Growth	-7.9					0	1.37	800 292-4726
Goldman Sachs Real Estate Sec A	Real Est	3.6	13.5		1	2	5.5	1.44	800 292-4726
Goldman Sachs Real Estate Sec B	Real Est	2.7	12.41		1	2	0	2.19	800 292-4726
Goldman Sachs Real Estate Sec C	Real Est	2.8	12.4		1	2	0	2.19	800 292-4726
Goldman Sachs Real Estate Sec Inst	Real Est	3.9	13.9		1	2	0	1.04	800 292-4726
Goldman Sachs Real Estate Sec Svc	Real Est	3.4	13.17		1	2	0	1.54	800 292-4726
Goldman Sachs Res Select A	Other	-7.3					0	1.5	800 292-4726
Goldman Sachs Res Select B	Other	-8					0	2.25	800 292-4726
Goldman Sachs Res Select C	Other	-8.1					0	2.25	800 292-4726
Goldman Sachs Res Select Instl	Other	-7					0	1.1	800 292-4726
Goldman Sachs Small Cap Value A	Small Co	-5.2	13.82	3.54	2	3	5.5	1.37	800 292-4726
Goldman Sachs Small Cap Value B	Small Co	-5.9	12.97	2.75	2	3	0	2.12	800 292-4726
Goldman Sachs Small Cap Value C	Small Co	-5.9	12.88	2.72	2	3	0	2.12	800 292-4726
Goldman Sachs Small Cap Value Inst	Small Co	-4.8	14.28	3.95	1	3	0	0.97	800 292-4726
Goldman Sachs Small Cap Value Svc	Small Co	-5.3	13.72	3.43	2	3	0	1.47	800 292-4726

Stock Fund Name	Objective	Annualized Return for			Rank		Max Load	Expense Ratio	Toll-Free/(Toll) Telephone
		1 Year	3 Years	5 Years	Overall	Risk			
Goldman Sachs Strategic Gr A	Growth	-9.2	-13.61		3	3	5.5	1.46	800 292-4726
Goldman Sachs Strategic Gr B	Growth	-9.7	-14.22		3	3	0	2.21	800 292-4726
Goldman Sachs Strategic Gr C	Growth	-9.7	-14.23		3	3	0	2.21	800 292-4726
Goldman Sachs Strategic Gr Inst	Growth	-8.7	-13.22		3	3	0	1.06	800 292-4726
Goldman Sachs Strategic Gr Svc	Growth	-8.9	-13.5		3	3	0	1.56	800 292-4726
Government Street Equity Fund	Growth	-8.8	-10	-0.72	3	3	0	0.81	800 443-4249
Grand Prix Fund A	Agg Growth	-17.4	-41.78	-4.08	5	5	5.25	1.67	800 432-4741
Grand Prix Super Core Fd A	Agg Growth	-3.5					5.25	1.59	800 432-4741
Grand Prix Super Core Fd C	Agg Growth	-4.2					0	2.15	800 432-4741
Granum Value Fund	Growth	-8.3	0.68	2.04	2	1	0	3.12	888 547-2686
Green Century Balanced	Balanced	-8.7	-12.14	2.08	3	5	0	2.35	800 934-7336
Green Century Equity	Growth	-9	-12.26	-1.87	3	3	0	1.5	800 934-7336
Greenspring Fund	Flexible	-1.6	8.77	2.39	1	2	0	1.19	800 366-3863
Guardian Asset Allocation A	AssetAlloc	-7.3	-7.26	-0.08	3	2	4.5	0.47	800 343-0817
Guardian Asset Allocation B	AssetAlloc	-8.1	-8.02		3	3	0	1.28	800 343-0817
Guardian Asset Allocation C	AssetAlloc	-8.5					0	1.27	800 343-0817
Guardian Baillie Giff Emerg Mkts A	Foreign	-8	-4.65	2.87	3	4	4.5	2.19	800 343-0817
Guardian Baillie Giff Emerg Mkts B	Foreign	-9.1	-5.86	1.04	3	4	0	3.51	800 343-0817
Guardian Baillie Giff Emerg Mkts C	Foreign	-9.1					0	3.34	800 343-0817
Guardian Baillie Giff Internatl A	Foreign	-13.7	-16.6	-6.59	5	2	4.5	1.45	800 343-0817
Guardian Baillie Giff Internatl B	Foreign	-14.8	-17.6		4	2	0	2.43	800 343-0817
Guardian Baillie Giff Internatl C	Foreign	-14.8					0	2.6	800 343-0817
Guardian Park Avenue Fund A	Growth	-9.8	-16.62	-5.13	4	4	4.5	0.83	800 343-0817
Guardian Park Avenue Fund B	Growth	-10.7	-17.39	-9.66	5	4	0	1.75	800 343-0817
Guardian Park Avenue Fund C	Growth	-11					0	1.76	800 343-0817
Guardian Park Avenue Small Cap A	Small Co	-8.9	-4	0.38	3	4	4.5	1.28	800 343-0817
Guardian Park Avenue Small Cap B	Small Co	-9.8	-4.87	-0.52	3	4	0	2.18	800 343-0817
Guardian Park Avenue Small Cap C	Small Co	-10					0	2.17	800 343-0817
Guardian S&P 500 Index A	Growth	-8.5					4.5	0.53	800 343-0817
Guardian S&P 500 Index B	Growth	-9.4					0	1.79	800 343-0817
Guardian S&P 500 Index C	Growth	-7.5					0	1.81	800 343-0817
Guardian UBS Large Cap Value A	Growth/Inc						4.5		800 343-0817
Guardian UBS Large Cap Value B	Growth/Inc						0		800 343-0817
Guardian UBS Large Cap Value C	Growth/Inc						0		800 343-0817
Guardian UBS Small Cap Value A	Small Co						4.5		800 343-0817
Guardian UBS Small Cap Value B	Small Co						0		800 343-0817
Guardian UBS Small Cap Value C	Small Co						0		800 343-0817
Guinness Atkinson Asia Focus Fund	Pacific	-9.7	-7.08	-3.81	4	4	0	1.98	800 915-6565
Guinness Atkinson China & HK Fund	Pacific	-8.3	-7.91	4.21	3	4	0	1.85	800 915-6565
Guinness Atkinson Glob Innov Fund	Growth	-2	-21.64		3	5	0	1.35	800 915-6565
H&Q IPO & Emerging Company A	Small Co	-10.2	-25.53		4	5	5.5	1.35	800 327-6679
H&Q IPO & Emerging Company B	Small Co	-10.4	-26		5	5	0	2.05	800 327-6679
HSBC Investor Balanced A	Balanced	0.1					4.75		800 782-8183
HSBC Investor Balanced B	Balanced	-0.7					0		800 782-8183
HSBC Investor Equity A	Growth	-12.6	-13.72	-5.62	4	3	0	0.94	800 782-8183
HSBC Investor Equity Adv	Growth	-12.4	-13.51	-5.33	4	3	0	0.69	800 782-8183
HSBC Investor Intl Equity Adv	Foreign	-15.8	-15.51	-3.45	4	3	0		800 782-8183
HSBC Investor Opportunity A	Agg Growth	-11.3	-6.79	3.12	3	4	5	1.75	800 782-8183
HSBC Investor Overseas Equity A	Foreign	-16.4	-16.1	-2.47	4	3	0	1.85	800 782-8183
HSBC Investor Small Cap Equity Y	Small Co	-10.7	-7.12	-0.72	3	4	0	1.05	800 782-8183
Hancock Horizon Burnkenroad A	Income	-7					5.25	1.72	888 346-6300
Hancock Horizon Burnkenroad D	Income	-7.1					0	1.4	888 346-6300
Hancock Horizon Growth A	Growth	-8.9					5.25	1.42	888 346-6300
Hancock Horizon Growth C	Growth	-9.5					0	2.17	888 346-6300
Hancock Horizon Growth Tr	Growth	-8.6					0	1.17	888 346-6300
Hancock Horizon Value A	Income	-9.5	3.45			2	5.25	1.25	888 346-6300
Hancock Horizon Value C	Income	-10.2	2.75			2	0	2	888 346-6300
Hancock Horizon Value Tr	Income	-9.3	3.7			2	0	1	888 346-6300

Stock Fund Name	Objective	Annualized Return for			Rank		Max Load	Expense Ratio	Toll-Free/(Toll) Telephone
		1 Year	3 Years	5 Years	Overall	Risk			
Harbor Capital Appreciation Inst	Growth	-12.4	-18.26	-1.71	3	4	0	0.66	800 422-1050
Harbor Capital Appreciation Inv	Growth						0		800 422-1050
Harbor Capital Appreciation Retire	Growth						0		800 422-1050
Harbor Global Equity Inst	Global	-13.5					0	1.2	800 422-1050
Harbor Global Equity Inv	Global						0		800 422-1050
Harbor Global Equity Retire	Global						0		800 422-1050
Harbor International Growth Fd	Foreign	-21.7	-27.46	-16.21	4	4	0	0.99	800 422-1050
Harbor International Growth Retire	Foreign						0	1.24	800 422-1050
Harbor International Inst	Foreign	-10	-4.08	0.02	3	3	0	0.87	800 422-1050
Harbor International Inv	Foreign						0		800 422-1050
Harbor International Retire	Foreign						0		800 422-1050
Harbor Large Cap Value Inst	Growth/Inc	-13.9	-1.28	0.59	3	3	0	0.77	800 422-1050
Harbor Large Cap Value Inv	Growth/Inc						0		800 422-1050
Harbor Large Cap Value Retire	Growth/Inc						0		800 422-1050
Harbor Mid Cap Growth Inst	Growth	-6.9					0	1.2	800 422-1050
Harbor Mid Cap Growth Inv	Growth						0		800 422-1050
Harbor Mid Cap Growth Retire	Growth						0		800 422-1050
Harbor Mid Cap Value Inv	Growth						0		800 422-1050
Harbor Mid Cap Value Retire	Growth						0		800 422-1050
Harbor Small Cap Growth Inst	Growth	3.6	-21.17	0.79	3	5	0	0.95	800 422-1050
Harbor Small Cap Growth Inv	Small Co						0		800 422-1050
Harbor Small Cap Growth Retire	Small Co						0		800 422-1050
Harbor Small Cap Value Inst	Small Co	2.7					0	1.2	800 422-1050
Harbor Small Cap Value Inv	Small Co						0		800 422-1050
Harbor Small Cap Value Retire	Small Co						0		800 422-1050
Harding Loevner Global Equity	Global	-8.6	-11.82	-2.49	3	3	0	1.25	877 435-8105
Harding Loevner Intl Equity	Foreign	-16.1	-10.25	-1.46	4	3	0	1	877 435-8105
Harris Insight Balanced A	Balanced	-3.7	1.72	2.06	1	1	5.5	1.13	800 982-8782
Harris Insight Balanced B	Balanced	-4.3					0	1.88	800 982-8782
Harris Insight Balanced Inst	Balanced	-3.3	2	2.47	1	1	0	0.88	800 982-8782
Harris Insight Balanced N	Balanced	-3.6	1.73	2.22	2	1	0	1.13	800 982-8782
Harris Insight Core Equity A	Growth	-5.4	-10.35	-1.55	3	2	5.5	1.35	800 982-8782
Harris Insight Core Equity B	Growth	-6.2					0	2.1	800 982-8782
Harris Insight Core Equity Instl	Growth	-5.3	-10.16	-1.35	3	2	0	1.1	800 982-8782
Harris Insight Core Equity N	Growth	-6.9	-10.85	-1.88	3	3	0	1.35	800 982-8782
Harris Insight Emerging Mkt A	Foreign	-5.1	-3.2	-0.5	3	4	5.5	1.95	800 982-8782
Harris Insight Emerging Mkt Inst	Foreign	-4.7	-2.97	-0.22	3	4	0	1.7	800 982-8782
Harris Insight Emerging Mkt N	Foreign	-5.1	-3.22	-0.54	3	4	0	1.95	800 982-8782
Harris Insight Equity Fund A	Growth/Inc	-13.4	-5.37		3	2	5.5	1.25	800 982-8782
Harris Insight Equity Fund B	Growth/Inc	-14.2					0	2	800 982-8782
Harris Insight Equity Fund Instl	Growth/Inc	-13.2	-5.15	-1.34	3	2	0	1	800 982-8782
Harris Insight Equity Fund N	Growth/Inc	-13.5	-5.41	-1.56	2	2	0	1.25	800 982-8782
Harris Insight Equity Income A	Income	-15.1	-10.16		4	2	5.5	1.18	800 982-8782
Harris Insight Equity Income B	Income	-15.8					0	1.93	800 982-8782
Harris Insight Equity Income Instl	Income	-14.9	-9.93	-3.5	4	2	0	0.93	800 982-8782
Harris Insight Equity Income N	Income	-15.2	-10.16	-3.75	4	2	0	1.18	800 982-8782
Harris Insight High Yld Select A	Converts	1.7	-7.58	-1.71	3	3	4.5	1.17	800 982-8782
Harris Insight High Yld Select Inst	Converts	2	-7.34	-1.48	3	3	0	0.92	800 982-8782
Harris Insight High Yld Select N	Converts	1.8	-7.57	-1.7	3	3	0	1.17	800 982-8782
Harris Insight Index B	Growth/Inc	-9.2					0	1.45	800 982-8782
Harris Insight Index Inst	Growth/Inc	-8.3	-11.16	-1.42	3	3	0	0.45	800 982-8782
Harris Insight Index N	Growth/Inc	-8.5	-11.38	-1.64	3	3	0	0.7	800 982-8782
Harris Insight International A	Foreign	-19.2	-11.44		4	3	5.5	1.65	800 982-8782
Harris Insight International Inst	Foreign	-15.4	-9.92	-5.83	3	3	0	1.4	800 982-8782
Harris Insight International N	Foreign	-15.7	-10.16	-6.12	3	3	0	1.65	800 982-8782
Harris Insight Sm-Cap Agg Gro Inst	Small Co	-4.5					0	1	800 982-8782
Harris Insight Small Cap Oppt A	Small Co	-4.2	1.32	5.62	2	4	5.5	1.45	800 982-8782
Harris Insight Small Cap Oppt B	Small Co	-4.9					0	2.2	800 982-8782

Stock Fund Name	Objective	Annualized Return for			Rank		Max Load	Expense Ratio	Toll-Free/(Toll) Telephone
		1 Year	3 Years	5 Years	Overall	Risk			
Harris Insight Small Cap Oppt Inst	Small Co	-3.9	1.58	5.86	2	4	0	1.2	800 982-8782
Harris Insight Small Cap Oppt N	Small Co	-4.1	1.34	5.61	2	4	0	1.45	800 982-8782
Harris Insight Small Cap Val A	Small Co	-5.6	10.96		2	3	5.5	1.24	800 982-8782
Harris Insight Small Cap Val B	Small Co	-6.3					0	1.99	800 982-8782
Harris Insight Small Cap Val Inst	Small Co	-5.4	11.24	4.99	1	3	0	0.99	800 982-8782
Harris Insight Small Cap Val N	Small Co	-5.6	10.98	4.74	1	3	0	1.24	800 982-8782
Hartford Advisers A	Growth/Inc	-1.4	-4.03	1.87	2	1	5.5	1.22	888 843-7824
Hartford Advisers B	Growth/Inc	-2.1	-4.67	1.17	2	1	0	1.93	888 843-7824
Hartford Advisers C	Growth/Inc	-1.9	-4.62		2	1	1	1.93	888 843-7824
Hartford Advisers Y	Growth/Inc	-0.7	-3.52	2.41	2	1	0		888 843-7824
Hartford Capital Apprec A	Agg Growth	-5.6	-3.95	7.4	2	4	5.5	1.28	888 843-7824
Hartford Capital Apprec B	Agg Growth	-6.3	-4.62	6.66	2	4	0	1.99	888 843-7824
Hartford Capital Apprec C	Agg Growth	-6.2	-4.54		2	4	1	1.99	888 843-7824
Hartford Capital Apprec Y	Agg Growth	-5	-3.39	7.99	2	4	0		888 843-7824
Hartford Dividend & Growth A	Growth/Inc	-8.6	-1.43	1.34	3	2	5.5	1.31	888 843-7824
Hartford Dividend & Growth B	Growth/Inc	-9.2	-2.12	0.66	3	2	0	2.03	888 843-7824
Hartford Dividend & Growth C	Growth/Inc	-9.2	-2.12		2	2	1	2.03	888 843-7824
Hartford Dividend & Growth Y	Growth/Inc	-8	-0.88	1.85	3	2	0		888 843-7824
Hartford Focus A	Growth	-6.8					5.5	1.63	888 843-7824
Hartford Focus B	Growth	-7.5					0	2.35	888 843-7824
Hartford Focus C	Growth	-7.4					1	2.35	888 843-7824
Hartford Focus Y	Growth	-6.4					0	1.2	888 843-7824
Hartford Global Communications A	Global	10.2					5.5	1.66	888 843-7824
Hartford Global Communications B	Global	9.5					0		888 843-7824
Hartford Global Communications C	Global	9.5					1	2.36	888 843-7824
Hartford Global Communications Y	Global	10.7					0		888 843-7824
Hartford Global Financial Service A	Financial	-12.9					5.5		888 843-7824
Hartford Global Financial Service B	Financial	-13.5					0		888 843-7824
Hartford Global Financial Service Y	Financial	-12.5					0		888 843-7824
Hartford Global Health A	Health	0.9	10.24		1	3	5.5	1.62	888 843-7824
Hartford Global Health B	Health	0.2	9.41		1	3	0	1.65	888 843-7824
Hartford Global Health C	Health	0.2	9.43		1	3	1	2.33	888 843-7824
Hartford Global Health Y	Health	1.4	10.91		1	3	0	1.19	888 843-7824
Hartford Global Leaders A	Global	-9.7	-11.86		3	3	5.5	1.48	888 843-7824
Hartford Global Leaders B	Global	-10.4	-12.53		4	3	0	2.23	888 843-7824
Hartford Global Leaders C	Global	-10.3	-12.48		4	3	1	2.19	888 843-7824
Hartford Global Technology A	Other	-1.1	-25.8		3	5	5.5	1.66	888 843-7824
Hartford Global Technology B	Other	-1.6	-26.39		3	5	0	1.66	888 843-7824
Hartford Global Technology C	Other	-1.6	-26.32		3	5	1	2.36	888 843-7824
Hartford Global Technology Y	Other	-0.5	-25.48		3	5	0	1.19	888 843-7824
Hartford Growth & Income A	Growth/Inc	-10.1	-10.6	-0.25	3	3	5.5	1.38	888 843-7824
Hartford Growth & Income B	Growth/Inc	-10.7	-11.26	-0.94	3	3	0	2.11	888 843-7824
Hartford Growth & Income C	Growth/Inc	-10.7	-11.24		4	3	1	2.09	888 843-7824
Hartford Growth (The) L	Growth	-2.6	-9.75	1.34	3	3	4.75	1.08	888 843-7824
Hartford Growth Fund A	Growth	-2.9	-9.85	1.28		3	5.5	1.45	888 843-7824
Hartford Growth Fund B	Growth	-3.5	-10.5	0.55		3	0	2.15	888 843-7824
Hartford Growth Fund C	Growth	-3.5	-10.5	0.55		3	1	2.15	888 843-7824
Hartford Growth Fund Y	Other	-2.4					0		888 843-7824
Hartford Growth Opport (The) L	Agg Growth	-8.1	-12.64	1.83	3	4	4.75	1.1	888 843-7824
Hartford Growth Opportunity A	Agg Growth	-8.4	-12.74	1.76		4	5.5	1.42	888 843-7824
Hartford Growth Opportunity B	Agg Growth	-9	-13.35	1.01		4	0	2.13	888 843-7824
Hartford Growth Opportunity C	Agg Growth	-9	-13.36	1.02		4	1	2.04	888 843-7824
Hartford Growth Opportunity Y	Agg Growth	-8					0	0.9	888 843-7824
Hartford Intl Capital Apprec A	Foreign	-6.6					5.5	1.65	888 843-7824
Hartford Intl Capital Apprec B	Foreign	-7.4					0	2.35	888 843-7824
Hartford Intl Capital Apprec C	Foreign	-7.2					1	2.35	888 843-7824
Hartford Intl Capital Apprec Y	Foreign	-6.2					0	1.2	888 843-7824
Hartford Intl Opportunity A	Foreign	-17.2	-14.58	-5.09	5	3	5.5	1.56	888 843-7824

Stock Fund Name	Objective	Annualized Return for			Rank		Max Load	Expense Ratio	Toll-Free/(Toll) Telephone
		1 Year	3 Years	5 Years	Overall	Risk			
Hartford Intl Opportunity B	Foreign	-17.8	-15.22	-5.71	5	3	0	2.3	888 843-7824
Hartford Intl Opportunity C	Foreign	-18	-15.3		5	3	1	2.28	888 843-7824
Hartford Intl Opportunity Y	Foreign	-17	-14.25	-4.63	5	3	0		888 843-7824
Hartford Intl Small Company A	Foreign	2.2					5.5	1.65	888 843-7824
Hartford Intl Small Company B	Foreign	1.9					0	2.35	888 843-7824
Hartford Intl Small Company C	Foreign	1.4					1	2.35	888 843-7824
Hartford Intl Small Company Y	Foreign	2.7					0	1.2	888 843-7824
Hartford Mid Cap Fd A	Growth	-5.2	2.29	14.63	1	3	5.5	1.38	888 843-7824
Hartford Mid Cap Fd B	Growth	-5.9	1.59	13.82	1	3	0	2.11	888 843-7824
Hartford Mid Cap Fd C	Growth	-5.9	1.61	1	3		1	2.09	888 843-7824
Hartford Mid Cap Value A	Growth	-7.3					5.5	1.69	888 843-7824
Hartford Mid Cap Value B	Growth	-8					0	2.38	888 843-7824
Hartford Mid Cap Value C	Growth	-7.9					1	2.37	888 843-7824
Hartford Sm Cap Gwth (The) L	Small Co	-9.7	-16.03	4.59	3	5	4.75	1.44	888 843-7824
Hartford Small Cap Growth A	Small Co	-9.7	-16.03	4.59		5	5.5	1.72	888 843-7824
Hartford Small Cap Growth B	Small Co	-10.2	-16.51	4.03		5	0	2.38	888 843-7824
Hartford Small Cap Growth C	Small Co	-10.3	-16.57	3.97		5	1	2.3	888 843-7824
Hartford Small Cap Growth Y	Small Co	-9.3					0		888 843-7824
Hartford Small Company A	Small Co	-10.7	-12.14	0.92	3	4	5.5	1.45	888 843-7824
Hartford Small Company B	Small Co	-11.4	-12.76	0.2	3	4	0	2.15	888 843-7824
Hartford Small Company C	Small Co	-11.4	-12.72		3	4	1	2.15	888 843-7824
Hartford Small Company Y	Small Co	-10.3	-11.69	1.44	3	4	0		888 843-7824
Hartford Stock A	Growth	-9.3	-12.5	-1.43	4	3	5.5	1.28	888 843-7824
Hartford Stock B	Growth	-9.9	-13.16	-2.14	3	3	0	2	888 843-7824
Hartford Stock C	Growth	-9.8	-13		3	3	1	1.99	888 843-7824
Hartford Stock Y	Growth	-8.8	-12	-0.93	3	3	0		888 843-7824
Hartford Value Fd A	Growth/Inc	-11.4					5.5	1.45	888 843-7824
Hartford Value Fd B	Growth/Inc	-11.9					0	2.15	888 843-7824
Hartford Value Fd C	Growth/Inc	-11.9					1	2.15	888 843-7824
Hartford Value Fd Y	Growth/Inc	-11					0	1	888 843-7824
Hartford Value Opportunities A	Growth/Inc	-6.8	-3.22	0.97		3	5.5	1.82	888 843-7824
Hartford Value Opportunities B	Growth/Inc	-7.6	-3.93	0.23		3	0	2.48	888 843-7824
Hartford Value Opportunities C	Growth/Inc	-7.5	-3.93	0.2		3	1	2.39	888 843-7824
Hartford Value Opportunities Y	Global	-6.4					0		888 843-7824
Heartland Select Value Fd	Growth	-11.4	10.44	6.58	1	3	0	1.46	888 505-5180
Heartland Value Fund	Small Co	-0.1	14.98	7.66	2	3	0	1.28	888 505-5180
Heartland Value Plus Fund	Growth/Inc	3.2	11.08	3.72	1	3	0	1.44	888 505-5180
Henderson European Focus A	Foreign	10.4					5.75	2	866 443-6337
Henderson European Focus B	Foreign	9.6					0	2.75	866 443-6337
Henderson European Focus C	Foreign	9.6					1	2.75	866 443-6337
Henderson Global Technology A	Technology	-6.1					5.75	2	866 443-6337
Henderson Global Technology B	Technology	-6.5					0	2.75	866 443-6337
Henderson Global Technology C	Technology	-6.5					1	2.75	866 443-6337
Henderson Internatl Opport A	Foreign	-6.5					5.75	2	866 443-6337
Henderson Internatl Opport B	Foreign	-7.2					0	2.75	866 443-6337
Henderson Internatl Opport C	Foreign	-7.2					1	2.75	866 443-6337
Henlopen Fund	Growth	-4.7	-7.98	3.58	3	5	0	1.6	800 922-0224
Hennessy Balanced Fund	Balanced	-4.8					0	1.84	800 966-4354
Hennessy Cornerstone Growth	Growth	-4.3	7.74	9.63	2	3	0	1.3	800 966-4354
Hennessy Cornerstone Value	Growth	-11.4	1.83	1.75	3	3	0	1.53	800 966-4354
Hennessy Total Return Fund	Balanced	-7.5					0	1.71	800 966-4354
Henssler Equity Fd	Growth	-8	-5.32		2	2	0	1.21	800 936-3863
Heritage Aggressive Growth A	Agg Growth	-3.3	1.6		2	4	4.75	1.45	800 421-4184
Heritage Aggressive Growth B	Agg Growth	-4	0.82		2	4	0	2.2	800 421-4184
Heritage Aggressive Growth C	Agg Growth	-4	0.82		2	4	0	2.2	800 421-4184
Heritage Capital Appreciation A	Agg Growth	-6.5	-7.38	3.52	3	4	4.75	1.29	800 421-4184
Heritage Capital Appreciation B	Agg Growth	-7.2	-7	3.52	3	4	0	2	800 421-4184
Heritage Capital Appreciation C	Agg Growth	-7.2	-7	3.5	2	4	0	2	800 421-4184

Stock Fund Name	Objective	Annualized Return for			Rank		Max Load	Expense Ratio	Toll-Free/(Toll) Telephone
		1 Year	3 Years	5 Years	Overall	Risk			
Heritage Growth & Income A	Growth/Inc	-3.3	-4.58	-2.47	2	2	4.75	1.35	800 421-4184
Heritage Growth Eq A	Growth	-10.7	-15.56	3.22	3	4	4.75	1.26	800 421-4184
Heritage Growth Eq B	Growth	-11.4	-16.19	2.45	4	4	0	2.01	800 421-4184
Heritage Growth Eq C	Growth	-11.4	-16.17	2.45	4	4	0	2.01	800 421-4184
Heritage Growth and Income Trust B	Growth/Inc	-4	-5.25	-3.18	2	2	0	2.1	800 421-4184
Heritage Growth and Income Trust C	Growth/Inc	-3.9	-5.21	-3.16	2	2	0	2.1	800 421-4184
Heritage Intl Equity A	Foreign	-10	-16.21	-6.36	4	2	4.75	1.85	800 421-4184
Heritage Intl Equity B	Foreign	-10.6	-16.8	-7.04	4	2	0	2.6	800 421-4184
Heritage Intl Equity C	Foreign	-10.6	-16.8	-7.04	3	2	0	2.6	800 421-4184
Heritage Mid Cap Stock A	Growth	-16.4	4.98	9.9	2	3	4.75	1.27	800 421-4184
Heritage Mid Cap Stock B	Growth	-17	4.17	9.07	2	3	0	2.02	800 421-4184
Heritage Mid Cap Stock C	Growth	-17	4.2	9.07	2	3	0	2.02	800 421-4184
Heritage Small Cap Stock A	Small Co	-15.5	0.45	-1.25	3	4	4.75	1.3	800 421-4184
Heritage Small Cap Stock B	Small Co	-16.1	-0.28	-1.98	3	4	0	2.05	800 421-4184
Heritage Small Cap Stock C	Small Co	-16.2	-0.28	-1.97	3	4	0	2.05	800 421-4184
Heritage Technology A	Technology	-23.9	-30.76		4	5	4.75	1.65	800 421-4184
Heritage Technology B	Technology	-24.5	-31.28		4	5	0	2.4	800 421-4184
Heritage Technology C	Technology	-24.5	-31.28		4	5	0	2.4	800 421-4184
Heritage Value Eq A	Growth/Inc	-18.7	-7.9	-4.37	3	3	4.75	1.45	800 421-4184
Heritage Value Eq B	Growth/Inc	-19.4	-8.59	-5.09	4	3	0	2.2	800 421-4184
Heritage Value Eq C	Growth/Inc	-19.4	-8.59	-5.09	4	3	0	2.2	800 421-4184
Hester Total Return Fund	Balanced	-5.5	-5.62	2.39	1	3	0	1.41	800 366-6223
Hibernia Capital Appreciation A	Growth	-9.7	-9.71	-0.91	3	3	4.5	1.27	800 263-1078
Hibernia Capital Appreciation B	Growth	-10.4	-10.4	-1.65	3	3	0	2.02	800 263-1078
Hibernia Mid Cap Equity Fund A	Growth	-8.7					4.5	1.55	800 263-1078
Hibernia Mid Cap Equity Fund B	Growth	-9.4	-1.91		2	3	0	2.3	800 263-1078
HighMark Balanced Fund Fid	Balanced	-3.2	-5.04	-1.14	2	1	0	0.95	800 433-6884
HighMark Balanced Fund Ret A	Balanced	-3.4	-5.2	-1.36	2	1	5.5	1.2	800 433-6884
HighMark Balanced Fund Ret B	Balanced	-4.1					0	1.85	800 433-6884
HighMark Balanced Fund Ret C	Balanced	-4.1	-5.87		1	1	0	1.85	800 433-6884
HighMark Core Equity Fund A	Global	-9.9					5.5	1.18	800 433-6884
HighMark Core Equity Fund B	Global	-10.6					0	1.83	800 433-6884
HighMark Growth Fund Fid	Growth	-7.2	-22.53	-9.94	3	4	0	0.95	800 433-6884
HighMark Growth Fund Retail A	Growth	-7.5	-22.69	-10.16	3	4	5.5	1.2	800 433-6884
HighMark Growth Fund Retail B	Growth	-8					0	1.85	800 433-6884
HighMark Growth Fund Retail C	Growth	-8	-23.19		4	4	0	1.85	800 433-6884
HighMark Intl Equity Fid	Foreign	-20	-17.3	-7.16	5	2	0	1.48	800 433-6884
HighMark Intl Equity Ret A	Foreign	-20.1	-17.55		5	2	5.5	1.71	800 433-6884
HighMark Intl Equity Ret B	Foreign	-20.7	-18		5	2	0	2.38	800 433-6884
HighMark Intl Equity Ret C	Foreign	-20.7	-18		5	2	0	2.38	800 433-6884
HighMark Large Cap Value Fid	Income	-12.6	-9.18	-4.66	4	3	0	0.95	800 433-6884
HighMark Large Cap Value Ret A	Income	-12.8	-9.27	-4.83	4	3	5.5	1.2	800 433-6884
HighMark Large Cap Value Ret B	Income	-13.4					0	1.85	800 433-6884
HighMark Large Cap Value Ret C	Income	-13.4	-10		3	3	0	1.85	800 433-6884
HighMark Sm Cap Value Fid	Small Co	1	5.21		1	3	0	1.47	800 433-6884
HighMark Sm Cap Value Ret A	Small Co	0.6	4.87		1	3	5.5	1.72	800 433-6884
HighMark Sm Cap Value Ret B	Small Co	-0.3	4.21		2	3	0	2.37	800 433-6884
HighMark Sm Cap Value Ret C	Small Co	-0.4	4.23		1	3	0	2.37	800 433-6884
HighMark Value Momentm Fund A	Growth/Inc	-8.5	-5.46	-0.7	3	3	5.5	1.2	800 433-6884
HighMark Value Momentm Fund B	Growth/Inc	-9.1					0	1.85	800 433-6884
HighMark Value Momentm Fund C	Growth/Inc	-9.1	-6.12		3	3	0	1.85	800 433-6884
HighMark Value Momentm Fund Fid	Growth/Inc	-8.3	-5.25	-0.47	3	3	0	0.95	800 433-6884
Hilliard-Lyons Growth Fund A	Growth	-13.5	-9.48	-3.35	3	3	4.75	1.3	800 444-1854
Hilliard-Lyons Senbanc Fund	Financial	15.6	23.94		1	1	2.25	1.75	800 444-1854
Hodges Fund	Growth	2.3	-5.2	-1.65	4	5	2.5	1.91	877 232-1222
Homestead Small Company	Small Co	-7.3	11.39	4.33	3	3	0	1.5	800 258-3030
Homestead Value Fund	Growth/Inc	-8.3	2.7	1.06	3	2	0	1.26	800 258-3030
Hotchkis and Wiley All Cap Value A	Income						0		800 796-5606

Stock Fund Name	Objective	Annualized Return for			Rank		Max Load	Expense Ratio	Toll-Free/(Toll) Telephone
		1 Year	3 Years	5 Years	Overall	Risk			
Hotchkis and Wiley Large Cap Val A	Growth/Inc	-4.9					5.25	1.3	800 796-5606
Hotchkis and Wiley Large Cap Val B	Growth/Inc	-5.6					0	2.05	800 796-5606
Hotchkis and Wiley Large Cap Val C	Growth/Inc	-5.6					0	2.05	800 796-5606
Hotchkis and Wiley Large Cap Val I	Growth/Inc	-4.7	6.8	2.91		3	0	1.05	800 796-5606
Hotchkis and Wiley Mid-Cap Val A	Growth	-1.1					5.25	1.4	800 796-5606
Hotchkis and Wiley Mid-Cap Val B	Growth	-1.9					0	2.15	800 796-5606
Hotchkis and Wiley Mid-Cap Val C	Growth	-1.8					0	2.15	800 796-5606
Hotchkis and Wiley Mid-Cap Val I	Growth	-0.9	14.41	12.09	1	3	0	1.15	800 796-5606
Hotchkis and Wiley Small Cap Val A	Small Co	3.9					5.25	1.5	800 796-5606
Hotchkis and Wiley Small Cap Val B	Small Co	3					0	2.25	800 796-5606
Hotchkis and Wiley Small Cap Val C	Small Co	3					0	2.25	800 796-5606
Hotchkis and Wiley Small Cap Val I	Small Co	4.1	25.92	5.49	1	3	0	1.25	800 796-5606
Huntington Dividend Capture A	Growth	0.6					5.75	1.9	800 253-0412
Huntington Dividend Capture B	Growth	0.1					0	2.4	800 253-0412
Huntington Dividend Capture Tr	Growth	1					0	1.65	800 253-0412
Huntington Growth A	Growth	-10.1	-11.09	-2.58	3	3	5.75	1.39	800 253-0412
Huntington Growth B	Growth	-10.6	-11.6		3	3	0	1.89	800 253-0412
Huntington Growth Tr	Growth	-9.9	-10.88	-2.41	3	3	0	1.14	800 253-0412
Huntington Income Equity A	Income	-11.2	-1.17	-0.86	3	2	5.75	1.41	800 253-0412
Huntington Income Equity B	Income	-11.7	-1.87		2	2	0	1.91	800 253-0412
Huntington Income Equity Tr	Income	-11	-1.04	-0.69	3	2	0	1.16	800 253-0412
Huntington International Equity A	Global	-10.1					5.75	2.37	800 253-0412
Huntington International Equity B	Global	-10.6					0	2.87	800 253-0412
Huntington International Equity Tr	Global	-9.9					0	2.12	800 253-0412
Huntington Mid Corp America A	Growth	-9.7					5.75	1.7	800 253-0412
Huntington Mid Corp America B	Growth	-10.2					0	2.2	800 253-0412
Huntington Mid Corp America Tr	Growth	-9.5					0	1.45	800 253-0412
Huntington New Economy A	Technology	-7.4					5.75	2.3	800 253-0412
Huntington New Economy B	Technology	-7.9					0	2.8	800 253-0412
Huntington New Economy Tr	Technology	-7.2					0	2.05	800 253-0412
Huntington Rotating Markets A	Growth	-12.5					1.5	2.26	800 253-0412
Huntington Rotating Markets Tr	Growth	-12.3					0	2.01	800 253-0412
Huntington Situs Small Cap B	Small Co						0		800 253-0412
Huntington Situs Small Cap Tr	Small Co						0		800 253-0412
Hussman Strategic Growth	Growth	7.5					0	1.42	800 487-7626
ICAP Discretionary Equity	Growth/Inc	-14.3	-4.32	-0.61	3	2	0	0.8	888 221-4227
ICAP Equity	Growth/Inc	-14.3	-3.72	0.01	2	2	0	0.8	888 221-4227
ICAP Euro Select Equity	European	-11.8	-6.75	-2.97	3	3	0	0.95	888 221-4227
ICAP Select Equity	Growth	-11.6	-3.64	2.97	2	2	0	0.8	888 221-4227
ICM-Isabelle Sm Cap Value Inst	Small Co	-21.9	-1.96	2.39	3	4	0	1.49	800 472-6114
ICM-Isabelle Sm Cap Value Inv	Small Co	-22.1	-2.31	2.1	3	4	0	1.74	800 472-6114
ICON Asia Region	Pacific	-6.2	-15.6	-3.81	3	2	0	1.66	800 764-0442
ICON Consumer Discretionary	Other	-22.5	2.5	0.17	3	4	0	1.29	800 764-0442
ICON Covered Call C	Other						0		800 764-0442
ICON Covered Call I	Other						0		800 764-0442
ICON Energy	Energy/Res	-4.9	7.29	11.13	1	4	0	1.35	800 764-0442
ICON Equity Income C	Income						0		800 764-0442
ICON Equity Income I	Income						0		800 764-0442
ICON Financial	Financial	-9.2	9.36	5.42	3	3	0	1.36	800 764-0442
ICON Healthcare	Health	-7.4	6.07	8	2	3	0	1.39	800 764-0442
ICON Industrials	Other	-25.5	-4.25	-4.62	3	3	0	1.3	800 764-0442
ICON Information Technology	Technology	-21.1	-15.58	13.4	4	5	0	1.31	800 764-0442
ICON Leisure & Consumer Staple	Other	-16.5	10.01	8.18	3	3	0	1.34	800 764-0442
ICON Long/Short C	Other						0		800 764-0442
ICON Long/Short I	Other						0		800 764-0442
ICON Materials	Other	-20.5	-4.12	-4.05	3	3	0	1.36	800 764-0442
ICON North Europe Region	European	-0.2	-10.55	-4.29	4	3	0	1.72	800 764-0442
ICON South Europe Region	European	-9	-5.2	-5.79	3	3	0	2.14	800 764-0442

Stock Fund Name	Objective	Annualized Return for			Rank		Max Load	Expense Ratio	Toll-Free/(Toll) Telephone
		1 Year	3 Years	5 Years	Overall	Risk			
ICON Telecommunications & Utilities	Utilities	-9.3	-7.04	0.81	3	2	0	1.5	800 764-0442
IDEX Alger Aggressive Growth A	Agg Growth	-11.6	-19.98	-1.43	4	4	5.5	1.55	888 233-4339
IDEX Alger Aggressive Growth B	Agg Growth	-12.4	-20.69	-2.14	4	4	0	2.2	888 233-4339
IDEX Alger Aggressive Growth C	Agg Growth	-12.4	-20.69		5	4	0	2.2	888 233-4339
IDEX Alger Aggressive Growth L	Agg Growth						0		888 233-4339
IDEX Alger Aggressive Growth M	Agg Growth	-12.3	-20.6	-2.02	4	4	1	2.1	888 233-4339
IDEX American Century Inc&Gr A	Growth/Inc	-8.7	-7.87			2	5.5	1.74	888 233-4339
IDEX American Century Inc&Gr B	Growth/Inc	-9.5	-8.51			2	0	2.39	888 233-4339
IDEX American Century Inc&Gr C	Growth/Inc	-9.5	-8.51			2	0	2.39	888 233-4339
IDEX American Century Inc&Gr L	Growth/Inc						0		888 233-4339
IDEX American Century Inc&Gr M	Growth/Inc	-9.3	-8.41			2	1	2.29	888 233-4339
IDEX American Century Intl A	Global	-16.5	-17.28	-7.7		3	5.5	1.76	888 233-4339
IDEX American Century Intl B	Global	-17.2	-17.92	-8.32		3	0	2.41	888 233-4339
IDEX American Century Intl C	Global	-17.1	-17.92			3	0	2.41	888 233-4339
IDEX American Century Intl L	Global						0		888 233-4339
IDEX American Century Intl M	Global	-17.1	-17.89	-8.27		3	1	2.31	888 233-4339
IDEX Asset Allocation-Conserv Pt A	AssetAlloc	2.5					5.5	0.45	888 233-4339
IDEX Asset Allocation-Conserv Pt B	AssetAlloc	1.8					0	1.09	888 233-4339
IDEX Asset Allocation-Conserv Pt C	AssetAlloc	1.8					0	1.09	888 233-4339
IDEX Asset Allocation-Conserv Pt L	AssetAlloc						0		888 233-4339
IDEX Asset Allocation-Conserv Pt M	AssetAlloc	1.9					1	0.99	888 233-4339
IDEX Asset Allocation-Growth Pt A	AssetAlloc	-10.2					5.5	0.45	888 233-4339
IDEX Asset Allocation-Growth Pt B	AssetAlloc	-10.9					0	1.1	888 233-4339
IDEX Asset Allocation-Growth Pt C	AssetAlloc	-10.9					0	1.1	888 233-4339
IDEX Asset Allocation-Growth Pt L	AssetAlloc						0		888 233-4339
IDEX Asset Allocation-Growth Pt M	AssetAlloc	-10.8					1	1	888 233-4339
IDEX Asset Allocation-Mod Gr Pt A	AssetAlloc	-12.2					5.5	0.44	888 233-4339
IDEX Asset Allocation-Mod Gr Pt B	AssetAlloc	-6.6					0	1.09	888 233-4339
IDEX Asset Allocation-Mod Gr Pt C	AssetAlloc	-6.6					0	1.09	888 233-4339
IDEX Asset Allocation-Mod Gr Pt L	AssetAlloc						0		888 233-4339
IDEX Asset Allocation-Mod Gr Pt M	AssetAlloc	-6.4					1	0.99	888 233-4339
IDEX Asset Allocation-Mod Pt A	AssetAlloc	-1.8					5.5	0.44	888 233-4339
IDEX Asset Allocation-Mod Pt B	AssetAlloc	-2.6					0	1.09	888 233-4339
IDEX Asset Allocation-Mod Pt C	AssetAlloc	-2.6					0	1.09	888 233-4339
IDEX Asset Allocation-Mod Pt L	AssetAlloc						0		888 233-4339
IDEX Asset Allocation-Mod Pt M	AssetAlloc	-2.5					1	0.99	888 233-4339
IDEX Great Companies America A	Growth	-4.1					5.5	1.55	888 233-4339
IDEX Great Companies America B	Growth	-4.9					0	2.2	888 233-4339
IDEX Great Companies America C	Growth	-4.9					0	2.2	888 233-4339
IDEX Great Companies America L	Growth						0		888 233-4339
IDEX Great Companies America M	Growth	-4.8					1	2.1	888 233-4339
IDEX Great Companies Global II A	Global	-7					5.5	1.55	888 233-4339
IDEX Great Companies Global II B	Global	-7.7					0	2.2	888 233-4339
IDEX Great Companies Global II C	Global	-7.7					0	2.2	888 233-4339
IDEX Great Companies Global II L	Global						0		888 233-4339
IDEX Great Companies Global II M	Global	-7.6					1	2.1	888 233-4339
IDEX Great Companies Tech A	Technology	-9.1					5.5	1.55	888 233-4339
IDEX Great Companies Tech B	Technology	-10.1					0	2.2	888 233-4339
IDEX Great Companies Tech C	Technology	-10.1					0	2.2	888 233-4339
IDEX Great Companies Tech L	Technology						0		888 233-4339
IDEX Great Companies Tech M	Technology	-9.8					1	2.1	888 233-4339
IDEX Isabelle Small Cap Value A	Small Co	-14.6					5.5	1.84	888 233-4339
IDEX Isabelle Small Cap Value B	Small Co	-15.2					0	2.49	888 233-4339
IDEX Isabelle Small Cap Value C	Small Co	-15.2					0	2.49	888 233-4339
IDEX Isabelle Small Cap Value L	Small Co						0		888 233-4339
IDEX Isabelle Small Cap Value M	Small Co	-15.2					1	2.39	888 233-4339
IDEX Janus Balanced A	Balanced	-1.1	-2.7	5.73	2	1	5.5	1.67	888 233-4339
IDEX Janus Balanced B	Balanced	-1.7	-3.29	5.09	2	1	0	2.32	888 233-4339

Stock Fund Name	Objective	Annualized Return for			Rank		Max Load	Expense Ratio	Toll-Free/(Toll) Telephone
		1 Year	3 Years	5 Years	Overall	Risk			
IDEX Janus Balanced C	Balanced	-1.7	-3.29	1		1	0	2.32	888 233-4339
IDEX Janus Balanced L	Balanced						0		888 233-4339
IDEX Janus Balanced M	Balanced	-1.5	-3.16	5.21	2	1	1	2.22	888 233-4339
IDEX Janus Global A	Global	-17.8	-20.8	-4.46	5	3	5.5	1.64	888 233-4339
IDEX Janus Global B	Global	-18.5	-21.48	-5.16	5	3	0	2.29	888 233-4339
IDEX Janus Global C	Global	-18.5	-21.42		5	3	0	2.29	888 233-4339
IDEX Janus Global L	Global						0		888 233-4339
IDEX Janus Global M	Global	-18.4	-21.37	-5.04	5	3	1	2.19	888 233-4339
IDEX Janus Growth & Income A	Growth/Inc	-8.3					5.5	1.92	888 233-4339
IDEX Janus Growth & Income B	Growth/Inc	-9					0	2.57	888 233-4339
IDEX Janus Growth & Income C	Growth/Inc	-9					0	2.57	888 233-4339
IDEX Janus Growth & Income L	Growth/Inc						0		888 233-4339
IDEX Janus Growth & Income M	Growth/Inc	-9					1	2.47	888 233-4339
IDEX Janus Growth A	Growth	-6.2	-23.64	-2.77	3	5	5.5	1.39	888 233-4339
IDEX Janus Growth B	Growth	-7	-24.35	-3.49	3	5	0	2.04	888 233-4339
IDEX Janus Growth C	Growth	-7	-24.25		3	5	0	2.04	888 233-4339
IDEX Janus Growth L	Growth						0		888 233-4339
IDEX Janus Growth M	Growth	-6.9	-24.23	-3.37	3	5	1	1.94	888 233-4339
IDEX Janus Growth T	Growth	-5.8	-23.26	-5.75	3	5	8.5	1.04	888 233-4339
IDEX Jennison Equity Opportunity A	Growth	-12.8	-8.13	-4.12	4	4	5.5	1.55	888 233-4339
IDEX Jennison Equity Opportunity B	Growth	-13.5	-8.84	-4.79	3	4	0	2.2	888 233-4339
IDEX Jennison Equity Opportunity C	Growth	-13.5	-8.84		4	4	0	2.2	888 233-4339
IDEX Jennison Equity Opportunity M	Growth	-13.4	-8.75	-4.7	3	4	1	2.1	888 233-4339
IDEX LKCM Strat Total Return A	Balanced	-1.9	-1.85	0.71	2	1	5.5	1.55	888 233-4339
IDEX LKCM Strategic Total Return B	Balanced	-2.4	-2.41	0.11	2	1	0	2.2	888 233-4339
IDEX LKCM Strategic Total Return C	Balanced	-2.4	-2.41		2	1	0	2.2	888 233-4339
IDEX LKCM Strategic Total Return L	Income						0		888 233-4339
IDEX LKCM Strategic Total Return M	Balanced	-2.3	-2.29	0.23	2	1	1	2.1	888 233-4339
IDEX Marsico Growth A	Growth	-10.7	-13.16		4	3	5.5	1.65	888 233-4339
IDEX Marsico Growth B	Growth	-11.6	-13.86		5	3	0	2.2	888 233-4339
IDEX Marsico Growth C	Growth	-11.6	-13.86		4	3	0	2.2	888 233-4339
IDEX Marsico Growth L	Growth						0		888 233-4339
IDEX Marsico Growth M	Growth	-11.4	-13.74		5	3	1	2.1	888 233-4339
IDEX PBHG Mid Cap Growth A	Growth	-14.5	-24.35		5	5	5.5	1.6	888 233-4339
IDEX PBHG Mid Cap Growth B	Growth	-15.3	-25.03		5	5	0	2.25	888 233-4339
IDEX PBHG Mid Cap Growth C	Growth	-15.3	-25.03		5	5	0	2.25	888 233-4339
IDEX PBHG Mid Cap Growth L	Growth						0		888 233-4339
IDEX PBHG Mid Cap Growth M	Growth	-15.1	-24.94		5	5	1	2.15	888 233-4339
IDEX Protected Principal Stock A	Growth/Inc						5.5		888 233-4339
IDEX Protected Principal Stock B	Growth/Inc						0		888 233-4339
IDEX Protected Principal Stock C	Growth/Inc						0		888 233-4339
IDEX Protected Principal Stock M	Growth/Inc						1		888 233-4339
IDEX Salomon All Cap A	Growth	-10.5	-3.54		3	4	5.5	1.55	888 233-4339
IDEX Salomon All Cap B	Growth	-11.3	-4.2		3	4	0	2.2	888 233-4339
IDEX Salomon All Cap C	Growth	-11.3	-4.2		3	4	0	2.2	888 233-4339
IDEX Salomon All Cap L	Growth						0		888 233-4339
IDEX Salomon All Cap M	Growth	-11.1	-4.07		3	4	1	2.1	888 233-4339
IDEX Salomon Investors Value A	Growth/Inc	-10.8	-1.47	-0.94	2	3	5.5	1.55	888 233-4339
IDEX Salomon Investors Value B	Growth/Inc	-11.5	-2.1	-1.59	3	3	0	2.2	888 233-4339
IDEX Salomon Investors Value C	Growth/Inc	-11.5	-2.1		2	3	0	2.2	888 233-4339
IDEX Salomon Investors Value L	Growth						0		888 233-4339
IDEX Salomon Investors Value M	Growth/Inc	-11.4	-2.02	-1.48	3	3	1	2.1	888 233-4339
IDEX T.Rowe Price Health Sci A	Health	2.6					5.5	1.94	888 233-4339
IDEX T.Rowe Price Health Sci B	Health	1.8					0	2.59	888 233-4339
IDEX T.Rowe Price Health Sci C	Health	1.8					0	2.59	888 233-4339
IDEX T.Rowe Price Health Sci M	Health	1.9					1	2.49	888 233-4339
IDEX T.Rowe Price Small Cap A	Small Co	-11.3	-10.82		3	4	5.5	1.6	888 233-4339
IDEX T.Rowe Price Small Cap B	Small Co	-12.1	-11.51		3	4	0	2.25	888 233-4339

Stock Fund Name	Objective	Annualized Return for			Rank		Max Load	Expense Ratio	Toll-Free/(Toll) Telephone
		1 Year	3 Years	5 Years	Overall	Risk			
IDEX T.Rowe Price Small Cap C	Small Co	-12.1	-11.51		4	4	0	2.25	888 233-4339
IDEX T.Rowe Price Small Cap L	Small Co						0		888 233-4339
IDEX T.Rowe Price Small Cap M	Small Co	-12	-11.42		3	4	1	2.15	888 233-4339
IDEX T.Rowe Price Tax-Eff Growth A	Income	-6.1	-3.6		2	2	5.5	1.6	888 233-4339
IDEX T.Rowe Price Tax-Eff Growth B	Income	-6.8	-4.25		2	2	0	2.25	888 233-4339
IDEX T.Rowe Price Tax-Eff Growth C	Income	-6.8	-4.25		2	2	0	2.25	888 233-4339
IDEX T.Rowe Price Tax-Eff Growth L	Growth/Inc						0		888 233-4339
IDEX T.Rowe Price Tax-Eff Growth M	Income	-6.6	-4.16		2	3	1	2.15	888 233-4339
IDEX Transamerica Convertible Sec A	Converts	5.8					4.75	1.74	888 233-4339
IDEX Transamerica Convertible Sec B	Converts	5.1					0	2.39	888 233-4339
IDEX Transamerica Convertible Sec C	Converts	5.1					0	2.39	888 233-4339
IDEX Transamerica Convertible Sec L	Converts						0		888 233-4339
IDEX Transamerica Convertible Sec M	Converts	5.3					1	2.29	888 233-4339
IDEX Transamerica Equity A	Growth	-6.6	-14.08		3	4	5.5	1.65	888 233-4339
IDEX Transamerica Equity B	Growth	-7.3	-14.71		3	4	0	2.2	888 233-4339
IDEX Transamerica Equity C	Growth	-7.3	-14.71		3	4	0	2.2	888 233-4339
IDEX Transamerica Equity L	Growth						0		888 233-4339
IDEX Transamerica Equity M	Growth	-7.3	-14.64		3	4	1	2.1	888 233-4339
IDEX Transamerica Growth Opp A	Small Co	-9.8	-12.18		3	5	5.5	1.6	888 233-4339
IDEX Transamerica Growth Opp B	Small Co	-10.3	-12.81		3	5	0	2.25	888 233-4339
IDEX Transamerica Growth Opp C	Small Co	-10.3	-12.81		3	5	0	2.25	888 233-4339
IDEX Transamerica Growth Opp L	Small Co						0		888 233-4339
IDEX Transamerica Growth Opp M	Small Co	-10.3	-12.74		3	5	1	2.15	888 233-4339
IDEX Transamerica Value Balanced A	Balanced	-3.5	1.03	0.32	1	2	5.5	1.57	888 233-4339
IDEX Transamerica Value Balanced B	Balanced	-4.2	0.34	-0.34	1	2	0	2.22	888 233-4339
IDEX Transamerica Value Balanced C	Balanced	-4.1	0.38		1	2	0	2.2	888 233-4339
IDEX Transamerica Value Balanced L	AssetAlloc						0		888 233-4339
IDEX Transamerica Value Balanced M	Balanced	-4.2	0.4	-0.27	1	2	1	2.12	888 233-4339
IMS Capital Value	Growth	7.8					0	1.59	800 298-1995
ING Balanced A	Balanced	-0.6	-3.08	1.68	2	1	5.75	1.39	877 463-6464
ING Balanced B	Balanced	-1.4	-3.81		1	1	0	2.14	877 463-6464
ING Balanced C	Balanced	-1.5	-3.83		2	1	0	2.14	877 463-6464
ING Balanced I	Balanced	-0.9	-3	1.93	2	1	0	1.14	877 463-6464
ING Classic Principl Protect I A	AssetAlloc	2.9	0.91		1	1	4.75	1.5	877 463-6464
ING Classic Principl Protect I B	AssetAlloc	2.2	0.14		1	1	0	2.25	877 463-6464
ING Classic Principl Protect II A	AssetAlloc	4.3	2.66		1	1	4.75	1.36	877 463-6464
ING Classic Principl Protect III A	AssetAlloc	5.3					4.75	1.5	877 463-6464
ING Classic Principl Protect III B	AssetAlloc	4.6	0.65		1	1	0	2.25	877 463-6464
ING Classic Principl Protect IV A	Growth	7					4.75	1.5	877 463-6464
ING Classic Principl Protect IV B	Growth	6.2					0	2.25	877 463-6464
ING Convertible A	Converts	7.8	-11.92	2.68	3	4	5.75	1.42	877 463-6464
ING Convertible B	Converts	7.2	-12.61	1.98	3	4	0	2.07	877 463-6464
ING Convertible C	Converts	7.2	-6.03	6.53	2	2	0	2.07	877 463-6464
ING Convertible Q	Converts	8.1	-11.61	3.04	3	4	0	1.15	877 463-6464
ING Corp Leaders Trust A	Growth/Inc	-5.8	-2.2	0.3	3	2	5.75	0.65	877 463-6464
ING Emerging Countries A	Foreign	-11.7	-10.82	-3.2	3	4	5.75	2.32	877 463-6464
ING Emerging Countries B	Foreign	-11.9					0	2.9	877 463-6464
ING Emerging Countries C	Foreign	-12.9	-11.59	-3.85	4	4	0	2.9	877 463-6464
ING Emerging Countries Q	Foreign	-12.2	-10.74	-2.95	3	4	0	1.97	877 463-6464
ING Equity & Bond A	Balanced	-0.7	-1.36	2.22	2	1	5.75	1.32	877 463-6464
ING Equity & Bond B	Balanced	-1.3	-2.16	1.51	2	1	0	1.97	877 463-6464
ING Equity & Bond C	Balanced	-1.3	-2.62	1.17	2	1	0	1.97	877 463-6464
ING Equity & Bond Q	Balanced	-0.6	-1.56	2.24	2	1	0	1.25	877 463-6464
ING Financial Services A	Financial	-7	10.58	-2.83	3	3	5.75	1.42	877 463-6464
ING Financial Services B	Financial	-7.7	9.75	-0.17	3	3	0	2.17	877 463-6464
ING Growth & Income A	Growth/Inc	-13.5	-15.25	-6.45	4	2	5.75	1.7	877 463-6464
ING Growth & Income B	Growth/Inc	-14.2	-15.93		5	2	0	2.45	877 463-6464
ING Growth & Income C	Growth/Inc	-14.2	-14.57		5	3	0	2.45	877 463-6464

Stock Fund Name	Objective	Annualized Return for			Rank		Max Load	Expense Ratio	Toll-Free/(Toll) Telephone
		1 Year	3 Years	5 Years	Overall	Risk			
ING Growth & Income I	Growth/Inc	-13.3	-15.03	-6.21	5	2	0	1.45	877 463-6464
ING Growth + Value A	Growth	-20.9	-27.5	-3.79	5	5	5.75	1.77	877 463-6464
ING Growth + Value B	Growth	-21.4	28.01	4.49	5	5	0	2.47	877 463-6464
ING Growth + Value C	Growth	-21.4	-28.03	-4.5	5	5	0	2.47	877 463-6464
ING Growth A	Growth	-11.1	-20	-4.62	4	4	5.75	1.21	877 463-6464
ING Growth B	Growth	-11.9	-20.62		5	3	0	1.96	877 463-6464
ING Growth C	Growth	-11.9	-20.66		4	3	0	1.96	877 463-6464
ING Growth I	Growth	-11	-19.82	-4.4	4	3	0	0.96	877 463-6464
ING Growth Opportunities A	Growth	-16	-28.1	-4.83	4	4	5.75	1.8	877 463-6464
ING Growth Opportunities B	Growth	-16.6	-28.6	-5.51	4	4	0	2.5	877 463-6464
ING Growth Opportunities C	Growth	-16.6	-28.6	-5.45	4	4	0	2.5	877 463-6464
ING Growth Opportunities T	Growth	-16.6	-28.55	-5.48	4	4	0	2.45	877 463-6464
ING Index Plus Large Cap A	Growth	-9.5					3	0.91	877 463-6464
ING Index Plus Large Cap B	Growth	-10.1	-12.71		3	3	0	1.66	877 463-6464
ING Index Plus Large Cap C	Growth	-9.9	-12.48		4	3	0	1.41	877 463-6464
ING Index Plus Large Cap I	Growth	-9.2					0	0.66	877 463-6464
ING Index Plus Mid Cap A	Growth	-9.1	0.5	5.24	2	3	3	1	877 463-6464
ING Index Plus Mid Cap B	Growth	-9.8	-0.27		3	3	0	1.75	877 463-6464
ING Index Plus Mid Cap C	Growth	-9.6	-0.02		3	3	0	1.5	877 463-6464
ING Index Plus Mid Cap I	Growth	-8.9	0.77	5.51	2	3	0	0.2	877 463-6464
ING Index Plus Protection A	Growth	6.8					4.75	1.5	877 463-6464
ING Index Plus Protection B	Growth	5.9					0	2.25	877 463-6464
ING Index Plus Small Cap A	Small Co	-9.6	3.35	1.73	3	3	3	1	877 463-6464
ING Index Plus Small Cap B	Small Co	-10.4	2.56		2	3	0	1.75	877 463-6464
ING Index Plus Small Cap C	Small Co	-10.1	2.83		3	3	0	1.5	877 463-6464
ING Index Plus Small Cap I	Small Co	-9.4	3.64	2	3	3	0	0.75	877 463-6464
ING International A	Foreign	-15.6	-12.96	-0.66	4	2	5.75	2.44	877 463-6464
ING International Growth A	Foreign	-21.2	-23.96	-9.05	5	3	5.75	1.6	877 463-6464
ING International Growth B	Foreign	-21.7	-24.48		5	3	0	2.35	877 463-6464
ING International Growth C	Foreign	-21.6	-24.44		5	3	0	2.35	877 463-6464
ING International Growth I	Foreign	-21.4	-23.85	-8.83	5	3	0	1.35	877 463-6464
ING International Small Cap Gr A	Foreign	-14.6	-16.76	3.93	4	3	5.75	1.94	877 463-6464
ING International Small Cap Gr B	Foreign	-15.2	-19.32	1.72	4	3	0	2.57	877 463-6464
ING International Small Cap Gr C	Foreign	-15.2	-19.35	1.69	3	3	0	2.57	877 463-6464
ING International Small Cap Gr Q	Foreign	-14.3	-18.75	2.49	4	3	0	1.59	877 463-6464
ING International Value A	Foreign	-16.8	-6.63	3.45	3	3	5.75	1.67	877 463-6464
ING International Value B	Foreign	-19	-7.87	1.46	3	3	0	2.37	877 463-6464
ING International Value C	Foreign	-19.1	-7.88	1.44	3	3	0	2.37	877 463-6464
ING Large Cap Gr A	Growth	-13.6	-28.46	-1.12	4	4	5.75	1.36	877 463-6464
ING Large Cap Gr B	Growth	-14.1	-28.96	-1.78	5	4	0	2.01	877 463-6464
ING Large Cap Gr C	Growth	-14.3	-29.01	-1.85	4	4	0	2.01	877 463-6464
ING Large Cap Gr Q	Growth	-13.2	-22.8	-0.93	4	5	0	1.26	877 463-6464
ING Large Company Value A	Growth/Inc	-15.3	-11.92	-2.91	4	3	5.75	0.88	877 463-6464
ING MagnaCap A	Growth	-12.5	-9.52	-2.49	3	3	5.75	1.34	877 463-6464
ING MagnaCap B	Growth	-13	-13.88	-5.59	4	3	0	2.01	877 463-6464
ING MagnaCap M	Growth	-12.8	-13.59	-5.29	4	3	3.5	1.79	877 463-6464
ING Mid Cap Opportunities A	Growth	-8.9	-19.01		3	4	5.75	1.94	877 463-6464
ING Mid Cap Opportunities B	Growth	-9.5	-19.53		3	4	0	2.64	877 463-6464
ING Mid Cap Opportunities C	Growth	-9.5	-19.55		3	4	0	2.64	877 463-6464
ING Precious Metals A	Prec Metal	-6.5	27.33	9.81	2	5	5.75	1.96	877 463-6464
ING Research Enhanced Idx A	Foreign	-9.7	-12.46		4	3	5.75	1.33	877 463-6464
ING Research Enhanced Idx B	Foreign	-10.4	-12.83		4	3	0	2.03	877 463-6464
ING Research Enhanced Idx C	Foreign	-10.4	-12.83		4	3	0	2.03	877 463-6464
ING Research Enhanced Idx I	Foreign	-9.4	-11.9		4	3	0	1	877 463-6464
ING Russia A	Foreign	25.9	29.42	16.5	1	5	5.75	2.16	877 463-6464
ING Senior Income A	Income	5.3					4.75	1.72	877 463-6464
ING Senior Income B	Income	4.7					0		877 463-6464
ING Senior Income C	Income	4.7					0		877 463-6464

Stock Fund Name	Objective	Annualized Return for			Rank		Max Load	Expense Ratio	Toll-Free/(Toll) Telephone
		1 Year	3 Years	5 Years	Overall	Risk			
ING Small Company A	Small Co	-12	-4.03	3.1	3	3	5.75	1.32	877 463-6464
ING Small Company B	Small Co	-12.6	-4.75		3	3	0	2.07	877 463-6464
ING Small Company C	Small Co	-12.8	-4.79		3	3	0	2.07	877 463-6464
ING Small Company I	Small Co	-11.7	-3.77	3.37	3	3	0	1.07	877 463-6464
ING SmallCap Opportunities A	Small Co	-24.5	-25.51	-1.32	5	5	5.75	1.86	877 463-6464
ING SmallCap Opportunities B	Small Co	-25	-26.03	-1.98	5	5	0	2.56	877 463-6464
ING SmallCap Opportunities C	Small Co	-25	-26.05	-2.02	5	5	0	2.56	877 463-6464
ING SmallCap Opportunities T	Small Co	-24.9	-25.96	-1.89	5	5	0	2.51	877 463-6464
ING Strategic Allocation Balanced A	AssetAlloc	-4.6					5.75	1.2	877 463-6464
ING Strategic Allocation Balanced B	AssetAlloc	-5.2	-4.08		2	1	0	1.95	877 463-6464
ING Strategic Allocation Balanced C	AssetAlloc	-5.3	-4.08		2	1	0	1.95	877 463-6464
ING Strategic Allocation Balanced I	AssetAlloc	-4.3	-3.12	-0.93	2	1	0	0.95	877 463-6464
ING Strategic Allocation Growth A	AssetAlloc	-8	-6.65	-2.68	3	2	5.75	0.65	877 463-6464
ING Strategic Allocation Growth B	AssetAlloc	-8.6	-7.33		3	2	0	0.65	877 463-6464
ING Strategic Allocation Growth C	AssetAlloc	-8.8	-7.33		3	2	0	0.65	877 463-6464
ING Strategic Allocation Growth I	AssetAlloc	-7.7	-6.4	-2.35	3	2	0	0.65	877 463-6464
ING Strategic Allocation Income A	AssetAlloc	-1.1	0.28	1.55	2	1	5.75	0.65	877 463-6464
ING Strategic Allocation Income B	AssetAlloc	-1.8	-0.41		1	1	0	0.65	877 463-6464
ING Strategic Allocation Income C	AssetAlloc	-1.8	-0.61		2	1	0	0.65	877 463-6464
ING Strategic Allocation Income I	AssetAlloc	-0.9	0.56	1.83	2	1	0	0.65	877 463-6464
ING Tax Efficient Eq A	Growth	-13.2	-11.85		3	3	5.75	1.4	877 463-6464
ING Tax Efficient Eq B	Growth	-13.8	-12.49		4	3	0	2.05	877 463-6464
ING Tax Efficient Eq C	Growth	-13.9	-12.5		4	3	0	2.05	877 463-6464
ING Value Opportunity A	Growth	-15.9	-8.55	-0.27	3	2	5.75	1.6	877 463-6464
ING Value Opportunity B	Growth	-16.6	-9.24		3	2	0	3.1	877 463-6464
ING Value Opportunity C	Growth	-16.6	-9.24		2	2	0	3.1	877 463-6464
ING Value Opportunity I	Growth	-15.7	-8.33	-0.04	3	2	0	1.1	877 463-6464
ING Worldwide Growth A	Global	-15.5	-21.16	-1.61	5	3	5.75	1.85	877 463-6464
ING Worldwide Growth B	Global	-16.1	-22.82	-3.12	4	3	0	2.5	877 463-6464
ING Worldwide Growth C	Global	-16	-22.8	-3.1	4	3	0	2.5	877 463-6464
ING Worldwide Growth Q	Global	-15.2	-22.03	-2.18	5	3	0	1.51	877 463-6464
INVESCO Advantage A	Agg Growth	-11.6					5.5	2.34	800 525-8085
INVESCO Advantage B	Agg Growth	-11.6					0	2.73	800 525-8085
INVESCO Advantage C	Agg Growth	-11.8					0	2.86	800 525-8085
INVESCO Advantage Globl Hlth&Sci A	Health	-3.5	-4.08	1.61	3	4	5.5	2.33	800 525-8085
INVESCO Advantage Globl Hlth&Sci B	Health	-4.9					0	3.43	800 525-8085
INVESCO Advantage Globl Hlth&Sci C	Health	-5.4					0	3.52	800 525-8085
INVESCO Balanced A	Balanced	-4.9					5.5	1.04	800 525-8085
INVESCO Balanced B	Balanced	-5.5					0	1.77	800 525-8085
INVESCO Balanced C	Balanced	-5.5	-7.7			2	0	2	800 525-8085
INVESCO Balanced Instl	Balanced	-4.5					0	0.96	800 525-8085
INVESCO Balanced Inv	Balanced	-4.8	-7	-0.23	3	2	0	1.22	800 525-8085
INVESCO Balanced K	Balanced	-5					0	1.39	800 525-8085
INVESCO Core Equity A	Income	-9.1					5.5	0.99	800 525-8085
INVESCO Core Equity B	Income	-10.1					0	1.62	800 525-8085
INVESCO Core Equity C	Income	-10.2	-8.32		3	2	0	1.9	800 525-8085
INVESCO Core Equity Inv	Income	-9.2	-7.49	-0.82	3	2	0	1.02	800 525-8085
INVESCO Core Equity K	Income	-10.1					0	1.18	800 525-8085
INVESCO Dynamics A	Agg Growth	-10.2					5.5	1.11	800 525-8085
INVESCO Dynamics B	Agg Growth	-10.8					0	2.09	800 525-8085
INVESCO Dynamics C	Agg Growth	-11.1	-21.89		3	5	0	1.96	800 525-8085
INVESCO Dynamics Instl	Agg Growth	-9.8	-20.92			5	0	0.84	800 525-8085
INVESCO Dynamics Inv	Agg Growth	-10.2	-21.19	-2.33	3	5	0	1.21	800 525-8085
INVESCO Dynamics K	Agg Growth	-10.4					0	1.36	800 525-8085
INVESCO Energy A	Energy/Res	-2.9					5.5	1.63	800 525-8085
INVESCO Energy B	Energy/Res	-3.8					0	2.28	800 525-8085
INVESCO Energy C	Energy/Res	-3.8	0.02		2	4	0	2.27	800 525-8085
INVESCO Energy Inv	Energy/Res	-3.2	0.7	8.34	2	4	0	1.53	800 525-8085

Stock Fund Name	Objective	Annualized Return for			Rank		Max Load	Expense Ratio	Toll-Free/(Toll) Telephone
		1 Year	3 Years	5 Years	Overall	Risk			
INVESCO Energy K	Energy/Res	-3					0	11.62	800 525-8085
INVESCO European A	European	-17.3					5.5	1.35	800 525-8085
INVESCO European B	European	-18.3					0	2.39	800 525-8085
INVESCO European C	European	-19.4	-29.75		5	4	0	2.64	800 525-8085
INVESCO European Inv	European	-17.7	-28.14	-12.68	5	4	0	1.74	800 525-8085
INVESCO European K	European	-17.9					0	2.12	800 525-8085
INVESCO Financial Services A	Financial	-6.8					5.5	1.37	800 525-8085
INVESCO Financial Services B	Financial	-7.5					0	2.02	800 525-8085
INVESCO Financial Services C	Financial	-7.9	0.2		3	3	0	2.07	800 525-8085
INVESCO Financial Services Inv	Financial	-6.9	0.98	1.66	3	3	0	1.27	800 525-8085
INVESCO Financial Services K	Financial	-7					0	1.63	800 525-8085
INVESCO Gold & Prec Met A	Prec Metal	-8.3					5.5	2.2	800 525-8085
INVESCO Gold & Prec Met B	Prec Metal	-8.6					0	2.85	800 525-8085
INVESCO Gold & Prec Met C	Prec Metal	-8.8	21.87		2	5	0	3.33	800 525-8085
INVESCO Gold & Prec Met Inv	Prec Metal	-8.3	19.94	3.91	2	4	0	2.1	800 525-8085
INVESCO Growth & Income A	Growth/Inc	-15.5					5.5	1.6	800 525-8085
INVESCO Growth & Income B	Growth/Inc	-16					0	2.3	800 525-8085
INVESCO Growth & Income C	Growth/Inc	-16.1	-27.08		5	5	0	2.25	800 525-8085
INVESCO Growth & Income Inv	Growth/Inc	-15.5	-26.53		5	5	0	1.5	800 525-8085
INVESCO Growth & Income K	Growth/Inc	-15.5					0	1.7	800 525-8085
INVESCO Growth A	Growth	-16.8					5.5	1.65	800 525-8085
INVESCO Growth B	Growth	-16.8					0	2.3	800 525-8085
INVESCO Growth C	Growth	-16.7	-34.96		5	5	0	3.03	800 525-8085
INVESCO Growth Inv	Growth	-15.8	-34.28	-14.93	5	5	0	1.55	800 525-8085
INVESCO Growth K	Growth	-15.7					0	2.32	800 525-8085
INVESCO Health Sciences A	Health	-7.5					5.5	1.41	800 525-8085
INVESCO Health Sciences B	Health	-8					0	2.06	800 525-8085
INVESCO Health Sciences C	Health	-8.8	-3		3	4	0	2.26	800 525-8085
INVESCO Health Sciences Inv	Health	-7.5	-1.9	2.12	3	4	0	1.31	800 525-8085
INVESCO Health Sciences K	Health	-8.1					0	1.71	800 525-8085
INVESCO Intl Blue Chip Value A	Foreign	-15.8					5.5	1.48	800 525-8085
INVESCO Intl Blue Chip Value B	Foreign	-16.3					0	2.6	800 525-8085
INVESCO Intl Blue Chip Value C	Foreign	-16.5	-10.25		4	3	0	2.75	800 525-8085
INVESCO Intl Blue Chip Value Inv	Foreign	-15.7	-11.94		3	3	0	1.99	800 525-8085
INVESCO Leisure A	Other	-7.3					5.5	1.5	800 525-8085
INVESCO Leisure B	Other	-8					0	2.15	800 525-8085
INVESCO Leisure C	Other	-8.3	-0.27		2	3	0	2.26	800 525-8085
INVESCO Leisure Inv	Other	-7.4	0.57	11.32	1	3	0	1.4	800 525-8085
INVESCO Leisure K	Other	-7.9					0	1.23	800 525-8085
INVESCO Mid-Cap Growth A	Growth	-8.5					5.5	1.65	800 525-8085
INVESCO Mid-Cap Growth B	Growth	-9.1					0	2.3	800 525-8085
INVESCO Mid-Cap Growth C	Growth	-9.5					0	2.3	800 525-8085
INVESCO Mid-Cap Growth Instl	Growth	-8.1	-5.83		2	4	0	1.3	800 525-8085
INVESCO Mid-Cap Growth Inv	Growth						0	2.54	800 525-8085
INVESCO Multi Sector A	Other						5.5	1.74	800 525-8085
INVESCO Multi Sector B	Other						0	2.46	800 525-8085
INVESCO Multi Sector C	Other						0	2.46	800 525-8085
INVESCO Real Estate Opp A	Real Est	5.2					5.5	2.35	800 525-8085
INVESCO Real Estate Opp B	Real Est	4.5					0	3	800 525-8085
INVESCO Real Estate Opp C	Real Est	3.9	9.71		1	2	0	2.37	800 525-8085
INVESCO Real Estate Opp Inv	Real Est	5.4	10.08	1.34	1	2	0	1.61	800 525-8085
INVESCO S&P 500 Instl	Growth	-9	-11.63	-1.5		3	0	0.35	800 525-8085
INVESCO S&P 500 Inv	Growth	-9.1	-12.02	-1.83	3	3	0	0.65	800 525-8085
INVESCO Small Company Growth A	Small Co	-12.6					5.5	1.24	800 525-8085
INVESCO Small Company Growth B	Small Co	-13.3					0	2.14	800 525-8085
INVESCO Small Company Growth C	Small Co	-14	-16.55		5	5	0	2.25	800 525-8085
INVESCO Small Company Growth Inv	Small Co	-12.5	-15.25	0.85	4	5	0	1.45	800 525-8085
INVESCO Small Company Growth K	Small Co	-12.7					0	1.17	800 525-8085

Stock Fund Name	Objective	Annualized Return for			Rank		Max Load	Expense Ratio	Toll-Free/(Toll) Telephone
		1 Year	3 Years	5 Years	Overall	Risk			
INVESCO Technology A	Technology	-17.3					5.5	1.47	800 525-8085
INVESCO Technology B	Technology	-18.1					0	2.12	800 525-8085
INVESCO Technology C	Technology	-18.3	-36.17		5	5	0	2.54	800 525-8085
INVESCO Technology Instl	Technology	-17	-35.1		4	5	0	0.74	800 525-8085
INVESCO Technology Inv	Technology	-17.8	-35.54	-5.04	4	5	0	1.37	800 525-8085
INVESCO Technology K	Technology	-17.9					0	1.28	800 525-8085
INVESCO Telecommunications A	Technology	-11.6					5.5	1.8	800 525-8085
INVESCO Telecommunications B	Technology	-11.9					0	2.45	800 525-8085
INVESCO Telecommunications C	Technology	-11.9	-42.39		4	5	0	2.6	800 525-8085
INVESCO Telecommunications Inv	Technology	-11	-41.81	-11.65	3	5	0	1.7	800 525-8085
INVESCO Telecommunications K	Technology	-11.3					0	2.21	800 525-8085
INVESCO Total Return A	AssetAlloc	-5					5.5	1.18	800 525-8085
INVESCO Total Return B	AssetAlloc	-5.5					0	1.86	800 525-8085
INVESCO Total Return C	AssetAlloc	-5.9	-4.76		2	1	0	2.59	800 525-8085
INVESCO Total Return Inv	AssetAlloc	-4.8	-3	-1.58	2	1	0	1.49	800 525-8085
INVESCO Utilities A	Utilities	-3.2					5.5	1.67	800 525-8085
INVESCO Utilities B	Utilities	-4					0	2.32	800 525-8085
INVESCO Utilities C	Utilities	-4.4	-17.82		3	3	0	2.04	800 525-8085
INVESCO Utilities Inv	Utilities	-3.2	-17.05	-4.41	3	3	0	1.3	800 525-8085
INVESCO Value Equity A	Growth/Inc	-9.9					5.5	1.39	800 525-8085
INVESCO Value Equity B	Growth/Inc	-10.4					0	1.95	800 525-8085
INVESCO Value Equity C	Growth/Inc	-10.6	-7.34		3	2	0	2.05	800 525-8085
INVESCO Value Equity Inv	Growth/Inc	-9.8	-6.59	-3.45	3	2	0	1.3	800 525-8085
IPO Plus Aftermarket Fund	Growth	-4.2	-33.03	-11.46	5	5	0	2.5	888 476-3863
IPS Millenium Fund	Growth	-17.4	-25.07	-0.11	5	5	0	1.15	800 249-6927
IPS New Frontier Fund	Agg Growth	-15.9					0	1.4	800 249-6927
ISI Strategy A	Growth	-2.5	-3.58	1.3	2	1	4.45	1.05	800 955-7175
Institutional Inv-Capital Apprec	Growth/Inc	-12.8					0	1.28	800 527-3713
Institutional Select S&P 500	Growth	-8.2	-10.93		3	3	0	0.15	800 266-5623
Integrity Fund of Funds	Growth/Inc	-8.9					0	1.6	800 276-1212
Ivy Developing Markets A	Foreign	-10.3	-7	-1.02	3	4	5.75	2.18	800 777-6472
Ivy Developing Markets B	Foreign	-11.1	-8.06	-1.96	3	4	0	2.98	800 777-6472
Ivy Developing Markets C	Foreign	-11.2	-8.1	-1.97	3	4	0	2.96	800 777-6472
Ivy European Opportunities A	European	-10.8	-12.75		3	4	5.75	2.11	800 777-6472
Ivy European Opportunities Adv	European	-10.8	-12.56		3	4	0	1.77	800 777-6472
Ivy European Opportunities B	European	-12	-13.58		4	4	0	2.87	800 777-6472
Ivy European Opportunities C	European	-11.9	-13.58		4	4	0	2.87	800 777-6472
Ivy Fund-Developing Markets Adv	Foreign	-10.2	-7.05	-0.85	3	4	0	1.84	800 777-6472
Ivy Fund-Global Sci/Tech A	Technology	-19.6	-43.03	-14.43	4	5	5.75	2.19	800 777-6472
Ivy Fund-Global Sci/Tech Adv	Technology	-19.2	-42.86	-14.3	4	5	0	2.02	800 777-6472
Ivy Fund-Global Sci/Tech B	Technology	-20.1	-43.43	-15.08	4	5	0	2.96	800 777-6472
Ivy Fund-Global Sci/Tech C	Technology	-20.2	-43.45	-15.06	4	5	0	3.03	800 777-6472
Ivy Fund-International Value A	Foreign	-15.2	-10.1	-4.75	4	3	5.75	1.77	800 777-6472
Ivy Fund-International Value Adv	Foreign	-16.2	-10.48	-4.94	4	3	0	1.51	800 777-6472
Ivy Fund-International Value B	Foreign	-17.2	-11.44	-5.94	4	3	0	2.5	800 777-6472
Ivy Fund-International Value C	Foreign	-17.3	-11.48	-5.94	4	3	0	2.5	800 777-6472
Ivy Fund-US Blue Chip Adv	Growth/Inc	-11.5	-12.82			3	0	1.22	800 777-6472
Ivy Fund-US Blue Chip B	Growth/Inc	-12.7	-13.83			3	0	2.31	800 777-6472
Ivy Fund-US Blue Chip C	Growth/Inc	-12.7	-13.9			3	0	2.38	800 777-6472
Ivy Global A	Global	-14.1	-14.51	-7.2	5	3	5.75	2.13	800 777-6472
Ivy Global Adv	Global	-13.8	-14.67	-7.21	5	3	0	1.99	800 777-6472
Ivy Global B	Global	-15.1	-15.67	-8.25	4	3	0	3.1	800 777-6472
Ivy Global C	Global	-15.6	-15.97	-8.58	4	3	0	3.17	800 777-6472
Ivy Global Natural Resources A	Energy/Res	-14.2	11.58	7.87	2	4	5.75	2.22	800 777-6472
Ivy Global Natural Resources B	Energy/Res	-15.3	10.72	7.08	1	4	0	2.94	800 777-6472
Ivy Global Natural Resources C	Energy/Res	-15.3	10.68	6.78	2	4	0	2.92	800 777-6472
Ivy Growth A	Growth	-13.6	-21.57	-9.3	5	4	5.75	1.62	800 777-6472
Ivy Growth Adv	Growth	-13.4	-21.64	-9.33	5	4	0	1.58	800 777-6472

Stock Fund Name	Objective	Annualized Return for			Rank		Max Load	Expense Ratio	Toll-Free/(Toll) Telephone
		1 Year	3 Years	5 Years	Overall	Risk			
Ivy Growth B	Growth	-14.4	-22.37	-10.19	5	4	0	2.61	800 777-6472
Ivy Growth C	Growth	-14.6	-22.46	-10.32	5	4	0	2.82	800 777-6472
Ivy International A	Foreign	-17.4	-16.67	-8.93	4	3	5.75	1.85	800 777-6472
Ivy International B	Foreign	-18.6	-17.6	-9.83	5	3	0	2.77	800 777-6472
Ivy International C	Foreign	-18.6	-17.6	-9.83	5	3	0	2.77	800 777-6472
Ivy International I	Foreign	-17.5	-16.53	-12.01	5	3	0	1.52	800 777-6472
Ivy International Sm Co A	Foreign	-21.8	-20.37	-6.94	4	3	5.75	2.24	800 777-6472
Ivy International Sm Co B	Foreign	-22.4	-20.94	-7.62	4	3	0	2.94	800 777-6472
Ivy International Sm Co C	Foreign	-22.4	-20.92	-7.59	4	3	0	2.95	800 777-6472
Ivy Pacific Opportunities A	Pacific	-14.9	-10.01	-0.11	4	3	5.75	2.2	800 777-6472
Ivy Pacific Opportunities Adv	Pacific	-15	-10.68	-0.63	4	3	0	2.06	800 777-6472
Ivy Pacific Opportunities B	Pacific	-16	-11.08	-1.12	4	3	0	2.96	800 777-6472
Ivy Pacific Opportunities C	Pacific	-15.9	-10.98	-1.07	4	3	0	2.94	800 777-6472
Ivy US Blue Chip A	Growth/Inc	-11.8	-13.16		5	3	5.75	1.57	800 777-6472
Ivy US Emerging Growth A	Small Co	-14	-27.19	-8.97	5	5	5.75	2.11	800 777-6472
Ivy US Emerging Growth Adv	Small Co	-13.6	-27.01	-8.73	5	5	0	1.94	800 777-6472
Ivy US Emerging Growth B	Small Co	-14.7	-27.8	-9.69	4	5	0	2.96	800 777-6472
Ivy US Emerging Growth C	Small Co	-14.6	-27.78	-9.66	4	5	0	2.94	800 777-6472
J Hancock 500 Index Fund R	Growth	-8.7	-11.36			3	0		800 257-3336
J Hancock Balanced A	Balanced	-6.8	-5.13	-1.63	2	1	5	1.31	800 257-3336
J Hancock Balanced B	Balanced	-7.4	-5.82	-2.25	2	1	0	2.01	800 257-3336
J Hancock Balanced C	Balanced	-7.4	-5.79		2	1	1	2.01	800 257-3336
J Hancock Balanced I	Balanced	-6.4					0	0.76	800 257-3336
J Hancock Biotechnology A	Health	5.9					5	1.6	800 257-3336
J Hancock Biotechnology B	Health	5.2					0	2.29	800 257-3336
J Hancock Biotechnology C	Health	5.2					1	2.29	800 257-3336
J Hancock Classic Value A	Growth	-2.7	14.31		1	3	5	1.25	800 257-3336
J Hancock Classic Value B	Growth						0	2.1	800 257-3336
J Hancock Classic Value C	Growth						0	2.1	800 257-3336
J Hancock Classic Value I	Growth						0	0.77	800 257-3336
J Hancock Core Equity A	Growth	-12.8	-11.46	-3.02	4	3	5	1.41	800 257-3336
J Hancock Core Equity B	Growth	-13.4	-12.07	-3.68	4	3	0	2.07	800 257-3336
J Hancock Core Equity C	Growth	-13.4	-12.08	-3.7	4	3	1	2.11	800 257-3336
J Hancock Core Equity I	Growth	-12.2					0	0.88	800 257-3336
J Hancock Dividend Perf Y	Growth/Inc	-11.5					0	0.7	800 257-3336
J Hancock Financial Indust A	Financial	-6.8	-2.77	-1.46	3	3	5	1.4	800 257-3336
J Hancock Financial Indust B	Financial	-7.4					0	2.05	800 257-3336
J Hancock Financial Indust C	Financial	-7.4	-3.43		3	3	1	2.1	800 257-3336
J Hancock Financial Indust I	Financial	-6.2					0	0.87	800 257-3336
J Hancock Focused Equity A	Agg Growth	-7.9					5	1.5	800 257-3336
J Hancock Focused Equity B	Agg Growth	-8.5					0	2.2	800 257-3336
J Hancock Focused Equity C	Agg Growth	-8.5					1	2.2	800 257-3336
J Hancock Focused Sm Cap Gr Y	Small Co	-13					0	0.9	800 257-3336
J Hancock Growth Trends A	Growth	-9.3					5	1.65	800 257-3336
J Hancock Growth Trends B	Growth	-9.9					0	2.35	800 257-3336
J Hancock Growth Trends C	Growth	-9.9					1	2.35	800 257-3336
J Hancock Health Sciences A	Health	-3.3	-1.1	3.87	2	2	5	1.5	800 257-3336
J Hancock Health Sciences B	Health	-4	-1.79	3.14	2	2	0	2.2	800 257-3336
J Hancock Health Sciences C	Health	-4	-1.79		2	2	1	2.2	800 257-3336
J Hancock Indep Div Core II I	Growth/Inc	-13					0	0.67	800 257-3336
J Hancock International A	Foreign	-15	-19.57	-10.21	4	2	5	1.88	800 257-3336
J Hancock International B	Foreign	-15.9	-20.17	-10.85	5	2	0	2.57	800 257-3336
J Hancock International C	Foreign	-15.9	-20.21		5	2	1	2.57	800 257-3336
J Hancock International I	Foreign	-14.5					0	1.6	800 257-3336
J Hancock Large Cap Equity A	Growth	-17.8	-14.11	-1.96	4	4	5	1.17	800 257-3336
J Hancock Large Cap Equity B	Growth	-18.5	-14.77	-2.7	4	4	0	1.98	800 257-3336
J Hancock Large Cap Equity C	Growth	-18.5	-14.77	-2.7	4	4	1	1.98	800 257-3336
J Hancock Large Cap Equity I	Growth	-17.5					0	0.75	800 257-3336

Stock Fund Name	Objective	Annualized Return for			Rank		Max Load	Expense Ratio	Toll-Free/(Toll) Telephone
		1 Year	3 Years	5 Years	Overall	Risk			
J Hancock Large Cap Growth A	Growth	-13.9	-26.07	-12.58	5	4	5	1.36	800 257-3336
J Hancock Large Cap Growth B	Growth	-14.5	-26.57	-13.17	4	4	0	2.05	800 257-3336
J Hancock Large Cap Growth C	Growth	-14.5	-26.58		5	4	1	2.06	800 257-3336
J Hancock Large Cap Spectrum A	Growth	-12.4					5	1.5	800 257-3336
J Hancock Large Cap Spectrum B	Growth	-13					0	2.2	800 257-3336
J Hancock Large Cap Spectrum C	Growth	-13					1	2.2	800 257-3336
J Hancock Mid Cap Growth A	Growth	-8.5	-19.85	-5.09	3	4	5	1.46	800 257-3336
J Hancock Mid Cap Growth B	Growth	-9.3	-20.46	-5.78	4	4	0	2.16	800 257-3336
J Hancock Mid Cap Growth C	Growth	-9.3	-20.44		4	4	1	2.16	800 257-3336
J Hancock Mid Cap Growth I	Growth	-7.9					0	0.96	800 257-3336
J Hancock Multi Cap Growth A	Growth	-4.8					5	1.39	800 257-3336
J Hancock Multi Cap Growth B	Growth	-5.4					0	2.1	800 257-3336
J Hancock Multi Cap Growth C	Growth	-5.4					1	2.1	800 257-3336
J Hancock Pac Basin Equities A	Pacific	-24.6	-17.03	-0.14	4	2	5	2.06	800 257-3336
J Hancock Pac Basin Equities B	Pacific	-25.2	-17.62	-0.82	4	2	0	2.77	800 257-3336
J Hancock Pac Basin Equities C	Pacific	-25.1	-17.62		3	2	1	2.77	800 257-3336
J Hancock Real Estate A	Real Est	1.4	13.05		1	2	5	1.65	800 257-3336
J Hancock Real Estate B	Real Est	0.8	12.25		1	2	0	2.35	800 257-3336
J Hancock Real Estate C	Real Est	0.8	12.25		1	2	1	2.35	800 257-3336
J Hancock Regional Bank A	Financial	-4	10.1	1.62	2	2	5	1.37	800 257-3336
J Hancock Regional Bank B	Financial	-4.7	9.33	0.93	2	2	0	2.07	800 257-3336
J Hancock Regional Bank C	Financial	-4.7	9.33		2	2	1	2.07	800 257-3336
J Hancock Small Cap Equity A	Small Co	-15.2	-12.6	4.62	3	5	5	1.36	800 257-3336
J Hancock Small Cap Equity B	Small Co	-15.8	-13.24	3.89	3	5	0	2.06	800 257-3336
J Hancock Small Cap Equity C	Small Co	-15.8	-13.22	3.89	3	5	1	2.06	800 257-3336
J Hancock Small Cap Equity I	Small Co	-14.5					0	0.87	800 257-3336
J Hancock Small Cap Growth A	Small Co	-13.5	-15.85	-1.84	4	5	5	1.28	800 257-3336
J Hancock Small Cap Growth B	Small Co	-14.2	-16.57	-2.6	4	5	0	2.03	800 257-3336
J Hancock Small Cap Growth C	Small Co	-14.2	-11.61		4	5	1	2.02	800 257-3336
J Hancock Small Cap Growth I	Small Co	-12.9	-15.38		5	5	0	0.87	800 257-3336
J Hancock Sovereign Investors A	Growth/Inc	-9.3	-4.83	-0.63	2	2	5	1.08	800 257-3336
J Hancock Sovereign Investors B	Growth/Inc	-9.9	-5.5	-1.36	3	2	0	1.78	800 257-3336
J Hancock Sovereign Investors C	Growth/Inc	-9.9	-5.5	-1.36	3	2	1	1.79	800 257-3336
J Hancock Strategic Growth A	Growth	-8.2					5	1.4	800 257-3336
J Hancock Strategic Growth B	Growth	-8.7					0	2.1	800 257-3336
J Hancock Strategic Growth C	Growth	-8.7					1	2.1	800 257-3336
J Hancock Technology A	Technology	-13	-36.82	-6.37	3	5	5	1.28	800 257-3336
J Hancock Technology B	Technology	-13.6	-37.24	-6.98	3	5	0	1.98	800 257-3336
J Hancock Technology C	Technology	-13.6	-37.24		4	5	1	1.99	800 257-3336
J Hancock Technology I	Technology	-11.7					0	0.84	800 257-3336
J Hancock US Glob Lead Gr A	Growth	-8	-2.72	1.78	2	2	5	1.38	800 257-3336
J Hancock US Glob Lead Gr B	Growth	-8.7					0	2.12	800 257-3336
J Hancock US Glob Lead Gr C	Growth	-8.7					1	2.12	800 257-3336
J Hancock US Glob Lead Gr I	Growth	-7.8					0	0.94	800 257-3336
JPMorgan Capital Growth A	Growth	-10.8	-5.09	-0.77	3	3	5.75	1.35	800 348-4782
JPMorgan Capital Growth B	Growth	-11.3	-5.58	-1.28	3	3	0	1.85	800 348-4782
JPMorgan Capital Growth C	Growth	-11.4	-5.62	0.66	3	3	0	1.85	800 348-4782
JPMorgan Capital Growth Sel	Growth	-10.4	-4.58	-0.28	3	3	0	0.93	800 348-4782
JPMorgan Disciplined Eq I	Growth	-8.8	-11.75	-2.25	3	3	0	0.45	800 348-4782
JPMorgan Disciplined Eq Sel	Growth	-9					0	0.72	800 348-4782
JPMorgan Diversified I	Balanced	-3.2	-4.23	1.1	2	1	0	0.65	800 348-4782
JPMorgan Dynamic Small Cap A	Small Co	-14.3	-9.58	1.65	4	4	5.75	1.5	800 348-4782
JPMorgan Dynamic Small Cap B	Small Co	-14.9	-10.16	0.97	4	4	0	2.12	800 348-4782
JPMorgan Dynamic Small Cap C	Small Co	-14.8	-10.16	0.96	4	4	0	2.12	800 348-4782
JPMorgan Dynamic Small Cap Sel	Small Co	-14	-9.21	1.96	3	4	0	1.1	800 348-4782
JPMorgan Equity Growth A	Growth	-9.1	-19.46	-4.45	4	4	0	1.25	800 348-4782
JPMorgan Equity Growth B	Growth	-9.8	-19.91	-4.75	4	4	0	1.98	800 348-4782
JPMorgan Equity Growth C	Growth	-9.7	-22.3	-6.49	4	4	0	1.98	800 348-4782

Stock Fund Name	Objective	Annualized Return for			Rank		Max Load	Expense Ratio	Toll-Free/(Toll) Telephone
		1 Year	3 Years	5 Years	Overall	Risk			
JPMorgan Equity Growth Sel	Growth	-8.9	-19.14	-4.21	4	4	0	1	800 348-4782
JPMorgan Equity Income A	Growth/Inc	-12.3	-10.68	-2.02	4	3	0	1.25	800 348-4782
JPMorgan Equity Income B	Growth/Inc	-12.7	-11.03	-2.2	4	3	0	1.75	800 348-4782
JPMorgan Equity Income C	Growth/Inc	-12.7	-11.06	-2.2	4	3	0	1.75	800 348-4782
JPMorgan Equity Income Sel	Growth/Inc	-12	-10.39	-1.67	3	3	0	0.9	800 348-4782
JPMorgan Fleming Emerg Mkt Eq A	Foreign	-11					5.75	2	800 348-4782
JPMorgan Fleming Emerg Mkt Eq B	Foreign	-11.2					0	2.5	800 348-4782
JPMorgan Fleming Emerg Mkt Eq I	Foreign	-10.4	-8.51	-3.68	3	4	0	1.45	800 348-4782
JPMorgan Fleming Emerg Mkt Eq Sel	Foreign	-10.7	-10.88	-6.79		4	0	1.75	800 348-4782
JPMorgan Fleming European A	European	-4.7	-6.62	0.75	3	3	5.75	1.5	800 348-4782
JPMorgan Fleming European B	European	-5.5	-4.29	1.96	3	3	0	2.25	800 348-4782
JPMorgan Fleming European C	European	-5.5	-7.33	0	3	3	0	2.25	800 348-4782
JPMorgan Fleming Intl Eq A	Foreign	-11.5					5.75	1.5	800 348-4782
JPMorgan Fleming Intl Eq B	Foreign	-11.9					0	2	800 348-4782
JPMorgan Fleming Intl Eq Sel	Foreign	-11.1	-11.41	-3.33	4	3	0	1	800 348-4782
JPMorgan Fleming Intl Growth A	Foreign	-12.3					5.75	2	800 348-4782
JPMorgan Fleming Intl Opps A	Foreign	-16.5					5.75	1.9	800 348-4782
JPMorgan Fleming Intl Opps B	Foreign	-16.9					0	2.4	800 348-4782
JPMorgan Fleming Intl Opps I	Foreign	-15.7	-13.77	-4.87	5	3	0	0.92	800 348-4782
JPMorgan Fleming Intl Value I	Foreign	-16.3	-14.91	-6.13	5	3	0	0.95	800 348-4782
JPMorgan Fleming Japan A	Pacific	-24.5	-20.94	-11.11	5	3	5.75	1.75	800 348-4782
JPMorgan Fleming Japan B	Pacific	-25.5	-21.6	-11.75	5	3	0	2.5	800 348-4782
JPMorgan Fleming Tx-Aware Int Opp A	Foreign	-15.7					5.75	1.8	800 348-4782
JPMorgan Fleming Tx-Aware Int Opp C	Foreign	-16.2					0	2.3	800 348-4782
JPMorgan Global 50 Sel	Global	-16	-17.42	-5.38	5	3	0	1.5	800 348-4782
JPMorgan Growth and Income A	Growth/Inc	-8.7	-7.75	-2.43	3	3	5.75	0.83	800 348-4782
JPMorgan Growth and Income B	Growth/Inc	-9.1	-8.21	-2.93	3	3	0	1.33	800 348-4782
JPMorgan Growth and Income C	Growth/Inc	-9.1	-8.19	-2.91	3	3	0	1.33	800 348-4782
JPMorgan Growth and Income Sel	Growth/Inc	-8.3	-6.91	-1.75	3	3	0	0.43	800 348-4782
JPMorgan Market Neutral Fund Inst	Other	-0.4	3.52			1	0	1.25	800 348-4782
JPMorgan Mid Cap Value Inst	Growth	5	16.01	15.78		2	0	0.75	800 348-4782
JPMorgan Select Mid Cap Equity	Growth	-3.2	1.12	6.82	1	3	0	0.8	800 348-4782
JPMorgan Select Small Cap Equity	Small Co	-13.6	-1.95	-1.98	3	3	0	0.5	800 348-4782
JPMorgan Small Cap Equity A	Small Co	-13.1	-2.75	1.19	3	3	5.75	1.38	800 348-4782
JPMorgan Small Cap Equity B	Small Co	-13.7	-3.5	0.3	3	3	0	2.12	800 348-4782
JPMorgan Small Cap Equity Sel	Small Co	-12.7	-2.22	1.6	3	3	0	0.85	800 348-4782
JPMorgan Tax Aware Disc Eq I	Growth	-8.8	-10.8	-1.59	3	3	0	0.55	800 348-4782
JPMorgan Tax Aware Lrg Cap Gr Sel	Growth	-7.9	-18.42	-3.33	3	4	0	0.85	800 348-4782
JPMorgan Tax Aware Lrg Cap Val Sel	Income	-9.6	-8.91	-3.85	3	2	0	0.85	800 348-4782
JPMorgan Tax Aware Sh Int Inc Inst	Other						0		800 348-4782
JPMorgan Tax Aware Sh Int Inc Sel	Other						0		800 348-4782
JPMorgan Tax Aware US Equity A	Growth	-9.4					5.75	1.1	800 348-4782
JPMorgan Tax Aware US Equity B	Growth	-9.8					0	1.6	800 348-4782
JPMorgan Tax Aware US Equity C	Growth	-9.9					0	1.6	800 348-4782
JPMorgan Tax Aware US Equity Inst	Growth	-9					0	0.7	800 348-4782
JPMorgan Tax Aware US Equity Sel	Growth	-9.1	-10.41	-0.97	3	3	0	0.84	800 348-4782
JPMorgan US Equity A	Growth	-7.5					5.75	1.05	800 348-4782
JPMorgan US Equity B	Growth	-8.1					0	1.75	800 348-4782
JPMorgan US Equity C	Growth	-8.2					0	1.75	800 348-4782
JPMorgan US Equity I	Growth	-7.1	-9.84	-2.29	3	3	0	0.64	800 348-4782
JPMorgan US Equity Sel	Growth	-7.3					0	0.79	800 348-4782
JPMorgan US Sm Comp Opps Sel	Small Co	-15.9	-19.55	-7.5	5	5	0	1.02	800 348-4782
JPMorgan US Small Company I	Small Co	-10.9	-5.82	-1.21	3	4	0	0.83	800 348-4782
JPMorgan Value Opportunity A	Growth	-4.8	-3.62	-2.16	2	3	5.75	1.39	800 348-4782
Jacob Internet Fund	Technology	50.6	-38.54		3	5	0	2.99	888 522-6239
James Advantage Golden Rainbow	Flexible	1	3.68	4.86	1	1	0	1.29	888 426-7640
James Advantage Large Cap Plus A	Growth	-10.6	-20.41			4	0	1.5	888 426-7640
James Advantage Market Neutral A	Growth	-6.9	1.91			1	4.2	1.95	888 426-7640

Stock Fund Name	Objective	Annualized Return for			Rank		Max Load	Expense Ratio	Toll-Free/(Toll) Telephone
		1 Year	3 Years	5 Years	Overall	Risk			
James Advantage Small Cap Value A	Small Co	3.6	10.08			3	4.2	1.5	888 426-7640
Jamestown Balanced Fund	Balanced	0					0	0.83	866 738-1129
Jamestown Equity Fund	Growth	-6.9					0	0.86	866 738-1129
Jamestown Intl Equity Fund	Foreign	-17.8	-18.73	-7.21	4	3	0	1.38	866 738-1129
Janus Adviser Aggressive Growth C	Agg Growth						0		800 525-3713
Janus Adviser Aggressive Growth I	Agg Growth	-5.3	-30	-4.41	3	5	0	1.16	800 525-3713
Janus Adviser Balanced C	Balanced						0		800 525-3713
Janus Adviser Balanced I	Balanced	-0.8	-1.6	6.95	1	1	0	1.17	800 525-3713
Janus Adviser Cap Appreciation C	Growth						0		800 525-3713
Janus Adviser Cap Appreciation I	Growth	-6.8	-13.73	5.51	3	3	0	1.18	800 525-3713
Janus Adviser Core Equity C	Income						0		800 525-3713
Janus Adviser Core Equity I	Income	-10.6	-9.46	4.95	3	2	0	1.7	800 525-3713
Janus Adviser Growth & Income C	Income						0		800 525-3713
Janus Adviser Growth & Income I	Growth/Inc	-8.6	-11.23	6.21	2	2	0	1.23	800 525-3713
Janus Adviser Growth Fd C	Income						0		800 525-3713
Janus Adviser Growth Fd I	Growth	-12.8	-17.35	-1.12	4	3	0	1.17	800 525-3713
Janus Adviser International C	Global						0		800 525-3713
Janus Adviser International I	Foreign	-16.7	-18.73	-1.59	5	3	0	1.24	800 525-3713
Janus Adviser International Value C	Global						0		800 525-3713
Janus Adviser Mid Cap Value C	Growth						0		800 525-3713
Janus Adviser Risk Mgd LgCap Core C	Growth						0		800 525-3713
Janus Adviser Risk Mgd LgCap Gr I	Growth						0		800 525-3713
Janus Adviser Worldwide C	Global						0		800 525-3713
Janus Adviser Worldwide I	Global	-17.1	-18.6	-2.5	5	3	0	1.2	800 525-3713
Janus Aspen Balanced Instl	Balanced	-0.6	-1.58	7.16		1	0	0.66	800 525-3713
Janus Balanced Fund	Balanced	-0.6	-1.85	6.28	1	1	0	0.85	800 525-3713
Janus Core Equity Fund	Growth/Inc	-11.5	-9.16	4.5	3	2	0	0.95	800 525-3713
Janus Enterprise Fund	Growth	-5.1	-27.23	-1.12	3	5	0	0.92	800 525-3713
Janus Fund	Growth	-11.6	-19.32	-1.72	4	4	0	0.84	800 525-3713
Janus Global Life Sciences Fund	Health	-12.8	-7.03		3	3	0	0.93	800 525-3713
Janus Global Technology	Technology	-11.2	-33.89		4	5	0	0.92	800 525-3713
Janus Growth & Income Fund	Growth/Inc	-9.8	-12.26	3.02	3	3	0	0.87	800 525-3713
Janus Mercury Fund	Agg Growth	-6	-22.64	2.35	3	4	0	0.89	800 525-3713
Janus Mid Cap Val Inv	Growth	-4.9	11.25		1	3	0	1.22	800 525-3713
Janus Olympus Fund	Growth	-12.9	-22.71	2.75	3	4	0	0.91	800 525-3713
Janus Orion Fund	Growth	-8.5					0	1.06	800 525-3713
Janus Overseas Fund	Foreign	-15.4	-19.5	-2.25	5	3	0	0.87	800 525-3713
Janus Risk - Managed Stock Fund	Growth						0		800 525-3713
Janus Small Cap Val Inst	Small Co	-9.7	10.17	9.58	2	3	0	1.08	800 525-3713
Janus Small Cap Val Inv	Small Co	-10	9.84	9.24	2	3	0		800 525-3713
Janus Special Equity Fund	Growth	-9.2	-7.55		3	3	0	0.92	800 525-3713
Janus Twenty Fund	Growth	-2.7	-22.53	-1.48	3	4	0	0.84	800 525-3713
Janus Venture Fund	Small Co	-11.8	-16.98	2.16	4	5	0	0.87	800 525-3713
Janus Worldwide Fund	Global	-16.6	-19.94	-3.37	5	3	0	0.87	800 525-3713
Jensen Portfolio	Growth/Inc	-7.2	-0.94	7.45	2	2	0	0.91	800 992-4144
Jhaveri Value Fund	Growth	-2.3					0	2.5	(440 356-1565)
JohnsonFamily Intl Value	Foreign	-7.2	-5.09	-0.2	3	2	4	1.83	800 276-8272
JohnsonFamily Large Cap Value	Growth	-9.1	0.34	0.46	3	3	4	1.39	800 276-8272
JohnsonFamily Small Cap Value	Small Co	-10.6	12.08	5.45	3	3	4	1.32	800 276-8272
Julius Baer International Equity A	Foreign	-4.7	-7.67	6.34	2	2	0	1.4	800 435-4659
Jundt Growth Fund A	Growth	2.6	-16.12	-3.77	3	3	5.75	2.53	800 370-0612
Jundt Growth Fund B	Growth	1.9	-16.73	-3.7	3	3	0	3.28	800 370-0612
Jundt Growth Fund C	Growth	1.9	-16.73	-3.7	3	3	0	3.28	800 370-0612
Jundt Growth Fund I	Growth	2.8	-15.9	-3.5	3	3	5.25	2.28	800 370-0612
Jundt Opportunity Fund A	Agg Growth	16	-20.55	1.01	3	4	5.75	3.1	800 370-0612
Jundt Opportunity Fund B	Agg Growth	15.1	-21.14	0.23	3	4	0	3.85	800 370-0612
Jundt Opportunity Fund C	Agg Growth	15	-21.16	0.22	3	4	0	3.85	800 370-0612
Jundt Twenty Five Fund A	Growth	-3.5	-19.62	-0.52	3	4	5.75	3.56	800 370-0612

| Stock Fund Name | Objective | Annualized Return for | | | Rank | | Max Load | Expense Ratio | Toll-Free/(Toll) Telephone |
		1 Year	3 Years	5 Years	Overall	Risk			
Jundt Twenty Five Fund B	Growth	-4.2	-20.23	-1.34	3	4	0	4.31	800 370-0612
Jundt Twenty Five Fund C	Growth	-4.3	-20.25	-1.3	3	4	0	4.31	800 370-0612
Jundt Twenty Five Fund I	Growth	-3.4	-19.44	-0.28	3	4	5.25	3.31	800 370-0612
Jundt US Emerging Growth A	Small Co	3.7	-15.24	2.72	3	4	5.75	2.62	800 370-0612
Jundt US Emerging Growth B	Small Co	2.9	-15.88	1.95	3	4	0	3.37	800 370-0612
Jundt US Emerging Growth C	Small Co	2.9	-15.88	1.94	3	4	0	3.37	800 370-0612
KOPP Emerging Growth Fund A	Growth	-8.2	-30.44	1.67	3	5	3.5	1.81	888 533-5677
KOPP Emerging Growth Fund I	Growth	-7.9					0	1.46	888 533-5677
Kalmar Growth With Value Small Cap	Small Co	-6.6	-0.1	0.85	2	4	0	1.23	800 282-2319
Keeley Small Cap Value Fund	Small Co	-9.5	9.42	4.4	3	3	4.5	1.72	888 933-5391
Kelmoore Strategy Eagle A	Income	0.6					5.5	2.25	877 328-9456
Kelmoore Strategy Eagle C	Income	0.6					0	3	877 328-9456
Kelmoore Strategy Fund A	Income	-1.1	-13.99		3	4	5.5	2	877 328-9456
Kelmoore Strategy Fund C	Income	-2.1	-14.71		3	4	5.5	2.75	877 328-9456
Kelmoore Strategy Liberty A	Growth/Inc	0.7					5.5	2.25	877 328-9456
Kelmoore Strategy Liberty C	Growth/Inc	0					0	3	877 328-9456
Kensington Real Estate Secs A	Real Est						5.75	1.45	800 253-2949
Kensington Real Estate Secs B	Real Est						0	2.2	800 253-2949
Kensington Real Estate Secs C	Real Est						0	2.2	800 253-2949
Kensington Select Income A	Real Est	13.2					5.75	1.6	800 253-2949
Kensington Select Income B	Real Est	12.4					0	2.35	800 253-2949
Kensington Select Income C	Real Est	12.4					0	2.35	800 253-2949
Kensington Strategic Realty A	Real Est	4.4	18.3		1	1	5.75	3.82	800 253-2949
Kensington Strategic Realty B	Real Est	3.6	17.42		1	1	0	4.57	800 253-2949
Kensington Strategic Realty C	Real Est	3.6	17.41		1	1	0	4.57	800 253-2949
Kinetics Internet Emerg Growth NL	Technology						0	2.74	800 930-3828
Kinetics Internet Fund A	Technology						5.75		800 930-3828
Kinetics Internet Fund NL	Technology	-4.8	-16.76	23.1	3	4	0	2.42	800 930-3828
Kinetics Medical Fund A	Health						5.75		800 930-3828
Kinetics Medical Fund NL	Health	4.2	-2.47		2	3	0	2	800 930-3828
Kinetics New Paradigm Fund A	Global						5.75	2.74	800 930-3828
Kinetics New Paradigm Fund C	Global						0		800 930-3828
Kinetics New Paradigm Fund NL	Global						0		800 930-3828
Kinetics Small Cap Opport A	Small Co						5.75		800 930-3828
Kinetics Small Cap Opport NL	Small Co						0		800 930-3828
Kirr Marbach Value Fund	Growth	-7	7.07		2	3	0	1.5	(812 376-9444)
Kobren Growth	Growth	-3.9	-4.58	1.18	2	2	0	0.96	800 456-2736
LEADER Balanced Inst	Balanced	6.2					0	1.11	800 219-4182
LEADER Balanced Inv	Balanced	5.9					5.5	1.45	800 219-4182
LEADER Balanced Inv B	Balanced						0		800 219-4182
LEADER Growth & Income Inst	Growth/Inc	-6.8	-11.5	-1.62	3	2	4	1	800 219-4182
LEADER Growth & Income Inv	Growth/Inc	-7	-11.67	-1.34	3	2	5.5	1.45	800 219-4182
LEADER Growth Equity Fund Inst	Income						0		800 219-4182
LEADER Growth Equity Fund Inv A	Growth/Inc						0		800 219-4182
LEADER Growth Equity Fund Inv B	Income						0		800 219-4182
LKCM Equity Fund	Growth	-6.5	-5.51	1.77	2	2	0	0.8	800 688-5526
LKCM International Fund	Foreign	-10.1	-15.75	-4.29	3	3	0	1.2	800 688-5526
LKCM Small Cap Equity	Small Co	-9.6	3.6	3.77	3	2	0	0.94	800 688-5526
Lake Forest Core Equity	Growth/Inc	-15.1					0	1.25	800 592-7722
Lakeshore Equity Fund	Other	-7					0	2.98	800 543-0407
Lazard Emerging Markets Inst	Foreign	-6.1	-4.69	-1.71	3	4	0	1.29	800 823-6300
Lazard Emerging Markets Open	Foreign	-6.1	-3.1	-1.93	3	4	0	1.6	800 823-6300
Lazard Equity Inst	Growth	-7.3	-5.58	-1.82	2	2	0	0.9	800 823-6300
Lazard Equity Open	Growth	-7.5	-5.83	-2.08	3	2	0	1.18	800 823-6300
Lazard Intl Equity Inst	Foreign	-8.5	-11.24	-5.03	4	2	0	0.9	800 823-6300
Lazard Intl Equity Open	Foreign	-8.6	-11.41	-5.25	4	2	0	1.19	800 823-6300
Lazard Intl Small Cap Inst	Foreign	-4.5	-1.18	0.17	3	3	0	0.95	800 823-6300
Lazard Intl Small Cap Open	Foreign	-4.9	-1.65	-0.35	3	2	0	1.43	800 823-6300

Stock Fund Name	Objective	Annualized Return for			Rank		Max Load	Expense Ratio	Toll-Free/(Toll) Telephone
		1 Year	3 Years	5 Years	Overall	Risk			
Lazard Mid Cap Inst	Growth	-8.6	1.34	2.08	2	2	0	1.05	800 823-6300
Lazard Small Cap Inst	Small Co	-11	6.46	1.18	3	3	0	0.8	800 823-6300
Lazard Small Cap Open	Small Co	-10.8	6.34	1	3	3	0	1.13	800 823-6300
Legg Mason American Lead Co Prim	Growth	-6.3	-2.64	0.8	2	3	0	1.91	800 822-5544
Legg Mason Balanced Fund Tr Prim	Balanced	-3.5	-2.62	-1.32	2	1	0	1.85	800 822-5544
Legg Mason Classic Valuation Fund	Growth	-15.2	-1.31		3	3	0	2	800 822-5544
Legg Mason Emerging Markets Prim	Foreign	-9.8	-7.92	1.4	3	4	0	2.5	800 822-5544
Legg Mason Financial Services A	Financial	-1.4	10.27		2	2	4.75	1.5	800 822-5544
Legg Mason Financial Services Prim	Financial	-2.1	9.43		2	2	0	2.25	800 822-5544
Legg Mason Focus Trust	Growth	31.4	-2.97	3.99	3	4	0	1.9	800 822-5544
Legg Mason International Eq Prim	Foreign	-7.5	-11.03	-7.2	3	2	0	2.25	800 822-5544
Legg Mason Opportunity Trust Prim	Growth	14.2	2.85		2	5	0	1.91	800 822-5544
Legg Mason Special Invest Tr Prim	Small Co	9.7	3.22	9.58	2	4	0	1.83	800 822-5544
Legg Mason US Sm-Cap Value Tr Prim	Small Co	-9.8	13.75		2	3	0	2	800 822-5544
Legg Mason Value Trust Prim	Growth	3.7	-4.92	5.2	2	4	0	1.71	800 822-5544
Leonetti Balanced Fund	Balanced	-7					0	1.86	800 366-6223
Leuthold Core Investment Fund	AssetAlloc	5.7	4.04	7.33	1	2	0	1.2	888 200-0409
Leuthold Grizzly Short Fund	Balanced	-2.9					0	1.25	888 200-0409
Leuthold Select Industries Fund	Growth	-12.1					0	1	888 200-0409
Liberty Acorn Foreign Forty A	Foreign	-8.3	-15.65		4	4	5.75	1.8	800 338-2550
Liberty Acorn Foreign Forty B	Foreign	-9	-16.17		4	4	0	2.45	800 338-2550
Liberty Acorn Foreign Forty C	Foreign	-8.9	-16.12		4	4	0	2.45	800 338-2550
Liberty Acorn Foreign Forty Z	Foreign	-7.9	-15.42		4	4	0	1.45	800 338-2550
Liberty Acorn Fund A	Small Co	-3.9	5.99	7.88	1	3	5.75	1.39	800 338-2550
Liberty Acorn Fund B	Small Co	-4.5	5.4	7.51	1	3	0	2.04	800 338-2550
Liberty Acorn Fund C	Small Co	-4.5	5.4	7.51	1	3	0	2.04	800 338-2550
Liberty Acorn Fund Z	Small Co	-3.3	6.54	8.22	1	3	0	0.8	800 338-2550
Liberty Acorn International Fund A	Foreign	-12.3	-14.27	-0.54	3	3	5.75	1.73	800 338-2550
Liberty Acorn International Fund B	Foreign	-13	-14.76	-0.88	4	3	0	2.38	800 338-2550
Liberty Acorn International Fund C	Foreign	-13	-14.76	-0.88	4	3	0	2.38	800 338-2550
Liberty Acorn International Fund Z	Foreign	-12	-13.9	-0.27	3	3	0	1.03	800 338-2550
Liberty Acorn Twenty Fund A	Growth	7.9	9.73		1	3	5.75	1.7	800 338-2550
Liberty Acorn Twenty Fund B	Growth	7.2	9.11		1	3	0	2.35	800 338-2550
Liberty Acorn Twenty Fund C	Growth	7.3	9.11		1	3	0	2.35	800 338-2550
Liberty Acorn Twenty Fund Z	Growth	8.3	10.09		1	3	0	1.26	800 338-2550
Liberty Acorn USA Fund A	Small Co	-5.8	7.71	3.7	2	3	5.75	1.84	800 338-2550
Liberty Acorn USA Fund B	Small Co	-6.5	7.13	3.35	2	3	0	2.49	800 338-2550
Liberty Acorn USA Fund C	Small Co	-6.5	7.37	3.49	2	3	0	2.49	800 338-2550
Liberty Acorn USA Fund Z	Small Co	-5.3	7.74	3.7	2	3	0	1.13	800 338-2550
Liberty Asset Allocation A	Balanced	-2.5	-5.82	-0.11	2	1	5.5	1.37	800 338-2550
Liberty Asset Allocation B	Balanced	-3	-6.44	-0.72	2	1	0	2.01	800 338-2550
Liberty Asset Allocation C	AssetAlloc						0	2.03	800 338-2550
Liberty Asset Allocation G	Balanced	-3.1	-6.5	-0.84	2	1	0	2.01	800 338-2550
Liberty Asset Allocation T	Balanced	-2.4	-5.83	-0.16	2	1	4.75	1.33	800 338-2550
Liberty Asset Allocation Z	Balanced	-2	-5.58	0.05	2	1	0	1.09	800 338-2550
Liberty Equity Growth A	Growth						5.5	1.17	800 338-2550
Liberty Equity Growth B	Growth						0	2.04	800 338-2550
Liberty Equity Growth C	Growth						0		800 338-2550
Liberty Equity Growth G	Growth						0	2.1	800 338-2550
Liberty Equity Growth T	Growth	-11.8	-14.66	-1.8	4	3	5.75	1.31	800 338-2550
Liberty Equity Growth Z	Growth	-11.3	-14.27	-1.37	4	3	0		800 338-2550
Liberty Equity Value A	Growth						5.75	1.37	800 338-2550
Liberty Equity Value B	Growth						0	2.21	800 338-2550
Liberty Equity Value C	Growth						0	2.21	800 338-2550
Liberty Equity Value T	Growth/Inc	-19	-8	-1.51	4	4	5.75	1.39	800 338-2550
Liberty Equity Value Z	Growth/Inc	-18.6	-7.62	-1.12	3	4	0		800 338-2550
Liberty European Thematic Equity Z	Foreign	-9.9					0	1.77	800 338-2550
Liberty Fund (The) A	Balanced	-3.6	-5.37	-0.86	2	1	5.75	1.13	800 338-2550

Stock Fund Name	Objective	Annualized Return for			Rank		Max Load	Expense Ratio	Toll-Free/(Toll) Telephone
		1 Year	3 Years	5 Years	Overall	Risk			
Liberty Fund (The) B	Balanced	-4.3	-6.09	-1.61	2	1	0	1.88	800 338-2550
Liberty Fund (The) C	Balanced	-4.4	-6.15	-1.63	2	1	0	1.88	800 338-2550
Liberty Fund (The) Z	Balanced	-3.5	-5.2		2	1	0	0.96	800 338-2550
Liberty Global Thematic Equity Fd Z	Global	-14.9					0	1.77	800 338-2550
Liberty Growth & Income Fund A	Growth	-16.2	-1.87	2.77	3	3	5.75	1.31	800 338-2550
Liberty Growth & Income Fund B	Growth	-16.8	-2.6	2	3	3	0	2.06	800 338-2550
Liberty Growth & Income Fund C	Growth	-16.8	-2.6	2	3	3	0	2.06	800 338-2550
Liberty Growth & Income Fund Z	Growth	-16					0	1.06	800 338-2550
Liberty Growth Stock Fund A	Growth	-13.6	-20.23	-4.83	5	4	5.75	1.31	800 338-2550
Liberty Growth Stock Fund B	Growth	-14.3	-20.8	-5.51	5	4	0	2.01	800 338-2550
Liberty Growth Stock Fund C	Growth	-14.3	-20.8	-5.48	5	4	0	2.01	800 338-2550
Liberty Growth Stock Fund Z	Growth	-12.9	-19.78	-4.25	5	4	0	0.88	800 338-2550
Liberty International Equity T	Foreign	-16.1	-18.1	-6.92	4	2	5.75	1.34	800 338-2550
Liberty International Equity Z	Foreign	-15.5	-17.62	-6.38	5	2	0	1.2	800 338-2550
Liberty Large Cap Core C	Growth						0	2.04	800 338-2550
Liberty Large Cap Core G	Growth/Inc	-13.9	-9.15	-2.91	3	3	0	2.11	800 338-2550
Liberty Large Cap Core T	Growth	-13.3	-8.52	-2.25		3	5.75	1.38	800 338-2550
Liberty Large Cap Core Z	Growth	-13	-8.19	-1.96		3	0	1	800 338-2550
Liberty Large Company Index A	Growth						5.75	0.75	800 338-2550
Liberty Large Company Index B	Growth						0	1.5	800 338-2550
Liberty Large Company Index C	Growth						0	1.5	800 338-2550
Liberty Large Company Index Z	Growth/Inc	-8.1	-11.19	-1.45	3	3	0	0.5	800 338-2550
Liberty Newport Asia Pacific A	Pacific	-19.2	-18.48		3	3	5.75	2.15	800 338-2550
Liberty Newport Asia Pacific B	Pacific	-19.8	-19.12		3	3	0	2.9	800 338-2550
Liberty Newport Asia Pacific C	Pacific	-19.9	-19.07		3	2	0	2.9	800 338-2550
Liberty Newport Asia Pacific Z	Pacific	-19					0	1.9	800 338-2550
Liberty Newport Europe Fund A	European	-9.6	-14.44		4	2	5.75	1.75	800 338-2550
Liberty Newport Europe Fund B	European	-10.3	-15.15		4	2	0	2.5	800 338-2550
Liberty Newport Europe Fund C	European	-11	-15.33		5	2	0	2.5	800 338-2550
Liberty Newport Europe Fund Z	European	-5.1					0	1.5	800 338-2550
Liberty Newport Global Equity A	Utilities	-3.1	-14.8	-4.21	3	3	5.75	1.57	800 338-2550
Liberty Newport Global Equity B	Utilities	-3.9	-15.46	-4.96	3	3	0	2.32	800 338-2550
Liberty Newport Global Equity C	Utilities	-3.9	-15.48	-4.96	3	3	0	2.32	800 338-2550
Liberty Newport Greater China A	Pacific	-13.9	-6.5	6.87	3	3	5.75	2.15	800 338-2550
Liberty Newport Greater China B	Pacific	-14.5	-7.24	6.08	3	3	0	2.9	800 338-2550
Liberty Newport Greater China C	Pacific	-14.6	-7.24	6.36	3	3	0	2.9	800 338-2550
Liberty Newport Greater China Z	Pacific	-13.2	-6.19	7.17	3	3	0	1.9	800 338-2550
Liberty Newport Japan Opportunity A	Pacific	-29.6	-31.44	-6.83	5	3	5.75	2	800 338-2550
Liberty Newport Japan Opportunity B	Pacific	-30	-32.06	-7.63	5	3	0	2.75	800 338-2550
Liberty Newport Japan Opportunity C	Pacific	-29.9	-32.06	-7.61	5	3	0	2.75	800 338-2550
Liberty Newport Japan Opportunity J	Foreign	-29.7					3	2.35	800 338-2550
Liberty Newport Japan Opportunity N	Foreign	-30.1	-32.04			3	0	2.85	800 338-2550
Liberty Newport Japan Opportunity Z	Pacific	-26.7	-30.53		5	4	0	1.75	800 338-2550
Liberty Newport Tiger Fund A	Pacific	-16.4	-11.35	3.89	4	3	5.75	1.8	800 338-2550
Liberty Newport Tiger Fund B	Pacific	-17.1	-12.05	3.04	4	3	0	2.55	800 338-2550
Liberty Newport Tiger Fund C	Pacific	-17.1	-12.06	3.04	4	3	1	2.55	800 338-2550
Liberty Newport Tiger Fund T	Pacific	-16.2	-11.16	4.08	4	3	5.75	1.55	800 338-2550
Liberty Newport Tiger Fund Z	Pacific	-16.2	-11.15		3	3	0	1.49	800 338-2550
Liberty Select Value Fund A	Growth	-11.6	1.8	4.46	3	2	5.75	1.22	800 338-2550
Liberty Select Value Fund B	Growth	-12.3	1.03	3.66	3	2	0	1.97	800 338-2550
Liberty Select Value Fund C	Growth	-12.3	1.03	3.68	3	2	0	1.92	800 338-2550
Liberty Select Value Fund Z	Growth	-11.5					0	0.95	800 338-2550
Liberty Small Cap C	Small Co						0		800 338-2550
Liberty Small Cap G	Small Co	-8.9	9.6			2	0		800 338-2550
Liberty Small Cap T	Small Co	-8.1	10.5	6.65	1	2	5.75	1.42	800 338-2550
Liberty Small Cap Z	Small Co	-12.3	9.17	5.88	3	2	0	0.92	800 338-2550
Liberty Small Company Equity A	Small Co						5.75		800 338-2550
Liberty Small Company Equity B	Growth						0	2.31	800 338-2550

Stock Fund Name	Objective	Annualized Return for			Rank		Max Load	Expense Ratio	Toll-Free/(Toll) Telephone
		1 Year	3 Years	5 Years	Overall	Risk			
Liberty Small Company Equity C	Small Co						0		800 338-2550
Liberty Small Company Equity G	Small Co	-13.1	-11.8	-3.62		4	0		800 338-2550
Liberty Small Company Equity T	Small Co	-12.2	-11.02	-2.89	3	4	5.75	1.42	800 338-2550
Liberty Small Company Equity Z	Small Co	-11.8	-10.64	-2.45	3	4	0		800 338-2550
Liberty Small Company Index C	Small Co						0		800 338-2550
Liberty Small Company Index Z	Small Co	-11.6	2.79	2.62	3	3	0	0.41	800 338-2550
Liberty Small-Cap Value Fund A	Small Co	-7.5	8.41	2.89	2	3	5.75	1.57	800 338-2550
Liberty Small-Cap Value Fund B	Small Co	-22.7	1.53	-1.36	3	3	0	2.32	800 338-2550
Liberty Small-Cap Value Fund C	Small Co	-22.3	1.73	-1.25	3	3	0	2.32	800 338-2550
Liberty Small-Cap Value Fund I	Small Co						0		800 338-2550
Liberty Small-Cap Value Fund Z	Small Co	-20.3	3.25	0.05	3	3	0	1.32	800 338-2550
Liberty Strategic Equity Fd A	Income						5.75	1.68	800 338-2550
Liberty Strategic Equity Fd B	Income						0	2.54	800 338-2550
Liberty Strategic Equity Fd C	Income						0	2.54	800 338-2550
Liberty Strategic Equity Fd G	Income	-14.8	-0.71	2.5		3	0		800 338-2550
Liberty Strategic Equity Fd T	Income	-14	0.1	3.24		3	5.75		800 338-2550
Liberty Strategic Equity Fd Z	Income	-13.6	0.56	3.68		3	0		800 338-2550
Liberty Tax-Managed Aggr Gr A	Agg Growth	-11.4					5.75	2.4	800 338-2550
Liberty Tax-Managed Aggr Gr B	Agg Growth	-11.9					0	3.1	800 338-2550
Liberty Tax-Managed Aggr Gr C	Agg Growth	-11.8					0	3.1	800 338-2550
Liberty Tax-Managed Aggr Gr Z	Agg Growth	-11.5					0	2.1	800 338-2550
Liberty Tax-Managed Growth Fund A	Growth	-6	-12.4	-2.68	3	3	5.75	1.41	800 338-2550
Liberty Tax-Managed Growth Fund B	Growth	-6.7	-13.08	-3.43	3	3	0	2.16	800 338-2550
Liberty Tax-Managed Growth Fund C	Growth	-6.7	-13.06	-3.41	3	3	1	2.16	800 338-2550
Liberty Tax-Managed Growth Fund E	Growth	-6	-12.48	-2.74	3	3	5	1.51	800 338-2550
Liberty Tax-Managed Growth Fund F	Growth	-6.6	-13.03	-3.41	3	3	0	2.16	800 338-2550
Liberty Tax-Managed Growth Fund Z	Growth	-5.8	-12.17		3	3	0	1.16	800 338-2550
Liberty Tax-Managed Growth II A	Growth	-6.2	-12.16		3	3	5.75	1.5	800 338-2550
Liberty Tax-Managed Growth II B	Growth	-7	-12.85		3	3	0	2.25	800 338-2550
Liberty Tax-Managed Growth II C	Growth	-7	-12.91		3	3	0	2.25	800 338-2550
Liberty Tax-Managed Growth II Z	Growth	-6	-11.99		3	3	0	1.25	800 338-2550
Liberty Tax-Managed Value Fund A	Growth	-16.7	-4.54		3	3	5.75	1.62	800 338-2550
Liberty Tax-Managed Value Fund B	Growth	-17.3	-5.2		3	3	0	2.32	800 338-2550
Liberty Tax-Managed Value Fund C	Growth	-17.3	-5.17		3	3	0	2.32	800 338-2550
Liberty Tax-Managed Value Fund Z	Growth	-16.4	-4.17		3	3	0	1.32	800 338-2550
Liberty Utilities A	Utilities	-26.6	-13.88	-2.79	4	4	4.75	1.22	800 338-2550
Liberty Utilities B	Utilities	-27.2	-14.49	-3.52	4	4	0	1.94	800 338-2550
Liberty Utilities C	Utilities	-27.2	-14.48	-3.52	4	4	0	1.94	800 338-2550
Liberty Utilities Z	Utilities	-26.6	-13.71		4	4	0	0.97	800 338-2550
Liberty Young Investor Fund A	Growth	-9.9					0	2.47	800 338-2550
Liberty Young Investor Fund Z	Growth	-10	-13.9	-3.89	4	4	0	1.76	800 338-2550
Light Revolution Fund	Technology	-10.2					4.75	2	800 463-3957
Lighthouse Opportunity Fund	Growth	-10.3	2.64	-3.85	3	4	0	2	866 811-0218
Lindner Communications Inv	Technology	4.7	-25.76	-10.08	3	4	0	1.55	800 995-7777
Lindner Growth & Income Inv	AssetAlloc	-6.1	-3.33	-4.53	2	2	0	1.25	800 995-7777
Lindner Large-Cap Growth Inv	Growth/Inc	-12.1	-20.01	-15	5	4	0	1.35	800 995-7777
Lindner Market Neutral Inv	Flexible	2.2	-0.41	2.5	1	1	0	2.18	800 995-7777
Lindner Small-Cap Growth Inv	Small Co	-18.6	-13.58	-8.01	5	4	0	1.06	800 995-7777
Longleaf Partners Fund	Growth	1.1	10.61	7.41	1	2	0	0.91	800 445-9469
Longleaf Partners Intl Fd	Foreign	-15.3	5.7		3	3	0	1.76	800 445-9469
Longleaf Partners Small-Cap Fund	Small Co	-2.7	8.83	6.29	2	3	0	0.95	800 445-9469
Loomis Sayles Aggressive Gr Inst	Growth	-10.5	-29.87	2.66	4	5	0	1.25	800 633-3330
Loomis Sayles Aggressive Gr Ret	Growth	-10.8	-30.1	2.37	4	5	0	1.25	800 633-3330
Loomis Sayles Growth Fund Inst	Growth	-7.8	-16.57	-3.24	3	4	0	0.85	800 633-3330
Loomis Sayles Growth Fund Ret	Growth	-8	-16.75	-3.47	3	4	0	1.1	800 633-3330
Loomis Sayles Intl Equity Inst	Foreign	-12.1	-16.73	-2.14	4	3	0	1	800 633-3330
Loomis Sayles Intl Equity Ret	Foreign	-12.2	-17.01	-2.31	3	3	0	1.25	800 633-3330
Loomis Sayles Small Cap Gr Inst	Small Co	-16.3	-30.55	-7.04	5	5	0	0.99	800 633-3330

Stock Fund Name	Objective	Annualized Return for			Rank		Max Load	Expense Ratio	Toll-Free/(Toll) Telephone
		1 Year	3 Years	5 Years	Overall	Risk			
Loomis Sayles Small Cap Gr Ret	Small Co	-16.6	-30.76	-7.3	5	5	0	1.25	800 633-3330
Loomis Sayles Small Cap Val Inst	Small Co	-9.1	8.57	4.95	2	2	0	0.9	800 633-3330
Loomis Sayles Small Cap Val Ret	Small Co	-9.3	8.31	4.69	2	2	0	1.15	800 633-3330
Loomis Sayles Value Inst	Growth/Inc	-9.8	-2.31	-1.77	3	2	0	0.85	800 633-3330
Loomis Sayles Worldwide Inst	AssetAlloc	6.1	-12.8	1.26	3	3	0	1	800 633-3330
Lord Abbett Affiliated Fund A	Growth/Inc	-8.4	-2.16	3.16	2	3	5.75	0.83	800 201-6984
Lord Abbett Affiliated Fund B	Growth/Inc	-8.9	-2.77	2.49	2	3	6.09	1.45	800 201-6984
Lord Abbett Affiliated Fund C	Growth/Inc	-9	-2.79	2.45	2	3	0	1.45	800 201-6984
Lord Abbett Affiliated Fund P	Growth/Inc	-8.4	-2.22	3.02	2	3	0	0.9	800 201-6984
Lord Abbett Affiliated Fund Y	Growth/Inc	-8	-1.8	3.52	1	3	0	0.45	800 201-6984
Lord Abbett All Value A	Growth/Inc	-5	0.63	4.91	1	2	5.75	1.52	800 201-6984
Lord Abbett All Value B	Growth/Inc	-5.6	0.01	4.29	1	2	5.75	2.18	800 201-6984
Lord Abbett All Value C	Growth/Inc	-5.5	0.08	4.3	1	2	0	2.18	800 201-6984
Lord Abbett All Value P	Growth/Inc	-5.1					0		800 201-6984
Lord Abbett All Value Y	Growth/Inc						0		800 201-6984
Lord Abbett America's Value A	Income	-9.2					5.75	2.43	800 201-6984
Lord Abbett America's Value B	Income	-9.8					0	3.04	800 201-6984
Lord Abbett America's Value C	Income	-9.9					0	3.04	800 201-6984
Lord Abbett America's Value P	Income	-9.3					0		800 201-6984
Lord Abbett America's Value Y	Income	-9					0		800 201-6984
Lord Abbett Developing Growth A	Small Co	-14.7	-9.44	-3.16	4	4	5.75	1.25	800 201-6984
Lord Abbett Developing Growth B	Small Co	-15.2	-10.01	-3.77	4	4	0	1.9	800 201-6984
Lord Abbett Developing Growth C	Small Co	-15.2	-9.91	-3.72	4	4	0	1.9	800 201-6984
Lord Abbett Developing Growth P	Small Co	-14.7	-9.5	-3.25	4	4	0	1.35	800 201-6984
Lord Abbett Developing Growth Y	Small Co	-14.4	-9.11	-2.81	4	4	0	0.9	800 201-6984
Lord Abbett Global-Equity A	Global	-3.4	-10.64	-3.58	3	2	5.75	2.29	800 201-6984
Lord Abbett Global-Equity B	Global	-4.1	-11.23	-4.23	3	2	0	2.92	800 201-6984
Lord Abbett Global-Equity C	Global	-4	-11.26	-4.23	3	2	0	2.92	800 201-6984
Lord Abbett Growth Opportunities A	Growth	-8.4	-7.66	3.14	3	4	5.75	1.8	800 201-6984
Lord Abbett Growth Opportunities B	Growth	-9	-8.24		3	4	0	2.43	800 201-6984
Lord Abbett Growth Opportunities C	Growth	-9	-8.24		3	4	0	2.43	800 201-6984
Lord Abbett Growth Opportunities P	Growth	-8.5					0		800 201-6984
Lord Abbett Growth Opportunities Y	Growth	-8.2	-7.42		3	4	0	1.43	800 201-6984
Lord Abbett International A	Foreign	-13.4	-22.03	-13.03	5	4	5.75	2.04	800 201-6984
Lord Abbett International B	Foreign	-14.2	-22.55	-13.63	5	4	0	2.69	800 201-6984
Lord Abbett International C	Foreign	-13.8	-22.44	-13.56	4	4	0	2.69	800 201-6984
Lord Abbett International P	Foreign	-13.5	-21.96		5	4	0	2.14	800 201-6984
Lord Abbett International Y	Foreign	-13.4	-21.78	-12.74	5	4	0	1.69	800 201-6984
Lord Abbett Invt Tr-Balanced A	Balanced	-1.6	1.14	3.54	1	1	5.75	0.38	800 201-6984
Lord Abbett Invt Tr-Balanced B	Balanced	-2.2	0.53	2.62	1	1	0	1	800 201-6984
Lord Abbett Invt Tr-Balanced C	Balanced	-2.2	0.6	2.83	1	1	0	1	800 201-6984
Lord Abbett Invt Tr-Balanced P	Balanced						0		800 201-6984
Lord Abbett Large-Cap Research A	Growth/Inc	-8.1	-2.35	2.75	2	3	5.75	1.45	800 201-6984
Lord Abbett Large-Cap Research B	Growth/Inc	-8.6	-2.97	2.08	2	3	0	2.06	800 201-6984
Lord Abbett Large-Cap Research C	Growth/Inc	-8.6	-2.89	2.12	2	3	0	2.06	800 201-6984
Lord Abbett Large-Cap Research P	Growth/Inc	-8	-2.31		2	3	0	1.51	800 201-6984
Lord Abbett Large-Cap Research Y	Growth/Inc	-7.8	-2.12		2	3	0	1.06	800 201-6984
Lord Abbett Lg Cap Growth A	Growth	-10.3	-25.19		4	4	5.75	2.22	800 201-6984
Lord Abbett Lg Cap Growth B	Growth	-10.9	-25.6		4	4	0	2.87	800 201-6984
Lord Abbett Lg Cap Growth C	Growth	-11.1	-25.69		5	4	0	2.76	800 201-6984
Lord Abbett Lg Cap Growth P	Growth	-10.1	-25.01		4	4	0	2.21	800 201-6984
Lord Abbett Lg Cap Growth Y	Growth	-11	-25.44		5	4	0	1.76	800 201-6984
Lord Abbett Mid-Cap Value A	Growth	-9.6	9.41	8.16	1	2	5.75	1.16	800 201-6984
Lord Abbett Mid-Cap Value B	Growth	-10.2	10.75	8.66	1	2	0	1.81	800 201-6984
Lord Abbett Mid-Cap Value C	Growth	-10.2	10.75	8.66	1	2	0	1.81	800 201-6984
Lord Abbett Mid-Cap Value P	Growth	-9.7	9.34	7.87	1	2	0	1.26	800 201-6984
Lord Abbett Mid-Cap Value Y	Growth	-9.3	9.76		1	2	0	0.81	800 201-6984
Lord Abbett Research-Small Cap A	Small Co	-4.2	12	6.84	1	3	5.75	1.41	800 201-6984

Stock Fund Name	Objective	Annualized Return for 1 Year	3 Years	5 Years	Rank Overall	Risk	Max Load	Expense Ratio	Toll-Free/(Toll) Telephone
Lord Abbett Research-Small Cap B	Small Co	-4.9	11.31	6.16	1	3	0	2.04	800 201-6984
Lord Abbett Research-Small Cap C	Small Co	-4.8	11.33	6.19	1	3	0	2.04	800 201-6984
Lord Abbett Research-Small Cap P	Small Co	-4.3	11.92		1	3	0	1.49	800 201-6984
Lord Abbett Research-Small Cap Y	Small Co	-4	12.41	7.21	1	3	0	1.04	800 201-6984
Lord Abbett Sec Tr-Alpha Series A	Growth	-11.2	-7.58	-3.33	4	3	5.75	0.37	800 201-6984
Lord Abbett Sec Tr-Alpha Series B	Growth	-11.8	-8.16	-3.95	4	3	0	1	800 201-6984
Lord Abbett Sec Tr-Alpha Series C	Growth	-11.8	-8.14	-3.95	4	3	0	1	800 201-6984
Lord Abbett Small Cap Blend A	Small Co	-10.7					5.75	1.6	800 201-6984
Lord Abbett Small Cap Blend B	Small Co	-11.3					0	2.25	800 201-6984
Lord Abbett Small Cap Blend C	Small Co	-11.3					0	2.25	800 201-6984
Lord Abbett Small Cap Blend P	Small Co	-10.5					0	1.7	800 201-6984
Lord Abbett Small Cap Blend Y	Small Co	-10.5					0	1.25	800 201-6984
Lou Holland Growth Fund	Growth/Inc	-8.7					0		800 522-2711
Lutheran Brotherhood Fund A	Growth/Inc	-10.2	-13.99	-3.97	4	3	5.5	1.09	800 847-4836
Lutheran Brotherhood Fund B	Growth/Inc	-10.9	-14.58	-4.65	4	3	0	1.84	800 847-4836
Lutheran Brotherhood Fund Inst	Growth/Inc	-9.7	-13.61	-3.64	3	3	0	0.51	800 847-4836
Lutheran Brotherhood Growth A	Growth	-10.1	-19.42		4	4	5.5	1.29	800 847-4836
Lutheran Brotherhood Growth B	Growth	-10.8	-20.03		5	4	0	2.04	800 847-4836
Lutheran Brotherhood Growth Inst	Growth	-8.7	-18.46		4	4	0	1.25	800 847-4836
Lutheran Brotherhood MidCap Gr A	Growth	-8.6	-7.99	5.15	2	4	5.5	1.89	800 847-4836
Lutheran Brotherhood MidCap Gr B	Growth	-9.3	-11.69	2.27	3	4	0	2.64	800 847-4836
Lutheran Brotherhood MidCap Gr I	Growth	-7.5	-10.17	3.79	3	4	0	0.78	800 847-4836
Lutheran Brotherhood Opp Gr A	Agg Growth	-13.9	-14.83	-6.83	5	4	5.5	1.83	800 847-4836
Lutheran Brotherhood Opp Gr B	Agg Growth	-14.5	-15.47	-7.53	5	4	0	2.59	800 847-4836
Lutheran Brotherhood Opp Gr Inst	Agg Growth	-12.8	-14.06	-6.2	5	4	0	0.79	800 847-4836
Lutheran Brotherhood Value A	Growth/Inc	-16.2	-8.66		2	2	5.5	1.22	800 847-4836
Lutheran Brotherhood Value B	Growth/Inc	-16.8	-9.33		3	2	0	1.97	800 847-4836
Lutheran Brotherhood Value Inst	Growth/Inc	-15.3	-7.9		3	2	0	0.2	800 847-4836
Lutheran Brotherhood World Gr A	Foreign	-14.9	-15.15	-5.67	5	3	5.5	2.38	800 847-4836
Lutheran Brotherhood World Gr B	Foreign	-15.4	-15.76	-6.37	4	3	0	3.23	800 847-4836
Lutheran Brotherhood World Gr Inst	Foreign	-13.8	-11.23	-2.95	4	3	0	1.24	800 847-4836
MFS Aggressive Growth Alloc R	Foreign						0		800 343-2829
MFS Capital Opportunities A	Agg Growth	-13.7	-18.94	-2.52	4	4	5.75	1.18	800 343-2829
MFS Capital Opportunities B	Agg Growth	-14.4	-19.55	-3.24	3	4	0	1.93	800 343-2829
MFS Capital Opportunities C	Agg Growth	-14.3	-19.53	-3.24	3	4	0	1.93	800 343-2829
MFS Capital Opportunities R	Growth						0		800 343-2829
MFS Conservative Allocation R	Foreign						0		800 343-2829
MFS Core Growth Fund A	Growth/Inc	-12.4					5.75	1.52	800 343-2829
MFS Core Growth Fund B	Growth/Inc	-13	-16.91	0.48	4	3	0	2.17	800 343-2829
MFS Core Growth Fund C	Growth/Inc	-13	-16.91	0.5	4	3	0	2.17	800 343-2829
MFS Core Growth Fund R	Growth						0		800 343-2829
MFS Emerging Growth Fund A	Agg Growth	-10	-23.92	-7.19	4	5	5.75	1.18	800 343-2829
MFS Emerging Growth Fund B	Agg Growth	-10.6	-24.48	-7.88	4	5	0	1.93	800 343-2829
MFS Emerging Growth Fund C	Agg Growth	-10.6	-24.48	-7.88	4	5	0	1.93	800 343-2829
MFS Emerging Growth Fund R	Growth						0		800 343-2829
MFS Emerging Mkt Equity Fund A	Foreign	-9.8	-3.81	-3.02	3	3	4.75	2.24	800 343-2829
MFS Emerging Mkt Equity Fund B	Foreign	-10.4	-4.32	-3.52	3	3	0	2.74	800 343-2829
MFS Emerging Mkt Equity Fund C	Foreign	-10.4	-4.34	-3.52	3	3	0	2.74	800 343-2829
MFS Global Asset Allocation Fund A	AssetAlloc	0.6	-3.33	-0.04	2	1	4.75	1.45	800 343-2829
MFS Global Asset Allocation Fund B	AssetAlloc	0.1	-3.83	-0.56	2	1	0	1.95	800 343-2829
MFS Global Asset Allocation Fund C	AssetAlloc	0.2	-3.79	-0.55	2	1	0	1.95	800 343-2829
MFS Global Equity Fund A	Global	-5.7	-6.69	-0.42	3	2	5.75	1.59	800 343-2829
MFS Global Equity Fund B	Global	-6.5	-7.41	-1.18	3	2	0	2.34	800 343-2829
MFS Global Equity Fund C	Global	-6.4	-7.4	-1.22	3	2	0	3.05	800 343-2829
MFS Global Equity Fund R	Global						0		800 343-2829
MFS Global Growth Fund A	Global	-9.3	-13.17	0.2	3	3	5.75	1.52	800 343-2829
MFS Global Growth Fund B	Global	-10	-13.82	-0.54	4	3	0	2.27	800 343-2829
MFS Global Growth Fund C	Global	-10	-13.83	-0.54	4	3	0	2.27	800 343-2829

Stock Fund Name	Objective	Annualized Return for			Rank		Max Load	Expense Ratio	Toll-Free/(Toll) Telephone
		1 Year	3 Years	5 Years	Overall	Risk			
MFS Global Growth Fund R	Global						0		800 343-2829
MFS Global Telecommunications Fd A	Technology	-10.8					5.75	1.71	800 343-2829
MFS Global Telecommunications Fd B	Technology	-11.3					0	2.36	800 343-2829
MFS Global Telecommunications Fd C	Technology	-11.3					0	2.36	800 343-2829
MFS Global Total Return Fund A	Balanced	6.5	1.59	3.5	1	1	4.75	1.51	800 343-2829
MFS Global Total Return Fund B	Balanced	5.9	0.95	2.83	2	1	0	2.16	800 343-2829
MFS Global Total Return Fund C	Balanced	5.9	0.94	2.83	2	1	0	2.16	800 343-2829
MFS Global Total Return Fund R	Global						0		800 343-2829
MFS Growth Allocation R	AssetAlloc						0		800 343-2829
MFS Growth Opportunities Fund A	Growth	-8.4	-17.46	-3.81	3	4	5.75	0.9	800 343-2829
MFS Growth Opportunities Fund B	Growth	-9.1	-18.07	-4.7	3	4	0	1.65	800 343-2829
MFS International Growth Fund A	Foreign	-8.6	-9.75	-3.97	3	2	4.75	2.01	800 343-2829
MFS International Growth Fund B	Foreign	-9	-10.17	-4.5	3	2	0	2.51	800 343-2829
MFS International Growth Fund C	Foreign	-9	-10.18	-4.5	3	2	0	2.51	800 343-2829
MFS Intl New Discovery A	Foreign	-7.9	-1.37	9.31	2	3	5.75	1.65	800 343-2829
MFS Intl New Discovery B	Foreign	-8.6					0	2.3	800 343-2829
MFS Intl New Discovery C	Foreign	-8.5					0	2.3	800 343-2829
MFS Intl New Discovery R	Foreign						0		800 343-2829
MFS Intl Value Fund A	Foreign	-4.9	-5.87	-0.76	3	2	4.75	2.08	800 343-2829
MFS Intl Value Fund B	Foreign	-5.4	-6.36	-1.26	3	2	0	2.58	800 343-2829
MFS Intl Value Fund C	Foreign	-5.4	-6.37	-1.27	3	2	0	2.6	800 343-2829
MFS Large Cap Growth Fund A	Growth	-10.9	-19.35	-3.6	3	4	5.75	1.24	800 343-2829
MFS Large Cap Growth Fund B	Growth	-11.5	-19.92	-4.3	3	4	0	1.98	800 343-2829
MFS Managed Sectors Fund A	Agg Growth	-9	-22.23	-4.87	4	4	5.75	1.36	800 343-2829
MFS Managed Sectors Fund B	Agg Growth	-9.4	-22.71	-5.46	4	4	0	2.01	800 343-2829
MFS Managed Sectors Fund C	Agg Growth	-9.5					0	2.01	800 343-2829
MFS Mass Investors Grwth Stock R	Growth						0		800 343-2829
MFS Mass Investors Trust Fund A	Growth/Inc	-9.9	-10.73	-4.01	4	2	5.75	0.91	800 343-2829
MFS Mass Investors Trust Fund B	Growth/Inc	-10.4	-11.28	-6.17	3	2	0	1.56	800 343-2829
MFS Mass Investors Trust Fund C	Growth/Inc	-10.5					0	1.56	800 343-2829
MFS Mass Investors Trust Fund R	Growth/Inc						0		800 343-2829
MFS Mid Cap Growth Fund A	Small Co	-15.7	-20.96	-0.19	3	5	5.75	1.26	800 343-2829
MFS Mid Cap Growth Fund B	Small Co	-16.4	-21.55	-0.94	3	5	0	2.01	800 343-2829
MFS Mid Cap Growth Fund C	Small Co	-16.3	-21.53	-0.93	3	5	0	2.01	800 343-2829
MFS Mid Cap Value Fund A	Growth	-8.9					5.75	1	800 343-2829
MFS Mid Cap Value Fund B	Growth	-9.4					0		800 343-2829
MFS Mid Cap Value Fund C	Growth	-9.4					0		800 343-2829
MFS Mid Cap Value Fund R	Growth						0		800 343-2829
MFS MidCap Growth Fund R	Growth						0		800 343-2829
MFS Moderate Allocation R	AssetAlloc						0		800 343-2829
MFS New Discovery Fund A	Small Co	-15.4					5.75	1.52	800 343-2829
MFS New Discovery Fund B	Small Co	-16					0	2.17	800 343-2829
MFS New Discovery Fund C	Small Co	-16					0	2.17	800 343-2829
MFS New Discovery Fund R	Small Co						0		800 343-2829
MFS New Endeavor Fund A	Growth	5.8					5.75	1.34	800 343-2829
MFS New Endeavor Fund B	Growth	5.2					0	2.05	800 343-2829
MFS New Endeavor Fund C	Growth	5.1					0	2.05	800 343-2829
MFS New Endeavor Fund R	Growth						0		800 343-2829
MFS Research Fund A	Growth	-10.8	-15.1	-3.83	4	3	5.75	0.99	800 343-2829
MFS Research Fund B	Growth	-11.4	-15.66	-4.45	4	3	0	1.64	800 343-2829
MFS Research Fund C	Growth	-11.4	-15.66	-4.45	4	3	0	1.64	800 343-2829
MFS Research Fund R	Growth						0		800 343-2829
MFS Research Gr & Income Fund A	Growth/Inc	-8.6					5.75	1.32	800 343-2829
MFS Research Gr & Income Fund B	Growth/Inc	-9.2	-8.19	-2.41	3	2	0	1.97	800 343-2829
MFS Research Gr & Income Fund C	Growth/Inc	-9.2					0	1.97	800 343-2829
MFS Research Gr & Income Fund R	Growth/Inc						0		800 343-2829
MFS Research International Fund A	Foreign	-9.3					5.75	1.76	800 343-2829
MFS Research International Fund B	Foreign	-9.9					0	2.41	800 343-2829

Stock Fund Name	Objective	Annualized Return for			Rank		Max Load	Expense Ratio	Toll-Free/(Toll) Telephone
		1 Year	3 Years	5 Years	Overall	Risk			
MFS Research International Fund C	Foreign	-9.9					0	2.41	800 343-2829
MFS Research International Fund R	Foreign						0		800 343-2829
MFS Strategic Growth Fund A	Growth	-6.9	-19.78	-1.5	3	4	5.75	1.37	800 343-2829
MFS Strategic Growth Fund B	Growth	-7.5	-20.3	-2.14	3	4	0	2.02	800 343-2829
MFS Strategic Growth Fund C	Growth	-7.5	-20.28	-2.14	3	4	0	2.02	800 343-2829
MFS Strategic Growth Fund R	Growth						0		800 343-2829
MFS Strategic Value A	Growth/Inc	-10.4	3.52	10.5	2	3	5.75	1.5	800 343-2829
MFS Strategic Value B	Growth/Inc	-11					0	2.15	800 343-2829
MFS Strategic Value C	Growth/Inc	-10.9					0	2.15	800 343-2829
MFS Strategic Value R	Income						0		800 343-2829
MFS Technology Fund A	Technology	-8					5.75	1.52	800 343-2829
MFS Technology Fund B	Technology	-8.6					0	2.17	800 343-2829
MFS Technology Fund C	Technology	-8.6					0	2.17	800 343-2829
MFS Technology Fund R	Technology						0		800 343-2829
MFS Total Return Fund A	Balanced	-1.2	4.36	4.91	1	1	4.75	0.88	800 343-2829
MFS Total Return Fund B	Balanced	-1.8	3.72	4.23	1	1	0	1.53	800 343-2829
MFS Total Return Fund C	Balanced	-1.8	3.7	4.23	1	1	0	1.53	800 343-2829
MFS Total Return Fund R	Balanced						0		800 343-2829
MFS Union Standard Equity Fund A	Growth	-9.9	-9.68	-7.2	3	2	5.75	1.22	800 343-2829
MFS Union Standard Equity Fund B	Growth	-10.6					0	1.87	800 343-2829
MFS Union Standard Equity Fund C	Growth	-10.4					0	1.87	800 343-2829
MFS Utilities Fund A	Utilities	4	-11.26	0.41	2	3	4.75	1.03	800 343-2829
MFS Utilities Fund B	Utilities	3.1	-11.94	-0.33	3	3	0	1.78	800 343-2829
MFS Utilities Fund C	Utilities	3.1	-11.93	-0.33	3	3	0	1.78	800 343-2829
MFS Utilities Fund R	Utilities						0		800 343-2829
MFS Value Fd A	Growth/Inc	-9.5	0.54	4.54	2	2	5.75	1.21	800 343-2829
MFS Value Fd B	Growth/Inc	-10.1	-0.11	3.85	3	2	0	1.86	800 343-2829
MFS Value Fd C	Growth/Inc	-10.1	-0.11	3.87	3	2	0	1.86	800 343-2829
MFS Value Fd R	Income						0		800 343-2829
MMA Praxis Core Stock Fund A	Growth	-10.6	-8.13	-2.45		2	5.25		800 977-2947
MMA Praxis Core Stock Fund B	Growth	-11.1	-8.67	-2.95	3	2	0	1.75	800 977-2947
MMA Praxis International A	Foreign	-17.1	-18.05	-6.5		3	5.25	2	800 977-2947
MMA Praxis International B	Foreign	-17.6	-18.53	-6.92	4	3	0	0.11	800 977-2947
MMA Praxis Value Index A	Growth/Inc	-9.2					5.25	0.95	800 977-2947
MMA Praxis Value Index B	Growth/Inc						0	1.5	800 977-2947
MSB Fund	Growth	-13.4	-2.58	2.74	3	2	0	1.45	800 661-3938
MSIF Active Intl Allocation A	Foreign	-12	-10.64	-3.64	4	2	0	0.8	800 354-8185
MSIF Active Intl Allocation B	Foreign	-12.3	-11.58	-4.29	4	2	0	1.05	800 354-8185
MSIF Asian Equity A	Pacific	-17.2	-14.39	0.81	3	4	0	1.04	800 354-8185
MSIF Asian Equity B	Pacific	-17.5	-14.58	0.5	3	4	0	1.3	800 354-8185
MSIF Emerging Markets A	Foreign	-10.2	-12.64	-0.69	3	4	0	1.65	800 354-8185
MSIF Emerging Markets B	Foreign	-10.4	-12.86	-0.96	3	4	0	1.89	800 354-8185
MSIF Equity Growth A	Growth	-9.8	-15.59	-2.18	3	3	0	0.81	800 354-8185
MSIF Equity Growth B	Growth	-10.1	-15.82	-2.41	4	3	0	1.06	800 354-8185
MSIF Euro Value Eq A	European	-8.5	-3.77	-3.58	3	3	0	1.01	800 354-8185
MSIF Euro Value Eq B	European	-8.7	-4.17	-3.93	3	2	0	1.27	800 354-8185
MSIF Focus Equity A	Agg Growth	-6.8	-15.51	-1.12	3	3	0	1	800 354-8185
MSIF Focus Equity B	Agg Growth	-7	-15.72	-1.36	3	3	0	1.25	800 354-8185
MSIF Global Value Equity A	Global	-19	-4.71	-2.12	3	2	0	1	800 354-8185
MSIF Global Value Equity B	Global	-19.2	-5	-2.39	3	2	0	1.25	800 354-8185
MSIF International Equity A	Foreign	-7.7	-1.06	2.79	3	2	0	1	800 354-8185
MSIF International Equity B	Foreign	-7.9	-1.42	2.45	2	2	0	1.25	800 354-8185
MSIF International Magnum A	Foreign	-13.8	-11.11	-6	3	2	0	1.01	800 354-8185
MSIF International Magnum B	Foreign	-14.2	-11.4	-6.28	3	2	0	1.27	800 354-8185
MSIF International Small Cap A	Foreign	-7.7	0.39	3.31	2	2	0	1.15	800 354-8185
MSIF Japanese Value Equity Port A	Pacific	-22.6	-20.78	-4.41	3	3	0	1.02	800 354-8185
MSIF Japanese Value Equity Port B	Pacific	-22.8	-20.92	-4.59	4	3	0	1.27	800 354-8185
MSIF Latin America A	Foreign	-8.4	-4.79	-1.55	3	4	0	1.77	800 354-8185

Stock Fund Name	Objective	Annualized Return for			Rank		Max Load	Expense Ratio	Toll-Free/(Toll) Telephone
		1 Year	3 Years	5 Years	Overall	Risk			
MSIF Latin America B	Foreign	-8.6	-5.03	-1.67	3	5	0	2.03	800 354-8185
MSIF Small Company Growth A	Small Co	-6.5	-10.36	9.59	3	5	0	1.1	800 354-8185
MSIF Small Company Growth B	Small Co	-6.8	-10.48	9.36	3	5	0	1.35	800 354-8185
MSIF Trust Balanced: ADV	Balanced	-2.3					0	0.83	800 354-8185
MSIF Trust Balanced: INST	Balanced	-2.1	-3.79	1.77	1	1	0	0.59	800 354-8185
MSIF Trust Balanced: INV	Balanced	-2.2					0	0.73	800 354-8185
MSIF Trust Equity: INST	Growth	-10.4	-14.3	-3.2	4	3	0	0.66	800 354-8185
MSIF Trust Mid Cap Core: INST	Growth	-10.8	-4.76	2.79	3	4	0	0.89	800 354-8185
MSIF Trust Mid Cap Core: INV	Growth	-10.9					0	1.04	800 354-8185
MSIF Trust Mid Cap Growth: ADV	Growth	-9.8					0	0.89	800 354-8185
MSIF Trust Mid Cap Growth: INST	Growth	-9.6	-17.85	1.15	3	4	0	0.64	800 354-8185
MSIF Trust Small Cap Core: INST	Small Co	-3.4	-2.43	1.96	2	3	0	0.89	800 354-8185
MSIF Trust Small Cap Growth: INST	Small Co	-7.2	-15.67		3	5	0	1.15	800 354-8185
MSIF Trust Value: ADV	Growth/Inc	-14.8					0	0.88	800 354-8185
MSIF Trust Value: INST	Growth/Inc	-14.6	2.43	-0.47	3	3	0	0.63	800 354-8185
MSIF Trust Value: INV	Growth/Inc	-14.8					0	0.78	800 354-8185
MSIF US Real Estate A	Real Est	3	12.69	4.71	2	2	0	0.98	800 354-8185
MSIF US Real Estate B	Real Est	2.7	12.33	6.49	1	2	0	1.23	800 354-8185
MSIF Value Equity A	Growth/Inc	-14.1	-3.45	1.02	3	3	0	0.7	800 354-8185
MUTUALS.com GW Aggressive Growth	Agg Growth	-9.2					0	1.96	800 688-8257
MUTUALS.com GW Alternative Growth	Growth/Inc	-6.3					0	2.12	800 688-8257
MUTUALS.com GW Balanced Growth	Balanced	-0.5					0	5.93	800 688-8257
MUTUALS.com GW Growth	Growth	-9.7					0	1.76	800 688-8257
MainStay Blue Chip Growth A	Growth	-15.6	-21.82		4	4	5.5	2.26	800 624-6782
MainStay Blue Chip Growth B	Growth	-16.2	-22.42		4	4	0	3.01	800 624-6782
MainStay Blue Chip Growth C	Growth	-16.2	-22.42		4	4	0	3.01	800 624-6782
MainStay Capital Appreciation A	Agg Growth	-14.9	-18.62	-4.53	5	3	5.5	1.36	800 624-6782
MainStay Capital Appreciation B	Agg Growth	-15.5	-19.26	-5.26	5	3	0	2.11	800 624-6782
MainStay Capital Appreciation C	Agg Growth	-15.6	-19.26		5	3	0	2.11	800 624-6782
MainStay Convertible Fund A	Converts	1	-0.9	5.17	1	2	5.5	1.39	800 624-6782
MainStay Convertible Fund B	Converts	0.2	-1.62	4.38	1	2	0	2.14	800 624-6782
MainStay Convertible Fund C	Converts	0.2	-1.62		1	2	0	2.14	800 624-6782
MainStay Equity Income A	Growth	-10.7	2.22		3	2	5.5	1.56	800 624-6782
MainStay Equity Income B	Growth	-11.4	1.47		3	2	0	2.31	800 624-6782
MainStay Equity Income C	Growth	-11.4	1.47		3	2	0	2.31	800 624-6782
MainStay Equity Index A	Growth/Inc	-9	-9.47	-0.5	2	3	3	1.07	800 624-6782
MainStay Growth Opportunities A	Growth	-13	-13.91		4	2	5.5	1.65	800 624-6782
MainStay Growth Opportunities B	Growth	-13.6	-14.56		4	2	0	2.4	800 624-6782
MainStay Growth Opportunities C	Growth	-13.6	-14.56		4	2	0	2.4	800 624-6782
MainStay Intl Equity A	Foreign	-1.4	-6.67	-1.33	3	2	5.5	2.35	800 624-6782
MainStay Intl Equity B	Foreign	-2.2					0	3.1	800 624-6782
MainStay Intl Equity C	Foreign	-2.2	-7.33		3	2	0	3.1	800 624-6782
MainStay MAP Fund A	Growth	-5.6	0.81		1	3	5.5	1.35	800 624-6782
MainStay MAP Fund B	Growth	-6.3	0.05		2	3	0	2.1	800 624-6782
MainStay MAP Fund C	Growth	-6.3	0.05		2	3	0	2.1	800 624-6782
MainStay MAP Fund I	Growth	-5.4	1.08	6.4	1	3	0	1.1	800 624-6782
MainStay Mid Cap Growth Fund A	Growth	-15.8					5.5	1.5	800 624-6782
MainStay Mid Cap Growth Fund B	Growth	-16.5					0	2.25	800 624-6782
MainStay Mid Cap Growth Fund C	Growth	-16.5					0	2.25	800 624-6782
MainStay Research Value A	Growth	-16.8	-8.93		3	3	5.5	1.7	800 624-6782
MainStay Research Value B	Growth	-17.5	-9.64		3	3	0	2.45	800 624-6782
MainStay Research Value C	Growth	-17.5	-9.64		2	3	0	2.45	800 624-6782
MainStay Select 20 Equity Fund A	Growth/Inc	-18.6					5.5	1.5	800 624-6782
MainStay Select 20 Equity Fund B	Growth/Inc	-19.3					0	2.25	800 624-6782
MainStay Select 20 Equity Fund C	Growth/Inc	-19.3					0	2.25	800 624-6782
MainStay Small Cap Growth A	Small Co	-14.5	-12.78		4	5	5.5	2.27	800 624-6782
MainStay Small Cap Growth B	Small Co	-15.1	-13.43		4	5	0	3.02	800 624-6782
MainStay Small Cap Growth C	Small Co	-15.1	-13.43		4	5	0	3.02	800 624-6782

Stock Fund Name	Objective	Annualized Return for			Rank		Max Load	Expense Ratio	Toll-Free/(Toll) Telephone
		1 Year	3 Years	5 Years	Overall	Risk			
MainStay Small Cap Value A	Small Co	-10.7	8.58		2	3	5.5	1.9	800 624-6782
MainStay Small Cap Value B	Small Co	-11.5	7.75		2	3	0	2.74	800 624-6782
MainStay Small Cap Value C	Small Co	-11.5	7.75		2	3	0	2.65	800 624-6782
MainStay Strategic Value A	AssetAlloc	-6	-0.51	1.03	1	2	5.5	1.7	800 624-6782
MainStay Strategic Value B	AssetAlloc	-6.7	-1.26	0.25	1	2	0	2.45	800 624-6782
MainStay Strategic Value C	AssetAlloc	-6.7	-1.22		1	2	0	2.45	800 624-6782
MainStay Total Return A	Flexible	-4.1	-8.33	0.48	3	2	5.5	1.36	800 624-6782
MainStay Total Return B	Flexible	-4.8	-8.98	-0.23	2	2	0	2.11	800 624-6782
MainStay Total Return C	Flexible	-4.8	-8.98		3	2	0	2.11	800 624-6782
MainStay US Large Cap Equity A	Growth/Inc	-13.9					5.5	1.5	800 624-6782
MainStay US Large Cap Equity B	Growth/Inc	-14.4					0	2.25	800 624-6782
MainStay US Large Cap Equity C	Growth/Inc	-14.4					0	2.25	800 624-6782
MainStay Value Fund A	Growth/Inc	-16.3	-3.54	-2.95	3	3	5.5	1.3	800 624-6782
MainStay Value Fund B	Growth/Inc	-16.9	-4.24	-3.68	3	3	0	2.05	800 624-6782
MainStay Value Fund C	Growth/Inc	-16.9	-4.33		3	3	0	2.05	800 624-6782
Mairs & Power Balanced Fund	Balanced	1.4	3.72	5.2	1	1	0	0.99	800 304-7404
Mairs & Power Growth Fund	Growth	-5.1	7.44	7.95	1	2	0	0.78	800 304-7404
Managers AMG Burridge Sm Cp Growth	Small Co						0	1.49	800 835-3879
Managers AMG Rorer Large Cap	Growth/Inc	-13.5					0	1.4	800 835-3879
Managers AMG Rorer Mid Cap	Growth/Inc	-5.2					0	1.4	800 835-3879
Managers AMG Systematic Value Inst	AssetAlloc	-3.4					0	0.9	800 835-3879
Managers Capital Appreciation	Growth	-14	-22.28	2.52	4	4	0	1.39	800 835-3879
Managers Emerging Markets Eq	Foreign	-7.2	-5.66	3.27	3	4	0	1.99	800 835-3879
Managers Essex Aggressive Growth	Agg Growth	0	-17.19		3	4	0	1.2	800 835-3879
Managers First Quad Tax-Managed Eq	Growth/Inc	-9.5					0	1	800 835-3879
Managers Frontier Growth Fund	Agg Growth	-11.2					0	1.24	800 835-3879
Managers Frontier Sml Comp Vl Fund	Small Co	-13.8					0	1.49	800 835-3879
Managers International Eq	Foreign	-15.7	-12.83	-5.65	3	2	0	1.54	800 835-3879
Managers Small Company	Growth	-5.8					0	1.45	800 835-3879
Managers Special Equity Fund	Small Co	-11.4	-8.09	2.87	3	4	0	1.31	800 835-3879
Managers US Stock Market Plus	Growth/Inc	-9	-10.92	-1.96	3	3	0	0.88	800 835-3879
Managers Value	Income	-16.3	-3	-0.28	3	3	0	1.28	800 835-3879
Marshall Equity Income Adv	Growth/Inc	-9.5	-2.58	-0.47	3	2	5.75	1.22	800 236-8554
Marshall Equity Income Inv	Growth/Inc	-9.5	-2.58	-0.47	3	2	0	1.22	800 236-8554
Marshall International Stock Adv	Foreign	-15.4	-13.58	-4.45	5	3	5.75	1.54	800 236-8554
Marshall International Stock Inst	Foreign	-15.2	-13.34		5	3	0	1.29	800 236-8554
Marshall International Stock Inv	Foreign	-15.4	-13.55	-4.42	4	3	0	1.54	800 236-8554
Marshall Large-Cap Gr & Inc Adv	Growth/Inc	-14.9	-14.42	-3.75	5	3	5.75	1.27	800 236-8554
Marshall Lg Cap Gr & Inc Inv	Growth/Inc	-14.9	-14.41	-3.75	5	3	0	1.27	800 236-8554
Marshall Mid-Cap Growth Adv	Growth	-11.2	-13.98	1.55	3	4	5.75	1.27	800 236-8554
Marshall Mid-Cap Growth Inv	Growth	-11.2	-13.98	1.55	3	4	0	1.27	800 236-8554
Marshall Mid-Cap Value Adv	Growth	-3.7	11.96	8.18	1	3	5.75	1.27	800 236-8554
Marshall Mid-Cap Value Inv	Growth	-3.7	11.96	8.18	1	3	0	1.27	800 236-8554
Marshall Small-Cap Growth Adv	Small Co	-10.2	-8.73	-1.1	3	5	5.75	1.71	800 236-8554
Marshall Small-Cap Growth Inv	Small Co	-10.2	-8.73	-1.1	3	5	0	1.71	800 236-8554
Marsico 21ST Century Fund	Growth	1.6	-8.5		3	4	0	1.7	888 860-8686
Marsico Focus Fund	Growth	-10.1	-10.27	2.14	3	3	0	1.27	888 860-8686
Marsico Growth Fund	Growth/Inc	-9.1	-10	2.41	3	3	0	1.3	888 860-8686
Marsico Intl Opportunities Fund	Foreign	-7.8					0	1.6	888 860-8686
Mason Street Aggr Gr Stk A	Agg Growth	-13.6	-11.69	3.39	3	4	4.75	1.3	888 627-6678
Mason Street Aggr Gr Stk B	Agg Growth	-14.1	-12.23	2.74	3	4	0	1.95	888 627-6678
Mason Street Asset Allocation A	AssetAlloc	-3.3	-2.25	4.49	1	1	4.75	1.35	888 627-6678
Mason Street Asset Allocation B	AssetAlloc	-3.8	-2.95	3.79	2	1	0	2	888 627-6678
Mason Street Gr & Inc Stk A	Growth/Inc	-12.8	-12.07	-5.29	4	3	4.75	1.2	888 627-6678
Mason Street Gr & Inc Stk B	Growth/Inc	-13.5	-12.63	-5.87	4	3	0	1.85	888 627-6678
Mason Street Gr Stk A	Growth	-11.5	-11.3	-0.38	4	3	4.75	1.3	888 627-6678
Mason Street Gr Stk B	Growth	-12.2	-11.83	-0.98	4	3	0	1.95	888 627-6678
Mason Street Index 500 Stk A	Growth	-8.7	-11.46	-1.68	3	3	4.75	0.85	888 627-6678

Stock Fund Name	Objective	Annualized Return for			Rank		Max Load	Expense Ratio	Toll-Free/(Toll) Telephone
		1 Year	3 Years	5 Years	Overall	Risk			
Mason Street Index 500 Stk B	Growth	-9.3	-11.97	-2.25	4	3	0	1.5	888 627-6678
Mason Street Intl Equity A	Foreign	-16.6	-8.01	-4.01	4	3	4.75	1.65	888 627-6678
Mason Street Intl Equity B	Foreign	-17.2	-8.64	-4.65	4	3	0	2.3	888 627-6678
MassMutual Aggressive Growth N	Agg Growth						0		800 542-6767
MassMutual Balanced Fund N	Balanced						0		800 542-6767
MassMutual Core Value Equity N	Growth						0		800 542-6767
MassMutual Diversified Bond N	Growth						0		800 542-6767
MassMutual Emerging Growth N	Foreign						0		800 542-6767
MassMutual Focused Value N	Growth						0		800 542-6767
MassMutual Fundamental Value N	Growth						0		800 542-6767
MassMutual Growth Equity N	Growth						0		800 542-6767
MassMutual Indexed Equity N	Other						0		800 542-6767
MassMutual Inst-Balanced S	Balanced	-2.1	-4.2	-1.2	2	1	0	0.6	800 542-6767
MassMutual Inst-Intl Equity S	Foreign	-24.9	-19.3	-6.67	5	4	0	1.5	800 542-6767
MassMutual Inst-Sm Cap Value Eq S	Small Co	-6.7	2.72	-0.01	2	3	0	0.69	800 542-6767
MassMutual Instl-Core Eqty Fund S	Growth/Inc	-8.7	-8.07	-3.95	3	3	0	0.59	800 542-6767
MassMutual International Equity N	Foreign						0		800 542-6767
MassMutual Large Cap Growth A	Growth						0		800 542-6767
MassMutual Large Cap Growth L	Growth						0		800 542-6767
MassMutual Large Cap Growth N	Growth						0		800 542-6767
MassMutual Large Cap Value Fund N	Growth						0		800 542-6767
MassMutual Mid Cap Growth Equity N	Growth						0		800 542-6767
MassMutual MidCap Gr Equity II N	Growth						0		800 542-6767
MassMutual OTC 100 Fund N	Growth						0		800 542-6767
MassMutual Overseas Fund N	Other						0		800 542-6767
MassMutual Short-Duration Bond N	Other						0		800 542-6767
MassMutual Small Cap Equity N	Small Co						0		800 542-6767
MassMutual Small Cap Growth N	Growth						0		800 542-6767
MassMutual Small Comp Growth L	Growth						0		800 542-6767
MassMutual Small Comp Value Y	Growth						0		800 542-6767
MassMutual Small Company Growth A	Small Co						0		800 542-6767
MassMutual Small Company Growth N	Growth						0		800 542-6767
MassMutual Small Company Value A	Small Co						0		800 542-6767
MassMutual Small Company Value L	Small Co						0		800 542-6767
MassMutual Small Company Value N	Growth						0		800 542-6767
MassMutual Small Company Y	Other						0		800 542-6767
MassMutual Value Equity N	Income						0		800 542-6767
MassMutual Value Equity Y	Income						0		800 542-6767
Massachusetts Investors Gr Stock A	Growth	-10.4	-17.26	-1.47	4	3	5.75	0.94	800 343-2829
Massachusetts Investors Gr Stock B	Growth	-11	-17.78	-2.12	4	3	0	1.59	800 343-2829
Massachusetts Investors Gr Stock C	Growth	-11					0	1.59	800 343-2829
Masters' Select Equity Fund	Growth	-4.8	-3.83	3.29	2	3	0	1.25	800 960-0188
Masters' Select International Fund	Foreign	-15.6	-10.97	3.18	3	3	0	1.32	800 960-0188
Mastrapasqua Growth Value Fund	Growth	-2.3					0	1.65	800 943-6786
Matrix Advisor Value Fund	Growth/Inc	-5	0.14	7.04	2	4	0	0.99	800 366-6223
Matterhorn Growth Fund	Growth	-19.4	-17.71	-5.73	4	4	0	3.48	800 637-3901
Matthew 25 Fund	Growth	1.2	6.8	6.19		2	0	1.25	888 625-3863
Matthews Asian Growth & Income Fd	Pacific	2.2	11.5	15.53	1	1	0	1.9	800 892-0382
Matthews Asian Technology Fund	Technology	-18.1	-24.51		5	5	0	2	800 892-0382
Matthews China Fund	Pacific	-8.5	7.7	4.32	2	4	0	2	800 892-0382
Matthews Japan Fund	Pacific	-23.6	-23.35		5	3	0	1.88	800 892-0382
Matthews Korea Fund	Pacific	-12.2	10.93	27.92	3	5	0	1.78	800 892-0382
Matthews Pacific Tiger Fund	Pacific	-10	-3.58	12.13	3	4	0	1.9	800 892-0382
McMorgan Balanced Fd NL	Balanced	-2.3	-2.79	1.73	2	1	0	0.6	800 788-9485
McMorgan Balanced Fd Z	Balanced	-2.5					0	0.85	800 788-9485
McMorgan Equity Investment Fd	Growth	-13.1	-12.34	-3.27	4	3	0	0.7	800 788-9485
McMorgan Equity Investment Z	Growth	-13.4					0	0.95	800 788-9485
Mellon Balanced Inv	Balanced	-1.6					0		800 499-3327

357

| Stock Fund Name | Objective | Annualized Return for | | | Rank | | Max | Expense | Toll-Free/(Toll) |
		1 Year	3 Years	5 Years	Overall	Risk	Load	Ratio	Telephone
Mellon Balanced M	Balanced	-1.4					0		800 499-3327
Mellon Emerging Markets Inv	Foreign	-4.3					0		800 499-3327
Mellon Emerging Markets M	Foreign	-4.2					0		800 499-3327
Mellon Income Stock Inv	Growth/Inc	-10.2					0		800 499-3327
Mellon Income Stock M	Growth/Inc	-10.2	-8.69	-2.93		2	0		800 499-3327
Mellon International M	Global	-14.6	-4.74			2	0		800 499-3327
Mellon Large Cap Stock M	Growth	-10.5	-12.18	-2.7		3	0		800 499-3327
Mellon Mid Cap Stock M	Growth	-11.7	-2.2	-0.75		3	0		800 499-3327
Mellon Small Cap Stock M	Small Co	-11.6	-1.67	2.41		3	0		800 499-3327
Members Balanced A	Balanced	-2.1	-2.33	2.79	1	1	5.75	1.1	800 877-6089
Members Balanced B	Balanced	-2.7	-3.02	2.06	2	1	0	1.85	800 877-6089
Members Capital Appreciation A	Growth	-10.5	-10.64	-0.54	3	3	5.75	1.2	800 877-6089
Members Capital Appreciation B	Growth	-11.2	-11.3	-1.28	3	3	0	1.95	800 877-6089
Members Growth & Income A	Growth/Inc	-12.5	-10.16	-1.6	4	3	5.75	1	800 877-6089
Members Growth & Income B	Growth/Inc	-13.2	-10.83	-2.37	4	3	0	1.75	800 877-6089
Members International A	Foreign	-8.6	-8.21	-6.2	3	2	5.75	1.6	800 877-6089
Members International B	Foreign	-9.3	-8.86	-6.88	4	2	0	2.35	800 877-6089
Members Multi-Cap Growth A	Growth	-6.2	-20.82			4	5.75	1.2	800 877-6089
Members Multi-Cap Growth B	Growth	-6.8	-21.41			4	0	1.95	800 877-6089
Mercury Global Holdings A	Global	-18	-21.94	-7.42	5	3	5.25	1.45	800 637-3863
Mercury Global Holdings B	Global	-18.8	-22.26	-8.07	5	3	0	2.49	800 637-3863
Mercury Global Holdings C	Global	-18.6	-22.23	-16.37	5	3	0	2.48	800 637-3863
Mercury Global Holdings I	Global	-17.9	-21.17	-14.96	5	3	5.25	1.69	800 637-3863
Merger Fund	Growth	-1	2.87	7.17	1	1	0	1.4	800 343-8959
Meridian Growth Fund	Small Co	-5.7	8.07	9.21	2	3	0	1.06	800 446-6662
Meridian Value Fund	Growth	-3.7	8.66	15.16	1	2	0	1.12	800 446-6662
Merrill Lynch Bal Capital A	Balanced	-7.1	-1.65	-3.91	2	1	5.25	0.84	800 637-3863
Merrill Lynch Bal Capital B	Balanced	-7.8	-2.41	-1.28	2	2	0	1.61	800 637-3863
Merrill Lynch Bal Capital C	Balanced	-7.8	-2.43	-4.49	2	1	0	1.62	800 637-3863
Merrill Lynch Bal Capital I	Balanced	-6.9	-1.41	-0.27	2	1	5.25	0.59	800 637-3863
Merrill Lynch Bal Capital R	Growth/Inc						0		800 637-3863
Merrill Lynch Basic Value A	Growth/Inc	-9.9	-2.83	-3.14	3	3	5.25	0.8	800 637-3863
Merrill Lynch Basic Value B	Growth/Inc	-10.6	-3.68	-0.34	3	3	0	1.57	800 637-3863
Merrill Lynch Basic Value C	Growth/Inc	-10.6	-3.7	-3.75	3	3	0	1.58	800 637-3863
Merrill Lynch Basic Value I	Growth/Inc	-9.6	-2.7	0.64	2	3	5.25	0.56	800 637-3863
Merrill Lynch Basic Value R	Growth/Inc						0		800 637-3863
Merrill Lynch Dev Cap Market A	Foreign	-11.9	-9.09	-3.27	3	4	5.25	1.9	800 637-3863
Merrill Lynch Dev Cap Market B	Foreign	-12.7	-9.82	-4.05	3	4	0	2.72	800 637-3863
Merrill Lynch Dev Cap Market C	Foreign	-12.6	-9.84	-4.08	3	4	0	2.73	800 637-3863
Merrill Lynch Dev Cap Market I	Foreign	-11.7	-8.88	-2.89	3	4	5.25	1.65	800 637-3863
Merrill Lynch Disciplined Eq A	Growth/Inc	-12.9	-7.41		3	2	4	1.46	800 637-3863
Merrill Lynch Disciplined Eq B	Growth/Inc	-13.6	-8.16		2	2	0	2.23	800 637-3863
Merrill Lynch Disciplined Eq C	Growth/Inc	-13.6	-8.13		3	2	0	2.24	800 637-3863
Merrill Lynch Dragon Fund A	Pacific	-21.4	-15.75	-1.77	3	4	5.25	1.76	800 637-3863
Merrill Lynch Dragon Fund B	Pacific	-22	-16.46	-2.56	4	4	0	2.51	800 637-3863
Merrill Lynch Dragon Fund C	Pacific	-22	-16.44	-2.7	4	4	0	2.53	800 637-3863
Merrill Lynch Dragon Fund I	Pacific	-21	-15.53	-1.88	3	4	5.25	1.54	800 637-3863
Merrill Lynch Equity Income A	Income	-7.9	-0.25	-3.62	3	2	5.25	1.33	800 637-3863
Merrill Lynch Equity Income B	Income	-8.6	-1.27	0.85	3	2	0	2.11	800 637-3863
Merrill Lynch Equity Income C	Income	-8.6	-1.06	-4.13	3	2	0	2.12	800 637-3863
Merrill Lynch Equity Income I	Income	-7.7	0	2.12	2	2	5.25	1.1	800 637-3863
Merrill Lynch Equity Income R	Income						0		800 637-3863
Merrill Lynch Eurofund A	European	-11.2	-4.84	-0.89	3	3	5.25	1.31	800 637-3863
Merrill Lynch Eurofund B	European	-12	-5.59	-1.71	3	3	0	2.08	800 637-3863
Merrill Lynch Eurofund C	European	-12	-5.61	-1.66	3	3	0	2.1	800 637-3863
Merrill Lynch Eurofund I	European	-11	-4.58	-0.64	3	3	5.25	1.06	800 637-3863
Merrill Lynch Eurofund R	Foreign						0		800 637-3863
Merrill Lynch Focus Value A	Growth/Inc	-8.1	-3.64	-1.82	2	4	5.25	1.49	800 637-3863

Stock Fund Name	Objective	Annualized Return for			Rank		Max Load	Expense Ratio	Toll-Free/(Toll) Telephone
		1 Year	3 Years	5 Years	Overall	Risk			
Merrill Lynch Focus Value B	Growth/Inc	-8.8	-4.33	3.58	2	4	0	2.26	800 637-3863
Merrill Lynch Focus Value C	Growth/Inc	-8.8	-4.37	-2.49	2	4	0	2.27	800 637-3863
Merrill Lynch Focus Value I	Growth/Inc	-7.8	-2.14	5.41	2	4	5.25	1.24	800 637-3863
Merrill Lynch Focus Value R	Growth						0		800 637-3863
Merrill Lynch Fundamental Gr A	Growth	-14.8	-16.53	-1.62	4	3	5.25	1.04	800 637-3863
Merrill Lynch Fundamental Gr B	Growth	-15.5	-17.17	-2.39	4	3	0	1.81	800 637-3863
Merrill Lynch Fundamental Gr C	Growth	-15.5	-17.19	-4.44	4	3	0	1.83	800 637-3863
Merrill Lynch Fundamental Gr I	Growth	-14.6	-16.32	-3.6	4	3	5.25	0.8	800 637-3863
Merrill Lynch Fundamental Gr R	Growth						0		800 637-3863
Merrill Lynch Glbl Allocation A	AssetAlloc	1.4	4	6.45	1	2	5.25	1.24	800 637-3863
Merrill Lynch Glbl Allocation B	AssetAlloc	0.8	3.72	5.95	1	2	0	2	800 637-3863
Merrill Lynch Glbl Allocation C	AssetAlloc	0.7	3.33	0.66	1	2	0	2.01	800 637-3863
Merrill Lynch Glbl Allocation I	AssetAlloc	1.8	4.24	1.31	1	2	5.25	0.98	800 637-3863
Merrill Lynch Glbl Allocation R	AssetAlloc						0		800 637-3863
Merrill Lynch Global Finan Svc R	Financial						0		800 637-3863
Merrill Lynch Global Growth R	Global						0		800 637-3863
Merrill Lynch Global Small Cap A	Global	-8.3	-1.39	12.47	2	3	5.25	1.54	800 637-3863
Merrill Lynch Global Small Cap B	Global	-9	-2.18	12	2	3	0	2.3	800 637-3863
Merrill Lynch Global Small Cap C	Global	-9	-2.18	11.83	2	3	0	2.32	800 637-3863
Merrill Lynch Global Small Cap I	Global	-8	-1.15	12.63	2	3	5.25	1.28	800 637-3863
Merrill Lynch Global Technology B	Global	-8	-35.5		3	5	0	2.36	800 637-3863
Merrill Lynch Global Technology R	Technology						0		800 637-3863
Merrill Lynch Global Value A	Global	-7.2	-9.4	-2.7	3	3	5.25	1.16	800 637-3863
Merrill Lynch Global Value B	Global	-8	-10.11	-3.47	3	3	0	1.92	800 637-3863
Merrill Lynch Global Value C	Global	-8	-10.1	-3.45	3	3	0	1.93	800 637-3863
Merrill Lynch Global Value I	Global	-7.1	-9.21	-2.49	3	3	5.25	0.91	800 637-3863
Merrill Lynch Global Value R	Global						0		800 637-3863
Merrill Lynch Healthcare A	Health	-6.2	1.84	5.34	2	3	5.25	1.5	800 637-3863
Merrill Lynch Healthcare B	Health	-7	1.01	8.58	2	3	0	2.26	800 637-3863
Merrill Lynch Healthcare C	Health	-7	1.04	3.91	2	3	0	2.28	800 637-3863
Merrill Lynch Healthcare I	Health	-5.9	2.06	9.68	2	3	5.25	1.24	800 637-3863
Merrill Lynch Healthcare R	Health						0		800 637-3863
Merrill Lynch Int Value A	Other	-17					5.25	1.31	800 637-3863
Merrill Lynch Int Value I	Foreign	-16.9	-6.46	-1.54	3	3	5.25	1.06	800 637-3863
Merrill Lynch Intl Equity A	Foreign	-12.1	-12.74	-5.2	3	2	5.25	1.54	800 637-3863
Merrill Lynch Intl Equity B	Foreign	-12.8	-13.41	-5.83	3	2	0	2.33	800 637-3863
Merrill Lynch Intl Equity C	Foreign	-12.8	-13.44	-5.87	3	2	0	2.32	800 637-3863
Merrill Lynch Intl Equity I	Foreign	-11.9	-12.55	-4.99	4	2	5.25	1.29	800 637-3863
Merrill Lynch Intl Index A	Foreign	-12.9	-14.67	-6.65	4	3	4	0.89	800 637-3863
Merrill Lynch Intl Index I	Global	-12.8	-14.47	-3.79	5	3	0	0.64	800 637-3863
Merrill Lynch Large Cap Value R	Growth						0		800 637-3863
Merrill Lynch Latin America A	Foreign	-7	-3.56	-0.71	3	4	5.25	1.98	800 637-3863
Merrill Lynch Latin America B	Foreign	-7.8	-4.33	-1.53	3	4	0	2.78	800 637-3863
Merrill Lynch Latin America C	Foreign	-7.8	-4.33	-1.52	3	4	0	2.78	800 637-3863
Merrill Lynch Latin America I	Foreign	-6.8	-3.33	-0.47	3	4	5.25	1.73	800 637-3863
Merrill Lynch Natural Resource A	Energy/Res	1.7	5.78	8	1	4	5.25	1.37	800 637-3863
Merrill Lynch Natural Resource B	Energy/Res	0.8	4.95	7.55	1	4	0	2.16	800 637-3863
Merrill Lynch Natural Resource C	Energy/Res	0.9	4.95	7.5	1	4	0	2.17	800 637-3863
Merrill Lynch Natural Resource I	Energy/Res	1.9	6.03	8.69	1	4	5.25	1.13	800 637-3863
Merrill Lynch Pacific A	Pacific	-16.8	-13.66	0.88	3	2	5.25	1.07	800 637-3863
Merrill Lynch Pacific B	Pacific	-17.5	-10.85	3.33	3	2	0	1.84	800 637-3863
Merrill Lynch Pacific C	Pacific	-17.6	-14.35	0.2	3	2	0	1.85	800 637-3863
Merrill Lynch Pacific I	Pacific	-16.7	-13.5	1.89	3	2	5.25	0.82	800 637-3863
Merrill Lynch Pacific R	Foreign						0		800 637-3863
Merrill Lynch Pan-Europe Gr I	European	-5.8	-12.27		3	3	5.25	1.29	800 637-3863
Merrill Lynch PanEurop Gr B	European	-6.7	-13.11		4	3	0	2.31	800 637-3863
Merrill Lynch PanEurop Gr C	European	-6.8	-13.24		4	3	0	2.31	800 637-3863
Merrill Lynch S & P Index A	Growth/Inc	-8.6	-11.6	-1.81	3	3	4	0.63	800 637-3863

Stock Fund Name	Objective	Annualized Return for			Rank		Max Load	Expense Ratio	Toll-Free/(Toll) Telephone
		1 Year	3 Years	5 Years	Overall	Risk			
Merrill Lynch S & P Index I	Growth	-8.4					0	0.38	800 637-3863
Merrill Lynch Small Cap Index A	Small Co	-8.6					4	1.3	800 637-3863
Merrill Lynch Small Cap Index I	Small Co	-8.4					0	0.5	800 637-3863
Merrill Lynch Small Cap Value A	Small Co	-8.2	8.27	5.04	2	4	5.25	1.3	800 637-3863
Merrill Lynch Small Cap Value B	Small Co	-8.9	7.45	7.62	2	4	0	2.06	800 637-3863
Merrill Lynch Small Cap Value C	Small Co	-8.9	7.45	4.25	2	4	0	2.08	800 637-3863
Merrill Lynch Small Cap Value I	Small Co	-8	8.55	8.72	2	4	5.25	1.04	800 637-3863
Merrill Lynch Util and Telecom A	Utilities	-6.8	-7.29	-3.35	3	2	4	1.08	800 637-3863
Merrill Lynch Util and Telecom B	Utilities	-7.5	-7.86	-0.91	2	2	0	1.59	800 637-3863
Merrill Lynch Util and Telecom C	Utilities	-7.5	-7.9	-3.75	3	2	0	1.65	800 637-3863
Merrill Lynch Util and Telecom I	Utilities	-6.5	-7.04	-0.08	3	2	4	0.83	800 637-3863
Merriman Growth & Income Fund	Growth/Inc	-0.8	-4.16	0.56	2	1	0	1.91	800 423-4893
Merriman Leveraged Growth Fund	Growth	-3.8	-4.62	4.04	2	2	0	2.39	800 423-4893
Midas Fund	Prec Metal	-9.9	15.14	-5.55	3	5	0	2.8	800 400-6432
Midas Special Equities Fund	Agg Growth	-11.4	-16.64	-11.91	4	3	0	3.8	800 400-6432
Millennium Growth Fund	Growth	-3.3	-27.55	-4.05	3	5	0	2.5	800 535-9169
Monetta Balanced Fund	Balanced	3.2	-8.75	-0.07	2	3	0	1.57	800 666-3882
Monetta Blue Chip Fund	Growth	-5.4	-30.39	-13.03	4	5	0	2.5	800 666-3882
Monetta Fund	Small Co	-2.7	-13.44	-3.68	4	4	0	1.65	800 666-3882
Monetta Mid-Cap Equity Fund	Growth	-1.3	-22.98	-8.55	3	5	0	1.89	800 666-3882
Monetta Select Technology Fund	Technology	-5	-20.73	-9.39	3	5	0	2.5	800 666-3882
Monterey OCM Gold Fund	Prec Metal	3.1	29.85	10.92	2	5	4.5	2.6	800 628-9403
Monterey PIA Equity Fund	Growth	-16.1	-0.77	1.86	3	3	4.5	1.8	800 628-9403
Montgomery Emerging Mkts Fd A	Foreign	-9					5.75	2.05	800 572-3863
Montgomery Emerging Mkts Fd B	Foreign	-6.8					0	2.8	800 572-3863
Montgomery Emerging Mkts Fd C	Foreign	-9.8					0	2.8	800 572-3863
Montgomery Emerging Mkts Fd R	Foreign	-8.9	-9.39	-4.86	3	4	0	1.9	800 572-3863
Montgomery Emerging Mkts Focus A	Foreign	-6.6					5.75	2.05	800 572-3863
Montgomery Emerging Mkts Focus B	Foreign	-7.2					0	2.8	800 572-3863
Montgomery Emerging Mkts Focus C	Foreign	-7.4					0	2.8	800 572-3863
Montgomery Gbl Tech Telco & Media R	Technology	0.1	-30.64	-7.84	3	5	0	1.89	800 572-3863
Montgomery Global Focus Fund A	Global	-15.9					5.75	1.6	800 572-3863
Montgomery Global Focus Fund R	Global	-16.2	-27.98	-13.43	5	4	0	1.8	800 572-3863
Montgomery Global Long-Short A	Other	-5					5.75	2.6	800 572-3863
Montgomery Global Long-Short B	Other	-5.8					0	3.35	800 572-3863
Montgomery Global Long-Short C	Other	-5.7					0	3.35	800 572-3863
Montgomery Global Long-Short R	Global	-4.9	-15.91	7.37	3	3	0	2.93	800 572-3863
Montgomery Global Opportunities R	Global	-16	-25.17	-10.43	5	4	0	1.91	800 572-3863
Montgomery Growth Fund P	Growth	-8.7	-16.67	-8.09	4	3	0	1.67	800 572-3863
Montgomery Growth Fund R	Growth	-8.6	-16.48	-7.92	4	3	0	1.42	800 572-3863
Montgomery Instl Emerging Mkts R	Foreign	-5.9	-7.54	-2.02	3	4	0	1.17	800 572-3863
Montgomery Intl Growth Fund P	Foreign	-12	-19.39	-10.66	5	3	0	1.9	800 572-3863
Montgomery Intl Growth Fund R	Foreign	-11.6	-19.1	-10.53	5	3	0	1.65	800 572-3863
Montgomery Mid Cap Fund R	Small Co	-8.9	-10.83	-3.02	3	4	0	1.75	800 572-3863
Montgomery Small Cap P	Small Co	-5.8	-12.75	-5.96	3	4	0	1.61	800 572-3863
Montgomery Small Cap R	Small Co	-5.6	-12.58	-5.38	3	4	0	1.35	800 572-3863
Morgan Stanley 21st Century A	Growth	-14.1	-16.57		5	3	5.25	1.41	800 869-6397
Morgan Stanley 21st Century B	Growth	-14.7	-17.28		5	3	0	2.17	800 869-6397
Morgan Stanley 21st Century C	Growth	-15.1	-17.28		5	3	0	2.17	800 869-6397
Morgan Stanley 21st Century D	Growth	-13.9	-16.44		5	3	0	1.17	800 869-6397
Morgan Stanley Aggr Equity A	Agg Growth	-14.2	-16.42		4	2	5.25	1.29	800 869-6397
Morgan Stanley Aggr Equity B	Agg Growth	-14.9	-17.07		4	2	0	2.05	800 869-6397
Morgan Stanley Aggr Equity C	Agg Growth	-14.8	-17.03		4	2	0	1.93	800 869-6397
Morgan Stanley Aggr Equity D	Agg Growth	-14	-16.21		4	2	0	1.05	800 869-6397
Morgan Stanley All Star Growth A	Growth	-13.1					5.25	1.37	800 869-6397
Morgan Stanley All Star Growth B	Growth	-13.8					0	2.12	800 869-6397
Morgan Stanley All Star Growth C	Growth	-13.8					0	2.12	800 869-6397
Morgan Stanley All Star Growth D	Growth	-13.1					0	1.12	800 869-6397

Stock Fund Name	Objective	Annualized Return for			Rank		Max Load	Expense Ratio	Toll-Free/(Toll) Telephone
		1 Year	3 Years	5 Years	Overall	Risk			
Morgan Stanley Allocator A	Income						5.25		800 869-6397
Morgan Stanley Allocator B	Income						0		800 869-6397
Morgan Stanley Allocator C	Income						0		800 869-6397
Morgan Stanley Allocator D	Income						0		800 869-6397
Morgan Stanley American Opp A	Growth	-13.6	-16	-1.22	4	2	5.25	0.81	800 869-6397
Morgan Stanley American Opp B	Growth	-14.4	-16.62	-1.87	4	2	0	1.61	800 869-6397
Morgan Stanley American Opp C	Growth	-14.4	-16.64	-2	4	2	0	1.61	800 869-6397
Morgan Stanley American Opp D	Growth	-13.5	-15.83	-1.02	4	2	0	0.55	800 869-6397
Morgan Stanley Balanced Growth A	Balanced	-5.3	1.64	2.24	2	1	5.25	1.07	800 869-6397
Morgan Stanley Balanced Growth B	Balanced	-6.1	0.8	1.41	2	1	0	1.83	800 869-6397
Morgan Stanley Balanced Growth C	Balanced	-6.1	0.6	1.3	2	1	0	1.83	800 869-6397
Morgan Stanley Balanced Growth D	Balanced	-5.1	1.92	2.5	2	1	0	0.83	800 869-6397
Morgan Stanley Balanced Income A	Balanced	2.3	5.98	4.62	1	1	5.25	1.16	800 869-6397
Morgan Stanley Balanced Income B	Balanced	1.6	5.08	3.75	1	1	0	1.91	800 869-6397
Morgan Stanley Balanced Income C	Balanced	1.5	4.83	3.6	2	1	0	1.91	800 869-6397
Morgan Stanley Balanced Income D	Balanced	2.6	6.2	4.83	1	1	0	0.91	800 869-6397
Morgan Stanley Biotechnology A	Health						5.25		800 869-6397
Morgan Stanley Biotechnology B	Health						0		800 869-6397
Morgan Stanley Biotechnology C	Health						0		800 869-6397
Morgan Stanley Biotechnology D	Health						0		800 869-6397
Morgan Stanley Capital Opp Trust A	Growth	-18.7	-32.29	-3.83	4	5	5.25	1.13	800 869-6397
Morgan Stanley Capital Opp Trust B	Growth	-19.3	-32.82	-4.46	4	5	0	2.02	800 869-6397
Morgan Stanley Capital Opp Trust C	Growth	-19.3	-32.79	-4.54	4	5	0	2.02	800 869-6397
Morgan Stanley Capital Opp Trust D	Growth	-18.5	-32.15	-3.66	4	5	0	1.02	800 869-6397
Morgan Stanley Convertbl Sec Tr A	Converts	3.7	1.4	4.41	1	1	5.25	1.06	800 869-6397
Morgan Stanley Convertbl Sec Tr B	Converts	2.9	0.26	3.35	1	1	0	1.81	800 869-6397
Morgan Stanley Convertbl Sec Tr C	Converts	2.9	0.57	3.6	1	1	0	1.81	800 869-6397
Morgan Stanley Convertbl Sec Tr D	Converts	3.9	1.69	4.69	1	1	0	0.81	800 869-6397
Morgan Stanley Devlp Growth Sec A	Small Co	-8.8	-15.08	-0.23	3	4	5.25	0.88	800 869-6397
Morgan Stanley Devlp Growth Sec B	Small Co	-9.5	-15.75	-1.01	3	4	0	1.7	800 869-6397
Morgan Stanley Devlp Growth Sec C	Small Co	-9.5	-15.73	-0.96	3	4	0	1.7	800 869-6397
Morgan Stanley Devlp Growth Sec D	Small Co	-8.6	-14.91	-0.01	3	4	0	0.7	800 869-6397
Morgan Stanley Dividend Gr Sec A	Growth/Inc	-11.6	-4.04	-2.04	3	2	5.25	0.73	800 869-6397
Morgan Stanley Dividend Gr Sec B	Growth/Inc	-12.3	-4.88	-2.75	3	2	0	1.49	800 869-6397
Morgan Stanley Dividend Gr Sec C	Growth/Inc	-12.3	-4.79	-2.79	3	2	0	1.48	800 869-6397
Morgan Stanley Dividend Gr Sec D	Growth/Inc	-11.4	-3.77	-1.79	3	2	0	0.49	800 869-6397
Morgan Stanley Equity Fund A	Growth	-12.8	-15.35		4	3	5.25	1.27	800 869-6397
Morgan Stanley Equity Fund B	Growth	-13.5	-15.98		5	3	0	2.04	800 869-6397
Morgan Stanley Equity Fund C	Growth	-13.6	-15.94		5	3	0	1.96	800 869-6397
Morgan Stanley Equity Fund D	Growth	-12.6	-14.61		5	3	0	1.04	800 869-6397
Morgan Stanley European Growth A	European	-11	-11.9	-3.06	4	3	5.25	1.27	800 869-6397
Morgan Stanley European Growth B	European	-11.7	-12.58	-3.81	3	3	0	2.1	800 869-6397
Morgan Stanley European Growth C	European	-11.8	-12.56	-3.77	3	3	0	2.1	800 869-6397
Morgan Stanley European Growth D	European	-10.8	-11.71	-2.85	4	3	0	1.1	800 869-6397
Morgan Stanley Fd of Fds Domst A	Growth	-11.3	-7.54	-0.6	3	3	5.25	0.57	800 869-6397
Morgan Stanley Fd of Fds Domst B	Growth	-12	-8.26	-1.36	3	3	0	1.34	800 869-6397
Morgan Stanley Fd of Fds Domst C	Growth	-12	-12.8	-1.27	3	3	0	1.34	800 869-6397
Morgan Stanley Fd of Fds Domst D	Growth	-11.2	-12.35	-0.38	3	3	0	0.34	800 869-6397
Morgan Stanley Fd of Fds Intl A	Foreign	-15.1	-14.39	-2.7	4	2	5.25	0.42	800 869-6397
Morgan Stanley Fd of Fds Intl B	Foreign	-15.8	-15.08	-3.47	3	2	0	1.26	800 869-6397
Morgan Stanley Fd of Fds Intl C	Foreign	-16	-15.05	-3.39	3	2	0	1.26	800 869-6397
Morgan Stanley Fd of Fds Intl D	Foreign	-14.9	-14.23	-2.5	4	2	0	0.26	800 869-6397
Morgan Stanley Financl Serv Tr A	Financial	-6.4	6.25	5.79	2	3	5.25	1.14	800 869-6397
Morgan Stanley Financl Serv Tr B	Financial	-7	5.42	4.98	3	3	0	1.93	800 869-6397
Morgan Stanley Financl Serv Tr C	Financial	-7	5.49	5	3	3	0	1.93	800 869-6397
Morgan Stanley Financl Serv Tr D	Financial	-6.2	6.5	6.08	2	3	0	0.93	800 869-6397
Morgan Stanley Fundamental Value A	Income						5.25		800 869-6397
Morgan Stanley Fundamental Value B	Income						0		800 869-6397

Stock Fund Name	Objective	Annualized Return for			Rank		Max Load	Expense Ratio	Toll-Free/(Toll) Telephone
		1 Year	3 Years	5 Years	Overall	Risk			
Morgan Stanley Fundamental Value C	Income						0		800 869-6397
Morgan Stanley Fundamental Value D	Income						0		800 869-6397
Morgan Stanley Glb Divnd Gr Sec A	Global	-12.6	-3.58	-0.46	3	3	5.25	1.16	800 869-6397
Morgan Stanley Glb Divnd Gr Sec B	Global	-13.3	-4.33	-1.2	3	3	0	1.93	800 869-6397
Morgan Stanley Glb Divnd Gr Sec C	Global	-13.3	-4.32	-1.21	3	3	0	1.93	800 869-6397
Morgan Stanley Glb Divnd Gr Sec D	Global	-12.5	-3.39	-0.25	3	3	0	0.93	800 869-6397
Morgan Stanley Glbl Utilities A	Utilities	-7.3	-10.96	0.84	3	2	5.25	1.06	800 869-6397
Morgan Stanley Glbl Utilities B	Utilities	-8	-11.63	0.11	3	2	0	1.82	800 869-6397
Morgan Stanley Glbl Utilities C	Utilities	-8	-11.57	0.13	3	2	0	1.67	800 869-6397
Morgan Stanley Glbl Utilities D	Utilities	-7.2	-10.75	1.1	3	2	0	0.82	800 869-6397
Morgan Stanley Global Advantage A	Growth	-11.7	-17.21	-6.91	5	3	5.25	1.18	800 869-6397
Morgan Stanley Global Advantage B	Growth	-12.6	-17.87	-7.63	5	3	0	1.93	800 869-6397
Morgan Stanley Global Advantage C	Growth	-12.5	-17.85	-7.58	5	3	0	1.93	800 869-6397
Morgan Stanley Global Advantage D	Growth	-11.6	-17.05	-6.73	5	3	0	0.93	800 869-6397
Morgan Stanley Growth Fund A	Growth	-9.4	-15.65	-1	3	3	5.25	1.18	800 869-6397
Morgan Stanley Growth Fund B	Growth	-10.2	-16.23	-1.58	4	3	0	1.94	800 869-6397
Morgan Stanley Growth Fund C	Growth	-10.2	-16.25	-1.65	3	3	0	1.73	800 869-6397
Morgan Stanley Growth Fund D	Growth	-9.2	-15.44	-0.78	3	3	0	0.94	800 869-6397
Morgan Stanley Health Sci Tr A	Health	-1.1	3.33	10.52	2	3	5.25	1.35	800 869-6397
Morgan Stanley Health Sci Tr B	Health	-1.9	2.5	9.64	2	3	0	2.16	800 869-6397
Morgan Stanley Health Sci Tr C	Health	-2.1	2.5	9.63	2	3	0	2.16	800 869-6397
Morgan Stanley Health Sci Tr D	Health	-0.9	3.52	10.67	2	3	0	1.16	800 869-6397
Morgan Stanley Income Builder A	Growth/Inc	-3.1	1.67	0.97	2	1	5.25	1.17	800 869-6397
Morgan Stanley Income Builder B	Growth/Inc	-3.9	0.44	-0.05	2	1	0	1.95	800 869-6397
Morgan Stanley Income Builder C	Growth/Inc	-3.9	0.81	0.2	2	1	0	1.93	800 869-6397
Morgan Stanley Income Builder D	Growth/Inc	-2.8	1.97	1.25	1	1	0	0.95	800 869-6397
Morgan Stanley Information Fd A	Technology	-15.3	-35.11	-1.59	3	5	5.25	1.32	800 869-6397
Morgan Stanley Information Fd B	Technology	-16.1	-35.67	-2.31	4	5	0	2.1	800 869-6397
Morgan Stanley Information Fd C	Technology	-16.1	-35.6	-2.31	4	5	0	1.88	800 869-6397
Morgan Stanley Information Fd D	Technology	-15.3	-35.02	-1.37	3	5	0	1.1	800 869-6397
Morgan Stanley International A	Foreign	-13.2	-12		4	2	5.25	1.46	800 869-6397
Morgan Stanley International B	Foreign	-14	-12.73		4	2	0	2.24	800 869-6397
Morgan Stanley International C	Foreign	-14.1	-12.72		4	2	0	2.24	800 869-6397
Morgan Stanley International D	Foreign	-13.1	-11.86		4	2	0	1.24	800 869-6397
Morgan Stanley Intl Small Cap A	Foreign	-9.7	-6.04	1.39	3	2	5.25	2.06	800 869-6397
Morgan Stanley Intl Small Cap B	Foreign	-10.4	-6.82	0.57	3	2	0	2.86	800 869-6397
Morgan Stanley Intl Small Cap C	Foreign	-10.4	-6.76	0.66	3	2	0	2.86	800 869-6397
Morgan Stanley Intl Small Cap D	Foreign	-9.5	-5.9	1.47	3	2	0	1.86	800 869-6397
Morgan Stanley Intl Value Equity A	Foreign	-8.2					5.25	1.88	800 869-6397
Morgan Stanley Intl Value Equity B	Foreign	-8.9					0	2.63	800 869-6397
Morgan Stanley Intl Value Equity C	Foreign	-9					0	2.63	800 869-6397
Morgan Stanley Intl Value Equity D	Foreign	-8					0	1.63	800 869-6397
Morgan Stanley Japan Fund A	Pacific	-22.4	-21.26	-4.74	3	3	5.25	1.55	800 869-6397
Morgan Stanley Japan Fund B	Pacific	-22.9	-21.96	-5.5	4	3	0	2.38	800 869-6397
Morgan Stanley Japan Fund C	Pacific	-23	-21.98	-5.54	5	3	0	2.32	800 869-6397
Morgan Stanley Japan Fund D	Pacific	-22.1	-21.14	-4.48	3	3	0	1.38	800 869-6397
Morgan Stanley KLD Social Index A	Other	-8.4					5.25	0.85	800 869-6397
Morgan Stanley KLD Social Index B	Other	-9.1					0	1.6	800 869-6397
Morgan Stanley KLD Social Index C	Other	-9					0	1.6	800 869-6397
Morgan Stanley KLD Social Index D	Other	-8.2					0	0.6	800 869-6397
Morgan Stanley Latin Amer Gr A	Foreign	-8.8	-5.61	-4.62	3	4	5.25	2.2	800 869-6397
Morgan Stanley Latin Amer Gr B	Foreign	-9.5	-6.3	-5.37	3	4	0	2.96	800 869-6397
Morgan Stanley Latin Amer Gr C	Foreign	-9.4	-6.25	-5.3	3	4	0	2.88	800 869-6397
Morgan Stanley Latin Amer Gr D	Foreign	-8.6	-5.41	-4.45	3	4	0	1.96	800 869-6397
Morgan Stanley Mid Cap Value A	Global	-10.6					5.25	1.51	800 869-6397
Morgan Stanley Mid Cap Value B	Global	-11.2					0	2.26	800 869-6397
Morgan Stanley Mid Cap Value C	Global	-11.2					0	2.26	800 869-6397
Morgan Stanley Mid Cap Value D	Global	-10.4					0	1.26	800 869-6397

Stock Fund Name	Objective	Annualized Return for			Rank		Max Load	Expense Ratio	Toll-Free/(Toll) Telephone
		1 Year	3 Years	5 Years	Overall	Risk			
Morgan Stanley Mkt Leader Tr A	Growth	-11.2	-14.77	0.76	3	3	5.25	1.13	800 869-6397
Morgan Stanley Mkt Leader Tr B	Growth	-12	-15.42	-0.02	4	3	0	1.92	800 869-6397
Morgan Stanley Mkt Leader Tr C	Growth	-12	-15.42	0.02	4	3	0	1.92	800 869-6397
Morgan Stanley Mkt Leader Tr D	Growth	-11	-14.58	1.02	3	3	0	0.92	800 869-6397
Morgan Stanley NASDAQ 100 A	Other	0.1					5.25	0.85	800 869-6397
Morgan Stanley NASDAQ 100 B	Other	-0.6					0	1.6	800 869-6397
Morgan Stanley NASDAQ 100 C	Other	-0.6					0	1.6	800 869-6397
Morgan Stanley NASDAQ 100 D	Other	0.4					0	0.6	800 869-6397
Morgan Stanley Natural Res Dev A	Energy/Res	-15.7	-5.26	-2.1	3	3	5.25	0.88	800 869-6397
Morgan Stanley Natural Res Dev B	Energy/Res	-16.3	-6.04	-2.91	3	3	0	1.86	800 869-6397
Morgan Stanley Natural Res Dev C	Energy/Res	-16.3	-6.04	-2.93	3	3	0	1.85	800 869-6397
Morgan Stanley Natural Res Dev D	Energy/Res	-15.5	-5.11	-1.93	3	3	0	0.86	800 869-6397
Morgan Stanley New Discoveries A	Growth	-10.8					5.25	1.49	800 869-6397
Morgan Stanley New Discoveries B	Growth	-11.4					0	2.28	800 869-6397
Morgan Stanley New Discoveries C	Growth	-12.6					0	2.28	800 869-6397
Morgan Stanley New Discoveries D	Growth	-10.6					0	1.28	800 869-6397
Morgan Stanley Next Generation A	Growth	-5.8	-11.91		3	4	5.25	1.97	800 869-6397
Morgan Stanley Next Generation B	Growth	-6.4	-12.56		3	4	0	2.73	800 869-6397
Morgan Stanley Next Generation C	Growth	-6.4	-12.56		3	4	0	2.73	800 869-6397
Morgan Stanley Next Generation D	Growth	-5.6	-11.75		3	4	0	1.73	800 869-6397
Morgan Stanley Pacific Growth A	Pacific	-17.1	-16.35	-1.48	4	3	5.25	1.74	800 869-6397
Morgan Stanley Pacific Growth B	Pacific	-18	-16.98	-2.2	3	3	0	2.55	800 869-6397
Morgan Stanley Pacific Growth C	Pacific	-18	-16.94	-2.14	3	3	0	2.5	800 869-6397
Morgan Stanley Pacific Growth D	Pacific	-17.1	-16.1	-1.19	4	3	0	1.55	800 869-6397
Morgan Stanley Real Estate A	Real Est	2.6	12.58		1	2	5.25	1.54	800 869-6397
Morgan Stanley Real Estate B	Real Est	1.8	11.66		1	2	0	2.36	800 869-6397
Morgan Stanley Real Estate C	Real Est	1.9	11.69		1	2	0	2.36	800 869-6397
Morgan Stanley Real Estate D	Real Est	2.9	12.78		1	2	0	1.36	800 869-6397
Morgan Stanley S&P 500 Index A	Growth/Inc	-8.6	-11.41	-1.73	3	3	5.25	0.72	800 869-6397
Morgan Stanley S&P 500 Index B	Growth/Inc	-9.3	-12.13	-2.5	4	3	0	1.53	800 869-6397
Morgan Stanley S&P 500 Index C	Growth/Inc	-9.3	-12.13	-2.5	4	3	0	1.53	800 869-6397
Morgan Stanley S&P 500 Index D	Growth/Inc	-8.4	-11.24	-1.52	3	3	0	0.53	800 869-6397
Morgan Stanley Sm-Mid Special Val A	Income	5.2					5.25		800 869-6397
Morgan Stanley Sm-Mid Special Val B	Income	4.4					0		800 869-6397
Morgan Stanley Sm-Mid Special Val C	Income	4.4					0		800 869-6397
Morgan Stanley Sm-Mid Special Val D	Income	5.5					0		800 869-6397
Morgan Stanley Small Cap Growth A	Small Co	-26.3	-32.35	-8.91	5	5	5.25	1.59	800 869-6397
Morgan Stanley Small Cap Growth B	Small Co	-26.9	-32.9	-9.57	5	5	0	2.35	800 869-6397
Morgan Stanley Small Cap Growth C	Small Co	-26.9	-32.86	-9.6	4	5	0	2.2	800 869-6397
Morgan Stanley Small Cap Growth D	Small Co	-26.2	-32.24	-8.69	5	5	0	1.35	800 869-6397
Morgan Stanley Special Value A	Small Co	-9.6	9.47	5.63	2	2	5.25	1.18	800 869-6397
Morgan Stanley Special Value B	Small Co	-10.2	8.64	4.83	2	2	0	1.94	800 869-6397
Morgan Stanley Special Value C	Small Co	-10.3	8.61	4.87	2	2	0	1.92	800 869-6397
Morgan Stanley Special Value D	Small Co	-9.4	9.73	5.88	2	2	0	0.94	800 869-6397
Morgan Stanley Strategist Fund A	Flexible	-6.8	-4.91	1.52	2	1	5.25	0.85	800 869-6397
Morgan Stanley Strategist Fund B	Flexible	-7.6	-5.86	0.64	2	2	0	1.63	800 869-6397
Morgan Stanley Strategist Fund C	Flexible	-7.6	-5.71	0.68	2	1	0	1.63	800 869-6397
Morgan Stanley Strategist Fund D	Flexible	-6.6	-4.69	1.75	2	1	0	0.63	800 869-6397
Morgan Stanley Tax-Managed Gr A	Growth	-11.8	-16.75		5	3	5.25	1.37	800 869-6397
Morgan Stanley Tax-Managed Gr B	Growth	-12.6	-17.37		4	3	0	2.12	800 869-6397
Morgan Stanley Tax-Managed Gr C	Growth	-12.9	-17.37		4	3	0	2.12	800 869-6397
Morgan Stanley Tax-Managed Gr D	Growth	-11.6	-16.55		5	3	0	1.12	800 869-6397
Morgan Stanley Technology Fund A	Technology	-16.4					5.25	1.54	800 869-6397
Morgan Stanley Technology Fund B	Technology	-17.4					0	2.32	800 869-6397
Morgan Stanley Technology Fund C	Technology	-18.3					0	2.32	800 869-6397
Morgan Stanley Technology Fund D	Technology	-16.4					0	1.32	800 869-6397
Morgan Stanley Total Mkt Index A	Growth	-8.2					5.25	0.9	800 869-6397
Morgan Stanley Total Mkt Index B	Growth	-8.8					0	1.65	800 869-6397

Stock Fund Name	Objective	Annualized Return for			Rank		Max Load	Expense Ratio	Toll-Free/(Toll) Telephone
		1 Year	3 Years	5 Years	Overall	Risk			
Morgan Stanley Total Mkt Index C	Growth	-8.8					0	1.57	800 869-6397
Morgan Stanley Total Mkt Index D	Growth	-7.9					0	0.65	800 869-6397
Morgan Stanley Total Return Tr A	Growth/Inc	-19.7	-17.92	-3.14	5	4	5.25	1.12	800 869-6397
Morgan Stanley Total Return Tr B	Growth/Inc	-20.3	-18.55	-3.81	5	4	0	1.91	800 869-6397
Morgan Stanley Total Return Tr C	Growth/Inc	-20.6	-18.57	-3.87	5	4	0	1.91	800 869-6397
Morgan Stanley Total Return Tr D	Growth/Inc	-19.5	-17.73	-2.93	5	4	0	0.91	800 869-6397
Morgan Stanley Utilities Fund A	Utilities	-5.3	-9.68	-0.76	3	2	5.25	0.87	800 869-6397
Morgan Stanley Utilities Fund B	Utilities	-6	-10.56	-1.63	3	2	0	1.63	800 869-6397
Morgan Stanley Utilities Fund C	Utilities	-6.1	-10.41	-1.55	3	2	0	1.63	800 869-6397
Morgan Stanley Utilities Fund D	Utilities	-5.1	-9.68	-0.7	3	2	0	0.63	800 869-6397
Morgan Stanley Val-Added Mkt Eq A	Growth/Inc	-7	0.46	3.12	1	2	5.25	0.84	800 869-6397
Morgan Stanley Val-Added Mkt Eq B	Growth/Inc	-7.6	-0.28	2.39	2	2	0	1.59	800 869-6397
Morgan Stanley Val-Added Mkt Eq C	Growth/Inc	-7.6	-0.28	2.37	2	2	0	1.54	800 869-6397
Morgan Stanley Val-Added Mkt Eq D	Growth/Inc	-6.7	0.68	3.35	1	3	0	0.6	800 869-6397
Morgan Stanley Value Fund A	Growth	-15	-0.78		3	3	5.25	1.45	800 869-6397
Morgan Stanley Value Fund B	Growth	-15.6	-1.53		3	3	0	2.21	800 869-6397
Morgan Stanley Value Fund C	Growth	-15.5	-1.48		3	3	0	2.21	800 869-6397
Morgan Stanley Value Fund D	Growth	-14.8	-0.54		3	3	0	1.21	800 869-6397
Mosaic Balanced Fund	Balanced	-2.2	3.1	4.45	1	1	0	1.2	800 336-3063
Mosaic Foresight Fund	Flexible	-6.3	0.86	3.45	2	1	0	1.25	800 336-3063
Mosaic Investors Fund	Growth	-8.2	-0.3	3.08	2	2	0	1	800 336-3063
Mosaic Mid-Cap Growth Fd	Growth	-2.4	8.72	8.25	1	2	0	1.25	800 336-3063
Muhlenkamp Fund	Growth	-7.6	7	5.84	2	4	0	1.17	800 860-3863
Munder Balanced A	Balanced	-2.5	-1.06	5.62	1	2	5.5	1.37	800 438-5789
Munder Balanced B	Balanced	-3	-1.85	4.79	1	2	0	2.12	800 438-5789
Munder Balanced C	Balanced	-3.1	-1.9	4.8	1	2	0	2.12	800 438-5789
Munder Balanced K	Balanced	-2.3	-1.21	5.51	1	2	0	1.52	800 438-5789
Munder Balanced Y	Balanced	-2.1	-0.96	5.79	1	2	0	1.12	800 438-5789
Munder Framlington Emerg Mkts A	Foreign	-3.4	-9	-1.82	3	4	5.5	1.99	800 438-5789
Munder Framlington Emerg Mkts B	Foreign	-3.9	-9.71	-2.58	3	4	0	2.73	800 438-5789
Munder Framlington Emerg Mkts C	Foreign	-4.1	-9.77	-2.77	3	4	0	2.73	800 438-5789
Munder Framlington Emerg Mkts K	Foreign	-3.2	-9.02	-2.06	3	4	0	1.99	800 438-5789
Munder Framlington Emerg Mkts Y	Foreign	-3	-8.96	-1.93	3	4	0	1.73	800 438-5789
Munder Framlington Healthcare A	Health	-2.7	-8.14	7.59	3	5	5.5	2.16	800 438-5789
Munder Framlington Healthcare B	Health	-3.5	-8.83	6.8	3	5	0	2.92	800 438-5789
Munder Framlington Healthcare C	Health	-3.4	-8.82	6.79	3	5	0	2.92	800 438-5789
Munder Framlington Healthcare K	Health	-2.8	-8.15	7.38	3	5	0	2.16	800 438-5789
Munder Framlington Healthcare Y	Health	-2.5	-7.91	7.87	3	5	0	1.92	800 438-5789
Munder Framlington Intl Growth A	Foreign	-14.1	-18.14	-6.11	5	3	5.5	1.69	800 438-5789
Munder Framlington Intl Growth B	Foreign	-15	-18.92	-7	5	3	0	2.44	800 438-5789
Munder Framlington Intl Growth C	Foreign	-14.8	-18.87	-6.96	5	3	0	2.44	800 438-5789
Munder Framlington Intl Growth K	Foreign	-14	-18.25	-6.21	5	3	0	1.69	800 438-5789
Munder Framlington Intl Growth Y	Foreign	-13.9	-18.05	-6	5	3	0	1.44	800 438-5789
Munder Future Technology A	Technology	-8.1	-38.93		4	5	5.5	2.56	800 438-5789
Munder Future Technology B	Technology	-9.1	-39.42		4	5	0	3.31	800 438-5789
Munder Future Technology II	Technology	-9.1	-39.45		4	5	0	3.31	800 438-5789
Munder Future Technology Y	Technology	-7.9	-38.78		4	5	0	2.31	800 438-5789
Munder Index 500 A	Growth/Inc	-8.8	-11.41	-1.63	3	3	2.5	0.64	800 438-5789
Munder Index 500 B	Growth/Inc	-9	-11.67	-1.95	3	3	0	1.39	800 438-5789
Munder Index 500 K	Growth/Inc	-8.7	-11.47	-1.71	3	3	0	0.73	800 438-5789
Munder Index 500 Y	Growth/Inc	-8.5	-11.24	-1.46	3	3	0	0.39	800 438-5789
Munder Instl S&P MidCap Index Y	Growth/Inc	-8.8	0.69	6.76	2	3	0	0.18	800 438-5789
Munder International Equity A	Foreign	-10.8	-14.43	-3.64	3	3	5.5	1.38	800 438-5789
Munder International Equity B	Foreign	-11.4	-15.06	-4.41	3	3	0	2.13	800 438-5789
Munder International Equity C	Foreign	-11.4	-15.07	-4.4	3	3	0	2.13	800 438-5789
Munder International Equity K	Foreign	-10.7	-14.35	-3.62	3	3	0	1.49	800 438-5789
Munder International Equity Y	Foreign	-10.4	-14.15	-3.37	4	3	0	1.13	800 438-5789
Munder Large Cap Value A	Growth/Inc	-9.2	-1.15	-2.06	3	2	5.5	1.28	800 438-5789

Stock Fund Name	Objective	Annualized Return for			Rank		Max Load	Expense Ratio	Toll-Free/(Toll) Telephone
		1 Year	3 Years	5 Years	Overall	Risk			
Munder Large Cap Value B	Growth/Inc	-9.8	-1.91	-2.81	3	2	0	2.03	800 438-5789
Munder Large Cap Value C	Growth/Inc	-9.8	-1.91	-2.79	3	2	0	2.03	800 438-5789
Munder Large Cap Value K	Growth/Inc	-9.2	-1.15	-2.08	3	2	0	1.32	800 438-5789
Munder Large Cap Value Y	Growth/Inc	-8.9	-0.92	-1.84	3	2	0	1.03	800 438-5789
Munder Micro-Cap Equity A	Small Co	-12.8	-0.84	7.09	3	5	5.5	1.66	800 438-5789
Munder Micro-Cap Equity B	Small Co	-13.4	-1.52	6.29	3	5	0	2.41	800 438-5789
Munder Micro-Cap Equity C	Small Co	-13.4	-1.52	6.29	3	5	0	2.41	800 438-5789
Munder Micro-Cap Equity K	Small Co	-12.8	-0.78	7.09	3	5	0	1.89	800 438-5789
Munder Micro-Cap Equity Y	Small Co	-12.6	-0.53	7.36	3	5	0	1.42	800 438-5789
Munder MidCap Select A	Growth	-4					5.5	1.43	800 438-5789
Munder MidCap Select B	Growth	-4.7					0	2.18	800 438-5789
Munder MidCap Select II	Growth	-4.7					0	2.18	800 438-5789
Munder MidCap Select Y	Growth	-3.7	-1.04			3	0	1.18	800 438-5789
Munder Multi-Season Growth A	Growth	-11.9	-12.57	-5.87	4	3	5.5	1.21	800 438-5789
Munder Multi-Season Growth B	Growth	-12.4	-13.3	-6.63	4	3	0	1.96	800 438-5789
Munder Multi-Season Growth C	Growth	-12.5	-13.16	-6.53	4	3	0	1.96	800 438-5789
Munder Multi-Season Growth K	Growth	-11.8	-12.5	-5.83	4	3	0	1.32	800 438-5789
Munder Multi-Season Growth Y	Growth	-11.6	-12.3	-5.62	4	3	0	0.96	800 438-5789
Munder Net Net Fund A	Technology	23.3	-37.1	-3.52	3	5	5.5	2.64	800 438-5789
Munder Net Net Fund B	Technology	22.4	-37.57		3	5	0	3.35	800 438-5789
Munder Net Net Fund C	Technology	22.4	-37.57		3	5	0	3.35	800 438-5789
Munder Net Net Fund Y	Technology	23.6	-36.95		3	5	0	2.35	800 438-5789
Munder Real Estate Equity A	Real Est	6.4	13.27	5.21	1	1	5.5	1.2	800 438-5789
Munder Real Estate Equity B	Real Est	5.6	12.33	4.38	2	1	0	1.95	800 438-5789
Munder Real Estate Equity C	Real Est	5.6	12.38	4.61	2	1	0	1.95	800 438-5789
Munder Real Estate Equity K	Real Est	6.3	13.27	5.19	1	1	0	1.43	800 438-5789
Munder Real Estate Equity Y	Real Est	6.7	13.49	5.46	1	1	0	0.95	800 438-5789
Munder Small Cap Value A	Small Co	-5.3	15.32	5.12	2	3	5.5	1.41	800 438-5789
Munder Small Cap Value B	Small Co	-5.8	14.5	4.36	2	3	0	2.16	800 438-5789
Munder Small Cap Value C	Small Co	-5.9	14.51	4.32	2	3	0	2.16	800 438-5789
Munder Small Cap Value K	Small Co	-5.2	15.33	5.09	2	3	0	1.6	800 438-5789
Munder Small Cap Value Y	Small Co	-4.9	15.64	5.37	2	3	0	1.16	800 438-5789
Munder Small Company Growth A	Small Co	-16.7	-13.83	-10.61	5	5	5.5	1.33	800 438-5789
Munder Small Company Growth B	Small Co	-17.3	-14.43	-11.51	5	5	0	2.08	800 438-5789
Munder Small Company Growth C	Small Co	-17.3	-14.48	-11.53	5	5	0	2.08	800 438-5789
Munder Small Company Growth K	Small Co	-16.6	-13.82	-10.88	5	5	0	1.59	800 438-5789
Munder Small Company Growth Y	Small Co	-16.4	-13.6	-10.65	5	5	0	1.08	800 438-5789
Mutual Beacon A	Growth/Inc	-7.5	3.66	4.45	2	2	5.75	1.15	800 632-2350
Mutual Beacon B	Growth/Inc	-8.1	3.02	3.81	2	2	0	1.8	800 632-2350
Mutual Beacon C	Growth/Inc	-8.1	2.99	3.77	2	2	1	1.79	800 632-2350
Mutual Beacon Z	Growth/Inc	-7.2	4.03	4.8	2	2	0	0.8	800 632-2350
Mutual Discovery A	Global	-7.7	1.68	3.81	2	1	5.75	1.39	800 632-2350
Mutual Discovery B	Global	-8.3	1.04	3.18	2	1	0	2.04	800 632-2350
Mutual Discovery C	Global	-8.3	1.03	3.16	2	1	1	2.03	800 632-2350
Mutual Discovery R	Global	-7.8	1.55	3.66	2	1	0	1.54	800 632-2350
Mutual Discovery Z	Global	-7.4	2.04	4.19	2	1	0	1.05	800 632-2350
Mutual European A	European	-8.8	0.11	6.4	2	2	5.75	1.4	800 632-2350
Mutual European B	European	-9.4	-0.54	5.76	2	2	0	2.06	800 632-2350
Mutual European C	European	-9.3	-0.51	5.79	2	2	1	2.02	800 632-2350
Mutual European Z	European	-8.4	0.48	6.84	2	2	0	1.2	800 632-2350
Mutual Financial Svcs A	Financial	-2.6	15.98	8.64	2	2	5.75	1.44	800 632-2350
Mutual Financial Svcs B	Financial	-3.2	15.19	8.19	2	2	0	2.09	800 632-2350
Mutual Financial Svcs C	Financial	-3.2	15.23	8.16	2	2	1	2.07	800 632-2350
Mutual Financial Svcs Z	Financial	-2.3	16.39	9.23	2	2	0	1.15	800 632-2350
Mutual Qualified A	Growth/Inc	-8.4	3.66	4.04	2	2	5.75	1.15	800 632-2350
Mutual Qualified B	Growth/Inc	-8.9	3	3.47	2	2	0	1.8	800 632-2350
Mutual Qualified C	Growth/Inc	-8.9	2.99	3.37	2	2	1	1.79	800 632-2350
Mutual Qualified Z	Growth/Inc	-8	4.04	4.4	2	2	0	0.81	800 632-2350

Stock Fund Name	Objective	Annualized Return for			Rank		Max Load	Expense Ratio	Toll-Free/(Toll) Telephone
		1 Year	3 Years	5 Years	Overall	Risk			
Mutual Shares A	Growth/Inc	-6.3	4.24	4.45	1	2	5.75	1.14	800 632-2350
Mutual Shares B	Growth/Inc	-7	3.56	3.85	2	2	0	1.79	800 632-2350
Mutual Shares C	Growth/Inc	-6.9	3.58	3.79	2	1	1	1.78	800 632-2350
Mutual Shares R	Growth/Inc	-6.5	4.12	4.28	1	2	0	1.29	800 632-2350
Mutual Shares Z	Growth/Inc	-6	4.61	4.82	1	2	0	0.79	800 632-2350
NI Numeric Inv Emerging Growth Fund	Small Co	-1.7	0.45	9.02	2	4	0	1.25	800 686-3742
NI Numeric Inv Growth Fund	Small Co	-6.9	-9.91	2.31	3	4	0	1.85	800 686-3742
NI Numeric Inv Mid Cap Fund	Growth	-8	-3.47	3.16	2	3	0	0.95	800 686-3742
NI Numeric Inv Small Cap Value	Small Co	-4.6	24.07		1	2	0	1.85	800 686-3742
Nations Asset Allocation Inv A	AssetAlloc	-3.8	-5.08	0.93	2	1	5.75	1.3	800 321-7854
Nations Asset Allocation Inv B	AssetAlloc	-4.7	-5.83	0.17	2	1	0	2.05	800 321-7854
Nations Asset Allocation Inv C	AssetAlloc	-4.7	-5.83	0.17	2	1	0	2.05	800 321-7854
Nations Capital Growth Inv A	Growth	-9.8	-16.67	-4.29	4	3	5.75	1.3	800 321-7854
Nations Capital Growth Inv B	Growth	-10.4	-17.3	-5	4	3	0	2.05	800 321-7854
Nations Capital Growth Inv C	Growth	-10.4	-17.3	-5	4	3	0	2.05	800 321-7854
Nations Capital Growth Pr A	Growth	-9.6	-16.46	-4.03	4	3	0	1.05	800 321-7854
Nations Classic Value Inv A	Financial	-16.4					5.75	1.23	800 321-7854
Nations Classic Value Inv B	Financial	-17.1					0	1.98	800 321-7854
Nations Classic Value Inv C	Financial	-17.1					0	1.98	800 321-7854
Nations Classic Value Pr A	Financial	-16.2					0	0.98	800 321-7854
Nations Convertible Sec Inv A	Converts	-2.4	-0.61	6.12	1	1	5.75	1.23	800 321-7854
Nations Convertible Sec Inv C	Converts	-3.2	-1.39	5.38	1	1	0	1.98	800 321-7854
Nations Global Value Inv A	Global	-13.6					5.75	1.65	800 321-7854
Nations Global Value Inv B	Global	-14.2					0	2.4	800 321-7854
Nations Global Value Inv C	Global	-14.3					0	2.4	800 321-7854
Nations Global Value Pr A	Global	-13.4					0	1.4	800 321-7854
Nations International Eq Inv A	Foreign	-12.8	-12.25	-2.83	4	3	5.75	1.46	800 321-7854
Nations International Eq Inv B	Foreign	-14.3	-13.21	-3.72	3	3	0	2.21	800 321-7854
Nations International Eq Inv C	Foreign	-13	-12.77	-3.45	3	3	0	2.21	800 321-7854
Nations International Eq Pr A	Foreign	-13.4	-12.32	-2.7	3	3	0	1.21	800 321-7854
Nations International Val Inv A	Foreign	-14.3	-4.87	4.8	3	3	5.75	1.4	800 321-7854
Nations International Val Inv B	Foreign	-15	-5.58	3.87	3	3	0	2.15	800 321-7854
Nations International Val Inv C	Foreign	-15	-5.58	3.93	3	3	0	2.15	800 321-7854
Nations International Val Pr A	Foreign	-14.2	-4.63	4.91	3	3	0	1.15	800 321-7854
Nations Large Cap Index Fund Inv A	Growth	-8.6	-11.41	-1.66	3	3	0	0.6	800 321-7854
Nations Large Cap Index Fund Pr A	Growth	-8.4	-11.17	-1.42	3	3	0	0.35	800 321-7854
Nations LifeGoal Bal Growth Inv A	Balanced	-2.7	0.34	3.77	1	1	5.75	0.5	800 321-7854
Nations LifeGoal Bal Growth Inv B	Balanced	-3.4	-0.41	2.77	1	1	0	1.25	800 321-7854
Nations LifeGoal Bal Growth Inv C	Balanced	-3.6	-0.46	2.79	1	1	0	1.25	800 321-7854
Nations LifeGoal Bal Growth Pr A	Balanced	-2.4	0.6	3.72	1	1	0	0.25	800 321-7854
Nations LifeGoal Bal Growth Pr B	Balanced	-3	0.07	3.2	1	1	0	0.75	800 321-7854
Nations LifeGoal Growth Inv A	Growth	-12.5	-8.39	0.46	3	3	5.75	1.2	800 321-7854
Nations LifeGoal Growth Inv B	Growth	-13.1	-9.09	-0.64	4	3	0	1.95	800 321-7854
Nations LifeGoal Growth Inv C	Growth	-13.1	-9.14	-0.68	4	3	0	1.95	800 321-7854
Nations LifeGoal Growth Pr A	Growth	-12.2	-8.25	0.32	3	3	0	0.95	800 321-7854
Nations LifeGoal Inc & Gr Inv A	Growth/Inc	1.8	3.33	4.15	1	1	5.75	0.5	800 321-7854
Nations LifeGoal Inc & Gr Inv B	Growth/Inc	1.1	2.27	2.87	2	1	0	1.25	800 321-7854
Nations LifeGoal Inc & Gr Inv C	Growth/Inc	1.2	2.56	3.02	2	1	0	1.25	800 321-7854
Nations LifeGoal Inc & Gr Pr A	Growth/Inc	2.1	3.6	3.91	1	1	0	0.25	800 321-7854
Nations Managed Index Inv A	Growth	-8.8	-10.3	-1.85	3	3	0	0.75	800 321-7854
Nations Managed Index Pr A	Growth	-8.5	-10.05	-1.58	3	3	0	0.5	800 321-7854
Nations Marsico 21st Century Inv A	Growth	2.5	-5.87		3	4	5.75	1.7	800 321-7854
Nations Marsico 21st Century Inv B	Growth	1.7	-6.62		2	4	0	2.45	800 321-7854
Nations Marsico 21st Century Inv C	Growth	1.7	-6.62		2	4	0	2.45	800 321-7854
Nations Marsico 21st Century Pr A	Growth	2.8	-5.66		3	4	0	1.45	800 321-7854
Nations Marsico Focused Eq Inv A	Growth	-9	-9.01	3.22	3	3	5.75	1.37	800 321-7854
Nations Marsico Focused Eq Inv B	Growth	-9.7	-9.71	2.47	3	3	0	2.12	800 321-7854
Nations Marsico Focused Eq Inv C	Growth	-9.6	-9.67	2.58	3	3	0	2.12	800 321-7854

Stock Fund Name	Objective	Annualized Return for			Rank		Max Load	Expense Ratio	Toll-Free/(Toll) Telephone
		1 Year	3 Years	5 Years	Overall	Risk			
Nations Marsico Focused Eq Pr A	Growth	-8.7	-8.77	3.22	3	3	0	1.12	800 321-7854
Nations Marsico Growth Inv A	Growth/Inc	-9.3	-9.85	1.71	3	3	5.75	1.41	800 321-7854
Nations Marsico Growth Inv B	Growth/Inc	-9.9	-10.55	0.97	3	3	0	2.16	800 321-7854
Nations Marsico Growth Inv C	Growth/Inc	-10	-10.56	0.96	3	3	0	2.16	800 321-7854
Nations Marsico Growth Pr A	Growth/Inc	-9	-9.65	1.88	3	3	0	1.16	800 321-7854
Nations Marsico Intl Oppt Inv A	Foreign	-7.7					5.75	1.75	800 321-7854
Nations Marsico Intl Oppt Inv B	Foreign	-8.3					0	2.5	800 321-7854
Nations Marsico Intl Oppt Inv C	Foreign	-8.3					0	2.5	800 321-7854
Nations Marsico Intl Oppt Pr A	Foreign	-7.5					0	1.5	800 321-7854
Nations MidCap Growth Fund Inv A	Agg Growth	-15.7	-16.07	-1.82	3	4	5.75	1.24	800 321-7854
Nations MidCap Growth Fund Inv B	Agg Growth	-16.5	-16.73	-2.56	3	4	0	1.99	800 321-7854
Nations MidCap Growth Fund Inv C	Agg Growth	-16.4	-16.69	-2.52	3	4	0	1.99	800 321-7854
Nations MidCap Growth Fund Pr A	Agg Growth	-15.6	-15.84	-1.55	3	4	0	0.99	800 321-7854
Nations MidCap Index Inv A	Growth	-9.7	0.39		2	3	0	0.6	800 321-7854
Nations MidCap Index Pr A	Growth	-9.5	0.61		3	3	0	0.35	800 321-7854
Nations MidCap Value Investor A	Growth	-7.2					5.75	1.46	800 321-7854
Nations MidCap Value Investor B	Growth	-7.9					0	2.21	800 321-7854
Nations MidCap Value Investor C	Growth	-7.9					0	2.21	800 321-7854
Nations Small Cap Index Inv A	Small Co	-11.5	2.52	0.93	3	3	0	0.65	800 321-7854
Nations Small Cap Index Pr A	Small Co	-11.4	2.79	1.25	3	3	0	0.4	800 321-7854
Nations Small Company Fund Inv A	Small Co	-17.4	-11.33	-0.78	4	4	5.75	1.4	800 321-7854
Nations Small Company Fund Inv B	Small Co	-18	-11.98	-1.46	4	4	0	2.15	800 321-7854
Nations Small Company Fund Inv C	Small Co	-18	-12	-1.43	4	4	0	2.15	800 321-7854
Nations Small Company Fund Pr A	Small Co	-17.2	-11.09	-0.51	4	4	0	1.15	800 321-7854
Nations SmallCap Value Inv A	Growth/Inc	-6.8					5.75	1.55	800 321-7854
Nations SmallCap Value Inv B	Growth/Inc	-7.5					0	2.3	800 321-7854
Nations SmallCap Value Inv C	Growth/Inc	-7.4					0	2.3	800 321-7854
Nations SmallCap Value Pr A	Growth/Inc	-6.5					0	1.3	800 321-7854
Nations Strategic Growth C	Growth	-12.2	-14.61		5	3	0	1.95	800 321-7854
Nations Strategic Growth Inv A	Growth	-11.5	-13.91		5	3	5.75	0.95	800 321-7854
Nations Strategic Growth Inv B	Growth	-12.2	-14.63		5	3	0	1.94	800 321-7854
Nations Strategic Growth Pr A	Growth	-11.4	-13.75		5	3	0	0.94	800 321-7854
Nations Value Fund Inv A	Growth/Inc	-11.9	-4.92	-2.04	3	2	5.75	1.24	800 321-7854
Nations Value Fund Inv B	Growth/Inc	-12.6	-5.62	-2.79	3	2	0	1.99	800 321-7854
Nations Value Fund Inv C	Growth/Inc	-12.6	-5.62	-2.72	3	2	0	1.99	800 321-7854
Nations Value Fund Pr A	Growth/Inc	-11.7	-4.67	-1.73	3	2	0	0.99	800 321-7854
Nationwide Internatl Index A	Foreign	-14.4	-14.43		5	3	5.75	0.76	800 848-0920
Nationwide Internatl Index B	Foreign	-15	-15		5	3	0	1.42	800 848-0920
Nationwide Internatl Index Inst	Foreign	-14.2	-14.19		5	3	0	0.36	800 848-0920
Nationwide Lrg Cap Gr A	Growth	-10.3	-20.39		5	4	5.75	1.44	800 848-0920
Nationwide Lrg Cap Gr B	Growth	-10.8	-21.16		5	4	0	1.94	800 848-0920
Nationwide Mid Cap Mkt Index A	Growth	-9.9	0.23		3	3	5.75	0.71	800 848-0920
Nationwide Mid Cap Mkt Index Inst	Growth	-9.5	0.68		2	3	0	0.31	800 848-0920
Nationwide S&P 500 Index A	Other	-8.6	-11.38		3	3	5.75	0.48	800 848-0920
Nationwide S&P 500 Index B	Other	-9.2	-12.06		3	3	0	1.23	800 848-0920
Nationwide S&P 500 Index Instl	Other	-8.3	-11.05		3	3	0	0.23	800 848-0920
Nationwide S&P 500 Index Instl-Svc	Other	-8.6	-11.24		3	3	0	0.48	800 848-0920
Nationwide S&P 500 Index L	Other	-8.4	-11.11		3	3	0	0.33	800 848-0920
Nationwide S&P 500 Index Svc	Other	-8.7	-11.43		3	3	0	0.63	800 848-0920
Nationwide Small Cap A	Small Co	-9.6	-0.22		3	3	5.75	0.69	800 848-0920
Nationwide Small Cap B	Small Co	-10	-0.88		3	3	0	2.1	800 848-0920
Nationwide Small Cap Index A	Small Co	-8.8	-3.39		3	4	5.75	0.76	800 848-0920
Nationwide Small Cap Index Inst	Small Co	-8.4	-2.93		3	4	0	0.29	800 848-0920
Navellier Millennium Mid Cap Gr A	Growth	-6.2					0	1.5	800 887-8671
Navellier Millennium Mid Cap Gr B	Growth	-6.9					0	2.25	800 887-8671
Navellier Millennium Mid Cap Gr C	Growth	-6.8					0	2.25	800 887-8671
Navellier Performance Aggr Growth	Agg Growth	-19.8	-12.57	0	4	3	0	1.49	800 887-8671
Navellier Performance Aggr Micro	Small Co	-20.9	-11.26	-1.03	4	5	0	1.49	800 887-8671

Stock Fund Name	Objective	Annualized Return for 1 Year	3 Years	5 Years	Rank Overall	Risk	Max Load	Expense Ratio	Toll-Free/(Toll) Telephone
Navellier Performance Aggr SmCp Eq	Small Co	-21.2	-26.46	-15.64	5	5	3	1.49	800 887-8671
Navellier Performance Lrg Cap Val	Growth	-16.6	-7.21	-3.22	3	2	0	1.4	800 887-8671
Navellier Performance Lrg Cp Grwth	Growth	-12.1	-16.8	3.66	4	4	0	1.49	800 887-8671
Navellier Performance Mid Cp Grwth	Growth	-8.2	-11.53	9.52	3	4	0	1.34	800 887-8671
Navellier Performance Sm Cap Val	Small Co	-20.1	3.68	0.42	3	3	0	1.49	800 887-8671
Needham Growth Fund	Growth	-7.9	-3.18	11.75	2	5	0	1.75	800 625-7071
Neuberger Berman AMT Balanced	Balanced	-5	-9.09	0.9	2	3	0	1.1	877 461-1899
Neuberger Berman Fasciano Adv	Global	-12.3					0	1.91	877 461-1899
Neuberger Berman Fasciano Inv	Small Co	-11.9	2.83	1.26	3	3	0	1.27	877 461-1899
Neuberger Berman Focus Adv	Growth	-16	-8.09	1.86	3	5	0	1.36	877 461-1899
Neuberger Berman Focus Inv	Growth	-15.6	-7.62	1.48	3	5	0	0.94	877 461-1899
Neuberger Berman Focus Tr	Growth	-15.8	-7.84	1.32	3	5	0	1.09	877 461-1899
Neuberger Berman Genesis Adv	Small Co	-3.9	11.66	8.1	1	2	0	1.38	877 461-1899
Neuberger Berman Genesis Inv	Small Co	-3.7	11.93	8.4	1	2	0	1.08	877 461-1899
Neuberger Berman Genesis Tr	Small Co	-3.7	11.89	8.33	1	2	0	1.11	877 461-1899
Neuberger Berman Guardian Adv	Growth/Inc	-10.8	-7.33	-4.26	3	3	0	1.32	877 461-1899
Neuberger Berman Guardian Inv	Growth/Inc	-10.5	-6.87	-3.7	3	3	0	0.93	877 461-1899
Neuberger Berman Guardian Tr	Growth/Inc	-10.6	-7	-3.81	3	3	0	1.05	877 461-1899
Neuberger Berman International	Foreign	-8.6	-11	-3.58	3	2	0	1.71	877 461-1899
Neuberger Berman Manhattan Adv	Agg Growth	-12.2	-21.44	-5.78	4	5	0	1.5	877 461-1899
Neuberger Berman Manhattan Inv	Agg Growth	-11.9	-20.21	-4.54	4	5	0	1.05	877 461-1899
Neuberger Berman Manhattan Tr	Agg Growth	-11.9	-20.89	-5.23	4	5	0	1.1	877 461-1899
Neuberger Berman Millennium Inv	Growth	-26.5	-24.28		5	5	0	1.75	877 461-1899
Neuberger Berman Millennium Tr	Growth	-26.5	-24.41		5	5	0	1.75	877 461-1899
Neuberger Berman Partners Adv	Growth	-9.9	-5.42	-2.22	3	3	0	1.27	877 461-1899
Neuberger Berman Partners Inv	Growth	-9.6	-4.91	-1.7	3	3	0	0.91	877 461-1899
Neuberger Berman Partners Tr	Growth	-9.7	-5.05	-1.77	3	3	0	1.07	877 461-1899
Neuberger Berman Real Estate Fund	Real Est	9.2					0		877 461-1899
Neuberger Berman Regency Tr	Other	-6.8	-1.88		1	2	0	1.52	877 461-1899
Neuberger Berman Socially Resp Inv	Growth	1.4	-0.13	1.45	2	3	0	1.13	877 461-1899
New Alternatives Fund	Other	-18.8	-4.74	-1.15	3	4	4.75	1.32	800 423-8383
New Century Balanced	Balanced	-5.8	-4.41	0.96	2	1	0	1.49	888 639-0102
New Century Capital	Growth	-12.5	-12.38	-1.32	5	3	0	1.29	888 639-0102
New Covenant Balanced Growth	Balanced	-1.6	-2.08	0.9		1	0	1.11	800 858-6127
New Covenant Balanced Income	Balanced	3.6	2.81	3.18		1	0	1.07	800 858-6127
New Covenant Growth	Global	-10.4	-10.39	-3.47		3	0	1.11	800 858-6127
New Market Fund	Growth	-4.9	-0.9			2	2.75	1.99	800 527-9525
New York Equity Fund	Growth	7.3	-26.94	-10.44	3	5	4.75	2	888 899-8344
Nicholas Equity Income Fund	Income	-15.8	-1.14	-2.39	3	2	0	0.9	800 227-5987
Nicholas Fund	Growth	-10.4	-9.47	-4.58	3	2	0	0.74	800 227-5987
Nicholas II Fund	Small Co	-7.6	-4.83	-3.31	2	3	0	0.65	800 227-5987
Nicholas Limited Edition	Small Co	-9.7	-4.4	-3.95	3	4	0	0.88	800 227-5987
Nicholas-Applegate Convertible I	Converts	-2.2	-8.02	5.59	2	3	0	1	800 551-8043
Nicholas-Applegate Emer Countries I	Foreign	-13.4	-15.53	-5.91	4	4	0	1.69	800 551-8043
Nicholas-Applegate Emerg Gr I	Small Co	-15.9	-19.3	-2.39	5	5	0	1.22	800 551-8043
Nicholas-Applegate Emerg Gr R	Global	-16	-19.46	-2.54		5	0	1.48	800 551-8043
Nicholas-Applegate Glb Select I	Global	-9.1	-12.64	10.41	3	4	0	1.23	800 551-8043
Nicholas-Applegate Gr Disc I	Small Co	-10.5	-8.91	3.87	3	5	0	1.57	800 551-8043
Nicholas-Applegate Growth Equity A	Growth	-16.6	-27.85	-5.17	5	5	5	1.76	800 225-1852
Nicholas-Applegate Growth Equity B	Growth	-17.2	-28.41	-5.92	5	5	0	2.55	888 743-7111
Nicholas-Applegate Growth Equity C	Growth	-17.2	-28.41	-5.92	5	5	1	2.55	888 743-7111
Nicholas-Applegate Growth Equity Z	Growth	-16.4	-27.66	-4.91	5	5	0	1.55	888 743-7111
Nicholas-Applegate Intl Core Gr I	Foreign	-13.1	-17.12	-4.2	5	2	0	1.37	800 551-8043
Nicholas-Applegate Intl Core Gr R	Foreign	-13.3	-17.32		5	2	0	1.62	800 551-8043
Nicholas-Applegate Intl Gr Opp I	Foreign	-12	-14.64	6.83	3	3	0	1.41	800 551-8043
Nicholas-Applegate Intl Struct I	Global	-7.9					0	1.37	800 551-8043
Nicholas-Applegate Lrg Cp Val I	Growth	-10.6	0.19	1.85	2	3	0	1.01	800 551-8043
Nicholas-Applegate Lrg Cp Val R	Growth	-10.8	-0.08	1.63		3	0		800 551-8043

Stock Fund Name	Objective	Annualized Return for			Rank		Max Load	Expense Ratio	Toll-Free/(Toll) Telephone
		1 Year	3 Years	5 Years	Overall	Risk			
Nicholas-Applegate Pacific Rim I	Pacific	-24.4	-12.88	8.6	4	3	0	1.78	800 227-7337
Nicholas-Applegate US Eq Gr I	Growth	-15.4	-27.05	-4.33	5	5	0	1	800 551-8043
Nicholas-Applegate US Eq Gr R	Growth	-15.6	-27.21	-4.45		5	0	1.25	800 551-8043
Nicholas-Applegate US Lg Cp Sl Gr I	Growth	-15.7	-30.66	-2.7	4	4	0	1.01	800 551-8043
Nicholas-Applegate US Lg Cp Sl Gr R	Growth	-16					0	1.25	800 551-8043
Nicholas-Applegate Val Opp I	Small Co	-3.7					0	1.3	800 551-8043
Nicholas-Applegate Worldwide Gr I	Global	-16.6	-23.44	-2.95	5	4	0	1.35	800 551-8043
Noah Fund	Growth	-10	-20.21	-4.5	4	4	0	2.2	800 794-6624
North Track DJ US Fin 100+ A	Financial	-5					5.25	1.17	800 826-4600
North Track DJ US Fin 100+ B	Financial	-5.6					0	1.92	800 826-4600
North Track DJ US Fin 100+ C	Financial	-5.7					1	1.92	800 826-4600
North Track DJ US Hlthcare 100+ A	Health	-2.8					5.25	1.17	800 826-4600
North Track DJ US Hlthcare 100+ B	Health	-3.5					0	1.92	800 826-4600
North Track DJ US Hlthcare 100+ C	Health	-3.4					0	1.92	800 826-4600
North Track Managed Growth A	Growth	-10.7	-0.69		2	3	5.25	1.73	800 826-4600
North Track Managed Growth B	Growth	-11.4	-2.2		1	3	0	2.48	800 826-4600
North Track Managed Growth C	Growth	-11.3	-1.31		2	3	1	2.48	800 826-4600
North Track PSE Tech 100 Index A	Technology	-4.6	-18.17	10.08	3	5	5.25	1.33	800 826-4600
North Track PSE Tech 100 Index B	Technology	-5.4	-18.8		3	5	0	2.09	800 826-4600
North Track PSE Tech 100 Index C	Technology	-5.4	-18.76		3	5	0	2.08	800 826-4600
North Track S&P 100 Plus A	Growth/Inc	-8.1	-13.94	-1.34	3	3	5.25	1.19	800 826-4600
North Track S&P 100 Plus B	Growth/Inc	-8.8	-14.59		4	3	0	1.94	800 826-4600
North Track S&P 100 Plus C	Growth/Inc	-8.8	-14.57		3	3	0	1.94	800 826-4600
NorthPointe Small Cap Value Inst	Small Co	-6.7					0	1	800 848-0920
Northeast Investors Growth	Growth	-8.6	-14.34	-2.22	4	3	0	1	800 225-6704
Northern Instl Balanced A	Balanced	-3.5	-3.43	2.95	2	1	0	0.61	800 637-1380
Northern Instl Balanced C	Balanced	-4	-4.16	2.79	2	1	0	0.85	800 637-1380
Northern Instl Balanced D	Balanced	-4.2	-4.21	2.62	2	1	0	1	800 637-1380
Northern Instl Diversified Gr A	Growth	-13.5	-14.48	-1.23	4	3	0	0.66	800 637-1380
Northern Instl Diversified Gr D	Growth	-14	-14.82	-1.64	4	3	0	1.05	800 637-1380
Northern Instl Equity Index A	Growth/Inc	-8.2	-10.99	-1.28	3	3	0	0.21	800 637-1380
Northern Instl Equity Index C	Growth/Inc	-8.5	-11.22	-1.53	3	3	0	0.45	800 637-1380
Northern Instl Equity Index D	Growth/Inc	-8.7	-11.28	-1.62	3	3	0	0.6	800 637-1380
Northern Instl Focused Growth A	Growth	-14.5	-16.73	-1.12	4	3	0	0.91	800 637-1380
Northern Instl Focused Growth C	Growth	-14.7	-16.91	-1.34	4	3	0	1.15	800 637-1380
Northern Instl Focused Growth D	Growth	-14.8	-17.05	-1.5	4	3	0	1.3	800 637-1380
Northern Instl Int'l Growth A	Foreign	-12.9	-14.28	-3.27	4	2	0	1.06	800 637-1380
Northern Instl Int'l Growth D	Other	-13.5					0	1.44	800 637-1380
Northern Instl Intl Equity Index A	Foreign	-12.5	-13.24	-4.96	5	3	0	0.55	800 637-1380
Northern Instl Intl Equity Index D	Foreign	-12.2	-13.77		5	2	1	0.94	800 637-1380
Northern Instl Mid Cap Growth A	Growth	-10.4	-9		3	4	0	0.94	800 637-1380
Northern Instl Mid Cap Growth C	Growth	-10.6					0	1.18	800 637-1380
Northern Instl Mid Cap Growth D	Growth	-10.8					0	1.33	800 637-1380
Northern Instl Small Co. Growth A	Small Co	-14.9	-15.83		5	4	0	0.92	800 637-1380
Northern Instl Small Co. Idx A	Small Co	-8.2	-1.32	0.28	3	4	0	0.31	800 637-1380
Northern Instl Small Co. Idx D	Small Co	-8.5	-1.54	-0.22	3	4	0	0.7	800 637-1380
Northern Technology	Technology	-6.9	-32.84	0.41	3	5	0	0.9	800 595-9111
Northern Trust Global Comm	Technology	-17.1					0	1.3	800 595-9111
Northern Trust Growth Equity	Growth	-14.2	-14.9	-1.59	4	3	0	1	800 595-9111
Northern Trust Grwth Opportunities	Growth	-17.2					0	1.25	800 595-9111
Northern Trust Income Equity	Income	-1.4	0.95	5.26	1	1	0	1	800 595-9111
Northern Trust Intl Growth Equity	Foreign	-13.3	-15.74	-4.41	5	3	0	1.25	800 595-9111
Northern Trust Intl Select Equity	Foreign	-16	-16.57	-5.2	5	3	0	1.25	800 595-9111
Northern Trust Large Cap Value	Growth	-8					0	1.1	800 595-9111
Northern Trust Midcap Growth	Growth	-11.3	-14.33	5	3	4	0	1	800 595-9111
Northern Trust Select Equity	Agg Growth	-13.5	-14.94	1.62	4	3	0	1	800 595-9111
Northern Trust Small Cap Growth	Small Co	-14.4	-11.11		5	5	0	1.25	800 595-9111
Northern Trust Small Cap Index	Small Co	-8.8	-1.64		2	4	0	0.65	800 595-9111

Stock Fund Name	Objective	Annualized Return for			Rank		Max Load	Expense Ratio	Toll-Free/(Toll) Telephone
		1 Year	3 Years	5 Years	Overall	Risk			
Northern Trust Small Cap Value	Small Co	-7.1	7.34	3.45	3	3	0	1	800 595-9111
Northern Trust Stock Index	Growth	-8.6	-11.31	-1.6	3	3	0	0.55	800 595-9111
Nuveen Balanced Muni & Stock A	Balanced	-3.7	-0.84	0.61	2	1	5.75	1.25	800 752-8700
Nuveen Balanced Muni & Stock B	Balanced	-4.4					0	2	800 752-8700
Nuveen Balanced Muni & Stock C	Balanced	-4.5					0	1.99	800 752-8700
Nuveen Balanced Muni & Stock R	Balanced	-3.5					0	1	800 752-8700
Nuveen Balanced Stock & Bond A	Balanced	-6.6	0.39	2.43	2	1	5.75	1.25	800 752-8700
Nuveen Balanced Stock & Bond B	Balanced	-7.3	-0.34	1.66	2	1	0	2	800 752-8700
Nuveen Balanced Stock & Bond C	Balanced	-7.3	-0.46	1.61	2	1	0	2	800 752-8700
Nuveen Balanced Stock & Bond R	Balanced	-6.3	0.45	2.56	2	1	0	1	800 752-8700
Nuveen European Value A	European	-13.3	-11.14	-3.91	3	3	5.75	1.55	800 752-8700
Nuveen European Value B	European	-14	-11.58	-4.42	3	3	0	2.3	800 752-8700
Nuveen European Value C	European	-14	-11.58	-4.42	3	3	0	2.3	800 752-8700
Nuveen European Value R	European	-13.1	-11	-3.72	4	3	0	1.3	800 752-8700
Nuveen Innovation Fund A	Agg Growth	-12.4	-27.96		4	5	5.75	1.96	800 752-8700
Nuveen Innovation Fund B	Agg Growth	-13.1	-28.48		4	5	0	2.7	800 752-8700
Nuveen Innovation Fund C	Agg Growth	-13.1	-28.51		4	5	0	2.71	800 752-8700
Nuveen Innovation Fund R	Agg Growth	-12.2	-27.78		4	5	0	1.7	800 752-8700
Nuveen International Value A	Foreign	-4	-11.07		3	3	5.75	2.12	800 752-8700
Nuveen International Value B	Foreign	-4.8	-11.76		3	3	0	2.86	800 752-8700
Nuveen International Value C	Foreign	-4.8	-11.76		3	3	0	2.86	800 752-8700
Nuveen International Value R	Foreign	-3.9	-10.91		3	3	0	1.86	800 752-8700
Nuveen Large Cap Value A	Growth	-14.8					5.75	1.33	800 752-8700
Nuveen Large Cap Value B	Growth	-15.4					0	2.08	800 752-8700
Nuveen Large Cap Value C	Growth	-15.4					0	2.07	800 752-8700
Nuveen Large Cap Value R	Growth	-14.6					0	2.07	800 752-8700
Nuveen Rittenhouse Growth Fund A	Growth	-8.6	-14.11	-3.95	4	3	5.75	1.35	800 752-8700
Nuveen Rittenhouse Growth Fund B	Growth	-9.3	-14.75	-4.66	3	3	0	2.1	800 752-8700
Nuveen Rittenhouse Growth Fund C	Growth	-9.3	-14.75	-4.66	3	3	0	2.1	800 752-8700
Nuveen Rittenhouse Growth Fund R	Growth	-8.4	-13.91	-3.72	4	3	0	1.1	800 752-8700
Oak Ridge Funds-Small Cap Equity A	Small Co	-7.4	-1.37	1.13	2	3	4.25	2	800 407-7298
Oak Ridge Funds-Small Cap Equity C	Small Co	-8.1	-2.35	0.23	2	3	0	2.75	800 407-7298
Oak Value Fund	Growth	-10.5	1.29	0.53	3	3	0	1.23	800 680-4199
Oakmark Equity & Income Fd	Balanced	2.1	12.69	11.06	1	1	0	0.98	800 625-6275
Oakmark Fund (The)	Growth	-8.5	8.88	1.56	2	2	0	1.15	800 625-6275
Oakmark International Fund	Foreign	-13.6	1.57	4.95	3	3	0	1.3	800 625-6275
Oakmark Intl Small Cap Fund	Foreign	-12.2	5.78	10.3	3	3	0	1.74	800 625-6275
Oakmark Select	Growth	-3.1	12.83	13.99	1	2	0	1.08	800 625-6275
Oakmark Small Cap	Small Co	-16.8	8	-1.26	3	3	0	1.27	800 625-6275
Oberweis Emerging Growth Portfolio	Small Co	2.4	-5.25	3.66	3	5	0	1.65	800 323-6166
Oberweis Micro Cap Portfolio	Small Co	18.8	8.82	10.4	2	5	0	1.98	800 323-6166
Oberweis Mid Cap Growth Portfolio	Small Co	-2.1	-24.58	1.85	3	5	0	2	800 323-6166
Old Dominion Investors Trust	Growth/Inc	-11.3	-7.16	-5.12	3	3	4	1.98	800 441-6580
Old Westbury International	Foreign	-15.5	-15.4	-7.37	5	2	0		800 607-2200
Olstein Financial Alert C	Growth	-16.8	3.81	10.18	3	4	0	2.2	800 799-2113
One Group Balanced A	Balanced	-1.9	-2.79	1.73	2	1	5.25	1.14	800 480-4111
One Group Balanced B	Balanced	-2.7	-3.54	0.97	2	1	0	1.89	800 480-4111
One Group Balanced C	Balanced	-2.7	-3.52		1	1	0	1.89	800 480-4111
One Group Balanced I	Balanced	-1.7	-2.56	2	2	1	0	0.89	800 480-4111
One Group Diversified Equity A	Growth/Inc	-10.9	-10.86	-2.04	4	3	5.25	1.23	800 480-4111
One Group Diversified Equity B	Growth/Inc	-11.4	-11.63	-2.81	4	3	0	1.98	800 480-4111
One Group Diversified Equity C	Growth/Inc	-11.5	-11.63	-2.81	4	3	0	1.98	800 480-4111
One Group Diversified Equity I	Growth/Inc	-10.6	-10.75	-1.86	4	3	0	0.98	800 480-4111
One Group Diversified Intl A	Foreign	-13.9	-13.81	-3.6	5	3	5.25	1.29	800 480-4111
One Group Diversified Intl B	Foreign	-14.5	-14.48	-4.29	5	3	0	2.04	800 480-4111
One Group Diversified Intl C	Foreign	-14.5	-14.47		5	3	0	2.04	800 480-4111
One Group Diversified Intl I	Foreign	-13.6	-13.63	-3.39	5	3	0	1.04	800 480-4111
One Group Diversified Mid Cap A	Growth	-12	-2.1	1.95	3	3	5.25	1.23	800 480-4111

Stock Fund Name	Objective	Annualized Return for			Rank		Max Load	Expense Ratio	Toll-Free/(Toll) Telephone
		1 Year	3 Years	5 Years	Overall	Risk			
One Group Diversified Mid Cap B	Growth	-12.6	-2.85	1.19	3	3	0	1.98	800 480-4111
One Group Diversified Mid Cap C	Growth	-12.6	-2.83		3	3	0	1.98	800 480-4111
One Group Diversified Mid Cap I	Growth	-11.7	-1.86	2.2	3	3	0	0.98	800 480-4111
One Group Equity Income A	Income	-10	-4.44	-1.52	3	2	5.25	1.24	800 480-4111
One Group Equity Income B	Income	-10.6	-5.13	-2.22	3	2	0	1.99	800 480-4111
One Group Equity Income C	Income	-10.6	-5.12	-2.22	3	2	0	1.99	800 480-4111
One Group Equity Income I	Income	-9.7	-4.19	-1.25	3	2	0	0.99	800 480-4111
One Group Equity Index A	Growth/Inc	-8.5	-11.33	-1.6	3	3	5.25	0.6	800 480-4111
One Group Equity Index B	Growth/Inc	-9.2	-11.99	-2.33	4	3	0	1.35	800 480-4111
One Group Equity Index C	Growth/Inc	-9.2	-12	-2.31	4	3	0	1.35	800 480-4111
One Group Equity Index I	Growth/Inc	-8.3	-11.09	-1.36	3	3	0	0.35	800 480-4111
One Group Health Sciences A	Health	-0.7					5.25	1.6	800 480-4111
One Group Health Sciences B	Health	-1.4					0	2.35	800 480-4111
One Group Health Sciences C	Health	-1.2					0	2.35	800 480-4111
One Group Health Sciences I	Health	-0.5					0	1.35	800 480-4111
One Group Intl Equity Index A	Foreign	-13.3	-14.65	-4.82	5	3	5.25	1.09	800 480-4111
One Group Intl Equity Index B	Foreign	-13.9	-15.22	-5.48	5	3	0	1.84	800 480-4111
One Group Intl Equity Index C	Foreign	-13.9	-15.23	-5.41	5	3	0	1.84	800 480-4111
One Group Intl Equity Index I	Foreign	-13	-14.38	-4.54	3	3	4.5	0.84	800 480-4111
One Group Investor Balanced A	Balanced	-0.5	-0.3	3.06	1	1	5.25	1.26	800 480-4111
One Group Investor Balanced B	Balanced	-1.3	-1.07	2.33	2	1	0	2.01	800 480-4111
One Group Investor Balanced C	Balanced	-1.3	-1.08	2.31	2	1	0	2.01	800 480-4111
One Group Investor Balanced I	Balanced	-0.3	-0.08	3.37	1	1	0	1.01	800 480-4111
One Group Investor Conserv Gr A	Growth/Inc	2.9	3	3.93	1	1	5.25	1.19	800 480-4111
One Group Investor Conserv Gr B	Growth/Inc	2.1	2.22	3.16	2	1	0	1.94	800 480-4111
One Group Investor Conserv Gr C	Growth/Inc	2.2	2.25	3.16	2	1	0	1.94	800 480-4111
One Group Investor Conserv Gr I	Growth/Inc	3.2	3.29	4.2	1	1	0	0.94	800 480-4111
One Group Investor Gr & Inc A	Growth/Inc	-4.8	-3.72	1.79	2	2	5.25	1.31	800 480-4111
One Group Investor Gr & Inc B	Growth/Inc	-5.5	-4.42	1.06	2	2	0	2.06	800 480-4111
One Group Investor Gr & Inc C	Growth/Inc	-5.6	-4.45	1.07	2	2	0	2.06	800 480-4111
One Group Investor Gr & Inc I	Growth/Inc	-4.6	-3.49	2.06	2	2	0	1.07	800 480-4111
One Group Investor Growth A	Growth	-9.3	-6.91	0.71	3	2	5.25	1.36	800 480-4111
One Group Investor Growth B	Growth	-10	-7.59	-0.02	3	2	0	2.11	800 480-4111
One Group Investor Growth C	Growth	-10	-7.59	-0.04	3	2	0	2.11	800 480-4111
One Group Investor Growth I	Growth	-9.1	-6.66	0.95	3	2	0	1.11	800 480-4111
One Group Large Cap Growth A	Growth	-8	-20.03	-5.21	4	4	5.25	1.24	800 480-4111
One Group Large Cap Growth B	Growth	-8.7	-20.62	-5.9	4	4	0	1.99	800 480-4111
One Group Large Cap Growth C	Growth	-8.7	-20.6	-5.9	4	4	0	1.99	800 480-4111
One Group Large Cap Growth I	Growth	-7.8	-19.82	-4.95	4	4	0	0.99	800 480-4111
One Group Large Cap Value A	Growth	-11.5	-7.71	-2.06	3	3	5.25	1.21	800 480-4111
One Group Large Cap Value B	Growth	-12.1	-8.74	-3.16	3	3	0	1.96	800 480-4111
One Group Large Cap Value C	Growth	-12.1	-8.39		3	3	0	1.96	800 480-4111
One Group Large Cap Value I	Growth	-11.3	-7.48	-1.85	3	3	0	0.96	800 480-4111
One Group Market Expansion Index A	Small Co	-10.5	1.5		3	3	5.25	0.82	800 480-4111
One Group Market Expansion Index B	Small Co	-11.2	0.7		3	3	0	1.57	800 480-4111
One Group Market Expansion Index C	Small Co	-11.3	0.75		3	3	0	1.57	800 480-4111
One Group Market Expansion Index I	Small Co	-10.3	1.72		2	3	0	0.57	800 480-4111
One Group Mid Cap Growth A	Small Co	-11.2	-8.32	5.08	3	4	5.25	1.24	800 480-4111
One Group Mid Cap Growth B	Small Co	-11.8	-9	4.29	3	4	0	1.99	800 480-4111
One Group Mid Cap Growth C	Small Co	-11.8	-9	4.28	3	4	0	1.99	800 480-4111
One Group Mid Cap Growth I	Small Co	-10.9	-8.08	5.34	3	4	0	0.99	800 480-4111
One Group Mid Cap Value A	Growth	-12.1	5.26	5.03	3	3	5.25	1.24	800 480-4111
One Group Mid Cap Value B	Growth	-12.8	4.44	4.2	2	3	0	1.99	800 480-4111
One Group Mid Cap Value C	Growth	-12.8	4.45		3	3	0	1.99	800 480-4111
One Group Mid Cap Value I	Growth	-11.9	5.51	5.28	3	3	0	0.99	800 480-4111
One Group Small Cap Growth A	Small Co	-11.6	-6.29	-0.17	3	4	5.25	1.27	800 480-4111
One Group Small Cap Growth B	Small Co	-12.4	-7	-1	3	4	0	2.02	800 480-4111
One Group Small Cap Growth C	Small Co	-12.3	-6.99	-0.95	3	4	0	2.02	800 480-4111

Stock Fund Name	Objective	Annualized Return for			Rank		Max Load	Expense Ratio	Toll-Free/(Toll) Telephone
		1 Year	3 Years	5 Years	Overall	Risk			
One Group Small Cap Growth I	Small Co	-11.4	-6.05	0.01	3	4	0	1.02	800 480-4111
One Group Small Cap Value A	Small Co	-12.7	14.43	4.26	3	3	5.25	1.24	800 480-4111
One Group Small Cap Value B	Small Co	-13.4	13.58	3.47	2	3	0	1.99	800 480-4111
One Group Small Cap Value C	Small Co	-13.4	13.6	3.45	3	3	0	1.99	800 480-4111
One Group Small Cap Value I	Small Co	-12.5	14.72	4.49	3	3	0	0.99	800 480-4111
One Group Technology A	Technology	-8.8					5.25	1.55	800 480-4111
One Group Technology B	Technology	-9.4					0	2.3	800 480-4111
One Group Technology C	Technology	-9.6					0	2.3	800 480-4111
One Group Technology I	Technology	-8.8					0	1.3	800 480-4111
Oppenheimer Capital Appr A	Agg Growth	-9	-12.44	2.2	3	3	5.75	1.03	800 525-7048
Oppenheimer Capital Appr B	Agg Growth	-9.7	-13.1	1.41	3	3	0	1.8	800 525-7048
Oppenheimer Capital Appr C	Agg Growth	-9.6	-13.09	1.41	3	3	0	1.8	800 525-7048
Oppenheimer Capital Appr N	Agg Growth	-9.1					0	1.36	800 525-7048
Oppenheimer Capital Appr Y	Agg Growth	-8.6	-12.11	2.58	3	3	0	0.66	800 525-7048
Oppenheimer Capital Income Fd A	Income	0.3	2.22	1.81	1	2	5.75	0.98	800 525-7048
Oppenheimer Capital Income Fd B	Income	-0.4	1.41	1.01	2	2	0	1.76	800 525-7048
Oppenheimer Capital Income Fd C	Income	-0.5	1.47	1.05	1	2	0	1.76	800 525-7048
Oppenheimer Capital Income Fd N	Income	0					0	1.25	800 525-7048
Oppenheimer Capital Preservation A	Other	3.5	5.12			1	3.5	1.71	800 525-7048
Oppenheimer Capital Preservation B	Other	2.8	4.42			1	0	2.37	800 525-7048
Oppenheimer Capital Preservation C	Other	2.8	4.41			1	0	2.35	800 525-7048
Oppenheimer Capital Preservation N	Other	3.7					0	1.52	800 525-7048
Oppenheimer Capital Preservation Y	Other	4.2	5.51			1	0	1.7	800 525-7048
Oppenheimer Convertible Sec A	Converts	5.8	-0.34	3.08	1	2	5.75	0.99	800 525-7048
Oppenheimer Convertible Sec B	Converts	4.8	-1.17	2.25	1	2	0	1.77	800 525-7048
Oppenheimer Convertible Sec C	Converts	4.8	-1.17	2.27	1	2	0	1.76	800 525-7048
Oppenheimer Convertible Sec M	Converts	4.8	-1	2.49	1	2	3.25	1.51	800 525-7048
Oppenheimer Convertible Sec N	Converts	5.4					0	1.43	800 525-7048
Oppenheimer Developing Mkts A	Foreign	-3.8	-2.33	6.78	1	4	5.75	1.81	800 525-7048
Oppenheimer Developing Mkts B	Foreign	-4.5	-3.06	6	2	4	0	2.58	800 525-7048
Oppenheimer Developing Mkts C	Foreign	-4.5	-3.06	5.98	2	4	0	2.57	800 525-7048
Oppenheimer Developing Mkts N	Foreign	-4					0	2.04	800 525-7048
Oppenheimer Disciplined Alloc A	AssetAlloc	0.7	-1.3	-0.05	2	1	5.75	1.19	800 525-7048
Oppenheimer Disciplined Alloc B	AssetAlloc	-0.2	-2.06	-0.81	2	1	0	1.94	800 525-7048
Oppenheimer Disciplined Alloc C	AssetAlloc	-0.2	-2.08	-0.82	2	1	0	1.94	800 525-7048
Oppenheimer Disciplined Alloc N	AssetAlloc	0.4					0	1.68	800 525-7048
Oppenheimer Discovery A	Small Co	-5.8	-9.83	-1.25	3	4	5.75	1.25	800 525-7048
Oppenheimer Discovery B	Small Co	-6.5	-10.5	-1.98	3	4	0	2.01	800 525-7048
Oppenheimer Discovery C	Small Co	-6.5	-10.5	-1.98	3	4	0	2.01	800 525-7048
Oppenheimer Discovery N	Small Co	-6					0	1.55	800 525-7048
Oppenheimer Discovery Y	Small Co	-5.5	-9.58	-0.97	3	4	0	1.14	800 525-7048
Oppenheimer Emerging Growth A	Small Co	1.2					5.75	1.63	800 525-7048
Oppenheimer Emerging Growth B	Small Co	0.3					0	2.45	800 525-7048
Oppenheimer Emerging Growth C	Small Co	0.4					0	2.44	800 525-7048
Oppenheimer Emerging Growth N	Small Co	0.9					0	2	800 525-7048
Oppenheimer Emerging Growth Y	Small Co	1.7					0	1.4	800 525-7048
Oppenheimer Emerging Tech A	Technology	-1.6	-37.38		4	5	5.75	2.12	800 525-7048
Oppenheimer Emerging Tech B	Technology	-2.1	-37.82		4	5	0	2.87	800 525-7048
Oppenheimer Emerging Tech C	Technology	-2.1	-37.82		4	5	0	2.87	800 525-7048
Oppenheimer Emerging Tech N	Technology	-2					0	2.39	800 525-7048
Oppenheimer Emerging Tech Y	Technology	-0.8	-36.92		4	5	0	1.73	800 525-7048
Oppenheimer Enterprise A	Growth	-6.1	-27.62	-7.48	4	5	5.75	1.67	800 525-7048
Oppenheimer Enterprise B	Growth	-6.7	-28.17	-8.16	4	5	0	2.43	800 525-7048
Oppenheimer Enterprise C	Growth	-6.8	-28.17	-8.14	4	5	0	2.43	800 525-7048
Oppenheimer Enterprise N	Growth	-6.4					0	1.91	800 525-7048
Oppenheimer Enterprise Y	Growth	-5.8	-27.41		4	5	0	1.3	800 525-7048
Oppenheimer Europe A	European	-17.2	-20.53		5	4	5.75	2.37	800 525-7048
Oppenheimer Europe B	European	-17.8	-21.12		5	4	0	3.13	800 525-7048

Stock Fund Name	Objective	Annualized Return for			Rank		Max Load	Expense Ratio	Toll-Free/(Toll) Telephone
		1 Year	3 Years	5 Years	Overall	Risk			
Oppenheimer Europe C	European	-17.7	-21.12		5	4	0	3.13	800 525-7048
Oppenheimer Europe N	European	-17.4					0	2.55	800 525-7048
Oppenheimer Europe Y	European	-16.6	-20.03		4	4	0	1.44	800 525-7048
Oppenheimer Global A	Global	-14.5	-9.24	4.2	3	3	5.75	1.24	800 525-7048
Oppenheimer Global B	Global	-15.2	-10.05	3.31	3	3	0	2.01	800 525-7048
Oppenheimer Global C	Global	-15.1	-9.93	3.41	3	3	0	2.01	800 525-7048
Oppenheimer Global N	Global	-14.6					0	1.51	800 525-7048
Oppenheimer Global Opportunities A	Global	-8.6	-12.75	4.76	4	4	5.75	1.4	800 525-7048
Oppenheimer Global Opportunities B	Global	-9.3	-13.42	3.97	4	4	0	2.16	800 525-7048
Oppenheimer Global Opportunities C	Global	-9.3	-13.41	3.97	4	4	0	2.14	800 525-7048
Oppenheimer Global Opportunities N	Global	-8.8					0	1.66	800 525-7048
Oppenheimer Global Opportunities Y	Global	-8.1					0	0.95	800 525-7048
Oppenheimer Global Y	Global	-14.3	-9.08		3	3	0	1.06	800 525-7048
Oppenheimer Gold/Spec Min A	Prec Metal	-11.8	19.76	9.09	2	4	5.75	1.45	800 525-7048
Oppenheimer Gold/Spec Min B	Prec Metal	-12.5	18.85	8.25	2	4	0	2.22	800 525-7048
Oppenheimer Gold/Spec Min C	Prec Metal	-12.4	18.89	8.27	2	4	0	2.22	800 525-7048
Oppenheimer Gold/Spec Min N	Prec Metal	-12					0	1.69	800 525-7048
Oppenheimer Growth A	Growth	-11.3	-18.73	-4.04	4	4	5.75	1.27	800 525-7048
Oppenheimer Growth B	Growth	-12	-19.37	-4.79	5	4	0	2.03	800 525-7048
Oppenheimer Growth C	Growth	-12	-19.37	-4.79	4	4	0	2.04	800 525-7048
Oppenheimer Growth N	Growth	-10.5					0	1.54	800 525-7048
Oppenheimer Growth Y	Growth	-11.1	-18.53	-3.81	4	4	0	0.98	800 525-7048
Oppenheimer Intl Growth A	Foreign	-22.2	-17.64	-5.13	5	4	5.75	1.42	800 525-7048
Oppenheimer Intl Growth B	Foreign	-22.8	-18.26	-5.86	5	4	0	2.17	800 525-7048
Oppenheimer Intl Growth C	Foreign	-22.8	-18.26	-5.86	5	4	0	2.17	800 525-7048
Oppenheimer Intl Growth N	Foreign	-22.4					0	1.74	800 525-7048
Oppenheimer Intl Small Comp N	Foreign	-8.2					0	2.32	800 525-7048
Oppenheimer Intl Small Company A	Foreign	-7.8	-14.8	-1.48	4	4	5.75	2.19	800 525-7048
Oppenheimer Intl Small Company B	Foreign	-8.6	-15.44	-2.25	4	4	0	2.96	800 525-7048
Oppenheimer Intl Small Company C	Foreign	-8.6	-15.46	-2.24	4	4	0	2.96	800 525-7048
Oppenheimer Main St A	Growth/Inc	-9.9	-10.02	-0.96	4	2	5.75	0.86	800 525-7048
Oppenheimer Main St B	Growth/Inc	-10.6	-10.73	-1.71	4	2	0	1.61	800 525-7048
Oppenheimer Main St C	Growth/Inc	-10.5	-10.71	-1.7	4	2	0	1.61	800 525-7048
Oppenheimer Main St N	Growth/Inc	-10					0	1.16	800 525-7048
Oppenheimer Main St Oppty A	Growth	-6.5					5.75	2.05	800 525-7048
Oppenheimer Main St Oppty B	Growth	-7.3					0	2.05	800 525-7048
Oppenheimer Main St Oppty C	Growth	-7.2					0	2.05	800 525-7048
Oppenheimer Main St Oppty N	Growth	-6.7					0	1.58	800 525-7048
Oppenheimer Main St Oppty Y	Growth	-6.1					0	1.04	800 525-7048
Oppenheimer Main St Small Cap A	Small Co	-6.8	5.04		3	4	5.75	1.37	800 525-7048
Oppenheimer Main St Small Cap B	Small Co	-7.5	4.24		3	4	0	2.12	800 525-7048
Oppenheimer Main St Small Cap C	Small Co	-7.5	4.25		3	4	0	2.12	800 525-7048
Oppenheimer Main St Small Cap N	Small Co	-7.1					0	1.65	800 525-7048
Oppenheimer Main St Small Cap Y	Small Co	-6.3	5.48		3	4	0	0.97	800 525-7048
Oppenheimer Main St Y	Growth/Inc	-9.8	-9.86	-0.79	4	2	0	0.73	800 525-7048
Oppenheimer Midcap A	Growth	-11.6	-22.62	-0.07	4	5	5.75	1.54	800 525-7048
Oppenheimer Midcap B	Growth	-12.2	-23.19	-0.78	4	5	0	2.3	800 525-7048
Oppenheimer Midcap C	Growth	-12.3	-23.21	-0.81	4	5	0	2.3	800 525-7048
Oppenheimer Midcap N	Growth	-11.8					0	1.83	800 525-7048
Oppenheimer Midcap Y	Growth	-11.2	-22.26	0.41	4	5	0	0.98	800 525-7048
Oppenheimer Multiple Strat A	AssetAlloc	-0.3	0.5	3.29	1	2	5.75	1.14	800 525-7048
Oppenheimer Multiple Strat B	AssetAlloc	-1.2	-0.34	2.43	1	2	0	1.95	800 525-7048
Oppenheimer Multiple Strat C	AssetAlloc	-1.2	-0.34	2.43	1	2	0	1.95	800 525-7048
Oppenheimer Multiple Strat N	AssetAlloc	-0.9					0	1.44	800 525-7048
Oppenheimer Quest Balanced Val A	Balanced	1.6	0.76	6.04	1	2	5.75	1.47	800 525-7048
Oppenheimer Quest Balanced Val B	Balanced	0.8	0.1	5.36	1	2	0	2.1	800 525-7048
Oppenheimer Quest Balanced Val C	Balanced	0.9	0.14	5.38	1	2	0	2.1	800 525-7048
Oppenheimer Quest Balanced Val N	Balanced	1.3					0	1.6	800 525-7048

Stock Fund Name	Objective	Annualized Return for			Rank		Max Load	Expense Ratio	Toll-Free/(Toll) Telephone
		1 Year	3 Years	5 Years	Overall	Risk			
Oppenheimer Quest Balanced Val Y	Balanced	1.9	1.22			2	0	0.91	800 525-7048
Oppenheimer Quest Capital Val A	Growth	-5.3	1.18	3.83	2	3	5.75	1.68	800 525-7048
Oppenheimer Quest Capital Val B	Growth	-6	0.53	3.18	2	3	0	2.31	800 525-7048
Oppenheimer Quest Capital Val C	Growth	-6.1	0.54	3.18	2	3	0	2.31	800 525-7048
Oppenheimer Quest Capital Val N	Growth	-5.5					0	1.8	800 525-7048
Oppenheimer Quest Global Val A	Global	-6.6	-6.53	-0.57	3	2	5.75	1.7	800 525-7048
Oppenheimer Quest Global Val B	Global	-7.3	-7.12	-1.15	3	2	0	2.34	800 525-7048
Oppenheimer Quest Global Val C	Global	-7.3	-7.12	-1.17	3	2	0	2.34	800 525-7048
Oppenheimer Quest Global Val N	Global	-6.9					0	1.84	800 525-7048
Oppenheimer Quest Opportunity Val A	Flexible	-7.7	-2.47	0.05	2	1	5.75	1.53	800 525-7048
Oppenheimer Quest Opportunity Val B	Flexible	-8.4	-3.1	-0.55	3	1	0	2.16	800 525-7048
Oppenheimer Quest Opportunity Val C	Flexible	-8.3	-3.08	-0.53	3	1	0	2.16	800 525-7048
Oppenheimer Quest Opportunity Val Y	Flexible	-7.5	-2.14	0.4	2	1	0	1.23	800 525-7048
Oppenheimer Quest Opporty Val N	Flexible	-8					0	1.67	800 525-7048
Oppenheimer Quest Value A	Growth	-8.9	-2.35	-1.83	3	2	5.75	1.62	800 525-7048
Oppenheimer Quest Value B	Growth	-9.6	-3.02	-2.45	3	2	0	2.25	800 525-7048
Oppenheimer Quest Value C	Growth	-9.6	-2.99	-2.43	3	2	0	2.25	800 525-7048
Oppenheimer Quest Value N	Growth	-9.2					0	1.78	800 525-7048
Oppenheimer Quest Value Y	Growth	-8.7	-2.04	-1.56	3	2	0	1.25	800 525-7048
Oppenheimer Real Asset A	AssetAlloc	26.3	4.19	4.57	2	4	5.75	1.76	800 525-7048
Oppenheimer Real Asset B	AssetAlloc	25.3	3.39	3.79	2	4	0	2.52	800 525-7048
Oppenheimer Real Asset C	AssetAlloc	25.4	3.39	3.79	2	4	0	2.52	800 525-7048
Oppenheimer Real Asset N	AssetAlloc	26.8					0	2.01	800 525-7048
Oppenheimer Real Asset Y	AssetAlloc	26.7	4.11	4.62	2	4	0	1.63	800 525-7048
Oppenheimer Small Cap Value A	Small Co	-9	4.91	1.95	2	3	5.75	1.86	800 525-7048
Oppenheimer Small Cap Value B	Small Co	-9.7	4.25	1.36	2	3	0	2.45	800 525-7048
Oppenheimer Small Cap Value C	Small Co	-9.7	4.25	1.37	2	3	0	2.45	800 525-7048
Oppenheimer Small Cap Value N	Small Co	-9.2					0	2.01	800 525-7048
Oppenheimer Total Return A	Flexible	-5.2	-8.4	-0.32	3	2	5.75	0.97	800 525-7048
Oppenheimer Total Return B	Flexible	-6	-9.15	-1.12	3	2	0	1.76	800 525-7048
Oppenheimer Total Return C	Flexible	-6.1	-9.16	-1.12	3	2	0	1.76	800 525-7048
Oppenheimer Total Return N	Flexible	-5.5					0	1.27	800 525-7048
Oppenheimer Total Return Y	Flexible	-5.1	-8.27	-0.2	3	2	0	0.91	800 525-7048
Oppenheimer Trinity Core A	Agg Growth	-9.3	-10.67		3	3	5.75	2.13	800 525-7048
Oppenheimer Trinity Core B	Agg Growth	-10.1	-11.41		4	3	0	2.91	800 525-7048
Oppenheimer Trinity Core C	Agg Growth	-10	-11.4		4	3	0	2.9	800 525-7048
Oppenheimer Trinity Core N	Agg Growth	-9.5					0	2.46	800 525-7048
Oppenheimer Trinity Core Y	Agg Growth	-8.8	-9.66		3	3	0	3.8	800 525-7048
Oppenheimer Trinity Lrg Cap Gr A	Growth	-7.9	-19.37		3	4	5.75	2.03	800 525-7048
Oppenheimer Trinity Lrg Cap Gr B	Growth	-8.5	-20.01		3	4	0	2.8	800 525-7048
Oppenheimer Trinity Lrg Cap Gr C	Growth	-8.5	-20.01		3	4	0	2.79	800 525-7048
Oppenheimer Trinity Lrg Cap Gr N	Growth	-8.2					0	2.29	800 525-7048
Oppenheimer Trinity Lrg Cap Gr Y	Growth	-7.4	-18.94		3	4	0	4.83	800 525-7048
Oppenheimer Trinity Value A	Growth	-12.9	-5.11		3	3	5.75	1.78	800 525-7048
Oppenheimer Trinity Value B	Growth	-13.6	-5.91		3	3	0	2.57	800 525-7048
Oppenheimer Trinity Value C	Growth	-13.6	-5.94		3	3	0	2.57	800 525-7048
Oppenheimer Trinity Value N	Growth	-13.1					0	2.1	800 525-7048
Oppenheimer Trinity Value Y	Growth	-12.4	-4.7		3	3	0	1.78	800 525-7048
Oppenheimer Value A	Growth	-4.8	-1.66	-1.73	2	3	5.75	1.23	800 525-7048
Oppenheimer Value B	Growth	-5.5	-2.41	-2.49	2	3	0	1.99	800 525-7048
Oppenheimer Value C	Growth	-5.5	-2.43	-2.49	2	3	0	1.99	800 525-7048
Oppenheimer Value N	Growth	-5.1					0	1.49	800 525-7048
Oppenheimer Value Y	Growth	-4.6	-1.36	-1.44	2	3	0	1.4	800 525-7048
OppenheimerFunds PLC U.S. Value Fd	Growth/Inc	-6.8	-20.28		4	5	0	2.5	800 535-9169
Optimum Q All Cap Core Adv	Growth						0	1.38	866 784-6867
Osterweis Fund	Growth	-1.6	-1.03	11.23	1	2	0	1.43	866 236-0050
PBHG Clipper Focus Fund PBHG Class	Other	-11.6	15.25			3	0	1.4	800 433-0051
PBHG Core Growth Fund	Growth	-8.9	-24.64	-4.54	4	5	0	1.31	800 433-0051

Stock Fund Name	Objective	Annualized Return for			Rank		Max Load	Expense Ratio	Toll-Free/(Toll) Telephone
		1 Year	3 Years	5 Years	Overall	Risk			
PBHG Disciplined Equity Fund	Growth	-13.2	-10.18	-11.08	4	3	5.75	0.99	800 433-0051
PBHG Emerging Growth Fund	Small Co	-14.1	-29.53	-13.91	4	5	0	1.26	800 433-0051
PBHG Focused Value Fund	Agg Growth	-11.8	-5.13		3	3	0	1.34	800 433-0051
PBHG Growth Adv	Small Co	-13.4	-25.76	-5.98	5	5	0	1.5	800 433-0051
PBHG Growth Fd	Small Co	-13.2	-25.6	-5.7	5	5	0	1.25	800 433-0051
PBHG Large Cap 20 Adv	Growth	-10.5					0	1.75	800 433-0051
PBHG Large Cap 20 Fd	Growth	-10.4	-24.98	1.91	4	4	0	1.23	800 433-0051
PBHG Large Cap Growth Adv	Growth	-10.2					0	1.6	800 433-0051
PBHG Large Cap Growth Fd	Growth	-10	-17.25	1.66	4	4	0	1.18	800 433-0051
PBHG Large Cap Value Adv	Growth	-16.4					0	1.34	800 433-0051
PBHG Large Cap Value Fd	Growth	-16.3	-3.79	5.53	3	3	0	1.16	800 433-0051
PBHG Limited Fd	Small Co	-6.3	-16.57	-0.05	3	5	0	1.33	800 433-0051
PBHG Mid-Cap Portfolio	Growth	-7	1.64	11.5	1	3	0	1.31	800 433-0051
PBHG Mid-Cap Portfolio Adv	Growth	-7.3	1.51	11.4		3	0	1.56	800 433-0051
PBHG New Opportunities Fund	Growth	-14.1	-20.67		4	5	0	1.34	800 433-0051
PBHG REIT PBHG Class	Real Est	3.3	13.75	6.9		2	0	1.47	800 433-0051
PBHG Select Equity	Growth	-12.4	-29.42	-1.13	4	5	0	1.26	800 433-0051
PBHG Small Cap Fd	Small Co	-18	-3.2	3.62	3	4	0	1.49	800 433-0051
PBHG Small Cap Value Adv	Small Co	-18.2					0	1.7	800 433-0051
PBHG Strategic Small Company	Small Co	-13	-9.59	3.29	3	5	0	1.5	800 433-0051
PBHG Tech & Comm Adv	Technology	-23.2					0	1.89	800 433-0051
PBHG Tech & Comm Fd	Technology	-23	-44.75	-9.48	4	5	0	1.25	800 433-0051
PF AIM Aggressive Growth Fund A	Agg Growth	-15.4					5.5	1.95	800 282-6693
PF AIM Aggressive Growth Fund B	Agg Growth	-15.8					0	2.45	800 282-6693
PF AIM Aggressive Growth Fund C	Agg Growth	-15.7					0	2.45	800 282-6693
PF AIM Blue Chip Fund A	Agg Growth	-9					5.5	1.9	800 282-6693
PF AIM Blue Chip Fund B	Agg Growth	-9.5					0	2.4	800 282-6693
PF AIM Blue Chip Fund C	Agg Growth	-9.5					0	2.4	800 282-6693
PF INVESCO Health Sciences Fund A	Health	-6.7					5.5	2.05	800 282-6693
PF INVESCO Health Sciences Fund B	Health	-7.1					0	2.55	800 282-6693
PF INVESCO Health Sciences Fund C	Health	-7					0	2.55	800 282-6693
PF INVESCO Technology Fund A	Technology	-18.8					5.5	2.05	800 282-6693
PF INVESCO Technology Fund B	Technology	-19.1					0	2.55	800 282-6693
PF INVESCO Technology Fund C	Technology	-19.2					0	2.55	800 282-6693
PF Janus Growth LT Fund A	Agg Growth	-6.4					5.5	1.7	800 282-6693
PF Janus Growth LT Fund B	Agg Growth	-6.7					0	2.2	800 282-6693
PF Janus Growth LT Fund C	Agg Growth	-6.9					0	2.2	800 282-6693
PF Janus Strategic Value Fund A	Agg Growth	-14.3					5.5	1.9	800 282-6693
PF Janus Strategic Value Fund B	Agg Growth	-14.7					0	2.4	800 282-6693
PF Janus Strategic Value Fund C	Agg Growth	-14.7					0	2.4	800 282-6693
PF Lazard International Value Fd A	Global	-9.4					5.5	1.8	800 282-6693
PF Lazard International Value Fd B	Global	-10					0	2.3	800 282-6693
PF Lazard International Value Fd C	Global	-9.9					0	2.3	800 282-6693
PF MFS Global Growth Fund A	Other	-11.2					5.5	2.05	800 282-6693
PF MFS Global Growth Fund B	Other	-11.7					0	2.55	800 282-6693
PF MFS Global Growth Fund C	Other	-11.5					0	2.55	800 282-6693
PF MFS Mid-Cap Growth Fund A	Growth	-18.6					5.5	1.85	800 282-6693
PF MFS Mid-Cap Growth Fund B	Growth	-18.9					0	2.35	800 282-6693
PF MFS Mid-Cap Growth Fund C	Growth	-19					0	2.35	800 282-6693
PF Putnam Equity Income A	Balanced	-9.8					5.5	1.9	800 282-6693
PF Putnam Equity Income B	Balanced	-10.3					0	2.4	800 282-6693
PF Putnam Equity Income C	Balanced	-10.1					0	2.4	800 282-6693
PF Putnam Research Fund A	Other	-11.3					5.5	1.95	800 282-6693
PF Putnam Research Fund B	Other	-11.8					0	2.45	800 282-6693
PF Putnam Research Fund C	Other	-11.8					0	2.45	800 282-6693
PF Salomon Bros Large-Cap Value A	Growth/Inc	-11.9					5.5	1.8	800 282-6693
PF Salomon Bros Large-Cap Value B	Growth/Inc	-12.3					0	2.3	800 282-6693
PF Salomon Bros Large-Cap Value C	Growth/Inc	-12.3					0	2.3	800 282-6693

Stock Fund Name	Objective	Annualized Return for			Rank		Max Load	Expense Ratio	Toll-Free/(Toll) Telephone
		1 Year	3 Years	5 Years	Overall	Risk			
PIMCO Asset Allocation A	AssetAlloc	-2.6	-0.78		1	1	5.5	1.39	800 227-7337
PIMCO Asset Allocation Admin	AssetAlloc	-2.2	-0.4		1	1	0	1.09	800 227-7337
PIMCO Asset Allocation B	AssetAlloc	-3.3	-1.53		1	1	0	2.14	800 227-7337
PIMCO Asset Allocation C	AssetAlloc	-3.2	-1.5		1	1	0	2.14	800 227-7337
PIMCO Asset Allocation Inst	AssetAlloc	-2	-0.25		1	1	0	0.84	800 227-7337
PIMCO CCM Capital Appreciation A	Growth	-10.5	-9.07	0.34	3	2	5.5	1.11	800 227-7337
PIMCO CCM Capital Appreciation Adm	Growth	-10.1	-8.84	0.46	3	2	0	0.96	800 227-7337
PIMCO CCM Capital Appreciation B	Growth	-11.2	-9.76	-0.41	3	2	0	1.86	800 227-7337
PIMCO CCM Capital Appreciation C	Growth	-11.2	-9.75	-0.4	3	2	0	1.86	800 227-7337
PIMCO CCM Capital Appreciation D	Growth	-10.5	-9.08	0.34	3	2	0	1.11	800 227-7337
PIMCO CCM Capital Appreciation I	Growth	-10.2	-8.69	0.66	3	2	0	0.71	800 227-7337
PIMCO CCM Emerg Cos Inst	Small Co	-5.5	7.55	3.49	2	4	0	1.51	800 927-4648
PIMCO CCM Emerging Companies Admin	Small Co	-5.7	7.29	3.24	2	4	0	1.75	800 227-7337
PIMCO CCM Mid Cap Fund A	Growth	-10.5	-7.08	0.96	3	2	5.5	1.11	800 227-7337
PIMCO CCM Mid Cap Fund Admin	Growth	-10.3	-7.01	1.12	3	2	0	0.96	800 227-7337
PIMCO CCM Mid Cap Fund B	Growth	-11.2	-7.79	0.2	3	2	0	1.86	800 227-7337
PIMCO CCM Mid Cap Fund C	Growth	-11.1	-7.78	0.2	3	2	0	1.86	800 227-7337
PIMCO CCM Mid Cap Fund D	Growth	-10.4	-7.05	1.05	3	2	0	1.1	800 227-7337
PIMCO CCM Mid Cap Fund Inst	Growth	-10.1	-6.73	1.37	3	2	0	0.71	800 227-7337
PIMCO Convertible Bond Admin	Converts	3.6	-5.08		2	2	0	0.9	800 227-7337
PIMCO Convertible Bond Inst	Converts	4.2	-4.83		2	2	0	0.65	800 227-7337
PIMCO NACM Core Equity Fund A	Growth						5.5	1.25	800 227-7337
PIMCO NACM Core Equity Fund Admin	Growth						0	1.05	800 227-7337
PIMCO NACM Core Equity Fund B	Growth						0	2	800 227-7337
PIMCO NACM Core Equity Fund C	Growth						0	2	800 227-7337
PIMCO NACM Core Equity Fund D	Growth						0	1.25	800 227-7337
PIMCO NACM Core Equity Fund Inst	Growth						0	0.8	800 227-7337
PIMCO NACM Flex-Cap Value A	Agg Growth						5.5	1.4	800 227-7337
PIMCO NACM Flex-Cap Value Admin	Agg Growth						0	1.2	800 227-7337
PIMCO NACM Flex-Cap Value B	Agg Growth						0	2.15	800 227-7337
PIMCO NACM Flex-Cap Value C	Agg Growth						0	2.15	800 227-7337
PIMCO NACM Flex-Cap Value D	Agg Growth						0	1.4	800 227-7337
PIMCO NACM Flex-Cap Value Inst	Agg Growth						0	0.95	800 227-7337
PIMCO NACM Global Fund A	Global						5.5	1.55	800 227-7337
PIMCO NACM Global Fund Admin	Global						0	1.35	800 227-7337
PIMCO NACM Global Fund B	Global						0	2.3	800 227-7337
PIMCO NACM Global Fund C	Global						0	2.3	800 227-7337
PIMCO NACM Global Fund D	Global						0	1.55	800 227-7337
PIMCO NACM Global Fund Inst	Global						0	1.1	800 227-7337
PIMCO NACM Growth Fund A	Agg Growth						5.5	1.25	800 227-7337
PIMCO NACM Growth Fund Admin	Agg Growth						0	1.05	800 227-7337
PIMCO NACM Growth Fund B	Agg Growth						0	2	800 227-7337
PIMCO NACM Growth Fund C	Agg Growth						0	2	800 227-7337
PIMCO NACM Growth Fund D	Agg Growth						0	1.25	800 227-7337
PIMCO NACM Growth Fund Inst	Agg Growth						0	0.8	800 227-7337
PIMCO NACM Int'l Fund A	Global						5.5	1.65	800 227-7337
PIMCO NACM Int'l Fund Admin	Global						0	1.45	800 227-7337
PIMCO NACM Int'l Fund B	Global						0	2.4	800 227-7337
PIMCO NACM Int'l Fund C	Global						0	2.4	800 227-7337
PIMCO NACM Int'l Fund D	Global						0	1.65	800 227-7337
PIMCO NACM Int'l Fund Inst	Global						0	1.2	800 227-7337
PIMCO NACM Pacific Rim Fd A	Global	-24.7	-13.26	8.13		3	5.5	1.85	800 227-7337
PIMCO NACM Pacific Rim Fd B	Global	-24.9	-13.78	7.42		4	0	2.6	800 227-7337
PIMCO NACM Pacific Rim Fd C	Global	-25.3	-13.93	7.32		4	0	2.6	800 227-7337
PIMCO NACM Pacific Rim Fd D	Global	-24.7	-13.26	8.13		3	0	1.85	800 227-7337
PIMCO NACM Pacific Rim Fd Inst	Global	-24.4	-12.88	8.6		3	0	1.4	800 227-7337
PIMCO NACM Value Fund A	Other						5.5	1.25	800 227-7337
PIMCO NACM Value Fund Admin	Other						0	1.05	800 227-7337

Stock Fund Name	Objective	Annualized Return for 1 Year	3 Years	5 Years	Rank Overall	Risk	Max Load	Expense Ratio	Toll-Free/(Toll) Telephone
PIMCO NACM Value Fund B	Other						0	2	800 227-7337
PIMCO NACM Value Fund C	Other						0	2	800 227-7337
PIMCO NACM Value Fund D	Other						0	1.25	800 227-7337
PIMCO NACM Value Fund Inst	Other						0	0.8	800 227-7337
PIMCO NFJ Equity Income Fund A	Income	-7.4	7.2			3	0	1.2	800 227-7337
PIMCO NFJ Equity Income Fund B	Income	-8.1	6.38			3	0	1.95	800 227-7337
PIMCO NFJ Equity Income Fund C	Income	-8.1	6.38			3	0	1.95	800 227-7337
PIMCO NFJ Equity Income Fund D	Income	-7.4	7.16			3	0	1.2	800 227-7337
PIMCO NFJ Small Cap Value Fund A	Small Co	0.1	16.17	5.62	1	2	5.5	1.25	800 227-7337
PIMCO NFJ Small Cap Value Fund Adm	Small Co	0.3	16.35	5.79	1	2	0	1.1	800 227-7337
PIMCO NFJ Small Cap Value Fund B	Small Co	-0.7	15.32	4.83	2	2	0	2	800 227-7337
PIMCO NFJ Small Cap Value Fund C	Small Co	-0.7	15.31	4.84	2	2	0	2	800 227-7337
PIMCO NFJ Small Cap Value Fund Inst	Small Co	0.7	16.75	6.09	1	2	0	0.85	800 927-4648
PIMCO PEA Growth & Income A	Growth	-13.4	-10.75	5.95	3	3	5.5	1.36	800 227-7337
PIMCO PEA Growth & Income Admin	Growth	-13.4	-10.64	6.11	3	3	0	1.11	800 227-7337
PIMCO PEA Growth & Income D	Growth	-13.4	-10.75	5.95	3	3	0	1.35	800 227-7337
PIMCO PEA Growth & Income Inst	Growth	-13.1	-10.32	6.44	3	3	0	0.86	800 227-7337
PIMCO PEA Growth Fund A	Growth	-17.4	-20.62	-5.04	5	4	5.5	1.16	800 227-7337
PIMCO PEA Growth Fund Admin	Growth	-17.3	-20.51	-5.01	5	4	0	1.01	800 227-7337
PIMCO PEA Growth Fund B	Growth	-18	-21.19	-5.78	5	4	0	1.91	800 227-7337
PIMCO PEA Growth Fund C	Growth	-18	-21.19	-5.78	4	4	0	1.91	800 227-7337
PIMCO PEA Growth Fund D	Growth	-17.3	-20.62	-5.08		4	0	1.16	800 227-7337
PIMCO PEA Growth Fund Inst	Growth	-17.1	-20.3	-4.71	5	4	0	0.76	800 227-7337
PIMCO PEA Innovation Fund A	Technology	-19.9	-36.85	-3.87	4	5	5.5	1.31	800 227-7337
PIMCO PEA Innovation Fund Admin	Technology	-19.6	-36.71	-3.7	4	5	0	1.16	800 227-7337
PIMCO PEA Innovation Fund B	Technology	-20.5	-37.32	-4.53	4	5	0	2.06	800 227-7337
PIMCO PEA Innovation Fund C	Technology	-20.4	-37.32	-4.51	4	5	0	2.06	800 227-7337
PIMCO PEA Innovation Fund D	Technology	-19.8	-36.82	-3.75	4	5	0	1.31	800 227-7337
PIMCO PEA Innovation Fund Inst	Technology	-19.6	-36.61	-3.56	4	5	0	0.91	800 227-7337
PIMCO PEA Opportunity Fund A	Agg Growth	-9.1	-12.92	-1.28	3	5	5.5	1.31	800 227-7337
PIMCO PEA Opportunity Fund Admin	Agg Growth	-9	-12.8	-1.21	3	5	0	1.16	800 227-7337
PIMCO PEA Opportunity Fund B	Agg Growth	-9.8	-13.57	-1.98	3	5	0	2.06	800 227-7337
PIMCO PEA Opportunity Fund C	Agg Growth	-9.8	-13.57	-1.98	3	5	0	2.06	800 227-7337
PIMCO PEA Opportunity Fund Inst	Agg Growth	-8.7	-12.63	-1.06	3	5	0	0.91	800 227-7337
PIMCO PEA Renaissance Fund A	Growth	-18.9	8.77	8.75	3	4	5.5	1.25	800 227-7337
PIMCO PEA Renaissance Fund Admin	Growth	-18.4	9.09	8.94	3	4	0	1.11	800 227-7337
PIMCO PEA Renaissance Fund B	Growth	-19.5	7.95	7.91	3	4	0	2	800 227-7337
PIMCO PEA Renaissance Fund C	Growth	-19.5	7.95	7.95	3	4	0	2	800 227-7337
PIMCO PEA Renaissance Fund D	Growth	-18.8	8.81	8.8	3	4	0	1.26	800 227-7337
PIMCO PEA Renaissance Fund Inst	Growth	-18.6	9.18	9.06	3	4	0	0.86	800 227-7337
PIMCO PEA Target Fund A	Growth	-11.7	-17.94	2.75	3	4	5.5	1.21	800 227-7337
PIMCO PEA Target Fund Admin	Growth	-11.4	-17.8	2.97	3	4	0	1.06	800 227-7337
PIMCO PEA Target Fund B	Growth	-12.3	-18.57	2.08	4	4	0	1.96	800 227-7337
PIMCO PEA Target Fund C	Growth	-12.3	-18.57	2.08	4	4	0	1.96	800 227-7337
PIMCO PEA Target Fund D	Growth	-11.7	-17.96	2.74		4	0	1.21	800 227-7337
PIMCO PEA Target Fund Inst	Growth	-11.4	-17.64	3.02	3	4	0	0.81	800 227-7337
PIMCO PEA Value Fund A	Growth	-15.6	7.79	6.16	3	4	5.5	1.1	800 227-7337
PIMCO PEA Value Fund Admin	Growth	-15.6	7.91	6.25	3	4	0	0.95	800 227-7337
PIMCO PEA Value Fund B	Growth	-16.3	6.98	5.37	3	4	0	1.85	800 227-7337
PIMCO PEA Value Fund C	Growth	-16.3	7	5.37	3	4	0	1.85	800 227-7337
PIMCO PEA Value Fund D	Growth	-15.5	7.86	6.21	3	4	0	1.1	800 227-7337
PIMCO PEA Value Fund Inst	Growth	-15.4	8.21	6.58	3	4	0	0.7	800 227-7337
PIMCO PPA T/E Strct Emg Mkts Inst	Foreign	5.2	-1.5		2	3	0	1.07	800 227-7337
PIMCO PPA Tax Efficient Eq A	Growth	-8	-10.91		3	3	5.5	1.11	800 227-7337
PIMCO PPA Tax Efficient Eq Admin	Growth	-7.8	-10.83		3	3	0	0.96	800 227-7337
PIMCO PPA Tax Efficient Eq B	Growth	-8.6	-11.59		4	3	0	1.86	800 227-7337
PIMCO PPA Tax Efficient Eq C	Growth	-8.6	-11.59		4	3	0	1.86	800 227-7337
PIMCO PPA Tax Efficient Eq D	Growth	-8	-10.94		3	3	0	1.11	800 227-7337

Stock Fund Name	Objective	Annualized Return for			Rank		Max Load	Expense Ratio	Toll-Free/(Toll) Telephone
		1 Year	3 Years	5 Years	Overall	Risk			
PIMCO PPA Tax Efficient Eq Inst	Growth	-7.6	-10.58		3	3	0	0.71	800 227-7337
PIMCO RCM Biotechnology D	Health	14.3	-4.7			5	0	1.6	800 227-7337
PIMCO RCM Emerging Markets D	Foreign	-12.1	-12.73	1.28	3	3	0	1.95	800 227-7337
PIMCO RCM Emerging Markets Inst	Foreign	-11.9	-12.41	1.56	3	3	0	1.5	800 227-7337
PIMCO RCM Europe D	European	-9.4	-19.92	-13.11	4	3	0	1.61	800 227-7337
PIMCO RCM Europe Inst	European	-10					0	1.35	800 227-7337
PIMCO RCM Global Healthcare D	Health	0.2	2.39		2	4	0	1.6	800 227-7337
PIMCO RCM Global Small Cap D	Global	-7.1	-14.44		4	4	0	1.85	800 227-7337
PIMCO RCM Global Small Cap Inst	Global	-6.8	-14.23			4	0	1.47	800 227-7337
PIMCO RCM Global Technology D	Technology	2.3	-27.16	8.43	3	5	0	1.75	800 227-7337
PIMCO RCM Global Technology Inst	Technology	2.7	-26.87	8.77	3	5	0	1.35	800 227-7337
PIMCO RCM Intl Growth Equity C	Global	-16.8					0	2.2	800 227-7337
PIMCO RCM Intl Growth Equity D	Foreign	-15.7	-21.69	-8.8	4	2	0	1.45	800 227-7337
PIMCO RCM Intl Growth Equity Inst	Foreign	-15	-21.42	-8.55	4	2	0	1.03	800 227-7337
PIMCO RCM Large-Cap Growth Admin	Growth/Inc	-5.7					0	1	800 227-7337
PIMCO RCM Large-Cap Growth D	Growth	-5.8	-15.42		3	3	0	1	800 227-7337
PIMCO RCM Large-Cap Growth Inst	Growth	-5.8	-15.27	-0.92		3	0	0.75	800 227-7337
PIMCO RCM Mid-Cap D	Growth	-7.3					0	1.02	800 227-7337
PIMCO RCM Mid-Cap Inst	Growth/Inc	-7.2					0	0.77	800 227-7337
PIMCO RCM Tax-Managed Growth D	Other	-5					0	1.46	800 227-7337
PIMCO RCM Tax-Managed Growth Inst	Growth/Inc	-4.6	-13.07		3		0	1.14	800 227-7337
PIMCO StocksPLUS Fund A	Growth/Inc	-6.1	-9.75	-0.69	3	3	3	1.05	800 227-7337
PIMCO StocksPLUS Fund Admin	Growth/Inc	-6	-9.61	-0.56	3	3	0	0.9	800 227-7337
PIMCO StocksPLUS Fund B	Growth/Inc	-6.7	-10.41	-1.42	3	3	0	1.8	800 227-7337
PIMCO StocksPLUS Fund C	Growth/Inc	-6.5	-10.16	-1.17	3	3	0	1.55	800 227-7337
PIMCO StocksPLUS Fund D	Growth/Inc	-6	-9.89	-0.8	3	3	0	1.05	800 227-7337
PIMCO StocksPLUS Fund Inst	Growth/Inc	-5.7	-9.25	-0.19	3	3	0	0.65	800 227-7337
PIMCO Strategic Balanced Admin	Balanced	1.2	-1.25	2.89	1	1	0	0.86	800 227-7337
PIMCO Strategic Balanced Inst	Balanced	1.5	-0.95	3.16	1	1	0	0.61	800 227-7337
Pacific Advisors Balanced Fund A	Balanced	3.2	1.18	3.77	1	1	5.75	1.57	800 282-6693
Pacific Advisors Income A	Growth/Inc	4.3	4.32	3.87	2	1	4.75	1.53	800 282-6693
Pacific Advisors Small Cap A	Small Co	-18.6	5.08	-5.99	3	4	5.75	1.73	800 282-6693
Pacific Capital Gr & Inc A	Growth/Inc	-11.3	-11.14	0.28	3	4	4	1.35	800 258-9232
Pacific Capital Gr & Inc B	Growth/Inc	-12	-11.67	-0.41	4	4	0	2.1	800 258-9232
Pacific Capital Gr & Inc Y	Growth/Inc	-11	-10.92	0.47	3	4	0	1.1	800 258-9232
Pacific Capital Growth Stock A	Growth	-11.5	-10.82	-4.45	4	5	4	1.33	800 258-9232
Pacific Capital Growth Stock B	Growth	-12.1					0	2.08	800 258-9232
Pacific Capital Growth Stock Y	Growth	-11.3	-19.26	-1.83	4	4	0	1.08	800 258-9232
Pacific Capital Intl Stock A	Foreign	-14.4	-24.17			3	5.25	1.85	800 258-9232
Pacific Capital Intl Stock B	Foreign	-14.5	-24.69			3	0	2.5	800 258-9232
Pacific Capital Intl Stock Y	Foreign	-13.6	-17.94		5	2	0	1.6	800 258-9232
Pacific Capital New Asia Gr A	Pacific	-21	-12.64	3.29	4	4	5.25	2.04	800 258-9232
Pacific Capital New Asia Gr B	Pacific	-21.5	-13.16	2.62	4	4	0	2.79	800 258-9232
Pacific Capital New Asia Gr Y	Pacific	-20.7	-12.43	3.54	4	4	0	1.79	800 258-9232
Pacific Capital Small Cap A	Small Co	-3.5	13.28			3	4	1.6	800 258-9232
Pacific Capital Small Cap B	Small Co	-4.2	12.59			3	0	2.4	800 258-9232
Pacific Capital Small Cap Y	Small Co	-3.2	16.55		1	3	0	1.35	800 258-9232
Pacific Capital Value A	Growth	-13.1	-12.15			3	4	1.3	800 258-9232
Pacific Capital Value B	Growth	-13.7	-12.66			3	0	2.06	800 258-9232
Pacific Capital Value Y	Growth	-12.9	-7.55		3	3	0	1.05	800 258-9232
Papp America-Abroad Fund	Growth	-15	-17.03	-4.55	4	4	0	1.11	800 421-4004
Papp America-Pacific Rim Fund	Growth	-7.7	-12.33	2.39	3	3	0	1.25	800 421-4004
Papp Stock Fund	Growth	-13.6	-12.91	-2.14	4	3	0	1.25	800 421-4004
Parnassus Equity Income Fund	Income	3.7	2.87	9.91	1	2	0	0.96	800 999-3505
Parnassus Fund	Growth	-8.3	-10.16	6.73	2	4	3.5	1	800 999-3505
Pax World Balanced Fund	Balanced	-0.8	-1.95	5.08	1	1	0	0.94	800 767-1729
Pax World Growth Fund	Growth	-4.7	-14.69	-3.6	3	2	0	1.53	800 767-1729
Payden & Rygel Growth & Income R	Growth/Inc	-10.4	-5.19	-1.34	3	3	0	0.75	800 572-9336

Stock Fund Name	Objective	Annualized Return for			Rank		Max Load	Expense Ratio	Toll-Free/(Toll) Telephone
		1 Year	3 Years	5 Years	Overall	Risk			
Payden Market Return R	Flexible	-7.6	-10.25	-1.82	3	3	0	0.45	800 572-9336
Payson Balanced Fund	Balanced	-13.2	-0.75	-0.14	3	2	4	1.44	800 805-8258
Payson Value Fund	Growth	-15.9	-9.5	-3.29	4	3	4	1.75	800 805-8258
Performance Large Cap Equity A	Growth	-9.6	-11.88	-3.25	3	2	5.25	1.15	800 737-3676
Performance Large Cap Equity Inst	Growth	-9.4	-11.66	-3	3	2	0	0.9	800 737-3676
Performance Mid Cap Equity A	Growth	-6.8	-0.42	1.08	2	3	5.25	1.38	800 737-3676
Performance Mid Cap Equity I	Growth	-6.6	-0.19	1.33	2	3	0	1.13	800 737-3676
Perkins Opportunity Fund	Small Co	-27.3	-11.03	-1.3	3	5	4.75	2.24	800 998-3190
Permanent Portfolio Aggress Gr	Agg Growth	-5.9	-3.22	4.65	2	4	0	1.41	800 531-5142
Permanent Portfolio Fund	AssetAlloc	15.7	10.44	7.04	1	1	0	1.46	800 531-5142
Perritt Micro Cap Opportunities	Small Co	-0.1	14.47	6.8	1	4	0	1.75	800 331-8936
Philadelphia Fund	Growth/Inc	-3	1.51	0.45	2	1	0	1.5	800 749-9933
Phoenix-Aberdeen Int'l Port. C	Foreign	-16.9	-16.87			3	0	2.92	800 243-4361
Phoenix-Aberdeen International A	Foreign	-16.3	-16.25	-7.57	4	3	5.75	2.17	800 243-4361
Phoenix-Aberdeen International B	Foreign	-17	-16.89	-8.24	5	3	0	2.92	800 243-4361
Phoenix-Aberdeen Worldwide Opp A	Global	-14.8	-11.51	-3.24	4	3	5.75	1.73	800 243-4361
Phoenix-Aberdeen Worldwide Opp B	Global	-15.5	-12.17	-3.97	5	3	0	2.48	800 243-4361
Phoenix-Aberdeen Worldwide Opp C	Global	-15.6	-12.21			2	0	2.48	800 243-4361
Phoenix-Capital West Mkt Ntrl A	Growth	0.4	6.63	1.59	2	1	5.5	2.3	800 243-4361
Phoenix-Capital West Mkt Ntrl B	Growth	-0.4	5.87	0.88	2	1	0	3	800 243-4361
Phoenix-Capital West Mkt Ntrl C	Growth	-0.4	5.87	0.84	2	1	0	3	800 243-4361
Phoenix-Duff & Phelps Core Eq A	Growth	-12.3	-16.42	-8.5	5	3	5.75	1.39	800 243-4361
Phoenix-Duff & Phelps Core Eq B	Growth	-13	-17.05	-9.19	5	3	0	2.14	800 243-4361
Phoenix-Duff & Phelps Core Eq C	Growth	-13	-17.07	-9.22	5	3	0	2.14	800 243-4361
Phoenix-Duff & Phelps Real Est A	Real Est	10.3	16.8	9.11	1	1	5.75	1.3	800 243-4361
Phoenix-Duff & Phelps Real Est B	Real Est	9.4	15.93	8.3	1	1	0	2.05	800 243-4361
Phoenix-Duff&Phelps Inst Gr Stock X	Growth	-12	-15.5	-1.87	4	3	0	0.7	800 243-4361
Phoenix-Duff&Phelps Inst Gr Stock Y	Growth	-12.3	-15.72	-2.12	4	3	0	0.95	800 243-4361
Phoenix-Engemann Aggressive Gr A	Agg Growth	-8.5	-23.23	-1.36	4	5	5.75	1.64	800 243-4361
Phoenix-Engemann Aggressive Gr B	Agg Growth	-9.3	-23.82	-2.1	4	5	0	2.39	800 243-4361
Phoenix-Engemann Aggressive Gr C	Agg Growth	-9.2					0	2.39	800 243-4361
Phoenix-Engemann Balanced Ret A	Balanced	1.6	-9.13	1.07	3	2	5.75	1.51	800 243-4361
Phoenix-Engemann Balanced Ret B	Balanced	0.9	-9.82	0.28	3	2	0	2.26	800 243-4361
Phoenix-Engemann Balanced Ret C	Balanced	0.8	-9.81	0.28	3	2	0	2.26	800 243-4361
Phoenix-Engemann Capital Gr A	Growth	-5.4	-22.73	-8.01	3	4	5.75	1.39	800 243-4361
Phoenix-Engemann Capital Gr B	Growth	-6.1	-23.3	-8.71	4	4	0	2.14	800 243-4361
Phoenix-Engemann Focus Gr A	Growth	1.4	-21.6	-4.08	3	4	5.75	1.55	800 243-4361
Phoenix-Engemann Focus Gr B	Growth	0.6	-22.19	-4.83	3	4	0	2.3	800 243-4361
Phoenix-Engemann Focus Gr C	Growth	0.6	-22.19	-4.83	3	4	0	2.3	800 243-4361
Phoenix-Engemann Nifty Fifty A	Growth	-7.8	-25.46	-8.91	3	4	5.75	1.6	800 243-4361
Phoenix-Engemann Nifty Fifty B	Growth	-8.4	-26.01	-9.58	4	4	0	2.35	800 243-4361
Phoenix-Engemann Nifty Fifty C	Growth	-8.4	-26.01	-9.58	4	4	0	2.35	800 243-4361
Phoenix-Engemann Sm & Mid-Cap Gr A	Agg Growth	2.1	-17.16	-0.22	3	5	5.75	1.59	800 243-4361
Phoenix-Engemann Sm & Mid-Cap Gr B	Agg Growth	1.4	-17.76	-0.95	3	5	0	2.34	800 243-4361
Phoenix-Engemann Sm & Mid-Cap Gr C	Agg Growth	1.3	-17.76	-0.95	3	5	0	2.34	800 243-4361
Phoenix-Hollister Apprec A	Small Co	-7.1	3.12	-0.93	3	3	5.5	1.41	800 243-4361
Phoenix-Hollister Apprec B	Small Co	-7.7	2.43	-1.61	3	3	0	2.11	800 243-4361
Phoenix-Hollister Apprec C	Small Co	-7.7	2.43	-1.62	3	3	0	2.11	800 243-4361
Phoenix-Hollister Sm Cap Value A	Small Co	-8.7	-3.06	7.9	3	3	5.75	1.15	800 243-4361
Phoenix-Hollister Sm Cap Value B	Small Co	-9.4	-3.79	7.09	3	3	0	2.15	800 243-4361
Phoenix-Hollister Sm Cap Value C	Small Co	-9.4	-3.79	7.12	3	3	0	2.15	800 243-4361
Phoenix-Hollister Value Equity A	Growth	-11.3	-5.42	1.58	3	3	5.75	1.25	800 243-4361
Phoenix-Hollister Value Equity B	Growth	-12	-6.13	0.8	3	3	0	2	800 243-4361
Phoenix-Hollister Value Equity C	Growth	-12	-6.13	0.81	3	3	0	2	800 243-4361
Phoenix-Kayne International A	Foreign						5.75	1.2	800 243-4361
Phoenix-Kayne International B	Foreign						0	1.95	800 243-4361
Phoenix-Kayne International C	Foreign						0	1.95	800 243-4361
Phoenix-Kayne International X	Foreign	-13.8					0	1.38	800 243-4361

Stock Fund Name	Objective	Annualized Return for			Rank		Max Load	Expense Ratio	Toll-Free/(Toll) Telephone
		1 Year	3 Years	5 Years	Overall	Risk			
Phoenix-Kayne Large Cap A	Growth						5.75	1	800 243-4361
Phoenix-Kayne Large Cap B	Growth						0	1.75	800 243-4361
Phoenix-Kayne Large Cap C	Growth						0	1.75	800 243-4361
Phoenix-Kayne Large Cap X	Growth/Inc	-9.7	-9.24	-1.66	3	2	0	0.95	800 243-4361
Phoenix-Kayne Small-Mid Cap A	Small Co						5.75	1.1	800 243-4361
Phoenix-Kayne Small-Mid Cap B	Small Co						0	1.85	800 243-4361
Phoenix-Kayne Small-Mid Cap C	Small Co						0	1.85	800 243-4361
Phoenix-Kayne Small-Mid Cap X	Small Co	-15.8	2.56		3	3	0	1.17	800 243-4361
Phoenix-Oakhurst Balanced A	Balanced	-1.6	-1.08	3.2	1	1	5.75	1.08	800 243-4361
Phoenix-Oakhurst Balanced B	Balanced	-2.4	-1.81	2.43	2	1	0	1.83	800 243-4361
Phoenix-Oakhurst Gr & Inc A	Growth/Inc	-9.9	-10.16	-0.92	3	3	5.75	1.22	800 243-4361
Phoenix-Oakhurst Gr & Inc B	Growth/Inc	-10.6	-10.83	-1.64	4	3	0	1.97	800 243-4361
Phoenix-Oakhurst Gr & Inc C	Growth/Inc	-10.6	-10.84	-1.65	4	3	0	1.97	800 243-4361
Phoenix-Oakhurst Inc & Gr A	Flexible	1.1	-0.05	1.97	1	1	5.75	1.28	800 243-4361
Phoenix-Oakhurst Inc & Gr B	Flexible	0.5	-0.77	1.19	2	1	0	2.03	800 243-4361
Phoenix-Oakhurst Inc & Gr C	Flexible	0.5	-0.83			1	0	2.03	800 243-4361
Phoenix-Oakhurst Mgd Assets A	AssetAlloc	-1	-3.27	0.46	2	1	5.5	1.6	800 243-4361
Phoenix-Oakhurst Mgd Assets B	AssetAlloc	-1.6	-3.93	-0.23	2	1	0	2.3	800 243-4361
Phoenix-Oakhurst Mgd Assets C	AssetAlloc	-1.7	-3.95	-0.25	2	1	0	2.3	800 243-4361
Phoenix-Oakhurst Strat Alloc A	Flexible	-1.2	-1.12	3.7	1	1	5.75	1.2	800 243-4361
Phoenix-Oakhurst Strat Alloc B	Flexible	-2	-1.86	2.91	2	1	0	1.95	800 243-4361
Phoenix-Oakhurst Strategy A	Growth	-10.7	-10.74	-8.31	4	3	5.5	1.37	800 243-4361
Phoenix-Oakhurst Strategy B	Growth	-11.3	-11.36	-8.93	4	3	0	2.07	800 243-4361
Phoenix-Oakhurst Strategy C	Growth	-11.3	-11.36	-8.93	4	3	0	2.07	800 243-4361
Phoenix-Seneca Gr A	Growth	-12.9	-15.38	-1.7	4	3	5.75	1.39	800 243-4361
Phoenix-Seneca Gr B	Growth	-13.6	-16.01		4	3	0	2.14	800 243-4361
Phoenix-Seneca Gr C	Growth	-13.6	-16		4	3	0	2.14	800 243-4361
Phoenix-Seneca Gr X	Growth	-12.6	-15.15	-1.42	4	3	0	1.14	800 243-4361
Phoenix-Seneca Mid-Cap EDGE A	Growth	-16.8	-14.18	2.77	4	4	5.75	1.4	800 243-4361
Phoenix-Seneca Mid-Cap EDGE B	Growth	-17.4	-14.83		4	4	0	2.15	800 243-4361
Phoenix-Seneca Mid-Cap EDGE C	Growth	-17.4	-14.83		4	4	0	2.15	800 243-4361
Phoenix-Seneca Mid-Cap EDGE X	Growth	-16.6	-13.97	3.08	3	4	0	1.15	800 243-4361
Phoenix-Seneca Real Est A	Real Est	4	12.91	5.12	1	2	5.75	2.04	800 243-4361
Phoenix-Seneca Real Est B	Real Est	3.2	11.99		1	2	0	2.79	800 243-4361
Phoenix-Seneca Real Est C	Real Est	3.3	12.01		1	2	0	2.79	800 243-4361
Phoenix-Seneca Real Est X	Real Est	5.4	14.44	6.61	1	2	0	1.79	800 243-4361
Phoenix-Seneca Strategic Theme A	Growth	-13.8	-22.26	-0.2	3	5	5.75	1.68	800 243-4361
Phoenix-Seneca Strategic Theme B	Growth	-14.3	-22.82	-0.9	3	5	0	2.43	800 243-4361
Phoenix-Seneca Strategic Theme C	Growth	-14.4	-22.83	-0.98	3	5	0	2.43	800 243-4361
Phoenix-Seneca Tax Sensitive Gr A	Growth	-14.1	-15.92			3	5.75	1.35	800 243-4361
Phoenix-Seneca Tax Sensitive Gr B	Growth	-14.8	-16.55			3	0	2.1	800 243-4361
Phoenix-Seneca Tax Sensitive Gr C	Growth	-14.8	-16.55			3	0	2.1	800 243-4361
Phoenix-Seneca Tax Sensitive Gr X	Growth	-13.9	-15.72			3	0		800 243-4361
Pictet Global Emerg Markets Inst	Foreign	-1.6	-3.33	0.36	2	4	0	1.7	(610 239-4835)
Pictet International Equity Inst	Foreign	-12.9					0	1	(610 239-4835)
Pictet International Small Co Inst	Small Co	-7.2	-12.75	4.24	3	3	0	1.2	(610 239-4835)
Pin Oak Aggressive Stock	Agg Growth	-19.5	-36.52	-6.5	4	5	0	0.99	888 462-5386
Pioneer Balanced Fund A	Balanced	-2.7	-1.25	-0.65	2	1	4.5	1.31	800 225-6292
Pioneer Balanced Fund B	Balanced	-3.5	-2.12	-1.52	2	1	0	2.2	800 225-6292
Pioneer Balanced Fund C	Balanced	-3.5	-2.37	-1.77	2	1	1	2.44	800 225-6292
Pioneer Core Equity A	Growth	-10.3	-12.41		3	3	5.75	1.75	800 225-6292
Pioneer Core Equity B	Growth	-11	-13.06		4	3	5.75	2.51	800 225-6292
Pioneer Core Equity C	Growth	-10.8	-12.99		4	3	1	2.44	800 225-6292
Pioneer Emerging Markets A	Foreign	-3.3	-9.64	-2.31	3	4	5.75	2.76	800 225-6292
Pioneer Emerging Markets B	Foreign	-4	-10.35	-3.1	3	4	0	3.59	800 225-6292
Pioneer Emerging Markets C	Foreign	-3.9	-10.19	-3.16	3	4	1	3.57	800 225-6292
Pioneer Emerging Markets Y	Foreign	-2.3	-8.82	-1.48	3	4	0	1.8	800 225-6292
Pioneer Equity Income A	Income	-10.4	-2.2	0.65	3	2	5.75	1.08	800 225-6292

Stock Fund Name	Objective	Annualized Return for			Rank		Max Load	Expense Ratio	Toll-Free/(Toll) Telephone
		1 Year	3 Years	5 Years	Overall	Risk			
Pioneer Equity Income B	Income	-11.2	-2.97	-0.14	3	2	0	1.87	800 225-6292
Pioneer Equity Income C	Income	-11.2	-3.04	-0.2	3	2	1	1.98	800 225-6292
Pioneer Equity Income Y	Income	-10	-1.8			2	0	0.66	800 225-6292
Pioneer Europe Fund A	European	-11.6	-16.6	-8.73	5	3	5.75	1.76	800 225-6292
Pioneer Europe Fund B	European	-12.5	-17.42	-9.57	4	3	0	2.64	800 225-6292
Pioneer Europe Fund C	European	-12.5	-17.39	-9.52	4	3	1	2.6	800 225-6292
Pioneer Europe Fund Y	Growth/Inc	-10.9	-16.1			3	0	1.19	800 225-6292
Pioneer Europe Select A	European	-1.5					5.75	1.75	800 225-6292
Pioneer Europe Select B	European	-2.7					0	2.33	800 225-6292
Pioneer Europe Select C	European	-2					1	2.07	800 225-6292
Pioneer Fund A	Growth/Inc	-12	-9.5	0.32	4	3	5.75	1.14	800 225-6292
Pioneer Fund B	Growth/Inc	-12.8	-10.3	-0.56	4	3	0	1.99	800 225-6292
Pioneer Fund C	Growth/Inc	-12.7	-10.22	-0.52	4	3	1	1.94	800 225-6292
Pioneer Fund Y	Growth/Inc	-11.6	-9.13		2	3	0	0.72	800 225-6292
Pioneer Growth Shares A	Growth	-11.5	-17.73	-8.41	4	3	5.75	1.18	800 225-6292
Pioneer Growth Shares B	Growth	-12.4	-18.41	-9.26	5	3	0	1.98	800 225-6292
Pioneer Growth Shares C	Growth	-12.2	-18.35	-9.21	4	3	1	1.87	800 225-6292
Pioneer Growth Shares Y	Growth	-10.9	-17.19	-7.73	4	3	0	0.61	800 225-6292
Pioneer Independence Fd	Growth	-5.4					0	1.5	800 225-6292
Pioneer International Equity A	Foreign	-15.8	-16.44	-6.28	5	3	5.75	1.75	800 225-6292
Pioneer International Equity B	Foreign	-16.5	-17.17	-7.11	4	3	0	2.62	800 225-6292
Pioneer International Equity C	Foreign	-16.7	-17.39	-7.29	4	3	1	2.91	800 225-6292
Pioneer International Value A	Foreign	-16.1	-17.71	-9.99	5	3	5.75	2	800 225-6292
Pioneer International Value B	Foreign	-17	-18.6	-10.88	4	3	0	2.98	800 225-6292
Pioneer International Value C	Foreign	-17	-18.67	-10.91	4	3	1	3.33	800 225-6292
Pioneer Mid Cap Value A	Growth	-6.8	5.41	3.37	1	3	5.75	1.24	800 225-6292
Pioneer Mid Cap Value B	Growth	-7.6	4.58	2.5	1	3	0	2.03	800 225-6292
Pioneer Mid Cap Value C	Growth	-7.6	4.5	2.43	2	3	1	2.11	800 225-6292
Pioneer Mid Cap Value Fund Y	Growth	-6.4	5.91			3	0	0.84	800 225-6292
Pioneer Mid-Cap Growth Fd A	Growth	-11.9	-10.97	-2.97	3	4	5.75	0.87	800 225-6292
Pioneer Mid-Cap Growth Fd B	Growth	-13.2	-12.14	-4.32	4	4	0	2.01	800 225-6292
Pioneer Mid-Cap Growth Fd C	Growth	-13.1	-12.25	-4.29	4	4	1	2.18	800 225-6292
Pioneer Protected Principal + II A	Balanced						5.75		800 225-6292
Pioneer Protected Principal + II B	Balanced						0		800 225-6292
Pioneer Protected Principal + II C	Balanced						1		800 225-6292
Pioneer Protected Principal Plus A	Balanced						5.75		800 225-6292
Pioneer Protected Principal Plus B	Balanced						0		800 225-6292
Pioneer Protected Principal Plus C	Balanced						0		800 225-6292
Pioneer Real Estate Shares A	Real Est	3.7	12.93	4.75	2	2	5.75	1.58	800 225-6292
Pioneer Real Estate Shares B	Real Est	2.8	12.01	3.93	2	2	0	2.36	800 225-6292
Pioneer Real Estate Shares C	Real Est	2.8	12.03	3.95	2	2	1	2.28	800 225-6292
Pioneer Real Estate Shares Y	Real Est	4.3					0	1.12	800 225-6292
Pioneer Small Cap Value Fund A	Small Co	-12	5.83	8.06	3	4	5.75	1.79	800 225-6292
Pioneer Small Cap Value Fund B	Small Co	-12.7	5.04	7.24	3	4	0	2.52	800 225-6292
Pioneer Small Cap Value Fund C	Small Co	-12.6					1	2.71	800 225-6292
Pioneer Small Company Fund A	Small Co	-19.4	-0.22	-0.89	3	4	5.75	1.58	800 225-6292
Pioneer Small Company Fund B	Small Co	-19.9	-0.93	-1.6	3	4	0	2.28	800 225-6292
Pioneer Small Company Fund C	Small Co	-20.2	-0.95	-1.81	3	4	1	2.45	800 225-6292
Pioneer Value Fund A	Growth/Inc	-10.5	-2.58	-2.64	3	3	5.75	1.01	800 225-6292
Pioneer Value Fund B	Growth/Inc	-11.5	-3.54	-3.75	3	3	0	2.07	800 225-6292
Pioneer Value Fund C	Growth/Inc	-11.4	-3.64	-3.72	3	3	1	2.15	800 225-6292
Polaris Global Value Fund	Global	-3.5	6.37		2	3	0	1.63	888 263-5594
Polynous Growth Fund	Growth	9.7	3.6	-7.12	3	5	4.5	1.9	800 924-3836
Portfolio 21	Growth	-9.5	-8.5		3	3	0	1.5	800 366-6223
Potomac Dow 30 Plus Inv	Growth/Inc	-15.2	-9.42		3	4	0	1.75	800 851-0511
Potomac OTC Plus Inv	Growth	-5.3	-38	-5.48	3	5	0	1.75	800 851-0511
Potomac OTC Short Inv	Growth	-15.5	10.67	-19.23	3	5	0	1.95	800 851-0511
Potomac Small Cap Plus Inv	Small Co	-17.3	-7.74		4	4	0	1.75	800 851-0511

Stock Fund Name	Objective	Annualized Return for			Rank		Max Load	Expense Ratio	Toll-Free/(Toll) Telephone
		1 Year	3 Years	5 Years	Overall	Risk			
Potomac U.S. Plus Inv	Growth	-17.3	-20.87	-8.21	5	4	0	1.9	800 851-0511
Potomac U.S. Short Inv	Growth	-0.9	8.16	-0.56	2	3	0	2.27	800 851-0511
Preferred Asset Allocation Fund	AssetAlloc	-3.1	-3.89	2	2	2	0	0.99	800 662-4769
Preferred International Value Fund	Foreign	-14.3	-4.48	-0.05	3	3	0	1.26	800 662-4769
Preferred Large Cap Growth Fund	Growth	-12.2	-18.39	-2.04	4	4	0	0.85	800 662-4769
Preferred Large Cap Value Fund	Growth/Inc	-9.2	-3.66	-0.78	2	2	0	0.77	800 662-4769
Preferred Small Cap Growth Fund	Small Co	-6	-16.03	-15.81	4	5	0	1.37	800 662-4769
Primary Income Fund	Income	-9.5	4.16	1.28	2	1	0	1	800 443-6544
Primary Trend Fund	Flexible	-8.6	4.04	1.42	2	2	0	1.52	800 443-6544
Principal Balanced Fund A	Balanced	-4.9	-4.63	-2.22	2	1	5.75	1.46	800 247-4123
Principal Balanced Fund B	Balanced	-5.6	-5.25	-2.89	2	1	0	2.21	800 247-4123
Principal Capital Value A	Growth/Inc	-7.1	-3.6	-3.93	3	2	5.75	1.01	800 247-4123
Principal Capital Value B	Growth/Inc	-7.8	-4.37	-4.7	3	2	0	1.83	800 247-4123
Principal Growth Fund A	Growth	-11.3	-19.44	-9.16	5	3	5.75	1.41	800 247-4123
Principal Growth Fund B	Growth	-11.9	-23.39	-12.09	5	4	0	2	800 247-4123
Principal International A	Foreign	-12.9	-14.61	-6.88	4	3	5.75	1.53	800 247-4123
Principal International B	Foreign	-13.7	-15.26	-7.53	4	3	0	2.24	800 247-4123
Principal Intl Emerg Mkts A	Foreign	-8.7	-8.98	-0.54	3	4	5.75	2.49	800 247-4123
Principal Intl Emerg Mkts B	Foreign	-9.5	-9.73	-1.31	3	4	0	3.19	800 247-4123
Principal Intl SmallCap A	Foreign	-13.5	-14.35	-0.54	4	3	5.75	2.31	800 247-4123
Principal Intl SmallCap B	Foreign	-14.4	-15.08	-1.42	3	3	0	3.15	800 247-4123
Principal Large Cap Stock Index A	Growth	-9.1	-11.6		3	3	1.5	0.9	800 247-4123
Principal Large Cap Stock Index B	Growth	-9.3	-11.9		4	3	0	1.25	800 247-4123
Principal MidCap A	Growth	-3.9	4.16	2.39	1	2	5.75	1.22	800 247-4123
Principal MidCap B	Growth	-4.4	3.6	1.88	2	2	0	1.81	800 247-4123
Principal Partners Blue Chip A	Growth/Inc	-10.8	-14.33	-6.99	4	3	5.75	1.55	800 247-4123
Principal Partners Blue Chip B	Growth/Inc	-11.4	-14.93	-7.66	4	3	0	2.08	800 247-4123
Principal Partners Equity Growth A	Growth	-12.4	-16.94		5	3	5.75	2.07	800 247-4123
Principal Partners Equity Growth B	Growth	-13.1	-17.6		5	3	0	2.83	800 247-4123
Principal Partners LrgCap Blend A	Growth	-9.5					5.75	1.9	800 247-4123
Principal Partners LrgCap Blend B	Growth	-10.2					0	2.75	800 247-4123
Principal Partners LrgCap Value A	Growth	-7.4					5.75	1.83	800 247-4123
Principal Partners LrgCap Value B	Growth	-8.2					0	2.6	800 247-4123
Principal Partners MidCap Gr A	Growth	-8.7					5.75	1.94	800 247-4123
Principal Partners MidCap Gr B	Growth	-8.9					0	2.69	800 247-4123
Principal Partners SmCap Growth A	Growth	-23.6					5.75	1.95	800 247-4123
Principal Partners SmCap Growth B	Growth	-24.2					0	2.69	800 247-4123
Principal Real Estate A	Real Est	6.8	15.24	7.83	1	1	5.75	1.7	800 247-4123
Principal Real Estate B	Real Est	6	14.39	7.08	1	1	0	2.34	800 247-4123
Principal SmallCap Fund A	Small Co	-17.4	-11.03	-3.1	4	4	5.75	1.98	800 247-4123
Principal SmallCap Fund B	Small Co	-18	-11.78	-3.87	3	4	0	2.74	800 247-4123
Principal Utilities Fund A	Utilities	-0.4	-7.17	-0.51	3	2	5.75	1.49	800 247-4123
Principal Utilities Fund B	Utilities	-1.3	-7.88	-1.26	3	2	0	2.4	800 247-4123
ProFunds-Bank UltraSector Inv	Financial	-10.8					0	1.95	888 776-3637
ProFunds-Bank UltraSector Svc	Financial	-11.4					0	2.8	888 776-3637
ProFunds-Basic Mat UltraSector Inv	Other	-26.5					0	1.27	888 776-3637
ProFunds-Basic Mat UltraSector Svc	Other	-26.8					0	2.95	888 776-3637
ProFunds-Bear Fund Inv	Growth	1.5	10.82	2.14	2	3	0	1.88	888 776-3637
ProFunds-Bear Fund Svc	Growth	0.5	9.83	1.12	2	3	0	2.95	888 776-3637
ProFunds-Biotech Ultra Sector Inv	Health	16.6					0	1.95	888 776-3637
ProFunds-Biotech Ultra Sector Svc	Health	15.5					0	2.95	888 776-3637
ProFunds-Bull Fund Inv	Growth	-10.9	-13.75	-0.46	4	3	0	1.79	888 776-3637
ProFunds-Bull Fund Svc	Growth	-11.7	-14.52	-5.17	5	3	0	2.8	888 776-3637
ProFunds-Energy UltraSector Inv	Energy/Res	-16.4					0	1.95	888 776-3637
ProFunds-Energy UltraSector Svc	Energy/Res	-16.9					0	2.95	888 776-3637
ProFunds-Europe 30 Inv	European	-9.1	-28.82		5	4	0	2.75	888 776-3637
ProFunds-Europe 30 Svc	European	-2.3	-27.64		4	4	0	3.36	888 776-3637
ProFunds-Financial UltraSector Inv	Financial	-13.2					0	1.95	888 776-3637

Stock Fund Name	Objective	Annualized Return for			Rank		Max Load	Expense Ratio	Toll-Free/(Toll) Telephone
		1 Year	3 Years	5 Years	Overall	Risk			
ProFunds-Financial UltraSector Svc	Financial	-13.8					0	2.95	888 776-3637
ProFunds-HlthCare UltraSector Inv	Health	-14.2					0	1.95	888 776-3637
ProFunds-HlthCare UltraSector Svc	Health	-15.2					0	2.95	888 776-3637
ProFunds-Internet UltraSector Inv	Technology	42.4					0	1.95	888 776-3637
ProFunds-Internet UltraSector Svc	Technology	41.8					0	2.95	888 776-3637
ProFunds-Mid Cap Growth Inv	Growth	-14.5					0	1.95	888 776-3637
ProFunds-Mid Cap Growth Svc	Growth	-15.4					0	2.94	888 776-3637
ProFunds-Mid Cap Inv	Growth	-12.8					0	1.95	888 776-3637
ProFunds-Mid Cap Svc	Growth	-13.7					0	2.79	888 776-3637
ProFunds-Mid Cap Value Inv	Growth	-13.2					0	1.95	888 776-3637
ProFunds-Mid Cap Value Svc	Growth	-13.9					0	2.77	888 776-3637
ProFunds-OTC Inv	Agg Growth	-1.9					0	1.91	888 776-3637
ProFunds-OTC Svc	Agg Growth	-2.9					0	2.95	888 776-3637
ProFunds-Pharm UltraSector Inv	Health	-17.5					0	1.95	888 776-3637
ProFunds-Pharm UltraSector Svc	Health	-18.1					0	2.95	888 776-3637
ProFunds-Real Est UltraSector Inv	Real Est	-5.1					0	1.95	888 776-3637
ProFunds-Real Est UltraSector Svc	Real Est	-6.1					0	2.95	888 776-3637
ProFunds-Semicond UltraSector Inv	Technology	-43.2					0	1.95	888 776-3637
ProFunds-Semicond UltraSector Svc	Technology	-43.7					0	2.95	888 776-3637
ProFunds-Small Cap Growth Inv	Growth	-10.7					0	1.95	888 776-3637
ProFunds-Small Cap Growth Svc	Growth	-11.7					0	2.85	888 776-3637
ProFunds-Small Cap Inv	Small Co	-10.9					0	1.95	888 776-3637
ProFunds-Small Cap Svc	Small Co	-12					0	2.76	888 776-3637
ProFunds-Small Cap Value Inv	Small Co	-19.6					0	1.95	888 776-3637
ProFunds-Small Cap Value Svc	Small Co	-20.6					0	2.85	888 776-3637
ProFunds-Tech UltraSector Inv	Technology	-18					0	1.95	888 776-3637
ProFunds-Tech UltraSector Svc	Technology	-18.1					0	2.95	888 776-3637
ProFunds-Telecom UltraSector Inv	Utilities	-28.2					0	1.95	888 776-3637
ProFunds-Telecom UltraSector Svc	Utilities	-28.7					0	2.95	888 776-3637
ProFunds-Ultra Bear Fund Inv	Agg Growth	-3.6	15.66	-3.87	3	5	0	1.79	888 776-3637
ProFunds-Ultra Bear Fund Svc	Agg Growth	-4.3	14.99	-4.4	3	5	0	2.8	888 776-3637
ProFunds-Ultra Bull Fund Inv	Agg Growth	-25.2	-29.8	-14.09	5	5	0	1.93	888 776-3637
ProFunds-Ultra Bull Fund Svc	Agg Growth	-25.6	-30.42	-14.9	5	5	0	2.87	888 776-3637
ProFunds-Ultra Japan Inv	Pacific	-53.7	-41.85		5	5	0	1.27	888 776-3637
ProFunds-Ultra Japan Svc	Pacific	-54.2	-41.36		5	5	0	2.27	888 776-3637
ProFunds-Ultra Mid Cap Inv	Agg Growth	-30.1	-13.94		5	5	0	1.31	888 776-3637
ProFunds-Ultra Mid Cap Svc	Agg Growth	-30.6	-14.74		5	5	0	2.31	888 776-3637
ProFunds-Ultra OTC Fund Inv	Agg Growth	-19.6	-62.39	-24.85	3	5	0	1.8	888 776-3637
ProFunds-Ultra OTC Fund Svc	Agg Growth	-20.2	-62.78	-25.62	3	5	0	2.8	888 776-3637
ProFunds-Ultra Short OTC Fund Inv	Agg Growth	-36.2	1.86		3	5	0	1.78	888 776-3637
ProFunds-Ultra Short OTC Fund Svc	Agg Growth	-36.7	0.98		3	5	0	2.92	888 776-3637
ProFunds-Ultra Small Cap Inv	Small Co	-25.1	-17.89		5	5	0	1.6	888 776-3637
ProFunds-Ultra Small Cap Svc	Small Co	-25.9	-18.73		5	5	0	2.34	888 776-3637
ProFunds-Utilities UltraSector Inv	Utilities	-23					0	1.35	888 776-3637
ProFunds-Utilities UltraSector Svc	Utilities	-23.8					0	2.35	888 776-3637
ProFunds-Wireless UltraSector Inv	Utilities	-30.5					0	1.95	888 776-3637
ProFunds-Wireless UltraSector Svc	Utilities	-31.4					0	2.95	888 776-3637
Profit Value Fund	Growth/Inc	-8.8					0	2.25	(301 650-0059)
Progressive Capital Accumulation	Growth	-4.9	-15.22	-3.5	3	3	0	2	(508 831-1171)
Provident Inv Counsel Growth I	Growth	-15.3	-24.46	-8.56	4	4	0	1	800 618-7643
Provident Inv Counsel Mid Cap B	Growth	-12	-13.08		4	5	0	2.14	800 618-7643
Provident Inv Counsel Sm Cap Gr I	Small Co	-8.7	-15.02	1.08	3	5	0	1	800 618-7643
Provident Inv Counsel Sm Co Gr A	Small Co	-9.2	-15.43	0.92	3	5	5.75	1.45	800 618-7643
Provident Inv Counsel Twenty Instl	Growth	-16.5	-29.42		5	5	0	1.3	800 618-7643
Prudent Bear	Growth	3.3	21.62	4.62	2	5	0	1.97	800 711-1848
Prudential 20/20 Focus Fd A	Growth	-9.4	-5.58		3	3	5	1.31	888 743-7111
Prudential 20/20 Focus Fd B	Growth	-10.1	-6.29		3	3	0	2.06	888 743-7111
Prudential 20/20 Focus Fd C	Growth	-10.1	-6.29		3	3	1	2.06	888 743-7111

Stock Fund Name	Objective	Annualized Return for			Rank		Max Load	Expense Ratio	Toll-Free/(Toll) Telephone
		1 Year	3 Years	5 Years	Overall	Risk			
Prudential 20/20 Focus Fd Z	Growth	-9.1	-5.32		3	3	0	1.06	888 743-7111
Prudential Active Balanced A	Balanced	-2	-2.85	2.1	1	2	5	1.21	888 743-7111
Prudential Active Balanced B	Balanced	-2.8	-3.54	1.37	2	2	0	1.96	888 743-7111
Prudential Active Balanced C	Balanced	-2.8	-3.54	1.37	2	2	1	1.96	888 743-7111
Prudential Active Balanced Z	Balanced	-1.9	-2.5	2.41	1	2	0	0.96	888 743-7111
Prudential Equity Fund A	Growth	-10	-7.08	-3.2	3	3	5	0.93	888 743-7111
Prudential Equity Fund B	Growth	-10.7	-7.78	-3.93	4	3	0	1.68	888 743-7111
Prudential Equity Fund C	Growth	-10.7	-7.76	-3.93	4	3	1	1.68	888 743-7111
Prudential Equity Fund Z	Growth	-9.8	-6.86	-2.95	3	3	0	0.68	888 743-7111
Prudential Europe Growth A	European	-13.4	-15.33	-7.29	4	4	5	1.63	888 743-7111
Prudential Europe Growth B	European	-14.1	-16.05	-8.01	5	4	0	2.38	888 743-7111
Prudential Europe Growth C	European	-14.1					1	2.38	888 743-7111
Prudential Europe Growth Z	European	-13.3	-15.18	-7.08	4	4	0	1.38	888 743-7111
Prudential Financial Services A	Financial	-4.9	7.42		2	3	5	1.45	888 743-7111
Prudential Financial Services B	Financial	-5.6	6.66		2	3	0	2.2	888 743-7111
Prudential Financial Services C	Financial	-5.6	6.66		2	3	1	2.2	888 743-7111
Prudential Financial Services Z	Financial	-4.6	7.73		2	3	0	1.2	888 743-7111
Prudential Global Gr Fund A	Global	-8.2	-15.35	-2.16	3	4	5	1.46	888 743-7111
Prudential Global Gr Fund B	Global	-8.6	-15.89	-2.79	3	4	0	2	888 743-7111
Prudential Global Gr Fund C	Global	-8.9	-15.94	-2.87	4	4	1	2.21	888 743-7111
Prudential Global Gr Fund Z	Global	-8	-15.16	-1.93	3	4	0	1.21	888 743-7111
Prudential Health Sci A	Health	6.8	4.63		1	3	5	1.37	888 743-7111
Prudential Health Sci B	Health	6	3.83		1	3	0	2.12	888 743-7111
Prudential Health Sci C	Health	6	3.83		1	3	1	2.11	888 743-7111
Prudential Health Sci Z	Health	7.1	4.91		1	3	0	1.11	888 743-7111
Prudential Intl Value Fund A	Foreign	-16.2	-10.9	-4.16	4	3	5	1.6	888 743-7111
Prudential Intl Value Fund B	Foreign	-16.9	-11.6	-4.91	3	3	0	2.35	888 743-7111
Prudential Intl Value Fund C	Foreign	-16.9	-11.58	-4.9	3	3	1	2.35	888 743-7111
Prudential Intl Value Fund Z	Foreign	-16.1	-10.72	-3.95	4	3	0	1.35	888 743-7111
Prudential Jennison Equity Opp A	Growth/Inc	-12.3	5.75	8.9	2	3	5	1.31	888 743-7111
Prudential Jennison Equity Opp B	Growth/Inc	-13	4.95	8.07	3	3	0	2.06	888 743-7111
Prudential Jennison Equity Opp C	Growth/Inc	-13	4.95	8.07	3	3	1	2.06	888 743-7111
Prudential Jennison Equity Opp Z	Growth/Inc	-12.1	6	9.16	2	3	0	1.06	888 743-7111
Prudential Jennison Gr Fd A	Growth	-12.6	-18.87	-2.62	4	4	5	1.08	888 743-7111
Prudential Jennison Growth Fund B	Growth	-13.3	-19.48	-3.35	5	4	0	1.83	888 743-7111
Prudential Jennison Growth Fund C	Growth	-13.3	-19.48	-3.35	5	4	1	1.83	888 743-7111
Prudential Jennison Growth Fund Z	Growth	-12.4	-18.67	-2.37	4	4	0	0.83	888 743-7111
Prudential Jennison Intl Growth A	Technology	-12.1	-22.33		5	4	5	1.73	888 743-7111
Prudential Jennison Intl Growth B	Technology	-12.7	-22.94		5	4	0	2.48	888 743-7111
Prudential Jennison Intl Growth C	Technology	-12.7	-22.94		5	4	1	2.48	888 743-7111
Prudential Jennison Intl Growth Z	Technology	-11.6	-22.17		5	4	0	1.48	888 743-7111
Prudential Natural Resources A	Energy/Res	-0.5	10.07	13.39	1	4	5	1.71	888 743-7111
Prudential Natural Resources B	Energy/Res	-1.3	9.25	12.52	1	4	0	2.46	888 743-7111
Prudential Natural Resources C	Energy/Res	-1.3	9.25	12.52	1	4	1	2.46	888 743-7111
Prudential Natural Resources Z	Energy/Res	-0.2	10.4	13.67	1	4	0	1.46	888 743-7111
Prudential Pacific Growth A	Pacific	-16.6	-20.73	-7.13	5	3	5	2.39	888 743-7111
Prudential Pacific Growth B	Pacific	-17.2	-21.53	-7.98	5	3	0	3.14	888 743-7111
Prudential Pacific Growth C	Pacific	-17.2	-21.41	-7.87	5	3	1	3.14	888 743-7111
Prudential Pacific Growth Z	Pacific	-16.6	-20.92	-7.11	5	3	0	2.14	888 743-7111
Prudential Real Estate Fd A	Real Est	9.4	15.53	5.78	1	1	5	1.79	888 743-7111
Prudential Real Estate Fd B	Real Est	8.6	14.68	5	1	1	0	2.54	888 743-7111
Prudential Real Estate Fd C	Real Est	7.8	14.4	4.84	1	2	1	2.54	888 743-7111
Prudential Real Estate Fd Z	Real Est	8.6	15.41	5.83	1	2	0	1.54	888 743-7111
Prudential Small Company Fund A	Small Co	-9.3	0.34	-3.08	3	4	5	1.22	888 743-7111
Prudential Small Company Fund B	Small Co	-10	-0.42	-3.81	3	4	0	1.97	888 743-7111
Prudential Small Company Fund C	Small Co	-10	-0.42	-3.81	3	4	1	1.97	888 743-7111
Prudential Small Company Fund Z	Small Co	-9	0.57	-2.85	3	4	0	0.97	888 743-7111
Prudential Stock Index A	Growth	-8.6	-11.24		3	3	3.25	0.65	888 743-7111

Stock Fund Name	Objective	Annualized Return for			Rank		Max Load	Expense Ratio	Toll-Free/(Toll) Telephone
		1 Year	3 Years	5 Years	Overall	Risk			
Prudential Stock Index B	Growth	-9.2	-11.89		3	3	0	1.4	888 743-7111
Prudential Stock Index C	Growth	-9.2	-11.86		3	3	1	1.4	888 743-7111
Prudential Stock Index I	Growth	-8.2	-10.91	-1.14	3	3	0	0.3	888 743-7111
Prudential Stock Index Z	Growth	-8.3	-11	-1.26	3	3	0	0.4	888 743-7111
Prudential Tax Managed Equity A	Growth	-8.4	-10.73		3	3	5	1.1	888 743-7111
Prudential Tax Managed Equity B	Growth	-9.1	-11.41		3	3	0	1.85	888 743-7111
Prudential Tax Managed Equity C	Growth	-9.1	-11.41		4	3	1	1.85	888 743-7111
Prudential Tax Managed Equity Z	Growth	-8.1	-10.47		3	3	0	0.85	888 743-7111
Prudential Tax-Managed Sm Cap A	Small Co	-9.4	4.58	0.11	2	3	5	1.32	888 743-7111
Prudential Tax-Managed Sm Cap B	Small Co	-10.1	3.77	-0.67	3	3	0	2.07	888 743-7111
Prudential Tax-Managed Sm Cap C	Small Co	-10.1	3.77	-0.67	2	3	1	2.07	888 743-7111
Prudential Tax-Managed Sm Cap Z	Small Co	-9	4.9	0.38	2	3	0	1.07	888 743-7111
Prudential Technology A	Technology	-6.7	-27.35		3	5	5	1.86	888 743-7111
Prudential Technology B	Technology	-7.4	-27.89		3	5	0	2.61	888 743-7111
Prudential Technology C	Technology	-7.4	-27.89		3	5	1	2.61	888 743-7111
Prudential Technology Z	Technology	-6.5	-27.16		3	5	0	1.61	888 743-7111
Prudential US Emerging Growth A	Small Co	-5.4	-14.89	4.24	3	5	5	1.31	888 743-7111
Prudential US Emerging Growth B	Small Co	-6.1	-15.51	3.45	3	5	0	2.06	888 743-7111
Prudential US Emerging Growth C	Small Co	-6.1	-15.51	3.45	3	5	1	2.06	888 743-7111
Prudential US Emerging Growth Z	Small Co	-5.1	-14.65	4.51	3	5	0	1.06	888 743-7111
Prudential Utility Fund A	Utilities	-4.4	-6.03	0.28	2	3	5	0.8	888 743-7111
Prudential Utility Fund B	Utilities	-5.2	-6.73	-0.46	2	3	0	1.55	888 743-7111
Prudential Utility Fund C	Utilities	-5.2	-6.73	-0.46	2	3	1	1.55	888 743-7111
Prudential Utility Fund Z	Utilities	-4.2	-5.79	0.54	2	3	0	0.55	888 743-7111
Prudential Value Fund A	Growth	-11.9	-0.41	-1.12	3	3	5	1.04	888 743-7111
Prudential Value Fund B	Growth	-12.6	-1.15	-1.87	3	3	0	1.79	888 743-7111
Prudential Value Fund C	Growth	-12.6	-1.15	-1.87	3	3	1	1.79	888 743-7111
Prudential Value Fund Z	Growth	-11.7	-0.17	-0.88	3	3	0	0.79	888 743-7111
Purisima Total Return Fund	Flexible	-12.1	-4.99	2.66	3	2	0	1.5	800 841-0199
Putnam Asset Alloc-Balanced R	Balanced	-4.3	-3.77	0.89		2	0	1.4	800 354-2228
Putnam Asset Alloc-Conserv R	AssetAlloc	3.4	2.1	3.06		1	0	1.58	800 354-2228
Putnam Asset Alloc-Growth R	AssetAlloc	-8.4	-6.74	-0.36		2	0		800 354-2228
Putnam Asset Alloc: Bal A	Balanced	-4.2	-3.56	1.12	2	2	5.75	1.11	800 354-2228
Putnam Asset Alloc: Bal B	Balanced	-5	-4.28	0.38	2	2	0	1.86	800 354-2228
Putnam Asset Alloc: Bal C	Balanced	-4.9	-4.29	0.36	2	2	0	1.86	800 354-2228
Putnam Asset Alloc: Bal M	Balanced	-4.7	-4.04	0.59	2	2	3.5	1.61	800 354-2228
Putnam Asset Allocation: Conserv A	AssetAlloc	3.6	2.33	3.31	1	1	5.75	1.29	800 354-2228
Putnam Asset Allocation: Conserv B	AssetAlloc	2.7	1.5	2.5	1	1	0	2.04	800 354-2228
Putnam Asset Allocation: Conserv C	AssetAlloc	2.6	1.5	2.52	1	1	0	2.04	800 354-2228
Putnam Asset Allocation: Conserv M	AssetAlloc	3	1.76	2.75	1	1	3.5	1.79	800 354-2228
Putnam Asset Allocation: Growth A	AssetAlloc	-8.2	-6.54	-0.14	3	2	5.75	1.25	800 354-2228
Putnam Asset Allocation: Growth B	AssetAlloc	-8.9	-7.23	-0.9	3	2	0	2	800 354-2228
Putnam Asset Allocation: Growth C	AssetAlloc	-8.9	-7.25	-0.89	3	2	0	2	800 354-2228
Putnam Asset Allocation: Growth M	AssetAlloc	-8.7	-7.01	-0.64	3	2	3.5	1.75	800 354-2228
Putnam Cap Appreciation A	Growth	-10.4	-9.63	-4.44	4	3	5.75	1	800 354-2228
Putnam Cap Appreciation B	Growth	-11	-10.28	-5.09	4	3	0	1.75	800 354-2228
Putnam Cap Appreciation C	Growth	-11	-10.23	-5.01	4	3	0	1.75	800 354-2228
Putnam Cap Appreciation M	Growth	-10.8	-10.07	-4.91	4	3	3.5	1.5	800 354-2228
Putnam Capital Opportunities A	Small Co	-18.9	4.48	3.56	2	5	5.75	1.1	800 354-2228
Putnam Capital Opportunities B	Small Co	-19.4	3.68	2.81	2	5	0	1.85	800 354-2228
Putnam Capital Opportunities C	Small Co	-19.5	3.7	2.81	3	5	0	1.85	800 354-2228
Putnam Capital Opportunities M	Small Co	-19.3	3.91	3.02	3	5	3.5	1.6	800 354-2228
Putnam Capital Opportunities R	Small Co	-19	4.25	3.33		5	0		800 354-2228
Putnam Classic Equity A	Growth/Inc	-9.8	-4.5	-2.41	3	3	5.75	0.97	800 354-2228
Putnam Classic Equity B	Growth/Inc	-10.4	-5.2	-3.14	3	2	0	1.72	800 354-2228
Putnam Classic Equity C	Growth/Inc	-10.3	-5.16	-3.1	3	2	0	1.72	800 354-2228
Putnam Classic Equity M	Growth/Inc	-10.2	-4.96	-2.91	3	2	3.5	1.47	800 354-2228
Putnam Convertible Inc-Gr Tr A	Converts	6.5	-1.58	0.77	2	2	5.75	1.01	800 354-2228

Stock Fund Name	Objective	Annualized Return for			Rank		Max Load	Expense Ratio	Toll-Free/(Toll) Telephone
		1 Year	3 Years	5 Years	Overall	Risk			
Putnam Convertible Inc-Gr Tr B	Converts	5.7	-2.31	0.02	2	2	0	1.76	800 354-2228
Putnam Convertible Inc-Gr Tr C	Converts	5.7	-2.31	0.02	2	2	0	1.76	800 354-2228
Putnam Convertible Inc-Gr Tr M	Converts	6	-2.06	0.3	2	2	3.5	1.51	800 354-2228
Putnam Discovery Growth Fund A	Agg Growth	-10.1	-23.17	-5	4	5	5.75	1.1	800 354-2228
Putnam Discovery Growth Fund B	Agg Growth	-10.8	-23.73	-5.71	4	5	0	1.85	800 354-2228
Putnam Discovery Growth Fund C	Agg Growth	-10.8	-23.73	-5.69	4	5	0	1.85	800 354-2228
Putnam Discovery Growth Fund M	Agg Growth	-10.5	-23.53	-5.46	4	5	3.5	1.6	800 354-2228
Putnam Equity Income A	Income	-7.1	1.39	2.04	2	2	5.75	0.97	800 354-2228
Putnam Equity Income B	Income	-7.8	0.64	1.29	2	2	0	1.72	800 354-2228
Putnam Equity Income C	Income	-7.8	0.64	1.29	2	2	0	1.72	800 354-2228
Putnam Equity Income M	Income	-7.6	0.89	1.54	2	2	3.5	1.47	800 354-2228
Putnam Equity Income R	Income	-7.3	1.13	1.79		2	0		800 354-2228
Putnam Europe Equity A	European	-12	-13.05	-5.28	5	3	5.75	1.23	800 354-2228
Putnam Europe Equity B	European	-12.7	-13.73	-5.98	5	3	0	1.98	800 354-2228
Putnam Europe Equity C	European	-12.7	-13.71	-5.98	5	3	0	1.98	800 354-2228
Putnam Europe Equity M	European	-12.4	-13.49	-5.7	5	3	3.5	1.73	800 354-2228
Putnam Fund for Gr & Inc A	Growth/Inc	-9.8	-3.87	-0.88	3	2	5.75	0.82	800 354-2228
Putnam Fund for Gr & Inc B	Growth/Inc	-10.5	-4.58	-1.61	3	2	0	1.57	800 354-2228
Putnam Fund for Gr & Inc C	Growth/Inc	-10.5	-4.58	-1.6	3	2	0	1.57	800 354-2228
Putnam Fund for Gr & Inc M	Growth/Inc	-10.2	-4.33	-1.37	3	2	3.5	1.32	800 354-2228
Putnam Fund for Gr & Inc R	Growth/Inc	-10	-4.12	-1.12		2	0		800 354-2228
Putnam George Fund R	AssetAlloc	-2.6	2.02	1.89		1	0		800 354-2228
Putnam Global Equity Fd A	Global	-9.6	-13.08	0.72	3	3	5.75	1.15	800 354-2228
Putnam Global Equity Fd B	Global	-10.2	-13.71	0.02	4	3	0	1.9	800 354-2228
Putnam Global Equity Fd C	Global	-10.4	-13.72	0.05	4	3	0	1.9	800 354-2228
Putnam Global Equity Fd M	Global	-10	-13.5	0.28	3	3	3.5	1.65	800 354-2228
Putnam Global Equity Fd R	Global	-9.7	-13.27	0.5		3	0		800 354-2228
Putnam Global Natural Resources A	Energy/Res	-8.7	-0.52	2.39	2	3	5.75	1.14	800 354-2228
Putnam Global Natural Resources B	Energy/Res	-9.4	-1.27	1.62	2	3	0	1.89	800 354-2228
Putnam Global Natural Resources C	Energy/Res	-9.4	-1.27	1.63	2	3	0	1.89	800 354-2228
Putnam Global Natural Resources M	Energy/Res	-9.2	-1.03	1.86	2	3	3.5	1.64	800 354-2228
Putnam Growth Opportunities A	Growth	-10	-25.53	-6	4	4	5.75	0.99	800 354-2228
Putnam Growth Opportunities B	Growth	-10.7	-26.08	-6.69	4	4	0	1.74	800 354-2228
Putnam Growth Opportunities C	Growth	-10.7	-26.1	-6.66	4	4	0	1.74	800 354-2228
Putnam Growth Opportunities M	Growth	-10.4	-25.92	-6.46	4	4	3.5	1.49	800 354-2228
Putnam Growth Opportunities R	Growth	-10.2	-25.69	-6.2		4	0		800 354-2228
Putnam Health Sciences Trust A	Health	-6.1	-5.95	1.1	2	2	5.75	0.96	800 354-2228
Putnam Health Sciences Trust B	Health	-6.8	-6.66	0.34	2	2	0	1.71	800 354-2228
Putnam Health Sciences Trust C	Health	-6.8	-6.66	0.35	2	2	0	1.71	800 354-2228
Putnam Health Sciences Trust M	Health	-6.6	-6.41	0.59	2	2	3.5	1.46	800 354-2228
Putnam Health Sciences Trust R	Health	-6.3	-6.17	0.84		2	0		800 354-2228
Putnam International Capital Opp A	Foreign	-18.6	-15.16	2.85	4	4	5.75	1.47	800 354-2228
Putnam International Capital Opp B	Foreign	-19.2	-15.8	2.06	4	4	0	2.22	800 354-2228
Putnam International Capital Opp C	Foreign	-19.2	-15.8	2.1	4	4	0	2.22	800 354-2228
Putnam International Capital Opp M	Foreign	-19	-15.58	2.31	3	4	3.5	1.97	800 354-2228
Putnam International Capital Opp R	Foreign	-18.8	-15.35	2.6		4	0		800 354-2228
Putnam International Equity A	Foreign	-13.7	-12.26	0.28	4	3	5.75	1.13	800 354-2228
Putnam International Equity B	Foreign	-14.4	-12.91	-0.45	4	3	0	1.88	800 354-2228
Putnam International Equity C	Foreign	-14.3	-12.9	-0.45	4	3	0	1.88	800 354-2228
Putnam International Equity M	Foreign	-14.1	-12.69	-0.2	4	3	3.5	1.63	800 354-2228
Putnam International Equity R	Foreign	-13.9	-12.48	0.05		3	0		800 354-2228
Putnam Intl Growth and Income A	Foreign	-12.7	-9.42	-2.74	4	3	5.75	1.29	800 354-2228
Putnam Intl Growth and Income B	Foreign	-13.4	-10.14	-3.49	4	3	0	2.04	800 354-2228
Putnam Intl Growth and Income C	Foreign	-13.3	-10.06	-3.41	4	3	0	2.04	800 354-2228
Putnam Intl Growth and Income M	Foreign	-13.2	-9.88	-3.22	4	3	3.5	1.79	800 354-2228
Putnam Intl New Opportunities A	Foreign	-8.1	-20.28	-3.2	3	3	5.75	1.48	800 354-2228
Putnam Intl New Opportunities B	Foreign	-8.8	-20.89	-3.93	5	3	0	2.23	800 354-2228
Putnam Intl New Opportunities C	Foreign	-8.8	-20.87	-3.91	3	3	0	2.23	800 354-2228

Stock Fund Name	Objective	Annualized Return for			Rank		Max Load	Expense Ratio	Toll-Free/(Toll) Telephone
		1 Year	3 Years	5 Years	Overall	Risk			
Putnam Intl New Opportunities M	Foreign	-8.6	-20.69	-3.68	3	3	3.5	1.98	800 354-2228
Putnam Investors Fund A	Growth	-8.3	-17.98	-4.66	4	3	5.75	0.89	800 354-2228
Putnam Investors Fund B	Growth	-8.9	-18.6	-5.37	4	3	0	1.64	800 354-2228
Putnam Investors Fund C	Growth	-8.9	-18.44	-5.25	4	3	0	1.64	800 354-2228
Putnam Investors Fund M	Growth	-8.7	-18.39	-5.13	4	3	3.5	1.39	800 354-2228
Putnam Investors Fund R	Growth	-8.5	-18.14	-4.87		3	0		800 354-2228
Putnam Mid Cap Value Fund A	Growth	-9.9	8.86		2	3	5.75	1.24	800 354-2228
Putnam Mid Cap Value Fund B	Growth	-10.5	8.08		2	3	0	1.99	800 354-2228
Putnam Mid Cap Value Fund C	Growth	-10.5	8.1		2	3	0	1.99	800 354-2228
Putnam Mid Cap Value Fund M	Growth	-10.2	8.35		2	3	3.5	1.74	800 354-2228
Putnam New Opportunities A	Agg Growth	-9.4	-24.12	-4.79	3	5	5.75	0.89	800 354-2228
Putnam New Opportunities B	Agg Growth	-10.2	-24.67	-5.45	3	5	0	1.64	800 354-2228
Putnam New Opportunities C	Agg Growth	-10.1	-24.69	-5.49	3	5	0	1.64	800 354-2228
Putnam New Opportunities M	Agg Growth	-9.9	-24.5	-5.26	3	5	3.5	1.39	800 354-2228
Putnam New Opportunities R	Agg Growth	-9.6	-24.3	-5.01		5	0		800 354-2228
Putnam New Value Fund A	Growth	-8.3	3.68	3.54	2	3	5.75	1.11	800 354-2228
Putnam New Value Fund B	Growth	-9	2.91	2.75	2	3	0	1.86	800 354-2228
Putnam New Value Fund C	Growth	-8.9	2.91	2.75	2	3	0	1.86	800 354-2228
Putnam New Value Fund M	Growth	-8.6	3.2	3.04	2	3	3.5	1.61	800 354-2228
Putnam OTC & Emerging Growth A	Small Co	-11.5	-33.17	-13.57	4	5	5.75	1.04	800 354-2228
Putnam OTC & Emerging Growth B	Small Co	-12.2	-33.67	-14.23	4	5	0	1.79	800 354-2228
Putnam OTC & Emerging Growth C	Small Co	-12.2	-33.67	-14.19	4	5	0	1.79	800 354-2228
Putnam OTC & Emerging Growth M	Small Co	-12	-33.5	-14	4	5	3.5	1.54	800 354-2228
Putnam Research Fund A	Growth	-10.6	-12.92	-0.08	3	3	5.75	1.05	800 354-2228
Putnam Research Fund B	Growth	-11.2	-13.58	-0.93	3	3	0	1.8	800 354-2228
Putnam Research Fund C	Growth	-11.3	-13.6	-0.83	3	3	0	1.8	800 354-2228
Putnam Research Fund M	Growth	-11	-13.35	-0.57	3	3	3.5	1.55	800 354-2228
Putnam Research Fund R	Growth	-10.7	-13.11	-0.33		3	0	1.29	800 354-2228
Putnam Small Cap Growth A	Small Co	-8.3	-5.37	13.31		5	5.75	1.55	800 354-2228
Putnam Small Cap Growth B	Small Co	-9	-6.08	12.46		5	0	2.3	800 354-2228
Putnam Small Cap Growth C	Small Co	-9.1	-6.09	12.43		5	0	2.3	800 354-2228
Putnam Small Cap Growth M	Small Co	-8.8	-5.83	12.75		5	0	2.05	800 354-2228
Putnam Small Cap Value A	Small Co	-13.4	9.46		2	3	5.75	1.25	800 354-2228
Putnam Small Cap Value B	Small Co	-14	8.67		2	3	0	2	800 354-2228
Putnam Small Cap Value C	Small Co	-14	8.66		2	3	0	2	800 354-2228
Putnam Small Capital Value Fund M	Small Co	-13.8	8.96			3	3.5	1.75	800 354-2228
Putnam Tax Smart Equity A	Growth	-7.3	-8.55		3	3	5.75	1.1	800 354-2228
Putnam Tax Smart Equity B	Growth	-8	-9.24		3	3	0	1.85	800 354-2228
Putnam Tax Smart Equity C	Growth	-8.1	-9.24		3	3	0	1.85	800 354-2228
Putnam Tax Smart Equity M	Growth	-7.8	-9.01		3	3	3.5	1.6	800 354-2228
Putnam Utilities Gr and Inc A	Utilities	-6.5	-9.52	-3.02	3	2	5.75	1.05	800 354-2228
Putnam Utilities Gr and Inc B	Utilities	-7.2	-10.21	-3.75	3	2	0	1.8	800 354-2228
Putnam Utilities Gr and Inc C	Utilities	-7.2	-10.18	-3.74	3	2	0	1.8	800 354-2228
Putnam Utilities Gr and Inc M	Utilities	-6.9	-9.96	-3.5	3	2	3.5	1.55	800 354-2228
Putnam Vista Fund A	Growth	-12.9	-21.32	-3.52	4	5	5.75	0.89	800 354-2228
Putnam Vista Fund B	Growth	-13.4	-21.91	-4.23	4	5	0	1.64	800 354-2228
Putnam Vista Fund C	Growth	-13.6	-21.94	-4.25	4	5	0	1.64	800 354-2228
Putnam Vista Fund M	Growth	-13.3	-21.71	-4	4	5	3.5	1.39	800 354-2228
Putnam Vista Fund R	Growth	-13	-21.5	-3.74		5	0		800 354-2228
Putnam Voyager A	Growth	-12	-17.89	-1.87	4	3	5.75	0.88	800 354-2228
Putnam Voyager B	Growth	-12.7	-18.51	-2.62	4	3	0	1.63	800 354-2228
Putnam Voyager C	Growth	-12.7	-18.51	-2.6	4	3	0	1.63	800 354-2228
Putnam Voyager M	Growth	-12.4	-18.3	-2.35	4	3	3.5	1.38	800 354-2228
Putnam Voyager R	Growth	-12.2	-18.1	-2.12		3	0	1.21	800 354-2228
Quaker Aggressive Growth A	Agg Growth	-0.8	-5.16	16.92	1	1	5.5	2.13	800 220-8888
Quaker Core Equity A	Growth	-8.8	-19.25	-6.55	4	4	0	1.99	800 220-8888
Quaker Mid Cap Value A	Growth	-14.9	1.46	1.1	3	4	5.5	2.13	800 220-8888
Quaker Small Cap Value A	Small Co	-5.6	9.66	5.16	2	3	5.5	2.6	800 220-8888

Stock Fund Name	Objective	Annualized Return for			Rank		Max Load	Expense Ratio	Toll-Free/(Toll) Telephone
		1 Year	3 Years	5 Years	Overall	Risk			
Quant Emg-Markets Instl	Foreign	2.9	-4.32		2	3	0	1.8	800 326-2151
Quant Emg-Markets Ord	Foreign	2.3	-4.82	0.04	2	3	0	2.31	800 326-2151
Quant Gr & Inc Inst	Growth	-11	-16.37	-1.76	4	3	0	1.16	800 326-2151
Quant Gr & Inc Ord	Growth	-11.4	-16.89	-2.33	4	3	0	1.67	800 326-2151
Quant Mid Cap Inst	Agg Growth	-16.4	-13.02	-0.46	4	4	0	1.58	800 326-2151
Quant Mid Cap Ord	Agg Growth	-16.6	-13.24	-0.78	4	4	0	1.91	800 326-2151
Quant Small Cap Inst	Small Co	-13	-6.7	1.5	3	3	0	1.92	800 326-2151
Quant Small Cap Ord	Small Co	-13.4	-7.17	0.98	3	3	0	1.96	800 326-2151
Quantitative Forgein Value Ordinary	Foreign	-5.5	1.94	-0.59	2	3	0	1.92	800 326-2151
Queens Road Large Cap Value Fund	Income						0		(704 714-7711)
Queens Road Small Cap Value Fund	Small Co						0	1.35	(704 714-7711)
RBC Large Cap Equity A	Income	-9.9					4.5	1.34	800 442-3688
RBC Large Cap Equity B	Income	-10.8					0	2	800 442-3688
RBC Mid Cap Equity A	Growth	-11.3					4.5	1.37	800 442-3688
RBC Mid Cap Equity B	Growth	-12					0	2.12	800 442-3688
RBC Mid Cap Equity C	Growth	-11	0.13	-2.64	3	3	0	1.12	800 442-3688
RBC Small Cap A	Small Co	-10.6					4.5	1.49	800 442-3688
RBC Small Cap B	Small Co	-11.3					0	2.24	800 442-3688
RBC Small Cap C	Small Co	-10.5					0	1.24	800 442-3688
RS Diversified Growth Fd	Growth	-14.9	-18.17	6.46	3	5	0	1.71	800 766-3863
RS Emerging Growth Fd	Small Co	-11.2	-22.98	4.46	3	5	0	1.59	800 766-3863
RS Global Natural Resources Fd	Energy/Res	8.3	11.85	5.58	1	3	0	1.88	800 766-3863
RS Internet Age Fund	Technology	17.4	-19.35		3	5	0	2.11	800 766-3863
RS MidCap Opportunities Fd	Growth/Inc	-3	-11.19	2.43	3	4	0	1.65	800 766-3863
RS Partners Fd	Small Co	10.1	20.62	6.29	1	3	0	1.88	800 766-3863
RS Smaller Company Growth	Small Co	-17.7	-8.15	2.39	3	5	0	1.91	800 766-3863
RS Value + Growth Fd	Growth	-7	-16.57	-2.27	3	3	0	1.61	800 766-3863
RSI Retirement Core Equity	Growth	-16	-16.96	-4.7	5	3	0	0.96	800 772-3615
RSI Retirement Emerg Growth Equity	Small Co	-21.9	-19.57	-5.19	4	5	0	1.97	800 772-3615
RSI Retirement International Equity	Foreign	-15.7	-13.61	-4.62	5	3	0	1.96	800 772-3615
RSI Retirement Value Equity	Growth	-10.6	-4.54	2.81	3	2	0	1.17	800 772-3615
Rainbow Fund	Growth/Inc	-13.5	-6.05	-11.07	3	2	0	3.66	(212 820-0502)
Rainier Balanced Portfolio	Balanced	-0.4	-2.6	2.6	1	1	0	1.19	800 280-6111
Rainier Core Equity Portfolio	Growth	-9.6	-10.01	-0.41	3	3	0	1.12	800 280-6111
Rainier Small/Mid Cap Equity Port	Small Co	-7.1	-2.95	1.2	2	3	0	1.26	800 280-6111
Red Oak Technology Select	Technology	-16.7	-40.84		4	5	0	0.98	888 462-5386
Regions Morg Keeg Sel Agg Gr A	Growth	-3.9					0	1.35	800 433-2829
Regions Morg Keeg Sel Agg Gr B	Growth	-4.2	1.95		2	3	0	1.65	800 433-2829
Regions Morg Keeg Sel Agg Gr C	Growth	-4.5					1	2.1	800 433-2829
Regions Morg Keeg Sel Bal A	Balanced	-1.6	-2.29	1.9	2	1	0	1.35	800 433-2829
Regions Morg Keeg Sel Bal B	Balanced	-1.9	-2.62	1.66	2	1	0	1.65	800 433-2829
Regions Morg Keeg Sel Bal C	Balanced	-2.4					1	2.1	800 433-2829
Regions Morg Keeg Sel Capital Gr A	Growth	-8.8	-9.32	-4.8	4	3	3.5	2	800 366-7426
Regions Morg Keeg Sel Growth A	Growth/Inc	-3	-15.35		3	3	0	1.29	800 433-2829
Regions Morg Keeg Sel Growth B	Growth/Inc	-3.2	-15.59	-2.29	3	3	0	1.59	800 433-2829
Regions Morg Keeg Sel Growth C	Growth/Inc	-3.6					1	2.04	800 433-2829
Regions Morg Keeg Sel Strat Eq A	Growth						0	1.29	800 433-2829
Regions Morg Keeg Sel Strat Eq B	Growth						0	1.59	800 433-2829
Regions Morg Keeg Sel Strat Eq C	Income						0	2.04	800 433-2829
Regions Morg Keeg Sel Val A	Growth/Inc	-14.2	-6.54	-2.58	3	2	5.5	1.25	800 433-2829
Regions Morg Keeg Sel Val B	Growth/Inc	-14.4	-6.79	-2.81	3	2	0	1.55	800 433-2829
Regions Morg Keeg Sel Val C	Income	-14.7					0	2	800 433-2829
Reserve Blue Chip Growth A	Growth	-10.4	-24.32	-4.66	3	5	4.5	0.92	800 637-1700
Reserve Informed Investors Gr R	Growth	-8.7	-18.53	5.13	4	4	4.5	1.01	800 637-1700
Reserve International Equity A	Foreign	-15.6	-19.69	-4.08	5	3	4.5	1.94	800 637-1700
Reserve Large Cap Growth R	Growth	-9.3	-16.1	-8.63	4	4	0	1.48	800 637-1700
Reserve Small Cap R	Small Co	-14.2	-16.3	11.25	3	5	4.5	1.56	800 637-1700
Reynolds Blue Chip Growth Fund	Growth	-6.3	-26.07	-6.45	3	5	0	1.77	800 773-9665

Stock Fund Name	Objective	Annualized Return for			Rank		Max Load	Expense Ratio	Toll-Free/(Toll) Telephone
		1 Year	3 Years	5 Years	Overall	Risk			
Reynolds Fund	Growth	21.7	-25.01		4	5	0	2	800 773-9665
Reynolds Opportunity Fund	Agg Growth	0	-27.6	-4.94	4	5	0	2.27	800 773-9665
Riggs Small Company Stock R	Small Co	-0.7	2.95	-1.97	2	4	5.75	1.75	800 934-3883
Riggs Small Company Stock Y	Small Co	-0.4	3.37		1	4	0	1.5	800 934-3883
Riggs Stock Fund R	Growth/Inc	-8.8	-13.17	-6.88	4	3	5.75	1.67	800 934-3883
Riggs Stock Fund Y	Growth/Inc	-8.7	-12.91		4	3	0	1.42	800 934-3883
Riverfront Balanced A	Balanced	-6.5	-8.19	0.08	2	2	4.5	2	800 424-2295
Riverfront Balanced B	Balanced	-7.2	-8.76	-0.65	3	2	0	2.75	800 424-2295
Riverfront Large Company Select A	Growth/Inc	-13.7	-20.07	-5.29	5	3	4.5	1.94	800 424-2295
Riverfront Large Company Select B	Growth/Inc	-14.4	-20.67	-5.99	5	3	0	2.69	800 424-2295
Riverfront Select Value A	Growth	-15.1	-13.25	-7.57	4	3	4.5	1.87	800 424-2295
Riverfront Select Value B	Growth	-15.8	-13.91	-8.25	5	3	0	2.62	800 424-2295
Riverfront Small Company A	Growth	-12	-26.37	-12.21	5	5	4.5	3.06	800 424-2295
Riverfront Small Company B	Growth	-12.6	-26.85	-12.84	5	5	0	3.81	800 424-2295
Rockland Small Cap Growth	Small Co	-10.9	-12.31		5	4	0	1.87	800 497-3933
Royce Low Priced Stock Fd	Small Co	-10.4	10.31	10.84	1	4	0	2.08	800 221-4268
Royce Micro-Cap Cons	Small Co	-9.3	9.33	6.5		4	2.49		800 221-4268
Royce Micro-Cap F	Small Co						1.48		800 221-4268
Royce Micro-Cap Fd	Small Co	-8.3	10.34	7.46	1	4	0	1.82	800 221-4268
Royce Opportunity F	Small Co	-9.6	6.75			5	1.29	1.29	800 221-4268
Royce Opportunity Fd	Small Co	-9.8	6.95	11.66	2	4	0	1.24	800 221-4268
Royce Opportunity Instl	Small Co	-9.4					1.04	1.04	800 221-4268
Royce PA Mutual Fd Cons	Small Co	-6.9	9.9	6.2	2	3	1.96	1.97	800 221-4268
Royce PA Mutual Fd Inv	Small Co	-5.9	11.14	7.21	2	3	0	0.99	800 221-4268
Royce Premier F	Small Co						1.29	1.29	800 221-4268
Royce Premier Fd	Small Co	-0.9	7.5	7.59	1	3	0	1.2	800 221-4268
Royce Premier Instl	Small Co						1.04	1.04	800 221-4268
Royce Special Equity Fd	Small Co	0.8	20.25	9.66		2	0	2.12	800 221-4268
Royce Technology Value Fd	Small Co	21.9					1.98	1.99	800 221-4268
Royce Total Return Cons	Small Co	-2.4					2.2	2.2	800 221-4268
Royce Total Return F	Small Co	-1.5					1.29	1.29	800 221-4268
Royce Total Return Fd	Growth/Inc	-1.5	13.48	7.7	1	2	0	1.24	800 221-4268
Royce Trust & GiftShares Cons	Small Co	-8.9	1.63	10.27	2	4	2.49	2.49	800 221-4268
Royce Trust & GiftShares Inv	Small Co	-8	4.29	12.44	1	4	0	1.78	800 221-4268
Royce Value Fd	Small Co	-1.4					1.48	1.49	800 221-4268
Royce Value Plus Fd	Small Co	2.6					1.48	1.49	800 221-4268
Runkel Value Fund	Other						0		(650 591-3042)
Russell Diversified Equity Fund C	Growth/Inc	-10.3	-12.34		5	3	0	2.03	800 832-6688
Russell Diversified Equity Fund E	Growth/Inc	-9.7	-11.73	-3.56	4	3	0	1.28	800 832-6688
Russell Diversified Equity Fund S	Growth/Inc	-9.4	-11.48	-3.29	4	3	0	1.03	800 832-6688
Russell Emerging Markets C	Foreign	-9.7	-8.85		3	4	0	3.12	800 832-6688
Russell Emerging Markets E	Foreign	-9.2	-8.15		3	4		2.38	800 832-6688
Russell Emerging Markets S	Foreign	-9					0	2.14	800 832-6688
Russell Equity Income C	Growth/Inc	-11.5	-5.87		3	2	0	2.36	800 832-6688
Russell Equity Income E	Growth/Inc	-10.8	-5.17	-3.99	3	2	0	1.61	800 832-6688
Russell Equity Income S	Growth/Inc	-10.6	-4.95	-3.74	3	2	0	1.37	800 832-6688
Russell Inst Equity I Fd E	Growth	-9.3	-11.26		4	3	0	0.92	800 832-6688
Russell Inst Equity I Fd I	Growth	-9	-11.05	-2.87	4	3	0	0.71	800 832-6688
Russell Inst Equity II Fd E	Growth	-8.4	-0.81		2	4	0	1.13	800 832-6688
Russell Inst Equity II Fd I	Growth	-8.3					0	1.13	800 832-6688
Russell Inst Equity III Fd E	Growth	-10.3	-3.22		3	3	0	1.18	800 832-6688
Russell Inst Equity III Fd I	Growth	-10.2	-4.5	-3.52	3	2	0	0.93	800 832-6688
Russell Inst Equity Q Fd E	Growth	-8.4	-10.22		3	3	0	0.89	800 832-6688
Russell Inst Equity Q Fd I	Growth	-8.1	-10.01	-0.47	3	3	0	0.7	800 832-6688
Russell Inst International E	Foreign	-13.5	-12.71		3	3	0	1.26	800 832-6688
Russell Inst International I	Foreign	-13.4	-12.5	-4.54	5	3	0	1.06	800 832-6688
Russell International Securities C	Foreign	-14.4	-13.56		5	3		2.46	800 832-6688
Russell International Securities E	Foreign	-13.7	-12.86	-4.88	5	3	0	1.72	800 832-6688

Stock Fund Name	Objective	Annualized Return for			Rank		Max Load	Expense Ratio	Toll-Free/(Toll) Telephone
		1 Year	3 Years	5 Years	Overall	Risk			
Russell International Securities S	Foreign	-13.5					0	1.47	800 832-6688
Russell LifePoints Aggr Strat C	Growth	-6.1	-5.2		2	2	0	1	800 832-6688
Russell LifePoints Aggr Strat D	Growth	-5.6	-5.34	-0.14	2	2	0	0.5	800 832-6688
Russell LifePoints Aggr Strat E	Growth	-5.4	-5.23	0.02	2	2	0	0.25	800 832-6688
Russell LifePoints Aggr Strat S	Growth	-5.2	-4.87		1	2	0	0	800 832-6688
Russell LifePoints Bal Strat C	Balanced	-1.4	-2.29		1	1	0	1	800 832-6688
Russell LifePoints Bal Strat D	Balanced	-0.9	-1.12	1.96	2	1	0	0.5	800 832-6688
Russell LifePoints Bal Strat E	Balanced	-0.7	-1.12	2.04	2	1	0	0.25	800 832-6688
Russell LifePoints Bal Strat S	Balanced	-0.3	-0.63		1	1	0	0	800 832-6688
Russell LifePoints Cons Strat C	Income	3.4	4.16		1	1	0	1	800 832-6688
Russell LifePoints Cons Strat D	Income	3.9	4.71	4.71	2	1	0	0.5	800 832-6688
Russell LifePoints Cons Strat E	Income	4.2	4.98	4.96	2	1	0	0.25	800 832-6688
Russell LifePoints Cons Strat S	Income	4.4					0	0	800 832-6688
Russell LifePoints Eq Aggr Strat C	Agg Growth	-9.8	-9.64		4	3	0	1	800 832-6688
Russell LifePoints Eq Aggr Strat D	Agg Growth	-9.4	-9.17	-1.98	4	3	0	0.5	800 832-6688
Russell LifePoints Eq Aggr Strat E	Agg Growth	-9.1	-8.9	-1.75	4	3	0	0.25	800 832-6688
Russell LifePoints Eq Aggr Strat S	Agg Growth	-8.9	-8.73		3	3	0	0	800 832-6688
Russell LifePoints Mod Strategy C	Growth/Inc	1.1	1.33		1	1	0	1	800 832-6688
Russell LifePoints Mod Strategy D	Growth/Inc	1.6	1.84	3.43	2	1	0	0.5	800 832-6688
Russell LifePoints Mod Strategy E	Growth/Inc	1.9	2.08	3.66	2	1	0	0.25	800 832-6688
Russell LifePoints Mod Strategy S	Growth/Inc	2.2					0	0	800 832-6688
Russell Quantitative Equity C	Growth	-9.4	-11.15		4	3	0	2.02	800 832-6688
Russell Quantitative Equity E	Growth	-8.8	-10.61	-1.23	3	3	0	1.27	800 832-6688
Russell Quantitative Equity S	Growth	-8.5	-10.33	-0.95	3	3	0	1.02	800 832-6688
Russell Real Estate Securities C	Real Est	4.1	12.63		1	2	0	2.19	800 832-6688
Russell Real Estate Securities E	Real Est	4.9	13.47	7.09	1	2	0	1.46	800 832-6688
Russell Real Estate Securities S	Real Est	5.1	13.75	7.37	1	2	0	1.19	800 832-6688
Russell Select Growth Fund C	Growth	-7.7					0	2.11	800 832-6688
Russell Select Growth Fund E	Growth	-6.8					0	1.16	800 832-6688
Russell Select Growth Fund I	Growth	-6.4					0	1.74	800 832-6688
Russell Select Growth Fund S	Growth	-6.6					0	0.97	800 832-6688
Russell Select Value C	Income	-10.6					0	2	800 832-6688
Russell Select Value E	Income	-9.8					0	1.04	800 832-6688
Russell Select Value I	Income	-9.5					0	1.48	800 832-6688
Russell Select Value S	Income	-9.6					0	0.87	800 832-6688
Russell Special Growth C	Agg Growth	-9.6	-2		2	4	0	2.31	800 832-6688
Russell Special Growth E	Agg Growth	-8.9	-1.27	1.95	2	4	0	1.56	800 832-6688
Russell Special Growth S	Agg Growth	-8.7					0	1.32	800 832-6688
Russell Tax Managed Global Eq C	Foreign	-10.6					0	1	800 832-6688
Russell Tax Managed Global Eq S	Foreign	-9.5					0	0	800 832-6688
Russell Tax-Managed Large Cap C	Growth	-10.6	-11.84		4	3	0	1.91	800 832-6688
Russell Tax-Managed Large Cap E	Growth	-9.7					0	1.16	800 832-6688
Russell Tax-Managed Large Cap S	Growth	-9.5					0	0.91	800 832-6688
Russell Tax-Managed Mid-Sm Cap C	Small Co	-9.4	-8.92		3	4	0	2.25	800 832-6688
Russell Tax-Managed Mid-Sm Cap E	Small Co	-8.7					0	1.5	800 832-6688
Russell Tax-Managed Mid-Sm Cap S	Small Co	-8.6	-8		3	4	0	1.25	800 832-6688
Rydex Banking Adv	Financial	-5.2	5.01	-2.39	3	3	0	1.91	800 820-0888
Rydex Banking Inv	Financial	-4.6	5.76	-1.82	3	3	0	1.5	800 820-0888
Rydex Basic Materials Adv	Other	-18.2	-4.07	-7.69	4	4	0	2	800 820-0888
Rydex Basic Materials Inv	Other	-18	-3.6	-7.5	4	4	0	1.41	800 820-0888
Rydex Consumer Products Adv	Other	-7.7	1.11		2	2	0	2.02	800 820-0888
Rydex Consumer Products Inv	Other	-7.2					0	1.56	800 820-0888
Rydex Dynamic-Tempest 500 C	Other	-4.4					0	2.5	800 820-0888
Rydex Dynamic-Tempest 500 H	Other				2	5	0	1.75	800 820-0888
Rydex Dynamic-Titan 500 C	Other	-27.1					0	2.64	800 820-0888
Rydex Dynamic-Titan 500 H	Other	-26.5	-31.17		5	5	0	1.89	800 820-0888
Rydex Dynamic-Velocity 100 C	Agg Growth	-19.8					0	2.5	800 820-0888
Rydex Dynamic-Velocity 100 H	Agg Growth	-19.2	-62.5		4	5	0	1.75	800 820-0888

Stock Fund Name	Objective	Annualized Return for			Rank		Max Load	Expense Ratio	Toll-Free/(Toll) Telephone
		1 Year	3 Years	5 Years	Overall	Risk			
Rydex Dynamic-Venture 100 C	Agg Growth	-36.5					0	2.5	800 820-0888
Rydex Dynamic-Venture 100 H	Agg Growth	-36	4.08		3	5	0	1.75	800 820-0888
Rydex Electronics Adv	Technology	-25.2	-32.39	3.39	4	5	0	1.75	800 820-0888
Rydex Energy Adv	Energy/Res	-5.1	-5.48	0.76	2	3	0	1.8	800 820-0888
Rydex Energy Inv	Energy/Res	-4.7	-5	1.14	2	3	0	1.32	800 820-0888
Rydex Energy Services Adv	Energy/Res	-8.6	-12.25	-6.41	3	5	0	1.97	800 820-0888
Rydex Energy Services Inv	Energy/Res	-8	-11.84	-6	3	5	0	1.54	800 820-0888
Rydex Financial Services Adv	Financial	-11.3	-1.97	-1.69	3	3	0	2.02	800 820-0888
Rydex Health Care Adv	Health	-1.3	-2.25	0.8	2	2	0	1.85	800 820-0888
Rydex Health Care Inv	Health	-0.8	-1.78	1.36	2	2	0	1.37	800 820-0888
Rydex Leisure Adv	Other	-16.8	-14.08	-7	4	4	0	2.26	800 820-0888
Rydex Leisure Inv	Other	-16.8	-13.66	-6.26	4	4	0	1.57	800 820-0888
Rydex OTC Adv	Agg Growth	-2.7	-30.64		3	5	0	1.6	800 820-0888
Rydex OTC Inv	Agg Growth	-2.2	-30.26	-1.28	3	5	0	1.08	800 820-0888
Rydex Retailing Adv	Other	-14.2	-7.98	-2.49	3	3	0	1.95	800 820-0888
Rydex Retailing Inv	Other	-14					0	1.44	800 820-0888
Rydex Series-Arktos C	Other	-14					0	2.38	800 820-0888
Rydex Series-Arktos Inv	Other	-13	16.39		2	5	0	1.35	800 820-0888
Rydex Series-Banking C	Financial	-5.6					0	2.4	800 820-0888
Rydex Series-Basic Materials C	Other	-18.8					0	2.6	800 820-0888
Rydex Series-Biotechnology Adv	Health	13.3	-9.52	13.48	3	5	0	1.72	800 820-0888
Rydex Series-Biotechnology C	Health	12.4					0	2.38	800 820-0888
Rydex Series-Biotechnology Inv	Health	13.8	-9.1	14.08	3	5	0	1.23	800 820-0888
Rydex Series-Consumer Products C	Other	-8.2					0	2.57	800 820-0888
Rydex Series-Electronics C	Technology	-25.7					0	2.49	800 820-0888
Rydex Series-Electronics Inv	Technology	-24.7	-32.04	3.95		5	0	1.29	800 820-0888
Rydex Series-Energy C	Energy/Res	-5.5					0	2.51	800 820-0888
Rydex Series-Energy Services C	Energy/Res	-8.8					0	2.57	800 820-0888
Rydex Series-Financial Service C	Financial	-12.1					0	2.52	800 820-0888
Rydex Series-Financial Service Inv	Financial	-11.5	-1.79	-1.41		3	0	1.51	800 820-0888
Rydex Series-Health Care C	Health	-1.9					0	2.54	800 820-0888
Rydex Series-Internet Adv	Technology	7.9					0	1.74	800 820-0888
Rydex Series-Internet C	Technology	7.4					0	2.36	800 820-0888
Rydex Series-Internet Inv	Technology	8.5					0	1.21	800 820-0888
Rydex Series-Large-Cap Europe C	Other	-17.1					0	2.69	800 820-0888
Rydex Series-Large-Cap Europe H	Other	-16.4	-21.41		5	4	0	1.76	800 820-0888
Rydex Series-Large-Cap Japan C	Other	-33.9					0	2.2	800 820-0888
Rydex Series-Large-Cap Japan H	Other	-33.7	-31.98		5	4	0	1.84	800 820-0888
Rydex Series-Leisure C	Other	-17.6					0	2.53	800 820-0888
Rydex Series-Medius C	Growth	-20.2					0	2.44	800 820-0888
Rydex Series-Medius H	Growth	-19.2					0	1.71	800 820-0888
Rydex Series-Mekros C	Small Co	-19.2					0	2.44	800 820-0888
Rydex Series-Mekros H	Small Co	-18.5					0	1.61	800 820-0888
Rydex Series-Nova Adv	Agg Growth	-17.9	-21.21		5	4	0	1.55	800 820-0888
Rydex Series-Nova C	Agg Growth	-18.3					0	2.27	800 820-0888
Rydex Series-Nova Inv	Agg Growth	-17.4	-20.76	-7.94	5	4	0	1.16	800 820-0888
Rydex Series-OTC C	Agg Growth	-3.1					0	2.24	800 820-0888
Rydex Series-Precious Metal C	Prec Metal	-13.7					0	2.38	800 820-0888
Rydex Series-Precious Metal Inv	Prec Metal	-12.9	16.07	2.31	2	5	0	1.39	800 820-0888
Rydex Series-Retailing C	Other	-15.2					0	2.7	-800 820-0888
Rydex Series-Sector Rotation C	Agg Growth	-11.7					0	2.44	800 820-0888
Rydex Series-Sector Rotation H	Agg Growth	-11.1					0	1.69	800 820-0888
Rydex Series-Technology C	Technology	-3.9					0	2.43	800 820-0888
Rydex Series-Telecomm C	Utilities	-1.7					0	2.43	800 820-0888
Rydex Series-Transportation C	Other	-12.3					0	2.59	800 820-0888
Rydex Series-Ursa Adv	Growth	1.9	11.78		2	3	0	1.85	800 820-0888
Rydex Series-Ursa C	Growth	1.5					0	2.47	800 820-0888
Rydex Series-Ursa Inv	Growth	2.5	12.47	-10.38	2	3	0	1.31	800 820-0888

Stock Fund Name	Objective	Annualized Return for			Rank		Max Load	Expense Ratio	Toll-Free/(Toll) Telephone
		1 Year	3 Years	5 Years	Overall	Risk			
Rydex Series-Utilities C	Utilities	-15.4					0	2.76	800 820-0888
Rydex Technology Adv	Technology	-3	-29.83	-2.75	3	5	0	1.93	800 820-0888
Rydex Technology Inv	Technology	-3.1	-29.67	-2.35	3	5	0	1.44	800 820-0888
Rydex Telecomm Adv	Utilities	-0.8	-38.65	-16.32	3	5	0	1.87	800 820-0888
Rydex Telecomm Inv	Utilities	-0.9	-38.46	-15.98	3	5	0	1.51	800 820-0888
Rydex Transportation Adv	Other	-11.7	-2.45	-9.66	3	3	0	2.23	800 820-0888
Rydex Transportation Inv	Other	-11.9	-1.45	-8.85	3	3	0	1.56	800 820-0888
Rydex Utilities Adv	Utilities	-12.2	-11.72		4	4	0	1.85	800 820-0888
Rydex Utilities Inv	Utilities	-11.6	-11.24		3	4	0	1.54	800 820-0888
SAFECO Balanced Fund	Balanced	-2.2	0.93	1.84	2	1	0	1.1	800 706-0700
SAFECO Balanced Fund A	Balanced	-2.4	0.71	1.79	2	1	5.75	1.35	800 706-0700
SAFECO Balanced Fund B	Balanced	-3.1	-0.05	1.05	2	1	0	2.1	800 706-0700
SAFECO Dividend Income Fund	Income	-10.2	-6.19	-5.58	3	2	0	1.08	800 706-0700
SAFECO Dividend Income Fund A	Income	-10.5	-6.45	-5.84	3	2	5.75	1.35	800 706-0700
SAFECO Dividend Income Fund B	Income	-11.2	-7.16	-6.57	3	2	0	2.1	800 706-0700
SAFECO Dividend Income Fund C	Income	-11.1	-7.42		3	2	0	2.1	800 706-0700
SAFECO Equity Fund A	Growth/Inc	-10.2	-12.44	-4.73	4	3	5.75	1.31	800 706-0700
SAFECO Equity Fund B	Growth/Inc	-10.8	-13.08	-5.45	4	3	0	2.06	800 706-0700
SAFECO Equity Fund C	Growth/Inc	-10.8	-13.03		3	3	0	2.06	800 706-0700
SAFECO Equity Fund INV	Growth/Inc	-10	-12.17	-4.45	4	3	0	0.94	800 706-0700
SAFECO Growth Opportunities	Small Co	-22.8	-3.6	-5.58	4	4	0	1.03	800 706-0700
SAFECO Growth Opportunities A	Small Co	-22.9	-3.89	-5.82	4	4	5.75	1.33	800 706-0700
SAFECO Growth Opportunities B	Small Co	-23.4	-4.53	-6.51	4	4	0	2.08	800 706-0700
SAFECO Growth Opportunities C	Small Co	-23.4	-4.53		3	4	0	2.08	800 706-0700
SAFECO International Fund A	Foreign	-15.9	-15.91	-6.41	5	3	5.75	1.65	800 706-0700
SAFECO International Fund B	Foreign	-16.2	-16.39	-7.07	4	3	0	2.4	800 706-0700
SAFECO International Stock Fund	Foreign	-15.7	-15.64	-6.09	5	3	0	1.46	800 706-0700
SAFECO Northwest Fund A	Growth	-5.7	-11.39	-0.08	3	4	5.75	1.35	800 706-0700
SAFECO Northwest Fund B	Growth	-6.4	-12.05	-0.78	3	4	0	2.1	800 706-0700
SAFECO Northwest Fund Inv	Growth	-5.4	-11.17	0.2	3	4	0	1.1	800 706-0700
SAFECO Small Company Value Fund	Small Co	0.5	9	-1.62	1	3	0	1.19	800 706-0700
SAFECO Small Company Value Fund A	Small Co	0	8.69	-2	1	3	5.75	1.4	800 706-0700
SAFECO Small Company Value Fund B	Small Co	-0.5	8	-2.7	1	3	0	2.15	800 706-0700
SAFECO U.S. Value Fund	Growth/Inc	-9.6	-4.41	-1.3	3	2	0	1.85	800 706-0700
SAFECO U.S. Value Fund A	Growth/Inc	-9.9	-4.66	-1.62	3	2	5.75	1.35	800 706-0700
SAFECO U.S. Value Fund B	Growth/Inc	-10.6	-5.37	-2.33	3	2	0	2.1	800 706-0700
SEI Asset Alloc-Divers Conserv A	Growth	3.2	0.28	3.06	1	1	0	0.12	800 342-5734
SEI Asset Alloc-Divers Conserv D	Growth	2.2	-0.7	2.02	2	1	0	1.12	800 342-5734
SEI Asset Alloc-Dvrs Glb Growth A	Global	-6.7	-8.23	-1.03	3	2	0	0.12	800 342-5734
SEI Asset Alloc-Dvrs Glb Growth D	Global	-7.7	-9.16	-2.04	3	2	0	1.12	800 342-5734
SEI Asset Alloc-Dvrs Glb Mod Gr A	Global	-1.6	-3.79	1.07	2	1	0	0.12	800 342-5734
SEI Asset Alloc-Dvrs Glb Mod Gr D	Global	-2.6	-4.75	-0.04	2	1	0	1.12	800 342-5734
SEI Asset Alloc-Dvrs Glb Stock A	Global	-11.8	-12.6	-3.25	5	3	0	0.12	800 342-5734
SEI Asset Alloc-Dvrs Glb Stock D	Global	-12.7	-13.48	-4.2	5	3	0	1.12	800 342-5734
SEI Asset Alloc-Dvrs Mod Gr A	Growth	-2	-4.25	0.93	2	1	0	0.12	800 342-5734
SEI Asset Alloc-Dvrs Mod Gr D	Growth	-2.9	-5.21	-0.05	2	1	0	1.12	800 342-5734
SEI Asset Alloc-Dvrs US Stock A	Growth	-9.4	-11.67	-2.5	4	3	0	0.12	800 342-5734
SEI Asset Alloc-Dvrs US Stock D	Growth	-10.3	-12.58	-3.47	5	3	0	1.12	800 342-5734
SEI Index Fds-S&P 500 Idx Fd A	Growth/Inc	-8.4	-11.25	-1.53	3	3	0	0.4	800 342-5734
SEI Index Fds-S&P 500 Idx Fd E	Growth/Inc	-8.3	-11.11	-1.29	3	3	0	0.25	800 342-5734
SEI Instl Managed Tr-Large Cap Gr A	Growth	-9.5	-22.1	-5.46	4	4	0	0.85	800 342-5734
SEI Instl Managed Tr-MidCap Portf A	Agg Growth	-7.5	0.05	1.12	2	3	0	1	800 342-5734
SEI Instl Managed Tr-T/M Lg Cap A	Growth	-9.5	-12.08	-2.52	4	3	0	0.85	800 342-5734
SEI Instl Managed Tr-T/M Sm Cap A	Small Co	-9.4					0	1.1	800 342-5734
SEI Instl Mgd Large Cap Value A	Growth/Inc	-10	-1.91	-0.39	3	2	0	0.85	800 342-5734
SEI Instl Mgd Tr Sm Cp Gwth A	Small Co	-7.8	-12.68	1.72	3	5	0	1.1	800 342-5734
SEI Instl Mgd Tr Small Cap Value A	Small Co	-7.8	9.96	2.56	2	3	0	1.1	800 342-5734
SEI Intl Tr-Emerging Mkts Eq Tr	Foreign	-11.6	-10.21	-4.74	3	4	0	1.95	800 342-5734

Stock Fund Name	Objective	Annualized Return for			Rank		Max Load	Expense Ratio	Toll-Free/(Toll) Telephone
		1 Year	3 Years	5 Years	Overall	Risk			
SEI Intl Tr-International Eq Tr	Foreign	-16.7	-15.66	-4.91	5	3	0	1.28	800 342-5734
SM&R Balanced Fund T	Balanced	-1	-2.33	2.66	2	1	5.75	1.25	800 231-4639
SM&R Equity Income T	Income	-9.6	-5.3	-2.77	3	2	5.75	1.07	800 231-4639
SM&R Growth Fund T	Growth	-10	-16.01	-5.38	4	3	5.75	1.1	800 231-4639
SSgA Aggressive Equity Fund	Growth	-4.8	-10.67		3	3	0	1.1	800 647-7327
SSgA Core Opportunities Fund	Growth/Inc	-9.7	-11.53	-0.07	3	3	0	1.1	800 647-7327
SSgA Disciplined Equity	Growth	-9	-11.42	-3.37	3	3	0	0.46	800 647-7327
SSgA Emerging Markets	Foreign	-8.5	-6.23	0.56	3	4	0	1.25	800 647-7327
SSgA IAM Shares Fund	Other	-10.2	-10.75		4	3	0	0.52	800 647-7327
SSgA International Stock Selection	Foreign	-9.9	-11.66	-4.29	4	2	0	1	800 647-7327
SSgA Intnl Growth Oppty Fund	Foreign	-16.7	-17.66	-4.51	4	3	0	1.1	800 647-7327
SSgA Life Solutions Balanced	Balanced	-0.2	-2.16	1.9	2	1	0	1.11	800 647-7327
SSgA Life Solutions Growth	Growth	-3.7	-6.09	0.14	2	2	0	1.25	800 647-7327
SSgA Life Solutions Inc & Growth	AssetAlloc	3.1	1.47	3.37	1	1	0	1.16	800 647-7327
SSgA S&P 500 Index	Growth	-8.3	-11	-1.23	3	3	0	0.16	800 647-7327
SSgA SmallCap Fund	Small Co	-10	-0.4	-2.02	3	3	0	1.08	800 647-7327
SSgA Special Equity	Small Co	-11.1	-12.66	-2.16	4	5	0	1.1	800 647-7327
SSgA Tuckerman Active REIT	Real Est	2.4	13.61	7.57	2	2	0	1	800 647-7327
STI Classic Balanced Flex	Balanced	-1.3	-1.12	1.96	2	1	0	2.09	800 428-6970
STI Classic Balanced Inv	Balanced	-0.9	-0.41	2.72	2	1	3.75	1.33	800 428-6970
STI Classic Balanced Tr	Balanced	-0.2	-0.11	3.04	2	1	0	1.02	800 428-6970
STI Classic Capital Apprec Flex	Growth	-11	-9.32	-1.31	3	2	0	2.35	800 428-6970
STI Classic Capital Apprec Inv	Growth	-10.5	-8.91	-0.82	3	2	3.75	1.88	800 428-6970
STI Classic Capital Apprec Tr	Growth	-10	-8.31	-0.2	3	2	0	1.22	800 428-6970
STI Classic Growth and Inc Flex	Growth/Inc	-11.4	-7.04	-1	3	2	0	1.93	800 428-6970
STI Classic Growth and Inc Inv	Growth/Inc	-10.9	-6.41	-0.28	3	2	3.75	1.18	800 428-6970
STI Classic Growth and Inc Tr	Growth/Inc	-10.8	-6.25	-0.17	3	2	0	0.99	800 428-6970
STI Classic Info and Tech Flex	Income	-25.4	-28.17		5	5	0	2.57	800 428-6970
STI Classic Info and Tech Tr	Income	-24.7					0	1.19	800 428-6970
STI Classic Inst Super Sh Inc Pl Tr	Growth						0		800 428-6970
STI Classic Intl Eq Flex	Foreign	-14.3	-11.89	-7.28	3	2	0	2.53	800 428-6970
STI Classic Intl Eq Index Flex	Foreign	-14.4	-15.9	-5.62	5	3	0	2.14	800 428-6970
STI Classic Intl Eq Index Inv	Foreign	-14	-15.38	-5.01	5	3	3.75	1.47	800 428-6970
STI Classic Intl Eq Index Tr	Foreign	-13.5	-15	-4.58	5	3	0	1.06	800 428-6970
STI Classic Intl Eq Inv	Foreign	-13.7	-11.25	-6.62	3	2	3.75	1.79	800 428-6970
STI Classic Intl Eq Tr	Foreign	-13.4	-10.96	-6.29	3	2	0	1.49	800 428-6970
STI Classic Life Vision Aggr Gr Tr	Other	-10.4	-4.91	-0.2	3	2	0	0.25	800 428-6970
STI Classic Life Vision Gr&Inc Tr	Growth/Inc	-5.5	-0.72	2.1	2	1	3.75	0.25	800 428-6970
STI Classic Mid-Cap Equity Flex	Agg Growth	-11.7	-10.39	-3.12	4	4	0	2.27	800 428-6970
STI Classic Mid-Cap Equity Inv	Agg Growth	-11.1	-9.82	-2.54	4	4	3.75	1.67	800 428-6970
STI Classic Mid-Cap Equity Tr	Agg Growth	-10.7	-9.42	-2.1	4	4	0	1.23	800 428-6970
STI Classic Sm Cap Gr Stock Flex	Small Co	-13.1	-4.49		3	4	0	2.31	800 428-6970
STI Classic Sm Cap Gr Stock Inv	Small Co	-12.4	-3.81		3	4	3.75	1.61	800 428-6970
STI Classic Sm Cap Gr Stock Tr	Small Co	-12.1	-3.47		3	4	0	1.25	800 428-6970
STI Classic Small Cap Val Eq Flex	Small Co	-6.1	14.5	2.66	2	2	0	2.31	800 428-6970
STI Classic Small Cap Val Eq Tr	Small Co	-5.2	15.8	3.75	2	2	0	1.25	800 428-6970
STI Classic Tax Sens Gr Stk Flex	Growth	-11.6	-15.27		5	3	0	2.31	800 428-6970
STI Classic Tax Sens Gr Stk Tr	Growth	-10.6	-14.36		4	3	0	1.25	800 428-6970
STI Classic Value Income Stock Flex	Income	-11.7	-1.72	-1.59	3	3	0	2.02	800 428-6970
STI Classic Value Income Stock Inv	Income	-11.1	-1.08	-0.9	3	3	3.75	1.28	800 428-6970
STI Classic Value Income Stock Tr	Income	-10.9	-0.59	-0.47	3	3	0	0.9	800 428-6970
STI Classic Vantage Fund Flex	Income	-13					0		800 342-5734
Salomon Brothers Balanced A	Balanced	3.2	3.12	3.16	1	1	5.75	0.95	800 725-6666
Salomon Brothers Balanced B	Balanced	2.4	2.35	2.33	1	1	0	1.7	800 725-6666
Salomon Brothers Balanced C	Balanced	2.4	2.35	2.33	1	1	0	1.95	800 725-6666
Salomon Brothers Balanced O	Balanced	3.4	2.81	2.83	1	1	0	0.7	800 725-6666
Salomon Brothers Capital A	Growth	-8.2	-1.81	7.7	2	3	5.75	1	800 725-6666
Salomon Brothers Capital B	Growth	-9	-2.58	7.04	2	3	0	1.81	800 725-6666

Stock Fund Name	Objective	Annualized Return for			Rank		Max Load	Expense Ratio	Toll-Free/(Toll) Telephone
		1 Year	3 Years	5 Years	Overall	Risk			
Salomon Brothers Capital C	Growth	-9	-2.58	6.99	2	3	0	1.75	800 725-6666
Salomon Brothers Capital O	Growth	-7.7	-1.39	8.22	2	3	0	0.63	800 725-6666
Salomon Brothers Capital Y	Growth	-7.7					0	0.61	800 725-6666
Salomon Brothers Investors Value A	Growth/Inc	-9.4	-3.66	2.45	2	3	5.75	0.91	800 725-6666
Salomon Brothers Investors Value B	Growth/Inc	-10.3	-4.51	1.58	3	3	0	1.82	800 725-6666
Salomon Brothers Investors Value C	Growth/Inc	-10.2	-4.45	1.62	3	3	0	1.75	800 725-6666
Salomon Brothers Investors Value O	Growth/Inc	-9.2	-3.41	2.7	2	3	0	0.63	800 725-6666
Salomon Brothers Opportunity	Growth	-12.3	-2.08	0.16	3	2	0	1.1	800 725-6666
Sand Hill Portfolio Manager Fund	Flexible	-5.4	-9.61	-2.04	3	2	0	1.85	800 527-9525
Santa Barbara Fds-Bender Growth C	Growth	-4.2	-19.6	8.36	3	5	0	2.6	800 723-8637
Santa Barbara Fds-Bender Growth Y	Growth	-3.1	-18.8	9.47	3	5	0	1.9	800 723-8637
Saratoga Adv Tr-Health & Biotech A	Health	-14.5	-9.94		4	5	5.75	2.5	800 807-3863
Saratoga Adv Tr-Health & Biotech B	Health	-15	-10.56		4	5	0	3.1	800 807-3863
Saratoga Adv Tr-Health & Biotech C	Health	-15.1					0	3.1	800 807-3863
Satuit Capital Micro Cap Fund	Growth	-2.6					5.75	2.8	800 527-9525
Schroder International Inv	Foreign	-19.5	-15.76	-5.57	5	3	0	0.99	800 464-3108
Schroder Mid Cap Value Inv	Growth	-6.1	-0.17	2.72	2	3	0	1.35	800 464-3108
Schroder Small Cap Value Inv	Small Co	-10.3	2.58	2.54	2	3	0	1.66	800 464-3108
Schroder US Large Cap Equity	Growth	-8.8	-13.4	-1.21	3	3	0	1.5	800 464-3108
Schroder US Opportunities Fund	Small Co	-11.3	4.5	4.76	2	3	0	1.49	800 464-3108
Schroder Ultra Fund	Small Co	4.4	51.82	66.06		3	0	2.03	800 464-3108
Schwab 1000 Inv	Growth/Inc	-7.9	-10.3	-0.81	3	3	0	0.46	800 266-5623
Schwab 1000 Sel	Growth/Inc	-7.8	-10.17	-0.72	3	3	0	0.35	800 266-5623
Schwab Balanced MarketMasters	Balanced	0.9	-2.39	3.41	1	1	0	1.1	800 266-5623
Schwab Communications Focus	Utilities	-6.3					0	0.89	800 266-5623
Schwab Core Equity	Growth	-8.1	-12.3	-0.34	3	2	0	0.75	800 266-5623
Schwab Financial Services Focus	Financial	-2.7					0	0.89	800 266-5623
Schwab Health Care Focus	Health	-9.9					0	0.89	800 266-5623
Schwab International Index Inv	Foreign	-12.3	-14.27	-4.79	5	3	0	0.58	800 266-5623
Schwab International MarketMasters	Foreign	-13.2	-11	1.17	3	3	0	1.65	800 266-5623
Schwab MarketTrack All Equity Port	Global	-9.4	-9.96	-1.95	4	3	0	0.5	800 266-5623
Schwab MarketTrack Balanced Port	AssetAlloc	-1.4	-2.06	2.06	2	1	0	0.5	800 266-5623
Schwab MarketTrack Conserv Port	AssetAlloc	2.7	1.89	3.7	1	1	0	0.5	800 266-5623
Schwab MarketTrack Growth Port	AssetAlloc	-5.4	-6	0.17	2	2	0	0.5	800 266-5623
Schwab S&P 500 E	Growth/Inc	-8.2					0	0.28	800 266-5623
Schwab S&P 500 Inv	Growth/Inc	-8.3	-11.08	-1.37	3	3	0	0.35	800 266-5623
Schwab S&P 500 Sel	Growth/Inc	-8.1	-10.92	-1.21	3	3	0	0.19	800 266-5623
Schwab Small-Cap Index Inv	Small Co	-7.8	-1.71	0.94	3	4	0	0.49	800 266-5623
Schwab Technology Focus	Technology	-7.4					0	0.89	800 266-5623
Schwab Total Stock Market Inv	Growth	-7.6	-9.71		3	3	0	0.4	800 266-5623
Schwab Total Stock Market Sel	Growth	-7.4	-9.59		3	3	0	0.27	800 266-5623
Schwab US MarketMasters	Growth	-4.3	-8.48	-0.1	3	3	0	1.25	800 266-5623
Schwartz Value Fund	Small Co	-10.3	9.38	1.02	3	3	0	2.05	888 726-0753
Scudder 21st Cent Growth A	Growth	-14.9					0	1.48	800 621-1048
Scudder 21st Cent Growth AARP	Growth	-14.8					0	1.2	800 621-1048
Scudder 21st Cent Growth B	Growth	-15.6					0	2.28	800 621-1048
Scudder 21st Cent Growth C	Growth	-15.6					1	2.25	800 621-1048
Scudder 21st Cent Growth I	Growth	-14.5					0		800 621-1048
Scudder 21st Cent Growth S	Growth	-14.8	-21.85	-2.7	4	5	0	1.2	800 621-1048
Scudder Aggressive Growth A	Agg Growth	-7.2	-18.73	-3.1	3	5	5.75	1.51	800 621-1048
Scudder Aggressive Growth B	Agg Growth	-8	-19.42	-3.95	3	5	0	2.48	800 621-1048
Scudder Aggressive Growth C	Agg Growth	-8					1	2.62	800 621-1048
Scudder Aggressive Growth I	Agg Growth	-6.9					0		800 621-1048
Scudder Asset Management Prem	AssetAlloc	-0.4	-3.02	2.35	2	1	0	0.93	800 621-1048
Scudder Balanced Fund AARP	Balanced	-2.8					0	0.77	800 621-1048
Scudder Balanced Fund S	Balanced	-2.8	-4.7	1.44	2	1	0	1.29	800 621-1048
Scudder Blue Chip A	Growth/Inc	-11.4	-12.71	-3.41	4	3	5.75	1.22	800 621-1048
Scudder Blue Chip B	Growth/Inc	-12.1	-13.42	-4.2	4	2	0	2.02	800 621-1048

394

Stock Fund Name	Objective	Annualized Return for			Rank		Max Load	Expense Ratio	Toll-Free/(Toll) Telephone
		1 Year	3 Years	5 Years	Overall	Risk			
Scudder Blue Chip C	Growth/Inc	-12.2	-13.36	-4.16	4	2	1	1.92	800 621-1048
Scudder Blue Chip I	Growth/Inc	-11.1	-12.32	-2.91	4	2	0	0.7	800 621-1048
Scudder Capital Growth A	Growth	-10.5	-16.53	-3.85	4	3	5.75	1.16	800 621-1048
Scudder Capital Growth AARP	Growth	-10.2	-16.32	-3.6	4	3	0	0.68	800 621-1048
Scudder Capital Growth B	Growth	-11.2	-17.19	-4.62	4	3	0	1.96	800 621-1048
Scudder Capital Growth C	Growth	-11.2	-17.17	-4.59	4	3	1	1.93	800 621-1048
Scudder Capital Growth I	Growth	-10.1					0	0.68	800 621-1048
Scudder Capital Growth Instl	Growth						0		800 621-1048
Scudder Capital Growth S	Growth	-10.2	-16.3	-3.6	3	3	0	0.88	800 621-1048
Scudder Contrarian A	Growth/Inc	-9.2	2.83	1.17	3	3	5.75	1.46	800 621-1048
Scudder Contrarian B	Growth/Inc	-10	1.92	0.28	3	3	0	2.45	800 621-1048
Scudder Contrarian C	Growth/Inc	-9.9	1.92	0.3	3	3	1	2.49	800 621-1048
Scudder Contrarian I	Growth/Inc	-8.8					0	0.85	800 621-1048
Scudder Development AARP	Small Co	-8.1					0	1.3	800 621-1048
Scudder Development S	Small Co	-8.1	-20.55	-8.46	3	5	0	1.3	800 621-1048
Scudder Dreman Financial Srvcs A	Financial	-2.5	4.79	2.45	2	3	5.75	1.45	800 621-1048
Scudder Dreman Financial Srvcs B	Financial	-3.4	4.23	1.8	2	3	0	2.24	800 621-1048
Scudder Dreman Financial Srvcs C	Financial	-3.4	3.99	1.65	2	3	1	2.17	800 621-1048
Scudder Dreman High Ret Eqty A	Growth/Inc	-12	7.17	3.5	2	3	5.75	1.27	800 621-1048
Scudder Dreman High Ret Eqty B	Growth/Inc	-12.7	6.3	2.64	2	3	0	2.03	800 621-1048
Scudder Dreman High Ret Eqty C	Growth/Inc	-12.7	6.33	2.68	2	3	1	2.36	800 621-1048
Scudder Dreman High Ret Eqty I	Growth/Inc	-11.6	7.66	3.95	2	3	0	0.8	800 621-1048
Scudder Dreman High Ret Eqty Instl	Growth/Inc						0		800 621-1048
Scudder Dreman Small Cap Val A	Small Co	-9.9	7.37	-1.14	3	3	5.75	1.58	800 621-1048
Scudder Dreman Small Cap Val B	Small Co	-10.6	6.49	-1.96	3	3	0	2.38	800 621-1048
Scudder Dreman Small Cap Val C	Small Co	-10.6	6.58	-1.87	3	3	1	2.46	800 621-1048
Scudder Dreman Small Cap Val I	Small Co	-9.3	8.09	-0.53	2	3	0	0.84	800 621-1048
Scudder Dreman Small Cap Val Instl	Small Co						0		800 621-1048
Scudder Dynamic Growth Fund A	Small Co	-10.2	-20.5	-10.89	3	5	5.75	1.1	800 621-1048
Scudder Dynamic Growth Fund B	Small Co	-10.6	-21.21	-11.78	3	5	0	2.25	800 621-1048
Scudder Dynamic Growth Fund C	Small Co	-10.7	-21.05	-11.6	3	5	1	1.89	800 621-1048
Scudder Dynamic Growth Fund I	Small Co	-9.4	-20.03	-10.35	3	5	0	0.7	800 621-1048
Scudder EAFE Equity Index Fund Prem	Foreign	-13.1	-13.82	-4.76	5	3	0	0.64	800 621-1048
Scudder Emerg Mkts Gr A	Foreign	-5.9					5.75	2.2	800 621-1048
Scudder Emerg Mkts Gr AARP	Foreign	-5.6					0	1.91	800 621-1048
Scudder Emerg Mkts Gr B	Foreign	-6.7					0	3	800 621-1048
Scudder Emerg Mkts Gr C	Foreign	-6.6					1	2.97	800 621-1048
Scudder Emerg Mkts Gr S	Foreign	-5.6	-8.91	-5.45	3	4	0	1.91	800 621-1048
Scudder Equity 500 Index Inv	Growth	-8.2	-11.14	-1.35	3	3	0	0.38	800 621-1048
Scudder Equity 500 Index Prem	Growth	-8.1	-10.93	-1.14	3	3	0	0.12	800 621-1048
Scudder European Equity A	European	-10.4					5.5	1.88	800 621-1048
Scudder European Equity B	European	-11.1					0	2.63	800 621-1048
Scudder European Equity C	European	-11.1					1	2.63	800 621-1048
Scudder European Equity Instl	European	-10.3	-11.83	13.09	3	3	0	1.63	800 621-1048
Scudder European Equity Inv	European	-10.5	-12		4	3	0	1.88	800 621-1048
Scudder Flag Inv Commnctn A	Technology	-6.5	-27.76	-6.91	3	5	5.5	1.27	800 621-1048
Scudder Flag Inv Commnctn B	Technology	-7.8	-28.48	-7.74	4	5	0	2.02	800 621-1048
Scudder Flag Inv Commnctn C	Technology	-7.8	-28.48			5	1	2.02	800,621-1048
Scudder Flag Inv Commnctn Instl	Technology	-6.1	-27.53			5	0	1.02	800 621-1048
Scudder Flag Inv Equity Part A	Growth	-7.8	1.03	1.71	2	3	5.5	1.93	800 621-1048
Scudder Flag Inv Equity Part B	Growth	-8.4	0.28	0.95	3	3	0	1.93	800 621-1048
Scudder Flag Inv Equity Part C	Growth/Inc	-8.5	0.26			3	1	1.93	800 621-1048
Scudder Flag Inv Equity Part Instl	Growth/Inc	-7.5	1.28	1.97		3	0	0.93	800 621-1048
Scudder Flag Inv Value Build A	Balanced	-4.4	0.56	2.58	2	3	5.5	1.11	800 621-1048
Scudder Flag Inv Value Build B	Balanced	-5.1	-0.16	1.8	2	3	0	1.86	800 621-1048
Scudder Flag Inv Value Build C	Balanced	-5.1	-0.16	1.77		3	1	1.86	800 621-1048
Scudder Flag Inv Value Build Instl	Balanced	-4.1	0.83	2.77	2	3	0	0.86	800 621-1048
Scudder Focus Value + Growth A	Growth	-10.7	-11.01	-3.31	4	3	5.75	1.43	800 621-1048

Stock Fund Name	Objective	Annualized Return for			Rank		Max Load	Expense Ratio	Toll-Free/(Toll) Telephone
		1 Year	3 Years	5 Years	Overall	Risk			
Scudder Focus Value + Growth B	Growth	-11.4	-11.74	-4.37	4	3	0	2.27	800 621-1048
Scudder Focus Value + Growth C	Growth	-11.4	-11.81	-4.11	4	3	1	2.36	800 621-1048
Scudder Global Biotechnology A	Health	11.8					5.75	1.5	800 621-1048
Scudder Global Biotechnology B	Health	11.1					0	2.25	800 621-1048
Scudder Global Biotechnology C	Health	11.1					1	2.25	800 621-1048
Scudder Global Discovery Fund A	Global	-7					5.75	1.89	800 621-1048
Scudder Global Discovery Fund AARP	Global	-6.8					0		800 621-1048
Scudder Global Discovery Fund B	Global	-7.8					0	2.55	800 621-1048
Scudder Global Discovery Fund C	Global	-7.8					1	2.53	800 621-1048
Scudder Global Discovery Fund S	Global	-6.8	-11.03	2.08	3	4	0	1.68	800 621-1048
Scudder Global Fund A	Global	-12.5					5.75	1.6	800 621-1048
Scudder Global Fund AARP	Global	-12.3					0	1.33	800 621-1048
Scudder Global Fund B	Global	-13.2					0	2.4	800 621-1048
Scudder Global Fund C	Global	-13.1					1	2.38	800 621-1048
Scudder Global Fund S	Global	-12.3	-9.33	-2.54	3	2	0	1.13	800 621-1048
Scudder Gold & Prec Metals A	Prec Metal	1	27.01	10.26	2	4	5.75	1.02	800 621-1048
Scudder Gold & Prec Metals AARP	Prec Metal	1.3					0	1.59	800 621-1048
Scudder Gold & Prec Metals B	Prec Metal	0.3	25.98	9.38	2	4	0	2.67	800 621-1048
Scudder Gold & Prec Metals C	Prec Metal	0.3	25.98	9.39	2	4	1	2.64	800 621-1048
Scudder Gold & Prec Metals S	Prec Metal	1.2	27.23	10.5	2	4	0	1.59	800 621-1048
Scudder Greater Europe Growth A	European	-12.9					5.75	1.64	800 621-1048
Scudder Greater Europe Growth AARP	European	-12.7					0	1.37	800 621-1048
Scudder Greater Europe Growth B	European	-13.6					0	2.44	800 621-1048
Scudder Greater Europe Growth C	European	-13.6					1	2.42	800 621-1048
Scudder Greater Europe Growth S	European	-12.7	-15.21	-5.79	5	3	0	1.37	800 621-1048
Scudder Growth & Income A	Growth/Inc	-9.6					5.75	1.02	800 621-1048
Scudder Growth & Income AARP	Growth/Inc	-9.2					0	1.83	800 621-1048
Scudder Growth & Income B	Growth/Inc	-10.3					0	1.83	800 621-1048
Scudder Growth & Income C	Growth/Inc	-10.3					1	1.8	800 621-1048
Scudder Growth & Income Instl	Growth/Inc						0		800 621-1048
Scudder Growth & Income S	Growth/Inc	-9.3	-10.38	-5.86	3	2	0	0.75	800 621-1048
Scudder Growth Fund A	Growth	-10.6	-20.67	-7.98	4	4	5.75	1.02	800 621-1048
Scudder Growth Fund B	Growth	-11.3	-21.44	-8.9	4	4	0	2.06	800 621-1048
Scudder Growth Fund C	Growth	-11.4	-21.35	-8.75	4	4	1	1.83	800 621-1048
Scudder Growth Fund I	Growth	-10.3	-20.37	-7.62	4	4	0	0.62	800 621-1048
Scudder Health Care Fund A	Health	0.3	0.28	8.75	2	3	5.75	1.4	800 621-1048
Scudder Health Care Fund AARP	Health	0.6					0	1.2	800 621-1048
Scudder Health Care Fund B	Health	-0.5	-0.56	7.84	2	3	0	2.19	800 621-1048
Scudder Health Care Fund C	Health	-0.4	-0.53	7.88	2	3	1	2.16	800 621-1048
Scudder Health Care Fund I	Health	0.7					0	0.95	800 621-1048
Scudder Health Care Fund S	Health	0.6	0.52	9.05	2	3	0	1.31	800 621-1048
Scudder Internatl Eqty A	Foreign	-14.6					5.75	1.37	800 621-1048
Scudder Internatl Eqty B	Foreign	-15.3					0	2.48	800 621-1048
Scudder Internatl Eqty C	Foreign	-15.3					1	2.48	800 621-1048
Scudder Internatl Eqty Inst I	Foreign	-14	-16.23	-7.24	4	2	0	1.25	800 621-1048
Scudder Internatl Eqty Inst2	Foreign	-14.2	-16.44	-7.33	5	2	0	1.45	800 621-1048
Scudder Internatl Eqty Inv	Foreign	-14.8	-16.76	-7.87	5	2	0	1.67	800 621-1048
Scudder Internatl Fd A	Foreign	-14.5					5.75	1.33	800 621-1048
Scudder Internatl Fd AARP	Foreign	-14.3					0	1.04	800 621-1048
Scudder Internatl Fd B	Foreign	-15.2					0	2.13	800 621-1048
Scudder Internatl Fd Barrett	Foreign	-14.2	-16.42	-4.12	5	2	0	0.96	800 621-1048
Scudder Internatl Fd C	Foreign	-15.2					1	2.11	800 621-1048
Scudder Internatl Fd I	Foreign	-14					0	1.12	800 621-1048
Scudder Internatl Fd S	Foreign	-14.3	-16.46	-4.21	5	2	0	1.07	800 621-1048
Scudder Internatl Sel Eqty A	Foreign	-14.9	-14.57	4.63		3	5.75	1.41	800 621-1048
Scudder Internatl Sel Eqty B	Foreign	-15.4	-15.35	3.75		3	0	2.16	800 621-1048
Scudder Internatl Sel Eqty C	Foreign	-15.6	-15.4	3.72		3	1	2.16	800 621-1048
Scudder Internatl Sel Eqty Instl	Foreign	-14.6	-14.5	4.8	4	3	0	1.16	800 621-1048

396

Stock Fund Name	Objective	Annualized Return for			Rank		Max Load	Expense Ratio	Toll-Free/(Toll) Telephone
		1 Year	3 Years	5 Years	Overall	Risk			
Scudder Internatl Sel Eqty Inv	Global	-14.9	-14.75			3	0	1.41	800 621-1048
Scudder Internatl Sel Eqty Prem	Foreign	-14.4	-14.32		4	3	0	1.16	800 621-1048
Scudder Japanese Equity A	Pacific	-22.3	-19.01	4.84	4	3	5.75	4.32	800 621-1048
Scudder Japanese Equity B	Pacific	-23	-19.62		4	3	0	5.35	800 621-1048
Scudder Japanese Equity C	Pacific	-22.9	-19.71			3	1	8.74	800 621-1048
Scudder Japanese Equity S	Pacific						0		800 621-1048
Scudder Large Company Growth A	Growth	-10.7					5.75	1.28	800 621-1048
Scudder Large Company Growth AARP	Growth	-10.5					0	2.08	800 621-1048
Scudder Large Company Growth B	Growth	-11.5					0	2.08	800 621-1048
Scudder Large Company Growth C	Growth	-11.4					1	2.05	800 621-1048
Scudder Large Company Growth I	Growth	-10.3					0	0.8	800 621-1048
Scudder Large Company Growth S	Growth	-10.5	-20.32	-4.84	4	4	0	0.8	800 728-3337
Scudder Large Company Value A	Growth	-10					5.75	1.16	800 621-1048
Scudder Large Company Value AARP	Growth	-9.9					0	0.89	800 621-1048
Scudder Large Company Value B	Growth	-10.8					0	1.95	800 621-1048
Scudder Large Company Value C	Growth	-10.8					1	1.93	800 621-1048
Scudder Large Company Value I	Growth	-9.6					0	0.68	800 621-1048
Scudder Large Company Value S	Growth	-9.8	-3.7	-1.12	3	2	0	0.89	800 621-1048
Scudder Latin America Fund A	Foreign	-5					5.75	2.18	800 621-1048
Scudder Latin America Fund AARP	Foreign	-4.6					0		800 621-1048
Scudder Latin America Fund B	Foreign	-5.5					0		800 621-1048
Scudder Latin America Fund C	Foreign	-5.8					1		800 621-1048
Scudder Latin America Fund S	Foreign	-4.7	-1.44	-0.92	2	4	0	1.9	800 621-1048
Scudder Lifecycle Long Range Inv	AssetAlloc	-0.9	-3.45	1.92	2	1	0	1.46	800 621-1048
Scudder Lifecycle Mid Range Inv	AssetAlloc	2.3	0.55	3.5	2	1	0	1.54	800 621-1048
Scudder Lifecycle Short Range Inv	AssetAlloc	4.8	4.26	4.65	2	1	0	1.79	800 621-1048
Scudder Micro Cap A	Small Co	-14.8	0.14	8.64		4	5.75		800 621-1048
Scudder Micro Cap B	Small Co	-15.4	-0.59	7.82		4	0		800 621-1048
Scudder Micro Cap C	Small Co	-15.4	-0.59	7.82		4	1		800 621-1048
Scudder Micro Cap Instl	Small Co	-14.7	0.35	8.88	3	4	0	1.98	800 621-1048
Scudder Micro Cap Inv	Small Co	-14.8	0.14	8.66	3	4	0	1.98	800 621-1048
Scudder Mid Cap A	Growth	-12.9	-10.56	3.7		4	5.75		800 621-1048
Scudder Mid Cap B	Growth	-13.7	-11.4	2.7		4	0		800 621-1048
Scudder Mid Cap C	Growth	-13.7	-11.4	2.7		4	1		800 621-1048
Scudder Mid Cap Instl	Growth	-12.7	-10.33	3.79	4	4	0	1.18	800 621-1048
Scudder Mid Cap Inv	Growth	-12.9	-10.56	3.7	4	4	0	1.43	800 621-1048
Scudder New Europe A	European	-12.6	-15.35	-2.62	4	3	5.75	1.38	800 621-1048
Scudder New Europe B	European	-13.3	-16.14	-6.48	5	3	0	2.22	800 621-1048
Scudder New Europe C	European	-13.4	-16.39	-6.63	5	3	1	2.2	800 621-1048
Scudder New Europe Instl	Foreign						0		800 621-1048
Scudder Pacific Opp A	Pacific	-14.5					5.75	1.8	800 621-1048
Scudder Pacific Opp AARP	Pacific	-14.3					0		800 621-1048
Scudder Pacific Opp B	Pacific	-15.2					0		800 621-1048
Scudder Pacific Opp C	Pacific	-15.1					1		800 621-1048
Scudder Pacific Opp S	Pacific	-14.3	-14.75	-2.41	4	4	0	1.79	800 621-1048
Scudder Pathway Conserv Port A	Income	1.3					5.75	0.25	800 621-1048
Scudder Pathway Conserv Port AARP	Income	1.6					0		800 621-1048
Scudder Pathway Conserv Port B	Income	0.6					0	1	800 621-1048
Scudder Pathway Conserv Port C	Income	0.6					1	1	800 621-1048
Scudder Pathway Conserv Port S	Income	1.5	0.16	0.68	2	1	0		800 621-1048
Scudder Pathway Growth Port A	Growth	-8					5.75	0.25	800 621-1048
Scudder Pathway Growth Port AARP	Growth	-7.8					0		800 621-1048
Scudder Pathway Growth Port B	Growth	-8.6					0	1	800 621-1048
Scudder Pathway Growth Port C	Growth	-8.6					1	1	800 621-1048
Scudder Pathway Growth S	Growth	-7.8	-9.21	-0.56	2	2	0		800 621-1048
Scudder Pathway Moderate Port A	Balanced	-2.7					5.75	0.25	800 621-1048
Scudder Pathway Moderate Port AARP	Balanced	-2.4					0		800 621-1048
Scudder Pathway Moderate Port B	Balanced	-3.4					0	1	800 621-1048

Stock Fund Name	Objective	Annualized Return for			Rank		Max Load	Expense Ratio	Toll-Free/(Toll) Telephone
		1 Year	3 Years	5 Years	Overall	Risk			
Scudder Pathway Moderate Port C	Balanced	-3.4					1	1	800 621-1048
Scudder Pathway Moderate Port S	Balanced	-2.5	-4.82	-0.42	2	1	0		800 621-1048
Scudder PreservationPlus Income A	Growth/Inc	4.2	5.33			1	2.75		800 621-1048
Scudder PreservationPlus Income C	Growth/Inc	3.4	4.54			1	1		800 621-1048
Scudder PreservationPlus Income Inv	Growth/Inc	4.4	5.58			1	0	1	800 621-1048
Scudder RREEF Real Est Sec A	Real Est	8.9	16.92			2	5.75		800 621-1048
Scudder RREEF Real Est Sec B	Real Est	8.1	16.03			2	0		800 621-1048
Scudder RREEF Real Est Sec C	Real Est	8.1	16.07			2	1		800 621-1048
Scudder RREEF Real Est Sec Instl	Real Est	9.1	17.3			2	0		800 621-1048
Scudder Retirement Fund-V	Flexible	-0.5	-1.89	2.16	2	1	5		800 621-1048
Scudder Retirement Fund-VI	Flexible	4.2	1.36	3.79	2	1	5		800 621-1048
Scudder Retirement Fund-VII	Flexible	10.8	5.15	5.25	1	1	5		800 621-1048
Scudder S&P 500 Index Fund AARP	Growth/Inc	-8.3					0	0.4	800 621-1048
Scudder S&P 500 Index Fund S	Growth/Inc	-8.3	-11.21	-1.44	3	3	0		800 621-1048
Scudder S&P 500 Stock Fund A	Growth	-8.7	-11.97		3	3	4.5	1.03	800 621-1048
Scudder S&P 500 Stock Fund B	Growth	-9.5	-12.63		4	3	0	1.81	800 621-1048
Scudder S&P 500 Stock Fund C	Growth	-9.4	-12.58		4	3	1	1.8	800 621-1048
Scudder Select 500 A	Growth	-10.2					5.75		800 621-1048
Scudder Select 500 AARP	Growth/Inc	-10					0	0.75	800 621-1048
Scudder Select 500 B	Growth/Inc	-11					0		800 621-1048
Scudder Select 500 C	Growth/Inc	-10.9					1		800 621-1048
Scudder Select 500 S	Growth/Inc	-10	-9.27		3	3	0	0.75	800 621-1048
Scudder Small Cap Fund A	Small Co	-16.6	-6.87	3.64		4	5.75		800 621-1048
Scudder Small Cap Fund B	Small Co	-17.2	-7.57	2.87		4	0		800 621-1048
Scudder Small Cap Fund C	Small Co	-17.2	-7.57	2.87		4	1		800 621-1048
Scudder Small Cap Fund Inv	Small Co	-16.6	-6.9	3.62	3	4	0	1.46	800 621-1048
Scudder Small Company Stock A	Small Co	-6.1					5.75	1.48	800 621-1048
Scudder Small Company Stock AARP	Small Co	-5.9	5.28	-1.45	3	3	0	1.19	800 621-1048
Scudder Small Company Stock B	Small Co	-6.9					0	2.28	800 621-1048
Scudder Small Company Stock C	Small Co	-6.9					1	2.25	800 621-1048
Scudder Small Company Stock S	Small Co	-5.9					0	1.19	800 621-1048
Scudder Small Company Value A	Small Co	-9.3					5.75		800 621-1048
Scudder Small Company Value B	Small Co	-10					0		800 621-1048
Scudder Small Company Value C	Small Co	-10					1		800 621-1048
Scudder Small Company Value S	Small Co	-9	11.91	0.38	2	3	0	1.23	800 621-1048
Scudder Target 2010	Flexible	13.1	5.33	7.2	1	1	5	1.01	800 621-1048
Scudder Target 2011	Flexible	12.9	3.95	6.13	1	1	5	0.95	800 621-1048
Scudder Target 2012	Flexible	10.8	0.17	3.75	2	1	5		800 621-1048
Scudder Target 2013	Flexible	2	-0.86	2.68	2	1	5		800 621-1048
Scudder Technology Fd A	Technology	-5.5	-27.78	0.17	3	5	5.75	1.16	800 621-1048
Scudder Technology Fd B	Technology	-6.5	-28.51	-0.84	3	5	0		800 621-1048
Scudder Technology Fd C	Technology	-6.3	-28.44	-0.72	3	5	1		800 621-1048
Scudder Technology Fd I	Technology	-5.1	-27.53	0.55	3	5	0		800 621-1048
Scudder Technology Fd Instl	Technology						0		800 621-1048
Scudder Technology Innovation A	Technology	-3.2					5.75		800 621-1048
Scudder Technology Innovation AARP	Technology	-2.9					0		800 621-1048
Scudder Technology Innovation B	Technology	-3.9					0		800 621-1048
Scudder Technology Innovation C	Technology	-3.9					1		800 621-1048
Scudder Technology Innovation S	Technology	-2.9	-32.17	0.44	3	5	0		800 621-1048
Scudder Top 50 US A	Growth	-9.9	-19.01	-5.87	5	3	5.5	3.09	800 621-1048
Scudder Top 50 US B	Growth	-10.6	-19.64	-6.62	5	3	0	3.84	800 621-1048
Scudder Top 50 US C	Growth	-10.5	-19.57			3	1	3.84	800 621-1048
Scudder Total Return Fund A	Balanced	-3.3	-5.24	0.25	2	1	5.75	0.99	800 621-1048
Scudder Total Return Fund B	Balanced	-4.1	-6.13	-0.69	2	1	0	1.98	800 621-1048
Scudder Total Return Fund C	Balanced	-4.1	-6.07	-0.64	2	1	1	1.87	800 621-1048
Scudder Total Return Fund I	Balanced	-2.9	-4.96	0.65	2	1	0	0.65	800 621-1048
Scudder Worldwide 2004	Growth	1.1	-0.46	2.1	2	1	5	1.7	800 621-1048
Security Capital Euro Real Est	Real Est	5.1	13.56		2	2	0	1.45	888 732-8748

Stock Fund Name	Objective	Annualized Return for 1 Year	3 Years	5 Years	Rank Overall	Risk	Max Load	Expense Ratio	Toll-Free/(Toll) Telephone
Security Capital U.S. Real Estate	Real Est	2	11.98	8.16	1	2	0	1.15	888 732-8748
Security Enhanced Index A	Growth	-9.7	-12.58		4	3	5.75	1.82	888 732-8748
Security Enhanced Index B	Growth	-10.7	-13.11		4	3	0	2.56	888 732-8748
Security Enhanced Index C	Growth	-10.7	-13.34		4	3	0	2.56	888 732-8748
Security Equity Fund A	Growth	-10.4	-12.46	-4.66	3	3	5.75	1.16	888 732-8748
Security Equity Fund B	Growth	-11.1	-13.27	-5.59	4	3	0	2	888 732-8748
Security Equity Fund C	Growth	-11.2	-13.25			3	0	2.01	888 732-8748
Security Equity Fund-Global B	Global	-16.6	-11.11	2.54	4	3	0	1.53	888 732-8748
Security Equity Select 25 A	Growth	-14.1	-13.32		4	3	5.75	1.64	888 732-8748
Security Equity Select 25 B	Growth	-14.6	-13.97		4	3	0	2.39	888 732-8748
Security Global Fund	Global	-16.8	-10.92	3.02	3	3	5.75	1.78	888 732-8748
Security Growth and Income A	Growth/Inc	-13.6	-7.45	-.7	3	2	5.75	1.42	888 732-8748
Security Growth and Income B	Growth/Inc	-14.1	-8.26	-7.88	4	2	0	2.17	888 732-8748
Security International A	Global	-19.9	-19.64		5	3	5.75	2.35	888 732-8748
Security International B	Global	-20.4	-20.3		5	3	0	3.23	888 732-8748
Security International C	Global	-20.5	-20.21		5	3	0	3.3	888 732-8748
Security Large Cap Growth A	Growth/Inc	-6.3	-16.64		3	3	5.75	1.86	.888 732-8748
Security Large Cap Growth B	Growth/Inc	-7	-17.37		3	3	0	2.61	888 732-8748
Security Large Cap Growth C	Growth/Inc	-6.8	-17.26		3	3	0	2.61	888 732-8748
Security Mid Cap Gwth A	Agg Growth	-4.6	-5.66	9.01	3	4	5.75	1.25	888 732-8748
Security Mid Cap Gwth B	Agg Growth	-5.3	-6.51	7.79	3	4	0	2.09	888 732-8748
Security Mid Cap Value A	Growth	-3.8	9.56	12.83	1	4	5.75	1.69	888 732-8748
Security Small Cap Growth A	Small Co	-7.6	-17.96	4.7	4	5	5.75	2.21	888 732-8748
Security Small Cap Growth B	Small Co	-8.2	-18.64	3.68	4	5	0	2.96	888 732-8748
Security Social Awareness A	Growth	-7.9	-12.41	-2.16	3	3	5.75	1.49	888 732-8748
Security Social Awareness B	Growth	-8.6	-13.19	-3.12	4	3	0	2.87	888 732-8748
Security Technology A	Technology	-1.9	-26.28		3	5	5.75	2.47	888 732-8748
Security Technology B	Technology	-2.8	-27.1		3	5	0	3.21	888 732-8748
Security Technology C	Technology	-2.8	-27.1		3	5	0	3.21	, 888 732-8748
Segall Bryant Gr & Income A	Growth	-11.2	-3.68		3	.3	4.75	1.39	800 277-3862
Selected American Shares	Growth/Inc	-6.4	-6.21	2.64	2	2	0	0.94	800 279-0279
Selected Special Shares	Small Co	-6.7	-7.88	0.32	3	3	0	1.18	800 279-0279
Seligman Capital Fund A	Agg Growth	-13.4	-15	1.82	3	5	4.75	1.15	800 221-2783
Seligman Capital Fund B	Agg Growth	-14	-15.6	1.06	4	5	0	1.83	800 221-2783
Seligman Capital Fund C	Agg Growth	-14.1	-15.6		4	5	1	1.83	800 221-2783
Seligman Capital Fund D	Agg Growth	-14.1	-15.61	1.06	4	5	0	1.83	800 221-2783
Seligman Common Stock Fund A	Growth/Inc	-15.8	-14.15	-7.08	5	2	4.75	1.18	800 221-2783
Seligman Common Stock Fund B	Growth/Inc	-16.4	-14.76	-7.74	5	2	0	1.93	800 221-2783
Seligman Common Stock Fund C	Growth/Inc	-16.5	-12.34		3	3	1	1.93	800 221-2783
Seligman Common Stock Fund D	Growth/Inc	-16.5	-14.81	-7.75	5	2	0	1.93	800 221-2783
Seligman Communications and Info A	Technology	-8.1	-21.53	1.2	3	5	4.75	1.44	800 221-2783
Seligman Communications and Info B	Technology	-8.8	-22.1	0.46	3	5	0	2.19	800 221-2783
Seligman Communications and Info C	Technology	-8.8	-22.1		3	5	1	2.19	800 221-2783
Seligman Communications and Info D	Technology	-8.8	-22.12	0.46	3	5	0	2.19.	800 221-2783
Seligman Emerging Markets A	Foreign	-9.8	-10.64	-5.91	3	4	4.75	3.14	800 221-2783
Seligman Emerging Markets B	Foreign	-10.4	-11.32	-6.62	4	4	0	3.89	800 221-2783
Seligman Emerging Markets C	Foreign	-10.4	-11.35		4	4	1	3.89	800 221-2783
Seligman Emerging Markets D	Foreign	-10.4	-11.35	-6.62	4	4	0	3.89	800 221-2783
Seligman Frontier Fund A	Small Co	-12.2	-10.77	-7.62	5	4	4.75	1.78	800 221-2783
Seligman Frontier Fund B	Small Co	-12.7	-11.41	-8.3	5	4	0	2.54	800 221-2783
Seligman Frontier Fund C	Small Co	-12.8	-11.48		5	4	1		800 221-2783
Seligman Frontier Fund D	Small Co	-12.8	-11.48	-8.33	5	4	0	2.54	800 221-2783
Seligman Global Growth A	Global	-13	-19.46	-6.29	4	3	4.75	1.79	800 221-2783
Seligman Global Growth B	Global	-13.6	-20.01	-6.95	5	3	0	2.54	800 221-2783
Seligman Global Growth C	Global	-13.6	-20.01		5	3	1		800 221-2783
Seligman Global Growth D	Global	-13.6	-20.01	-6.95	5	3	0	2.54	800 221-2783
Seligman Global Small Co A	Global	-18.5	-15.92	-9.39	4	3	4.75	1.81	800 221-2783
Seligman Global Small Co B	Global	-19.2	-16.57	-10.08	4	3	0	2.56	800 221-2783

Stock Fund Name	Objective	Annualized Return for			Rank		Max Load	Expense Ratio	Toll-Free/(Toll) Telephone
		1 Year	3 Years	5 Years	Overall	Risk			
Seligman Global Small Co C	Global	-19.2	-16.57		4	3	1		800 221-2783
Seligman Global Small Co D	Global	-19.2	-16.57	-10.07	5	3	0	2.56	800 221-2783
Seligman Global Tech A	Technology	-15.7	-26.64	-0.5	4	5	4.75	1.67	800 221-2783
Seligman Global Tech B	Technology	-16.4	-27.23	-1.28	4	5	0	2.42	800 221-2783
Seligman Global Tech C	Technology	-16.4	-27.16		4	5	1	2.42	800 221-2783
Seligman Global Tech D	Technology	-16.4	-27.21	-1.26	4	5	0	2.42	800 221-2783
Seligman Growth Fund A	Growth	-11.6	-21.48	-5.91	4	4	4.75	1.33	800 221-2783
Seligman Growth Fund B	Growth	-11.9	-22.05	-6.58	4	4	0	2	800 221-2783
Seligman Growth Fund C	Growth	-11.9	-22.05		4	4	1	2	800 221-2783
Seligman Growth Fund D	Growth	-12.2	-22.05	-6.58	4	4	0	2	800 221-2783
Seligman Income Fund A	Flexible	-2.5	-3.97	-2.56	2	1	4.75	1.25	800 221-2783
Seligman Income Fund B	Flexible	-3.3	-4.67	-3.31	2	1	0	2	800 221-2783
Seligman Income Fund D	Flexible	-3.3	-4.67	-3.31	2	1	0	2	800 221-2783
Seligman Intl Growth Fund A	Foreign	-15.2	-18.62	-14.08	5	3	4.75	1.29	800 221-2783
Seligman Intl Growth Fund B	Foreign	-16	-19.19	-14.69	5	3	0	3.13	800 221-2783
Seligman Intl Growth Fund D	Foreign	-15.8	-19.12	-14.66	4	3	0	3.13	800 221-2783
Seligman Large-Cap Value A	Growth	-18.1	-4.26	-3.12	3	3	4.75	1.53	800 221-2783
Seligman Large-Cap Value B	Growth	-18.7	-4.98	-3.83	3	3	0	2.28	800 221-2783
Seligman Large-Cap Value D	Growth	-18.8	-5.01	-3.87	3	3	0	2.28	800 221-2783
Seligman Small-Cap Value A	Small Co	-7.4	11.75	3.35	2	3	4.75	1.74	800 221-2783
Seligman Small-Cap Value B	Small Co	-8	10.97	2.6	2	3	0	2.49	800 221-2783
Seligman Small-Cap Value D	Small Co	-8	10.92	2.6	2	3	0	2.49	800 221-2783
Sentinel Balanced A	Balanced	-1.6	0.19	1.61	2	1	5	1.15	800 282-3863
Sentinel Balanced B	Balanced	-2.4	-0.56	0.83	2	1	4	1.93	800 282-3863
Sentinel Common Stock A	Growth/Inc	-8.4	-4.37	-0.54	3	2	5	1.06	800 282-3863
Sentinel Common Stock B	Growth/Inc	-9.4	-5.2	-1.37	3	2	4	1.86	800 282-3863
Sentinel International Equity A	Foreign	-15	-8.99	-2.58	4	3	5	1.26	800 282-3863
Sentinel Mid Cap Growth A	Growth	-8.4	-15.14	-0.11	3	5	5	1.27	800 282-3863
Sentinel Small Company Fd A	Small Co	-6.2	8.25	10.41	1	3	5	1.21	800 282-3863
Sentinel Small Company Fd B	Small Co	-7	7.25	9.39	1	3	4	2.12	800 282-3863
Sentinel World B	Foreign	-16	-9.98	-3.58	4	3	4	2.21	800 282-3863
Sentry Fund	Growth	-9.1	-8.64	-6.26	3	3	0	0.91	800 533-7827
Sequoia Fund	Growth	-2.8	8.24	4.58	2	1	0	1	800 686-6884
Sextant Growth Fund	Growth	-6.4	-4.86	5.98	2	4	0	0.78	800 728-8762
Sextant International Fund	Foreign	-12.7	-12.58	-2.5	3	4	0	1.17	800 728-8762
Shadow Stock Fund	Small Co	-11.2	8.26	5.29	2	3	0	1.03	866 409-2550
Shaker Fund A	Growth	-17.9			-		5.75	2.15	888 314-9048
Shaker Fund B	Growth	-17.9					0	2.25	888 314-9048
Shaker Fund C	Growth	-17.9					0	2.2	888 314-9048
Shaker Fund I	Growth	-17.4					0	1.65	888 314-9048
Shelby Fund A	Growth	-10.7	-17.96		4	4	4.75	2.03	800 774-3529
Shelby Fund Y	Growth	-10.4	-17.8	-2.97	4	4	0	1.78	800 774-3529
Shelby Large Cap Fund A	Growth	-7.3	-9.66	0.42	3	3	4.75	1.64	800 774-3529
Shepherd Large Cap Growth Fund	Growth	-14.9	-39.64	-15.01	5	5	3.75	2.25	800 416-2053
Sierra Club Balanced Fund	Balanced						0	1.84	800 222-5852
Sierra Club Stock Fund	Growth/Inc	-8.3	-10.18		3	3	0	1.5	800 222-5852
Signal Income Fund A	Income						0		888 426-9709
Signal Income Fund B	Income						0		888 426-9709
Signal Large Cap Growth A	Growth						0		888 426-9709
Signal Large Cap Growth B	Growth						0		888 426-9709
Signal Tax Exempt Income A	Other						0		888 426-9709
Signal Tax Exempt Income B	Other						0		888 426-9709
Signal Tax Exempt Income I	Other						0		888 426-9709
Simms International Equity Fd	Foreign	-24.6	-23.05		5	3	0	1.15	877 438-7467
Sit Balanced Fund	Balanced	-2.7	-10.28	-0.92	3	2	0	1	800 332-5580
Sit Developing Mkts Growth Fund	Foreign	-11.4	-14.63	-4.71	4	3	0	2	800 332-5580
Sit International Growth Fund	Foreign	-18.3	-25.26	-10.92	5	3	0	1.5	800 332-5580
Sit Large Cap Growth	Growth	-7.6	-21.33	-6.12	3	4	0	1	800 332-5580

Stock Fund Name	Objective	Annualized Return for			Rank		Max Load	Expense Ratio	Toll-Free/(Toll) Telephone
		1 Year	3 Years	5 Years	Overall	Risk			
Sit Mid Cap Growth Fund	Growth	-9.7	-21.46	-3.72	3	5	0	1.15	800 332-5580
Sit Small Cap Growth Fund	Small Co	-7.2	-15.33	6.33	3	4	0	1.5	800 332-5580
Skyline Special Equities	Small Co	-9.7	11.98	1.68	3	3	0	1.49	800 458-5222
SmBarney Aggressive Growth A	Agg Growth	-1.1	-5.58	12.61	2	4	5	1.17	800 451-2010
SmBarney Aggressive Growth B	Agg Growth	-1.5	-6.23	11.78	2	4	0	1.99	800 451-2010
SmBarney Aggressive Growth L	Agg Growth	-1.8	-6.29	11.75	2	4	1	1.94	800 451-2010
SmBarney Allocation Balanced Port A	Balanced	1.8					5	0.6	800 451-2010
SmBarney Allocation Balanced Port B	Balanced	1	-0.11	1.98	1	1	0	1.35	800 451-2010
SmBarney Allocation Balanced Port L	Balanced	1.2	-0.05	2.04	1	1	1	1.35	800 451-2010
SmBarney Allocation Global Port A	AssetAlloc	-11.5					5	0.63	800 451-2010
SmBarney Allocation Global Port B	AssetAlloc	-12.1					0	1.39	800 451-2010
SmBarney Allocation Global Port L	AssetAlloc	-12.1	-12.99	-5.67	4	3	0	1.39	800 451-2010
SmBarney Allocation Growth Port A	Growth	-3.8					5	0.6	800 451-2010
SmBarney Allocation Growth Port B	Growth	-4.5					0	1.35	800 451-2010
SmBarney Allocation Growth Port L	Growth	-4.6					1	1.35	800 451-2010
SmBarney Allocation High Growth A	Growth	-8					5	0.6	800 451-2010
SmBarney Allocation High Growth B	Growth	-8.8					0	1.35	800 451-2010
SmBarney Allocation High Growth L	Growth	-8.7					1	1.35	800 451-2010
SmBarney Appreciation Fund A	Growth	-5	-4.04	2.04	2	2	5	0.92	800 451-2010
SmBarney Appreciation Fund B	Growth	-5.8	-4.86	1.13	2	2	0	1.76	800 451-2010
SmBarney Appreciation Fund L	Growth	-5.7	-4.8	1.21	2	2	1	1.72	800 451-2010
SmBarney Appreciation Fund Y	Growth	-4.7	-3.72	3.24	1	2	0	0.58	800 451-2010
SmBarney Balanced Fund A	Balanced	0.8	-5.63	0.1	2	2	5	1.02	800 451-2010
SmBarney Balanced Fund B	Balanced	0.5	-6.09	-0.4	2	2	0	1.47	800 451-2010
SmBarney Balanced Fund L	Balanced	0.1	-6.33		2	2	1	1.73	800 451-2010
SmBarney Balanced Fund O	Balanced	0.4	-6.03	-0.35	2	2	0	1.39	800 451-2010
SmBarney Capital & Income A	Flexible	2.8	-0.17	1.63	1	2	5	1.08	800 451-2010
SmBarney Capital & Income B	Flexible	2.3	-0.7	1.12	1	2	0	1.62	800 451-2010
SmBarney Capital & Income L	Flexible	2					1	1.88	800 451-2010
SmBarney Capital & Income O	Flexible	2.4	-0.65	1.13	1	2	0	1.6	800 451-2010
SmBarney Capital & Income Y	Flexible	3.2					0	0.7	800 451-2010
SmBarney Convertible A	Converts	9.2	4.33	2.39	1	2	5	1.25	800 451-2010
SmBarney Convertible B	Converts	8.7	3.79	1.88	1	2	0	1.81	800 451-2010
SmBarney Convertible O	Converts	8.6	3.74	1.87	1	2	0	1.83	800 451-2010
SmBarney Convertible Y	Converts	9.6					0	0.79	800 451-2010
SmBarney Divers Large Cap Gr A	Growth	-6.9	-14.07	-3.16	3	3	5	1.05	800 451-2010
SmBarney Divers Large Cap Gr B	Growth	-7.6	-14.72		4	3	0		800 451-2010
SmBarney Financial Services L	Financial	-8.6	2.08		2	3	0	2.28	800 451-2010
SmBarney International Fund 1	Foreign	-17.2	-27.8	-6.71	5	4	8.5	1.42	800 451-2010
SmBarney International Fund A	Foreign	-17.9	-28.3	-7.28	5	4	5	2.17	800 451-2010
SmBarney International Fund B	Foreign	-18.8	-28.92	-8.02	5	4	0	2.9	800 451-2010
SmBarney Large Cap Growth A	Growth	0.2					5	1.13	800 451-2010
SmBarney Large Cap Growth B	Growth	-0.5					0	1.89	800 451-2010
SmBarney Large Cap Growth L	Growth	-0.5					0	1.89	800 451-2010
SmBarney Large Cap Value A	Growth/Inc	-15	-6.96	-3.18	3	3	5	0.89	800 451-2010
SmBarney Large Cap Value B	Growth/Inc	-15.7	-7.71	-3.97	3	3	0	1.74	800 451-2010
SmBarney Large Cap Value L	Growth/Inc	-15.6	-7.69	-3.95	3	3	1	1.71	800 451-2010
SmBarney Large Cap Value Y	Growth/Inc	-14.6					0	0.58	800 451-2010
SmBarney Muni Fds-Ltd Term B	Other						0		800 451-2010
SmBarney Sh Term High Grade Bd B	Other						0		800 451-2010
SmBarney Small Cap Core A	Small Co	-9.9	-1	1.07	3	3	5	1.23	800 451-2010
SmBarney Small Cap Core B	Small Co	-10.6	-1.77		3	3	0	1.97	800 451-2010
SmBarney Small Cap Core L	Small Co	-10.6	-1.77		3	3	0	1.98	800 451-2010
SmBarney Small Cap Growth 1	Small Co	-11.9					0	1.28	800 451-2010
SmBarney Small Cap Growth A	Small Co	-11.6	-17.94		5	5	5	1.34	800 451-2010
SmBarney Small Cap Growth B	Small Co	-12.3	-18.57		5	5	0	2.07	800 451-2010
SmBarney Small Cap Growth L	Small Co	-11.9	-18.35		5	5	0	1.93	800 451-2010
SmBarney Small Cap Growth Y	Small Co	-10.8	-17.42		4	5	0	0.8	800 451-2010

Stock Fund Name	Objective	Annualized Return for			Rank		Max Load	Expense Ratio	Toll-Free/(Toll) Telephone
		1 Year	3 Years	5 Years	Overall	Risk			
SmBarney Small Cap Value A	Small Co	-6.8	10.81		2	3	5	1.2	800 451-2010
SmBarney Small Cap Value B	Small Co	-7.5	9.98		2	3	0	1.97	800 451-2010
SmBarney Small Cap Value L	Small Co	-7.5	9.99		2	3	1	1.96	800 451-2010
Smith Barney Financial Services A	Financial	-7.9	2.85		2	3	5	1.5	800 451-2010
Smith Barney Financial Services B	Financial	-8.6	2.08		2	3	0	2.25	800 451-2010
Smith Barney Fundamental Value A	Growth	-11.8	-6.37	5.51	3	3	5	1.02	800 451-2010
Smith Barney Fundamental Value B	Growth	-12.5	-7.12	4.7	3	3	0	1.83	800 451-2010
Smith Barney Fundamental Value L	Growth	-12.5	-7.09	4.7	3	3	1	1.82	800 451-2010
Smith Barney Fundamental Value Y	Growth	-11.4					0	0.71	800 451-2010
Smith Barney Group Spectrum A	Growth	-11.5					5	1.22	800 451-2010
Smith Barney Group Spectrum B	Growth	-12.3					0	1.96	800 451-2010
Smith Barney Group Spectrum L	Growth	-12.2					0	1.94	800 451-2010
Smith Barney Growth & Income 1	Growth/Inc	-7.6	-10.21	-2.74	3	3	8.5	2	800 451-2010
Smith Barney Growth & Income A	Growth/Inc	-7.8	-6.55	2.24	2	3	5	1.17	800 451-2010
Smith Barney Growth & Income B	Growth/Inc	-8.9	-11.33	-3.87	4	3	0	2	800 451-2010
Smith Barney Growth & Income L	Growth/Inc	-8.3					0	1.85	800 451-2010
Smith Barney Hansberger Gl Value A	Global	-14.6	-10.14	-4.78	4	3	5	1.49	800 451-2010
Smith Barney Hansberger Gl Value B	Global	-15.3	-10.83	-5.65	3	3	0	2.29	800 451-2010
Smith Barney Hansberger Gl Value L	Global	-15.2	-10.81	-5.65	3	3	1	2.29	800 451-2010
Smith Barney Hansberger Gl Value Y	Global	-14.1	-9.66	-4.29	4	3	0	1.06	800 451-2010
Smith Barney Health Sciences A	Health	-7.2	-3.37		2	2	5	1.5	800 451-2010
Smith Barney Health Sciences B	Health	-8	-4.11		2	2	0	2.25	800 451-2010
Smith Barney Health Sciences L	Health	-8	-4.09		2	2	0	2.25	800 451-2010
Smith Barney Intl All Cap Growth A	Foreign	-13.4	-20.19	-10.01	5	3	5	1.21	800 451-2010
Smith Barney Intl All Cap Growth B	Foreign	-14.2	-21.39	-10.75	5	3	0	2.06	800 451-2010
Smith Barney Intl All Cap Growth L	Foreign	-14.3	-20.85	-10.75	4	3	1	2.04	800 451-2010
Smith Barney Intl All Cap Growth Y	Foreign	-13.1	-19.87	-9.67	4	3	0	0.94	800 451-2010
Smith Barney Intl Large Cap A	Foreign	-13.6	-16.57	-6	3	2	4.75	1.75	800 451-2010
Smith Barney Large Cap Core 1	Growth	-9.2	-13.69	-0.56	3	3	8.5	0.7	800 451-2010
Smith Barney Large Cap Core A	Growth	-9.9	-14.25	-1.07	3	3	5	1.34	800 451-2010
Smith Barney Large Cap Core B	Growth	-10.8	-14.93	-1.83	4	3	0	2.04	800 451-2010
Smith Barney Mid Cap Core A	Growth	-10.7	-5.42		3	3	5	1.16	800 451-2010
Smith Barney Mid Cap Core B	Growth	-11.3	-6.12		3	3	0	1.9	800 451-2010
Smith Barney Mid-Cap Core 1	Growth	-10.8	-4.87		3	3	1	1.89	800 451-2010
Smith Barney Prem Sel AllCap Gr A	Growth	-12.9					5	1.18	800 451-2010
Smith Barney Prem Sel AllCap Gr B	Growth	-13.6					0	1.93	800 451-2010
Smith Barney Prem Sel Lrg Cap A	Growth	-21.7	-15.08		4	3	5	1.16	800 451-2010
Smith Barney Prem Sel Lrg Cap B	Growth	-22.3	-15.75		5	3	0	1.93	800 451-2010
Smith Barney Prem Select Gbl Gwth A	Other	-6.3					0	1.36	800 451-2010
Smith Barney Prem Select Gbl Gwth B	Other	-6.9					0	1.93	800 451-2010
Smith Barney S&P 500 Index A	Growth	-8.6	-11.28	-2.37	3	3	0	0.59	800 451-2010
Smith Barney S&P 500 Index D	Growth	-8.3	-11.08		3	3	0	0.36	800 451-2010
Smith Barney Security & Growth	Growth/Inc	-3					0	0.97	800 451-2010
Smith Barney Small Cap Gr Opp A	Small Co	-13.6					0	1.35	800 451-2010
Smith Barney Soc Awareness Fund A	Balanced	-2.1	-4.79	1.37	2	2	5	1.24	800 451-2010
Smith Barney Soc Awareness Fund B	Balanced	-2.8	-5.57	0.56	2	2	0	1.99	800 451-2010
Smith Barney Soc Awareness Fund L	Balanced	-2.8	-5.5	0.6	2	2	1	1.98	800 451-2010
Smith Barney Technology A	Technology	-7.5	-30.28		4	5	5	1.5	800 451-2010
Smith Barney Technology B	Technology	-8.4	-30.89		4	5	0	2.25	800 451-2010
Smith Barney Technology L	Technology	-8.4	-30.89		4	5	0	2.25	800 451-2010
Smith Barney Telecom-Income	Utilities	-7.6	-19.82	-5.33	4	5	0	0.9	800 451-2010
Sound Shore Fund	Growth	-8.6	2.91	1.69	2	3	0	0.98	800 754-8758
SouthTrust Growth Fund	Growth	-5	-9.58		3	3	4.5	1.22	800 843-8618
SouthTrust Value Fund	Growth/Inc	-9.8	-4.12	0.56	2	3	4.5	1.02	800 843-8618
Spectra Fund N	Agg Growth	-12.1	-20.17	-0.84	4	4	0	1.9	800 711-6141
Standish Internatl Eqty Instl	Foreign	-5	-2.91	0.05	3	2	0	1	800 221-4795
Standish Internatl Small Cap	Foreign	-1.1	2.16		1	2	0	1.25	800 221-4795
Standish Select Value Instl	Growth	-7.8	-1.5	-0.46	3	2	0	0.71	800 221-4795

Stock Fund Name	Objective	Annualized Return for			Rank		Max Load	Expense Ratio	Toll-Free/(Toll) Telephone
		1 Year	3 Years	5 Years	Overall	Risk			
Standish Small Cap Equity Fund	Small Co	-9.9	-14.76	-0.1	3	4	0	0.74	800 221-4795
Standish Small Cap Growth Instl	Small Co	-10.7	-14.38	5	3	5	0	1	800 221-4795
Standish Small Cap Tax-Sensitive	Small Co	-9.8	-13.73	3.02	3	5	0	1	800 221-4795
Standish Tax-Sensitive Equity	Growth	-10.1	-9.18	-4.84	3	3	0	0.75	800 221-4795
State Farm Balanced Fund	Balanced	0.3	-3.64	1.72	2	1	0	0.15	800 447-0740
State Farm Equity & Bond Inst	Growth	-2.5					0	0.67	800 447-0740
State Farm Equity A	Growth	-7.8					3	1.27	800 447-0740
State Farm Equity B	Growth	-8.2					0	1.67	800 447-0740
State Farm Equity Inst	Growth	-7.4					0	0.77	800 447-0740
State Farm Growth Fund	Growth	-6.7	-9.51	-0.07	3	2	0	0.13	800 447-0740
State Farm Intl Equity A	Other	-14					3	1.5	800 447-0740
State Farm Intl Equity B	Other	-14.3					0	1.89	800 447-0740
State Farm Intl Equity Inst	Other	-13.5					0	1	800 447-0740
State Farm Intl Index A	Other	-13.4					3	1.14	800 447-0740
State Farm Intl Index B	Other	-13.8					0	1.55	800 447-0740
State Farm Intl Index Inst	Other	-12.9					0	0.65	800 447-0740
State Farm S&P 500 Index A	Other	-8.7					3	0.8	800 447-0740
State Farm S&P 500 Index B	Other	-9.1					0	1.19	800 447-0740
State Farm S&P 500 Index Inst	Other	-8.4					0	0.3	800 447-0740
State Farm Small Cap Equity A	Small Co	-13.6					3	1.48	800 447-0740
State Farm Small Cap Equity B	Small Co	-13.9					0	1.88	800 447-0740
State Farm Small Cap Equity Inst	Small Co	-13.1					0	0.98	800 447-0740
State Farm Small Cap Index A	Small Co	-9.3					3	0.94	800 447-0740
State Farm Small Cap Index B	Small Co	-9.6					0	1.35	800 447-0740
State Farm Small Cap Index Inst	Small Co	-8.6					0	0.45	800 447-0740
State Street Research Asst Allc A	Flexible	-5.8	0.85	3.24	1	2	5.75	1.1	800 882-0052
State Street Research Asst Allc B	Flexible	-5.5	0.56	2.75	2	2	0	0.1	800 882-0052
State Street Research Asst Allc B1	Flexible	-6.4	0.11	2.49	2	2	0	1.1	800 882-0052
State Street Research Asst Allc C	Flexible	-6.5	0.11	2.49	2	2	0	1.1	800 882-0052
State Street Research Asst Allc S	Flexible	-5.5	1.14	3.52	1	2	0	1.1	800 882-0052
State Street Research Aurora A	Small Co	-15.3	8.89	8.17	3	4	5.75	1.13	800 882-0052
State Street Research Aurora B	Small Co	-15	8.59	7.67	3	4	0	1.13	800 882-0052
State Street Research Aurora B1	Small Co	-15.9	8.11	7.4	3	4	0	1.13	800 882-0052
State Street Research Aurora C	Small Co	-15.9	8.1	7.4	3	4	0	1.13	800 882-0052
State Street Research Aurora S	Small Co	-15	9.16	8.58	3	4	0	1.13	800 882-0052
State Street Research Emerg Gro A	Small Co	-2.7	-4.26	2.04	3	4	5.75	1.1	800 882-0052
State Street Research Emerg Gro B	Small Co	-3.4	-4.5	1.58	3	4	0	1.1	800 882-0052
State Street Research Emerg Gro B1	Small Co	-3.5	-4.88	1.36	3	4	0	1.1	800 882-0052
State Street Research Emerg Gro C	Small Co	-3.3	-4.82	1.39	3	4	0	1.1	800 882-0052
State Street Research Emerg Gro S	Small Co	-2.4	-3.95	2.33	3	4	0	1.1	800 882-0052
State Street Research Glb Res A	Energy/Res	7.7	15.38	8.16	1	5	5.75	1.31	800 882-0052
State Street Research Glb Res B	Energy/Res	6.9	14.67	7.44	1	5	0	1.31	800 882-0052
State Street Research Glb Res B1	Energy/Res	6.8	14.64	7.37	1	5	0	1.31	800 882-0052
State Street Research Glb Res C	Energy/Res	6.9	14.65	7.41	1	5	0	1.31	800 882-0052
State Street Research Glb Res S	Energy/Res	8.3	15.97	8.58	1	5	0	1.31	800 882-0052
State Street Research Inst LgCap An	Growth						0	0.45	800 882-0052
State Street Research Invest Tr A	Growth	-9.2	-15.02	-3.43	4	3	5.75	0.8	800 882-0052
State Street Research Invest Tr B	Growth	-9	-15.14	-3.74	4	3	0	1	800 882-0052
State Street Research Invest Tr B1	Growth	-9.9	-15.63	-4.12	4	3	0	1.8	800 882-0052
State Street Research Invest Tr C	Growth	-9.8	-15.6	-4.12	4	3	0	1.8	800 882-0052
State Street Research Invest Tr S	Growth	-8.9	-14.76	-3.16	4	3	0	0.8	800 882-0052
State Street Research Legacy A	Growth	-8.7	-11.89	-1.44	4	3	5.75	1.03	800 882-0052
State Street Research Legacy B	Growth	-8.5	-12.09	-1.85	4	3	0	0.73	800 882-0052
State Street Research Legacy B1	Growth	-9.2	-12.5		4	3	0	1.03	800 882-0052
State Street Research Legacy C	Growth	-9.2	-12.5	-2.16	3	3	0	1.03	800 882-0052
State Street Research Legacy S	Growth	-8.4	-11.48	-1.08	3	3	0	1.03	800 882-0052
State Street Research Lg Cap An A	Growth	-7.6	-10.18	0.39	3	3	5.75	1	800 882-0052
State Street Research Lg Cap An B	Growth	-7.6	-10.64	-0.22	3	3	0	1	800 882-0052

403

Stock Fund Name	Objective	Annualized Return for 1 Year	3 Years	5 Years	Rank Overall	Risk	Max Load	Expense Ratio	Toll-Free/(Toll) Telephone
State Street Research Lg Cap An B1	Growth	-8.2	-10.85	-0.38	3	3	0	1	800 882-0052
State Street Research Lg Cap An C	Growth	-8.2	-10.81	-0.34	3	3	0	1	800 882-0052
State Street Research Lg Cap An S	Growth	-7.5	-9.99	0.61	3	3	0	1	800 882-0052
State Street Research LgCap Val A	Growth/Inc	-11.8	-2	-0.1	3	3	5.75	0.99	800 882-0052
State Street Research LgCap Val B	Growth/Inc	-12.4	-2.72	-0.82	3	3	0	1.99	800 882-0052
State Street Research LgCap Val B1	Growth/Inc	-12.4	-2.72	-0.84	3	3	0	1.99	800 882-0052
State Street Research LgCap Val C	Growth/Inc	-12.4	-2.74	-0.82	3	3	0	1.99	800 882-0052
State Street Research LgCap Val S	Growth/Inc	-11.5	-1.7	0.17	3	3	0	0.99	800 882-0052
State Street Research MidCap Gr A	Agg Growth	-6.8	-14.05	-3.14	3	4	5.75	1.48	800 882-0052
State Street Research MidCap Gr B	Agg Growth	-6.4	-14.25	-3.58	3	4	0	0.48	800 882-0052
State Street Research MidCap Gr B1	Agg Growth	-7	-14.56	-3.77	3	4	0	1.48	800 882-0052
State Street Research MidCap Gr C	Agg Growth	-7.4	-14.63	-3.83	3	4	0	1.48	800 882-0052
State Street Research MidCap Gr S	Agg Growth	-6.4	-13.77	-2.87	3	4	0	1.48	800 882-0052
State Street Research MidCp Val A	Growth	-18.9	9.1	3.37	3	4	5.75	0.95	800 882-0052
State Street Research MidCp Val B	Growth	-18.8	8.65	2.79	3	4	0	0.95	800 882-0052
State Street Research MidCp Val B1	Growth	-19.4	8.35	2.6	3	4	0	1.95	800 882-0052
State Street Research MidCp Val C	Growth	-19.4	8.41	2.66	3	4	0	1.95	800 882-0052
State Street Research MidCp Val S	Growth	-18.6	9.49	3.68	3	4	0	0.95	800 882-0052
Stonebridge Aggressive Growth Fd	Agg Growth	-0.2					0	2.9	800 639-3935
Stonebridge Growth Fund	Growth	-7.4	-14.41	-7.08	3	3	0	1.5	800 639-3935
Strategic Partners Consv Gr A	Growth	2.1	2.2		1	1	5	1.62	800 225-1852
Strategic Partners Consv Gr B	Growth	1.3	1.42		1	1	0	2.37	800 225-1852
Strategic Partners Consv Gr C	Growth	1.3	1.42		1	1	1	2.37	800 225-1852
Strategic Partners Consv Gr Z	Growth	2.3	2.43		1	1	0	1.37	800 225-1852
Strategic Partners Focused Gr A	Growth	-9.7					5	1.61	800 225-1852
Strategic Partners Focused Gr B	Growth	-10.4					0	2.36	800 225-1852
Strategic Partners Focused Gr C	Growth	-10.4					1	2.36	800 225-1852
Strategic Partners Focused Gr Z	Growth	-9.4					0	1.36	800 225-1852
Strategic Partners Focused Val A	Technology	-10.4					5	1.52	800 225-1852
Strategic Partners Focused Val B	Technology	-11					0	2.27	800 225-1852
Strategic Partners Focused Val C	Technology	-11					1	1.27	800 225-1852
Strategic Partners Focused Val Z	Technology	-10.2					0	1.27	800 225-1852
Strategic Partners High Growth A	Growth	-9.6	-7.24		3	3	5	1.57	800 225-1852
Strategic Partners High Growth B	Growth	-10.3	-7.92		3	3	0	2.32	800 225-1852
Strategic Partners High Growth C	Growth	-10.3	-7.92		3	3	1	2.32	800 225-1852
Strategic Partners High Growth Z	Growth	-9.3	-7		3	3	0	1.32	800 225-1852
Strategic Partners Int'l Eq A	Financial	-9.4	-11.83		3	2	5	2	800 225-1852
Strategic Partners Int'l Eq B	Financial	-10	-12.48		4	2	0	2.75	800 225-1852
Strategic Partners Int'l Eq C	Financial	-10	-12.48		4	2	1	2.75	800 225-1852
Strategic Partners Intl Equity	Foreign	-9.2	-11.06	-5.01	4	2	5	1.09	800 442-8748
Strategic Partners Large Cap Gr A	Financial	-11.7	-20.85		4	5	5	1.6	800 225-1852
Strategic Partners Large Cap Gr B	Financial	-12.4	-21.46		4	5	0	2.35	800 225-1852
Strategic Partners Large Cap Gr C	Financial	-12.4	-21.46		4	5	1	2.35	800 225-1852
Strategic Partners Large Cap Val A	Financial	-7.5	1.58		2	3	5	1.6	800 225-1852
Strategic Partners Large Cap Val B	Financial	-8.3	0.78		2	3	0	2.35	800 225-1852
Strategic Partners Large Cap Val C	Financial	-8.3	0.78		2	3	1	2.35	800 225-1852
Strategic Partners Mid-Cap Value A	Technology	-3.8					5	1.66	800 225-1852
Strategic Partners Mid-Cap Value B	Technology	-4.6					0	2.41	800 225-1852
Strategic Partners Mid-Cap Value C	Technology	-4.6					1	2.41	800 225-1852
Strategic Partners Mid-Cap Value Z	Technology	-3.7					0	1.41	800 225-1852
Strategic Partners Moderate Gr A	Growth	-3.2	-2.54		1	2	5	1.48	800 225-1852
Strategic Partners Moderate Gr B	Growth	-3.9	-3.25		1	2	0	2.23	800 225-1852
Strategic Partners Moderate Gr C	Growth	-3.9	-3.25		1	2	1	2.23	800 225-1852
Strategic Partners Moderate Gr Z	Growth	-3	-2.31		1	2	0	1.23	800 225-1852
Strategic Partners New Era Gr A	Technology	-8.1					5	1.67	800 225-1852
Strategic Partners New Era Gr B	Technology	-8.8					0	2.42	800 225-1852
Strategic Partners New Era Gr C	Technology	-8.8					1	2.42	800 225-1852
Strategic Partners New Era Gr Z	Technology	-7.7					0	1.42	800 225-1852

Stock Fund Name	Objective	Annualized Return for			Rank		Max Load	Expense Ratio	Toll-Free/(Toll) Telephone
		1 Year	3 Years	5 Years	Overall	Risk			
Strategic Partners Small Cap Gr A	Financial	-17.2	-17		5	4	5	1.85	800 225-1852
Strategic Partners Small Cap Gr B	Financial	-17.9	-17.66		5	4	0	2.6	800 225-1852
Strategic Partners Small Cap Gr C	Financial	-17.9	-17.66		5	4	1	2.6	800 225-1852
Strategic Partners Small Cap Val A	Financial	-3.5	10.71		1	2	5	1.86	800 225-1852
Strategic Partners Small Cap Val B	Financial	-4.2	9.9		1	2	0	2.61	800 225-1852
Strategic Partners Small Cap Val C	Financial	-4.2	9.9		1	2	1	2.61	800 225-1852
Strategic Partners Total Return A	Financial	11.5	10.08		1	1	5	1.05	800 225-1852
Strategic Partners Total Return B	Financial	10.9	9.52		1	1	0	1.55	800 225-1852
Strategic Partners Total Return C	Financial	10.9	9.52		1	1	1	1.55	800 225-1852
Stratton Growth Fund	Growth/Inc	-13.5	3.54	1.26	3	3	0	1.18	800 634-5726
Stratton Monthly Dividend REIT Shs	Real Est	5.5	17.05	7.69	1	1	0	0.99	800 634-5726
Stratton Small-Cap Value Fund	Small Co	-2.5	11.75	3.06	2	3	0	1.59	800 634-5726
Strong Advisor Common Stock A	Growth	-3.4					5.75	1.52	800 368-1683
Strong Advisor Common Stock B	Growth	-4.2					0	2.26	800 368-1683
Strong Advisor Common Stock C	Growth	-4.3					0	2.28	800 368-1683
Strong Advisor Common Stock Z	Growth	-3.3	-3.97	4.57	1	4	0	1.29	800 368-1683
Strong Advisor Endeavor Lrg Cap A	Growth	-8.3					5.75	2.03	800 368-1683
Strong Advisor Endeavor Lrg Cap B	Growth	-8.6					0	1.95	800 368-1683
Strong Advisor Endeavor Lrg Cap C	Growth	-8.6					0	2.48	800 368-1683
Strong Advisor Focus A	Growth	-11.2					5.75	2.93	800 368-1683
Strong Advisor Focus B	Growth	-11.7					0	2.49	800 368-1683
Strong Advisor Focus C	Growth	-11.7					0	3.94	800 368-1683
Strong Advisor International Core A	Global	-8.6					5.75	2.21	800 368-1683
Strong Advisor International Core B	Global	-8.4					0	2.38	800 368-1683
Strong Advisor International Core C	Global	-8.8					0	2.27	800 368-1683
Strong Advisor Large Company Core A	Growth/Inc						5.75		800 368-1683
Strong Advisor Large Company Core B	Growth/Inc						0		800 368-1683
Strong Advisor Large Company Core C	Growth/Inc						0		800 368-1683
Strong Advisor Large Company Core K	Growth/Inc						0		800 368-1683
Strong Advisor Mid Cap Growth A	Growth	-11.4					5.75	1.62	800 368-1683
Strong Advisor Mid Cap Growth B	Growth	-12.3					0	2.57	800 368-1683
Strong Advisor Mid Cap Growth C	Growth	-12.2					0	2.49	800 368-1683
Strong Advisor Mid-Cap Growth Z	Growth	-11.8	-20.87	-1.21	3	5	0	1.87	800 368-1683
Strong Advisor Select Fund A	Growth	-4.5					5.75	1.6	800 368-1683
Strong Advisor Select Fund B	Growth	-5.1					0	2.39	800 368-1683
Strong Advisor Select Fund C	Growth	-5.1					0	2.22	800 368-1683
Strong Advisor Small Cap Value A	Small Co	-6					5.75	1.58	800 368-1683
Strong Advisor Small Cap Value B	Small Co	-6.8					0	2.41	800 368-1683
Strong Advisor Small Cap Value C	Small Co	-6.8					0	2.58	800 368-1683
Strong Advisor Small Cap Value Z	Small Co	-5.9	10.82	11.74	2	3	0	1.49	800 368-1683
Strong Advisor Technology A	Technology	1.6					5.75	3.28	800 368-1683
Strong Advisor Technology B	Technology	1.3					0	2.5	800 368-1683
Strong Advisor Technology C	Technology	1.3					0	2.5	800 368-1683
Strong Advisor U.S. Value B	Income	-8.4					0	2.15	800 368-1683
Strong Advisor U.S. Value C	Income	-8.3					0	2.16	800 368-1683
Strong Advisor U.S. Value Z	Income	-8	-6.99	0.11	3	2	0	1.91	800 368-1683
Strong Advisor US Sm/Mid-Cap Gr A	Growth	-5.3					5.75	3.18	800 368-1683
Strong Advisor US Sm/Mid-Cap Gr B	Growth	-5					0	3.22	800 368-1683
Strong Advisor US Sm/Mid-Cap Gr C	Growth	-4.9					0	3.19	800 368-1683
Strong Advisor US Value A	Income	-7.9					5.75	1.3	800 368-1683
Strong Advisor US Value K	Income	-8.4					0	1.1	800 368-1683
Strong Aggressive Portfolio	Balanced	-6	-10.93		3	2	0	0.25	800 368-1683
Strong All Cap Value Fund	Growth	-7.7					0	3.56	800 368-1683
Strong Asia Pacific Fund	Pacific	-16.8	-9.73	2.64	3	3	0	2.09	800 368-1683
Strong Balanced Fund	Balanced	-1.8	-7.41	-0.02	2	1	0	1.3	800 368-1683
Strong Blue Chip Inv	Growth	-18.2	-22.26	-4.45	5	3	0	1.51	800 368-1683
Strong Conservative Portfolio	Balanced	0.1					0	0.4	800 368-1683
Strong Discovery Fund	Agg Growth	-2.1	-0.16	2.66	1	3	0	1.5	800 368-1683

405

Stock Fund Name	Objective	Annualized Return for			Rank		Max Load	Expense Ratio	Toll-Free/(Toll) Telephone
		1 Year	3 Years	5 Years	Overall	Risk			
Strong Dividend Income Fd	Income	-11.8	-3.66	2.89	3	2	0	1.44	800 368-1683
Strong Dividend Income K	Income	-12.3					0	2.12	800 368-1683
Strong Dow 30 Value Fund	Growth	-11.1	-5.54	0.13	3	3	0	1.41	800 368-1683
Strong Endeavor Fund	Growth	-8.9					0	2.65	800 368-1683
Strong Energy	Energy/Res	-6.2	-0.34	3.6	2	4	0	2	800 368-1683
Strong Enterprise Adv	Small Co	-8.1	-16.67		3	5	0	2	800 368-1683
Strong Enterprise Inv	Small Co	-8.5	-16.66		4	5	0	1.96	800 368-1683
Strong Growth & Income Adv	Growth/Inc	-8.5	-14.66	-1.03	3	3	0	1.2	800 368-1683
Strong Growth & Income Instl	Growth/Inc	-8	-14.07		4	3	0	0.63	800 368-1683
Strong Growth & Income Inv	Growth/Inc	-8.7	-14.64	-0.93	3	3	0	1.34	800 368-1683
Strong Growth & Income K	Growth/Inc	-8.6					0	0.99	800 368-1683
Strong Growth 20 Adv	Growth	-11.7	-26.17	1.67	4	4	0	1.6	800 368-1683
Strong Growth 20 Inv	Growth	-12	-26.23	1.68	4	4	0	1.91	800 368-1683
Strong Growth Adv	Growth	-7.1	-20.48	0.71	3	4	0	1.56	800 368-1683
Strong Growth C	Growth						0		800 368-1683
Strong Growth Instl	Growth	-6.5	-19.8		4	4	0	0.92	800 368-1683
Strong Growth Inv	Growth	-7.1	-20.37	0.88	3	4	0	1.59	800 368-1683
Strong Index 500 Fund	Growth/Inc	-8.4	-11.26	-1.53	3	3	0	0.95	800 368-1683
Strong Large Cap Core Fund	Growth	-16.1	-10.91		4	3	0	2.46	800 368-1683
Strong Large Cap Growth Fund	Growth	-8.9	-20.41	-2.06	4	4	0	1.24	800 368-1683
Strong Large Company Growth Inv	Growth						0		800 368-1683
Strong Mid Cap Disciplined	Agg Growth	-2.5	7.78		1	3	0	1.48	800 368-1683
Strong Moderate Portfolio	Balanced	-2.4	-6.62		2	1	0	0.37	800 368-1683
Strong Multi-Cap Value Inv	Growth	-16.3	-3.85	-7.46	3	3	0	1.65	800 368-1683
Strong Opportunity Adv	Growth	-11.5	-7.13	3.22	2	4	0	1.58	800 368-1683
Strong Opportunity Inv	Growth	-11.4	-6.91	3.49	2	4	0	1.41	800 368-1683
Strong Overseas Fund	Foreign	-12.6	-19.37		4	3	0	2.12	800 368-1683
Strong Small Company Value Fund	Small Co	13.8					0	2.55	800 368-1683
Strong Strategic Value Fund	Growth	-9.6					0	1.95	800 368-1683
Strong Technology 100 Fund	Technology	-5.6					0	2.63	800 368-1683
Strong U.S. Emerging Growth	Agg Growth	-8.5	-14.66		4	5	0	1.91	800 368-1683
Strong Value Fund	Growth	-3.9	-0.32	1.61	2	2	0	1.65	800 368-1683
Summit Apex Balanced Index Fund	Balanced	-1	-2.93		1	1	0	0.14	888 259-7565
Summit Apex EAFE Internatl Index	Foreign	-13.8					0	1.25	888 259-7565
Summit Apex Everest Fund	Income	-12	2.47		2	3	0	0.9	888 259-7565
Summit Apex Nasdaq 100 Index	Agg Growth	-1.6	-29.78		4	5	0	0.65	888 259-7565
Summit Apex Russell 2000 Sm Cp Idx	Small Co	-8.8	-1.73		3	4	0	0.75	888 259-7565
Summit Apex S&P 500 Index	Growth/Inc	-8.5	-11.25		3	3	0	0.48	888 259-7565
Summit Apex S&P MidCap 400 Index	Growth	-9.7	0.17		3	3	0	0.59	888 259-7565
Summit Apex Total Social Impact	Balanced	-8.4					0	0.75	888 259-7565
SunAmerica Agg Gr Lifestage A	AssetAlloc	-11.2	-12.08		5	2	5.75	0.2	800 858-8850
SunAmerica Agg Gr Lifestage B	AssetAlloc	-11.8	-12.56		5	2	0	0.85	800 858-8850
SunAmerica Agg Gr Lifestage I	AssetAlloc	-11.1	-16.78		5	3	0	0.1	800 858-8850
SunAmerica Agg Gr Lifestage II	AssetAlloc	-11.7					0	0.85	800 858-8850
SunAmerica Bal Assets A	Balanced	-5.2	-10.28	-1.38	3	2	5.75	0.48	800 858-8850
SunAmerica Bal Assets B	Balanced	-5.9	-10.85	-1.89	3	2	0	2.11	800 858-8850
SunAmerica Blue Chip Growth A	Growth	-11.7	-17.23	-2.81	4	3	5.75	1.47	800 858-8850
SunAmerica Blue Chip Growth B	Growth	-12.4	-17.85	-3.5	4	3	0	2.12	800 858-8850
SunAmerica Consrv Gr Lifestage A	AssetAlloc	-1.2	-2.62		2	1	5.75	0.2	800 858-8850
SunAmerica Consrv Gr Lifestage B	AssetAlloc	-1.8	-3.2		1	1	0	0.85	800 858-8850
SunAmerica Consrv Gr Lifestage I	AssetAlloc	-1	-5.99		2	1	0	0.1	800 858-8850
SunAmerica Consrv Gr Lifestage II	AssetAlloc	-1.7					0	0.85	800 858-8850
SunAmerica Focused 2000 Gr A	Growth	-5.4	-10.24	2.37	3	5	5.75	2.18	800 858-8850
SunAmerica Focused 2000 Gr B	Growth	-6	-10.76	1.58	3	5	0	2.76	800 858-8850
SunAmerica Focused 2000 Gr II	Growth	-6.1	-10.85	1.5	3	5	0	3.01	800 858-8850
SunAmerica Focused 2000 Val A	Small Co	-6.2	8.92	5.48	1	3	5.75	1.78	800 858-8850
SunAmerica Focused 2000 Val B	Small Co	-6.7	8.25	4.8	1	3	0	2.43	800 858-8850
SunAmerica Focused 2000 Val II	Small Co	-6.6	8.3	4.83	1	3	0	2.43	800 858-8850

Stock Fund Name	Objective	Annualized Return for			Rank		Max Load	Expense Ratio	Toll-Free/(Toll) Telephone
		1 Year	3 Years	5 Years	Overall	Risk			
SunAmerica Focused Div Strategy A	Agg Growth	-10.2	3.47		3	3	5.75	0.95	800 858-8850
SunAmerica Focused Div Strategy B	Agg Growth	-10.8	2.75		3	3	0	1.6	800 858-8850
SunAmerica Focused Div Strategy II	Agg Growth	-10.8	2.79		3	3	0	1.6	800 858-8850
SunAmerica Focused Gr & Inc A	Growth	-3.6	-8.67	1.89	3	4	5.75	1.45	800 858-8850
SunAmerica Focused Gr & Inc B	Growth	-4.2	-9.27	1.22	3	4	0	2.1	800 858-8850
SunAmerica Focused Gr & Inc II	Growth	-4.3	-9.27	1.2	3	4	0	2.1	800 858-8850
SunAmerica Focused Lrg-Cp Gr A	Growth	-5.8	-12.93		3	3	5.75	1.56	800 858-8850
SunAmerica Focused Lrg-Cp Gr B	Growth	-6.3	-13.49		3	3	0	2.21	800 858-8850
SunAmerica Focused Lrg-Cp Gr II	Growth	-6.3	-13.49		3	3	0	2.21	800 858-8850
SunAmerica Focused Lrg-Cp Val A	Growth	-2.3	-2.81	1.18	2	3	5.75	1.78	800 858-8850
SunAmerica Focused Lrg-Cp Val B	Growth	-3	-3.45	0.56	2	3	0	2.43	800 858-8850
SunAmerica Focused Lrg-Cp Val II	Growth	-2.9	-3.43	0.56	2	3	0	2.43	800 858-8850
SunAmerica Focused Multi-Cp Gr A	Agg Growth	-13.4	-16.57	2.04	4	4	5.75	1.78	800 858-8850
SunAmerica Focused Multi-Cp Gr B	Agg Growth	-14	-17.12	1.37	4	4	0	2.43	800 858-8850
SunAmerica Focused Multi-Cp Gr II	Agg Growth	-14	-17.1	1.37	4	4	0	2.43	800 858-8850
SunAmerica Focused Multi-Cp Val A	Growth	-8.9	5.78		2	3	5.75	1.55	800 858-8850
SunAmerica Focused Multi-Cp Val B	Growth	-9.5	5.11		2	3	0	2.2	800 858-8850
SunAmerica Focused Multi-Cp Val II	Growth	-9.4	5.11		2	3	0	2.2	800 858-8850
SunAmerica Growth & Income A	Growth	-13.3	-15.83	-3.58	5	3	5.75	1.44	800 858-8850
SunAmerica Growth & Income B	Growth	-13.9	-16.39	-4.2	5	3	0	2.07	800 858-8850
SunAmerica Growth & Income II	Growth	-14	-16.42	-4.21	5	3	1	2.09	800 858-8850
SunAmerica Growth Opportunities A	Growth	-13.6	-23.8	0.23	3	5	5.75	1.46	800 858-8850
SunAmerica Growth Opportunities B	Growth	-14.2	-24.35	-0.5	3	5	0	2.13	800 858-8850
SunAmerica Intl Equity A	Foreign	-16	-18.3	-8.85	4	3	5.75	1.96	800 858-8850
SunAmerica Intl Equity B	Foreign	-16.4	-18.78	-9.41	5	3	0	2.56	800 858-8850
SunAmerica Intl Equity II	Foreign	-16.4	-18.78	-9.41	4	3	0	2.56	800 858-8850
SunAmerica Mod Gr Lifestage B	AssetAlloc	-7.4	-7.59		3	2	0	0.85	800 858-8850
SunAmerica Mod Gr Lifestage I	AssetAlloc	-7.7	-11		3	2	0	0.1	800 858-8850
SunAmerica Mod Gr Lifestage II	AssetAlloc	-7.4					0	0.85	800 858-8850
SunAmerica New Century A	Small Co	-9.4	-19.53	-0.66	3	4	5.75	1.43	800 858-8850
SunAmerica New Century B	Small Co	-10.1	-20.07	-1.31	4	4	0	2.14	800 858-8850
SunAmerica New Century II	Small Co	-9.8	-21.05	-2.04	4	4	1	2.14	800 858-8850
SunAmerica Science & Tech A	Technology	-5	-30.37		4	5	5.75	1.5	800 858-8850
SunAmerica Science & Tech B	Technology	-5.8	-30.87		4	5	0	2.15	800 858-8850
SunAmerica Science & Tech I	Technology	-5	-30.3		4	5	0	1.4	800 858-8850
SunAmerica Science & Tech II	Technology	-6					0	2.15	800 858-8850
SunAmerica Stock Index A	Growth	-8.7	-11.77		3	3	5.75	0.75	800 858-8850
SunAmerica Stock Index B	Growth	-9.3	-12.17		4	3	0	1.4	800 858-8850
SunAmerica Stock Index II	Growth	-9.2					0	1.4	800 858-8850
SunAmerica Tax Managed Equity A	Growth	-10.7	-11.61		4	3	5.75	1.45	800 858-8850
SunAmerica Value A	Growth	0	3.47	3.45	1	2	5.75	1.78	800 858-8850
SunAmerica Value B	Growth	-0.7	2.81	2.81	1	2	0	2.43	800 858-8850
SunAmerica Value II	Growth	-0.7	2.83	2.81	1	2	0	2.43	800 858-8850
T. Rowe Price Balanced Fd	Balanced	-0.4	-1.02	2.72	1	1	0	0.84	800 638-5660
T. Rowe Price Blue Chip Growth Adv	Growth	-6.4	-10.96	-0.4	3	3	0	0.98	800 638-5660
T. Rowe Price Blue Chip Growth Fd	Growth	-6.4	-10.98	-0.42	3	3	0	1.01	800 638-5660
T. Rowe Price Blue Chip Growth R	Growth	-6.6	-11.03	-0.46		3	0	1.35	800 638-5660
T. Rowe Price Cap Appreciation	Growth/Inc	0.5	11.66	9.52	1	1	0	0.87	800 638-5660
T. Rowe Price Cap Opportunity	Growth	-8.1	-9.69	-3.33	3	3	0	1.56	800 638-5660
T. Rowe Price Developing Tech	Technology	-6.7					0	1.5	800 638-5660
T. Rowe Price Diversified Sm-Cap Gr	Small Co	-10.7	-10.58	-2.7	3	5	0	1.25	800 638-5660
T. Rowe Price Dividend Growth	Growth/Inc	-8.8	-2.54	-0.46	3	2	0	0.89	800 638-5660
T. Rowe Price Emerging Mkts Stk	Foreign	-7.4	-8.36	0.77	3	4	0	1.5	800 638-5660
T. Rowe Price Equity Income Fd	Income	-8.1	1.98	2.97	2	2	0	0.81	800 638-5660
T. Rowe Price Equity Income R	Growth	-8.3	1.89	2.91		2	0	1.18	800 638-5660
T. Rowe Price Equity Index 500	Growth/Inc	-8.2	-11.07	-1.32	3	3	0	0.4	800 638-5660
T. Rowe Price European Stk	European	-9	-11.72	-4.09	4	3	0	1.16	800 638-5660
T. Rowe Price Extended Eq Mkt Indx	Growth/Inc	-4.9	-7.16	-0.52	3	4	0	0.4	800 638-5660

Stock Fund Name	Objective	Annualized Return for			Rank		Max Load	Expense Ratio	Toll-Free/(Toll) Telephone
		1 Year	3 Years	5 Years	Overall	Risk			
T. Rowe Price Financial Services	Financial	-3.4	7.12	6.2	2	3	0	1.04	800 638-5660
T. Rowe Price Global Stock Fd	Global	-10.4	-11.48	-1.52	4	3	0	1.2	800 638-5660
T. Rowe Price Global Technology	Technology	-3.7					0	1.5	800 638-5660
T. Rowe Price Growth & Inc	Growth/Inc	-10.6	-4.42	-1.23	3	3	0	0.86	800 638-5660
T. Rowe Price Growth Stock Adv	Growth	-5.5	-8.27	1.48		3	0	0.91	800 638-5660
T. Rowe Price Growth Stock Fd	Growth	-5.4	-8.17	1.56	2	3	0	0.8	800 638-5660
T. Rowe Price Growth Stock R	Growth	-5.7	-8.27	1.48		3	0	1.35	800 638-5660
T. Rowe Price Health Sciences	Health	2.2	5.17	8.34	2	4	0	1.09	800 638-5660
T. Rowe Price Instl Emer Mkt Eqty	Foreign						0	1.1	800 638-5660
T. Rowe Price Instl Foreign Eq	Foreign	-13.2	-14.55	-4.76		3	0	0.76	800 638-5660
T. Rowe Price Instl Lrg Cap Gr	Growth	-3					0	0.65	800 638-5660
T. Rowe Price Instl Mid-Cap Eq Gr	Growth	-7.2					0	0.66	800 638-5660
T. Rowe Price Intl Discovery	Foreign	-2.4	-14.91	6.88	2	3	0	1.47	800 638-5660
T. Rowe Price Intl Equity Index Fd	Foreign	-11.8					0	0.5	800 638-5660
T. Rowe Price Intl Gr & Inc Adv	Foreign	-9.5	-6.37			2	0	1.15	800 638-5660
T. Rowe Price Intl Gr & Inc Fd	Foreign	-9.6	-6.41			2	0	1.25	800 638-5660
T. Rowe Price Intl Gr & Inc R	Foreign	-9.8	-6.45			2	0	1.4	800 638-5660
T. Rowe Price Intl Stock Adv	Foreign	-14.1	-15.09	-5.15	5	3	0	1.15	800 638-5660
T. Rowe Price Intl Stock Fd	Foreign	-13.8	-15	-5.11	5	3	0	0.98	800 638-5660
T. Rowe Price Intl Stock R	Foreign	-14.1	-15.09	-5.16		3	0	1.4	800 638-5660
T. Rowe Price Japan Fund	Pacific	-25.9	-25.6	-3.7	5	3	0	1.51	800 638-5660
T. Rowe Price Latin America	Foreign	-6.5	-1.26	-0.28	2	4	0	1.61	800 638-5660
T. Rowe Price Media & Telecomm	Technology	6.5	-12.33	6.29	3	5	0	1.23	800 638-5660
T. Rowe Price Mid-Cap Growth Adv	Growth	-7.4	-2.14	5.46	2	4	0	1.1	800 638-5660
T. Rowe Price Mid-Cap Growth Fd	Growth	-7.2	-2	5.54	2	4	0	0.91	800 638-5660
T. Rowe Price Mid-Cap Growth R	Growth	-7.5	-2.1	5.49		4	0	1.4	800 638-5660
T. Rowe Price Mid-Cap Value Adv	Global	-6.8	11.65	7.4		3	0	1.07	800 638-5660
T. Rowe Price Mid-Cap Value Fd	Global	-6.8	11.66	7.41	2	3	0	0.97	800 638-5660
T. Rowe Price Mid-Cap Value R	Global	-7	11.58	7.36		3	0	1.4	800 638-5660
T. Rowe Price New Amer Growth	Growth	-5.5	-11.43	-4.71	3	4	0	1.04	800 638-5660
T. Rowe Price New Asia Fd	Pacific	-13.9	-12.22	4.3	4	4	0	1.23	800 638-5660
T. Rowe Price New Era	Energy/Res	-8.2	1.76	3.81	2	3	0	0.75	800 638-5660
T. Rowe Price New Horizons	Small Co	-5.8	-5.29	2.06	3	5	0	0.97	800 638-5660
T. Rowe Price Personal Strategy Bal	Balanced	0	1.06	3.39	1	1	0	0.97	800 638-5660
T. Rowe Price Personal Strategy Gr	Growth	-3.7	-1.89	2.22	1	2	0	1	800 638-5660
T. Rowe Price Personal Strategy Inc	Balanced	2.8	3.56	4.29	1	1	0	0.8	800 638-5660
T. Rowe Price Real Estate	Real Est	5.8	14.4	7.5	1	1	0	1	800 638-5660
T. Rowe Price Retirement 2010	Other						0	0.74	800 638-5660
T. Rowe Price Retirement 2020	Other						0	0.81	800 638-5660
T. Rowe Price Retirement 2030	Other						0	0.84	800 638-5660
T. Rowe Price Retirement 2040	Other						0	0.84	800 638-5660
T. Rowe Price Retirement Income	Other						0	0.63	800 638-5660
T. Rowe Price Science & Tech Adv	Technology	-5.6	-31.64	-6.2	3	5	0	1.07	800 638-5660
T. Rowe Price Science & Tech Fd	Technology	-5.7	-31.66	-6.23	3	5	0	1.22	800 638-5660
T. Rowe Price Small Cap Stock Adv	Small Co	-8.1	4.05	4.11	2	3	0	1.2	800 638-5660
T. Rowe Price Small Cap Stock Fd	Small Co	-7.9	4.2	4.19	2	3	0	0.98	800 638-5660
T. Rowe Price Small Cap Value Adv	Small Co	-3.8	14.48	5.96	1	2	0	1.04	800 638-5660
T. Rowe Price Small Cap Value Fd	Small Co	-3.7	14.64	6.04	1	2	0	0.92	800 638-5660
T. Rowe Price Spectrum Growth	Growth	-8.7	-6.04	0.68	2	3	0	0.85	800 638-5660
T. Rowe Price Spectrum Intl	Foreign	-11.5	-12.97	-2.81	3	3	0	1.14	800 638-5660
T. Rowe Price Tax Eff Balanced	Balanced	2.9	-0.51	4.62		1	0	1.08	800 638-5660
T. Rowe Price Tax Eff Growth	Growth	-6.3	-10.74		3	3	0	1.1	800 638-5660
T. Rowe Price Tax Eff Mult-Cap Gr	Growth	-8.8					0	1.25	800 638-5660
T. Rowe Price Total Eq Mkt Index	Growth/Inc	-7.6	-9.85	-1.37	3	3	0	0.4	800 638-5660
T. Rowe Price Value Adv	Growth/Inc	-11.7	0.3	2.37	2	3	0	1.07	800 638-5660
T. Rowe Price Value Fd	Growth/Inc	-11.7	0.46	2.45	2	3	0	1.02	800 638-5660
TCW Galileo Aggressive Gr Eq I	Agg Growth	5.4					0	1.24	800 386-3829
TCW Galileo Aggressive Gr Eq K	Agg Growth						0		800 386-3829

Stock Fund Name	Objective	Annualized Return for			Rank		Max Load	Expense Ratio	Toll-Free/(Toll) Telephone
		1 Year	3 Years	5 Years	Overall	Risk			
TCW Galileo Aggressive Gr Eq N	Agg Growth	5	-25.17		3	5	0	1.63	800 386-3829
TCW Galileo Asia Pacific Equities I	Pacific	-18.1	-10.06	7.92	4	4	0	2.14	800 386-3829
TCW Galileo Convertible Sec I	Converts	-2.8					0	1.09	800 386-3829
TCW Galileo Diversified Value N	Growth	-10.1	-2.6	-0.89	3	3	0	0.9	800 386-3829
TCW Galileo Emerging Markets Eq I	Foreign	-11.4	-9.11	-1.05	3	4	0	1.64	800 386-3829
TCW Galileo European Gr Equities I	European	-16.4	-20.69	-8.84	5	4	0	1.84	800 386-3829
TCW Galileo Income and Growth N	Growth/Inc	-7.5	6.34	5.96	1	2	0	1.21	800 386-3829
TCW Galileo Large Cap Growth I	Growth	-4.6	-23.64	-2.04	3	4	0	1.53	800 386-3829
TCW Galileo Large Cap Growth N	Growth	-4.8	-23.73	-1.62	3	4	0	1.53	800 386-3829
TCW Galileo Large Cap Value I	Growth	-13.5					0	0.74	800 386-3829
TCW Galileo Large Cap Value K	Growth						0		800 386-3829
TCW Galileo Large Cap Value N	Growth	-14.1	-6.95	1.26	3	3	0	1.38	800 386-3829
TCW Galileo Opportunity I	Small Co	-13.2	6.12	6.73	3	5	0	1.2	800 386-3829
TCW Galileo Opportunity K	Small Co						0		800 386-3829
TCW Galileo Opportunity N	Small Co	-13.4	5.78	6.37	3	3	0	1.37	800 386-3829
TCW Galileo Select Equities I	Growth	-0.3					0	0.87	800 386-3829
TCW Galileo Select Equities N	Growth	-0.6	-15.82	2.72	3	5	0	1.21	800 386-3829
TCW Galileo Select Intl Equity K	Growth						0		800 386-3829
TCW Galileo Select Intl Gr Equity I	Foreign	-15.7	-19.98		5	3	0	1.18	800 386-3829
TCW Galileo Small Cap Growth I	Small Co	-17.5					0	1.25	800 386-3829
TCW Galileo Small Cap Growth N	Small Co	-17.6	-29.76	-7.69	4	5	0	1.53	800 386-3829
TCW Galileo Small Cap Value I	Small Co	-20.6					0	1.51	800 386-3829
TCW Galileo Small Cap Value K	Small Co						0		800 386-3829
TCW Galileo Small Cap Value N	Small Co	-20.6					0	1.52	800 386-3829
TCW Galileo Technology N	Technology	-10.1					0	1.98	800 386-3829
TCW Galileo Value Opportunities I	Growth	-12.5					0	1	800 386-3829
TCW Galileo Value Opportunities K	Growth						0		800 386-3829
TCW Galileo Value Opportunities N	Growth	-12.7					0	1.29	800 386-3829
TIAA-CREF Equity Index Fund	Growth	-7.8	-10.06		3	3	0	0.26	800 842-2252
TIAA-CREF Growth & Income	Growth/Inc	-10.1	-12.48	-1.35	3	3	0	0.43	800 842-2252
TIAA-CREF Growth Equity	Growth	-9.6	-21.57	-5.54	3	4	0	0.45	800 842-2252
TIAA-CREF Inst Infltn Lnk Bd Retail	Other						0		800 842-2252
TIAA-CREF International Equity	Foreign	-11.7	-15.07	-2.5	3	3	0	0.49	800 842-2252
TIAA-CREF Managed Allocation	AssetAlloc	0.5	-5.7	1.7	2	2	0	0	800 842-2252
TIAA-CREF Social Choice Equity	Growth	-6.7	-9.94		3	3	0	0.27	800 842-2252
Target Large Cap Growth	Growth	-11	-21.07	0.66	3	5	0	0.81	800 442-8748
Target Large Cap Value	Growth	-7	2.25	0.55	2	3	0	0.8	800 442-8748
Target Small Cap Growth	Small Co	-16.4	-15.75	-5.7	5	4	0	0.99	800 442-8748
Target Small Cap Value	Small Co	-2.7	12.06	5.9	1	3	0	0.88	800 442-8748
Teberg Fund (The)	Growth/Inc	8.5					0	2.5	866 209-1964
Templeton Capital Accumulator	Growth	-13.4	-5.41	0.05	3	3	9	1.11	800 632-2350
Templeton Developing Markets A	Foreign	-1.5	-2.68	-0.47	2	3	5.75	2.24	800 632-2350
Templeton Developing Markets Adv	Foreign	-0.9	-2.27	-0.11	2	3	0	1.89	800 632-2350
Templeton Developing Markets B	Foreign	-2.1	-3.29		2	3	0	2.88	800 632-2350
Templeton Developing Markets C	Foreign	-2.2	-3.29	-1.13	2	3	1	2.89	800 632-2350
Templeton Developing Markets R	Foreign	-1.8	-2.87	-0.68	2	3	0	2.39	800 632-2350
Templeton Foreign A	Foreign	-12.2	-2.64	0.93	3	2	5.75	1.22	800 632-2350
Templeton Foreign Adv	Foreign	-12	-2.41	0.28	3	2	0	0.97	800 632-2350
Templeton Foreign B	Foreign	-12.8	-3.35		3	2	0	1.97	800 632-2350
Templeton Foreign C	Foreign	-12.9	-3.35	0.2	3	2	1	1.97	800 632-2350
Templeton Foreign R	Foreign	-12.3	-2.85	0.68	3	2	0	1.47	800 632-2350
Templeton Foreign Smaller Co A	Foreign	-9.9	-1.92	0.28	3	3	5.75	1.63	800 632-2350
Templeton Foreign Smaller Co Adv	Foreign	-9.7	-1.68	0.53	3	3	0	1.35	800 632-2350
Templeton Foreign Smaller Co B	Foreign	-10.7	-2.72		2	3	0	2.38	800 632-2350
Templeton Foreign Smaller Co C	Foreign	-10.8	-2.72		3	3	1	2.31	800 632-2350
Templeton Global Long-Short A	Other	-10.4					5.75	2.85	800 632-2350
Templeton Global Long-Short B	Other	-11.1					0	3.51	800 632-2350
Templeton Global Opport Trust A	Global	-15.1	-8.66	-2.1	3	3	5.75	1.46	800 632-2350

Stock Fund Name	Objective	Annualized Return for			Rank		Max Load	Expense Ratio	Toll-Free/(Toll) Telephone
		1 Year	3 Years	5 Years	Overall	Risk			
Templeton Global Opport Trust B	Global	-15.7	-9.33		3	3	0	2.2	800 632-2350
Templeton Global Opport Trust C	Global	-15.7	-9.47	-2.87	4	3	1	2.21	800 632-2350
Templeton Global Smaller Cos A	Global	-14	-2.33	-3.75	3	3	5.75	1.44	800 632-2350
Templeton Global Smaller Cos Adv	Global	-13.7	-2.1	-5.83	3	3	0	1.19	800 632-2350
Templeton Global Smaller Cos B	Global	-14.6	-3.08		3	3	0	2.18	800 632-2350
Templeton Global Smaller Cos C	Global	-14.7	-3.08	-4.45	3	3	1	2.14	800 632-2350
Templeton Growth A	Global	-6.9	1.39	3.64	2	2	5.75	1.12	800 632-2350
Templeton Growth Adv	Global	-6.7	1.65	1.48	2	2	0	0.87	800 632-2350
Templeton Growth B	Global	-7.6	0.64		2	2	0	1.87	800 632-2350
Templeton Growth C	Global	-7.6	0.66	2.87	3	2	1	1.87	800 632-2350
Templeton Growth R	Global	-7.2	1.12	3.33	2	2	0	1.37	800 632-2350
Templeton Inst-Emerg Markets Mkt	Foreign	-0.8	-2.22	0.81	2	3	0	1.46	800 632-2350
Templeton Inst-Foreign Eq Prim	Foreign	-13.2					0	0.82	800 632-2350
Templeton Inst-Foreign Eq Svc	Foreign	-13.2	-6.87		3	3	0	0.81	800 632-2350
Templeton International (ex EM) A	European	-13.4	-4.04	-2.64	3	3	5.75	1.81	800 632-2350
Templeton International (ex EM) Adv	European	-13.1	-3.72	-2.72	3	3	0	1.46	800 632-2350
Templeton International (ex EM) C	European	-13.9	-4.61	-3.2	3	3	1	2.45	800 632-2350
Templeton World A	Global	-10.3	-3.56	0.79	3	2	5.75	1.1	800 632-2350
Templeton World B	Global	-11	-4.29		3	2	0	1.84	800 632-2350
Templeton World C	Global	-11.1	-4.29	0.04	3	2	1	1.85	800 632-2350
Texas Capital-Value & Growth	Growth/Inc	-11.2	11.76	-3.58	3	4	4.5	1.92	800 880-0324
The Contrarian Fd	Global	9.4	6.9	3.37	1	2	0	1.72	800 766-3863
The Information Age Fd	Technology	14.2	-26.92	4.04	3	5	0	1.68	800 766-3863
The Japan Fund S	Pacific	-22	-21.83	2.49	3	3	0	1.08	866 995-2726
Third Avenue Real Estate Value	Real Est	8	17.14			1	0	1.5	800 443-1021
Third Avenue Sm Cap Value Fund	Small Co	-7.6	8.84	5.44	1	3	0	1.23	800 443-1021
Third Avenue Value Fund	Growth	-11.2	0.65	5.2	2	2	0	1.07	800 443-1021
Third Millenium Russia Fund	Foreign	23.5	19.12		1	5	5.75		800 527-9525
Thomas White American Enterprise	Growth	-14	-7.3		3	2	0	1.47	800 811-0535
Thomas White American Oppor	Growth	-7.5	3.04		2	2	0	1.54	800 811-0535
Thomas White International	Foreign	-14.1	-9.93	-2.75	4	2	0	1.66	800 811-0535
Thompson Plumb Balanced	Balanced	-4	3.87	7.08	1	2	0	1.17	800 841-0199
Thompson Plumb Growth	Growth	-9.8	6.98	8.52	2	4	0	1.2	800 841-0199
Thornburg Core Growth A	Growth	7.5					4.5	1.44	800 847-0200
Thornburg Core Growth C	Growth	6.1					0	2.19	800 847-0200
Thornburg International Value A	Foreign	-12.2	-5.82	4.29	3	2	4.5	0.85	800 847-0200
Thornburg International Value C	Foreign	-13					0	1.61	800 847-0200
Thornburg Value Fund A	Growth	-6.7	-7.62	3.89	2	3	4.5	0.49	800 847-0200
Thornburg Value Fund B	Growth/Inc	-7.5	-8.43			3	0	0.33	800 847-0200
Thornburg Value Fund C	Growth	-7.4	-8.33	3.12	2	3	0	0.27	800 847-0200
Thornburg Value Fund I	Growth	-6.2	-7.21	4.44	2	3	0	1.03	800 847-0200
Thurlow Growth Fd	Growth	-1.8					0	1.99	888 848-7569
Timothy Plan Small Cap Value A	Small Co	-18.1	0.38	0.89	3	3	5.5	1.97	800 846-7526
Timothy Plan Small Cap Value B	Small Co	-18.6	-0.35	0.08	3	3	0	2.72	800 846-7526
Tocqueville Alexis Fund	Growth	-1.9	-1.61	3.56	2	2	0	1.26	800 697-3863
Tocqueville Fund	Growth	-10.3	-1.4	0.02	3	3	0	1.4	800 697-3863
Tocqueville Gold Fund	Prec Metal	-1.2	32.79		2	5	0	1.57	800 697-3863
Tocqueville Intl Value Fund	Foreign	-17.8	-3.25	0.34	3	3	4	1.74	800 697-3863
Tocqueville Small Cap Value Fund	Small Co	-3.6	4.19	9.67	3	4	0	1.42	800 697-3863
Torray Fund	Growth/Inc	-7.2	-2.12	2.22	2	3	0	1.07	800 443-3036
Touchstone Emerging Growth A	Small Co	-9.8	4.19	11.34	2	4	5.75	1.5	800 638-8194
Touchstone Emerging Growth B	Small Co	-11					0	2.25	800 638-8194
Touchstone Emerging Growth C	Small Co	-11	3.16	10.41	2	4	0	2.25	800 638-8194
Touchstone Enhanced 30 A	Growth	-9.4	-7.67		3	3	5.75	1	800 638-8194
Touchstone Enhanced 30 B	Growth	-10.2					0	1.75	800 638-8194
Touchstone Enhanced 30 C	Growth	-9.7	-8.22		3	3	0	1.75	800 638-8194
Touchstone Intl Equity Fund A	Foreign	-25.5	-23.96	-11.16	4	3	5.75	1.6	800 638-8194
Touchstone Intl Equity Fund B	Foreign	-26.3					0	2.35	800 638-8194

Stock Fund Name	Objective	Annualized Return for			Rank		Max Load	Expense Ratio	Toll-Free/(Toll) Telephone
		1 Year	3 Years	5 Years	Overall	Risk			
Touchstone Intl Equity Fund C	Foreign	-26.3	-24.48	-11.84	4	3	0	2.35	800 638-8194
Touchstone Strat Tr Gr Opps A	Growth	-1.4	-18.78	2.7	3	4	5.75	1.82	800 638-8194
Touchstone Strat Tr Gr Opps B	Growth	-2.6					0	3.16	800 638-8194
Touchstone Strat Tr Gr Opps C	Growth	-2.4	-19.64		3	4	0	2.98	800 638-8194
Touchstone Strat Tr Lrg Cap Gr A	Growth	-15.9	-23.16	-10.66	5	4	5.75	1.31	800 638-8194
Touchstone Strat Tr Lrg Cap Gr B	Growth	-16.7					0	2.41	800 638-8194
Touchstone Strat Tr Lrg Cap Gr C	Growth	-16.4	-23.92	-11.58	5	4	0	2.41	800 638-8194
Touchstone Strat Tr Sm Cap Gr A	Small Co						5.75	1.95	800 638-8194
Touchstone Strat Tr Sm Cap Gr B	Small Co						0	2.7	800 638-8194
Touchstone Strat Tr Sm Cap Gr C	Small Co						0	2.7	800 638-8194
Touchstone Value Plus A	Growth	-12	-5.87	0.6	3	3	5.75	1.3	800 638-8194
Touchstone Value Plus B	Growth	-12.6					0	2.05	800 638-8194
Touchstone Value Plus C	Growth	-12.6	-6.69	-0.28	3	3	0	2.05	800 638-8194
Trainer Wortham First Mutual	Growth	-15.3	-18.55	-1.56	5	4	0	1.94	800 441-6580
Transamerica Premier Agg Grwth A	Agg Growth	-2.3	-18.25	2.47		5	5.25	1.5	800 892-7587
Transamerica Premier Agg Grwth Inv	Agg Growth	-2.4	-18.21	2.54	3	5	0	1.5	800 892-7587
Transamerica Premier Balanced A	Balanced	-3.5	-1.9	5.34		1	5.25	1.55	800 892-7587
Transamerica Premier Balanced Inv	Balanced	-3.2	-1.55	5.66	1	1	0	1.55	800 892-7587
Transamerica Premier Core Eq A	Other	-13.3	-7.79	0.27		3	0	1.3	800 892-7587
Transamerica Premier Core Eq Inv	Other	-13.2	-7.71	0.35		3	0	1.2	800 892-7587
Transamerica Premier Equity A	Growth	-7.4	-14.91	-2		4	5.25	1.6	800 892-7587
Transamerica Premier Equity Inv	Growth	-7.2	-14.69	-1.78	3	4	0	1.6	800 892-7587
Transamerica Premier Growth Opp A	Small Co	-14	-17.35	7.38		5	5.25	1.6	800 892-7587
Transamerica Premier Growth Opp Inv	Small Co	-14.2	-17.35	7.46	4	5	0	1.5	800 892-7587
Transamerica Premier Index A	Growth	-8.5	-11.18	-1.47		3	5.25		800 892-7587
Transamerica Premier Index Inv	Growth	-8.3	-10.97	-3.39	3	3	0	0.25	800 892-7587
Turner Core Value	Growth/Inc	-11	4.16	2.99	3	3	0	1.1	800 224-6312
Turner Core Value Fund	Growth	-8.4	-17.82	6.38	3	5	0	1.04	800 224-6312
Turner Future Financial Svcs	Financial	-4.6	7.04	1.82	2	3	0	2.29	800 224-6312
Turner Large Cap Value	Growth/Inc	-10.8	-5.32	0.77	3	2	0	3.56	800 224-6312
Turner Micro Cap Growth Fund	Small Co	-12.5	7.46	31.08	3	4	0	1.4	800 224-6312
Turner Small Cap Growth Fund	Small Co	-6.3	-15.64	0.71	3	5	0	0.96	800 224-6312
Turner Small Cap Value	Small Co	-17.8	5.8	7.54	3	4	0	1.28	800 224-6312
Turner Strategic Value & High Inc I	Growth/Inc						0		800 224-6312
Turner Technology Fund	Technology	-9.3	-40.14		4	5	0	1.58	800 224-6312
Turner Top 20 Fund	Growth	-8.9	-33.15		4	5	0	1.32	800 224-6312
Tweedy Browne American Value	Growth	-11.5	1.73	1.15	3	2	0	1.36	800 432-4789
Tweedy Browne Global Value	Global	-15.5	-2.47	2.68	3	2	0	1.37	800 432-4789
UBS Enhanced NASDAQ 100 A	Agg Growth	-0.9	-28.82		3	5	5.5	1.28	888 793-8637
UBS Enhanced NASDAQ 100 B	Agg Growth	-1.8	-29.37		3	5	0	2.03	888 793-8637
UBS Enhanced NASDAQ 100 C	Agg Growth	-1.8	-29.37		3	5	1	2.03	888 793-8637
UBS Enhanced NASDAQ 100 Y	Agg Growth	-0.9	-28.67		3	5	0	1.03	888 793-8637
UBS Enhanced S&P 500 A	Growth	-9.2	-11.52		4	3	3	0.98	888 793-8637
UBS Enhanced S&P 500 B	Growth	-9.6	-11.9		4	3	0	1.38	888 793-8637
UBS Enhanced S&P 500 C	Growth	-9.6	-11.89		4	3	1	1.38	888 793-8637
UBS Enhanced S&P 500 Y	Growth	-9	-11.31		3	3	0	0.73	888 793-8637
UBS Financial Services A	Financial	-6.5	3.1	-1.07	3	3	5.5	1.15	888 793-8637
UBS Financial Services B	Financial	-7.4	2.29	-1.83	3	3	0	1.92	888 793-8637
UBS Financial Services C	Financial	-7.3	2.31	-1.82	3	3	1	1.9	888 793-8637
UBS Financial Services Y	Financial	-6.5					0	1.04	888 793-8637
UBS Global Allocation A	Global	1.1	5.08	3.31	1	1	5.5	1.35	888 793-8637
UBS Global Allocation B	Global	0.3					0	1.99	888 793-8637
UBS Global Allocation C	Global	0.3					1	1.99	888 793-8637
UBS Global Allocation Y	Global	1.3	5.25	3.54	1	1	0	0.99	888 793-8637
UBS Global Equity A	Global	-9.5	-4.45	-1.22	3	3	5.5	1.25	888 793-8637
UBS Global Equity B	Global	-10.2					0	2	888 793-8637
UBS Global Equity C	Global	-10.2					1	2	888 793-8637
UBS Global Equity Y	Global	-9.2	-4.16	-0.91	3	3	0	1	888 793-8637

Stock Fund Name	Objective	Annualized Return for			Rank		Max Load	Expense Ratio	Toll-Free/(Toll) Telephone
		1 Year	3 Years	5 Years	Overall	Risk			
UBS International Equity A	Foreign	-13.5	-9.43	-4.25	4	2	5.5	1.25	888 793-8637
UBS International Equity B	Foreign	-10.4					0	2.37	888 793-8637
UBS International Equity C	Foreign	-14.4					1	2.3	888 793-8637
UBS International Equity Y	Foreign	-13.5	-9.3	-4.04	4	2	0	1.2	888 793-8637
UBS PACE International Emerg Mkts A	Foreign	-12.7					5.5	1.87	888 793-8637
UBS PACE International Emerg Mkts B	Foreign	-13.6					0	2.66	888 793-8637
UBS PACE International Emerg Mkts C	Foreign	-13.6					1	2.67	888 793-8637
UBS PACE International Emerg Mkts P	Foreign	-12.6	-13.13	-5.84	4	4	0	1.5	888 793-8637
UBS PACE International Equity A	Foreign	-14.6					5.5	1.52	888 793-8637
UBS PACE International Equity B	Foreign	-15.3					0	2.37	888 793-8637
UBS PACE International Equity C	Foreign	-15.3					1	2.3	888 793-8637
UBS PACE International Equity P	Foreign	-14.4	-16	-5.83	4	3	0	1.3	888 793-8637
UBS PACE International Equity Y	Foreign	-14.2					0	1.2	888 793-8637
UBS PACE Large Company Gr Equity A	Growth	-8					5.5	1.2	888 793-8637
UBS PACE Large Company Gr Equity B	Growth	-8.8					0	2.02	888 793-8637
UBS PACE Large Company Gr Equity C	Growth	-8.8					1	1.99	888 793-8637
UBS PACE Large Company Gr Equity P	Growth	-7.9	-20.71	-5.95	4	4	0	0.99	888 793-8637
UBS PACE Large Company Gr Equity Y	Growth	-7.7					0	0.88	888 793-8637
UBS PACE Large Company Value A	Growth/Inc	-10.3					5.5	1.14	888 793-8637
UBS PACE Large Company Value B	Growth/Inc	-11					0	1.92	888 793-8637
UBS PACE Large Company Value C	Growth/Inc	-11					1	1.92	888 793-8637
UBS PACE Large Company Value P	Growth/Inc	-10	-3.45	-1.98	3	2	0	0.89	888 793-8637
UBS PACE Large Company Value Y	Growth/Inc	-10					0	0.84	888 793-8637
UBS PACE Small/Medium Comp Gr Eq A	Growth	-4					5.5	1.3	888 793-8637
UBS PACE Small/Medium Comp Gr Eq B	Growth	-4.9					0	2.8	888 793-8637
UBS PACE Small/Medium Comp Gr Eq C	Growth	-4.8					1	2.8	888 793-8637
UBS PACE Small/Medium Comp Gr Eq P	Growth	-3.7	-10.66	7.13	3	5	0	0.98	888 793-8637
UBS PACE Small/Medium Comp Value A	Small Co	-21.4					5.5	1.37	888 793-8637
UBS PACE Small/Medium Comp Value B	Small Co	-22.1					0	2.16	888 793-8637
UBS PACE Small/Medium Comp Value C	Small Co	-22.1					1	2.15	888 793-8637
UBS PACE Small/Medium Comp Value P	Small Co	-14.7	10.01	1.21	3	3	0	1.05	888 793-8637
UBS PACE Small/Medium Comp Value Y	Small Co	-21.2					0	1.13	888 793-8637
UBS S&P 500 Index Fund A	Growth	-8.7	-11.42	-1.75	3	3	5.5	0.63	888 793-8637
UBS S&P 500 Index Fund C	Growth	-9.4	-12.75		4	3	1	1.38	888 793-8637
UBS S&P 500 Index Fund Y	Growth	-8.4	-11.19	-1.56	3	3	0	0.39	888 793-8637
UBS Tactical Allocation A	AssetAlloc	-9	-9.9	-0.56	3	3	5.5	0.95	888 793-8637
UBS Tactical Allocation B	AssetAlloc	-9.6	-10.58	-2.41	3	3	0	1.71	888 793-8637
UBS Tactical Allocation C	AssetAlloc	-9.6	-10.58	-1.22	3	3	1	1.69	888 793-8637
UBS Tactical Allocation Y	AssetAlloc	-8.6	-9.61	-0.14	3	3	0	0.61	888 793-8637
UBS US Balanced Fund A	Balanced	0.2	5.5	3.18	1	1	5.5	1.05	888 793-8637
UBS US Balanced Fund B	Balanced	-0.6					0	1.8	888 793-8637
UBS US Balanced Fund C	Balanced	-0.5					1	1.8	888 793-8637
UBS US Balanced Fund Y	Balanced	0.5	5.79	3.5	1	1	0	0.8	888 793-8637
UBS US Equity A	Growth/Inc	-7.2	-0.78	-0.71	2	3	5.5	1.05	888 793-8637
UBS US Equity B	Growth/Inc	-7.7					0	1.8	888 793-8637
UBS US Equity C	Growth/Inc	-7.7					1	1.8	888 793-8637
UBS US Equity Y	Growth/Inc	-7	-0.54	-0.42	2	3	0	0.8	888 793-8637
UBS US Large Cap Growth Fund A	Growth	-9.6	-20.23		4	4	5.5	1.05	888 793-8637
UBS US Large Cap Growth Fund B	Growth	-10.1					0	1.8	888 793-8637
UBS US Large Cap Growth Fund C	Growth	-10.2					1	1.8	888 793-8637
UBS US Large Cap Growth Fund Y	Growth	-9.3	-19.98	-6.95		4	0	0.8	888 793-8637
UBS US Small Cap Growth A	Small Co	-6.1	-3.33			4	5.5	1.4	888 793-8637
UBS US Small Cap Growth B	Small Co	-6.8					0	2.15	888 793-8637
UBS US Small Cap Growth C	Small Co	-6.8					1	2.15	888 793-8637
UBS US Small Cap Growth Y	Small Co	-5.9	-3.08	4.82	3	4	0	1.15	888 793-8637
UBS US Value Equity A	Income	-6.7					5.5	1.1	888 793-8637
UBS US Value Equity B	Income	-7.3					0	1.85	888 793-8637
UBS US Value Equity C	Income	-7.3					1	1.85	888 793-8637

Stock Fund Name	Objective	Annualized Return for			Rank		Max Load	Expense Ratio	Toll-Free/(Toll) Telephone
		1 Year	3 Years	5 Years	Overall	Risk			
UBS US Value Equity Y	Income	-6.4					0	0.85	888 793-8637
UMB Scout Balanced Fund	Balanced	-4	0.53	-0.5	2	1	0	0.85	800 996-2862
UMB Scout Small Cap Fund	Small Co	-3.1	9.67	4.73	1	1	0	0.99	800 996-2862
UMB Scout Stock Fund	Growth/Inc	-8.7	-7.21	-1.76	3	2	0	0.85	800 996-2862
UMB Scout WorldWide Fund	Foreign	-7.1	-8.17	-0.28	3	2	0	1.12	800 996-2862
US Global Accolade Bonnel Growth	Growth	-21	-21.01	1.23	4	3	0	1.77	800 873-8637
US Global Accolade East European	European	25.1	15.4	10.41	1	4	0	6.43	800 873-8637
US Global Accolade MegaTrends	Flexible	-13.6	-9.23	-1.91	3	3	0	2.37	800 873-8637
US Global Inv All American Equity	Growth/Inc	-18.9	-17.71	-7	5	3	0	2.19	800 873-8637
US Global Inv China Region Opport	Pacific	-11	-10.32	-2.7	3	3	0	3.54	800 873-8637
US Global Inv Global Resources	Energy/Res	-7.4	7.66	2.93	2	4	0	3.83	800 873-8637
US Global Inv Gold Shares	Prec Metal	-21.9	21.57	2.25				3.57	800 873-8637
US Global Inv World Prec Minerals	Prec Metal	-22.4	16.1	-2.08	3	5	0	2.27	800 873-8637
USAA Aggressive Growth Fund	Agg Growth	-10.8	-21.46	-2.12	4	5	0	1.2	800 382-8722
USAA Balanced Strategy	Balanced	-2.7	1.4	4.42	1	1	0	1	800 382-8722
USAA Cornerstone Strategy Fund	Flexible	-2.6	-1.66	-0.08	2	1	0	1.19	800 382-8722
USAA Emerging Markets	Foreign	-8.8	-6.83	-3.85	3	4	0	2.44	800 382-8722
USAA First Start Growth Fund	Growth	-14	-24.12	-8.26	5	4	0	1.46	800 382-8722
USAA Growth & Income Fund	Growth/Inc	-8.9	-6.5	-1.6	3	2	0	1.11	800 382-8722
USAA Growth & Tax Strategy	Balanced	1.5	-3.93	0.61	2	1	0	0.9	800 382-8722
USAA Growth Fund	Growth	-12.8	-22.07	-8.08	4	4	0	1	800 382-8722
USAA Income Fund	Corp-Inv	11.2	10.25	7	1	1	0	0.51	800 382-8722
USAA Income Stock Fund	Income	-14.4	-4.04	-0.68	3	2	0	0.83	800 382-8722
USAA International Fund	Foreign	-7.7	-8.02	-2.83	3	2	0	1.42	800 382-8722
USAA Precious Metals and Minerals	Prec Metal	-5.1	32.17	13.88	2	5	0	1.49	800 382-8722
USAA S&P 500 Index Members	Growth/Inc	-8.3	-11.03	-1.26	3	3	0	0.27	800 382-8722
USAA Science & Technology Fund	Technology	-7.4	-28.17	-6.75	3	5	0	2.18	800 382-8722
USAA Small Cap Stock Fund	Small Co	-8.4	-5.9		2	4	0	1.4	800 382-8722
USAA World Growth Fund	Global	-9.3	-12.43	-3.43	4	3	0	1.56	800 382-8722
Undiscovered Mgrs Behavior Gr Inst	Growth	5.3	-15.94		3	4	0	1.3	888 242-3514
Undiscovered Mgrs Behavior Gr Inv	Growth	5	-16.32		3	4	0	1.65	888 242-3514
Undiscovered Mgrs Behavior Val Inst	Growth	-3.7	6.24		2	4	0	1.4	888 242-3514
Undiscovered Mgrs REIT Inst	Real Est	4.2	14.38	9.01	1	1	0	1.4	888 242-3514
Undiscovered Mgrs Spec Sm Cap Instl	Small Co	-11.5	6.69	3.91	3	2	0	1.2	888 242-3514
United Assoc S&P 500 Index 1	Other	-8.6	-11.16		3	3	0	0.06	888 766-8043
Valley Forge Fund	Growth	-10.2	5.34	3.14	3	2	0	1.26	800 548-1942
Value Line Asset Allocation	AssetAlloc	-7.2	-3.54	2.91			0	1.09	800 223-0818
Value Line Convertible Fund	Converts	1.3	-3.79	1.64			0	1.4	800 223-0818
Value Line Emerging Opportunities	Small Co	-7.4	2.04	13.31			0	1.35	800 223-0818
Value Line Fund	Growth/Inc	-14.9	-14.55	-3.25			0	1.11	800 223-0818
Value Line Income & Growth Fund	Income	-2.3	-2.91	6			0	1.15	800 223-0818
Value Line Leveraged Growth	Agg Growth	-16.9	-14.73	-0.72			0	1.25	800 223-0818
Value Line Special Situations	Growth	-9.1	-9.25	5.45			0	1.2	800 223-0818
Van Eck Asia Dynasty A	Pacific	-17.2	-15.13	3.47	4	4	4.75	3.36	800 221-2220
Van Eck Asia Dynasty B	Pacific	-18.2	-15.67	2.72	4	4	0	4.15	800 221-2220
Van Eck Global Hard Assets A	Prec Metal	-12	2.14	-0.44	2	3	4.75	2.61	800 221-2220
Van Eck Global Hard Assets B	Prec Metal	-12.9	1.37	-1.12	2	3	0	3.57	800 221-2220
Van Eck Global Hard Assets C	Prec Metal	-13.3	1.37	-1.39	2	3	0	3.71	800 221-2220
Van Eck Global Leaders A	Balanced	-10.1	-19.1	-7.41	4	3	4.75	2	800 221-2220
Van Eck Intl Investors Gold A	Prec Metal	-7.9	25.94	5.13	2	5	5.75	1.96	800 221-2220
Van Eck Mid Cap Value A	Growth/Inc	-10.8	-16.41	-8.67	5	4	4.75	1.79	800 221-2220
Van Kampen Aggressive Growth A	Agg Growth	-12.8	-24.89	2.81	4	4	5.75	1.43	800 421-5666
Van Kampen Aggressive Growth B	Agg Growth	-13.5	-25.48	2.02	4	4	0	2.18	800 421-5666
Van Kampen Aggressive Growth C	Agg Growth	-13.5	-25.48	2.06	4	4	0	2.18	800 421-5666
Van Kampen American Value A	Small Co	-9.5	-5.61	-0.2	3	3	5.75	1.46	800 421-5666
Van Kampen American Value B	Small Co	-10.3	-6.33	-0.97	3	3	0	2.21	800 421-5666
Van Kampen American Value C	Small Co	-9.7	-6.11	-0.83	3	3	0	2.21	800 421-5666
Van Kampen Asian Equity A	Pacific	-21	-17.26	-0.11	3	4	5.75	2.13	800 421-5666

Stock Fund Name	Objective	Annualized Return for			Rank		Max Load	Expense Ratio	Toll-Free/(Toll) Telephone
		1 Year	3 Years	5 Years	Overall	Risk			
Van Kampen Asian Equity B	Pacific	-21.6	-17.66	-0.71	5	4	0	2.92	800 421-5666
Van Kampen Asian Equity C	Pacific	-21.7	-17.69	-0.75	5	4	0	2.92	800 421-5666
Van Kampen Comstock A	Growth/Inc	-8.8	2.72	5.17	2	3	5.75	0.87	800 421-5666
Van Kampen Comstock B	Growth/Inc	-9.4	-0.34	2.97	2	3	0	1.65	800 421-5666
Van Kampen Comstock C	Growth/Inc	-9.4	-0.33	2.95	2	3	0	1.65	800 421-5666
Van Kampen Comstock R	Growth/Inc						0		800 421-5666
Van Kampen Emerging Growth A	Agg Growth	-13.9	-22.85	2.14	4	4	5.75	0.93	800 421-5666
Van Kampen Emerging Growth B	Agg Growth	-14.6	-23.44	1.36	4	4	0	1.7	800 421-5666
Van Kampen Emerging Growth C	Agg Growth	-14.5	-23.42	1.37	4	4	0	1.7	800 421-5666
Van Kampen Emerging Markets A	Foreign	-10.5	-13.24	-1.21	3	4	5.75	2.47	800 421-5666
Van Kampen Emerging Markets B	Foreign	-11.1	-13.78	-1.9	4	4	0	3.1	800 421-5666
Van Kampen Emerging Markets C	Foreign	-11	-13.73	-1.83	4	4	0	3.1	800 421-5666
Van Kampen Enterprise A	Growth	-13.5	-19.46	-6.17	5	3	5.75	1.05	800 421-5666
Van Kampen Enterprise B	Growth	-14.2	-20.07	-6.9	5	3	0	1.8	800 421-5666
Van Kampen Enterprise C	Growth	-14.1	-20.01	-6.86	5	3	0	1.8	800 421-5666
Van Kampen Equity & Income A	Income	-2.5	2.91	6.28	1	1	5.75	0.82	800 421-5666
Van Kampen Equity & Income B	Income	-3.2	-0.79	3.64	1	1	0	1.58	800 421-5666
Van Kampen Equity & Income C	Income	-3.3	-0.69	3.7	1	1	0	1.58	800 421-5666
Van Kampen Equity Growth A	Growth	-12	-16.62	-2.56	4	3	5.75	1.58	800 421-5666
Van Kampen Equity Growth B	Growth	-12.6	-17.25	-3.27	4	3	0	2.33	800 421-5666
Van Kampen Equity Growth C	Growth	-12.3	-17.12	-3.18	4	3	0	2.33	800 421-5666
Van Kampen European Value Equity A	European	-10	-4.79		3	3	5.75	2.5	800 421-5666
Van Kampen European Value Equity B	European	-10.4	-5.13		2	3	0	3.1	800 421-5666
Van Kampen European Value Equity C	European	-9.9	-5.01		3	3	0	3.25	800 421-5666
Van Kampen Exchange	Growth	-15	-13.42	1.36	2	3	0	1.6	800 421-5666
Van Kampen Focus Equity A	Agg Growth	-12	-17.3	-2.62	4	3	5.75	1.55	800 421-5666
Van Kampen Focus Equity B	Agg Growth	-12.7	-17.98	-3.37	4	3	0	2.27	800 421-5666
Van Kampen Focus Equity C	Agg Growth	-12.7	-17.96	-3.35	4	3	0	2.27	800 421-5666
Van Kampen Global Eqty Allocatn A	Global	-12	-10.75	-2.95	3	2	5.75	1.68	800 421-5666
Van Kampen Global Eqty Allocatn B	Global	-12.6	-11.42	-3.68	4	2	0	2.4	800 421-5666
Van Kampen Global Eqty Allocatn C	Global	-12.6	-11.4	-3.66	4	2	0	2.4	800 421-5666
Van Kampen Global Franchise A	Global	-6.7	10.85		2	2	5.75	1.8	800 421-5666
Van Kampen Global Franchise B	Global	-7.3	10		1	2	0	3.82	800 421-5666
Van Kampen Global Franchise C	Global	-7.4	10		1	2	0	3.84	800 421-5666
Van Kampen Global Value Equity A	Global	-19.9	-5.2	-2.47	3	2	5.75	1.64	800 421-5666
Van Kampen Global Value Equity B	Global	-20.6	-5.82	-4.44	3	2	0	2.39	800 421-5666
Van Kampen Global Value Equity C	Global	-20.3	-5.7	-4.33	3	2	0	2.39	800 421-5666
Van Kampen Growth A	Growth	-12.8	-14.89	2	4	4	5.75	1.43	800 421-5666
Van Kampen Growth B	Growth	-13.5	-15.52	0.92	3	4	0	2.18	800 421-5666
Van Kampen Growth C	Growth	-13.4	-15.47	0.93	3	4	0	2.18	800 421-5666
Van Kampen Growth and Income A	Growth/Inc	-9.3	-1.09	4.12	2	2	5.75	0.82	800 421-5666
Van Kampen Growth and Income B	Growth/Inc	-10	-1.85	3.31	2	2	0	1.59	800 421-5666
Van Kampen Growth and Income C	Growth/Inc	-9.9	-1.8	3.35	2	2	0	1.59	800 421-5666
Van Kampen Growth and Income R	Growth/Inc						0		800 421-5666
Van Kampen Harbor A	Converts	-0.2	-6.41	4.17	2	2	5.75	0.99	800 421-5666
Van Kampen Harbor B	Converts	-0.9	-7	3.49	2	2	0	1.75	800 421-5666
Van Kampen Harbor C	Converts	-0.9	-7.12	3.37	2	2	0	1.75	800 421-5666
Van Kampen Intl Magnum A	Foreign	-18.5	-13.9	-8.19	5	2	5.75	1.6	800 421-5666
Van Kampen Intl Magnum B	Foreign	-19.5	-14.44	-8.82	5	2	0	2.35	800 421-5666
Van Kampen Intl Magnum C	Foreign	-19.5	-14.48	-8.82	5	2	0	2.35	800 421-5666
Van Kampen Latin American A	Foreign	-8.4	-5.2	-1.76	3	4	5.75	2.2	800 421-5666
Van Kampen Latin American B	Foreign	-8.9	-5.88	-2.43	3	4	0	2.95	800 421-5666
Van Kampen Latin American C	Foreign	-8.9	-5.86	-2.43	3	4	0	2.95	800 421-5666
Van Kampen Mid Cap Growth A	Growth	-10.6	-18.67		4	4	5.75	1.58	800 421-5666
Van Kampen Mid Cap Growth B	Growth	-11.2	-19.23		4	4	0	2.33	800 421-5666
Van Kampen Mid Cap Growth C	Growth	-11.1	-19.21		4	4	0	2.33	800 421-5666
Van Kampen Pace A	Growth	-9.8	-13.97	-5.66	4	3	5.75	0.87	800 421-5666
Van Kampen Pace B	Growth	-10.6	-14.71	-6.44	4	3	0	1.62	800 421-5666

Stock Fund Name	Objective	Annualized Return for			Rank		Max Load	Expense Ratio	Toll-Free/(Toll) Telephone
		1 Year	3 Years	5 Years	Overall	Risk			
Van Kampen Pace C	Growth	-10.4	-14.66	-6.4	4	3	0	1.62	800 421-5666
Van Kampen Real Estate Sec A	Real Est	1.9	12.23	6.54	1	2	4.75	1.67	800 421-5666
Van Kampen Real Estate Sec B	Real Est	1.2	11.36	5.73	2	2	0	2.42	800 421-5666
Van Kampen Real Estate Sec C	Real Est	1.2	11.4	5.75	2	2	0	2.42	800 421-5666
Van Kampen Select Growth A	Growth	-11.8					5.75	1.48	800 421-5666
Van Kampen Select Growth B	Growth	-12.5					0	2.23	800 421-5666
Van Kampen Select Growth C	Growth	-12.5					0	2.23	800 421-5666
Van Kampen Small Cap Growth A	Small Co	-8					5.75	1.72	800 421-5666
Van Kampen Small Cap Growth B	Small Co	-8.6					0	2.47	800 421-5666
Van Kampen Small Cap Growth C	Small Co	-8.6					0	2.47	800 421-5666
Van Kampen Small Cap Value A	Small Co	-10.4	10.14		2	3	5.75	1.63	800 421-5666
Van Kampen Small Cap Value B	Small Co	-11.1	9.32		2	3	0	2.38	800 421-5666
Van Kampen Small Cap Value C	Small Co	-11	9.31		2	3	0	2.38	800 421-5666
Van Kampen Tax-Mgnd Equity Gr A	Growth	-12.2	-16.87		5	3	5.75	2.2	800 421-5666
Van Kampen Tax-Mgnd Equity Gr B	Growth	-12.8	-17.53		5	3	0	2.95	800 421-5666
Van Kampen Tax-Mgnd Equity Gr C	Growth	-12.6	-17.5		5	3	0	2.95	800 421-5666
Van Kampen Technology A	Technology	-18.6	-43.85		4	5	5.75	1.65	800 421-5666
Van Kampen Technology B	Technology	-19.2	-44.28		4	5	0	2.4	800 421-5666
Van Kampen Technology C	Technology	-19.2	-44.28		4	5	0	2.4	800 421-5666
Van Kampen Utility A	Utilities	-5.9	-7.83	1.62	3	3	5.75	1.27	800 421-5666
Van Kampen Utility B	Utilities	-6.5	-8.51	0.85	3	3	0	2.02	800 421-5666
Van Kampen Utility C	Utilities	-6.6	-8.52	0.86	3	3	0	2.02	800 421-5666
Van Kampen Value A	Growth	-15.1	-0.26	-2.27	3	3	5.75	1.45	800 421-5666
Van Kampen Value B	Growth	-15.7	-1.1	-3.02	3	3	0	2.22	800 421-5666
Van Kampen Value C	Growth	-15.3	-0.92	-2.93	3	3	0	2.22	800 421-5666
Van Kampen Value Opportunities A	Growth/Inc	-7.7					5.75	2.96	800 421-5666
Van Kampen Value Opportunities B	Growth/Inc	-8.4					0	3.71	800 421-5666
Van Kampen Value Opportunities C	Growth/Inc	-8.4					0	3.71	800 421-5666
Van Wagoner Emerging Growth Fund	Agg Growth	-21.3	-44.43	-11.93	4	5	0	1.84	800 228-2121
Van Wagoner Micro-Cap Growth Fund	Small Co	-10.5	-27.5	1.41	4	5	0	1.95	800 228-2121
Van Wagoner Mid-Cap Growth Fund	Agg Growth	-31.7	-45.15	-19.69	5	5	0	1.95	800 228-2121
Van Wagoner Post-Venture Fund	Agg Growth	-41.6	-51.59	-20.1	5	5	0	1.95	800 228-2121
Van Wagoner Technology Fund	Technology	-39.3	-51	-17.57		5	0	1.95	800 228-2121
Vanguard 500 Index Adm	Growth	-8					0	0.12	800 662-7447
Vanguard 500 Index Inv	Growth/Inc	-8.1	-10.9	-1.09	3	3	0	0.18	800 662-7447
Vanguard Asset Allocation Adm	AssetAlloc	-3.1					0	0.32	800 662-7447
Vanguard Asset Allocation Inv	AssetAlloc	-3.2	-3.39	1.9	2	2	0	0.42	800 662-7447
Vanguard Balanced Index Inv	Balanced	0.1	-1.6	2.89	1	1	0	0.22	800 662-7447
Vanguard Calvert Social Index Fd	Growth	-6.7	-12.76		3	3	0	0.25	800 662-7447
Vanguard Capital Opportunity Inv	Growth	-2.7	-9.33	15.82	3	4	0	0.58	800 662-7447
Vanguard Convertible Securities	Converts	6.9	-0.05	4.83	1	2	0	0.95	800 662-7447
Vanguard Dividend Growth Fd	Growth/Inc	-14.3	-9.49	-2.04	4	2	0	0.37	800 662-7447
Vanguard Emerging Mkts Stk Idx Fd	Foreign	-8.4	-5.95	0.38	3	4	0	0.57	800 662-7447
Vanguard Energy Inv	Energy/Res	1	5.9	7.07	1	3	0	0.4	800 662-7447
Vanguard Equity Income Inv	Income	-9.4	-0.36	1.72	3	2	0	0.46	800 662-7447
Vanguard European Stock Index Inv	European	-9.3	-11.52	-4.62	5	3	0	0.33	800 662-7447
Vanguard Explorer Fund Adm	Small Co	-8.1					0	0.61	800 662-7447
Vanguard Explorer Fund Inv	Small Co	-8.2	-2.22	5.69	2	4	0	0.7	800 662-7447
Vanguard Extended Market Index Inst	Growth	-4.4	-6.79	-0.05	3	4	0	0.1	800 662-7447
Vanguard Extended Market Index Inv	Growth	-4.6	-6.94	-0.2	3	4	0	0.25	800 662-7447
Vanguard Global Equity Fund	Global	-7.2	1.17	4.13	1	3	0	1.19	800 662-7447
Vanguard Growth & Income Adm	Growth/Inc	-9.5					0	0.34	800 662-7447
Vanguard Growth & Income Inv	Growth/Inc	-9.6	-10.46	-0.97	4	3	0	0.45	800 662-7447
Vanguard Growth Equity	Growth	-8	-22.96	-3.12	3	4	0	0.58	800 662-7447
Vanguard Growth Index Inv	Growth	-7.6	-15.86	-2.06	3	3	0	0.22	800 662-7447
Vanguard Health Care Inv	Health	-3.6	6.08	13.09	1	2	0	0.29	800 662-7447
Vanguard Instl Index Fd	Growth/Inc	-8	-10.78	-0.97	3	3	0	0.05	800 662-7447
Vanguard International Explorer Fd	Other	-8.2	-10.28	6.28		3	0	0.75	800 662-7447

Stock Fund Name	Objective	Annualized Return for			Rank		Max Load	Expense Ratio	Toll-Free/(Toll) Telephone
		1 Year	3 Years	5 Years	Overall	Risk			
Vanguard International Growth Inv	Foreign	-12.1	-12.92	-3.39	3	3	0	0.61	800 662-7447
Vanguard International Value Fund	Foreign	-16	-8.27	-2.29	4	3	0	0.65	800 662-7447
Vanguard LifeStrategy Conserv Gr Fd	Income	1.9	1.43	4.03	1	1	0	0.28	800 662-7447
Vanguard LifeStrategy Growth Fd	Growth	-5.1	-6.46	0.47	2	2	0	0.27	800 662-7447
Vanguard LifeStrategy Income Fd	Income	5.5	5.46	5.62	1	1	0	0.27	800 662-7447
Vanguard LifeStrategy Mod Growth Fd	Growth/Inc	-1.2	-2.27	2.66	1	1	0	0.28	800 662-7447
Vanguard Mid-Cap Index Inv	Growth	-9.7	1	7.25		3	0	0.26	800 662-7447
Vanguard Morgan Growth Inv	Growth	-6	-12.51	-0.83	3	4	0	0.48	800 662-7447
Vanguard PRIMECAP Inv	Growth	-6.9	-11.17	5.07	3	4	0	0.5	800 662-7447
Vanguard Pacific Stock Index Inv	Pacific	-19.4	-17.25	-3.25	4	2	0	0.37	800 662-7447
Vanguard Precious Metals Fd	Prec Metal	-9.5	25.8	12.38	2	4	0	0.63	800 662-7447
Vanguard REIT Index Inv	Real Est	4.4	13.88	6.58	2	2	0	0.28	800 662-7447
Vanguard STAR Fund	Balanced	-1	1.8	4	1	1	0	0.04	800 662-7447
Vanguard Selected Value Fund	Growth	-9	8.67	1.77	2	3	0	0.74	800 662-7447
Vanguard Small-Cap Grwth Index Fd	Small Co	-5.4	-1.55	2.41		4	0	0.27	800 662-7447
Vanguard Small-Cap Index Inst	Small Co	-8.7	-0.84	1.12	2	4	0	0.1	800 662-7447
Vanguard Small-Cap Index Inv	Small Co	-8.9	-1.03	0.98	3	4	0	0.27	800 662-7447
Vanguard Small-Cap Value Index Fd	Small Co	-16.2	7.9	3.47	3	3	0	0.27	800 662-7447
Vanguard Strategic Equity Fd	Agg Growth	-2.1	11.5	9.91	1	4	0	0.05	800 662-7447
Vanguard Tax-Managed Balanced Fd	Balanced	1.8	-1.19	3.91	1	1	0	0.18	800 662-7447
Vanguard Tax-Managed Gr & Inc Inv	Growth/Inc	-7.9	-10.77	-1	3	3	0	0.18	800 662-7447
Vanguard Tax-Managed Intl Fd	Foreign	-12.4	-13.18		3	3	0	0.35	800 662-7447
Vanguard Tax-Mgd Cap Appr Inv	Growth	-8.3	-12.94	-0.32	3	3	0	0.18	800 662-7447
Vanguard Total Intl Stock Index Fd	Foreign	-11.9	-12.58	-3.91	3	3	0	0.37	800 662-7447
Vanguard Total Stock Mkt Index Adm	Growth/Inc	-7.3					0	0.15	800 662-7447
Vanguard Total Stock Mkt Index Inst	Growth/Inc	-7.3	-9.61	-0.73	3	3	0	0.08	800 662-7447
Vanguard Total Stock Mkt Index Inv	Growth/Inc	-7.3	-9.71	-0.83	3	3	0	0.2	800 662-7447
Vanguard US Growth Adm	Growth	-12.6					0	0.36	800 662-7447
Vanguard US Growth Inv	Growth	-12.7	-26.48	-10.82	5	4	0	0.23	800 662-7447
Vanguard Value Index Inv	Growth	-8.3	-6.03	-0.79	3	3	0	0.23	800 662-7447
Vanguard Wellesley Income Inv	Flexible	6.7	10.42	7.08	1	1	0	0.03	800 662-7447
Vanguard Wellington Inv	Balanced	-1.2	4.78	4.55	1	1	0	0.36	800 662-7447
Vanguard Windsor-I Inv	Growth/Inc	-7.9	1.32	1.72	2	3	0	0.45	800 662-7447
Vanguard Windsor-II Inv	Growth/Inc	-8.2	-0.02	0.34	3	2	0	0.4	800 662-7447
Victory Balanced A	Balanced	-3.2	-1.8	2.04	2	1	5.75	1.15	800 539-3863
Victory Convertible Fund A	Converts	2.6	0.32	3.18	1	1	2	1.32	800 539-3863
Victory Diversified Stock A	Growth	-7.6	-3.58	3.77	2	3	5.75	1.09	800 539-3863
Victory Established Value A	Growth	-7.8					5.75	1.14	800 539-3863
Victory Growth Fund A	Growth	-8.7	-13.38	-1.93	4	3	5.75	1.21	800 539-3863
Victory International Fund A	Foreign	-15.9	-17.55	-7.41	4	3	5.75	1.92	800 539-3863
Victory Portf-Balanced C	Balanced						0		800 539-3863
Victory Portf-Balanced R	Balanced	-3.6	-2.12		1	1	0	2	800 539-3863
Victory Portf-Diversified Stk C	Growth	-8.3					0	1.9	800 539-3863
Victory Portf-Diversified Stk R	Growth	-8.1	-3.99		3	3	0	1.49	800 539-3863
Victory Portf-Established Value C	Growth						0		800 539-3863
Victory Portf-Established Value R	Growth	-8.1					0	1.35	800 539-3863
Victory Portf-Growth Fund C	Growth						0		800 539-3863
Victory Portf-Growth Fund R	Growth	-8.9	-13.68		3	3	0	1.93	800 539-3863
Victory Portf-Intl Growth R	Foreign	-16.2	-17.8		4	3	0	2.37	800 539-3863
Victory Portf-Real Estate Fd C	Real Est	1.2					0	2.2	800 539-3863
Victory Portf-Real Estate Fd R	Real Est	1.7	10.58		1	1	0	2	800 539-3863
Victory Portf-Sm Co Opportunity C	Small Co						0		800 539-3863
Victory Portf-Sm Co Opportunity R	Small Co	-7.1					0	1.52	800 539-3863
Victory Portf-Special Value C	Growth						0		800 539-3863
Victory Portf-Special Value R	Growth	-9.7	5.55		2	3	0	2	800 539-3863
Victory Portf-Stock Index Fund R	Growth	-8.8	-11.67		3	3	0	1.19	800 539-3863
Victory Portf-Value Fund C	Growth						0		800 539-3863
Victory Portf-Value Fund R	Growth/Inc	-11.6	-7.5		3	3	0	1.87	800 539-3863

Stock Fund Name	Objective	Annualized Return for			Rank		Max Load	Expense Ratio	Toll-Free/(Toll) Telephone
		1 Year	3 Years	5 Years	Overall	Risk			
Victory Real Estate Fd A	Real Est	2	10.96	6.33	1	1	5.75	1.77	800 539-3863
Victory Sm Co Opportunity A	Small Co	-6.8	5.34		2	3	5.75	1.18	800 539-3863
Victory Special Value A	Growth	-9.5	5.83	2.43	3	3	5.75	1.25	800 539-3863
Victory Stock Index Fund A	Growth	-8.6	-11.5	-1.75	3	3	5.75	0.72	800 539-3863
Victory Value Fund A	Growth/Inc	-11.2	-7.19	0.32	3	3	5.75	1.19	800 539-3863
Vintage Aggressive Gr	Agg Growth	-11.8	-16.6	-5.75	3	4	0	1.42	800 438-6375
Vintage Balanced	Balanced	-6.1	-8.02	-0.68	3	2	0	1.25	800 438-6375
Vintage Equity Fund S	Growth	-12	-15.84	-4.44	4	3	4.25	1.41	800 438-6375
Vintage Equity Fund T	Growth	-11.8	-15.66	-5.38	5	3	0	1.16	800 438-6375
Vision International Equity A	Foreign	-11.8	-7.41		3	2	4.5	1.73	800 836-2211
Vision International Equity B	Foreign	-12.6					0	2.63	800 836-2211
Vision Large Cap Core A	Growth	-13.4	-15.08	-4.54	4	4	5.5	1.31	800 836-2211
Vision Large Cap Core B	Growth	-14.3					0	2.16	800 836-2211
Vision Large Cap Growth A	Growth	-10.3	-10.96		3	2	5.5	1.32	800 836-2211
Vision Large Cap Growth B	Growth	-11.2	-11.8		3	2	0	2.21	800 836-2211
Vision Large Cap Value A	Growth	-10.7	-4.76	-2.06	3	3	5.5	1.12	800 836-2211
Vision Large Cap Value B	Growth	-11.5	-5.74		3	3	0	2.21	800 836-2211
Vision Mid Cap Stock A	Growth	-10.1	-1.64	1.61	3	3	5.5	1.29	800 836-2211
Vision Mid Cap Stock B	Growth	-11	-2.52		3	3	0	2.24	800 836-2211
Vision Mngd Alloc-Aggressive Gr A	Agg Growth	-8.5	-6.51		3	2	5	1	800 836-2211
Vision Mngd Alloc-Aggressive Gr B	AssetAlloc	-9.4					0	2	800 836-2211
Vision Mngd Alloc-Conserv Gr A	Growth	2.7	2.04		1	1	5	2	800 836-2211
Vision Mngd Alloc-Conserv Gr B	AssetAlloc	1.7					0	2	800 836-2211
Vision Mngd Alloc-Moderate Gr A	Growth	-3.3	-2.41		2	1	5	1	800 836-2211
Vision Mngd Alloc-Moderate Gr B	AssetAlloc	-4.3					0	2	800 836-2211
Vision Small Cap Stock Fund A	Small Co	1	2.56	4.48	2	4	5.5	2.12	800 836-2211
Vision Small Cap Stock Fund B	Small Co	0.3					0	2.12	800 836-2211
Volumetric Fund	Growth	-7.3	-1.12	-1.07	3	2	0	1.9	800 541-3863
Vontobel Eastern European Eq A	European	20.5	3.87	-3.79	2	4	0	3.46	800 527-9525
Vontobel International Equity A	Foreign	-7	-13.09	-3.87	4	2	0	1.89	800 527-9525
Vontobel U.S. Value Equity Fund	Growth	-1.3	13.96	6.29	2	2	0	1.75	800 527-9525
W&R Asset Strategy Fund C	Flexible	1.4	-0.45	8.11	1	1	0	2.2	888 923-3355
W&R Asset Strategy Fund Y	Flexible	2.3	0.39	9.52	1	1	0	1.33	888 923-3355
W&R Core Equity Fund C	Growth/Inc	-11.4	-12.27	-2.45	3	2	0	2.05	888 923-3355
W&R Core Equity Fund Y	Growth/Inc	-10.5	-11.48	-1.72	3	2	0	1.17	888 923-3355
W&R International Growth Fund C	Foreign	-16.5	-20.44	-4.04	3	2	0	2.62	888 923-3355
W&R International Growth Fund Y	Foreign	-15.2	-19.5	-2.95	4	2	0	1.52	888 923-3355
W&R Large Cap Growth A	Growth	-6.5					5.75	1.02	888 923-3355
W&R Large Cap Growth B	Growth	-8.2					0	2.78	888 923-3355
W&R Large Cap Growth C	Growth	-7.5					0	2.37	888 923-3355
W&R Large Cap Growth Y	Growth	-6.4					0	1.5	888 923-3355
W&R Mid Cap Growth Fund A	Growth	-6.5					5.75	1.17	888 923-3355
W&R Mid Cap Growth Fund B	Growth	-7.9					0	2.3	888 923-3355
W&R Mid Cap Growth Fund C	Growth	-7.4					0	2.1	888 923-3355
W&R Mid Cap Growth Fund Y	Growth	-6.4					0	0.83	888 923-3355
W&R Science & Technology Fund C	Technology	-5.8	-11.66	11.17	3	3	0	2.45	888 923-3355
W&R Science & Technology Fund Y	Technology	-4.6	-10.66		3	3	0	1.39	888 923-3355
W&R Small Cap Growth Fund C	Small Co	-6.7	-8.88	5.92	2	4	0	2.2	888 923-3355
W&R Small Cap Growth Fund Y	Small Co	-5.8	-8.02	6.86	2	4	0	1.31	888 923-3355
W&R Tax Managed Equity A	Growth	0.3					5.75	1.62	888 923-3355
W&R Tax Managed Equity B	Growth	-0.8					0	2.56	888 923-3355
W&R Tax Managed Equity C	Growth	-0.8					0	2.76	888 923-3355
WF Montgomery Mid Cap Growth A	Growth	-8.1					5.75	1.4	800 222-8222
WM Balanced Portfolio A	Balanced	0.7	-0.91	5.75	1	1	5.5	1.02	800 222-5852
WM Balanced Portfolio B	Balanced	0	-1.69	4.92	1	1	0	1.78	800 222-5852
WM Balanced Portfolio C	Balanced	-0.1					0		800 222-5852
WM Conservative Balanced C	Balanced	3.6					0		800 222-5852
WM Conservative Gr Portfolio A	Growth	-2.9	-4.92	5.32	1	2	5.5	1.03	800 222-5852

417

Stock Fund Name	Objective	Annualized Return for			Rank		Max Load	Expense Ratio	Toll-Free/(Toll) Telephone
		1 Year	3 Years	5 Years	Overall	Risk			
WM Conservative Gr Portfolio B	Growth	-3.7	-5.61	4.49	1	2	0	1.79	800 222-5852
WM Conservative Gr Portfolio C	Growth/Inc	-3.7					0		800 222-5852
WM Equity Income A	Income	-4.9	5.2	4.82	1	2	5.5		800 222-5852
WM Equity Income B	Income	-5.8	4.25	3.93	1	2	0		800 222-5852
WM Equity Income C	Income	-5.7					0		800 222-5852
WM Flexible Inc Portfolio A	Dvsfd Bond	6.6	5.29	6.11	1	1	4.5	1.06	800 222-5852
WM Flexible Inc Portfolio B	Dvsfd Bond	5.7	4.53	5.33	1	1	0	1.79	800 222-5852
WM Growth & Income Fd A	Growth/Inc	-7	-6.16	1.55	2	3	5.5		800 222-5852
WM Growth & Income Fd B	Growth/Inc	-7.9	-7.05	0.66	2	3	0		800 222-5852
WM Growth & Income Fd C	Growth/Inc	-7.8					0		800 222-5852
WM Growth Fd A	Growth	-9.5	-24	1.34	3	4	5.5	1.68	800 222-5852
WM Growth Fd B	Growth	-10.4	-24.62	0.54	3	4	0	2.31	800 222-5852
WM International Gr A	Foreign	-13	-16.44	-6.29	4	3	5.5		800 222-5852
WM International Gr B	Foreign	-14	-17.25	-7.16	5	3	0		800 222-5852
WM International Gr C	Foreign	-13.6					0		800 222-5852
WM Mid Cap Stock A	Growth	-5.5	7.29		1	2	5.5	1.36	800 222-5852
WM Mid Cap Stock B	Growth	-6.6	6.32		1	2	0	2.16	800 222-5852
WM Mid Cap Stock C	Growth	-6.5					0		800 222-5852
WM REIT Fund A	Real Est						5.5		800 222-5852
WM REIT Fund B	Real Est						0		800 222-5852
WM REIT Fund C	Real Est						0		800 222-5852
WM Small Cap Stock Fund A	Small Co	-5.3	-18.55	-2.66	3	5	5.5		800 222-5852
WM Small Cap Stock Fund B	Small Co	-6.4	-19.32	-3.56	3	5	0		800 222-5852
WM Small Cap Stock Fund C	Small Co	-5.8					0		800 222-5852
WM Strategic Gr Portfolio A	Growth	-6.6	-7.91	4.25	2	3	5.5	1.08	800 222-5852
WM Strategic Gr Portfolio B	Growth	-7.3	-8.61	3.5	2	3	0	1.84	800 222-5852
WM Strategic Gr Portfolio C	Growth	-7.2					0		800 222-5852
WM West Coast Equity Fd A	Growth	-7.4	-1.67	10.61	2	4	5.5	1.05	800 222-5852
WM West Coast Equity Fd B	Growth	-8.3	-2.47	9.69	3	4	0	1.88	800 222-5852
WM West Coast Equity Fund Class C	Growth	-8.2					0		800 222-5852
WPG Large Cap Growth	Growth	-10	-13.08	-4	4	4	0	1	800 223-3332
WPG Quantitative Equity	Growth/Inc	-9.8	-9.22	-1.18	3	3	0	1.67	800 223-3332
WPG Tudor Fund	Agg Growth	-5.1	-10.24	-3.75	3	5	0	1.58	800 223-3332
WST Growth Fd Inst	Growth/Inc	-14.8	-16.67	-6.66	5	3	0	1.75	800 430-3863
WST Growth Fd Inv	Growth/Inc	-15.2	-17.12	-7.13	5	3	3.93	2.25	800 430-3863
WWW Internet A	Technology	2	-40.61	-9.6	3	5	0	3.01	888 999-8331
Waddell & Reed Adv Accumulative A	Growth	-13.1	-8.83	2.62	2	2	5.75	1.08	888 923-3355
Waddell & Reed Adv Accumulative B	Growth	-14.1	-9.81		3	2	0	2.17	888 923-3355
Waddell & Reed Adv Accumulative C	Growth	-13.9	-9.74		3	2	0	2.08	888 923-3355
Waddell & Reed Adv Accumulative Y	Growth	-12.7	-8.52	3.02	3	2	0	0.85	888 923-3355
Waddell & Reed Adv Asset Strat A	Flexible	1.8	0.4	9.58	1	1	5.75	1.42	888 923-3355
Waddell & Reed Adv Asset Strat B	Flexible	0.9	-0.47	7.16	1	1	0	2.27	888 923-3355
Waddell & Reed Adv Asset Strat C	Flexible	1	-0.44	7.19	1	1	0	2.27	888 923-3355
Waddell & Reed Adv Asset Strat Y	Flexible	2.2	0.78	8.14	1	1	0	1.02	888 923-3355
Waddell & Reed Adv Cntinentl Inc B	Balanced	-3.2	-3.08	3.25	1	1	0	2.1	888 923-3355
Waddell & Reed Adv Cntinentl Inc C	Balanced	-3.2	-3.12	4.29	1	1	0	2.19	888 923-3355
Waddell & Reed Adv Cntinentl Inc Y	Balanced	-2.1	-2.04	2.24	2	1	0	0.91	888 923-3355
Waddell & Reed Adv Cont Inc A	Balanced	-2.1	-2.18	1.89	2	1	5.75	1.19	888 923-3355
Waddell & Reed Adv Core Invest A	Growth/Inc	-10.1	-11.43	-0.85	3	2	5.75	1.02	888 923-3355
Waddell & Reed Adv Core Invest B	Growth/Inc	-11.2	-12.4	-0.56	3	2	0	2.14	888 923-3355
Waddell & Reed Adv Core Invest C	Growth/Inc	-11.2	-12.35	-0.56	3	2	0	2.11	888 923-3355
Waddell & Reed Adv Core Invest Y	Growth/Inc	-10	-11.21	-0.61	3	2	0	0.76	888 923-3355
Waddell & Reed Adv Intl Gr A	Foreign	-14.8	-17.67	-6.38	4	2	5.75	1.56	888 923-3355
Waddell & Reed Adv Intl Gr B	Foreign	-16	-18.75		5	2	0	2.94	888 923-3355
Waddell & Reed Adv Intl Gr C	Foreign	-15.6	-18.48		5	2	0	2.55	888 923-3355
Waddell & Reed Adv Intl Gr Y	Foreign	-14.4	-17.3	-4.32	4	2	0	1.13	888 923-3355
Waddell & Reed Adv New Concepts A	Agg Growth	-6.1	-11.22	2.52	3	4	5.75	1.47	888 923-3355
Waddell & Reed Adv New Concepts B	Agg Growth	-7.3	-12.34		3	4	0	2.72	888 923-3355

Stock Fund Name	Objective	Annualized Return for			Rank		Max Load	Expense Ratio	Toll-Free/(Toll) Telephone
		1 Year	3 Years	5 Years	Overall	Risk			
Waddell & Reed Adv New Concepts C	Agg Growth	-7.2	-12.25		3	4	0	2.67	888 923-3355
Waddell & Reed Adv New Concepts Y	Agg Growth	-5.4	-10.77	2.97	3	4	0	1.04	888 923-3355
Waddell & Reed Adv Ret Shares A	Growth/Inc	-2.6	-11.25	1.61	3	4	5.75	1.21	888 923-3355
Waddell & Reed Adv Ret Shares B	Growth/Inc	-3.9	-12.19		3	4	0	2.22	888 923-3355
Waddell & Reed Adv Ret Shares C	Growth/Inc	-3.9	-12.17		3	4	0	2.22	888 923-3355
Waddell & Reed Adv Ret Shares Y	Growth/Inc	-2.4	-10.97	2.22	3	4	0	0.92	888 923-3355
Waddell & Reed Adv Sci & Tech A	Technology	-5.5	-12.82	10.23	3	3	5.75	1.35	888 923-3355
Waddell & Reed Adv Sci & Tech B	Technology	-6.9	-14.05		4	3	0	2.76	888 923-3355
Waddell & Reed Adv Sci & Tech C	Technology	-6.8	-14.02		4	3	0	2.73	888 923-3355
Waddell & Reed Adv Sci & Tech Y	Technology	-5	-12.49	10.61	3	3	0	1.01	888 923-3355
Waddell & Reed Adv Small Cap Gr A	Small Co	1.9	-6.46		2	3	5.75	1.62	888 923-3355
Waddell & Reed Adv Small Cap Gr B	Small Co	0.9	-7.25		2	3	0	2.67	888 923-3355
Waddell & Reed Adv Small Cap Gr C	Small Co	1.2	-7.04		2	3	0	2.44	888 923-3355
Waddell & Reed Adv Small Cap Gr Y	Small Co	2.7	-6.08		2	3	0	1.09	888 923-3355
Waddell & Reed Adv Tax Managed A	Growth	-0.7	-12.55		3	2	5.75	1.34	888 923-3355
Waddell & Reed Adv Tax Managed B	Growth	-1.6	-13.33		3	2	0	2.21	888 923-3355
Waddell & Reed Adv Tax Managed C	Growth	-1.6	-13.46		3	2	0	2.26	888 923-3355
Waddell & Reed Adv Tax Managed Y	Growth	-0.4	-12.33		2	2	0	1.2	888 923-3355
Waddell & Reed Adv Value A	Growth	-9.2					5.75	1.43	888 923-3355
Waddell & Reed Adv Value B	Growth	-10.2					0	2.41	888 923-3355
Waddell & Reed Adv Value C	Growth	-10.1					0	2.25	888 923-3355
Waddell & Reed Adv Value Y	Growth	-8.8					0	1.07	888 923-3355
Waddell & Reed Adv Vanguard A	Growth	-7.1	-15.09	2.62	3	3	5.75	1.19	888 923-3355
Waddell & Reed Adv Vanguard B	Growth	-8.5	-16.17		4	3	0	2.47	888 923-3355
Waddell & Reed Adv Vanguard C	Growth	-8.5	-16.17		4	3	0	2.46	888 923-3355
Waddell & Reed Adv Vanguard Y	Growth	-6.8	-14.82	2.93	2	3	0	0.87	888 923-3355
Waddell & Reed InvestEd Balanced A	Growth						0		888 923-3355
Waddell & Reed InvestEd Balanced B	Growth						0		888 923-3355
Waddell & Reed InvestEd Balanced C	Growth						0		888 923-3355
Waddell & Reed InvestEd Conserv A	Growth						0		888 923-3355
Waddell & Reed InvestEd Conserv B	Growth						0		888 923-3355
Waddell & Reed InvestEd Conserv C	Growth						0		888 923-3355
Waddell & Reed InvestEd Growth C	Growth						0		888 923-3355
Walden Social Balanced	Growth/Inc	-1.5	-0.08		1	1	0	1	877 792-5336
Walden Social Equity Fund	Growth	-5.7	-3.18		2	2	0	1	877 792-5336
Wall Street Fund	Growth	-7.6	-16.39	3	3	5	4	1.68	800 443-4693
Wasatch Core Growth Fund	Small Co	-21.5	13.68	11.06	3	4	0	1.32	800 551-1700
Wasatch Micro Cap Fund	Small Co	-2.7	23.37	22.16	1	4	0	2.32	800 551-1700
Wasatch Small Cap Growth	Small Co	-7	9.25	12.48	2	4	0	1.36	800 551-1700
Wasatch Small Cap Value	Small Co	-16.6	14.58	14.83	2	4	0	1.92	800 551-1700
Wasatch Ultra Growth	Agg Growth	-3.2	11.97	12.41	2	5	0	1.79	800 551-1700
Wayne Hummer Core Portfolio	Growth	-10.6	-14.9		3	3	2	0.75	800 621-4477
Wayne Hummer Growth Fund	Growth	-13.3	-6.37	3	3	2	2	1.04	800 621-4477
Weitz Hickory Fund	Growth	-15	-7.96	-1.71	3	4	0	1.29	800 232-4161
Weitz Partners Value Fund	Growth	-3.7	3.41	7.88	1	2	0	1.09	800 232-4161
Weitz Value Fund	Growth	-3.6	4.41	7.92	1	3	0	1.07	800 232-4161
Wells Fargo Asset Allocation A	AssetAlloc	-1.2	-4.28	2.1	2	2	5.75	1.15	800 222-8222
Wells Fargo Asset Allocation B	AssetAlloc	-2	-5		2	2	0	1.9	800 222-8222
Wells Fargo Asset Allocation C	AssetAlloc	-2	-5.01	1.34	2	2	0	1.9	800 222-8222
Wells Fargo Asset Allocation I	AssetAlloc	-1	-4.2	2.16	2	2	0	0.99	800 222-8222
Wells Fargo Diversified Equity A	Growth	-11.4	-9.8	-0.93	4	3	5.75	1.25	800 222-8222
Wells Fargo Diversified Equity B	Growth	-12	-10.47	-1.67	4	3	0	2	800 222-8222
Wells Fargo Diversified Equity C	Growth	-12.1	-10.49	-1.64	4	3	0	2	800 222-8222
Wells Fargo Diversified Equity I	Growth	-11.1	-9.63	-0.82	4	3	0	1	800 222-8222
Wells Fargo Diversified Sm Cap I	Small Co	-10.2	2.02	0.88	3	3	0	1.2	800 222-8222
Wells Fargo Equity Income A	Growth/Inc	-13	-5.37	-1.17	3	2	5.75	1.1	800 222-8222
Wells Fargo Equity Income B	Growth/Inc	-13.6	-6.09	-1.92	3	2	0	1.85	800 222-8222
Wells Fargo Equity Income C	Growth/Inc	-13.6	-6.07	-1.91	3	2	0	1.85	800 222-8222

Stock Fund Name	Objective	Annualized Return for			Rank		Max Load	Expense Ratio	Toll-Free/(Toll) Telephone
		1 Year	3 Years	5 Years	Overall	Risk			
Wells Fargo Equity Income I	Growth/Inc	-12.8	-5.15	-1.02	3	2	0	0.85	800 222-8222
Wells Fargo Equity Index A	Growth/Inc	-8.6	-11.38	-1.72	3	3	5.75	0.67	800 222-8222
Wells Fargo Equity Index B	Growth/Inc	-9.3	-12.03		4	3	0	1.41	800 222-8222
Wells Fargo Growth Balanced A	Balanced	-8	-2.77	3.37	3	2	5.75	1.15	800 222-8222
Wells Fargo Growth Balanced B	Balanced	-8.7	-3.5	2.6	2	2	0	1.9	800 222-8222
Wells Fargo Growth Balanced C	Balanced	-8.7	-3.5	2.64	2	2	0	1.9	800 222-8222
Wells Fargo Growth Balanced I	Balanced	-7.8	-2.56	3.58	3	2	0	0.93	800 222-8222
Wells Fargo Growth Equity A	Growth	-11.9	-10.02	-0.83	4	3	5.75	1.5	800 222-8222
Wells Fargo Growth Equity B	Growth	-12.6	-10.74	-1.6	4	3	0	2.25	800 222-8222
Wells Fargo Growth Equity C	Growth	-12.6	-10.72	-1.42	4	3	0	2.25	800 222-8222
Wells Fargo Growth Equity I	Growth	-11.7	-9.83	-0.66	4	3	0	1.25	800 222-8222
Wells Fargo Growth Fund A	Growth	-13.2	-16.71	-4.82	4	3	5.75	1.12	800 222-8222
Wells Fargo Growth Fund B	Growth	-13.9	-17.32	-5.5	5	3	0	1.87	800 222-8222
Wells Fargo Growth Fund I	Growth	-13.2	-16.62	-10.05	5	3	0	1	800 222-8222
Wells Fargo Index Allocation A	AssetAlloc	-9.3	-11.97	-2.16	4	3	5.75	1.3	800 222-8222
Wells Fargo Index Allocation B	AssetAlloc	-10	-12.61		4	3	0	2.05	800 222-8222
Wells Fargo Index Allocation C	AssetAlloc	-10	-12.64		4	3	0	2.05	800 222-8222
Wells Fargo Index I	Growth/Inc	-8	-10.89	-1.2	3	3	0	0.25	800 222-8222
Wells Fargo International Equity A	Foreign	-19.2	-15.49	-3.33	3	3	5.75	1.5	800 222-8222
Wells Fargo International Equity B	Foreign	-19.8	-16.1	-4	5	3	0	2.25	800 222-8222
Wells Fargo International Equity C	Foreign	-19.8	-16.1	-4	5	3	0	2.25	800 222-8222
Wells Fargo International Equity I	Foreign	-19	-15.25	-3.1	4	3	0	1.5	800 222-8222
Wells Fargo Large Co Growth A	Growth	-8.5	-15.71	0.78	3	4	5.75	1.2	800 222-8222
Wells Fargo Large Co Growth B	Growth	-9	-16.17	0.2	3	4	0	1.75	800 222-8222
Wells Fargo Large Co Growth C	Growth	-8.9	-16.16	0.23	3	4	0	1.75	800 222-8222
Wells Fargo Large Co Growth I	Growth	-8.3	-15.52	0.96	3	4	0	0.97	800 222-8222
Wells Fargo Mid-Cap Growth B	Growth	-8.6					0	2.15	800 222-8222
Wells Fargo Mid-Cap Growth C	Growth	-8.6					0	2.15	800 222-8222
Wells Fargo Moderate Balanced I	Balanced	-2.2	1.51	4.79	2	1	0	0.88	800 222-8222
Wells Fargo Outlook 2010 A	AssetAlloc	-1.6	-1.2	2.41	2	1	5.75	1.3	800 222-8222
Wells Fargo Outlook 2010 B	AssetAlloc	-2.1	-1.69	1.9	2	1	0	1.8	800 222-8222
Wells Fargo Outlook 2010 C	AssetAlloc	-2.2	-1.71	1.88	2	1	0	1.8	800 222-8222
Wells Fargo Outlook 2010 I	AssetAlloc	-1.3	-0.98	2.54	2	1	0	1	800 222-8222
Wells Fargo Outlook 2020 A	AssetAlloc	-4.7	-5.44	0.54	2	1	5.75	1.3	800 222-8222
Wells Fargo Outlook 2020 B	AssetAlloc	-5.3	-5.94	0.02	2	1	0	1.8	800 222-8222
Wells Fargo Outlook 2020 C	AssetAlloc	-5.2	-5.9	0.02	2	1	0	1.8	800 222-8222
Wells Fargo Outlook 2020 I	AssetAlloc	-4.5	-5.2	0.72	2	1	0	1	800 222-8222
Wells Fargo Outlook 2030 A	AssetAlloc	-6	-7.82	-0.46	3	2	5.75	1.3	800 222-8222
Wells Fargo Outlook 2030 B	AssetAlloc	-6.5	-8.27	-0.96	3	2	0	1.8	800 222-8222
Wells Fargo Outlook 2030 C	AssetAlloc	-6.4	-8.25	-0.97	3	2	0	1.8	800 222-8222
Wells Fargo Outlook 2030 I	AssetAlloc	-5.7	-7.57	-0.28	2	2	0	1	800 222-8222
Wells Fargo Outlook 2040 A	AssetAlloc	-7.8	-10.82	-1.77	3	3	5.75	1.3	800 222-8222
Wells Fargo Outlook 2040 B	AssetAlloc	-8.2	-11.24	-2.25	4	3	0	1.8	800 222-8222
Wells Fargo Outlook 2040 C	AssetAlloc	-8.2					0	1.8	800 222-8222
Wells Fargo Outlook 2040 I	AssetAlloc	-7.5	-10.57	-1.57	3	3	0	1	800 222-8222
Wells Fargo Outlook Today A	AssetAlloc	1.6	2.64	3.7	2	1	5.75	1.3	800 222-8222
Wells Fargo Outlook Today B	AssetAlloc	1.1	2.12	3.16	2	1	0	1.8	800 222-8222
Wells Fargo Outlook Today C	AssetAlloc	1	2.12	3.14	2	1	0	1.8	800 222-8222
Wells Fargo Outlook Today I	AssetAlloc	1.9	2.95	3.87	2	1	0	1	800 222-8222
Wells Fargo SIFE Spec Fincl Svc A	Financial	-8.3	3.66	0.93	3	3	5.75	1.35	800 222-8222
Wells Fargo SIFE Spec Fincl Svc B	Financial	-9	2.72	-0.08	3	3	0	2.1	800 222-8222
Wells Fargo SIFE Spec Fincl Svc C	Financial	-9	2.68	-0.14	3	3	1	2.1	800 222-8222
Wells Fargo Sm Cap Opports I	Small Co	-11.3	4.78	5.04	2	3	0	1.2	800 222-8222
Wells Fargo Small Cap Growth A	Small Co	-18.6	-22.42	-4.88	4	5	5.75	1.4	800 222-8222
Wells Fargo Small Cap Growth B	Small Co	-19.2	-23.03	-5.59	4	5	0	2.15	800 222-8222
Wells Fargo Small Cap Growth C	Small Co	-19.3					0	2.15	800 222-8222
Wells Fargo Small Cap Growth I	Small Co	-18.5	-22.32	-4.61	4	5	0	1.2	800 222-8222
Wells Fargo Small Co Growth I	Small Co	-11.3	-8.05	-2.58	3	4	0	1.25	800 222-8222

Stock Fund Name	Objective	Annualized Return for			Rank		Max Load	Expense Ratio	Toll-Free/(Toll) Telephone
		1 Year	3 Years	5 Years	Overall	Risk			
Wells Fargo Small Co Value A	Small Co	-11.5	13.16	4.91		3	5.75	1.4	800 222-8222
Wells Fargo Small Co Value B	Small Co	-12.2	12.27	4.11		3	0	2.15	800 222-8222
Wells Fargo Small Co Value C	Small Co	-12.2	12.27	4.11		3	1	2.2	800 222-8222
Wells Fargo Small Co Value 1	Small Co	-11.4	13.33	5.07		3	0	1.2	800 222-8222
Wells Fargo Specialized Tech A	Technology	2.6					5.75	1.75	800 222-8222
Wells Fargo Specialized Tech B	Technology	1.9					0	2.5	800 222-8222
Wells Fargo Specialized Tech C	Technology	1.6					0	2.5	800 222-8222
Wells Fargo Strategic Gr Alloc I	Balanced	-10.4	-5.34	2.27	3	2	0	1	800 222-8222
Wells Fargo Strategic Income I	AssetAlloc	2.4	4.54	5.54	2	1	0	0.8	800 222-8222
Wells Fargo WealthBuilder Gr & Inc	Growth/Inc	-13.1	-12.64	-3.04	5	3	1.5	1.25	800 222-8222
Wells Fargo WealthBuilder Gr Bal	Balanced	-8.1	-5.54	-0.14	3	2	1.5	1.25	800 222-8222
Wells Fargo WealthBuilder Growth	Growth	-15.4	-13.75	-2.7	5	3	1.5	1.25	800 222-8222
Wells S&P REIT Index A	Real Est	3.7	14.18	5.26	2	2	4	0.99	800 282-1581
Wells S&P REIT Index B	Real Est	2.9	13.4		1	1	0	0.98	800 282-1581
Wells S&P REIT Index C	Real Est	2.9	13.36		1	1	0	0.98	800 282-1581
WesMark Balanced Fund	Balanced	-3.4	-5.58		2	2	4.75	1.27	800 341-7400
WesMark Growth Fund	Growth	-4.8	-7.7	2.89	2	3	4.75	1.2	800 341-7400
WesMark Small Company Growth	Small Co	-11.4					4.75	1.89	800 341-7400
Westcore Blue Chip	Growth/Inc	-12.6	-5.79	-1.93	3	3	0	1.15	800 392-2673
Westcore Growth and Income	Growth/Inc	-11.7	-10.09	2.25	3	3	0	1.15	800 392-2673
Westcore MIDCO Growth	Agg Growth	-2.1	-6.7	4.26	2	4	0	1.15	800 392-2673
Westcore Small-Cap Opportunity	Small Co	-11.8	6.36	-0.67	3	4	0	1.3	800 392-2673
Westport Fund I	Growth	-8.2					0	1.5	(203 227-3601)
Westport Fund R	Growth	-8	0.94	8.11		3	0	1.5	(203 227-3601)
Westport Select Cap I	Small Co	-7.5	4.34	10.94	2	3	0	1.09	(203 227-3601)
Westport Select Cap R	Small Co	-7.7	4.19	10.8		3	0	1.38	(203 227-3601)
White Oak Growth Stock	Agg Growth	-8.4	-25.67	-3.79	4	5	0	0.95	888 462-5386
William Blair Growth N	Growth	-14.9	-14.08	-2.41	4	4	0	1.18	800 742-7272
William Blair Intl Growth N	Foreign	-13.1	-9.61	5.86	3	2	0	1.6	800 742-7272
William Blair Mutual-Small Cap Gr N	Small Co	-2.7	10.91			5	0	1.95	800 742-7272
William Blair Value Discovery N	Small Co	-13.1	9.38	5.54	3	3	0	1.49	800 742-7272
Wilmington Large Cap Core	Growth	-9.8	-15.52	-4.05	4	3	0	0.8	800 336-9970
Wilmington Large Cap Growth Equity	Growth	-8.1	-23.87	-6.87	3	4	0	0.71	800 336-9970
Wilshire Target-5000 Index Instl	Growth	-7.8	-9.96		3	3	0	0.34	888 200-6796
Wilshire Target-5000 Index Inv	Growth	-8.2	-10.26		3	3	0	0.64	888 200-6796
Wilshire Target-Large Co Gr Inst	Growth	-4.9	-13.17	0.45	3	3	0	0.51	888 200-6796
Wilshire Target-Large Co Gr Inv	Growth	-5.1	-13.44	0.17	3	3	0	0.83	888 200-6796
Wilshire Target-Large Co Val Inst	Growth	-10.8	0.79	-0.98	3	2	0	0.68	888 200-6796
Wilshire Target-Large Co Val Inv	Growth	-10.9	0.64	-0.11	3	2	0	0.95	888 200-6796
Wilshire Target-Small Co Gr Inst	Small Co	-8.4	-6.32	-3.37	3	4	0	1.44	888 200-6796
Wilshire Target-Small Co Gr Inv	Small Co	-8.4	-6.51	-3.58	3	4	0	1.72	888 200-6796
Wilshire Target-Small Co Val Inst	Small Co	-9.5	10.73	1.18	3	3	0	0.95	888 200-6796
Wilshire Target-Small Co Val Inv	Small Co	-9.6	10.51	0.98	3	3	0	1.18	888 200-6796
Winslow Green Growth Fund	Agg Growth	-5	-9.83	10.83	3	5	0	1.45	888 314-9049
Wisdom Fund B	Growth/Inc	-4.6	3.72			1	0	2.75	877 352-0020
Wisdom Fund C	Growth/Inc	-4.6	3.72			1	0	2.75	877 352-0020
Wisdom Fund Instl	Growth/Inc	-3.6	4.75			1	0	1.75	877 352-0020
Wisdom Fund Inv	Growth/Inc	-4	4.17			1	5.75	2	877 352-0020
Women's Equity Fund	Growth	-6.9	-2.58	2.37	2	2	0	1.5	866-811-0221
Wright Intl Blue Chip Equity	Foreign	-10	-14.33	-5.99	3	3	0	1.43	800 232-0013
Wright Major Blue Chip Equity	Growth	-12.2	-14.48	-4.59	4	3	0	1.05	800 232-0013
Wright Selected Blue Chip Eq	Growth/Inc	-13.7	-5.2	-2.54	3	3	0	1.25	800 232-0013
Yacktman Focused Fund	Growth	17.6	22.82	3.68	1	3	0	1.25	800 525-8258
Yacktman Fund	Growth/Inc	14.3	23.05	6.05	1	2	0	1.17	800 525-8258

BOND FUNDS

Bond Fund Name	Objective	Annualized Return for			Rank		Max Load	Expense Ratio	Toll-Free/(Toll) Telephone
		1 Year	3 Years	5 Years	Overall	Risk			
1838 Fixed Income Fund	Corp-Inv	10.8	10.19	4.5	3	2	0	0.6	877 367-1838
1st Source Monogram Income	Corp-Inv	9.6	9.21	6.37	2	2	4	0.93	800 766-8938
AAL Bond Fund A	Corp-Inv	11.3	10.08	6.62	3	3	4.5	0.91	800 553-6319
AAL Bond Fund B	Corp-Inv	10.3	9.11	5.63	4	3	0	1.8	800 553-6319
AAL Bond Fund I	Corp-Inv	11.8	10.56	7.07	2	3	0	0.46	800 553-6319
AAL Bond Index Fund I	Intl Bond	11.2	10.68		1	2	0	1.36	800 553-6319
AAL High Yield Bond A	Corp-HY	13	4.07	-0.22	4	5	4.5	1.17	800 553-6319
AAL High Yield Bond B	Corp-HY	12	3.24	-1	4	5	0	1.93	800 553-6319
AAL High Yield Bond I	Corp-HY	13.3	4.37	0.08	4	5	0	0.68	800 553-6319
AAL Municipal Bond Fund A	Muni Natl	9.6	9.57	5.53	3	3	4.5	0.82	800 553-6319
AAL Municipal Bond Fund B	Muni Natl	8.7	8.67	4.66	4	3	0	1.62	800 553-6319
AAL Municipal Bond Fund I	Muni Natl	9.9	9.9	5.84	2	3	0	0.51	800 553-6319
AAL US Government Target 2006	Govt-Mtg	10.8	9.64	4.5	4	4	4.75	0.9	800 553-6319
AAM DFA Two-Year Government	Government	5.3					0	0.34	800 342-6684
AAM Two-Year Corporate Fixed Inc	Corp-Inv	5.3					0	0.34	800 342-6684
ABN AMRO Bond Fund N	Dvsfd Bond	8.6	9	6.55	3	2	0	0.74	800 992-8151
ABN AMRO Investment Grade Bond I	Corp-Inv	9.5	8.73	6.49	2	2	0	0.68	800 992-8151
ABN AMRO Muni Bond N	Muni Natl	7.6	7.92	5.3	3	3	0	0.5	800 992-8151
AFBA 5Star High Yield I	Corp-HY	13.4	8.55	3.2	4	4	0	1.05	800 243-9865
AHA Full Mat Fixed Income	Corp-Inv	11.1	9.09	6.95	4	3	0	0.3	800 445-1341
AHA Limited Mat Fixed Income	Corp-Inv	5.4	5.99	5.78	3	1	0	0.24	800 445-1341
AIC Sirach Bond Inst	Corp-Inv	8.5					0	0.5	866 234-5426
AIM Floating Rate B	Corp-HY	2.6	2.45	3.5	5	1	0	1.38	800 347-4246
AIM Floating Rate C	Corp-HY	2.4	2.12		4	2	0	1.63	800 347-4246
AIM Global Income Fund B	Intl Bond	13.2	6.83	2.41	4	4	0	2	800 347-4246
AIM Global Income Fund C	Intl Bond	13	6.79	2.41	4	4	0	2	800 347-4246
AIM High Income Muni A	Muni Natl	8	7.51	3.41	3	2	4.75	1.07	800 347-4246
AIM High Income Muni B	Muni Natl	7.2	6.7	2.66	3	2	0	1.82	800 347-4246
AIM High Income Muni C	Muni Natl	7.2	6.7	2.66	3	2	0	1.82	800 347-4246
AIM High Yield Fund A	Corp-HY	5.9	-6.5	-6.83	5	5	4.75	1.07	800 347-4246
AIM High Yield Fund B	Corp-HY	5.1	-7.19	-7.54	5	5	0	1.82	800 347-4246
AIM High Yield Fund C	Corp-HY	5.1	-7.19	-7.53	5	5	0	1.82	800 347-4246
AIM High Yield II A	Corp-HY	4.1	-6.58		5	5	4.75	1.3	800 347-4246
AIM High Yield II B	Corp-HY	3.3	-7.32		5	5	0	2.05	800 347-4246
AIM High Yield II C	Corp-HY	3.3	-7.25		5	5	0	2.05	800 347-4246
AIM Income Fund A	Corp-Inv	11	5.91	2.18	4	4	4.75	0.95	800 347-4246
AIM Income Fund B	Corp-Inv	10.2	5.12	1.4	5	4	0	1.71	800 347-4246
AIM Income Fund C	Corp-Inv	10	5.12	1.39	5	4	0	1.71	800 347-4246
AIM Interm Govt Fund A	Government	9.2	8.69	6.15	3	3	4.75	0.93	800 347-4246
AIM Interm Govt Fund B	Government	8.5	7.91	5.36	4	3	0	1.69	800 347-4246
AIM Interm Govt Fund C	Government	8.4	7.91	5.36	4	3	0	1.69	800 347-4246
AIM Ltd Maturity Treas Ret A	Government	4.4	6.13	5.32	3	1	1	0.56	800 347-4246
AIM Municipal Bond Fund A	Muni Natl	9.4	7.88	5.08	3	3	4.75	0.81	800 347-4246
AIM Municipal Bond Fund B	Muni Natl	8.5	7.08	4.29	3	3	0	1.89	800 347-4246
AIM Municipal Bond Fund C	Muni Natl	8.7	7.08	4.29	3	3	0	1.89	800 347-4246
AIM Short Term Bond C	Dvsfd Bond						0	1.85	800 347-4246
AIM Strategic Income A	Intl Bond	8	3.7	-0.28	4	4	4.75	1.51	800 347-4246
AIM Strategic Income B	Intl Bond	7.4	3.08	-0.93	4	4	0	2.16	800 347-4246
AIM Strategic Income C	Intl Bond	7.2	3.06		4	4	0	2.16	800 347-4246
AIM Tax-Free Intermediate	Muni Natl	9.6	8.5	5.91	2	3	1	0.38	800 347-4246
AIM Total Return Bond Fund A	Corp-Inv	11.1					4.75	1	800 347-4246
AIM Total Return Bond Fund B	Corp-Inv	10.3					0	1.75	800 347-4246
AIM Total Return Bond Fund C	Corp-Inv	10.3					0	1.75	800 347-4246
AMF Adjustable Rate Mortgage	Govt-Mtg	2.7	4.94	4.91	3	1	0	0.45	800 982-1846
AMF Intermediate Mortgage Fund	Govt-Mtg	4.7	7.62	5.86	3	1	0	0.47	800 982-1846

Bond Fund Name	Objective	Annualized Return for			Rank		Max Load	Expense Ratio	Toll-Free/(Toll) Telephone
		1 Year	3 Years	5 Years	Overall	Risk			
AMF Short-U.S. Government Fund	Government	4.7	6.45	5.53	3	1	0	0.47	800 982-1846
AMF U.S. Government Mortgage Fund	Govt-Mtg	6.6	8.25	6.2	3	2	0	0.47	800 982-1846
AMF Ultra Short Fund	Dvsfd Bond	2.3					0	0.5	800 982-1846
API Trust-Treasuries Trust Fund	Government	5.9	6.79	5.16	4	3	0	0.85	800 544-6060
ARK Fds-Income Inst	Dvsfd Bond	11	10.02	6.44	3	3	0	0.83	800 275-3863
ARK Fds-Income Retail A	Dvsfd Bond	10.7	9.85	6.28	3	3	4.5	1.03	800 275-3863
ARK Fds-Income Retail B	Dvsfd Bond	10.1	9.14	5.65	3	3	0	1.73	800 275-3863
ARK Fds-Intermed Fix Inc Inst	Dvsfd Bond	12.2	9.75	6.73	2	3	0	0.82	800 275-3863
ARK Fds-MD Tax-Free Inst	Muni State	9	8.75	5.37	2	3	0	0.81	800 275-3863
ARK Fds-MD Tax-Free Retail A	Muni State	8.8	8.57	5.2	3	3	4.5	1.02	800 275-3863
ARK Fds-PA Tax-Free Fd Inst	Muni State	9.9	9.21	5.28	2	3	0	0.98	800 275-3863
ARK Fds-PA Tax-Free Fd Retail A	Muni State	9.7	9.05	5.12	2	3	4.5	1.84	800 275-3863
ARK Fds-Short-Term Bond Inst	Corp-Inv	5.7	5.75	4.87	3	1	0	0.97	800 275-3863
ARK Fds-Short-Term Treas Inst	Government	4.2	6.12	5.29	2	1	0	0.63	800 275-3863
ARK Fds-Short-Term Treas Retail A	Government	3.9	5.9	5.07	3	1	0	0.91	800 275-3863
ARK Fds-US Gov Bond Inst	Government	8.9	9.01	5.98	3	3	0	0.98	800 275-3863
ARK Fds-US Gov Bond Retail A	Government	8.8	8.88	5.87	3	2	4.5	1.18	800 275-3863
ASAF Federated High Yield Bond A	Corp-HY	8.1	2.6	1.26	5	5	4.25	1.5	800 752-6342
ASAF Federated High Yield Bond B	Corp-HY	7.6	2.04	0.71	5	5	0	2	800 752-6342
ASAF Federated High Yield Bond C	Corp-HY	7.6	2.08	0.75	5	5	1	2	800 752-6342
ASAF Federated High Yield Bond X	Corp-HY	7.6	2.04	0.71	5	5	0	2	800 752-6342
ASAF PIMCO Total Return Bond A	Dvsfd Bond	7.8	8.67	6.29	4	3	4.25	1.5	800 752-6342
ASAF PIMCO Total Return Bond B	Dvsfd Bond	7.2	8.1	5.79	4	3	0	2	800 752-6342
ASAF PIMCO Total Return Bond C	Dvsfd Bond	7.1	8.1	5.76	4	3	1	2	800 752-6342
ASAF PIMCO Total Return Bond X	Dvsfd Bond	7.2	8.11	5.78	4	3	0	2	800 752-6342
AXA Premier Core Bond A	Dvsfd Bond	11.3					4.5	1.49	866 231-8585
AXA Premier Core Bond B	Dvsfd Bond	10.8					0	2.24	866 231-8585
AXA Premier Core Bond C	Dvsfd Bond	10.7					0	2.24	866 231-8585
AXA Premier Core Bond Z	Dvsfd Bond	11.5					0	1.24	866 231-8585
AXP Bond Fund A	Corp-Inv	9	8.71	5.36	3	2	4.75	0.94	800 328-8300
AXP Bond Fund B	Corp-Inv	8.2					0	1.71	800 328-8300
AXP CA Tax Exempt Fund A	Muni CA	9.2	8.42	5.23	5	4	4.75	0.83	800 328-8300
AXP CA Tax Exempt Fund B	Muni CA	8.1					0	1.59	800 328-8300
AXP Extra Income A	Corp-HY	7.6	0.68	-0.94	5	5	4.75	1.06	800 328-8300
AXP Extra Income B	Corp-HY	6.8					0	1.82	800 328-8300
AXP Federal Income A	Government	4.9	6.94	4.9	3	1	4.75	0.91	800 328-8300
AXP Federal Income B	Government	4.1					0	1.67	800 328-8300
AXP Global Bond A	Intl Bond	20.8	10.18	5.53	3	4	4.75	1.33	800 328-8300
AXP Global Bond B	Intl Bond	19.7					0	2.09	800 328-8300
AXP High Yield Tax Exempt A	Muni Natl	8.8	8.13	5.09	4	3	4.75	0.79	800 328-8300
AXP High Yield Tax Exempt B	Muni Natl	8					0	1.54	800 328-8300
AXP Insured Tax Exempt A	Muni Natl	9.6	8.71	5.45	4	4	4.75	0.81	800 328-8300
AXP Insured Tax Exempt B	Muni Natl	8.8	7.9	4.66	5	4	0	1.58	800 328-8300
AXP Intermediate Tax Exempt A	Muni Natl	9.3					4.75	0.87	800 328-8300
AXP Intermediate Tax Exempt B	Muni Natl	8.5					0	1.63	800 328-8300
AXP MA Tax Exempt Fund A	Muni State	8.7	8.25	4.88	4	3	4.75	0.92	800 328-8300
AXP MA Tax Exempt Fund B	Muni State	7.9					0	1.67	800 328-8300
AXP MI Tax Exempt Fund A	Muni State	10.9	9	5.28	3	3	4.75	0.9	800 328-8300
AXP MI Tax Exempt Fund B	Muni State	9.9					0	1.65	800 328-8300
AXP MN Tax Exempt Fund A	Muni State	9.3	8.46	5.28	3	3	4.75	0.83	800 328-8300
AXP MN Tax Exempt Fund B	Muni State	8.5					0	1.58	800 328-8300
AXP NY Tax Exempt Fund A	Muni NY	10.4	8.94	5.45	3	4	4.75	0.88	800 328-8300
AXP NY Tax Exempt Fund B	Muni NY	9.6					0	1.64	800 328-8300
AXP OH Tax Exempt Fund A	Muni State	8.8	8.09	5.07	3	3	4.75	0.89	800 328-8300
AXP OH Tax Exempt Fund B	Muni State	8	7.29	4.29	5	3	0	1.65	800 328-8300
AXP Selective Fund A	Corp-Inv	6.4	7.57	5.38	5	2	4.75	0.95	800 328-8300
AXP Selective Fund B	Corp-Inv	5.7	6.79	4.62	4	2	0	1.72	800 328-8300
AXP Tax Exempt Bond Fund A	Muni Natl	10.3	9.33	5.53	4	4	4.75		800-328-8300

Bond Fund Name	Objective	Annualized Return for			Rank		Max Load	Expense Ratio	Toll-Free/(Toll) Telephone
		1 Year	3 Years	5 Years	Overall	Risk			
AXP Tax Exempt Bond Fund B	Muni Natl	9.4					0	1.57	800 328-8300
Access Cap Strat Community Inv Fd	Government	6.5	9.08			4	0		
Accessor Interm Fixed Inc Adv	Dvsfd Bond	14.2	11.98	7.44	3	4	0	0.67	800 759-3504
Accessor Mortgage Sec Adv	Govt-Mtg	5.5	8.75	6.45	1	2	0	0.84	800 759-3504
Accessor Mortgage Sec Inv	Govt-Mtg	5.1	8.1		2	2	0	1.31	800 759-3504
Accessor Sh-Interm Fixed Inc Adv	Corp-Inv	7.2	7.58	5.79	3	2	0	0.64	800 759-3504
Activa Intermediate Bond Fund	Dvsfd Bond	10	9.92		2	3	0	0.7	800 346-2670
Adv Inn Cir TS&W Fixed Inc Inst	Corp-Inv	10.5	9.43	5.19	2	3	0		866 450-3722
Advantus Bond Fund A	Corp-Inv	12.2	10.78	6.51	3	3	4.5	1.14	800 665-6005
Advantus Bond Fund B	Corp-Inv	11.2	9.94	5.76	3	3	0	1.89	800 665-6005
Advantus Bond Fund C	Corp-Inv	11.3	9.93	6.08	3	3	0	1.89	800 665-6005
Advantus Mortgage Securities A	Govt-Mtg	8.3	10.38	7.67	2	2	4.5	0.96	800 665-6005
Advantus Mortgage Securities B	Govt-Mtg	7.5	9.56	6.87	3	2	0	1.71	800 665-6005
Advantus Mortgage Securities C	Govt-Mtg	7.5	9.52	6.86	3	2	0	1.71	800 665-6005
Alabama Tax Free Bond	Muni State	8.8	7.87	5.37	2	2	0	0.65	800 443-4249
AllianceBernstein Amer Govt Inc A	Intl Bond	23.9	12.33	12.25	3	5	4.25	1.57	800 247-4154
AllianceBernstein Amer Govt Inc B	Intl Bond	23.1	11.44	11.28	3	5	0	2.28	800 247-4154
AllianceBernstein Amer Govt Inc C	Intl Bond	23	11.52	11.33	3	5	0	2.33	800 247-4154
AllianceBernstein Bond-Corp Bond A	Corp-Inv	13.9	10	4.99	3	5	4.25	1.16	800 247-4154
AllianceBernstein Bond-Corp Bond B	Corp-Inv	13.1	9.11	5.01	3	5	0	1.89	800 247-4154
AllianceBernstein Bond-Corp Bond C	Corp-Inv	13.1	11.59	6.41	3	5	0	1.87	800 247-4154
AllianceBernstein Bond-Quality A	Dvsfd Bond	10.4	9.24		1	2	4.25	0.98	800 247-4154
AllianceBernstein Bond-Quality B	Dvsfd Bond	9.6	8.72		1	2	0	1.68	800 247-4154
AllianceBernstein Bond-Quality C	Dvsfd Bond	9.6	8.65		1	2	0	1.68	800 247-4154
AllianceBernstein Bond-US Govt A	Government	10.8	9.41	6.66	3	3	4.25	1.05	800 247-4154
AllianceBernstein Bond-US Govt B	Government	10	8.6	6.58	3	3	0	1.78	800 247-4154
AllianceBernstein Bond-US Govt C	Government	10	8.65	6.61	3	3	0	1.77	800 247-4154
AllianceBernstein CA Muni	Muni CA	6.5	6.66	4.91	3	2	0	0.66	800 247-4154
AllianceBernstein Emg Mkt Debt A	Intl Bond	33.4	19.42	11.9	2	5	4.25	1.88	800 247-4154
AllianceBernstein Emg Mkt Debt B	Intl Bond	32.3	18.44	11.02	2	5	0	2.58	800 247-4154
AllianceBernstein Emg Mkt Debt C	Intl Bond	32.4	18.6	11.15	2	5	0	2.56	800 247-4154
AllianceBernstein Gbl Str Inc A	Intl Bond	15.7	5.65	5.59	3	4	4.25	1.53	800 247-4154
AllianceBernstein Gbl Str Inc Adv	Intl Bond	16.1	5.75	5.66	3	4	0	1.24	800 247-4154
AllianceBernstein Gbl Str Inc B	Intl Bond	14.9	4.91	4.95	3	4	0	2.24	800 247-4154
AllianceBernstein Gbl Str Inc C	Intl Bond	14.9	4.91	4.94	3	4	0	2.23	800 247-4154
AllianceBernstein Govt Short Dur	Government	5	6.61	6.25	3	1	0	0.74	800 247-4154
AllianceBernstein High Yield Adv	Corp-HY	8.1	-0.28	-1.39	5	5	0	1.16	800 247-4154
AllianceBernstein High Yield Fund A	Corp-HY	7.8	-0.64	-2.2	5	5	4.25	1.43	800 247-4154
AllianceBernstein High Yield Fund B	Corp-HY	7.6	-1.19	-2.7	5	5	0	2.15	800 247-4154
AllianceBernstein High Yield Fund C	Corp-HY	7.2	-1.29	-2.75	5	5	0	2.14	800 247-4154
AllianceBernstein Multi-Mkt StrA	Intl Bond	6.6	5.51	4.69	4	1	4.25	1.49	800 247-4154
AllianceBernstein Multi-Mkt StrB	Intl Bond	5.8	4.71	3.87	4	1	0	2.24	800 247-4154
AllianceBernstein Multi-Mkt StrC	Intl Bond	5.8	4.7	4.53	4	1	0	2.2	800 247-4154
AllianceBernstein Muni Inc II-AZ A	Muni State	7	7.96	5.99	3	3	4.25	0.78	800 247-4154
AllianceBernstein Muni Inc II-AZ B	Muni State	6.3	7.16	5.16	4	3	0	1.48	800 247-4154
AllianceBernstein Muni Inc II-AZ C	Muni State	6.2	7.25	5.2	3	3	0	1.48	800 247-4154
AllianceBernstein Muni Inc II-FL A	Muni State	9.8	9.15	6.17	1	2	4.25	0.78	800 247-4154
AllianceBernstein Muni Inc II-FL B	Muni State	9.1	8.43	5.41	2	2	0	1.48	800 247-4154
AllianceBernstein Muni Inc II-FL C	Muni State	9	8.42	5.41	2	2	0	1.48	800 247-4154
AllianceBernstein Muni Inc II-MA A	Muni State	7.4	8.24	5.62	3	3	4.25	0.82	800 247-4154
AllianceBernstein Muni Inc II-MA B	Muni State	6.8	7.53	4.86	5	3	0	1.52	800 247-4154
AllianceBernstein Muni Inc II-MA C	Muni State	6.8	7.53	4.83	5	3	0	1.52	800 247-4154
AllianceBernstein Muni Inc II-MI A	Muni State	9.2	9.49	6.83	1	3	4.25	1.01	800 247-4154
AllianceBernstein Muni Inc II-MI B	Muni State	8.6	8.75	6.03	2	3	0	1.71	800 247-4154
AllianceBernstein Muni Inc II-MI C	Muni State	8.6	8.75	6.03	2	3	0	1.71	800 247-4154
AllianceBernstein Muni Inc II-MN A	Muni State	9.4	8.88	6.36	1	3	4.25	0.9	800 247-4154
AllianceBernstein Muni Inc II-MN B	Muni State	8.7	8.09	5.54	3	3	0	1.6	800 247-4154
AllianceBernstein Muni Inc II-MN C	Muni State	8.6	8.13	5.55	3	3	0	1.6	800 247-4154

Bond Fund Name	Objective	Annualized Return for			Rank		Max Load	Expense Ratio	Toll-Free/(Toll) Telephone
		1 Year	3 Years	5 Years	Overall	Risk			
AllianceBernstein Muni Inc II-NJ A	Muni State	6.3	7.36	5.26	4	4	4.25	0.87	800 247-4154
AllianceBernstein Muni Inc II-NJ B	Muni State	5.6	6.58	4.42	5	4	0	1.57	800 247-4154
AllianceBernstein Muni Inc II-NJ C	Muni State	5.6	6.58	4.42	5	4	0	1.57	800 247-4154
AllianceBernstein Muni Inc II-OH A	Muni State	7.7	8.27	5.55	3	3	4.25	0.85	800 247-4154
AllianceBernstein Muni Inc II-OH B	Muni State	7	7.54	4.84	4	3	0	1.55	800 247-4154
AllianceBernstein Muni Inc II-OH C	Muni State	7	7.5	4.84	3	3	0	1.55	800 247-4154
AllianceBernstein Muni Inc II-PA A	Muni State	8.3	9.02	6.11	2	3	4.25	0.95	800 247-4154
AllianceBernstein Muni Inc II-PA B	Muni State	7.6	8.27	5.29	3	3	0	1.65	800 247-4154
AllianceBernstein Muni Inc II-PA C	Muni State	7.6	8.27	5.29	3	3	0	1.65	800 247-4154
AllianceBernstein Muni Inc II-VA A	Muni State	9	8.41	5.83	2	3	4.25	0.72	800 247-4154
AllianceBernstein Muni Inc II-VA B	Muni State	8.3	7.69	5.04	3	3	0	1.42	800 247-4154
AllianceBernstein Muni Inc II-VA C	Muni State	8.3	7.67	5.05	4	3	0	1.42	800 247-4154
AllianceBernstein Muni Inc-NY A	Muni NY	7.8	7.88	4.95	4	3	4.25	0.56	800 247-4154
AllianceBernstein Muni Income-CA A	Muni CA	8.9	7.75	5.16	4	3	4.25	0.76	800 247-4154
AllianceBernstein Muni Income-CA B	Muni CA	8.2	7.05	4.91	5	3	0	1.46	800 247-4154
AllianceBernstein Muni Income-CA C	Muni CA	8.1	7.04	4.9	5	3	0	1.46	800 247-4154
AllianceBernstein Muni Income-NY B	Muni NY	6.8	7.08	4.66	4	3	0	1.29	800 247-4154
AllianceBernstein Muni Income-NY C	Muni NY	6.8	7.07	4.66	5	3	0	1.28	800 247-4154
AllianceBernstein Muni-Insd CA A	Muni CA	11.3	9.68	6.38	3	4	4.25	1.04	800 247-4154
AllianceBernstein Muni-Insd CA B	Muni CA	10.4	8.85	5.61	4	4	0	1.75	800 247-4154
AllianceBernstein Muni-Insd CA C	Muni CA	10.3	8.85	5.61	4	4	0	1.74	800 247-4154
AllianceBernstein Muni-Insd Natl A	Muni Natl	8.6	8.77	5.28	3	3	4.25	1.04	800 247-4154
AllianceBernstein Muni-Insd Natl B	Muni Natl	7.9	8.07	4.45	5	3	0	1.75	800 247-4154
AllianceBernstein Muni-Insd Natl C	Muni Natl	7.8	8.02	4.44	5	3	0	1.74	800 247-4154
AllianceBernstein Muni-National A	Muni Natl	5	7.04	3.95	4	3	4.25	0.65	800 247-4154
AllianceBernstein Muni-National B	Muni Natl	4.3	6.29	3.74	5	3	0	1.34	800 247-4154
AllianceBernstein Muni-National C	Muni Natl	4.3	6.3	3.75	5	3	0	1.33	800 247-4154
AllianceBernstein NY Muni	Muni NY	7.2	7.09	5.12	3	2	0	0.66	800 247-4154
AllianceBernstein Sh-Dur Dvrs Muni	Muni Natl	2.8	4.33	3.72	3	1	0	0.71	800 247-4154
AllianceBernstein St Dur CA Muni	Muni CA	2.4	3.77	3.41	3	1	0	0.79	800 247-4154
AllianceBernstein St Dur NY Muni	Muni NY	2.6	3.99	3.45	3	1	0	0.77	800 247-4154
AmSouth Bond Fund A	Corp-Inv	11.9	10.43	7.38	3	3	4	0.99	800 451-8379
AmSouth Bond Fund B	Corp-Inv	11.1	9.6	6.5	3	3	0	1.73	800 451-8379
AmSouth Bond Fund Tr	Corp-Inv	12.2	10.63	7.51	2	3	0	0.84	800 451-8379
AmSouth FL T/E Fund A	Muni State	8.3	7.82	5.21	3	3	4	0.9	800 451-8379
AmSouth FL T/E Fund B	Muni State	7.6	7.03			3	0	1.64	800 451-8379
AmSouth FL T/E Fund Tr	Muni State	8.5	8	5.38	2	3	0	0.75	800 451-8379
AmSouth Govt Income Fd A	Government	8.4	8.83	6.53	2	2	4	0.99	800 451-8379
AmSouth Govt Income Fd B	Government	7.6	8.06	5.74		2	0	1.74	800 451-8379
AmSouth Govt Income Fd Tr	Government	8.6	9.02	6.76		2	0	0.84	800 451-8379
AmSouth Limited Term Bd A	Corp-Inv	6.4	7.59	6.87	2	1	4	1	800 451-8379
AmSouth Limited Term Bd B	Corp-Inv	5.7	6.79	5.24		1	0	1.75	800 451-8379
AmSouth Limited Term Bd Tr	Corp-Inv	6.7	7.78	7.08	2	1	0	0.86	800 451-8379
AmSouth Muni Bond A	Muni Natl	8.4	8.17	5.29	3	3	4	0.89	800 451-8379
AmSouth Muni Bond B	Muni Natl	7.6	7.37	5.11		3	0	1.64	800 451-8379
AmSouth Muni Bond Tr	Muni Natl	8.6	8.36	5.5	2	3	0	0.74	800 451-8379
AmSouth Tennessee T/E Fund A	Muni State	7.9	7.55	4.58	4	3	4	1.09	800 451-8379
AmSouth Tennessee T/E Fund B	Muni State	7	6.7	3.79	5	3	0	1.84	800 451-8379
AmSouth Tennessee T/E Fund Tr	Muni State	8	7.7	4.74	3	3	0	0.94	800 451-8379
American AAdvant Interm Bd Inst	Dvsfd Bond	10.2	10.6	7.04	2	2	0	0.54	800 967-9009
American AAdvant Short Tm Inst	Corp-Inv	5.7	7.16	5.55	3	1	0	0.51	800 967-9009
American AAdvant Short Tm PlanAhd	Corp-Inv	5.4	6.91	5.29	3	1	0	0.75	800 967-9009
American Century AZ Muni Bond Inv	Muni State	9.3	8.85	6.17	1	3	0	0.51	800 378-9878
American Century CA H/Y Muni Inv	Muni CA	11.1	9.64	6.26	2	3	0	0.54	800 378-9878
American Century CA Int-Term T/F	Muni CA	9	8.24	5.79	3	3	0	0.51	800 378-9878
American Century CA Lg Term T/F	Muni CA	10.4	9.9	6.08	3	4	0	0.51	800 378-9878
American Century CA Ltd-Term T/F	Muni CA	5.9	6.25	4.91	3	2	0	0.51	800 378-9878
American Century Diversified Bd I	Dvsfd Bond	9.7					0	0.44	800 378-9878

425

Bond Fund Name	Objective	Annualized Return for			Rank		Max Load	Expense Ratio	Toll-Free/(Toll) Telephone
		1 Year	3 Years	5 Years	Overall	Risk			
American Century FL Muni Bond	Muni State	9.9	8.82	6.25	1	3	0	0.51	800 378-9878
American Century Ginnie Mae Adv	Govt-Mtg	5.2	7.98	5.98	2	1	0	0.84	800 378-9878
American Century Ginnie Mae Inv	Govt-Mtg	5.4	8.24	6.23	2	1	0	0.58	800 378-9878
American Century Govt Bond Adv	Government	15.4	10.78	7.45	3	4	0	0.76	800 378-9878
American Century High Yld Muni A	Muni Natl						4.5	0.89	800 378-9878
American Century High Yld Muni B	Muni Natl						0	1.64	800 378-9878
American Century High Yld Muni C	Muni Natl						0	1.39	800 378-9878
American Century High Yld Muni Inv	Muni Natl	9.4	8.9	6.01	1	2	0	0.64	800 378-9878
American Century High-Yield A	Muni Natl						4.5	1.15	800 378-9878
American Century High-Yield Adv	Corp-HY	8.8					0	1.15	800 378-9878
American Century High-Yield B	Muni Natl						0	1.9	800 378-9878
American Century High-Yield C	Muni Natl						0	1.65	800 378-9878
American Century High-Yield Inv	Corp-HY	8.8	0.76	-0.38	4	5	0	0.9	800 378-9878
American Century Ifl-Adj Tres Inv	Government	16.1	12.02	9.43	2	4	0	0.51	800 378-9878
American Century Infl Adj Bd Adv	Dvsfd Bond						0	0.51	800 378-9878
American Century Infl Adj Bd Inst	Dvsfd Bond						0	0.51	800 378-9878
American Century Intl Bond Inv	Intl Bond	32.9	12.33	7.2	3	5	0	0.84	800 378-9878
American Century Sh-Term Govt Inv	Government	4.4	6.45	5.26	3	1	0	0.58	800 378-9878
American Century Tax-Free Bond Inv	Muni Natl	9.3	8.81	6.09	1	3	0	0.51	800 378-9878
American Century Tgt Mat 2005 Inv	Government	14	15.92	10.39	2	4	0	0.59	800 378-9878
American Century Tgt Mat 2010 Inv	Government	28.7	19.69	12	2	5	0	0.59	800 378-9878
American Century Tgt Mat 2015 Inv	Government	37.8	20.85	12.3	3	5	0	0.59	800 378-9878
American Century Tgt Mat 2020 Inv	Government	43.5	22.8	12.89	3	5	0	0.59	800 378-9878
American Century Tgt Mat 2025 Inv	Government	48.2	25.82	17.64	2	5	0	0.59	800 378-9878
American Century VP Int'l III	Dvsfd Bond						0	0.86	800 378-9878
American Funds Bnd Fd of Amer A	Corp-Inv	12.5	9.52	6.41	1	3	3.75	0.7	800 421-4120
American Funds Bnd Fd of Amer B	Corp-Inv	11.7	7.75		3	4	0	1.47	800 421-4120
American Funds Bnd Fd of Amer C	Corp-Inv	11.6					0	1.55	800 421-4120
American Funds Bnd Fd of Amer F	Corp-Inv	12.5	9.41	6.3	2	3	0	0.77	800 421-4120
American Funds Bnd Fd of Amer R1	Dvsfd Bond	11.6	8.65	5.54		3	0	2.53	800 421-4120
American Funds Bnd Fd of Amer R2	Dvsfd Bond	11.6	8.69	5.59		3	0	1.67	800 421-4120
American Funds Bnd Fd of Amer R3	Dvsfd Bond	12.1	9.11	6		3	0	1.2	800 421-4120
American Funds Bnd Fd of Amer R4	Dvsfd Bond	12.5	9.46	6.34		3	0	0.77	800 421-4120
American Funds Bnd Fd of Amer R5	Dvsfd Bond						0	0.42	800 421-4120
American Funds Cap World Bond A	Intl Bond	25.1	11.81	6.87	3	4	3.75	1.08	800 421-4120
American Funds Cap World Bond B	Intl Bond	24.3	10.91		1	4	0	1.84	800 421-4120
American Funds Cap World Bond C	Intl Bond	24.1					0	1.9	800 421-4120
American Funds Cap World Bond F	Intl Bond	25.1	11.66	6.75	3	4	0	1.16	800 421-4120
American Funds Cap World Bond R1	Intl Bond	24.2	10.98	6.08		4	0	1.81	800 421-4120
American Funds Cap World Bond R2	Intl Bond	24.2	11	6.11		4	0	1.76	800 421-4120
American Funds Cap World Bond R3	Intl Bond	24.7	11.44	6.53		4	0	1.37	800 421-4120
American Funds Cap World Bond R4	Intl Bond	25.4	11.91	6.94		4	0	1.04	800 421-4120
American Funds Cap World Bond R5	Intl Bond						0	0.74	800 421-4120
American Funds Endowments Bd Port	Corp-Inv	13.1	10.75	7.3	1	3	0	0.7	800 421-4120
American Funds High Inc Muni Bnd A	Muni Natl	7.2	7.62	4.7	3	2	3.75	0.77	800 421-4120
American Funds High Inc Muni Bnd B	Muni Natl	6.4	5.58		4	2	0	1.59	800 421-4120
American Funds High Inc Muni Bnd C	Muni Natl	6.3					0	1.59	800 421-4120
American Funds High Inc Muni Bnd F	Muni Natl	7	7.42	4.57	3	2	0	0.88	800 421-4120
American Funds High Income Tr A	Corp-HY	13.1	6.16	3.91	4	5	3.75	0.88	800 421-4120
American Funds High Income Tr B	Corp-HY	12.2	3.77		4	5	0	1.59	800 421-4120
American Funds High Income Tr C	Corp-HY	12.1					0	1.67	800 421-4120
American Funds High Income Tr F	Corp-HY	13	6.04	3.81	4	5	0	0.93	800 421-4120
American Funds High Income Tr R1	Corp-HY	12.1	5.3	3.04		5	0	1.66	800 421-4120
American Funds High Income Tr R2	Corp-HY	12.2	5.36	3.1		5	0	1.61	800 421-4120
American Funds High Income Tr R3	Corp-HY	12.6	5.75	3.5		5	0	1.22	800 421-4120
American Funds High Income Tr R4	Corp-HY	12.9	6.08	3.83		5	0	0.89	800 421-4120
American Funds High Income Tr R5	Corp-HY	13.4	6.45	4.16		5	0	0.59	800 421-4120
American Funds Intm Bd Fd Amer A	Corp-Inv	6.7	8.27	6.26	3	1	3.75	0.76	800 421-4120

Bond Fund Name	Objective	Annualized Return for			Rank		Max Load	Expense Ratio	Toll-Free/(Toll) Telephone
		1 Year	3 Years	5 Years	Overall	Risk			
American Funds Intm Bd Fd Amer B	Corp-Inv	6	6.53		2	1	0	1.46	800 421-4120
American Funds Intm Bd Fd Amer C	Corp-Inv	5.9					0	1.55	800 421-4120
American Funds Intm Bd Fd Amer F	Corp-Inv	6.7	8.18	6.17	3	1	0	0.79	800 421-4120
American Funds Intm Bd Fd Amer R1	Dvsfd Bond	5.8	7.41	5.41		1	0	1.55	800 421-4120
American Funds Intm Bd Fd Amer R2	Dvsfd Bond	5.9	7.48	5.48		1	0	1.5	800 421-4120
American Funds Intm Bd Fd Amer R3	Dvsfd Bond	6.3	7.9	5.88		1	0	1.11	800 421-4120
American Funds Intm Bd Fd Amer R4	Dvsfd Bond	6.7	8.25	6.25		1	0	0.78	800 421-4120
American Funds Intm Bd Fd Amer R5	Dvsfd Bond	7	8.58	6.57		1	0	0.48	800 421-4120
American Funds Ltd Term T/E Bond A	Muni Natl	8.5	7.87	3.66	3	2	3.75	0.7	800 421-4120
American Funds Ltd Term T/E Bond B	Muni Natl	7.7	6.04		3	2	0	1.4	800 421-4120
American Funds Ltd Term T/E Bond C	Muni Natl	7.6					0	1.52	800 421-4120
American Funds Ltd Term T/E Bond F	Muni Natl	8.4	7.65	5.2	3	2	0	0.82	800 421-4120
American Funds T/E Bd of America A	Muni Natl	9.3	8.91	5.76	1	3	3.75	0.63	800 421-4120
American Funds T/E Bd of America B	Muni Natl	8.5	6.82		5	3	0	1.38	800 421-4120
American Funds T/E Bd of America C	Muni Natl	8.3					0	1.51	800 421-4120
American Funds T/E Bd of America F	Muni Natl	9.1	8.75	5.65	2	3	0	0.78	800 421-4120
American Funds Tax Exempt of CA A	Muni CA	9.2	8.52	5.75	3	3	3.75	0.68	800 421-4120
American Funds Tax Exempt of CA B	Muni CA	8.4	7.75		4	3	0	1.42	800 421-4120
American Funds Tax Exempt of CA C	Muni CA	8.3					0	1.55	800 421-4120
American Funds Tax Exempt of CA F	Muni CA	9.1	8.34	5.62	3	3	0	0.83	800 421-4120
American Funds Tax Exempt of MD A	Muni State	9.2	8.19	5.3	1	2	3.75	0.75	800 421-4120
American Funds Tax Exempt of MD B	Muni State	8.4	7.37		4	2	0	1.49	800 421-4120
American Funds Tax Exempt of MD C	Muni State	8.2					0	1.64	800 421-4120
American Funds Tax Exempt of MD F	Muni State	9	7.96	5.15	2	2	0	0.99	800 421-4120
American Funds Tax Exempt of VA A	Muni State	9.6	8.82	5.66	1	3	3.75	0.73	800 421-4120
American Funds Tax Exempt of VA B	Muni State	8.8	8		3	3	0	1.48	800 421-4120
American Funds Tax Exempt of VA C	Muni State	8.6					0	1.62	800 421-4120
American Funds Tax Exempt of VA F	Muni State	9.4	8.49	5.45	3	3	0	1.23	800 421-4120
American Funds US Govt Sec A	Government	9	9.17	6.63	3	2	3.75	0.8	800 421-4120
American Funds US Govt Sec B	Government	8.2	8.1		1	2	0	1.5	800 421-4120
American Funds US Govt Sec C	Government	8.1					0	1.57	800 421-4120
American Funds US Govt Sec F	Government	9	9.08	6.55	3	2	0	0.83	800 421-4120
American Funds US Govt Sec R1	Govt-Mtg	8	8.32	5.8		2	0	1.57	800 421-4120
American Funds US Govt Sec R2	Govt-Mtg	8	8.4	5.87		2	0	1.52	800 421-4120
American Funds US Govt Sec R3	Govt-Mtg	8.6	8.82	6.29		2	0	1.13	800 421-4120
American Funds US Govt Sec R4	Govt-Mtg	8.9	9.18	6.65		2	0	0.8	800 421-4120
American Funds US Govt Sec R5	Govt-Mtg	9.4	9.52	6.99		2	0	0.5	800 421-4120
American Independence Intrm Bd Fd	Dvsfd Bond	11.1	10.13	7.21	2	2	0	0.76	800 342-1223
American Independence KS T/E Bond	Muni State	8.1	7.96	4.98	3	2	0	0.6	800 342-1223
American Independence Shrt Tm Bd Fd	Dvsfd Bond	3.3	5.79	5.58	3	1	0	0.65	800 342-1223
American Performance Bond Fund	Corp-Inv	11.8	10.83	7.41	1	2	4	0.88	800 762-7085
American Performance Interm Bond	Dvsfd Bond	8.2	8.63	6.53	2	1	3	0.88	800 762-7085
American Performance Interm T/F	Muni Natl	7.7	7.88	5.24	3	3	3	0.63	800 762-7085
American Performance Sh-Term Inc	Dvsfd Bond	5	7.34	6.32	2	1	2	0.45	800 762-7085
Analysts Inv-Fixed Income	Dvsfd Bond	6.4	13.59	6.69	5	5	0	1.5	
Aquila Churchill T/F Fd of KY A	Muni State	9.2	7.79	5.19	2	2	4	0.71	800 437-1020
Aquila Churchill T/F Fd of KY C	Muni State	8.4	6.91	4.29	3	2	0	1.56	800 437-1020
Aquila Churchill T/F Fd of KY Y	Muni State	9.5	7.98	5.34	2	2	0	0.56	800 437-1020
Aquila Hawaiian Tax Free Trust A	Muni State	8.7	8.61	5.44	2	3	4	0.69	800 437-1020
Aquila Hawaiian Tax Free Trust C	Muni State	7.9	7.98	4.74	3	3	0	1.5	800 437-1020
Aquila Hawaiian Tax Free Trust Y	Muni State	9	8.83	5.66	2	3	0	0.5	800 437-1020
Aquila Narragansett Ins T/F Inc A	Muni State	10.5	9.14	5.8	1	3	4	0.48	800 437-1020
Aquila Narragansett Ins T/F Inc C	Muni State	9.6	8.19	4.87	4	3	0	1.33	800 437-1020
Aquila Narragansett Ins T/F Inc Y	Muni State	10.8	9.31	5.95	1	3	0	0.33	800 437-1020
Aquila Tax-Free Fd For Utah A	Muni State	11.7	9.58	5.54	2	3	4	0.41	800 437-1020
Aquila Tax-Free Fd For Utah C	Muni State	10.6	8.58	4.54	3	3	0	1.3	800 437-1020
Aquila Tax-Free Fd For Utah Y	Muni State	11.7	9.86	5.73	1	3	0	0.3	800 437-1020
Aquila Tax-Free Fd of Colorado A	Muni State	10.2	8.66	5.8	1	3	4	0.73	800 437-1020

Bond Fund Name	Objective	Annualized Return for			Rank		Max Load	Expense Ratio	Toll-Free/(Toll) Telephone
		1 Year	3 Years	5 Years	Overall	Risk			
Aquila Tax-Free Fd of Colorado C	Muni State	9.1	7.55	4.79	3	3	0	1.68	800 437-1020
Aquila Tax-Free Fd of Colorado Y	Muni State	10.3	8.68	5.86	1	3	0	0.68	800 437-1020
Aquila Tax-Free Tr of Arizona A	Muni State	10.1	8.58	5.62	1	3	4	0.7	800 437-1020
Aquila Tax-Free Tr of Arizona C	Muni State	9.2	7.67	4.7	3	3	0	1.55	800 437-1020
Aquila Tax-Free Tr of Arizona Y	Muni State	10.3	8.72	5.79	1	3	0	0.55	800 437-1020
Aquila Tax-Free Tr of Oregon A	Muni State	10.1	8.9	5.87	1	3	4	0.7	800 437-1020
Aquila Tax-Free Tr of Oregon C	Muni State	9.2	7.95	4.95	3	3	0	1.55	800 437-1020
Aquila Tax-Free Tr of Oregon Y	Muni State	10.5	9.09	6.05	1	3	0	0.55	800 437-1020
Aquinas Fixed Income Fund	Corp-Inv	12.1	10	6.62	2	3	0	1	800 423-6369
Ariel Premier Bond Inst	Dvsfd Bond	10.5	9.46	6.58	3	2	0	0.45	800 292-7435
Ariel Premier Bond Inv	Dvsfd Bond	10.3					0	0.85	800 292-7435
Armada Bond A	Dvsfd Bond	10.6	9.26	6.28	3	3	4.75	0.96	800 622-3863
Armada Bond B	Dvsfd Bond	9.6	8.5	5.24	4	3	0	1.67	800 622-3863
Armada Bond Inst	Dvsfd Bond	10.7	9.52	6.45	3	3	3.75	0.71	800 622-3863
Armada GNMA A	Govt-Mtg	5.1	7.75	5.84	3	1	4.75	1.01	800 622-3863
Armada GNMA Inst	Govt-Mtg	5.4	8	6.08	2	1	0	0.76	800 622-3863
Armada Intermediate Bond A	Corp-Inv	10.7	9.09	6.37	2	2	4.75	0.82	800 622-3863
Armada Intermediate Bond B	Corp-Inv	10	8.32	5.5	3	2	0	1.53	800 622-3863
Armada Intermediate Bond C	Corp-Inv	10	8.39		1	2	0	1.53	800 622-3863
Armada Intermediate Bond Inst	Corp-Inv	11	9.4	6.69	2	2	0	0.56	800 622-3863
Armada Limited Maturity Bond A	Dvsfd Bond	5.2	6.36	5.5	3	1	2.75	0.73	800 622-3863
Armada Limited Maturity Bond H	Dvsfd Bond	3.5					0	1.48	800 622-3863
Armada Limited Maturity Bond Inst	Dvsfd Bond	5.6	6.62	5.63	3	1	0	0.53	800 622-3863
Armada MI Municipal Bond A	Muni State	8.3	7.88	5.21	3	3	4	0.79	800 622-3863
Armada MI Municipal Bond B	Muni State	7.6	7.08	4.28	4	3	0	1.5	800 622-3863
Armada MI Municipal Bond Inst	Muni State	8.5	8.11	5.44	2	3	0	0.59	800 622-3863
Armada OH Tax-Exempt Bond A	Muni State	8.3	7.91	5.36	3	3	3	0.8	800 622-3863
Armada OH Tax-Exempt Bond Inst	Muni State	8.6	8.1	5.53	2	3	0	0.6	800 622-3863
Armada PA Municipal Bond A	Muni State	8.5	7.76	5.45	3	3	3	0.84	800 622-3863
Armada PA Municipal Bond Inst	Muni State	8.7	7.95	5.55	2	3	0	0.64	800 622-3863
Armada Total Return Advantage A	Dvsfd Bond	13.8	11.1	7.5	2	3	4.75	0.8	800 622-3863
Armada Total Return Advantage Inst	Dvsfd Bond	14.2	11.3	7.76	2	3	0	0.55	800 622-3863
Armada US Govt Income A	Government	5.8	8.16	3.66		1	4.75	1.01	800 622-3863
Armada US Govt Income B	Government	5.2	7.45	3.25		1	0	1.72	800 622-3863
Armada US Govt Income C	Government	4.3					0	1.72	800 622-3863
Armada US Govt Income H	Government	4.7					0	1.69	800 622-3863
Armada US Govt Income Inst	Government	6.2	8.66	5.91	3	1	0	0.76	800 622-3863
Atlantic Whitehall Income Fund	Corp-Inv	9.3	6.83	4.91	5	3	0	1.28	800 994-2533
Atlas USG & Mortgage Secs A	Govt-Mtg	6	8.66	6.12	2	2	3	1.06	800 933-2852
BB&K Bond Opportunity Fund	Intl Bond	11.8	7.33	4.66	4	4	0	0.89	800 882-8383
BB&T Interm Corp Bond A	Corp-Inv	13.7	10.26			3	5.75	1.11	800 228-1872
BB&T Interm Corp Bond B	Corp-Inv	12.9	9.83			3	0	1.84	800 228-1872
BB&T Interm Corp Bond C	Corp-Inv	12.8					0	1.89	800 228-1872
BB&T Interm Corp Bond Tr	Corp-Inv	14	10.92		1	3	0	0.96	800 228-1872
BB&T Interm US Govt Bd A	Government	10.4	9.89	6.95	3	3	5.75	1.1	800 228-1872
BB&T Interm US Govt Bd B	Government	9.5	9.06	6.16	2	3	0	1.85	800 228-1872
BB&T Interm US Govt Bd Tr	Government	10.7	10.15	7.21	3	3	0	0.95	800 228-1872
BB&T Kentucky Interm Tax-Free A	Muni State						3	1.53	800 228-1872
BB&T Kentucky Interm Tax-Free Inst	Muni State						0	1.03	800 228-1872
BB&T Maryland Interm Tax-Free A	Muni State						3	1.5	800 228-1872
BB&T Marylnd Interm Tax-Free Instl	Muni State						0	1	800 228-1872
BB&T NC Interm Tax Free A	Muni State	8.5	8.31	5.34	3	3	3	1.43	800 228-1872
BB&T NC Interm Tax-Free Tr	Muni State	8.7	8.46	5.49	2	3	0	0.93	800 228-1872
BB&T SC Interm Tax Free Tr	Muni State	8.9	8.69	5.41	3	3	0	1.03	800 228-1872
BB&T SC Interm Tax-Free A	Muni State	8.8	8.58	5.36	3	3	3	1.53	800 228-1872
BB&T Short US Govt Inc A	Government	4.9	6.8	5.38	3	1	3	1.03	800 228-1872
BB&T Short US Govt Inc Tr	Government	5.2	7.05	5.74	3	1	0	0.93	800 228-1872
BB&T VA Interm Tax Free A	Muni State	8.6	8.41			3	3	1.53	800 228-1872

428

Bond Fund Name	Objective	Annualized Return for			Rank		Max Load	Expense Ratio	Toll-Free/(Toll) Telephone
		1 Year	3 Years	5 Years	Overall	Risk			
BB&T VA Interm Tax Free Tr	Muni State	8.7	9.48			3	0	0.71	800 228-1872
BB&T West VA Interm Tax-Free A	Muni State	8.9	8.52	2.16		4	3	1.43	800 228-1872
BB&T West VA Interm Tax-Free Tr	Muni State	9.2	8.91	5.54		3	0	0.78	800 228-1872
BBH Inflation Index Sec	Government	18.6	13.3	10.25	2	4	0	0.65	800 625-5759
BBH T/F Sh-Int Fix/Inc	Muni Natl	5	5.58	4.29	2	1	0	0.82	800 625-5759
BNY Hamilton Enhanced Income Inst	Dvsfd Bond	2.8					0	0.25	800 426-9363
BNY Hamilton Interm Gov Inst	Government	10.5	10.01	6.82	3	3	0	0.79	800 426-9363
BNY Hamilton Interm Gov Inv	Government	10.3	9.76	6.58	3	3	0	1.04	800 426-9363
BNY Hamilton Interm Inv Grade Inst	Corp-Inv	10.2	9.19	6.24	3	3	0	0.79	800 426-9363
BNY Hamilton Interm Inv Grade Inv	Corp-Inv	10.1	9.02	6	3	3	0	1.04	800 426-9363
BNY Hamilton Interm NY T/E Inst	Muni NY	8.8	8.06	5.28	3	3	0	0.79	800 426-9363
BNY Hamilton Interm NY T/E Inv	Muni NY	8.4	7.82	5.09	3	3	0	1.04	800 426-9363
BNY Hamilton Interm Tax Exempt Inst	Muni Natl	9.3	8.5	5.4	3	3	0	0.79	800 426-9363
BNY Hamilton Interm Tax Exempt Inv	Muni Natl	9	9.43	5.83	3	4	0	1.04	800 426-9363
BNY Hamilton US Bond Mkt Indx Inst	Dvsfd Bond	11.5	9.83		1	2	0	0.35	800 426-9363
Babson Bond-L Portfolio	Corp-Inv	7.9	8.65	5.91	4	3	0	0.97	866 409-2550
Babson Bond-S Portfolio	Corp-Inv	7	8.21	5.96	4	2	0	0.68	866 409-2550
Babson Tax-Free Income Fund	Muni Natl	10.4	9.14	5.66	3	3	0	0.98	866 409-2550
Baird Intermediate Bond Inst	Dvsfd Bond	10.5					0	0.3	800 338-1579
Barclays Gbl Inv Bd Index Fund	Dvsfd Bond	11.5	10.98	7.54	2	3	0	0.23	888 204-3956
Bear Stearns H/Y Total Return A	Corp-HY	7.7	4.29	0.7	4	5	4.5	0.39	800 766-4111
Bear Stearns H/Y Total Return B	Corp-HY	7.1	3.7	0.11	5	5	0	0.38	800 766-4111
Bear Stearns H/Y Total Return C	Corp-HY	7	3.5	0.02	5	5	0	0.38	800 766-4111
Bear Stearns Income Portfolio A	Corp-Inv	9.9	9.77	6.38	3	3	4.5	0.71	800 766-4111
Bear Stearns Income Portfolio B	Corp-Inv	9.2					0	0.71	800 766-4111
Bear Stearns Income Portfolio C	Corp-Inv	9.2	8.82	5.55	3	3	0	0.71	800 766-4111
Bear Stearns Income Portfolio Y	Corp-Inv	10.3	9.82	6.54	3	3	0	0.71	800 766-4111
Bernstein Diversified Muni	Muni Natl	7	7.19	5.16	3	2	0	0.64	
Bernstein Intermediate Duration	Government	10.1	8.89	6.09	2	2	0	0.6	
Bernstein Short Duration Plus	Government	5.1	6.54	5.59	2	1	0	0.67	
Bishop Street HI Muni Bond Inst	Muni State	10.4	9.89	6.37	1	3	0	0.7	800 262-9565
Bishop Street High Grade Inc Inst	Corp-Inv	14.2	10.42	7.04	3	3	0	0.76	800 262-9565
BlackRock Core Bd Tot Rtn I	Corp-Inv	11	10.84	7.66	2	3	0	0.55	800 441-7762
BlackRock Core Bond Blrk	Corp-Inv	11.4	11.08	7.84	2	3	0	0.4	800 441-7762
BlackRock Core Bond Inv A	Corp-Inv	10.4	10.36	7.2	3	3	4	0.9	800 441-7762
BlackRock Core Bond Inv B	Corp-Inv	9.7	9.55	6.4	3	3	0	1.65	800 441-7762
BlackRock Core Bond Inv C	Corp-Inv	9.7	9.58	6.41	3	3	0	1.65	800 441-7762
BlackRock Core Bond Svc	Corp-Inv	10.6	10.51	7.36	2	3	0	0.85	800 441-7762
BlackRock DE Tax Free Inc A	Muni State	9.4	8.51	5.58	4	3	4	1.18	800 441-7762
BlackRock DE Tax Free Inc B	Muni State	8.6	7.7	4.54	5	3	0	1.92	800 441-7762
BlackRock DE Tax Free Inc C	Muni State	8.6	7.7	4.54	5	3	0	1.9	800 441-7762
BlackRock DE Tax Free Inc Inst	Muni State	9.9	9.01	6.09	2	3	0	0.7	800 441-7762
BlackRock GNMA Portfolio A	Govt-Mtg	5.3	8.68	6.3	3	2	4	1.07	800 441-7762
BlackRock GNMA Portfolio B	Govt-Mtg	4.5	7.87	5.51	3	2	0	1.8	800 441-7762
BlackRock GNMA Portfolio C	Govt-Mtg	4.5	7.83	5.5	3	2	0	1.79	800 441-7762
BlackRock GNMA Portfolio Inst	Govt-Mtg	5.9	9.07	6.62	2	2	0	0.6	800 441-7762
BlackRock GNMA Portfolio Svc	Govt-Mtg	5.5	8.69	6.4	2	2	0	0.9	800 441-7762
BlackRock Govt Inc Inv A	Government	13.2	12.66	8.32	3	4	4.5	1.07	800 441-7762
BlackRock Govt Inc Inv B	Government	12.5	11.88	7.53	3	4	0	1.82	800 441-7762
BlackRock Govt Inc Inv C	Government	12.4	11.82	7.5	3	4	0	1.81	800 441-7762
BlackRock High Yield Bond A	Corp-HY	10.4	4.92		4	5	5	1.17	800 441-7762
BlackRock High Yield Bond B	Corp-HY	9.5	4.09		4	5	0	1.92	800 441-7762
BlackRock High Yield Bond C	Corp-HY	9.5	4.13		4	5	0	1.91	800 441-7762
BlackRock High Yield Bond Serv	Corp-HY	10.4	4.83		4	5	0	1	800 441-7762
BlackRock Interm Bd Blrk	Dvsfd Bond	12	10.51	7.67	1	2	0	0.45	800 441-7762
BlackRock Interm Bd Inst	Dvsfd Bond	11.7	10.91	7.84	1	2	0	0.6	800 441-7762
BlackRock Interm Bd Inv A	Dvsfd Bond	11.2	10.41	7.34	1	2	4	0.95	800 441-7762
BlackRock Interm Bd Inv B	Dvsfd Bond	10.4	9.09	6.28	2	2	0	1.7	800 441-7762

429

Bond Fund Name	Objective	Annualized Return for			Rank		Max Load	Expense Ratio	Toll-Free/(Toll) Telephone
		1 Year	3 Years	5 Years	Overall	Risk			
BlackRock Interm Bd Inv C	Dvsfd Bond	10.4					0	1.7	800 441-7762
BlackRock Interm Bd Svc	Dvsfd Bond	11.5	10.63	7.55	1	2	0	0.9	800 441-7762
BlackRock Interm Govt Bond Inst	Government	9.6	9.75	7.26	2	2	0	0.6	800 441-7762
BlackRock Interm Govt Bond Inv A	Government	9.1	9.31	6.83	2	2	4	1.07	800 441-7762
BlackRock Interm Govt Bond Inv C	Government	8.2	8.44	5.98	3	2	0	1.81	800 441-7762
BlackRock Interm Govt Bond Svc	Government	9.2	9.41	6.94	2	2	0	0.9	800 441-7762
BlackRock Intl Bond Inst	Intl Bond	14.8	10.39	8.46	1	2	0	0.9	800 441-7762
BlackRock Intl Bond Inv A	Intl Bond	14.4	9.91	7.98	1	2	5	1.37	800 441-7762
BlackRock Intl Bond Inv B	Intl Bond	13.5	9.08	7.19	3	2	0	2.11	800 441-7762
BlackRock Intl Bond Inv C	Intl Bond	13.5	9.15	7.21	3	2	0	2.11	800 441-7762
BlackRock Intl Bond Svc	Intl Bond	14.5	10.08	8.13	1	2	0	1.2	800 441-7762
BlackRock KY Tax Free Inc B	Muni State	5.5	5.87	3.52	4	3	0	1.91	800 441-7762
BlackRock KY Tax Free Inc C	Muni State	5.5	5.88	3.5	4	2	0	1.9	800 441-7762
BlackRock KY Tax Free Inc Inst	Muni State	6.8	8.41	5.5	3	3	0	0.7	800 441-7762
BlackRock KY Tax Free Inc Svc	Muni State	6.6	6.8	4.45	3	2	0	1	800 441-7762
BlackRock Low Duration Blrk	Corp-Inv	5.6	7.33	6.4	2	1	0	0.4	800 441-7762
BlackRock Low Duration Inst	Corp-Inv	5.5	7.2	6.25	2	1	0	0.55	800 441-7762
BlackRock Low Duration Inv A	Corp-Inv	5	6.73	5.76	3	1	3	0.9	800 441-7762
BlackRock Low Duration Inv B	Corp-Inv	4.3	5.95	5	3	1	0	1.65	800 441-7762
BlackRock Low Duration Inv C	Corp-Inv	4.3	5.95	5	3	1	0	1.65	800 441-7762
BlackRock Low Duration Svc	Corp-Inv	5.2	6.88	5.91	2	1	0	0.85	800 441-7762
BlackRock Mgd Income Inst	Dvsfd Bond	11	11	7.5	2	3	0	0.65	800 441-7762
BlackRock Mgd Income Inv A	Dvsfd Bond	10.5	10.49	7.01	2	3	4.5	1.12	800 441-7762
BlackRock Mgd Income Inv B	Dvsfd Bond	9.6	9.21	5.95	3	3	0	1.87	800 441-7762
BlackRock Mgd Income Svc	Dvsfd Bond	10.6	10.67	7.2	2	3	0	0.95	800 441-7762
BlackRock NJ Tax Free Inst	Muni State	9					0	0.6	800 441-7762
BlackRock NJ Tax Free Inv A	Muni State	8.6	8.43	5.37	3	3	4	1.07	800 441-7762
BlackRock NJ Tax Free Inv B	Muni State	7.8	7.62	4.58	4	3	0	1.81	800 441-7762
BlackRock NJ Tax Free Svc	Muni State	8.6	8.58	5.53	3	3	0	0.9	800 441-7762
BlackRock OH Tax Free Inc Inst	Muni State	9.2	9.6	6.2	1	3	0	0.6	800 441-7762
BlackRock OH Tax Free Inc Inv A	Muni State	8.6	9.09	5.75	3	3	4	1.06	800 441-7762
BlackRock OH Tax Free Inc Inv B	Muni State	7.8	8.3	4.96	4	3	0	1.81	800 441-7762
BlackRock OH Tax Free Inc Inv C	Muni State	7.9	8.33		4	3	0	1.8	800 441-7762
BlackRock OH Tax Free Inc Svc	Muni State	8.9	9.32	5.95	3	3	0	0.9	800 441-7762
BlackRock PA Tax Free Inst	Muni State	7.9	8.11	5.41	3	3	4	0.6	800 441-7762
BlackRock PA Tax Free Inv A	Muni State	7.3	7.58	4.91	4	3	4	1.08	800 441-7762
BlackRock PA Tax Free Inv B	Muni State	6.5	6.84	4.16	5	3	0	1.82	800 441-7762
BlackRock PA Tax Free Inv C	Muni State	6.6					0	1.81	800 441-7762
BlackRock PA Tax Free Svc	Muni State	7.5	7.76	5.08	3	3	0	0.9	800 441-7762
BlackRock Tax Free Inc Inst	Muni Natl	7	7.83	4.9	4	3	0	0.6	800 441-7762
BlackRock Tax Free Inc Inv A	Muni Natl	6.5	7.33	4.41	5	3	4	1.07	800 441-7762
BlackRock Tax Free Inc Inv B	Muni Natl	5.7	6.54	3.62	5	3	0	1.82	800 441-7762
BlackRock Tax Free Inc Inv C	Muni Natl	5.7	6.54	3.62	5	3	0	1.82	800 441-7762
BlackRock Tax Free Inc Svc	Muni Natl	6.5	7.48	4.57	5	3	0	0.9	800 441-7762
BlackRock-High Yield Bond Inst	Corp-HY	10.8	5.41		4	5	0	0.7	800 441-7762
BlackRock-Interm Govt Bond Inv B	Government	8.2	8.44	5.99	3	2	0	1.81	800 441-7762
Bremer Bond Fund	Dvsfd Bond	9.3	9.05	6.09	3	2	0	0.93	800 595-5552
Brown Advisory Interm Bond A	Corp-Inv	8.9	8.98	6.57	2	2	5.5	0.7	800 540-6807
Brown Advisory Interm Bond Instl	Corp-Inv	9.2	9.25	6.84	1	2	0	0.45	800 540-6807
Brown Advisory Maryland Bond Instl	Muni State	8.9					0	0.25	800 540-6807
Brundage Story & Rose Short-Interm	Corp-Inv	9.6	9.22	6.59	2	2	0	0.65	800 543-8721
Buffalo High Yield Fund	Corp-HY	14.4	10.06	4.29	4	4	0	1.04	800 492-8332
CCMI Bond Fund	Dvsfd Bond						0	0.85	800 386-3111
CDC Nvest Bond Income A	Corp-Inv	8.8	8.01	5.4	3	3	4.5	1.17	800 225-5478
CDC Nvest Bond Income B	Corp-Inv	8.1	7.25	4.63	4	3	0	1.93	800 225-5478
CDC Nvest Bond Income C	Corp-Inv	8	7.21	4.61	4	3	1	1.93	800 225-5478
CDC Nvest Bond Income Y	Corp-Inv	9.4	8.52	5.8	3	3	0	0.67	800 225-5478
CDC Nvest Govt Securities A	Government	16.3	11.22	7.11	3	4	4.5	1.25	800 225-5478

Bond Fund Name	Objective	Annualized Return for			Rank		Max Load	Expense Ratio	Toll-Free/(Toll) Telephone
		1 Year	3 Years	5 Years	Overall	Risk			
CDC Nvest Govt Securities B	Government	15.5	10.42	6.33	3	4	0	2	800 225-5478
CDC Nvest Govt Securities Y	Government	16.4	11.4	7.29	3	4	0	0.87	800 225-5478
CDC Nvest High Income A	Corp-HY	6.4	-6.16	-5.11	5	5	4.5	1.58	800 225-5478
CDC Nvest High Income B	Corp-HY	5.4	-6.83	-5.8	5	5	0	2.33	800 225-5478
CDC Nvest High Income C	Corp-HY	5.6	-6.84	-5.8	5	5	1	2.33	800 225-5478
CDC Nvest Ltd Term U.S. Govt A	Government	7.1	7.65	5.54	3	2	3	1.35	800 225-5478
CDC Nvest Ltd Term U.S. Govt B	Government	6.3	6.95	4.88	3	2	0	2	800 225-5478
CDC Nvest Ltd Term U.S. Govt C	Government	6.4	6.98	4.9	3	2	1	2	800 225-5478
CDC Nvest Ltd Term U.S. Govt Y	Government	7.3	8.08	5.98	3	2	0	0.88	800 225-5478
CDC Nvest MA Tax-Free Income A	Muni State	10.5	7.79	4.62	3	3	4.25	1.34	800 225-5478
CDC Nvest MA Tax-Free Income B	Muni State	9.8	7.12	3.95	4	3	0	1.99	800 225-5478
CDC Nvest Municipal Income A	Muni Natl	7.4	7.12	4.5	4	3	4.5	1.05	800 225-5478
CDC Nvest Municipal Income B	Muni Natl	6.7	6.37	3.75	5	3	0	1.8	800 225-5478
CDC Nvest Strategic Income A	Corp-Inv	26.2	11.71	7.41	3	5	4.5	1.33	800 225-5478
CDC Nvest Strategic Income B	Corp-Inv	25.3	10.85	6.62	3	5	0	2.08	800 225-5478
CDC Nvest Strategic Income C	Corp-Inv	25.2	10.86	6.61	3	5	1	2.08	800 225-5478
CG Cap Mkts Interm Fixed Inc	Corp-Inv	8.1	9.32	6.67	2	3	0	0.72	800 444-4273
CG Cap Mkts Intl Fixed Invt	Intl Bond	24.6	9.3	5.26	4	5	0	0.93	800 444-4273
CG Cap Mkts Long Term Bond	Corp-Inv	19.2	12.86	7.75	3	4	0	1.16	800 444-4273
CG Cap Mkts Mortgage Backed	Govt-Mtg	2.8	8.25	6.13	2	2	0	0.8	800 444-4273
CG Cap Mkts Municipal Bond Invt	Muni Natl	10.6	10.02	5.74	3	4	0	0.91	800 444-4273
CNI Charter CA Tax-Exempt Bond I	Muni CA	7.9	7.12		3	3	0	0.5	888 889-0799
CNI Charter Corporate Bond Inst	Corp-Inv	11.2	10.01		1	2	0	0.75	888 889-0799
CNI Charter Government Bond Inst	Govt-Mtg	9.1	8.91		1	2	0	0.7	888 889-0799
CNI Charter High Yield Bond Inst	Corp-HY	8.2	6.33		4	5	0	1	888 889-0799
CRA Qualified Investment Fd	Dvsfd Bond	12.1	10.02		2	3	0	0.99	877 272-1977
CSI Fixed Income	Government	9.1					0	1.48	800 527-9525
Calamos High Yield A	Muni Natl	8.1	8.39			5	0	1.75	800 823-7386
Calamos High Yield B	Muni Natl	7.4					0	2.5	800 823-7386
Calamos High Yield C	Muni Natl	7.4					0	2.5	800 823-7386
California Insured Intermediate Fd	Muni CA	8.2	7.74	5.69	4	4	0	0.55	800 225-8778
California Tax-Free Income Fd	Muni CA	9.8	8.64	5.7	4	4	0	0.62	800 225-8778
California US Government Sec Fd	Government	9.9	9.08	6.55	3	3	0	0.65	800 225-8778
Calvert CA Muni Interm A	Muni State	8.7					2.75	0.86	800 368-2745
Calvert Income Fund A	Corp-Inv	9.8	10.86	9.06	3	4	3.75		800 368-2745
Calvert Income Fund B	Corp-Inv	9					0	1	800 368-2745
Calvert Income Fund C	Corp-Inv	9					0	2.09	800 368-2745
Calvert Income Fund I	Corp-Inv	10.5					0		800 368-2745
Calvert Natl Muni Interm A	Muni Natl	10.2	8.69	5.75	3	3	2.75	0.91	800 368-2745
Calvert Social Inv Bond A	Corp-Inv	9.7	10.66	6.95	4	4	3.75	0.2	800 368-2745
Calvert Tax Free Reserve-Lmtd A	Muni Natl	2.9	3.87	3.7	3	1	1	0.61	800 368-2745
Calvert Tax Free Reserve-Long A	Muni Natl	11.8	9.99	6.04	3	4	3.75		800 368-2745
Calvert Tax Free Reserve-VT A	Muni State	10.2	8.57	5.16	3	3	3.75		800 368-2745
Canandaigua Bond Fund	Muni Natl	8	8.52	5.98	2	2	0	0.5	888 693-9276
Citizens Income	Corp-Inv	9.4	6.78	4.54	4	3	0	1.39	800 223-7010
Citizens Ultra Short Bond Fund	Dvsfd Bond						0	0.85	800 223-7010
Colorado Bond Shares Tax-Exempt A	Muni State	6.1	7.01	6.17	2	1	4.75	0.66	800 572-0069
Columbia Fixed Income Securities A	Dvsfd Bond						4.75		800 338-2550
Columbia Fixed Income Securities B	Dvsfd Bond						0		800 338-2550
Columbia Fixed Income Securities D	Dvsfd Bond						0		800 338-2550
Columbia Fixed Income Securities Z	Corp-Inv	9.2	10	6.75	3	2	0	0.67	800 338-2550
Columbia High Yield A	Corp-HY						4.75		800 338-2550
Columbia High Yield B	Corp-HY						0		800 338-2550
Columbia High Yield D	Corp-HY						0		800 338-2550
Columbia High Yield Z	Corp-HY	6.3	6.37	4.63	4	4	0	0.84	800 338-2550
Columbia National Muni Bond A	Muni Natl						4.75		800 338-2550
Columbia National Muni Bond B	Muni Natl						0		800 338-2550
Columbia National Muni Bond D	Muni Natl						0		800 338-2550

431

Bond Fund Name	Objective	Annualized Return for			Rank		Max Load	Expense Ratio	Toll-Free/(Toll) Telephone
		1 Year	3 Years	5 Years	Overall	Risk			
Columbia National Muni Bond Z	Muni Natl	10.8	9.52		1	3	0	0.65	800 338-2550
Columbia Oregon Municipal Bond A	Muni State						4.75		800 338-2550
Columbia Oregon Municipal Bond B	Muni State						0		800 338-2550
Columbia Oregon Municipal Bond C	Muni State						0		800 338-2550
Columbia Oregon Municipal Bond Z	Muni Natl	10	10.68	6.71	3	4	0	0.58	800 338-2550
Columbia Short Term Bond A	Government						4.75	1.26	800 338-2550
Columbia Short Term Bond B	Government						0	2.03	800 338-2550
Columbia Short Term Bond D	Government						0	2.03	800 338-2550
Columbia Short Term Bond G	Government						0	1.83	800 338-2550
Columbia Short Term Bond T	Government						4.75	1.16	800 338-2550
Columbia Short Term Bond Z	Government	5.8	6.99	5.69	3	1	0	0.75	800 338-2550
Commerce Bond Instl	Corp-Inv	8	9.16	6.37	4	3	3.5	0.73	800 995-6365
Commerce Bond Svc	Corp-Inv	7.8	8.88	3.35	4	3	3.5	0.98	800 995-6365
Commerce MO Tax Free Inst	Muni State	9.4	8.69	5.82	1	3	3.5	0.65	800 995-6365
Commerce National Tax Free Inst	Muni Natl	10.1	8.93	6	1	3	3.5	0.7	800 995-6365
Commerce Short Term Govt Bd Inst	Govt-Mtg	6	7.5	6.08	3	2	3.5	0.68	800 995-6365
Commerce Short Term Govt Bd Svc	Govt-Mtg	5.8	7.26	3.54	4	2	3.5	0.93	800 995-6365
Conseco Fixed Inc Fund A	Corp-Inv	10.2	10.08	6.69	3	3	5	1.25	800 825-1530
Conseco Fixed Inc Fund B	Corp-Inv	9.7	9.6	6.41	3	3	0	1.6	800 825-1530
Conseco Fixed Inc Fund C	Corp-Inv	9.7	9.64	6.45	3	3	0	1.6	800 825-1530
Conseco Fixed Inc Fund Y	Corp-Inv	10.8	10.69	7.36	2	3	0	0.6	800 825-1530
Conseco High Yield Fund A	Corp-HY	14.9	5.62	3.08	4	5	5.75	1.4	800 825-1530
Conseco High Yield Fund B	Corp-HY	14.4	5.05	2.52	4	5	0	1.9	800 825-1530
Conseco High Yield Fund C	Corp-HY	14.4	5.11	2.54	4	5	0	1.9	800 825-1530
Conseco High Yield Fund Y	Corp-HY	15.6	6.23	3.56	4	5	0	0.9	800 825-1530
Country Trust Bond A	Dvsfd Bond	10.5					4.25	0.85	800 245-2100
Country Trust Bond Y	Corp-Inv	10.7	10.51	7.49	2	2	0	0.85	800 245-2100
Country Trust Short-Term Bond A	Dvsfd Bond	4.9					2.5	0.85	800 245-2100
Country Trust Short-Term Bond Y	Dvsfd Bond	5	6.58	5.59		1	0	0.85	800 245-2100
Country Trust Tax Exempt Bond Y	Muni Natl	7.6	7.46	5.08	4	3	0	1.66	800 245-2100
Credit Suisse Fixed Income Adv	Corp-Inv	6.3	7.45	5.04	4	3	0	0.95	800 494-6847
Credit Suisse Fixed Income Com	Corp-Inv	6.5	7.66	5.21	4	3	0	0.94	800 494-6847
Credit Suisse Global Fixed Inc A	Intl Bond	15.9					4.75	1.2	800 494-6847
Credit Suisse Global Fixed Inc Adv	Intl Bond	15.6	9.98	6.58	3	3	0	1.44	800 494-6847
Credit Suisse Global Fixed Inc Com	Intl Bond	16.2	9.83	7.16	3	3	0	0.94	800 494-6847
Credit Suisse High Income A	Dvsfd Bond	9.2	5.08			5	4.75	1.1	800 494-6847
Credit Suisse High Income B	Dvsfd Bond	8.4	4.2			5	0	1.85	800 494-6847
Credit Suisse High Income C	Dvsfd Bond	8.4	4.2			5	0	1.85	800 494-6847
Credit Suisse High Income Com	Dvsfd Bond	9.1					0	1.1	800 494-6847
Credit Suisse Inst Fixed Inc	Corp-Inv	6.6	7.92	5.76	3	3	0	0.45	800 494-6847
Credit Suisse Inst High Yield	Corp-HY	6.7	1	0.04	5	5	0	0.7	800 494-6847
Credit Suisse Invt Grade Bond C	Government	7.9					0	1.6	800 494-6847
Credit Suisse Invt Grade Bond Com	Government	8.9	8.38	6.28	3	3	0	0.6	800 494-6847
Credit Suisse Muni Bond A	Muni Natl	10.1					4.75	0.95	800 494-6847
Credit Suisse NY Muni A	Muni NY	5.5					4.75	0.85	800 494-6847
Credit Suisse NY Muni Com	Muni NY	5.6	7.28	5.08	3	2	0	0.6	800 494-6847
Croft-Leominster Income	Corp-Inv	21.4	11.93	6.37	3	4	0	1.1	800 551-0990
DFA Five-Year Global Fixed Income	Intl Bond	8.3	7.04	6.3	2	2	0	0.38	800 342-6684
DFA Five-Year Government	Government	13.5	9.42	7.34	2	3	0	0.26	800 342-6684
DFA Intermediate Govt Fx Inc	Government	17.8	13.97	9.01	2	4	0	0.16	800 342-6684
DFA One-Yr Fixed Income	Corp-Inv	3.6	5.07	5.04	3	1	0	0.2	800 342-6684
DFA Two-Year Global Fixed Income	Intl Bond	5.1	5.74	5.5	3	1	0	0.26	800 342-6684
DLB Fixed Income	Dvsfd Bond	10					0	0.55	888 722-2766
Davis Government Bond A	Govt-Mtg	7.9	9.82	6.04	4	3	4.75	1.22	800 279-0279
Davis Government Bond B	Govt-Mtg	7	7.75	4.5	4	2	0	1.94	800 279-0279
Davis Government Bond C	Govt-Mtg	7	7.67	4.41	4	2	0	1.96	800 279-0279
Davis Government Bond Y	Govt-Mtg	7.9	8.83		1	2	0	0.96	800 279-0279
Delaware American Govt Bond A	Government	10.8	10.18	6.75	3	3	4.5	1.05	800 523-1918

Bond Fund Name	Objective	Annualized Return for			Rank		Max Load	Expense Ratio	Toll-Free/(Toll) Telephone
		1 Year	3 Years	5 Years	Overall	Risk			
Delaware American Govt Bond B	Government	10.1	9.4	6	3	3	0	1.75	800 523-1918
Delaware American Govt Bond C	Government	10.1	9.4	6.03	3	3	0	1.75	800 523-1918
Delaware American Govt Bond I	Government	11.2	10.5	7.05	3	3	0	0.75	800 523-1918
Delaware Corporate Bond A	Corp-Inv	18	13.9		1	4	4.5	0.8	800 523-1918
Delaware Corporate Bond B	Corp-Inv	17.2	13.07		1	4	0	1.55	800 523-1918
Delaware Corporate Bond C	Corp-Inv	17.2	13.07		1	4	0	1.55	800 523-1918
Delaware Corporate Bond I	Corp-Inv	18.3					0	0.55	800 523-1918
Delaware Delchester Fund A	Corp-HY	15.8	-2.1	-5.37	5	5	4.5	1.32	800 523-1918
Delaware Delchester Fund B	Corp-HY	15.3	-2.72	-5.83	5	5	0	2.04	800 523-1918
Delaware Delchester Fund C	Corp-HY	15.3	-2.74	-5.83	5	5	0	2.04	800 523-1918
Delaware Delchester Fund I	Corp-HY	16.1	-1.84	-5.12	5	5	0	1.04	800 523-1918
Delaware Diversified Income A	Dvsfd Bond	16.4	13.1	9.34	1	3	4.5	1	800 523-1918
Delaware Diversified Income B	Dvsfd Bond						0	1.75	800 523-1918
Delaware Diversified Income C	Dvsfd Bond						0	1.75	800 523-1918
Delaware Diversified Income I	Dvsfd Bond						0	0.75	800 523-1918
Delaware Extended Duration Bd A	Dvsfd Bond	23.4	16.96		1	4	4.5	0.8	800 523-1918
Delaware Extended Duration Bd B	Dvsfd Bond	22.4	16.07		1	4	0	1.55	800 523-1918
Delaware Extended Duration Bd C	Dvsfd Bond	22.4	16.07		1	4	0	1.55	800 523-1918
Delaware Extended Duration Bd I	Dvsfd Bond	23.7					0	0.55	800 523-1918
Delaware High Yield Opport A	Corp-HY	16.6	3.77	1.67	4	5	4.5	1.13	800 523-1918
Delaware High Yield Opport B	Corp-HY	15.5	2.93	0.45	4	5	0	1.83	800 523-1918
Delaware High Yield Opport C	Corp-HY	15.8	3.02	0.48	4	5	0	1.83	800 523-1918
Delaware High Yield Opport I	Corp-HY	16.7	4	1.97	4	5	0	0.83	800 523-1918
Delaware Limited Term Govt A	Govt-Mtg	7.2	8.38	6.44	2	2	2.75	0.75	800 523-1918
Delaware Limited Term Govt B	Govt-Mtg	6.3	7.45	5.51	3	2	0	1.6	800 523-1918
Delaware Limited Term Govt C	Govt-Mtg	6.3	7.45	5.54	3	2	0	1.6	800 523-1918
Delaware Limited Term Govt I	Govt-Mtg	7.3	8.56	6.59	2	2	0	0.6	800 523-1918
Delaware MN HY Muni Bond A	Muni State	11	9.38	5.08	1	2	4.5	0.75	800 523-1918
Delaware MN HY Muni Bond B	Muni State	10.3					0	1.5	800 523-1918
Delaware MN HY Muni Bond C	Muni State	10.3					0	1.5	800 523-1918
Delaware Natl High Yield Muni A	Muni Natl	6.3	6.86	4	3	2	4.5	0.97	800 523-1918
Delaware Natl High Yield Muni B	Muni Natl	5.4	6.04	3.29	3	2	0	1.72	800 523-1918
Delaware Natl High Yield Muni C	Muni Natl	5.5	6.04	3.29	3	2	0	1.72	800 523-1918
Delaware Pooled Tr-Core + Fxd Inc	Dvsfd Bond						0	0.93	800 523-1918
Delaware Pooled Tr-Core Fixed	Dvsfd Bond	10	*9.01		1	3	0	0.83	800 523-1918
Delaware Pooled Tr-Glbl Fxd Income	Intl Bond	32.4	15.08	8.41	3	5	0	1.1	800 523-1918
Delaware Pooled Tr-High Yield Bond	Corp-HY	16.9	5.32	2	4	5	0	1.04	800 523-1918
Delaware Pooled Tr-Int Fix Inc	Dvsfd Bond	10.3					0	1.1	800 523-1918
Delaware Pooled Tr-Intl Fixed Inc	Intl Bond	33.2	13.83	7.41	3	5	0	1.1	800 523-1918
Delaware Strategic Income A	Corp-Inv	21	8.97	3.83	3	4	5.75	1.84	800 523-1918
Delaware Strategic Income B	Corp-Inv	20.4	8.16	3.04	3	4	0	2.59	800 523-1918
Delaware Strategic Income C	Corp-Inv	20.4	8.16	2.89	3	4	0	2.59	800 523-1918
Delaware Strategic Income I	Corp-Inv	21.3	9.25	3.95	3	4	0	1.59	800 523-1918
Delaware Tax Free Arizona A	Muni State	6.4	7.73	4.33	3	3	4.5	0.75	800 523-1918
Delaware Tax Free Arizona B	Muni State	5.7	6.96	3.56	4	3	0	1.5	800 523-1918
Delaware Tax Free Arizona C	Muni State	5.7	6.92	3.54	4	3	0	1.5	800 523-1918
Delaware Tax Free Arizona Insured A	Muni State	9.7	8.77	5.57	2	3	4.5	0.9	800 523-1918
Delaware Tax Free Arizona Insured B	Muni State	9	8	3.22	3	3	0	1.65	800 523-1918
Delaware Tax Free Arizona Insured C	Muni State	9	8.01	4.82	3	3	0	1.65	800 523-1918
Delaware Tax Free CA Insured A	Muni CA	11.2	9.06	5.55	4	4	4.5	0.92	800 523-1918
Delaware Tax Free CA Insured B	Muni CA	10.2	8.24	4.76	5	4	0	1.67	800 523-1918
Delaware Tax Free CA Insured C	Muni CA	10.4	8.3	3.04	5	4	0	1.67	800 523-1918
Delaware Tax Free California A	Muni CA	11.1	10.44	5.73	3	4	4.5	0.5	800 523-1918
Delaware Tax Free California B	Muni CA	10.2	9.63	4.92	3	4	0	1.25	800 523-1918
Delaware Tax Free California C	Muni CA	10.3	9.61	4.94	3	4	0	1.25	800 523-1918
Delaware Tax Free Colorado A	Muni State	9.1	8.67	4.84	3	3	4.5	0.94	800 523-1918
Delaware Tax Free Colorado B	Muni State	8.3					0	1.7	800 523-1918
Delaware Tax Free Colorado C	Muni State	8.2	7.86	4.08	4	3	0	1.7	800 523-1918

Bond Fund Name	Objective	Annualized Return for			Rank		Max Load	Expense Ratio	Toll-Free/(Toll) Telephone
		1 Year	3 Years	5 Years	Overall	Risk			
Delaware Tax Free Florida A	Muni State	10.7	9.36	5.4	2	3	4.5	0.75	800 523-1918
Delaware Tax Free Florida B	Muni State	9.8	8.58	4.62	3	3	0	1.5	800 523-1918
Delaware Tax Free Florida C	Muni State	10	8.64	4.66	3	3	0	1.5	800 523-1918
Delaware Tax Free Florida Ins A	Muni State	10.2	9.08	5.55	2	3	4.5	0.9	800 523-1918
Delaware Tax Free Florida Ins B	Muni State	9.4	8.25	4.78	4	3	0	1.65	800 523-1918
Delaware Tax Free Idaho A	Muni State	9.7	9.32	5.2	2	3	4.5	1	800 523-1918
Delaware Tax Free Idaho B	Muni State	8.9	8.51	4.49	3	3	0	1.75	800 523-1918
Delaware Tax Free Idaho C	Muni State	9	8.55	4.44	3	3	0	1.75	800 523-1918
Delaware Tax Free Insured A	Muni Natl	10.9	9.52	5.62	2	4	4.5	0.92	800 523-1918
Delaware Tax Free Insured B	Muni Natl	10	8.67	4.82	3	4	0	1.7	800 523-1918
Delaware Tax Free Insured C	Muni Natl	10	8.67	4.79	3	4	0	1.7	800 523-1918
Delaware Tax Free MN Insured A	Muni State	10.7	8.85	5.62	2	3	4.5	0.96	800 523-1918
Delaware Tax Free MN Insured B	Muni State	9.9					0	1.71	800 523-1918
Delaware Tax Free MN Insured C	Muni State	10	8.07	4.87	3	3	0	1.71	800 523-1918
Delaware Tax Free MN Interm A	Muni State	10.6	8.09	4.98	1	2	2.75	0.85	800 523-1918
Delaware Tax Free MN Interm B	Muni State	9.7					0	1.7	800 523-1918
Delaware Tax Free MN Interm C	Muni State	9.7	7.17	4.11	2	2	0	1.7	800 523-1918
Delaware Tax Free Minnesota A	Muni State	10.7	9.27	5.41	1	3	4.5	0.97	800 523-1918
Delaware Tax Free Minnesota B	Muni State	9.9					0	1.73	800 523-1918
Delaware Tax Free Minnesota C	Muni State	10	8.48	4.65	3	3	0	1.73	800 523-1918
Delaware Tax Free Missouri Ins A	Muni State	9.6	8.38	5.3	2	3	4.5	0.96	800 523-1918
Delaware Tax Free Missouri Ins B	Muni State	8.8	7.58	4.54	3	3	0	1.71	800 523-1918
Delaware Tax Free Missouri Ins C	Muni State	8.8	7.59	2.99	4	3	0	1.71	800 523-1918
Delaware Tax Free New York A	Muni NY	10.6	9.57	5.38	2	3	4.5	0.5	800 523-1918
Delaware Tax Free New York B	Muni NY	9.7	8.76	4.62	3	3	0	1.25	800 523-1918
Delaware Tax Free New York C	Muni NY	9.8	8.77	4.62	3	3	0	1.25	800 523-1918
Delaware Tax Free Oregon Insured A	Muni State	9.6	9.39	5.54	3	4	4.5	0.85	800 523-1918
Delaware Tax Free Oregon Insured B	Muni State	8.7	8.6	4.78	3	4	0	1.6	800 523-1918
Delaware Tax Free Oregon Insured C	Muni State	8.8	8.63	3.25	3	4	0	1.6	800 523-1918
Delaware Tax Free Pennsylvania A	Muni State	11	9.02	5.12	3	3	4.5	0.89	800 523-1918
Delaware Tax Free Pennsylvania B	Muni State	10.1	8.16	4.15	3	3	0	1.69	800 523-1918
Delaware Tax Free Pennsylvania C	Muni State	10.1	8.16	4.19	3	3	0	1.69	800 523-1918
Delaware Tax Free USA A	Muni Natl	10.5	9.27	5.15	3	3	4.5	0.86	800 523-1918
Delaware Tax Free USA B	Muni Natl	9.6	8.43	4.32	3	3	0	1.65	800 523-1918
Delaware Tax Free USA C	Muni Natl	9.6	8.43	4.32	3	3	0	1.65	800 523-1918
Delaware Tax Free USA Interm A	Muni Natl	11	9.02	6.11	1	3	2.75	0.8	800 523-1918
Delaware Tax Free USA Interm B	Muni Natl	10.1	8.11	5.21	2	3	0	1.65	800 523-1918
Delaware Tax Free USA Interm C	Muni Natl	10.1	8.11	5.21	2	3	0	1.65	800 523-1918
Diversified Inst Core Bond	Dvsfd Bond	10.8	9.75	6.53		3	0	0.99	
Diversified Inst High Quality Bd	Corp-Inv	5.8	7.45	6.16		1	0	1	
Diversified Inst High Yield Bd	Corp-HY	12.1	5.44	2.27		5	0	1.1	
Diversified Inv Core Bond	Dvsfd Bond	10.3	9.35	6.16		3	0	0.99	
Diversified Inv High Quality Bd	Corp-Inv	5.5	7.05	5.78		1	0	1	
Diversified Inv High Yield Bd	Corp-HY	11.9	5.16	2		5	0	1.1	
Dodge & Cox Income Fund	Corp-Inv	11.5	11.77	7.98	1	2	0	0.45	800 621-3979
Domini Social Bond Fund	Corp-Inv	8.6					0	0.95	800 762-6814
Dreyfus A Bonds Plus	Corp-Inv	10.6	8.8	5.87	3	3	0	0.93	800 782-6620
Dreyfus Basic US Mortgage Sec Fd	Govt-Mtg	6.4	9.02	6.45	2	2	0	0.65	800 782-6620
Dreyfus Bond Market Index Basic	Corp-Inv	11.6	10.68	7.46	2	3	0	0.15	800 782-6620
Dreyfus Bond Market Index Inv	Corp-Inv	11.3	10.42	7.21	2	3	0	0.4	800 782-6620
Dreyfus CA Intermediate Muni	Muni CA	9.1	8.34	5.74	3	3	0	0.76	800 782-6620
Dreyfus CA Tax Exempt Bond	Muni CA	10.3	9.63	6.01	3	4	0	0.7	800 782-6620
Dreyfus CT Intermediate Muni	Muni State	8.8	7.75	5.26	3	2	0	0.78	800 782-6620
Dreyfus FL Intermediate Muni	Muni State	9.9	8.08	5.37	2	3	0	0.78	800 782-6620
Dreyfus Founders Government Sec F	Government	8.4	8.48	5.8	4	3	0	1	800 645-6561
Dreyfus GNMA Fund	Govt-Mtg	6.4	8.83	6.12	2	2	0	0.84	800 782-6620
Dreyfus General CA Muni Bond	Muni CA	8.6	8.76	5.05	5	4	0	0.75	800 782-6620
Dreyfus General Municipal Bond	Muni Natl	7.7	7.53	4.25	5	4	0	0.86	800 782-6620

434

Bond Fund Name	Objective	1 Year	3 Years	5 Years	Overall	Risk	Max Load	Expense Ratio	Toll-Free/(Toll) Telephone
Dreyfus General NY Muni Bond	Muni NY	10.1	9.13	5.59	3	3	0	0.89	800 782-6620
Dreyfus Infl Adjusted Sec - Inst	Muni Natl						0		800 782-6620
Dreyfus Infl Adjusted Sec - Inv	Muni Natl						0		800 782-6620
Dreyfus Insured Muni Bond	Muni Natl	10	8.96	5.62	3	4	0	0.84	800 782-6620
Dreyfus Interm Term Income Instl	Corp-Inv	10.9					0	0.45	800 782-6620
Dreyfus Interm Term Income Inv	Corp-Inv	10.6	9.66	7.86	2	3	0	0.69	800 782-6620
Dreyfus Intermediate Muni Bd	Muni Natl	8.1	7.24	4.79	4	2	0	0.73	800 782-6620
Dreyfus Lifetime Income Inv	Dvsfd Bond	5.3					0	1.12	800 782-6620
Dreyfus Lifetime Income Rest	Dvsfd Bond	5.9					0	0.72	800 782-6620
Dreyfus MA Intermediate Muni Bd	Muni State	9.7	8.17	5.49	3	3	0	0.75	800 782-6620
Dreyfus MA Tax Exempt Bond	Muni State	10.6	9.25	5.7	2	3	0	0.81	800 782-6620
Dreyfus Municipal Bond	Muni Natl	7.8	8.14	4.45	5	4	0	0.71	800 782-6620
Dreyfus NJ Intermediate Muni Bd	Muni State	9.8	8.07	5.48	2	3	0	0.77	800 782-6620
Dreyfus NJ Municipal Bond	Muni State	10.1	9.21	5.55	2	3	4.5	0.85	800 782-6620
Dreyfus NY Tax Exempt Bond	Muni NY	9.6	9.01	5.71	2	3	0	0.69	800 782-6620
Dreyfus NY Tax Exempt Intermed	Muni NY	8.7	8.39	5.54	3	3	0	0.8	800 782-6620
Dreyfus PA Intermediate Muni	Muni State	8.3	8.93	5.82	1	2	0	0.8	800 782-6620
Dreyfus Premier CA Muni A	Muni CA	11.2	9.64	5.33	4	4	4.5	0.93	800 782-6620
Dreyfus Premier CA Muni B	Muni CA	10.6	9.08	4.78	4	4	0	1.43	800 782-6620
Dreyfus Premier CA Muni C	Muni CA	10.3	8.84	4.57	4	4	0	1.67	800 782-6620
Dreyfus Premier CT Muni A	Muni State	9.8	9.08	5.58	3	3	4.5	0.9	800 782-6620
Dreyfus Premier CT Muni B	Muni State	9.3	8.51	5.03	4	3	0	1.42	800 782-6620
Dreyfus Premier CT Muni C	Muni State	9	8.24	4.76	5	3	0	1.65	800 782-6620
Dreyfus Premier Core Bond A	Dvsfd Bond	9.7	8.33	6.26	3	3	4.5	1.08	800 782-6620
Dreyfus Premier Core Bond B	Dvsfd Bond	9.3	7.84		2	3	0	1.52	800 782-6620
Dreyfus Premier Core Bond C	Dvsfd Bond	9	7.57		3	3	0	1.77	800 782-6620
Dreyfus Premier Core Bond R	Dvsfd Bond	10.2					0	0.65	800 782-6620
Dreyfus Premier Corporate Bond A	Corp-HY						0		800 782-6620
Dreyfus Premier Corporate Bond B	Corp-HY						0		800 782-6620
Dreyfus Premier Corporate Bond C	Corp-HY						0		800 782-6620
Dreyfus Premier Corporate Bond R	Corp-HY						0		800 782-6620
Dreyfus Premier FL Muni A	Muni State	9.3	9.56	5.42	2	3	4.5	0.94	800 782-6620
Dreyfus Premier FL Muni B	Muni State	8.7	9.02	4.9	3	3	0	1.45	800 782-6620
Dreyfus Premier FL Muni C	Muni State	8.5	8.75	4.61	3	3	0	1.67	800 782-6620
Dreyfus Premier GNMA A	Govt-Mtg	5.7	7.99	5.95	2	2	4.5	1.04	800 782-6620
Dreyfus Premier GNMA B	Govt-Mtg	5.1	7.41	5.4	3	2	0	1.55	800 782-6620
Dreyfus Premier GNMA C	Govt-Mtg	4.9	7.12	5.12	2	2	0	1.79	800 782-6620
Dreyfus Premier Lmtd Term Hi Inc A	Corp-HY	1.5	-1.55	-1.53	5	5	4.5	0.95	800 782-6620
Dreyfus Premier Lmtd Term Hi Inc B	Corp-HY	1	-1.98	-2	5	5	0	1.45	800 782-6620
Dreyfus Premier Lmtd Term Hi Inc C	Corp-HY	0.7	-2.22	-2.22	5	5	0	1.7	800 782-6620
Dreyfus Premier Lmtd Term Hi Inc R	Corp-HY	1.6	-1.29	-1.27	5	5	0	0.7	800 782-6620
Dreyfus Premier Lmtd Term Inc A	Corp-Inv	10	9.72	6.58	3	3	3	0.85	800 782-6620
Dreyfus Premier Lmtd Term Inc B	Corp-Inv	9.4	9.21	6.08	3	3	0	1.35	800 782-6620
Dreyfus Premier Lmtd Term Inc C	Corp-Inv	9.5	9.18	6.05	3	3	0	1.35	800 782-6620
Dreyfus Premier Lmtd Term Inc R	Corp-Inv	10.3	9.99	6.86	3	3	0	0.6	800 782-6620
Dreyfus Premier MA Muni A	Muni State	10.9	9.34	5.62	3	3	4.5	0.97	800 782-6620
Dreyfus Premier MA Muni B	Muni State	10.3	8.77	5.05	3	3	0	1.48	800 782-6620
Dreyfus Premier MA Muni C	Muni State	10.1	8.49	4.78	3	3	0	1.72	800 782-6620
Dreyfus Premier MD Muni A	Muni State	11.1	7.84	4.66	3	3	4.5	0.92	800 782-6620
Dreyfus Premier MD Muni B	Muni State	10.6	7.29	4.12	3	3	0	1.43	800 782-6620
Dreyfus Premier MD Muni C	Muni State	10.2	6.99	3.75	3	3	0	1.67	800 782-6620
Dreyfus Premier MI Muni A	Muni State	9.7	8.77	5.42	3	3	4.5	0.93	800 782-6620
Dreyfus Premier MI Muni B	Muni State	9.2	8.25	4.91	4	3	0	1.44	800 782-6620
Dreyfus Premier MI Muni C	Muni State	8.9	7.96	4.62	3	3	0	1.68	800 782-6620
Dreyfus Premier MN Muni A	Muni State	10.7	9.19	5.69	2	3	4.5	0.93	800 782-6620
Dreyfus Premier MN Muni B	Muni State	10.1	8.63	5.13	2	3	0	1.44	800 782-6620
Dreyfus Premier MN Muni C	Muni State	9.9	8.33	4.86	3	3	0	1.69	800 782-6620
Dreyfus Premier Managed Inc A	Dvsfd Bond	11.5	9.64	5.61	3	2	4.5	0.95	800 782-6620

435

Bond Fund Name	Objective	Annualized Return for			Rank		Max Load	Expense Ratio	Toll-Free/(Toll) Telephone
		1 Year	3 Years	5 Years	Overall Risk				
Dreyfus Premier Managed Inc B	Dvsfd Bond	10.7	8.81	4.83	3	2	0	1.7	800 782-6620
Dreyfus Premier Managed Inc C	Dvsfd Bond	10.7	8.81	4.83	3	2	0	1.7	800 782-6620
Dreyfus Premier Managed Inc R	Dvsfd Bond	11.8	9.85	5.86	3	2	0	0.7	800 782-6620
Dreyfus Premier Muni Bond A	Muni Natl	7.2	7.3	3.6	5	3	4.5	0.92	800 782-6620
Dreyfus Premier Muni Bond B	Muni Natl	6.6	6.74	3.06	5	3	0	1.43	800 782-6620
Dreyfus Premier Muni Bond C	Muni Natl	6.5	6.5	2.81	5	3	0	1.66	800 782-6620
Dreyfus Premier NC Muni A	Muni State	11.1	8.99	5.33	3	3	4.5	0.95	800 782-6620
Dreyfus Premier NC Muni B	Muni State	10.4	8.43	4.79	3	3	0	1.45	800 782-6620
Dreyfus Premier NC Muni C	Muni State	10.2	8.18	4.5	4	3	0	1.68	800 782-6620
Dreyfus Premier NJ Muni Bond Inc B	Muni State						0	1.19	800 782-6620
Dreyfus Premier NJ Muni Bond Inc C	Muni State						0	1.44	800 782-6620
Dreyfus Premier NY Muni A	Muni NY	10.7	9.64	5.73	3	4	4.5	0.95	800 782-6620
Dreyfus Premier NY Muni B	Muni NY	10.1	9.1	5.19	3	4	0	1.46	800 782-6620
Dreyfus Premier NY Muni C	Muni NY	9.9	8.83	4.95	4	4	0	1.69	800 782-6620
Dreyfus Premier OH Muni A	Muni State	9.1	8.49	5.32	3	3	4.5	0.92	800 782-6620
Dreyfus Premier OH Muni B	Muni State	8.5	7.99	4.8	4	3	0	1.42	800 782-6620
Dreyfus Premier OH Muni C	Muni State	8.3	7.69	4.48	4	3	0	1.65	800 782-6620
Dreyfus Premier PA Muni A	Muni State	10.5	8.46	5.11	3	4	4.5	0.93	800 782-6620
Dreyfus Premier PA Muni B	Muni State	9.9	7.95	4.57	4	4	0	1.43	800 782-6620
Dreyfus Premier PA Muni C	Muni State	9.7	7.67	4.41	4	4	0	1.66	800 782-6620
Dreyfus Premier Select Int Muni A	Muni Natl						4.5		800 782-6620
Dreyfus Premier Select Int Muni B	Muni Natl						0		800 782-6620
Dreyfus Premier Select Int Muni C	Muni Natl						0		800 782-6620
Dreyfus Premier Select Int Muni Z	Muni Natl	8.5	9.07	5.99	1	2	0	0.45	800 782-6620
Dreyfus Premier Select Muni A	Muni Natl						4.5		800 782-6620
Dreyfus Premier Select Muni B	Muni Natl						0		800 782-6620
Dreyfus Premier Select Muni C	Muni Natl						0		800 782-6620
Dreyfus Premier Select Muni D	Muni Natl	9.9	9.49	5.67	2	3	0	0.45	800 782-6620
Dreyfus Premier Sh-Intmd Muni Bd A	Muni Natl						2		800 782-6620
Dreyfus Premier Sh-Intmd Muni Bd B	Muni Natl						0		800 782-6620
Dreyfus Premier Sh-Intmd Muni Bd D	Muni Natl	3.6	4.61	3.97	3	1	0	0.68	800 782-6620
Dreyfus Premier Sh-Intmd Muni Bd P	Muni Natl						0		800 782-6620
Dreyfus Premier Short-Term Income D	Corp-Inv	2.8	6.03	5.33	4	1	0	0.8	800 782-6620
Dreyfus Premier TX Muni A	Muni State	10.5	10	5.76	2	4	4.5	0.85	800 782-6620
Dreyfus Premier TX Muni B	Muni State	9.9	9.47	5.24	3	4	0	1.35	800 782-6620
Dreyfus Premier TX Muni C	Muni State	9.7	9.19	4.98	3	4	0	1.6	800 782-6620
Dreyfus Premier VA Muni A	Muni State	9.9	8.92	5.2	3	4	4.5	0.94	800 782-6620
Dreyfus Premier VA Muni B	Muni State	9.4	8.38	4.66	5	4	0	1.45	800 782-6620
Dreyfus Premier VA Muni C	Muni State	9.1	8.14	4.41	5	4	0	1.68	800 782-6620
Dreyfus Premier Yield Advantage A	Corp-HY						0		800 782-6620
Dreyfus Premier Yield Advantage B	Corp-HY						0		800 782-6620
Dreyfus Premier Yield Advantage D	Dvsfd Bond	1.4					0	0.75	800 782-6620
Dreyfus Premier Yield Advantage P	Corp-HY						0		800 782-6620
Dreyfus Premier Yield Advantage S	Corp-HY						0		800 782-6620
Dreyfus Sh-Interm Govt	Government	5.3	6.79	5.66	3	1	0	0.6	800 782-6620
Dreyfus UST Interm Term	Government	10.2	10.16	6.9	4	3	0	0.8	800 782-6620
Dreyfus UST Long Term	Government	15.8	11.65	7.25	3	4	0	0.8	800 782-6620
Dupree Interm Government Bond	Government	10.3	10.27	6.91	3	3	0	0.12	800 866-0614
Dupree KY Tax Free Income	Muni State	9.6	7.08	4.87	2	2	0	0.15	800 866-0614
Dupree KY Tax Free Short-to-Med	Muni State	7.3	6.61	4.71	3	1	0	0.18	800 866-0614
Dupree NC Tax Free Income	Muni State	10.4	8.25	5.29	2	3	0	0.14	800 866-0614
Dupree NC Tax Free Sh-to-Med	Muni State	8.6	6.95	5.2	2	2	0	0.12	800 866-0614
Dupree TN Tax-Free Income	Muni State	10.6	7.94	5.94	1	3	0	0.14	800 866-0614
Dupree TN Tax-Free Sh-to-Med	Muni State	8.8	6.61	4.86	3	2	0	0.13	800 866-0614
E*TRADE Bond Fund	Corp-Inv	10.2	7		3	3	0	0.65	800 786-2575
EARNEST Partners Fixed Income Fund	Corp-Inv	12.4	10.33	7.29	3	3	0	0.9	800 773-3863
Eaton Vance AL Muni A	Muni State	8.8	9.25	5.32	4	4	4.75	0.81	800 262-1122
Eaton Vance AL Muni B	Muni State	8	8.31	4.46	5	4	0	1.56	800 262-1122

Bond Fund Name	Objective	Annualized Return for			Rank		Max Load	Expense Ratio	Toll-Free/(Toll) Telephone
		1 Year	3 Years	5 Years	Overall	Risk			
Eaton Vance AR Muni A	Muni State	8.7	8.74	5.37	3	3	4.75	0.78	800 262-1122
Eaton Vance AR Muni B	Muni State	7.8	7.95	4.61	5	3	0	1.53	800 262-1122
Eaton Vance AZ Muni A	Muni State	9.7	8.39	4.63	4	4	4.75	0.78	800 262-1122
Eaton Vance AZ Muni B	Muni State	9	7.5	3.81	5	4	0	1.53	800 262-1122
Eaton Vance CA Ltd Mat Muni A	Muni CA	8.7	8.57	5.17	4	4	2.25	1	800 262-1122
Eaton Vance CA Ltd Mat Muni B	Muni CA	7.8	7.7	4.37	5	4	0	1.75	800 262-1122
Eaton Vance CA Muni A	Muni CA	11.1	10.25	5.59	3	4	4.75	0.91	800 262-1122
Eaton Vance CA Muni B	Muni CA	10.8	9.93	5.28	3	4	0	1.24	800 262-1122
Eaton Vance CO Muni A	Muni State	8.8	9.23	5.05	4	4	4.75	0.78	800 262-1122
Eaton Vance CO Muni B	Muni State	8	8.31	4.23	5	4	0	1.53	800 262-1122
Eaton Vance CT Muni A	Muni State	9	9.22	5.62	2	3	4.75	0.8	800 262-1122
Eaton Vance CT Muni B	Muni State	8.2	8.31	4.75	4	3	0	1.55	800 262-1122
Eaton Vance FL Ins Muni A	Muni State	10.9	10.19	5.88	3	4	4.75	0.72	800 262-1122
Eaton Vance FL Ins Muni B	Muni State	10.1	9.27	5	3	4	0	1.47	800 262-1122
Eaton Vance FL Ltd Mat Muni A	Muni State	9.4	8.58	5.24	2	3	2.25	0.91	800 262-1122
Eaton Vance FL Ltd Mat Muni B	Muni State	8.5	7.8	4.46	4	3	0	1.66	800 262-1122
Eaton Vance FL Ltd Mat Muni C	Muni State	8.6	7.91	4.53	4	3	2.25	1.66	800 262-1122
Eaton Vance FL Muni A	Muni State	9.5	9.75	5.45	2	3	4.75	0.82	800 262-1122
Eaton Vance FL Muni B	Muni State	8.8	8.83	4.62	4	3	0	1.57	800 262-1122
Eaton Vance Float-Rate High Inc Adv	Govt-Mtg	3.6					0	1.15	800 262-1122
Eaton Vance Float-Rate High Inc B	Govt-Mtg	2.9					0	1.9	800 262-1122
Eaton Vance Float-Rate High Inc C	Govt-Mtg	2.8					0	1.91	800 262-1122
Eaton Vance Float-Rate High Inc I	Govt-Mtg	3.8					0	0.94	800 262-1122
Eaton Vance Floating Rate Adv	Govt-Mtg	2.5					0	1.13	800 262-1122
Eaton Vance Floating Rate B	Govt-Mtg	1.6					0	1.89	800 262-1122
Eaton Vance Floating Rate C	Govt-Mtg	1.8					0	1.89	800 262-1122
Eaton Vance Floating Rate I	Govt-Mtg	2.7					0	0.89	800 262-1122
Eaton Vance GA Muni A	Muni State	10.1	9.68	5.29	3	4	4.75	0.84	800 262-1122
Eaton Vance GA Muni B	Muni State	9.3	8.64	4.36	5	4	0	1.59	800 262-1122
Eaton Vance Govt Obligation A	Govt-Mtg	7	8.69	6.33	3	2	4.75	1.27	800 262-1122
Eaton Vance Govt Obligation B	Govt-Mtg	6.2	7.69	5.44	3	2	0	0.27	800 262-1122
Eaton Vance Govt Obligation C	Govt-Mtg	6.2	7.87	5.48	3	2	0	2.01	800 262-1122
Eaton Vance HI Muni A	Muni State	8.5	9.25	5.2	3	4	4.75	0.94	800 262-1122
Eaton Vance HI Muni B	Muni State	7.7	8.3	4.3	5	4	0	1.7	800 262-1122
Eaton Vance High Income Fund B	Corp-HY	10.7	-1.77	-0.05	4	5	4.75	1.79	800 262-1122
Eaton Vance High Income Fund C	Corp-HY	10.7					0	1.82	800 262-1122
Eaton Vance High Yield Muni A	Corp-HY	10.1					4.75	1.07	800 262-1122
Eaton Vance High Yield Muni B	Corp-HY	9.2					0	1.82	800 262-1122
Eaton Vance High Yield Muni C	Corp-HY	9.3	7.24		4	3	0	1.82	800 262-1122
Eaton Vance Income Fd of Boston A	Corp-HY	10.5	0.73	2.35	4	5	4.75	1.07	800 262-1122
Eaton Vance Income Fd of Boston I	Corp-HY	10.8	0.92	2.45	4	5	0	0.85	800 262-1122
Eaton Vance KS Muni A	Muni State	9.3	9.77	5.73	3	4	4.75	0.99	800 262-1122
Eaton Vance KS Muni B	Muni State	8.6	8.84	4.9	4	4	0	1.74	800 262-1122
Eaton Vance KY Muni A	Muni State	9.2	8.3	4.74	3	3	4.75	0.79	800 262-1122
Eaton Vance KY Muni B	Muni State	8.4	7.4	3.91	5	3	0	1.54	800 262-1122
Eaton Vance LA Muni A	Muni State	9.3	9.66	5.17	3	4	4.75	0.8	800 262-1122
Eaton Vance LA Muni B	Muni State	8.4	8.73	4.32	5	4	0	1.56	800 262-1122
Eaton Vance MA Ltd Mat Muni A	Muni State	9.6	8.32	5.04	2	3	2.25	0.91	800 262-1122
Eaton Vance MA Ltd Mat Muni B	Muni State	8.7	7.46	4.2	4	3	0	1.66	800 262-1122
Eaton Vance MA Ltd Mat Muni C	Muni State	8.8	7.65	4.36	4	3	0	1.66	800 262-1122
Eaton Vance MA Muni A	Muni State	10.4	9.99	5.65	2	4	4.75	0.8	800 262-1122
Eaton Vance MA Muni B	Muni State	9.6	9.05	4.74	3	4	0	1.55	800 262-1122
Eaton Vance MD Muni A	Muni State	9.6	9.08	4.75	2	4	4.75	0.78	800 262-1122
Eaton Vance MD Muni B	Muni State	8.8	8.16	3.89	3	3	0	1.52	800 262-1122
Eaton Vance MI Muni A	Muni State	9.1	9.61	5.23	3	4	4.75	0.8	800 262-1122
Eaton Vance MI Muni B	Muni State	8.4	8.67	4.36	4	4	0	1.55	800 262-1122
Eaton Vance MN Muni A	Muni State	6.2	7.62	4.29	3	3	4.75	0.75	800 262-1122
Eaton Vance MN Muni B	Muni State	5.5	6.7	3.47	4	3	0	1.5	800 262-1122

Bond Fund Name	Objective	Annualized Return for			Rank		Max Load	Expense Ratio	Toll-Free/(Toll) Telephone
		1 Year	3 Years	5 Years	Overall	Risk			
Eaton Vance MO Muni A	Muni State	9.5	9.57	5.42	2	3	4.75	0.79	800 262-1122
Eaton Vance MO Muni B	Muni State	8.6	8.59	4.48	3	3	0	1.55	800 262-1122
Eaton Vance MS Muni A	Muni State	8.8	8.75	5.28	2	3	4.75	0.83	800 262-1122
Eaton Vance MS Muni B	Muni State	7.9	7.83	4.41	4	3	0	1.58	800 262-1122
Eaton Vance Municipal Bond A	Muni Natl	10.1	10.67	5.45	3	4	4.75	0.9	800 262-1122
Eaton Vance Municipal Bond B	Muni Natl	9.2	9.75	4.62	4	4	0	1.65	800 262-1122
Eaton Vance Municipal Bond I	Muni Natl	10.2	10.96	5.59	2	4	0	0.66	800 262-1122
Eaton Vance NC Muni A	Muni State	7.4	8.17	4.8	5	3	4.75	0.83	800 262-1122
Eaton Vance NC Muni B	Muni State	6.7	7.21	3.97	5	3	0	1.56	800 262-1122
Eaton Vance NJ Ltd Mat Muni A	Muni State	8.4	7.7	4.87	3	3	2.25	0.94	800 262-1122
Eaton Vance NJ Ltd Mat Muni B	Muni State	7.5	6.86	4.07	4	3	0	1.69	800 262-1122
Eaton Vance NJ Muni A	Muni State	10	9.96	5.53	3	4	4.75	0.83	800 262-1122
Eaton Vance NJ Muni B	Muni State	9.2	9.01	4.65	4	4	0	1.58	800 262-1122
Eaton Vance NY Ltd Mat Muni A	Muni NY	9.1	8.5	5.48	3	3	2.25	0.89	800 262-1122
Eaton Vance NY Ltd Mat Muni B	Muni NY	8.4	7.67	4.67	4	3	0	1.64	800 262-1122
Eaton Vance NY Ltd Mat Muni C	Muni NY	8.2					0	1.64	800 262-1122
Eaton Vance NY Muni A	Muni NY	9.9	10.5	6.29	3	4	4.75	0.82	800 262-1122
Eaton Vance NY Muni B	Muni NY	9.3	9.75	5.5	4	4	0	0.81	800 262-1122
Eaton Vance Nat Ltd Mat Muni A	Muni Natl	9.7	7.99	4.82	2	2	2.25	0.88	800 262-1122
Eaton Vance Nat Ltd Mat Muni B	Muni Natl	9	7.2	4.03	3	2	0	1.63	800 262-1122
Eaton Vance Nat Ltd Mat Muni C	Muni Natl	8.8	7.33	4.08	3	2	0	1.63	800 262-1122
Eaton Vance National Muni A	Muni Natl	12.2	9.57	4.73	5	4	4.75	0.82	800 262-1122
Eaton Vance National Muni B	Muni Natl	11.7	9.09	4.16	5	4	0	1.23	800 262-1122
Eaton Vance National Muni C	Muni Natl	11.4					0	1.56	800 262-1122
Eaton Vance National Muni I	Muni Natl	12.4	9.75		3	4	0	0.56	800 262-1122
Eaton Vance OH Ltd Mat Muni A	Muni State	8.6	7.59	4.5	3	3	2.25	1.11	800 262-1122
Eaton Vance OH Ltd Mat Muni B	Muni State	7.8	6.8	3.74	5	3	0	1.86	800 262-1122
Eaton Vance OH Muni A	Muni State	8.4	8.46	4.66	4	4	4.75	0.8	800 262-1122
Eaton Vance OH Muni B	Muni State	7.7	7.53	3.79	4	4	0	1.58	800 262-1122
Eaton Vance OR Muni A	Muni State	7	8.18	5.05	4	4	4.75	0.82	800 262-1122
Eaton Vance OR Muni B	Muni State	6.2	7.23	4.17	5	4	0	1.57	800 262-1122
Eaton Vance PA Ltd Mat Muni A	Muni State	8.7	7.96	4.83	3	3	2.25	0.92	800 262-1122
Eaton Vance PA Ltd Mat Muni B	Muni State	7.9	7.16	4.04	4	3	0	1.67	800 262-1122
Eaton Vance PA Ltd Mat Muni C	Muni State	7.9	7.33	4.15	4	3	2.25	1.67	800 262-1122
Eaton Vance PA Muni A	Muni State	9	9.02	4.61	2	3	4.75	0.85	800 262-1122
Eaton Vance PA Muni B	Muni State	8.2	8.07	3.72	3	3	0	1.6	800 262-1122
Eaton Vance Prime Rate Reserves	Govt-Mtg	2.2					0	1.27	800 262-1122
Eaton Vance RI Muni A	Muni State	9.2	9.57	5.5	3	4	4.75	0.72	800 262-1122
Eaton Vance RI Muni B	Muni State	8.3	8.6	4.62	5	4	0	1.47	800 262-1122
Eaton Vance SC Muni A	Muni State	7.8	8.83	4.84	3	3	4.75	0.78	800 262-1122
Eaton Vance SC Muni B	Muni State	6.9	7.73	3.85	5	3	0	1.54	800 262-1122
Eaton Vance Sr Floating-Rate Adv	Govt-Mtg	2.2					0	1.2	800 262-1122
Eaton Vance Sr Floating-Rate Cl	Govt-Mtg	2.1	2.29	3.83	4	1	0	1.42	800 262-1122
Eaton Vance Sr Floating-Rate Instl	Govt-Mtg	2.7	2.97	4.41	4	1	0	0.74	800 262-1122
Eaton Vance Strategic Inc A	Intl Bond	11	6.8	5.23	3	4	4.75	1.17	800 262-1122
Eaton Vance Strategic Inc B	Intl Bond	10.1	5.95	4.34	4	4	0	1.92	800 262-1122
Eaton Vance Strategic Inc C	Intl Bond	10.2	6	4.37	4	4	0	1.93	800 262-1122
Eaton Vance TN Muni A	Muni State	9.9	9.25	5.62	2	3	4.75	0.74	800 262-1122
Eaton Vance TN Muni B	Muni State	9.1	8.33	4.76	4	3	0	1.49	800 262-1122
Eaton Vance VA Muni A	Muni State	8.6	8.74	5.11	4	4	4.75	0.82	800 262-1122
Eaton Vance VA Muni B	Muni State	8	7.83	4.25	4	3	0	1.57	800 262-1122
Eaton Vance WV Muni A	Muni State	10.3	9.56	5.46	3	4	4.75	0.74	800 262-1122
Eaton Vance WV Muni B	Muni State	9.4	8.59	4.58	5	4	0	1.49	800 262-1122
Eclipse Bond Fund	Corp-Inv	11	9.52	6.4	3	3	0	0.75	866 232-5477
Eclipse Bond Fund Svc	Corp-Inv	10.8					0	1	866 232-5477
Eclipse Core Bond Plus Fd	Dvsfd Bond	11.7					0	0.7	866 232-5477
Eclipse Indexed Bond Fd NL	Corp-Inv	11.3	10.33	7.09	2	3	0	0.5	866 232-5477
Eclipse Indexed Bond Fd Svc	Corp Inv	11					0	0.75	866 232-5477

438

Bond Fund Name	Objective	Annualized Return for 1 Year	3 Years	5 Years	Rank Overall Risk		Max Load	Expense Ratio	Toll-Free/(Toll) Telephone
Eclipse Short Term Bond Fund	Corp-Inv	5	6.63	5.61	3	1	0	0.6	866 232-5477
Eclipse Short Term Bond Fund Svc	Corp-Inv	4.8					0	0.85	866 232-5477
Eclipse Tax Free Bond Fund	Muni Natl	8.3					0	0.65	866 232-5477
Eclipse Ultra Short Term Income	Government	3	4.98	5	3	1	0	0.2	866 232-5477
Elfun Income Fund	Corp-Inv	11.8	10.96	8.27	1	2	0	0.19	800 242-0134
Elfun Tax Exempt Income	Muni Natl	10.4	9.75	6.33	1	3	0	0.19	800 242-0134
Empire Builder Tax Free Bond B	Muni State	10.5					0	1.2	800 847-5886
Empire Builder Tax Free Bond Prem	Muni State	10.8					0	0.86	800 847-5886
Enterprise Government Sec A	Govt-Mtg	7.6	9.36	6.59	2	2	4.75	1.27	800 432-4320
Enterprise Government Sec B	Govt-Mtg	7	8.6	5.91	3	2	0	1.82	800 432-4320
Enterprise Government Sec C	Govt-Mtg	6.9	8.58	5.32	3	2	1	1.82	800 432-4320
Enterprise Government Sec Y	Govt-Mtg	8.1					0	0.82	800 432-4320
Enterprise High-Yield Bond A	Corp-HY	7.2	4.95	2.68	4	5	4.75	1.3	800 432-4320
Enterprise High-Yield Bond B	Corp-HY	6.6	4.11	1.97	4	5	0	1.85	800 432-4320
Enterprise High-Yield Bond C	Corp-HY	6.5	4.33	2.12	4	5	1	1.85	800 432-4320
Enterprise High-Yield Bond Y	Corp-HY	7.7					0	0.85	800 432-4320
Enterprise Tax-Exempt Income A	Muni Natl	10.8	8.63	5.44	3	3	4.75	1.1	800 432-4320
Enterprise Tax-Exempt Income B	Muni Natl	10.2	8.07	4.9	4	3	0	1.65	800 432-4320
Enterprise Tax-Exempt Income C	Muni Natl	10.2	8.14	4.95	4	3	1	1.65	800 432-4320
Enterprise Tax-Exempt Income Y	Muni Natl	11.3					0	0.65	800 432-4320
Enterprise-Total Return A	Dvsfd Bond	10.2					4.75	1.35	800 432-4320
Enterprise-Total Return B	Dvsfd Bond	9.6					0	1.9	800 432-4320
Enterprise-Total Return C	Dvsfd Bond	9.6					1	1.9	800 432-4320
Enterprise-Total Return Y	Dvsfd Bond	10.7					0	0.9	800 432-4320
EquiTrust Series High Grade Bond	Corp-Inv	8.6	9.55	6.03	3	2	0	1.68	877 860-2904
EquiTrust Strat Yield Port Trad	Corp-HY	6.2	7.54	4.58	5	3	0	1.94	877 860-2904
Eureka Investment Grade Bond A	Dvsfd Bond	10.8	9.83	6.66		3	3.5	1.24	888 890-8121
Eureka Investment Grade Bond B	Dvsfd Bond	9.8	8.84	5.75		3	0	2.2	888 890-8121
Eureka Investment Grade Bond Tr	Dvsfd Bond	11.1	10.13	6.95		3	0	0.99	888 890-8121
Evergreen Adj Rate Fund A	Govt-Mtg	3.5	5.73	5.57	3	1	3.25	0.65	800 343-2898
Evergreen Adj Rate Fund B	Govt-Mtg	2.7	4.95	5.11	3	1	0	1.42	800 343-2898
Evergreen Adj Rate Fund C	Govt-Mtg	2.7	4.95	5.11	3	1	1	1.42	800 343-2898
Evergreen Adj Rate Fund I	Govt-Mtg	3.8	5.98	5.7	2	1	0	0.43	800 343-2898
Evergreen Adj Rate Fund IS	Govt-Mtg	3.5	5.71	5.44	3	1	0	0.67	800 343-2898
Evergreen CT Muni Bond A	Muni State	9.1	8.58	5.4	2	3	4.75	0.96	800 343-2898
Evergreen CT Muni Bond B	Muni State	8.3	7.79	4.61	4	3	0	1.71	800 343-2898
Evergreen CT Muni Bond C	Muni State	8.3					1	1.76	800 343-2898
Evergreen CT Muni Bond I	Muni State	9.4	8.85	5.66	2	3	0	0.71	800 343-2898
Evergreen Core Bond A	Dvsfd Bond	11.1	10.83	7.69	1	2	4.75	0.69	800 343-2898
Evergreen Core Bond B	Dvsfd Bond	10.3	10.27	7.36	1	2	0	1.44	800 343-2898
Evergreen Core Bond C	Dvsfd Bond	10.3	10.27	7.36	1	2	1	1.41	800 343-2898
Evergreen Core Bond I	Dvsfd Bond	11.4	11.02	7.79	1	2	0	0.44	800 343-2898
Evergreen Core Bond IS	Dvsfd Bond	11.1	10.75	6.95	2	2	0	0.69	800 343-2898
Evergreen Diversified Bond A	Corp-Inv	12.8	10.11	5.92	2	3	4.75	1.07	800 343-2898
Evergreen Diversified Bond B	Corp-Inv	11.9	9.31	5.17	3	3	0	1.82	800 343-2898
Evergreen Diversified Bond C	Corp-Inv	11.9	9.31	5.16	3	3	1	1.83	800 343-2898
Evergreen Diversified Bond I	Corp-Inv	13	10.4	6.08	2	3	0	0.86	800 343-2898
Evergreen FL High Income Muni A	Muni State	5.7	6.7	3.81	3	1	4.75	0.97	800 343-2898
Evergreen FL High Income Muni B	Muni State	5	5.9	3.04	4	1	0	1.72	800 343-2898
Evergreen FL High Income Muni C	Muni State	5	5.9	3.04	4	1	1	1.72	800 343-2898
Evergreen FL High Income Muni I	Muni State	6	6.95	4.05	3	1	0	0.72	800 343-2898
Evergreen FL Muni Bond A	Muni State	7.8	7.51	4.61	3	2	4.75	0.77	800 343-2898
Evergreen FL Muni Bond B	Muni State	6.9	6.58	3.7	4	2	4.75	1.61	800 343-2898
Evergreen FL Muni Bond C	Muni State	6.9	6.58	3.68	4	2	1	1.6	800 343-2898
Evergreen FL Muni Bond I	Muni State	8	7.65	4.73	3	2	0	0.6	800 343-2898
Evergreen Fixed Income II I	Dvsfd Bond	11.6	10.83	7.61		2	0	0.41	800 343-2898
Evergreen Fixed Income II IS	Dvsfd Bond	11.3	10.58	7.37	2	2	0	0.42	800 343-2898
Evergreen GA Muni Bond A	Muni State	9.3	8.65	5.41	2	3	4.75	0.87	800 343-2898

Bond Fund Name	Objective	Annualized Return for			Rank		Max Load	Expense Ratio	Toll-Free/(Toll) Telephone
		1 Year	3 Years	5 Years	Overall	Risk			
Evergreen GA Muni Bond B	Muni State	8.5	7.84	4.62	4	3	0	1.62	800 343-2898
Evergreen GA Muni Bond C	Muni State	8.5	8.33	5.23		3	1	1.61	800 343-2898
Evergreen GA Muni Bond I	Muni State	9.6	8.92	5.67	2	3	0	0.62	800 343-2898
Evergreen High Grade Muni A	Muni Natl	10.9	9.39	5.51	3	4	4.75	0.91	800 343-2898
Evergreen High Grade Muni B	Muni Natl	10	8.58	4.74	4	4	0	1.66	800 343-2898
Evergreen High Grade Muni C	Muni Natl	10	8.58	4.87	4	4	1	1.66	800 343-2898
Evergreen High Grade Muni I	Muni Natl	11.1	9.66	5.79	2	4	0	0.66	800 343-2898
Evergreen High Income Muni A	Muni Natl	3.9					4.75	0.93	800 343-2898
Evergreen High Income Muni B	Muni Natl	3.1					0	1.68	800 343-2898
Evergreen High Income Muni C	Muni Natl	3.1	5.4	3.33	4	1	1	1.68	800 343-2898
Evergreen High Income Muni I	Muni Natl	4.2	6.51	4.58	3	1	0	0.68	800 343-2898
Evergreen High Yield Bond A	Corp-HY	9.7	6.07	2.75	4	4	4.75	1.18	800 343-2898
Evergreen High Yield Bond B	Corp-HY	8.9	5.28	2	4	4	0	1.91	800 343-2898
Evergreen High Yield Bond C	Corp-HY	8.9	5.28	2.02	4	4	1	1.92	800 343-2898
Evergreen High Yield Bond I	Corp-HY	10	6.33	3.02	4	4	0	0.91	800 343-2898
Evergreen Intermediate Municipal I	Muni Natl	6.9	6.5	3.93	4	2	0	0.66	800 343-2898
Evergreen Intermediate Municipal IS	Muni Natl	6.6	6.23	3.66	4	2	0	0.91	800 343-2898
Evergreen Interntl Bond I	Intl Bond	33.9	14.85	8.88	3	5	0	0.71	800 343-2898
Evergreen Interntl Bond IS	Intl Bond	33.5	14.56	8.64	3	5	4.75	0.96	800 343-2898
Evergreen Limited Duration A	Dvsfd Bond	4.7					3.25	0.47	800 343-2898
Evergreen Limited Duration B	Dvsfd Bond	3.8					0	1.37	800 343-2898
Evergreen Limited Duration C	Dvsfd Bond	3.8					1	1.37	800 343-2898
Evergreen Limited Duration I	Dvsfd Bond	4.8	7.04	5.96	3	1	0	0.37	800 343-2898
Evergreen Limited Duration IS	Dvsfd Bond	4.6	6.78			1	0	0.62	800 343-2898
Evergreen MD Muni Bond A	Muni State	7.8	8.1	5.19	3	2	4.75	0.9	800 343-2898
Evergreen MD Muni Bond B	Muni State	7	7.3	4.25	4	2	0	1.65	800 343-2898
Evergreen MD Muni Bond C	Muni State	7	7.3		4	2	1	1.65	800 343-2898
Evergreen MD Muni Bond I	Muni State	8.1	8.38	5.45	2	2	0	0.65	800 343-2898
Evergreen Municipal Bond A	Muni Natl	10					4.75	0.82	800 343-2898
Evergreen Municipal Bond B	Muni Natl	9.2	8.07	4.08	4	3	0	1.57	800 343-2898
Evergreen Municipal Bond C	Muni Natl	9.2					1	1.57	800 343-2898
Evergreen Municipal Bond I	Muni Natl	10.3	9.15			3	0	0.57	800 343-2898
Evergreen NC Muni Bond A	Muni State	9.7	8.48	5.12	2	3	4.75	0.7	800 343-2898
Evergreen NC Muni Bond B	Muni State	8.9	7.67	4.33	3	3	0	1.45	800 343-2898
Evergreen NC Muni Bond C	Muni State	8.9	8.16	4.94		3	1	1.45	800 343-2898
Evergreen NC Muni Bond I	Muni State	10	8.75	5.37	1	3	0	0.45	800 343-2898
Evergreen NJ Muni Bond A	Muni State	8.3	8.21	5.25	3	3	4.75	0.77	800 343-2898
Evergreen NJ Muni Bond B	Muni State	7.4	7.26	4.33	5	3	0	1.6	800 343-2898
Evergreen NJ Muni Bond C	Muni State	7.4	7.86	5.04		3	1	1.58	800 343-2898
Evergreen NJ Muni Bond I	Muni State	8.5	8.33	5.37	3	3	0	0.6	800 343-2898
Evergreen Offit CA Municipal A	Muni State	10.2	9.19	6.54		4	4.75	0.93	800 343-2898
Evergreen Offit CA Municipal B	Muni State	9.8	9.05	6.45		3	0	1.68	800 343-2898
Evergreen Offit CA Municipal C	Muni State	9.8	9.05	6.45		3	1	1.69	800 343-2898
Evergreen Offit CA Municipal I	Muni State	10.4	9.25	6.57		4	0	0.7	800 343-2898
Evergreen Offit High Yield A	Corp-HY						4.75	1.24	800 343-2898
Evergreen Offit High Yield I	Corp-HY						0	0.51	800 343-2898
Evergreen Offit Mortgage Sec A	Govt-Mtg	5.5	8.58	6.28		2	4.75	0.84	800 343-2898
Evergreen Offit Mortgage Sec I	Govt-Mtg	6	8.77	6.41		2	0	0.59	800 343-2898
Evergreen Offit NY Municipal A	Muni State	11	9.67	6.66		3	4.75	0.82	800 343-2898
Evergreen Offit NY Municipal B	Muni State	10.6	9.66	6.65		3	0	1.58	800 343-2898
Evergreen Offit NY Municipal C	Muni State	10.6	9.66	6.65		3	1	1.57	800 343-2898
Evergreen Offit NY Municipal I	Muni NY	11.2	9.88	6.78	2	3	0	0.58	800 343-2898
Evergreen Offit National Muni A	Muni Natl	11.4	10.41	7.44		3	4.75	0.75	800 343-2898
Evergreen Offit National Muni B	Muni Natl	11.1	10.32	7.37		3	0	1.57	800 343-2898
Evergreen Offit National Muni C	Muni Natl	11.1	10.32	7.37		3	1	1.48	800 343-2898
Evergreen Offit National Muni I	Muni Natl	11.8	10.52	7.5		3	0	0.51	800 343-2898
Evergreen Offit US Govt Secs I	Govt-Mtg	8.9	9.36	6.95		3	0	0.51	800 343-2898
Evergreen PA Muni Bond A	Muni State	9.1	8.44	5.26	1	3	4.75	0.64	800 343-2898

Bond Fund Name	Objective	Annualized Return for			Rank		Max Load	Expense Ratio	Toll-Free/(Toll) Telephone
		1 Year	3 Years	5 Years	Overall	Risk			
Evergreen PA Muni Bond B	Muni State	8.4	7.74	4.65	3	3	0	1.4	800 343-2898
Evergreen PA Muni Bond C	Muni State	8.4	7.73	4.62	4	3	1	1.4	800 343-2898
Evergreen PA Muni Bond I	Muni State	9.4	8.73	5.62	1	3	0	0.4	800 343-2898
Evergreen SC Muni Bond A	Muni State	9.5	8.83	5.49	2	3	4.75	0.86	800 343-2898
Evergreen SC Muni Bond B	Muni State	8.7	8.02	4.58	4	3	0	1.6	800 343-2898
Evergreen SC Muni Bond C	Muni State	8.7	8.51	5.32		3	1	1.58	800 343-2898
Evergreen SC Muni Bond I	Muni State	9.8	9.1	5.76	1	3	0	0.61	800 343-2898
Evergreen Select High Yield Fd I	Corp-HY	7.1	7.92		2	4	0	0.67	800 343-2898
Evergreen Select High Yield Fd IS	Corp-HY	6.8	7.66		2	4	0	0.93	800 343-2898
Evergreen Short-Intermed Bond A	Dvsfd Bond						3.25	0.67	800 343-2898
Evergreen Short-Intermed Bond B	Dvsfd Bond						0	1.57	800 343-2898
Evergreen Short-Intermed Bond C	Dvsfd Bond						1	1.57	800 343-2898
Evergreen Short-Intermed Bond I	Dvsfd Bond	11.3	10.52	7.75	1	2	0	0.57	800 343-2898
Evergreen Short-Intermed Bond IS	Dvsfd Bond	11	10.25	7.63	1	2	0	0.82	800 343-2898
Evergreen Short-Intermed Muni A	Muni Natl	6.8	6.4	4.79	3	1	3.25	0.78	800 343-2898
Evergreen Short-Intermed Muni B	Muni Natl	5.8	5.45	3.85	3	1	0	1.68	800 343-2898
Evergreen Short-Intermed Muni C	Muni Natl	5.8	6.08	4.65		1	1	1.7	800 343-2898
Evergreen Short-Intermed Muni I	Muni Natl	6.9	6.5	4.91	3	1	0	0.68	800 343-2898
Evergreen Strategic Income A	Dvsfd Bond	18.9	11.38	6.16	2	4	4.75	1.19	800 343-2898
Evergreen Strategic Income B	Dvsfd Bond	18	10.55	5.33	3	4	0	1.95	800 343-2898
Evergreen Strategic Income C	Dvsfd Bond	18	10.56	5.36	3	4	1	1.95	800 343-2898
Evergreen Strategic Income I	Dvsfd Bond	19.2	11.66	6.63	2	4	0	0.95	800 343-2898
Evergreen US Govt A	Government	9	9.18	6.5	3	2	4.75	0.93	800 343-2898
Evergreen US Govt B	Government	8.2	8.38	5.7	4	2	0	1.68	800 343-2898
Evergreen US Govt C	Government	8.2	8.38	5.87	4	2	1	1.68	800 343-2898
Evergreen US Govt I	Government	9.3	9.46	6.75	3	2	0	0.68	800 343-2898
Evergreen VA Muni Bond A	Muni State	8.7	8.49	5.55	1	3	4.75	0.87	800 343-2898
Evergreen VA Muni Bond B	Muni State	7.9	7.67	4.76	4	3	0	1.62	800 343-2898
Evergreen VA Muni Bond C	Muni State	7.9	8.17	5.38		3	1	1.61	800 343-2898
Evergreen VA Muni Bond I	Muni State	8.9	8.75	5.83	1	3	4.75	0.62	800 343-2898
Excelsior Institutional Income	Dvsfd Bond	10.3	9.9	6.94	3	3	0		800 881-9358
Excelsior Instl Tot Ret Bd Instl I	Corp-Inv	12.4	11.18	7.75	3	3	0	0.5	800 881-9358
Excelsior Intermed Trm Mgd Inc Fd	Corp-Inv	10.1	9.99	6.96	3	2	0	0.9	800 881-9358
Excelsior Intermed Trm T/E Fd	Muni Natl	8.8	8.23	5.54	2	3	0	0.8	800 881-9358
Excelsior Long-Term T/E Fd	Muni Natl	9	9.06	4.9	4	4	0	0.7	800 881-9358
Excelsior Managed Income Fd	Corp-Inv	11.3	10.58	7.2	2	3	0	0.9	800 881-9358
Excelsior NY Interm Term T/E Fd	Muni NY	8.1	8.14	5.38	2	3	0	0.8	800 881-9358
Excelsior Shrt Trm Govt Sec Fd	Government	5.5	7.05	5.75	3	1	0	0.59	800 881-9358
Excelsior Shrt Trm T/E Sec Fd	Muni Natl	1.4	3.66	3.39	3	1	0	0.8	800 881-9358
Expedition Invst Gr Bd A	Government	13.2	11.09	7.58	2	3	4	1.11	800 992-2085
Expedition Invst Gr Bd B	Govt-Mtg	12.4	10.33	7.41	2	3	0	1.86	800 992-2085
Expedition Invst Gr Bd Instl	Government	13.4	11.36	7.83	2	3	0	0.86	800 992-2085
FBR MD Tax Free Fund	Muni State	8.5	7.86	5.15	3	2	0	0.93	888 888-0025
FBR Total Return Bond Fund	Government	-3.1	5.62	4.29	4	4	0	0.9	888 888-0025
FBR VA Tax Free Fund	Muni State	10.2	9.02	5.44	2	3	0	0.93	888 888-0025
FFTW International Portfolio	Intl Bond	21.6					0	0.6	888 367-3389
FFTW Limited Duration Portfolio	Government	5.5					0	0.3	888 367-3389
FFTW US Short-Term Portfolio	Corp-Inv	0.6	3.52	4.08	4	1	0	0.1	888 367-3389
FFTW Worldwide Core Portfolio	Intl Bond	9.8	8.91	7.24	3	2	0	0.45	888 367-3389
FFTW Worldwide Portfolio	Intl Bond	16	8.75	6.05	4	4	0	0.6	888 367-3389
FPA New Income Fund	Corp-Inv	1.2	9.26	6.5	3	2	3.5	0.14	800 982-4372
Fairport Governmnt Securities Fd	Government	11.5	8.08	5.78	3	3	0	0.89	800 332-6459
Federated Adj Rate Sec Instl	Govt-Mtg	2.8	5.09	4.74	2	1	0	0.6	800 341-7400
Federated Adj Rate Sec Instl-Svc	Govt-Mtg	2.6	4.83	4.48	3	1	0	0.86	800 341-7400
Federated Bond Fund A	Corp-Inv	12.7	9.61	5.4	3	4	4.5	1.05	800 341-7400
Federated Bond Fund B	Corp-Inv	11.9	8.82	4.61	3	4	0	1.85	800 341-7400
Federated Bond Fund C	Corp-Inv	11.8	8.75	4.59	3	4	0	1.08	800 341-7400
Federated Bond Fund F	Corp-Inv	12.7	9.64	5.42	2	4	1	1.09	800 341-7400

Bond Fund Name	Objective	Annualized Return for			Rank		Max Load	Expense Ratio	Toll-Free/(Toll) Telephone
		1 Year	3 Years	5 Years	Overall	Risk			
Federated CA Municipal Income A	Muni CA	9.4	8.67		4	4	4.5	0.5	800 341-7400
Federated CA Municipal Income B	Muni CA	8.6					0	1.25	800 341-7400
Federated Fund for US Govt Sec A	Govt-Mtg	5.8	8.48	6.23	3	2	4.5	0.91	800 341-7400
Federated Fund for US Govt Sec B	Govt-Mtg	5.2	7.66	5.42	2	2	0	1.66	800 341-7400
Federated Fund for US Govt Sec C	Govt-Mtg	5.2	7.66	5.42	2	2	0	1.66	800 341-7400
Federated GNMA Trust Instl	Govt-Mtg	5.8	8.34	6.37	2	2	0	0.63	800 341-7400
Federated GNMA Trust Instl-Svc	Govt-Mtg	5.7	8.17	6.2	2	1	0	0.79	800 341-7400
Federated Gov UltraShort Instl	Government	1.7					0	0.25	800 341-7400
Federated Gov UltraShort Instl-Svc	Government	1.6	3.77		4	1	0	0.35	800 341-7400
Federated Govt Inc Securities A	Govt-Mtg	9.9	9.63	6.7	3	3	4.5	0.98	800 341-7400
Federated Govt Inc Securities B	Govt-Mtg	9.1	8.81	5.91	3	3	0	1.73	800 341-7400
Federated Govt Inc Securities C	Govt-Mtg	9.1	8.82	5.91	3	3	1	1.73	800 341-7400
Federated Govt Inc Securities F	Govt-Mtg	9.9	9.64	6.7	3	3	1	0.97	800 341-7400
Federated High Income Bond A	Corp-HY	8.8	2.33	0.61	5	5	4.5	1.23	800 341-7400
Federated High Income Bond B	Corp-HY	7.8	1.52	-0.14	5	5	0	1.99	800 341-7400
Federated High Income Bond C	Corp-HY	8	1.57	-0.13	5	5	0	1.99	800 341-7400
Federated High Yield Trust	Corp-HY	7	0.92	-0.39	5	5	0	0.93	800 341-7400
Federated Income Trust Instl	Govt-Mtg	6.4	9.02	6.66	1	2	0	0.57	800 341-7400
Federated Income Trust Instl-Svc	Govt-Mtg	6.2	8.82	6.44	2	2	0	0.79	800 341-7400
Federated Instl High Yld Bond Instl	Corp-HY						0	0.7	800 341-7400
Federated Interm Income Instl	Corp-Inv	13	10.74	7.13	2	3	0	0.55	800 341-7400
Federated Interm Income Instl-Svc	Corp-Inv	12.7					0	0.8	800 341-7400
Federated Interm Muni Trust	Muni Natl	7.8	7.87	5	3	3	0	0.6	800 341-7400
Federated International Bond A	Intl Bond	31.7	10.75	4.67	3	5	4.5	1.8	800 341-7400
Federated International Bond B	Intl Bond	30.8	9.96	3.91	3	5	0	2.52	800 341-7400
Federated International Bond C	Intl Bond	30.8	9.93	3.93	3	5	0	2.52	800 341-7400
Federated International High Inc A	Intl Bond	22.2	16.64	9.46	2	5	4.5	1.16	800 341-7400
Federated International High Inc B	Intl Bond	21.4	15.83	8.66	2	5	0	1.91	800 341-7400
Federated International High Inc C	Intl Bond	21.4	15.83	8.66	2	5	0	1.91	800 341-7400
Federated Limited Dur Gov Instl	Government	4.9					0	0.3	800 341-7400
Federated Limited Dur Gov Instl-Svc	Government	4.7	6.32	5.29	3	1	0	0.55	800 341-7400
Federated Limited Dur Instl	Dvsfd Bond	2.1	5.23	4.88	4	1	0	0.65	800 341-7400
Federated Limited Dur Instl-Svc	Dvsfd Bond	1.8	5.04	4.66	4	1	0	0.35	800 341-7400
Federated Limited Term Fund A	Corp-Inv	0.4	4.29	3.74	4	1	1	1.09	800 341-7400
Federated Limited Term Fund F	Corp-Inv	0.4	4.41	3.83	4	1	1	0.99	800 341-7400
Federated Limited Term Muni A	Muni Natl	4.5	4.88	3.85	3	1	1	0.98	800 341-7400
Federated Limited Term Muni F	Muni Natl	4.8	5.12	4.08	3	1	0	0.73	800 341-7400
Federated MI Interm Muni Tr	Muni State	10.6	8.9	5.95	1	3	3	0.51	800 341-7400
Federated Mngd Income Port Instl	Dvsfd Bond	9	6.2	5.08	4	2	0	0.91	800 341-7400
Federated Mngd Income Port Sel	Dvsfd Bond	8.1	5.42	4.36	4	2	0	1.61	800 341-7400
Federated Mortgage Fund Instl	Government	5.9	9.41	7.2	2	2	0	0.3	800 341-7400
Federated Mortgage Fund Instl-Svc	Government	5.6	9.09	6.88	2	2	0	0.6	800 341-7400
Federated Muni Opportunities A	Muni Natl	7.9	6.84	3.47	4	2	4.5	1.08	800 341-7400
Federated Muni Opportunities B	Muni Natl	6.9	6.04	2.66	4	2	0	1.83	800 341-7400
Federated Muni Opportunities C	Muni Natl	7	6.04	2.66	4	2	0	1.08	800 341-7400
Federated Muni Opportunities F	Muni Natl	7.9	6.84	3.47	4	2	1	1.08	800 341-7400
Federated Muni Securities Fd A	Muni Natl	10.6	9.25	5	3	4	4.5	0.86	800 341-7400
Federated Muni Securities Fd B	Muni Natl	9.7	8.49	4.2	5	4	0	1.76	800 341-7400
Federated Muni Securities Fd C	Muni Natl	9.7	8.3	4.08	5	4	0	1.76	800 341-7400
Federated Muni Ultrashrt A	Muni Natl	2.7					0	0.8	800 341-7400
Federated Muni Ultrashrt Instl	Muni Natl	3.2					0	0.35	800 341-7400
Federated NC Muni Inc A	Muni State	11.3	9.48	6.01	2	4	4.5	0.79	800 341-7400
Federated NY Muni Income Fd A	Muni NY	8.8	8.11	4.91	4	3	4.5	0.91	800 341-7400
Federated NY Muni Income Fd B	Muni State						0	1.66	800 341-7400
Federated OH Muni Income Fd F	Muni State	10	8.49	5.13	3	3	1	0.91	800 341-7400
Federated PA Muni Income Fund A	Muni State	10.7	9.32	5.33	2	3	4.5	0.75	800 341-7400
Federated PA Muni Income Fund B	Muni State	9.9					0	1.52	800 341-7400
Federated Sh Term Inc Instl	Corp-Inv	2.4	5.63	5.25	3	1	0	0.56	800 341-7400

Bond Fund Name	Objective	Annualized Return for			Rank		Max Load	Expense Ratio	Toll-Free/(Toll) Telephone
		1 Year	3 Years	5 Years	Overall	Risk			
Federated Sh Term Inc Instl-Svc	Corp-Inv	2.2	5.37	5	3	1	0	0.81	800 341-7400
Federated Sh Term Muni Instl	Muni Natl	5	5.49	4.42	3	1	0	0.45	800 341-7400
Federated Sh Term Muni Instl-Svc	Muni Natl	4.7	5.24	4.17	3	1	0	0.7	800 341-7400
Federated Strategic Income Fund A	Dvsfd Bond	14.4	8.58	5.12	3	4	4.5	1.26	800 341-7400
Federated Strategic Income Fund B	Dvsfd Bond	13.5	7.82	4.33	3	4	0	2.01	800 341-7400
Federated Strategic Income Fund C	Dvsfd Bond	13.5	7.8	4.33	3	4	0	2.01	800 341-7400
Federated Strategic Income Fund F	Dvsfd Bond	14.4	8.56	5.11	3	4	1	1.26	800 341-7400
Federated Tot Ret Bd A	Dvsfd Bond	10.1					4.5	0.85	800 341-7400
Federated Tot Ret Bd B	Dvsfd Bond	9.5					0	1.35	800 341-7400
Federated Tot Ret Bd C	Dvsfd Bond	9.5					0	1.35	800 341-7400
Federated Tot Ret Bd Instl	Corp-Inv	10.6	10.39	7.44	1	2	0	0.35	800 341-7400
Federated Tot Ret Bd Instl-Svc	Corp-Inv	10.3	10.06	7.12	1	2	0	0.65	800 341-7400
Federated Tot Ret Gov Bd Instl	Government	13.8	11.86	8.15	3	4	0	0.3	800 341-7400
Federated Tot Ret Gov Bd Instl-Svc	Government	13.5	11.51	7.83	3	4	0	0.6	800 341-7400
Federated USG Bond Fund	Government	21.7	13.3	8.85	3	5	0	0.91	800 341-7400
Federated USG Sec:1-3yrs Instl	Government	4	6.04	5.25	3	1	0	.54	800 341-7400
Federated USG Sec:1-3yrs Instl-Svc	Government	3.7	5.76	5	3	1	0	0.79	800 341-7400
Federated USG Sec:2-5yrs Instl	Government	10.3	9.92	7.2	2	2	0	0.57	800 341-7400
Federated USG Sec:2-5yrs Instl-Svc	Government	10	9.66	6.94	2	2	0	0.82	800 341-7400
Federated Ultra Short Bd A	Dvsfd Bond						2		800 341-7400
Federated Ultra Short Bd Instl	Dvsfd Bond	1.7	4.7		3	1	0	0.35	800 341-7400
Federated Ultra Short Bd Instl-Svc	Dvsfd Bond	1.3	4.24	4.75	4	1	0	0.8	800 341-7400
Fidelity Adv Emerging Mkts Inc A	Intl Bond	25.2	16.96	12.3	1	5	4.75	1.45	800 522-7297
Fidelity Adv Emerging Mkts Inc B	Intl Bond	24.2	16.16	10.88	1	5	0	2.22	800 522-7297
Fidelity Adv Emerging Mkts Inc I	Intl Bond	25.5	17.3	12	1	5	0	1.17	800 522-7297
Fidelity Adv Emerging Mkts Inc T	Intl Bond	25	16.89	11.59	1	5	3.5	1.5	800 522-7297
Fidelity Adv Float-Rate Hi-Inc A	Corp-HY	3.7					3.75	1.11	800 522-7297
Fidelity Adv Float-Rate Hi-Inc B	Corp-HY	3.1					0	1.65	800 522-7297
Fidelity Adv Float-Rate Hi-Inc C	Corp-HY	3					0	1.74	800 522-7297
Fidelity Adv Float-Rate Hi-Inc I	Corp-HY	3.8					0	0.95	800 522-7297
Fidelity Adv Float-Rate Hi-Inc T	Corp-HY	3.6					0	1.2	800 522-7297
Fidelity Adv Govt Investment A	Government	12.5	10.51	7.33	3	3	4.75	0.84	800 522-7297
Fidelity Adv Govt Investment B	Government	11.8	9.75	6.55	3	3	0	1.61	800 522-7297
Fidelity Adv Govt Investment C	Government	11.6	9.48	6.36	3	3	0	1.68	800 522-7297
Fidelity Adv Govt Investment I	Government	12.7	10.71	7.49	3	3	0	0.7	800 522-7297
Fidelity Adv Govt Investment T	Government	12.5	10.27	7.13	3	3	3.5	0.97	800 522-7297
Fidelity Adv Hi Income Advantage A	Corp-HY	21	3.6	1.52	4	5	4.75	1.01	800 522-7297
Fidelity Adv Hi Income Advantage B	Corp-HY	20.2	2.81	0.77	4	5	0	1.77	800 522-7297
Fidelity Adv Hi Income Advantage C	Corp-HY	20.2	2.27	0.41	4	5	0	1.84	800 522-7297
Fidelity Adv Hi Income Advantage I	Corp-HY	21.4	3.79	1.68	4	5	0	0.85	800 522-7297
Fidelity Adv Hi Income Advantage T	Corp-HY	21.1	3.2	1.25	4	5	3.5	1.09	800 522-7297
Fidelity Adv High Income A	Intl Bond	11.7	5.05			5	4.75	1.02	800 522-7297
Fidelity Adv High Income B	Intl Bond	11	4.17			5	0	1.83	800 522-7297
Fidelity Adv High Income I	Intl Bond	11.8	5.25			5	0	0.94	800 522-7297
Fidelity Adv Inflation-Protect Bd I	Dvsfd Bond						0		800 522-7297
Fidelity Adv Inflation-Protect Bd T	Dvsfd Bond						0		800 522-7297
Fidelity Adv Interm Bond A	Corp-Inv	11.9	10.34	7.33	1	2	3.75	0.85	800 522-7297
Fidelity Adv Interm Bond B	Corp-Inv	11	9.5	6.5	1	2	0	1.65	800 522-7297
Fidelity Adv Interm Bond C	Corp-Inv	10.9	9.39	6.5	1	2	0	1.72	800 522-7297
Fidelity Adv Interm Bond I	Corp-Inv	12.1	10.55	7.49	1	2	0	0.69	800 522-7297
Fidelity Adv Interm Bond T	Corp-Inv	11.8	10.21	7.2	1	2	2.75	0.98	800 522-7297
Fidelity Adv Invt Grade Bond A	Dvsfd Bond						4.75	0.79	800 522-7297
Fidelity Adv Invt Grade Bond B	Dvsfd Bond						0	1.56	800 522-7297
Fidelity Adv Invt Grade Bond C	Dvsfd Bond						0	1.62	800 522-7297
Fidelity Adv Invt Grade Bond I	Dvsfd Bond						0	0.63	800 522-7297
Fidelity Adv Invt Grade Bond T	Dvsfd Bond						0	0.9	800 522-7297
Fidelity Adv Mortgage Secs A	Govt-Mtg	6.8	9.18	6.73	2	1	4.75	0.86	800 522-7297
Fidelity Adv Mortgage Secs B	Govt-Mtg	6	8.33	5.88	1	1	0	1.61	800 522-7297

Bond Fund Name	Objective	Annualized Return for			Rank		Max Load	Expense Ratio	Toll-Free/(Toll) Telephone
		1 Year	3 Years	5 Years	Overall	Risk			
Fidelity Adv Mortgage Secs C	Govt-Mtg	6	8.25	5.84	3	1	0	1.69	800 522-7297
Fidelity Adv Mortgage Secs I	Govt-Mtg	7	9.32	6.87	2	1	0	0.79	800 522-7297
Fidelity Adv Mortgage Secs T	Govt-Mtg	6.7	9	6.59	2	1	3.5	0.97	800 522-7297
Fidelity Adv Muni Income A	Muni Natl	11.6	9.89	6.42	1	3	4.75	0.71	800 522-7297
Fidelity Adv Muni Income B	Muni Natl	10.8	9.06	5.63	2	3	0	1.46	800 522-7297
Fidelity Adv Muni Income C	Muni Natl	10.7	8.73	5.41	3	3	0	1.56	800 522-7297
Fidelity Adv Muni Income I	Muni Natl	11.8	10.07	6.58	1	3	0	0.56	800 522-7297
Fidelity Adv Muni Income T	Muni Natl	11.4	9.77	6.36	1	3	3.5	0.8	800 522-7297
Fidelity Adv Short-Fixed Income A	Corp-Inv	7.2	7.36	6.01	2	1	1.5	0.82	800 522-7297
Fidelity Adv Short-Fixed Income C	Corp-Inv	6.3	6.13	4.98	3	1	0	1.67	800 522-7297
Fidelity Adv Short-Fixed Income I	Corp-Inv	7.4	7.58	6.21	2	1	0	0.65	800 522-7297
Fidelity Adv Short-Fixed Income T	Corp-Inv	7.2	7.37	6	2	1	1.5	0.83	800 522-7297
Fidelity Adv Strategic Income A	Corp-Inv	17.6	10.49	7.32	2	4	4.75	1.07	800 522-7297
Fidelity Adv Strategic Income B	Corp-Inv	16.7	9.69	6.3	3	4	0	1.81	800 522-7297
Fidelity Adv Strategic Income C	Corp-Inv	16.7	9.4	6.28	3	4	0	1.89	800 522-7297
Fidelity Adv Strategic Income I	Corp-Inv	17.8	10.66	7.48	2	4	0	0.94	800 522-7297
Fidelity Adv Strategic Income T	Corp-Inv	17.5	10.43	7.01	2	4	3.5	1.14	800 522-7297
Fidelity Capital & Income	Corp-HY	25.1	2.43	3.02	4	5	0	0.81	800 343-3548
Fidelity GNMA Fund	Govt-Mtg	6.1	8.48	6.45	2	1	0	0.59	800 343-3548
Fidelity Government Income Fund	Government	12.5	10.61	7.42	3	3	0	0.56	800 343-3548
Fidelity High Income	Corp-HY	14.7	0.61	0.23	4	5	0	0.76	800 343-3548
Fidelity Inflation-Protected Bd	Dvsfd Bond						0	0.86	800 343-3548
Fidelity Inst Short-Interm Govt I	Government	7.9	8.52	6.75	1	2	0		800 343-3548
Fidelity Intermediate Bond	Corp-Inv	11.4	10.4	7.53	1	2	0	0.63	800 343-3548
Fidelity Intermediate Government	Government	10.5	9.92	7.3	1	2	0	0.59	800 343-3548
Fidelity Investment Grade Bond Fd	Corp-Inv	11.8	10.65	7.33	1	2	0	0.66	800 343-3548
Fidelity Mortgage Securities	Govt-Mtg	7.1	9.33	6.87	2	1	0	0.63	800 343-3548
Fidelity New Markets Income	Intl Bond	26	17.39	11.83	1	5	0	1	800 343-3548
Fidelity Short-Term Bond	Corp-Inv	7.6	7.75	6.36	1	1	0	0.57	800 343-3548
Fidelity Spartan AZ Muni Income	Muni State	11.1	9.68	6.4	1	3	0	0.55	800 343-3548
Fidelity Spartan CA Muni Inc	Muni CA	10	9.24	6.24	2	4	0	0.48	800 343-3548
Fidelity Spartan CT Muni Income	Muni State	10.7	9.59	6.33	1	3	0	0.5	800 343-3548
Fidelity Spartan FL Muni Income	Muni State	10.4	9.57	6.16	1	3	0	0.5	800 343-3548
Fidelity Spartan Govt Income	Government	12.7	10.85	7.73	3	3	0	0.56	800 343-3548
Fidelity Spartan Intermd Muni Inc	Muni Natl	9.6	8.85	6.08	1	3	0	0.46	800 343-3548
Fidelity Spartan Invest Grade Bd	Corp-Inv	12	10.98	7.66	1	2	0	0.59	800 343-3548
Fidelity Spartan MA Muni Inc	Muni State	10.7	9.67	6.28	1	3	0	0.5	800 343-3548
Fidelity Spartan MD Muni Income	Muni State	9.8	9.08	6.04	1	3	0	0.55	800 343-3548
Fidelity Spartan MI Muni Inc	Muni State	11.5	9.92	6.33	1	3	0	0.51	800 343-3548
Fidelity Spartan MN Muni Inc	Muni State	9.7	8.94	5.79	1	3	0	0.53	800 343-3548
Fidelity Spartan Municipal Inc	Muni Natl	10.3	9.83	6.54	1	3	0	0.47	800 343-3548
Fidelity Spartan NJ Muni Income	Muni State	10	9.39	6.33	2	3	0	0.5	800 343-3548
Fidelity Spartan NY Muni Inc	Muni NY	12.1	10.43	6.7	1	3	0	0.48	800 343-3548
Fidelity Spartan OH Muni Inc	Muni State	11.3	9.82	6.34	1	3	0	0.52	800 343-3548
Fidelity Spartan PA Muni Inc	Muni State	10.1	9.25	6.15	1	3	0	0.53	800 343-3548
Fidelity Spartan Sh-Interm Muni	Muni Natl	5.8	6.37	4.98	3	1	0	0.5	800 343-3548
Fidelity Spartan Tax Free Bond	Dvsfd Bond	12.1					0	0.66	800 343-3548
Fidelity Strategic Income Fund	Dvsfd Bond	18	10.72	7.63	1	4	3	0.87	800 343-3548
Fidelity Target Timeline 2003	Corp-Inv	3.6	7.2	5.51	3	1	0	0.7	800 343-3548
Fidelity US Bond Index	Corp-Inv	12	10.86	7.74	1	2	0	0.51	800 343-3548
Fidelity Ultra Short Bond Fund	Dvsfd Bond						0	0.87	800 343-3548
Fifth Third Bond Fund A	Corp-Inv	10.2	8.24	5.69	4	4	4.75	1.06	800 282-5706
Fifth Third Bond Fund Inst	Corp-Inv	10.8	10.35	6.63		3	0	0.81	800 282-5706
Fifth Third Intermediate Bond A	Corp-Inv	9.7	1.08	1.65	4	5	3.5	1.02	800 282-5706
Fifth Third Intermediate Bond Inst	Corp-Inv	10.6	9.8	6.75		2	0	0.77	800 282-5706
Fifth Third Intermediate Muni A	Muni Natl	7.8	7.16	5.4	4	5	3.5	1	800 282-5706
Fifth Third Michigan Muni A	Muni State	5.6	6.21	4.58	3	1	4.75	0.84	800 282-5706
Fifth Third Michigan Muni Inst	Muni State	5.7	6.37	4.71	3	1	0	0.69	800 282-5706

Bond Fund Name	Objective	Annualized Return for			Rank		Max Load	Expense Ratio	Toll-Free/(Toll) Telephone
		1 Year	3 Years	5 Years	Overall	Risk			
Fifth Third Muni Bond A	Muni Natl	9.8	8.91	5.7	3	3	0	1.05	800 282-5706
Fifth Third Muni Bond Inst	Muni Natl	10.2	9.18	5.95	2	3	0	0.8	800 282-5706
Fifth Third Ohio Muni A	Muni State	7.6	7.53	3.08	4	3	4.75	1.04	800 282-5706
Fifth Third Ohio Muni C	Muni State	6.8	6.79	4.08	4	2	0	1.79	800 282-5706
Fifth Third Ohio Muni I	Muni State	7.9	7.82		3	3	0	0.79	800 282-5706
Fifth Third Short Term Bond A	Corp-Inv	5.4	6.79	5.61	3	1	0	0.9	800 282-5706
Fifth Third Short Term Bond Instl	Corp-Inv	5.5	6.94	5.75	3	1	0	0.75	800 282-5706
Fifth Third US Govt Bond A	Government	9.1	8.91	6.49	2	2	4.75	1	800 282-5706
Fifth Third US Govt Bond C	Government	8.4	8	5.7	3	2	0	1.74	800 282-5706
Fifth Third US Govt Bond Instl	Government	9.4	9.16		2	2	0	0.75	800 282-5706
First American AZ Tax Free A	Muni State	11	9.89		1	3	4.25	0.75	800 677-3863
First American AZ Tax Free C	Muni State	10.6	9.46		1	3	1	1.15	800 677-3863
First American AZ Tax Free Y	Muni State	11.3	10.16		1	3	0	0.5	800 677-3863
First American CA Interm T/F A	Muni CA	8.6	8	6.37	3	3	2.25	0.85	800 677-3863
First American CA Interm T/F Y	Muni CA	8.8	8.11	6.44	3	3	0	0.7	800 677-3863
First American CA Tax Free A	Muni State	11.5	10.02		2	4	4.25	0.75	800 677-3863
First American CA Tax Free C	Muni State	11.1	9.67		2	4	1	1.15	800 677-3863
First American CA Tax Free Y	Muni State	11.7	10.33		2	4	0	0.5	800 677-3863
First American CO Interm T/F A	Muni State	9.2	8.8	5.7	2	3	2.25	0.85	800 677-3863
First American CO Interm T/F Y	Muni State	9.3	8.91	5.73	2	3	0	0.7	800 677-3863
First American CO Tax Free A	Muni State	11.3	10.6		2	4	4.25	0.75	800 677-3863
First American CO Tax Free C	Muni State	10.9	10.16		2	4	1	1.15	800 677-3863
First American CO Tax Free Y	Muni State	11.5	10.9		2	4	0	0.5	800 677-3863
First American Core Bond A	Corp-Inv	10.2	9.71	6.63	2	3	4.25	0.94	800 677-3863
First American Core Bond B	Corp-Inv	9.5	9.08	5.96	4	3	0	1.7	800 677-3863
First American Core Bond C	Corp-Inv	9.4	8.84		2	3	1	1.15	800 677-3863
First American Core Bond S	Corp-Inv	10.2					0	0.95	800 677-3863
First American Core Bond Y	Corp-Inv	10.4	9.98	7.82	3	3	0	0.7	800 677-3863
First American Corp Bond A	Corp-Inv	12.4	10.32		1	4	4.25	1	800 677-3863
First American Corp Bond B	Corp-Inv	11.6	9.43		1	4	0	1.75	800 677-3863
First American Corp Bond C	Corp-Inv	11.7	9.44		1	4	1	1.75	800 677-3863
First American Corp Bond S	Corp-Inv	12.5					0	1	800 677-3863
First American Corp Bond Y	Corp-Inv	12.7	10.55		1	4	0	0.75	800 677-3863
First American High Inc A	Dvsfd Bond	9.9	9.49		4	5	4.25	1.2	800 677-3863
First American High Inc B	Dvsfd Bond	9.1	8.98		4	5	0	1.95	800 677-3863
First American High Inc C	Dvsfd Bond	9	8.71		4	5	1	1.95	800 677-3863
First American High Inc S	Dvsfd Bond	10					0	0.95	800 677-3863
First American High Inc Y	Dvsfd Bond	10.1	10.02		3	5	0	0.95	800 677-3863
First American Intrm Govt Bd A	Government						2.25	0.75	800 677-3863
First American Intrm Govt Bd Y	Government						0	0.6	800 677-3863
First American Intrm Tax Free A	Muni Natl	9.6	8.73	5.75	1	3	2.25	0.85	800 677-3863
First American Intrm Tax Free Y	Muni Natl	9.8	8.66	6.23	1	3	0	0.7	800 677-3863
First American Intrm Trm Bd A	Corp-Inv	10.1	8.52	6.29	3	2	2.25	0.75	800 677-3863
First American Intrm Trm Bd S	Corp-Inv	10.2					0	0.75	800 677-3863
First American Intrm Trm Bd Y	Corp-Inv	10.4	8.74	6.42	3	2	0	0.6	800 677-3863
First American MN Interm T/F A	Muni State	8.7	8.27	5.54	1	2	2.25	0.85	800 677-3863
First American MN Interm T/F Y	Muni State	8.9	8.35	5.54	1	2	0	0.7	800 677-3863
First American MN Tax Free A	Muni State	9.9	8.69	5.58	1	3	4.25	0.95	800 677-3863
First American MN Tax Free C	Muni State	9.5	8.25		2	3	1	1.35	800 677-3863
First American MN Tax Free Y	Muni State	10.2	8.97	5.84	1	3	0	0.7	800 677-3863
First American MO Tax Free A	Muni State	10.4	8.91	5.58	2	3	4.25	0.95	800 677-3863
First American MO Tax Free C	Muni State	9.9					1	1.35	800 677-3863
First American MO Tax Free Y	Muni State	10.6	9.3	5.88	1	3	0	0.7	800 677-3863
First American NE Tax Free A	Muni State	10.7					4.25	0.75	800 677-3863
First American NE Tax Free C	Muni State	10.2					1	1.15	800 677-3863
First American NE Tax Free Y	Muni State	10.9					0	0.5	800 677-3863
First American OH Tax Free Fund A	Muni State	11.2					4.25	0.75	800 677-3863
First American OH Tax Free Fund C	Muni State	9.7					1	1.15	800 677-3863

Bond Fund Name	Objective	Annualized Return for 1 Year	Annualized Return for 3 Years	Annualized Return for 5 Years	Rank Overall	Rank Risk	Max Load	Expense Ratio	Toll-Free/(Toll) Telephone
First American OH Tax Free Fund Y	Muni State	11.5					0	0.5	800 677-3863
First American OR Interm T/F A	Muni State	8.9	8.09		2	3	2.5	0.85	800 677-3863
First American OR Interm T/F Y	Muni State	9.2	8.22	6.12	1	3	0	0.7	800 677-3863
First American Shrt Trm Bd A	Corp-Inv	5.8	7.01	6	3	1	2.25	0.75	800 677-3863
First American Shrt Trm Bd S	Corp-Inv	5.7					0	0.75	800 677-3863
First American Shrt Trm Bd Y	Corp-Inv	5.9	7.17	6.75	2	1	0	0.6	800 677-3863
First American Tax Free A	Muni Natl	11.1	9.19	5.44	3	3	2.25	0.95	800 677-3863
First American Tax Free C	Muni Natl	10.6					1	1.35	800 677-3863
First American Tax Free Y	Muni Natl	11.4	9.96	6.05	2	3	0	0.7	800 677-3863
First American U.S. Govt Mortgage A	Government	6.2	8.58	6.26	2	2	4.25	0.95	800 677-3863
First American U.S. Govt Mortgage B	Government	5.3	7.62	5.79	3	2	0	1.7	800 677-3863
First American U.S. Govt Mortgage C	Government	5.4					1	1.7	800 677-3863
First American U.S. Govt Mortgage S	Government	6.2	8.46	6.57	2	2	0	0.95	800 677-3863
First American U.S. Govt Mortgage Y	Government	6.4	7.99	6.04	3	2	0	0.7	800 677-3863
First Fds-Bond Portfolio A	Corp-Inv	12.8	10.07	6.65	3	3	3.75	0.86	800 442-1941
First Fds-Bond Portfolio C	Corp-Inv	12.6	9.61	6.13	3	3	0	1.41	800 442-1941
First Fds-Bond Portfolio I	Corp-Inv	13.2	10.43	6.86	3	3	0	0.62	800 442-1941
First Fds-Tennessee Tax Free I	Muni State	8	8.02	5.45	3	2	0	0.64	800 442-1941
First Fds-Tennessee Tax Free II	Muni State	7.7	7.75	5.24	3	2	2.5	0.88	800 442-1941
First Fds-Tennessee Tax Free III	Muni State	7.6	7.51	4.95	3	2	0	1.14	800 442-1941
First Focus Bond Instl	Corp-Inv	13.4	10.34	6.33	3	3	0	0.95	800 662-4203
First Focus Nebraska Tax Free Inst	AssetAlloc	9.3	8.27	5.37		3	0	0.91	800 662-4203
First Focus Sh Inter Bond Inst	Corp-Inv	10.5	8.43	5.91	4	3	0	0.77	800 662-4203
First Hawaii-Interm Muni Fund	Muni State	7.8	6.75	4.91	3	2	0	0.79	(808 599-2400)
First Hawaii-Muni Bond	Muni State	9.4	8	5.2	2	2	0	0.94	(808 599-2400)
First Inv Fund for Income A	Corp-HY	8.8	2.39	1.35	4	5	5.75	1.32	800 423-4026
First Inv Government A	Govt-Mtg	6.1	8.06	5.87	3	2	5.75	1.1	800 423-4026
First Inv Insd Interm T/E A	Muni Natl	11.8	10.26	7.33	1	4	5.75	0.75	800 423-4026
First Inv Insd Interm T/E B	Muni Natl	11	9.5	6.45	2	4	0	1.5	800 423-4026
First Inv Insd NY Tax Free A	Muni NY	11.9	9.86	6.15	3	4	5.75	0.99	800 423-4026
First Inv Insd NY Tax Free B	Muni NY	11	9.05	5.38	4	4	0	1.74	800 423-4026
First Inv Insd Tax Ex A	Muni Natl	11.3	9.71	6	3	4	5.75	1.02	800 423-4026
First Inv Insd Tax Ex B	Muni Natl	10.4	8.84	5.2	4	4	0	1.75	800 423-4026
First Inv Insd Tax Ex II A	Muni Natl	13.5	11.56	7.88	2	4	5.75	1	800 423-4026
First Inv Insd Tax Ex II B	Muni Natl	12.6					0	1.75	800 423-4026
First Inv Investment Grade A	Corp-Inv	13.7	10.67	6.78	3	3	5.75	1.1	800 423-4026
First Inv Multi Ins T/F-AZ A	Muni Natl	11.3	9.44	6.34	2	3	5.75	0.75	800 423-4026
First Inv Multi Ins T/F-AZ B	Muni Natl	10.4	8.75	5.61	3	3	0	1.5	800 423-4026
First Inv Multi Ins T/F-CA A	Muni CA	12.3	10.26	6.87	3	4	5.75	0.75	800 423-4026
First Inv Multi Ins T/F-CA B	Muni CA	11.4	9.56	6.11	3	4	0	1.5	800 423-4026
First Inv Multi Ins T/F-CO A	Muni Natl	11.9	10.3	6.84	1	3	5.75	0.6	800 423-4026
First Inv Multi Ins T/F-CO B	Muni Natl	11	9.46	6.04	2	3	0	1.35	800 423-4026
First Inv Multi Ins T/F-CT A	Muni Natl	10.8	9.24	6.12	2	3	5.75	0.8	800 423-4026
First Inv Multi Ins T/F-CT B	Muni Natl	10	8.41	5.3	3	3	0	1.55	800 423-4026
First Inv Multi Ins T/F-FL A	Muni Natl	11.8	10.14	6.5	3	4	5.75	0.85	800 423-4026
First Inv Multi Ins T/F-FL B	Muni Natl	11	9.41	5.74	3	4	0	1.6	800 423-4026
First Inv Multi Ins T/F-GA A	Muni Natl	12.5	10.69	6.95	2	4	5.75	0.6	800 423-4026
First Inv Multi Ins T/F-GA B	Muni Natl	11.6	9.97	6.17	3	4	0	1.35	800 423-4026
First Inv Multi Ins T/F-MA A	Muni State	11.4	10.09	6.42	3	4	5.75	0.8	800 423-4026
First Inv Multi Ins T/F-MA B	Muni State	10.6	9.26	5.62	3	4	0	1.55	800 423-4026
First Inv Multi Ins T/F-MD A	Muni Natl	11	9.65	6.41	3	4	5.75	0.75	800 423-4026
First Inv Multi Ins T/F-MD B	Muni Natl	10.2	8.93	5.66	3	4	0	1.5	800 423-4026
First Inv Multi Ins T/F-MI A	Muni State	11.1	9.35	6.01	2	3	5.75	0.91	800 423-4026
First Inv Multi Ins T/F-MI B	Muni State	10.2	8.64	5.26	3	3	0	1.66	800 423-4026
First Inv Multi Ins T/F-MN A	Muni State	10.8	9.36	6.36	1	3	5.75	0.6	800 423-4026
First Inv Multi Ins T/F-MN B	Muni State	10	8.67	5.62	2	3	0	1.35	800 423-4026
First Inv Multi Ins T/F-MO A	Muni Natl	12.2	10.28	6.94	2	4	5.75	0.6	800 423-4026
First Inv Multi Ins T/F-MO B	Muni Natl	11.5	9.49	6.12	2	4	0	1.35	800 423-4026

Bond Fund Name	Objective	Annualized Return for			Rank		Max Load	Expense Ratio	Toll-Free/(Toll) Telephone
		1 Year	3 Years	5 Years	Overall	Risk			
First Inv Multi Ins T/F-NC A	Muni Natl	11.3	10.08	6.71	1	4	5.75	0.75	800 423-4026
First Inv Multi Ins T/F-NC B	Muni Natl	10.5	9.3	5.9	3	4	0	1.5	800 423-4026
First Inv Multi Ins T/F-OR A	Muni Natl	11	9.51	6.33	2	4	5.75	0.75	800 423-4026
First Inv Multi Ins T/F-OR B	Muni Natl	10.2	8.82	5.59	3	3	0	1.5	800 423-4026
First Inv Multi Ins T/F-PA A	Muni Natl	10.9	9.75	6.29	2	3	5.75	0.91	800 423-4026
First Inv Multi Ins T/F-PA B	Muni Natl	10.2	9.02	5.54	3	3	0	1.66	800 423-4026
First Inv Multi Ins T/F-VA A	Muni Natl	11	9.47	6.23	2	3	5.75	0.85	800 423-4026
First Inv Multi Ins T/F-VA B	Muni Natl	10.2	8.74	5.45	3	3	0	1.6	800 423-4026
First Inv NJ Ins Tax-Free A	Muni State	10.9	9.27	6.08	3	4	5.75	0.96	800 423-4026
First Inv NJ Ins Tax-Free B	Muni State	10.1	8.5	5.25	4	4	0	1.71	800 423-4026
First Inv Ohio Ins Tax-Free A	Muni State	11.8	9.91	6.58	3	4	5.75	0.75	800 423-4026
First Inv Ohio Ins Tax-Free B	Muni State	11	9.21	5.82	3	4	0	1.5	800 423-4026
Flex-funds U.S. Government Bond	Government	8.4	5.9	5.38	4	4	0	1.1	800 325-3539
Florida Tax-Free Short Term	Muni State	4.8					0	0.4	800 557-7555
Forum Investors Bond Fund	Corp-Inv	11.3	12.09	7.12	3	4	3.75	0.95	800 943-6786
Forum Maine TaxSaver Bond Fund	Muni State	7.6	7.42	5.16	3	2	2.5	0.95	800 943-6786
Forum NH TaxSaver Bond Fund	Muni State	6.2	6.91	4.82	3	2	2.5	0.95	800 943-6786
Forum TaxSaver Bond Fund	Muni Natl	7.5	7.62	5.03	3	2	3.75	0.95	800 943-6786
Franklin AGE High Income A	Corp-HY	10.7	3.79	1.06	5	5	4.25	0.76	800 632-2350
Franklin AGE High Income Adv	Corp-HY	10.2	3.93	1.19	5	5	0	0.62	800 632-2350
Franklin AGE High Income B	Corp-HY	10.2	3.31		5	5	0	1.27	800 632-2350
Franklin AGE High Income C	Corp-HY	10.1	3.25	0.64	5	5	1	1.26	800 632-2350
Franklin AGE High Income R	Corp-HY	10.2	3.58	0.75	5	5	0	1.12	800 632-2350
Franklin Adjustable US Govt Sec A	Govt-Mtg	3.1	5.19	4.79	2	1	2.25	0.92	800 632-2350
Franklin Alabama Tax-Free Inc A	Muni State	10.7	8.77	5.3	1	3	4.25	0.72	800 632-2350
Franklin Alabama Tax-Free Inc C	Muni State	10.1	8.18	4.75	2	3	1	1.26	800 632-2350
Franklin Arizona Tax-Free Inc A	Muni State	9.8	7.95	4.84	3	3	4.25	0.65	800 632-2350
Franklin Arizona Tax-Free Inc B	Muni State	9.2					0	1.2	800 632-2350
Franklin Arizona Tax-Free Inc C	Muni State	9.2	7.37	4.29	4	3	1	1.18	800 632-2350
Franklin CT Tax-Free Inc A	Muni State	10	9.32	5.3	3	3	4.25	0.7	800 632-2350
Franklin CT Tax-Free Inc C	Muni State	9.3	8.73	4.73	3	3	1	1.23	800 632-2350
Franklin California H/Y Muni A	Muni CA	8.2	8.25	4.83	3	3	4.25	0.65	800 632-2350
Franklin California H/Y Muni B	Muni CA	7.6	7.73		4	3	0	1.2	800 632-2350
Franklin California H/Y Muni C	Muni CA	7.5	7.63	4.25	4	3	1	1.19	800 632-2350
Franklin California Ins Tax-Free A	Muni CA	10.6	9.18	5.95	2	3	4.25	0.59	800 632-2350
Franklin California Ins Tax-Free B	Muni CA	10.1					0	1.15	800 632-2350
Franklin California Ins Tax-Free C	Muni CA	10	8.6	5.4	3	3	1	1.13	800 632-2350
Franklin California Inter T/F A	Muni CA	8.4	7.9	5.61	2	3	2.25	0.67	800 632-2350
Franklin California Tx-Fr Inc A	Muni CA	9	8.83	5.55	3	3	4.25	0.56	800 632-2350
Franklin California Tx-Fr Inc Adv	Muni CA	9.1	8.84	5.55		3	0	0.49	800 632-2350
Franklin California Tx-Fr Inc B	Muni CA	8.4	8.18		5	3	0	1.14	800 632-2350
Franklin California Tx-Fr Inc C	Muni CA	8.4	8.24	4.95	5	3	1	1.14	800 632-2350
Franklin Colorado Tax-Free Inc A	Muni State	9.1	9.07	5.34	3	3	4.25	0.68	800 632-2350
Franklin Colorado Tax-Free Inc C	Muni State	8.5	8.46	4.78	4	3	1	1.22	800 632-2350
Franklin Double Tax-Free Inc A	Muni State	9.1	8.59	5.49	3	3	4.25	0.75	800 632-2350
Franklin Double Tax-Free Inc C	Muni State	8.5	8.01	4.94	3	3	1	1.27	800 632-2350
Franklin FL Ins Tax-Free Inc A	Muni State	10.6	9.75	5.95	1	3	4.25	0.76	800 632-2350
Franklin Federal Interm Tax-Free A	Muni Natl	10.5	8.86	5.62	2	3	2.25	0.74	800 632-2350
Franklin Federal Tax-Free Inc A	Muni Natl	8.6	8.22	5.33	3	3	4.25	0.59	800 632-2350
Franklin Federal Tax-Free Inc Adv	Muni Natl	8.7	8.25	5.34		3	0	0.51	800 632-2350
Franklin Federal Tax-Free Inc B	Muni Natl	8	7.59		4	3	0	1.16	800 632-2350
Franklin Federal Tax-Free Inc C	Muni Natl	8.1	7.59	4.74	3	3	1	1.15	800 632-2350
Franklin Floating Rate Dly-Acc A	Govt-Mtg	2.4					2.25	1.16	800 632-2350
Franklin Floating Rate Dly-Acc Adv	Govt-Mtg	2.6					0	0.91	800 632-2350
Franklin Floating Rate Dly-Acc B	Govt-Mtg	1.7					0	1.76	800 632-2350
Franklin Floating Rate Dly-Acc C	Govt-Mtg	2					1	1.46	800 632-2350
Franklin Floating Rate Trust A	Govt-Mtg	0					0	1.35	800 632-2350
Franklin Florida Tax-Free Inc A	Muni State	10.6	9.5	5.96	1	3	4.25	0.6	800 632-2350

Bond Fund Name	Objective	Annualized Return for			Rank		Max Load	Expense Ratio	Toll-Free/(Toll) Telephone
		1 Year	3 Years	5 Years	Overall	Risk			
Franklin Florida Tax-Free Inc B	Muni State	10	9.02		1	3	0	1.16	800 632-2350
Franklin Florida Tax-Free Inc C	Muni State	10	8.91	5.37	2	3	1	1.16	800 632-2350
Franklin Georgia Tax-Free Inc A	Muni State	9.7	8.82	5.44	2	3	4.25	0.74	800 632-2350
Franklin Georgia Tax-Free Inc C	Muni State	9.3	8.25	4.83	4	3	1	1.28	800 632-2350
Franklin High Yield Tax-Free Inc A	Muni Natl	6.2	6.46	3.81	4	2	4.25	0.61	800 632-2350
Franklin High Yield Tax-Free Inc B	Muni Natl	5.6	5.91		3	2	0	1.18	800 632-2350
Franklin High Yield Tax-Free Inc C	Muni Natl	5.6	5.92	3.27	4	2	1	1.18	800 632-2350
Franklin Insured Tax-Free Inc A	Muni Natl	10.4	9.39	5.94	1	3	4.25	0.64	800 632-2350
Franklin Insured Tax-Free Inc B	Muni Natl	9.8					0	1.2	800 632-2350
Franklin Insured Tax-Free Inc C	Muni Natl	9.8	8.77	5.37	2	3	1	1.18	800 632-2350
Franklin Kentucky Tax-Free Inc A	Muni State	8.9	8.99	5.26	3	3	4.25	0.6	800 632-2350
Franklin Louisiana Tax-Free Inc A	Muni State	9.4	9.16	5.58	1	3	4.25	0.73	800 632-2350
Franklin Louisiana Tax-Free Inc C	Muni State	8.9	8.58	5.01	3	3	1	1.27	800 632-2350
Franklin MA Ins Tax-Free A	Muni State	10.4	9.66	5.95	1	3	4.25	0.68	800 632-2350
Franklin MA Ins Tax-Free C	Muni State	9.8	9.05	5.37	3	3	1	1.22	800 632-2350
Franklin MI Ins Tax-Free Inc A	Muni State	10.5	9.27	6.15	1	3	4.25	0.64	800 632-2350
Franklin MI Ins Tax-Free Inc B	Muni State	10					0	1.19	800 632-2350
Franklin MI Ins Tax-Free Inc C	Muni State	10	8.69	5.58	1	3	1	1.17	800 632-2350
Franklin MN Ins Tax-Free Inc A	Muni State	9.8	9.22	5.66	1	3	4.25	0.67	800 632-2350
Franklin MN Ins Tax-Free Inc C	Muni State	9.3	8.6	5.09	2	3	1	1.19	800 632-2350
Franklin Maryland Tax-Free Inc A	Muni State	9.5	9.34	5.75	1	3	4.25	0.7	800 632-2350
Franklin Maryland Tax-Free Inc C	Muni State	9	8.75	5.25	2	3	1	1.24	800 632-2350
Franklin Missouri Tax-Free Inc A	Muni State	10.1	9.56	5.66	1	3	4.25	0.66	800 632-2350
Franklin Missouri Tax-Free Inc C	Muni State	9.5	8.96	5.09	2	3	1	1.2	800 632-2350
Franklin NC Tax-Free Inc A	Muni State	9.9	9.34	5.67	2	3	4.25	0.67	800 632-2350
Franklin NC Tax-Free Inc C	Muni State	9.3	8.8	5.09	3	3	1	1.21	800 632-2350
Franklin NY Ins Tax-Free Inc A	Muni NY	10.6	8.83	5.62	1	3	4.25	0.71	800 632-2350
Franklin NY Ins Tax-Free Inc C	Muni NY	10	8.26	4.98	2	3	1	1.25	800 632-2350
Franklin NY Interm Tax-Free A	Muni NY	10.6	9.25	6.23	2	3	2.25	0.82	800 632-2350
Franklin NY Tax-Free Inc A	Muni NY	10.1	8.83	5.91	1	3	4.25	0.59	800 632-2350
Franklin New Jersey Tax-Free Inc A	Muni State	9.3	9.09	5.75	2	3	4.25	0.65	800 632-2350
Franklin New Jersey Tax-Free Inc B	Muni State	8.7	8.6		3	3	0	1.2	800 632-2350
Franklin New Jersey Tax-Free Inc C	Muni State	8.7	8.52	5.2	3	3	1	1.17	800 632-2350
Franklin New York Tax-Free Inc Adv	Muni NY	10.2	8.91	5.95		2	0	0.52	800 632-2350
Franklin New York Tax-Free Inc B	Muni NY	9.5	8.24		2	3	0	1.17	800 632-2350
Franklin New York Tax-Free Inc C	Muni NY	9.6	8.22	5.33	2	2	1	1.17	800 632-2350
Franklin Ohio Ins Tax-Free Inc A	Muni State	9.9	8.98	5.83	1	3	4.25	0.65	800 632-2350
Franklin Ohio Ins Tax-Free Inc B	Muni State	9.4					0	1.21	800 632-2350
Franklin Ohio Ins Tax-Free Inc C	Muni State	9.3	8.41	5.26	2	3	1	1.19	800 632-2350
Franklin Oregon Tax-Free Inc A	Muni State	9.3	8.66	5.29	3	3	4.25	0.66	800 632-2350
Franklin Oregon Tax-Free Inc C	Muni State	8.7	8.06	4.74	5	3	1	1.2	800 632-2350
Franklin PA Tax-Free Inc A	Muni State	10.3	9.26	5.66	1	3	4.25	0.67	800 632-2350
Franklin PA Tax-Free Inc B	Muni State	9.8					0	1.22	800 632-2350
Franklin PA Tax-Free Inc C	Muni State	9.7	8.68	5.11	2	3	1	1.2	800 632-2350
Franklin Short-Int US Govt Sec A	Government	6.8	7.69	5.96	1	1	2.25	0.83	800 632-2350
Franklin Short-Int US Govt Sec Adv	Government	6.8	7.79	5.99	2	1	0	0.74	800 632-2350
Franklin Strategic Income A	Dvsfd Bond	15.4	9.23	5.78	3	4	4.25	0.88	800 632-2350
Franklin Strategic Income Adv	Dvsfd Bond	15.8	9.52	6	3	4	0	0.63	800 632-2350
Franklin Strategic Income B	Dvsfd Bond	14.9	8.81		3	4	0	1.28	800 632-2350
Franklin Strategic Income C	Dvsfd Bond	15					1	1.26	800 632-2350
Franklin Strategic Income R	Dvsfd Bond	15.1	8.92	5.48	3	4	0	1.13	800 632-2350
Franklin Strategic Mortgage A	Govt-Mtg	6.8	9.72	7.33	1	1	4.25	0.57	800 632-2350
Franklin Templeton Hard Curr A	Intl Bond	22.9	7.53	3.66	4	4	2.25	1.55	800 632-2350
Franklin Templeton Hard Curr Adv	Intl Bond	23.4	7.92	4	3	4	0	1.14	800 632-2350
Franklin Tennessee Muni Bond A	Muni State	10.7	10.24	5.71	2	4	4.25	0.6	800 632-2350
Franklin Total Return Fund A	Dvsfd Bond	11					4.25	1.01	800 632-2350
Franklin Total Return Fund Adv	Dvsfd Bond	11.2					0	0.76	800 632-2350
Franklin Total Return Fund B	Dvsfd Bond	10.5					0	1.4	800 632-2350

Bond Fund Name	Objective	Annualized Return for			Rank		Max Load	Expense Ratio	Toll-Free/(Toll) Telephone
		1 Year	3 Years	5 Years	Overall	Risk			
Franklin Total Return Fund C	Dvsfd Bond	10.6					1	1.4	800 632-2350
Franklin Total Return Fund R	Dvsfd Bond	10.6	9.91		1	2	0	1.26	800 632-2350
Franklin US Government Sec A	Govt-Mtg	6.2	8.58	6.41	2	2	4.25	0.71	800 632-2350
Franklin US Government Sec Adv	Govt-Mtg	6.5	8.75	6.54	2	2	0	0.6	800 632-2350
Franklin US Government Sec B	Govt-Mtg	5.8	8.02		1	2	0	1.25	800 632-2350
Franklin US Government Sec C	Govt-Mtg	5.7	8	5.83	3	2	1	1.24	800 632-2350
Franklin US Government Sec R	Govt-Mtg	5.8	8.16	5.98	2	1	0	1.1	800 632-2350
Franklin Virginia Tax-Free Inc A	Muni State	9.5	8.59	5.28	3	3	4.25	0.67	800 632-2350
Franklin Virginia Tax-Free Inc C	Muni State	8.9	8	4.7	4	3	1	1.21	800 632-2350
Fremont Bond Fund	Corp-Inv	12.2	11.58	8.5	1	3	0	0.58	800 548-4539
Fremont CA Intermediate Tx Fr	Muni CA	8.1	6.7	4.99	3	2	0	0.53	800 548-4539
Frontegra Total Return Bond	Dvsfd Bond	10.4	9.98	7.61	2	3	0		888 825-2100
GE Fixed Income Fund A	Corp-Inv	10	9.76	7.17	2	2	5.75	0.8	800 242-0134
GE Fixed Income Fund B	Corp-Inv	10.1	9.25	6.54	3	2	0	1.55	800 242-0134
GE Fixed Income Fund Y	Corp-Inv	11.2	10.33	7.7	2	2	0	0.55	800 242-0134
GE Government Securities A	Government	12.7	10.57	7.28	2	4	5.75	1.1	800 242-0134
GE Government Securities B	Government	12	9.73	6.55	3	4	0	1.6	800 242-0134
GE Institutional Income	Corp-Inv	11.6	10.75	7.46	2	2	0	0.24	800 242-0134
GE S&S Long Term Bond	Corp-Inv	12.1	11.08	7.62	1	2	0	0.14	800 242-0134
GE S&S Short Term Bond	Government	6.7	7.92	7.9	2	1	2.5		800 242-0134
GE Short-Term Government A	Government	4.8					5.75	0.7	800 242-0134
GE Short-Term Government B	Government	4.3	6.24	5.16	3	1	0	1.3	800 242-0134
GE Short-Term Government Y	Government	5.2	7.25	6.16	2	1	0	0.45	800 242-0134
GE Tax Exempt Income Fund A	Muni Natl	10.7	9.23	5.78	2	3	5.75	0.83	800 242-0134
GE Tax Exempt Income Fund B	Muni Natl	9.8	8.41	5.04	3	3	0	1.58	800 242-0134
GE Tax Exempt Income Fund Y	Muni Natl	15.3	10.86	6.91	2	4	0	0.58	800 242-0134
Gabelli Comstock Partners Strat A	Intl Bond	5.8	5.24	-2.37	4	5	4.5		800 422-3554
Gabelli Comstock Partners Strat C	Intl Bond	5.2	4.62	-2.97	4	5	0		800 422-3554
Gabelli Comstock Partners Strat O	Intl Bond	6.2	5.53	-2.1	5	5	4.5	2.02	800 422-3554
Gabelli Westwood Interm Bond Fund	Corp-Inv	11	9.66	6.37	3	3	0	1.06	800 937-8909
Gartmore Bond Fund A	Corp-Inv	12.9	10.57	6.51	3	3	5.75	1.07	800 848-0920
Gartmore Bond Fund B	Corp-Inv	12.4	9.97	5.95	3	3	0	1.64	800 848-0920
Gartmore Bond Fund D	Corp-Inv	13.3	10.83	7.01	3	3	4.5	0.84	800 848-0920
Gartmore Govt Bond Fund A	Government	11.1	10.68	7.25	3	3	4.5	1.03	800 848-0920
Gartmore Govt Bond Fund B	Government	10.6	10.05	6.53	3	3	0	1.63	800 848-0920
Gartmore Govt Bond Fund D	Government	11.3	10.94	7.58	3	3	4.5	0.79	800 848-0920
Gartmore High Yield A	Intl Bond	6.5	0.35		5	5	4.5	1.1	800 848-0920
Gartmore High Yield B	Intl Bond	5.9	-0.34		5	5	0	1.77	800 848-0920
Gartmore High Yield C	Intl Bond	5.7					1	1.7	800 848-0920
Gartmore High Yield Instl-Svc	Intl Bond	6.9	0.61		5	5	0	0.7	800 848-0920
Gartmore Morley Enhanced A	Dvsfd Bond	2	3.02		4	1	4.5	0.9	800 848-0920
Gartmore Morley Enhanced IS	Dvsfd Bond	2.2	3.2		4	1	0	0.7	800 848-0920
Gartmore Morley Enhanced Inst	Dvsfd Bond	2.4	3.43		4	1	0	0.45	800 848-0920
Gartmore Tax-Free Inc A	Muni Natl	9.5	8.59	5.17	2	3	5.75	0.99	800 848-0920
Gartmore Tax-Free Inc B	Muni Natl	8.9	8	4.7	4	3	0	1.59	800 848-0920
Gartmore Tax-Free Inc D	Muni Natl	9.8	8.91	5.63	2	3	4.5	0.73	800 848-0920
Glenmede Core Fixed-Income Port	Government	11.3	10.4	7.42	2	3	0	0.11	800 442-8299
Glenmede Intermediate Muni	Muni Natl	8.7	7.65	5.7	1	2	0	0.27	800 442-8299
Glenmede NJ Muni Fund	Muni State	8.3	8.07	5.69	2	2	0	0.27	800 442-8299
Golden Oak Interm Term Income A	Corp-Inv	11.6	10.31	6.83	3	3	4.5	0.9	800 545-6331
Golden Oak Interm Term Income I	Corp-Inv	11.8	10.53	7.11	2	3	0	0.65	800 545-6331
Golden Oak MI Tax-Free Bond A	Muni State	6.7	7.23	4.92	3	2	4.5	0.9	800 545-6331
Golden Oak MI Tax-Free Bond I	Muni State	7.1	7.46	5.16	3	2	0	0.65	800 545-6331
Goldman Sachs Core Fixed Inc A	Corp-Inv	10.9	10.39	7.08	2	2	4.5	0.9	800 292-4726
Goldman Sachs Core Fixed Inc B	Corp-Inv	10.1	9.52	6.26	3	2	0	1.69	800 292-4726
Goldman Sachs Core Fixed Inc C	Corp-Inv	10.1	9.52	6.25	3	2	0	1.69	800 292-4726
Goldman Sachs Core Fixed Inc Inst	Corp-Inv	11.5	10.83	7.5	1	2	0	0.54	800 292-4726
Goldman Sachs Core Fixed Inc Svc	Corp-Inv	10.9	10.25	6.96	2	2	0	1.08	800 292-4726

Bond Fund Name	Objective	Annualized Return for			Rank		Max Load	Expense Ratio	Toll-Free/(Toll) Telephone
		1 Year	3 Years	5 Years	Overall	Risk			
Goldman Sachs Enhanced Inc A	Dvsfd Bond	2.1					0	0.72	800 292-4726
Goldman Sachs Enhanced Inc Admin	Dvsfd Bond	2.3					0	0.57	800 292-4726
Goldman Sachs Enhanced Inc Instl	Dvsfd Bond	2.5					0	0.32	800 292-4726
Goldman Sachs Glb Income A	Intl Bond	10	7.24	5.58	4	2	4.5	0.89	800 292-4726
Goldman Sachs Glb Income B	Intl Bond	9.4	6.69	5.04	5	2	0	0.49	800 292-4726
Goldman Sachs Glb Income C	Intl Bond	9.5	6.73	5.05	5	2	0	0.99	800 292-4726
Goldman Sachs Glb Income Inst	Intl Bond	10.7	7.92	6.25	3	2	0	0.69	800 292-4726
Goldman Sachs Glb Income Svc	Intl Bond	10.2	7.41	5.71	4	2	0	1.19	800 292-4726
Goldman Sachs Govt Income A	Government	9.4	10.08	7	3	2	4.5	0.94	800 292-4726
Goldman Sachs Govt Income B	Government	8.6	9.24	6.19	3	2	0	1.54	800 292-4726
Goldman Sachs Govt Income C	Government	8.6	9.25	6.19	3	2	0	1.69	800 292-4726
Goldman Sachs Govt Income Inst	Government	9.8	10.49	7.2	3	2	0	0.58	800 292-4726
Goldman Sachs Govt Income Svc	Government	9.3	9.98	6.69	3	2	0	1.04	800 292-4726
Goldman Sachs High Yield Fd A	Corp-HY	10.1	4.82	2.93	4	5	4.5	1.16	800 292-4726
Goldman Sachs High Yield Fd B	Corp-HY	9.3	3.56	2.04	5	5	0	1.91	800 292-4726
Goldman Sachs High Yield Fd C	Corp-HY	9.3	4.08	2.31	4	5	0	1.91	800 292-4726
Goldman Sachs High Yield Fd Inst	Corp-HY	10.6	5.23	3.47	4	5	0	0.76	800 292-4726
Goldman Sachs High Yield Fd Svc	Corp-HY	10	4.66	2.93	4	5	0	1.26	800 292-4726
Goldman Sachs High Yield Muni A	Muni Natl	7.6	8.58		2	3	4.5	0.94	800 292-4726
Goldman Sachs High Yield Muni B	Muni Natl	6.8	7.73		3	3	0	1.69	800 292-4726
Goldman Sachs High Yield Muni C	Muni Natl	6.8	7.76		3	3	0	1.69	800 292-4726
Goldman Sachs High Yield Muni Inst	Muni Natl	8.1	9.09		2	3	0	0.54	800 292-4726
Goldman Sachs Municipal Income A	Muni Natl	8.9	8.92	5.2	3	3	4.5	0.79	800 292-4726
Goldman Sachs Municipal Income B	Muni Natl	8.1	8.24	4.46	4	3	0	1.39	800 292-4726
Goldman Sachs Municipal Income C	Muni Natl	8	8.21	4.45	4	3	0	1.54	800 292-4726
Goldman Sachs Municipal Income Inst	Muni Natl	9.3	9.49	5.58	1	3	0	0.39	800 292-4726
Goldman Sachs Municipal Income Svc	Muni Natl	8.7	9.05	5.19	3	3	0	0.89	800 292-4726
Goldman Sachs Short Dur Gov A	Govt-Mtg	5.5	7.83	5.92	2	1	2	0.89	800 292-4726
Goldman Sachs Short Dur Gov B	Govt-Mtg	4.9	7.21	5.29	3	1	0	1.86	800 292-4726
Goldman Sachs Short Dur Gov C	Govt-Mtg	4.6	7	5.08	3	1	0	1.86	800 292-4726
Goldman Sachs Short Dur Gov Inst	Govt-Mtg	5.9	8.27	6.32	2	1	0	0.95	800 292-4726
Goldman Sachs Short Dur Gov Svc	Govt-Mtg	5.3	7.71	5.79	2	1	0	0.99	800 292-4726
Goldman Sachs Short Dur T/F A	Muni Natl	4.7	5.63	4.2	2	1	2	0.99	800 292-4726
Goldman Sachs Short Dur T/F B	Muni Natl	4.1	4.83	3.45	4	1	0	1.74	800 292-4726
Goldman Sachs Short Dur T/F C	Muni Natl	3.9	4.66	3.31	4	1	0	1.74	800 292-4726
Goldman Sachs Short Dur T/F Inst	Muni Natl	5.1	5.91	4.5	2	1	0	0.96	800 292-4726
Goldman Sachs Short Dur T/F Svc	Muni Natl	4.4					0	0.89	800 292-4726
Goldman Sachs Ult Shrt Dur Gov A	Govt-Mtg	1.7	4.66	4.57	3	1	1.5	0.97	800 292-4726
Goldman Sachs Ult Shrt Dur Gov Inst	Govt-Mtg	2.2	5.09	5	2	1	0	0.48	800 292-4726
Goldman Sachs Ult Shrt Dur Gov Svc	Govt-Mtg	1.7	4.61	4.48	3	1	0	0.99	800 292-4726
Government Street Bond Fund	Corp-Inv	8.7	9.5	6.51	3	2	0	0.71	800 443-4249
Guardian High Yield Bond Fd A	Corp-HY	7.8					4.5	0.85	800 343-0817
Guardian High Yield Bond Fd B	Corp-HY	7					0	2.38	800 343-0817
Guardian High Yield Bond Fd C	Corp-HY	6.8					0	2.31	800 343-0817
Guardian Investment Quality Bond A	Corp-Inv	10.8	10.25	7.01	2	3	4.5	0.85	800 343-0817
Guardian Investment Quality Bond B	Corp-Inv	10					0	0.85	800 343-0817
Guardian Investment Quality Bond C	Corp-Inv	10					0	1.93	800 343-0817
Guardian Tax-Exempt A	Muni Natl	12.1	10.21	6.44	2	4	4.5	0.91	800 343-0817
Guardian Tax-Exempt C	Muni Natl	11.2					0	1.95	800 343-0817
HSBC Investor Bond A	Corp-Inv	10.6	10.35	7.71	2	3	0	1.07	800 782-8183
HSBC Investor Fixed Income Adv	Corp-Inv	11.2	11.02	7.21	2	3	0	0.61	800 782-8183
HSBC Investor Limited Maturity A	Dvsfd Bond	9.3					4.75		800 782-8183
HSBC Investor Limited Maturity B	Dvsfd Bond	8.4					0		800 782-8183
HSBC Investor Limited Maturity C	Dvsfd Bond	8.5					0		800 782-8183
HSBC Investor Limited Maturity Y	Dvsfd Bond	9.5					0		800 782-8183
HSBC Investor NY Tax Free Bond A	Muni NY	10.3	8.85	5.87	2	3	0	0.96	800 782-8183
HSBC Investor NY Tax Free Bond B	Muni State	9.5	8.09	4.86		3	0		800 782-8183
HSBC Investor NY Tax Free Bond Y	Muni NY	10.6	8.96	5.75	2	3	0	0.71	800 782-8183

Bond Fund Name	Objective	Annualized Return for			Rank		Max Load	Expense Ratio	Toll-Free/(Toll) Telephone
		1 Year	3 Years	5 Years	Overall	Risk			
Hancock Horizon Strat Inc Bond A	Corp-Inv	8.8	8.46			2	4	1	888 346-6300
Hancock Horizon Strat Inc Bond C	Corp-Inv	7.9	7.76			2	0	1.75	888 346-6300
Hancock Horizon Strat Inc Bond Tr	Corp-Inv	9	8.73			2	0	0.75	888 346-6300
Harbor Bond Inst	Corp-Inv	12	11.49	8.41	1	2	0	0.56	800 422-1050
Harbor Bond Retire	Dvsfd Bond						0	0.83	800 422-1050
Harbor Short Duration Inst	Corp-Inv	3.5	5.37	5.2	3	1	0	0.28	800 422-1050
Harris Insight Bond A	Dvsfd Bond	9.2	9.91	6.82	3	3	4.5	0.85	800 982-8782
Harris Insight Bond B	Dvsfd Bond	8.4					0	1.6	800 982-8782
Harris Insight Bond Inst	Dvsfd Bond	9.5	10.17	7.08	3	3	0	0.6	800 982-8782
Harris Insight Bond N	Dvsfd Bond	9.2	9.91	6.82	3	3	0	0.85	800 982-8782
Harris Insight Interm Govt Bd A	Government	11.5	10.74	7.55	3	3	3.5	0.75	800 982-8782
Harris Insight Interm Govt Bd B	Government	10.6					0	1.5	800 982-8782
Harris Insight Interm Govt Bd Inst	Government	11.7	10.94	7.79	2	3	0	0.5	800 982-8782
Harris Insight Interm Govt Bd N	Government	11.5	10.74	7.55	3	3	0	0.75	800 982-8782
Harris Insight Intermed T/E Bd A	Muni Natl	9.9	9.33	6.4	1	3	3.5	1.05	800 982-8782
Harris Insight Intermed T/E Bd B	Muni Natl	9					0	1.8	800 982-8782
Harris Insight Intermed T/E Bd I	Muni Natl	10.2	9.59	6.66	1	3	0	0.8	800 982-8782
Harris Insight Intermed T/E Bd N	Muni Natl	9.9	9.33	6.41	1	3	0	1.05	800 982-8782
Harris Insight Short/Int Bd A	Corp-Inv	8.6	8.74	6.37	3	2	3.5	0.85	800 982-8782
Harris Insight Short/Int Bd B	Corp-Inv	7.8					0	1.6	800 982-8782
Harris Insight Short/Int Bd Inst	Corp-Inv	8.9	9	6.62	3	2	0	0.6	800 982-8782
Harris Insight Short/Int Bd N	Corp-Inv	8.6	8.73	6.34	3	2	0	0.85	800 982-8782
Harris Insight Tax Exempt Bd A	Muni Natl	12.2	11.25	7	2	4	4.5	1.05	800 982-8782
Harris Insight Tax Exempt Bd B	Muni Natl	11.4					0	1.8	800 982-8782
Harris Insight Tax Exempt Bd Inst	Muni Natl	12.5	11.51	7.25	2	4	0	0.8	800 982-8782
Harris Insight Tax Exempt Bd N	Muni Natl	12.2	11.25	7	2	4	0	1.05	800 982-8782
Hartford High Yield A	Corp-HY	8.8					4.5	1.35	888 843-7824
Hartford High Yield B	Corp-HY	8.2	3.14		4	5	4.5	2.08	888 843-7824
Hartford High Yield C	Corp-HY	8.2	3.18		5	5	1	2.08	888 843-7824
Hartford Income A	Dvsfd Bond						4.5	1.3	888 843-7824
Hartford Income B	Dvsfd Bond						0	2.03	888 843-7824
Hartford Income C	Dvsfd Bond						1	1.93	888 843-7824
Hartford Inflation Plus A	Government						4.5	1.3	888 843-7824
Hartford Inflation Plus B	Government						0	2.03	888 843-7824
Hartford Inflation Plus C	Government						1	1.93	888 843-7824
Hartford Short Duration A	Dvsfd Bond						4.5	1.25	888 843-7824
Hartford Short Duration B	Dvsfd Bond						0	1.98	888 843-7824
Hartford Short Duration C	Dvsfd Bond						0	1.88	888 843-7824
Hartford Tax-Free CA A	Muni State						4.5	1.21	888 843-7824
Hartford Tax-Free CA B	Muni State						0	1.94	888 843-7824
Hartford Tax-Free CA C	Muni State						1	1.84	888 843-7824
Hartford Tax-Free MN A	Muni State	9.4	8.32	5.41		3	4.5	1.15	888 843-7824
Hartford Tax-Free MN B	Muni State	8.5	7.51	4.53		3	0	1.85	888 843-7824
Hartford Tax-Free MN C	Muni State	8.6	7.5	4.58		3	1	1.85	888 843-7824
Hartford Tax-Free NY A	Muni State						4.5	1.21	888 843-7824
Hartford Tax-Free NY B	Muni State						0	1.94	888 843-7824
Hartford Tax-Free NY C	Muni State						1	1.84	888 843-7824
Hartford Tax-Free National A	Muni Natl	10.8	9.32	5.74		4	4.5	1.15	888 843-7824
Hartford Tax-Free National B	Muni Natl	10	8.27	4.7		4	0	1.85	888 843-7824
Hartford Tax-Free National C	Muni Natl	9.9	8.39	4.75		4	1	1.85	888 843-7824
Hartford Tax-Free National Y	Other	11.6					0		888 843-7824
Hartford Total Return Bond A	Corp-Inv	13.4	10.81	7.08	1	2	4.5	1.25	888 843-7824
Hartford Total Return Bond B	Corp-Inv	12.6	10.02	6.29	1	2	0	1.95	888 843-7824
Hartford Total Return Bond C	Corp-Inv	12.6	10.07		1	2	1	1.95	888 843-7824
Hartford Total Return Bond Y	Corp-Inv	14	11.33	7.66	1	2	0		888 843-7824
Hartford US Governmnt Securities A	Government	11.2	10.57	7.25		3	4.5	1.2	888 843-7824
Hartford US Governmnt Securities B	Government	10.4	9.58	6.25		3	0	1.9	888 843-7824
Hartford US Governmnt Securities C	Government	10.5	9.58	6.26		3	1	1.9	888 843-7824

Bond Fund Name	Objective	Annualized Return for			Rank		Max Load	Expense Ratio	Toll-Free/(Toll) Telephone
		1 Year	3 Years	5 Years	Overall	Risk			
Hartford US Governmnt Securities E	Government	11.6	10.74	7.33	2	3	4.5	0.79	888 843-7824
Heritage Income Tr-High Yld Bd A	Corp-HY	12.4	6.78	1.87	4	4	3.75	1.12	800 421-4184
Heritage Income Tr-High Yld Bd B	Corp-HY	11.6	6.17	1.31	4	4	0	1.65	800 421-4184
Heritage Income Tr-High Yld Bd C	Corp-HY	11.7	6.17	1.34	4	4	0	1.65	800 421-4184
Heritage Income Tr-Intmed Govt A	Government	8.8	8.6	6.5	3	2	3.75	0.9	800 421-4184
Heritage Income Tr-Intmed Govt B	Government	8.5	8.25	6.16	3	2	0	1.2	800 421-4184
Heritage Income Tr-Intmed Govt C	Government	8.4	8.27	6.21	3	2	0	1.2	800 421-4184
Hibernia LA Muni Income A	Muni State	9.5	9.11	5.91	1	3	3	0.76	800 263-1078
Hibernia LA Muni Income B	Muni State	8.7					0	1.61	800 263-1078
Hibernia Total Return Bond Fund	Corp-Inv	10.8	9.17	6.25	2	3	3	1.01	800 263-1078
Hibernia US Government Income	Government	8.7	8.97	6.59	3	2	3	0.69	800 263-1078
HighMark Bond Fund A	Corp-Inv	10.6	10.02	6.87	2	2	3.25	0.77	800 433-6884
HighMark Bond Fund B	Corp-Inv	9.7	8.72	6.09	3	2	0	1.76	800 433-6884
HighMark Bond Fund Fid	Corp-Inv	10.7	9.93	6.8	2	2	0	0.77	800 433-6884
HighMark CA Int Tax Free Bond A	Muni CA	7.6	7.75	5.74	3	3	2.25	0.49	800 433-6884
HighMark CA Int Tax Free Bond B	Muni CA	6.6	6.61		5	3	0	1.49	800 433-6884
HighMark CA Int Tax Free Bond Fid	Muni CA	7.7	7.79	5.75	3	3	0	0.49	800 433-6884
HighMark National Interm T/F Fid	Muni Natl						0		800 433-6884
Homestead Short Term Bond	Corp-Inv	5.2	6.53	5.66	3	1	0	0.83	800 258-3030
Homestead Short Term Govt	Government	4.4	5.67	4.98	3	1	0	0.92	800 258-3030
Huntington Fixed Income Sec A	Corp-Inv	11	9.91	6.29	3	3	4.75	1.32	800 253-0412
Huntington Fixed Income Sec B	Corp-Inv	10.5	9.15		1	3	0	1.82	800 253-0412
Huntington Fixed Income Sec Tr	Corp-Inv	11.4	10.02	6.46	3	3	0	1.07	800 253-0412
Huntington Intermediate Govt Inc A	Government	9.2	9.31	6.55	3	3	4.75	1.34	800 253-0412
Huntington Intermediate Govt Inc Tr	Government	9.3	9.5	6.8	3	3	0	1.09	800 253-0412
Huntington MI Tax Free A	Muni State	7.7	7.07	4.79	4	3	4.75	1.47	800 253-0412
Huntington MI Tax Free Tr	Muni State	7.9	7.36	5.04	3	3	2	1.22	800 253-0412
Huntington Mortgage Secs A	Govt-Mtg	5	8.84	6.34	3	1	4.75	1.39	800 253-0412
Huntington Mortgage Secs Tr	Govt-Mtg	5.1	9.1	6.58	2	1	0	1.14	800 253-0412
Huntington OH Tax Free A	Muni State	7.8	7.17	4.9	3	2	4.75	1.36	800 253-0412
Huntington OH Tax Free Tr	Muni State	8	7.45	5.25	3	2	0	1.11	800 253-0412
Huntington Short-Interm Fxd Inc Tr	Corp-Inv	6.6	7.15	5.69	4	2	0	1.06	800 253-0412
ICON Bond C	Dvsfd Bond						0	1.9	800 764-0442
ICON Bond I	Dvsfd Bond						0	1.3	800 764-0442
ICON Short-Term Fixed Income	Corp-Inv	1	2.04	3	4	1	0	1.4	800 764-0442
IDEX Federated Tax Exempt A	Muni Natl	10.7	9.01	4.83	3	4	4.75	1.35	888 233-4339
IDEX Federated Tax Exempt B	Muni Natl	9.9	8.32	4.16	4	4	0	2	888 233-4339
IDEX Federated Tax Exempt C	Muni Natl	9.9	8.31		3	4	0	2	888 233-4339
IDEX Federated Tax Exempt L	Muni Natl						0		888 233-4339
IDEX Federated Tax Exempt M	Muni Natl	10.3	8.72	4.55	3	4	1	1.6	888 233-4339
IDEX Janus Flexible Income A	Corp-HY	13.7	9.75	6.54	2	3	4.75	1.84	888 233-4339
IDEX Janus Flexible Income B	Corp-HY	12.8	8.94	5.79	3	3	0	2.49	888 233-4339
IDEX Janus Flexible Income C	Corp-HY	12.8	8.94		2	3	0	2.49	888 233-4339
IDEX Janus Flexible Income L	Dvsfd Bond						0		888 233-4339
IDEX Janus Flexible Income M	Corp-HY	13	9.09	5.92	3	3	1	2.39	888 233-4339
IDEX PIMCO Total Return A	Corp-Inv	10.7					4.75	1.65	888 233-4339
IDEX PIMCO Total Return B	Corp-Inv	10					0	2.3	888 233-4339
IDEX PIMCO Total Return C	Corp-Inv	10					0	2.3	888 233-4339
IDEX PIMCO Total Return L	Corp-Inv						0		888 233-4339
IDEX PIMCO Total Return M	Corp-Inv	10.1					1	2.2	888 233-4339
IDEX Transamerica Consv Hi-Yd Bd A	Corp-HY	8.8	6.54	3.66	4	4	4.75	1.36	888 233-4339
IDEX Transamerica Consv Hi-Yd Bd B	Corp-HY	7.9	5.8	2.95	4	4	0	2.01	888 233-4339
IDEX Transamerica Consv Hi-Yd Bd C	Corp-HY	7.9	5.8		4	4	0	2.01	888 233-4339
IDEX Transamerica Consv Hi-Yd Bd L	Dvsfd Bond						0		888 233-4339
IDEX Transamerica Consv Hi-Yd Bd M	Corp-HY	8	5.91	3.06	4	4	1	1.91	888 233-4339
ING Bond A	Corp-Inv	11.7	10.16	6.88	2	2	4.75	1	877 463-6464
ING Bond B	Corp-Inv	10.8	9.36		1	2	0	1.72	877 463-6464
ING Bond C	Corp-Inv	10.9	9.36		3	2	0	1.75	877 463-6464

452

Bond Fund Name	Objective	Annualized Return for			Rank		Max Load	Expense Ratio	Toll-Free/(Toll) Telephone
		1 Year	3 Years	5 Years	Overall	Risk			
ING Bond I	Corp-Inv	12	10.47	7.15	1	2	0	0.75	877 463-6464
ING GNMA Income A	Govt-Mtg	8.2	9.44	7.08	3	3	4.75	1.21	877 463-6464
ING Government A	Government	8.7	8.52	6.33	3	2	4.75	0.65	877 463-6464
ING Government B	Government	7.9	7.71		2	2	0	0.65	877 463-6464
ING Government C	Government	8.1	7.75		4	2	0	0.65	877 463-6464
ING Government I	Government	9	8.81	6.57	3	2	0	0.65	877 463-6464
ING High Yield Bond A	Corp-HY	5.8	5.13		4	5	4.75	1	877 463-6464
ING High Yield Bond B	Corp-HY	5	3.04		5	5	0	1.65	877 463-6464
ING High Yield Bond C	Corp-HY	5.1	3		5	5	0	1.65	877 463-6464
ING High Yield Opportunity A	Corp-HY	1.5	-3.18	-1.36	5	5	5.75	1.32	877 463-6464
ING High Yield Opportunity B	Corp-HY	0.7	-3.74	-1.8	5	5	0	1.97	877 463-6464
ING High Yield Opportunity C	Corp-HY	0.8	-3.74	-1.92	5	5	0	1.97	877 463-6464
ING High Yield Opportunity Q	Corp-HY	1.6	-2.91	-1.2	5	5	0		877 463-6464
ING Intermediate Bond A	Dvsfd Bond	11.9	12.91		1	3	4.75	1.36	877 463-6464
ING Intermediate Bond B	Dvsfd Bond	11	12.13		1	3	0	2.01	877 463-6464
ING Intermediate Bond C	Dvsfd Bond	11	12.09		3	4	0	2.01	877 463-6464
ING National Tax-Exempt Bond A	Muni Natl	11.1	9.39			3	4.75	1.52	877 463-6464
ING National Tax-Exempt Bond B	Muni Natl	10.4	8.64			3	0	1.84	877 463-6464
ING National Tax-Exempt Bond C	Muni Natl	10.4	8.58			3	0	1.83	877 463-6464
ING Strategic Bond A	Dvsfd Bond	10.6	6	4.42	4	4	5.75	0.97	877 463-6464
ING Strategic Bond B	Dvsfd Bond	10.2	5.58	4.05	5	4	0	1.38	877 463-6464
ING Strategic Bond C	Dvsfd Bond	10.3	5.62	4.07	5	4	0	1.38	877 463-6464
ING Strategic Bond Q	Dvsfd Bond	10.9	6.29	4.66	4	4	0	1.38	877 463-6464
INVESCO High Yield A	Corp-HY	19					5.5	1.09	800 525-8085
INVESCO High Yield B	Corp-HY	18.9					0	1.81	800 525-8085
INVESCO High Yield C	Corp-HY	18	-6.91		4	5	0	2	800 525-8085
INVESCO High Yield Inv	Corp-HY	19.3	-6.2	-3.93	4	5	0	1.26	800 525-8085
INVESCO High Yield K	Corp-HY	18.5					0	1.45	800 525-8085
INVESCO Select Income A	Corp-Inv	13.7					5.5	1.07	800 525-8085
INVESCO Select Income B	Corp-Inv	13.1					0	1.86	800 525-8085
INVESCO Select Income C	Corp-Inv	13.1	3.27			4	0	1.8	800 525-8085
INVESCO Select Income Inv	Corp-Inv	13.9	3.97	2.72	4	4	0	1.05	800 525-8085
INVESCO Select Income K	Corp-Inv	13.7					0	1.25	800 525-8085
INVESCO Tax-Free Bond A	Muni Natl	10.8					5.5	1.1	800 525-8085
INVESCO Tax-Free Bond B	Muni Natl	10.2					0	1.8	800 525-8085
INVESCO Tax-Free Bond C	Muni Natl	10.6	13		3	5	0	1.65	800 525-8085
INVESCO Tax-Free Bond Inv	Muni Natl	11.3	9.36	5.83	3	4	0	0.9	800 525-8085
INVESCO US Govt Securities A	Government	9.2					5.5	1.06	800 525-8085
INVESCO US Govt Securities B	Government	8.7					0	1.72	800 525-8085
INVESCO US Govt Securities C	Government	8.7	8.34		3	3	0	1.75	800 525-8085
INVESCO US Govt Securities Inv	Government	9.5	9.18	6.38	4	3	0	1	800 525-8085
ISI Managed Municipal Fund	Muni Natl	9.4	8.91	5.61	2	3	3	0.9	800 955-7175
ISI North American Govt Bond Fund A	Government	14.1	10.46	8.02	3	4	3	1.13	800 955-7175
ISI Total Return US Treasury	Government	14.9	10.3	7.48	3	4	3	0.81	800 955-7175
Idaho Tax-Exempt Fund	Muni State	9.5	8.59	5.62	3	3	0	0.78	800 728-8762
Ivy Bond A	Corp-Inv	12.8	10	3.47	3	4	4.75	1.46	800 777-6472
Ivy Bond Adv	Corp-Inv	12.5	10.05	3.5	3	4	0	1.39	800 777-6472
Ivy Bond B	Corp-Inv	10.9	8.61	2.33	4	4	0	2.3	800 777-6472
Ivy Bond C	Corp-Inv	10.8	8.58	2.35	4	3	0	2.26	800 777-6472
J Hancock Bond Fund A	Corp-Inv	12.2	10.22	6.87	2	3	4.5	1.11	800 257-3336
J Hancock Bond Fund B	Corp-Inv	11.5	9.47	6.25	3	3	0	1.81	800 257-3336
J Hancock Bond Fund C	Corp-Inv	11.5	9.41		2	3	1	1.8	800 257-3336
J Hancock Bond Fund I	Corp-Inv	12.7					0	0.68	800 257-3336
J Hancock CA Tax Free Income A	Muni CA	8.9	8.39	5.55	4	4	4.5	0.75	800 257-3336
J Hancock CA Tax Free Income B	Muni CA	8	7.54	4.82	5	4	0	1.6	800 257-3336
J Hancock CA Tax Free Income C	Muni CA	8	7.45		5	4	1	1.6	800 257-3336
J Hancock Government Inc A	Govt-Mtg	11.1	10.25	7.09	3	3	4.5	1.02	800 257-3336
J Hancock Government Inc B	Govt-Mtg	10.3	9.43	6.32	3	3	0	1.75	800 257-3336

Bond Fund Name	Objective	Annualized Return for			Rank		Max Load	Expense Ratio	Toll-Free/(Toll) Telephone
		1 Year	3 Years	5 Years	Overall	Risk			
J Hancock Government Inc C	Govt-Mtg	10.3	9.41			3	1	1.77	800 257-3336
J Hancock High Income A	Corp-HY	10.9					5	1.24	800 257-3336
J Hancock High Income B	Corp-HY	10.1					0	1.9	800 257-3336
J Hancock High Income C	Corp-HY	10.1					1	1.9	800 257-3336
J Hancock High Income I	Corp-HY	11.2					0	0.98	800 257-3336
J Hancock High Yield Bond A	Corp-HY	10.8	4.08	0.56	4	5	4.5	0.99	800 257-3336
J Hancock High Yield Bond B	Corp-HY	10	3.31	-0.39	4	5	0	1.67	800 257-3336
J Hancock High Yield Bond C	Corp-HY	10	3.31	1.08	4	5	1	1.74	800 257-3336
J Hancock High Yield Muni Bond A	Muni Natl	5	6.09	3.45	4	2	4.5	1.08	800 257-3336
J Hancock High Yield Muni Bond B	Muni Natl	4.2	5.32	2.47	4	2	0	1.82	800 257-3336
J Hancock High Yield Muni Bond C	Muni Natl	4.2	5.29			2	1	1.83	800 257-3336
J Hancock Invest Gr Bond A	Government	12.5	10.42	7.62	1	3	3	1.05	800 257-3336
J Hancock Invest Gr Bond B	Government	11.6	9.59	6.79	2	3	0	1.77	800 257-3336
J Hancock Invest Gr Bond C	Government	11.6	9.57		1	3	1	1.8	800 257-3336
J Hancock MA Tax Free Income A	Muni State	10.9	9.57	5.9	2	3	4.5	0.77	800 257-3336
J Hancock MA Tax Free Income B	Muni State	10.1	8.82	5.49	3	3	0	1.47	800 257-3336
J Hancock MA Tax Free Income C	Muni State	10.1	8.77			3	1	1.47	800 257-3336
J Hancock NY Tax Free Income A	Muni NY	9	9.11	5.83	3	4	4.5	0.83	800 257-3336
J Hancock NY Tax Free Income B	Muni NY	8.3	8.35	5.21	5	4	0	1.53	800 257-3336
J Hancock NY Tax Free Income C	Muni NY	8.3	8.34			4	1	1.53	800 257-3336
J Hancock Strategic Income A	Dvsfd Bond	16.5	8.48	5.87	3	4	4.5	0.89	800 257-3336
J Hancock Strategic Income B	Dvsfd Bond	15.7	7.74	5.41	3	4	0	1.59	800 257-3336
J Hancock Strategic Income C	Dvsfd Bond	15.7	7.71	5.12	3	4	1	1.59	800 257-3336
J Hancock Strategic Income I	Dvsfd Bond	17					0	0.6	800 257-3336
J Hancock Tax Free Bond A	Muni Natl	7.9	7.7	4.8	5	4	4.5	0.85	800 257-3336
J Hancock Tax Free Bond B	Muni Natl	7.1	6.91	4.09	5	4	0	1.61	800 257-3336
J Hancock Tax Free Bond C	Muni Natl	7.1	6.83		5	4	1	1.71	800 257-3336
JPMorgan Bond I	Dvsfd Bond	10.9	10.28	7.04	1	2	0	0.49	800 348-4782
JPMorgan Bond II A	Corp-Inv	11.2	10.38	7	2	2	4.5	0.75	800 348-4782
JPMorgan Bond II B	Corp-Inv	10.3	9.67	6.59	3	2	0	1.5	800 348-4782
JPMorgan Bond II Sel	Corp-Inv	11.3	10.42	7.03	2	2	0	0.6	800 348-4782
JPMorgan CA Bond A	Muni CA	8.2					4.5	0.6	800 348-4782
JPMorgan CA Bond I	Muni CA	8.4	8.09	5.9	3	3	0	0.5	800 348-4782
JPMorgan Fleming Emer Mkt Debt Sel	Intl Bond	24.4	15.47	11.01	2	5	0	1.25	800 348-4782
JPMorgan Global Strategic Inc I	Intl Bond	9.6	7.45	4.63	3	3	0	0.65	800 348-4782
JPMorgan Intermediate T/F Inc Sel	Muni Natl	9.4	8.63	6	2	3	0	0.66	800 348-4782
JPMorgan NJ Tax-Free Income A	Muni State	9.9					5.75	1	800 348-4782
JPMorgan NJ Tax-Free Income B	Muni State	9.3					0	1.5	800 348-4782
JPMorgan NJ Tax-Free Income Sel	Muni State	10	9.49	6.3	2	4	0	0.75	800 348-4782
JPMorgan NY Interm T/F Income A	Muni NY	9.3	8.48	5.87	2	3	4.5	0.75	800 348-4782
JPMorgan NY Interm T/F Income B	Muni NY	8.4	7.79	5.48	4	3	0	1.55	800 348-4782
JPMorgan NY Interm T/F Income Sel	Muni NY	9.3	8.51	5.9	1	3	0	0.72	800 348-4782
JPMorgan Short Term Bond I	Corp-Inv	5.6	6.83	5.94	2	1	0	0.3	800 348-4782
JPMorgan Short Term Bond II A	Corp-Inv	5	6.58	5.41	3	1	1.5	0.75	800 348-4782
JPMorgan Short Term Bond II Sel	Corp-Inv	5.2	6.91	5.62	3	1	4.5	0.5	800 348-4782
JPMorgan Strategic Income A	Dvsfd Bond	9.8	8.02		3	4	4.5	1.25	800 348-4782
JPMorgan Strategic Income B	Dvsfd Bond	9.3	5.54		4	4	0	1.75	800 348-4782
JPMorgan Strategic Income C	Dvsfd Bond	9.3	5.54		4	4	0	1.75	800 348-4782
JPMorgan Tax Aware Enhanc Inc A	Other	1.7					5.75	0.75	800 348-4782
JPMorgan Tax Aware Enhanc Inc I	Other	1.9	3.74		4	1	0	0.25	800 348-4782
JPMorgan Tax Aware Enhanc Inc Sel	Other	2.1	-39.71			5	0	0.5	800 348-4782
JPMorgan Tax Free Income A	Muni Natl	10.4	9.31	5.99	3	4	4.5	0.75	800 348-4782
JPMorgan Tax Free Income B	Muni Natl	9.3	8.58	5.57	4	4	0	1.64	800 348-4782
JPMorgan Tax Free Income Sel	Muni Natl	10.4	9.43	6.04	3	4	0	0.75	800 348-4782
JPMorgan US Treasury Income A	Government	12.7	10.17	7.29	3	4	4.5	0.75	800 348-4782
JPMorgan US Treasury Income B	Government	11.8	9	6.21	4	4	0	1.64	800 348-4782
Jamestown VA Tax Exempt	Muni State	8.4					0	0.68	866 738-1129
Janus Adviser Flexible Income C	Corp-Inv						0		800 525-3713

Bond Fund Name	Objective	Annualized Return for			Rank		Max Load	Expense Ratio	Toll-Free/(Toll) Telephone
		1 Year	3 Years	5 Years	Overall	Risk			
Janus Adviser Flexible Income I	Corp-Inv	13.7	7.54	3.31	3	3	0	1.2	800 525-3713
Janus Federal Tax-Exempt	Muni Natl	11.5	8.64	5.11	4	4	0	0.68	800 525-3713
Janus Flexible Income Fund	Dvsfd Bond	13.7	9.9	6.42	2	3	0	0.79	800 525-3713
Janus High-Yield Bond Fund	Corp-HY	6.6	5.03	3.52	4	4	0	1.03	800 525-3713
Janus Short-Term Bond Fund	Corp-Inv	4.6	6.34	5.45	3	1	0	0.66	800 525-3713
JohnsonFamily Int Fixed Income	Corp-Inv	10.2	9.75	6.2	2	2	2.75	0.85	800 276-8272
Julius Baer Global Income Fund A	Intl Bond	18.6	11.33	7.26	3	4	0	1.48	800 435-4659
Kansas Insured Intermediate Fd	Muni State	1.9	4.75	3.81	3	1	2.75	0.75	800 276-1262
Kansas Municipal Fund	Muni State	-0.4	4.48	3.35	3	1	4.25	0.95	800 276-1262
LEADER Intermediate Govt Bond Inst	Government	11.1	11.06	6.83	3	3	4	0.82	800 219-4182
LEADER Intermediate Govt Bond Inv	Government	10.8	10.21	6.23	3	3	5.5	1.12	800 219-4182
LEADER Intermediate Govt Bond Inv B	Dvsfd Bond						0		800 219-4182
LEADER Short Term Bond Fd B	Dvsfd Bond						0		800 219-4182
LEADER Short Term Bond Fd Inv	Muni Natl	8.3					4.75	1.31	800 219-4182
LEADER Tax-Exempt Bond Inst	Muni Natl	8.2					0		800 219-4182
LEADER Tax-Exempt Bond Inv	Muni Natl	7.9					5.5	1.16	800 219-4182
LEADER Tax-Exempt Bond Inv B	Dvsfd Bond						0		800 219-4182
LKCM Fixed Income Fund	Dvsfd Bond	7.8	9.39	6.66		2	0	0.65	800 688-5526
Lazard Bond Inst	Corp-Inv	8.9	8.01	5.41	3	2	0	0.91	800 823-6300
Lazard Bond Open	Corp-Inv	8.7	7.86	5.17	3	2	0	1.1	800 823-6300
Lazard High Yield Fund Instl	Corp-HY	0	-4.5	-4.07	5	5	0	0.75	800 823-6300
Lazard Strategic Yield Inst	Corp-HY	2.9	2.27	1.73	4	3	0	0.93	800 823-6300
Lazard Strategic Yield Open	Corp-HY	2.3	1.71	1.34	4	3	0	1.46	800 823-6300
Lebenthal NY Municipal Bond A	Muni NY	9.9	9.52	5.75	2	4	4.5	0.88	800 221-5822
Lebenthal New Jersey Muni Bond	Muni State	9.6	9.89	5.94	1	3	4.5	1.47	800 221-5822
Lebenthal Taxable Municipal Bond	Corp-Inv	16.3	14.1	8.55	3	4	4.5	1.35	800 221-5822
Legg Mason Global Income Trust	Intl Bond	17.2	7.82	4.13	3	4	0	1.97	800 822-5544
Legg Mason High Yield Prim	Corp-HY	5.5	-2.43	-2.41	5	5	0	1.36	800 822-5544
Legg Mason Investmnt Grade Inc Prim	Corp-Inv	16.7	11.73	7.58	1	3	0	1.3	800 822-5544
Legg Mason MD Tax Free Inc Primary	Muni State	10.2	8.96	5.71	1	3	0	0.93	800 822-5544
Legg Mason PA Tax-Free Inc Prim	Muni State	10.4	8.91	5.91	2	3	2.75	0.7	800 822-5544
Legg Mason Tax-Free Interm Income	Muni Natl	7.9	7.53	5.74	3	2	2	0.7	800 822-5544
Legg Mason US Gov Interm-Term Prim	Government	7.7	8	5.87	3	2	0	1.3	800 822-5544
Liberty CT Interm Muni Bond Fd A	Muni Natl						5.75	1.25	800 338-2550
Liberty CT Interm Muni Bond Fd B	Muni Natl						0	2.11	800 338-2550
Liberty CT Interm Muni Bond Fd C	Muni Natl						0	2.11	800 338-2550
Liberty CT Interm Muni Bond Fd G	Muni State	8					0	1.77	800 338-2550
Liberty CT Interm Muni Bond Fd T	Muni State	8.8					4.75	1.08	800 338-2550
Liberty CT Interm Muni Bond Fd Z	Muni State	9	8.5	5.48		3	0	0.92	800 338-2550
Liberty CT Tax-Exempt Fund A	Muni State	10.5	9.75	6.41	1	3	4.75	0.79	800 338-2550
Liberty CT Tax-Exempt Fund B	Muni State	9.7	8.96	5.62	3	3	0	1.54	800 338-2550
Liberty CT Tax-Exempt Fund C	Muni State	10	9.27	5.94	2	3	0	1.24	800 338-2550
Liberty California Tax-Exempt A	Muni CA	11	9.98	6.34	3	4	4.75	0.93	800 338-2550
Liberty California Tax-Exempt B	Muni CA	10.1	9.09	5.51	4	4	0	1.68	800 338-2550
Liberty California Tax-Exempt C	Muni CA	10.4	9.41	5.84	4	4	0	1.38	800 338-2550
Liberty Contrarian Income A	Corp-Inv	10.4	9.66	7.29	2	2	4.75	0.8	800 338-2550
Liberty Contrarian Income B	Corp-Inv	9.5	5.63			3	0	1.55	800 338-2550
Liberty Contrarian Income C	Corp-Inv	9.5	5.69			3	0	1.55	800 338-2550
Liberty Contrarian Income I	Dvsfd Bond	10.8	10.07			2	0	0.38	800 338-2550
Liberty Contrarian Income Z	Corp-Inv	10.8	9.75			3	0	0.55	800 338-2550
Liberty Corporate Bond A	Corp-Inv						4.75		800 338-2550
Liberty Corporate Bond B	Corp-Inv						0		800 338-2550
Liberty Corporate Bond C	Corp-Inv						0	1.97	800 338-2550
Liberty Corporate Bond Z	Corp-Inv	13.4	10.86	7.34	2	3	0		800 338-2550
Liberty FL Intermediate Muni Bond A	Muni State						4.75	1.22	800 338-2550
Liberty FL Intermediate Muni Bond B	Muni State						0		800 338-2550
Liberty FL Intermediate Muni Bond C	Muni State						0	1.97	800 338-2550
Liberty FL Intermediate Muni Bond Z	Muni State	8.5	8.18	5.25		3	0	0.94	800 338-2550

Bond Fund Name	Objective	Annualized Return for			Rank		Max Load	Expense Ratio	Toll-Free/(Toll) Telephone
		1 Year	3 Years	5 Years	Overall	Risk			
Liberty Federal Securities Fund A	Government	9.9	10.19	6.62	3	3	4.75	1.2	800 338-2550
Liberty Federal Securities Fund B	Government	9.1	9.19	5.62	4	3	0	1.98	800 338-2550
Liberty Federal Securities Fund C	Government	9.2	9.35	5.78	3	3	0	1.98	800 338-2550
Liberty Federal Securities Fund Z	Government	10.2	9.46			3	0	0.98	800 338-2550
Liberty Floating Rate Advantage A	Dvsfd Bond	3.9					3.5	2.79	800 338-2550
Liberty Floating Rate Advantage B	Dvsfd Bond	3.6	5.26		4	4	0	3.14	800 338-2550
Liberty Floating Rate Advantage C	Dvsfd Bond	3.4	5.13		4	4	0	3.29	800 338-2550
Liberty Floating Rate Advantage Z	Dvsfd Bond	4.3	5.98		4	4	0	2.49	800 338-2550
Liberty Floating Rate Fund A	Govt-Mtg	3	4.34		5	3	3.5	1.43	800 338-2550
Liberty Floating Rate Fund B	Govt-Mtg	2.7	3.97		4	3	0	1.5	800 338-2550
Liberty Floating Rate Fund C	Govt-Mtg	2.5	3.81		5	3	0	1.65	800 338-2550
Liberty Floating Rate Fund Z	Govt-Mtg	3.4	4.42		4	3	0	0.8	800 338-2550
Liberty High Yield Municipal Z	Muni Natl	7.8	7.28	4.45	3	3	0	0.47	800 338-2550
Liberty High Yield Securities A	Corp-HY	6.1	-1.25	-0.61	5	5	4.75	1.31	800 338-2550
Liberty High Yield Securities B	Corp-HY	5.3	-2.12	-1.6	5	5	0	2.06	800 338-2550
Liberty High Yield Securities C	Corp-HY	5.4	-1.97	-1.45	5	5	0	1.91	800 338-2550
Liberty High Yield Securities Z	Corp-HY	6.3	-1.11			5	0		800 338-2550
Liberty Income Fund A	Govt-Mtg	11.8					4.75	1.33	800 338-2550
Liberty Income Fund B	Dvsfd Bond	10.9	10.36	6.73		3	0	2	800 338-2550
Liberty Income Fund C	Dvsfd Bond	11	10.41	6.75		3	0	1.33	800 338-2550
Liberty Income Fund Z	Corp-Inv	8.9	10.16	6.61	3	3	0	0.51	800 338-2550
Liberty Intermediate Bond Fund A	Govt-Mtg	9.6	10.25	7.12		3	4.75	0.96	800 338-2550
Liberty Intermediate Bond Fund B	Govt-Mtg	8.8					0	2	800 338-2550
Liberty Intermediate Bond Fund C	Govt-Mtg	9					0	1.85	800 338-2550
Liberty Intermediate Bond Fund Z	Corp-Inv	9.9	10.6	7.33	2	3	0	1	800 338-2550
Liberty Intermediate Govt Income A	Government						4.75		800 338-2550
Liberty Intermediate Govt Income B	Government						0		800 338-2550
Liberty Intermediate Govt Income C	Government						0		800 338-2550
Liberty Intermediate Govt Income G	Dvsfd Bond	8.2	8.4			2	0	1.91	800 338-2550
Liberty Intermediate Govt Income T	Government	9	9.22	6.7	3	2	4.75	0.98	800 338-2550
Liberty Intermediate Govt Income Z	Government	9.3	9.5	6.96	3	2	0	0.69	800 338-2550
Liberty Intermediate T/E Bond Fd A	Corp-Inv						4.75	1.19	800 338-2550
Liberty Intermediate T/E Bond Fd B	Corp-Inv						0	1.81	800 338-2550
Liberty Intermediate T/E Bond Fd C	Corp-Inv						0	1.81	800 338-2550
Liberty MA Interm Muni Bond Fd A	Muni State						4.75		800 338-2550
Liberty MA Interm Muni Bond Fd B	Muni State						0		800 338-2550
Liberty MA Interm Muni Bond Fd C	Muni State						0		800 338-2550
Liberty MA Interm Muni Bond Fd G	Muni State	8.4					0		800 338-2550
Liberty MA Interm Muni Bond Fd T	Muni State	9.1					4.75		800 338-2550
Liberty MA Interm Muni Bond Fd Z	Muni State	9.2	8.6	5.61		3	0		800 338-2550
Liberty MA Tax-Exempt A	Muni State	12.2	10.8	6.51	2	4	4.75	0.94	800 338-2550
Liberty MA Tax-Exempt B	Muni State	11.4	9.99	5.73	3	4	0	1.69	800 338-2550
Liberty MA Tax-Exempt C	Muni State	11.7	10.31	6.04	3	4	0	1.39	800 338-2550
Liberty Managed Municipals B	Muni Natl						0		800 338-2550
Liberty Managed Municipals Z	Muni Natl	11.8	10.27	6.29	2	4	0	0.75	800 338-2550
Liberty NJ Intermediate Muni Bond A	Muni Natl						4.75	1.28	800 338-2550
Liberty NJ Intermediate Muni Bond B	Muni Natl						0	2.03	800 338-2550
Liberty NJ Intermediate Muni Bond C	Muni Natl						0	2.03	800 338-2550
Liberty NJ Intermediate Muni Bond G	Muni Natl	9.6					0		800 338-2550
Liberty NJ Intermediate Muni Bond T	Muni State	9.8					3.89	0.9	800 338-2550
Liberty NJ Intermediate Muni Bond Z	Muni State	10					0	1.74	800 338-2550
Liberty NY Intermediate Muni Bond A	Muni State						4.75	1.29	800 338-2550
Liberty NY Intermediate Muni Bond B	Muni State						0	2.08	800 338-2550
Liberty NY Intermediate Muni Bond C	Muni State						0	2.08	800 338-2550
Liberty NY Intermediate Muni Bond G	Muni State	10.3					0		800 338-2550
Liberty NY Intermediate Muni Bond T	Muni NY	10.7	9.27	5.79	3	4	4.75	0.97	800 338-2550
Liberty NY Intermediate Muni Bond Z	Muni NY	11.1	9.57	6.07	2	4	0	0.78	800 338-2550
Liberty NY Tax-Exempt Fund A	Muni NY	11.1	10.58	6.5	3	4	4.75	0.79	800 338-2550

Bond Fund Name	Objective	Annualized Return for			Rank		Max Load	Expense Ratio	Toll-Free/(Toll) Telephone
		1 Year	3 Years	5 Years	Overall	Risk			
Liberty NY Tax-Exempt Fund B	Muni NY	10.3	9.64	5.63	4	4	0	1.54	800 338-2550
Liberty NY Tax-Exempt Fund C	Muni NY	10.6	9.94	5.95	3	4	0	1.24	800 338-2550
Liberty PA Intermediate Muni Bond A	Muni Natl						4.75	1.39	800 338-2550
Liberty PA Intermediate Muni Bond B	Muni Natl						0		800 338-2550
Liberty PA Intermediate Muni Bond C	Muni Natl						0		800 338-2550
Liberty PA Intermediate Muni Bond Z	Muni Natl	10.2	9.94	5.37		4	0		800 338-2550
Liberty Quality Plus Bond A	Corp-HY	12.8	10.72			3	4.75	1.28	800 338-2550
Liberty Quality Plus Bond B	Corp-HY	12	9.92			3	0	1.94	800 338-2550
Liberty Quality Plus Bond C	Corp-HY						0	1.96	800 338-2550
Liberty Quality Plus Bond T	Government	12.6	10.64	7.19	3	3	4.75	0.98	800 338-2550
Liberty Quality Plus Bond Z	Government	12.8	10.89	7.38	3	3	0	0.69	800 338-2550
Liberty RI Intermediate Muni Bond A	Muni State						4.75	1.19	800 338-2550
Liberty RI Intermediate Muni Bond B	Muni State						0	1.96	800 338-2550
Liberty RI Intermediate Muni Bond C	Muni State						0	1.96	800 338-2550
Liberty RI Intermediate Muni Bond G	Muni State	8.5					0		800 338-2550
Liberty RI Intermediate Muni Bond T	Muni State	9.4	8.99	5.79		3	4.75		800 338-2550
Liberty SteinRoe Instl Float Rate	Govt-Mtg	3.4	-0.46			3	0	0.75	800 338-2550
Liberty Strategic Income Fund A	Dvsfd Bond	16.4	7.92	4.78	3	4	4.75	1.22	800 338-2550
Liberty Strategic Income Fund B	Dvsfd Bond	15.5	7.12	4	3	4	0	1.98	800 338-2550
Liberty Strategic Income Fund C	Dvsfd Bond	15.7	7.54	4.34	3	4	0	1.83	800 338-2550
Liberty Strategic Income Fund Z	Dvsfd Bond	16.2	7.91			4	0	0.99	800 338-2550
Liberty Tax-Exempt Fund A	Muni Natl	12	9.59	5.66	3	4	4.75	0.95	800 338-2550
Liberty Tax-Exempt Fund B	Muni Natl	11.2	8.75	4.79	4	4	0	1.7	800 338-2550
Liberty Tax-Exempt Fund C	Muni Natl	11.4	8.91	4.95	4	4	0	1.7	800 338-2550
Liberty Tax-Exempt Insured Fund A	Muni Natl	12.2	10.74	6.62	3	4	4.75	1.04	800 338-2550
Liberty Tax-Exempt Insured Fund B	Muni Natl	11.4	10.81	6.33	3	4	0	1.81	800 338-2550
Liberty Tax-Exempt Insured Fund C	Muni Natl	11.7	10.13	6.08	3	4	0	1.81	800 338-2550
Liberty US Treasury Index B	Government						0		800 338-2550
Liberty US Treasury Index C	Government						0	1.43	800 338-2550
Liberty US Treasury Index Z	Government	13.3	10.39	7.55	3	4	0	0.42	800 338-2550
Limited Term New York Muni Fd A	Muni NY	6	6.28	4.53	3	2	3.5	0.78	800 525-7048
Limited Term New York Muni Fd B	Muni NY	5.2	5.46	3.79	4	2	0	1.54	800 525-7048
Limited Term New York Muni Fd C	Muni NY	5.2	5.37	3.72	4	2	0	1.53	800 525-7048
Limited Term New York Muni Fd X	Muni NY	6.3	6	4.2	3	2	0	1.31	800 525-7048
Loomis Sayles Bond Inst	Corp-Inv	25.5	12.47	8.35	3	4	0	0.75	800 633-3330
Loomis Sayles Bond Ret	Corp-Inv	25.1	12.16	8.09	3	4	0	1	800 633-3330
Loomis Sayles Global Bond Inst	Intl Bond	28.6	14.48	9.69	2	4	0	0.9	800 633-3330
Loomis Sayles Global Bond Ret	Intl Bond	28.2	14.21	9.46	2	4	0	0.9	800 633-3330
Loomis Sayles Invstmnt Gr Bd Inst	Corp-Inv	21.4	13.03	9.32	1	4	0	0.55	800 633-3330
Loomis Sayles US Govt Sec Inst	Government	15.4	11.99	8.3	3	4	0	0.5	800 633-3330
Lord Abbett Bond Debenture A	Corp-HY	7.8	4.79	3.2	4	4	4.75	0.98	800 201-6984
Lord Abbett Bond Debenture B	Corp-HY	7	4.36	2.66	5	4	0	1.64	800 201-6984
Lord Abbett Bond Debenture C	Corp-HY	7	4.34	2.68	5	4	0	1.64	800 201-6984
Lord Abbett Bond Debenture P	Corp-HY	7.6	4.69		4	4	0	1.09	800 201-6984
Lord Abbett Bond Debenture Y	Corp-HY	8.2	5.45	3.77	4	4	0	0.64	800 201-6984
Lord Abbett Core Fixed Income A	Dvsfd Bond	10.9					4.75	1.5	800 201-6984
Lord Abbett Core Fixed Income B	Dvsfd Bond	10.1					0	2.15	800 201-6984
Lord Abbett Core Fixed Income C	Dvsfd Bond	10.1					0	2.15	800 201-6984
Lord Abbett Core Fixed Income P	Dvsfd Bond	10.8					0	1.6	800 201-6984
Lord Abbett Core Fixed Income Y	Dvsfd Bond	11.4	11.5	8.51	1	3	0	1.15	800 201-6984
Lord Abbett Global-Income A	Intl Bond	20.1	9.76	4.44	3	4	4.75	1.44	800 201-6984
Lord Abbett Global-Income B	Intl Bond	19.3	9.07	3.79	3	4	0	2.06	800 201-6984
Lord Abbett Global-Income C	Intl Bond	19.4	9.13	3.81	3	4	0	2.06	800 201-6984
Lord Abbett Global-Income P	Intl Bond	20.1	9.58		2	4	0	1.51	800 201-6984
Lord Abbett High Yield A	Corp-HY	6.7	4.83		4	5	4.75	1.24	800 201-6984
Lord Abbett High Yield B	Corp-HY	6	4.2		5	5	0	1.85	800 201-6984
Lord Abbett High Yield C	Corp-HY	6	4.2		5	5	0	1.85	800 201-6984
Lord Abbett High Yield Y	Corp-HY	7.2	5.16		4	5	0	0.85	800 201-6984

Bond Fund Name	Objective	Annualized Return for			Rank		Max Load	Expense Ratio	Toll-Free/(Toll) Telephone
		1 Year	3 Years	5 Years	Overall	Risk			
Lord Abbett Invt Tr-High Yield P	Corp-HY						0		800 201-6984
Lord Abbett Invt Tr-Ltd US Gov A	Government	7.5	7.71	6.5	2	1	3.25	1.09	800 201-6984
Lord Abbett Invt Tr-Ltd US Gov C	Government	6.5	6.62	5.37	3	1	0	1.78	800 201-6984
Lord Abbett Tax Free Inc-CA A	Muni CA	10.6	9.91	5.7	3	4	3.25	1	800 201-6984
Lord Abbett Tax Free Inc-CA C	Muni CA	9.9	9.31	5.04	4	4	0	1.64	800 201-6984
Lord Abbett Tax Free Inc-CT A	Muni State	11.2	9.83	5.73	2	3	3.25	1.09	800 201-6984
Lord Abbett Tax Free Inc-FL A	Muni State	11.1	9.64	5.38	3	4	3.25	1.09	800 201-6984
Lord Abbett Tax Free Inc-FL C	Muni State	10.3	8.84	4.69	4	4	0	1.71	800 201-6984
Lord Abbett Tax Free Inc-GA A	Muni State	11.4	10.75	6.7	2	4	3.25	0.68	800 201-6984
Lord Abbett Tax Free Inc-HI A	Muni State	9.5	8.81	5.17	4	3	3.25	1.04	800 201-6984
Lord Abbett Tax Free Inc-MI A	Muni State	11.7	10.92	6.63	2	4	3.25	0.75	800 201-6984
Lord Abbett Tax Free Inc-MN A	Muni State	10.7	9.98	5.98	1	3	3.25	0.77	800 201-6984
Lord Abbett Tax Free Inc-MO A	Muni State	11.3	9.73	5.86	1	3	3.25	1.03	800 201-6984
Lord Abbett Tax Free Inc-NJ A	Muni State	9.5	9.24	5.36	3	3	3.25	1.05	800 201-6984
Lord Abbett Tax Free Inc-NY A	Muni NY	11.5	10.33	6.2	2	4	3.25	1.03	800 201-6984
Lord Abbett Tax Free Inc-NY C	Muni NY	10.6	9.67	5.53	3	4	0	1.65	800 201-6984
Lord Abbett Tax Free Inc-Natl A	Muni Natl	11.1	9.71	5.66	3	4	3.25	1.03	800 201-6984
Lord Abbett Tax Free Inc-Natl B	Muni Natl	10.4	9	5	4	4	0	1.64	800 201-6984
Lord Abbett Tax Free Inc-Natl C	Muni Natl	10.3	9	4.95	4	4	0	1.64	800 201-6984
Lord Abbett Tax Free Inc-PA A	Muni State	10.6	9.83	5.87	3	4	3.25	1.08	800 201-6984
Lord Abbett Tax Free Inc-TX A	Muni State	12.1	10.35	5.67	3	4	3.25	1.08	800 201-6984
Lord Abbett Tax Free Inc-WA A	Muni State	10.8	9.74	5.65	2	3	3.25	0.74	800 201-6984
Lord Abbett Total Return A	Dvsfd Bond	11					4.75	1.54	800 201-6984
Lord Abbett Total Return B	Dvsfd Bond	10.2					0	2.15	800 201-6984
Lord Abbett Total Return C	Dvsfd Bond	10.3					0	2.15	800 201-6984
Lord Abbett Total Return P	Dvsfd Bond	10.9					0	1.6	800 201-6984
Lord Abbett Total Return Y	Dvsfd Bond	11.4	11.5		1	3	0	1.15	800 201-6984
Lord Abbett U.S. Govt Secs A	Government	10	9.92	6.86	3	3	4.75	1.09	800 201-6984
Lord Abbett U.S. Govt Secs B	Government	9.4	9.17	6.19	3	3	0	1.7	800 201-6984
Lord Abbett U.S. Govt Secs C	Government	9.3	9.21	6.13	3	3	0	1.7	800 201-6984
Lutheran Brotherhood High Yld A	Corp-HY	5.6	-3.52	-2.58	5	5	4.5	0.78	800 847-4836
Lutheran Brotherhood High Yld B	Corp-HY	4.8	-4.2	-3.29	5	5	0	1.78	800 847-4836
Lutheran Brotherhood High Yld Inst	Corp-HY	6.1	-3.27	-2.16	5	5	0	0.54	800 847-4836
Lutheran Brotherhood Income A	Corp-Inv	9.4	9.27	6.23	3	3	5.5	0.58	800 847-4836
Lutheran Brotherhood Income B	Corp-Inv	8.6	8.49	5.45	4	3	0	1.64	800 847-4836
Lutheran Brotherhood Income Inst	Corp-Inv	9.7	9.57	6.53	3	3	0	0.45	800 847-4836
Lutheran Brotherhood Ltd Mat Bd A	Dvsfd Bond	6.6	7.83		2	1	4.5	0.85	800 847-4836
Lutheran Brotherhood Ltd Mat Bd B	Dvsfd Bond	6.5	7.8		2	1	0	1.05	800 847-4836
Lutheran Brotherhood Ltd Mat Bd I	Dvsfd Bond	6.9	8.13		2	1	0	0.57	800 847-4836
Lutheran Brotherhood Muni A	Muni Natl	9.5	9.25	5.98	2	3	4.5	0.47	800 847-4836
Lutheran Brotherhood Muni B	Muni Natl	8.8	8.48	5.58	3	3	0	1.48	800 847-4836
Lutheran Brotherhood Muni Inst	Muni Natl	9.8	9.46	6.65	2	3	0	0.42	800 847-4836
MDL Broad Market Fixed Income	Corp-Inv	8.5	9.33	6.66	2	3	0	0.9	877 635-3863
MFS AL Municipal Bond A	Muni State	10.6	9.48	6	1	3	4.75	0.88	800 343-2829
MFS AL Municipal Bond B	Muni State	9.8	8.66	5.21	3	3	0	1.63	800 343-2829
MFS AR Municipal Bond A	Muni State	10.2	9.46	6.08	1	3	4.75	0.72	800 343-2829
MFS AR Municipal Bond B	Muni State	9.3	8.59	5.28	3	3	0	1.5	800 343-2829
MFS Bond A	Corp-Inv	14.8	11.13	6.45	2	3	4.75	0.93	800 343-2829
MFS Bond B	Corp-Inv	14	10.34	5.7	2	3	0	1.64	800 343-2829
MFS Bond C	Corp-Inv	14	10.35	5.71	2	3	0	1.64	800 343-2829
MFS Bond R	Dvsfd Bond						0		800 343-2829
MFS CA Municipal Bond A	Muni CA	10.4	9.64	6.12	3	4	4.75	0.67	800 343-2829
MFS CA Municipal Bond B	Muni CA	9.7	8.83	5.32	4	4	0	1.45	800 343-2829
MFS CA Municipal Bond C	Muni CA	9.6	8.75	5.2	4	4	0	1.57	800 343-2829
MFS FL Municipal Bond Fund A	Muni State	10.2	9.42	5.88	2	3	4.75	0.63	800 343-2829
MFS FL Municipal Bond Fund B	Muni State	9.3	8.55	5.04	3	3	0	1.43	800 343-2829
MFS GA Municipal Bond Fund A	Muni State	10.6	9.48	5.83	3	4	4.75	0.93	800 343-2829
MFS GA Municipal Bond Fund B	Muni State	9.8	8.68	5.07	4	4	0	1.68	800 343-2829

Bond Fund Name	Objective	Annualized Return for			Rank		Max Load	Expense Ratio	Toll-Free/(Toll) Telephone
		1 Year	3 Years	5 Years	Overall	Risk			
MFS Government Ltd Maturity Fund A	Government	4.8	6.41	5.49	3	1	2.5	0.81	800 343-2829
MFS Government Ltd Maturity Fund B	Government	4	5.58	4.63	3	1	0	1.59	800 343-2829
MFS Government Ltd Maturity Fund C	Government	3.9	5.48	4.55	3	1	0	1.66	800 343-2829
MFS Government Mortgage Fund A	Govt-Mtg	5.6	8.14	5.99	3	2	4.75	0.91	800 343-2829
MFS Government Mortgage Fund B	Govt-Mtg	4.8	7.33	5.21	3	2	0	1.66	800 343-2829
MFS Government Securities Fund A	Government	9.5	9.64	6.75	3	3	4.75	0.95	800 343-2829
MFS Government Securities Fund B	Government	8.8	8.94	6.05	3	3	0	1.61	800 343-2829
MFS Government Securities Fund C	Government	8.8	8.91	6.04	4	3	0	1.61	800 343-2829
MFS Government Securities Fund R	Govt-Mtg						0		800 343-2829
MFS High Income Fund A	Corp-HY	10.1	1.79	1.21	4	5	4.75	1.06	800 343-2829
MFS High Income Fund B	Corp-HY	9.3	1.14	0.56	5	5	0	1.76	800 343-2829
MFS High Income Fund C	Corp-HY	9	1.08	0.51	4	5	0	1.76	800 343-2829
MFS High Income Fund R	Corp-HY						0		800 343-2829
MFS High Yield Opportunities Fd A	Corp-HY	11.4	5.41		4	5	4.75	1.01	800 343-2829
MFS High Yield Opportunities Fd B	Corp-HY	10.5	4.73		4	5	0	1.66	800 343-2829
MFS High Yield Opportunities Fd C	Corp-HY	10.5	4.74		4	5	0	1.66	800 343-2829
MFS Interm Invst Grade Bond A	Corp-Inv	11.7	10.84			2	4.75	0.41	800 343-2829
MFS Interm Invst Grade Bond B	Corp-Inv	10.8	10.46			2	0	1.63	800 343-2829
MFS Interm Invst Grade Bond C	Corp-Inv	10.8	10.46			2	0	1.63	800 343-2829
MFS Interm Invst Grade Bond R	Corp-Inv						0		800 343-2829
MFS Limited Maturity Fund A	Corp-Inv	5.7	7.04	5.54	3	1	2.5	0.81	800 343-2829
MFS Limited Maturity Fund B	Corp-Inv	4.9	6.19	4.74	3	1	0	1.6	800 343-2829
MFS Limited Maturity Fund C	Corp-Inv	4.8	6.08	4.65	3	1	0	1.67	800 343-2829
MFS Limited Maturity Fund R	Dvsfd Bond						0		800 343-2829
MFS MA Municipal Bond Fund A	Muni State	10.7	9.55	5.79	2	4	4.75	1.57	800 343-2829
MFS MA Municipal Bond Fund B	Muni State	10	8.86	5.12	3	4	0	1.57	800 343-2829
MFS MD Municipal Bond Fund A	Muni State	9.7	9.22	5.66	2	3	4.75	0.95	800 343-2829
MFS MD Municipal Bond Fund B	Muni State	9	8.51	4.98	3	3	0	1.6	800 343-2829
MFS MS Municipal Bond Fund A	Muni State	10.1	9.02	5.9	1	3	4.75	0.65	800 343-2829
MFS MS Municipal Bond Fund B	Muni State	9.1	8.16	5.05	3	3	0	1.46	800 343-2829
MFS Municipal Bond Fund A	Muni Natl	10.7	9.66	5.98	2	3	4.75	0.58	800 343-2829
MFS Municipal Bond Fund B	Muni Natl	9.8	8.81	5.15	3	3	0	1.37	800 343-2829
MFS Municipal High Income Fund A	Muni Natl	7.3	7.36	4.46	4	2	4.75	0.76	800 343-2829
MFS Municipal High Income Fund B	Muni Natl	6.4	6.46	3.6	4	2	0	1.55	800 343-2829
MFS Municipal High Income Fund C	Muni Natl	6.2	6.16	3.39	3	2	0	1.76	800 343-2829
MFS Municipal Income Fund A	Muni Natl	8.9	8.23	5.17	4	3	4.75	0.91	800 343-2829
MFS Municipal Income Fund B	Muni Natl	8.1	7.41	4.38	5	3	0	1.66	800 343-2829
MFS Municipal Income Fund C	Muni Natl	8.1	7.4	4.37	5	3	0	1.66	800 343-2829
MFS Municipal Lmtd Maturity Fund A	Muni Natl	7.6	7.04	5	3	2	2.5	0.85	800 343-2829
MFS Municipal Lmtd Maturity Fund B	Muni Natl	6.9	6.23	4.2	4	2	0	1.59	800 343-2829
MFS Municipal Lmtd Maturity Fund C	Muni Natl	6.7	6.13	4.12	4	2	0	1.69	800 343-2829
MFS NC Municipal Bond Fund A	Muni State	10.2	9.21	5.54	2	3	4.75	0.92	800 343-2829
MFS NC Municipal Bond Fund B	Muni State	9.5	8.48	4.87	3	3	0	1.57	800 343-2829
MFS NC Municipal Bond Fund C	Muni State	9.4	8.48	4.84	3	3	0	1.57	800 343-2829
MFS NY Municipal Bond Fund A	Muni NY	10.8	9.71	6.01	2	4	4.75	0.88	800 343-2829
MFS NY Municipal Bond Fund B	Muni NY	9.9	8.82	5.16	4	4	0	1.63	800 343-2829
MFS NY Municipal Bond Fund C	Muni NY	10	8.93	5.57	3	4	0	1.63	800 343-2829
MFS PA Municipal Bond Fund A	Muni State	10.7	9.91	6.41	2	3	4.75	0.36	800 343-2829
MFS PA Municipal Bond Fund B	Muni State	9.8	9	5.54	3	3	0	1.2	800 343-2829
MFS Research Bond A	Dvsfd Bond	14.2	12.31		1	3	4.75	0.7	800 343-2829
MFS Research Bond B	Dvsfd Bond	13.3	11.59		1	3	0	1.55	800 343-2829
MFS Research Bond C	Dvsfd Bond	13.2	11.58		1	3	0	1.55	800 343-2829
MFS Research Bond R	Dvsfd Bond						0		800 343-2829
MFS SC Municipal Bond Fund A	Muni State	10.3	9.3	5.45	2	3	4.75	0.94	800 343-2829
MFS SC Municipal Bond Fund B	Muni State	9.6	8.59	4.76	3	3	0	1.59	800 343-2829
MFS Strategic Income Fund A	Dvsfd Bond	13.3	6.65	4.33	3	4	4.75	0.95	800 343-2829
MFS Strategic Income Fund B	Dvsfd Bond	12.7	5.95	3.68	3	4	0	1.61	800 343-2829
MFS Strategic Income Fund C	Dvsfd Bond	12.6	5.91	3.66	3	4	0	1.61	800 343-2829

Bond Fund Name	Objective	Annualized Return for 1 Year	3 Years	5 Years	Rank Overall	Risk	Max Load	Expense Ratio	Toll-Free/(Toll) Telephone
MFS TN Municipal Bond Fund A	Muni State	9.9	9.15	5.49	1	3	4.75	0.94	800 343-2829
MFS TN Municipal Bond Fund B	Muni State	9.2	8.41	4.82	3	3	0	1.59	800 343-2829
MFS VA Municipal Bond Fund A	Muni State	9.9	8.74	5.4	1	3	4.75	0.92	800 343-2829
MFS VA Municipal Bond Fund B	Muni State	9.2	8.02	4.73	3	3	0	1.57	800 343-2829
MFS VA Municipal Bond Fund C	Muni State	9.2	8.02	4.71	3	3	0	1.57	800 343-2829
MFS WV Municipal Bond Fund A	Muni State	9.8	9.15	5.5	2	3	4.75	0.93	800 343-2829
MFS WV Municipal Bond Fund B	Muni State	9.1	8.48	4.82	3	3	0	1.58	800 343-2829
MMA Praxis Intermediate Income A	Dvsfd Bond	11	9.02	5.95		3	3.75	1.2	800 977-2947
MMA Praxis Intermediate Income B	Corp-Inv	10.5	8.58	5.62	3	3	0	1.2	800 977-2947
MSIF Emerging Markets Debt A	Intl Bond	21.5	16.73	5.96	1	5	0	1.12	800 354-8185
MSIF Emerging Markets Debt B	Intl Bond	21	15	5	1	5	0	1.37	800 354-8185
MSIF Trust Core Plus Fix Inc Adv	Corp-Inv	7.3					0	0.75	800 354-8185
MSIF Trust Core Plus Fix Inc Inst	Corp-Inv	7.6	10.33	6.79	3	2	0		800 354-8185
MSIF Trust Core Plus Fix Inc Inv	Corp-Inv	7.4					0	0.65	800 354-8185
MSIF Trust High Yield: ADV	Corp-HY	4.4					0	0.85	800 354-8185
MSIF Trust High Yield: INST	Corp-HY	4.2	-3.79	-1.9	5	5	0		800 354-8185
MSIF Trust High Yield: INV	Corp-HY	4.3					0	0.74	800 354-8185
MSIF Trust Int. Duration: INST	Dvsfd Bond	8.8	10.26	7.01	2	2	0	0.53	800 354-8185
MSIF Trust International FIP: INST	Intl Bond	28.7	10.02	6.16	3	5	0	0.6	800 354-8185
MSIF Trust Invest Grd Fxd Inc Inst	Corp-Inv	8.2	10.77	7.04	3	2	0		800 354-8185
MSIF Trust Limited Duration: INST	Corp-Inv	4.1	7.01	5.83	3	1	0	0.44	800 354-8185
MSIF Trust Municipal: INST	Muni Natl	7.3	9.68	6.05	1	3	0	0.5	800 354-8185
MSIF Trust U.S. Core Fixed Income	Corp-Inv	8.1	10.83	6.83	3	2	0		800 354-8185
MainStay Global High Yield A	Intl Bond	23.5	17.69		2	5	4.5	1.91	800 624-6782
MainStay Global High Yield B	Intl Bond	22.7	16.87		2	5	0	1.7	800 624-6782
MainStay Global High Yield C	Intl Bond	22.7	16.87		1	5	0	2.45	800 624-6782
MainStay Government Fund A	Government	10.6	9.52	6.65	3	3	4.5	1.16	800 624-6782
MainStay Government Fund B	Government	9.7	8.72	5.87	4	3	0	1.9	800 624-6782
MainStay Government Fund C	Government	9.7	8.72		3	3	0	1.91	800 624-6782
MainStay High Yield Corp Bond A	Corp-HY	12.8	4.12	5.04	4	5	4.5	1.03	800 624-6782
MainStay High Yield Corp Bond B	Corp-HY	12.2	3.39	2.77	4	5	0	1.78	800 624-6782
MainStay High Yield Corp Bond C	Corp-HY	12.2	3.41		4	5	0	1.78	800 624-6782
MainStay Intl Bond A	Intl Bond	23.6	9.31	3.85	3	4	4.5	1.69	800 624-6782
MainStay Intl Bond B	Intl Bond	22.7					0	2.45	800 624-6782
MainStay Intl Bond C	Intl Bond	22.7	8.52		3	4	0	2.45	800 624-6782
MainStay Strategic Income A	Dvsfd Bond	13.6	7.79	4.83	3	4	4.5	1.44	800 624-6782
MainStay Strategic Income B	Dvsfd Bond	12.6	6.99	4.04	3	4	0	2.19	800 624-6782
MainStay Strategic Income C	Dvsfd Bond	12.6	7		4	4	0	2.19	800 624-6782
MainStay Tax Free Bond Fund A	Muni Natl	9	8.74	4.79	3	3	4.5	1.03	800 624-6782
MainStay Tax Free Bond Fund B	Muni Natl	8.7	8.47	4.5	3	3	0	1.28	800 624-6782
MainStay Tax Free Bond Fund C	Muni Natl	8.7	8.47		3	3	0	1.28	800 624-6782
Managers Bond Fund	Corp-Inv	16	12.39	8.3	1	4	0	0.98	800 835-3879
Managers Global Bond Fund	Intl Bond	29.1	10.39	6.04	3	4	0	1.55	800 835-3879
Managers Interm Bond	Corp-Inv	-2.4	4.45	3.87	4	3	0	1.26	800 835-3879
Managers Interm Duration US Gov	Government	6.6	9.47	6.58	2	2	0	0.88	800 835-3879
Managers Short Dur Govt Fund	Government	3.3	5.83	4.88	3	1	0	0.78	800 835-3879
Managers Total Return Bond Fund	Dvsfd Bond						0	0.99	800 835-3879
Marshall Government Income Adv	Govt-Mtg	5.2	7.55	5.45	3	2	4.75	1.1	800 236-8554
Marshall Government Income Inv	Govt-Mtg	5.4	7.79	5.74	2	2	0	0.86	800 236-8554
Marshall Intermediate Bond Adv	Dvsfd Bond	9.6	8.26	6.04	3	2	4.75	0.72	800 236-8554
Marshall Intermediate Bond Inv	Dvsfd Bond	9.9	8.5	6.34	2	2	0	0.72	800 236-8554
Marshall Intermediate Tax Free Inv	Muni Natl	9.3	8.36	5.57	2	3	0	0.62	800 236-8554
Marshall Short-Term Income Adv	Corp-Inv	5.6					0	0.79	800 236-8554
Marshall Short-Term Income Inv	Corp-Inv	5.8	6.59	5.45	3	1	0	0.56	800 236-8554
Mason Street High Yield Bd A	Corp-HY	5.8	3.08	-0.2	5	5	4.75	1.3	888 627-6678
Mason Street High Yield Bd B	Corp-HY	5.2	2.52	-0.78	5	5	0	1.95	888 627-6678
Mason Street Muni Bond A	Muni Natl	10.6	9.88	6.63	2	3	4.75	0.85	888 627-6678
Mason Street Muni Bond B	Muni Natl	9.9	9.3	6.3	2	3	0	1.5	888 627-6678

Bond Fund Name	Objective	Annualized Return for			Rank		Max Load	Expense Ratio	Toll-Free/(Toll) Telephone
		1 Year	3 Years	5 Years	Overall	Risk			
Mason Street Select Bond A	Dvsfd Bond	10.3	8.74	6.41	2	3	4.75	0.85	888 627-6678
Mason Street Select Bond B	Dvsfd Bond	10.3	8.5	6.17	3	3	0	1.5	888 627-6678
MassMutual Blue Chip Growth A	Govt-Mtg						0		800 542-6767
MassMutual Blue Chip Growth N	Govt-Mtg						0		800 542-6767
MassMutual Blue Chip Growth Y	Govt-Mtg						0		800 542-6767
MassMutual Core Bond Fund N	Dvsfd Bond						0		800 542-6767
MassMutual Inst-Core Bond S	Dvsfd Bond	11	10.16	7.01	2	2	0	0.59	800 542-6767
MassMutual Inst-Short-Term Bd S	Dvsfd Bond	9.5	7.51	6.24	2	2	0	0.54	800 542-6767
MassMutual Large Cap Growth Y	Govt-Mtg						0		800 542-6767
MassMutual Value Equity L	Govt-Mtg						0		800 542-6767
McMorgan Fixed Income NL	Dvsfd Bond	14.2	11.42	7.21		4	0	0.5	800 788-9485
McMorgan Fixed Income Z	Dvsfd Bond	13.8					0	0.75	800 788-9485
McMorgan Interm Fixed Income	Dvsfd Bond	10.2	9.98	7.01	3	3	0	0.5	800 788-9485
Mellon Bond Inv	Dvsfd Bond	8.6					0		800 499-3327
Mellon Bond M	Dvsfd Bond	8.8					0		800 499-3327
Mellon Intermediate Bond M	Dvsfd Bond	15.6					0		800 499-3327
Mellon National Interm Muni Bd M	Dvsfd Bond	4.6					0		800 499-3327
Mellon National Sh-Trm Muni Bd M	Muni Natl	1.8					0		800 499-3327
Mellon Penn Interm Muni Bond M	Muni Natl	4.3					0		800 499-3327
Mellon Sh-Trm U.S. Gov Securities M	Dvsfd Bond	4.2					0		800 499-3327
Members Bond A	Corp-Inv	9.2	8.8	6.45	2	2	4.75	0.9	800 877-6089
Members Bond B	Corp-Inv	8.5	7.96	5.59	3	2	0	1.65	800 877-6089
Members High Income A	Corp-HY	8.7	2.85	1.9	4	5	4.75	1	800 877-6089
Members High Income B	Corp-HY	7.9	2.12	1.19	5	5	0	1.75	800 877-6089
Mercury Low Duration I	Corp-Inv	5.5	6.5	5.44	3	1	3	0.57	866 637-2879
Merrill Lynch Aggregate Bd Idx A	Dvsfd Bond	11.1	9.52	6.41	2	2	0	0.6	800 637-3863
Merrill Lynch Aggregate Bd Idx I	Dvsfd Bond	11.2	9.73	6.61	2	2	0	0.35	800 637-3863
Merrill Lynch Bond Fund High Inc A	Corp-HY	9.7	2.41	-0.02	5	5	4	0.86	800 637-3863
Merrill Lynch Bond Fund High Inc B	Corp-HY	9.1	1.81	-0.55	5	5	0	1.37	800 637-3863
Merrill Lynch Bond Fund High Inc C	Corp-HY	9	1.82	-0.57	5	5	0	1.43	800 637-3863
Merrill Lynch Bond Fund High Inc I	Corp-HY	10.1	2.64	0.23	5	5	4	0.6	800 637-3863
Merrill Lynch Bond Fund Interm A	Corp-Inv	11.2	10.02	4.2	3	2	1	0.94	800 637-3863
Merrill Lynch Bond Fund Interm B	Corp-Inv	10.6	9.48	6.16	3	2	0	1.35	800 637-3863
Merrill Lynch Bond Fund Interm C	Corp-Inv	10.6	9.58	3.93	3	2	0	1.36	800 637-3863
Merrill Lynch Bond Fund Interm I	Corp-Inv	11.4	10.17	6.79	1	2	1	0.83	800 637-3863
Merrill Lynch CA Insured Muni A	Muni CA	9.9	9.46	3.2	3	4	4	0.84	800 637-3863
Merrill Lynch CA Insured Muni B	Muni CA	9.4	9.01	5.29	3	4	0	1.25	800 637-3863
Merrill Lynch CA Insured Muni C	Muni CA	9.3	8.91	2.89	4	4	0	1.35	800 637-3863
Merrill Lynch CA Insured Muni I	Muni CA	9.9	9.6	5.83	3	4	4	0.75	800 637-3863
Merrill Lynch Core Bond A	Corp-Inv	11.1	10.25	6.25	3	3	4	0.86	800 637-3863
Merrill Lynch Core Bond B	Corp-Inv	10.5	9.64	5.69	3	3	0	1.38	800 637-3863
Merrill Lynch Core Bond C	Corp-Inv	10.5	9.6	5.65	3	3	0	1.44	800 637-3863
Merrill Lynch Core Bond I	Corp-Inv	11.3	10.47	6.49	2	3	4	0.6	800 637-3863
Merrill Lynch Core Bond R	Corp-Inv						0		800 637-3863
Merrill Lynch FL Muni A	Muni State	9.7	9.11	3.31	2	3	4	0.86	800 637-3863
Merrill Lynch FL Muni B	Muni State	9.2	8.66	4.82	2	3	0	1.26	800 637-3863
Merrill Lynch FL Muni C	Muni State	9.1	8.58	3	2	3	0	1.36	800 637-3863
Merrill Lynch FL Muni I	Muni State	9.8	9.22	5.36	1	3	4	0.76	800 637-3863
Merrill Lynch Low Duration R	Dvsfd Bond						0		800 637-3863
Merrill Lynch Muni Insd A	Muni Natl	10.7	9.76	5.69	2	3	4	0.7	800 637-3863
Merrill Lynch Muni Insd B	Muni Natl	10.1	9.25	5.17	2	3	0	1.21	800 637-3863
Merrill Lynch Muni Insd C	Muni Natl	10.1	9.15	5.09	3	3	0	1.26	800 637-3863
Merrill Lynch Muni Insd I	Muni Natl	10.9	10.01	5.94	2	3	4	0.45	800 637-3863
Merrill Lynch Muni Interm-Trm A	Muni Natl	9.7	8.85	3.7	4	4	1	1.01	800 637-3863
Merrill Lynch Muni Interm-Trm B	Muni Natl	9.4	8.52	5.55	3	4	0	1.22	800 637-3863
Merrill Lynch Muni Interm-Trm C	Muni Natl	9.5	8.65	3.56	4	4	0	1.22	800 637-3863
Merrill Lynch Muni Interm-Trm I	Muni Natl	9.9	8.94	5.91	3	4	1	0.9	800 637-3863
Merrill Lynch Muni Ltd Mat A	Muni Natl	3.2	4.54	2.41	4	1	1	0.5	800 637-3863

Bond Fund Name	Objective	Annualized Return for			Rank		Max Load	Expense Ratio	Toll-Free/(Toll) Telephone
		1 Year	3 Years	5 Years	Overall	Risk			
Merrill Lynch Muni Ltd Mat B	Muni Natl	2.9	4.25	3.6	3	1	0	0.76	800 637-3863
Merrill Lynch Muni Ltd Mat C	Muni Natl	2.9	4.21	2.24	4	1	0	0.76	800 637-3863
Merrill Lynch Muni Ltd Mat I	Muni Natl	3.2	4.62	3.97	3	1	1	0.4	800 637-3863
Merrill Lynch Muni Natl A	Muni Natl	9.4	9.33	5.28	2	3	4	0.83	800 637-3863
Merrill Lynch Muni Natl B	Muni Natl	9.1	8.86	4.79	3	3	0	1.34	800 637-3863
Merrill Lynch Muni Natl C	Muni Natl	9	8.82	4.74	3	3	0	1.39	800 637-3863
Merrill Lynch Muni Natl I	Muni Natl	9.9	9.72	5.58	1	3	4	0.57	800 637-3863
Merrill Lynch NJ Muni A	Muni State	7.9	8.73	1.83	4	3	4	0.9	800 637-3863
Merrill Lynch NJ Muni B	Muni State	7.4	8.43	4.16	5	4	0	1.3	800 637-3863
Merrill Lynch NJ Muni C	Muni State	7.4	8.17	1.52	5	3	0	1.4	800 637-3863
Merrill Lynch NJ Muni I	Muni State	7.9	8.99	4.7	4	3	4	0.79	800 637-3863
Merrill Lynch NY Muni A	Muni NY	8.1	9.18	2.35	4	4	4	0.69	800 637-3863
Merrill Lynch NY Muni B	Muni NY	7.6	8.71	4.45	5	4	0	0.59	800 637-3863
Merrill Lynch NY Muni C	Muni NY	7.6	8.63	2.04	5	4	0	1.19	800 637-3863
Merrill Lynch NY Muni I	Muni NY	8.1	9.27	4.99	4	4	4	0.58	800 637-3863
Merrill Lynch PA Muni A	Muni State	9.9	9.16	3.04	3	3	4	0.95	800 637-3863
Merrill Lynch PA Muni B	Muni State	9.4	8.69	5.09	3	3	0	1.35	800 637-3863
Merrill Lynch PA Muni C	Muni State	9.2	8.58	2.7	3	3	0	1.45	800 637-3863
Merrill Lynch PA Muni I	Muni State	9.9	9.24	5.62	2	3	4	0.84	800 637-3863
Merrill Lynch Short-Term US Govt A	Govt-Mtg	4.2	5.7	5.16	3	1	4	1.17	800 637-3863
Merrill Lynch Short-Term US Govt B	Govt-Mtg	3.9	5.32	4.73	3	1	0	1.7	800 637-3863
Merrill Lynch Short-Term US Govt C	Govt-Mtg	3.9	5.32	2.85	4	1	0	1.73	800 637-3863
Merrill Lynch Short-Term US Govt I	Govt-Mtg	4.2	5.82	3.16	3	1	4	0.92	800 637-3863
Merrill Lynch U.S. Govt Mortgage A	Govt-Mtg	6.3	8.88	6.41	2	2	4	1	800 637-3863
Merrill Lynch U.S. Govt Mortgage B	Govt-Mtg	5.8	8.3	5.86	3	2	0	1.52	800 637-3863
Merrill Lynch U.S. Govt Mortgage C	Govt-Mtg	5.7	8.23	5.79	3	2	0	1.57	800 637-3863
Merrill Lynch U.S. Govt Mortgage I	Govt-Mtg	6.5	9.11	6.66	2	2	4	0.75	800 637-3863
Merrill Lynch U.S. Govt Mortgage R	Govt-Mtg						0		800 637-3863
Merrill Lynch U.S. High Yield R	Dvsfd Bond						0		800 637-3863
Merrill Lynch World Income A	Intl Bond	16.5	7.69	-2.64	4	5	4	1.18	800 637-3863
Merrill Lynch World Income B	Intl Bond	15.8	7.17	0.28	4	5	0	1.71	800 637-3863
Merrill Lynch World Income C	Intl Bond	15.6	7.05	-3	4	5	0	1.76	800 637-3863
Merrill Lynch World Income I	Intl Bond	16.4	7.87	1.01	4	5	4	0.93	800 637-3863
Merriman High Yield Fund	Corp-HY	11.5	4.16	4.83	4	4	0	1.87	800 423-4893
Metropolitan West Low Dur Bd Fd	Dvsfd Bond	1.5	2.5	3.87	4	2	0	0.58	800 441-6580
Metropolitan West Tot Ret Bd Fd	Dvsfd Bond	4.8	5.26	5.32	3	4	0	0.65	800 441-6580
Monetta Intermediate Bond Fund	Corp-Inv	11.9	8.93	6.65	3	3	0	0.76	800 666-3882
Montana Tax Free Fund B	Muni State	-1.6	4.04	2.35	4	2	0	1.3	800 276-1212
Monterey PIA Short-Term Govt	Government	2.9	5.63	5.2	3	1	1.25	0.33	800 628-9403
Montgomery Sh Dur Govt Bond R	Government	5.4	7.04	6	3	1	0	0.6	800 572-3863
Montgomery Total Return Bond Fund A	Dvsfd Bond	6.9					4.5	0.9	800 572-3863
Montgomery Total Return Bond Fund B	Dvsfd Bond	6.8					0	1.65	800 572-3863
Montgomery Total Return Bond Fund C	Dvsfd Bond	6.8					0	1.65	800 572-3863
Montgomery Total Return Bond Fund R	Dvsfd Bond	6.7	9.16	6.88	3	3	0	0.7	800 572-3863
Morgan Stanley CA T/F Income A	Muni CA	9.6	8.67	5.45	3	4	4.25	0.8	800 869-6397
Morgan Stanley CA T/F Income B	Muni CA	9.5	8.52	5.34	4	4	0		800 869-6397
Morgan Stanley CA T/F Income C	Muni CA	8.9	8.08	4.92	5	4	0	1.34	800 869-6397
Morgan Stanley CA T/F Income D	Muni CA	9.8	8.91	5.73	3	4	0	0.59	800 869-6397
Morgan Stanley Federal Sec Tr A	Government	7	8.48	6.13	3	3	4.25	0.91	800 869-6397
Morgan Stanley Federal Sec Tr B	Government	6	7.66	5.16	4	3	0	1.56	800 869-6397
Morgan Stanley Federal Sec Tr C	Government	6.1	7.62	5.17	4	3	0	1.56	800 869-6397
Morgan Stanley Federal Sec Tr D	Government	7	8.52	6.08	3	3	0	0.71	800 869-6397
Morgan Stanley Flex Inc Tr B	Dvsfd Bond	12.8	0.88	-0.56	5	4	0	1.42	800 869-6397
Morgan Stanley Flexable Inc Tr A	Dvsfd Bond	13.4	1.54	0.07	4	4	4.25	0.78	800 869-6397
Morgan Stanley Flexable Inc Tr C	Dvsfd Bond	12.7	0.9	-0.56	5	4	0	1.37	800 869-6397
Morgan Stanley Flexable Inc Tr D	Dvsfd Bond	13.8	1.76	0.34	4	4	0	0.58	800 869-6397
Morgan Stanley Hawaii Muni Trust	Muni State	9.8	9.55	5.57	3	3	3	1.85	800 869-6397
Morgan Stanley High Yield Sec A	Corp-HY	1.8	-17.35	-12.6	5	5	4.25	0.77	800 869-6397

Bond Fund Name	Objective	Annualized Return for			Rank		Max Load	Expense Ratio	Toll-Free/(Toll) Telephone
		1 Year	3 Years	5 Years	Overall	Risk			
Morgan Stanley High Yield Sec B	Corp-HY	1.2	-17.82	-13.1	4	5	0	1.37	800 869-6397
Morgan Stanley High Yield Sec C	Corp-HY	1.7	-17.78	-13.14	4	5	0	1.47	800 869-6397
Morgan Stanley High Yield Sec D	Corp-HY	2	-17.12	-12.4	5	5	0	0.62	800 869-6397
Morgan Stanley Limited Duration Fd	Corp-Inv	3.3	6.12	5.33	3	1	0	0.92	800 869-6397
Morgan Stanley Ltd Dur US Tres Trst	Government	3.4	5.82	4.95	3	1	0	0.7	800 869-6397
Morgan Stanley Ltd Trm Muni Tr	Muni Natl	10	8.33	5.57	2	3	0	0.88	800 869-6397
Morgan Stanley Multi-St Muni AZ	Muni State	10.1	8.52	5.46	3	3	4	0.71	800 869-6397
Morgan Stanley Multi-St Muni FL	Muni State	10.4	8.75	5.54	3	3	4	0.65	800 869-6397
Morgan Stanley Multi-St Muni NJ	Muni State	9.1	8.46	5.37	2	3	4	0.69	800 869-6397
Morgan Stanley Multi-St Muni PA	Muni State	9.1	8.8	5.45	1	3	4	0.68	800 869-6397
Morgan Stanley NY Tax Free Inc A	Muni NY	10.6	9.52	5.71	1	3	4.25	0.94	800 869-6397
Morgan Stanley NY Tax Free Inc B	Muni NY	9.5	8.76	5.03	3	3	0	1.46	800 869-6397
Morgan Stanley NY Tax Free Inc C	Muni NY	9.7	8.83	5.05	3	3	0	1.46	800 869-6397
Morgan Stanley NY Tax Free Inc D	Muni NY	10.4	9.52	5.78	2	3	0	0.71	800 869-6397
Morgan Stanley Prime Inc Trust	Govt-Mtg	2.5					0	1.29	800 869-6397
Morgan Stanley Quality Inc Tr A	Corp-Inv	8.1	8.56	5.45	3	2	4.25	1.21	800 869-6397
Morgan Stanley Quality Inc Tr B	Corp-Inv	7.7	7.58	4.62	4	2	0	1.84	800 869-6397
Morgan Stanley Quality Inc Tr C	Corp-Inv	7.7	7.61	4.65	3	2	0	1.84	800 869-6397
Morgan Stanley Quality Inc Tr D	Corp-Inv	8.5	8.38	5.45	3	2	0	0.99	800 869-6397
Morgan Stanley T/E Sec Trust A	Muni Natl	10.2	8.73	5.66	2	3	4.25	0.72	800 869-6397
Morgan Stanley T/E Sec Trust B	Muni Natl	9.7	8.27	5.23	3	3	0	1.11	800 869-6397
Morgan Stanley T/E Sec Trust C	Muni Natl	9.6	8.16	5.12	3	3	0	1.21	800 869-6397
Morgan Stanley T/E Sec Trust D	Muni Natl	10.3	9.24	6.04	1	3	0	0.51	800 869-6397
Morgan Stanley US Govt Sec Tr A	Govt-Mtg	9.8	9.41	6.91	3	3	4.25	0.73	800 869-6397
Morgan Stanley US Govt Sec Tr B	Govt-Mtg	9.5	9.21	6.67	3	3	0	1.29	800 869-6397
Morgan Stanley US Govt Sec Tr C	Govt-Mtg	9.2	8.83	6.34	3	3	0	1.29	800 869-6397
Morgan Stanley US Govt Sec Tr D	Govt-Mtg	10	9.66	7.08	3	3	0	0.54	800 869-6397
Mosaic Government Fd	Government	7.3	8.69	6.16	3	2	0	1.15	800 336-3063
Mosaic Intermediate Income Fd	Dvsfd Bond	7.8	8.88	4.7	3	2	0	1.08	800 336-3063
Mosaic Tax Free National Fd	Muni Natl	10.8	9.25	5.76	3	4	0	1.07	800 336-3063
Mosaic Tax Free Tr-AZ	Muni State	9.2	8.61	5.21	3	3	0	1.11	800 336-3063
Mosaic Tax Free Tr-MO	Muni State	9.6	8.89	5.38	4	4	0	1.09	800 336-3063
Mosaic Tax Free Tr-VA	Muni State	9.8	9.02	5.37	3	3	0	1.02	800 336-3063
Munder Bond A	Corp-Inv	11.7	9.24	6.04	4	3	4	0.95	800 438-5789
Munder Bond B	Corp-Inv	10.7	8.41	5.32	4	3	0	1.7	800 438-5789
Munder Bond C	Corp-Inv	10.8	8.41	5.25	4	3	0	1.7	800 438-5789
Munder Bond K	Corp-Inv	11.6	9.27	6.07	3	3	0	1.05	800 438-5789
Munder Bond Y	Corp-Inv	11.8	9.55	6.33	3	3	0	0.8	800 438-5789
Munder Intermediate Bond A	Corp-Inv	10	8.75	6.33	3	2	4	0.94	800 438-5789
Munder Intermediate Bond B	Corp-Inv	9.2	8.16	5.63	3	2	0	1.69	800 438-5789
Munder Intermediate Bond C	Corp-Inv	9.1	8.3	5.69	4	2	0	1.69	800 438-5789
Munder Intermediate Bond K	Corp-Inv	10	8.98	6.42	3	2	0	0.97	800 438-5789
Munder Intermediate Bond Y	Corp-Inv	10.3	9.27	6.71	2	2	0	0.71	800 438-5789
Munder International Bond Fund A	Intl Bond	29.6	9.75		3	5	4	1.14	800 438-5789
Munder International Bond Fund B	Intl Bond	28.4	8.93	5.41	3	5	0	1.89	800 438-5789
Munder International Bond Fund K	Intl Bond	28.5	9.52	6.08	3	5	0	1.25	800 438-5789
Munder International Bond Fund Y	Intl Bond	29.3	9.91	6.4	3	5	0	0.89	800 438-5789
Munder MI Tax-Free Bond A	Muni State	10.8	9.66	5.82	2	4	4	1.17	800 438-5789
Munder MI Tax-Free Bond B	Muni State	9.8	8.8	5.08	4	4	0	1.92	800 438-5789
Munder MI Tax-Free Bond C	Muni State	9.8	8.73	5.03	4	4	0	1.92	800 438-5789
Munder MI Tax-Free Bond K	Muni State	10.8	9.61	5.82	2	4	0	1.17	800 438-5789
Munder MI Tax-Free Bond Y	Muni State	10.9	9.89	6.11	2	4	0	0.92	800 438-5789
Munder Tax Free Bond A	Muni Natl	10.6	9.38	5.95	3	4	4	1.14	800 438-5789
Munder Tax Free Bond B	Muni Natl	9.8	8.55	4.94	4	4	0	1.89	800 438-5789
Munder Tax Free Bond K	Muni Natl	10.5	9.38	5.7	3	4	0	1.14	800 438-5789
Munder Tax Free Bond Y	Muni Natl	10.8	9.61	5.96	3	4	0	0.89	800 438-5789
Munder Tax-Free Short Int Bond A	Muni Natl	6.6	6.79	4.78	3	2	4	1.01	800 438-5789
Munder Tax-Free Short Int Bond B	Muni Natl	5.8	6	4.17	4	2	0	1.76	800 438-5789

463

Bond Fund Name	Objective	Annualized Return for			Rank		Max Load	Expense Ratio	Toll-Free/(Toll) Telephone
		1 Year	3 Years	5 Years	Overall	Risk			
Munder Tax-Free Short Int Bond K	Muni Natl	6.6	6.75	4.78	3	2	0	1.01	800 438-5789
Munder Tax-Free Short Int Bond Y	Muni Natl	6.8	7.05	5.05	3	2	0	0.76	800 438-5789
Munder US Government Income A	Government	9.5	10.14	6.91	3	3	4	0.94	800 438-5789
Munder US Government Income B	Government	8.6	9.33	6.33	4	3	0	1.69	800 438-5789
Munder US Government Income C	Government	8.7	9.38	6.33	4	3	0	1.69	800 438-5789
Munder US Government Income K	Government	9.4	10.16	6.91	3	3	0	1.01	800 438-5789
Munder US Government Income Y	Government	9.8	10.43	7.17	3	3	0	0.69	800 438-5789
ND Tax-Free Fund B	Muni State	-2.1	3.56	2.39	4	2	0	1.3	800 276-1212
Nations Bond Inv A	Dvsfd Bond	9.6	9.48	6.36	3	2	3.25	0.92	800 321-7854
Nations Bond Inv B	Dvsfd Bond	8.8	8.66	5.57	4	2	0	1.67	800 321-7854
Nations Bond Inv C	Dvsfd Bond	8.8	8.66	5.55	4	2	0	1.67	800 321-7854
Nations Bond Pr A	Dvsfd Bond	10	9.77	6.62	3	2	0	0.67	800 321-7854
Nations CA Muni Bond Inv A	Muni CA	9.8	8.5	5.54	3	3	4.75	0.85	800 321-7854
Nations CA Muni Bond Inv C	Muni CA	9	7.79		4	3	0	1.6	800 321-7854
Nations FL Interm Muni Inv A	Muni State	7.3	7.16	4.86	3	2	3.25	0.75	800 321-7854
Nations FL Interm Muni Inv B	Muni State	6.5	.6.34	4.16	4	2	0	1.5	800 321-7854
Nations FL Interm Muni Inv C	Muni State	6.5	6.29	4.13	4	2	0	1.5	800 321-7854
Nations FL Interm Muni Pr A	Muni State	7.5	7.38	5.12	3	2	0	0.5	800 321-7854
Nations FL Muni Bond Inv A	Muni State	9.8	9.11	5.82	1	3	4.75	0.85	800 321-7854
Nations FL Muni Bond Inv B	Muni State	9	8.31	4.98	3	3	0	1.6	800 321-7854
Nations FL Muni Bond Inv C	Muni State	8.9	8.23	4.91	4	3	0	1.6	800 321-7854
Nations FL Muni Bond Pr A	Muni State	10.1	9.39	5.98	1	3	0	0.6	800 321-7854
Nations GA Interm Muni Inv A	Muni State	6.9	7.2	4.88	3	2	3.25	0.75	800 321-7854
Nations GA Interm Muni Inv B	Muni State	6.1	6.45	4.2	4	2	0	1.5	800 321-7854
Nations GA Interm Muni Inv C	Muni State	6.1	6.4	4.11	4	2	0	1.5	800 321-7854
Nations GA Interm Muni Pr A	Muni State	7.2	7.48	5.04	3	2	0	0.5	800 321-7854
Nations Government Secs Inv A	Government	12.5	10.32	6.83	3	3	4.75	0.97	800 321-7854
Nations Government Secs Inv B	Government	11.7	9.52	6.12	3	3	0	1.72	800 321-7854
Nations Government Secs Inv C	Government	11.6	9.57	6.04	3	4	0	1.72	800 321-7854
Nations Government Secs Pr A	Government	12.8	10.61	7.12	3	3	0	0.72	800 321-7854
Nations High Yield Bond Inv A	Corp-HY	12.9	8.16		3	5	4.75	1.17	800 321-7854
Nations High Yield Bond Inv B	Corp-HY	11.9	7.37		3	5	0	1.92	800 321-7854
Nations High Yield Bond Inv C	Corp-HY	11.9	7.28		3	5	0	1.92	800 321-7854
Nations High Yield Bond Pr A	Corp-HY	13.1	8.5		3	5	0	0.92	800 321-7854
Nations Interm Bond A	Muni Natl	10.2	9.27	6.41	1	2	3.25	0.96	800 321-7854
Nations Interm Bond B	Muni Natl	9.5	8.46		2	2	0	1.71	800 321-7854
Nations Interm Bond C	Muni Natl	9.4	10.75	7.13	3	4	0	1.71	800 321-7854
Nations Interm Bond Pr A	Muni Natl	12.6	10.21		1	3	0	0.71	800 321-7854
Nations Interm Muni Inv A	Muni Natl	8.3	7.62	5.08	3	2	3.25	0.75	800 321-7854
Nations Interm Muni Inv B	Muni Natl	7.5	6.82	4.34	4	2	0	1.5	800 321-7854
Nations Interm Muni Inv C	Muni Natl	7.5	6.78	4.33	4	2	0	1.5	800 321-7854
Nations Interm Muni Pr A	Muni Natl	8.7	7.91	5.36	3	2	0	0.5	800 321-7854
Nations KS Muni Inc Inv A	Muni Natl	7.1					4.75	0.85	800 321-7854
Nations KS Muni Inc Inv B	Muni Natl	6.3					0	1.6	800 321-7854
Nations KS Muni Inc Inv C	Muni Natl	5.5					0		800 321-7854
Nations KS Muni Inc Pr A	Muni Natl	7.3					0	0.6	800 321-7854
Nations MD Interm Muni Inv A	Muni State	7.9	7.46	5.12	3	2	3.25	0.75	800 321-7854
Nations MD Interm Muni Inv B	Muni State	7	6.67	4.37	4	2	0	1.5	800 321-7854
Nations MD Interm Muni Inv C	Muni State	7	6.66	4.34	4	2	0	1.5	800 321-7854
Nations MD Interm Muni Pr A	Muni State	8	7.74	5.34	3	2	0	0.5	800 321-7854
Nations Muni Income Fd Inv A	Muni Natl	7.9	7.57	4.58	4	3	4.75	0.85	800 321-7854
Nations Muni Income Fd Inv B	Muni Natl	7	6.76	3.83	5	3	0	1.6	800 321-7854
Nations Muni Income Fd Inv C	Muni Natl	7	6.76	3.83	5	3	0	1.6	800 321-7854
Nations Muni Income Fd Pr A	Muni Natl	8.1	7.83	4.83	4	3	0	0.6	800 321-7854
Nations NC Interm Muni Inv A	Muni State	8.4	7.66	5.09	3	2	3.25	0.75	800 321-7854
Nations NC Interm Muni Inv B	Muni State	7.6	6.83	4.33	4	2	0	1.5	800 321-7854
Nations NC Interm Muni Inv C	Muni State	7.6	6.86	4.33	4	2	0	1.5	800 321-7854
Nations NC Interm Muni Pr A	Muni State	8.7	7.9	5.33	2	2	0	0.5	800 321-7854

Bond Fund Name	Objective	Annualized Return for			Rank		Max Load	Expense Ratio	Toll-Free/(Toll) Telephone
		1 Year	3 Years	5 Years	Overall	Risk			
Nations SC Intermed Muni Inv A	Muni State	7.5	7.45	5.04	3	2	3.25	0.75	800 321-7854
Nations SC Intermed Muni Inv B	Muni State	6.7	6.66	4.29	4	2	0	1.5	800 321-7854
Nations SC Intermed Muni Inv C	Muni State	6.7	6.67	4.29	4	2	0	1.5	800 321-7854
Nations SC Intermed Muni Pr A	Muni State	7.8	7.71	5.28	3	2	0	0.5	800 321-7854
Nations Sh-Interm Govt Inv A	Government	9.4	9.17	6.48	2	2	3.25	0.89	800 321-7854
Nations Sh-Interm Govt Inv B	Government	8.6	8.44	5.76	3	2	0	1.64	800 321-7854
Nations Sh-Interm Govt Inv C	Government	8.6	8.46	5.75	3	2	0	1.64	800 321-7854
Nations Sh-Interm Govt Pr A	Government	9.7	9.52	6.76	2	2	0	0.64	800 321-7854
Nations Sh-Interm Govt Pr B	Government	9.4	8.99	4.16	3	2	0	1.14	800 321-7854
Nations Sh-Term Inc Inv A	Corp-Inv	5	6.8	5.62	3	1	1	0.75	800 321-7854
Nations Sh-Term Inc Inv B	Corp-Inv	4.2	5.98	5	3	1	0	1.5	800 321-7854
Nations Sh-Term Inc Inv C	Corp-Inv	4.2	5.98	4.9	3	1	0	1.5	800 321-7854
Nations Sh-Term Inc Pr A	Corp-Inv	5.2	7	5.83	3	1	0	0.5	800 321-7854
Nations Sh-Term Muni Inc Inv A	Muni Natl	4.6	5.11	4.37	3	1	1	0.65	800 321-7854
Nations Sh-Term Muni Inc Inv B	Muni Natl	3.8	4.33	3.79	2	1	0	1.4	800 321-7854
Nations Sh-Term Muni Inc Inv C	Muni Natl	3.8	4.34	3.68	2	1	0	1.4	800 321-7854
Nations Sh-Term Muni Inc Pr A	Muni Natl	4.8	5.37	4.62	3	1	0	0.4	800 321-7854
Nations Strategic Inc Fd Inv A	Dvsfd Bond	9.8	8.93	5.21	3	2	4.75	1.08	800 321-7854
Nations Strategic Inc Fd Inv B	Dvsfd Bond	9	8.11	4.49	4	2	0	1.83	800 321-7854
Nations Strategic Inc Fd Inv C	Dvsfd Bond	9	8.13	4.45	4	2	0	1.83	800 321-7854
Nations Strategic Inc Fd Pr A	Dvsfd Bond	10.1	9.19	5.49	3	2	0	0.83	800 321-7854
Nations TN Interm Muni Inv A	Muni State	8.2	7.96	5.24	3	2	3.25	0.75	800 321-7854
Nations TN Interm Muni Inv B	Muni State	7.4	7.16	4.5	4	2	0	1.5	800 321-7854
Nations TN Interm Muni Inv C	Muni State	7.3	7.12	4.45	4	2	0	1.5	800 321-7854
Nations TN Interm Muni Pr A	Muni State	8.5	8.24	5.58	2	2	0	0.5	800 321-7854
Nations TX Interm Muni Inv A	Muni State	8.7	7.7	5.2	3	2	3.25	0.75	800 321-7854
Nations TX Interm Muni Inv B	Muni State	7.9	6.91	4.46	3	2	0	1.5	800 321-7854
Nations TX Interm Muni Inv C	Muni State	7.9	6.87	4.41	3	2	0	1.5	800 321-7854
Nations TX Interm Muni Pr A	Muni State	9	7.98	5.45	2	2	0	0.5	800 321-7854
Nations VA Interm Muni Inv A	Muni State	8.1	7.7	5.23	3	2	3.25	0.75	800 321-7854
Nations VA Interm Muni Inv B	Muni State	7.3	6.88	4.48	4	2	0	1.5	800 321-7854
Nations VA Interm Muni Inv C	Muni State	7.3	6.88	4.45	4	2	0	1.5	800 321-7854
Nations VA Interm Muni Pr A	Muni State	8.4	7.95	5.48	2	2	0	0.5	800 321-7854
Nationwide Bond Index A	Dvsfd Bond	10.8	10		3	5	5.75	0.71	800 848-0920
Nationwide Bond Index Inst	Dvsfd Bond	11.3	10.5		1	3	0	0.31	800 848-0920
Nebraska Municipal Fund	Muni State	1.6	5.91		3	2	4.25	0.95	800 276-1262
Neuberger Berman High Income Bond	Corp-HY	7.6	7.82	5.54	4	3	0	1.25	877 461-1899
Neuberger Berman Ltd Mat Bd Inv	Corp-Inv	5.4	6.95	5.08	3	1	0	0.69	877 461-1899
Neuberger Berman Ltd Mat Bd Tr	Corp-Inv	5.2	6.83	4.98	3	1	0	0.8	877 461-1899
Neuberger Berman Muni Sec	Muni Natl	10	8.76	5.79	2	3	0	0.65	877 461-1899
New Covenant Income	Dvsfd Bond	10.8	10.23	6.54		2	0	0.82	800 858-6127
Nicholas Income Fund	Corp-HY	-4.1	0.56	-1.34	5	5	0	0.56	800 227-5987
Nicholas-Applegate High Yld Bond I	Corp-HY	9.9	4.12	3.75	4	5	0	0.79	800 551-8043
North Carolina Tax Free Bond	Muni State	9.4	9.09	5.45	2	3	0	0.85	800 543-8721
North Track Government A	Government	6.4	7.66	5.74	3	2	3.5	1.33	800 826-4600
North Track Government C	Government	5.6	6.9		1	2	0	2.08	800 826-4600
North Track Tax Exempt A	Muni Natl	11	9.52	4.71	3	4	3.5	1.31	800 826-4600
North Track WI Tax Exempt A	Muni State	9.8	8.82	5.16	2	3	3.5	1	800 826-4600
North Track WI Tax Exempt B	Muni State						0	1.72	800 826-4600
North Track WI Tax Exempt C	Muni State						0	1.73	800 826-4600
Northeast Investors Trust	Corp-HY	-0.8	1.61	-0.11	4	5	0	0.65	800 225-6704
Northern Instl Bond A	Corp-Inv	11	9.64	6.83	3	2	0	0.35	800 637-1380
Northern Instl Bond C	Corp-Inv	10.7	9.38	6.58	3	2	0	0.6	800 637-1380
Northern Instl Bond D	Corp-Inv	10.4	9.06	6.16	3	2	0	0.75	800 637-1380
Northern Instl Core Bond A	Dvsfd Bond	10.9					0	0.36	800 637-1380
Northern Instl Core Bond C	Dvsfd Bond	10.5					0	0.6	800 637-1380
Northern Instl Core Bond D	Dvsfd Bond	10.5					0	0.75	800 637-1380
Northern Instl Int'l Bond A	Intl Bond	22	9.25	4.91	4	4	0	0.96	800 637-1380

Bond Fund Name	Objective	Annualized Return for			Rank		Max Load	Expense Ratio	Toll-Free/(Toll) Telephone
		1 Year	3 Years	5 Years	Overall	Risk			
Northern Instl Intermediate Bond A	Muni Natl	11.6	9.71	6.69	1	2	0	0.36	800 637-1380
Northern Instl Intermediate Bond D	Muni Natl	11.2	9.33		1	2	0	0.75	800 637-1380
Northern Instl Short Interm Bond A	Corp-Inv	7.3	7.49	6.28	3	1	0	0.36	800 637-1380
Northern Instl Short Interm Bond D	Corp-Inv	7	7.24	7.13	3	1	0	0.75	800 637-1380
Northern Instl US Govt Sec A	Government	7.5	8.27	6.66	2	2	0	0.36	800 637-1380
Northern Instl US Govt Sec D	Government	7.1	8.52	6.57	1	2	0	0.75	800 637-1380
Northern Instl US Treasury Index A	Government	14	10.65	7.83	3	4	0	0.26	800 637-1380
Northern Instl US Treasury Index C	Government	13.8	11.65		2	4	0	0.5	800 637-1380
Northern Instl US Treasury Index D	Government	13.6	11.13	7.86	3	4	0	0.65	800 637-1380
Northern Trust AZ Tax Exempt	Muni State	10.2	9.46		2	4	0	0.85	800 595-9111
Northern Trust CA Intermediate T/E	Muni State	8.9	7.42	4.87	3	4	0	0.85	800 595-9111
Northern Trust CA T/E Bond	Muni CA	11.3	9.91	6.38	3	4	0	0.85	800 595-9111
Northern Trust FL Interm T/E Bond	Muni State	9.2	8.06	5.54	2	3	0	0.85	800 595-9111
Northern Trust Fixed Income	Corp-Inv	10.5	9.21	6.12	2	2	0	0.9	800 595-9111
Northern Trust Global Fixed Inc	Intl Bond	19.1	9.13	5.15	3	4	0	1.15	800 595-9111
Northern Trust HY Fixed Inc Fund	Corp-HY	10.8	5.32		4	5	0	0.9	800 595-9111
Northern Trust High Yield Muni Fd	Corp-HY	8.8	8.24		3	2	0	0.85	800 595-9111
Northern Trust Intermed Tax Exempt	Muni Natl	9.6	8.51	5.67	1	3	0	0.85	800 595-9111
Northern Trust Short-Int U.S. Govt	Govt-Mtg	6.8	-12.74	-7	5	5	0	0.9	800 595-9111
Northern Trust Tax Exempt	Muni Natl	11.1	9.83	6.12	2	3	0	0.85	800 595-9111
Northern Trust US Govt	Government	9.7	9.46	6.95	2	2	0	0.9	800 595-9111
Nuveen AZ Muni Bond A	Muni State	9.2	8.8	5.19	3	3	4.2	0.92	800 752-8700
Nuveen AZ Muni Bond B	Muni State	8.4					0	1.67	800 752-8700
Nuveen AZ Muni Bond C	Muni State	8.6	8.21	4.62	5	3	0	1.47	800 752-8700
Nuveen AZ Muni Bond R	Muni State	9.4	8.94	5.37	3	3	0	0.72	800 752-8700
Nuveen All Amer Muni A	Muni Natl	8.3	8.58	4.83	4	3	4.2		800 752-8700
Nuveen All Amer Muni B	Muni Natl	7.4					0	1.56	800 752-8700
Nuveen All Amer Muni C	Muni Natl	7.6	8	4.26	5	3	0	1.36	800 752-8700
Nuveen All Amer Muni R	Muni Natl	8.5					0	0.61	800 752-8700
Nuveen CA Insd Muni Bond Fund A	Muni CA	10.5	9.05	5.61	3	4	4.2	0.85	800 752-8700
Nuveen CA Insd Muni Bond Fund B	Muni CA	9.5	8.21		4	4	0	1.6	800 752-8700
Nuveen CA Insd Muni Bond Fund C	Muni CA	9.8	8.48	5.03	4	4	0	1.4	800 752-8700
Nuveen CA Insd Muni Bond Fund R	Muni CA	10.7	9.27	5.82	3	4	0	0.65	800 752-8700
Nuveen CA Muni Bond Fund A	Muni CA	8.6	7.23	4.66	4	3	4.2	0.86	800 752-8700
Nuveen CA Muni Bond Fund B	Muni CA	7.8					0	1.61	800 752-8700
Nuveen CA Muni Bond Fund C	Muni CA	7.9	6.63	4.08	5	3	0	1.41	800 752-8700
Nuveen CA Muni Bond Fund R	Muni CA	8.7	7.37	4.83	4	3	0	0.66	800 752-8700
Nuveen CO Muni Bond A	Muni State	8.7	8.74	4.58	3	3	4.2	0.94	800 752-8700
Nuveen CO Muni Bond B	Muni State	8	7.91	3.83	4	3	0	1.69	800 752-8700
Nuveen CO Muni Bond C	Muni State	8.2	8.06	4.03	4	3	0	1.48	800 752-8700
Nuveen CO Muni Bond R	Muni State	8.9	8.98	4.8	3	3	0	0.74	800 752-8700
Nuveen CT Muni Bond A	Muni State	11.1	9.44	5.79	1	3	4.2	0.84	800 752-8700
Nuveen CT Muni Bond B	Muni State	10.2					0	1.59	800 752-8700
Nuveen CT Muni Bond C	Muni State	10.4	8.82	5.21	2	3	0	1.39	800 752-8700
Nuveen CT Muni Bond R	Muni State	11.3					0	0.64	800 752-8700
Nuveen FL Muni Bond A	Muni State	7.6	7.25	4.61	4	3	4.2		800 752-8700
Nuveen FL Muni Bond B	Muni State	6.8					0	1.59	800 752-8700
Nuveen FL Muni Bond C	Muni State	7	6.67	4.03	5	3	0	1.39	800 752-8700
Nuveen FL Muni Bond R	Muni State	7.9	7.45	4.79	4	3	0	0.64	800 752-8700
Nuveen GA Muni Bond A	Muni State	10.8	9.43	5.37	3	3	4.2	0.91	800 752-8700
Nuveen GA Muni Bond B	Muni State	9.9	8.64	4.59	3	3	0	1.66	800 752-8700
Nuveen GA Muni Bond C	Muni State	10	8.83	4.79	3	3	0	1.45	800 752-8700
Nuveen GA Muni Bond R	Muni State	11	9.66	5.61	2	3	0	0.71	800 752-8700
Nuveen High Yield Muni Bond A	Muni Natl	7.6	9.08		2	3	4.2	1.08	800 752-8700
Nuveen High Yield Muni Bond B	Muni Natl	6.8	8.35		3	3	0	1.83	800 752-8700
Nuveen High Yield Muni Bond C	Muni Natl	6.9	8.55		3	3	0	1.63	800 752-8700
Nuveen High Yield Muni Bond R	Muni Natl	7.7	9.25		2	3	0	0.87	800 752-8700
Nuveen Insured Municipal Bond A	Muni Natl	10.4	8.76	5.54	2	3	4.2	0.8	800 752-8700

Bond Fund Name	Objective	Annualized Return for			Rank		Max Load	Expense Ratio	Toll-Free/(Toll) Telephone
		1 Year	3 Years	5 Years	Overall	Risk			
Nuveen Insured Municipal Bond B	Muni Natl	9.6					0	1.55	800 752-8700
Nuveen Insured Municipal Bond C	Muni Natl	9.8	8.16	4.99	3	3	0	1.35	800 752-8700
Nuveen Insured Municipal Bond R	Muni Natl	10.6	8.91	5.74	1	3	0		800 752-8700
Nuveen Interm Duration Muni Bond A	Muni Natl	6.7	7.44	4.83	3	2	3	0.79	800 752-8700
Nuveen Interm Duration Muni Bond B	Muni Natl	5.9					0	1.54	800 752-8700
Nuveen Interm Duration Muni Bond C	Muni Natl	6.2	7.01	4.33	4	2	0	1.34	800 752-8700
Nuveen Interm Duration Muni Bond R	Muni Natl	7.1	7.65	5.03	3	2	0		800 752-8700
Nuveen KS Muni Bond A	Muni State	10	9.35	5.36	2	3	4.2	0.87	800 752-8700
Nuveen KS Muni Bond B	Muni State	9.2	8.52	4.55	3	3	0	1.62	800 752-8700
Nuveen KS Muni Bond C	Muni State	9.4	8.73	4.75	4	3	0	1.42	800 752-8700
Nuveen KS Muni Bond R	Muni State	10.3	9.57	5.55	3	3	0	0.67	800 752-8700
Nuveen KY Muni Bond A	Muni State	9	8.55	5.09	2	3	4.2	0.87	800 752-8700
Nuveen KY Muni Bond B	Muni State	8.2	7.74	4.32	4	3	0	1.62	800 752-8700
Nuveen KY Muni Bond C	Muni State	8.5	7.98	4.54	3	3	0	1.42	800 752-8700
Nuveen KY Muni Bond R	Muni State	9.2	8.77	5.29	2	3	0	0.68	800 752-8700
Nuveen LA Muni Bond A	Muni State	10.5	9.77	5.49	3	4	4.2	0.87	800 752-8700
Nuveen LA Muni Bond B	Muni State	9.8					0	1.62	800 752-8700
Nuveen LA Muni Bond C	Muni State	9.9	9.18	4.91	3	4	0	1.42	800 752-8700
Nuveen LA Muni Bond R	Muni State	11.2					0	0.67	800 752-8700
Nuveen LtdTerm Muni A	Muni Natl	7	6.98	4.8	3	2	2.5	0.7	800 752-8700
Nuveen LtdTerm Muni C	Muni Natl	6.5					0	1.04	800 752-8700
Nuveen LtdTerm Muni R	Muni Natl	7.2					0	0.5	800 752-8700
Nuveen MA Insured Muni Bond A	Muni State	10.1	8.64	5.46	3	3	4.2	0.9	800 752-8700
Nuveen MA Insured Muni Bond B	Muni State	9.2					0	1.67	800 752-8700
Nuveen MA Insured Muni Bond C	Muni State	9.5	8.06	4.9	4	3	0	1.46	800 752-8700
Nuveen MA Insured Muni Bond R	Muni State	10.2	8.85	5.66	3	3	0	0.73	800 752-8700
Nuveen MA Muni Bond Fund A	Muni State	10.2	8.52	5.29	2	3	4.2	0.93	800 752-8700
Nuveen MA Muni Bond Fund B	Muni State	9.5					0	1.68	800 752-8700
Nuveen MA Muni Bond Fund C	Muni State	9.7	7.95	4.75	3	3	0	1.48	800 752-8700
Nuveen MA Muni Bond Fund R	Muni State	10.5	8.73	5.51	1	3	0	0.73	800 752-8700
Nuveen MD Muni Bond Fund A	Muni State	10.8	9.31	5.45	2	3	4.2	0.96	800 752-8700
Nuveen MD Muni Bond Fund B	Muni State	9.8					0	1.71	800 752-8700
Nuveen MD Muni Bond Fund C	Muni State	10.1	8.67	4.87	3	3	0	1.51	800 752-8700
Nuveen MD Muni Bond Fund R	Muni State	10.9	9.46	5.62	2	3	0	0.76	800 752-8700
Nuveen MI Muni Bond A	Muni State	10.4	9.5	5.5	2	3	4.2		800 752-8700
Nuveen MI Muni Bond B	Muni State	9.6					0	1.62	800 752-8700
Nuveen MI Muni Bond C	Muni State	9.7	8.89	4.91	3	3	0	1.42	800 752-8700
Nuveen MI Muni Bond R	Muni State	10.6					0	0.67	800 752-8700
Nuveen MO Muni Bond A	Muni State	9.6	8.91	5.33	2	3	4.2	0.86	800 752-8700
Nuveen MO Muni Bond B	Muni State	8.8					0	1.61	800 752-8700
Nuveen MO Muni Bond C	Muni State	9	8.33	4.74	3	3	0	1.41	800 752-8700
Nuveen MO Muni Bond R	Muni State	9.8					0	0.66	800 752-8700
Nuveen NC Muni Bond A	Muni State	10.8	9.66	5.58	2	3	4.2	0.86	800 752-8700
Nuveen NC Muni Bond B	Muni State	10					0	1.61	800 752-8700
Nuveen NC Muni Bond C	Muni State	10.2	9.06	5	3	3	0	1.41	800 752-8700
Nuveen NC Muni Bond R	Muni State	11	10.15	5.95	1	3	0	0.65	800 752-8700
Nuveen NJ Muni Bond A	Muni State	9.1	8.99	5.63	1	3	4.2	0.87	800 752-8700
Nuveen NJ Muni Bond B	Muni State	8.2					0	1.62	800 752-8700
Nuveen NJ Muni Bond C	Muni State	8.4	8.39	5.04	4	3	0	1.44	800 752-8700
Nuveen NJ Muni Bond R	Muni State	9.2	9.14	5.79	1	3	0	0.69	800 752-8700
Nuveen NM Muni Bond A	Muni State	8.7	8.31	4.79	3	3	4.2	0.94	800 752-8700
Nuveen NM Muni Bond B	Muni State	7.9					0	1.69	800 752-8700
Nuveen NM Muni Bond C	Muni State	8.1					0	1.48	800 752-8700
Nuveen NM Muni Bond R	Muni State	8.9					0	0.74	800 752-8700
Nuveen NY Insured Muni Bond A	Muni NY	11.9	9.3	5.95	2	3	4.2	0.87	800 752-8700
Nuveen NY Insured Muni Bond B	Muni NY	11.1					0	1.62	800 752-8700
Nuveen NY Insured Muni Bond C	Muni NY	11.3	8.74	5.38	3	3	0	1.42	800 752-8700
Nuveen NY Insured Muni Bond R	Muni NY	12.2	9.51	6.16	1	3	0		800 752-8700

Bond Fund Name	Objective	Annualized Return for			Rank		Max Load	Expense Ratio	Toll-Free/(Toll) Telephone
		1 Year	3 Years	5 Years	Overall	Risk			
Nuveen NY Muni Bond A	Muni NY	10.2	8.81	5.79	2	3	4.2	0.65	800 752-8700
Nuveen NY Muni Bond B	Muni NY	9.4					0	1.41	800 752-8700
Nuveen NY Muni Bond C	Muni NY	9.6	8.25	5.24	3	3	0	1.21	800 752-8700
Nuveen NY Muni Bond R	Muni NY	10.5	9.02	6.01	1	3	0	0.46	800 752-8700
Nuveen OH Muni Bond A	Muni State	10.7	8.74	5.29	3	3	4.2		800 752-8700
Nuveen OH Muni Bond B	Muni State	9.9					0	1.61	800 752-8700
Nuveen OH Muni Bond C	Muni State	10	8.16	4.73	3	3	0	1.41	800 752-8700
Nuveen OH Muni Bond R	Muni State	10.9	8.91	5.5	2	3	0	0.66	800 752-8700
Nuveen PA Muni Bond A	Muni State	9.4	9.5	5.17	2	3	4.2	0.94	800 752-8700
Nuveen PA Muni Bond B	Muni State	8.6					0	1.67	800 752-8700
Nuveen PA Muni Bond C	Muni State	8.7	8.88	4.58	3	3	0	1.49	800 752-8700
Nuveen PA Muni Bond R	Muni State	9.5	9.64	5.34	1	3	0	0.74	800 752-8700
Nuveen TN Muni Bond A	Muni State	11.1	9.52	5.54	2	3	4.2	0.83	800 752-8700
Nuveen TN Muni Bond B	Muni State	10.3					0	1.58	800 752-8700
Nuveen TN Muni Bond C	Muni State	10.5	8.93	4.99	3	3	0	1.38	800 752-8700
Nuveen TN Muni Bond R	Muni State	11.3					0	0.63	800 752-8700
Nuveen VA Muni Bond A	Muni State	9.3	8.38	5.17	3	3	4.2	0.87	800 752-8700
Nuveen VA Muni Bond B	Muni State	8.5					0	1.62	800 752-8700
Nuveen VA Muni Bond C	Muni State	8.7	7.75	4.59	5	3	0	1.42	800 752-8700
Nuveen VA Muni Bond R	Muni State	9.5	8.52	5.37	2	3	0	0.67	800 752-8700
Nuveen WI Muni Bond A	Muni State	9.4	9.48	5.29	3	4	4.2	0.92	800 752-8700
Nuveen WI Muni Bond B	Muni State	8.5	8.64	4.48	5	4	0	1.67	800 752-8700
Nuveen WI Muni Bond C	Muni State	8.8	8.88	4.7	4	4	0	1.49	800 752-8700
Nuveen WI Muni Bond R	Muni State	9.6					0	0.72	800 752-8700
Ocean State Tax-Exempt Fund	Muni State	7.6	7.03	4.66	3	2	4		800 992-2207
Oklahoma Municipal Fund	Muni State	3.8	6.87		3	2	4.25	0.7	800 276-1262
One Group AZ Municipal Bond A	Muni State	9.5	8.3	5.08	2	3	4.5	0.84	800 480-4111
One Group AZ Municipal Bond B	Muni State	8.6	7.58	4.59	3	3	0	1.49	800 480-4111
One Group AZ Municipal Bond I	Muni State	9.7	8.52	5.54	1	3	0	0.59	800 480-4111
One Group Bond A	Dvsfd Bond	10.3	10.96	7.54	2	3	4.5	0.84	800 480-4111
One Group Bond B	Dvsfd Bond	9.6	10.11	6.79	3	3	0	1.5	800 480-4111
One Group Bond C	Dvsfd Bond	9.6	10.22		2	3	0	1.5	800 480-4111
One Group Bond I	Dvsfd Bond	10.6	11.21	7.83	2	3	0	0.6	800 480-4111
One Group Government Bond A	Government	11.1	10.59	7.12	3	3	4.5	0.86	800 480-4111
One Group Government Bond B	Government	10.4	9.84	6.45	3	3	0	1.52	800 480-4111
One Group Government Bond C	Government	10.5	9.85		2	3	0	1.52	800 480-4111
One Group Government Bond I	Government	11.4	10.85	7.41	3	3	0	0.62	800 480-4111
One Group High Yield Bond A	Corp-HY	9.6	4.95		5	5	4.5	1.14	800 480-4111
One Group High Yield Bond B	Corp-HY	8.8	4.25		5	5	0	1.79	800 480-4111
One Group High Yield Bond C	Corp-HY	8.8	4.25		5	5	0	1.79	800 480-4111
One Group High Yield Bond I	Corp-HY	9.8	5.21		5	5	0	0.89	800 480-4111
One Group Inc Bond Fund A	Corp-Inv	10.2	9.51	6.58	3	2	4.5	0.89	800 480-4111
One Group Inc Bond Fund B	Corp-Inv	9.5	8.77	5.83	3	2	0	1.54	800 480-4111
One Group Inc Bond Fund C	Corp-Inv	9.5	8.83		1	2	0	1.54	800 480-4111
One Group Inc Bond Fund I	Corp-Inv	10.4	9.76	6.8	1	3	0	0.64	800 480-4111
One Group Interm Tax Free A	Muni Natl	9.4	8.41	5.34	3	3	4.5	0.84	800 480-4111
One Group Interm Tax Free B	Muni Natl	8.7	7.71	4.69	5	3	0	1.49	800 480-4111
One Group Interm Tax Free I	Muni Natl	9.6	8.66	5.44	2	3	0	0.53	800 480-4111
One Group Intermediate Bond A	Corp-Inv	9.3	9.77	7.12	1	2	4.5	0.82	800 480-4111
One Group Intermediate Bond B	Corp-Inv	8.5	9.08	6.44	2	2	0	1.48	800 480-4111
One Group Intermediate Bond C	Corp-Inv	8.5	9.08		1	2	0	1.48	800 480-4111
One Group Intermediate Bond I	Corp-Inv	9.4	10.02	7.38	1	2	0	0.58	800 480-4111
One Group KY Municipal A	Muni State	9	7.9	5.2	3	3	4.5	0.86	800 480-4111
One Group KY Municipal B	Muni State	8.4	7.2	4.53	3	3	0	1.51	800 480-4111
One Group KY Municipal I	Muni State	9.3	8.17	5.48	2	3	0	0.61	800 480-4111
One Group LA Muni Bond A	Muni State	9.3	8.07	5.25	3	3	4.5	0.86	800 480-4111
One Group LA Muni Bond B	Muni State	8.5	7.37	4.58	3	3	0	1.51	800 480-4111
One Group LA Muni Bond I	Muni State	9.6	8.34	5.51	2	3	4.5	0.61	800 480-4111

Bond Fund Name	Objective	Annualized Return for			Rank		Max Load	Expense Ratio	Toll-Free/(Toll) Telephone
		1 Year	3 Years	5 Years	Overall	Risk			
One Group MI Muni Bond A	Muni State	9.9	8.96	5.33	2	3	4.5	0.84	800 480-4111
One Group MI Muni Bond B	Muni State	9.2	8.27	4.7	3	3	0	1.49	800 480-4111
One Group MI Muni Bond I	Muni State	10.2	9.22	5.59	1	3	0	0.6	800 480-4111
One Group Mortgage Backed Sec A	Govt-Mtg	6.5					4.5	0.4	800 480-4111
One Group Mortgage Backed Sec I	Govt-Mtg	6.6					0	0.4	800 480-4111
One Group Muni Income A	Muni Natl	7.7	7.48	4.67	3	2	4.5	0.84	800 480-4111
One Group Muni Income B	Muni Natl	7	6.79	4.08	4	2	0	1.49	800 480-4111
One Group Muni Income C	Muni Natl	7	6.78	4.08	4	2	0	1.49	800 480-4111
One Group Muni Income I	Muni Natl	8	7.75	5.03	3	2	0	0.59	800 480-4111
One Group OH Municipal A	Muni State	8.9	8.16	5.23	3	3	4.5	0.85	800 480-4111
One Group OH Municipal B	Muni State	8.1	7.44	4.48	4	3	0	1.5	800 480-4111
One Group OH Municipal I	Muni State	9.1	8.42	5.42	1	3	0	0.6	800 480-4111
One Group Short Term Bond A	Government	5.5	6.98	5.86	2	1	3	0.8	800 480-4111
One Group Short Term Bond B	Government	5.1	6.42	5.34	3	1	0	1.3	800 480-4111
One Group Short Term Bond I	Government	5.8	7.25	6.12	2	1	0	0.55	800 480-4111
One Group Short Term Muni Bond A	Muni Natl	5.4	5.48	4.3	3	1	3	0.8	800 480-4111
One Group Short Term Muni Bond B	Muni Natl	4.9	4.95	3.81	3	1	0	1.34	800 480-4111
One Group Short Term Muni Bond I	Muni Natl	5.8	5.75	4.58	3	1	0	0.55	800 480-4111
One Group Tax Free Bond A	Muni Natl	10.4	9.21	5.78	2	3	4.5	0.83	800 480-4111
One Group Tax Free Bond B	Muni Natl	9.7	8.5	5.08	3	3	0	1.48	800 480-4111
One Group Tax Free Bond I	Muni Natl	10.6	9.47	6.04	2	3	0	0.58	800 480-4111
One Group Treasury & Agency A	Government	9.3	9	6.7	2	2	3	0.65	800 480-4111
One Group Treasury & Agency B	Government	8.8	8.48	6.16	3	2	0	1.15	800 480-4111
One Group Treasury & Agency I	Government	9.6	9.26	6.96	2	2	0	0.4	800 480-4111
One Group Ultra Sh Term Bond A	Corp-Inv	3.2	5.33	5.2	3	1	3	0.65	800 480-4111
One Group Ultra Sh Term Bond B	Corp-Inv	2.8	4.87	4.62	3	1	0	1.15	800 480-4111
One Group Ultra Sh Term Bond I	Corp-Inv	3.4	5.61	5.37	3	1	0	0.4	800 480-4111
One Group WV Municipal Bond A	Muni State	9.2	8.21	5.25	3	3	4.5	0.84	800 480-4111
One Group WV Municipal Bond B	Muni State	8.4	7.53	4.58	4	3	0	1.49	800 480-4111
One Group WV Municipal Bond I	Muni State	9.4	8.48	5.54	2	3	0	0.59	800 480-4111
One Group-Short Term Bond C	Government	5	6.28	5.15		1	0	1.81	800 480-4111
One Group-Short Term Muni Bond C	Muni Natl	5	4.86	3.62		1	0	1.3	800 480-4111
One Group-Ultra Sh Term Bond C	Corp-Inv	2.8	4.71	4.42		1	0	1.15	800 480-4111
Oppenheimer AMT-Free NY Munis A	Muni NY	7	7.79	4.7	5	4	4.75	0.88	800 525-7048
Oppenheimer AMT-Free NY Munis B	Muni NY	6.2	6.96	3.89	5	4	0	1.65	800 525-7048
Oppenheimer AMT-Free NY Munis C	Muni NY	6.1	6.95	3.89	5	4	0	1.65	800 525-7048
Oppenheimer Bond A	Corp-Inv	13.7	9.52	5.67	3	3	4.75	1.31	800 525-7048
Oppenheimer Bond B	Corp-Inv	12.8	8.67	4.88	3	3	0	2.04	800 525-7048
Oppenheimer Bond C	Corp-Inv	13	8.73	4.91	3	3	0	1.82	800 525-7048
Oppenheimer Bond N	Corp-Inv	13.3					0	1.44	800 525-7048
Oppenheimer Bond Y	Corp-Inv	14.2	10.35	6.24	3	3	0	0.63	800 525-7048
Oppenheimer CA Municipal A	Muni CA	5.6	7.7	4.26	5	4	4.75	0.86	800 525-7048
Oppenheimer CA Municipal B	Muni CA	4.8	6.91	3.5	5	4	0	1.62	800 525-7048
Oppenheimer CA Municipal C	Muni CA	4.8	6.92	3.5	5	4	0	1.62	800 525-7048
Oppenheimer Champion Income A	Corp-HY	7.4	2.33	1.52	5	5	4.75	1.07	800 525-7048
Oppenheimer Champion Income B	Corp-HY	6.6	1.56	0.77	5	5	0	1.89	800 525-7048
Oppenheimer Champion Income C	Corp-HY	6.6	1.56	0.76	5	5	0	1.89	800 525-7048
Oppenheimer Champion Income N	Corp-HY	7.1					0	1.36	800 525-7048
Oppenheimer High Yield A	Corp-HY	7.2	1.76	0.64	5	5	4.75	1.1	800 525-7048
Oppenheimer High Yield B	Corp-HY	6.4	0.96	-0.14	5	5	0	1.86	800 525-7048
Oppenheimer High Yield C	Corp-HY	6.4	0.98	-0.11	5	5	0	1.86	800 525-7048
Oppenheimer High Yield N	Corp-HY	7					0	1.35	800 525-7048
Oppenheimer High Yield Y	Corp-HY	7.2	1.84	-0.76	5	5	0	1.01	800 525-7048
Oppenheimer Intl Bond A	Intl Bond	26.6	14.17	9.19	2	4	4.75	1.45	800 525-7048
Oppenheimer Intl Bond B	Intl Bond	25.7	13.33	8.4	3	4	0	2.23	800 525-7048
Oppenheimer Intl Bond C	Intl Bond	25.6	13.33	8.43	3	4	0	2.23	800 525-7048
Oppenheimer Intl Bond N	Intl Bond	26					0	1.69	800 525-7048
Oppenheimer Limited Term Govt A	Government	4.7	6.5	5.53	3	1	3.5	0.89	800 525-7048

Bond Fund Name	Objective	Annualized Return for			Rank		Max Load	Expense Ratio	Toll-Free/(Toll) Telephone
		1 Year	3 Years	5 Years	Overall	Risk			
Oppenheimer Limited Term Govt B	Government	3.9	5.7	4.73	3	1	0	1.65	800 525-7048
Oppenheimer Limited Term Govt C	Government	4	5.7	4.75	3	1	0	1.65	800 525-7048
Oppenheimer Limited Term Govt N	Government	4.4					0	1.14	800 525-7048
Oppenheimer Limited Term Govt Y	Government	5.2	6.87	5.9	2	1	0	0.52	800 525-7048
Oppenheimer Limited Term Muni A	Muni Natl	7.6	7.21	4.44	4	3	3.5	0.9	800 525-7048
Oppenheimer Limited Term Muni B	Muni Natl	6.8	6.38	3.66	5	3	0	1.66	800 525-7048
Oppenheimer Limited Term Muni C	Muni Natl	6.7	6.37	3.64	5	3	0	1.66	800 525-7048
Oppenheimer Municipal Bond A	Muni Natl	8.7	7.58	4.16	5	4	4.75	0.88	800 525-7048
Oppenheimer Municipal Bond B	Muni Natl	7.8	6.75	3.35	5	4	0	1.65	800 525-7048
Oppenheimer Municipal Bond C	Muni Natl	7.8	6.74	3.35	5	4	4.75	1.63	800 525-7048
Oppenheimer NJ Municipal A	Muni State	6	7.99	3.81	5	4	4.75	0.84	800 525-7048
Oppenheimer NJ Municipal B	Muni State	5.4	7.2	3.08	5	4	0	1.6	800 525-7048
Oppenheimer NJ Municipal C	Muni State	5.2	7.2	3.04	5	4	0	1.6	800 525-7048
Oppenheimer PA Municipal A	Muni State	11.3	9.75	4.95	3	3	4.75	0.85	800 525-7048
Oppenheimer PA Municipal B	Muni State	10.4	8.92	4.16	3	3	0	1.61	800 525-7048
Oppenheimer PA Municipal C	Muni State	10.4	8.93	4.17	3	3	0	1.61	800 525-7048
Oppenheimer Sen-Floating Rate A	Govt-Mtg	4.4	3.77		4	2	4.75	1.42	800 525-7048
Oppenheimer Sen-Floating Rate B	Govt-Mtg	4	3.25		4	2	0	1.92	800 525-7048
Oppenheimer Sen-Floating Rate C	Govt-Mtg	4	3.31		4	2	0	1.77	800 525-7048
Oppenheimer Strat Income A	Dvsfd Bond	13.2	7.5	4.86	3	4	4.75	1.04	800 525-7048
Oppenheimer Strat Income B	Dvsfd Bond	12.6	6.69	4.12	3	4	0	1.79	800 525-7048
Oppenheimer Strat Income C	Dvsfd Bond	12.7	6.74	4.13	3	4	0	1.79	800 525-7048
Oppenheimer Strat Income N	Dvsfd Bond	13.2					0	1.26	800 525-7048
Oppenheimer Strat Income Y	Dvsfd Bond	13.3	7.59	5.12	3	4	0	1.06	800 525-7048
Oppenheimer US Govt Trust A	Government	10	9.31	6.58	3	3	4.75	1.05	800 525-7048
Oppenheimer US Govt Trust B	Government	9.2	8.49	5.78	3	3	0	1.81	800 525-7048
Oppenheimer US Govt Trust C	Government	9.2	8.5	5.79	3	3	0	1.81	800 525-7048
Oppenheimer US Govt Trust N	Government	9.6					0	1.29	800 525-7048
Oppenheimer US Govt Trust Y	Government	10.6	9.72	6.8	2	3	0	0.99	800 525-7048
Osterweis Strategic Income Fund	Dvsfd Bond						0	1.5	800 366-6223
PBHG IRA Capital Preservation	Dvsfd Bond	4.2	5.38			1	0	1.25	800 433-0051
PF PIMCO Managed Bond Fund A	Dvsfd Bond	13.6					4.5	1.55	800 282-6693
PF PIMCO Managed Bond Fund B	Dvsfd Bond	13.1					0	2.05	800 282-6693
PF PIMCO Managed Bond Fund C	Dvsfd Bond	13.1					0	2.05	800 282-6693
PIMCO CA Interm Muni Bond A	Muni Natl	4	6.74		4	2	3	0.85	800 227-7337
PIMCO CA Interm Muni Bond Admin	Muni Natl	4.2	6.87			2	0	0.72	800 227-7337
PIMCO CA Interm Muni Bond D	Muni Natl	4.1	6.75			2	0	0.85	800 227-7337
PIMCO CA Interm Muni Bond Inst	Muni Natl	4.5	7.16		3	2	0	0.47	800 227-7337
PIMCO CA Municipal A	Muni Natl	7.1	8.39		3	4	3	0.85	800 227-7337
PIMCO CA Municipal D	Muni Natl	7.1	8.43		3	4	0	0.85	800 227-7337
PIMCO CA Municipal Inst	Muni Natl	7.5	8.83		2	4	0	0.47	800 227-7337
PIMCO Emerging Markets Bond A	Intl Bond	28	25.17	16.62	1	5	4.5	1.25	800 227-7337
PIMCO Emerging Markets Bond Admin	Intl Bond	28.3	25.41	16.82	1	5	0	1.1	800 227-7337
PIMCO Emerging Markets Bond B	Intl Bond	27.1	24.28	15.75	1	5	0	2	800 227-7337
PIMCO Emerging Markets Bond C	Intl Bond	27.1	24.28	15.8	1	5	0	2	800 227-7337
PIMCO Emerging Markets Bond D	Intl Bond	28.1	25.23	16.66	1	5	0	1.25	800 227-7337
PIMCO Emerging Markets Bond Inst	Intl Bond	28.6	25.73	17.12	1	5	0	0.84	800 227-7337
PIMCO Foreign Bond Fund A	Intl Bond	9.7	8.63	6.87	1	2	4.5	0.95	800 227-7337
PIMCO Foreign Bond Fund Admin	Intl Bond	10.1	8.88	7.11	1	2	0	0.75	800 227-7337
PIMCO Foreign Bond Fund B	Intl Bond	9	7.8	6.05	2	2	0	1.7	800 227-7337
PIMCO Foreign Bond Fund C	Intl Bond	8.9	7.79	6.04	2	2	0	1.7	800 227-7337
PIMCO Foreign Bond Fund D	Intl Bond	9.7	8.64	6.88	1	2	0	0.95	800 227-7337
PIMCO Foreign Bond Fund Inst	Intl Bond	10.2	9.07	7.33	1	2	0	0.5	800 227-7337
PIMCO GNMA A	Govt-Mtg	6.3	9.81	7.62	2	2	4.5	1	800 227-7337
PIMCO GNMA B	Govt-Mtg	5.5	8.92	6.78		2	0	1.65	800 227-7337
PIMCO GNMA C	Govt-Mtg	5.5	8.94	6.79		2	0	1.65	800 227-7337
PIMCO GNMA D	Govt-Mtg	6.3	9.77	7.61		2	0	1	800 227-7337
PIMCO GNMA Inst	Govt-Mtg	6.8	10.25	8.05	2	2	0	0.5	800 227-7337

Bond Fund Name	Objective	Annualized Return for			Rank		Max Load	Expense Ratio	Toll-Free/(Toll) Telephone
		1 Year	3 Years	5 Years	Overall	Risk			
PIMCO Global Bond Fd Admin	Intl Bond	25.5	11.76	7.11	3	4	0	0.8	800 227-7337
PIMCO Global Bond Fd Inst	Intl Bond	25.8	12	7.33	3	4	0	0.55	800 227-7337
PIMCO Global Bond Fund II A	Intl Bond	11.6	9.88	7.03	1	2	4.5	0.95	800 227-7337
PIMCO Global Bond Fund II B	Intl Bond	10.7	9.11	6.26	2	2	0	1.7	800 227-7337
PIMCO Global Bond Fund II C	Intl Bond	10.7	9.11	6.26	2	2	0	1.7	800 227-7337
PIMCO Global Bond Fund II Inst	Intl Bond	12	10.39	7.5	1	2	0	0.55	800 227-7337
PIMCO High Yield Fund A	Corp-HY	11.5	5.9	3.91	4	5	4.5	0.9	800 227-7337
PIMCO High Yield Fund Admin	Corp-HY	11.7	6.04	4.07	4	5	0	0.75	800 227-7337
PIMCO High Yield Fund B	Corp-HY	10.7	5.11	3.14	4	5	0	1.65	800 227-7337
PIMCO High Yield Fund C	Corp-HY	10.7	5.11	3.14	4	5	0	1.65	800 227-7337
PIMCO High Yield Fund D	Corp-HY	11.5	5.9	3.93	4	5	0	0.9	800 227-7337
PIMCO High Yield Fund Inst	Corp-HY	11.9	6.32	4.33	4	5	0	0.5	800 227-7337
PIMCO Investment Grade Corp Inst	Dvsfd Bond	18.2	13.76		1	4	0	0.5	800 227-7337
PIMCO Long Term US Govt A	Government	22.8	15.27	9.85	3	5	4.5	0.9	800 227-7337
PIMCO Long Term US Govt Admin	Government	22.9	15.42	10	3	5	0	0.75	800 227-7337
PIMCO Long Term US Govt B	Government	21.8	14.42	9.02	3	5	0	1.65	800 227-7337
PIMCO Long Term US Govt C	Government	21.8	14.42	9.02	3	5	0	1.65	800 227-7337
PIMCO Long Term US Govt Inst	Government	23.2	15.73	10.28	3	5	0	0.5	800 227-7337
PIMCO Low Duration Fund A	Dvsfd Bond	6.6	7.5	6.12	2	1	3	0.9	800 227-7337
PIMCO Low Duration Fund Admin	Dvsfd Bond	6.8	7.71	6.34	2	1	0	0.68	800 227-7337
PIMCO Low Duration Fund B	Dvsfd Bond	5.8	6.66	5.32	2	1	0	1.65	800 227-7337
PIMCO Low Duration Fund C	Dvsfd Bond	6	6.91	5.57	3	1	0	1.4	800 227-7337
PIMCO Low Duration Fund D	Dvsfd Bond	6.7	7.65	6.29	2	1	0	0.75	800 227-7337
PIMCO Low Duration Fund Inst	Dvsfd Bond	7	7.95	6.59	2	1	0	0.42	800 227-7337
PIMCO Low Duration Fund-II Admin	Dvsfd Bond	6	7.45	6.04	2	1	0	0.75	800 227-7337
PIMCO Low Duration Fund-II Inst	Dvsfd Bond	6.3	7.7	6.32	2	1	0	0.5	800 227-7337
PIMCO Low Duration Fund-III Admin	Dvsfd Bond	7.4	7.9	6.33	1	1	0	0.75	800 227-7337
PIMCO Low Duration Fund-III Inst	Dvsfd Bond	7.7	8.21	6.62	1	1	0	0.5	800 227-7337
PIMCO Moderate Duration Inst	Dvsfd Bond	11.8	11.05	8.16	1	2	0	0.45	800 227-7337
PIMCO Municipal Bond A	Muni Natl	5.6	8.8	5.41	4	3	3	0.85	800 227-7337
PIMCO Municipal Bond B	Muni Natl	4.8	8.01	4.66	5	3	0	1.6	800 227-7337
PIMCO Municipal Bond C	Muni Natl	5.1	8.26	4.91	4	3	0	1.35	800 227-7337
PIMCO Municipal Bond D	Muni Natl	5.7	8.81	5.42	4	3	0	0.85	800 227-7337
PIMCO Municipal Bond Inst	Muni Natl	6	9.23	5.82	2	3	0	0.49	800 227-7337
PIMCO NY Muni Bond A	Muni Natl	7.3	10.23		2	3	3	0.85	800 227-7337
PIMCO NY Muni Bond D	Muni Natl	7.3	10.25		3	3	0	0.85	800 227-7337
PIMCO NY Muni Bond Inst	Muni Natl	7.7	10.66		3	3	0	0.47	800 227-7337
PIMCO Real Return Asset Inst	Dvsfd Bond	27.6					0	0.65	800 227-7337
PIMCO Real Return Fund A	Corp-Inv	17.4	13.1	10.61	2	4	3	0.9	800 227-7337
PIMCO Real Return Fund Admin	Corp-Inv	17.6	13.26	10.77	1	4	0	0.7	800 227-7337
PIMCO Real Return Fund B	Corp-Inv	16.5	12.22	9.76	2	4	0	1.65	800 227-7337
PIMCO Real Return Fund C	Corp-Inv	16.8	12.51	10.05	2	4	0	1.4	800 227-7337
PIMCO Real Return Fund D	Corp-Inv	17.4	13.11	10.61	1	4	0	0.9	800 227-7337
PIMCO Real Return Fund Inst	Corp-Inv	17.9	13.59	11.08	1	4	0	0.45	800 227-7337
PIMCO Short Duration Muni Inc D	Muni Natl	1.6	3.97			1	0	0.8	800 227-7337
PIMCO Short Duration Muni Inc Inst	Muni Natl	2	4.37		4	1	0	0.39	800 227-7337
PIMCO Short Term Fund A	Corp-Inv	3.3	4.55	4.73	4	1	2	0.85	800 227-7337
PIMCO Short Term Fund Admin	Corp-Inv	3.5	4.78	4.92	4	1	0	0.7	800 227-7337
PIMCO Short Term Fund B	Corp-Inv	2.6	3.81	3.97	4	1	0	1.6	800 227-7337
PIMCO Short Term Fund C	Corp-Inv	3	4.23	4.41	4	1	0	1.15	800 227-7337
PIMCO Short Term Fund D	Corp-Inv	3.4	4.7	4.86	4	1	0	0.75	800 227-7337
PIMCO Short Term Fund Inst	Corp-Inv	3.8	5.01	5.16	4	1	0	0.45	800 227-7337
PIMCO Total Return Fund A	Corp-Inv	11	11.16	8.02	2	3	4.5	0.9	800 227-7337
PIMCO Total Return Fund Admin	Corp-Inv	11.3	11.41	8.26	2	3	0	0.68	800 227-7337
PIMCO Total Return Fund B	Corp-Inv	10.2	10.33	7.21	3	3	0	1.65	800 227-7337
PIMCO Total Return Fund C	Corp-Inv	10.2	10.33	7.21	3	3	0	1.65	800 227-7337
PIMCO Total Return Fund D	Corp-Inv	11.2	11.35	8.19	2	3	0	0.75	800 227-7337
PIMCO Total Return Fund Inst	Corp-Inv	11.6	11.69	8.52	1	3	0	0.42	800 227-7337

Bond Fund Name	Objective	Annualized Return for			Rank		Max Load	Expense Ratio	Toll-Free/(Toll) Telephone
		1 Year	3 Years	5 Years	Overall Risk				
PIMCO Total Return Fund-II Admin	Corp-Inv	11.4	11.24	7.99	2	3	0	0.75	800 227-7337
PIMCO Total Return Fund-II Inst	Corp-Inv	11.6	11.49	8.24	2	3	0	0.5	800 227-7337
PIMCO Total Return Fund-III Admin	Corp-Inv	12.5	11.77	8.15	1	3	0	0.75	800 227-7337
PIMCO Total Return Fund-III Inst	Corp-Inv	12.7	12.1	8.46	1	3	0	0.5	800 227-7337
PIMCO Total Return Mortgage A	Govt-Mtg	7.3	10.16	7.51	2	2	4.5	0.9	800 227-7337
PIMCO Total Return Mortgage B	Govt-Mtg	6.5	9.34	6.71	2	2	0	1.65	800 227-7337
PIMCO Total Return Mortgage C	Govt-Mtg	6.5	9.33	6.7	2	2	0	1.65	800 227-7337
PIMCO Total Return Mortgage D	Govt-Mtg	7.3	10.16	7.5	2	2	0	0.9	800 227-7337
PIMCO Total Return Mortgage Inst	Govt-Mtg	7.7	10.59	7.94	1	2	0	0.5	800 227-7337
Pacific Advisors Govt Secs A	Government	9.4	7.01	6.17	4	4	4.75	1.18	800 282-6693
Pacific Capital Divers Fixed Inc A	Dvsfd Bond	13.7	11.25	7.25	3	3	4	0.96	800 258-9232
Pacific Capital Divers Fixed Inc B	Dvsfd Bond	12.9	8.86	5.69		4	0	1.7	800 258-9232
Pacific Capital Divers Fixed Inc Y	Dvsfd Bond	14	11.39	7.4	3	4	0	0.71	800 258-9232
Pacific Capital Sh-Int US Govt A	Government	7.2	7.86	5.95	3	1	2.25	0.82	800 258-9232
Pacific Capital Sh-Int US Govt Y	Government	7.4	8.22	6.01	3	2	2.25	0.57	800 258-9232
Pacific Capital T/F Secs A	Muni Natl	9.7	8.88	3.52	3	3	4	0.94	800 258-9232
Pacific Capital T/F Secs B	Muni Natl	8.9	8.08	4.75	3	3	0	1.69	800 258-9232
Pacific Capital T/F Secs Y	Muni Natl	10	9.14	5.92	1	3	0	0.69	800 258-9232
Pacific Capital T/F Sh-Interm A	Muni Natl	6	6.37	4.37	3	2	2.25	0.99	800 258-9232
Pacific Capital T/F Sh-Interm Y	Muni Natl	6.3	6.65	4.66	3	2	0	0.74	800 258-9232
Pacific Capital Ultra Short Govt A	Government	2.8					1.75	0.62	800 258-9232
Pacific Capital Ultra Short Govt B	Government	2.1					0	1.37	800 258-9232
Pacific Capital Ultra Short Govt Y	Government	3.1					0	0.37	800 258-9232
Parnassus CA Tax-Exempt Fund	Muni CA	7.7	7.95	5.51	4	4	0	0.73	800 999-3505
Parnassus Fixed-Income Fund	Corp-Inv	15.3	11.78	6.69	2	3	0	0.81	800 999-3505
Pax World High Yield Fund	Intl Bond	6.2	4.17		5	5	0	1.57	800 767-1729
Payden & Rygel CA Muni Inc R	Muni Natl	7.8	7.91		4	3	0	0.5	800 572-9336
Payden & Rygel Core Bond R	Corp-Inv	12.7	11.83	7.67	2	3	0	0.44	800 572-9336
Payden & Rygel Global Fixed Inc R	Intl Bond	11.6	8.17	6.83	3	2	0	0.51	800 572-9336
Payden & Rygel Global Short Bond R	Intl Bond	8.5	7.42	6.28	1	1	0	0.5	800 572-9336
Payden & Rygel High Income R	Corp-HY	8.6	5.2	3.62	4	5	0	0.57	800 572-9336
Payden & Rygel Limited Maturity R	Corp-Inv	2.7	4.91	5.05	2	1	0	0.4	800 572-9336
Payden & Rygel Opportunity Bond R	Dvsfd Bond	11.4	10.91	7.37	1	3	0	0.5	800 572-9336
Payden & Rygel Short Bond R	Corp-Inv	6.4	7.76	6.49	2	1	0	0.4	800 572-9336
Payden & Rygel Short Dur T/E R	Muni Natl	3.6	4.75	4.01	3	1	0	0.5	800 572-9336
Payden & Rygel Tax Exempt Bd R	Muni Natl	9.7	8.63	5.83	1	3	0	0.5	800 572-9336
Payden & Rygel US Government R	Government	8.1	8.75	6.8	2	2	0	0.4	800 572-9336
Performance Intmed-Term Govt A	Government	10.3	10.28	6.58	3	2	2	1.01	800 737-3676
Performance Intmed-Term Govt Inst	Government	10.6	10.57	6.87	2	2	0	0.76	800 737-3676
Performance Short-Term Govt A	Government	4.2	6.15	5.29	2	1	2	0.98	800 737-3676
Performance Short-Term Govt Inst	Government	4.5	6.44	5.55	3	1	0	0.73	800 737-3676
Permanent Portfolio Treasury	Government	0.4	2.2	2.91	4	1	0	1.01	800 531-5142
Permanent Portfolio Versatile Bd	Corp-Inv	3.4	4.86	4.5	3	1	0	1.11	800 531-5142
Phoenix-Duff & Phelps Core Bd A	Government	7.6	8.38	5.2	4	2	4.75	1.14	800 243-4361
Phoenix-Duff & Phelps Core Bd B	Government	7	7.58	4.44	5	2	0	1.9	800 243-4361
Phoenix-Duff & Phelps Core Bd C	Government	6.9	7.58			2	0	1.9	800 243-4361
Phoenix-Duff&Phelps Instl Mgd Bd X	Corp-Inv	9.6	10.52	6.37	2	3	0	0.55	800 243-4361
Phoenix-Duff&Phelps Instl Mgd Bd Y	Corp-Inv	9.3	10.25	6.12	3	3	0	0.8	800 243-4361
Phoenix-Goodwin California T/E A	Muni CA	10.1	9.32	5.75	3	4	4.75	1.12	800 243-4361
Phoenix-Goodwin California T/E B	Muni CA	9.2	8.49	4.95	5	4	0	1.87	800 243-4361
Phoenix-Goodwin Emerg Mkts Bd A	Intl Bond	21	13.11	6.78	2	5	4.75	1.18	800 243-4361
Phoenix-Goodwin Emerg Mkts Bd B	Intl Bond	20.2	12.25	5.98	3	5	0	1.93	800 243-4361
Phoenix-Goodwin Emerg Mkts Bd C	Intl Bond	20.1	12.24		1	5	0	1.93	800 243-4361
Phoenix-Goodwin High Yield A	Corp-HY	6	-1.92	-2.16	5	5	4.75	1.36	800 243-4361
Phoenix-Goodwin High Yield B	Corp-HY	5.2	-2.66	-2.89	5	5	0	2.11	800 243-4361
Phoenix-Goodwin High Yield C	Corp-HY	5.2	-2.66		5	5	0	2.11	800 243-4361
Phoenix-Goodwin Multi-Sec F/I A	Dvsfd Bond	14.5	9.23	4.41	3	4	4.75	1.25	800 243-4361
Phoenix-Goodwin Multi-Sec F/I B	Dvsfd Bond	13.6	8.38	3.64	3	4	0	2	800 243-4361

472

Bond Fund Name	Objective	Annualized Return for			Rank		Max Load	Expense Ratio	Toll-Free/(Toll) Telephone
		1 Year	3 Years	5 Years	Overall	Risk			
Phoenix-Goodwin Multi-Sec F/I C	Dvsfd Bond	13.6	8.41	3.68	3	4	0	2	800 243-4361
Phoenix-Goodwin Multi-Sec ST A	Dvsfd Bond	11.5	9.51	6.21	1	2	2.25	1.14	800 243-4361
Phoenix-Goodwin Multi-Sec ST B	Dvsfd Bond	11	9	5.66	1	2	0	1.64	800 243-4361
Phoenix-Goodwin Multi-Sec ST C	Dvsfd Bond	11.2	9.38		1	2	0	1.39	800 243-4361
Phoenix-Goodwin Tax Exempt A	Muni Natl	10.4	9.21	5.16	3	4	4.75	1.09	800 243-4361
Phoenix-Goodwin Tax Exempt B	Muni Natl	9.6	8.4	4.37	4	4	0	1.7	800 243-4361
Phoenix-Kayne CA Int T/F Bd X	Muni Natl	8	7.69	5.33	3	3	0	0.75	800 243-4361
Phoenix-Kayne Interm Tot Ret Bd X	Corp-Inv	9.4					0	0.96	800 243-4361
Phoenix-Seneca Bond A	Dvsfd Bond	11.3	9.22		2	3	4.75	1.12	800 243-4361
Phoenix-Seneca Bond B	Dvsfd Bond	10.6	8.43		3	3	0	1.87	800 243-4361
Phoenix-Seneca Bond C	Dvsfd Bond	10.5	8.39		3	3	0	1.87	800 243-4361
Phoenix-Seneca Bond X	Dvsfd Bond	11.7	9.57	6.88	1	3	0	0.87	800 243-4361
Pioneer America Income Trust A	Government	8.6	8.75	6.33	3	3	4.5	1.2	800 225-6292
Pioneer America Income Trust B	Government	7.7	7.82	5.48	4	3	0	1.93	800 225-6292
Pioneer America Income Trust C	Government	7.7	7.83	5.65	4	3	1	1.81	800 225-6292
Pioneer Bond Fund A	Corp-Inv	11.5	10.48	6.45	2	2	4.5	1.2	800 225-6292
Pioneer Bond Fund B	Corp-Inv	10.5	9.58	5.57	3	3	0	2.05	800 225-6292
Pioneer Bond Fund C	Corp-Inv	10.5	9.46	5.36	3	3	1	2.18	800 225-6292
Pioneer Bond Fund Y	Corp-Inv	12					0	0.71	800 225-6292
Pioneer High Yield A	Corp-HY	11.1	12.07	11.69	3	5	4.5	1	800 225-6292
Pioneer High Yield B	Corp-HY	10.3	11.18	10.97		5	0	1.75	800 225-6292
Pioneer High Yield C	Corp-HY	10.3	11.09	11.14		5	1	1.75	800 225-6292
Pioneer High Yield Y	Corp-HY	11.4	12.11	11.78	3	5	0	0.75	800 225-6292
Pioneer Strategic Income A	Dvsfd Bond	17.8					4.5	1	800 225-6292
Pioneer Strategic Income B	Dvsfd Bond	16.8	11.25		1	4	0	1.66	800 225-6292
Pioneer Strategic Income C	Dvsfd Bond	16.9	11.24		1	4	1	1.44	800 225-6292
Pioneer Tax Free Income Fund A	Muni Natl	7.1	7.95	4.88	5	4	4.5	0.91	800 225-6292
Pioneer Tax Free Income Fund B	Muni Natl	6.2	7.11	4.15	5	4	0	1.66	800 225-6292
Pioneer Tax Free Income Fund C	Muni Natl	6.3	7.16	4.16	5	4	1	1.61	800 225-6292
Pioneer Tax Free Income Fund Y	Muni Natl	5.8					0	0.66	800 225-6292
Preferred Fixed Income Fund	Corp-Inv	12.5	10.61	6.94	2	3	0	0.69	800 662-4769
Preferred Short-Term Government	Government	6	6.7	5.44	3	1	0	0.54	800 662-4769
Principal Bond Fund A	Corp-Inv	10.2	10.1	5.62	3	3	4.75	1.06	800 247-4123
Principal Bond Fund B	Corp-Inv	9.4	9.27	4.86	3	3	0	1.72	800 247-4123
Principal Govt Securities Income A	Govt-Mtg	7	8.65	6.37	3	2	4.75	0.91	800 247-4123
Principal Govt Securities Income B	Govt-Mtg	6.1	7.82	5.54	2	2	0	1.7	800 247-4123
Principal Limited Term Bond A	Corp-Inv	7.9	7.82	5.91	3	2	1.5	0.95	800 247-4123
Principal Limited Term Bond B	Corp-Inv	7.4	7.3	5.46	3	2	0	1.38	800 247-4123
Principal Tax Exempt Bond Fund A	Muni Natl	10.6	8.86	5.36	2	3	4.75	0.8	800 247-4123
Principal Tax Exempt Bond Fund B	Muni Natl	9.8	8.23	4.91	3	3	0	1.51	800 247-4123
Prudential Global Tot Ret A	Intl Bond	17.6	7.98	4.37	4	4	4	1.45	888 743-7111
Prudential Global Tot Ret B	Intl Bond	16.7	7.32	3.79	4	4	0	2.21	888 743-7111
Prudential Global Tot Ret C	Intl Bond	17	7.41	3.85	4	4	1	1.96	888 743-7111
Prudential Global Tot Ret Z	Intl Bond	18	8.27	4.66	3	4	0	1.21	888 743-7111
Prudential Government Inc A	Government	11.4	10.33	7.13	3	3	4	0.98	888 743-7111
Prudential Government Inc B	Government	10.7	9.75	6.5	3	3	0	1.55	888 743-7111
Prudential Government Inc C	Government	10.8	9.83	6.49	3	3	1	1.48	888 743-7111
Prudential Government Inc Z	Government	11.6	10.58	7.26	3	3	0	0.73	888 743-7111
Prudential High Yield Fd A	Corp-HY	8.8	2.33	0.48	5	5	4	0.88	888 743-7111
Prudential High Yield Fd B	Corp-HY	8	1.85	-0.02	5	5	0	1.37	888 743-7111
Prudential High Yield Fd C	Corp-HY	8	1.85	0.11	5	5	1	1.38	888 743-7111
Prudential High Yield Fd Z	Corp-HY	8.8	2.66	0.75	5	5	0	0.63	888 743-7111
Prudential Muni-CA A	Muni CA	10.6	9.56	6.09	3	4	3	0.97	888 743-7111
Prudential Muni-CA B	Muni CA	10.4	9.33	5.83	3	4	0	1.22	888 743-7111
Prudential Muni-CA C	Muni CA	10.1	9.06	5.58	3	4	1	1.47	888 743-7111
Prudential Muni-CA Income A	Muni CA	12.4	9.69	6.19	2	4	3	0.87	888 743-7111
Prudential Muni-CA Income B	Muni CA	10	8.77	5.45	4	4	0	1.12	888 743-7111
Prudential Muni-CA Income C	Muni CA	9.8	8.51	5.19	4	4	1	1.37	888 743-7111

Bond Fund Name	Objective	Annualized Return for			Rank		Max Load	Expense Ratio	Toll-Free/(Toll) Telephone
		1 Year	3 Years	5 Years	Overall	Risk			
Prudential Muni-CA Income Z	Muni CA	10.6	9.32	5.99	3	4	0	0.62	888 743-7111
Prudential Muni-CA Z	Muni CA	10.8	9.8	6.33	3	4	0	0.72	888 743-7111
Prudential Muni-FL A	Muni State	10	8.91	5.7	2	3	3	1.01	888 743-7111
Prudential Muni-FL B	Muni State	9.7	8.64	5.41	3	3	0	1.26	888 743-7111
Prudential Muni-FL C	Muni State	9.4	8.38	5.08	3	3	1	1.51	888 743-7111
Prudential Muni-FL Z	Muni State	10.2	9.17	5.87	1	3	0	0.76	888 743-7111
Prudential Muni-High Income A	Muni Natl	7.8	6.48	3.83	3	2	3	0.84	888 743-7111
Prudential Muni-High Income B	Muni Natl	7.6	6.21	3.56	3	2	0	1.09	888 743-7111
Prudential Muni-High Income C	Muni Natl	7.3	5.95	3.18	4	2	1	1.34	888 743-7111
Prudential Muni-High Income Z	Muni Natl	8.1	6.74	3.95	3	2	0	0.59	888 743-7111
Prudential Muni-Insured A	Muni Natl	10.8	9.56	6.04	2	4	3	0.87	888 743-7111
Prudential Muni-Insured B	Muni Natl	10.5	9.27	5.75	2	4	0	1.12	888 743-7111
Prudential Muni-Insured C	Muni Natl	10.2	9.01	5.4	3	4	1	1.37	888 743-7111
Prudential Muni-Insured Z	Muni Natl	11.1	9.8	6.16	2	4	0	0.62	888 743-7111
Prudential Muni-NJ A	Muni State	9.8	9.43	5.91	2	3	3	0.91	888 743-7111
Prudential Muni-NJ B	Muni State	9.5	9.16	5.62	2	3	0	1.16	888 743-7111
Prudential Muni-NJ C	Muni State	9.2	8.9	5.37	3	3	1	1.4	888 743-7111
Prudential Muni-NJ Z	Muni State	10	9.67	6.2	2	3	0	0.65	888 743-7111
Prudential Muni-NY A	Muni NY	10	9.33	5.83	3	4	3	0.91	888 743-7111
Prudential Muni-NY B	Muni NY	9.7	9.09	5.54	3	4	0	1.16	888 743-7111
Prudential Muni-NY C	Muni NY	9.4	8.83	5.29	4	4	1	1.41	888 743-7111
Prudential Muni-NY Z	Muni NY	10.2	9.63	6.08	2	4	0	0.66	888 743-7111
Prudential Muni-PA A	Muni State	10.4	9.13	5.29	3	3	3	0.96	888 743-7111
Prudential Muni-PA B	Muni State	10.2	8.85	5.08	3	3	0	1.21	888 743-7111
Prudential Muni-PA C	Muni State	10	8.58	4.75	4	3	1	1.46	888 743-7111
Prudential National Muni A	Muni Natl	10.4	9.38	5.66	2	3	3	0.89	888 743-7111
Prudential National Muni B	Muni Natl	10.2	9.11	5.37	3	3	0	1.14	888 743-7111
Prudential National Muni C	Muni Natl	9.9	8.84	5.12	3	3	1	1.39	888 743-7111
Prudential National Muni Z	Muni Natl	10.6	9.65		1	3	0	0.64	888 743-7111
Prudential Sh Term Corp Bond Fd A	Corp-Inv	9.3	8.16	6.34	1	2	3.25	1	888 743-7111
Prudential Sh Term Corp Bond Fd B	Corp-Inv	8.6	7.54	5.71	3	2	0	1.75	888 743-7111
Prudential Sh Term Corp Bond Fd C	Corp-Inv	8.9	7.66	5.79	3	2	1	1.5	888 743-7111
Prudential Sh Term Corp Bond Fd Z	Corp-Inv	9.7	8.5	6.54	1	2	0	0.75	888 743-7111
Prudential Total Return Bond A	Dvsfd Bond	10.6	9.24	5.71	3	3	4	1.18	888 743-7111
Prudential Total Return Bond B	Dvsfd Bond	9.8	8.58	5.11	4	3	0	1.68	888 743-7111
Prudential Total Return Bond C	Dvsfd Bond	10	8.75	5.2	3	3	1	1.68	888 743-7111
Prudential Total Return Bond Z	Dvsfd Bond	10.8	9.51	5.95	3	3	0	0.93	888 743-7111
Putnam AZ Tax Exempt Income A	Muni State	9.4	8.64	5.34	3	3	4.75	0.88	800 354-2228
Putnam AZ Tax Exempt Income B	Muni State	8.6	7.94	4.69	4	3	0	1.53	800 354-2228
Putnam AZ Tax Exempt Income M	Muni State	9	8.31	5.04	3	3	3.25	1.18	800 354-2228
Putnam American Government Income A	Government	8.7	8.93	6.2	3	3	4.75	0.97	800 354-2228
Putnam American Government Income B	Government	7.9	8.09	5.37	3	3	0	1.74	800 354-2228
Putnam American Government Income C	Government	7.8	8.09	5.36	4	3	0	1.74	800 354-2228
Putnam American Government Income M	Government	8.4	8.61	5.9	4	3	3.25	1.24	800 354-2228
Putnam CA Tax Exempt Income A	Muni CA	9.2	8.66	5.42	3	4	4.75	0.75	800 354-2228
Putnam CA Tax Exempt Income B	Muni CA	8.4	7.96	4.75	4	4	0	1.4	800 354-2228
Putnam CA Tax Exempt Income C	Muni CA	8.4	7.83	4.58	4	4	0	1.55	800 354-2228
Putnam CA Tax Exempt Income M	Muni CA	8.8	8.31	5.08	5	4	3.25	1.05	800 354-2228
Putnam Diversified Income Trust A	Dvsfd Bond	13.5	7.4	3.45	3	4	4.75	0.94	800 354-2228
Putnam Diversified Income Trust B	Dvsfd Bond	12.5	6.55	2.68	4	4	0	1.7	800 354-2228
Putnam Diversified Income Trust C	Dvsfd Bond	12.5	6.58	2.68	4	4	0	1.7	800 354-2228
Putnam Diversified Income Trust M	Dvsfd Bond	13.2	7.09	3.2	3	4	3.25	1.2	800 354-2228
Putnam FL Tax Exempt Income A	Muni State	9.1	9.06	5.54	2	3	4.75	0.84	800 354-2228
Putnam FL Tax Exempt Income B	Muni State	8.4	8.34	4.86	3	3	0	1.49	800 354-2228
Putnam FL Tax Exempt Income M	Muni State	8.7	8.69	5.21	3	3	3.25	1.14	800 354-2228
Putnam Global Income A	Intl Bond	20.1	9.74	5.15	3	4	4.75	1.23	800 354-2228
Putnam Global Income B	Intl Bond	19.2	8.92	4.36	3	4	0	1.99	800 354-2228
Putnam Global Income C	Intl Bond	19.2	8.91	4.36	3	4	0	1.99	800 354-2228

| Bond Fund Name | Objective | Annualized Return for | | | Rank | | Max Load | Expense Ratio | Toll-Free/(Toll) Telephone |
		1 Year	3 Years	5 Years	Overall	Risk			
Putnam Global Income M	Intl Bond	19.8	9.43	4.88	3	4	3.25	1.49	800 354-2228
Putnam High Yield Advantage A	Corp-HY	10	2.52	-0.57	5	5	4.75	1	800 354-2228
Putnam High Yield Advantage B	Corp-HY	9.1	1.6	-1.4	5	5	0	1.75	800 354-2228
Putnam High Yield Advantage M	Corp-HY	9.9	2.45	-0.72	5	5	3.25	1.25	800 354-2228
Putnam High Yield Trust A	Corp-HY	9.6	2.66	-0.11	5	5	4.75	1.01	800 354-2228
Putnam High Yield Trust B	Corp-HY	8.7	1.87	-0.84	5	5	0	1.76	800 354-2228
Putnam High Yield Trust C	Corp-HY	8.7	1.82	-0.92		5	0	1.76	800 354-2228
Putnam High Yield Trust M	Corp-HY	9.4	2.39	-0.34	5	5	3.25	1.24	800 354-2228
Putnam High Yield Trust R	Corp-HY	9.4	2.41	-0.34		5	0		800 354-2228
Putnam Income Fund A	Corp-Inv	9.7	9.67	5.29	3	2	4.75	0.94	800 354-2228
Putnam Income Fund B	Corp-Inv	8.8	8.8	4.48	4	2	0	1.7	800 354-2228
Putnam Income Fund C	Corp-Inv	8.8	8.77	4.48	4	2	0	1.7	800 354-2228
Putnam Income Fund M	Corp-Inv	9.5	9.36	5.07	3	2	3.25	1.2	800 354-2228
Putnam Income Fund R	Dvsfd Bond	9.5	9.4	5.03		2	0		800 354-2228
Putnam Intermed US Govt Income A	Government	6.4	8.05	6.2	3	2	3.25	0.96	800 354-2228
Putnam Intermed US Govt Income B	Government	5.7	7.38	5.55	3	2	0	1.56	800 354-2228
Putnam Intermed US Govt Income C	Government	5.6	7.16	5.33	2	2	0	1.71	800 354-2228
Putnam Intermed US Govt Income M	Government	6.4	7.86	6.05	3	2	2	1.11	800 354-2228
Putnam MA Tax Exempt Income A	Muni State	9.4	8.98	5.57	3	3	4.75	0.82	800 354-2228
Putnam MA Tax Exempt Income B	Muni State	8.7	8.26	4.86	4	3	0	1.47	800 354-2228
Putnam MA Tax Exempt Income M	Muni State	9.2	8.65	5.25	3	3	3.25	1.12	800 354-2228
Putnam MI Tax Exempt Income A	Muni State	8	8.43	4.84	3	3	4.75	0.87	800 354-2228
Putnam MI Tax Exempt Income B	Muni State	7.3	7.79	4.16	4	3	0	1.52	800 354-2228
Putnam MI Tax Exempt Income M	Muni State	7.7	8.16	4.54	4	3	3.25	1.17	800 354-2228
Putnam MN Tax Exempt Income A	Muni State	9.1	8.68	5.12	2	3	4.75	0.88	800 354-2228
Putnam MN Tax Exempt Income B	Muni State	8.3	7.95	4.44	3	3	0	1.53	800 354-2228
Putnam MN Tax Exempt Income M	Muni State	8.8	8.36	4.79	3	3	3.25	1.18	800 354-2228
Putnam Municiapl Income Fund M	Muni Natl	6.1	6.86	4.15	5	3	3.25	1.2	800 354-2228
Putnam Municipal Income Fund A	Muni Natl	6.3	7.08	4.41	4	3	4.75		800 354-2228
Putnam Municipal Income Fund B	Muni Natl	5.8	6.48	3.79	5	3	0	1.55	800 354-2228
Putnam Municipal Income Fund C	Muni Natl	5.6	6.32	3.56	5	3	0	1.7	800 354-2228
Putnam NJ Tax Exempt Income A	Muni State	8	8.4	5.08	3	3	4.75	0.85	800 354-2228
Putnam NJ Tax Exempt Income B	Muni State	7.3	7.7	4.41	5	3	0	1.51	800 354-2228
Putnam NJ Tax Exempt Income M	Muni State	7.8	8.1	4.75	4	3	3.25	1.16	800 354-2228
Putnam NY Tax Exempt Income A	Muni NY	9.1	9	5.55	3	4	4.75	0.81	800 354-2228
Putnam NY Tax Exempt Income B	Muni NY	8.4	8.27	4.87	5	4	0	1.46	800 354-2228
Putnam NY Tax Exempt Income C	Muni NY	8.2	8.09	4.63	5	4	0	1.61	800 354-2228
Putnam NY Tax Exempt Income M	Muni NY	8.8	8.68	5.25	4	4	3.25	1.11	800 354-2228
Putnam NY Tax Exempt Opport A	Muni NY	8.8	9.08	5.33	3	3	4.75	0.87	800 354-2228
Putnam NY Tax Exempt Opport B	Muni NY	7.9	8.32	4.63	4	3	0	1.52	800 354-2228
Putnam NY Tax Exempt Opport C	Muni NY	7.9	8.24	4.53	4	3	0	1.67	800 354-2228
Putnam NY Tax Exempt Opport M	Muni NY	8.4	8.75	5.04	4	3	3.25	1.17	800 354-2228
Putnam OH Tax Exempt Income A	Muni State	9.4	8.83	5.24	3	3	4.75	0.88	800 354-2228
Putnam OH Tax Exempt Income B	Muni State	8.8	8.17	4.58	4	3	0	1.53	800 354-2228
Putnam OH Tax Exempt Income M	Muni State	9	8.55	4.95	3	3	3.25	1.18	800 354-2228
Putnam PA Tax Exempt Income A	Muni State	9	8.92	4.95	2	3	4.75	0.87	800 354-2228
Putnam PA Tax Exempt Income B	Muni State	8.3	8.23	4.28	3	3	0	1.52	800 354-2228
Putnam PA Tax Exempt Income M	Muni State	8.8	8.59	4.66	3	3	3.25	1.17	800 354-2228
Putnam Tax Exempt Income A	Muni Natl	7.9	8.23	4.92	4	3	4.75	0.78	800 354-2228
Putnam Tax Exempt Income B	Muni Natl	7.3	7.54	4.25	5	3	0	1.45	800 354-2228
Putnam Tax Exempt Income C	Muni Natl	7.1	7.4	4.03	5	3	0	1.6	800 354-2228
Putnam Tax Exempt Income M	Muni Natl	7.7	7.87	4.62	4	3	3.25	1.1	800 354-2228
Putnam Tax-Free High Yield A	Muni Natl	4.4	5.07	3.12	4	2	4.75	0.88	800 354-2228
Putnam Tax-Free High Yield B	Muni Natl	3.9	4.54	2.58	4	2	0	1.36	800 354-2228
Putnam Tax-Free High Yield C	Muni Natl	3.6	4.25	2.29	4	2	0	1.68	800 354-2228
Putnam Tax-Free High Yield M	Muni Natl	4.1	4.75	2.81	4	2	3.25	1.18	800 354-2228
Putnam Tax-Free Inc:Insured C	Muni Natl	9.2	8.55	4.91	3	3	0	1.63	800 354-2228
Putnam Tax-Free Insured A	Muni Natl	10.1	9.39	5.76	2	4	4.75	0.83	800 354-2228

Bond Fund Name	Objective	Annualized Return for 1 Year	Annualized Return for 3 Years	Annualized Return for 5 Years	Rank Overall	Rank Risk	Max Load	Expense Ratio	Toll-Free/(Toll) Telephone
Putnam Tax-Free Insured B	Muni Natl	9.4	8.82	5.38	3	4	0	1.38	800 354-2228
Putnam Tax-Free Insured M	Muni Natl	9.7	9.02	5.49	3	3	3.25	1.13	800 354-2228
Putnam US Govt Income Tr A	Govt-Mtg	4.8	7.7	5.83	3	2	4.75	0.85	800 354-2228
Putnam US Govt Income Tr B	Govt-Mtg	4	6.9	5.04	2	2	0	1.61	800 354-2228
Putnam US Govt Income Tr C	Govt-Mtg	4	6.91	5.04	2	2	0	1.61	800 354-2228
Putnam US Govt Income Tr M	Govt-Mtg	4.5	7.45	5.58	3	2	3.25	1.11	800 354-2228
Putnam US Govt Income Tr R	Govt-Mtg	4.5	7.41	5.57		2	0		800 354-2228
Quaker Fixed Income A	Corp-Inv	2.2	7.54	4.91	4	3	4	1.88	800 220-8888
RBC Government Income A	Government	10					2.75	0.93	800 442-3688
RBC Government Income B	Government	9.5					0	1.43	800 442-3688
RBC Government Income C	Government	10.2	9.56	4.45	3	2	0	0.63	800 442-3688
RBC NC Tax Free Bond A	Muni State	8.1					2.75	1.1	800 442-3688
RBC NC Tax Free Bond B	Muni State	7.7					0	1.6	800 442-3688
RBC NC Tax Free Bond C	Muni State	8.4	7.87	3.49	3	3	0	0.85	800 442-3688
RSI Retirement Active Manage Bond	Govt-Mtg	6.9	10.73	7.01	4	3	0	0.78	800 772-3615
RSI Retirement Intermediate Bond	Corp-Inv	3.2	7.08	5.34	3	1	0	1.13	800 772-3615
RSI Retirement Short Term Invest	Corp-Inv	1.2	3.41	3.87	4	1	0	0.8	800 772-3615
Rainier Interm Fixed Inc Portfolio	Corp-Inv	11.5	9.83	7.26	1	2	0	0.55	800 280-6111
Regions Morg Keeg Sel Fix Inc A	Corp-Inv	10.2	9.94	6.9	2	2	0	0.97	800 433-2829
Regions Morg Keeg Sel Fix Inc B	Corp-Inv	9.8	9.69	6.7	3	2	0	1.27	800 433-2829
Regions Morg Keeg Sel Fix Inc C	Corp-Inv	9.4					1	1.72	800 433-2829
Regions Morg Keeg Sel Hi Inc A	Corp-HY	12.5	15.47			4	2.5	1.24	800 433-2829
Regions Morg Keeg Sel Hi Inc C	Corp-HY	12	14.92			4	0		800 433-2829
Regions Morg Keeg Sel Hi Inc I	Corp-HY	12.8	15.77			4	0		800 433-2829
Regions Morg Keeg Sel Intrm Bd A	Corp-Inv	9.8	11.13			2	0	1.24	800 433-2829
Regions Morg Keeg Sel Intrm Bd C	Corp-Inv	9.3	10.69			2	0		800 433-2829
Regions Morg Keeg Sel Intrm Bd I	Corp-Inv	10.2	11.42			2	0		800 433-2829
Regions Morg Keeg Sel Ltd Mat Gv A	Government	4.4	6.45	5.25	3	1	0	0.99	800 433-2829
Regions Morg Keeg Sel Ltd Mat Gv B	Government	4.2	6.29	5.33	3	1	0	1.24	800 433-2829
Regions Morg Keeg Sel Ltd Mat Gv C	Government	3.6					1	1.74	800 433-2829
Reynolds Govt Bond Fund	Government	1.6	4.16	4.15	4	1	0	0.9	800 773-9665
Riggs Bond R	Dvsfd Bond	10.8	9.5		2	3	0	0.94	800 934-3883
Riggs Interm Tax-Free Bond R	Muni Natl	11.2	8.82		1	3	0	0.95	800 934-3883
Riggs Short Tax-Free Bond R	Muni Natl	5.9	6.29		3	2	0	0.94	800 934-3883
Riggs US Govt Securities R	Government	10.8	9.21	6.78	3	3	4.75	0.97	800 934-3883
Riggs US Govt Securities Y	Government	11.1	9.42		2	3	0	0.72	800 934-3883
Riverfront US Government Inc A	Government	8.7	8.83	6.32	3	2	4.5	1.18	800 424-2295
Riverfront US Government Inc B	Government	7.8	8	5.49	3	2	0	1.93	800 424-2295
Rochester Fund Municipals A	Muni NY	4.6	7.45	4.4	5	4	4.75	0.72	800 525-7048
Rochester Fund Municipals B	Muni NY	3.6	6.53	3.5	5	4	0	1.58	800 525-7048
Rochester Fund Municipals C	Muni NY	3.6	6.54	3.5	5	4	0	1.58	800 525-7048
Rochester Fund Municipals Y	Muni NY	4.6	7.54		5	4	0	0.58	800 525-7048
Rochester National Municipals A	Muni State	2.6	7.33	4.21	5	4	4.75		800 525-7048
Rochester National Municipals B	Muni State	1.8	6.54	3.43	5	4	0		800 525-7048
Rochester National Municipals C	Muni State	1.9	6.53	3.43	4	4	0		800 525-7048
Russell Diversified Bond C	Corp-Inv	9.9	9.24		2	2	0	1.66	800 832-6688
Russell Diversified Bond E	Corp-Inv	10.7	10.09	6.98	2	2	0	0.91	800 832-6688
Russell Diversified Bond S	Corp-Inv	11	10.33	7.21	2	2	0	0.66	800 832-6688
Russell Inst Fixed Inc I E	Corp-Inv	11.2	10.38		1	2	0	0.61	800 832-6688
Russell Inst Fixed Inc I I	Corp-Inv	11.5	10.66	7.51	1	2	0	0.39	800 832-6688
Russell Inst Fixed Inc III E	Corp-Inv	11.8	10.11		1	3	0	0.93	800 832-6688
Russell Inst Fixed Inc III I	Corp-Inv	12	10.35	7.13	1	3	0	0.72	800 832-6688
Russell Multistrategy Bond C	Corp-Inv	10.7	9.02		1	2	0	1.85	800 832-6688
Russell Multistrategy Bond E	Corp-Inv	11.4	9.83		1	3	0	1.17	800 832-6688
Russell Multistrategy Bond S	Corp-Inv	11.8					0	0.92	800 832-6688
Russell Short-Term Bond C	Corp-Inv	5.3	6.42		2	1	0	1.52	800 832-6688
Russell Short-Term Bond E	Corp-Inv	6.1	7.21		1	1	0	0.77	800 832-6688
Russell Short-Term Bond S	Corp-Inv	6.3	7.49	6.19	2	1	0	0.52	800 832-6688

Bond Fund Name	Objective	Annualized Return for			Rank		Max Load	Expense Ratio	Toll-Free/(Toll) Telephone
		1 Year	3 Years	5 Years	Overall	Risk			
Russell Tax Exempt Bond C	Muni Natl	7.3	6.7		4	2	0	1.56	800 832-6688
Russell Tax Exempt Bond E	Muni Natl	8	8.48		3	2	0	0.83	800 832-6688
Russell Tax Exempt Bond S	Muni Natl	8.3					0	0.57	800 832-6688
Rydex Series-Juno C	Government	-22.4					0	2.47	800 820-0888
Rydex Series-Juno Inv	Government	-21.7	-11.07	-5.08	5	5	0	1.41	800 820-0888
Rydex Series-US Govt Bond C	Government	27.4					0	1.79	800 820-0888
Rydex Series-US Govt Bond Inv	Government	28.5	13.34	7.16	4	5	0	0.88	800 820-0888
SAFECO California Tax Free Bd A	Muni CA	11.2	10.47	5.42	3	4	4.5	1.06	800 706-0700
SAFECO California Tax Free Bd B	Muni CA	10.1	9.57	4.62	4	4	0	1.77	800 706-0700
SAFECO California Tax Free Inc Bd	Muni CA	11.6	10.83	5.78	3	4	0	1.5	800 706-0700
SAFECO High Yield Bond Fund	Corp-HY	-2.9	-3.16	-1.94	5	5	0	1.07	800 706-0700
SAFECO High Yield Bond Fund A	Corp-HY	-3.1	-3.39	-2.16	5	5	4.5	1.31	800 706-0700
SAFECO High Yield Bond Fund B	Corp-HY	-3.8	-4.07	-2.85	5	5	0	2.06	800 706-0700
SAFECO Inter Term US Treasury Fd	Government	11.4	9.52	6.95	3	3	0	0.95	800 706-0700
SAFECO Intermed Term Muni Bd Fd	Muni Natl	9.5	8.17	5.5	3	3	0	0.9	800 706-0700
SAFECO Intermed US Treasury Fd A	Government	10.9	9.16	6.62	2	3	4.5	1.2	800 706-0700
SAFECO Intermed US Treasury Fd B	Government	10.5	8.52	5.95	4	3	0	1.95	800 706-0700
SAFECO Managed Bond Fund	Dvsfd Bond	8.6	9.14	5.23	3	2	0	0.9	800 706-0700
SAFECO Managed Bond Fund A	Dvsfd Bond	8.4	8.83	5.63	4	3	4.5	1.15	800 706-0700
SAFECO Managed Bond Fund B	Dvsfd Bond	7.6	8.08	4.87	4	2	0	1.9	800 706-0700
SAFECO Municipal Bond Fund	Muni Natl	12.1	10.77	6.25	2	4	0	1.67	800 706-0700
SAFECO Municipal Bond Fund A	Muni Natl	11.8	10.42	5.91	3	4	4.5	0.89	800 706-0700
SAFECO Municipal Bond Fund B	Muni Natl	11	9.61	5.12	3	4	0	1.68	800 706-0700
SAFECO US Govt Fund NL	Govt-Mtg	8.7	9.23	6.53	2	2	0	0.95	800 706-0700
SEI Asset Alloc-Divers Consv Inc A	Dvsfd Bond	4	3.31	5	4	4	0	0.12	800 342-5734
SEI Asset Alloc-Divers Consv Inc D	Dvsfd Bond	3	2.6	3.43	5	4	0	1.12	800 342-5734
SEI Daily Inc Tr-Corp Daily Inc A	Dvsfd Bond	2.7	5.45	5.28	3	1	0	0.35	800 342-5734
SEI Daily Inc Tr-GNMA Bond A	Govt-Mtg	6.2	8.64	6.49	2	1	0	0.59	800 342-5734
SEI Daily Inc Tr-Int Dur Gov Bd A	Government	10.9	9.99	7.4	2	2	0	0.5	800 342-5734
SEI Daily Inc Tr-Sh Dur Gov Bd A	Government	5	6.65	5.82	2	1	0	0.45	800 342-5734
SEI Index-Bond Index Portf A	Corp-Inv	11	10.39	7.33	2	3	0	0.38	800 342-5734
SEI Instl Mgd High Yield Bond A	Corp-HY	9.2	5.12	2.25	4	4	0	1.11	800 342-5734
SEI Instl Mgd Tr-Core Fixed Inc A	Dvsfd Bond	11	10.28	7.25	3	3	0	0.59	800 342-5734
SEI Intl Tr-Emerging Mkts Debt Tr	Intl Bond	26					0	1.35	800 342-5734
SEI Intl Tr-Intl Fixd Income Trust	Intl Bond	26.3	8.09	5.08	4	5	0	1	800 342-5734
SEI T/E Tr-Interm Term Muni A	Muni Natl	9.2	8.33	5.74	2	3	0	0.35	800 342-5734
SEI Tax-Exempt Tr-PA Muni Bond B	Muni State	10.3	8.85	6.04	1	3	0	0.65	800 342-5734
SM&R Government Bond Fund T	Government	8.4	9.06	6.29	3	2	4.5	0.93	800 231-4639
SM&R Tax-Free Fund T	Muni Natl	8.7	8.61	5.61	2	3	4.5	0.75	800 231-4639
SSgA Bond Market Fund	Corp-Inv	11.1	10.44	7.17	2	3	0	0.49	800 647-7327
SSgA High Yield Bond	Corp-HY	8.3	3.49	4.67	4	5	0	0.75	800 647-7327
SSgA Intermediate Fund	Government	10.9	9.93	7.16	2	2	0	0.6	800 647-7327
SSgA Yield Plus Fund	Corp-Inv	1.6	3.27	4.03	4	1	0	0.53	800 647-7327
STI Classic FL Tax Exempt Bnd Flex	Muni State	9.6	8.51	5.42	4	4	0	1.42	800 428-6970
STI Classic FL Tax Exempt Bnd Inv	Muni State	10	9.02	5.94	3	4	3.75	0.92	800 428-6970
STI Classic FL Tax Exempt Bnd Tr	Muni State	10.2	9.27	6.13	2	4	0	0.71	800 428-6970
STI Classic GA Tax Exempt Bnd Flex	Muni State	8.5	7.82	4.83	5	3	0	1.42	800 428-6970
STI Classic GA Tax Exempt Bnd Inv	Muni State	9	8.35	5.32	3	3	3.75	0.92	800 428-6970
STI Classic GA Tax Exempt Bnd Tr	Muni State	9.3	8.57	5.55	2	3	0	0.71	800 428-6970
STI Classic High Income Flex	Dvsfd Bond	6.8	4.3	5.04	5	5	4.75	1.4	800 428-6970
STI Classic Inv Grade Bond Flex	Corp-Inv	10.3	8.98	5.42	4	4	0	1.7	800 428-6970
STI Classic Inv Grade Bond Inv	Corp-Inv	10.8	9.49	5.94	3	4	3.75	1.22	800 428-6970
STI Classic Inv Grade Bond Tr	Corp-Inv	11.2	9.92	6.37	3	4	0	0.81	800 428-6970
STI Classic Inv Grade T/E Bnd Flex	Muni Natl	5.4	7.17	5.13	3	3	0	1.7	800 428-6970
STI Classic Inv Grade T/E Bnd Inv	Muni Natl	5.9	7.69	5.62	3	3	3.75	1.22	800 428-6970
STI Classic Inv Grade T/E Bnd Tr	Muni Natl	6.3	8.1	6.05	2	3	3.75	0.81	800 428-6970
STI Classic Ltd-Trm Fed Mtg Flex	Govt-Mtg	6	7.41	5.59	2	1	0	1.31	800 428-6970
STI Classic Ltd-Trm Fed Mtg Inv	Govt-Mtg	6.3	7.75	5.9	3	1	3.75	0.96	800 428-6970

Bond Fund Name	Objective	Annualized Return for			Rank		Max Load	Expense Ratio	Toll-Free/(Toll) Telephone
		1 Year	3 Years	5 Years	Overall	Risk			
STI Classic Ltd-Trm Fed Mtg Tr	Govt-Mtg	6.4	7.98	6.17	2	1	0	0.71	800 428-6970
STI Classic MD Municipal Bond Flex	Muni State	8.4	7.91	4.83	5	3	0	1.64	800 428-6970
STI Classic MD Municipal Bond Tr	Muni State	9.4	8.9	5.74	2	3	0	0.72	800 428-6970
STI Classic Sh-Term Bond Flex	Corp-Inv	2.9	5.37	4.38	4	2	0	1.26	800 428-6970
STI Classic Sh-Term Bond Inv	Corp-Inv	3.3	5.75	4.75	4	1	2	0.91	800 428-6970
STI Classic Sh-Term Bond Tr	Corp-Inv	3.5	5.92	4.94	4	1	0	0.7	800 428-6970
STI Classic Sh-Term US Treas Flex	Government	3.2	5.04	4.57	3	1	0	1.11	800 428-6970
STI Classic Sh-Term US Treas Inv	Government	3.4	5.23	4.76	3	1	1	0.86	800 428-6970
STI Classic Sh-Term US Treas Tr	Government	3.6	5.41	4.91	3	1	0	0.7	800 428-6970
STI Classic US Govt Secs Flex	Government	7.6	8.34	5.7	4	3	0	1.72	800 428-6970
STI Classic US Govt Secs Inv	Government	8.2	8.88	6.23	3	3	3.75	1.22	800 428-6970
STI Classic US Govt Secs Tr	Government	8.6	9.3	6.63	3	3	0	0.82	800 428-6970
STI Classic VA Interm Muni Bnd Inv	Muni State	7.1	7.58	4.94	4	3	3.75	0.79	800 428-6970
STI Classic VA Interm Muni Bnd Tr	Muni State	7.1	7.65	4.95	3	3	0	0.75	800 428-6970
STI Classic VA Muni Bond Flex	Muni State	8.3	7.91	4.38	5	3	0	1.69	800 428-6970
STI Classic VA Muni Bond Tr	Muni State	9.2	8.83	5.3	3	3	0	0.77	800 428-6970
Salomon Brothers High Yld Bd A	Corp-HY	14.1	7.7	3.2	3	5	4.75	1.24	800 725-6666
Salomon Brothers High Yld Bd B	Corp-HY	13.2	6.84	2.41	4	5	0	2.05	800 725-6666
Salomon Brothers High Yld Bd C	Corp-HY	13.5	7.16	2.64	4	5	0	1.72	800 725-6666
Salomon Brothers High Yld Bd O	Corp-HY	14.5	8.01	3.47	3	5	0	0.88	800 725-6666
Salomon Brothers NY Tax Free Inc A	Muni NY	11	9.25	5.83	3	4	4.5	1.05	800 331-1792
Salomon Brothers Natl Tax Free A	Muni Natl	11.4	9.59	6.37	3	4	0	1.8	800 331-1792
Salomon Brothers Strategic Bd A	Dvsfd Bond	14.8	9.38	6.07	2	3	4.75	1.43	800 725-6666
Salomon Brothers Strategic Bd B	Dvsfd Bond	14	8.66	5.3	3	3	0	2.05	800 725-6666
Salomon Brothers Strategic Bd C	Dvsfd Bond	14.2	8.92	5.57	3	3	0	1.76	800 725-6666
Salomon Brothers Strategic Bd O	Dvsfd Bond	15	9.66	6.36	2	3	0	1.03	800 725-6666
Salomon Brothers US Government A	Government	8.3	8.5	6.78	2	2	4.75	1.11	800 725-6666
Salomon Brothers US Government B	Government	7.4	7.75	5.99	2	2	0	1.55	800 725-6666
Salomon Brothers US Government C	Government	7.8	8.08	6.23	3	2	0	1.3	800 725-6666
Salomon Brothers US Government O	Government	8.6	8.88	7.08	2	2	0	0.55	800 725-6666
Schwab CA Long-Term Tax-Free	Muni CA	10.8	10.19	6.07	2	4	0	0.49	800 266-5623
Schwab CA Short/Interm Tax-Free	Muni CA	6.2	6.41	4.91	3	2	0	0.49	800 266-5623
Schwab Long-Term Tax Free Bond	Muni Natl	12	11	6	2	4	0	0.49	800 266-5623
Schwab Short-Term Bond Market	Government	8.1	8.11	6.44	2	1	0	0.35	800 266-5623
Schwab Short/Intermediate Tax Free	Muni Natl	7.6	7.04	5.08	3	2	0	0.49	800 266-5623
Schwab Total Bond Market Fd	Government	11.3	10.51	7.21	2	2	0	0.34	800 266-5623
Schwab YieldPlus Inv	Corp-Inv	0.8	1.73		5	1	0	0.55	800 266-5623
Schwab YieldPlus Sel	Corp-Inv	0.9	2.16		5	1	0	0.4	800 266-5623
Scudder Emerg Mkts Debt Instl	Intl Bond	22.2	16.07	7.17	1	5	0	1	800 621-1048
Scudder Emerg Mkts Inc A	Intl Bond	26					4.5	1.93	800 621-1048
Scudder Emerg Mkts Inc AARP	Intl Bond	26.3					0	1.65	800 621-1048
Scudder Emerg Mkts Inc B	Intl Bond	25					0	2.73	800 621-1048
Scudder Emerg Mkts Inc C	Intl Bond	24.9					1	2.7	800 621-1048
Scudder Emerg Mkts Inc S	Intl Bond	26.4	18.98	7.17	1	5	0	1.64	800 621-1048
Scudder Fixed Income A	Dvsfd Bond	11	10.9	7.57		2	4.5	0.55	800 621-1048
Scudder Fixed Income B	Dvsfd Bond	10.1	10.05	6.75		2	0		800 621-1048
Scudder Fixed Income C	Dvsfd Bond	10.1	10.05	6.75		2	1		800 621-1048
Scudder Fixed Income Instl	Corp-Inv	10.7	11	7.95	2	2	0	0.55	800 621-1048
Scudder Fixed Income Inv	Corp-Inv	10.5	10.8	7.49	2	2	0	0.79	800 621-1048
Scudder GNMA Fund AARP	Govt-Mtg	5.9	8.31	6.26	2	2	0	0.69	800 621-1048
Scudder GNMA Fund S	Govt-Mtg	5.9	8.76	6.41	3	2	0	0.7	800 621-1048
Scudder Global Bond Fund A	Intl Bond	17.5					4.5	1.62	800 621-1048
Scudder Global Bond Fund AARP	Intl Bond	17.8					0	1.13	800 621-1048
Scudder Global Bond Fund B	Intl Bond	16.4					0	2.06	800 621-1048
Scudder Global Bond Fund C	Intl Bond	16.4					1	1.83	800 621-1048
Scudder Global Bond Fund S	Intl Bond	17.8	10.27	6.54	3	3	0	1.12	800 621-1048
Scudder High Income Fund A	Corp-HY	6.6	2.37	0.54	4	5	4.5	1.09	800 621-1048
Scudder High Income Fund B	Corp-HY	5.9	1.58	-0.23	5	5	0	1.91	800 621-1048

Bond Fund Name	Objective	Annualized Return for			Rank		Max Load	Expense Ratio	Toll-Free/(Toll) Telephone
		1 Year	3 Years	5 Years	Overall	Risk			
Scudder High Income Fund C	Corp-HY	5.9	1.54	-0.27	5	5	1	1.95	800 621-1048
Scudder High Income Fund I	Corp-HY	7.1	2.79	0.91	4	5	0	0.64	800 621-1048
Scudder High Income Fund Instl	Corp-HY						0		800 621-1048
Scudder High Income Opport A	Corp-HY	7.7					4.5	1.23	800 621-1048
Scudder High Income Opport AARP	Corp-HY	8.1					0	0.9	800 621-1048
Scudder High Income Opport B	Corp-HY	6.7					0	1.98	800 621-1048
Scudder High Income Opport C	Corp-HY	6.9					1	1.95	800 621-1048
Scudder High Income Opport S	Corp-HY	7.9	3.37	1.63	5	5	0	0.9	800 621-1048
Scudder High Income Plus Instl	Corp-HY	9.7	4.84	4.75		5	0	0.68	800 621-1048
Scudder High Income Plus Inv	Corp-HY	9.5	-2.31		5	5	0	0.68	800 621-1048
Scudder High Income Plus Prem	Corp-HY	9.8					0	0.53	800 621-1048
Scudder High Yield T/F A	Muni Natl	8.1	8.49	5.49	3	3	4.5	0.89	800 621-1048
Scudder High Yield T/F AARP	Muni Natl	8.2					0	0.89	800 621-1048
Scudder High Yield T/F B	Muni Natl	7.2	7.67	4.62	4	3	0	1.82	800 621-1048
Scudder High Yield T/F C	Muni Natl	7.3	7.7	4.63	4	3	1	1.82	800 621-1048
Scudder High Yield T/F Instl	Muni Natl						0		800 621-1048
Scudder High Yield Tax Free S	Muni Natl	8.2	8.56	5.65	2	3	0	0.8	800 728-3337
Scudder Income Fund A	Corp-Inv	10.3					4.5	1.07	800 621-1048
Scudder Income Fund AARP	Corp-Inv	10.6					0	0.9	800 621-1048
Scudder Income Fund B	Corp-Inv	9.4					0	1.82	800 621-1048
Scudder Income Fund C	Corp-Inv	9.6					1	1.72	800 621-1048
Scudder Income Fund I	Corp-Inv	10.7					0	0.62	800 621-1048
Scudder Income Fund S	Corp-Inv	10.6	9.02	5.87	3	3	0	0.9	800 621-1048
Scudder Managed Muni Bonds A	Muni Natl	9.4	9.11	.6	3	4	4.5	0.77	800 621-1048
Scudder Managed Muni Bonds AARP	Muni Natl	9.6					0		800 621-1048
Scudder Managed Muni Bonds B	Muni Natl	8.5	8.25	5.16	5	4	0	1.55	800 621-1048
Scudder Managed Muni Bonds C	Muni Natl	8.5	8.24	5.15	5	4	1	1.57	800 621-1048
Scudder Managed Muni Bonds Instl	Muni Natl						0		800 621-1048
Scudder Managed Muni Bonds S	Muni Natl	9.5	9.33	6.2	3	4	0	0.56	800 728-3337
Scudder Mass Tax-Free A	Muni State	9.5					4.5	1.02	800 621-1048
Scudder Mass Tax-Free AARP	Muni State	9.7					0	0.75	800 621-1048
Scudder Mass Tax-Free B	Muni State	8.6					0	1.82	800 621-1048
Scudder Mass Tax-Free C	Muni State	8.6					1	1.79	800 621-1048
Scudder Mass Tax-Free S	Muni State	9.7	9.46	6.15	3	4	0	1.02	800 621-1048
Scudder Medium Term Tax-Free S	Muni Natl	8.9	8.22	5.59	3	3	0		800 728-3337
Scudder Medium-Term Tax Free A	Muni Natl	8.8					4.5	0.92	800 621-1048
Scudder Medium-Term Tax Free AARP	Muni Natl	9					0		800 621-1048
Scudder Medium-Term Tax Free B	Muni Natl	7.9					0	1.76	800 621-1048
Scudder Medium-Term Tax Free C	Muni Natl	7.8					1	1.73	800 621-1048
Scudder Muni Bond Instl	Muni Natl	8.5	7.95	5.44	2	2	0	0.55	800 621-1048
Scudder Muni Bond Inv	Muni Natl	8.5	7.82	5.24	2	2	0	0.8	800 621-1048
Scudder PreservationPlus Instl	Dvsfd Bond	5.6	5.66	5.7	3	1	0	0.4	800 621-1048
Scudder PreservationPlus Inv	Dvsfd Bond	5.4	5.42			1	0	0.65	800 621-1048
Scudder Short Duration A	Dvsfd Bond	5.3	6.25	5.83		1	2.75		800 621-1048
Scudder Short Duration B	Dvsfd Bond	4.5	5.46	5.04		1	0		800 621-1048
Scudder Short Duration C	Dvsfd Bond	4.4	5.44	5.03		1	1		800 621-1048
Scudder Short Duration Instl	Corp-Inv	5.5	6.5	6.07	3	1	0	0.55	800 621-1048
Scudder Short-Term Bond A	Corp-Inv	5.4					4.5	1.03	800 621-1048
Scudder Short-Term Bond AARP	Corp-Inv	5.7					0	0.75	800 621-1048
Scudder Short-Term Bond B	Corp-Inv	4.7					0	1.83	800 621-1048
Scudder Short-Term Bond C	Corp-Inv	4.6					1	1.8	800 621-1048
Scudder Short-Term Bond S	Corp-Inv	5.7	6.5	5.04	3	1	0	0.75	800 621-1048
Scudder Short-Term Muni Bond A	Muni Natl	5	5.4	4.33		1	2		800 621-1048
Scudder Short-Term Muni Bond B	Muni Natl	4.2	4.62	3.56		1	0		800 621-1048
Scudder Short-Term Muni Bond C	Muni Natl	4.2	4.62	3.56		1	0		800 621-1048
Scudder Short-Term Muni Bond Instl	Muni Natl	5.3	5.65	4.66	3	1	0	0.55	800 621-1048
Scudder Short-Term Muni Bond Inv	Muni Natl	5.1					0	0.92	800 621-1048
Scudder State Tax Free Inc-CA A	Muni CA	9	8.81	5.73	4	4	4.5	0.86	800 621-1048

Bond Fund Name	Objective	Annualized Return for			Rank		Max Load	Expense Ratio	Toll-Free/(Toll) Telephone
		1 Year	3 Years	5 Years	Overall	Risk			
Scudder State Tax Free Inc-CA B	Muni CA	8.2	7.96	4.88	5	4	0	1.68	800 621-1048
Scudder State Tax Free Inc-CA C	Muni CA	8.1	7.9	4.88	5	4	1	1.68	800 621-1048
Scudder State Tax Free Inc-CA S	Muni State	9.1					0		800 621-1048
Scudder State Tax Free Inc-FL A	Muni State	10.4	9.43	5.73	3	4	4.5	0.89	800 621-1048
Scudder State Tax Free Inc-FL B	Muni State	9.4	8.52	4.84	3	4	0	1.63	800 621-1048
Scudder State Tax Free Inc-FL C	Muni State	9.4	8.46	4.83	4	4	1	1.63	800 621-1048
Scudder State Tax Free Inc-NY A	Muni NY	9.4	9.22	5.71	3	4	4.5	0.92	800 621-1048
Scudder State Tax Free Inc-NY B	Muni NY	8.5	8.35	4.87	5	4	0	1.69	800 621-1048
Scudder State Tax Free Inc-NY C	Muni NY	8.6	8.4	4.91	5	4	1	1.67	800 621-1048
Scudder State Tax Free Inc-NY S	Muni State	9.6					0		800 621-1048
Scudder Strategic Income A	Dvsfd Bond	12.6	6.7	3.08	4	4	4.5	1.18	800 621-1048
Scudder Strategic Income B	Dvsfd Bond	11.7	5.66	2.1	4	4	0	1.95	800 621-1048
Scudder Strategic Income C	Dvsfd Bond	11.9	5.91	2.31	4	4	1	1.77	800 621-1048
Scudder U.S. Govt Securities A	Govt-Mtg	5.7	8.25	6.19	3	2	4.5	1.09	800 621-1048
Scudder U.S. Govt Securities B	Govt-Mtg	4.8	7.37	5.26	2	2	0	1.65	800 621-1048
Scudder U.S. Govt Securities C	Govt-Mtg	4.9	7.42	5.36	2	2	1	1.59	800 621-1048
Scudder U.S. Govt Securities I	Govt-Mtg	5.9	8.5	6.45	2	2	0	0.52	800 621-1048
Scudder US Bond Index Prem	Dvsfd Bond	11.4	10.73	7.55	1	2	0	0.14	800 621-1048
Security Diversified Income A	Govt-Mtg	10.5	9.72	6.32	3	3	4.75	0.95	888 732-8748
Security Diversified Income B	Govt-Mtg	9.8	8.9	5.45	3	3	0	1.71	888 732-8748
Security High Yield Income A	Corp-HY	5.7	4.71	2.12	5	5	4.75	1.48	888 732-8748
Security High Yield Income B	Corp-HY	4.9	3.93	1.34	5	5	0	2.23	888 732-8748
Security Municipal Bond A	Muni Natl	10.5	9.52	6.04	3	4	4.75	1	888 732-8748
Security Municipal Bond B	Muni Natl	9.8	8.69	5.21	4	4	0	1.75	888 732-8748
Selected US Govt Income	Government	6.8	7.99	5.05	4	2	0	1.3	800 279-0279
Seligman High Yield Bond A	Corp-HY	7	-6.71	-5.42	4	5	4.75	1.09	800 221-2783
Seligman High Yield Bond B	Corp-HY	6.1	-7.46	-6.15	5	5	0	1.84	800 221-2783
Seligman High Yield Bond C	Corp-HY	6.4	-7.44		5	5	1		800 221-2783
Seligman High Yield Bond D	Corp-HY	6.4	-7.5	-6.16	5	5	0	1.84	800 221-2783
Seligman Muni Series-CA H/Y A	Muni CA	8.2	8.71	5.36	3	3	4.75	0.69	800 221-2783
Seligman Muni Series-CA H/Y D	Muni CA	7.2	7.67	4.37	5	3	0	1.6	800 221-2783
Seligman Muni Series-CA Qlty A	Muni CA	9.4	9.65	5.78	3	4	4.75	0.86	800 221-2783
Seligman Muni Series-CA Qlty C	Muni CA	8.5	8.52		5	4	1	1.77	800 221-2783
Seligman Muni Series-CA Qlty D	Muni CA	8.5	8.65	4.79	5	4	0	1.77	800 221-2783
Seligman Muni Series-CO A	Muni State	9.3	9.33	5.54	2	3	4.75	0.96	800 221-2783
Seligman Muni Series-CO D	Muni State	8.4	8.38	4.57	4	3	0	1.84	800 221-2783
Seligman Muni Series-FL A	Muni State	9.2	9.48	5.75	2	3	4.75	0.69	800 221-2783
Seligman Muni Series-FL C	Muni State	8.3	8.58		4	3	1	1.44	800 221-2783
Seligman Muni Series-FL D	Muni State	8.4	8.65	4.92	4	3	0	1.44	800 221-2783
Seligman Muni Series-GA A	Muni State	8	8.63	5.24	4	3	4.75	0.95	800 221-2783
Seligman Muni Series-GA C	Muni State	6.6	7.48		4	3	1	1.85	800 221-2783
Seligman Muni Series-GA D	Muni State	7	7.62	4.32	5	3	0	1.85	800 221-2783
Seligman Muni Series-LA A	Muni State	8.7	8.77	5.46	2	3	4.75	0.89	800 221-2783
Seligman Muni Series-LA C	Muni State	7.3	7.7		4	3	1		800 221-2783
Seligman Muni Series-LA D	Muni State	7.7	7.84	4.51	4	3	0	1.79	800 221-2783
Seligman Muni Series-MA A	Muni State	11.3	10.76	6.12	2	4	4.75	0.89	800 221-2783
Seligman Muni Series-MA C	Muni State	10.4	9.8		3	4	1		800 221-2783
Seligman Muni Series-MA D	Muni State	10.4	10.74	5.71	3	4	0	1.79	800 221-2783
Seligman Muni Series-MD A	Muni State	7.3	7.91	5.12	3	2	4.75	0.91	800 221-2783
Seligman Muni Series-MD D	Muni State	6.3	6.95	4.17	4	2	0	1.81	800 221-2783
Seligman Muni Series-MI A	Muni State	10.1	9.07	5.79	1	3	4.75	0.7	800 221-2783
Seligman Muni Series-MI C	Muni State	8.6	7.98		3	3	1		800 221-2783
Seligman Muni Series-MI D	Muni State	9.1	8.14	4.87	3	3	0	1.6	800 221-2783
Seligman Muni Series-MN A	Muni State	9.2	8.85	5.54	2	3	4.75	0.89	800 221-2783
Seligman Muni Series-MN C	Muni State	8.2	7.87		4	3	1		800 221-2783
Seligman Muni Series-MN D	Muni State	8.2	7.87	4.61	4	3	0	1.77	800 221-2783
Seligman Muni Series-MO A	Muni State	10.2	9.76	5.79	2	4	4.75	0.92	800 221-2783
Seligman Muni Series-MO C	Muni State	9	8.71		4	4	1	1.85	800 221-2783

Bond Fund Name	Objective	Annualized Return for			Rank		Max Load	Expense Ratio	Toll-Free/(Toll) Telephone
		1 Year	3 Years	5 Years	Overall	Risk			
Seligman Muni Series-MO D	Muni State	9.2	8.77	4.83	4	4	0	1.84	800 221-2783
Seligman Muni Series-NC A	Muni State	9.3	8.89	5.37	2	3	4.75	1.12	800 221-2783
Seligman Muni Series-NC C	Muni State	8	7.91		4	3	1	1.87	800 221-2783
Seligman Muni Series-NC D	Muni State	8.5	8.08	4.59	4	3	0	1.87	800 221-2783
Seligman Muni Series-NJ A	Muni State	8.4	8.89	5.2	3	3	4.75	1.14	800 221-2783
Seligman Muni Series-NJ C	Muni State	7.4	7.99		4	3	1	1.87	800 221-2783
Seligman Muni Series-NJ D	Muni State	7.6	8.02	4.41	4	3	0	1.89	800 221-2783
Seligman Muni Series-NY A	Muni NY	10.5	9.8	5.99	2	3	4.75	0.7	800 221-2783
Seligman Muni Series-NY C	Muni NY	9.3	8.75		3	3	1		800 221-2783
Seligman Muni Series-NY D	Muni NY	9.5	8.83	5.03	3	3	0	1.6	800 221-2783
Seligman Muni Series-Natl A	Muni Natl	8	8.21	4.82	3	3	4.75		800 221-2783
Seligman Muni Series-Natl C	Muni Natl	7.2	7.25		5	3	1		800 221-2783
Seligman Muni Series-Natl D	Muni Natl	7.1	7.28	3.89	5	3	0		800 221-2783
Seligman Muni Series-OH A	Muni State	9	8.91	5.57	2	3	4.75	0.7	800 221-2783
Seligman Muni Series-OH C	Muni State	7.9	7.87		4	3	1		800 221-2783
Seligman Muni Series-OH D	Muni State	8	7.94	4.63	4	3	0	1.6	800 221-2783
Seligman Muni Series-OR A	Muni State	8.7	8.91	5.62	2	3	4.75	0.88	800 221-2783
Seligman Muni Series-OR C	Muni State	7.3	7.83		5	3	1		800 221-2783
Seligman Muni Series-OR D	Muni State	7.7	7.98	4.66	5	3	0	1.78	800 221-2783
Seligman Muni Series-PA A	Muni State	9.7	9.16	5.54	3	3	4.75	1.32	800 221-2783
Seligman Muni Series-PA D	Muni State	8.8	8.31	4.7	3	3	0	2.06	800 221-2783
Seligman Muni Series-SC A	Muni State	8.8	9.09	5.38	2	3	4.75	0.88	800 221-2783
Seligman Muni Series-SC D	Muni State	7.8	8.07	4.41	4	3	0	0.88	800 221-2783
Seligman US Govt Securities A	Government	11.6	9.96	6.7	3	4	4.75	1.1	800 221-2783
Seligman US Govt Securities B	Government	10.6	9.08	5.91	4	4	0	1.85	800 221-2783
Seligman US Govt Securities D	Government	10.6	9.01	5.87	4	4	0	1.85	800 221-2783
Sentinel Bond A	Corp-Inv	11.4	10.13	6.12	3	3	4	0.98	800 282-3863
Sentinel Bond B	Corp-Inv	10.3	9.17	5.2	3	3	4	1.82	800 282-3863
Sentinel Government Securities	Government	9.2	9.66	6.84	3	3	4	0.85	800 282-3863
Sentinel High Yield Bond A	Corp-HY	9.8	6.44	2.93	3	4	4	1.28	800 282-3863
Sentinel High Yield Bond B	Corp-HY	9.2	5.96	2.5	3	4	4	1.68	800 282-3863
Sentinel NY Tax Free Fund	Muni NY	11.2	10.15	6.33	1	3	4	0.93	800 282-3863
Sentinel PA Tax Free Income	Muni State	10.3	9.08	5.44	3	4	4	1.19	800 282-3863
Sentinel Short Maturity Govt	Govt-Mtg	4.1	6.58	5.46	3	1	1	1.15	800 282-3863
Sentinel Tax Free Income A	Muni Natl	10.4	8.98	5.65	3	4	4	0.95	800 282-3863
Sextant Bond Income Fund	Muni Natl	16.5	13.06	7.7	2	4	0	0.34	800 728-8762
Sextant Short-Term Bond Fund	Dvsfd Bond	7.3	7.54	6.07	2	1	0	0.51	800 728-8762
Sit Bond Fund	Dvsfd Bond	7.1	9.14	6.2	4	2	0	0.8	800 332-5580
Sit MN Tax Free Income	Muni State	6.7	7.45	4.63	3	1	0	0.8	800 332-5580
Sit Tax Free Income Fund	Muni Natl	5.8	7.16	4.24	2	2	0	0.76	800 332-5580
Sit US Government Fund	Government	4.2	7.36	5.9	2	1	0	0.8	800 332-5580
SmBarney AZ Municipals A	Muni State	4.1	6.46	4.04	3	2	4	0.94	800 451-2010
SmBarney AZ Municipals B	Muni State	3.4	5.87	3.47	4	2	0	1.48	800 451-2010
SmBarney AZ Municipals L	Muni State	3.4					1	1.48	800 451-2010
SmBarney Adjustable Rate Inc A	Govt-Mtg	0.2	0.54	0.47		1	0	1.1	800 451-2010
SmBarney Adjustable Rate Inc B	Govt-Mtg	2.1	4.29	4.2	4	1	0	1.78	800 451-2010
SmBarney Adjustable Rate Inc L	Govt-Mtg	2.4	4.54	4.37	4	1	0	1.29	800 451-2010
SmBarney Allocation Conservative A	Dvsfd Bond	5.1	2.89	3.16	5	4	4.5	0.6	800 451-2010
SmBarney Allocation Conservative B	Dvsfd Bond	4.5	2.33	2.62	5	4	0	1.35	800 451-2010
SmBarney Allocation Conservative L	Dvsfd Bond	4.6	2.43	2.7	5	4	1	1.35	800 451-2010
SmBarney Allocation Income Port A	Dvsfd Bond	7.6	4.51	3.12	5	4	4.5	0.6	800 451-2010
SmBarney Allocation Income Port B	Dvsfd Bond	7.1	4	2.62	5	3	0	1.35	800 451-2010
SmBarney Allocation Income Port L	Dvsfd Bond	7.2	4.05	2.66	5	3	1	1.35	800 451-2010
SmBarney Divers Strategic Inc A	Dvsfd Bond	10.6	5.11	3.56	4	3	4.5	1	800 451-2010
SmBarney Divers Strategic Inc B	Dvsfd Bond	10.3	4.63	3.04	4	3	0	1.53	800 451-2010
SmBarney Divers Strategic Inc L	Dvsfd Bond	10.3	4.58	3.06	4	3	1	1.49	800 451-2010
SmBarney Divers Strategic Inc Y	Dvsfd Bond	11.2	5.5	3.91	4	3	0	0.7	800 451-2010
SmBarney Florida Municipals A	Muni State	7.2	8.3	4.99	4	3	4	0.73	800 451-2010

Bond Fund Name	Objective	Annualized Return for			Rank		Max Load	Expense Ratio	Toll-Free/(Toll) Telephone
		1 Year	3 Years	5 Years	Overall	Risk			
SmBarney Florida Municipals B	Muni State	6.7	7.75	4.45	5	3	0	1.25	800 451-2010
SmBarney Florida Municipals L	Muni State	6.6	7.7	4.4	4	3	1	1.31	800 451-2010
SmBarney Georgia Municipals A	Muni State	8	8.64	4.91	4	4	4	0.75	800 451-2010
SmBarney Georgia Municipals B	Muni State	7.4					0	1.3	800 451-2010
SmBarney Georgia Municipals L	Muni State	7.4					1	1.35	800 451-2010
SmBarney Global Gov Bond A	Intl Bond	10.6	7.63	5.45	2	2	4.5	1.23	800 451-2010
SmBarney Global Gov Bond B	Intl Bond	10	7.11	4.92	3	2	0	1.8	800 451-2010
SmBarney Global Gov Bond L	Intl Bond	10.2	7.23	5.03	4	2	1	1.69	800 451-2010
SmBarney Global Gov Bond Y	Intl Bond	10.9	8.08	5.87	2	2	0	0.86	800 451-2010
SmBarney High Income A	Corp-HY	10	-0.07	-0.96	5	5	4.5	1.06	800 451-2010
SmBarney High Income B	Corp-HY	9.5	-0.57	-1.47	5	5	0	1.56	800 451-2010
SmBarney High Income L	Corp-HY	9.4	-0.53	-1.39	5	5	1	1.49	800 451-2010
SmBarney High Income Y	Corp-HY	10.4	0.28	-0.59	5	5	0	0.72	800 451-2010
SmBarney Investment Grade Bd A	Corp-Inv	20.1	13.89	7.08	3	4	4.5	1	800 451-2010
SmBarney Investment Grade Bd B	Corp-Inv	19.5	13.32	6.54	3	4	0	1.51	800 451-2010
SmBarney Investment Grade Bd L	Corp-Inv	19.5	13.41	6.59	3	4	1	1.41	800 451-2010
SmBarney Investment Grade Bd Y	Corp-Inv	20.5					0	0.68	800 451-2010
SmBarney MA Municipals A	Muni State	7.9	9.57	5.34	3	3	4	0.84	800 451-2010
SmBarney MA Municipals B	Muni State	7.5	8.98	4.8	3	3	0	1.42	800 451-2010
SmBarney MA Municipals L	Muni State	7.4					1	1.42	800 451-2010
SmBarney Managed Government A	Govt-Mtg	5.8	7.86	5.62	2	2	4.5	1.04	800 451-2010
SmBarney Managed Government B	Govt-Mtg	5.3	7.32	5.07	4	2	0	1.54	800 451-2010
SmBarney Managed Government L	Govt-Mtg	5.3	7.37	5.17	3	2	1	1.46	800 451-2010
SmBarney Managed Government Y	Govt-Mtg	6.2					0	0.7	800 451-2010
SmBarney Managed Municipals 1	Muni Natl	4.6					0		800 451-2010
SmBarney Managed Municipals A	Muni Natl	4.7	8.27	4.33	5	4	4	0.68	800 451-2010
SmBarney Managed Municipals B	Muni Natl	4.1	7.73	3.79	5	4	0	1.2	800 451-2010
SmBarney Managed Municipals L	Muni Natl	4.1					1	1.25	800 451-2010
SmBarney Managed Municipals Y	Muni Natl	4.9					0	0.5	800 451-2010
SmBarney Muni Fds-Ltd Term A	Muni Natl	7.3	7.76	4.82	2	3	2	0.72	800 451-2010
SmBarney Muni Fds-Ltd Term O	Muni Natl	7.1	7.53	4.58	3	3	1	1.32	800 451-2010
SmBarney Muni Fds-NY A	Muni NY	7.1	8.25	5.17	3	3	4	0.64	800 451-2010
SmBarney Muni Fds-NY B	Muni NY	6.5	7.66	4.62	3	3	0	1.22	800 451-2010
SmBarney Muni Fds-NY L	Muni NY	6.5	7.66	4.5	3	3	1	1.25	800 451-2010
SmBarney Muni Fds-National A	Muni Natl	5.6	7.66	4.62	5	3	4	0.68	800 451-2010
SmBarney Muni Fds-National B	Muni Natl	5.1	7.12	4.08	5	3	0	1.18	800 451-2010
SmBarney Muni Fds-National L	Muni Natl	5.1	7.07	4.03	5	3	1	1.25	800 451-2010
SmBarney Muni Fds-PA A	Muni State	7.9	9.59	5.28	3	4	4	0.54	800 451-2010
SmBarney Muni Fds-PA B	Muni State	7.3	9.02	4.71	4	4	0	1.08	800 451-2010
SmBarney Muni Fds-PA L	Muni State	7.2	8.94	4.66	4	4	1	1.16	800 451-2010
SmBarney Muni High Inc A	Muni Natl	4	5.07	2.77	4	2	4	0.82	800 451-2010
SmBarney Muni High Inc B	Muni Natl	3.5	4.54	2.25	3	2	0	1.32	800 451-2010
SmBarney Muni High Inc L	Muni Natl	3.4					1	1.35	800 451-2010
Smith Barney CA Municipals A	Muni CA	5	7.95	4.67	4	3	4	0.68	800 451-2010
Smith Barney CA Municipals B	Muni CA	4.3	7.37	4.12	5	3	0	1.21	800 451-2010
Smith Barney CA Municipals L	Muni CA	4.3					1	1.24	800 451-2010
Smith Barney Govt Securities 1	Government	10.4					0		800 451-2010
Smith Barney Govt Securities A	Government	10.3	9.31	6.03	3	3	4.5	0.91	800 451-2010
Smith Barney Govt Securities B	Government	9.8	8.76	5.5	4	3	0	1.48	800 451-2010
Smith Barney Govt Securities L	Government	9.8					1	1.42	800 451-2010
Smith Barney Govt Securities Y	Government	10.6					0	0.6	800 451-2010
Smith Barney Intrm Mat CA Muni A	Muni CA	5.6	6.9	4.95	2	3	2	0.65	800 451-2010
Smith Barney Intrm Mat CA Muni L	Muni CA	5.3	-13	-8.15	5	5	1	0.89	800 451-2010
Smith Barney Intrm Mat CA Muni Y	Muni CA	5.9					0	0.37	800 451-2010
Smith Barney Intrm Mat NY Muni A	Muni NY	8.2	8.31	5.48	3	3	2	0.65	800 451-2010
Smith Barney Intrm Mat NY Muni L	Muni NY	7.9					1	0.92	800 451-2010
Smith Barney NJ Municipals A	Muni State	5.2	7.96	4.32	3	3	4	0.76	800 451-2010
Smith Barney NJ Municipals B	Muni State	4.7	7.41	3.77	4	3	0	1.29	800 451-2010

Bond Fund Name	Objective	Annualized Return for			Rank		Max Load	Expense Ratio	Toll-Free/(Toll) Telephone
		1 Year	3 Years	5 Years	Overall	Risk			
Smith Barney NJ Municipals L	Muni State	4.6	7.36	3.74	4	2	1	1.33	800 451-2010
Smith Barney OR Municipals A	Muni State	7.4					.4	0.82	800 451-2010
Smith Barney OR Municipals B	Muni State	6.8					0	1.35	800 451-2010
Smith Barney OR Municipals L	Muni State	6.7					1	1.39	800 451-2010
Smith Barney Sh Term High Gr Bd A	Government	6.3	7.12	5.25	3	1	0	0.99	800 451-2010
Smith Barney Total Return Bond A	Dvsfd Bond	11.9	11.85	6.59	3	4	0	1.05	800 451-2010
Smith Barney Total Return Bond B	Dvsfd Bond	11.2	11.25	6.04	3	4	0	1.58	800 451-2010
Smith Barney Total Return Bond L	Dvsfd Bond	11.2	11.33		3	4	0	1.52	800 451-2010
Smith Barney US Govt Securities A	Govt-Mtg	6	7.96	5.86	3	2	4.5	0.84	800 451-2010
Smith Barney US Govt Securities B	Govt-Mtg	5.4	7.45	5.33	2	2	0	1.34	800 451-2010
Smith Barney US Govt Securities L	Govt-Mtg	5.3	7.41	5.33	3	2	1	1.32	800 451-2010
Smith Barney US Govt Securities Y	Govt-Mtg	6.2					0	0.55	800 451-2010
South Dakota Tax Free Fund B	Muni State	-0.5	4.5		4	2	0	1.3	800 276-1212
SouthTrust AL Tax-Free Income Fund	Muni State	10.1	9.07		1	3	3.5	0.61	800 843-8618
SouthTrust Bond Fund	Corp-Inv	13	9.66	6.54	3	3	3.5	0.87	800 843-8618
SouthTrust Income Fund	Dvsfd Bond	7.5	7.16	5.75	3	1	3.5	0.66	800 843-8618
Standish Controll Maturity Instl	Corp-Inv	6.1	7.41	6.07	2	1	0	0.3	800 221-4795
Standish Fixed Income Instl	Corp-Inv	10.8	9.93	6.34	2	2	0	0.36	800 221-4795
Standish Global Fixed Inc Instl	Intl Bond	10.6	7.99	5.73	3	2	0	0.54	800 221-4795
Standish High Grade Bond	Dvsfd Bond	10.4					0	0.4	800 221-4795
Standish Interm Tax Ex Instl	Muni Natl	8.9	7.98	5.49	2	3	0	0.63	800 221-4795
Standish Internatl Fix Inc Fd II	Intl Bond	26.4	9.1		3	5	0	0.55	800 221-4795
Standish Internatl Fix Inc Instl	Intl Bond	10.5	7.2	6	3	2	0	0.52	800 221-4795
Standish Internatl Fix Inc Svc	Intl Bond	10	5.8		4	2	0	0.78	800 221-4795
Standish MA Interm Tax Ex Instl	Muni State	8.3	7.82	5.3	3	3	0	0.65	800 221-4795
Standish Shrt Trm Asset Res Instl	Corp-Inv	3.1	4.65	4.87	4	1	0	0.36	800 221-4795
State Farm Bond Inst	Corp-Inv	11.3					0	0.23	800 447-0740
State Farm Interim Fund	Dvsfd Bond	7.6	7.08	4.49	4	3	0	0.16	800 447-0740
State Farm Muni Bond Fund	Muni Natl	8.9	7.66	4.54	4	3	0	0.17	800 447-0740
State Farm Tax Advant Bond A	Other	12.7					3	0.71	800 447-0740
State Farm Tax Advant Bond B	Other	12.3					0	1.11	800 447-0740
State Farm Tax Advant Bond Inst	Other	13.5					0	0.21	800 447-0740
State Street Research Govt Inc A	Government	10.1	9.41	6.75	3	3	4.5	0.92	800 882-0052
State Street Research Govt Inc B	Government	9.4	8.69	6	4	3	0	1.92	800 882-0052
State Street Research Govt Inc B1	Government	9.4	8.71	5.94	4	3	0	1.92	800 882-0052
State Street Research Govt Inc C	Government	9.4	8.68	6	4	3	0	1.92	800 882-0052
State Street Research Govt Inc S	Government	10.4	9.77	7.05	3	3	0	0.92	800 882-0052
State Street Research High Inc A	Corp-HY	8.5	-2.79	-3.85	5	5	4.5	0.99	800 882-0052
State Street Research High Inc B	Corp-HY	7.8	-3.66	-4.66	5	5	0	1.99	800 882-0052
State Street Research High Inc B1	Corp-HY	7.5	-3.49	-4.61	5	5	0	1.99	800 882-0052
State Street Research High Inc C	Corp-HY	7.8	-3.66	-4.7	5	5	0	0.99	800 882-0052
State Street Research High Inc S	Corp-HY	8.9	-2.74	-3.75	5	5	0	0.99	800 882-0052
Strong Advisor Bond A	Dvsfd Bond	9.3	8.21	6.48	3	3	0	1.02	800 368-1683
Strong Advisor Bond B	Dvsfd Bond	8.6					0	1.84	800 368-1683
Strong Advisor Bond C	Dvsfd Bond	8.6					0	1.8	800 368-1683
Strong Advisor Bond Instl	Dvsfd Bond	10.1					0	0.32	800 368-1683
Strong Advisor Bond K	Dvsfd Bond	9.6					0	0.74	800 368-1683
Strong Advisor Bond Z	Dvsfd Bond	9.2	8.34	6.76	3	3	0	1.08	800 368-1683
Strong Advisor Muni Bond A	Muni Natl	10.2	8.89	5.41		3	4.5		800 368-1683
Strong Advisor Muni Bond B	Muni Natl	9.2	8.02	4.62		3	0		800 368-1683
Strong Advisor Muni Bond C	Muni Natl	9.6	8.13	4.69		3	0		800 368-1683
Strong Advisor Muni Bond Instl	Muni Natl	10.8	9.26	5.76		3	0		800 368-1683
Strong Advisor Short Duration Bd A	Intl Bond	2.7					2.25	1.25	800 368-1683
Strong Advisor Short Duration Bd B	Intl Bond	1.8					0	2.04	800 368-1683
Strong Advisor Short Duration Bd C	Intl Bond	1.8					0	2.03	800 368-1683
Strong Advisor Short Duration Bd Z	Intl Bond	2.6	4.13	4.41	4	1	0	1.16	800 368-1683
Strong Advisor Strategic Income A	Corp-HY	8.3					4.5	1.59	800 368-1683
Strong Advisor Strategic Income B	Corp-HY	6.8					0	2.4	800 368-1683

Bond Fund Name	Objective	Annualized Return for			Rank		Max Load	Expense Ratio	Toll-Free/(Toll) Telephone
		1 Year	3 Years	5 Years	Overall	Risk			
Strong Advisor Strategic Income C	Corp-HY	6.9					0	2.38	800 368-1683
Strong Corporate Bond Adv	Corp-Inv	13.8	8.69	5.5	3	4	0	1.15	800 368-1683
Strong Corporate Bond Instl	Corp-Inv	14.3	9.34		3	4	0	0.59	800 368-1683
Strong Corporate Bond Inv	Corp-Inv	13.8	8.84	5.7	3	4	0	0.98	800 368-1683
Strong Corporate Income	Corp-Inv						0	1.19	800 368-1683
Strong Government Securities Adv	Govt-Mtg	11.4	10.6	7.29	2	3	0	1.1	800 368-1683
Strong Government Securities C	Govt-Mtg						0		800 368-1683
Strong Government Securities Inst	Govt-Mtg	12.1	11.34		1	3	0	0.43	800 368-1683
Strong Government Securities Inv	Govt-Mtg	11.7	10.86	7.58	2	3	0	0.84	800 368-1683
Strong High Yield Bond Adv	Corp-HY	6.1	-1.02	-0.02	5	5	0	1.2	800 368-1683
Strong High Yield Bond Instl	Corp-HY	7.1					0	0.46	800 368-1683
Strong High Yield Bond Inv	Corp-HY	6.2	-0.73	0.25	5	5	0	0.96	800 368-1683
Strong High-Yield Muni Bond Inv	Muni Natl	-6.2	-4.17	-3.39	5	4	0	0.91	800 368-1683
Strong Intermediate Muni Bond Fd	Muni Natl	9.6					0	1.43	800 368-1683
Strong Minnesota Tax-Free C	Muni State						0		800 368-1683
Strong Minnesota Tax-Free Inv	Muni State						0		800 368-1683
Strong Municipal Bond Fund Inv	Muni Natl	7.8	6.25	3.08	5	3	0	1.08	800 368-1683
Strong Short-Term Bond Adv	Corp-Inv	4.2	4.21	3.93	4	1	0	1.11	800 368-1683
Strong Short-Term Bond Instl	Corp-Inv	4.8	4.92		4	1	0	0.35	800 368-1683
Strong Short-Term Bond Inv	Corp-Inv	4.4	4.5	4.21	4	1	0	0.92	800 368-1683
Strong Short-Term H/Y Bond Adv	Corp-HY	6	2.7	3.47	5	4	0	1.18	800 368-1683
Strong Short-Term H/Y Bond Fd	Corp-HY	6.1	2.91	3.72	5	4	0	0.93	800 368-1683
Strong Short-Term H/Y Municipal	Muni Natl	4.8	4.57	3.56	3	1	0	0.77	800 368-1683
Strong Short-Term Income	Dvsfd Bond						0	1.28	800 368-1683
Strong Short-Term Muni Bond Inv	Muni Natl	5.3	5.54	4.45	3	1	0		800 368-1683
Strong Ultra Short Fund Adv	Corp-Inv	2.2	3.41	3.79	4	1	0	1.11	800 368-1683
Strong Ultra Short Fund Inst	Corp-Inv	2.9					0	0.36	800 368-1683
Strong Ultra Short Fund Inv	Corp-Inv	2.4	3.68	4.15	4	1	0	0.81	800 368-1683
Strong Ultra Short Municipal Instl	Muni Natl	3.6					0	0.36	800 368-1683
Strong Ultra Short Municipal Inv	Muni Natl	3.2	3.43	3.37	3	1	0	0.69	800 368-1683
Strong Wisconsin Tax-Free C	Muni State						0		800 368-1683
Strong Wisconsin Tax-Free Inv	Muni State	10.9					0	1.14	800 368-1683
Summit Apex Bond	Corp-Inv	7.5	8.38		3	2	0	0.72	888 259-7565
Summit Apex Lehman Aggrg Bd Idx	Corp-Inv	9.4	9.57		1	3	0	0.6	888 259-7565
Summit Apex Short-Term Govt	Government	4.9	6.58		2	1	0	0.73	888 259-7565
SunAmerica Core Bond A	Corp-Inv	10.4	8.63	5.33	3	3	4.75	1.33	800 858-8850
SunAmerica Core Bond B	Corp-Inv	9.6	7.83	4.62	4	3	0	1.98	800 858-8850
SunAmerica Core Bond II	Corp-Inv	9.8	8	4.75	4	2	0	1.98	800 858-8850
SunAmerica GNMA A	Govt-Mtg	10.9	10.09	7.54	2	3	4.75	0.76	800 858-8850
SunAmerica GNMA B	Govt-Mtg	10.1	9.43	6.86	3	3	0	1.64	800 858-8850
SunAmerica High Yield A	Corp-HY	6	-3.39	-3.56	5	5	4.75	1.48	800 858-8850
SunAmerica High Yield B	Corp-HY	5.3	-3.91	-4.13	5	5	0	2.12	800 858-8850
SunAmerica High Yield II	Corp-HY	5.4	-3.95	-4.08	5	5	1	2.17	800 858-8850
SunAmerica Sr Floating Rate B	Govt-Mtg	4.4	2.85		4	2	0	1.45	800 858-8850
SunAmerica Sr Floating Rate C	Govt-Mtg	4.3	2.81		5	2	0	1.5	800 858-8850
SunAmerica Sr Floating Rate D	Govt-Mtg	4.6					0	1.25	800 858-8850
SunAmerica Strategic Bond A	Dvsfd Bond	15.1	3.7	1.61	4	4	4.75	1.52	800 858-8850
SunAmerica Strategic Bond B	Dvsfd Bond	14	3.37	1.14	4	4	0	2.19	800 858-8850
SunAmerica Tax Exempt Insd A	Muni Natl	9.6	8.42	5.09	4	4	4.75	1.29	800 858-8850
SunAmerica Tax Exempt Insd B	Muni Natl	8.8	7.54	4.32	5	4	0	2.04	800 858-8850
SunAmerica US Gov Sec A	Government	13.6	10.92	7.4	2	3	4.75	1.41	800 858-8850
SunAmerica US Gov Sec B	Government	12.8	9.99	6.59	3	3	0	2.09	800 858-8850
T. Rowe Price CA Tax Free	Muni CA	10	9.09	5.99	3	4	0	0.53	800 638-5660
T. Rowe Price Corporate Income	Corp-Inv	12.8	11.01	6.08	3	4	0	0.8	800 638-5660
T. Rowe Price Emer Europe & Mdtr	Intl Bond	14.3					0	1.75	800 638-5660
T. Rowe Price Emerging Mkts Bd	Intl Bond	22	17.12	8.93	1	5	0	1.1	800 638-5660
T. Rowe Price FL Ins Intrm T/F	Muni State	8.9	8.35	5.63	1	3	0	0.54	800 638-5660
T. Rowe Price GA Tax Free	Muni State	10.3	9.35	5.87	2	3	0	0.65	800 638-5660

Bond Fund Name	Objective	Annualized Return for			Rank		Max Load	Expense Ratio	Toll-Free/(Toll) Telephone
		1 Year	3 Years	5 Years	Overall	Risk			
T. Rowe Price GNMA Fd	Govt-Mtg	7.1	9.08	6.61	1	2	0	0.69	800 638-5660
T. Rowe Price High Yield Adv	Corp-HY	10.3	5.71	3.66	4	4	0	1.02	800 638-5660
T. Rowe Price High Yield Fd	Corp-HY	10.5	5.94	3.93	4	4	0	0.81	800 638-5660
T. Rowe Price Infla-Protect Bond	Government						0	0.5	800 638-5660
T. Rowe Price Instl High Yield	Corp-HY	12.4					0	0.5	800 638-5660
T. Rowe Price Intl Bond Adv	Intl Bond	27	9.83	5.86	3	5	0	1.05	800 638-5660
T. Rowe Price Intl Bond Fd	Intl Bond	27.2	10.08	5.2	3	5	0	0.93	800 638-5660
T. Rowe Price MD Sh-Term T/F	Muni State	4	5.25	4.25	3	1	0	0.53	800 638-5660
T. Rowe Price MD Tax Free	Muni State	10.6	9.51	6.12	1	3	0	0.47	800 638-5660
T. Rowe Price NJ Tax Free	Muni State	10.2	9.56	5.87	1	3	0	0.59	800 638-5660
T. Rowe Price NY Tax Free	Muni NY	10.6	9.66	5.98	2	3	0	0.56	800 638-5660
T. Rowe Price New Income Adv	Corp-Inv	10.4	10.18	6.05		2	0	0.9	800 638-5660
T. Rowe Price New Income Fd	Corp-Inv	10.5	10.23	6.46	3	2	0	0.73	800 638-5660
T. Rowe Price New Income R	Corp-Inv	10.2	10.13	6.03		2	0	1.15	800 638-5660
T. Rowe Price Short-Term Bond	Corp-Inv	6.7	7.84	6.2	2	1	0	0.55	800 638-5660
T. Rowe Price Spectrum Income	Dvsfd Bond	11.5	8.72	5.94	3	2	0	0.8	800 638-5660
T. Rowe Price Summit GNMA	Govt-Mtg	7.1	9.09	6.58	1	2	0	0.6	800 638-5660
T. Rowe Price Summit Muni Inc	Muni Natl	10.4	9.76	6.01	1	3	0	0.5	800 638-5660
T. Rowe Price Summit Muni Intrm	Muni Natl	8.9	8.61	5.82	1	2	0	0.5	800 638-5660
T. Rowe Price Tax Free High Yld	Muni Natl	7.7	7.51	4.2	3	2	0	0.71	800 638-5660
T. Rowe Price Tax Free Income Adv	Muni Natl	10	9.33	5.86		3	0	0.9	800 638-5660
T. Rowe Price Tax Free Income Fd	Muni Natl	10.2	9.41	5.9	1	3	0	0.55	800 638-5660
T. Rowe Price Tax Free Insd Interm	Muni Natl	9	8.61	5.83	2	3	0	0.56	800 638-5660
T. Rowe Price Tax Free Sh-Interm	Muni Natl	6.1	6.7	5.03	3	1	0	0.52	800 638-5660
T. Rowe Price U.S. Bond Index	Dvsfd Bond	11.2					0	0.3	800 638-5660
T. Rowe Price US Treas Interm	Government	12.9	10.86	7.7	3	4	0	0.64	800 638-5660
T. Rowe Price US Treas Long	Government	19.6	12.49	8.48	3	4	0	0.67	800 638-5660
T. Rowe Price VA Tax Free	Muni State	10.8	9.65	6.17	1	3	0	0.52	800 638-5660
TCW Galileo Core Fixed Income I	Dvsfd Bond	13.3	10.07	6.95	1	3	0	0.78	800 386-3829
TCW Galileo Core Fixed Income N	Dvsfd Bond	13.2	9.8	6.25	2	2	0	1	800 386-3829
TCW Galileo Emerging Mkt Income I	Intl Bond	28					0	1.02	800 386-3829
TCW Galileo High Yield Bond I	Corp-HY	6.9					0	0.88	800 386-3829
TCW Galileo High Yield Bond N	Corp-HY	6.5	3.12	1.84	5	5	0	1.26	800 386-3829
TCW Galileo Short Term Bond I	Govt-Mtg	3					0	1	800 386-3829
TCW Galileo Total Return Bond I	Govt-Mtg	9.2	11.73	7.54	2	2	0	0.66	800 386-3829
TCW Galileo Total Return Bond N	Govt-Mtg	8.9	11.5	7.04	2	2	0	0.94	800 386-3829
TIAA-CREF BondPlus Fund	Government	12.6	11.14	7.87	2	3	0	0.3	800 842-2252
TIAA-CREF Short Term Bond	Government	9	9.26		1	1	0	0.3	800 842-2252
TIAA-CREF Tax Exempt Bond	Muni Natl	11.7	9.96		2	3	0	0.3	800 842-2252
Target Intermediate-Term Bond	Corp-Inv	10.2	9.68	7.25	1	2	0	0.66	800 442-8748
Target International Bond	Intl Bond	21.7	8.25	3.81	4	5	0	1.68	800 442-8748
Target Mortgage Backed Secs	Govt-Mtg	6.1	8.5	6.37	2	1	0	0.84	800 442-8748
Target Total Return Bond	Dvsfd Bond	11.6	10.88	7.66	2	3	0	0.75	800 442-8748
Templeton Global Bond A	Intl Bond	29.3	15.3	7.91	3	4	4.25	1.09	800 632-2350
Templeton Global Bond Adv	Intl Bond	29.5	15.57	8.17	3	4	0	0.84	800 632-2350
Templeton Global Bond C	Intl Bond	28.7	14.83	7.5	3	4	1	1.44	800 632-2350
Templeton Inst-Emerg Fixed Inc Mkt	Intl Bond	16.1					0	2.89	800 632-2350
Thompson Plumb Bond	Corp-Inv	8	9.24	6.07	3	4	0	0.8	800 841-0199
Thornburg Interm Muni-FL A	Muni State	7.6	7.41	5.12	3	2	2	0.85	800 847-0200
Thornburg Interm Muni-NM A	Muni State	7.8	6.83	4.87	3	2	2	0.97	800 847-0200
Thornburg Interm Muni-NM D	Muni State	7.6	6.54		3	2	0	1.25	800 847-0200
Thornburg Interm Muni-Natl A	Muni Natl	8.8	7.84	4.92	2	3	2	0.98	800 847-0200
Thornburg Interm Muni-Natl C	Muni Natl	8.4	7.45	4.5	3	3	0	1.39	800 847-0200
Thornburg Interm Muni-Natl I	Muni Natl	9.2	8.17	5.24	1	3	0	0.6	800 847-0200
Thornburg Ltd Term Income Fd A	Corp-Inv	11	9.68	6.91	2	2	1.5	0.93	800 847-0200
Thornburg Ltd Term Income Fd C	Corp-Inv	10.9	9.34	6.58	2	2	0	1.21	800 847-0200
Thornburg Ltd Term Income Fd I	Corp-Inv	11.6	10.11	7.3	1	2	0	0.69	800 847-0200
Thornburg Ltd Term Muni-CA A	Muni CA	5.7	5.83	4.5	3	2	1.5	1	800 847-0200

Bond Fund Name	Objective	Annualized Return for			Rank		Max Load	Expense Ratio	Toll-Free/(Toll) Telephone
		1 Year	3 Years	5 Years	Overall	Risk			
Thornburg Ltd Term Muni-CA C	Muni CA	5.4	5.42	4.11	4	2	0	1.29	800 847-0200
Thornburg Ltd Term Muni-CA I	Muni CA	6	6.21	4.87	3	2	0	0.65	800 847-0200
Thornburg Ltd Term Muni-Natl A	Muni Natl	7.2	6.96	5.08	3	2	1.5	0.93	800 847-0200
Thornburg Ltd Term Muni-Natl C	Muni Natl	7	6.62	4.62	3	2	0	1.16	800 847-0200
Thornburg Ltd Term Muni-Natl I	Muni Natl	7.6	7.36	5.4	2	2	0	0.58	800 847-0200
Thornburg Ltd Term US Govt Fd A	Government	10.7	9.77	7	2	2	1.5	0.98	800 847-0200
Thornburg Ltd Term US Govt Fd C	Government	10.3	9.4	6.59	2	2	0	1.36	800 847-0200
Thornburg Ltd Term US Govt Fd I	Government	11	10.08	7.33	1	2	0	0.99	800 847-0200
Thornburg NY Interm Muni A	Muni State	7.1	7.29	5.08	3	2	2	0.87	800 847-0200
Touchstone Core Bond Fund A	Dvsfd Bond	10	9.39	6.37	3	2	4.75	0.9	800 638-8194
Touchstone Core Bond Fund B	Dvsfd Bond	9.2					0	1.65	800 638-8194
Touchstone Core Bond Fund C	Dvsfd Bond	9.2	8.6	5.33	4	3	0	1.65	800 638-8194
Touchstone High Yield A	Corp-HY	9.7	7.33		3	4	4.75	1.05	800 638-8194
Touchstone High Yield B	Corp-HY	8.7					0	1.8	800 638-8194
Touchstone High Yield C	Corp-HY	8.8	6.55		3	4	0	1.8	800 638-8194
Touchstone Interm US Govt Bd A	Government	8.9	8.86	6.19	3	3	4.75	0.99	800 638-8194
Touchstone Interm US Govt Bd B	Government	7.7					0	1.83	800 638-8194
Touchstone Interm US Govt Bd C	Government	8					0	1.85	800 638-8194
Touchstone T/F Interm Fd A	Muni Natl	9	8	5.37	2	3	4.75	0.99	800 638-8194
Touchstone T/F Interm Fd B	Muni Natl	7.9					0	1.74	800 638-8194
Touchstone T/F Interm Fd C	Muni Natl	8.1	7.12	4.57	4	3	0	1.74	800 638-8194
Touchstone T/F Tr-Ohio Insd A	Muni State	10.4	8.69	5.58	3	4	4.75	0.75	800 638-8194
Touchstone T/F Tr-Ohio Insd B	Muni State	9.5					0	1.5	800 638-8194
Touchstone T/F Tr-Ohio Insd C	Muni State	9.7	8.05	4.73	4	4	0	1.5	800 638-8194
Trainer Wortham Total Return Bond	Dvsfd Bond	8.9	8.36		2	2	0	1	800 441-6580
Transamerica Premier Bond A	Dvsfd Bond	4.4	6.37	4.96		4	4.75	1.4	800 892-7587
Transamerica Premier Bond Inv	Dvsfd Bond	4.4	6.46	5.08	4	4	0	1.4	800 892-7587
Transamerica Premier Hi Yld Bd Inst	Corp-HY	7.4	3.41			5	0	0.65	800 892-7587
Trust for Credit Uns-Govt Sec	Govt-Mtg	3.1	5.58	5.45	3	1	0		800 342-5828
Trust for Credit Uns-Mortgage	Govt-Mtg	5.5	7.75	6.29	1	1	0		800 342-5828
Turner Core Fixed Income	Corp-Inv	10.5	9.9	7.16	3	3	0	1.01	800 224-6312
Turner Short Duration FI II	Government	3.1	5.95		2	1	0	0.96	800 224-6312
Turner Strategic HY Bond	Corp-HY	8.7	-11.25	-5.04	5	5	0	0.68	800 224-6312
Turner Ultra Short Dur FI I	Government	1.2	4.08	4.7	4	1	0	0.87	800 224-6312
Turner Ultra Short Dur FI II	Government	1	3.97	4.45	4	1	0	1.1	800 224-6312
UBS Global Bond A	Intl Bond	23.7					4.5	1.15	888 793-8637
UBS Global Bond B	Intl Bond	22.7					0	1.6	888 793-8637
UBS Global Bond Y	Intl Bond	23.9	11.08	6.32	3	4	0	0.6	888 793-8637
UBS High Yield A	Corp-HY	9.5	3.62			5	4.5	0.95	888 793-8637
UBS High Yield B	Corp-HY	8.7					0	1.7	888 793-8637
UBS High Yield C	Corp-HY	9					1	1.45	888 793-8637
UBS High Yield Y	Corp-HY	9.9	3.85	1.82		5	5.5	0.7	888 793-8637
UBS PACE Global Fixed Income A	Intl Bond	22.4					4.5	1.3	888 793-8637
UBS PACE Global Fixed Income B	Intl Bond	21.5					0	2.07	888 793-8637
UBS PACE Global Fixed Income C	Intl Bond	21.8					1	1.81	888 793-8637
UBS PACE Global Fixed Income P	Intl Bond	22.8	9.41	5.75	3	4	0	1.01	888 793-8637
UBS PACE Global Fixed Income Y	Intl Bond	23.2					0	1.02	888 793-8637
UBS PACE Government Fixed Income A	Government	5.4					4.5	1	888 793-8637
UBS PACE Government Fixed Income B	Government	4.2					0	1.79	888 793-8637
UBS PACE Government Fixed Income C	Government	4.5					1	1.53	888 793-8637
UBS PACE Government Fixed Income P	Government	5.3	8.93	6.71	1	2	0	0.78	888 793-8637
UBS PACE Government Fixed Income Y	Government	5.4					0	0.68	888 793-8637
UBS PACE Intermediate Fixed Inc A	Corp-Inv	2.6					4.5	1	888 793-8637
UBS PACE Intermediate Fixed Inc B	Corp-Inv	1.9					0	1.76	888 793-8637
UBS PACE Intermediate Fixed Inc C	Corp-Inv	2.1					1	1.5	888 793-8637
UBS PACE Intermediate Fixed Inc P	Corp-Inv	3	6.26	4.91	4	3	0	0.73	888 793-8637
UBS PACE Intermediate Fixed Inc Y	Corp-Inv	3					0	1.5	888 793-8637
UBS PACE Municipal Fixed Income A	Muni Natl	7.5					4.5	0.9	888 793-8637

Bond Fund Name	Objective	Annualized Return for			Rank		Max Load	Expense Ratio	Toll-Free/(Toll) Telephone
		1 Year	3 Years	5 Years	Overall	Risk			
UBS PACE Municipal Fixed Income C	Muni Natl	6.9					1	1.42	888 793-8637
UBS PACE Municipal Fixed Income P	Muni Natl	7.6	7.54	4.91	3	2	0	0.68	888 793-8637
UBS PACE Municipal Fixed Income Y	Muni Natl	8					0	0.66	888 793-8637
UBS PACE Strategic Fixed Income A	Corp-Inv	12.9					4.5	1.14	888 793-8637
UBS PACE Strategic Fixed Income B	Corp-Inv	12.1					0	1.9	888 793-8637
UBS PACE Strategic Fixed Income C	Corp-Inv	12.4					1	1.65	888 793-8637
UBS PACE Strategic Fixed Income P	Corp-Inv	13.3	11.65	7.58	2	3	0	0.85	888 793-8637
UBS PACE Strategic Fixed Income Y	Corp-Inv	13.2					0	0.89	888 793-8637
UBS US Bond A	Corp-Inv	10.1	10.28	7.01	3	3	4.5	0.85	888 793-8637
UBS US Bond B	Corp-Inv	9.2					0	1.6	888 793-8637
UBS US Bond C	Corp-Inv	9.5					1	1.35	888 793-8637
UBS US Bond Y	Corp-Inv	10.3	10.72	7.37	3	3	0	0.6	888 793-8637
UMB Scout Bond Fund	Corp-Inv	9.9	9.35	6.65	2	2	0	0.86	800 996-2862
US Global Inv Near-Term Tax Free	Muni Natl	7.2	6.91	4.91	3	2	0	2.63	800 873-8637
US Global Inv Tax Free Fund	Muni Natl	9.3	9.01	5.41	3	3	0	1.56	800 873-8637
USAA California Bond	Muni CA	11.3	9.6	5.91	3	4	0	0.54	800 382-8722
USAA Florida Tax-Free Income	Muni State	11.4	10.19	5.87	2	3	0	0.63	800 382-8722
USAA GNMA Trust	Govt-Mtg	6.5	9.02	6	3	2	0	0.46	800 382-8722
USAA High-Yield Opportunities Fund	Corp-HY	11.3	3.89		4	5	0	1	800 382-8722
USAA Intermediate-Term Bond Fund	Dvsfd Bond	11.3	9.44		2	3	0	0.65	800 382-8722
USAA New York Bond Fund	Muni NY	11.5	10.39	6.16	2	4	0	0.68	800 382-8722
USAA Short-Term Bond	Corp-HY	3.5	4.69	4.51	4	3	0	0.56	800 382-8722
USAA T/E Short Term Bond Fund	Muni Natl	5.5	5.75	4.65	3	1	0	0.54	800 382-8722
USAA Tax-Exempt Interm-Term	Muni Natl	8.8	8.55	5.59	1	2	0	0.48	800 382-8722
USAA Tax-Exempt Long Term Fund	Muni Natl	13.5	10.61	6.16	3	4	0	0.53	800 382-8722
USAA Virginia Bond	Muni State	11.3	9.8	6.04	2	4	0	0.59	800 382-8722
Value Line Aggressive Inc Tr	Corp-HY	9.8	-0.86	-2.37			0	1.37	800 223-0818
Value Line NY Tax Exempt	Muni NY	9.4	8.98	5.58			0	1.29	800 223-0818
Value Line Tax Exempt Natl Bond	Muni Natl	8.6	8.6	5.19			0	0.91	800 223-0818
Value Line US Govt Securities	Government	11	10.48	7.13			0	0.94	800 223-0818
Van Kampen CA Insured Tax Free A	Muni CA	10.6	9.59	5.92	3	4	3.25	0.9	800 421-5666
Van Kampen CA Insured Tax Free B	Muni CA	9.8	8.77	5.16	4	4	0	1.65	800 421-5666
Van Kampen CA Insured Tax Free C	Muni CA	9.8	8.8	5.16	4	4	0	1.65	800 421-5666
Van Kampen Corporate Bond A	Corp-Inv	10.9	9.85	5.55	3	3	4.75	1.07	800 421-5666
Van Kampen Corporate Bond B	Corp-Inv	10.1	8.99	4.71	3	3	0	1.83	800 421-5666
Van Kampen Corporate Bond C	Corp-Inv	10.1	8.98	4.71	3	3	0	1.83	800 421-5666
Van Kampen Govt Secs A	Government	9.3	9.52	6.62	3	3	4.75	1.02	800 421-5666
Van Kampen Govt Secs B	Government	8.4	8.77	5.84	4	3	0	1.77	800 421-5666
Van Kampen Govt Secs C	Government	8.4	8.75	5.87	4	3	0	1.77	800 421-5666
Van Kampen High Income Corp A	Corp-HY	4.4	-2.66	-2.25	5	5	4.75	1.06	800 421-5666
Van Kampen High Income Corp B	Corp-HY	3.3	-3.45	-3.14	5	5	0	1.82	800 421-5666
Van Kampen High Income Corp C	Corp-HY	3.6	-3.45	-3.12	5	5	0	1.82	800 421-5666
Van Kampen High Yield A	Corp-HY	4.4	-3.2	-2.25	5	5	4.75	1.32	800 421-5666
Van Kampen High Yield B	Corp-HY	3.6	-3.97	-3.02	5	5	0	2.08	800 421-5666
Van Kampen High Yield C	Corp-HY	3.6	-3.99	-3.02	5	5	0	2.08	800 421-5666
Van Kampen High Yield Muni A	Muni Natl	6.9	6.45	4.25	3	2	4.75	0.89	800 421-5666
Van Kampen High Yield Muni B	Muni Natl	6.1	5.67	3.49	2	2	0	1.65	800 421-5666
Van Kampen High Yield Muni C	Muni Natl	6.1	5.67	3.5	2	2	0	1.65	800 421-5666
Van Kampen Insured Tax Free A	Muni Natl	11	9.71	5.82	3	4	4.75	0.86	800 421-5666
Van Kampen Insured Tax Free B	Muni Natl	10.2	8.88	5	4	4	0	1.65	800 421-5666
Van Kampen Insured Tax Free C	Muni Natl	10.2	8.89	4.99	4	4	0	1.65	800 421-5666
Van Kampen Intmed Muni Income A	Muni Natl	9.5	7.86	5.23	2	3	3.25	1.23	800 421-5666
Van Kampen Intmed Muni Income B	Muni Natl	9.1	7.23	4.53	2	3	0	1.98	800 421-5666
Van Kampen Intmed Muni Income C	Muni Natl	8.7	7.07	4.44	3	3	0	1.98	800 421-5666
Van Kampen Limited Mat Govt A	Govt-Mtg	3.6	6.03	4.95	3	1	2.25	1.01	800 421-5666
Van Kampen Limited Mat Govt B	Govt-Mtg	3.1	5.58	4.41	3	1	0	1.5	800 421-5666
Van Kampen Limited Mat Govt C	Govt-Mtg	3	5.61	4.45	3	1	0	1.5	800 421-5666
Van Kampen Muni Income A	Muni Natl	10.5	8.49	4.53	3	4	4.75	0.86	800 421-5666

Bond Fund Name	Objective	Annualized Return for			Rank		Max Load	Expense Ratio	Toll-Free/(Toll) Telephone
		1 Year	3 Years	5 Years	Overall	Risk			
Van Kampen Muni Income B	Muni Natl	9.7	7.66	3.74	5	4	0	1.59	800 421-5666
Van Kampen Muni Income C	Muni Natl	9.7	7.63	3.72	4	4	0	1.59	800 421-5666
Van Kampen NY Tax Free Inc A	Muni NY	11.2	10.25	6.16	2	4	4.75	1.13	800 421-5666
Van Kampen NY Tax Free Inc B	Muni NY	10.4	9.42	5.26	3	4	0	1.88	800 421-5666
Van Kampen NY Tax Free Inc C	Muni NY	10.5	9.47	5.29	3	4	0	1.88	800 421-5666
Van Kampen PA Tax Free Inc A	Muni State	9.1	8.24	4.76	3	3	4.75	1.02	800 421-5666
Van Kampen PA Tax Free Inc B	Muni State	8.4	7.41	3.97	5	3	0	1.77	800 421-5666
Van Kampen PA Tax Free Inc C	Muni State	8.6	7.53	4	4	3	0	1.77	800 421-5666
Van Kampen Prime Rate Income Trust	Govt-Mtg	1	0.2	1.84	4	3	0	1.43	800 421-5666
Van Kampen Senior Floating Rate Fd	Govt-Mtg	-1	-2.62	0.4	5	2	0	1.69	800 421-5666
Van Kampen Strat Muni Inc A	Muni Natl	6.7	5.8	3.24	3	2	4.75	0.85	800 421-5666
Van Kampen Strat Muni Inc B	Muni Natl	5.9	5	2.45	4	2	0	1.62	800 421-5666
Van Kampen Strat Muni Inc C	Muni Natl	6.6	5.24	2.58	4	2	0	1.62	800 421-5666
Van Kampen US Govt A	Govt-Mtg	4.7	8.43	5.82	3	1	4.75	0.88	800 421-5666
Van Kampen US Govt B	Govt-Mtg	3.8	7.58	4.96	2	1	0	1.68	800 421-5666
Van Kampen US Govt C	Govt-Mtg	3.9	7.58	4.96	3	1	0	1.68	800 421-5666
Van Kampen Wrldwde High Inc A	Intl Bond	13.2	2.31	-0.16	4	5	4.75		800 421-5666
Van Kampen Wrldwde High Inc B	Intl Bond	12.6	1.31	-1.03	4	5	0	2.3	800 421-5666
Van Kampen Wrldwde High Inc C	Intl Bond	12.6	1.31	-1.03	4	5	0	2.3	800 421-5666
Vanguard CA Interm-Term T-E Adm	Muni Natl	9.3					0	0.13	800 662-7447
Vanguard CA Interm-Term T-E Inv	Muni CA	9.2	8.55	6.25	3	4	0	0.17	800 662-7447
Vanguard CA Long-Term Tax-Exempt Inv	Muni CA	10.8	9.88	6.67	3	4	0	0.17	800 662-7447
Vanguard FL Long-Term Tax-Exempt Inv	Muni State	12.1	10.74	6.96	2	4	0	0.17	800 662-7447
Vanguard GNMA Adm	Govt-Mtg	7.8					0	0.17	800 662-7447
Vanguard GNMA Inv	Govt-Mtg	7.7	9.41	7.07	2	2	0	0.22	800 662-7447
Vanguard High-Yield Corporate Inv	Corp-HY	7.7	4.7	3.22	4	4	0	0.26	800 662-7447
Vanguard High-Yld Tax-Exempt Inv	Muni Natl	8.3	8.83	5.58	3	3	0	0.17	800 662-7447
Vanguard Ins Long-Term T/E Inv	Muni Natl	11.4	10.25	6.67	2	4	0	0.17	800 662-7447
Vanguard Int-Term T/E Inv	Muni Natl	8	8.3	5.79	3	3	0	0.17	800 662-7447
Vanguard Interm-Term Bond Index Inv	Corp-Inv	15.7	12.83	8.49	2	4	0	0.21	800 662-7447
Vanguard Interm-Term Corporate Inv	Corp-Inv	13.5	12.07	7.78	2	3	0	0.02	800 662-7447
Vanguard Interm-Term Treasury Adm	Government	15.4	13.41	9.18	3	4	0	0.15	800 662-7447
Vanguard Interm-Term Treasury Inv	Government	15.3	12.44	8.59	3	4	0	0.28	800 662-7447
Vanguard Long-Term Bond Index Fd	Dvsfd Bond	22.3	15.19	9.49	2	4	0	0.2	800 662-7447
Vanguard Long-Term Corporate Inv	Corp-Inv	20.6	15.13	8.5	2	4	0	0.3	800 662-7447
Vanguard Long-Term T/E Inv	Muni Natl	11.2	10.26	6.51	3	4	0	0.17	800 662-7447
Vanguard Long-Term Treasury Adm	Government	23.1	13.06	8.97	3	5	0	0.15	800 662-7447
Vanguard Long-Term Treasury Inv	Government	23	14	9.46	3	5	0	0.28	800 662-7447
Vanguard Ltd-Tm Tx-Exmpt Inv	Muni Natl	5.9	6.42	5	3	1	0	0.17	800 662-7447
Vanguard MA Tax-Exempt Fd	Govt-Mtg	9.1	6.69			4	0	0.14	800 662-7447
Vanguard NJ Long-Term Tax-Exempt Inv	Muni State	10.7	10.01	6.58	1	3	0	0.17	800 662-7447
Vanguard NY Long-Term Tax-Exmpt Inv	Muni NY	11.7	10.28	6.7	2	4	0	0.17	800 662-7447
Vanguard OH Long-Term Tax-Exmpt Fd	Muni State	11.3	10.16	6.57	2	4	0	0.14	800 662-7447
Vanguard PA Long-Term Tax-Exmpt Inv	Muni State	11.2	10.08	6.61	1	3	0	0.17	800 662-7447
Vanguard Short-Term Bond Index Inv	Corp-Inv	7.3	8.32	6.69	2	1	0	0.21	800 662-7447
Vanguard Short-Term Corporate Inv	Corp-Inv	6.3	7.78	6.3	3	1	0	0.23	800 662-7447
Vanguard Short-Term Federal Inv	Government	6.8	8.47	6.71	2	1	0	0.26	800 662-7447
Vanguard Short-Term T/E Inv	Muni Natl	3.2	4.25	3.87	3	1	0	0.17	800 662-7447
Vanguard Short-Term Treasury Adm	Government	7.3	8.81	6.96	1	2	0	0.15	800 662-7447
Vanguard Short-Term Treasury Inv	Government	7.2	8.02	6.46	2	1	0	0.28	800 662-7447
Vanguard Total Bond Mrkt Index Inst	Dvsfd Bond	9.9	10.09	7.29	2	2	0	0.1	800 662-7447
Vanguard Total Bond Mrkt Index Inv	Dvsfd Bond	9.8	10.16	7.29	2	2	0	0.22	800 662-7447
Victory Fund For Income A	Government	7.1					2	1.04	800 539-3863
Victory Intermediate Inc A	Dvsfd Bond	10	9.74	6.82	2	2	2	1.26	800 539-3863
Victory NY Muni Bond A	Muni NY	12.5	9.14	6.08	3	4	2	1.49	800 539-3863
Victory National Muni A	Muni Natl	9.1	9.59	6.58	1	3	2	1.21	800 539-3863
Victory OH Muni Bond A	Muni State	9.1	9.1	5.88	2	3	2	1.11	800 539-3863
Victory Portf-Fund For Income C	Government	6.5					0	1.7	800 539-3863

Bond Fund Name	Objective	Annualized Return for			Rank		Max Load	Expense Ratio	Toll-Free/(Toll) Telephone
		1 Year	3 Years	5 Years	Overall	Risk			
Victory Portf-Fund For Income R	Government	7	8.48	6.51	2	2	0	1.07	800 539-3863
Vintage Bond Fund	Dvsfd Bond	6.3	8.16	3.64	4	2	0	0.95	800 438-6375
Vintage Limited Term Bond	Corp-Inv	1.8	5.75	4.36	4	1	0	0.92	800 438-6375
Vintage Municipal Bond	Muni Natl	9.2	7.98	5.26	3	3	3.75	0.85	800 438-6375
Vision Instl Ltd Dur US Govt	Government	5.2	6.33	5.37	3	1	3	0.69	800 836-2211
Vision Intermediate Term Bond A	Corp-Inv	8.6	8.81	5.83	3	2	4.5	0.78	800 836-2211
Vision NY Municipal Income Fund A	Muni NY	9.4	8.91	5.38	3	3	4.5	0.87	800 836-2211
Vision PA Muni Income Fund A	Muni State	9	8.02	5.25	2	3	4.5	1.01	800 836-2211
Vision US Government Securities A	Government	10.3	9.75	6.74	3	2	4.5	0.94	800 836-2211
W&R High Income Fund C	Corp-HY	7.3	6.32	3.25	4	4	0	1.82	888 923-3355
W&R High Income Fund Y	Corp-HY	8.3	7.54		3	4	0	0.79	888 923-3355
W&R Limited-Term Bond Fund C	Corp-Inv	4.7	7.16	5.12	3	1	0	1.94	888 923-3355
W&R Limited-Term Bond Fund Y	Corp-Inv	5.6	8.24	6.23	3	1	0	1.04	888 923-3355
W&R Municipal Bond Fund C	Muni Natl	8.9	8.75	4.25	3	3	0	2.13	888 923-3355
WM CA Ins Interm Muni A	Muni CA	8.9	8.27	5.83	3	3	4.5	0.72	800 222-5852
WM CA Ins Interm Muni B	Muni CA	8	7.48	5.04	3	3	0	1.47	800 222-5852
WM CA Ins Interm Muni C	Muni Natl	8					0		800 222-5852
WM CA Municipal Bond A	Muni CA	9.5	9.11	5.65	3	4	4.5	0.84	800 222-5852
WM CA Municipal Bond B	Muni CA	8.7	8.32	4.86	5	4	0	1.58	800 222-5852
WM CA Municipal Bond C	Muni State	8.7					0		800 222-5852
WM Conservative Balanced A	Dvsfd Bond	4.4					5.5	1.15	800 222-5852
WM Conservative Balanced B	Dvsfd Bond	3.6					0	1.88	800 222-5852
WM High Yield Fund A	Corp-HY	13.9	5.84	5.44	3	5	4.5	1.08	800 222-5852
WM High Yield Fund B	Corp-HY	12.9	4.48	2.33	4	5	0	1.77	800 222-5852
WM High Yield Fund C	Corp-HY	12.9					0		800 222-5852
WM Income Fund A	Corp-Inv	12.3	10.64	7.2	1	3	4.5		800 222-5852
WM Income Fund B	Corp-Inv	11.5	9.83	6.45	2	3	0		800 222-5852
WM Income Fund C	Dvsfd Bond	11.4					0		800 222-5852
WM Short Term Income Fund A	Corp-Inv	7	7.71	6.29	3	1	3.5	0.82	800 222-5852
WM Short Term Income Fund B	Corp-Inv	6.2	6.96	5.49	4	1	0	1.54	800 222-5852
WM Short Term Income Fund C	Dvsfd Bond	6.2					0		800 222-5852
WM Tax Exempt Bond A	Muni Natl	10.8	9.3	5.59	3	4	4.5	0.9	800 222-5852
WM Tax Exempt Bond B	Muni Natl	10	8.48	4.8	3	4	0	1.62	800 222-5852
WM Tax Exempt Bond C	Muni Natl	10					0		800 222-5852
WM US Govt Securities A	Govt-Mtg	6.5	8.59	6.3	1	2	4.5	0.94	800 222-5852
WM US Govt Securities B	Govt-Mtg	5.7	7.82	5.5	2	2	0	1.66	800 222-5852
WM US Govt Securities C	Government	5.8					0		800 222-5852
WPG Core Bond Fund	Government	12.6	10.5	7.33	2	3	0	0.5	800 223-3332
WPG Intermediate Muni Bond	Muni Natl	9.1	7.37	5.2	3	3	0	0.85	800 223-3332
Waddell & Reed Adv Bond Fund A	Corp-Inv	11.2	9.77	8.5	2	3	5.75	1.01	888 923-3355
Waddell & Reed Adv Bond Fund B	Corp-Inv	10.4	9.21	7.4	2	3	0	1.87	888 923-3355
Waddell & Reed Adv Bond Fund C	Corp-Inv	10.4	9.33	7.53	2	3	0	1.87	888 923-3355
Waddell & Reed Adv Bond Fund Y	Corp-Inv	11.6	10.31	7.51	2	3	0	0.73	888 923-3355
Waddell & Reed Adv Global Bond A	Intl Bond	9.6	6.61	3.18	3	3	5.75	1.18	888 923-3355
Waddell & Reed Adv Global Bond B	Intl Bond	8.5	5.32	2.04	4	3	0	2.13	888 923-3355
Waddell & Reed Adv Global Bond C	Intl Bond	8.5	5.24	2.81	4	3	0	2.31	888 923-3355
Waddell & Reed Adv Global Bond Y	Intl Bond	10.1	6.2	3.22	3	3	0	0.85	888 923-3355
Waddell & Reed Adv Gov Sec A	Government	9.2	10.08	6.99	3	3	4.25	1.04	888 923-3355
Waddell & Reed Adv Gov Sec B	Government	8.3	9.06	6.63	3	3	0	1.98	888 923-3355
Waddell & Reed Adv Gov Sec C	Government	8.3	8.97	6.4	3	3	0	1.85	888 923-3355
Waddell & Reed Adv Gov Sec Y	Government	9.5	9.77	7.08	3	3	0	0.79	888 923-3355
Waddell & Reed Adv High Income A	Corp-HY	5.6	3.31	4.99	4	4	5.75	1.08	888 923-3355
Waddell & Reed Adv High Income B	Corp-HY	4.5	3.25	3.99	5	4	0	1.99	888 923-3355
Waddell & Reed Adv High Income C	Corp-HY	4.5	2.75	3.72	5	4	0	1.97	888 923-3355
Waddell & Reed Adv High Income Y	Corp-HY	5.9	3.93	2.99	4	4	0	0.81	888 923-3355
Waddell & Reed Adv Ltd Term Bd A	Dvsfd Bond						0		888 923-3355
Waddell & Reed Adv Ltd Term Bd B	Dvsfd Bond						0		888 923-3355
Waddell & Reed Adv Ltd Term Bd C	Dvsfd Bond						0		888 923-3355

Bond Fund Name	Objective	Annualized Return for			Rank		Max Load	Expense Ratio	Toll-Free/(Toll) Telephone
		1 Year	3 Years	5 Years	Overall	Risk			
Waddell & Reed Adv Ltd Term Bd Y	Dvsfd Bond						0		888 923-3355
Waddell & Reed Adv Muni Bond A	Muni Natl	10.3	8.19	7.08	3	4	4.25	0.89	888 923-3355
Waddell & Reed Adv Muni Bond B	Muni Natl	9.3	7.61	5.55	3	4	0	1.72	888 923-3355
Waddell & Reed Adv Muni Bond C	Muni Natl	9.3	7.49	5.49	4	4	0	1.74	888 923-3355
Waddell & Reed Adv Muni Hi Inc A	Muni Natl	6.7	6.78	3.93	3	2	4.25	1.03	888 923-3355
Waddell & Reed Adv Muni High Inc B	Muni Natl	5.8	5.63	3.43	4	2	0	1.91	888 923-3355
Waddell & Reed Adv Muni High Inc C	Muni Natl	5.8	5.65	3.43	4	2	0	1.84	888 923-3355
Wasatch-Hoisington US Treasury	Government	26.7	14.3	9.27	4	5	0	0.95	800 551-1700
Wayne Hummer Income Fund	Corp-Inv	9.8	9.1	6.25	3	2	0	1.15	800 621-4477
Weitz Fixed Income Fund	Corp-Inv	6.6	7.87	5.29	3	2	0	0.75	800 232-4161
Wells Fargo CA Limit Term T/F A	Muni CA	5.5	5.82	4.54	2	2	4.5	1.02	800 222-8222
Wells Fargo CA Limit Term T/F I	Muni CA	5.8	6		4	2	0	0.77	800 222-8222
Wells Fargo CA Tax-Free A	Muni CA	8.9	8.86	5.82	3	3	4.5	0.91	800 222-8222
Wells Fargo CA Tax-Free B	Muni CA	8.2	8.02	5.04	5	3	0	1.67	800 222-8222
Wells Fargo CA Tax-Free C	Muni CA	8.2	8.02		5	3	0	1.64	800 222-8222
Wells Fargo CA Tax-Free I	Muni CA	9.2	9.06	6	3	3	0	0.64	800 222-8222
Wells Fargo CO Tax-Free A	Muni State	10.7	10.44	6.09	3	4	4.5	0.96	800 222-8222
Wells Fargo CO Tax-Free B	Muni State	9.8	9.61	5.28	3	4	0	1.75	800 222-8222
Wells Fargo CO Tax-Free I	Muni State	10.7	10.5	6.12	3	4	0	0.72	800 222-8222
Wells Fargo Diversified Bond I	Dvsfd Bond	8.1	8.4	6.49	4	3	0	0.88	800 222-8222
Wells Fargo High Yield Bond A	Corp-HY						4.5	1.15	800 222-8222
Wells Fargo High Yield Bond B	Corp-HY						0	1.9	800 222-8222
Wells Fargo High Yield Bond C	Corp-HY						1	1.9	800 222-8222
Wells Fargo Income A	Corp-Inv	10.6	9.57	6.17	4	3	4.5	1.06	800 222-8222
Wells Fargo Income B	Corp-Inv	9.9	8.81	5.41	4	3	0	1.91	800 222-8222
Wells Fargo Income I	Corp-Inv	11.1	9.91	6.41	3	3	0	0.78	800 222-8222
Wells Fargo Income Plus A	Govt-Mtg	11.5					5.75	1.4	800 222-8222
Wells Fargo Income Plus B	Govt-Mtg	10.6					0	2.25	800 222-8222
Wells Fargo Income Plus C	Govt-Mtg	10.6					0	2.19	800 222-8222
Wells Fargo Inflation Prot Bond A	Dvsfd Bond						4.5	1.14	800 222-8222
Wells Fargo Inflation Prot Bond B	Dvsfd Bond						0	1.89	800 222-8222
Wells Fargo Inflation Prot Bond C	Dvsfd Bond						0	1.89	800 222-8222
Wells Fargo Inflation Prot Bond I	Dvsfd Bond						0		800 222-8222
Wells Fargo Intermediate Gov Inc A	Government	10	9.39	6.8	3	3	4.5	1.1	800 222-8222
Wells Fargo Intermediate Gov Inc B	Government	9.1	8.57	5.94	4	3	0	1.8	800 222-8222
Wells Fargo Intermediate Gov Inc C	Government	9.1					0	1.69	800 222-8222
Wells Fargo Intermediate Gov Inc I	Government	10.2	9.67	7	3	3	0	0.74	800 222-8222
Wells Fargo Limited Term Gov Inc A	Government	7.3	8.13	6	3	2	4.5	1.06	800 222-8222
Wells Fargo Limited Term Gov Inc B	Government	6.5	7.33	5.24	4	2	0	1.78	800 222-8222
Wells Fargo Limited Term Gov Inc I	Government	7.7	8.48	3.83	3	2	0	0.81	800 222-8222
Wells Fargo MN Tax-Free A	Muni State	10.4	9.66	5.62	1	3	4.5	0.97	800 222-8222
Wells Fargo MN Tax-Free B	Muni State	9.6	8.84	4.84	2	3	0	1.68	800 222-8222
Wells Fargo MN Tax-Free I	Muni State	10.5	9.67	5.63	1	3	0	0.63	800 222-8222
Wells Fargo NE Tax-Free I	Muni Natl	9.6					3	0.89	800 222-8222
Wells Fargo Nat'l Ltd T/F I	Muni Natl	8.2					0	0.6	800 222-8222
Wells Fargo National Tax-Free A	Muni Natl	8.7	9.08	5.65	3	3	4.5	0.92	800 222-8222
Wells Fargo National Tax-Free B	Muni Natl	7.9	8.27	4.59	5	3	0	1.66	800 222-8222
Wells Fargo National Tax-Free C	Muni Natl	7.9					0	1.66	800 222-8222
Wells Fargo National Tax-Free I	Muni Natl	9	9.27	5.54	3	3	0	0.6	800 222-8222
Wells Fargo Stable Income A	Corp-Inv	3	4.8	4.69	4	1	1.5	1	800 222-8222
Wells Fargo Stable Income B	Corp-Inv	2.2	4.05	3.91	4	1	0	1.82	800 222-8222
Wells Fargo Stable Income I	Corp-Inv	3.1	5.05	4.88	3	1	0	0.79	800 222-8222
WesMark Bond Fund	Dvsfd Bond	4.8	8.61	5.55	4	2	3.75	0.95	800 341-7400
WesMark West Virginia Muni Bond	Muni State	7.9	8.24		2	3	3.75	0.86	800 341-7400
Westcore CO Tax Exempt	Muni State	8.8	8.25	5.37	2	2	0	0.65	800 392-2673
Westcore Flexible Income	Corp-Inv	5.7	8.16	5.09	4	4	0	0.85	800 392-2673
Westcore Plus Bond Fund	Corp-Inv	10.5	9.81	6.87	3	2	0	0.55	800 392-2673
Western Asset Interm Duration	Corp-Inv	8.8	9.66	7.17	2	3	0	0.45	800 577-8589

Bond Fund Name	Objective	Annualized Return for			Rank		Max Load	Expense Ratio	Toll-Free/(Toll) Telephone
		1 Year	3 Years	5 Years	Overall	Risk			
Western Asset Tr-Core Plus F	Dvsfd Bond	11.6					0	0.7	800 577-8589
Western Asset Tr-Core Plus Inst	Dvsfd Bond	11.8	12.03			4	0	0.45	800 577-8589
Western Asset Tr-Core Port Inst	Corp-Inv	10.9	11.73	8.02	2	4	0	0.5	800 577-8589
Western Asset Tr-Core Portf F	Dvsfd Bond	10.4	11.36			3	0	0.75	800 577-8589
William Blair Income N	Corp-Inv	9	9.33	6.79	1	2	0	0.94	800 742-7272
Wilmington Muni Bond	Muni Natl	8	7.79	5.26	3	3	0	0.75	800 336-9970
Wilmington Short/Interm Bond I	Corp-Inv	11.7	9.96	7.33	1	2	0	0.61	800 336-9970
Wright Current Income Fd-Standard	Govt-Mtg	5.5	8	6	3	1	0	0.91	800 232-0013
Wright Total Return Bond Fund	Corp-Inv	11.6	9.02	6.04	3	3	0	0.9	800 232-0013
Wright US Gov Near-Term Fd	Government	4.8	6.24	5.16	3	1	0	0.91	800 232-0013
Wright US Treasury Fund	Government	9.1	8.09	6.11	4	3	0	0.92	800 232-0013

GLOSSARY OF FUND INVESTMENT TERMS

Adviser.   Organization or person hired by a mutual fund to provide professional management and guidance.

Aggressive Growth Fund.   Mutual fund that seeks high growth by employing aggressive investment strategies. Such funds typically own shares of small, emerging companies that offer the potential for rapid growth.

Alpha.   Excess return provided by an investment that is uncorrelated with the general stock market.

Annual Report.   Yearly summary sent by mutual funds to shareholders, showing which securities are owned and discussing performance over the period under review.

Ask or Offer Price.   Lowest amount a seller is willing to take for shares of a stock or closed-end fund. In the case of no-load funds, it represents the net asset value plus any sales charges.

Asset Allocation.   Act of spreading an investment portfolio across various categories, such as stocks, bonds, and money market funds.

Assets.   Investment holdings owned by a fund.

Automatic Reinvestment.   Shareholder-authorized purchase of additional shares using fund dividends and capital gains distributions.

Average Maturity.   Length of time before a bond issuer must return the holder's principal. Bonds are issued for a variety of maturities, from 30 days to more than 30 years. Bond mutual funds attempt to maintain a portfolio of securities with different maturities. When taken together, the overall fund's average maturity can then be measured.

Balanced Fund.   Mutual fund that invests in a blended portfolio of stocks, bonds, and cash.

Bear Market.   Period of time in which prices on the stock market are generally falling.

Beta.   Coefficient measure of a stock's or mutual fund's relative volatility in relation to the Standard & Poor's 500 Index, which has a beta of 1.

Bid Price. Highest amount a buyer is willing to pay for shares of a stock or mutual fund. Also referred to as the redemption price. This is the same as net asset value, except for funds with back-end sales loads.

Blue Chip. Common stock of a nationally known company with a long record of profit growth and dividend payments, along with a reputation for quality products and services.

Blue-Sky Laws. State laws governing the registration and distribution of mutual fund shares. All 50 states and the District of Columbia regulate mutual funds.

Bond. Any interest-bearing or discounted government or corporate obligation to pay a specified sum of money, usually at regular intervals.

Bond Fund. Mutual fund that holds bonds of various maturities and safety ratings.

Book Value. What a company would be worth if all assets were sold (assets minus liability). Also, the price at which an asset is carried on a balance sheet.

Bottom-Up Investing. Process used to search for individual stocks without regard for overall economic trends.

Broker. Person who acts as an intermediary between a buyer and seller.

Bull Market. Period of time in which security prices are generally rising.

Buy-and-Hold Strategy. Technique that calls for accumulating and keeping shares of a mutual fund for many years, regardless of price swings.

Call. Option contract giving the holder the right to purchase a specified security at a stated price during a specific time period.

Capital Appreciation. Increase in the market value of a mutual fund's securities. This is reflected in the increased net asset value of a fund's shares.

Capital Depreciation. Decline in the value of a given investment, including the net asset value of a fund's shares.

Capital Gains Distribution. Payment to fund shareholders of profits realized for securities sold at a premium to their original cost. For tax purposes, shares held more than 12 months are treated as long-term capital gains, with a maximum tax rate of 20 percent. However, gains from securities held less than 12 months are taxed as ordinary income by the Internal Revenue Service.

Cash Equivalent. Investment that can easily be turned into cash. Examples include certificates of deposit and money market funds.

Cash Position. Percentage of a fund's portfolio invested in cash and cash equivalents, minus current liabilities.

Certificate of Deposit. Instrument issued by a bank or savings and loan that pays a specific amount of interest for a set time period. If you take your money out before the maturity date, you must pay an early-withdrawal penalty.

Check-Writing Privilege. Service offered by most discount brokers and large fund families allowing shareholders to write checks against their money market fund holdings. This cash continues to earn interest until a check clears.

Classes of Shares (i.e., Class A, Class B). Trend among fund organizations to provide multiple purchase options for the same fund. This is a way of disguising sales load in various ways. Class A shares, for example, might require payment of an up-front load.

Class B shares, on the other hand, might impose a 12b-1 fee and redemption fee instead.

Closed-End Fund.   Investment company that issues a limited number of shares and is traded on a stock exchange. The value of such funds is determined by market supply and demand; shares are not necessarily traded at net asset value.

Commercial Paper.   Short-term, unsecured promissory notes issued by corporations to finance immediate credit needs.

Commission.   Fee paid by investors to a broker or other sales agent for the purchase of investment products. Also referred to as a sales load.

Common Stock.   Security representing ownership of a corporation's assets that generally carries voting rights. Common stock dividends, however, are always paid after the company has met its obligations for bonds, debentures, and preferred stock.

Compounding.   Earnings on top of earnings.

Contractual Plan.   Program for the accumulation of mutual fund shares in which an investor agrees to invest a fixed amount on a regular basis for a specific number of years.

Contrarian.   Investor who does the opposite of the majority at any particular time.

Convertible Securities.   Securities that can be exchanged for other securities of the issuer under certain conditions; usually, the exchange is from preferred stock or bonds into common stock.

Corporate Bond Fund.   Mutual fund that holds bonds of various maturities and safety ratings·issued by a private or publicly traded company.

Credit Risk.   Possibility that a bond issuer will default on the payment of interest and return of principal. Risk is minimized by investing in bonds issued by large blue-chip corporations or government agencies.

Current Assets.   In a mutual fund, cash plus cash equivalents, minus current liabilities.

Current Liabilities.   Obligations due within one year or less.

Custodian.   Person or organization (usually a bank or trust company) that holds the securities and other assets of a mutual fund.

Debenture.   Bond secured only by the general credit of a corporation.

Distribution.   Dividends paid from net investment income plus realized capital gains.

Diversification.   Act of spreading risk by putting assets into several different investment categories (i.e., stocks, bonds, and cash).

Diversified Investment Company.   Under the Investment Company Act, a company (or fund) that, with respect to 75 percent of total assets, has not invested more than 5 percent nor holds more than 10 percent of the outstanding voting securities of any one company.

Dividend.   Distribution of earnings to shareholders.

Dividend Yield.   Cash dividend paid per share each year, divided by the current share price.

Dollar-Cost Averaging.   Process of accumulating positions in mutual funds over time by investing a set amount of money on a regular basis. This allows the investor to buy more shares when prices are down and fewer when they are up.

Dow Jones Industrial Average.   Oldest and most widely quoted stock market indicator. It represents the price direction of 30 blue-chip stocks on the New York Stock Exchange. However, it doesn't always give an accurate view of what's happening with the market as a whole, because it completely ignores small-cap and mid-cap stocks.

Earnings.   Net income after all charges, divided by the number of outstanding shares.

Equity Income Fund.   Mutual fund that seeks to produce a high level of income without undue risk by investing primarily in a combination of dividend-paying stocks, corporate bonds, and convertibles.

Exchange Privilege.   Option enabling fund shareholders to shift investments from one fund to another, usually at no cost.

Ex-Dividend Date.   Day on which a mutual fund's declared distributions are deducted from the fund's net asset value and distributed to shareholders.

Expense Ratio.   Percent of assets taken from a fund to cover all operating costs.

Family of Funds.   Group of mutual funds managed and distributed by the same company; each fund typically has its own investment objective.

Fixed-Income Security.   Preferred stock or debt instrument, such as a bond, with a stated percentage or dollar amount of income paid at regular intervals.

401(k) Plan.   Employer-sponsored retirement plan enabling employees to defer taxes on a portion of their salaries by making a contribution. In some cases, employers will match part or all of an employee's contribution.

403(b) Plan.   Employer-sponsored retirement plan enabling employees of universities, public schools, and nonprofit organizations to defer taxes on a portion of their salaries by earmarking it for the retirement plan.

Front-End Load.   Sales fee charged to investors of some funds at the time shares are purchased.

Fund Family.   Group of mutual funds managed and distributed by the same company.

Fund Symbol.   Letter code used to identify a fund on the exchange.

General Government Bond (Short/Intermediate Term).   Mutual fund that seeks to provide current income and stability of principal by investing in a blend of U.S. government-backed securities. The average maturity of bonds in this type of portfolio is usually ten years or less.

Global Stock Fund.   Mutual fund that seeks growth by investing primarily in stocks of companies located around the world, including the United States.

Government Agency Issues.   Debt securities issued by governmental enterprises, federal agencies, and international institutions.

Growth Fund.   Mutual fund that seeks long-term growth without undue risk by investing in the stocks of solid U.S.-based companies.

Growth and Income Fund.   Mutual fund that seeks both growth of capital and current income by investing in dividend-paying stocks with the potential for growth.

Growth Stock.   Stock of a corporation that shows greater-than-average gains in earnings.

Hedge Fund. Mutual fund that hedges its market commitments by holding securities likely to increase in value, while selling short other securities likely to decrease. The sole objective is capital appreciation.

High-Yield Bond Fund. Mutual fund that invests in corporate bonds that pay high interest and typically have low credit ratings. Such securities are also known as junk bonds.

Income. Dividends, interest, and/or short-term capital gains paid to a mutual fund's shareholders.

Income Fund. Mutual fund for which the primary objective is to generate current income.

Index Fund. Mutual fund that seeks to match the returns of a particular market index, such as the Standard & Poor's 500 or Russell 2000. These funds essentially allow investors to "buy the market" but not outperform it.

Individual Retirement Account (IRA). Tax-deferred account established to hold funds until retirement.

Inflation. Persistent upward movement in the general price level of goods and services; its effect is to reduce the purchasing power of money.

Institutional Investor. Organization (a mutual fund, bank, or insurance company) that trades a large volume of securities.

Interest Rate Risk. Chance that market rates will rise above the fixed rate of a bond, thus reducing the bond's principal value and total return. (The opposite is also true. If rates fall, the principal value of the bond will rise.) Interest rate risk can be minimized by investing in short-term bond funds.

International Equity Fund. Mutual fund that seeks growth by investing in securities of companies located in developing markets outside of the United States, such as in Japan, New Zealand, Australia, Canada, and Western Europe. International equity funds entail an added degree of risk because of political instability, currency fluctuations, foreign taxes, and differences in financial reporting standards.

Investment Company. Corporation, trust, or partnership that invests pooled shareholder dollars in securities, in line with the organization's objective. Mutual funds, also known as "open-end" investment companies, are the most popular type of investment company.

Investment Company Act of 1940. Federal statute enacted by Congress in 1940, requiring the registration and regulation of investment companies (mutual funds).

Investment Management Company. Organization hired to advise the directors and trustees of a mutual fund in selecting and supervising assets in the fund's portfolio.

Investment Objective. Investors' long-term goal; the reason for placing money in a mutual fund in the first place.

Keogh Plan. Tax-favored retirement program for the self-employed and their employees.

Large-Cap Growth Fund. Mutual fund that invests in established, growing companies with market capitalizations of $5 billion or more.

Large-Cap Value Fund. Mutual fund that invests in established companies with market capitalizations of $5 billion or more, when their securities are available at what the manager deems to be bargain prices.

Liquidity. Ability to redeem all or part of mutual fund shares, on any business day, for the closing net asset value.

Load. Sales commission assessed by some mutual funds to compensate the person who sells them (usually a stockbroker or financial planner). There are two types of loads: (1) front-end loads are taken at the time of the initial purchase; (2) back-end loads are collected when fund shares are redeemed. Loads typically range from 2 to 8 percent.

Long-Term Fund. Mutual fund designed for capital appreciation over an extended period of time.

Management Fee. Amount paid by a mutual fund for the services of an investment adviser.

Market Capitalization. Calculated by multiplying the number of shares outstanding by the per-share price of a stock. Equities can be categorized into several different classes, including micro-cap, small-cap, mid-cap, and large-cap. The general guidelines for these classifications are as follows:

- **Micro-Cap**—stock market capitalizations of $0 to $500 million.
- **Small-Cap**—stock market capitalizations of $500 million to $2 billion.
- **Mid-Cap**—stock market capitalizations of $2 billion to $5 billion.
- **Large-Cap**—stock market capitalizations of $5 billion or more.

Market Order. Order to buy or sell a security at the best available price.

Mid-Cap Growth Fund. Mutual fund that invests in growing medium-sized companies with market capitalizations generally between $1 billion and $5 billion.

Mid-Cap Value Fund. Mutual fund that invests in medium-sized companies with market capitalizations generally between $1 billion and $5 billion, when securities are available at what the manager deems to be bargain prices.

Money Market Fund. Highly liquid mutual fund that invests in short-term securities and seeks to maintain a stable net asset value of $1 per share (although this is not guaranteed).

Mortgage-Backed Securities Fund. Mutual fund that invests in mortgage pass-through instruments, such as those issued by the Government National Mortgage Association (GNMA).

Municipal Fund. Fund that deals in bonds issued by a state, city, municipality, or revenue district. Municipal bonds, also known as munis, are exempt from federal and, in some cases, state and local income taxes.

Mutual Fund. Investment company that raises money from shareholders and puts it to work in stocks, options, bonds, or money market securities. Offers investors diversification, professional management, liquidity, and convenience.

NASDAQ Composite. An index (formerly National Association of Securities Dealers Automated Quotation System) weighted by market value and representing domestic companies that are sold over-the-counter.

National Association of Securities Dealers (NASD). Self-regulatory organization with authority over firms that distribute mutual fund shares and other securities.

Net Asset Value (NAV). Market worth of one share of a mutual fund. Calculated by adding up the fund's total assets, subtracting any liabilities, and dividing the resulting figure by the number of shares outstanding.

No-Load Fund. Mutual fund for which shares are bought and sold at the prevailing net asset value, without any sales charges or commissions.

Open-End Fund. Mutual fund that stands ready to issue and redeem an unlimited number of shares as requested by investors.

Operating Expenses. Costs paid from a fund's assets, before earnings are distributed to shareholders, to cover overhead and operations.

Over-the-Counter Market. Universe of securities, both stocks and bonds, not listed on a national or regional exchange (like the New York Stock Exchange or NASDAQ stock market). Over-the-counter transactions are primarily conducted through an informal network or by auction.

Payroll Deduction Plan. Arrangement that some employers offer employees to accumulate mutual fund shares. Employees authorize their employer to deduct a specified amount from their salaries at stated times, and to transfer the proceeds to a fund.

Pension Plan. Retirement program based on a defined formula providing employees with benefits paid during the remainder of their lifetime, upon reaching a stated age.

Pension Rollover. Opportunity to take distributions from a qualified pension or profit-sharing plan and reinvest the proceeds in an individual retirement account (IRA) within 60 days from the date of distribution.

Performance Record. Statistical record of the returns a fund and/or fund manager has produced over a stated time period.

Pooling. Concept behind mutual funds; the assets of various investors with common goals are brought together and invested in a single diversified portfolio.

Portfolio. Collection of investment securities owned by an individual or institution—perhaps including stocks, bonds, and money market instruments.

Portfolio Manager. Person responsible for investing a fund's pool of assets in accordance with the provisions set forth in the prospectus.

Portfolio Turnover. Measure of trading activity in a fund. Shows how frequently a manager buys and sells securities in the portfolio.

Preferred Stock. Equity instrument that generally carries a fixed dividend that must be satisfied before dividends are paid to holders of common shares.

Price-to-Earnings Ratio. Price of a stock divided by its earnings per share.

Principal. Initial amount of money invested in a fund.

Professional Management. Ability to hire an experienced professional to decide which securities in the fund's portfolio should be bought and sold. A major advantage to mutual fund investing.

Prospectus. Official document describing a mutual fund's investment objectives, policies, services, fees, and past performance history.

Proxy Statement.   Information about fund matters, sent to shareholders of record annually for a vote. (Sadly, many fund investors don't even bother to vote. As a result, fund trustees can easily get their way on such matters as raising operating expenses and changing investment policies, when these outcomes may not be in the best interest of shareholders.)

Prudent Man Rule.   Law governing the investment of trust funds in states that give broad discretion to trustees.

Qualified Plans.   Retirement plans that meet the requirements of Sections 401(k), 403(a), or 403(b) of the Internal Revenue Code and/or the Self-Employed Individuals Tax Retirement Act.

Record Date.   Date by which shareholders must own shares in a fund in order to receive the announced distribution.

Redemption.   Act of selling shares in a mutual fund.

Redemption-In-Kind.   Redemption of investment company shares for which payment is made in portfolio securities rather than cash.

Registered Investment Company.   Investment company that has filed a registration statement with the Securities and Exchange Commission (SEC) under the requirements of the Investment Company Act of 1940.

Reinvestment.   Process of using mutual fund dividends and capital gains distributions to automatically buy additional shares, thus increasing overall holdings.

Return on Investment.   Amount of money an investment earns over a given period of time. This figure is often expressed as a percentage.

Risk.   Accepted possibility that an investment will fluctuate in value.

Risk/Reward Tradeoff.   Principle stating that an investment must offer higher potential returns to compensate for the likelihood of increased volatility. Investors are normally willing to accept higher risk on long-term investments, because the effects of price volatility generally diminish over time. Conversely, they seek lower risk with short-term investments, where accessibility and preservation of principal override the need for maximum return.

Rollover.   Shifting of assets from one qualified retirement plan to another without incurring a penalty.

Roth IRA.   Tax-deferred account in which contributions are nondeductible, but earnings grow tax-free. Eligibility for the Roth IRA gradually phases out at income levels of $95,000 to $110,000 for individuals, and $150,000 to $160,000 for married couples.

Sales Load.   Amount charged for the sale of mutual fund shares by a stockbroker or other financial professional. The cost is usually added to the fund's net asset value.

Sector Fund.   Mutual fund that invests in the securities of a single industry or country-specific region.

Securities and Exchange Commission (SEC).   Federal agency charged with regulating the registration and distribution of mutual fund shares.

Senior Securities.   Notes, bonds, debentures, or preferred stocks that have a claim to assets and earnings that supercedes claims by holders of common stock.

Series Funds.   Funds organized with separate portfolios of securities, each with its own unique investment objective.

Shareholder.   Investor who owns shares in a mutual fund.

Short Sale.   Sale of a security that is borrowed, not owned, in the hope that the price will go down so it can be repurchased at a lower price, therefore generating a profit through the underlying spread.

Short-Term Funds.   Mutual funds that invest in securities with the intention of holding them for one year or less (i.e., money market funds).

Small-Cap Growth Fund.   Mutual fund that invests in small, fast-growing companies with market capitalizations generally under $1 billion.

Small-Cap Value Fund.   Mutual fund that invests in small, growing companies with market capitalizations generally under $1 billion, whose securities are available at what the manager deems to be bargain prices.

Small-Company or Small-Cap Fund.   Mutual fund that seeks capital appreciation by investing in the stocks of small, fast-growing companies.

Standard & Poor's Composite Index of 500 Stocks (S&P 500).   Index that tracks the performance of 500 widely held common stocks, weighted by market value. It includes mostly blue-chip names and represents some two-thirds of the U.S. stock market's total value.

Statement of Additional Information (SAI).   Supplement to a prospectus; contains updated and more complete information about a mutual fund. (Also referred to as "Part B" of the registration statement.)

Stock.   Representation of ownership in a corporation. Usually issued in terms of shares.

Systematic Withdrawal Plan.   Program in which fund shareholders receive regular automatic distributions from their investments. Shares are redeemed to meet the shareholders' income needs, and payments are sent out monthly, quarterly, or annually, as specified.

Tax-Deferred Income.   Dividends, interest, and capital gains received from investments held in qualified retirement plans, such as IRAs, Keoghs, 401(k)s, and 403(b)s. This income is not subject to current taxation. Instead, it is taxed upon withdrawal.

Time Horizon.   Length of time money is to be invested in a fund. Time horizon helps to pinpoint the types of investments that should be included in a portfolio mix. The longer the time horizon, the more risk one can afford to take, because of the ability to weather any short-term declines in the market.

Total Return.   Measure of a fund's overall performance during a given period of time. Encompasses all aspects affecting return, including dividends, capital gains distributions, and changes in net asset value.

Transfer Agent.   Organization or person hired by a mutual fund to prepare and maintain records on shareholders' accounts.

Treasury Bill.   Non-interest-bearing security issued at a discount to its value by the U.S. Treasury. Maturity is one year or less.

Turnover Ratio.   Measure of how frequently a manager buys and sells securities in the portfolio. The higher the number, the more trading that occurs.

12b-1 Fee.   Mutual fund expense used to pay for marketing and distribution costs.

Underwriter.   Organization or person acting as the distributor of a mutual fund's shares to broker/dealers and investors.

U.S. Government Bond.   Bond issued by the U.S. Treasury or other government agency. Considered among the safest investments available, because they are backed by the full faith and credit of the U.S. government.

Value Fund.   Mutual fund with the objective of buying stocks in companies whose shares are considered to be undervalued, as measured by price-to-earnings ratio, book value, or other valuation benchmark.

Variable Annuity.   Investment contract sold by an insurance company. Accumulates capital, often through mutual fund investments, which is later converted to an income stream, usually at retirement.

Volatility.   Measure of risk that refers to how a fund's share price moves up or down compared to its underlying index.

Warrant.   Option to buy a specific number of shares of stock at a stated price during a limited time period.

Wash Sale.   Purchase and sale of a security either simultaneously or within a short time period. Wash sales that take place within 30 days of the underlying purchase do not qualify for a tax loss deduction under rules set forth by the Internal Revenue Service.

Withdrawal Plan.   Program in which shareholders receive income on principal payments at regular intervals from their mutual fund investments.

Yield.   Measure of the net income (dividends and interest minus expenses) earned by the securities in a fund portfolio during a specific period of time.

Yield to Maturity.   The rate of return offered on a debt security if held to maturity.

INDEX